# Biometrics

**Books in the IEEE Press Series on Computational Intelligence**

# Biometrics
## Theory, Methods, and Applications

Edited by

**Nikolaos V. Boulgouris**
**Konstantinos N. Plataniotis**
**Evangelia Micheli-Tzanakou**

**IEEE Computational Intelligence Society**, *Sponsor*
**IEEE Press Series on Computational Intelligence**
David B. Fogel, *Series Editor*

IEEE PRESS

A John Wiley & Sons, Inc., Publication

*Library of Congress Cataloging-in-Publication Data is available.*

ISBN 978-0470-24782-2

10 9 8 7 6 5 4 3 2 1

# Contents

# Preface

The objective of biometric systems is the recognition or authentication of individuals based on some physical or behavioral characteristics that are intrinsically unique for each individual. Nowadays, biometric systems are fundamental components of advanced security architectures. The applications of biometrics range from access control, military, and surveillance to banking and multimedia copyright protection. Recently, biometric information has started to become an essential element in government issued authentication and travel documents. The large-scale deployment of biometrics sensors in a variety of electronic devices, such as mobile phones, laptops, and personal digital assistants (PDA), has further accelerated the pace at which the demand for biometric technologies has been growing. The immense interest in the theory, technology, applications, and social implications of biometric systems has created an imperative need for the systematic study of the use of biometrics in security and surveillance infrastructures.

This edited volume provides an extensive survey of biometrics theory, methods, and applications, making it a good source of information for researchers, security experts, policy makers, engineers, and graduate students. The volume consists of 26 chapters which cover most aspects of biometric systems. The first few chapters address particular recognition techniques that can be used in conjunction with a variety of biometric traits. The following chapters present technologies tailored to specific biometric traits, such as face, hand geometry, fingerprints, signature, electrocardiogram, electroencephalogram, and gait. The remaining chapters focus on both theoretical issues as well as issues related to the emerging area of privacy-enhancing biometric solutions.

**An overview of recent developments in discriminant analysis for dimensionality reduction** is presented in the first chapter. Specifically, a unified framework is presented for generalized linear discriminant analysis (LDA) via a transfer function. It is shown that various LDA-based algorithms differ in their transfer functions. This framework explains the properties of various algorithms and their relationship. Furthermore, the theoretical properties of various algorithms and their relationship are also presented. An emerging extension of the classical LDA is the **multilinear discriminant analysis (MLDA) for biometric signal recognition**. Biometric signals are mostly multidimensional objects, known as tensors. Recently, there has been a growing interest in MLDA solutions. In Chapter 2, the fundamentals of existing MLDA solutions are presented and then categorized according to the multilinear projection employed. At the same time, their connections with traditional linear solutions are pointed out. The next two chapters present classification issues in biometric identification. The problem of classification is extremely important because it essentially sets the framework regarding the way decisions are made once feature extraction and dimensionality reduction have taken place. A variety of classification approaches can be taken. One of these approaches is to use neural networks (NN). Chapter 3 is **a comparative survey on biometric identity authentication techniques based on neural networks**. This chapter presents a survey on representative NN-based methodologies for biometric identification. In particular, it captures the evolution of some of the representative NN-based methods in order to provide an outline of the application of neural nets in biometric systems. A specific, but far from uncommon, case of classification is that involving fusion of biometrics. The main task here is the **design of classifiers for fusion-based biometric verification**, which is addressed in Chapter 4. The chapter provides guidelines for optimal ensemble generation, where each classifier in the ensemble is a base classifier. Examples are shown for support vector machines and correlation filters. The chapter also focuses on decision fusion rules and the effect of classifier output diversity on their decision fusion accuracy is also analyzed.

Chapters 5–20 present systems based on specific biometric modalities. Methods for face recognition/verification are presented in Chapters 5–8. One of the most important problems in face recognition is feature selection. Chapter 5 presents a **person-specific characteristic feature selection for face recognition**. In this chapter, a new methodology for face recognition is introduced that detects and extracts unique features on a person's face and then uses those features for the purpose of recognition. Chapter 6 presents a different approach by performing **face verification based on elastic graph matching**. Using elastic graph matching, a face is represented as a connected graph. This approach endows the recognition process with robustness against geometric distortions of the facial image. Another challenging task in the area of face-based biometric systems is the efficient use of video sequences for face authentication. Chapter 7 presents a method for the **combination of geometrical and statistical models for video-based face authentication**. In this chapter, it is shown that it is possible to describe object appearance using a combination of analytically derived geometrical models and statistical data analysis. Specifically, a framework that is robust to large changes in facial pose and lighting conditions is presented for face recognition from video sequences. The method can handle situations where the pose and lighting conditions in the training and testing data are completely disjoint. Chapter 8 is about a **biologically inspired model for the simultaneous recognition of identity and expression**. This work builds upon the fact that faces can provide a wide range of information about a person's identity, race, sex, age and emotional state. In most cases, humans easily derive such information by processes that appear rapid and automatic. However, upon closer inspection, one finds these processes to be diverse and complex. This chapter examines the perception of identity and emotion. Next, it develops a computational model that is applied for identification based on face images with differing expression as well as for the classification of expressions.

Chapters 9–11 present some more advanced methods for face recognition. The first two of these chapters go beyond the conventional approach and are based on the realization that face recognition does not have to rely on an image taken using a conventional camera. **Face recognition using infrared cameras** is a very interesting extension of conventional face recognition. In Chapter 9, a near-infrared (NIR) face-based approach is presented for multimodal biometric fusion. The NIR face is fused with the visible light (VL) face or iris modality. This approach has several advantages, including the fact that NIR face recognition overcomes problems arising from uncontrolled illumination in VL images and achieves significantly better results than when VL faces are used. Furthermore, the fusion of NIR face with VL face or iris is a natural combination for multibiometric solutions. A different, multimodal system based on the fusion of **2D and 3D face and hand geometry data** is presented in Chapter 10. This topic is of particular interest because recent advances in multimodal biometrics as well as the emergence of affordable 3D imaging technologies have created great potential for techniques that involve 3D data. The main advantage is the simultaneous acquisition of a pair of depth and color images of biometric information using low-cost sensors. Although the above face-based methodologies offer improved performance, they are not directly improving the resilience of visual biometric systems to the change that these biometrics undergo through time. Aging is a crucial factor for recognition applications and, in the case of face recognition, can be dealt with by using **learning facial aging models.** Such facial models studied in Chapter 11 can be used for the prediction of one's appearance across ages and, therefore, are of great importance for performing reliable face recognition across age progression. Chapter 12 is about **super-resolution** techniques, which can be used in conjunction with face recognition technologies.

The next three chapters are devoted to iris and fingerprint recognition. The technologies that are used in **iris recognition** systems are presented in Chapter 13. Iris recognition is an extremely reliable technique for identification of individuals, and this chapter reviews both its theoretical and practical aspects. Fingerprint recognition is another very important technology that has been reliably used in biometric systems for a many years. Chapter 14, entitled **learning in fingerprints**, gives a short introduction of the basic concepts and terminology. Furthermore, it provides a detailed review of the existing literature by discussing the most salient learning-based approaches applied to feature extraction, matching, and classification of fingerprints. Chapter 15 makes a **comparison of classification and indexing-based approaches for fingerprint recognition**. This chapter presents a comparison of two key approaches for fingerprint identification. These approaches are based on classification followed by verification and indexing followed by verification. The fingerprint classification approach is based on a feature-learning algorithm, while the indexing approach is based on features derived from triplets of minutiae.

Chapters 16 and 17 present methods using electrocardiograms (ECG). ECG is essentially a medical diagnostic technique but more recently it has fulfilled a rather unlikely role, as a provider of security and privacy in the form of a biometric. Chapter 16, entitled **Electrocardiogram (ECG) Biometric for Robust Identification and Secure Communication**, examines the various implications and technical challenges of using the ECG as a biometric. Specifically, novel signal processing techniques are surveyed and proposed that seek to not only establish the status of the ECG as an indisputable biometric trait, but also reinforce its versatile utility, such as in alleviating the resource consumption in certain communication networks. Chapter 17 discusses **the heartbeat as a living biometric**. Although previous research on the topic focused mainly on analysis of the electrocardiogram, this chapter extends the ECG results by applying processing methods to a larger and more diverse set of individuals, demonstrating that performance remains high for a larger and a more diverse population. Alternative sensing methods, using blood pressure and pulse oximetry, are presented and their corresponding performance is documented. The chapter also discusses the phenomenology and sensing modalities for monitoring cardiovascular function and, finally, examines the fusion of heartbeat information across the three modalities and quantifies its performance.

Chapters 18 and 19 explore methodologies mainly based on electroencephalograms (EEG). In Chapter 18, a method is proposed using **physiological signals for key features in high-security biometric systems**. The experimental protocol that is common for EEG and ECG recording is explained. EEG and ECG features as well as the authentication algorithms are presented and their efficiency is individually assessed. A fusion process carried out to achieve higher performance is also presented. Chapter 19 presents a **multiresolution analysis of the effect of face familiarity on human event-related potentials**. This method works by processing of the electroencephalograms (EEGs) in response to familiar and unfamiliar face stimuli. Stimuli were presented in successive trials and consisted of (a) multiple presentations of frontal, gray-scale images of one person known to the subject and (b) unique unknown images taken from multiple face databases. Coherent oscillations in phase were observed in the lower delta activity of ERPs in response to known stimuli but not in response to unknown stimuli.

Chapters 20 and 21 present methods and applications based on signature recognition and gait recognition. Although several approaches can be used in authentication systems, the most commonly used authentication method in everyday transactions is based on signature. The specific points of concern regarding **online signature-based authentication** have to do more with template security issues and countermeasures. Chapter 20 focuses on the security issues related to biometric templates, with application to signature based authentication systems. The main privacy and security issues are briefly summarized and some approaches that are used for the protection of biometric templates are discussed. Data hiding techniques are used to design a security scalable authentication system. The enrollment and the authentication procedure are detailed. In contrast to the signature, which is an established method for authentication, gait recognition is an emerging technology that is particularly attractive for biometric identification because the capturing of gait can take place in an unobtrusive manner. Chapter 21 presents the fundamental approaches for **unobtrusive biometric identification based on gait** and provides directions for future research.

Chapters 22–26 deal with biometric applications including issues related to the concept of biometric capacity. Chapter 22, presents a completely new framework for biometric authentication in secure environments as well as a relevant application based on gait recognition. The proposed framework is based on **distributed source coding for biometrics**. In this new framework, the problem of biometric recognition is formulated as the dual of data communication over noisy channels. In such a system, the enrollment and authentication procedures are considered as the encoding and decoding stages of a communication system. The above approach is highly relevant to information theory. Further application of information theory in biometrics can be found in the assessment of the information content of biometric traits. The discriminating ability of biometric features is usually estimated by means of experimentation. However, the information carried by biometrics, their uniqueness, and their fusion prospects can be studied based on concepts from information theory. This is the topic of Chapter 23, which deals with **measuring information content in biometric features**. Next, in Chapter 24, a summary is presented of the theoretical results and design experience obtained during the development of a next generation physical access security system (PASS). The main feature of this PASS is its efficient **decision-making support** of security personnel enhanced with the situational awareness paradigm and intelligent tools.

Despite the increasing use of biometric features for authentication and identification purposes in a broad variety of institutional and commercial systems, the adoption of biometric techniques is restrained by a rising concern regarding the protection of the biometrics templates. In fact, people are not generally keen to give out biometric traits unless they are assured that their biometrics cannot be stolen or used without their consent. Recent results showed that it is feasible to generate a unique identifier by combining biometric traits. This approach makes it impossible to recover the original biometric features and, thus, ensures the privacy of the biometrics. Chapter 25, entitled **Privacy in Biometrics**, reviews the privacy issues related to the use of biometrics, presents some of the most advanced techniques available up to date, provides a comparative analysis, and gives an overview of future trends. A particular system that builds privacy into an information system is presented in the final chapter, entitled **Biometric Encryption**. In this chapter, the emerging area of privacy-enhancing biometric technologies, referred to as "untraceable biometrics," makes it possible to enhance both privacy and security in a positive-sum model.

By its nature, an edited volume covers only a limited number of works and initiatives in the area of biometric systems. Researchers and practitioners are introducing new developments at a very fast pace, and it would be impossible to cover all of them in a single volume. However, we believe that the collection of chapters presented here cover sufficiently well the theory, methods, and applications of biometrics. Readers who wish to further explore the fascinating area of biometrics can find additional information using the bibliographic links that are provided in each one of the chapters of this volume.

We thank all those who have helped to make this edited volume possible, especially the contributors who spent much of their precious time and energy in preparing their chapters. We are really grateful for their enthusiasm and devotion to this project. We thank the contributors and other experts who served as reviewers. Special thanks should go to Dr. Qinghan Xiao, the reviewer assigned by IEEE Press, for providing lots of useful suggestions for the improvement of the book. Our deep feelings of appreciation go to John Wiley & Sons for the impeccable processing of the authors' contributions and the final production of the book. Last, but certainly not least, we would like to thank Jeanne Audino of IEEE Press for her professionalism and her continuous support and assistance during all stages of the preparation and publication of the manuscript.

Nikolaos V. Boulgouris
Konstantinos N. Plataniotis
Evangelia Micheli-Tzanakou

*London, United Kingdom*
*Toronto, Ontario, Canada*
*New Brunswick, New Jersey*
*July 2009*

# Contributors

**ANDY ADLER,**  Carleton University, Ottawa, Ontario, Canada

**FOTEINI AGRAFIOTI,**  University of Toronto, Toronto, Ontario, Canada

**SAVVAS ARGYROPOULOS,**  Informatics and Telematics Institute, Thessaloniki, Greece

**VINEETH BALASUBRAMANIAN,**  Arizona State University, Tempe, Arizona

**BIR BHANU,**  University of California, Riverside, California

**JOHN BLACK,**  Arizona State University, Tempe, Arizona

**OLEG BOULANOV,**  University of Calgary, Calgary, Alberta, Canada

**NIKOLAOS V. BOULGOURIS,**  King's College, London, United Kingdom

**NIKOLAOS BOURBAKIS,**  Wright State University, Dayton, Ohio

**FRANCIS MINHTHANG BUI,**  University of Toronto, Toronto, Ontario, Canada

**PATRIZIO CAMPISI,**  University of Rome, Rome, Italy

**MARCO CAPARRINI,**  Starlab, Barcelona, Spain

**ANN CAVOUKIAN,**  Office of Information and Privacy Commissioner Ontario, Toronto, Ontario, Canada

**IVAN CESTER,**  Starlab, Barcelona, Spain

**RAMA CHELLAPPA,**  University of Maryland, College Park, Maryland

**STELVIO CIMATO,**  University of Milan, Milan, Italy

**BRETT DEMARCO,**  Rutgers University, New Brunswick, New Jersey

**MARCO GAMASSI,**  University of Milan, Milan, Italy

**DIMITRIOS HATZINAKOS,**  University of Toronto, Toronto, Ontario, Canada

**XIAXI HUANG,**  King's College, London, United Kingdom

**DIMOSTHENIS IOANNIDIS,**  Informatics and Telematics Institute, Thessaloniki, Greece

**JOHN M. IRVINE,**  Science Applications International Corporation (SAIC), Arlington, Virginia

**STEVEN A. ISRAEL,**  Science Applications International Corporation (SAIC), Arlington, Virginia

**SHUIWANG JI,**  Arizona State University, Tempe, Arizona

**RAGHUDEEP KANNAVARA,**  Wright State University, Dayton, Ohio

**SREEKAR KRISHNA,**  Arizona State University, Tempe, Arizona

**B. V. K. VIJAYA KUMAR,**   Carnegie Mellon University, Pittsburgh, Pennsylvania

**ZHEN LEI,**   National Laboratory of Pattern Recognition, Institute of Automation, Chinese Academy of Sciences, Beijing, China

**STAN Z. LI,**   National Laboratory of Pattern Recognition, Institute of Automation, Chinese Academy of Sciences, Beijing, China

**YUNG-HUI LI,**   Carnegie Mellon University, Pittsburgh, Pennsylvania

**SHENGCAI LIAO,**   National Laboratory of Pattern Recognition, Institute of Automation, Chinese Academy of Sciences, Beijing, China

**HAIPING LU,**   University of Toronto, Toronto, Ontario, Canada

**ALESSANDRA LUMINI,**   Biometric System Laboratory, University of Bologna, Bologna, Italy

**EMANUELE MAIORANA,**   University of Rome, Rome, Italy

**SOTIRIS MALASSIOTIS,**   Informatics and Telematics Institute, Thessaloniki, Greece

**DAVIDE MALTONI,**   Biometric System Laboratory, University of Bologna, Bologna, Italy

**ALEIX M. MARTINEZ,**   Ohio State University, Columbus, Ohio

**EVANGELIA MICHELI-TZANAKOU**,   Rutgers University, New Brunswick, New Jersey

**LORIS NANNI,**   Biometric System Laboratory, University of Bologna, Bologna, Italy

**ALESSANDRO NERI,**   University of Rome, Rome, Italy

**DONALD NETH,**   Ohio State University, Columbus, Ohio

**SETHURAMAN PANCHANATHAN,**   Arizona State University, Tempe, Arizona

**SUNG WON PARK,**   Carnegie Mellon University, Pittsburgh, Pennsylvania

**IOANNIS PITAS,**   University of Thessaloniki, Thessaloniki, Greece

**VINCENZO PIURI,**   University of Milan, Milan, Italy

**KONSTANTINOS N. PLATANIOTIS,**   University of Toronto, Toronto, Ontario, Canada

**NARAYANAN RAMANATHAN,**   University of Maryland, College Park, Maryland

**ALEJANDRO RIERA,**   Starlab, Barcelona, Spain

**AMIT K. ROY-CHOWDHURY,**   University of California, Riverside, California

**GIULIO RUFFINI,**   Starlab, Barcelona, Spain

**ROBERTO SASSI,**   University of Milan, Milan, Italy

**MARIOS SAVVIDES,**   Carnegie Mellon University, Pittsburgh, Pennsylvania

**FABIO SCOTTI,**   University of Milan, Milan, Italy

**VLAD P. SHMERKO,**   University of Calgary, Calgary, Alberta, Canada

**AURELI SORIA-FRISCH,** Starlab, Barcelona, Spain

**ALEX STOIANOV,** Office of Information and Privacy Commissioner Ontario, Toronto, Ontario, Canada

**ADRIAN STOICA,** Jet Propulsion Laboratory, NASA, USA

**MICHAEL G. STRINTZIS,** Informatics and Telematics Institute, Thessaloniki, Greece

**XUEJUN TAN,** University of California, Riverside, California

**ANASTASIOS TEFAS,** University of Thessaloniki, Thessaloniki, Greece

**FILARETI TSALAKANIDOU,** Informatics and Telematics Institute, Thessaloniki, Greece

**DIMITRIOS TZOVARAS,** Informatics and Telematics Institute, Thessaloniki, Greece

**ANASTASIOS N. VENETSANOPOULOS,** University of Toronto, Toronto, Ontario, Canada

**KRITHIKA VENKATARAMANI,** Carnegie Mellon University, Pittsburgh, Pennsylvania

**RONG WANG,** University of California, Riverside, California

**RUI WANG,** National Laboratory of Pattern Recognition, Institute of Automation, Chinese Academy of Sciences, Beijing, China

**BRENDA K. WIEDERHOLD,** Science Applications International Corporation (SAIC), Arlington, Virginia

**MARK D. WIEDERHOLD,** Science Applications International Corporation (SAIC), Arlington, Virginia

**YILEI XU,** University of California, Riverside, California

**SVETLANA N. YANUSHKEVICH,** University of Calgary, Calgary, Alberta, Canada

**JIEPING YE,** Arizona State University, Tempe, Arizona

**RICHARD YOUMARAN,** Carleton University, Ottawa, Ontario, Canada

# Chapter 1

# Discriminant Analysis for Dimensionality Reduction: An Overview of Recent Developments

**Jieping Ye and Shuiwang Ji**

## 1.1 INTRODUCTION

Many biometric applications such as face recognition involve data with a large number of features [1–3]. Analysis of such data is challenging due to the *curse-of-dimensionality* [4, 5], which states that an enormous number of samples are required to perform accurate predictions on problems with a high dimensionality. Dimensionality reduction, which extracts a small number of features by removing irrelevant, redundant, and noisy information, can be an effective solution [6]. The commonly used dimensionality reduction methods include supervised approaches such as linear discriminant analysis (LDA) [7, 8], unsupervised ones such as principal component analysis (PCA) [9], and additional spectral and manifold learning methods [10–14]. When the class label information is available, supervised approaches, such as LDA, are usually more effective than unsupervised ones such as PCA for classification.

Linear discriminant analysis (LDA) is a classical statistical approach for supervised dimensionality reduction and classification [8, 15–18]. LDA computes an optimal transformation (projection) by minimizing the within-class distance and maximizing the between-class distance simultaneously, thus achieving maximum

*Biometrics: Theory, Methods, and Applications.* Edited by Boulgouris, Plataniotis, and Micheli-Tzanakou
Copyright © 2010 the Institute of Electrical and Electronics Engineers, Inc.

class discrimination. The optimal transformation in LDA can be readily computed by applying an eigendecomposition on the so-called scatter matrices. It has been used widely in many applications involving high-dimensional data [19–24]. However, classical LDA requires the so-called *total scatter matrix* to be nonsingular. In many applications involving high-dimensional and low sample size data, the total scatter matrix can be singular since the data points are from a very high-dimensional space, and in general the sample size does not exceed this dimension. This is the well-known *singularity or undersampled problem* encountered in LDA.

In recent years, many LDA extensions have been proposed to deal with the singularity problem, including PCA+LDA [19, 23], regularized LDA (RLDA) [21], null space LDA (NLDA) [20], orthogonal centroid method (OCM) [25], uncorrelated LDA (ULDA) [24], orthogonal LDA (OLDA) [24], and LDA/GSVD [26]. A brief overview of these algorithms is given in Section 1.2. Different algorithms have been applied successfully in various domains, such as PCA+LDA in face recognition [19, 23], OCM in text categorization [25], and RLDA in microarray gene expression data analysis [21]. However, there is a lack of a systematic study to explore the commonalities and differences of these algorithms, as well as their intrinsic relationship. This has been a challenging task, since different algorithms apply completely different schemes when dealing with the singularity problem.

Many of these LDA extensions involve an eigenvalue problem, which is computationally expensive to solve especially when the sample size is large. LDA in the binary-class case, called Fisher LDA, has been shown to be equivalent to linear regression with the class label as output. Such regression model minimizes the sum-of-squares error function whose solution can be obtained efficiently by solving a system of linear equations. However, the equivalence relationship is limited to the binary-class case.

In this chapter, we present a unified framework for generalized LDA via a transfer function. We show that various LDA-based algorithms differ in their transfer functions. The unified framework elucidates the properties of various algorithms and their relationship. We then discuss recent development on establishing the equivalence relationship between multivariate linear regression (MLR) and LDA in the multiclass case. In particular, we show that MLR with a particular class indicator matrix is equivalent to LDA under a mild condition, which has been shown to hold for most high-dimensional data. We further show how LDA can be performed in the semisupervised setting, where both labeled and unlabeled data are provided, based on the equivalence relationship between MLR and LDA. We also extend our discussion to the kernel-induced feature space and present recent developments on multiple kernel learning (MKL) for kernel discriminant analysis (KDA).

The rest of this chapter is organized as follows. We give an overview of classical LDA and its generalization in Section 1.2. A unified framework for generalized LDA as well as the theoretical properties of various algorithms and their relationship is presented in Section 1.3. Section 1.4 discusses the least squares formulation for LDA. We then present extensions of the discussion to semisupervised learning and kernel-induced feature space in Sections 1.5 and 1.6, respectively. This chapter concludes in Section 1.8.

## 1.2  OVERVIEW OF LINEAR DISCRIMINANT ANALYSIS

We are given a data set that consists of $n$ samples $\{(x_i, y_i)\}_{i=1}^{n}$, where $x_i \in \mathbb{R}^d$ denotes the $d$-dimensional input, $y_i \in \{1, 2, \ldots, k\}$ denotes the corresponding class label, $n$ is the sample size, and $k$ is the number of classes. Let

$$X = [x_1, x_2, \ldots, x_n] \in \mathbb{R}^{d \times n}$$

be the data matrix and let $X_j \in \mathbb{R}^{d \times n_j}$ be the data matrix of the $j$th class, where $n_j$ is the sample size of the $j$th class and $\sum_{j=1}^{k} n_j = n$. Classical LDA computes a linear transformation $G \in \mathbb{R}^{d \times \ell}$ that maps $x_i$ in the $d$-dimensional space to a vector $x_i^L$ in the $\ell$-dimensional space as follows:

$$x_i \in \mathbb{R}^d \rightarrow x_i^L = G^T x_i \in \mathbb{R}^{\ell}, \qquad \ell < d.$$

In LDA, three scatter matrices, called the *within-class*, *between-class*, and *total* scatter matrices are defined as follows [8]:

$$S_w = \frac{1}{n} \sum_{j=1}^{k} \sum_{x \in X_j} (x - c^{(j)})(x - c^{(j)})^T, \tag{1.1}$$

$$S_b = \frac{1}{n} \sum_{j=1}^{k} n_j (c^{(j)} - c)(c^{(j)} - c)^T, \tag{1.2}$$

$$S_t = \frac{1}{n} \sum_{i=1}^{n} (x_i - c)(x_i - c)^T, \tag{1.3}$$

where $c^{(j)}$ is the *centroid* of the $j$th class and $c$ is the *global centroid*. It can be verified from the definitions that $S_t = S_b + S_w$ [8]. Define three matrices $H_w$, $H_b$, and $H_t$ as follows:

$$H_w = \frac{1}{\sqrt{n}} [X_1 - c^{(1)}(e^{(1)})^T, \ldots, X_k - c^{(k)}(e^{(k)})^T], \tag{1.4}$$

$$H_b = \frac{1}{\sqrt{n}} [\sqrt{n_1}(c^{(1)} - c), \ldots, \sqrt{n_k}(c^{(k)} - c)], \tag{1.5}$$

$$H_t = \frac{1}{\sqrt{n}} (X - ce^T), \tag{1.6}$$

where $e^{(j)}$ and $e$ are vectors of all ones of length $n_j$ and $n$, respectively. Then the three scatter matrices, defined in Eqs. (1.1)–(1.3), can be expressed as

$$S_w = H_w H_w^T, \qquad S_b = H_b H_b^T, \qquad S_t = H_t H_t^T. \tag{1.7}$$

It follows from the properties of matrix trace that

$$\text{trace}(S_w) = \frac{1}{n} \sum_{j=1}^{k} \sum_{x \in X_j} \|x - c^{(j)}\|_2^2, \tag{1.8}$$

$$\text{trace}(S_b) = \frac{1}{n} \sum_{j=1}^{k} n_j \| c^{(j)} - c \|_2^2. \tag{1.9}$$

Thus trace($S_w$) measures the distance between the data points and their corresponding class centroid, and trace($S_b$) captures the distance between the class centroids and the global centroid.

In the lower-dimensional space resulting from the linear transformation $G$, the scatter matrices become

$$S_w^L = G^T S_w G, \qquad S_b^L = G^T S_b G, \qquad S_t^L = G^T S_t G. \tag{1.10}$$

An optimal transformation $G$ would maximize trace($S_b^L$) and minimize trace($S_w^L$) simultaneously, which is equivalent to maximizing trace($S_b^L$) and minimizing trace($S_t^L$) simultaneously, since $S_t^L = S_w^L + S_b^L$. The optimal transformation, $G^{LDA}$, of LDA is computed by solving the following optimization problem [8, 16]:

$$G^{LDA} = \arg\max_{G} \left\{ \text{trace}\left( S_b^L \left( S_t^L \right)^{-1} \right) \right\}. \tag{1.11}$$

It is known that the optimal solution to the optimization problem in Eq. (1.11) can be obtained by solving the following generalized eigenvalue problem [8]:

$$S_b x = \lambda S_t x. \tag{1.12}$$

More specifically, the eigenvectors corresponding to the $k - 1$ largest eigenvalues form columns of $G^{LDA}$. When $S_t$ is nonsingular, it reduces to the following regular eigenvalue problem:

$$S_t^{-1} S_b x = \lambda x. \tag{1.13}$$

When $S_t$ is singular, the classical LDA formulation discussed above cannot be applied directly. This is known as the *singularity* or *undersampled* problem in LDA. In the following discussion, we consider the more general case when $S_t$ may be singular. The transformation, $G^{LDA}$, then consists of the eigenvectors of $S_t^+ S_b$ corresponding to the nonzero eigenvalues, where $S_t^+$ denotes the pseudo-inverse of $S_t$ [27]. Note that when $S_t$ is nonsingular, $S_t^+$ equals $S_t^{-1}$.

The above LDA formulation is an extension of the original Fisher linear discriminant analysis (FLDA) [7], which deals with binary-class problems, that is, $k = 2$. The optimal transformation, $G^F$, of FLDA is of rank one and is given by [15, 16]

$$G^F = S_t^+ (c^{(1)} - c^{(2)}). \tag{1.14}$$

Note that $G^F$ is invariant of scaling. That is, $\alpha G^F$, for any $\alpha \neq 0$, is also a solution to FLDA.

When the dimensionality of data is larger than the sample size, which is the case for many high-dimensional and low sample size data, all of the three scatter matrices are singular. In recent years, many algorithms have been proposed to deal with this singularity problem. We first review these LDA extensions in the next subsection. To elucidate their commonalities and differences, a general framework is presented in Section 1.3 that unifies many of these algorithms.

## 1.2.1   Generalizations of LDA

A common way to deal with the singularity problem is to apply an intermediate dimensionality reduction, such as PCA [9], to reduce the data dimensionality before classical LDA is applied. The algorithm is known as PCA+LDA, or subspace LDA [19, 28]. In this two-stage PCA+LDA algorithm, the discriminant stage is preceded by a dimensionality reduction stage using PCA. The dimensionality, $p$, of the subspace transformed by PCA is chosen such that the "reduced" total scatter matrix in this subspace is nonsingular, so that classical LDA can be applied. The optimal value of $p$ is commonly estimated through cross-validation.

Regularization techniques can also be applied to deal with the singularity problem of LDA. The algorithm is known as regularized LDA (RLDA) [21]. The key idea is to add a constant $\mu > 0$ to the diagonal elements of $S_t$ as $S_t + \mu I_d$, where $I_d$ is the identity matrix of size $d$. It is easy to verify that $S_t + \mu I_d$ is positive definite [27], hence nonsingular. Cross-validation is commonly applied to estimate the optimal value of $\mu$. Note that regularization is also the key to many other learning algorithms including Support Vector Machines (SVM) [29].

In reference 20, the null space LDA (NLDA) was proposed, where the between-class distance is maximized in the null space of the within-class scatter matrix. The singularity problem is thus avoided implicitly. The efficiency of the algorithm can be improved by first removing the null space of the total scatter matrix. It is based on the observation that the null space of the total scatter matrix is the intersection of the null spaces of the between-class and within-class scatter matrices. In contrast, the orthogonal centroid method (OCM) [25] maximizes the between-class distance only and thereby omits the within-class information. The optimal transformation of OCM is given by the top eigenvectors of the between-class scatter matrix $S_b$.

In reference 24, a family of generalized discriminant analysis algorithms were presented. Uncorrelated LDA (ULDA) and orthogonal LDA (OLDA) are two representative algorithms from this family. The features in the reduced space of ULDA are uncorrelated, while the transformation, $G$, of OLDA has orthonormal columns, that is, $G^T G = I_\ell$. The LDA/GSVD algorithm proposed in reference 26, which overcomes the singularity problem via the generalized singular value decomposition (GSVD)[27], also belongs to this family. Discriminant analysis with an orthogonal transformation has also been studied in reference 30.

## 1.3   A UNIFIED FRAMEWORK FOR GENERALIZED LDA

The LDA extensions discussed in the last section employ different techniques to deal with the singularity problem. In this section, we present a four-step general framework for various generalized LDA algorithms. The presented framework unifies most of the generalized LDA algorithms. The properties of various algorithms as well as their relationships are elucidated from this framework. The unified framework consists of four steps described below:

1. Compute the eigenvalues, $\{\lambda_i\}_{i=1}^d$, of $S_t$ in Eq. (1.3) and the corresponding eigenvectors $\{u_i\}_{i=1}^d$, with $\lambda_1 \geq \cdots \geq \lambda_d$. Then $S_t$ can be expressed as $S_t = \sum_{i=1}^d \lambda_i u_i u_i^T$.

2. Given a transfer function $\Phi : \mathbb{R} \to \mathbb{R}$, let $\tilde{\lambda}_i = \Phi(\lambda_i)$, for all $i$. Construct the matrix $\tilde{S}_t$ as $\tilde{S}_t = \sum_{i=1}^d \tilde{\lambda}_i u_i u_i^T$.

3. Compute the eigenvectors, $\{\phi_i\}_{i=1}^q$, of $\tilde{S}_t^+ S_b$ corresponding to the nonzero eigenvalues, where $q = \text{rank}(S_b)$, $\tilde{S}_t^+$ denotes the pseudo-inverse of $\tilde{S}_t$ [27]. Construct the matrix $G$ as $G = [\phi_1, \ldots, \phi_q]$.

4. Optional orthogonalization step: Compute the QR decomposition [27] of $G$ as $G = QR$, where $Q \in \mathbb{R}^{d \times q}$ has orthonormal columns and $R \in \mathbb{R}^{q \times q}$ is upper triangular.

With this four-step procedure, the final transformation is given by either the matrix $G$ from step 3, if the optional orthogonalization step is not applied, or the matrix $Q$ from step 4 if the transformation matrix is required to be orthogonal. In this framework, different transfer functions, $\Phi$, in step 2 lead to different generalized LDA algorithms, as summarized below:

- In PCA+LDA, the intermediate dimensionality reduction stage by PCA keeps the top $p$ eigenvalues of $S_t$; thus it applies the following linear step function: $\Phi(\lambda_i) = \lambda_i$, for $1 \leq i \leq p$, and $\Phi(\lambda_i) = 0$, for $i > p$. The optional orthogonalization step is not employed in PCA+LDA.

- In regularized LDA (RLDA), a regularization term is applied to $S_t$ as $S_t + \mu I_d$, for some $\mu > 0$. It corresponds to the use of the following transfer function: $\Phi(\lambda_i) = \lambda_i + \mu$, for all $i$. The optional orthogonalization step is not employed in RLDA.

- In uncorrelated LDA (ULDA), the optimal transformation consists of the top eigenvectors of $S_t^+ S_b$ [24]. The corresponding transfer function is thus given by $\Phi(\lambda_i) = \lambda_i$, for all $i$. The same transfer function is used in orthogonal LDA (OLDA). The difference between ULDA and OLDA is that OLDA performs the optional orthogonalization step while it is not applied in ULDA.

- In orthogonal centroid method (OCM), the optimal transformation is given by the top eigenvectors of $S_b$ [25]. The transfer function is thus given by $\Phi(\lambda_i) = 1$, for all $i$. Since the eigenvectors of $S_b$ forms an orthonormal set, the optional orthogonalization step is not necessary in OCM.

It has been shown [31] that the regularization in RLDA is effective for nonzero eigenvalues only. Thus, we can apply the following transfer function for RLDA:

$$\Phi(\lambda_i) = \begin{cases} \lambda_i + \mu & \text{for } 1 \leq i \leq t, \\ 0 & \text{for } i > t, \end{cases}$$

**Table 1.1.** Transfer Functions for Different LDA Extensions

| | PCA+LDA | RLDA | ULDA/OLDA | OCM |
|---|---|---|---|---|
| $\Phi(\lambda_i) =$ | $\begin{cases} \lambda_i \text{ for } 1 \leq i \leq p \\ 0 \text{ for } i > p \end{cases}$ | $\begin{cases} \lambda_i + \mu \text{ for } 1 \leq i \leq t \\ 0 \quad\quad \text{ for } i > t \end{cases}$ | $\lambda_i$ | 1 |

where $t = \text{rank}(S_t)$. The transfer functions for different LDA extensions are summarized in Table 1.1.

In null space LDA (NLDA) [20, 32], the data are first projected onto the null space of $S_w$, which is then followed by classical LDA. It is not clear which transfer function $\Phi$ corresponds to the projection onto the null space of $S_w$. In reference 33, the equivalence relationship between NLDA and OLDA was established under a mild condition

$$C1 : \text{rank}(S_t) = \text{rank}(S_b) + \text{rank}(S_w), \tag{1.15}$$

which has been shown to hold for many high-dimensional data. Thus, for high-dimensional data, we can use the following transfer function for NLDA: $\Phi(\lambda_i) = \lambda_i$, for all $i$.

## 1.3.1 Analysis

The unified framework from the last section summarizes the commonalities and differences of various LDA-based algorithms. This unification of diverse algorithms into a common framework sheds light on the understanding of the key features of various algorithms as well as their relationship.

It is clear from Table 1.1 that ULDA is reduced to the OCM algorithm [25] when $S_t$ is a multiple of the identity matrix. Recent studies on the geometric representation of high-dimensional and small sample size data show that under mild conditions, the covariance matrix $S_t$ tends to a scaled identity matrix when the data dimension $d$ tends to infinity with the sample size $n$ fixed [34]. This implies that all the eigenvalues of $S_t$ are the same. In other words, the data behave as if the underlying distribution is spherical. In this case, OCM is equivalent to ULDA. This partially explains the effectiveness of OCM when working on high-dimensional data.

We can observe from Table 1.1 that when the reduced dimensionality, $p$, in the PCA stage of PCA+LDA is chosen to be the rank of $S_t$—that is, the PCA stage keeps all the information—then the transfer functions for PCA+LDA and ULDA are identical. That is, PCA+LDA is equivalent to ULDA in this case. It can also be observed from Table 1.1 that the transfer function for RLDA equals the one for ULDA when $\mu = 0$. Thus, ULDA can be considered as a special case of both PCA+LDA and RLDA.

It follows from the above discussion that when $\mu = 0$ in RLDA, and $p = \text{rank}(S_t)$ in PCA+LDA, they both reduce to ULDA. It has been shown that, under condition C1 in Eq. (1.15), the transformation matrix of ULDA lies in the null space of $S_w$ [33]. That is, $G^T S_w = 0$. Furthermore, it was shown in reference 31 that if $G^T S_w = 0$

holds, then the transformation matrix $G$ maps all data points from the same class to a common vector. This is an extension of the result in reference 32, which assumes that all classes in the data set have the same number of samples. Thus it follows that the ULDA transformation maps all data points from the same class to a common vector, provided that condition C1 is satisfied. This leads to a perfect separation between different classes in the dimensionality-reduced space. However, it may also result in overfitting. RLDA overcomes this limitation by choosing a nonzero regularization value $\mu$, while PCA+LDA overcomes this limitation by setting $p < \text{rank}(S_t)$.

The above analysis shows that the regularization in RLDA and the PCA dimensionality reduction in PCA+LDA are expected to alleviate the overfitting problem, provided that appropriate values for $\mu$ and $p$ can be estimated. Selecting an optimal value for a parameter such as $\mu$ in RLDA and $p$ in PCA+LDA from a given candidate set is called *model selection* [17]. Existing studies have focused on the estimation from a small candidate set, as it involves expensive matrix computations for each candidate value. However, a large candidate set is desirable in practice to achieve good performance. This has been one of the main reasons for their limited applicability in practice. To overcome this problem, an efficient model selection algorithm for RLDA was proposed in reference 31 and this algorithm can estimate an optimal value for $\mu$ from a large number of candidate values efficiently.

## 1.4    A LEAST SQUARES FORMULATION FOR LDA

In this section, we discuss recent developments on connecting LDA to multivariate linear regression (MLR). We first discuss the relationship between linear regression and LDA in the binary-class case. We then present multivariate linear regression with a specific class indicator matrix. This indicator matrix plays a key role in establishing the equivalence relationship between MLR and LDA in the multiclass case.

### 1.4.1    Linear Regression versus Fisher LDA

Given a data set of two classes, $\{(x_i, y_i)\}_{i=1}^n$, $x_i \in \mathbb{R}^d$ and $y_i \in \{-1, 1\}$, the linear regression model with the class label as the output has the following form:

$$f(x) = x^T w + b, \tag{1.16}$$

where $w \in \mathbb{R}^d$ is the weight vector, and $b$ is the bias of the linear model. A popular approach for estimating $w$ and $b$ is to minimize the sum-of-squares error function, called least squares, as follows:

$$L(w, b) = \frac{1}{2} \sum_{i=1}^n \|f(x_i) - y_i\|^2 = \frac{1}{2} \|X^T w + be - y\|^2, \tag{1.17}$$

where $X = [x_1, x_2, \ldots, x_n]$ is the data matrix, $e$ is the vector of all ones, and $y$ is the vector of class labels. Assume that both $\{x_i\}$ and $\{y_i\}$ have been centered, that is,

$\sum_{i=1}^{n} x_i = 0$ and $\sum_{i=1}^{n} y_i = 0$. It follows that

$$y_i \in \{-2n_2/n, 2n_1/n\},$$

where $n_1$ and $n_2$ denote the number of samples from the negative and positive classes, respectively. In this case, the bias term $b$ in Eq. (1.16) becomes zero and we construct a linear model $f(x) = x^T w$ by minimizing

$$L(w) = \frac{1}{2} ||X^T w - y||^2. \tag{1.18}$$

It can be shown that the optimal $w$ minimizing the objective function in Eq. (1.18) is given by [16, 17]

$$w = \left( X X^T \right)^{+} X y.$$

Note that the data matrix $X$ has been centered and thus $X X^T = n S_t$ and $X y = \frac{2n_1 n_2}{n} (c^{(1)} - c^{(2)})$. It follows that

$$w = \frac{2n_1 n_2}{n^2} S_t^{+} (c^{(1)} - c^{(2)}) = \frac{2n_1 n_2}{n^2} G^F,$$

where $G^F$ is the optimal solution to FLDA in Eq. (1.14). Hence linear regression with the class label as the output is equivalent to Fisher LDA, as the projection in FLDA is invariant of scaling. More details on this equivalence relationship can be found in references 15, 16, and 35.

## 1.4.2 Relationship Between Multivariate Linear Regression and LDA

In the multiclass case, we are given a data set consisting of $n$ samples $\{(x_i, y_i)\}_{i=1}^{n}$, where $x_i \in \mathbb{R}^d$ and $y_i \in \{1, 2, \ldots, k\}$ denotes the class label of the $i$th sample and $k > 2$. To apply the least squares formalism to the multiclass case, the 1-of-$k$ binary coding scheme is usually used to associate a vector-valued class code to each data point [15, 17]. In this coding scheme, the class indicator matrix, denoted as $Y_1 \in \mathbb{R}^{n \times k}$, is defined as follows:

$$Y_1(ij) = \begin{cases} 1 & \text{if } y_i = j, \\ 0 & \text{otherwise.} \end{cases} \tag{1.19}$$

It is known that the solution to least squares problem approximates the conditional expectation of the target values given the input [15]. One justification for using the 1-of-$k$ scheme is that, under this coding scheme, the conditional expectation is given by the vector of posterior class probabilities. However, these probabilities are usually approximated rather poorly [15]. There are also some other class indicator matrices considered in the literature. In particular, the indicator matrix $Y_2 \in \mathbb{R}^{n \times k}$, defined as

$$Y_2(ij) = \begin{cases} 1 & \text{if } y_i = j, \\ -1/(k-1) & \text{otherwise,} \end{cases} \tag{1.20}$$

has been introduced to extend support vector machines (SVM) for multiclass classi-fication [36] and to generalize the kernel target alignment measure [37], originally proposed in reference 38.

In multivariate linear regression, a $k$-tuple of discriminant functions

$$f(x) = (f_1(x), f_2(x), \ldots, f_k(x))$$

is considered for each $x \in \mathbb{R}^d$. Denote $\tilde{X} = [\tilde{x}_1, \ldots, \tilde{x}_n] \in \mathbb{R}^{d \times n}$ and $\tilde{Y} = (\tilde{Y}_{ij}) \in \mathbb{R}^{n \times k}$ as the centered data matrix $X$ and the centered indicator matrix $Y$, respectively. That is, $\tilde{x}_i = x_i - \bar{x}$ and $\tilde{Y}_{ij} = Y_{ij} - \bar{Y}_j$, where $\bar{x} = \frac{1}{n} \sum_{i=1}^{n} x_i$ and $\bar{Y}_j = \frac{1}{n} \sum_{i=1}^{n} Y_{ij}$. Then MLR computes the weight vectors, $\{w_j\}_{j=1}^{k} \in \mathbb{R}^d$, of the $k$ linear models, $f_j(x) = x^T w_j$, for $j = 1, \ldots, k$, via the minimization of the following sum-of-squares error function:

$$L(W) = \frac{1}{2} \|\tilde{X}^T W - \tilde{Y}\|_F^2 = \frac{1}{2} \sum_{j=1}^{k} \sum_{i=1}^{n} \|f_j(\tilde{x}_i) - \tilde{Y}_{ij}\|^2, \tag{1.21}$$

where $W = [w_1, w_2, \ldots, w_k]$ is the weight matrix and $\| \cdot \|_F$ denotes the Frobenius norm of a matrix [27]. The optimal $W$ is given by [15, 17]

$$W = \left(\tilde{X}\tilde{X}^T\right)^+ \tilde{X}\tilde{Y}, \tag{1.22}$$

which is dependent on the centered class indicator matrix $\tilde{Y}$.

Both $Y_1$ and $Y_2$ defined in Eqs. (1.19) and (1.20), as well as the one in reference 39, could be used to define the centered indicator matrix $\tilde{Y}$. An interesting connection between the linear regression model using $Y_1$ and LDA can be found in reference 17 (page 112). It can be shown that if $X^L = W_1^T \tilde{X}$ is the transformed data by $W_1$, where $W_1 = \left(\tilde{X}\tilde{X}^T\right)^+ \tilde{X}\tilde{Y}_1$ is the least squares solution in Eq. (1.22) using the centered indicator matrix $\tilde{Y}_1$, then LDA applied to $X^L$ is identical to LDA applied to $\tilde{X}$ in the original space. In this case, linear regression is applied as a preprocessing step before the classification and is in general not equivalent to LDA. The second indicator matrix $Y_2$ has been used in SVM, and the resulting model using $Y_2$ is also not equivalent to LDA in general. This is also the case for the indicator matrix in reference 39. One natural question is whether there exists a class indicator matrix $\tilde{Y} \in \mathbb{R}^{n \times k}$, with which multivariate linear regression is equivalent to LDA. If this is the case, then LDA can be formulated as a least squares problem in the multiclass case, and the generalizations of least squares can be readily applied to LDA.

In MLR, each $\tilde{x}_i$ is transformed to

$$(f_1(\tilde{x}_i), \ldots, f_k(\tilde{x}_i))^T = W^T \tilde{x}_i,$$

and the centered data matrix $\tilde{X} \in \mathbb{R}^{d \times n}$ is transformed to $W^T \tilde{X} \in \mathbb{R}^{k \times n}$, thus achiev-ing dimensionality reduction if $k < d$. Note that the transformation matrix $W$ in MLR is dependent on the centered class indicator matrix $\tilde{Y}$ as in Eq. (1.22). To derive a class indicator matrix for MLR with which the transformation matrix is related to that of LDA, it is natural to apply the class discrimination criterion used in LDA. We thus look for $\tilde{Y}$, which solves the following optimization problem:

$$\max_{\tilde{Y}} \qquad \text{trace}\left((W^T S_b W)(W^T S_t W)^+\right)$$
$$\text{subject to} \qquad W = \left(\tilde{X}\tilde{X}^T\right)^+ \tilde{X}\tilde{Y}, \tag{1.23}$$

where the pseudo-inverse is used as the matrix $\tilde{X}\tilde{X}^T$ can be singular.

In reference 40, a new class indicator matrix, called $Y_3$, is constructed and it was shown that $Y_3$ solves the optimization problem in Eq. (1.23). This new class indicator matrix $Y_3 = (Y_3(ij))_{ij} \in \mathbb{R}^{n \times k}$ is defined as follows:

$$Y_3(ij) = \begin{cases} \sqrt{\frac{n}{n_j}} - \sqrt{\frac{n_j}{n}} & \text{if } y_i = j, \\ -\sqrt{\frac{n_j}{n}} & \text{otherwise,} \end{cases} \tag{1.24}$$

where $n_j$ is the sample size of the $j$th class, and $n$ is the total sample size. Note that $Y_3$ defined above has been centered (in terms of rows), and thus $\tilde{Y}_3 = Y_3$. More importantly, it was shown in reference 40 that, under condition C1 in Eq. (1.15), multivariate linear regression with $Y_3$ as the class indicator matrix is equivalent to LDA. We outline the main result below and the detailed proof can be found in reference 40.

Recall that in LDA, the optimal transformation matrix ($G^{LDA}$) consists of the top eigenvectors of $S_t^+ S_b$ corresponding to the nonzero eigenvalues. On the other hand, since $\tilde{X}\tilde{X}^T = nS_t$ and $\tilde{X}Y_3 = nH_b$, where $S_t$ and $H_b$ are defined in Eqs. (1.3) and (1.5), respectively, the optimal weight matrix $W^{MLR}$ for MLR in Eq. (1.22) can be expressed as

$$W^{MLR} = \left(\tilde{X}\tilde{X}^T\right)^+ \tilde{X}Y_3 = (nS_t)^+ nH_b = S_t^+ H_b. \tag{1.25}$$

It can be shown that the transformation matrix $G^{LDA}$ of LDA, which consists of the top eigenvectors of $S_t^+ S_b$, and the projection matrix for MLR that is given in Eq. (1.25) are related as follows [40]:

$$W^{MLR} = \left[G^{LDA}\Sigma, 0\right] Q^T,$$

where $\Sigma$ is a diagonal matrix and $Q$ is an orthogonal matrix.

The K-Nearest-Neighbor (K-NN) algorithm [16] based on the Euclidean distance is commonly applied as the classifier in the dimensionality-reduced space of LDA. If we apply $W^{MLR}$ for dimensionality reduction before K-NN, the matrix $W^{MLR}$ is invariant of an orthogonal transformation, since any orthogonal transformation preserves all pairwise distance. Thus $W^{MLR}$ is essentially equivalent to $\left[G^{LDA}\Sigma, 0\right]$ or $G^{LDA}\Sigma$, as the removal of zero columns does not change the pairwise distance either. Thus the essential difference between $W^{MLR}$ and $G^{LDA}$ is the diagonal matrix $\Sigma$. Interestingly, it was shown in reference 40 that the matrix $\Sigma$ is an identity matrix under the condition C1 defined in Eq. (1.15). This implies that multivariate linear regression with $Y_3$ as the class indicator matrix is equivalent to LDA provided that the condition C1 is satisfied. Thus LDA can be formulated as a least squares problem in the multiclass case. Experimental results in reference 40 show that condition C1 is likely to hold for high-dimensional and undersampled data.

## 1.5  SEMISUPERVISED LDA

Semisupervised learning, which occupies the middle ground between supervised learning (in which all training examples are labeled) and unsupervised learning (in which no labeled data are given), has received considerable attention recently [41–43]. The least square LDA formulation from the last section results in Laplacian-regularized LDA [44]. Furthermore, it naturally leads to semisupervised dimensionality reduction by incorporating the unlabeled data through the graph Laplacian.

### 1.5.1  Graph Laplacian

Given a data set $\{x_i\}_{i=1}^n$, a weighted graph can be constructed where each node in the graph corresponds to a data point in the data set. The weight $S_{ij}$ between two nodes $x_i$ and $x_j$ is commonly defined as follows:

$$S_{ij} = \begin{cases} \exp\left(-\frac{\|x_i - x_j\|^2}{\sigma}\right), & x_i \in N_\kappa(x_j) \text{ or } x_j \in N_\kappa(x_i), \\ 0 & \text{otherwise,} \end{cases} \quad (1.26)$$

where both $\kappa$ and $\sigma > 0$ are parameters to be specified, and $x_i \in N_\kappa(x_j)$ implies that $x_i$ is among the $\kappa$ nearest neighbors of $x_j$ [45]. Let $S$ be the similarity matrix whose $(i, j)$th entry is $S_{ij}$. To learn an appropriate representation $\{z_i\}_{i=1}^n$ which preserves locality structure, it is common to minimize the following objective function [45]:

$$\sum_{i,j} \|z_i - z_j\|^2 S_{ij}. \quad (1.27)$$

Intuitively, if $x_i$ and $x_j$ are close to each other in the original space—that is, $S_{ij}$ is large—then $\|z_i - z_j\|$ tends to be small if the objective function in Eq. (1.27) is minimized. Thus the locality structure in the original space is preserved.

Define the Laplacian matrix $L$ as $L = D - S$, where $D$ is a diagonal matrix whose diagonal entries are the column sums of $S$. That is, $D_{ii} = \sum_{j=1}^n S_{ij}$. Note that $L$ is symmetric and positive semidefinite. It can be verified that

$$\frac{1}{2} \sum_{i=1}^n \sum_{j=1}^n \|z_i - z_j\|^2 S_{ij} = \text{trace}(ZLZ^T), \quad (1.28)$$

where $Z = [z_1, \ldots, z_n]$.

## 1.5.2   A Regularization Framework
## for Semisupervised LDA

In semisupervised LDA, information from unlabeled data is incorporated into the formulation via a regularization term defined as in Eq. (1.28). Mathematically, semisupervised LDA computes an optimal weight matrix $W^*$, which solves the following optimization problem:

$$W^* = \arg \min_{W} \left\{ \| \tilde{X}^T W - Y_3 \|_F^2 + \gamma \text{trace}(W^T \tilde{X} L \tilde{X}^T W) \right\}, \qquad (1.29)$$

where $\gamma \geq 0$ is a tuning parameter and $Y_3$ is the class indicator matrix defined in Eq. (1.24). Since the Laplacian regularizer in Eq. (1.29) does not depend on the label information, the unlabeled data can be readily incorporated into the formulation. Thus the locality structures of both labeled and unlabeled data points are captured through the transformation $W$. It is clear that $W^*$ is given by

$$W^* = \left( \gamma \tilde{X} L \tilde{X}^T + \tilde{X} \tilde{X}^T \right)^+ n H_b. \qquad (1.30)$$

## 1.6   EXTENSIONS TO KERNEL-INDUCED
## FEATURE SPACE

The discussion so far focuses on linear dimensionality reduction and regression. It has been shown that both discriminant analysis and regression can be adapted to nonlinear models by using the kernel trick [46–48]. Mika et al. [49] extended the Fisher discriminant analysis to its kernel version in the binary-class case. Following the work in reference 50, Baudat and Anouar [51] proposed the generalized discriminant analysis (GDA) algorithm for multiclass problems. The equivalence relationship between kernel discriminant analysis (KDA) and kernel regression has been studied in reference 35 for binary-class problems. The analysis presented in this chapter can be applied to extend this equivalence result to multiclass problems.

A symmetric function $\kappa : \mathcal{X} \times \mathcal{X} \rightarrow \mathbb{R}$, where $\mathcal{X}$ denotes the input space, is called a kernel function if it satisfies the finitely positive semidefinite property [46]. That is, for any $x_1, \ldots, x_n \in \mathcal{X}$, the kernel *Gram* matrix $K \in \mathbb{R}^{n \times n}$, defined by $K_{ij} = \kappa(x_i, x_j)$, is positive semidefinite. Any kernel function $\kappa$ implicitly maps the input set $\mathcal{X}$ to a high-dimensional (possibly infinite) Hilbert space $\mathcal{H}_\kappa$ equipped with the inner product $(\cdot, \cdot)_{\mathcal{H}_\kappa}$ through a mapping $\phi_\kappa$ from $\mathcal{X}$ to $\mathcal{H}_\kappa$:

$$\kappa(x, z) = (\phi_\kappa(x), \phi_\kappa(z))_{\mathcal{H}_\kappa}.$$

In KDA, three scatter matrices are defined in the feature space $\mathcal{H}_\kappa$ as follows:

$$S_w^\phi = \frac{1}{n} \sum_{j=1}^{k} \sum_{x \in X_j} \left( \phi(x) - c_j^\phi \right) \left( \phi(x) - c_j^\phi \right)^T, \qquad (1.31)$$

$$S_b^\phi = \frac{1}{n} \sum_{j=1}^{k} n_j \left( c_j^\phi - c^\phi \right) \left( c_j^\phi - c^\phi \right)^T, \tag{1.32}$$

$$S_t^\phi = \frac{1}{n} \sum_{j=1}^{k} \sum_{x \in X_j} \left( \phi(x) - c^\phi \right) \left( \phi(x) - c^\phi \right)^T, \tag{1.33}$$

where $c_j^\phi$ is the centroid of the $j$th class and $c^\phi$ is the global centroid in the feature space. Similar to the linear case, the transformation $\mathcal{G}$ of KDA can be computed by solving the following optimization problem:

$$\mathcal{G} = \arg \max_{\mathcal{G}} \left\{ \operatorname{trace} \left( \left( \mathcal{G}^T S_t^\phi \mathcal{G} \right)^+ \mathcal{G}^T S_b^\phi \mathcal{G} \right) \right\}. \tag{1.34}$$

It follows from the Representer Theorem [47] that columns of $\mathcal{G}$ lie in the span of the images of training data in the feature space. That is,

$$\mathcal{G} = \phi(X)B, \tag{1.35}$$

for some matrix $B \in \mathbb{R}^{n \times (k-1)}$, where

$$\phi(X) = [\phi(x_1), \dots, \phi(x_n)]$$

is the data matrix in the feature space. Substituting Eq. (1.35) into Eq. (1.34), we can obtain the matrix $B$ by solving the following optimization problem:

$$B = \arg \max_{B} \left\{ \operatorname{trace} \left( \left( B^T S_t^K B \right)^+ B^T S_b^K B \right) \right\}, \tag{1.36}$$

where $S_b^K = KY_3 Y_3^T K$, $S_t^K = K^2$, and $K = \phi(X)^T \phi(X)$ is the kernel matrix.

It can be verified that $S_b^K$ and $S_t^K$ are the between-class and total scatter matriices, respectively, when each column in $K$ is considered as a data point in the $n$-dimensional space. It follows from Theorem 5.3 in reference 33 that the condition C1 in Eq. (1.15) is satisfied if all the training data points are linearly independent. Therefore, if the kernel matrix $K$ is nonsingular (hence its columns are linearly independent), then kernel discriminant analysis (KDA) and kernel regression using $Y_3$ as the class indicator matrix are essentially equivalent. This extends the equivalence result between KDA and kernel regression in the binary-class case, originally proposed in reference 35, to the multiclass setting.

To overcome the singularity problem in kernel discriminant analysis (KDA), a number of techniques have been developed in the literature. Regularization was employed in reference 52. The QR decomposition was employed in reference 51 to avoid the singularity problem by removing the zero eigenvalues. Lu et al. [53, 54] extended the direct LDA (DLDA) algorithm [55] to kernel direct LDA based on the kernel trick. PCA+LDA was discussed in reference 56, and a *complete* algorithm was proposed to derive discriminant vectors from the null space of the within-class scatter matrix and its orthogonal complement. Recently, similar ideas were extended to the feature space based on kernel PCA [57].

Another challenging issue in applying KDA is the selection of an appropriate kernel function. Recall that kernel methods work by embedding the input data into some high-dimensional feature space. The key fact underlying the success of kernel methods is that the embedding into feature space can be determined uniquely by specifying a kernel function that computes the dot product between data points in the feature space. In other words, the kernel function implicitly defines the nonlinear mapping to the feature space and expensive computations in the high-dimensional feature space can be avoided by evaluating the kernel function. Thus one of the central issues in kernel methods is the selection of kernels.

To automate kernel-based learning algorithms, it is desirable to integrate the tuning of kernels into the learning process. This problem has been addressed from different perspectives recently. Lanckriet et al. [58] pioneered the work of multiple kernel learning (MKL) in which the optimal kernel matrix is obtained as a linear combination of prespecified kernel matrices. It was shown [58] that the coefficients in MKL can be determined by solving convex programs in the case of Support Vector Machines (SVM). While most existing work focuses on learning kernels for SVM, Fung et al. [59] proposed to learn kernels for discriminant analysis. Based on ideas from MKL, this problem was reformulated as a semidefinite program (SDP) [60] in reference 61 for binary-class problems.

By optimizing an alternative criterion, an SDP formulation for the KDA kernel learning problem in the multiclass case was proposed in reference 62. To reduce the computational cost of the SDP formulation, an approximate scheme was also developed. Furthermore, it was shown that the regularization parameter for KDA can also be learned automatically in this framework [62]. Although the approximate SDP formulation in reference 62 is scalable in terms of the number of classes, interior point algorithms [63] for solving SDP have an inherently large time complexity and thus it can not be applied to large-scale problems. To improve the efficiency of this formulation, a quadratically constrained quadratic program (QCQP) [63] formulation was proposed in reference 64 and it is more scalable than the SDP formulations.

## 1.7   OTHER LDA EXTENSIONS

Sparsity has recently received much attention for extending existing algorithms to induce sparse solutions [65–67]. $L_1$-norm penalty has been used in regression [68], known as LASSO, and SVM [69, 70] to achieve model sparsity. Sparsity often leads to easy interpretation and good generalization ability of the resulting model. Sparse Fisher LDA has been proposed in reference 35, for binary-class problems. Based on the equivalence relationship between LDA and MLR, a multiclass sparse LDA formulation was proposed in reference 71 and an entire solution path for LDA was also obtained through the LARS algorithm [72].

The discussions in this chapter focus on supervised approaches. In the unsupervised setting, LDA can be applied to find the discriminant subspace for clustering, such as K-means clustering. In this case, an iterative algorithm can be derived alternating between clustering and discriminant subspace learning via LDA [73–75].

Interestingly, it can be shown that this iterative procedure can be simplified and is essentially equivalent to kernel K-means with a specific kernel Gram matrix [76].

When the data in question are given as high-order representations such as 2D and 3D images, it is natural to encode them using high-order tensors. Discriminant tensor factorization, which is a two-dimensional extension of LDA, for a collection of two-dimensional images has been studied [77]. It was further extended to higher-order tensors in reference 78. However, the computational convergency of these iterative algorithms [77, 78] is not guaranteed. Recently, a novel discriminant tensor factorization procedure with the convergency property was proposed [79]. Other recent extensions on discriminant tensor factorization as well as their applications to image analysis can be found in reference 80.

## 1.8  CONCLUSION

In this chapter, we provide a unified view of various LDA algorithms and discuss recent developments on connecting LDA to multivariate linear regression. We show that MLR with a specific class indicator matrix is equivalent to LDA under a mild condition, which has been shown to hold for many high-dimensional and small sample size data. This implies that LDA reduces to a least squares problem under this condition, and its solution can be obtained by solving a system of liner equations. Based on this equivalence result, we show that LDA can be applied in the semisupervised setting. We further extend the discussion to the kernel-induced feature space and present recent developments on kernel learning. Finally, we discuss several other recent developments on discriminant analysis, including sparse LDA, unsupervised LDA, and tensor LDA.

## REFERENCES

1. A. K. Jain, P. Flynn, and A. A. Ross, *Handbook of Biometrics*, Springer, New York, 2007.
2. A. K. Jain and S. Z. Li, *Handbook of Face Recognition*, Springer-Verlag, New York, 2005.
3. A. K. Jain, A. A. Ross, and S. Prabhakar, An introduction to biometric recognition, *IEEE Trans. Circuits Syt. Video Technol.* **14**(1):4–20, 2004.
4. R. E. Bellman, *Adaptive Control Processes: A Guided Tour*, Princeton University Press, Princeton, NJ, 1961.
5. D. Donoho, High-dimensional data analysis: The curses and blessings of dimensionality, in *American Mathematical Society Lecture—Math Challenges of the 21st Century*, August 2000.
6. S. Yan, D. Xu, B. Zhang, H.-J. Zhang, Q. Yang, and S. Lin, Graph embedding and extensions: A general framework for dimensionality reduction. *IEEE Trans. Pattern Anal. Mach. Intell.* **29**(1):40–51, 2007.
7. R. A. Fisher, The use of multiple measurements in taxonomic problems. *Ann. Eugenics* **7**:179–188, 1936.
8. K. Fukunaga, *Introduction to Statistical Pattern Recognition*, 2nd edition, Academic Press Professional, San Diego, 1990.
9. I. T. Jolliffe, *Principal Component Analysis*, 2nd edition, Springer-Verlag, New York, 2002.
10. M. Belkin and P. Niyogi, Laplacian eigenmaps for dimensionality reduction and data representation, *Neural Comput.* **15**(6):1373–1396, 2003.

11. C. J. C. Burges. Geometric methods for feature extraction and dimensional reduction, in O. Maimon and L. Rokach, editors, *Mining and Knowledge Discovery Handbook: A Complete Guide for Practitioners and Researchers*, Springer, New York, 2005, pp. 59–92.
12. S. T. Roweis and L. K. Saul, Nonlinear dimensionality reduction by locally linear embedding, *Science* **290**(5500):2323–6, 2000.
13. L. K. Saul, K. Q. Weinberger, J. H. Ham, F. Sha, and D. D. Lee, Spectral methods for dimensionality reduction, in O. Chapelle B. Schöelkopf and A. Zien, editors, *Semisupervised Learning*, MIT Press, Cambridge, MA, 293–308, 2006.
14. J. B. Tenenbaum, V. d. Silva, and J. C. Langford, A global geometric framework for nonlinear dimensionality reduction, *Science* **290**(5500):279–294, 2000.
15. C. M. Bishop, *Pattern Recognition and Machine Learning*, Springer, New York, 2006.
16. R. O. Duda, P. E. Hart, and D. Stork, *Pattern Classification*, John Wiley & Sons, New York, 2000.
17. T. Hastie, R. Tibshirani, and J.H. Friedman, *The Elements of Statistical Learning: Data Mining, Inference, and Prediction*, Springer, New York, 2001.
18. A. M. Martinez and M. Zhu, Where are linear feature extraction methods applicable? *IEEE Trans. Pattern Anal. Mach. Intell.* **27**(12):1934–1944, 2005.
19. P. N. Belhumeour, J. P. Hespanha, and D. J. Kriegman, Eigenfaces vs. Fisherfaces: Recognition using class specific linear projection. *IEEE Trans. Pattern Anal. Mach. Intell.* **19**(7):711–720, 1997.
20. L. F. Chen, H. Y. M. Liao, M. T. Ko, J. C. Lin, and G. J. Yu, A new lda-based face recognition system which can solve the small sample size problem, *Pattern Recognit* **33**:1713–1726, 2000.
21. Y. Guo, T. Hastie, and R. Tibshirani, Regularized linear discriminant analysis and its application in microarrays, *Biostatistics* **8**(1):86–100, 2007.
22. A. M. Martinez and A. C. Kak, PCA versus LDA, *IEEE Trans. Pattern Anal. Mach. Intell.* **23**(2):228–233, 2001.
23. X. Wang and X. Tang, A unified framework for subspace face recognition. *IEEE Trans. Pattern Anal. Mach. Intell.* **26**(9):1222–1228, 2004.
24. J. Ye, Characterization of a family of algorithms for generalized discriminant analysis on undersampled problems, *J. Mach. Learning Res.* **6**:483–502, 2005.
25. H. Park, M. Jeon, and J. B. Rosen, Lower dimensional representation of text data based on centroids and least squares, *BIT* **43**(2):1–22, 2003.
26. P. Howland, M. Jeon, and H. Park, Structure preserving dimension reduction for clustered text data based on the generalized singular value decomposition, *SIAM J. Matrix Anal. Appl.* **25**(1):165–179, 2003.
27. G. H. Golub and C. F. Van Loan, *Matrix Computations*, 3rd edition, The Johns Hopkins University Press, Baltimore, 1996.
28. W. Zhao, R. Chellappa, and P. Phillips, Subspace linear discriminant analysis for face recognition, Technical Report CAR-TR-914, Center for Automation Research, University of Maryland, 1999.
29. V. N. Vapnik. *Statistical Learning Theory*, John Wiley & Sons, New York, 1998.
30. L. Duchene and S. Leclerq, An optimal transformation for discriminant and principal component analysis, *IEEE Trans. Pattern Anal. Mach. Intell.* **10**(6):978–983, 1988.
31. J. Ye, T. Xiong, Q. Li, R. Janardan, J. Bi, V. Cherkassky, and C. Kambhamettu, Efficient model selection for regularized linear discriminant analysis, in *Proceedings of the 15th ACM International Conference on Information and Knowledge Management*, 2006, pp. 532–539.
32. H. Cevikalp, M. Neamtu, M. Wilkes, and A. Barkana, Discriminative common vectors for face recognition, *IEEE Trans. Pattern Anal. Mach. Intell.* **27**(1):4–13, 2005.
33. J. Ye and T. Xiong, Computational and theoretical analysis of null space and orthogonal linear discriminant analysis, *J. Mach. Learning Res.* **7**:1183–1204, 2006.
34. P. Hall, J. S. Marron, and A. Neeman, Geometric representation of high dimension, low sample size data, *J. R. Stat. Soc. Ser. B* **67**:427–444, 2005.
35. S. Mika, *Kernel Fisher Discriminants*, Ph.D. thesis, University of Technology, Berlin, 2002.
36. Y. Lee, Y. Lin, and G. Wahba, Multicategory support vector machines, theory, and application to the classification of microarray data and satellite radiance data, *J. Am. Stat. Assoc.* **99**:67–81, 2004.

37. Y. Guermeur, A. Lifchitz, and R. Vert, A kernel for protein secondary structure prediction, in *Kernel Methods in Computational Biology*, The MIT Press, Cambridge, MA, 2004, pp. 193–206.

38. N. Cristianini, J. Kandola, A. Elisseeff, and J. Shawe-Taylor, On kernel target alignment, in *Advances in Neural Information Processing Systems*, The MIT Press, Cambridge, MA, 2001.

39. C. Park and H. Park, A relationship between LDA and the generalized minimum squared error solution, *SIAM J. Matrix Anal. Appl.* **27**(2):474–492, 2005.

40. J. Ye, Least squares linear discriminant analysis, in *Proceedings of the 24th International Conference on Machine Learning*, 2007, pp. 1087–1093.

41. O. Chapelle, B. Schölkopf, and A. Zien, editors. *Semi-Supervised Learning*. MIT Press, Cambridge, MA, 2006.

42. D. Zhou, O. Bousquet, T. Lal, J. Weston, and B. Schölkopf, Learning with local and global consistency, in *Advances in Neural Information Processing Systems*, 2003, pp. 321–328.

43. X. Zhu, Z. Ghahramani, and J. Lafferty, Semi-supervised learning using Gaussian fields and harmonic functions, in *Proceedings of the 20th International Conference on Machine Learning*, 2003, pp. 912–919.

44. J. Chen, J. Ye, and Q. Li, Integrating global and local structures: A least squares framework for dimensionality reduction, in *IEEE Computer Society Conference on Computer Vision and Pattern Recognition*, 2007, pp. 1–8.

45. M. Belkin and P. Niyogi, Laplacian eigenmaps and sepctral techniques for embedding and clustering, *Adv. Neural Inf. Processing Sys.* **15**:585–591, 2001.

46. N. Cristianini and J. S. Taylor, *An Introduction to Support Vector Machines and other Kernel-Based Learning Methods*, Cambridge University Press, New York, 2000.

47. S. Schölkopf and A. Smola, *Learning with Kernels: Support Vector Machines,Regularization, Optimization and Beyond*, MIT Press, Cambridge, MA, 2002.

48. J. Shawe-Taylor and N. Cristianini, *Kernel Methods for Pattern Analysis*, Cambridge University Press, New York, 2004.

49. S. Mika, G. Rätsch, J. Weston, B. Schölkopf, and K.-R. Müller, Fisher discriminant analysis with kernels, in Y.-H. Hu, J. Larsen, E. Wilson, and S. Douglas, editors, *Neural Networks for Signal Processing IX*, IEEE, New York, 1999, pp. 41–48.

50. B. Schölkopf, A. J. Smola, and K-R. Müller, Nonlinear component analysis as a kernel eigenvalue problem, *Neural Comput.* **10**(5):1299–1319, 1998.

51. G. Baudat and F. Anouar, Generalized discriminant analysis using a kernel approach, *Neural Comput.* **12**(10):2385–2404, 2000.

52. S. Mika, G. Rätsch, J. Weston, B. Schölkopf, A. Smola, and K.-R. Müller, Constructing descriptive and discriminative nonlinear features: Rayleigh coefficients in kernel feature spaces, *IEEE Trans. Pattern Anal. Mach. Intell.* **25**(5):623–633, 2003.

53. J. Lu, K. N. Plataniotis, and A. N. Venetsanopoulos, Face recognition using kernel direct discriminant analysis algorithms, *IEEE Trans. Neural Networks* **14**(1):117– 126, 2003.

54. J. Lu, K. N. Plataniotis, A. N. Venetsanopoulos, and J. Wang, An efficient kernel discriminant analysis method, *Pattern Recognit.* **38**(10):1788–1790, 2005.

55. H. Yu and J. Yang, A direct LDA algorithm for high-dimensional data with applications to face recognition, *Pattern Recognit.* **34**:2067–2070, 2001.

56. J. Yang and J. Yang, Why can LDA be performed in PCA transformed space? *Pattern Recognit.* **36**(2):563–566, 2003.

57. J. Yang, A. F. Frangi, J. Yang, D. Zhang, and Z. Jin, KPCA plus LDA: A complete kernel fisher discriminant framework for feature extraction and recognition. *IEEE Trans. Pattern Anal. Mach. Intell.* **27**(2):230–244, 2005.

58. G. R. G. Lanckriet, N. Cristianini, P. Bartlett, L. E. Ghaoui, and M. I. Jordan, Learning the kernel matrix with semidefinite programming, *J. Mach. Learning Res.* **5**:27–72, 2004.

59. G. Fung, M. Dundar, J. Bi, and B. Rao, A fast iterative algorithm for Fisher discriminant using heterogeneous kernels, in *Proceedings of the Twenty-First International Conference on Machine Learning*, 2004.

60. L. Vandenberghe and S. Boyd, Semidefinite programming, *SIAM Rev.* **38**(1):49–95, 1996.

61. S.-J. Kim, A. Magnani, and S. Boyd, Optimal kernel selection in kernel Fisher discriminant analysis, in *Proceedings of the Twenty-Third International Conference on Machine Learning*, 2006, pp. 465–472.
62. J. Ye, J. Chen, and S. Ji, Discriminant kernel and regularization parameter learning via semidefinite programming, in *Proceedings of the Twenty-Fourth International Conference on Machine Learning*, 2007, pp. 1095–1102.
63. S. Boyd and L. Vandenberghe, *Convex Optimization*, Cambridge University Press, New York, 2004.
64. J. Ye, S. Ji, and J. Chen, Learning the kernel matrix in discriminant analysis via quadratically constrained quadratic programming, in *Proceedings of the 13th ACM SIGKDD International Conference on Knowledge Discovery and Data Mining*, 2007, pp. 854–863.
65. A. d'Aspremont, L. E. Ghaoui, M. I. Jordan, and G. R. G. Lanckriet, A direct formulation for sparse PCA using semidefinite programming, *SIAM Rev.* **49**(3):434–448, 2007.
66. I. T. Jolliffe and M. Uddin, A modified principal component technique based on the lasso, *J. Comput. Graph. Stat.* **12**:531–547, 2003.
67. H. Zou, T. Hastie, and R. Tibshirani, Sparse principal component analysis, *J. Comput. Graph. Stat.* **15**(2):265–286, 2006.
68. R. Tibshirani, Regression shrinkage and selection via the lasso, *J. Royal Stat. Soc. Ser. B* (1):267–288, 1996.
69. L. Wang and X. Shen, On $L_1$-norm multiclass support vector machines: Methodology and theory, *J. Am. Stat. Assoc.* **102**(478):583–594, 2007.
70. J. Zhu, S. Rosset, T. Hastie, and R. Tibshirani, 1-Norm support vector machines, in *Advances in Neural Information Processing Systems*, 2003.
71. J. Ye, J. Chen, R. Janardan, and S. Kumar, Developmental stage annotation of *Drosophila* gene expression pattern images via an entire solution path for LDA, in *ACM Transactions on Knowledge Discovery from Data, Special Issue on Bioinformatics*, 2008.
72. B. Efron, T. Hastie, I. Johnstone, and R. Tibshirani, Least angle regression (with discussion). *Ann. Stat.*, **32**(2):407–499, 2004.
73. F. De la Torre and T. Kanade, Discriminative cluster analysis, in *Proceedings of the Twenty-Third International Conference on Machine Learning*, 2006, pp. 241–248.
74. C. Ding and T. Li, Adaptive dimension reduction using discriminant analysis and k-means clustering, in *Proceedings of the Twenty-Fourth International Conference on Machine Learning*, 521–528, 2007.
75. J. Ye, Z. Zhao, and H. Liu, Adaptive distance metric learning for clustering, in *IEEE Conference on Computer Vision and Pattern Recognition*, 2007.
76. J. Ye, Z. Zhao, and M. Wu, Discriminative $k$-means for clustering, in *Proceedings of the Annual Conference on Advances in Neural Information Processing Systems*, 2007, pp. 1649–1656.
77. J. Ye, R. Janardan, and Q. Li, Two-dimensional linear discriminant analysis, in *Proceedings of the Annual Conference on Advances in Neural Information Processing Systems*, 2004, pp. 1569–1576.
78. S. Yan, D. Xu, Q. Yang, L. Zhang, X. Tang, and H. Zhang, Discriminant analysis with tensor representation, in *Proceedings of the International Conference on Computer Vision and Pattern Recogniton*, 2005.
79. H. Wang, S. Yan, T. Huang, and X. Tang, A convergent solution to tensor subspace learning, in *Proceedings of the International Joint Conference on Artificial Intelligence*, 2007.
80. D. Tao, X. Li, X. Wu, and S. J. Maybank, General tensor discriminant analysis and gabor features for gait recognition. *IEEE Trans. Pattern Anal. Mach. Intell.* **29**(10):1700–1715, 2007.

# Chapter 2

# A Taxonomy of Emerging Multilinear Discriminant Analysis Solutions for Biometric Signal Recognition

**Haiping Lu, Konstantinos N. Plataniotis, and Anastasios N. Venetsanopoulos**

## 2.1 INTRODUCTION

Many biometric signals, such as fingerprint, palmprint, ear, face images, and gait silhouettes sequences, are naturally multidimensional objects, which are formally referred to as tensor objects. The elements of a tensor are to be addressed by a number of indices [1]. The number of indices used in the description defines the order of the tensor object, and each index defines one "mode."

Gray-level biometric images,[1] such as face images, are naturally second-order tensors with the column and row modes [2, 3]. Color biometric images are naturally third-order tensors with the column, row, and color modes [4, 5]. Three-dimensional gray-level faces are naturally third-order tensors with the column, row, and depth modes [6, 7], and the popular Gabor faces [8] are third-order tensors with the column, row, and Gabor modes. In many surveillance applications, the (sequential) biometric signals observed in surveillance video sequences [9] are naturally higher-order tensors. Binary gait silhouette sequences, the input to most (if not all) gait recognition

---

[1] The discussion here applies to images in general; however, since this book is on biometrics, we put emphasis on biometric signals in this chapter.

*Biometrics: Theory, Methods, and Applications.* Edited by Boulgouris, Plataniotis, and Micheli-Tzanakou

algorithms [10–12], as well as other gray-level biometric video sequences, can be viewed as third-order tensors with the column, row, and time modes. Naturally, color biometric video sequences are fourth-order tensors with the addition of a color mode.

For illustration, Figure 2.1 shows the natural representations of three commonly used biometric signals, a second-order face tensor with the column and row modes in Figure 2.1a, a third-order Gabor face [2, 8, 13] tensor with the column, row, and Gabor modes in Figure 2.1b, and a third-order gait silhouette sequence tensor [14] with the column, row, and time modes in Figure 2.1c.

The tensor space where a typical biometric tensor object is specified is often high-dimensional, and recognition methods operating directly on this space suffer from the so-called curse of dimensionality [15]. On the other hand, the classes of a particular biometric signal, such as face images, are usually highly constrained and belong to

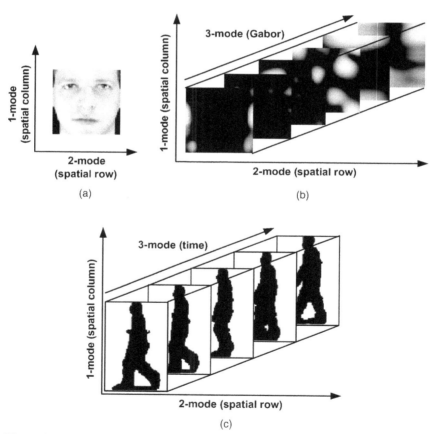

**Figure 2.1.** Biometric data represented naturally as tensors: **(a)** A 2-D face tensor, **(b)** a 3-D Gabor-face tensor, and **(c)** a 3-D gait (silhouette) tensor.

a subspace, a manifold of intrinsically low dimension [15, 16]. Feature extraction or dimensionality reduction is thus an attempt to transform a high-dimensional data set into a low-dimensional space of equivalent representation while retaining most of the underlying structure [17]. Traditionally, feature extraction algorithms operate on one-dimensional objects, that is, first-order tensors (vectors); and any tensor object with order greater than one, such as images and videos, have to be reshaped (vectorized) into vectors first before processing. However, it is well understood that reshaping breaks the natural structure and correlation in the original data, removing redundancies and/or higher-order dependencies present in the original data set and losing potentially more compact or useful representations that can be obtained in the original form.

By recognizing the fact that tensor objects are naturally multidimensional objects instead of one-dimensional objects, multilinear feature extraction algorithms [2, 14, 18–20] operating directly on the tensorial representations rather than their vectorized versions are emerging, partly due to the recent development in multilinear algebra [1, 21, 22]. The multilinear principal component analysis (MPCA) framework [14][2] attempts to determine a multilinear projection that projects the original tensor objects into a lower-dimensional tensor subspace while preserving the variation in the original data. It can be further extended through the combination with classical approaches [14, 18, 25] and has achieved good results when applied to the gait recognition problem. Nonetheless, MPCA is an unsupervised method and the class information is not used in the feature extraction process. There has been a growing interest in the development of supervised multilinear feature extraction algorithms. A two-dimensional linear discriminant analysis (2DLDA) was proposed in reference 26; and later a more general extension, the Discriminant Analysis with Tensor Representation (DATER),[3] was proposed in reference 2. They maximize a tensor-based scatter ratio criterion and the application to the face recognition problem showed better recognition results than linear discriminant analysis (LDA). In reference 19, a so-called general tensor discriminant analysis (GTDA) algorithm is proposed by maximizing a scatter difference criterion, and it is used as a preprocessing step in tensorial gait data classification [19]. All these methodologies are based on the tensor-to-tensor projection (TTP). The so-called Tensor Rank-one Discriminant Analysis (TR1DA) algorithm [27, 28], which uses the scatter difference criterion, obtains a number of rank-one projections from the repeatedly calculated residues of the original tensor data and it can be viewed as a tensor-to-vector projection (TVP). This "greedy" approach is a heuristic method originally proposed in reference 29 for tensor approximation. In reference 30, an uncorrelated multilinear discriminant analysis (UMLDA) approach is proposed to extract uncorrelated features through TVP. The extensions of linear graph-embedding algorithms were also introduced similarly in references 31–35.

---

[2]An earlier version with a slightly different approach appears in reference 23 and a different formulation is in reference 24.

[3]Here, we adopt the name that was used when the algorithm was first proposed, which is more commonly referred to in the literature.

In this chapter, we focus primarily on the development of supervised multi-linear methodologies, in particular the multilinear discriminant analysis (MLDA) algorithms, the multilinear extensions of the well-known LDA algorithm. The objective is to answer the following two questions regarding MLDA so that the interested researchers/practitioners can grasp multilinear concepts with ease and clarity for practical usage and further research/development:

1. What are the various multilinear projections and how are they related to traditional linear projection?
2. What are the relationships (similarities and differences) among the existing MLDA variants?

First in Section 2.2, basic multilinear algebra is reviewed and the commonly used tensor distance measure is shown to be equivalent to the Euclidean distance for vectors. Next, Section 2.3 discusses various multilinear projections including linear projection: from vector to vector, from tensor to tensor, and from tensor to vector, based on which the two general categories of MLDA are introduced. Commonly used separation criteria and initialization methods are then discussed and the underlying connections between the LDA and the MLDA variants are revealed. Subsequently, a taxonomy of the existing MLDA variants is suggested. Finally, empirical studies are presented in Section 2.4, and conclusions are drawn in Section 2.5.

## 2.2 MULTILINEAR BASICS

Before discussions on the multilinear discriminant analysis solutions for biometric signals, it is necessary to review some basic multilinear algebra, including the notations and some basic multilinear operations. To pursue further in this topic, references 1, 21, 22, 29, and 36 are excellent references. In addition, the equivalent vector interpretation of a commonly used tensor distance measure is derived.

### 2.2.1 Notations

The notations in this chapter follow the conventions in the multilinear algebra, pattern recognition, and adaptive learning literature. Vectors are denoted by lowercase bold-face letters (e.g., $\mathbf{x}$), matrices by uppercase boldface (e.g., $\mathbf{U}$), and tensors by script letters (e.g., $\mathcal{A}$). Their elements are denoted with indices in brackets. Indices are denoted by lowercase letters and span the range from 1 to the uppercase letter of the index (e.g., $n = 1, 2, \ldots, N$). Throughout this chapter, the discussion is restricted to real-valued vectors, matrices, and tensors since the biometric applications that we are interested in involve real data only, such as gray-level/color face images and binary gait silhouette sequences.

## 2.2.2 Basic Multilinear Algebra

An $N$th-order tensor is denoted as $\mathcal{A} \in \mathbb{R}^{I_1 \times I_2 \times \cdots \times I_N}$. It is addressed by $N$ indices $i_n, n = 1, \ldots, N$, and each $i_n$ addresses the $n$-mode of $\mathcal{A}$. The $n$-mode product of a tensor $\mathcal{A}$ by a matrix $\mathbf{U} \in \mathbb{R}^{J_n \times I_n}$, denoted by $\mathcal{A} \times_n \mathbf{U}$, is a tensor with entries:

$$(\mathcal{A} \times_n \mathbf{U})(i_1, \ldots, i_{n-1}, j_n, i_{n+1}, \ldots, i_N) = \sum_{i_n} \mathcal{A}(i_1, \ldots, i_N) \cdot \mathbf{U}(j_n, i_n). \quad (2.1)$$

The scalar product of two tensors $\mathcal{A}, \mathcal{B} \in \mathbb{R}^{I_1 \times I_2 \times \cdots \times I_N}$ is defined as

$$\langle \mathcal{A}, \mathcal{B} \rangle = \sum_{i_1} \sum_{i_2} \cdots \sum_{i_N} \mathcal{A}(i_1, i_2, \ldots, i_N) \cdot \mathcal{B}(i_1, i_2, \ldots, i_N), \quad (2.2)$$

and the Frobenius norm of $\mathcal{A}$ is defined as $\| \mathcal{A} \|_F = \sqrt{\langle \mathcal{A}, \mathcal{A} \rangle}$. The "$n$-mode vectors" of $\mathcal{A}$ are defined as the $I_n$-dimensional vectors obtained from $\mathcal{A}$ by varying the index $i_n$ while keeping all the other indices fixed. A rank-1 tensor $\mathcal{A}$ equals to the outer product of $N$ vectors: $\mathcal{A} = \mathbf{u}^{(1)} \circ \mathbf{u}^{(2)} \circ \cdots \circ \mathbf{u}^{(N)}$, which means that

$$\mathcal{A}(i_1, i_2, \ldots, i_N) = \mathbf{u}^{(1)}(i_1) \cdot \mathbf{u}^{(2)}(i_2) \cdot \ldots \cdot \mathbf{u}^{(N)}(i_N) \quad (2.3)$$

for all values of indices. Unfolding $\mathcal{A}$ along the $n$-mode is denoted as $\mathbf{A}_{(n)} \in \mathbb{R}^{I_n \times (I_1 \times \cdots \times I_{n-1} \times I_{n+1} \times \cdots \times I_N)}$, and the column vectors of $\mathbf{A}_{(n)}$ are the $n$-mode vectors of $\mathcal{A}$.

Figures 2.2b, 2.2c, and 2.2d give visual illustrations of the 1-mode, 2-mode, and 3-mode vectors of the third-order tensor $\mathcal{A}$ in Figure 2.2a, respectively. Figure 2.3a shows the 1-mode unfolding of the tensor $\mathcal{A}$ in Figure 2.2a and Figure 2.3b demonstrates how the 1-mode multiplication $\mathcal{A} \times_1 \mathbf{B}$ is obtained. The product $\mathcal{A} \times_1 \mathbf{B}$ is computed as the inner product between the 1-mode vector of $\mathcal{A}$ and the rows of $\mathbf{B}$. In the 1-mode multiplication, each 1-mode vector of $\mathcal{A}$ ($\in \mathbb{R}^8$) is projected by $\mathbf{B} \in \mathbb{R}^{3 \times 8}$ to obtain a vector ($\in \mathbb{R}^3$), as the differently shaded vectors indicate in Figure 2.3b.

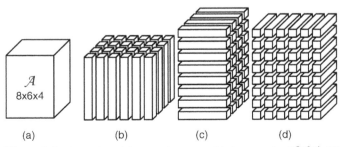

**Figure 2.2.** Illustration of the $n$-mode vectors: **(a)** A tensor $\mathcal{A} \in \mathbb{R}^{8 \times 6 \times 4}$, **(b)** the 1-mode vectors, **(c)** the 2-mode vectors, and **(d)** the 3-mode vectors.

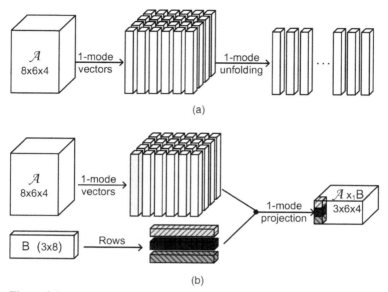

**Figure 2.3.** Visual illustration of (**a**) the $n$-mode (1-mode) unfolding and (**b**) the $n$-mode (1-mode) multiplication.

## 2.2.3   Tensor Distance Measure

To measure the distance between tensors $\mathcal{A}$ and $\mathcal{B}$, the Frobenius norm is used in reference 2: $dist(\mathcal{A}, \mathcal{B}) = \parallel \mathcal{A} - \mathcal{B} \parallel_F$. Let $vec(\mathcal{A})$ be the vector representation (vectorization) of $\mathcal{A}$, then it is straightforward to show the following:

**Proposition 1.**   $dist(\mathcal{A}, \mathcal{B}) = \parallel vec(\mathcal{A}) - vec(\mathcal{B}) \parallel_2$

That is, the Frobenius norm of the difference between two tensors equals to the Euclidean distance of their vectorized representations, since the Frobenius norm is a point-based measurement as well [37] and it does not take the structure of a tensor into account.

## 2.3   MULTILINEAR DISCRIMINANT ANALYSIS

The linear discriminant analysis (LDA) [38] is a classical algorithm that has been successfully applied and extended to various biometric signal recognition problems [15, 39–42]. The recent advancement in multilinear algebra [1, 21] led to a number of multilinear extensions of the LDA, multilinear discriminant analysis (MLDA), being proposed for the recognition of biometric signals using their natural tensorial representation [2, 19, 28, 30].

In general, MLDA seeks a multilinear projection that maps the input data from one space to another (lower-dimensional, more discriminative) space. Therefore, we need to understand what is a multilinear projection before proceeding to the MLDA solutions. In this section, we first propose a categorization of the various multilinear projections in terms of the input and output of the projection: the traditional vector-to-vector projection (VVP), the tensor-to-tensor projection (TTP), and the tensor-to-vector (TVP) projection.[4] Based on the categorization of multilinear projections, we discuss two general formulations of MLDA: the MLDA based on the tensor-to-tensor projection (MLDA-TTP) and the MLDA based on the tensor-to-vector projection (MLDA-TVP). Commonly used separation criteria and initialization methods are then presented. Furthermore, the relationships between the LDA, MLDA-TTP, and MLDA-TVP are investigated and a taxonomy of the existing MLDA variants is suggested.

### 2.3.1   Vector-to-Vector Projection (VVP)

Linear projection is a standard transform used widely in various applications [38, 43]. A linear projection takes a vector $\mathbf{x} \in \mathbb{R}^I$ and projects it to $\mathbf{y} \in \mathbb{R}^P$ using a projection matrix $\mathbf{U} \in \mathbb{R}^{I \times P}$:

$$\mathbf{y} = \mathbf{U}^T \mathbf{x}. \tag{2.4}$$

In typical pattern recognition applications, $P \ll I$. Therefore, linear projection is a vector-to-vector projection (VVP) and it requires the vectorization of an input before projection. Figure 2.4a illustrates the VVP of a tensor object $\mathcal{A}$. The classical LDA algorithm employs VVP.

### 2.3.2   Tensor-to-Tensor Projection (TTP)

Besides the traditional VVP, we can also project a tensor to another tensor (of the same order), which is named as tensor-to-tensor projection (TTP) in this chapter. An $N$th-order tensor $\mathcal{X}$ resides in the tensor (multilinear) space $\mathbb{R}^{I_1} \otimes \mathbb{R}^{I_2} \cdots \otimes \mathbb{R}^{I_N}$, where $\otimes$ denotes the Kronecker product [43]. Thus the tensor (multilinear) space can be viewed as the Kronecker product of $N$ vector (linear) spaces $\mathbb{R}^{I_1}, \mathbb{R}^{I_2}, \ldots, \mathbb{R}^{I_N}$. For the projection of a tensor $\mathcal{X}$ in a tensor space $\mathbb{R}^{I_1} \otimes \mathbb{R}^{I_2} \cdots \otimes \mathbb{R}^{I_N}$ to another tensor $\mathcal{Y}$ in a lower-dimensional tensor space $\mathbb{R}^{P_1} \otimes \mathbb{R}^{P_2} \cdots \otimes \mathbb{R}^{P_N}$, where $P_n < I_n$ for all $n$, $N$ projection matrices $\{\mathbf{U}^{(n)} \in \mathbb{R}^{I_n \times P_n}, n = 1, \ldots, N\}$ are used so that

$$\mathcal{Y} = \mathcal{X} \times_1 \mathbf{U}^{(1)^T} \times_2 \mathbf{U}^{(2)^T} \cdots \times_N \mathbf{U}^{(N)^T}. \tag{2.5}$$

Figure 2.4b demonstrates the TTP of a tensor object $\mathcal{A}$ to a smaller tensor of size $P_1 \times P_2 \times P_3$. How this multilinear projection is carried out can be understood better by referring to the illustration on the $n$-mode multiplication in Figure 2.3b. Many multilinear algorithms [2, 14, 19] have been developed through solving such a TTP.

---

[4]Multilinear projections are closely related to multilinear/tensor decompositions, which are included in the Appendix for completeness. They share some mathematical similarities but they are from different perspectives.

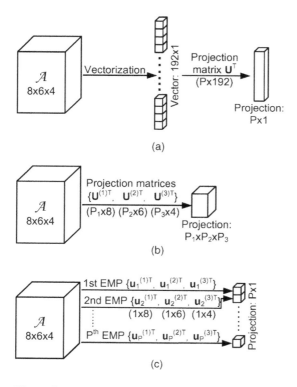

**Figure 2.4.** Illustration of **(a)** vector-to-vector projection (VVP), **(b)** tensor-to-tensor projection (TTP), and **(c)** tensor-to-vector projection (TVP).

## 2.3.3  Tensor-to-Vector Projection (TVP)

In our recent work [30], we introduced a multilinear projection from a tensor space to a vector space, called the tensor-to-vector projection (TVP). The projection from a tensor to a scalar is considered first. A tensor $\mathcal{X} \in \mathbb{R}^{I_1 \times I_2 \times \cdots \times I_N}$ is projected to a point $y$ as

$$y = \mathcal{X} \times_1 \mathbf{u}^{(1)^T} \times_2 \mathbf{u}^{(2)^T} \cdots \times_N \mathbf{u}^{(N)^T}, \tag{2.6}$$

which can also be written as the following inner product:

$$y = \left\langle \mathcal{X}, \mathbf{u}^{(1)} \circ \mathbf{u}^{(2)} \circ \cdots \circ \mathbf{u}^{(N)} \right\rangle. \tag{2.7}$$

Let $\mathcal{U} = \mathbf{u}^{(1)} \circ \mathbf{u}^{(2)} \circ \cdots \circ \mathbf{u}^{(N)}$, then we have $y = \langle \mathcal{X}, \mathcal{U} \rangle$. Such a multilinear projection $\left\{ \mathbf{u}^{(1)^T}, \mathbf{u}^{(2)^T}, \ldots, \mathbf{u}^{(N)^T} \right\}$, named an elementary multilinear projection (EMP), is the projection of a tensor on a single multilinear projection direction, and it consists of one projection vector in each mode.

The projection of a tensor object $\mathcal{X}$ to $\mathbf{y} \in \mathbb{R}^P$ in a $P$-dimensional vector space consists of $P$ EMPs

$$\left\{ \mathbf{u}_p^{(1)^T}, \mathbf{u}_p^{(2)^T}, \ldots, \mathbf{u}_p^{(N)^T} \right\}, \qquad p = 1, \ldots, P, \tag{2.8}$$

which can be written compactly as $\left\{ \mathbf{u}_p^{(n)^T}, n = 1, \ldots, N \right\}_{p=1}^P$. Thus, this TVP is written as

$$\mathbf{y} = \mathcal{X} \times_{n=1}^N \left\{ \mathbf{u}_p^{(n)^T}, n = 1, \ldots, N \right\}_{p=1}^P, \tag{2.9}$$

where the $p$th component of $\mathbf{y}$ is obtained from the $p$th EMP as

$$\mathbf{y}(p) = \mathcal{X} \times_1 \mathbf{u}_p^{(1)^T} \times_2 \mathbf{u}_p^{(2)^T} \cdots \times_N \mathbf{u}_p^{(N)^T}. \tag{2.10}$$

Figure 2.4c shows the TVP of a tensor object $\mathcal{A}$ to a vector of size $P \times 1$. A number of recent multilinear algorithms [27, 28, 30, 35][5] have been proposed with the objective of solving such a TVP.

## 2.3.4  MLDA-TTP

The multilinear extension of the LDA using the TTP is named MLDA-TTP hereafter. To formulate MLDA-TTP, the following definitions are introduced first.

**Definition 1.** Let $\{\mathcal{A}_m, m = 1, \ldots, M\}$ be a set of $M$ tensor samples in $\mathbb{R}^{I_1} \otimes \mathbb{R}^{I_2} \cdots \otimes \mathbb{R}^{I_N}$. The between-class scatter of these tensors is defined as

$$\Psi_{B_A} = \sum_{c=1}^C N_c \parallel \bar{\mathcal{A}}_c - \bar{\mathcal{A}} \parallel_F^2, \tag{2.11}$$

and the within-class scatter of these tensors is defined as

$$\Psi_{W_A} = \sum_{m=1}^M \parallel \mathcal{A}_m - \bar{\mathcal{A}}_{c_m} \parallel_F^2, \tag{2.12}$$

where $C$ is the number of classes, $N_c$ is the number of samples for class $c$, $c_m$ is the class label for the $m$th sample $\mathcal{A}_m$, the mean tensor is $\bar{\mathcal{A}} = \frac{1}{M} \sum_m \mathcal{A}_m$ and the class mean tensor is $\bar{\mathcal{A}}_c = \frac{1}{N_c} \sum_{m, c_m=c} \mathcal{A}_m$.

Next, the $n$-mode scatter matrices are defined accordingly.

**Definition 2.** The $n$-mode between-class scatter matrix of these samples is defined as

$$\mathbf{S}_{B_A}^{(n)} = \sum_{c=1}^C N_c \cdot \left( \bar{\mathbf{A}}_{c(n)} - \bar{\mathbf{A}}_{(n)} \right) \left( \bar{\mathbf{A}}_{c(n)} - \bar{\mathbf{A}}_{(n)} \right)^T, \tag{2.13}$$

---

[5]TVP is referred to as the rank-one projections in some works [27, 28, 35].

and the $n$-mode within-class scatter matrix of these samples is defined as

$$\mathbf{S}_{W_A}^{(n)} = \sum_{m=1}^{M} \left(\mathbf{A}_{m(n)} - \bar{\mathbf{A}}_{c_{m(n)}}\right)\left(\mathbf{A}_{m(n)} - \bar{\mathbf{A}}_{c_{m(n)}}\right)^{T}, \qquad (2.14)$$

where $\bar{\mathbf{A}}_{c(n)}$ is the $n$-mode unfolded matrix of $\bar{\mathcal{A}}_c$.

From the definitions above, the following properties are derived:

**Property 1.** *Since* $trace(\mathbf{A}\mathbf{A}^T) =\parallel \mathbf{A} \parallel_F^2$ *and* $\parallel \mathcal{A} \parallel_F^2 = \parallel \mathbf{A}_{(n)} \parallel_F^2$, *we have trace* $\left(\mathbf{S}_{B_A}^{(n)}\right) = \sum_{c=1}^{C} N_c \parallel \bar{\mathbf{A}}_{c(n)} - \bar{\mathbf{A}}_{(n)} \parallel_F^2 = \Psi_{B_A}$ *and trace* $\left(\mathbf{S}_{W_A}^{(n)}\right) = \sum_{m=1}^{M} \parallel \mathbf{A}_{m(n)} - \bar{\mathbf{A}}_{c_{m(n)}} \parallel_F^2 = \Psi_{W_A}$ *for all* $n$.

The formal definition of the problem to be solved in MLDA-TTP is then described below:

A set of $M$ training tensor objects $\{\mathcal{X}_1, \mathcal{X}_2, \ldots, \mathcal{X}_M\}$ is available. Each tensor object $\mathcal{X}_m \in \mathbb{R}^{I_1 \times I_2 \times \cdots \times I_N}$ assumes values in the tensor space $\mathbb{R}^{I_1} \otimes \mathbb{R}^{I_2} \cdots \otimes \mathbb{R}^{I_N}$, where $I_n$ is the $n$-mode dimension of the tensor. The objective of MLDA-TPP is to find a multilinear mapping $\{\mathbf{U}^{(n)} \in \mathbb{R}^{I_n \times P_n}, n = 1, \ldots, N\}$ from the original tensor space $\mathbb{R}^{I_1} \otimes \mathbb{R}^{I_2} \cdots \otimes \mathbb{R}^{I_N}$ into a tensor subspace $\mathbb{R}^{P_1} \otimes \mathbb{R}^{P_2} \cdots \otimes \mathbb{R}^{P_N}$ (with $P_n < I_n$, for $n = 1, \ldots, N$):

$$\mathcal{Y}_m = \mathcal{X}_m \times_1 \mathbf{U}^{(1)^T} \times_2 \mathbf{U}^{(2)^T} \cdots \times_N \mathbf{U}^{(N)^T}, \qquad m = 1, \ldots, M, \qquad (2.15)$$

based on the optimization of a certain separation criterion, such that an enhanced separability between different classes is achieved.

The MLDA-TTP objective is to determine the $N$ projection matrices $\{\mathbf{U}^{(n)} \in \mathbb{R}^{I_n \times P_n}, n = 1, \ldots, N\}$ that maximize some class separation criterion, which is often in terms of $\Psi_{B_y}$ and $\Psi_{W_y}$. By making use of Property 1, the problem can be converted to $N$ subproblems in terms of $\mathbf{S}_{B_y}^{(n)}$ and $\mathbf{S}_{W_y}^{(n)}$, which employs the commonly-used alternating projection principal [1, 2, 14]. The pseudo-code implementation of a general MLDA-TTP algorithm is shown in Figure 2.5. In each iteration $k$, for mode $n$, the input tensor samples are projected using the current projection matrices in all modes except $n$ to obtain a set of $N$th-order tensor samples, whose $n$-mode unfolding matrices are used to obtain $\mathbf{S}_{B_y}^{(n)}$ and $\mathbf{S}_{W_y}^{(n)}$.

### 2.3.5 MLDA-TVP

The multilinear extension of the LDA using the TVP is named MLDA-TVP and the formal definition of the problem to be solved in MLDA-TVP is described below:

A set of $M$ training tensor objects $\{\mathcal{X}_1, \mathcal{X}_2, \ldots, \mathcal{X}_M\}$ is available. Each tensor object $\mathcal{X}_m \in \mathbb{R}^{I_1 \times I_2 \times \cdots \times I_N}$ assumes values in the tensor space $\mathbb{R}^{I_1} \otimes \mathbb{R}^{I_2} \cdots \otimes \mathbb{R}^{I_N}$, where $I_n$ is the $n$-mode dimension of the tensor. The objective of MLDA-TVP is to find a set of $P$ EMPs $\{\mathbf{u}_p^{(n)} \in \mathbb{R}^{I_n \times 1}, n = 1, \ldots, N\}_{p=1}^{P}$ mapping from the original

**Input:** A set of tensor samples $\{\mathcal{X}_m \in \mathbb{R}^{I_1 \times I_2 \times \cdots \times I_N}, m = 1, \ldots, M\}$ with class labels $\mathbf{c} \in \mathbb{R}^M$, $P_n$ for $n = 1, \ldots, N$.

**Output:** Low-dimensional representations $\{\mathcal{Y}_m \in \mathbb{R}^{P_1 \times P_2 \times \cdots \times P_N}, m = 1, \ldots, M\}$ of the input tensor samples maximizing a separation criterion.

**Algorithm:**

**Step 1:** Initialize $\mathbf{U}_0^{(n)}$ for $n = 1, \ldots, N$.

**Step 2 (Local optimization):**

- For $k = 1 : K$
  - For $n = 1 : N$
    * Calculate $\{\mathcal{Y}_m = \mathcal{X}_m \times_1 \mathbf{U}_k^{(1)^T} \cdots \times_{n-1} \mathbf{U}_k^{(n-1)^T} \times_{n+1}$ $\mathbf{U}_{k-1}^{(n+1)^T} \cdots \times_N \mathbf{U}_{k-1}^{(N)^T}, m = 1, \ldots, M\}$.
    * Calculate $\mathbf{S}_{B_y}^{(n)}$ and $\mathbf{S}_{W_y}^{(n)}$.
    * Set the matrix $\mathbf{U}_k^{(n)}$ to optimize a separation criterion.
  - If $k > 2$ and $\mathbf{U}_k^{(n)}$ converges for all $n$, set $\mathbf{U}^{(n)} = \mathbf{U}_k^{(n)}$ and break.

**Step 3 (Projection):** The feature tensor after projection is obtained as $\{\mathcal{Y}_m = \mathcal{X}_m \times_1 \mathbf{U}^{(1)^T} \times_2 \mathbf{U}^{(2)^T} \cdots \times_N \mathbf{U}^{(N)^T}, m = 1, \ldots, M\}$.

**Figure 2.5.** The pseudo-code implementation of a general MLDA-TTP.

tensor space $\mathbb{R}^{I_1} \otimes \mathbb{R}^{I_2} \ldots \otimes \mathbb{R}^{I_N}$ into a vector subspace $\mathbb{R}^P$ (with $P < \prod_{n=1}^N I_n$):

$$\mathbf{y}_m = \mathcal{X}_m \times_{n=1}^N \left\{ \mathbf{u}_p^{(n)^T}, n = 1, \ldots, N \right\}_{p=1}^P, \qquad m = 1, \ldots, M, \quad (2.16)$$

based on the optimization of a certain separation criteria, such that an enhanced separability between different classes is achieved.

The MLDA-TVP objective is to determine the $P$ projection bases in each mode $\left\{ \mathbf{u}_p^{(n)} \in \mathbb{R}^{I_n \times 1}, n = 1, \ldots, N, p = 1, \ldots, P \right\}$ that maximize a class separation criterion. In MLDA-TVP, since the projected space is a vector space, the definition of scatter matrices in classical LDA can be followed. For the samples projected by the $p$th EMP $\{y_{m_p}, m = 1, \ldots, M\}$, where $y_{m_p}$ is the projection of the $m$th sample by the $p$th EMP, the between-class scatter matrix and the within-class scatter matrix are defined as

$$S_{B_p}^{\mathbf{y}} = \sum_{c=1}^C N_c (\bar{y}_{c_p} - \bar{y}_p)^2 \qquad (2.17)$$

and

$$S_{W_p}^{\mathbf{y}} = \sum_{m=1}^M (y_{m_p} - \bar{y}_{c_{m_p}})^2, \qquad (2.18)$$

respectively, where $\bar{y}_p = \frac{1}{M} \sum_m y_{m_p}$, $\bar{y}_{c_p} = \frac{1}{N_c} \sum_{m, c_m = c} y_{m_p}$. Figure 2.6 is the pseudo-code implementation of a general MLDA-TVP algorithm. To solve the problem, the alternating projection principal is again employed. In each iteration $k$, for

---

**Input:** A set of tensor samples $\{\mathcal{X}_m \in \mathbb{R}^{I_1 \times I_2 \times \cdots \times I_N}, m = 1, \ldots, M\}$ with class labels $\mathbf{c} \in \mathbb{R}^M$, the projected feature dimension $P$.

**Output:** Low-dimensional representations $\{\mathbf{y}_m \in \mathbb{R}^P, m = 1, \ldots, M\}$ of the input tensor samples maximizing a separation criterion.

**Algorithm:**

   **Step 1 (Stepwise optimization):**

     For $p = 1 : P$

- For $n = 1, \ldots, N$, initialize $\mathbf{u}_p^{(n)} \in \mathbb{R}^{I_n}$.
- For $k = 1 : K$
  - For $n = 1 : N$
    * Calculate $\{\mathbf{y}_m = \mathcal{X}_{m_p} \times_1 \mathbf{u}_{p_k}^{(1)^T} \cdots \times_{n-1} \mathbf{u}_{p_k}^{(n-1)^T} \times_{n+1} \mathbf{u}_{p_{k-1}}^{(n+1)^T} \cdots \times_N \mathbf{u}_{p_{k-1}}^{(N)^T}, m = 1, \ldots, M\}$.
    * Calculate the between-class and the within-class scatter matrices by treating $\{\mathbf{y}_m\}$ as the input vector samples, as in classical LDA.
    * Compute the vector $\mathbf{u}_{p_k}^{(n)}$ that optimizes a separation criterion.
  - If $k > 2$ and $\mathbf{u}_{p_k}^{(n)}$ converges for all $n$, set $\mathbf{u}_p^{(n)} = \mathbf{u}_{p_k}^{(n)}$ and break.

   **Step 2 (Projection):** The feature vector after projection is obtained as $\{\mathbf{y}_m(p) = \mathcal{X}_m \times_1 \mathbf{u}_p^{(1)^T} \cdots \times_N \mathbf{u}_p^{(N)^T}, p = 1, \ldots, P, m = 1, \ldots, M\}$.

---

**Figure 2.6.** The pseudo-code implementation of a general MLDA-TVP.

mode $n$, the input tensor samples are projected using the current projection vectors in all modes except $n$ to obtain a set of vector samples and the problem is then converted to a number of classical LDA problems.

## 2.3.6 Separation Criteria and Initialization Methods

Both MLDA-TTP and MLDA-TVP need to specify a class separation criterion to be optimized. One commonly used separation criterion is the ratio of the between-class scatter $\Psi_{B_y}$ or $S_{B_p}^{\mathbf{y}}$ and the within-class scatter $\Psi_{W_y}$ or $S_{W_p}^{\mathbf{y}}$: $\left(\frac{\Psi_{B_y}}{\Psi_{W_y}}\right)$ for MLDA-TTP or $\left(\frac{S_{B_p}^{\mathbf{y}}}{S_{W_p}^{\mathbf{y}}}\right)$ for MLDA-TVP [39], hereafter named SRatio.

Another separation criterion is the (weighted) difference between the between-class scatter $\Psi_{B_y}$ or $S_{B_p}^{\mathbf{y}}$ and the within-class scatter $\Psi_{W_y}$ or $S_{W_p}^{\mathbf{y}}$: $(\Psi_{B_y} - \zeta\Psi_{W_y})$ for MLDA-TTP or $(S_{B_p}^{\mathbf{y}} - \zeta \cdot S_{W_p}^{\mathbf{y}})$ for MLDA-TVP [44], hereafter named SDiff, where $\zeta$ is a parameter tuning the weight between the between-class and within-class scatters.

Since MLDA algorithms rely on the alternating projection principal, they are generally iterative and there is a need in choosing an initialization method. Commonly used initialization methods for MLDA-TTP are: pseudo-identity matrices (truncated identity matrices) and random matrices. Commonly used initialization methods for MLDA-TVP are: all ones and random vectors. There are also initialization methods based on projections obtained from the $n$-mode vectors of the input tensor samples [30, 45].

### 2.3.7  Relationships Between the LDA, MLDA-TTP, and MLDA-TVP

To study the relationships between the LDA, MLDA-TTP, and MLDA-TVP, it is beneficial to investigate what are the relationships between VVP, TTP, and TVP first. It is easy to verify that VVP is the special case of TTP and TVP with $N = 1$. On the other hand, each projected element in TTP can be viewed as the projection of an EMP formed by taking one column from each of the projection matrices and thus the projected tensor is obtained through $\prod_{n=1}^{N} I_n$ interdependent EMPs in effect, while in TVP the $P$ EMPs obtained sequentially are not interdependent generally.

Furthermore, recall that the projection using an EMP $\left\{ \mathbf{u}^{(1)^T}, \mathbf{u}^{(2)^T}, \ldots, \mathbf{u}^{(N)^T} \right\}$ can be written as $y = \langle \mathcal{X}, \mathcal{U} \rangle$; it is then straightforward to show

**Proposition 2.** $y = \langle \mathcal{X}, \mathcal{U} \rangle = \langle vec(\mathcal{X}), vec(\mathcal{U}) \rangle = [vec(\mathcal{U})]^T vec(\mathcal{X})$.

Thus, an EMP is equivalent to a linear projection of $vec(\mathcal{X})$, the vectorized representation of $\mathcal{X}$, on a vector $vec(\mathcal{U})$. Since $\mathcal{U} = \mathbf{u}^{(1)} \circ \mathbf{u}^{(2)} \circ \cdots \circ \mathbf{u}^{(N)}$, Proposition 2 indicates that the EMP is in effect a linear projection with constraint on the projection vector such that it is the vectorized representation of a rank-one tensor. Compared with a projection vector of size $I \times 1$ in VVP specified by $I$ parameters ($I = \prod_{n=1}^{N} I_n$ for an $N$th-order tensor), an EMP in TVP can be specified by $\sum_{n=1}^{N} I_n$ parameters. Hence, to project a tensor of size $\prod_{n=1}^{N} I_n$ to a vector of size $P \times 1$, the TVP needs to estimate only $P \cdot \sum_{n=1}^{N} I_n$ parameters, while the VVP needs to estimate $P \cdot \prod_{n=1}^{N} I_n$ parameters. The implication in pattern recognition problem is that the TVP has fewer parameters to estimate while being more constrained on the solutions, and the VVP has less constraint on the solutions sought while having more parameters to estimate.

The connections between the MLDA algorithms and the LDA algorithm can be revealed through the relationships among VVP, TTP, and TVP. From the analysis above, LDA is a special case of MLDA-TTP and MLDA-TVP when $N = 1$, with the scatter ratio as the separation criterion. On the other hand, the MLDA-TTP is looking for interdependent EMPs while the EMPs sought sequentially in the MLDA-TVP are not interdependent generally. Furthermore, for the same projected vector size, the MLDA-TVP has fewer parameters to estimate while the projection to be solved are more constrained, and LDA has more parameters to estimate while the projection is less constrained.

### 2.3.8  A Taxonomy of MLDA Variants

With the two general formulations of MLDA, a taxonomy of the existing MLDA variants is given in Table 2.1, followed by brief descriptions of the four MLDA variants listed in the view of this taxonomy.

**Table 2.1.** A Taxonomy of MLDA Variants

| MLDA Variants | Projection Type | Separation Criterion | Reference |
|---|---|---|---|
| DATER | TTP | SRatio | 2 |
| GTDA | TTP | SDiff | 19 |
| TR1DA | TVP | SDiff | 27, 28 |
| UMLDA | TVP | SRatio | 30 |

From the taxonomy suggested in Table 2.1, it can been seen that the Discriminant Analysis with Tensor Representation (DATER) algorithm [2] is a specific realization of the MLDA-TTP, with the objective of maximizing the scatter ratio and using the pseudo-identity matrices for initialization. The General Tensor Discriminant Analysis (GTDA) algorithm [46] is an MLDA-TTP variant maximizing the scatter difference, where in each step of the iteration and in each mode, the tuning parameter $\zeta$ is determined to be the maximum eigenvalue of a mode-wise scatter ratio (which means that a different weighting between the between-class and within-class scatter is used in each mode and each iteration). The initialization in GTDA is done by setting the initial projection matrix to be all ones. The Tensor Rank-One Discriminant Analysis (TR1DA) algorithm [27, 28] is an MLDA-TVP variant maximizing the scatter difference. In each iteration, TR1DA calculates the residues of all tensor samples using the obtained EMPs, which is a heuristic greedy approach used in tensor approximation problem [29], and the residues are used as the input tensor samples in the next iteration. The selection of $\zeta$ in TR1DA is not addressed in references 27 and 28, and random initialization is employed in this MLDA variant. The uncorrelated multilinear discriminant analysis (UMLDA) algorithm [30, 47] is an MLDA-TVP variant maximizing the scatter ratio, while pursuing uncorrelated features, and a regularization procedure with parameter $\eta$ was introduced to increase the estimated within-class scatter, resulting in better generalization. The initialization method used in reference 30 is based on the $n$-mode vectors.

## 2.4  EMPIRICAL COMPARISON OF MLDA VARIANTS ON FACE RECOGNITION

In this section, empirical performance comparison of MLDA variants is carried out on 2-D face images (second-order tensors). For experiments on third-order tensors, please refer to references 14 and 30 for results on gait silhouette sequences and refer to references 2 and 19 for results on the Gabor face/gait images. Two public face databases with a large number of samples per subject available for testing were used. One is the PIE (Pose, Illumination, and Expression) database from CMU [48] and the other is the extended Yale face database B (YaleB) [49, 50].

For the MLDA variants, all the face images are cropped and normalized to $32 \times 32$ pixels (represented as second-order tensors), with 256 gray levels per pixel.[6] A random subset with $L$ ($= 5, 10, 20, 30$) samples per subject was taken with labels to form the training set, and the rest of the database was considered to be the testing set. For each given $L$, the results averaged over 20 random splits[7] are reported in this chapter. The nearest-neighbor classifier with the Euclidean distance measure was employed in classification for simplicity. The MLDA-TTP variants (DATER and GTDA) produce features in tensor representation, which cannot be handled directly by the selected classifier. Since from Section 2.2.3 the tensor distance measured by the Frobenius norm is equivalent to the Euclidean distance between vectorized representations, the tensor features from MLDA-TTP are rearranged to vectors for easy classification and comparison, which is described in detail in Section 2.4.1. Besides the four MLDA variants listed in Table 2.1, the Fisherface algorithm [39], which is a classical LDA approach, and the uncorrelated LDA (ULDA) algorithm [51] are included for comparison between LDA and MLDA. For LDA and ULDA, a $32 \times 32$ face image is represented as a $1024 \times 1$ vector for input.

In the experiments, the number of iterations for the MLDA variants was set to 10. For DATER, GTDA, and TR1DA, up to 300 features were tested. For UMLDA, up to 100 features were tested. The maximum number of features tested for LDA and ULDA was $C - 1$, where $C$ is the number of subjects (classes) in training. For the TR1DA algorithm, we tested several values of $\zeta$ for each $L$ and the best one for each $L$ was used: $\zeta = 2$ for $L = 5$, $\zeta = 0.8$ for $L = 10$, and $\zeta = 0.6$ for $L = 20, 30$. For UMLDA, a fixed regularization parameter $\eta = 5 \times 10^4$ was empirically chosen and all initial projection vectors are set to all ones (**1**) for simplicity.

## 2.4.1  Feature Rearrangement for MLDA-TTP

The MLDA-TTP algorithms produce features in tensorial representation. For tensor distance calculation, the Frobenius norm is commonly used [2]. By Proposition 1, it is equivalent to calculate the Euclidean distance of their vectorized representation. Therefore, in this study we rearrange the tensor features obtained by MLDA-TTP to vectors for easy comparison. The MLDA-TTP algorithms obtain the highest-dimension projection ($P_n = I_n$ for $n = 1, \ldots, N$) first and then the TTP is viewed as $\prod_{n=1}^{N} I_n$ EMPs. The discriminability of each such EMP is calculated on the training set and the EMPs are arranged in descending discriminability so that a feature vector is obtained, as in reference 14 for the MPCA algorithm. The MLDA-TVP algorithms produce feature vectors directly so there is no such rearrangement necessary.

## 2.4.2  Face Recognition Results on PIE Database

The CMU PIE database contains 68 individuals with face images captured by 13 synchronized cameras and 21 flashes, under varying pose, illumination, and expression.

---

[6]The $32 \times 32$ face data was obtained from http://www.cs.uiuc.edu/homes/dengcai2/Data/FaceData.html.

[7]The reason for randomly selecting the training set and repeating 20 times is to reduce the dependency of the performance on a particular set of training data.

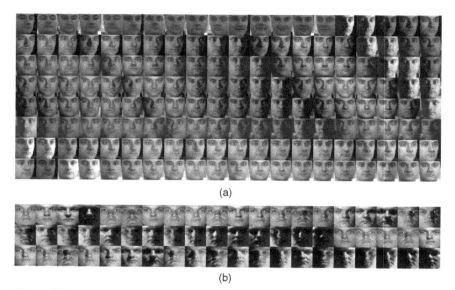

(a)

(b)

**Figure 2.7.** Sample face images of one subject from (**a**) the CMU PIE database and (**b**) the YaleB database.

As in references 31 and 32, we chose the five near frontal poses (C05, C07, C09, C27, C29) and used all the images under different illumination, lighting, and expressions. Thus, there are about 170 samples per subject and there are a total number of 11,554 face images. Figure 2.7a shows 160 sample face images for a subject in this database.

Figure 2.8 shows the detailed face recognition results on the CMU PIE database for various values of $L$. The correct classification rates (CCRs) for each algorithm in comparison are plotted against the number of features used. To examine the discriminability of the most discriminative features extracted by each algorithm in detail, the horizontal axis (the number of features) is shown in log scale. The best results for each algorithm on the PIE database are reported in Table 2.2, where the best CCR for each $L$ is highlighted with bold fonts.

From the detailed results, it can be seen that the first a few features extracted by the UMLDA algorithm consistently outperforms all the other algorithms, although the number of useful features extracted by UMLDA is limited compared to other MLDA variants [30]. In contrast, the heuristic TR1DA algorithm, built upon a greedy approximation approach, performs the worst in most cases, especially when the number of samples per subject is small (e.g., $L = 5, 10$). Similarly, the DATER algorithm outperforms the GTDA greatly on the PIE database. Thus, the MLDA variants based on scatter ratio have achieved much better results than the MLDA variants based on the scatter difference in this experiment, with the added benefit that there is no need to choose a tuning parameter $\zeta$.

For the comparison between MLDA-TTP and MLDA-TVP, we focus on the scatter ratio-based variants: UMLDA and DATER. As mentioned above, the most discriminative features extracted by UMLDA seem to outperform the most discriminative

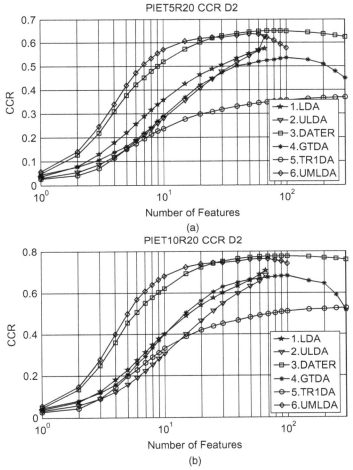

**Figure 2.8.** Detailed face recognition results on the CMU PIE database with (**a**) $L = 5$, (**b**) $L = 10$, (**c**) $L = 20$, and (**d**) $L = 30$.

features extracted by DATER. However, UMLDA has limited number of useful features in comparison. The results in Table 2.2 show that their performances are close on the PIE database.

Regarding the comparison between LDA and MLDA, we concentrate on the scatter-ratio-based methods: LDA and ULDA versus DATER and UMLDA. In this experiment, DATER and UMLDA outperform LDA and ULDA greatly, especially when $L$ is small. When $L = 30$—that is, the number of training samples for each subject is large—the performance gap is reduced. This comparison demonstrates that treating gray-level face images in their natural 2-D representation is advantageous against vectorized representation, especially when the number of training samples per subject is small.

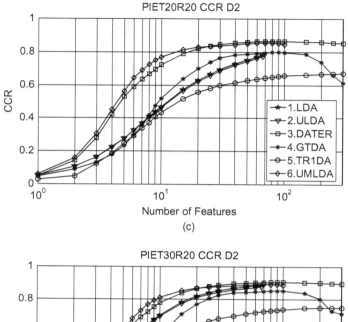

**Figure 2.8.** (*Continued*)

**Table 2.2.** Face Recognition Results on PIE Database

| $L$ | Fisherface (LDA) | ULDA | DATER | GTDA | TR1DA | UMLDA |
|----|------|------|------|------|------|------|
| 5  | 0.574 | 0.626 | **0.651** | 0.537 | 0.370 | 0.639 |
| 10 | 0.708 | 0.684 | **0.776** | 0.684 | 0.525 | 0.763 |
| 20 | 0.785 | 0.774 | **0.866** | 0.801 | 0.672 | 0.856 |
| 30 | 0.891 | 0.880 | **0.906** | 0.856 | 0.749 | 0.894 |

### 2.4.3  Face Recognition Results on YaleB Database

The Extended Yale face database B (YaleB) consists of 2414 frontal face images of 38 individuals, which were captured under various laboratory-controlled lighting conditions. There are about 64 samples per subject and 60 sample face images for a subject are shown in Figure 2.7b.

Figure 2.9 shows the detailed face recognition results on the YaleB database; and the best results for each algorithm on the YaleB database are reported in Table 2.3, in a similar way as Section 2.4.2 for various values of $L$.

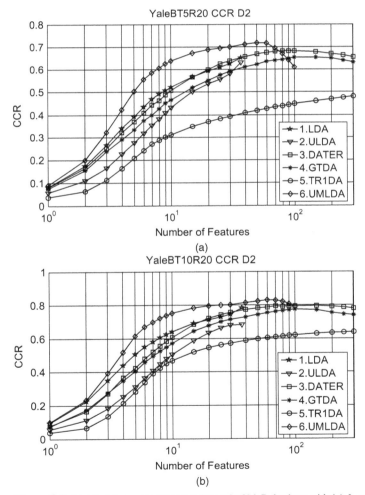

**Figure 2.9.** Detailed face recognition results on the YaleB database with (**a**) $L = 5$, (**b**) $L = 10$, (**c**) $L = 20$, and (**d**) $L = 30$.

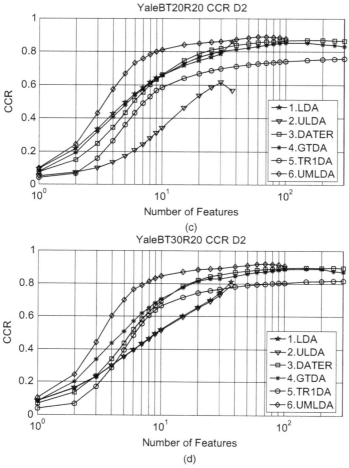

**Figure 2.9.** (*Continued*)

From the detailed results in Figure 2.9, it can be seen that the first a few features extracted by the UMLDA algorithm again consistently outperforms all the other algorithms. The heuristic TR1DA algorithm performs the worst for $L = 5, 10$. From Table 2.3, the DATER algorithm outperforms the GTDA slightly on the YaleB

**Table 2.3.** Face Recognition Results on YaleB Database

| $L$ | Fisherface (LDA) | ULDA | DATER | GTDA | TR1DA | UMLDA |
|---|---|---|---|---|---|---|
| 5 | 0.653 | 0.632 | 0.685 | 0.657 | 0.480 | **0.720** |
| 10 | 0.783 | 0.695 | 0.797 | 0.777 | 0.640 | **0.831** |
| 20 | 0.858 | 0.628 | 0.870 | 0.856 | 0.758 | **0.892** |
| 30 | 0.812 | 0.792 | 0.900 | 0.894 | 0.819 | **0.921** |

database but the performance gap is quite small. Overall, the MLDA variants based on scatter ratio again obtained better results than the MLDA variants based on scatter difference.

As in Section 2.4.2, we focus on the scatter-ratio-based variants, UMLDA and DATER, for the comparison between MLDA-TTP and MLDA-TVP. From Figure 2.9 and Table 2.3, UMLDA consistently outperforms DATER significantly on this database, especially for a smaller $L$, although the performance of UMLDA deteriorates when the number of features exceeds a certain number. Thus, on this database the UMLDA, an MLDA-TVP approach extracting uncorrelated features, shows its advantage against the MLDA-TTP approach, where the features can be viewed to be extracted through interdependent EMPs.

Regarding the comparison between LDA and MLDA, there is an interesting observation from this experiment. For the Fisherface (LDA) approach, when $L$ increases from 20 to 30, the recognition rate ironically decreases, as seen in Table 2.3. For the ULDA, when $L$ increases from 10 to 20, the recognition rate surprisingly decreases too, as in Table 2.3. This is in contrary with our belief that more training samples should result in better recognition performance. On the other hand, all the four MLDA variants do not have this problem on this database, with recognition rate increasing as $L$ increases, showing that MLDA approaches are more stable and consistent. Furthermore, the UMLDA algorithm outperforms the LDA and ULDA significantly, especially for a larger $L$, demonstrating again the benefits of extracting features directly from the natural 2-D representation of face images rather than from their vectorized representation.

## 2.4.4  Discussions

In summary, through the comparison in Figures 2.8 and 2.9 and in Tables 2.2 and 2.3, it can be seen that by treating face images in their natural 2-D representation, the MLDA solution UMLDA achieves very good recognition results consistently on two very challenging face databases, for various number of training samples per subjects ($L = 5, 10, 20,$ and $30$). It is also observed that the MLDA variants based on scatter ratio generally outperform the MLDA variants based on scatter difference; and with scatter ratio as the separation criterion, the overall performance of MLDA-TVP is better than that of MLDA-TTP. In addition, MLDA variants are shown to be more stable and consistent than LDA approaches.

Considering the short period of research and development in multilinear learning solutions for biometric signal recognition, the empirical evaluation results presented here are very encouraging and we believe that there is still great potential in further development of multilinear learning algorithms that operate directly on natural tensorial representations. The materials provided in this chapter represent a good starting point for newcomers to this field; and the taxonomy of various multilinear projections and MLDA variants, together with discussions on their connections, is also beneficial for researchers already working in this field.

## 2.5 CONCLUSIONS

This chapter provides a comprehensive introduction to the area of multilinear learning algorithms, in particular the multilinear discriminant analysis (MLDA) algorithms, for the recognition of biometric signals, most of which are naturally tensor objects. Three typical projections are introduced first: the vector-to-vector projections (VVP), the tensor-to-tensor projections (TTP) and the tensor-to-vector projections (TVP), and two general MLDA solutions are formulated: the MLDA-TTP and the MLDA-TVP. The choices of the separation criteria and the initialization methods are then presented and the relationships between LDA, MLDA-TTP, and MLDA-TVP are discussed. A taxonomy of MLDA variants is subsequently suggested; and it not only helps us to understand the existing mutlilinear algorithms, but also benefits us in the development of new multilinear algorithms. Finally, the MLDA variants are experimentally evaluated on the CMU PIE database and the extended Yale database B to demonstrate their performance on the popular face recognition problem. The experimental results indicate that the MLDA solutions, and multilinear learning algorithms in general, are promising emerging areas for research and applications.

## ACKNOWLEDGMENTS

We would like to thank Cai Deng from the University of Illinois at Urbana-Champaign for making the standard-size face data available. We also would like to acknowledge all those who contributed to the research described in this chapter.

## APPENDIX: MULTILINEAR DECOMPOSITIONS

There are two types of decompositions used most in multilinear applications: the canonical decomposition (CANDECOMP) [21, 22, 53], which is also known as the parallel factors (PARAFAC) decomposition [21, 22, 54], and the TUCKER decomposition [21, 22, 55].

With the CANDECOMP decomposition, a tensor $\mathcal{A}$ can be decomposed into a linear combination of $P$ rank-1 tensors:

$$\mathcal{A} = \sum_{p=1}^{P} \lambda_p \mathbf{u}_p^{(1)} \circ \mathbf{u}_p^{(2)} \circ \cdots \circ \mathbf{u}_p^{(N)}, \tag{B.1}$$

where $P \leq \prod_{n=1}^{N} I_n$. With the TUCKER decomposition, a tensor $\mathcal{A}$ can be expressed as the product:

$$\mathcal{A} = \sum_{p_1=1}^{P_1} \sum_{p_2=1}^{P_2} \cdots \sum_{p_N=1}^{P_N} \mathcal{S}(p_1, p_2, \ldots, p_N) \mathbf{u}_{p_1}^{(1)} \circ \mathbf{u}_{p_2}^{(2)} \circ \cdots \circ \mathbf{u}_{p_N}^{(N)}$$

$$= \mathcal{S} \times_1 \mathbf{U}^{(1)} \times_2 \mathbf{U}^{(2)} \times \cdots \times_N \mathbf{U}^{(N)}, \tag{B.2}$$

where $P_n \leq I_n$ for $n = 1, \ldots, N$, $\mathcal{S} = \mathcal{A} \times_1 \mathbf{U}^{(1)^T} \times_2 \mathbf{U}^{(2)^T} \ldots \times_N \mathbf{U}^{(N)^T}$, and $\mathbf{U}^{(n)} = \left( \mathbf{u}_1^{(n)} \mathbf{u}_2^{(n)} \ldots \mathbf{u}_{P_n}^{(n)} \right)$ is an $I_n \times P_n$ matrix with orthonormal column vectors. The CONDECOMP decomposition is in fact a special case of the TUCKER decomposition.

## REFERENCES

1. L. D. Lathauwer, B. D. Moor, and J. Vandewalle, On the best rank-1 and rank-$(R_1, R_2, \ldots, R_N)$ approximation of higher-order tensors, *SIAM J. Matrix Anal. Appl.* **21**(4):1324–1342, 2000.
2. S. Yan, D. Xu, Q. Yang, L. Zhang, X. Tang, and H. Zhang, Multilinear discriminant analysis for face recognition, *IEEE Trans. Image Processing*, **16**(1):212–220, 2007.
3. H. Lu, J. Wang, and K. N. Plataniotis, A review on face and gait recognition: System, data and algorithms, in Advanced Signal Processing Handbook, 2nd edition, S. Stergiopoulos, editor, CRC Press, Boca Raton, FL, 2009, 000–000.
4. Y.-D. Kim and S. Choi, Color face tensor factorization and slicing for illumination-robust recognition, in *Proceedings of the International Conference. on Biometrics*, August 2007, pp. 19–28.
5. K. N. Plataniotis and A. N. Venetsanopoulos, *Color Image Processing and Applications*, Springer-Verlag, Berlin, 2000.
6. K. W. Bowyer, K. Chang, and P. Flynn, A survey of approaches and challenges in 3D and multi-modal 3D + 2D face recognition, *Comput. Vis. Image Understanding* **101**(1):1–15, 2006.
7. S. Z. Li, C. Zhao, X. Zhu, and Z. Lei, 3D + 2D face recognition by fusion at both feature and decision levels, in *Proceedings of the IEEE International Workshop on Analysis and Modeling of Faces and Gestures*, October 2005.
8. C. Liu and H. Wechsler, Independent component analysis of gabor features for face recognition, *IEEE Trans. Neural Networks* **14**(4):919–928, 2003.
9. R. Chellappa, A. Roy-Chowdhury, and S. Zhou, *Recognition of Humans and Their Activities Using Video*, Morgan & Claypool Publishers, San Rafael, CA, 2005.
10. H. Lu, K. N. Plataniotis, and A. N. Venetsanopoulos, A layered deformable model for gait analysis, in *Proceedings of the IEEE International Conference on Automatic Face and Gesture Recognition*, April 2006, pp. 249–254.
11. N. V. Boulgouris, D. Hatzinakos, and K. N. Plataniotis, Gait recognition: a challenging signal processing technology for biometrics, *IEEE Signal Processing Mag.* **22**(6):000–000, 2005.
12. H. Lu, K. N. Plataniotis, and A. N. Venetsanopoulos, A full-body layered deformable model for automatic model-based gait recognition, *EURASIP Journal on Advances in Signal Processing: Special Issue on Advanced Signal Processing and Pattern Recognition Methods for Biometrics*, Vol. 2008, 2008, article ID 261317, 13 pages, doi:10.1155/2008/261317.
13. Z. Lei, R. Chu, R. He, S. Liao, and S. Z. Li, Face recognition by discriminant analysis with gabor tensor representation, in *Proceedings of the. International Conference on Biometrics*, August 2007, pp. 87–95.
14. H. Lu, K. N. Plataniotis, and A. N. Venetsanopoulos, MPCA: Multilinear principal component analysis of tensor objects, *IEEE Trans. Neural Networks*, **19**(1):18–39, 2008.
15. G. Shakhnarovich and B. Moghaddam, Face recognition in subspaces, in S. Z. Li and A. K. Jain, editors, *Handbook of Face Recognition*, Springer-Verlag, Berlin, 2004, pp. 141–168.
16. J. Zhang, S. Z. Li, and J. Wang, Manifold learning and applications in recognition, in Y. P. Tan, K. H. Yap, and L. Wang, editors, *Intelligent Multimedia Processing with Soft Computing*, Springer-Verlag, Berlin, 2004, pp. 281–300.
17. M. H. C. Law and A. K. Jain, Incremental nonlinear dimensionality reduction by manifold learning, *IEEE Trans. Pattern Anal. Mach. Intell.* **28**(3):377–391, 2006.
18. H. Lu, K. N. Plataniotis, and A. N. Venetsanopoulos, Gait recognition through MPCA plus LDA, in *Proceedings of the Biometrics Symposium 2006*, September 2006, pp. 1–6, doi:10.1109 BCC.2006.4341613.

19. D. Tao, X. Li, X. Wu, and S. J. Maybank, General tensor discriminant analysis and gabor features for gait recognition, *IEEE Trans. Pattern Anal. Mach. Intell.*, **29**(10):1700–1715, 2007.

20. H. Lu, K. N. Plataniotis, and A. N. Venetsanopoulos, Uncorrelated multilinear principal component analysis through successive variance maximization, in *Proceedings of the International Conference on Machine Learning*, July 2008, pp. 616–623.

21. L. D. Lathauwer, B. D. Moor, and J. Vandewalle, A multilinear singualr value decomposition, *SIAM J. Matrix Anal. Appl.* **21**(4):1253–1278, 2000.

22. B. W. Bader and T. G. Kolda, Algorithm 862: Matlab tensor classes for fast algorithm prototyping, *ACM Trans. Math. Software*, **32**(4):635–653, 2006.

23. H. Lu, K. N. Plataniotis, and A. N. Venetsanopoulos, Multilinear principal component analysis of tensor objects for recognition, in *Proceedings of the International Conference on Pattern Recognition*, Vol. 2, August 2006, pp. 776–779.

24. D. Xu, S. Yan, L. Zhang, H.-J. Zhang, Z. Liu, and H.-Y. Shum, Concurrent subspaces analysis, in *Proceedings of the IEEE Computer Society Conf. on Computer Vision and Pattern Recognition*, Vol. II, June 2005, pp. 203–208.

25. H. Lu, K. N. Plataniotis, and A. N. Venetsanopoulos, Boosting LDA with regularization on MPCA features for gait recognition, in *Proceedings of the Biometrics Symposium 2007*, September 2007, doi:10.1109/BCC.2007.4430542.

26. J. Ye, R. Janardan, and Q. Li, Two-dimensional linear discriminant analysis, in *Advances in Neural Information Processing Systems (NIPS)*, 2004, pp. 1569–1576.

27. Y. Wang and S. Gong, Tensor discriminant analysis for view-based object recognition, in *Proceedings of the International Conference on Pattern Recognition*, Vol. 3, August 2006, pp. 33–36.

28. D. Tao, X. Li, X. Wu, and S. J. Maybank, Elapsed time in human gait recognition: A new approach, in *Proceedings IEEE International Conference on Acoustics, Speech and Signal Processing*, Vol. 2, April 2006, pp. 177–180.

29. T. G. Kolda, Orthogonal tensor decompositions, *SIAM J. Matrix Anal. Appl.*, **23**(1):243–255, 2001.

30. H. Lu, K. N. Plataniotis, and A. N. Venetsanopoulos, Uncorrelated multilinear discriminant analysis with regularization for gait recognition, in *Proceedings of the Biometrics Symposium 2007*, September 2007, doi:10.1109/BCC.2007.4430540.

31. X. He, D. Cai, and P. Niyogi, Tensor subspace analysis, in *Advances in Neural Information Processing Systems 18 (NIPS)*, 2005.

32. G. Dai and D. Y. Yeung, Tensor embedding methods, in *Proceedings of the Twenty-First National Conference on Artificial Intelligence*, July 2006, pp. 330–335.

33. S. Yan, D. Xu, B. Zhang, H. J. Zhang, Q. Yang, and S. Lin, Graph embedding and extensions: A general framework for dimensionality reduction, *IEEE Trans. Pattern Anal. Mach. Intell.* **29**(1):40–51, 2007.

'. D. Xu, S. Lin, S. Yan, and X. Tang, Rank-one projections with adaptive margins for face recognition, *IEEE Trans. Syst., Man, Cybern. B* **37**(5):1226–1236, Oct. 2007.

ᴣ. Hua, P. A. Viola, and S. M. Drucker, Face recognition using discriminatively trained orthogonal ᴟk one tensor projections, in *Proceedings of the IEEE Computer Society Conference on Computer ᴵon and Pattern Recognition*, June 2007, pp. 1–8.

Lathauwer and J. Vandewalle, Dimensionality reduction in higher-order signal processing and $R_1, R_2, ..., R_N$) reduction in multilinear algebra, *Lin. Algebra Appl.* **391**:31–55, 2004.

A. C. Kot, and Y. Q. Shi, Distance-reciprocal distortion measure for binary document images, *ignal Processing Lett.* **11**(2):228–231, 2004.

ᴵuda, P. E. Hart, and D. G. Stork, *Pattern Classification, 2nd edition*, Wiley Interscience, ᴵk, 2001.

humeur, J. P. Hespanha, and D. J. Kriegman, Eigenfaces vs. fisherfaces: Recognition using ific linear projection, *IEEE Trans. Pattern Anal. Mach. Intell.* **19**(7):711–720, 1997.

ᴺ. Plataniotis, and A. N. Venetsanopoulos, Face recognition using lda based algorithms, ᵴ. *Neural Networks* **14**(1):195–200, 2003.

B. Bhanu, Individual recognition using gait energy image, *IEEE Trans. Pattern Anal.* ᴵ. **28**(2):316–322, 2006.

42. J. Lu, K. N. Plataniotis, and A. N. Venetsanopoulos, Face recognition using kernel direct discriminant analysis algorithms, *IEEE Trans. Neural Networks*, **14**(1):117–126, 2003.
43. T. K. Moon and W. C. Stirling, *Mathematical methods and Algorithms for Signal Processing*, Prentice-Hall, Upper Saddle River, NJ, 2000.
44. Q. Liu, X. Tang, H. Lu, and S. Ma, Face recognition using kernel scatter-difference-based discriminant analysis, *IEEE Trans. Neural Networks* **17**(4):1081–1085, 2006.
45. Z. Liang, High-dimensional discriminant analysis and its application to color face images, in *Proceedings of the International Conference on Pattern Recognition*, Vol. 2, August 2006, pp. 917–920.
46. D. Tao, X. Li, X. Wu, and S. J. Maybank, Human carrying status in visual surveillance, in *Proc. IEEE Computer Society Conference on Computer Vision and Pattern Recognition*, Vol. 2, 2006, pp. 1670–1677.
47. H. Lu, K. N. Plataniotis, and A. N. Venetsanopoulos, Uncorrelated multilinear discriminant analysis with regularization and aggregation for tensor object recognition, *IEEE Trans. Neural Networks*, 2009, to appear.
48. T. Sim, S. Baker, and M. Bsat, The CMU pose, illumination, and expression database, *IEEE Trans. Pattern Anal. Mach. Intell.* **25**(12):1615–1618, 2003.
49. A. Georghiades, P. Belhumeur, and D. Kriegman, From few to many: Illumination cone models for face recognition under variable lighting and pose, *IEEE Trans. Pattern Anal. Machine Intell.* **23**(6):643–660, 2001.
50. K. C. Lee, J. Ho, and D. Kriegman, Acquiring linear subspaces for face recognition under variable lighting, *IEEE Trans. Pattern Anal. Mach. Intell.*, **27**(5):684–698, 2005.
51. J. Ye, Characterization of a family of algorithms for generalized discriminant analysis on undersampled problems, *J. Mach. Learning Res.* **6**:483–502, 2005.
52. D. Cai, X. He, J. Han, and H. J. Zhang, Orthogonal laplacianfaces for face recognition, *IEEE Trans. Image Processing* **15**(11):3608–3614, 2006.
53. J. D. Carroll and J. J. Chang, Analysis of individual differences in multidimensional scaling via an *n*-way generalization of "eckart-young" decomposition, *Psychometrika* **35**:283–319, 1970.
54. R. A. Harshman, Foundations of the parafac procedure: Models and conditions for an "explanatory" multi-modal factor analysis, in *UCLA Working Papers in Phonetics*, Vol. 16, 1970, pp. 1–84.
55. L. R. Tucker, Some mathematical notes on three-mode factor analysis, *Psychometrika*, **31**:279–311, 1966.

# Chapter 3

# A Comparative Survey on Biometric Identity Authentication Techniques Based on Neural Networks

**Raghudeep Kannavara and Nikolaos Bourbakis**

## 3.1 INTRODUCTION

Biometrics is the study of methods for uniquely identifying or authenticating humans based on intrinsic physical or behavioral traits. *Identification* means characteristics are selected from a database, to produce a list of possible or likely matches. *Authentication* means that when a person makes a claim that he or she is that specific person, just that specific person's characteristics are being checked to see if they match. The two important operations in a biometric system are *enrollment* and *test*. During enrollment the biometric of the individual is stored as a database, and during test the biometric information of the individual is detected and compared with the stored database. Various biometric techniques are currently used, as shown in Figure 3.1.

In this chapter, we select representative works on neural networks that describe biometric-based methodologies on voice, iris, finger, palm, and face. We do not cover all the work done in the field of neural networks (NN)-based biometrics, but we select a small set of NN-based methods from different forms of biometrics in order to capture the evolution of some of the most representative neural networks based methods. The objective is to provide to the readers the general idea behind NN-based biometrics and their future [1–26].

*Biometrics: Theory, Methods, and Applications.* Edited by Boulgouris, Plataniotis, and Micheli-Tzanakou
Copyright © 2010 the Institute of Electrical and Electronics Engineers, Inc.

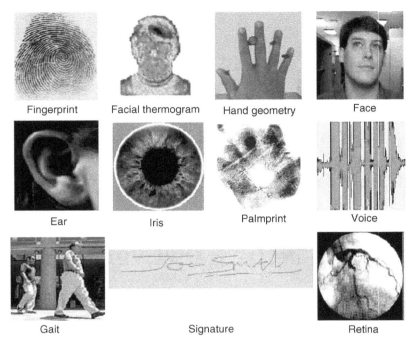

Fingerprint    Facial thermogram    Hand geometry    Face

Ear    Iris    Palmprint    Voice

Gait    Signature    Retina

**Figure 3.1.** Examples of biometric characteristics [26].

The overall organization of the chapter consists of seven main sections that reflect on the grouping of the methodologies into clusters of the same or similar biometric. Each of the first seven sections provides a brief description of the methodologies presented in the selected works and their advantages and disadvantages. In the eighth section, we provide a comparative study of the selected methodologies in order to show the status of their current performance and the potential improvement to their maximum level. Finally, Section 3.9 presents the conclusion of this study.

## 3.2    VOICE BIOMETRIC

Voice-based authentication methodologies are the easiest to implement because they do not need a considerable amount of investment on hardware. Existing hardware can be used along with required software to implement a voice-based identification system. This section contains the review of representative works that describe voice-based identity verification systems.

### 3.2.1    Speaker Verification by Means of Artificial Neural Networks

The two general approaches to speaker verification are text-dependent and text-independent. In a text-dependent speaker verification system, a predefined utterance by the user is used for training the system and testing/using it. In text-independent speaker verification, the text to be uttered is not prescribed. Effectively, language does not matter. Reference and test signals are required to have identical wording. Intra-speaker variations are induced by emotional state of the speaker, health, and aging, whereas inter-speaker variations are caused by different speaking habits such as rhythm and intonation or dialects.

Prior to comparison of the reference and test speech, some kind of time alignment has to be performed between the two. This aligning of speech signals can be done by dynamic time warping (DTW). Once this alignment is done, corresponding frames of the test and reference signals can be directly compared to each other. For each pair consisting of a test and reference signal, a distance called *local distance* is computed. The global distance is then computed by averaging the local distances over the length of the signal.

In reference 1, artificial neural network (ANN)-based distance measure for the discrimination task is investigated. The test and reference speech signals are time-aligned with the DTW algorithm that uses Euclidean cepstral distance as optimization criterion. For each frame of the aligned signals, features are extracted. These extracted features are then fed to the ANN, which yields a local distance for this pair of frames. These local distances are weighted and averaged over time to obtain the global distance, which is compared to a predetermined threshold for classification.

The ANN used in this study is a fully connected multilayer perceptron with hyperbolic tangent activation function. For training, back-propagation algorithm is used along with the adaptive learning rate. Since the feature vector has 24 cepstral coefficients, we need 24 input nodes and 1 output node. Two hidden layers having 60 nodes in the first and 18 in the second produced optimal results. The calculated distances should be the same even if the reference and test feature vectors are interchanged. This invariance was built using the absolute difference between the feature vectors. Linear transformation is used to normalize the data in order to have zero mean and diagonal covariance matrixes.

Further transitional information using the first and second derivatives of the cepstrum coefficients was fed to the ANN along with the cepstrum coefficients. For this purpose, the number of input nodes had to be tripled. Though this increased the Fisher ratio for local distances, the global distances were distorted, leading to poor performance. To overcome this issue, the authors propose the use of parallel ANN. To the first ANN, only the cepstrum coefficients are presented; to the second ANN, the first derivatives of the cepstrum coefficients are presented; and to the third, the second derivatives of the cepstrum coefficients are presented. Though the cepstrum coefficients or instantaneous features bear more information, the combination of their derivatives along with the cepstrum coefficients provides useful results.

The test set considered here is 30 male speakers. Ten sessions per speaker were recorded within a time frame of several months using different telephones. The total duration of the collected speech is about 3 h, and the LPC cepstrum coefficients were extracted from 37.5-ms-long speech frames with a frame shift of 15 ms. The ANNs were trained with some 500,000 feature pairs from 20 speakers and tested with the remaining 10 speakers along with the 20 speakers.

The authors claim that the above-presented method showed good generalization and is virtually speaker-independent. They further claim that new speakers do not require a retraining of the ANNs. But further details on how generalization is achieved are not provided. Also, the training set used is very small and if thousands of users are involved, generalization may not hold good.

## 3.2.2   Speaker Specific Mapping for Text-Independent Speaker Recognition

In reference 2, the authors propose a mapping approach for the task of text-independent speaker recognition. The mapping property of a multilayer feed-forward neural network (MLFFNN) is used to generate a model for each speaker. In the mapping approach, speaker-specific information is captured by mapping a set of parameter vectors specific to linguistic information in the speech to a set of parameter vectors having linguistic and speaker information.

Linear prediction (LP) coding-derived cepstral coefficients are used to derive suitable vectors for mapping approach. LP analysis is used to obtain clues about parameters that contain predominantly linguistic information or linguistic and speaker information. After selecting the parameter vectors suitable for mapping, the next task is to derive the mapping function itself. The nonlinear speaker-specific mapping function can be captured using the MLFFNN, where the mean-squared error is minimized using a gradient descent algorithm.

For testing, the input parameter vector is presented to each MLFFNN, and the difference between the desired output vector and the actual output vector of the MLFFNN is used as a distance for that frame. The total accumulated distance is then averaged over all test frames to give an indication of the proximity of test utterance. Euclidean distance between the output of the network and the desired output parameter vector was used for evaluating the performance of a speaker model relative to the models of other speakers. A background model (BG) is generated using the parameter vectors extracted from speech utterances of a large number of speakers registered with the system. The MLFFNN is trained with the pooled input and output parameter vectors from all the speakers. These weights from the BG model are then used to train each speaker model. This avoids the bias that any arbitrary initial weights may introduce while generating a speaker model. The relative score for the test signal is obtained using the difference between the average distance for the BG model and the speaker model. Also, investigation on the frequency content shows that speaker-specific information is available in the higher frequencies.

The authors claim that the proposed mapping approach performs as efficiently as the GMM-based approaches for all the 630 speakers in the database. But the number of free parameters is much less as compared to the Gaussian Mixture Models-based approach.

### 3.2.3   Neural Network for Improved Text-Independent Speaker Identification

In reference 3, the authors present a neural network array (NNA) that combines a binary partitioned approach having pattern index information with decision trees. The authors verify that the NNA can not only reduce the computation cost of training and recognition, but also reduce the classification error. Speaker identification with radial basis function neural network array (RBFNNA) is considered as an application of the NNA. The advantage of using NNA is that the architecture is expandable when a new entry is added; the main disadvantage of NNs needing to retain the entire network for the new catalog is partly overcome by the NNA.

The authors present a fast searching algorithm for distinguishing neural networks (NN) catalogs by a cascading a decision and pruning criteria. The subnet is trained by two catalogs. In recognition stage, a subnet could accept one catalog and reject the other catalog. If a catalog is accepted, we consider that it was similar to the correct catalog and the other must be incorrect. The search path for the algorithm is from the top row to the bottom row. All the subnets that reject the unknown catalog will be pruned.

The database used consisted of speech utterances of Chinese words, by 20 male postgraduate students under normal lab conditions. The speech signal was sampled at 8 kHz with 16 bits ADC. Sixteen orders of linear predictive cepstral coefficients (LPCC) of each frame is adopted as the speaker's features. The frames consist of 256 sample points with 128 overlapping sample points.

The authors use the RBFNN because it has the same underlying structure of the Gaussian mixture models usually used in similar applications and also because the RBFNNs have efficient training algorithms where the number of nodes in the hidden layer can be automatically determined by orthogonal least squares. The number of nodes in the first layer is 16, in the output layer it is 1, and in the hidden layer it is automatically determined.

The authors conclude that the larger the number of speakers, the higher the error rate for identification. To reduce the error rate, additional information of the catalog index can be used. Although NNA could deal with any classifying problem, its application for speaker identification is limited. The authors conclude that, additionally, the NNAs are more suitable for difficult tasks like automatic classification of EEG or biomedical signals where the signals are corrupted to a higher degree.

### 3.2.4   Speaker Identification Using Neural Networks and Wavelets

Reference 4 presents an offline system that uses wavelets to generate multiresolution time–frequency features that characterize the speech waveform to successfully identify a speaker in the presence of competing speakers. The authors say that this system is successful for short utterances and has also been applied to inter-speaker speech recognition.

The "cocktail party" effect describes the phenomenon in which humans can selectively focus attention to one sound source among competing sound sources. For the hearing impaired, the ability to achieve this effect is somewhat more difficult, because amplifying sound also translates into amplifying noise, which conventional hearing aids normally do. The primary objective of this research relates to noise in the ambient listening environment, such as with competing speakers. Therefore, before the signal processing can be applied to the sound signal arriving at the user's ears, a method must be first developed to differentiate speech and noise; that is, the noise is speech from a competing speaker.

The phonemes of speech encompass a wide variety of characteristics, in both time and frequency domains. Frequency analysis using fixed-time window techniques such as the short-time Fourier transforms are fixed window resolution operators in which the time duration of the analysis is inversely proportional to the bandwidth of the filters, meaning that high-frequency localization results in poor time resolution and vice versa. The multiresolution analysis of speech models the cochlear mechanism of spectral decomposition during the initial stage of sound transduction, wherein a time-varying signal is spatially distributed in patterns along the basilar membrane. It has been shown that the nervous system processes spatially distributed patterns more efficiently than varying temporal signals.

The original speech waveform sampled at 8 kHz is convolved with the high-pass and low-pass quadrature mirror filters. The resulting convolution coefficients are subsampled or decimated by a factor of two and they represent the coefficients for that octave. Once the time–frequency features have been obtained for the various speech waveforms, the objective is to use these features in a pattern recognition scheme and in a manner that avoids the undesirability of the local convergence. The ALOPEX (algorithms of pattern extraction) is a method developed to effectively find the global maxima and minima without local convergence, in a manner that does not require inefficient scanning.

Three male and three females, including those with American, Chinese, and European accents, were used as subjects. Subjects were asked to speak into a unidirectional microphone, leaving an approximately 1-cm gap between the mouth and the microphone. The sampling rate and analog-to-digital conversion resolution were 8 kHz at 8 bits, respectively. Each speaker was asked to articulate a series of 10 words, three times each. After the input speech is preprocessed, it is made available to the wavelet transform. The signal detail coefficients, which are time–frequency features, are generated for four octaves. Each octave has 64 bins spanning 896 ms. Signals shorter than 896 ms are padded to that duration. The wavelet transform consists of convolutions of quadrature mirror filters. Because linear convolution is inefficient, a frequency-based convolution was implemented. A problem with frequency-based convolution is that FFT processes the input signal as if it is periodic, therefore resulting in side-lobe artifacts. Also, memory overhead is high to process the entire length of the waveform at one time. To circumvent these limitations, an overlapping windowing technique is used, in which the sampled waveform is processed in windows of 256 bytes with overlaps of 32 bytes, in which each 8-bit sample is stored in a byte.

Before the next window is processed, the resulting wavelet coefficients for the current window are swapped to a disk. The current window that is read is processed entirely, but not all of the coefficients are written to the disk, because the coefficients closest to the boundary contain the artifacts associated with the FFT. The coefficients from the next window overwrite the artifact area of the previous window. The overlap values are determined as a ratio of windows overlapping each other by a factor of 1/8. As described above, the mean values of the coefficients are taken for a window subdivided by two. To calculate the time resolution that these subdivisions represent, the actual size of the window is truncated by the overlap of the preceding window. In this case, we have a 32-bit overlap for the signal. These coefficients are mapped to a 256-parameter vector and the ANN consists of 256 input nodes.

The cocktail party effect was simulated by digital mixing with the input waveform from another speaker. Tests were also conducted with input waveforms corrupted with 20-dB white noise. Training data were not used as testing data. Three methods of pattern recognition were implemented: ALOPEX template matching method, artificial neural network method using ALOPEX training algorithm, and artificial neural network using a back-propagation learning algorithm. The neural network topology used in each neural network implementation consisted of 256 nodes in the input, 10 nodes in the hidden layer, and three nodes in the output layer. Each node of the output layer represents one of the three templates (speakers). For the NN topology, the ALOPEX method showed better convergence than did the back-propagation method.

Due to computational overhead, the implementation of the cocktail party preprocessor into a digital hearing aid is presently unlikely. However, a feasible method of speaker identification in the presence of competing noise has been demonstrated, which is a complication that all speaker-and-speech recognition systems are susceptible to.

## 3.3    IRIS SCAN BIOMETRIC

Iris recognition is a method of biometric authentication that uses pattern recognition techniques based on high-resolution images of the iris of the individual's eyes. Iris scan-based security systems offer robust and reliable authentication as compared to other biometric methodologies. In this section we review representative works describing iris scan systems for identity authentication.

### 3.3.1    Fast Iris Detection for Personal Verification Using Modular Neural Nets

El-Bakry [5] presents the application of fast and cooperative modular neural nets (MNN) to automatically identify human irises in a given image. Image acquisition of the irises cannot be expected to yield an image containing only the irises. Therefore, prior to iris pattern matching, it is important to localize the portion of the acquired image corresponding to the iris. The work also aims to solve the problem of requiring large databases to build an automatic system in order to detect the location of the irises in the acquired image.

The MNN proposed in this work attempts to reduce the effects of overlearning or underlearning capabilities of the NN by using a divide-and-conquer approach, where large tasks are decomposed into smaller subtasks, each handled by a fast, simple, and efficient module. A fast searching algorithm for iris detection that reduces the computational complexity of the NNs is presented.

In the initial proposed algorithm, the first step is histogram equalization of the acquired image. Then, the classifier receives an input of $20 \times 20$ pixel region of the gray scale image and generates an output region ranging from $-1$ to $1$, signifying the presence or absence of an iris, respectively. The classifier is applied at every pixel position in the input image. To achieve rotation invariance, the NN is trained for images rotated from 0 degrees to 355 degrees by a step of 5 degrees. To detect irises in a larger window size, the input image is repeatedly reduced in size. Thus, the classification has some invariance to rotation, translation, and scaling.

To enhance the detection decision, the detection results of the neighboring windows are used to confirm the decision at a given location. This will reduce the false detection as neighboring windows may reveal non-iris characteristics of the data. A threshold on the number of neighboring windows can be used for this task. Images in the databases were divided into three groups, which resulted in three NNs. Each group consisted of 400 patterns (200 irises and 200 non-irises). Each group is used to train one neural network. Each network consists of 13 hidden neurons. The output layer consists of only one neuron. Using the enhanced detection, the author claims up to 96% detection rate.

El-Bakry [5] also presents a fast algorithm using a 2D cross-correlation technique between the reference and the input images in a sliding window. This window is represented by the neural nets weights situated between the input unit and the hidden layer. The author proposes the use of fast Fourier transforms to speed up the calculation of the cross-correlation results. The author also proposes image normalization in the frequency space by normalizing the weights in the neural network. As compared to time domain normalization, which requires $(N - n + 1)^2 n^2$ operations, the proposed frequency domain normalization requires $2n^2$ operations, where $N \times N$ is the image size and $n \times n$ is the sliding window size. The theoretical speedup factor $K$ obtained is

$$K = [q(N - n + 1)^2 \mathrm{n}^2]/[(q + 1)N^2 \log_2 N^2 + qN^2]$$

The images were tested for the presence of iris at different scales by building a pyramid of the input image, which generates a set of images at different resolutions. The iris detector is applied at each resolution, and this process takes much more time. To overcome this in Fourier space, the new scales need not be computed. This is because if $f(x, y)$ is the original image and $g(x, y)$ is the subsampled image by a factor of 2, then

$$g(x, y) = \mathrm{FT}(2x, 2y).$$

El-Bakry [5] further investigates the number of computation steps required by the neural nets on varying image sizes. It is found that as the size of the image increases, the number of computations does not increase linearly; that is, the number of computations for a $100 \times 100$ image is far greater as compared to a $50 \times 50$ image. To overcome this disadvantage, the author proposes decomposing the image into subimages and then testing these subimages separately. Further improvement can be achieved by using parallel processors on these subimages. Thus the speedup ratio increases and the running time decreases.

El-Bakry [5] claims that the simulation results show that the proposed algorithm is an efficient method for finding locations of irises when the size of the iris is unknown. Also rotated, scaled, occluded, noised, and mirrored irises are detected correctly at different illumination levels. The proposed method is also suitable for detecting the presence or absence of any other object in an image.

### 3.3.2  Iris Recognition by a Rotation Spreading Neural Network

Murakami et al. [6, 7] present a rotation spreading neural network (R-SAN net). This neural net can recognize the orientation of an object irrespective of its shape and its shape irrespective of its orientation. Thus, it is suitable for shape and orientation recognition of a concentric circular pattern because it uses polar conversion. The authors propose to experiment with R-SAN net to simultaneously recognize the orientation and shape of the iris images of people who have had their irises registered.

The input pattern of $300 \times 300$ pixels is transformed to polar coordinates. This transformed pattern is input into the spreading layer, and the spread pattern is obtained. In the learning stage, the memory matrix of the orientation and shape are obtained by generalized inverse learning. The number of learning patterns is the product of the number of learning shapes and the number of learning orientations. The spread image corresponding to the respective spreading weight is obtained by multiplication of the transformed image with the spreading weight, which is the periodic Gaussian curve function predetermined at equal intervals in various directions. The spread image is summed in each direction and combined to produce the spread pattern vector. A population vector is created to indicate the orientation of the object.

In the recollection stage, the output of orientation recognition neurons is obtained by multiplying the spread pattern and orientation memory matrix, and the output of shape recognition neurons is obtained by the spread pattern and shape memory matrix. The recognition experiments were performed in three sessions; the number of subjects was 3, 5, and 10, respectively. For each subject, six iris patterns oriented at six orientations were generated from one iris image, and these were used for learning the R-SAN net. The pupil position was detected using a partial eye template for the eye image taken by a compact close-up camera. Murakami et al. [6, 7] conclude that iris recognition is possible in any arbitrary orientation without depending on zoom of the camera. In an experiment with unlearned test iris patterns, the R-SAN net combined with minimum distance as the shape recognition criterion rejected the unregistered iris patterns.

## 3.4   FINGERPRINT BIOMETRIC

Fingerprint identification is the process of comparing given and known skin ridge impressions from fingers to determine if the impressions are from the same finger, thus identifying or verifying the owner of the given fingerprint. In this section we review representative works describing fingerprint biometric, which is by far the most commonly used biometric.

### 3.4.1   Fingerprints Classification Using Artificial Neural Nets: A Combined Structural and Statistical Approach

Nagaty [8] describes a fingerprint classification algorithm using multilayer artificial neural networks (ANN). A method for coarse level classification of the fingerprint images by combining both the structural features and statistical measure of fingerprint patterns is introduced. Fingerprints are classified into six categories: arches, tented arches, left loops, right loops, whorls, and twin loops.

After preprocessing and normalization of the fingerprint image, its block directional image is calculated and is used to extract both statistical and structural features required for classification. The classification algorithm consists of four major steps:

1. Compute the block directional image.
2. Extract the structural features of the pattern.
3. Compute the statistical measures of the pattern.
4. Design a multilayer ANN composed of six subnet works for the six fingerprint classes and use a multivariate input vector, which is a combination of the structural features and statistical measures.

In the first step of calculating the block directional image, the fingerprint image is divided into a number of squares and the local orientation is computed in these squares. Later on, the spurious directions in the block directional image are smoothened. A set of horizontal and vertical operators are used iteratively for the smoothening purpose. These block directions of the directional image are converted into binary blocks so that the resultant curves can be traced using a line tracing algorithm.

The transformed block directional image is composed of ones, which act as a link between various curves of the pattern. The pattern is scanned from left to right and from top to bottom by using a set of feature masks. Each mask is assigned a symbol, and each connected curve consists of a string of symbols that represent the curve without any loss of information. The alphabetic symbols used to represent the curve strings are then transformed to map an input vector to the ANN. Every symbol is transformed to a binary string.

Method of moments is used to extract the statistical features for a fingerprint from its characteristic string, which can be described using a second moment. The Euclidean distance measure is used to measure the distance between the second moment of the unknown pattern and mean second moment of each class. A three-layer feed-forward ANN that has six subnetworks (one for each class) is used. The input layer has 180 independent variables of the binary string and six Euclidean distances—that is, a total of 186 elements. Each subnet is trained independently on its data set by using error back-propagation learning.

The database used was the Egyptian Criminal Evidence Fingerprint database, which contains 30,000 fingerprints; of these, 1500 fingerprints of good quality were selected. Each subnet was trained on 100 patterns, which carries the characteristics of its class. Nagaty [8] claims that in a six-class problem the network achieved 95% classification accuracy; he also reports that in a four-class problem where whorls and twin loops together formed one category, the classification accuracy was 99%.

### 3.4.2 Fingerprint Classification by Directional Image Partitioning

Cappelli et al. [9] present a new fingerprint classification method that uses dynamic masks for directional image partitioning. The authors claim that this approach is translation- and rotation-invariant and does not require the singularities to be detected. The directional image is a discrete matrix whose elements represent the local average directions of the fingerprint ridge lines, which summarize the information contained in the fingerprint pattern. It is reliable even in the presence of noise and damaged areas. A compact version of the directional image by grouping similar elements into "homogeneous" regions is generated, thus eliminating redundancy and giving useful synthetic representation that can be exploited for the classification task. The authors conduct a literature review on the following:

1. Syntactic methods, where patterns are described by means of terminal symbols and production rules.

2. Approaches based on singularities, where heuristics criteria based on the number and position of the singularities are important for classification.

3. Neural approaches, where multilayer perceptrons or Kohonen self-organizing networks are used.

4. Other methods based on geometrical shape, curve fitting, and hidden Markov model classifier.

5. PCASYS approach by NIST, where the feature extraction is done using principal component analysis and classification is done by using a probabilistic neural network.

6. A structural approach based on relational graphs, where dynamic clustering algorithms are used to segment the image processed with directional masks to create homogeneous regions, thus building a relational graph.

In the new approach, Cappelli et al. [9] propose a guided segmentation of the directional image with the aim of reducing the degrees of freedom during the partitioning process. To achieve this, a set of dynamic masks directly derived from the most common fingerprint classes are used to guide the partitioning. Initially, averaging is done using a 3 × 3 window to smoothen the image, and later on the singularities are strengthened. This image is then partitioned using dynamic masks. Dynamic masks are characterized by a set of vertices defining the borders of the regions that determine the segmentation. The creation of prototype masks is thus completed. For each possible fingerprint pattern, at least one well-fitting dynamic mask is created. Therefore, the masks are derived from the classes of a well-known classifier.

Cappelli et al. [9] define two methodologies for fingerprint retrieval. The first methodology assumes an error-free classification, so the search is restricted to the database fingerprints resembling analogous classification characteristics. The second methodology allows for misclassification to be taken into consideration, and the search is carried out incrementally over the whole database. This method requires that a human expert terminates the search. For experiments, the authors used two databases:

1. Db4: contains 2000 fingerprints, uniformly distributed in five classes

2. Db14: contains 27,000 fingerprint pairs randomly taken

Cappelli et al. [9] conclude that the proposed method is suitable for both  (a) continuous classification where each fingerprint is characterized with a numerical vector, whose components denote the similarity degree with respect to a predefined set of class prototypes, and (b) exclusive classification techniques where fingerprints are partitioned into some predefined classes according to their macro-features.

## 3.5  PALM PRINT BIOMETRIC

Palm print recognition implements many of the same matching characteristics of fingerprint recognition. Palm biometrics is represented by the information presented in a friction ridge impression. This information combines ridge flow, ridge characteristics, and ridge structure of the raised portion of the epidermis. The data represented by these impressions allow identification or authentication of individuals by comparing with a database. In this section we review representative works that describe biometric identification based on palm prints.

### 3.5.1  Biometric Identification through Hand Geometry Measurements

Macros et al. [10] present a method in defining and implementing a biometric system based on hand geometry identification. Hand features are extracted from a color photograph of the user's hand. Various pattern recognition techniques are explored for classification and verification. The authors claim up to 97% success rate in classification.

Hand geometry is appropriate for medium security applications. There are certain advantages in using hand geometry, as listed below:

1. Medium cost
2. Low computational cost algorithms
3. Low template size
4. Easy and attractive to users, leading to nearly null user rejection
5. Lack of relation to police, justice, and criminal records

The hand geometry identification system presented in this work works in two phases:

1. An enrollment phase where several photographs are taken from the user, and features extracted from them are stored in a central database.
2. The verification phase where a single photograph is taken, and features extracted from it are compared with the data base.

The comparison phase can be configured in two ways:

1. As a classifier, where the extracted features are compared with the features of all the users' templates in the database to recognize the user.
2. As a verifier, where the user states his/her identity and only a particular sample belonging to that user is compared.

The process starts with the image capture of the user's palm. The captured image is a 640- × 480-pixel color photograph in JPEG format. The image also contains a lateral view of the hand due to the placement of a mirror, to be able to measure heights. This captured color image is then converted to a black and white image. Any deviations due to hand positioning are then corrected by resizing or rotating this image. An edge detector—that is, Sobel function—is applied to extract the contour of the hand. In the measurement phase, features based on the following are extracted: widths of the four fingers; the height of the middle finger, little finger, and the palm; inter-finger distances/deviations, and inter-finger angles. To account for weight loss or gain by the user, all distances are taken relative to a determined measure.

A total of 31 features are extracted: 21 widths, 3 heights, 4 deviations, and 3 angles. Using the Fisher ratio, redundant features were eliminated, and the total number of features was reduced to 25. For the purpose of classification and verification, the features vectors are compared against templates in the database. For this purpose, four methods were evaluated:

1. *Euclidean Distance*: This is the most common approach of all where Euclidean distances between the user's feature vectors and the feature vectors in the database are calculated.
2. *Hamming Distance*: Based on the assumption that the feature vector distribution follows the Gaussian distribution, hamming distances are calculated for classification.

**3.** *Gaussian Mixture Models (GMM)*: A simple probability density function is calculated through training to estimate the probability if a sample belongs to a class or not.

**4.** *Radial Basis Functions Neural Networks (RBFNN)*: A two-layer neural network is trained using the feature vectors from all the users for classification purpose. But if it is to be used for a user verification purpose, each user has to have his or her own NN, but this NN has to be trained using all the feature vectors from all the users in the database. This could be against some restrictions. Therefore, Marcos et al. [10] consider only a classification scheme for the RBFNN.

The database was created using 10 photographs of 20 people of different ages, sex, color, profession, and living style, taken over three months. For enrollment, three to five samples were considered sufficient. Experiments were carried out for both verification and classification approaches.

Marcos et al. [10] conclude that in both the approaches, the GMM performed better with 97% of success for classification and an error rate below 10% for verification. Reducing the feature vectors to nine features leads to great loss in success rate. The database size used is limited and the authors conclude with a remark on conducting further work using a larger database with easier implementation approaches to generalize the results obtained.

## 3.5.2   Personal Authentication Using Palm-Prints Features

Cheng et al. [11] propose a scanner-based personal authentication system by using the palm print features. The identification process is composed of two stages: enrollment and verification. In the enrollment stage, many hand images of an individual are collected and preprocessed for feature extraction and creation of a template. In the verification stage, the test sample is also preprocessed for feature extraction and then matched with the templates to decide whether it is a genuine sample or not.

The preprocessing is done by image thresholding, border tracing, wavelet-based segmentation, and ROI location. Sobel and other morphological operators are used for feature extraction, and the reference templates are generated. In verification, template matching along with back-propagation neural nets are used to measure similarity between the reference and test samples. To create the feature vectors, the mean values of pixels in the grids are calculated. These values are sequentially arranged row by row to form the feature vectors. The authors use three different grid sizes—$32 \times 32$, $16 \times 16$ and $8 \times 8$—to obtain the multiresolution feature vectors. Template matching using the correlation function is used to perform the verification task to decide whether the query sample is genuine or not. Also, in the case of neural nets, a three-layer-based network that includes a hidden and an output layer is used. The number of neurons in each layer is 80, 40, and 1, respectively.

To create the database, 30 hand images of each person are obtained three times within three weeks. In the enrollment stage, the first 10 images are used to train, and 20 other images are used for verification. Implementation and coding was done using C and Matlab on a Windows platform. For the template matching method, Cheng et al. [11] report 91% accuracy rate, whereas for the neural network based method, using the back-propagation and scaled conjugate gradient algorithm, the authors report 98% accuracy.

## 3.6   FACIAL BIOMETRIC

Face recognition systems work by comparing the acquired facial image of an individual with a database to identify or authenticate the individual. In this section we review representative works that describe face recognition systems based on neural networks.

### 3.6.1   Face Recognition with Radial Basis Function (RBF) Neural Networks

Er et al. [12] present an efficient design approach for the radial basis function neural networks (RBFNN) classifier to deal with small training sets of high dimension. The face features are first extracted using the principal component analysis (PCA) and are then processed with Fisher's linear discriminant to lower the dimensionality. The authors also propose a hybrid algorithm for training the RBFNNs.

The face recognition problem has the following issues as compared to any other pattern classification problem:

1. Overfitting: If the input dimension for network is comparable to the size of the training set, it results in poor generalization.

2. Overtraining: High dimension of the network input results in slow convergence.

3. Small Sample Effect: Small samples can easily contaminate the design and evaluation of the proposed system.

4. If the number of training patterns is less than the number of features plus one, the sample covariance matrix is singular and unusable.

The proposed method tries to solve the above problems and deals with small training sets of high dimensionality. The proposed method consists of the following parts:

1. Reducing the number of input variables: Features are extracted using the PCA and the dimensionality is reduced using Fischer's linear discriminator.

2. A new clustering algorithm concerning category information and training samples: To avoid undesired and highly dominant averaging phenomenon associated with unsupervised learning algorithms, Er et al. [12] propose using

a supervised clustering algorithm that takes into consideration the category information of the training data.

3. Two criteria to estimate the width of the RBF to control generalization:

   • *Majority Criterion*: In any class, each datum should have more than 50% confidence level for the class to which it belongs.
   • *Overlapping Criterion*: The key idea of this approach is to consider not only the intra-data distribution, but also the inter-data variations.

   The number of inputs is made equal to that of features (i.e., the dimension of the input space) and the number of outputs to be equal to that of classes.

4. A hybrid learning algorithm to train the RBF: The hybrid algorithm combines the gradient and the linear least squares paradigm to adjust the parameters.

A total of 300 face images from the ORL database were used. The training set consisted of 10 images for each of the 30 individuals, selected to represent different poses and expressions. Another 300 images were used as the testing set. Er et al. [12] claim that the results demonstrated that the success rate of recognition is 100%.

### 3.6.2    A State-of-the-Art Neural Network for Robust Face Verification

Bengio et al. [13], propose the use of skin color as an additional feature for robust face verification. This new feature set is tested on a benchmark database, namely XM2VTS, using a simple discriminant artificial neural network. The bounding box for the face is computed using the coordinates of the located eyes, assuming perfect face detection. The face is then cropped and the extracted subimage is down-sized to a $30 \times 40$ image. After enhancement and smoothing, the face then becomes a feature vector of dimension 1200. The skin color pixels are filtered from the subimage corresponding to the extracted face, using a look-up table of skin color pixels. For better results, the face bounding box should thus avoid as much hair as possible.

The histograms for RGB pixel components are calculated. These histograms are characteristic to a specific person and also can be used as discriminant among different people. The illumination during image acquisition is controlled. For each color channel, a histogram is built using 32 discrete bins. Hence, the feature vector produced by the concatenation of the histograms (R, G, and B) has 96 components. For verification, the authors choose multilayer perceptrons (MLP). For each client, the MLP is trained to classify the input as the given client or an imposter. The input to the MLP is a feature vector extracted from the face image with or without skin color. The MLP is trained using both client and imposter images.

The database used for this purpose is the multimodal XM2VTS database, and its associated experimental protocol is the Lausanne Protocol. The XM2VTS database contains synchronized image and speech data recorded on 295 subjects during four sessions taken at one-month intervals. On each session, two recordings were made, each consisting of a speech shot and a head rotation shot. The 295 subjects were divided into a set of 200 clients, 25 evaluation impostors, and 70 test impostors.

For experimenting and comparison, the authors compared an MLP using 1200 inputs corresponding to the downsized 30 × 40 gray-scale face images and an MLP using 1296 inputs corresponding to the same face image and skin color. For each client model the training database consisted of four images of the client and four images of the imposter training set. The database was enlarged by rotating and scaling these images. These training sets were later divided into three subsets, one for training, one for validation, and a third as a test set. A 90-hidden-unit MLP was the chosen architecture. The authors conclude that the results using the skin color information achieve state-of-the art results and have enhanced performance.

### 3.6.3   Face Recognition: A Convolution Neural Network Approach

Back et al. [14] present a hybrid neural network solution. The system combines local image sampling, a self-organizing map neural network, and a convolutional neural network. The authors present results using the Karhunen–Loeve transform in place of the self-organizing map and a multilayer perceptron in place of the convolutional network. The convolutional network extracts larger features in a hierarchical set of layers. The authors are interested in face recognition with varying facial detail, expression, pose, and so on, and do not consider invariance to high degree of scaling or rotation.

Initially, local sampling of the image is done. The authors evaluate two methods to perform local sampling:

1. The first method is to create a vector from a local window on the image using intensity values at each point in the window.

2. The second method creates a representation of the local sample by forming a vector out of the intensity of the center pixel and the difference in intensity between the center pixel and all the other pixels within the square window.

A self-organizing map (SOM) is trained on the vectors from the previous stage. Back et al. [14] also experiment with replacing the SOM with Karhunen–Loeve transform. The same window as in the first step is stepped over all of the images in the test, and training sets and the generated vectors are passed through the SOM at each step, thereby creating new training and test sets in the output space created by self-organizing map.

A convolutional neural network is trained on the newly created training set. The network consists of a set of layers, each of which contains one or more planes. Multiple planes are used to detect multiple features. Back et al. [14] also experimented with training a standard multilayer perceptron for comparison, but it resulted in poorer performance since the MLP does not have inbuilt variance to minor translation and local deformation.

With respect to computational complexity, the SOM takes considerable time to train. But the system can be extended to cover new classes without retraining. It also took considerable time to train the convolutional network. To overcome this issue, the author suggests breaking the convolutional block into two: the initial feature extraction layer and the final feature extraction and classification layer. Replacing the second part with another type of classifier such as a nearest-neighbor classifier greatly reduces the training time for the NN when adding new classes.

On the whole, the self-organizing map provides a quantization of the image samples into a topological space where inputs that are nearby in the original space are also nearby in the output space, which results in invariance to minor changes in the image samples. Also, the convolution NN provides for partial invariance to translation, rotation, scale and deformation. Substituting the Karhunen–Loeve transform for the self-organizing map produced slightly worse results. With five images per person from the ORL database, Back et al. [14] claim that the proposed method resulted in 3.8% error.

## 3.6.4   A Local–Global Graph Approach for Facial Expression Recognition

Kakumanu and co-workers [15, 16] present a local global graph approach for recognizing facial expressions from static images irrespective of varying illumination, shadows, and cluttered backgrounds.

Initially a neural network to detect skin in real-world images, based on color constancy method, is presented. Later, the local–global graph (LGG) method is presented here for detecting faces and facial expressions with a maximum confidence from skin segmented images. The LGG approach first extracts the most important facial features and then interrelates them for face and facial expressions; that is, it combines local information with the global information. Facial expression recognition from the detected face images is obtained by comparing the LG expression graphs with the existing LG expression models present in the LGG database.

### 3.6.4.1   Neural Network

An NN is used for adapting skin color under various illumination conditions. First, the images are color-corrected based on the illuminant estimate of the NN. The skin regions in the NN-stabilized images are then detected using a simple threshold operation. The advantage of the NN method for color adaptation is that it does not have any inherent assumptions about the object surfaces in the image or the illumination sources because the input to the network is only the color from the image. Initially, the NN is trained so as to adapt to the skin color using random images from a database consisting of images collected under various illumination conditions both indoor and outdoor and containing skin colors of different ethnic groups. The color correction step assigns achromatic (gray) to skin pixels. The second skin detection stage classifies the skin and non-skin pixels using a threshold based on the achromatic value of the color-corrected images.

It should be noted that building an accurate classifier that can detect all the skin types under all possible illuminations, shadows, cluttered backgrounds, and makeup, using visible spectrum, is still an unsolved question.

### 3.6.4.2   Local Region Graph (Facial Feature Region Graph)

A local graph is built to encode the spatial relationships of the line segments that are a result of a curve-fitting procedure on the segmented regions produced by the neural network. Each facial region is represented by a local graph; and to identify the segmented regions as facial regions, we need to match the local graph of the segmented regions to the stored model local graphs in the database.

It is also important to identify the geometrical positions and placements of the facial features along with identifying those features. The authors use the Voronoi tessellation method, the Delaunay triangulation, and the local–global graphs as the basic representation of the image structure. Matching two graphs involves establishing point correspondences between two graph node sets that maximize the likelihood between two graphs, given the spatial constraints. The extra step needed for recognizing facial expressions is that we need to compare the image LG graph with the existing expression LG graphs.

The proposed LGG method does not require any training samples. The graph method is invariant to scale, to rotations, and, to a certain extent, to pose, and it is shown to perform robustly under various illumination conditions when combined with the neural-constancy-based skin detection. Five facial features are used to represent an expression, and the authors propose to use other features such as furrows and cheeks, and they also indicate facial motion during an expression.

## 3.6.5   Comparison of Neural Network Algorithms for Face Recognition

Dong et al. [17] present a comparison of neural methods of recognizing faces using three different compression techniques, namely, wavelets, moments, and F-CORE coefficients. Different types of faces were used as inputs: normal with different facial expressions; clear of noise and noise-contaminated; and smiling and serious ones; also, the effects of occlusion or missing parts of the faces were considered.

The images were obtained from different individuals with a JVC camcorder. The images were saved in a TGA format. With custom-made software, using the Laplacian pyramid structure, the images were reduced in size and further compressed by several methods. The compression was done in order to extract features that could be used as inputs to a NN. Before compression took place, some processing was also done on the images to normalize the data for better comparisons later on. Since the images were taken under different luminance and background conditions, a masking process is used to segment the face from its background.

### 3.6.5.1   F-CORE Method

The Fourier-based compression reconstruction technique was developed by Micheli–Tzanakou and Binge. After performing the DFT and finding the power spectrum of an image, it sorts the coefficients from maximum to minimum. Once this is accomplished, a user-selectable percent of these coefficients is stored along with their coordinates in the power spectrum. The rest of the coefficients are set to zero. If the reconstruction is desired, the saved coefficients are put back in the original position and the so-formed power spectrum is used in an inverse DFT. The image so formed is then used as a first "guess" of an image that is refined to perfection by algebraic reconstruction techniques. In order to do that, the sums of each column and of each row in the image are also saved. A multiplicative algebraic technique is used until perfection of the image is achieved.

### 3.6.5.2  Invariant Moments

The system has been designed for the representation of gray-scale images by invariant moments. A set of moments that are invariant to translation, rotation, and scaling is computed, so these can be used as inputs to a neural network for the recognition of human faces from various images. The type of invariant moments that has been used in this system is known as Hu's moments.

Using a 2D continuous function $f(x, y)$, moment of order $(p + q)$ is defined as

$$m_{pq} = \iint x^p y^q f(x, y) \, dx \, dy$$

for $p = 0, 1, 2, 3, \ldots$ and $q = 0, 1, 2, 3, \ldots$.

Correspondingly, the central moments can be defined as

$$\mu_{pq} = \iint (x - x')^p (y - y')^q f(x, y) \, dx \, dy$$

Here, $x' = m_{10}/m_{00}$ and $y' = m_{01}/m_{00}$.

The third-order central moments are calculated and normalized. From these normalized central moments, the seven invariant moments are computed.

### 3.6.5.3  Wavelet Decomposition

The principal drawback with Fourier transforms is its inability to analyze a signal locally. To overcome this, wavelet transform is used and is built by dilating and translating a unique function $g(x)$. This decomposition defines an orthogonal multiresolution representation called a *wavelet representation*. It is computed with a pyramidal algorithm based on convolutions with quadrature mirror filters. A wavelet transform can be interpreted as decomposition into a set of frequency channels having the same bandwidth on a logarithmic scale. The resolution of the wavelet transform varies with scale parameter. Large scale implies coarse resolution in spatial domain and fine in frequency domain, whereas small scale implies coarse resolution in frequency domain and fine in spatial domain. The multiresolution decomposition is critically sampled; that is, the number of samples in the representation is equal to the number of samples in the signal. This allows one to violate the Nyquist criteria without discarding information. The 2D images of the preprocessed faces are subjected to a wavelet analysis. The wavelet transform is based on dilations and translations of a unique function known as "wavelet," defined by

$$g_{q,p(t)} = \frac{1}{\sqrt{|q|}} g\left(\frac{(t-p)}{q}\right),$$

where $g(t)$ is the wavelet prototype, corresponding to scale $q$ and position, or space, $p$.

### 3.6.5.4 Neurocomputing

The architecture or interconnection schemes employed by neural network designs is varied as the applications, although some have seen a special concentration through the years. Two types of training are commonly seen: supervised and unsupervised. In supervised learning, there exists information about the correct solution (desired transformation) of the network for each example pattern presented to it. In unsupervised learning, no a priori information about the desired transformation exists, and the training must be solely based on the properties of the patterns. Dong et al. [17] comment that it is better to begin thinking of neuron-computing as an alternative to the many years of sequentially dominated processing. Neural networks are a specialized form of parallel distributed processing (PDP) systems and can be useful as a machine, but they must be looked at as a machine and not as a biological blueprint.

### 3.6.5.5 Feature Extraction

A good feature extraction routine will compress the input space to a lower dimensionality while still maintaining a large portion of the information contained in the original pattern space. In unsupervised situations, the only information available to the feature extraction module is the statistical distribution of the patterns. In such a scenario, it is impossible to quantitatively analyze the effectiveness of a feature extraction routine in improving pattern classification. However, there are operators designed to maintain high information content in the features (as compared to the original measurement pattern) with a minimal number of dimensions. For a classification problem the operator's input to the network is a feature vector, whereas the outputs are represented so that one output node per class or template is assigned, and for a feature vector from class I the desired output is shown for one neuron being *on* while the rest of the output neurons are *off*.

### 3.6.5.6 Multilayer Perceptron

Common network architectures consist of multiple layers of neurons, where each neuron in layer 1 is connected to all neurons in layer 2. The input layer receives external stimuli, and the output layer generates the output of the network. The hidden layer and all the interconnections are responsible for the neuron computation. As the number of neurons increases, problem complexity increases as does the time to train the network. Only after training is the network capable of performing the task it was designed to do.

### 3.6.5.7   *The Back-Propagation Algorithm*

The back-propagation is a learning scheme where the error is back-propagated layer by layer and used to update the weights. The algorithm is a gradient descent method that minimizes the error between the desired output and the actual output calculated by the MLP. The gradient descent method updates an arbitrary weight, $w$, in the network by the following rule:

$$w(n + 1) = w(n) + w(n),$$

where $\Delta w(n) = -k(\partial E/\partial w(n))$ and, where $n$ is the iteration number and $k$ is a scaling constant.

There are many variations to the basic algorithm that have been proposed to speed the convergence of the system. Convergence is defined as a reduction in the overall error below a minimum threshold. It is the point at which the network is said to be fully trained. One method used in Dong et al. [17] is the inclusion of momentum term in the update equation as shown below:

$$w(n + 1) = w(n) - k(\partial E/\partial w(n)) + a\Delta w(n),$$

where $k$ is the learning rate and is taken as 0.25 and $a$ is a constant momentum term.

### 3.6.5.8   *The ALOPEX Algorithm*

The ALOPEX process is an optimization procedure that has been successfully demonstrated in a wide variety of applications. It incorporates a stochastic element to avoid local extremes in search of the global optimum of the cost function. The cost function is problem-dependent and is generally a function of a large number of parameters. ALOPEX iteratively updates all parameters simultaneously based on cross-correlation of local changes, $\Delta X_i$, and the global response change $\Delta R$, plus an additive noise. All parameters $X_i$ are changed simultaneously at each iteration according to the equation

$$X_i = X_i(n - 1) + \gamma \Delta X_i(n)\Delta R + r_i(n).$$

The basic concept is that this cross-correlation provides a direction of movement for the next iteration. The general ALOPEX updating equation is explained as follows. $X_i(n)$ are the parameters to be updated, $n$ is the iteration number, and $R(\ )$ is the cost function, of which the best solution in terms of $X_i$ is sought. Gamma, $\gamma$, is a scaling constant, $r_i(n)$ is a random number from a Gaussian distribution whose mean and standard deviation are varied, and $\Delta X_i(n)$ and $\Delta R$ are found by

$$\Delta X_i = X_i(n - 1) - X_i(n - 2),$$
$$R(n) = R(n - 1) - R(n - 2).$$

The calculation of $R(n)$ is problem-dependent and can be modified easily. Additional constraints include a maximal change permitted for $X_i$, for one iteration. This bounded step size prevents the algorithm from drastic changes from one iteration to the next. These drastic changes often lead to long periods of oscillations without convergence.

### *3.6.5.9    Results*

After preprocessing, the feature vectors are fed to the NN as inputs. Several options were used, such as the performance of effectiveness of the features used, the convergence of the algorithms, their recognition ability, and their performance on noisy and incomplete images. All three methods of compression converge to the same level eventually, but the wavelets seem to perform in a much smoother way and much faster than the rest.

When the NN was tested with the images used in training, recognition for ALOPEX was 99%. The training with back-propagation was inferior and so was its testing. Also, the number of iterations that back-propagation needed for convergence was much higher than the ones needed for ALOPEX. Features also played and important role in the recognition rate of the neural network. For tilted and smiling faces or profiles, invariant moments performed better. The F-CORE coefficients were most robust to noise and partially occluded faces.

## 3.7  COMBINING BIOMETRIC TECHNIQUES

Combining two or more biometric technologies yields better performance and reliability, reducing false rejections and false acceptance rates by the biometric systems. In this section we review representative works that describe combining two biometric technologies.

## 3.7.1  Fusion of Face and Speech Data for Person Identity Verification

Identity authentication task is a binary classification problem: reject or accept identity claim. Combining/fusing information based on a different modality like speech, face, and/or fingerprint increases the performance and robustness of identity authentication systems. Abdeljaoued et al. [18] propose to evaluate different binary classification schemes like support vector machine, multilayer perceptrons, C4.5 decision tree, Fisher's linear discriminant, and Bayesian classifier, to carry on the fusion. The authors concentrate on the biometric identity verification problem, where the user states his or her identity; this is verified with a database to accept or reject the claim.

The first method investigated is the elastic graph matching (EGM) method. Each face is represented by a set of feature vectors positioned on nodes of a coarse, rectangular grid placed on the image. As features, the modulus of complex Gabor responses from filters with six orientations and three resolutions are used. Comparing two faces corresponds to matching and adapting a grid taken from one image to the features of the other image, taking into account both the feature vectors of each node and the deformation information attached to the edges. The matching is done in two steps, initially a rigid matching is performed, and then this rigidly matched grid is deformed to minimize the distances between the reference and input feature vectors. The contributions from each node are considered equally, which may be of disadvantage since the contributions of each node to the distance are different. The second method investigated is the speaker verification method. Both text-dependent and text-independent methods are investigated.

In the text-independent speaker verification, liner prediction cepstral coefficients are calculated from the audio signal. The 12 LPC coefficients along with the signal energy yield the 13-dimensional feature vector. Covariance matrix for these features is calculated, and during testing the covariance matrix for the input signals is calculated, and their arithmetic harmonic sphericity measure is used as similarity measure.

In the case of text-dependent speaker verification, hidden Markov models (HMM) are explored. When a user claims a certain identity, the HMM of the claimed identity will be used to compute the likelihood of the feature vector being generated by the client—that is, the true claimed identity. Similarly, the HMM modeling the world (or impostors) will be used to compute the likelihood of the feature vector being generated by an impostor. The decision is then made by comparing the likelihood ratio to a predefined threshold. All models were trained based on the maximum likelihood criterion using the Baum–Welch algorithm and verified using the Viterbi algorithm to calculate the likelihood. Having computed the match using the above methods, a verification decision is made based on the fusion of the above-computed results. For classification purposes, the following methods are evaluated.

### 3.7.1.1  Support Vector Machines

The support vector machine is based on the structural risk minimization. Better generalization capabilities are achieved through a minimization of the bound on the generalization error. The computational complexity of the SVM during the training depends on the number of data points rather than on their dimensionality. At the run time, the classification is a simple weighted sum.

### 3.7.1.2  Minimum-Cost Bayesian Classifier

The results from distributed detection and distributed estimation are used, since the data from multisensors is used. This multimodal person authentication problem reduces to using the Bayesian classifiers. The quality of the probability fusion and decision models depends on the modeling of the likelihood function.

### 3.7.1.3  Fisher's Linear Discriminant

Fisher's, linear discriminator maximizes the ratio of interclass variance to intraclass variance.

### 3.7.1.4  C4.5 Decision Trees

In a decision tree, at each node a test on a particular attribute of the data is performed. The path of the root node to a particular leaf is then a series of tests on the attributes that classifies the data to the class defined by the particular leaf.

### 3.7.1.5 Multilayer Perceptron

A multilayer perceptron with one hidden layer is used for classification purpose. The hidden layer is composed of 10 hidden units. Training will be performed with the classical back-propagation algorithm.

To achieve fair evaluation of the different approaches, the authors compared the performance of different fusion schemes on a large database of 295 subjects with a specified testing protocol. Among the evaluated classifiers mentioned above, Abdeljaoued et al. [18] claim that the SVM polynomial and the Bayesian classifiers gave the best results, therefore outperforming the single modalities. In the case of the Bayesian classifier, data modeling is necessary, whereas the SVM technique does not assume any particular data distribution.

## 3.7.2  Combining Face and Iris Biometrics for Identity Verification

Jain et al. [19] present two different strategies for fusing face and iris classifiers. The first method is to compute a weighted and/or unweighted sum to be compared with a threshold, and the second method is to use distance measure of the feature vectors on classifiers like Fisher discriminator or neural networks with radial basis functions.

The accuracy of face recognition is affected by illumination, pose, and facial expression. In the case of an iris, image acquisition must meet stringent quality so that poor-quality images are rejected. Also, an iris can change over time—that is, due to diseases. Some of the above problems can only be solved, or at least their impact reduced, by fusing several biometric identification systems, such as face and iris recognizers. The advantage in fusing various modalities of biometric data is that people with specific disabilities will be able to use the biometric identification system. Among the face recognition techniques, appearance-based approaches are the most popular—for example, principal component analysis (PCA), independent component analysis (ICA), and linear discriminant analysis (LDA) using the eigenface method as the face matcher. In the case of iris verification, dyadic wavelets are used are used to filter the acquired iris image.

In the weighted sum method for fusion of data, since the performance of different classifiers is different, it is necessary to use different weights to combine the individual classifiers. In the case of the Fisher discriminant analysis, the face and iris matcher outputs are treated as feature vector $X = (x_1, x_2)$, and known classifiers are used to determine the separation boundary. In the case of the RBFNN, since it is a verification problem, every subject has his or her own neural network. The feature vectors $(x_1, x_2)$ are fed to the NN for classification.

Two databases were created. The first database consisted of 2096 iris images corresponding to 210 subjects, captured by an iris acquisition system developed at NLPR. There are at least five images for one eye. Iris images of left and right eyes are known to be different. Since not every individual provided iris images of both the eyes, there are 303 different classes from 210 subjects. The images were acquired during two different sessions, one month apart. The second database was created to illustrate the enrollment failure and its effect on the overall verification accuracy by using some of the poor-quality iris images that would normally be rejected in an operational iris verification system. Forty subjects and 400 iris images (10 images per subject) were used.

In the case of database 1, the performance of the fusion is worse than the performance of the iris stand-alone system except for the weighted sum rule. In the case of database 2, which includes some poor-quality iris images that will be rejected by an operational iris verification system, the images are accepted and correctly classified by the fused classifier, which means that the enrollment failure rate can be decreased by fusion while maintaining a high accuracy.

## 3.8    COMPARATIVE SURVEY

In this section we set up comparative survey tables to compare the various methods reviewed above.

### 3.8.1    Comparative Survey Tables

In Table 3.1 all methodologies are listed. In each cell a "1" is designated if this feature is available or a "0" is designated if this feature is not available. In Table 3.2 for each feature, a weight is assigned which reflects its importance from the user's view (weights table). For example, computational complexity is much more important to the engineer than to the user, because coding, construction, and implementation of the device is done by the engineer since the lesser the computational complexity, the easier it is to code and implement the software.

We grade each methodology, if possible, with a value ($x_i$) between 1 and 10 (scores table). If we don't grade one characteristic, we make it 0, which means that the characteristic is not available or we don't have enough information. Finally in Table 3.3, using the formula $T = \sum_{i=1}^{N} w_i x_i / N + b$, a total score of each methodology is calculated, where $i$ refers to a specific characteristic, $N$ is the total number of characteristics for each system, and $b$ is bias (for now, $b = 0$). Below are some examples to show how the weights are assigned in the tables.

**Method Complexity**

   Highest complexity: 10

   Least complexity: 1

**Invasive**

   Highly invasive: 10

   Noninvasive: 1

**Product**

   Product: 10

   Not a product: 1

**Table 3.1.** Methodology Versus Features Table

| | F1 | F2 | F3 | F4 | F5 | F6 | F7 | F8 | F9 | F10 | F11 | F12 | F13 | F14 | F15 | F16 | F17 | F18 | F19 |
|------|----|----|----|----|----|----|----|----|----|-----|-----|-----|-----|-----|-----|-----|-----|-----|-----|
| M1   | 1  | 1  | 1  | 1  | 1  | 0  | 1  | 1  | 1  | 1   | 1   | 1   | 0   | 1   | 1   | 1   | 1   | 1   | 1   |
| M2   | 1  | 1  | 1  | 1  | 1  | 0  | 1  | 1  | 1  | 1   | 1   | 1   | 0   | 1   | X   | 1   | 1   | 1   | 1   |
| M3   | 1  | 1  | 1  | 1  | 1  | 0  | 1  | 1  | 1  | 1   | 1   | 1   | 0   | 1   | 1   | 1   | 1   | 1   | 1   |
| M4   | 1  | 1  | 1  | 1  | 1  | 0  | 1  | 1  | 1  | 1   | 1   | 1   | 0   | 1   | 1   | 1   | 1   | 1   | 1   |
| M5   | 1  | 1  | 1  | 1  | 1  | 0  | 1  | 1  | 1  | 1   | 1   | 1   | 0   | 1   | 1   | 1   | 1   | 1   | 1   |
| M6   | 1  | 1  | 1  | 1  | 1  | 0  | 1  | 1  | 1  | 1   | 1   | 1   | 0   | 1   | X   | 1   | 1   | 1   | 1   |
| M7   | 1  | 1  | 1  | 1  | 1  | 0  | 1  | 1  | 1  | 1   | 1   | 1   | 0   | 1   | X   | 1   | 1   | 1   | 1   |
| M8   | 1  | 1  | 1  | 1  | 1  | 0  | 1  | 1  | 1  | 1   | 1   | 1   | 0   | 1   | X   | 1   | 1   | 1   | 1   |
| M9   | 1  | 1  | 1  | 1  | 1  | 0  | 1  | 1  | 1  | 1   | 1   | 1   | 0   | 1   | X   | 1   | 1   | 1   | 1   |
| M10  | 1  | 1  | 1  | 1  | 1  | 0  | 1  | 1  | 1  | 1   | 1   | 1   | 0   | 1   | 1   | 1   | 1   | 1   | 1   |
| M11  | 1  | 1  | 1  | 1  | 1  | 0  | 1  | 1  | 1  | 1   | 1   | 1   | 0   | 1   | 1   | 1   | 1   | 1   | 1   |
| M12  | 1  | 1  | 1  | 1  | 1  | 0  | 1  | 1  | 1  | 1   | 1   | 1   | 0   | 1   | X   | 1   | 1   | 1   | 1   |
| M13  | 1  | 1  | 1  | 1  | 1  | 0  | 1  | 1  | 1  | 1   | 1   | 1   | 0   | 1   | 1   | 1   | 1   | 1   | 1   |
| M14  | 1  | 1  | 1  | 1  | 1  | 0  | 1  | 1  | 1  | 1   | 1   | 1   | 0   | 1   | X   | 1   | 1   | 1   | 1   |
| M15  | 1  | 1  | 1  | 1  | 1  | 0  | 1  | 1  | 1  | 1   | 1   | 1   | 0   | 1   | X   | 1   | 1   | 1   | 1   |
| M16  | 1  | 1  | 1  | 1  | 1  | 0  | 1  | 1  | 1  | 1   | 1   | 1   | 0   | 1   | 1   | 1   | 1   | 1   | 1   |
| M17  | 1  | 1  | 1  | 1  | 1  | 0  | 1  | 1  | 1  | 1   | 1   | 1   | 0   | 1   | X   | 1   | 1   | 1   | 1   |

**Table 3.2.** Weights Table

|  | F1 | F2 | F3 | F4 | F5 | F6 | F7 | F8 | F9 | F10 | F11 | F12 | F13 | F14 | F15 | F16 | F17 | F18 | F19 |
|---|---|---|---|---|---|---|---|---|---|---|---|---|---|---|---|---|---|---|---|
| User's perspective | 2 | 1 | 1 | 10 | 9 | 10 | 1 | 10 | 10 | 10 | 10 | 3 | 2 | 10 | 10 | 10 | 9 | 9 | 9 |
| Administrator's perspective | 7 | 1 | 1 | 10 | 9 | 10 | 1 | 8 | 10 | 10 | 10 | 3 | 9 | 7 | 10 | 8 | 9 | 9 | 9 |
| Engineer's perspective | 9 | 10 | 7 | 10 | 9 | 10 | 10 | 8 | 10 | 10 | 10 | 9 | 7 | 8 | 10 | 7 | 10 | 9 | 9 |
| Average | 6 | 4 | 3 | 10 | 9 | 10 | 4 | 8.7 | 10 | 10 | 10 | 5 | 6 | 8.3 | 10 | 8.3 | 9.3 | 9 | 9 |

Weights from Table 3.2:

| Features | F1 | F2 | F3 | F4 | F5 | F6 | F7 | F8 | F9 | F10 | F11 | F12 | F13 | F14 | F15 | F16 | F17 | F18 | F19 |
|---|---|---|---|---|---|---|---|---|---|---|---|---|---|---|---|---|---|---|---|
| Weights | 6 | 4 | 3 | 10 | 9 | 10 | 4 | 8.7 | 10 | 10 | 10 | 5 | 6 | 8.3 | 10 | 8.3 | 9.3 | 9 | 9 |

**Table 3.3.** Scores Table

| | F1 | F2 | F3 | F4 | F5 | F6 | F7 | F8 | F9 | F10 | F11 | F12 | F13 | F14 | F15 | F16 | F17 | F18 | F19 | Total | Final Total |
|---|---|---|---|---|---|---|---|---|---|---|---|---|---|---|---|---|---|---|---|---|---|
| M1 | 7 | 8 | 5 | 7 | 8 | 0 | 8 | 9 | 7 | 6 | 6 | 9 | 0 | 1 | 7 | 9 | 7 | 7 | 8 | 849.1 | 44.69 |
| M2 | 8 | 6 | 6 | 8 | 9 | 0 | 6 | 7 | 7 | 6 | 6 | 7 | 0 | 1 | 7 | 6 | 8 | 6 | 8 | 809.1 | 42.58 |
| M3 | 7 | 7 | 6 | 8 | 9 | 0 | 7 | 8 | 8 | 9 | 8 | 8 | 0 | 1 | 8 | 6 | 7 | 8 | 8 | 903.5 | 47.55 |
| M4 | 6 | 8 | 7 | 7 | 8 | 0 | 9 | 7 | 7 | 6 | 6 | 9 | 0 | 1 | 9 | 8 | 7 | 8 | 8 | 856.4 | 45.07 |
| M5 | 6 | 8 | 7 | 7 | 8 | 0 | 8 | 8 | 8 | 8 | 9 | 9 | 0 | 1 | 9 | 7 | 6 | 8 | 8 | 903.5 | 47.55 |
| M6 | 7 | 7 | 6 | 6 | 8 | 0 | 7 | 7 | 7 | 6 | 6 | 8 | 0 | 1 | 7 | 7 | 7 | 7 | 8 | 795.1 | 41.85 |
| M7 | 7 | 7 | 6 | 7 | 8 | 0 | 8 | 7 | 7 | 6 | 6 | 8 | 0 | 1 | 8 | 7 | 7 | 7 | 8 | 809.1 | 42.58 |
| M8 | 6 | 8 | 7 | 8 | 9 | 0 | 8 | 8 | 8 | 8 | 8 | 8 | 0 | 1 | 8 | 6 | 8 | 8 | 8 | 907.8 | 47.78 |
| M9 | 8 | 7 | 6 | 8 | 8 | 0 | 6 | 7 | 7 | 6 | 6 | 7 | 0 | 1 | 6 | 6 | 8 | 6 | 8 | 794.1 | 41.79 |
| M10 | 7 | 7 | 8 | 8 | 8 | 0 | 7 | 9 | 7 | 6 | 7 | 8 | 0 | 1 | 7 | 9 | 7 | 7 | 8 | 865.1 | 45.53 |
| M11 | 7 | 7 | 5 | 8 | 8 | 0 | 7 | 9 | 6 | 6 | 6 | 8 | 0 | 1 | 7 | 9 | 7 | 7 | 8 | 826.1 | 43.48 |
| M12 | 7 | 8 | 6 | 8 | 8 | 0 | 8 | 8 | 8 | 8 | 8 | 8 | 0 | 1 | 8 | 6 | 8 | 8 | 8 | 901.8 | 47.46 |
| M13 | 7 | 7 | 7 | 6 | 8 | 0 | 7 | 8 | 9 | 9 | 9 | 7 | 0 | 1 | 8 | 6 | 7 | 8 | 8 | 892.5 | 46.97 |
| M14 | 6 | 7 | 7 | 6 | 7 | 0 | 8 | 7 | 6 | 6 | 7 | 7 | 0 | 1 | 7 | 7 | 7 | 7 | 8 | 782.1 | 41.16 |
| M15 | 7 | 8 | 8 | 7 | 7 | 0 | 8 | 7 | 6 | 6 | 7 | 6 | 0 | 1 | 7 | 7 | 7 | 7 | 8 | 800.1 | 42.11 |
| M16 | 7 | 7 | 8 | 7 | 8 | 0 | 7 | 9 | 6 | 6 | 7 | 7 | 0 | 1 | 7 | 7 | 7 | 7 | 8 | 823.5 | 43.34 |
| M17 | 7 | 7 | 8 | 7 | 8 | 0 | 7 | 7 | 7 | 6 | 6 | 7 | 0 | 1 | 7 | 7 | 7 | 7 | 8 | 806.1 | 42.43 |

### Training Time (Preprocessing Stage)

High training time: 10

Low training time: 1

### Computational Requirements

High: 10

Low: 1

Similarly, the rest of the scores are assigned, with 10 standing for highest score and 1 standing for the lowest score applicable for that feature. The methods with their abbreviations are given below:

| Method | Abbreviation |
| --- | --- |
| Speaker verification by means of ANNs | M1 |
| Biometric identification through hand geometry measurements | M2 |
| Fast iris detection for personal verification using modular neural nets | M3 |
| Fusion of face and speech data for person identity verification | M4 |
| Combining face and iris biometrics for identity verification | M5 |
| Face recognition with radial basis function (RBF) neural networks | M6 |
| A state-of-the-art neural network for robust face verification | M7 |
| Fingerprints classification using artificial neural networks: A combined structural and statistical approach | M8 |
| Personal authentication using palm-prints features | M9 |
| Speaker-specific mapping for text-independent speaker recognition | M10 |
| Neural network for improved text-independent speaker identification | M11 |
| Fingerprint classification by directional image partitioning | M12 |
| Iris recognition by a rotation spreading neural network | M13 |
| Face recognition: A convolution neural network approach | M14 |
| A local global graph approach for facial expression recognition (includes an ANN-based approach for image chromatic adaptation for skin color detection) | M15 |
| Speaker identification using neural networks and wavelets | M16 |
| Comparison of neural network algorithms for face recognition | M17 |

The features with their abbreviations are given below:

| | | |
| --- | --- | --- |
| F1 | Simplicity | The methodology is simple. |
| F2 | Complexity | The number of operations to be performed by the methodology for achieving the desirable solution. |
| F3 | Originality | The methodology is based on original algorithms and or mathematical formulas or the synergistic combination of simple methods composing a new original method. |

| F4 | Real application | The methodology is applicable to solve real problems of high importance. |
| F5 | Real-Time (Processing Time) | The methodology can be implemented in real time. It can produce results as soon as the input data is fed to the methodology. |
| F6 | Product | The methodology is a commercial product. |
| F7 | Computational requirements | The computational power required by the methodology to produce desirable results. |
| F8 | Friendliness (to user) | The methodology offers a user-friendly interface. |
| F9 | Performance and test on real cases | Sufficient results and performance statistics are presented to back up methodology's efficiency on real cases. |
| F10 | Reliability | The methodology produces reliable results. |
| F11 | Robustness | The methodology produces acceptable results under any circumstances. |
| F12 | Training time (preprocessing stage) | The methodology requires extra time for preprocessing the data set (i.e., NN training). |
| F13 | Cost | The amount of money needed for the purchase or usage of the methodology. |
| F14 | Invasive | The methodology requires a preprocessing stage, such as a surgical operation, in order to produce its results. |
| F15 | Security levels | Security level that the methodology can provide. |
| F16 | Requires training to User | The methodology requires that the user be trained. |
| F17 | Further improvements | The methodology has the potential of further enhancement. |
| F18 | Implementation | The methodology has already been implemented in a useable environment. |
| F19 | Prototype | The methodology has been successfully implemented at the experimental stage and produced desirable results. |

## 3.9  CONCLUSION

In the previous sections we provided a comparative study on neural-nets-based biometric methodologies from a selective set of works. We also set up comparative survey tables to compare the various works and methods that we reviewed. We find that iris scan and fingerprint scan offer the better performance as compared to face-based, voice-based, and palm-print-based biometrics. We also see that combined biometrics yield better results as compared to relying on just one biometric measure. It is also important to mention here that our comparative study does not intend to identify one or more methods as being better than others (which requires running these methods under the same conditions or on the same data sets), but to indicate the status of the current performance of these methods and their potential improvements if this is desirable.

# REFERENCES

1. U. Niesen and B. Pfister, Speaker Verification by Means of ANNs, reprint from Proceedings of ESANN 2004, April 28–30, Brugges, Belgium.

2. H. Misra, B. Yegnanarayana, and S. Ikbal, Speaker specific mapping for text independent speaker recognition, *Speech Commun.* **39**:301–310, 2003.

3. X. Yue, D. Ye, C. Zheng, and X. Wu, Neural networks for improved text-independent speaker identification, *IEEE Eng. Med. Biol. Mag.* **21**(2):53–58, 2002.

4. F. Phan, E. Micheli-Tzanakou, and S. Sideman, Speaker identification using neural networks and wavelets, *IEEE Eng. Med. Biol. Mag.* **19**(1):92–101, 2000.

5. H. El-Bakry, Fast iris detection for personal verification using modular neural nets, in *Fuzzy Days 2001,* LNCS 2206, Springer-Verlag, Berlin, 2001, pp. 269–283.

6. M. Murakami, K. Nakamura, and H. Takano, Iris recognition by a rotation spreading neural network, in *Neural Networks, 2004,* Proceedings, 2004 IEEE International Joint Conference, Vol. 4, 25–29 July 2004 pp. 2589–2594.

7. M. Murakami, K. Nakamura, and H. Takano, Real-time iris recognition by a rotation spreading neural network, *SICE 2003 Annual Conference*, Vol. 1, 4–6 August 2003, pp. 283–289.

8. K. A. Nagaty, Fingerprints classification using artificial neural networks: a combined structural and statistical approach, *Neural Networks* **14**:1293–1305, 2001.

9. R. Cappelli, A. Lumini, D. Maio, and D. Maltoni, Fingerprint classification by directional image partitioning, *IEEE Trans. Pattern Anal. Mach. Intell.* **21**(5):402–421, 1999.

10. R. Sanchez-Reillo, C. Sanchez-Avila, and A. Gonzalez-Marcos, Biometric identification through hand geometry measurements, *IEEE Trans. Pattern Anal. Mach. Intell.* **22**(10):1168–1171, 2000.

11. H. L. Cheng, K. C. Fan, C. C. Han, and C. L. Lin, Personal authentication using palm-prints features, *Pattern Recognit.* **36**:371–381, 2003.

12. M. J. Er, S. Wu, and J. Lu, Face recognition with radial basis function (RBF) neural networks, in *Proceedings of the 38th IEEE Conference on Decision and Control,* Vol. 3, 1999, pp. 2162–2167.

13. S. Bengio, C. Marcel, and S. Marcel, *A State-of-the-Art Neural Network for Robust Face Verification,* Dalle Molle Institute for Perceptual Artificial Intelligence (IDIAP), P. O. Box 592, CH-1920 Martigny, Switzerland.

14. S. Lawrence, C. Lee Giles, A. C. Tsoi, and A. D. Back, Face recognition: A convolution neural-network approach, *IEEE Trans. Neural Networks,* **8**(1):98–113, 1997.

15. P. Kakumanu and N. Bourbakis, A local global graph approach for facial expression recognition, in *18th IEEE International Conference on Tools with Artificial Intelligence, 2006* (ICTAI 2006), November 2006, pp. 685–692.

16. N. Bourbakis, R. Bryll, P. Kakumanu, and S. Makrogiannis, An ANN based approach for image chromatic adaptation for skin color detection, in *16th IEEE International Conference on Tools with Artificial Intelligence, 2004,* (ICTAI 2004), 15–17 November 2004, pp. 478–485.

17. J. Dong, E. Micheli-Tzanakou, R. Ramanujan, R. Ray, A. Sharma, and E. Uyeda, Comparison of neural network algorithms for face recognition, *Simulation* **64**(1):15–27, 1995.

18. S. Ben-Yacoub, Y. Abdeljaoued, and E. Mayoraz, Fusion of face and speech data for person identity verification, *IEEE Trans. Neural Networks* **10**(5):1065–1074, 1999.

19. A. K. Jain, T. Tan, and Y. Wang, Combining face and iris biometrics for identity verification, in *4th International Conference on AVBPA,* June 2003.

20. A. Ross, J. Reisman, and A. Jain, Fingerprint matching using feature space correlation, in *Proceedings of Post-ECCV Workshop on Biometric Authentication,* 2002, pp. 48–57.

21. M. Tico and P. Kuosmanen, Fingerprint matching using an orientation-based minutiae descriptor, *IEEE Trans. Pattern Anal. Mach. Intell.* **25**(8):1009–1014, 2003.

22. R. Sanchez-Reillo and C. Sanchez-Avila, *RBF Neural Networks for Hand-Based Biometric Recognition,* Springer, Berlin, 2001.

23. S. Yong, W. Kin Lai and G. Goghill, *Weightless Neural Networks for Typing Biometrics Authentication,* Springer, Berlin, 2004.

24. M. Brady, Biometric recognition using a classification neural network, U.S. patent, 1999.
25. G. K. Venayagamoorthy, V. Moonasar, and K. Sandrasegaran, Voice Recognition Using Neural Networks, in *Proceedings of the 1998 South African Symposium on Communications and Signal Processing, 1998*, COMSIG '98, Rondebosch, South Africa, 7–8 September 1998, pp. 29–32.
26. A. K., Jain, A., Ross, and S., Prabhakar, An introduction to biometric recognition, *IEEE Trans. Circuits Sys. Video Techno.* **14**(1):4–20, 2004.

# Chapter 4

# Designing Classifiers for Fusion-Based Biometric Verification

**Kritha Venkataramani and B. V. K. Vijaya Kumar**

## 4.1  INTRODUCTION

The natural variability of biometric features presents challenges to recognition. In some practical situations, there may be a large variability present in the intra-person features and perhaps small differences between the inter-person features. Pose, illumination, and occlusion present major challenges in face recognition. For example, in the Face Recognition Grand Challenge (FRGC) [1] Experiment 4, involving the matching of studio-quality gallery images to probe images corresponding to uncontrolled illumination, the baseline principal component analysis (PCA) method has a correct verification rate of only 12% at 0.1% false accept rate (FAR). Challenges in fingerprint recognition are due to (a) elastic distortion caused by applying pressure on the finger on a sensor surface and (b) varying environmental conditions such as dryness, moisture, dirt, and so on, present in fingers. Varying eyelid occlusion in iris images causes difficulty in iris recognition. To mitigate the effect of such impairments, multiple sources of information/experts/classifiers can be fused to improve accuracy.

Dasarathy [2] provides different classifications of fusion based on the application, objective, input–output characteristics, and sensor-suite configuration. Among the input–output characteristics, classification is based on data, features, or classifier outputs. Multimodal fusion (e.g., fusion of face and finger) and multisensor fusion (e.g., visual and infrared camera data) are examples of data fusion. Sensor-suite

*Biometrics: Theory, Methods, and Applications.* Edited by Boulgouris, Plataniotis, and Micheli-Tzanakou
Copyright © 2010 the Institute of Electrical and Electronics Engineers, Inc.

configurations fall into serial or parallel sensor fusion. This chapter focuses on parallel classifier output fusion for biometric verification.

Kuncheva [3] reviews different classifier fusion strategies. Classifier decisions or scores can be fused. In addition to combining outputs from all classifiers, classifier selection can be done depending on the accuracy of the classifiers on the test sample. The most common decision fusion examples are Majority voting and weighted-Majority voting [3]. Other decision fusion methods such as Naive Bayes [4] and Behavior Knowledge Space [5] estimate the posterior probability of the decision vector. Examples of papers on score fusion are references 6 and 7. These are mainly empirical in nature, where the error rates of simple fusion rules such as the sum or the product of scores are compared on databases to find the best fusion rule. There is some theoretical analysis as to when fusion accuracy can be improved for linear and order-statistic score combiners [8] and Majority voting [3, 9].

Ho et al. [10] introduced the concept of dynamic classifier selection (DCS) as an alternative to classifier ensemble combination where the most appropriate classifier is chosen to make the decision. Classifier selection is typically done by estimating the local accuracy (around the test point) of the classifiers in the test phase. This is attempted by finding the $K$ nearest neighbors to the test input in the training or validation set and then computing the competence of the classifiers on these $K$ objects [11]. There are several variations of this approach [12, 13].

The classifier ensemble generation/selection is much more important than the selection or fusion. This is because none of these methods are effective in reducing the ensemble fusion error when the classifier ensemble has poor diversity. There is a lack of theory on generating classifier ensembles that have the desired statistical dependence on their outputs. Some methods have been attempted to generate classifier ensembles that have desirable statistical dependence for sum score fusion and Majority fusion [14], but have not been successful. There are some classifier ensemble selection strategies that select diverse classifiers from among randomly generated classifiers [15–17]. Such selection strategies are suboptimal in general, and fail to take into account the complete statistical dependence between all classifier outputs.

This chapter provides guidelines for optimal ensemble generation, where each classifier in the ensemble is of the same type (base classifier). This approach is applicable to most base classifiers. Examples are shown here for support vector machines [18] and correlation filters [19]. While background and references for different base classifiers are not provided here, the readers are referred to other sources for such information [3, 20].

Decision fusion rules are focused on in this chapter since the space of decision fusion rules is large and fixed. For $N$ classifiers, there are $2^{2^N}$ decision fusion rules. There is some similarity between common decision fusion rules such as the Majority rule and typical score fusion rules such as the Sum rule. Hence, some of the ideas presented here are applicable to score fusion too. Section 4.2 analyzes the effect of classifier output diversity on their decision fusion accuracy. It is found that the Or, And, and Majority decision rules are important because of the likeliness of one of them being the best fusion rule when the individual classifiers have the same accuracy. Section 4.3 analyzes the Or rule fusion in detail. The diversity between classifier outputs for which Or fusion is effective in increasing accuracy is analyzed. Similar analysis for other fusion rules can be carried out [21]. Guidelines for the design of classifier ensembles for the important decision fusion rules are provided and demonstrated on biometric data in Sections 4.4 to 4.6. The conclusion and important contributions are provided in Section 4.7.

## 4.2 ROLE OF STATISTICAL DEPENDENCE ON CLASSIFIER ENSEMBLE FUSION

In the literature, the statistical dependence that is useful for a particular fusion rule is studied [3, 9]. A unified analysis of how all fusion rules are affected by statistical dependence is not present. This is investigated in this section by studying which decision fusion rule is the best over each value of statistical dependence for a given number of classifiers [21, 22]. This analysis is directly useful to determine the best decision fusion rule for a given set of classifiers, without searching over a large space of rules. It is also useful in ensemble generation, because statistical dependence is easier to control in ensemble design than fusion accuracy. The link between statistical dependence and ensemble generation is explained in Sections 4.4, 4.5, and 4.6.

The statistical dependence between classifier decisions implies a statistical dependence between classifier scores. A link between diversity measures of decisions and scores is provided in this section. The role of statistical dependence is investigated by evaluating the accuracy of three-classifier decision fusion rules on three jointly Gaussian scores with various covariances. For jointly Gaussian scores with known means and variances of individual classifiers, the correlation coefficient between pairs of classifier scores completely characterizes the statistical dependence. Hence, it is used as the classifier score diversity measure [3]. It is linked to the $Q$ statistic, which is found to be a good diversity measure for classifier decisions [3].

The effect of statistical dependence between classifiers on the fusion performance is analyzed by finding the minimum probability of error for the best fusion rule for different statistical dependences between the classifiers. For $N$ classifiers and two classes, there are $2^{2^N}$ decision fusion rules. The optimal decision fusion rule for independent classifiers is monotonic [23]. For statistically dependent classifiers, the optimum decision fusion is nonmonotonic in general. However, there are large regions of statistical dependence in which monotonic rules are optimal [21]. It is beyond the scope of this chapter to explain this result, and we focus only on monotonic rules here to limit the computational complexity. For two, three, and four classifiers, there are 6, 20, and 168 monotonic rules, respectively [23]. For a large number of classifiers, the number of monotonic rules becomes too large, and searching for the best rule becomes computationally infeasible. The performance of all the monotonic rules for three classifiers are analyzed at different statistical dependence between classifiers to study if there are any important decision rules.

We assume that there are two classes, authentics and impostors, which need to be discriminated in verification applications. Let $H_0$ and $H_1$ be the two hypotheses denoting impostors and authentics, respectively. Three synthetic classifier scores, $s$, are generated from the following joint Gaussian distributions, with equal variances and same pairwise correlation coefficient.

$$p(\mathbf{s}|H_1) \sim N\left(\begin{bmatrix} 1 \\ 1 \\ 1 \end{bmatrix}, \begin{bmatrix} 1 & \rho_a & \rho_a \\ \rho_a & 1 & \rho_a \\ \rho_a & \rho_a & 1 \end{bmatrix}\right), \qquad -0.5 \le \rho_a \le 1, \qquad (4.1)$$

$$p(\mathbf{s}|H_0) \sim N\left(\begin{bmatrix} 0 \\ 0 \\ 0 \end{bmatrix}, \begin{bmatrix} 1 & \rho_i & \rho_i \\ \rho_i & 1 & \rho_i \\ \rho_i & \rho_i & 1 \end{bmatrix}\right), \qquad -0.5 \le \rho_i \le 1. \qquad (4.2)$$

The correlation coefficient for authentic scores, $\rho_a$, can be different from that of the impostor scores, $\rho_i$. The limits on the correlation coefficient ensure that the covariance matrix is positive semidefinite. $\rho_a$ and $\rho_i$ are varied from $-0.5$ to 1 in steps of 0.1; and for each combination of $(\rho_a, \rho_i)$, 10,000 authentic and 10,000 impostor scores are generated from their respective joint Gaussian distributions.

There are 20 monotonic rules for three-classifier decision fusion. One rule declares everything as authentic; one rule declares everything as impostor. These two rules need not be considered since either the FAR or FRR is 100%. The other 18 rules are shown in Figure 4.1. The single-classifier and two-classifier rules are not considered because they will not have more accuracy than three-classifier rules. This is because there is information to be gained from fusion of all classifiers. In addition to the three-classifier And, Or, and Majority rules, there are six three-classifier rules where Or (And) fusion of two classifiers is followed by And (Or) fusion of the third classifier. Only one each of the latter type of decision rules need to be considered since individual classifiers are identical and have same pairwise correlation coefficient.

The minimum probability of error, assuming equiprobable priors for authentics and impostors, is found for the five three-classifier monotonic fusion rules for each combination of $(\rho_a, \rho_i)$. The thresholds on the classifier scores are chosen jointly (by brute force) to minimize the probability of error. It may happen that the thresholds are different for each classifier. Details on finding this joint set of thresholds are given in reference 22. Figure 4.2 shows the minimum probability of error for the best decision fusion rule at each value of $(\rho_a, \rho_i)$ and Figure 4.3 shows the best decision fusion rule as a function of $(\rho_a, \rho_i)$. It can be seen from Figure 4.2 that the minimum probability of error is different for different statistical dependence values. Hence it is desirable to design classifiers to have a particular statistical dependence that leads to the smallest probability of error. The maximum error probability in Figure 4.2 is for the case of maximum 'positive' correlation ($\rho_a = 1$, $\rho_i = 1$), with the probability of error on fusion equal to the minimum probability of error for the single classifier, which is 31% for this experiment. Here, the best thresholds for fusion rules are such that only one classifier is used and the other two are ignored. All other points in the figure are smaller, showing that the fusion of multiple classifiers improves the

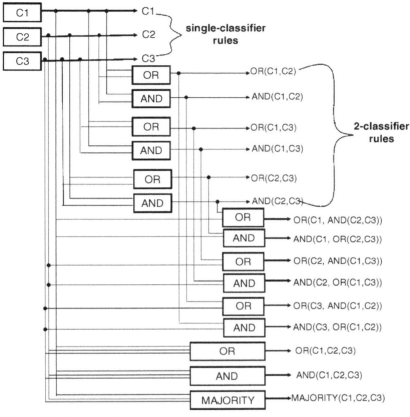

**Figure 4.1.** Eighteen of the twenty monotonic rules for three-classifier fusion. The other two rules declare everything as authentic and impostor, respectively.

accuracy over the individual classifiers. The probability of error surface has its minima at the corners of the plot—that is, at $(\rho_a = -0.5, \rho_i = -0.5)$, $(\rho_a = 1, \rho_i = -0.5)$, $(\rho_a = -0.5, \rho_i = 1)$ for which the And, Majority, and Or rules, respectively, are the best with the probability of error of 7%, 11%, and 7%, respectively. In other words, the And and the Or rules are the best rules since they can achieve the smallest probability of error at their *optimal* conditional dependence.

From Figure 4.3, it can be seen that the And, Or, and Majority rules are the important fusion rules to focus on since one of these three is the best rule at any given $(\rho_a, \rho_i)$. In general, from the figure, the best decision fusion rule appears to be as follows:

$$\text{best rule} = \begin{cases} \text{And,} & \rho_a > 0, \rho_i < \rho_a, \\ \text{Majority,} & \rho_a \leq 0, \rho_i \leq 0, \\ \text{Or,} & \rho_i > 0, \rho_i > \rho_a. \end{cases} \tag{4.3}$$

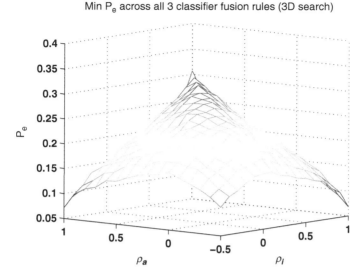

**Figure 4.2.** Minimum probability of error of three classifiers for the best fusion rule as a function of statistical dependence.

It is also seen in Figure 4.3 that there are multiple fusion rules having the best performance at and around the boundaries of the regions given in Eq. (4.3). This boundary region has a slow rate of decrease in error from the single-classifier error, as observed from Figure 4.2. Hence, this region of the classifier statistical dependence is not desirable.

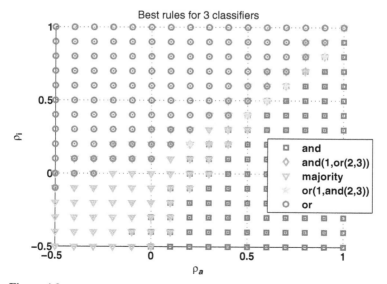

**Figure 4.3.** The best fusion rule as a function of statistical dependence.

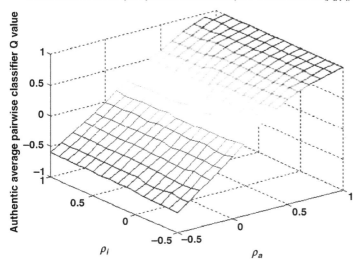

**Figure 4.4.** Authentic $Q$ values at the optimal thresholds of the best decision rule at different authentic ($\rho_a$) and impostor ($\rho_i$) score correlation coefficients.

There is a link between the diversity of classifier decisions and the diversity of classifier scores. The $Q$ statistic, is a good diversity measure for classifier decisions [3]. The pairwise classifier $Q$ statistic is defined by

$$Q = \frac{N_{11}N_{00} - N_{10}N_{01}}{N_{11}N_{00} + N_{10}N_{01}}. \tag{4.4}$$

Here, $N_{ab}$ is the number of number of data points in the evaluation dataset for which the first classifier declares $a = 0, 1$ and the second classifier declares $b = 0, 1$. The $Q$ value is zero for statistically independent decisions and has limits of $-1$ and $1$. The $Q$ value has the same sign as the correlation coefficient of classifier decisions $\rho_d$. It can also be proved that $|\rho_d| \leq |Q|$. The best decision rule's authentic and impostor $Q$ values at the optimal thresholds of the three-classifier scores are shown as a function of the correlation coefficient of the scores in Figures 4.4 and 4.5. The authentic (impostor) $Q$ values plotted are the average pairwise classifier authentic (impostor) $Q$ values. It can be observed that the sign of the authentic (impostor) $Q$ value is the same as the sign of the authentic (impostor) correlation coefficient between scores. Furthermore, the magnitude of the $Q$ values increase (decrease) as the magnitude of the correlation coefficients increase (decrease). Hence there is a direct relation between the $Q$ values of decisions (at the best thresholds) and the $\rho$ of scores. Taking into account Eq. (4.3) and the above result, the sign of the diversity measures, Q and $\rho$, are useful in predicting the best decision fusion rule.

From this section, it is found that Or, And, and Majority are the important decision rules because one of them is the best decision fusion rule (for individual classifiers

**Impostor Q value (at best thresholds) as a function of $(\rho_a, \rho_i)$**

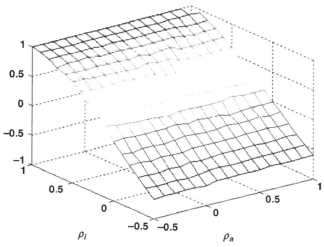

**Figure 4.5.** Impostor $Q$ values at the optimal thresholds of the best decision rule at different authentic $(\rho_a)$ and impostor $(\rho_i)$ score correlation coefficients.

having the same accuracy and same pairwise statistical dependence). Furthermore, the sign of the diversity measures—correlation coefficient of scores, $\rho$, and $Q$ value of decisions—is a good measure for predicting the best decision fusion rule for a given set of classifiers. While this is observed for three classifiers in this section, it is extended to the general case of $N$ classifiers in the next section.

## 4.3    ANALYSIS OF OR RULE FUSION

The statistical dependence that improves accuracy of the important decision fusion rules, Or, And, and Majority, can be studied in detail for the general case of $N$ classifier fusion. This analysis is necessary for optimal ensemble generation. The Majority decision rule has been investigated in references 3 and 9. Since the Or decision rule is complementary to the And decision rule, the results of the analysis for these two rules will be complementary. Hence, only one of these two rules need to be studied. Or rule fusion is analyzed in this section.

The conditional dependence where the error rates are minimized, for given individual classifier error rates, is termed as *optimal* conditional dependence. Ensembles having *optimal* conditional dependence are unlikely to be obtained due to the difficulties in ensemble generation for a given database. Hence, the *favorable/ unfavorable* conditional dependences for the Or rule are analyzed. The conditional dependence where the error rates are smaller (larger) than the corresponding values of conditionally independent classifiers is referred to as favorable (unfavorable) conditional dependence.

Analysis of conditional dependence on 2-classifier Or fusion and 2-classifier And fusion were presented in references 24 and 25, respectively. Accuracy improvement of the general case of $N > 2$ classifier Or fusion over that of conditionally independent classifiers is analyzed in this section. The error rates on authentics and impostors are considered separately with a view to decrease each of them over the corresponding values of conditionally independent classifiers.

The false reject rate (FRR) for the Or rule at favorable conditional dependence is first considered. Let $u_j$ be the decision made by the $j$th classifier. Let $\mathbf{u}$ be the vector of decisions from the $N$ classifiers. For Or rule fusion of $N$ classifiers, the $P_{FR}$ is given by

$$P_{FR} = P\left(\mathbf{u} = \begin{bmatrix} 0 & 0 & \cdots & 0 \end{bmatrix} | H_1\right). \tag{4.5}$$

The probability of detection ($P_D$), the complement of $P_{FR}$, can be written as follows.

$$P_D = 1 - P_{FR} = 1 - P\left(\mathbf{u} = \begin{bmatrix} 0 & 0 & \cdots & 0 \end{bmatrix} | H_1\right)$$

$$= P\left(\bigcup_{j=1}^{N}(u_j = 1 | H_1)\right)$$

$$= \sum_{j=1}^{N} P(u_j = 1 | H_1) - \sum_{j=1}^{N}\sum_{k \neq j} P(u_j = 1 \cap u_k = 1 | H_1)$$

$$+ \sum_{j=1}^{N}\sum_{k \neq j}\sum_{l \neq j,l \neq k} P(u_j = 1 \cap u_k = 1 \cap u_l = 1 | H_1)$$

$$- \cdots + (-1)^{N-1} P(u_1 = 1 \cap u_2 = 1 \cap \cdots \cap u_N = 1 | H_1). \tag{4.6}$$

Minimizing FRR is the same as maximizing $P_D$. From the above equation, we can maximize $P_D$ by maximizing all the terms in the right-hand side (RHS) with a positive sign in front of them, that is, the first, third, fifth, and other odd-order terms, and minimizing all the terms with a negative sign in front of them, that is, the second, fourth, and other even-order terms. When each of the even (odd) terms are larger (smaller) than their corresponding values at conditional independence, then it is certain that *favorable* authentic conditional dependence for Or rule fusion is achieved. At conditional independence, the probability of the intersection of events is equal to the product of the individual events. The $k$th-order probabilities in Eq. (4.6) should be as follows for *favorable* authentic conditional dependence, where the RHS terms are their values at conditional independence.

Second-order probability:

$$P(u_{i_1} = 1, u_{i_2} = 1|H_1) \leq P(u_{i_1} = 1|H_1)P(u_{i_2} = 1|H_1),$$

$$i_1 \neq i_2, 1 \leq i_1, i_2 \leq N.$$

Third-order probability:

$$P(u_{i_1} = 1, u_{i_2} = 1, u_{i_3} = 1|H_1) \geq \prod_{j=1}^{3} P(u_{i_j} = 1|H_1),$$

$$i_1 \neq i_2 \neq i_3, 1 \leq i_1, i_2, i_3 \leq N. \qquad (4.7)$$

$k$th-order probability:

$$P(u_{i_1} = 1, \ldots, u_{i_k} = 1|H_1) \leq \prod_{j=1}^{k} P(u_{i_j} = 1|H_1), \qquad \text{if } k \text{ is even,}$$

$$\geq \prod_{j=1}^{k} P(u_{i_j} = 1|H_1), \qquad \text{if } k \text{ is odd,}$$

$$i_j \neq i_l, 1 \leq j, l, \leq k, 1 \leq i_j, i_l \leq N.$$

We can quantify the conditional dependence through correlation coefficients of the normalized decisions. The normalized decisions with zero mean and unit variance, $z_h(i)$, are given by

$$z_h(i) = \frac{u_i - P(u_i = 1|H_h)}{\sqrt{P(u_i = 1|H_h)(1 - P(u_i = 1|H_h))}}, \qquad h = 0, 1. \qquad (4.8)$$

The second and higher-order correlation coefficients of these normalized variables are defined as follows.

Second-order coefficient:

$$\rho_h(i_1, i_2) = E\left(z_h(i_1)z_h(i_2)\right), i_1 \neq i_2, 1 \leq i_1, i_2 \leq N, h = 0, 1$$

$$= E\left(\frac{\left(u_{i_1} - P(u_{i_1} = 1|H_h)\right)\left(u_{i_2} - P(u_{i_2} = 1|H_h)\right)}{\prod_{j=1}^{2} \sqrt{P(u_{i_j} = 1|H_h)(1 - P(u_{i_j} = 1|H_h))}} \Bigg| H_h\right). \qquad (4.9)$$

Third-order coefficient:

$$\rho_h(i_1, i_2, i_3) = E\left(z_h(i_1)z_h(i_2)z_h(i_3)\right),$$

$$i_1 \neq i_2 \neq i_3, 1 \leq i_1, i_2, i_3 \leq N, h = 0, 1$$

$$= E\left(\frac{\prod_{j=1}^{3}\left(u_{i_j} - P(u_{i_j} = 1|H_h)\right)}{\prod_{j=1}^{3}\left(\sqrt{P(u_{i_j} = 1|H_h)(1 - P(u_{i_j} = 1|H_h))}\right)} \Bigg| H_h\right). \qquad (4.10)$$

$k$th-order coefficient:

$$\rho_h(i_1, i_2, i_3, \ldots, i_k) = E\left(z_h(i_1)z_h(i_2)z_h(i_3) \cdots z_h(i_k)\right),$$

$$i_j \neq i_l, 1 \leq j, l, \leq k, 1 \leq i_j, i_l \leq N. \qquad (4.11)$$

The sign of the $k$th-order authentic correlation coefficients at *favorable* authentic conditional dependence are obtained as follows by taking into account the desired inequalities in Eq. (4.7). For the sake of convenience in demonstration, let

$$q_j = \frac{1}{\sqrt{P(u_{i_j} = 1|H_1)(1 - P(u_{i_j} = 1|H_1))}}. \qquad (4.12)$$

At *favorable* authentic conditional dependence, the sign of the second-order authentic correlation coefficient of the normalized decisions is negative, as demonstrated below.

$$\rho_1(i_1, i_2) = q_1 q_2 E\left(\left(\left(u_{i_1}u_{i_2} - \sum_{m=1}^{2}\sum_{n=1, n\neq m}^{2} u_{i_m} P(u_{i_n} = 1|H_1)\right)\right)|H_1\right)$$

$$+ q_1 q_2 \prod_{j=1}^{2} P(u_{i_j} = 1|H_1)$$

$$= q_1 q_2 \left\{ E\left(u_{i_1}u_{i_2}|H_1\right) - P(u_{i_1} = 1|H_1)P(u_{i_2} = 1|H_1)\right\}$$

$$\leq 0 \quad \text{since } E\left(u_{i_1}u_{i_2}|H_1\right) \leq \prod_{j=1}^{2} P(u_{i_j} = 1|H_1) \text{ from Eq. (4.7)} \qquad (4.13)$$

The sign of the third-order authentic correlation coefficient is positive at *favorable* conditional dependence, as demonstrated below.

$$\rho_1(i_1, i_2, i_3) = q_1 q_2 q_3 \left\{ E(u_{i_1}u_{i_2}u_{i_3}|H_1) + 2\prod_{j=1}^{3} P(u_{i_j} = 1|H_1) \right.$$

$$\left. - \sum_{j=1}^{3}\sum_{m=1, m\neq j}^{3}\sum_{n=1, n\neq m, j}^{3} E(u_{i_j}u_{i_m}|H_1)P(u_{i_n} = 1|H_1)\right\}$$

$$\geq q_1 q_2 q_3 \left\{ E(u_{i_1}u_{i_2}u_{i_3}|H_1) + 2\prod_{j=1}^{3} P(u_{i_j} = 1|H_1) - 3\prod_{j=1}^{3} P(u_{i_j} = 1|H_1)\right\}$$

$$\text{since } E\left(u_{i_1}u_{i_2}|H_1\right) \leq \prod_{j=1}^{2} P(u_{i_j} = 1|H_1) \text{ from Eq. (4.7)}$$

$$\geq 0 \quad \text{since } E\left(u_{i_1}u_{i_2}u_{i_3}|H_1\right) \geq \prod_{j=1}^{3} P(u_{i_j} = 1|H_1) \text{ from Eq. (4.7).}$$

$$(4.14)$$

Following the same procedure, it can be shown that even-order authentic correlation coefficients are negative and odd-order authentic correlation coefficients are positive at *favorable* conditional dependence for the Or rule. For the two classifier case, the second-order correlation coefficient has the same sign as the $Q$ statistic, which should be negative for authentics and has an upper limit of $-1$ for the optimal authentic conditional dependence, thus agreeing with our previous analysis of two classifier Or fusion [24].

It should be noted that the above constraints on the sign of the authentic correlation coefficients is only a sufficient condition for favorable conditional dependence. Since the probability of detection [Eq. (4.6)] is composed of all the $k$th-order probabilities, $k = 2, 3, \ldots, N$, the relative weightage of these terms plays a role in the favorable conditional dependence for the Or rule. It is possible that there is favorable conditional dependence for the Or rule even when some of the even-order correlation coefficients are positive and some of the odd-order correlation coefficients are negative.

The role of conditional dependence on the false acceptance rate (FAR) of the Or rule is now considered. For the Or rule fusion of $N$ classifiers, the $P_{FA}$ is given by

$$P_{FA} = 1 - P\left(\mathbf{u} = \begin{bmatrix} 0 & 0 & \ldots & 0 \end{bmatrix} | H_0\right). \tag{4.15}$$

Similar to Eq. (4.6), we can write the FAR for the OR rule as

$$P_{FA} = 1 - P\left(\mathbf{u} = \begin{bmatrix} 0 & 0 & \cdots & 0 \end{bmatrix} | H_0\right)$$

$$= P\left(\bigcup_{j=1}^{N} (u_j = 1 | H_0)\right)$$

$$= \sum_{j=1}^{N} P(u_j = 1 | H_0) - \sum_{j=1}^{N} \sum_{k \neq j} P(u_j = 1 \cap u_k = 1 | H_0)$$

$$+ \sum_{j=1}^{N} \sum_{k \neq j} \sum_{l \neq j, l \neq k} P(u_j = 1 \cap u_k = 1 \cap u_l = 1 | H_0)$$

$$- \cdots + (-1)^{N-1} P(u_1 = 1 \cap u_2 = 1 \cap \cdots \cap u_N = 1 | H_0). \tag{4.16}$$

For *favorable* impostor conditional dependence, the $P_{FA}$ should be smaller than the corresponding value at conditional independence; and for "optimal" impostor conditional dependence, the $P_{FA}$ should be minimized. Minimizing the $P_{FA}$ would mean minimizing the odd terms and maximizing the even terms in the RHS of Eq. (4.16). Following a similar analysis for the favorable authentic conditional dependence, this would imply that the odd-order impostor correlation coefficients should be negative, and the even-order impostor correlation coefficients should be positive for *favorable* conditional dependence on impostors. For the two-classifier case, the second-order impostor correlation coefficient should be positive for impostors, thus agreeing with our previous analysis of two-classifier Or fusion [24]. The second-order impostor

$Q$ value has an upper limit of 1 for the *optimal* conditional dependence on impostor [24].

The limits for the $k$th-order conditional probabilities and correlation coefficients at *optimal* conditional dependence for Or rule fusion are difficult to obtain. This is because the limits for the $k$th-order conditional probabilities depend on the individual classifier error probabilities as well as the $l = 2, 3, \ldots, (k-1)$th-order conditional probability limits. The solution is intractable because of the interdependencies between the variables.

This section determines the sign of diversity measures that are *favorable* for the Or fusion rule. The analysis of *favorable* statistical dependence for the And and the Majority fusion rules can be done in a similar manner [21]. The next three sections use this information to provide guidelines for obtaining *favorable* classifier ensembles for fusion with the Or, And, and Majority fusion rules, respectively.

## 4.4 ENSEMBLE DESIGN FOR OR RULE FUSION

Classifier ensemble design is the key idea of this chapter that is different from the ideas proposed in literature. Most of the ensemble design methods such as Bagging [26] and Random Subspaces [27] aim to produce independent classifiers. However, in practice, they are not statistically independent but have positive statistical dependence [28]. As found in Section 4.2, this would lead to poor fusion accuracy. Even Adaboost and other boosting methods [26] aimed at producing diverse classifiers have also been shown to exhibit positive statistical dependence [28]. There have been some attempts at obtaining diverse classifier ensembles, but these have had limited success [14, 16, 17, 29].

The *optimal* statistical dependence between classifiers for the different decision fusion rules found in the previous sections are linked to *optimal* ensemble generation in this and the following two sections. The findings of this section and next two sections show the data distribution and the base classifier effectively decide the best decision fusion rule and the optimal ensemble design strategy for that fusion rule. The ensemble design proposed in this chapter is general to any base classifier and hence is an important contribution. The proposed ensemble design is applied to real biometric data, and its power over the best single classifiers as well as over other ensemble generation methods is demonstrated.

Guidelines for optimal ensemble generation for Or fusion are provided in this section. If the authentic data are in clusters, the ensemble design principle for the Or rules is to design each classifier to separate each authentic cluster from the entire set of impostors. One of the challenges in applying this to real data is being able to identify these authentic clusters and be able to separate images/features of one cluster from others. Each classifier would then have a large FRR but very low FAR. The authentic decision region for the Or rule is the union of the authentic decision regions of all the classifiers, which would lower the FRR drastically from those of individual classifiers. The impostor decision region for the Or rule is the intersection of the impostor decision regions of all the classifiers; and if this covers most of the impostors for well-designed ensembles, then there will still be a low FAR. Hence, it is important for each individual classifier's impostor decision region to cover most of the impostors. By this design, the classifier outputs would have *favorable* conditional dependence for fusion with the Or rule, which has been detailed in the last section. The ensemble design strategies tuned to Or fusion are applied to the CMU PIE face database [30] and the NIST 24 fingerprint database [31] here.

## 4.4.1 Ensemble Design For Faces

The CMU PIE [30] data set contains face images of 65 people with 13 poses for each person and 21 different illuminations without background lighting for each pose. Sample images of different poses are shown in Figure 4.6. Sample images of different illuminations for the frontal pose are shown in Figure 4.7. The performance of the proposed ensemble generated for effective Or rule fusion is compared to the best single classifier, Adaboost and Bagging [26], which are common ensemble generation techniques.

It is possible to obtain illumination tolerance on the PIE database [32] using the unconstrained minimum average correlation energy (UMACE) filter [33]. If the UMACE filter is the base classifier, this reduces the requirements on the classifier ensemble to obtain good accuracy on both pose and illumination variation. The UMACE filter is not very tolerant to pose variation. The UMACE filter is quite specific to the training images used in its design. In other words, if a UMACE filter is built from images of one pose, it would falsely reject authentic images from other poses. However,

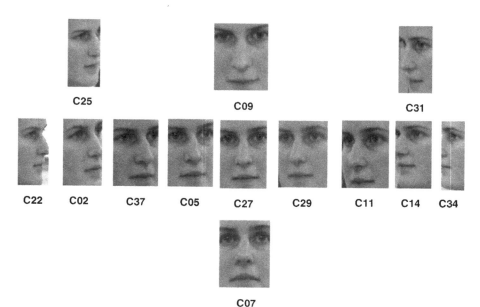

**Figure 4.6.** Images of different face poses of a person.

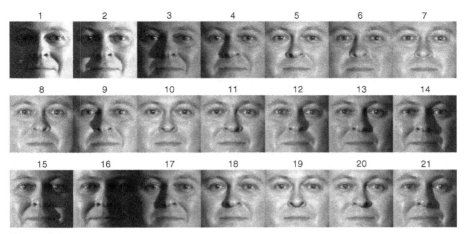

**Figure 4.7.** Images of different illuminations on the frontal pose of a person.

since images from impostor images are different from the authentic training images, the UMACE filter is expected to correctly reject impostor images of all poses. Following the ensemble design strategy for the Or rule outlined at the beginning of this section, generating one UMACE classifier for each pose and applying the Or fusion to the classifier decisions would be very effective in achieving a high overall accuracy.

For obtaining tolerance to illumination in each pose, three extreme illumination images of that pose are used to train a pose-specific UMACE filter. Only the authentic images are used in training. The remaining images of the data set—that is, images other than the training images—form the test set. For each person, there are $[(21 - 3(\text{training}) = 18)$ illuminations* 13 poses] $= 234$ authentic test images and [21 illuminations * 13 poses * 64 impostors] $= 17,472$ impostor test images. The peak-to-sidelobe ratio (PSR) is used as the performance metric for the UMACE filter, and a decision is obtained by thresholding the PSR [19]. To obtain statistically meaningful results of fusion, authentic and impostor decisions from all persons are used. In other words, statistical analysis of the test error and diversity of the ensemble is done on (234 authentics per person * 65 persons) $= 15,210$ authentic *ensemble decisions* (ensemble composed of 13 classifiers) and (17,472 impostors per person * 65 persons) $= 1,135,680$ impostor ensemble decisions.

On face verification with the Or rule classifier ensemble, each test image is correlated with each of the 13 UMACE filters of the claimant. Thirteen match scores (PSRs) are obtained from the UMACE ensemble. A threshold on the match scores produces a decision. The same threshold is used on all 13 match scores from the 13-classifier ensemble to obtain 13 decisions. The 13 decisions from the classifier ensemble are fused with the Or fusion rule. In other words, if one of the decisions is an authentic decision, then the Or rule decision is authentic. The individual classifiers for the 13-classifier Or rule ensemble are quite poor, with an equal error rate (EER) of nearly 45%. This is because each of them are tuned to only one pose and show errors in the other 12 poses.

The same training and test sets are used in comparing the performance of the 13 classifier Or rule ensemble design to the performance of the best single UMACE classifier and other classifier ensembles. Different pose images are registered with respect to each other so that at least one of the eyes is aligned. The best single UMACE filter is trained on all 39 (13 poses * 3 illuminations) authentic training images of a person. The performance is also compared to Adaboost [26]. The Adaboost algorithm for generating UMACE classifiers is provided in Table 4.1.

There are some intrinsic problems associated in applying Adaboost with UMACE classifiers. Adaboost is designed to work with weak learners; however, the UMACE classifier is a strong classifier. A single UMACE filter may have difficulty in fitting to all poses in the training data. However, in a few iterations, the classifier focuses on a subset (due to reweighting) of the authentic training images. Since the UMACE filter is highly tuned to the training images, the error on the weighted training set becomes zero in a few iterations, thus stopping the algorithm. For many persons in

**Table 4.1.** The Adaboost Algorithm for the UMACE Base Classifier

---

**Let** the lexicographically ordered Fourier transform of the authentic training images be $x_i$, $i = 1, 2, \ldots, M$.

**Let** $D$ be a diagonal matrix having the average spectral density of the training images along the diagonal.

**Initialize** the training image weights $w_i^1 = 1/M$, $i = 1, 2, \ldots, M$.

**For** $l = 1, 2, \ldots, N$

   1. Compute the UMACE filter in the frequency domain

$$h_l = D^{-1} \sum_{i=1}^{M} w_i^l x_i.$$

   2. Calculate the PSR $p_i$ on correlating the filter $h_l$ with each of the training images $x_i$.

   3. Let the decision of $h_l$ on the training image $x_i$, $i = 1, \ldots, M$ be

$$d_i = h_l(x_i) = \begin{cases} 1, & p_i \neq \tau, \\ 0, & p_i < \tau \end{cases}$$

   4. Calculate the weighted error of $h_l$:

$$\epsilon_l = \sum_{i=1}^{M} w_i^l (1 - d_i)$$

   5. If $\epsilon_l = 0$, stop Adaboost algorithm. Set $N = l$. Set $\beta_l = \delta \ll \frac{1}{M-1}$, $\delta > 0$.

   6. Otherwise, if $\epsilon_l > 0$, Set $\beta_l = \frac{\epsilon_l}{1-\epsilon_l}$

   7. Set the new weights of the training images to be $w_i^{l+1} = \dfrac{w_i^l \beta_l^{d_i}}{\sum\limits_{i=1}^{M} w_i^l \beta_l^{d_i}}$

**Output** the final decision

$$d_f(x) = \begin{cases} 1 & \text{if } \sum_{l=1}^{N} \log(1/\beta_l) d_l(x) \geq \frac{1}{2} \sum_{l=1}^{N} \log(1/\beta_l) \\ 0 & \text{otherwise} \end{cases}$$

---

the database, there are fewer than 13 UMACE classifiers in the ensemble, with as few as one UMACE classifier. The other problem is deciding whether each UMACE should have the same match score (PSR) threshold to make decisions and whether this threshold should be defined before designing the Adaboost ensemble. While the number of classifiers and their accuracy vary for each person in Adaboost, the individual classifier EERs for a sample (40th) person were between 5% and 12%. Hence, in general, these are strong classifiers with good accuracy.

In Bagging [26], Bootstrap classifiers are obtained by training on Bootstrap subsets of the training set. The Bootstrap subsets are obtained by random sampling with replacement from the original training set. With the same authentic training set as used previously, 13 Bootstrap classifiers are generated. The classifier decisions are combined using Majority decision fusion in Bagging. However, Majority rule need not be the best decision fusion rule for the given Bagging ensemble. Hence the other important decision rules, And fusion and Or fusion are also evaluated.

Second-order $Q$ values on the classifier decisions are used as diversity measures for the classifier ensembles. The $Q$ values are computed for a given threshold on the match score (PSR). The pairwise $Q$ values for the $^{13}C_2$ pairs of decisions are averaged at a given match score (PSR) threshold. The average $Q$ values at different match score thresholds for the 13 classifier OR rule ensemble are shown in Figure 4.8. From Figure 4.8, it can be observed that for PSR thresholds greater than 10, the *favorable* conditional dependence between classifiers for Or rule fusion—that is, positive $Q$ value for impostors and negative $Q$ value for authentics—is obtained. At a PSR value greater than 20, the impostor image decisions are all zero, which results in a pairwise

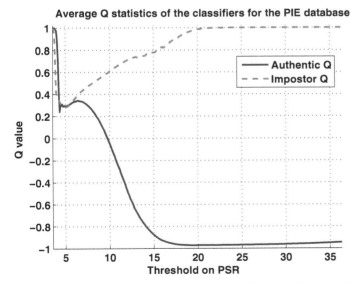

**Figure 4.8.** Average pairwise authentic and imposter $Q$ values of the ensemble designed for the OR rule on the PIE database.

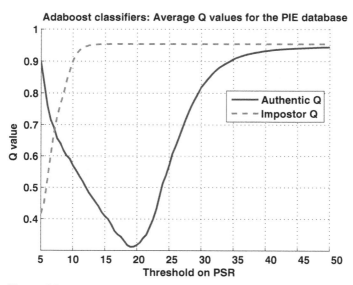

**Figure 4.9.** Average pairwise authentic and imposter $Q$ values for the Adaboost ensemble on the PIE database.

impostor $Q$ value of 1. Above a PSR threshold of 20, the individual authentic image decision is 1 for images of the same pose as the pose used in training the classifier and is 0 for most images of other poses. This would result in an authentic $Q$ value close to $-1$ because most of the pairwise classifier decisions are different. There would be only a small variation between the second-order $Q$ values of the $^{13}C_2$ different pairs of classifiers because of the symmetry between the pairs of classifiers.

The average pairwise classifier authentic and impostor Q values over all persons are positive for the Adaboost ensemble as shown in Figure 4.9. The plot is obtained by first averaging pairwise $Q$ values for each person at a given threshold, and then averaging over all persons at that threshold. This averaging is different from that of other classifier ensembles because the number of classifiers in the Adaboost ensemble is person-dependent. The average pairwise classifier $Q$ values are positive for the Bagging ensemble too, as seen in Figure 4.10. The positive $Q$ values on both authentics and impostors are *unfavorable* for fusion.

The performance curves for the OR rule ensemble and the best single classifier are "Global ROCs." In other words, for a threshold $\tau$ on the match score (PSR), the proportion of authentic scores from all persons [which would be 15,210 (234 authentic scores per person *65 people) authentic scores] that are below this threshold $\tau$ would be an FRR point. The proportion of impostor scores from all persons [which would be 1,135,680 (17,472 impostor scores per person * 65 persons) impostor scores] that are above this thresholds $\tau$ would be the corresponding FAR point in this ROC.

It should be noted that the ROC for the Adaboost is obtained differently. The Adaboost ROCs of each person are combined by averaging the FRRs of each persons

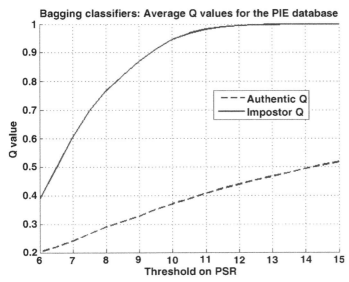

**Figure 4.10.** Average pairwise authentic and imposter $Q$ values of the Bagging ensemble on the PIE database.

ROC at a given FAR. This is done because the weights for the weighted decision fusion vary from person to person. Furthermore, there are different numbers of classifiers obtained by Adaboost for each person. The decision fusion ROCs for the Bagging ensemble are also averaged same as of Adaboost. This is because there is no correspondence between the classifiers of different persons. For a sample person, it is observed that the individual classifier EERs of the Adaboost ensemble are between 5% and 12%.

The test set ROC of one UMACE filter per person, which is trained on all 39 authentic images, is displayed on Figure 4.11. The test set ROCs after fusion of proposed Or rule ensemble, the Adaboost and bagging ensembles are displayed in Figure 4.12. The equal error rate (EER) for the Or rule ensemble after Or fusion, the Adaboost ensemble after the corresponding weighted Majority fusion, the Bagging ensemble after Majority rule fusion and Or rule fusion, and the best single classifier are 0.75%, 6.2%, 9.3%, 4.7%, and 7.5%, respectively. It is important to note that the Or rule fusion is significantly better than Majority rule fusion for the Bagging ensemble. Majority fusion that is done in Bagging need not be the best fusion rule. The superiority of the proposed Or rule ensemble is proved here since its Or fusion accuracy is an order of magnitude more accurate than the others. The Or fusion is also the best decision fusion rule for the Or rule ensemble because their statistical dependence is optimal to the Or fusion rule. While the individual classifiers in the Adaboost and Bagging ensembles are superior to the individual classifiers of the Or rule ensemble, the positive pairwise classifier $Q$ values are not favorable for fusion. Hence their fusion accuracy does not improve as significantly as observed for the Or rule ensemble.

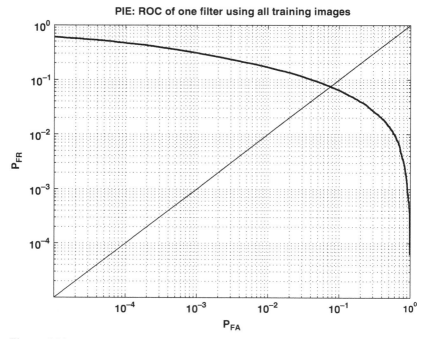

**Figure 4.11.** ROC of a single classifier per person trained on all authentic training poses and illuminations.

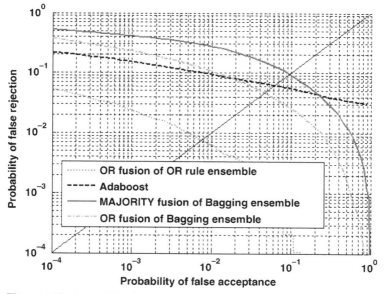

**Figure 4.12.** ROCs of the 13 classifier Or rule ensemble fusion, the Adaboost ensemble fusion, and Bagging ensemble fusion.

## 4.4.2  Ensemble Design for Fingerprints

The generation of ensembles tuned for Or rule fusion are demonstrated on the NIST 24 plastic distortion fingerprint database [31] in this section [24]. In the plastic distortion database, fingers are twisted and rolled. Ten fingers of 10 people—that is, 100 fingers in total—are present here. Sample images of a finger from the NIST 24 plastic distortion database are shown in Figure 4.13. Partial, blurred, and distorted images are present in this dataset. All 300 images from each finger are used here, without any preprocessing done on the images. Down-sampled (by averaging) images of size 128 × 128 are used for evaluation because of faster processing time. Reasonable accuracy is present even at this resolution [34].

The comparison of an ensemble tuned for Or rule fusion, the best single classifier, and Bagging [26] is provided here. Twenty uniformly sampled images from the 300 images of a finger, starting from the first image, are used as the authentic training set; and the first image from each of the remaining 99 fingers are used as the impostor training set to design unconstrained optimal trade-off (UOTF) filters [35]. The rest of the images are used in the test set. The UOTF filters have been shown to have better performance than the UMACE filters [34], and hence are used here. All the training images are normalized to unit energy. While more details of the filter can be obtained from reference 35, the UOTF filter provides a trade-off between distortion tolerance and discrimination. Boosting is not possible with the UOTF base classifier. This is because the UOTF classifier is a strong classifier and has no training set errors.

For improved Or rule fusion, the multiple classifiers are designed to classify different regions of distortion in the authentic space. The following guidelines can be used to generate a set of multiple UOTF filters for the Or fusion rule by partitioning

**Figure 4.13.** Distorted and partial fingerprints of a sample finger in the NIST 24 plastic distortion data set.

the authentic training set. The entire impostor training set is used to design each of the multiple filters. The authentic training images are divided into multiple subsets of similar plastic distortion in the following way.

1. Pick an image, say the first image of the training set, to build a filter.
2. Build a filter and cross-correlate the filter with the rest of the training images.
3. Pick the image that is most different from the current filter(s) by choosing the one with lowest PSR to build the next filter.
4. Cross-correlate the rest of the training set with all the current filters. For each image, store the maximum PSR across different filters (in order to compare between different images in step 3).
5. Repeat step 3 until the required number of filters have been built or when all images have a sufficiently high PSR (greater than a specified threshold).
6. The remaining images are used to update the closest filter (the filter for which the maximum PSR is obtained).

Figure 4.14 shows the authentic and impostor $Q$ values for each pair of classifiers for the best set of thresholds for Or fusion found for each point on the Or rule ROC curve. The $x$ axis for the plot is the index of the threshold set. The impostor $Q$ values are positive, which is favorable for the Or rule. It can be seen that the authentic $Q$ values are negative at the higher indices of the threshold set, which is favorable for the Or rule. Only three classifiers are used in this Or rule ensemble because the authentic $Q$ values for each of the three classifier pairs is negative only at the higher

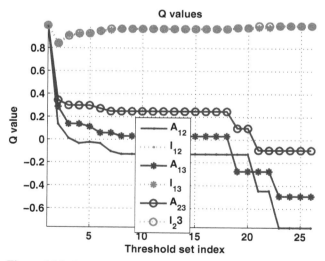

**Figure 4.14.** Pairwise authentic and imposter $Q$ values for the ensemble designed for Or fusion on the NIST 24 plastic distortion database. The best set of thresholds on the classifiers are found for a given FAR/FRR point on the Or rule fusion ROC. The $x$ axis represents the index for these threshold sets.

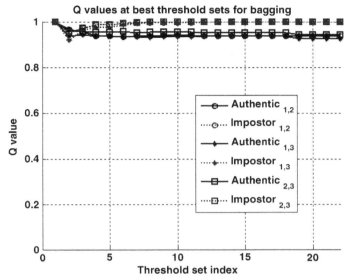

**Figure 4.15.** Pairwise authentic and imposter $Q$ values for the Bagging ensemble on the NIST 24 plastic distortion database. The best set of thresholds are found for a given FAR/FRR point on the Majority rule fusion ROC. The $x$ axis in this figure represents the index for these threshold sets.

indices of the threshold set. Using more classifiers in the ensemble would result in a positive authentic $Q$ value for at least one pair of classifiers. In other words, additional classifiers may be similar to one of the three classifiers present in the ensemble, which is not desirable for fusion. The EER of each of the three classifiers in this ensemble is above 10%.

In the Bagging ensemble, three bootstrap [26] classifiers are generated as a fair comparison to the proposed three-classifier Or rule ensemble. The diversity of the Bagging ensemble is poor, as reflected from the positive authentic and impostor $Q$ values observed in Figure 4.15.

The comparison of the performance of the best single classifier, the Bagging ensemble fusion, and the Or fusion of the designed ensemble for Or rule fusion is shown in Figure 4.16. The EER of the best single classifier, which is trained on the entire training set, is 2.8%. While the Majority rule is used for fusion in Bagging, the performance of Or rule fusion is comparable for this Bagging ensemble. The EER values after Majority fusion and Or fusion of the Bagging ensemble are 3.1% and 2.9%, respectively. Since the authentic and impostor $Q$ values in the Bagging ensemble are close to 1, the classifier decisions are similar. There is not much improvement on fusion of the Bagging ensemble because of the lack of diversity in the decisions. It was found that the Or rule is the best fusion rule for the ensemble designed for the Or rule [21, 24], and has an EER of 1.8%. This shows that the designed ensemble for Or rule fusion is more accurate than the best possible single (UOTF) classifier as well as Bagging.

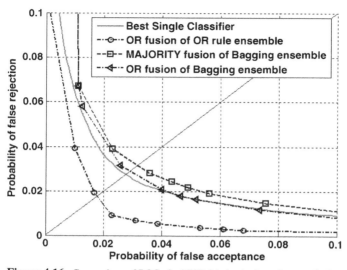

**Figure 4.16.** Comparison of ROCs for NIST 24 plastic distortion set: the best single OTF classifier using the entire authentic training set; Or fusion ROC of the ensemble designed for Or rule fusion; MAJORITY fusion ROC for the Bagging ensemble; and Or fusion ROC of the Bagging ensemble.

## 4.5  ENSEMBLE DESIGN FOR AND RULE FUSION

The And rule is the complement of the Or rule, and hence the ensemble design strategy for the And rule is the complement of the ensemble design strategy for the Or rule. If the impostor data are in clusters, the ensemble design principle for the And rule is to design each classifier to separate each impostor cluster from the entire set of authentics. Each classifier would then have a large FAR but very low FRR. The authentic decision region for the And rule is the intersection of the authentic decision regions of all the classifiers, and the impostor decision region for the And rule is the union of the impostor decision regions of all the classifiers. For well-designed ensembles, the authentic decision region for the And rule covers most of the authentics, and the impostor decision region for the And rule covers most of the impostors.

Accurate And fusion on the PIE pose and illumination database would require each individual classifier to have a high accuracy on authentic images of all poses and illuminations and a reasonable accuracy on impostor images. Pose is a difficult problem in faces, and this is a tough requirement on a base classifier. Hence successful ensemble design for And fusion is not possible on the PIE database.

For the NIST 24 plastic distortion fingerprint database, ensembles tuned for And rule fusion are demonstrated. The UOTF filter [35] used as base classifier in Or rule ensemble generation in the last section is not a suitable base classifier for And rule fusion. Due to its design specifications, it is mainly affected by changes in the authentic training set but hardly affected due to changes in the impostor training set [21]. Hence it is not possible to achieve diversity in impostor decisions for the ensemble with the UOTF as a base classifier.

A two-class support vector machine (SVM) is a base classifier that uses impostor training data. Due to this fact, we will now design a classifier ensemble for the AND rule on the NIST 24 plastic distortion set using the SVM as a base classifier. The training and test set for the NIST 24 database remains unchanged from Section 4.4.2.

For the proposed ensemble design, the cosine distance metric is used for dividing the impostor training data into different subsets. For each finger, the $k$-means clustering algorithm is used to obtain three clusters from the impostor training set consisting of 99 images. The initial cluster centroids are chosen at random. During the $k$-means clustering iterations, if one of the clusters loses all its members, it is removed. The $k$-means clustering is repeated five times with a different set of initial cluster centroids in order to obtain a "good" set of clusters. One impostor cluster and the entire authentic training set (consisting of 20 authentic images) are used to train a SVM classifier. Three SVM classifiers, one for each impostor cluster, form the And rule ensemble. The proposed And rule ensemble design is compared to Bagging with three Bootstrap SVM classifiers. Adaboost [26] is not feasible for the NIST 24 plastic distortion data set, even for the SVM base classifier. This is because there are no training errors made by an SVM classifier that uses all training images. Hence no further classifiers are made in Adaboost.

The diversity in the classifier decisions is measured using the pairwise classifier $Q$ values. The $Q$ values are given in Figure 4.17 and Figure 4.18, for the proposed And

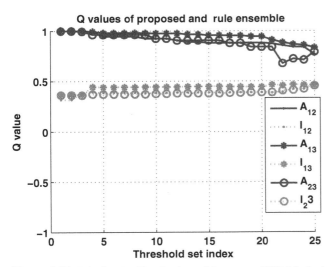

**Figure 4.17.** Pairwise classifier $Q$ values of the proposed SVM And rule ensemble on the NIST 24 plastic distortion database. These are shown as a function of the best threshold set for And fusion. Dashed (solid) lines are impostor (authentic) $Q$ values.

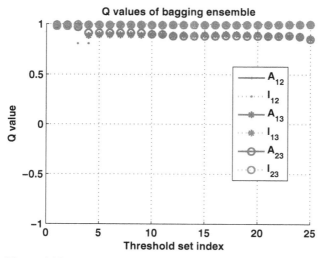

**Figure 4.18.** Pairwise $Q$ values of the Bagging ensemble of SVM classifiers on the NIST 24 plastic distortion database. An optimal set of thresholds are selected for And fusion, for which the $Q$ values are shown. Dashed (solid) lines are impostor (authentic) $Q$ values.

rule ensemble and the Bagging ensemble, respectively. The authentic and impostor pairwise classifier $Q$ values are shown as a function of the optimal set of thresholds for the And rule. The authentic and impostor $Q$ values are positive in both figures. The Bagging ensemble has authentic and impostor $Q$ values close to 1, which implies similar decisions by the classifiers and low diversity. The impostor $Q$ values of the proposed ensemble are lower and close to 0.5, which signifies more diversity on the impostor decisions than the Bagging ensemble. The most favorable conditional dependence for And fusion is negative impostor $Q$ values and positive authentic $Q$ values. While this target has not been reached, more diversity than for the Bagging classifier ensemble has been achieved by our proposed design. The Cosine distance metric used in the proposed ensemble generaton does not capture the classification strategy of the SVM and is hence a poor metric for clustering images. Due to the difficulty in obtaining good clusters of impostors, it is tough to obtain very diverse decisions on impostors.

The ROCs of 15 monotonic decision rules applied the three SVM classifiers in the proposed And rule ensemble are shown in Figure 4.19. The ROCs are obtained by finding a set of optimal thresholds on the three classifier scores for each decision fusion rule. It is observed that the And rule is the best rule with an EER of 1.2%. The performance of the monotonic fusion rules on the Bagging classifier ensemble is displayed in Figure 4.20. Here, the ROCs of many the decision fusion rules are comparable. The EERs of the Or rule and the Majority rule are 2.4% and 2.6% and hence are comparable. Thus the better diversity on impostor decisions in the And rule ensemble have enabled a better fusion accuracy than the Bagging ensemble.

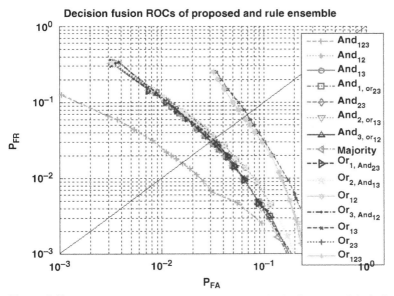

**Figure 4.19.** ROCs of the 15 monotonic decision fusion rules for the proposed And rule ensemble with SVM classifiers on NIST 24 plastic distortion database. And fusion of three classifiers is the best decision fusion rule.

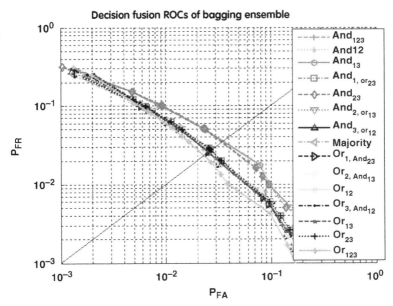

**Figure 4.20.** ROCs of the 15 monotonic decision fusion rules for the Bagging ensemble with SVM classifiers on NIST 24 plastic distortion database. Majority fusion and Or fusion of three classifiers are comparable.

## 4.6   ENSEMBLE GENERATION FOR MAJORITY RULE FUSION

Ensembles favorable to the Majority rule fusion are generated in this section. The classifiers in the Majority rule ensemble are expected to make diverse decisions on both authentics and impostors. Furthermore, the individual classifiers are expected to make a majority of correct decisions on both authentics and impostors. Hence the classifier ensemble design for the Majority rule is tougher than the design for Or and And rules.

For the majority decision rule to be correct, more than half the classifiers should make a correct decision. If the training data can be divided into $N$ subsets, each classifier should be trained on a different set of $\lceil \frac{N+1}{2} \rceil$ subsets for an optimal coverage of the training set. This provides the most significant Majority decision fusion improvement over the individual classifier and the optimal diversity for the majority rule. Table 4.2 shows an example of the training subsets used in training each classifier for Majority fusion of three classifiers. The base classifier on the PIE database [30] suitable for Majority fusion has the tough requirement that it has to be accurate on a Majority of authentic poses and a majority of impostor poses. Different classifiers are required to be accurate on a different subset of the authentic and impostor data. These stringent requirements on the ensemble for Majority rule fusion cannot result in design of a successful Majority rule classifier ensemble for the PIE database. However, this principle is used in training classifier ensembles for the NIST 24 fingerprint database [31].

The training image subsets are based on the similarity in distortion. One method of authentic set division has been described in the Or rule ensemble generation in Section 4.4.2, which is also used here. Two of the three authentic training subsets are used to train each classifier in the Majority rule ensemble as described in Table 4.2. The training and test sets are the same as in Section 4.4.2. The UOTF classifier [35] is the base classifier, the same as in the Or rule ensemble in Section 4.4.2. The EERs of the individual classifiers are 6.1%, 9.8%, and 6.8%.

The diversity of the ensemble can be measured by the correlation coefficients between pairwise classifier scores given in Table 4.3. The authentic score correlation coefficients are negative between classifiers 1 and 2, as well as between classifiers 2

**Table 4.2.** Training of Each Classifier for Majority Decision Fusion of a Three-Classifier Set[a]

|              | Subset 1  | Subset 2  | Subset 3  |
|--------------|-----------|-----------|-----------|
| Classifier 1 | Used      | Used      | Not used  |
| Classifier 2 | Not used  | Used      | Used      |
| Classifier 3 | Used      | Not used  | Used      |

[a] Each training subset is used in the training sets of two classifiers. This results in maximum accuracy since at least two classifiers produce a correct decision on that training subset. Each classifier is trained on a different set of two training subsets for maximum diversity and most significant improvement over the individual classifier.

**Table 4.3.** Pairwise Correlation Coefficients of UOTF Filter PSRs

| Classifier Pairs | 1,2 | 2,3 | 1,3 |
|---|---|---|---|
| Authentic $\rho$ | −0.17 | −0.17 | 0.80 |
| Impostor $\rho$ | 0.72 | 0.70 | 0.87 |

and 3. This is favorable for the majority rule. However, there is positive correlation between classifiers 1 and 3. The decisions made by classifiers 1 and 3 are not sufficiently
different for an optimal ensemble. The impostor correlation coefficients are all positive. For *favorable* conditional dependence for Majority rule fusion, all pairwise
correlation coefficients should be negative for authentics as well as impostors.
The conditional dependence between authentics is promising for the majority rule.
However, the desired conditional dependence on impostors is not achieved for the
Majority rule. The UOTF filters reject impostors well. Due to this, the impostor
correlation coefficients between all classifiers will be positive. The Majority rule will
not be the best decision fusion rule for this classifier set because of these reasons.

The ROCs of the Majority fusion rule and the best decision fusion rule for this
ensemble are displayed in Figure 4.21. Comparison is made with the ROCs of the
best single classifier and Bagging, which have been found in Section 4.4.2. From the

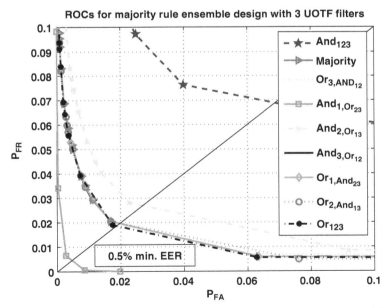

**Figure 4.21.** ROCs on fusion of the ensemble designed for Majority rule on the NIST 24 plastic
distortion set are compared to the ROC of the Bagging ensemble fusion and the ROC of the best
single classifier. $And_{1,OR_{2,3}}$: The result of Or fusion of classifiers 2 and 3 is fused with classifier 1 by
the And rule.

figure, it is observed that fusion with the Majority rule ensemble is better than Bagging and the best single classifier. The EER of the Majority rule is 2%. The best decision fusion rule is a combination of Or/And fusion between the classifiers and has an EER of 0.5%. This rule combines classifiers 2 and 3 by the Or rule, the result of which is then combined with classifier 1 by the And rule. This result is reasonable based on the classifier score diversity. Since classifiers 2 and 3 have negative dependence on authentics and positive dependence on impostors, Or fusion is best for them ($Or_{23}$). The authentic conditional dependence between $Or_{23}$ and classifier 1 will be positive. This is because of the positive correlation coefficient between classifiers 1 and 3. Hence $Or_{1,Or_{23}} = Or_{123}$ will not be the best rule. The only other monotonic rule is $And_{1,Or_{2,3}}$, which turns out to be the best decision fusion rule.

## 4.7 CONCLUSIONS

Statistical dependence has been shown to play a significant role in classifier ensemble fusion accuracy. It has been found that Or, And, and Majority decision fusion rules are the important decision fusion rules (for verification applications) since one of them is the best decision fusion rule for classifiers of the same accuracy and same pairwise classifier conditional dependence. Analysis of Or rule fusion has been presented to find the *favorable* conditional dependence between classifiers that would improve accuracy over conditionally independent classifier fusion with the Or rule. Similar analysis can be done for other major decision fusion rules. The most important contribution of this research has been providing guidelines for designing classifier ensembles that have their output diversity favorable for fusion with the Or, And, and Majority decision fusion rules. Successful design of such classifier ensembles have been demonstrated on biometric data for improving verification accuracy. This desirable diversity improves accuracy over not only the best single classifier, but also over fusion of commonly generated ensembles such as Bagging and Boosting, wherever possible.

## ACKNOWLEDGMENT

This research is funded in part by CyLab at Carnegie Mellon University.

## REFERENCES

1. P. J. Phillips, P. J. Flynn, T. Scruggs, K. W. Bowyer, J. Chang, K. Hoffman, J. Marques, J. Min, and W. Worek, Overview of the face recognition grand challenge, in *Proceedings of IEEE Conference on Computer Vision and Pattern Recognition*, 2005.
2. B. V. Dasarathy, *Decision Fusion*, IEEE Computer Society Press, New York, 1994.
3. L. I. Kuncheva, *Combining Pattern Classifiers: Methods and Algorithms*, John Wiley & Sons, Hoboken, NJ, 2004.

4. P. Domingos and M. Pazzani, On the optimality of the simple Bayes classifier under zero-one loss, *Machine Learning* **29**(2–3) p:103–130, 1997.

5. Y. S. Huang and C. Y. Suen, A method of combining multiple experts for the recognition of unconstrained handwritten numerals, *IEEE Trans. Pattern Anal. Mach. Intelli.*, **17**:90–93, 1995.

6. A. Ross and A. K. Jain, Information fusion in biometrics, *Pattern Recognit. Lett.* **24** (13):2115–2125, 2003.

7. J. Kittler, M. Hatef, R. P. Duin, and J. Matas, On combining classifiers, *IEEE Trans. Pattern Anal. Mach. Intelli.* **20**(3):226–239, 1998.

8. K. Tumer and J. Ghosh, Robust combining of disparate classifiers through order statistics, *Pattern Anal. Appl.* **5**:189–200, 2002.

9. M. Demirekler and H. Altincay, Plurality voting-based multiple classifier systems: statistically independent with respect to dependent classifier sets, *Pattern Recognit.* **35**:2365–2379, 2002.

10. T. K. Ho, J. J. Hull, and S. N. Srihari, Decision combination in multiple classifier systems, *IEEE Trans. Pattern Anal. Mach. Intelli.* **16**(1):66–75, 1994.

11. K. Woods, W. P. Kegelmeyer, Jr., and K. Bowyer, Combination of multiple classifiers using local accuracy estimates, *IEEE Trans. Pattern Anal. Mach. Intelli.* **19**(4):405–410, 1997.

12. G. Giacinto and F. Roli, Dynamic classifier selection based on multiple classifier behaviour, *Pattern Recognit.* **34**:179–181, 2001.

13. H. W. Shin and S. Y. Sohn, Selected tree classifier combination based on both accuracy and error diversity, *Pattern Recognit.* **38**:191–197, 2005.

14. G. Brown and J. Wyatt, Negative correlation learning and the ambiguity family of ensemble methods, in T. Windeatt and F. Roli, editors, *Multiple Classifier Systems, Lecture Notes in Computer Science*, Vol. 2709, Springer-Verlag, New York, 2003, pp. 266–275.

15. N. Oza and K. Tumer, Input decimation ensembles: Decorrelation through dimensionality reduction, in J. Kittler and F. Roli, editors, *Multiple Classifier Systems, Lecture Notes in Computer Science*, Vol. 2096, Springer-Verlag, New York, 2001, pp. 238–247.

16. G. Giacinto and F. Roli, An approach to the automatic design of multiple classifier systems, *Pattern Recognit. Lett.* **22**(1):25–33, 2001.

17. D. D. Margineantu and T. G. Dietterich, Pruning adaptive boosting, in M. Kaufmann, editor, *Proceedings of the 14th International Conference on Machine Learning*, 1997, pp. 378–387.

18. C. J. C. Burges, A tutorial on support vector machines for pattern recognition, *Data Mining and Knowledge Discovery* **2**(2):121–167, 1998.

19. B. V. K. Vijaya Kumar, Tutorial survey of composite filter designs for optical correlators, *Applied Optics* **31**, 4773–4801, 1992.

20. R. O. Duda, P. E. Hart, and D. G. Stork, *Pattern Classification*, 2nd edition, John Wiley & Sons, New York, 2001.

21. K. Venkataramani, Optimal classifier ensembles for improved biometric verification, Carnegie Mellon, Ph.D. dissertation, January 2007.

22. K. Venkataramani and B. V. K. Vijaya Kumar, Role of statistical dependence between classifier scores in determining the best decision fusion rule for improved biometric verification, in *International Workshop on Multimedia Content Representation, Classification and Security (MRCS)*, Istanbul, Turkey, September 2006.

23. P. K. Varshney, *Distributed Detection and Data Fusion*, Springer-Verlag, New York, 1997.

24. K. Venkataramani and B. V. K. Vijaya Kumar, Or rule fusion of conditionally dependent correlation filter based classifiers for improved biometric verification, in *OPR XVII, Proceedings of the SPIE*, Vol. 6245, April 2006, pp. 105–116.

25. K. Venkataramani and B. V. K. Vijaya Kumar, Conditionally dependent classifier fusion using and rule for improved biometric verification, in *International Conference on Advances on Pattern Recognition*, Lecture Notes in Computer Science, Vol. 3687, Springer-Verlag, New York, 2005, pp. 277–286.

26. T. Hastie et al., *The Elements of Statistical Learning*, 1st edition, Springer, New York, 2003.

27. T. K. Ho, The random subspace method for constructing decision forests, *IEEE Trans. Pattern Anal. Mach. Intelli.* **20**(8):832–844, 1998.

28. M. Skurichina, L. I. Kuncheva, and R. P. Duin, Bagging and boosting for the nearest mean classifier: Effects of sample size on diversity and accuracy, in F. Roli and J. Kittler, editors, *Multiple Classifier Systems, Lecture Notes in Computer Science*, Vol. 2364, Springer-Verlag, New York, 2002, pp. 62–71.

29. K. Tumer and J. Ghosh, Error correlation and error reduction in ensemble classifiers, *Connection Sci.* **8**(3/4):385–404, 1996.

30. T. Sim, S. Baker, and M. Bsat, The CMU pose, illumination, and expression (PIE) database of human faces, Robotics Institute, Carnegie Mellon University, Technical Report CMU-RI-TR-01-02, January 2001.

31. C. I. Watson, NIST special database 24—Live-scan digital video fingerprint database, July 1998.

32. M. Savvides, B. V. K. Vijaya Kumar, and P. Khosla, Face verification using correlation filters, in *Proceedings of the Third IEEE Automatic Identification Advanced Technologies*, Tarrytown, NY, March 2002, pp. 56–61.

33. A. Mahalanobis, B. V. K. Vijaya Kumar, S. Song, S. Sims, and J. Epperson, Unconstrained correlation filters, *Appl. Opt.* **33**(17):3751–3759, 1994.

34. K. Venkataramani and B. V. K. Vijaya Kumar, Performance of composite correlation filters in fingerprint verification, *Opt. Eng.* **43**(8):1820–1827, 2004.

35. B. V. K. Vijaya Kumar, D. W. Carlson, and A. Mahalanobis, Optimal trade-off synthetic discriminant function filters for arbitrary devices, *Opt. Lett.* **19**(19):1556–1558, 1994.

# Chapter 5

# Person-Specific Characteristic Feature Selection for Face Recognition

**Sreekar Krishna, Vineeth Balasubramanian, John Black, and Sethuraman Panchanathan**

## 5.1 INTRODUCTION

Fingerprint recognition and/or iris recognition have proven to be very robust when the cooperation of the human subject can be assumed, both during enrollment and during test. This makes them ideal for limiting entry into secured areas (such as buildings) to known and trusted individuals. However, these biometrics are not very useful for recognizing people in public places, where there is little or no motivation to cooperate with the system.

In contrast, face recognition has the potential for recognizing people at a distance, without their knowledge or cooperation. For decades, banking, retail, commercial, and industrial buildings have been populated with surveillance cameras that capture video streams of all people passing through critical areas. More recently, as a result of threats to public safety, some public places (such as in Glasgow and London) have been heavily populated with video surveillance cameras. On average, a person moving through London is captured on video over five times a day. This offers an unprecedented basis for developing and testing face recognition as a biometric for security and surveillance.

Given this great potential, it is not surprising that many private corporations have attempted to develop and deploy face recognition systems, as an adjunct to existing video security and surveillance systems. However, the performance of these systems

---

*Biometrics: Theory, Methods, and Applications.* Edited by Boulgouris, Plataniotis, and Micheli-Tzanakou
Copyright © 2010 the Institute of Electrical and Electronics Engineers, Inc.

has been disappointing. Depending on how such a system is adjusted, miscreants might easily pass through the system undetected, or innocent people might be incessantly inconvenienced by false alarms.

One of the most difficult problems that face recognition researchers encounter in surveillance applications is that face databases of miscreants typically contain only frontal and profile views of each person's face, with no intermediate views. Surveillance videos captured of the same person with the same camera in the same lighting conditions might have face images that look quite different, due to pose angle variations, making it very difficult to compare captured face images to those in a database. Combine this problem with the fact that miscreants are highly motivated to disguise their identity, along with the fact that face databases often contains thousands of faces, and the problem seems insurmountable.

Given all of these complicating factors, it is premature to rely upon face recognition systems for detecting miscreants in public places. On the other hand, the use of face recognition in controlled access applications (where users are highly motivated to cooperate and where face database images can be both captured and tested with the same camera under the same illumination conditions) is certainly within the limitations of current face recognition algorithms.

### 5.1.1 Employing Face Recognition to Facilitate Social Interactions

However, there is a real-world application for face recognition that is moderately challenging, but still potentially within the realm of possibility. When people who are blind enter a room, they might find it awkward to initiate social interactions because they don't know how many people are in the room, who those people are, or where they are standing.[1,2] A robust, wearable face recognition device could solve this problem.

This problem is simplified considerably by the fact that on a day-to-day basis most people encounter a limited number of people whom they need to recognize. It

---

[1] In order to understand the assistive technology requirements of people who are blind, we conducted two focus group studies [one in Tempe, Arizona (9 participants) and another in Tucson, Arizona (11 participants)] which included:

1. Students and adult professionals who are blind.
2. Parents of individuals who are blind.
3. Professionals who work in the area of blindness and visual impairments.

There was unanimous agreement among participants that a technology that would help people with visual impairment to recognize people or hear them described would significantly enhance their social life.

[2] To quote some candidates opinion about face recognition technology in a social setting:

- "It would be nice to walk into a room and immediately get to know who are all in front of me before they start a conversation."
- One young man said, "It would be great to walk into a bar and identify beautiful women."

is further simplified by the fact that people typically don't attempt to disguise their appearance in social situations. When a new person is encountered, the system could employ face detection to extract and save a sequence of face images captured during a conversation. This would provide a wide variety of facial expressions and pose angles that could be stored in a database and used for training a face recognition algorithm.

As people use such an assistive device over an extended period of time, they will learn both its abilities and its limitations. Conjectural information from the system can then be combined with the user's other sensory abilities (especially hearing) to jointly ascertain the identity of the person. This synergy between the user and the system relaxes some of the stringent requirements normally placed on face recognition systems.

However, such an assistive technology application still poses some significant challenges for researchers. One problem is the extreme variety in lighting conditions encountered during normal daily activities. While there are standards for indoor office lighting that tend to provide diffuse and adequate lighting, lighting in other public places might vary considerably. For example, large windows can significantly alter lighting conditions, and incandescent lighting is much more yellow than flourescent lighting. Outdoor lighting can be quite harsh in full sunlight, and it can be much more blue and diffuse in shadows. A person who is blind might not be aware of extreme lighting conditions, so the system would need to either (1) be tolerant of extreme variations or (2) recruit the user to ameliorate those extreme conditions.

In summary, the development of an assistive face recognition system for people who are blind provides a more tractable problem for face recognition researchers than security and surveillance applications. It imposes a somewhat less stringent set of requirements because (1) the number of people to be recognized is generally smaller, (2) facial disguise is not a serious concern, (3) multiple pose angles and facial expressions of a person can be captured as training images, and (4) the person recognition process can be a collaborative process between the system and the user.

In an attempt to provide such an assistive face recognition system, we have developed a new methodology for face recognition that detects and extracts unique features on a person's face and then uses those features to recognize that person. Contrast this with conventional face recognition algorithms that might avoid the use of a few distinguishing features because that approach might make the system very vulnerable to disguise.

## 5.2  FACE RECOGNITION IN HUMANS

For decades, scientists in various research areas have studied how humans recognize faces. Developmental psychologists have studied how human infants start to recognize faces, cognitive psychologists have studied how adolescents and adults perform face recognition, neuroscientists have studied the visual pathways and cortical regions used for recognizing faces, and neuropsychologists have attempted to integrate knowledge from neurobiological studies with face recognition research. Computer vision researchers are relatively new to this area, and have attempted to develop face recognition algorithms using image processing methods. Only recently have computer vision researchers been motivated to better understand the process by which humans recognize faces, in order to use that knowledge to develop robust computational models. Their new interest has led to more interdisciplinary face recognition research, which will likely aid our understanding of face recognition.

New studies have shown that humans, to a large extent, rely on both the featural and configural information in face images to recognize faces [1]. Featural information provides details about the various facial features, such as the shape and size of the nose, the eyes, and the chin. Configural information defines the locations of the facial features, with respect to each other. Psychologists Vicki Bruce and Andrew Young [2] agree with this dual representation, saying that humans create a view-centric description of a human face by relying upon feature-by-feature perceptual input, which is then combined into a structural model of the face.

Sadar et al. [3] showed that characteristic facial features are important for recognizing famous faces. For example, when they erased eyebrows from famous people's faces, face recognition by human participants was adversely affected. Young [4] showed that human participants were confused when asked to recognize faces that combined facial features from different famous faces. These studies suggest that the details of facial features are important in the recognition of faces.

However, Sinha et al. [5] showed that the relative locations of the facial features was also very important for the recognition of faces. They collected face images of famous personalities and then changed the aspect ratio of those images, such that the height was greatly compressed while the width was emphasized. Surprisingly, all the resulting face images were still recognizable, despite their contorted appearance, as long as the relative locations of the features were maintained within the distorted image. This study suggests that humans can flexibly use the configural information when recognizing faces.

Another important area of research in the human perception of faces has been in understanding the medical condition of face blindness, called *prosopagnosia*. People with prosopagnosia are unable to recognize faces including their own. Until recently it was assumed that prosopagnosia was acquired often as a result of a localized stroke. However, new evidence suggests that a substantial portion of the general population have a congenital form of prosopagnosia [6]. Kennerknecht et al. [7] conducted a survey of 789 students in 2006 which showed that 17 (2.5%) suffered from congenital prosopagnosia. These students went about their daily life without realizing their disorder in face recognition.

Other studies at the perception research centers at Harvard and University College of London have shown that prosopagnosics recognize people using unique personal characteristics, such as hair style, gait, clothing, and voice. These findings suggest that the detection of unique personal characteristics might provide a basis for face recognition systems to better recognize people. Since current methods of face recognition have met with only limited success, it makes sense to explore the use of this alternative approach.

Research in own-race bias (ORB) in face recognition [8] has also revealed some interesting results regarding human face recognition capabilities. David Turk et al. found that when humans are presented with new objects or new faces, they initially learn to recognize those objects and faces based on their distinctive features. Then, as familiarity increases, they incorporate configural information, moving toward holistic recognition. This study suggests that distinctive features are important during the initial stages of face recognition and that configural information subsequently provides additional useful information.

Distinctive facial features can take many different forms. For example, after a first encounter with a person who has a handlebar moustache, we readily recognize that person by the presence of his distinctive feature. Similarly, a person with a large black mole on her face will be remembered by first-time acquaintances by that feature. Given the current limited understanding of how humans recognize faces, it makes sense to use these observations as the basis for a new approach to face recognition.

The research described in this chapter is based on the approach of identifying distinctive facial features that can be used to distinguish each person's face from other faces in a face database. In recognition of the role played by configural information in the later stages of face recognition, it also takes into account the location of these features with respect to each other. The results of our research suggest that this approach can be very effective for distinguishing one person's face from other faces.

## 5.3  OUR APPROACH TO FACE RECOGNITION

Having introduced the potential for using characteristic person-specific features for face recognition, we now turn our attention toward the development of a method for discovering such features and for using them to index face images. Then we propose a novel methodology for face recognition, using person-specific feature extraction and representation. For each person in a face database, a learning algorithm discovers a set of distinguishing features (each feature consisting of a unique local image characteristic and a corresponding face location) that are unique to that person. This set of characteristic facial features can then be compared to the normalized face image of any person, to determine the presence or absence of those features. Because a unique set of features is used to identify each person in the database, this method effectively employs a different feature space for each person, unlike other face recognition algorithms that assign all of the face images in the database to a locality in a shared feature space. Face recognition is then accomplished by a sequence of steps, in which query face images is mapped into a locality within the feature space of each person in the database, and its position is compared to the cluster of points in that space that represents that person. The feature space in which the query face images are closest to the cluster is used to identify the query face images.

Having introduced the conceptual theory behind a person-specific characteristic feature extraction approach to face recognition, we now propose in the subsequent sections a method for detecting and extracting such features from face images and for constructing a feature space that is unique to each person in the database.

## 5.4 FEATURE EXTRACTORS

### 5.4.1 What Is a Feature?

The task of face recognition is inherently a multiclass classification problem. For every face image $X$, there is an associated label $y$ that is the name of the class—that is, the name of the person depicted in the image. While $X$ represents the image of the person, there is no inherent constraint on whether the image is a color RGB, HUV, or YCbCr image, or a gray-scale image with a gray-scale range of 0 to 255, or even spectral representation that is extracted from the face image using Fourier transform or wavelets. Irrespective of the image representation, the basis vectors spanning that representation are called features. The feature space spanned by these basis vectors is partitioned by the decision boundaries that ultimately define the different classes in the multiclass problem of face recognition. In this work, we choose a particular set of Gabor filters as feature detectors, and we choose each of those feature detectors for each person in the database, and that set of Gabor filters spans a unique feature space for that person.

### 5.4.2 Gabor Features

Gabor filters are a family of functions (sometimes called Gabor wavelets) that are derived from a mother kernel (a Gabor function) by varying the parameters of the kernel. As with any wavelet filters, the Gabor filters extract local spatial frequency content from the underlying image. Gabor filters specifically capture the spatial location and spatial orientation of the intensity variations in the image underneath the filter's location. By varying the spatial frequency and the spatial scope of the filters, it is possible to extract a Gabor coefficient that partially describes the nature of the image underneath it. The coefficients obtained by filtering a locality in a face image with a set of different Gabor filters are called Gabor features.

#### 5.4.2.1 Use of Gabor Filters in Face Recognition

Gabor filters have been widely used to represent the receptive field sensitivity of simple cell feature detectors in the human primary visual cortex. Recognizing this fact, Gabor features have been widely used by face recognition researchers. Over the last few years, the extensive use of Gabor wavelets as generators of feature spaces for face recognition has led to objective studies of the strength of Gabor features for this application. For example, Yang and co-workers [9] reviewed the strength of Gabor features for face recognition using an evaluation method that combined both alignment precision and recognition accuracy. Their experiments confirmed that Gabor features are robust to image variations caused by the imprecision of facial feature localization. As indicated by Gökberk et al. [10], several studies have concentrated on examining the importance of the Gabor kernel parameters for face analysis. These include: the weighting of Gabor kernel-based features using the simplex algorithm for face recognition [11], the extraction of facial subgraphs for head pose estimation [12], the analysis of Gabor kernels using univariate statistical techniques for discriminative region finding [13], the weighting of elastic graph nodes using quadratic optimization for authentication [14], the use of principal component analysis (PCA) to determine the importance of Gabor features [15], boosting Gabor features [9], and Gabor frequency/orientation selection using genetic algorithms [16].

A relevant work on Gabor filters for face recognition that is closely related to the research presented here is by Wiskott et al. [17]. Their work [17–21] proposes a framework for face recognition that is based on modeling human face images as labeled graph. Termed *elastic bunch graph matching* (EBGM), the technique has become a cornerstone in face recognition research. Each node of the graph is represented by a group of Gabor filters/wavelets (called "jets") which are used to model the intensity variations around their locations. The edges of the graph are used to model the relative location of the various jets. Since the jets represent the underlying image characteristics, it is desirable to place them on fiducial points on the face. This is achieved by *manually* marking the locations of the facial fiducial points using a small set of controlled graphs that represent "general face knowledge," which represents an average geometry for the human face. In our work, a genetic algorithm is used to obtain the spatial location of the fiducial points. Besides automating the process of locating these points, our work identifies spatial locations on the face image that are unique to every single person, rather than relying on an average geometry.

Closely following the work of Wiskott et al., Lyons et al. [22] proposed a technique that uses Gabor filter coefficients extracted at (1) automatically located rectangular grid points or (2) manually selected image feature points. These coefficients are then used to bin face images based on sex, race, and expression. The technique relies on a combined principal component analysis (PCA) dimensionality reduction and linear discriminant analysis (LDA) classification over the extracted Gabor coefficients, to achieve a pooling of images. While the classification task is not related directly to *identifying* individuals from face images, this technique also demonstrates the ability of Gabor filters to extract features that can encode subtle variations on facial images, providing a basis for face identification.

### 5.4.2.2 Gabor Filters

Mathematically, Gabor filters can be defined as follows:

$$\Psi_{\omega,\theta}(x, y) = \frac{1}{2\pi\sigma_x\sigma_y} \cdot G_\theta(x, y) \cdot S_{\omega,\theta}(x, y), \tag{5.1}$$

$$G_\theta(x, y) = \exp\left\{-\left(\frac{(x\cos\theta + y\sin\theta)^2}{2\sigma_x^2} + \frac{(-x\sin\theta + y\cos\theta)^2}{2\sigma_y^2}\right)\right\}, \tag{5.2}$$

$$S_{\omega,\theta}(x, y) = \left[\exp\left\{i\left(\omega x\cos\theta + \omega y\sin\theta\right)\right\} - \exp\left\{-\frac{\omega^2\sigma^2}{2}\right\}\right], \tag{5.3}$$

where

- $G_\theta (x, y)$ represents a Gaussian function.
- $S_{\omega,\theta} (x, y)$ represents a sinusoid function.
- $(x, y)$ is the spatial location where the filter is centered with respect to the image axis.
- $\omega$ is the frequency parameter of a 2D sinusoid.
- $\sigma_{dir}^2$ represents the variance of the Gaussian (and thus the filter) along the specified direction. *dir* can be either $x$ or $y$. The variance controls the region around the center where the filter has influence.

From the definition of Gabor filters, as given in Eq. (5.1), it is seen that the filters are generated by multiplying two components: a Gaussian Function $G_\theta (x, y)$ [Eq. (5.2)] and a Sinusoid $S_{\omega,\theta} (x, y)$ [Eq. (5.3)]. The following discussions detail the two components of Eq. (5.1).

### 5.4.2.3  Gaussian Function

The 2D Gaussian function defines the spatial spread of the Gabor filter. This spread is defined by the variance parameters of the Gaussian, along the $x$ and $y$ direction together with the orientation parameter $\theta$. Figure 5.1a shows a 3D representation of the Gaussian mask generated with $\sigma_x = 10$ and $\sigma_y = 15$ and rotation angle $\theta = 0$. The image in Figure 5.1b shows the region of spatial influence of an elliptical mask on an image, where the variance in the $x$ direction is larger than the variance in the $y$ direction.

Typically the Gaussian filter has the same variance along both the $x$ and $y$ directions, that is, $\sigma_x = \sigma_y = \sigma$. Under such conditions the rotation parameter $\theta$ does not play any role as the spread will be circular.

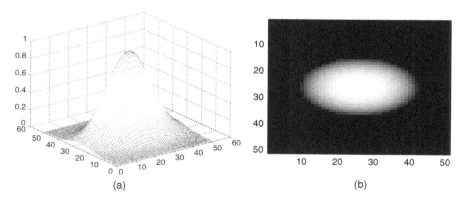

(a)                                                    (b)

**Figure 5.1.** (a) 3D representation of a Gaussian mask; $\sigma_x = 10$, $\sigma_y = 15$ and $\theta = 0$. (b) Image of the Gaussian mask $\sigma_x = 10$, $\sigma_y = 15$ and $\theta = 0$.

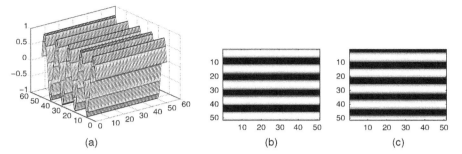

**Figure 5.2. (a)** 3D representation of a sinusoid $S_{\omega,\theta}$. **(b)** Image representation of the real part of the complex sinusoid $\Re\{S_{\omega,\theta}\}$. **(c)** Image representation of the imaginary part of complex sinusoid $\Im\{S_{\omega,\theta}\}$.

### 5.4.2.4 Sinusoid

The 2D complex sinusoid defined by Eq. (5.3) generates the two sinusoidal components of the Gabor filters which (when applied to an image) extracts the local frequency content of the intensity variations in the signal. The complex sinusoid has two components (the real and the imaginary parts) which are two 2D sinusoids that are phase-shifted by $\frac{\pi}{2}$ radians. Figure 5.2a shows the 3D representation of a sinusoidal signal (either real or imaginary) at $\omega = 0.554$ radians and $\theta = 0$ radians, while Figures 5.2b and 5.2c show an image of the real and imaginary parts of the same complex sinusoid, respectively. It can be seen that the two filters are similar, except for the $\pi/2$-radian phase shift.

Multiplying the Gaussian and the sinusoid generates the complex Gabor filter, as defined in Eq. (5.1). If $\sigma_x = \sigma_y = \sigma$, then the real and imaginary parts of this complex filter can be described as follows.

$$\Re\left\{\Psi_{\omega,\theta}\left(x,y\right)\right\} = \frac{1}{2\pi\sigma^2} \cdot G_\theta\left(x,y\right) \cdot \Re\left\{S_{\omega,\theta}\left(x,y\right)\right\}, \tag{5.4}$$

$$\Im\left\{\Psi_{\omega,\theta}\left(x,y\right)\right\} = \frac{1}{2\pi\sigma^2} \cdot G_\theta\left(x,y\right) \cdot \Im\left\{S_{\omega,\theta}\left(x,y\right)\right\}. \tag{5.5}$$

Figure 5.3a shows the 3D representation of a Gabor filter (either real or imaginary) at $\omega = 0.554$ radians, $\theta = 0$ radians, and $\sigma = 10$, and Figures 5.3b and 5.3c show an image with the real and imaginary parts of the complex filter.

In order to extract a Gabor feature at a location $(x, y)$ of an image $I$, the real and imaginary parts of the filter are applied separately to the same location in the image, and a magnitude is computed from the two results. Thus, the Gabor filter coefficient at a location $(x, y)$ in an image $I$ with a Gabor filter $\Psi_{\omega,\theta}$ is given by

$$C_\Psi(x,y) = \sqrt{(I(x,y) * \Re\{\Psi_{\omega,\theta}(x,y)\})^2 + (I(x,y) * \Im\{\Psi_{\omega,\theta}(x,y)\})^2}. \tag{5.6}$$

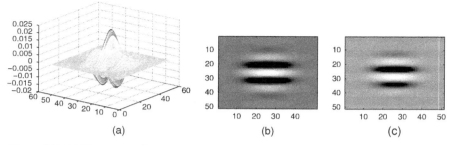

**Figure 5.3.** (a) 3D representation of a Gabor filter $\Psi_{\omega,\theta}$. (b) Image representation of the real part of Gabor filter $\Re\{\Psi_{\omega,\theta}\}$. (c) Image representation of the imaginary part of Gabor filter $\Im\{\Psi_{\omega,\theta}\}$.

In our experiments, a *Gabor filter bank* was created by varying three parameters of $\Psi_{\omega,\theta}$: (1) the frequency parameter $\omega$, (2) the orientation parameter $\theta$, and (3) the variance parameter $\sigma$. We chose five values for each of these parameters thereby generating 125 different Gabor filters.

- $\omega = \left(2^{(-f+2)/2} \cdot \pi\right)$, where $f = \{0, 1, 2, 3, 4\}$.
- $\theta = \left(\frac{\pi}{2} \cdot \frac{1}{5} \cdot t\right)$, where $t = \{0, 1.25, 2.5, 3.75, 5\}$.
- $\sigma = \{5, 10, 15, 20, 25\}$.

## 5.5  THE LEARNING ALGORITHM

The proposed method uses the above-described Gabor filters to find distinguishing features (and corresponding feature locations) within a face image. That is, for each person in the database, the algorithm finds a set of Gabor filters which, when applied at their corresponding $(x, y)$ locations within the image, will produce coefficients that are unique for that individual. This means that all of the 125 Gabor filters in the filter bank are applied at each and every location of each of the individual's face images and are then tested for their ability to distinguish every individual. Given a $128 \times 128$ face image, there will be $128 \times 128 \times 125 \times n$ filter coefficients that will be generated per face image per person, where $n$ is the number of characteristic features to be extracted for each person. This must be computed for every person in the training set, which further increases the search space. To search such a vast space of parameter values (the size of the Gaussian mask, the frequency of the complex sinusoid, the orientation of the entire Gabor filter, and the $(x, y)$ location where the filter is placed), it is important that some scheme for effective search be incorporated into the system. To this end, we have chosen Genetic Algorithms to conduct the search. For each person in the training set, all of the face images that depict to that person are indexed as positives, while all of the other face images in the database are indexed as negatives. Dedicated genetic algorithm-based search is conducted with these positive and negative images, with the aim of finding a set of Gabor filters and filter locations that distinguish all the positives from the negatives.

## 5.5.1 Genetic Algorithms

When the parameter space is vast (as it is in our case) a genetic algorithm (GA) searches for the optimum solution by randomly picking parameter sets and evolving newer ones from the best performers. This happens over many generations, hopefully resulting in the optimum set of parameters. To start the search, the GA generates a random set of *parents*. Each parent is characterized by the presence of a *chromosome*. The chromosome internally encodes all the parameters that are used by the parent to perform the intended operation. In our case, the intended operation is face recognition. The parent uses the parameters that are found in its chromosome to derive the Gabor features on the positive and negative images.

Based on the ability of these features to distinguish a face from all others in the database, the parent is ranked within its population. This rank is also referred to as the *fitness of the parent*. The ranking of all the parents, based on their fitness, marks the end of a generation, and a new generation needs to be created. New generations are formed based on three important aspects of GAs: *retention*, *crossover*, and *mutation*. A portion of the newer generation is derived from the older generation, using the above-mentioned methods; and the rest of the new generation is created randomly, maintaining the same overall number of parents between generations. Once a new population has been formed, the process of ranking parents occurs (as explained earlier) and a new generation is born out of that ranking. This iterative process continues until the parents in a certain generation are fit enough to achieve the given task (with the desired amount of success) or until the desired number of generations have evolved.

### 5.5.1.1 Use of Genetic Algorithms in Face Recognition

GAs have been used in face recognition to search for optimal sets of features from a pool of potentially useful features that have been extracted from the face images. Liu et al. [23] used a GA along with kernel principal component analysis (KPCA) for face recognition. In their approach, KPCA was first used to extract facial image features. After feature extraction using the KPCA, GAs were employed to select the optimal feature subset for recognition—or more precisely the optimal nonlinear components. Xu et al. [24] used GAs along with independent component analysis to recognize faces. After obtaining all the independent components using the Fast ICA algorithm, a genetic algorithm was introduced to select optimal independent components.

Wong and Lam [25] proposed an approach for reliable face detection using genetic algorithms with eigenfaces. After histogram normalization of face images and computation of eigenfaces, the $k$ most significant eigenfaces were selected for the computation of the fitness function. The fitness function was based on the distance between the projection of a test image and that of the training-set face images. Since GAs are computationally intensive, the search space for possible face regions was limited to possible eye regions alone.

Karungaru et al. [26] performed face recognition using template matching. Template matching was performed using a genetic algorithm to automatically test several positions around the target and to adjust the size of the template as the matching process progressed. The template was a symmetrical T-shaped region between the eyes, which covered the eyes, nose, and mouth.

Ozkan [27] used genetic algorithms for feature selection in face recognition. In this work, the scale invariant feature transform (SIFT) [28] was used to extract features. Since SIFT was originally designed for object recognition in general, genetic algorithms were used to identify SIFT features, which are more suitable to face recognition.

Huang and Weschler [29] developed an approach to identify eye location in face images using navigational routines, which were automated by learning and evolution using genetic algorithms. Specifically, eye localization was divided into two steps: (i) the derivation of the saliency attention map and (ii) the possible classification of salient locations as eye regions. The saliency map was derived using a consensus between navigation routines that were encoded as finite-state automata (FSA) exploring the facial landscape and evolved using GAs. The classification stage was concerned with the optimal selection of features and the derivation of decision trees for confirmation of eye classification using genetic algorithms.

Sun and Yin [30] applied genetic algorithms for feature selection in 3D face recognition. An individual face model was created from a generic model and two views of a face. Genetic algorithms were used to select optimal features from a feature space composed of geometrical structures, the labeled curvature types of each vertex in the individualized 3D model.

Sun et al. [31] approached the problem of gender classification using a genetic algorithm to select features. A genetic algorithm was used to select a subset of features from a low-dimensional representation, which was obtained by applying PCA and removing eigenvectors that did not seem to encode information about gender.

As is evident from these citations, many feature-based approaches toward face recognition use genetic algorithms for feature selection. However, these approaches employ a single feature space derived from a set of face images. We believe that it is more effective to employ aimed at extracting person-specific features and that an effective way to do this is by using genetic algorithms. As observed by Turk et al. [8], humans initially learn to recognize faces based on person-specific characteristic features. This suggests that better recognition performance might be achieved by representing each person's face in a person-specific feature space that is learned using GAs.

The following paragraphs describe how we employed GAs to solve the problem of finding person-specific Gabor features aimed at face recognition.

### 5.5.1.2 The Chromosome

Each parent per generation encodes the parameters of a set of Gabor filters in the form of a chromosome. In our implementation, each Gabor filter is represented by five parameters. If there are $n$ Gabor filters, parameters for all of these filters are

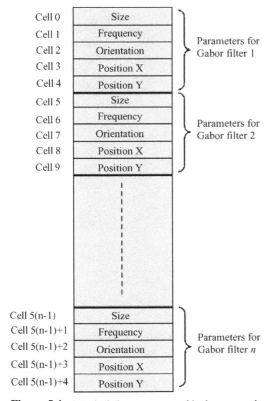

**Figure 5.4.** A typical chromosome used in the proposed method.

encoded into the chromosome in a serial manner, as shown in Figure 5.4. Thus the length of the chromosome is $5n$. The number of Gabor filters being used per face image determines the length of the chromosome. As shown in Figure 5.4, each parameter in the chromosome is encoded as a gene. The boundaries of these genes defines the regions where the chromosome undergoes both the crossover and mutation. The genes can be considered as the primary element of the parent responsible in the evolution.

### 5.5.1.3  Creation of the First Generation

Figure 5.5 depicts the first generation of parents, which are created randomly. Each parent's chromosome is filled randomly with parameter values where, each parameter value is within the allowed range for that parameter. Thus, in our experiment, each parent potentially has the parameters needed for it to perform face recognition using Gabor filters for feature extraction.

Once these parents are created, each parent in the gene pool is evaluated based on its capacity to perform face recognition. To this end, a fitness function

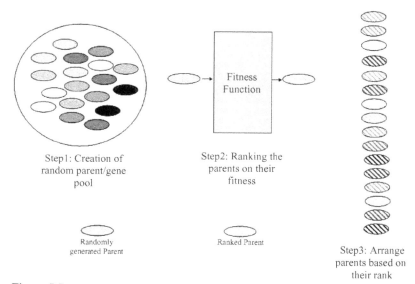

Step1: Creation of random parent/gene pool

Step2: Ranking the parents on their fitness

Fitness Function

Randomly generated Parent

Ranked Parent

Step3: Arrange parents based on their rank

**Figure 5.5.** Stages in the creation of the First Generation of parents.

is defined, which takes into account the ability of each parent to distinguish an individual from all others based on the most distinguishing features on the individual's face.

This fitness function also takes into account the similarity of the extracted features, and it discourages the selection of features that are highly correlated with each other. This ensures that the face images will be searched for multiple distinguishing characteristics. Section 5.6.3.1 explains in detail the fitness function used in our experiments. The parents with the best fitness are ranked higher and have the highest probability of being picked for using genetics the next generation. At the end of the rank ordering process, the parents are arranged in a descending order, based on their fitness. This rank ordering determines the probability of each parent being used to create the subsequent generation. If a parent has a higher fitness, it will have a higher probability of being cloned into the next generation, or of otherwise being involved in reproduction.

### 5.5.1.4  *Creation of the Newer Generations*

The newer generations are created from the older population using *clones, mutants,* and *crossovers* of the fittest parents. To better search for the optimal parameter set, new random parents are created every generation. This reduces the likelihood that the algorithm will get stuck in a local minimum in the search space.

Figure 5.6 shows how crossover creates a newer generation, using the fittest parents from the older generation.

The number of offsprings created from mutation, cloning, and crossover are determined by parameters of the genetic algorithm. The number of clones, mutants,

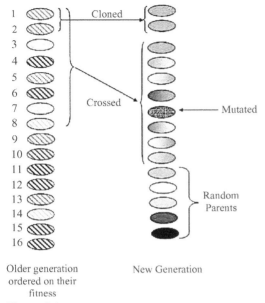

Older generation
ordered on their
fitness

New Generation

**Figure 5.6.** Deriving newer parents from the current generation.

and crossovers are controlled by the following parameters:

1. *Cloning Rate.* This parameter controls the number of parents from the previous generation that will be retained without undergoing any changes in their genetic structure.

2. *Crossover Rate.* This parameter controls the number of offsprings that will be born from crossing the parents from the previous generation.

3. *Mutation Rate.* This parameter determines how many of the crossed offsprings will then be mutated.

4. *Cloning Distribution Variance.* After determining the number of offsprings be to cloned, the index of the parents for cloning are chosen using a normal distribution random number generator, with the mean zero and variance equal to this parameter. Since the parents from the previous generation have been rank ordered in descending order of fitness, the zeroth parent will be the top performer (which coincides with the mean of the random number generator, and has the highest probability of getting picked).

5. *Crossover Distribution Variance.* This parameter (which is similar to the Cloning Distribution Variance) is used to choose the index of the parents who will undergo Crossover.

## 5.5.1.5  Crossover

As discussed earlier, the parents for crossover are selected by a random number generator. Between these parents, the points of crossover are determined by choosing

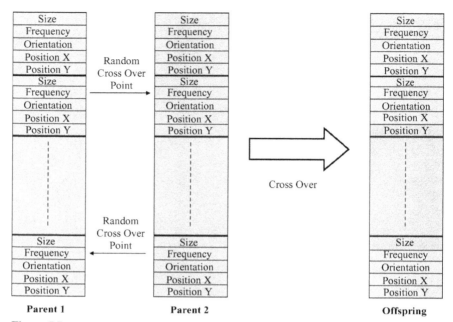

**Figure 5.7.** Typical crossing of two parents to create an offspring.

locations of crossover randomly. As seen in the Figure 5.7, these locations are arbitrary gene boundary locations and at these locations the gene content from the two parents gets mixed. The offspring thus created now contains parts of the genes coming from the contributing parents. The motivation for this step is the fact that, as more and more generations pass, the fittest parents undergoing crossover will already contain the better sets of parameters, and their crossing might bring together the better sets of parameter values from both the parents.

### 5.5.1.6  Mutation

In addition to the process of crossover at gene boundaries in the chromosome, the values of some parameters within the genes might be changed randomly. This is illustrated in the Figure 5.8. Such mutations help in exploring the local parameter space more thoroughly. Mutations can be seen as small perturbations to the larger search that explores the vast parameter space, searching for the global minima.

## 5.6  METHODOLOGY

Most feature-based face recognition methods use feature detectors that are not tailored specifically for face recognition, and they make no attempt to selectively choose feature detectors based specifically on their usefulness for face recognition. The method

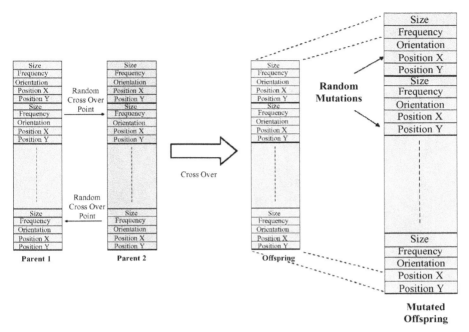

**Figure 5.8.** Mutation of a newly created offspring.

described in this paper uses Gabor wavelets as feature detectors, but evaluates the usefulness of each particular feature detector (and a corresponding $(x, y)$ location) for distinguishing between the faces within our face database. Given the very large number of possible Gabor feature detectors and locations, we use a genetic algorithm (GA) to explore the space of possibilities, with a fitness function that propagates parents with a higher ability to distinguish between the faces in the database. By selecting the Gabor feature detectors and locations that are most useful for distinguishing each person from all of the other people in the database, we define a unique (i.e., person-specific) feature space for each person.

### 5.6.1  The FacePix(30) Database

All experiments were conducted with face images from the FacePix(30) database [32]. FacePix(30) was compiled to contain face images with pose and illumination angles annotated in $1°$ increments. Figure 5.9 shows the apparatus that is used for capturing the face images. A video camera and a spotlight are mounted on separate annular rings, which rotate independently around a subject seated in the center. Angle markings on the rings are captured simultaneously with the face image in a video sequence, from which the required frames are extracted.

This database has face images of 30 people across a spectrum of pose and illumination angles. For each person in the database, there are three sets of images. (1) The

**Figure 5.9.** The data capture setup for FacePix(30).

*pose angle set* contains face images of each person at pose angles from $+90°$ to $-90°$. (2) The *no-ambient-light set* contains frontal face images with a spotlight placed at angles ranging from $+90°$ to $-90°$ with no ambient light. (3) The *ambient-light set* contains frontal face images with a spot light placed at angles placed at angels from $+90°$ to $-90°$ in the presence of ambient light. Thus, for each person, there are three face images available for every angle, over a range of $180°$. Figure 5.10 provides two examples extracted from the database, showing pose angles and illumination angles ranging from $-90°$ to $+90°$ in steps of $10°$. For earlier work using images from this database, please refer to reference 33. Work is currently in progress to make this database publicly available.

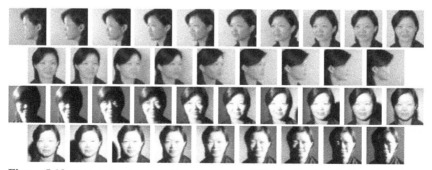

**Figure 5.10.** Sample face images with varying pose and illumination from the FacePix (30) database.

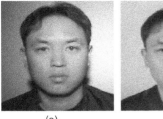  

(a)                    (b)                    (c)

**Figure 5.11.** Sample frontal images of one person from the FacePix (30) database.

We selected at random two images out of each set of three frontal ($0°$) (Figure 5.11) images for training, and used the remaining image for testing. The genetic algorithms used the training images to find a set of Gabor feature detectors that were able to distinguish each person's face from all of the other people in the training set. These feature detectors were then used to recognize the test images.

In order to evaluate the performance of our system, we used the same set of training and testing images with face classification algorithm based on low-dimensional representation of face images extracted through principal component analysis [34]. Specifically, the performance of the implementation of PCA-based face recognition followed by reference 35 was used in our experiments.

## 5.6.2  The Gabor Features

Each Gabor feature corresponds to a particular Gabor wavelet (i.e., a particular special frequency, a particular orientation, and a particular Gaussian-defined spatial extent) applied to a particular $(x, y)$ location within a normalized face image. (Given that 125 different Gabor filters were generated, by varying $\omega$, $\sigma$, and $\theta$ in 5 steps each, and given that each face image contained $128 \times 128 = 16,384$ pixels, there was a pool of $125 \times 16384 = 2,048,000$ potential Gabor features to choose from.) We used an $N$-dimensional vector to represent each person's face in the database, where $N$ represents the predetermined number of Gabor features that the genetic algorithm (GA) selected from this pool. Figure 5.12 shows an example face image, marked with five locations where Gabor features will be extracted (i.e., $N = 5$). Given any normalized face image, real number Gabor features are extracted at these locations using Eq. (5.6). This process can be envisioned as a projection of a 16,384-dimensional face image onto an $N$-dimensional subspace, where each dimension is represented by a single Gabor feature detector.

Thus, the objective of the proposed methodology is to extract an $N$-dimensional real-valued person-specific feature vector to characterize each person in the database. The $N$ $(x, y)$ locations (and the spatial frequency and spatial extent parameters of the $N$ Gabor wavelets used at these locations) are chosen by a GA, with a fitness function that takes into account the ability of each Gabor feature detector to distinguish one face from all the other faces in the database.

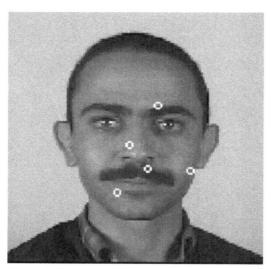

**Figure 5.12.** A face image marked with five locations where unique Gabor features were extracted.

## 5.6.3 The Genetic Algorithm

Every genetic algorithm (GA) is controlled in its progress through generations with a few control parameters such as

- the number of generations of evolution ($n_g$)
- the number of parents per generation ($n_p$)
- the number of parents cloned per generation ($n_c$)
- the number of parents generated through crossover ($n_{co}$)
- the number of mutations in every generation ($n_m$)

In our experiments, the GA used the following empirically chosen GA parameters: $n_g = 50$, $n_p = 100$, $n_c = 6$, $n_{co} = 35$ and $n_m = 5$.

### 5.6.3.1 The Fitness Function

The fitness function of a GA determines the nature of the search conducted over the parameter space. For face recognition applications, the fitness function is the capacity of a parent to classify the individuals accurately. In our proposed method, the fitness function needs to take both the Gabor features and the corresponding feature locations into consideration when evaluating face classification. We define here a fitness function that has two components to it. One determines the capacity of the parent to isolate an individual's face image from the others in the database, and the other evaluates whether the feature is redundant with other extracted features (i.e., whether a feature detector produces coefficients that are highly correlated with the coefficients produced by another feature detector.) Thus the fitness $F$ can be defined as

$$F = w_D D - w_C C, \qquad (5.7)$$

where $D$ is the distance measure weighted by $w_D$, and $C$ represents the correlation measure which measure the similarity between the coefficients that have been extracted. The correlation measure $C$ is weighted by the factor $w_C$.

If a parent extracts features from a face image that distinguish one individual from all the others very well (compared to the other parents within the same generation), then the distance measure $D$ will be the largest for that parent, making its fitness $F$ large. If the correlation between the extracted features is small, $C$ will be small, which also makes the fitness $F$ large. Thus, the correlation measure serves as a *penalty* for extracting the same feature from the face image multiple times, even though that particular feature might be the best distinguishing feature on that face.

The correlation between coefficients was used instead of spatial separation to counter the problem of similar features being extracted, because the Gabor filters might not be able to represent the underlying image characteristic completely. If there are some large image features on the face (such as beard) that require multiple Gabor features within a certain spatial locality, setting a hard lower limit on this spatial separation might lead to insufficient representation of that large image feature, in terms of the Gabor filters.

Consider a parent searching for a unique set of $M$ Gabor filters to distinguish one individual's face from all other faces. Let this set of filters be referred to as $S$. Thus, $S = \{G_1, G_2, \ldots, G_M\}$, where $G_m$ represents the $m$th Gabor filter.

If the set of all individuals in the database is referred to as $I = \{i_1, i_2, \ldots, i_j\}$ with $J$ number of individuals, then for every individual $i$ in $I$ a set $S_i$ has to be extracted. To achieve this, all the images in the database depicting individual $i$ are marked as positives, and the ones not depicting that individual are marked as negatives. Let the set of positive images be referred to as $P_i$ (with $L$ number of images) and let the set of negatives be referred to as $N$ (with $K$ number of images). Thus, $S_i = \{G_{1i}, G_{2,i}, \ldots, G_{mi}\}$, $P_i = \{p_{1i}, p_{2i}, \ldots, p_{li}\}$, and $N_i = \{n_{1i}, n_{2i}, \ldots, n_{ki}\}$ are the sets of Gabor filters, positive images, and negatives images set, respectively, for the individual $i$.

**The Distance Measure D.** A parent trying to recognize an individual $i$ with a Gabor filter set $S_i$ can be thought of as a transformation that projects all of the face images from the image space to a $M$-dimensional space, where the dimensions are defined by the $M$ Gabor filters in the set $S_i$. Thus, all of the images in the two sets $P_i$ and $N_i$ can be considered as points on this $M$-dimensional space. Since the goal of the genetic algorithm is to find the set $S_i$ that best distinguishes the individual $i$ from others, in our method we search for the $M$-dimensional space (defined by a parent) that best separates the points formed by the sets $P_i$ and $N_i$. Figure 5.13 is an illustration of hypothetical set of face images projected on a two-dimensional space defined by a set of 2 Gabor filters $S_i = \{G_0, G_1\}$. As shown in the figure, the measure $D$ is the minimum of all the Euclidian distances between every positive and negative points.

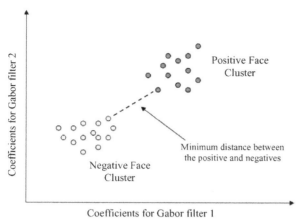

**Figure 5.13.** Distance measure $D$ for the fitness function.

Thus, $D$ can be defined as follows:

$$D = \min_{\forall \ l,k} [\delta_M(\phi_M(p_{li}), \phi_M(n_{ki}))], \qquad (5.8)$$

where $\delta_M(A, B) = \sqrt{(a_1 - b_1)^2 + (a_2 - b_2)^2 + \cdots + (a_m - b_m)^2}$ is the $M$-dimensional Euclidian distance between $A$ and $B$. $a_x$ and $b_x$ correspond to the xth-coordinate of $A$ and $B$, respectively.

$\phi_M(X)$ is the transformation function that projects image $X$ from the image space to the $M$-dimensional space defined by the set of Gabor filters.

**The Correlation Measure $C$.** In the proposed method, in addition to having every parent selecting the Gabor filter set $S_i$ that can best distinguish the individual $i$ from all the others in the database, it is necessary to ensure that this set of Gabor filters does not include filters that extract identical image features. If there were no such constraint, the algorithm might find one very distinguishing image feature on the face image and, over generations of evolution, all of its Gabor filters might converge to this one image feature. To avoid this, the correlation measure $C$ determines the correlation between the image features extracted at all the locations pointed to by the chromosome. To test for correlations between the Gabor features at the different spatial locations, we use the entire set of 125 Gabor filters to thoroughly characterize the textural context at these locations.

Assuming that there are $M$ Gabor features that we are looking for on the face image of individual $i$, let $(x_m, y_m)$, $m = 1, 2, \ldots, M$, be the $M$ points that have been selected genetically in the chromosome. To find the correlations of the image features extracted at each of these points, the $N$ Gabor filters $G_i$, $i = 1, 2, \ldots, N$, are used to characterize each of the points. Let the coefficients of such a characterization be represented by a matrix $A$. Thus, matrix A is $M \times N$ in dimension, where the rows correspond to the $M$ locations and $N = 125$ refers to the Gabor filter coefficients.

Thus,

$$A = \begin{bmatrix} g_{(1,1)} & g_{(1,2)} & \cdots & g_{(1,N)} \\ g_{(2,1)} & g_{(2,2)} & \cdots & g_{(2,N)} \\ \vdots & \vdots & \vdots & \vdots \\ g_{(m,1)} & g_{(m,2)} & \cdots & g_{(m,N)} \end{bmatrix}, \tag{5.9}$$

where $g_{(m,n)}$ is the coefficient obtained by applying the $n$th Gabor filter to the image at the point $(x_m, y_m)$.

The correlation measure can now be defined in terms of matrix $A$ as follows:

$$C = \log\left(\det\left(\text{diag}(B)\right)\right) - \log\left(\det(B)\right), \tag{5.10}$$

where diag($B$) returns the diagonal matrix corresponding to $B$, and $B$ is the covariance matrix defined by $B = \frac{1}{N-1}(AA^T)$.

Examining the Eq. (5.10), it can be seen that the first log term gets closer to the second log term when the off diagonal elements of B reduces. The diagonal elements of the matrix $B$ corresponds to the variance of the $M$ image locations, whereas the off diagonal elements correspond to the covariance between pairs of locations. Thus, as the covariance between the image points decreases, the value of the overall correlation parameter decreases.

**Normalization of *D* and *C*.** In order to have an equal representation of both the distance measure $D$ and the correlation term $C$ in the fitness function, it is necessary to normalize the range of values that they can take. For each generation, before the fitness values are used to rank the parents, parameters $D$ and $C$ are normalized to range between 0 and 1.

$$D_{\text{norm}} = \frac{D - D_{\text{Min}}}{D_{\text{Max}} - D_{\text{Min}}}, \tag{5.11}$$

$$C_{\text{norm}} = \frac{C - C_{\text{Min}}}{C_{\text{Max}} - C_{\text{Min}}}, \tag{5.12}$$

where Max represents the maximum value of $D$ or $C$ in a single generation across all the parents and Min refers to the minimum value.

**Weighting Factors *w_D* and *w_C*.** The influence of the two components of the fitness function are controlled by the weighting factors $w_D$ and $w_C$. We used the relation $w_C = 1 - w_D$ to control the two parameters simultaneously. With this relationship, a value of $w_D \approx 1$ will subdue the effect of the correlation measure, causing the genetic algorithm to choose the Gabor filters on the most prominent image feature alone. On the other hand, $w_D \approx 0$ will subdue the distance measure, deviating the genetic algorithm from the main goal of face recognition. Thus an optimal value for the weight $w_D$ has to be estimated empirically, to suit the face image database in question.

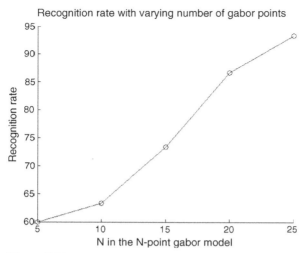

**Figure 5.14.** The recognition rate versus the number Gabor feature detectors.

## 5.7 RESULTS

To evaluate the relative importance of the two terms ($D$ and $C$) in the fitness function, we ran the proposed algorithm on the training set several times with five feature detectors per chromosome, while changing the weighting factors in the fitness function for each run, setting $w_D$ to 0, .25, .50, .75, and 1.00, and computing $w_C = (1 - w_D)$. Figure 5.15 shows the recognition rate achieved in each case.

We then ran the proposed algorithm on the training set five times, while changing the number of Gabor feature detectors per parent chromosome for each run to 5, 10, 15, 20, and 25. In all the trials, we have $w_D = 0.5$. Figure 5.14 shows the recognition rate achieved in each case.

### 5.7.1 Discussion of Results

Figure 5.14 shows that the recognition rate of the proposed algorithm when trained with 5, 10, 15, 20, and 25 Gabor feature detectors increases monotonically as the number of Gabor feature detectors ($N$) is increased. This can be attributed to the fact that increasing the number of Gabor features essentially increases the number of dimensions for the Gabor feature detector space, allowing for greater spacing between the positive and the negative clusters.

Figure 5.15 shows that for $N = 5$ the recognition rate was optimal when the distance measure $D$ and the correlation measure $C$ were weighted equally, in computing the fitness function $F$. The dip in the recognition rate for $w_D = 0.75$ and $w_D = 1.0$ indicates the significance of using the correlation factor $C$ in the fitness function. The penalty introduced by $C$ ensures that the GA searches for Gabor

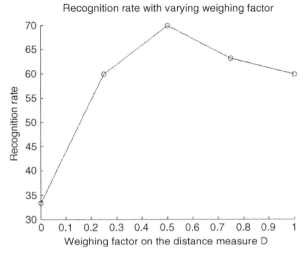

**Figure 5.15.** Recognition rate with varying $w_D$.

features with different textural patterns. If no such penalty were imposed, the GA might select Gabor features that are clustered on one salient facial feature, such as a mole.

The best recognition results for the proposed algorithm (93.3%) were obtained with 25 Gabor feature detectors. The best recognition performance for the PCA algorithm was reached at about 15 components and was flattened out beyond that point, providing a recognition rate for the same set of faces that was less than 83.3%. This indicates that for the face images used in this experiment (which included substantial illumination variations) the proposed method performed substantially better than the PCA algorithm.

## 5.7.2  Person-Specific Feature Extraction

When the FacePix(30) face database was built, all but one person were captured without eyeglasses or a hat. Figures 5.16a and 5.16b show the results of extracting 10 and 20 distinguishing features from that person's face images. The important things to note about these results are as follows:

1. At least half of the extracted Gabor features (8 of the 10) and (10 of the 20) are located on (or near) the eyeglasses.

2. As the number of Gabor features was increased from 10 to 20, more Gabor features are seen toward the boundaries of the images. This is because the genetic algorithm chooses Gabor feature locations based on a Gaussian probability distribution that is centered over the image, and it decreases toward the boundaries of the images.

 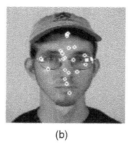

(a)                              (b)

**Figure 5.16.** Ten and 20 person-specific features extracted for a particular individual in the database

These results suggest that person-specific feature extraction might be useful for face recognition in small face databases, such as those typical of a social interaction assistance device for people who are blind.

## 5.8  CONCLUSIONS AND FUTURE WORK

As mentioned earlier, the proposed person-specific approach to evolutionary feature selection in face images is well-suited for applications such as those that enhance social interaction for people who are blind, because people do not generally disguise their appearance in normal social situations, and even when some significant change occurs (such as a man shaving off his beard), the system can continue to evolve as it captures new images with each encounter.

A wearable social interaction assistant prototype has been implemented using a pair of eyeglasses equipped with a tiny unobtrusive video camera in the nose bridge [36] and is shown in Figure 5.17. The analog video output from this camera is passed through a video digitizer, and the resulting digital stream is then fed into a portable laptop computer. A video stream of any person standing in front of the eyeglasses is captured. A face detection algorithm, based on Adaboost [37], is then used to (a) identify the frames of the video where a face is present and (b) localize that face within that frame. This detected face is then cropped and compared to indexed faces in a face database.

The performance of the proposed approach for identifying person-specific features relies, to a large extent, on obtaining near-frontal views of faces. To offset this limitation, there is ongoing work [38] to perform person-independent head pose estimation on the face images obtained from this platform. It is expected that this will help us select face images from the video stream with near-frontal views, which will improve the performance of our algorithm in identifying person-specific features.

Another factor that limits the performance of our algorithm is illumination variations in the captured images. Especially problematic are variations between outdoor–indoor and day–night settings. (Of course, this limitation is not unique to our algorithm.) As a strategy to provide additional light unobtrusively under adverse

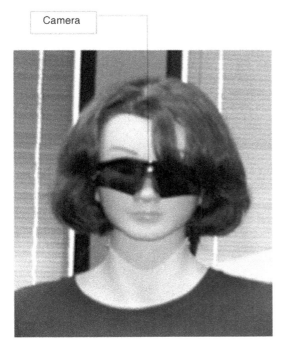

Camera

**Figure 5.17.** Wearable face recognition platform.

lighting conditions, we are employing infrared LED illuminators in conjunction with an infrared-sensitive camera.

In summary, while there have been many different feature-based approaches to face recognition over the last two decades of research, we have proposed a novel methodology based on the discovery and extraction of person-specific characteristic features to improve face recognition performance for small face databases. This approach is aimed at facilitating social interaction in casual settings. The use of Gabor features, in tandem with a genetic algorithm to discover characteristic person-specific features, has been inspired by the human visual system and is based on knowledge that has been developed about the process by which humans recognize faces. We believe that more needs to be learned about human face recognition; and we also believe that as more is learned, the knowledge can be put to use to develop more robust face recognition algorithms.

## REFERENCES

1. A. Schwaninger, C.-C. Carbon, H. Leder, *Expert Face Processing: Specialization and Constraints*, In G. Schwarzer & H. Leder, Development of face processing, Goettingen: Hogrefe, pp. 81–97.
2. V. Bruce and A. Young, *In the Eye of the Beholder: The Science of Face Perception*, Oxford University Press, New York, 2006.

3. J. Sadr, I. Jarudi, and P. Shinha, The role of eyebrows in face recognition, *Perception* **32**:285–293, 2003.

4. A. W. Young, D. Hellawell, and D. C. Hay, Configurational information in face perception, *Perception* **16**:747–759, 1987.

5. P. Sinha, B. J. Balas, Y. Ostrovsky, and R. Russell, Face recognition by humans: 19 results all computer vision researchers should know about, *Proc. IEEE* **94**(11):1948–62, 2006.

6. H. R. McConachie, Developmental prosopagnosia: A single case report, *Cortex* **12**:76–82, 1976.

7. I. Kennerknecht, T. Gruter, B. Welling, S. Wentzek, J. Horst, S. Edwards, and M. Gruter, First report of prevalence of non-syndromic hereditary prosopagnosia (hpa), *Am. J. Med. Genet. Part A* **140**:1617–1622, 2006.

8. D. J. Turk, T. C. Handy, and M. S. Gazzaniga, Can perceptual expertise account for the own-race bias in face recognition? A split brain study. *Cognit. Neuropsychol.* **22**(7):877–883, 2005.

9. P. Yang, S. Shan, W. Gao, S.Z. Li, and D. Zang, Face recognition using ada-boosted Gabor features, in *Proceedings of the 16th International Conference on Face and Gesture Recognition*, 2004.

10. B. Gökberk, M. O. Irfanoglu, L. Akarun, and E. Alpaydin, Learning the best subset of local features for face recognition, *Pattern Recognit.* **40**(5):1520, 2007.

11. L. Wiskott, Phantom faces for face analysis, *Pattern Recognit.* **30**(6):837, 1997.

12. N. Kruger, M. Potzsch, and C. Malsburg, Determination of face position and pose with a learned representation based on labelled graphs, *Image Vis. Comput.* **15**:665, 1997.

13. P. Kalocsai, C. Malsburg, and J. Horn, Face recognition by statistical analysis of feature detectors, *Image Vis. Comput.* **18**(4):273, 2000.

14. A. Tefas, C. Kotropoulos, and I. Pitas, Using support vector machines to enhance the performance of elastic graph matching for frontal face authentication, *IEEE Trans. Pattern Anal. Mach. Intell.* **23**(7):735, 2001.

15. D. H. Liu, K. M. Lam, and L. S. Shen, Optimal sampling of Gabor features for face recognition, *Pattern Recognit. Lett.* **25**(2):267, 2004.

16. X. Wang and H. Oi, Face recognition using optimal non-orthogonal wavelet basis evaluated by information complexity, in *Proceedings of the 16th International Conference on Pattern Recognition*, 2002, p. 164.

17. L. Wiskott, J.-M. Fellous, N. Krüger, and C. von der Malsburg, *Face Recognition by Elastic Bunch Graph Matching*. Springer-Verlag, Heidelberg, 1997, pp. 456–463.

18. C. von der Malsburg, Nervous structures with dynamical links, *Ber. Bunsenges. Phys. Chem.* **89**:703–710, 1985.

19. E Bienenstock and C. von der Malsburg, A neural network for invariant pattern recognition, *Europhy. Lett.* **4**:121–126, 1987.

20. L. Wiskott, J.-M. Fellous, N. Krüger, and C. von der Malsburg, *Face Recognition and Gender Determination*, International Workshop on Automatic Face- and Gesture-Recognition, Zürich, June 26–28, 1995.

21. L. Wiskott and C. von der Malsburg, *Face Recognition by Dynamic Link Matching*. The UTCS Neural Networks Research Group, Austin, TX, http://www.cs.utexas.edu/users/nn/webpubs/htmlbook96/, 1996.

22. M.J. Lyons, M.J. Lyons, J. Budynek, J. Budynek, and S. Akamatsu, Automatic classification of single facial images, *Trans. Pattern Anal. Mach. Intell.* **21**:1357–1362, 1999.

23. Y. Zhang and C. Liu, Face recognition using kernel principal component analysis and genetic algorithms, in *12th IEEE Workshop on Neural Networks for Signal Processing*, September 2002, p. 337.

24. Y. Xu, B. Li, and B. Wang, Face recognition by fast independent component analysis and genetic algorithm, in *Fourth International Conference on Computer and Information*, 14–16 September 2004, p. 194.

25. K. Wong and K. Lam, A reliable approach for human face detection using genetic algorithm, in *IEEE International Symposium on Circuits and Systems*, Vol. 4, 1999, p. 499.

26. S. Karungaru, M. Fukumi, and N. Akamatsu, Face recognition using genetic algorithm based template matching, in *International Symposium on Communications and Information Technologies*, October 26–29, 2004.

27. D. Ozkan, Feature selection for face recognition using a genetic algorithm, Technical report, Department of Computer Engineering, Bilkent University, Ankara, Turkey. 2006.

28. D. G. Lowe, Distinctive image features from scale-invariant keypoints, *Int. J. Comput. Vis.* **20**:91–110, 2003.

29. J. Huang and H. Wechsler, Eye location using genetic algorithm, in *2nd International Conference on Audio and Video-Based Biometric Person Authentication*, 1999.

30. Y. Sun and L. Yin, A genetic algorithm based feature selection approach for 3d face recognition, in *Biometrics Consortium Conference*, September 19–21, 2005.

31. Z. Sun, X. Yuan, G. Bebis, and S. Louis, "Neural-network-based gender classification using genetic search for eigen-feature selection," Neural Networks, 2002. IJCNN '02. Proceedings of the 2002 International Joint Conference on, 2002, pp. 2433–2438.

32. J. Black, M. Gargesha, K. Kahol, and S. Panchanathan, A framework for performance evaluation of face recognition algorithms, *ITCOM, Internet Multimedia Systems II, Boston*, July 2002.

33. G. Little, S. Krishna, J. Black, and S. Panchanathan, A methodology for evaluating robustness of face recognition algorithms with respect to variations in pose and illumination angle, in *Proceedings of IEEE International Conference on Acoustics, Speech and Signal Processing*, Philadelphia, 2005, pp. 89–92.

34. L. Sirovich and M. Kirby, Low-dimensional procedure for the characterization of human faces, *J. Opt. Soc. Am. A* **4**:519, 1987.

35. M. Turk and A. Pentland, Face recognition using eigenfaces, in *Proceedings of IEEE Conference on Computer Vision and Pattern Recognition*, 1991, pp. 586–591.

36. S. Krishna, G. Little, J. Black, and S. Panchanathan, A wearable face recognition system for individuals with visual impairments, in *Assets '05: Proceedings of the 7th International ACM SIGACCESS Conference on Computers and Accessibility*, ACM Press, New York, 2005, pp. 106–113.

37. P. Viola and M. Jones. Robust real-time object detection. Technical report, COMPAQ Cambridge Research Laboratory, Cambridge, MA, February 2001.

38. V. Balasubramanian, J. Ye, and S. Panchanathan, Biased manifold embedding: A framework for person-independent head pose estimation, in *IEEE Computer Society Conference on Computer Vision and Pattern Recognition (CVPR'07)*, Minneapolis, MN, June 2007.

# Chapter 6

# Face Verification Based on Elastic Graph Matching

**Anastasios Tefas and Ioannis Pitas**

## 6.1 INTRODUCTION

Many techniques for face recognition have been developed, whose principles span several disciplines, such as image processing, pattern recognition, computer vision, and neural networks [1, 2]. The increasing interest on face recognition is mainly driven by application demands, such as nonintrusive identification and verification for credit cards and automatic teller machine transactions, nonintrusive access control to buildings, identification for law enforcement, and so on. Machine analysis of faces provides solutions to the following problems:

- *Face Recognition.* Given a test face and a set of reference faces in a database, find the $N$ most similar reference faces to the test face.
- *Face Verification.* Given a test face and a reference one, decide if the test face is identical to the reference face.

Face recognition has been studied more extensively than face verification. The two problems are conceptually different. On the one hand, a face recognition system usually assists a human expert to determine the identity of a test face by computing all similarity scores between the test face and each human face stored in the system database and by ranking them. On the other hand, a face verification system should decide itself if a test face is assigned to a *client* (i.e., one who claims a person's identity) or to an *impostor* (i.e., one who pretends to be someone else). The evaluation criteria for face recognition and face verification systems are different. The performance of face recognition systems is quantified in terms of the percentage of correctly identified

*Biometrics: Theory, Methods, and Applications.* Edited by Boulgouris, Plataniotis, and Micheli-Tzanakou
Copyright © 2010 the Institute of Electrical and Electronics Engineers, Inc.

faces within the $N$ best matches [3]. The performance of face verification systems is measured in terms of the *false rejection rate* (FRR) achieved at a fixed *false acceptance rate* (FAR) or vice versa.

Two main categories for face recognition techniques can be identified: those employing geometrical features (e.g., reference 4) and those using gray-level facial image information (e.g., the eigenface approach [5]). A different approach that uses both gray-level information and shape information has been proposed in reference 6. This pattern matching algorithm is called *dynamic link architecture* (DLA). An implementation of DLA based on Gabor wavelets is described in reference 7. The DLA is a general object recognition technique that represents an object by projecting its image onto a rectangular elastic grid, where a Gabor wavelet bank response is measured at each node. A simplified implementation of DLA, the so-called elastic graph matching (EGM), is often preferred for locating objects in a scene with a known references [6, 8, 9].

A comparative study of three algorithms for face recognition, namely, the eigenfaces [5, 10], the auto-association and classification neural networks [11], and the elastic graph matching [6], can be found in reference 9. The outcome of this study reveals that the elastic graph matching achieves a better performance than the other methods, because it is more robust to illumination, facial pose, and face expression variations. The eigenfaces and the neural network algorithms require the images to be of the same scale and viewing angle. Moreover, the aforementioned methods are very sensitive to illumination variations. The problem of compensating for changes in illumination conditions is crucial for the face recognition algorithms [12, 13]. The interested reader may refer to references 14 and 15 for the treatment of varying image recording conditions.

In elastic graph matching, an object is represented as a connected graph. Each graph node is located at certain spatial image coordinates **x**. At each graph node, a feature vector, called *jet*, is attached. The jet elements can be the local brightness values that represent the image region around the node. However, it is desirable to have more complex types of jets that are derived from a multiscale image analysis [6]. The representation of an object in the EGM framework can be summarized in the following steps:

- Group all the features that correspond to the same graph node of the object into a jet.
- Group all the nodes and jets that belong to the object in order to form the object graph.
- Define neighborhood relationships for each graph node.

The research on elastic graph matching and its applications has been an active research topic since its invention. A different topology cost for a particular pair of nodes, which was based on the radius of the Apollonius sphere defined by the Euclidean distances between the nodes being matched, was proposed in reference 16. Three major extensions to elastic graph matching that allowed for handling larger face image galleries, tolerated larger variations in facial pose, and increased its matching accuracy were introduced in reference 17. Procedures that increase the robustness of elastic graph matching in translations, deformations and changes in background were proposed in reference 18.

In reference 17, the graph structure has been enhanced by introducing a stack-like structure, the so-called *bunch graph*, and has been tested for face recognition. In the bunch graph structure, for every node, a set of jets has been measured for different face instances (e.g., with opened or closed mouth/eyes). This way, the bunch graph representation could cover a variety of possible changes in the appearance of a face. In reference 8, the bunch graph structure has been used for determining facial characteristics such as beard, presence of glasses, or person's sex.

A variant of the standard EGM, the so-called *morphological elastic graph matching* (MEGM), has been proposed for frontal face verification and tested for various recording conditions [15, 19, 20]. In MEGM, the Gabor features have been replaced by multiscale morphological features obtained through dilation–erosion of the facial image by a structuring function [21]. In references 19 and 20 the standard coarse-to-fine approach [7] for elastic matching has been replaced by a simulated annealing method that optimizes a cost function of the jet similarity distances subject to node deformation constraints. The multiscale morphological analysis has been proven to be suitable for facial image analysis and MEGM has given comparable verification results with the standard EGM approach, without having to compute the computationally expensive Gabor filter bank output. Another variant of EGM has been presented in reference 22, where morphological signal decomposition has been used instead of the standard Gabor analysis [7]. In reference 23 the use of EGM has been extended in order to treat the problem of hand posture recognition.

Discriminant techniques have been employed in order to enhance the recognition and verification performance of the EGM. The use of linear discriminating techniques at the feature vectors for selecting the most discriminating features has been proposed in references 7, 19, and 20. Several schemes that aim at weighting the graph nodes according to their discriminatory power have been proposed [19, 20, 24, 25]. In reference 24 the selection of the weighting coefficients has been based on a non-linear function that depends on a small set of parameters. These parameters have been determined on the training set by maximizing a criterion using the SIMPLEX linear programming method. In references 19, 20, and 22, the set of node weighting coefficient was not calculated by some criterion optimization but by using the first- and second-order statistics of the node similarity values. A Bayesian approach for determining which nodes are more reliable has been used in reference 8. A more sophisticated scheme for weighting the nodes of the elastic graph by constructing a modified class of support vector machines [26], has been proposed in reference 25. In reference 25, it has been also shown that the verification performance of the EGM can be highly improved by proper node weighting strategies.

The remainder of this chapter is organized as follows. In Section 6.2 the algorithm of elastic graph matching is described in detail. The various facial region modeling methods that can be used with EGM are presented in Section 6.3. The incorporation of discriminant analysis techniques in EGM is described in Section 6.4. In Section 6.5, the extension of EGM to discriminant graph structures is presented.

Finally, the performance evaluation of the EGM algorithm and its variants in face verification is presented in Section 6.6.

## 6.2  THE ELASTIC GRAPH MATCHING ALGORITHM

In the first step of the EGM algorithm, a sparse graph suitable for face representation is selected [7, 17, 19]. The facial image region is analyzed and a set of local descriptors is extracted at each graph node. The analysis is usually performed by building an information pyramid using scale-space techniques. In the standard EGM, a 2D Gabor-based filter bank has been used for image analysis [6]. The output of multiscale morphological dilation–erosion operations or the morphological signal decomposition at several scales are nonlinear alternatives to the Gabor filters for multiscale analysis, and both have been successfully used for facial image analysis [19, 20, 22, 27]. At each graph node $l$ that is located at image coordinates $\mathbf{x}^l$, a jet (feature vector) $\mathbf{j}(\mathbf{x})$ is formed:

$$\mathbf{j}(\mathbf{x}^l) = [f_1(\mathbf{x}^l), \ldots, f_M(\mathbf{x}^l)]^T, \tag{6.1}$$

where $f_i(\mathbf{x}^l)$ denotes the output of a local operator applied to the image $f$ at the $i$th scale or at the $i$th scale-orientation pair, and $M$ is the jet dimensionality. The next step of the EGM is to translate and deform the reference graph on the test image in order to find the correspondences of the reference graph nodes on the test image. This is accomplished by minimizing a cost function that employs node jet similarities and, in the same time, preserves the node neighborhood relationships. Let the superscripts $t$ and $r$ denote a test and a reference facial image (or graph), respectively. The $L_2$ norm between the feature vectors at the $l$th graph node of the reference and the test graph is used as a similarity measure between jets, that is,

$$C_f\left(\mathbf{j}\left(\mathbf{x}_t^l\right), \mathbf{j}\left(\mathbf{x}_r^l\right)\right) = \left\|\mathbf{j}\left(\mathbf{x}_r^l\right) - \mathbf{j}\left(\mathbf{x}_t^l\right)\right\|. \tag{6.2}$$

Alternatively, one may use other distance metrics, like the Mahalanobis distance, or the normalized jet correlation.

Let $\mathcal{V}$ be the set of all graph nodes of a certain facial image. The graphs are usually considered to be rectangular graphs that are topologically equivalent to a rectangular subset of $\mathcal{Z}^2$ ($\mathcal{Z}$ is the set of integers). Thus, all nodes, except from the boundary nodes, have exactly four connected neighborhood nodes. Figure 6.1 shows a typical rectangular graph as well as a graph with special structure adapted to facial images. Let $\mathcal{H}(l)$ be the four-connected neighborhood of node $l$. In order to quantify the node neighborhood relationships using a metric, the local node deformation is used:

$$C_d\left(\mathbf{x}_t^l, \mathbf{x}_r^l\right) = \sum_{\xi \in \mathcal{H}(l)} \left\|\left(\mathbf{x}_t^l - \mathbf{x}_r^l\right) - \left(\mathbf{x}_t^\xi - \mathbf{x}_r^\xi\right)\right\|. \tag{6.3}$$

The objective is to find a set of vertices $\{\mathbf{x}_t^l, l \in \mathcal{V}\}$ in the test image that minimize the cost function:

$$C\left(\{\mathbf{x}_t^l\}\right) = \sum_{l \in \mathcal{V}} \left\{C_f\left(\mathbf{j}\left(\mathbf{x}_t^l\right), \mathbf{j}\left(\mathbf{x}_r^l\right)\right) + \lambda C_d\left(\mathbf{x}_t^l, \mathbf{x}_r^l\right)\right\}. \tag{6.4}$$

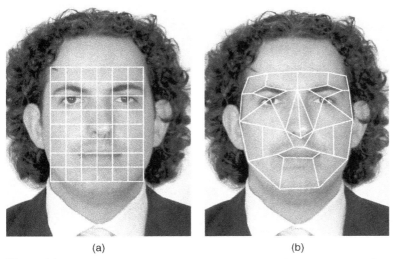

(a)                                        (b)

**Figure 6.1.**  The reference grid can be either **(a)** rectangular or **(b)** placed on certain facial landmarks.

The jet of the $l$th node that has been produced after the matching procedure of the graph of the reference person $r$ in the image of the test image of person $t$ is denoted as $\mathbf{j}(\mathbf{x}_t^l)$. This notation is used due to the fact that different reference graphs $r$ result to different test jets $\mathbf{j}(\mathbf{x}_t^l)$. Thus, the jet of the $l$th node of the test graph $t$ is a function of the reference graph $r$. The notation $\mathbf{j}(\mathbf{x}_r^l)$ is used only when the $l$th node is in a preselected position of a facial image.

The optimization of Eq. (6.4) has been interpreted as a simulated annealing with additional penalties imposed by the graph deformations in reference 19. Accordingly, Eq. (6.4) can be simplified to the minimization of

$$D_t(r) = \sum_{l \in \mathcal{V}} \left\{ C_f \left( \mathbf{j}\left(\mathbf{x}_t^l\right), \mathbf{j}\left(\mathbf{x}_r^l\right) \right) \right\} \qquad \text{subject to}$$
$$\mathbf{x}_t^l = \mathbf{x}_r^l + \mathbf{s} + \delta_l, \quad ||\delta_l|| \leq \delta_{\max}, \tag{6.5}$$

where $\mathbf{s}$ is a global translation of the graph and $\delta_l$ denotes a local perturbation of the graph nodes. The choices of $\lambda$ in Eq. (6.4) and of $\delta_{\max}$ in Eq. (6.5) control the rigidity/plasticity of the graph [7, 19]. Obviously, both functions (6.4) and (6.5) define a similarity measure between two faces. After the matching procedure, the distance $D_t(r)$ is used as a quantitative measure for the similarity of two faces [7, 15, 19]. Figure 6.2 illustrates the graph matching procedure for a rectangular graph.

## 6.3  FACIAL REGION MODELING

The facial region modeling is an important step of the EGM. Many image analysis techniques have been proposed in the literature for this purpose. The objective of the

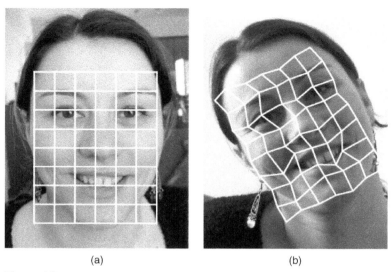

(a)          (b)

**Figure 6.2.** (a) The reference grid and (b) the test grid after the elastic graph matching.

facial region modeling step is the construction of a feature jet at each node of the elastic graph. The extracted feature vectors should have certain properties in order to be:

(a) *Descriptive*: The feature vectors should describe sufficiently the region around the graph node.

(b) *Robust*: The feature vectors should be robust against geometrical transformations and illumination changes and should pose variations that are very common in facial biometrics.

(c) *Discriminative*: The feature vectors should ideally be able to capture only or primarily the discriminative power of the region around the graph node.

(d) *Easily Computable*: The computation cost for calculating the feature vector at each graph node should be low in order to be suitable for real-time applications.

Toward the above objectives, many transformations have been proposed for extracting the feature vectors in EGM. In the remainder of this section the most representative image analysis tools that have been proposed for facial region modeling in EGM will be presented in more detail.

## 6.3.1 Gabor Wavelet Transformation

The most popular image analysis technique used in EGM is the Gabor wavelet transform (GWT) [6, 7]. The GWT kernel functions, commonly used for extracting the jets, are defined as follows:

$$\psi_{\mu,\upsilon}(\mathbf{x}) = \frac{\|\mathbf{k}_{\mu,\upsilon}\|^2}{\sigma^2} \exp\left(-\frac{\|\mathbf{k}_{\mu,\upsilon}\|^2 \|\mathbf{x}\|^2}{2\sigma^2}\right) \times \left[\exp(i\mathbf{k}_{\mu,\upsilon}\mathbf{x}) - \exp\left(-\frac{\sigma^2}{2}\right)\right],$$

$$(6.6)$$

where $\mu = 0, \ldots, L - 1, \upsilon = 0, \ldots, M - 1$. $L$ and $M$ denote the number of directions and the number of scales respectively. The characteristics of Gabor kernels are determined by the wave vector, which is defined as follows:

$$\mathbf{k}_{\mu,\upsilon} = \frac{k_{max}}{\lambda^{\upsilon}} \exp\left(i\mu\frac{\pi}{L}\right). \qquad (6.7)$$

$k_{max}$ is the maximum frequency and $\lambda$ is the spacing factor between kernels in the frequency domain. By this sampling, the frequency domain is evenly covered within a reasonable band-pass radius. The kernels are DC-free (i.e., the integral $\int \psi_{\mu,\upsilon}(\mathbf{x})\,d\mathbf{x}$ vanishes). Since this is a wavelet transform, the family of kernels is self-similar in the sense that all kernels can be generated from one mother wavelet by dilation and rotation. In Figure 6.3, the magnitude of two Gabor filters with different orientation and scale are depicted.

Given a face image $f(\mathbf{x})$, the typical jet at $\mathbf{x}_0$ is a vector composed of the magnitude parts of Gabor wavelet coefficients calculated by the convolution of the image and GWT kernel functions centered at $\mathbf{x}_0$, that is,

$$j_{\mu,\upsilon}(\mathbf{x}_0) = f(\mathbf{x}) * *\psi_{\mu,\upsilon}(\mathbf{x} - \mathbf{x}_0), \qquad (6.8)$$

$$\mathbf{j}(\mathbf{x}_0) = [j_{0,0}, j_{1,0}, \ldots, j_{L-1,M-1}]^T, \qquad (6.9)$$

where $j_{\mu,\upsilon}$ is the simplified notation of $j_{\mu,\upsilon}(\mathbf{x}_0)$, and $T$ is the vector transposition operator.

Usually, 3–5 different spatial frequencies and 6–8 different orientations are used for building the information pyramid. Gabor wavelets are chosen for their technical properties and biological relevance. Since they are DC-free, they provide robustness against varying illumination of the facial region. A limited robustness against geometric transforms can be also noticed. A disadvantage of the large in scale kernels is their sensitivity to background variations. Another disadvantage is the computation cost of the convolution used for calculating the response of the filters.

**Figure 6.3.** The magnitude of Gabor filters at different scales and orientations.

## 6.3.2 Multiscale Morphology

An alternative to linear techniques for generating an information pyramid is scale-space morphology. In the following, a brief description of the feature extraction procedure in morphological elastic graph matching (MEGM) is given. In MEGM, the image representation part of elastic graph matching [6] that is based on Gabor wavelets is substituted by the *multiscale morphological dilation–erosion*. Let $\mathcal{R}$ and $\mathcal{Z}$ denote the set of real and integer numbers, respectively. Given an image $f(\mathbf{x}) : \mathcal{D} \subseteq \mathcal{Z}^2 \rightarrow \mathcal{R}$ and a structuring function $g(\mathbf{x}) : \mathcal{G} \subseteq \mathcal{Z}^2 \rightarrow \mathcal{R}$, the dilation of the image $f(\mathbf{x})$ by $g(\mathbf{x})$ is defined by [28, 31]

$$(f \oplus g)(\mathbf{x}) = \max_{\mathbf{z} \in \mathcal{G}, \, \mathbf{x} - \mathbf{z} \in \mathcal{D}} \{f(\mathbf{x} - \mathbf{z}) + g(\mathbf{z})\} . \qquad (6.10)$$

Its complementary operation, the erosion is given by

$$(f \ominus g)(\mathbf{x}) = \min_{\mathbf{z} \in \mathcal{G}, \, \mathbf{x} + \mathbf{z} \in \mathcal{D}} \{f(\mathbf{x} + \mathbf{z}) - g(\mathbf{z})\} . \qquad (6.11)$$

The multiscale dilation–erosion of the image $f(\mathbf{x})$ by $g_\sigma(\mathbf{x})$ is defined by [21]

$$(f \star g_\sigma)(\mathbf{x}) = \begin{cases} (f \oplus g_\sigma)(\mathbf{x}) & \text{if } \sigma > 0, \\ f(\mathbf{x}) & \text{if } \sigma = 0, \\ (f \ominus g_{|\sigma|})(\mathbf{x}) & \text{if } \sigma < 0. \end{cases} \qquad (6.12)$$

where $\sigma$ denotes the scale parameter of the structuring function. In reference 19, it was shown that the choice of structuring function does not lead to statistically significant changes in the face verification performance. However, it affects the computational complexity of feature calculation.

Such morphological operations can highlight and capture important information for key facial features, such as eyebrows, eyes, nose tip, nostrils, lips, and face contour, but can be affected by different illumination conditions and noise [19]. To compensate for these conditions, the normalized multiscale dilation–erosion has been also proposed for facial image analysis [27, 30]. It is well known that the different illumination conditions affect the facial region in a nonuniform manner. However, it can safely be assumed that the illumination changes are locally uniform inside the area of the structuring element used for multiscale analysis. The proposed morphological features are calculated by subtracting the mean value of the intensity of the image $f$ inside the area of structuring element from the corresponding maximum (dilation) or minimum (erosion) of the area. Formally, the normalized multiscale morphological analysis is given by

$$(f \star g_\sigma)(\mathbf{x}) = \begin{cases} (f \oplus g_\sigma)(\mathbf{x}) - m_-(f, \mathbf{x}, G_\sigma) & \text{if } \sigma > 0, \\ f(\mathbf{x}) & \text{if } \sigma = 0, \\ (f \ominus g_{|\sigma|})(\mathbf{x}) - m_+(f, \mathbf{x}, G_\sigma) & \text{if } \sigma < 0, \end{cases} \qquad (6.13)$$

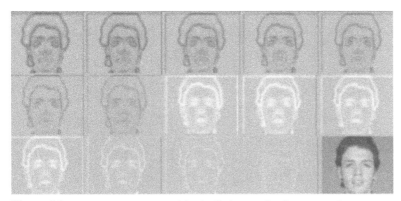

**Figure 6.4.** Output of normalized multiscale dilation–erosion for seven scales.

where $m_-(f, \mathbf{x}, \mathcal{G}_\sigma)$ and $m_+(f, \mathbf{x}, \mathcal{G}_\sigma)$ are the mean values of the image $f(\mathbf{x} - \mathbf{z})$, $\mathbf{x} - \mathbf{z} \in \mathcal{D}$ and $f(\mathbf{x} + \mathbf{z})$, $\mathbf{x} + \mathbf{z} \in \mathcal{D}$ inside the support area of the structuring element $\mathcal{G}_\sigma = \{\mathbf{z} \in \mathcal{G} : ||\mathbf{z}|| < \sigma\}$, respectively. Another implementation for the operators $m_+(f, \mathbf{x}, \mathcal{G}_\sigma)$ and $m_-(f, \mathbf{x}, \mathcal{G}_\sigma)$ would be the median of the values of the image inside the support area of the structuring element. The output of these morphological operations forms the jet $\mathbf{j}(\mathbf{x}^l)$, at the graph node $l$ that is located in the image coordinates $\mathbf{x}^l$:

$$\mathbf{j}(\mathbf{x}^l) = ((f \star g_{\sigma_\Lambda})(\mathbf{x}^l), \ldots, (f \star g_{\sigma_1})(\mathbf{x}^l), f(\mathbf{x}^l), (f \star g_{\sigma_{-1}})(\mathbf{x}^l), \ldots, (f \star g_{\sigma_{-\Lambda}})(\mathbf{x}^l)),$$

$$(6.14)$$

where $\Lambda$ is the number of different scales used. Figure 6.4 depicts the output of normalized dilation erosion for various scales used. The lower right image is the original image extracted from the XM2VTS database. The first seven images, starting from the upper left corner, are the normalized eroded images and the remaining nine are the normalized dilated images.

### 6.3.3  Morphological Signal Decomposition

Another option for analyzing a gray-scale facial image region $f(\mathbf{x})$ is by employing the morphological signal decomposition (MSD) [22]. Given $f(\mathbf{x}) : \mathcal{D} \subseteq \mathcal{Z}^2 \to \mathcal{Z}$ and a structuring function $g(\mathbf{x}) : \mathcal{G} \subseteq \mathcal{Z}^2 \to \mathcal{Z}$, the *gray-scale dilation* of the image $f(\mathbf{x})$ by the structuring function $g(\mathbf{x})$ is noted by $(f \oplus g)(\mathbf{x})$ and its dual operation, the *gray-scale erosion*, is defined as $(f \ominus g)(\mathbf{x})$, [29, 31]. Let $f(\mathbf{x})$ be approximated by

$$\hat{f}_K(\mathbf{x}) = \sum_{i=1}^{K} f_i(\mathbf{x}),$$

$$(6.15)$$

where $f_i(\mathbf{x})$ denotes the $i$th component and $K$ is the total number of components. MSD provides a simple method to determine the components and can then be implemented recursively as follows.

**Step 1.** Initialization: $\hat{f}_0(\mathbf{x}) = 0$.

**Step 2.** Find the $i$th level of decomposition. Starting with $n_i = 1$, increment $n_i$ until

$$\left[(f - \hat{f}_{i-1}) \ominus (n_i + 1)g\right](\mathbf{x}) \le 0. \tag{6.16}$$

**Step 3.** Calculate the $i$th component by

$$f_i(\mathbf{x}) = \left\{ \underbrace{\left[(f - \hat{f}_{i-1}) \ominus n_i\, g\right] \oplus n_i\, g}_{l_i(\mathbf{x})} \right\}(\mathbf{x}). \tag{6.17}$$

**Step 4.** Calculate the reconstructed image at the $i$th decomposition level:

$$\hat{f}_i(\mathbf{x}) = \hat{f}_{i-1}(\mathbf{x}) + f_i(\mathbf{x}). \tag{6.18}$$

**Step 5.** Let $\mathcal{M}(f - \hat{f}_i)$ be a measure of the approximation of the image $f(\mathbf{x})$ by its reconstruction $\hat{f}_i(\mathbf{x})$ at the $i$th decomposition level. Let also $L$ be the maximum number of image components used for reconstruction. Increment $i$ and go to Step 2 until $i > L$ or, alternatively, until $\mathcal{M}(f - \hat{f}_i) < T$, where $T$ is a predefined threshold.

Figure 6.5 shows the response of the MSD analysis applied to a facial image. There are several reasons supporting the use of MSD as a feature extraction algorithm, namely:

1. The decomposition of a complex object yields simple components that conform with our intuition. For example, if a cylinder is used as structuring function, the component is the maximal inscribable cylinder. In addition, the method is object-independent, in the sense that it employs generic structuring functions that do not depend on the object that is approximated [32].

2. It allows arbitrary amounts of detail to be computed and also allows the abstraction from details [32].

3. The representation is unique.

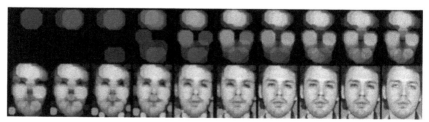

**Figure 6.5.** Output of morphological signal decomposition.

4. Gray-scale erosions and dilations with a flat structuring function that are more suited for MSD can be computed very efficiently using running min/max selection algorithms [31].

## 6.3.4 Warping Robust Gabor Features

Another work on increasing the robustness of Gabor features has been presented in reference 33. The proposed feature vectors are based on the standard Gabor wavelet coefficients and they are devised so as to become robust against image rotation and scaling. In order to extract the robust jets, the Gabor wavelet coefficients are represented by an $L \times M$ Gabor wavelet matrix:

$$\Phi = \begin{bmatrix} j_{0,0} & \cdots & j_{0,M-1} \\ \vdots & \ddots & \vdots \\ j_{L-1,0} & \cdots & j_{L-1,M-1} \end{bmatrix} \tag{6.19}$$

and then an $L \times M$ 2-D DFT is applied to matrix $\Phi$, thus producing matrix $\Omega = [c_{\mu,\upsilon}]$. The proposed robust jet comprises of the normalized magnitude parts of the complex elements of $\Omega$ as follows:

$$\mathbf{j}(\mathbf{x}_0) = \frac{1}{\rho}[|c_{0,0}|, |c_{1,0}|, \ldots, |c_{L-1,M-1}|]^T, \tag{6.20}$$

where

$$\rho = \left( \sum_{\mu=0}^{L-1} \sum_{\upsilon=0}^{M-1} |c_{\mu,\upsilon}|^2 \right)^{1/2}.$$

It can be proven that the above jets are robust against rotation and scaling of the test image. The robustness has its source to the shift invariance property of the magnitude of the DFT coefficients and the self-similarity property of the Gabor kernels. That is, rotation and scaling of the test image corresponds to convolution with symmetric Gabor kernels, which is a translation on the Gabor matrix given in Eq. (6.19) that maps to DFT coefficients having the same magnitude as the original ones. Thus, the robust Gabor feature vector remains unaltered.

In the matching procedure, the cost function given in Eq. (6.4) is modified in order to take into account the estimated warping. That is, a $2 \times 2$ warping-matrix $\mathbf{A}$ that describes the in-plane pose change caused by rotation, scaling, and skew is used as follows:

$$C\left(\left\{\mathbf{x}_t^l\right\}\right) = \sum_{l \in \mathcal{V}} \left\{ C_f\left(\mathbf{j}\left(\mathbf{x}_t^l\right), \mathbf{j}\left(\mathbf{x}_r^l\right)\right) + \lambda C_d\left(\mathbf{A}^{-1}\mathbf{x}_t^l, \mathbf{x}_r^l\right) \right\}. \tag{6.21}$$

Estimating the four parameters of the skew-matrix $\mathbf{A}$ increases the computational complexity of the matching procedure, because four more parameters should be optimized using simulated annealing.

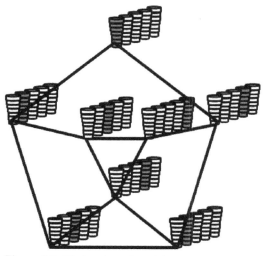

**Figure 6.6.** The bunch graph model.

### 6.3.5 Bunch Graphs

Another variant of EGM, the so-called elastic bunch graph matching (EBGM), has been proposed in reference 17 (Figure 6.6). The idea behind EBGM is that a single graph is appropriate for modeling only a single image, whereas a class of images should be modeled using a bunch graph. That is, at each graph node a bunch of jets should be assigned. Each jet corresponds to the different feature that can be extracted at the specific node, when the face is under different appearance conditions. Faces, for example, may have a beard or glasses, may have different expressions, or may be of different age, sex, or race. Another change with respect to the standard EGM is the use of facial landmarks (e.g., eyes, nose, mouth, etc.), for placing the nodes of the graph. Of course, the landmarks should be detected using a face and facial feature detector.

The face bunch graph has a stack-like structure and combines graphs of individual sample faces. It is crucial that the individual graphs all have the same structure and that the nodes refer to the same fiducial points. All jets referring to the same fiducial point (e.g., all left-eye jets) are bundled together in a bunch, from which one can select any jet as an alternative description. The left-eye bunch might contain a male eye, a female eye, both closed or open, and so on. Each fiducial point is represented by such a set of alternatives; and, from each bunch, any jet can be selected independently of the ones selected from the other bunches. This provides enhanced combinatorial power that renders it so general, even if it is constituted from few graphs only.

Another variation that EBGM introduces is the use of the phase of the complex Gabor wavelet transform instead of the magnitude. That is, the authors claimed that the transform phase has greater capability in finding the exact locations of the fiducial points than the transform magnitude. The major change in the matching algorithm is the matching between a test jet and a bunch of reference jets, where the maximum similarity is proposed to be used according to Eq. (6.2).

## 6.4 DISCRIMINANT ELASTIC GRAPH MATCHING

Since the invention of EGM, many efforts have been made toward the exploitation of the discriminant information of faces. The idea is to import discriminant analysis to each step of the EGM. However, most of the proposed methods are dealing with discriminant analysis, either at feature level [7, 33] or at graph level [25]. A complete methodology for applying discriminant analysis techniques to all phases of EGM for face verification has been proposed in reference 30 and is presented in this section in detail. This methodology is called discriminant elastic graph matching (DEGM) and can be applied to all EGM algorithms like those in 7 and 19. More precisely, in the DEGM, each node is considered as a local expert and discriminant feature selection techniques are employed for enhancing its verification performance. The deformation of each node is considered to provide a second local similarity measure that can quantify the relationships between its neighboring nodes. The new local similarity value at each node is produced by discriminant weighting of both the feature vector similarity measure and the node deformation. Finally, a discriminant node weighting step is used in order to form the similarity measure between face graphs.

By examining carefully the elastic graph matching procedure from a pattern recognition perspective, the following questions arise: Do all jet dimensions possess discriminant information? Does the node deformation possess any discriminant information? Are all the graph nodes equally significant for performing facial image verification?

In order to answer all these questions, DEGM has been proposed as a general framework that enhances the verification performance of the EGM algorithm in a supervised manner [30]. In more detail, discriminant techniques are used for selecting the most discriminant features of every facial image class. The jet similarity measure is combined with the node deformation in a discriminant manner, in order to form a local discriminant similarity measure between nodes. The use of node deformation can be explained intuitively as follows. The face graph has nodes that may correspond to facial landmarks (the landmarks correspond to facial points) whose deformation can be considered either as rigid or elastic for a particular face. For example, nodes corresponding to a person's face scars that are in some rigid region like forehead or nose cannot be easily moved, whereas some nodes corresponding to landmarks in lips can be moved much more freely.

If the information about the elasticity/rigidity of each facial region was available a priori, we could have incorporated it in the grid matching procedure. However, this information is person-specific, and thus it should be retrieved using a training procedure and be taken into account when forming the local similarity measure between grid nodes. The last step of DEGM is to learn which nodes contain significant discriminant information and, thus, to use proper weights when forming the similarity measure between entire faces. This step is motivated by the fact that certain facial features (e.g., beauty spots) are more discriminant than others for certain persons.

## 6.4.1   Feature Vector Discriminant Analysis

The first step of the DEGM is to learn a face- and node-specific discriminant function $\mathbf{g}_r^l$, for the $l$th node of the reference face $r$ that transforms the jets $\mathbf{j}(\mathbf{x}_t^l)$:

$$\check{\mathbf{j}}\left(\mathbf{x}_t^l\right) = \mathbf{g}_r^l\left(\mathbf{j}\left(\mathbf{x}_t^l\right)\right). \tag{6.22}$$

The transform $\mathbf{g}_r^l$ can be any linear or nonlinear discriminant feature transformation, like the ones used for face recognition and verification [5, 19, 34–36]. We will use linear techniques in the remainder of the section. Alternatively, nonlinear techniques could also be used.

Before calculating the linear transformations, all the jets that have been produced during the graph matching of the reference person $r$ to all other facial images in the training set are normalized in order to have zero mean and unit magnitude. Let $\hat{\mathbf{j}}(\mathbf{x}_t^l)$ be the normalized jet at $l$th node. Let $\mathcal{F}_C^l$ and $\mathcal{F}_I^l$ be the sets of the normalized jets of the $l$th node that correspond to genuine and impostor claims related to person $r$, respectively. In the Fisher linear discriminant analysis (FLDA), the within-class and between-class scatter matrices are used to formulate criteria of class separability [37]. For a two-class problem the within class scatter for the vectors $\hat{\mathbf{j}}(\mathbf{x}_t^l)$ is defined as

$$\mathbf{F}_W^l = \hat{P}_C \frac{1}{N\left(\mathcal{F}_C^l\right)} \sum_{\hat{\mathbf{j}}\left(\mathbf{x}_t^l\right) \in \mathcal{F}_C^l} \left(\hat{\mathbf{j}}\left(\mathbf{x}_t^l\right) - \mathbf{m}\left(\mathcal{F}_C^l\right)\right)\left(\hat{\mathbf{j}}\left(\mathbf{x}_t^l\right) - \mathbf{m}\left(\mathcal{F}_C^l\right)\right)^T$$

$$+ \hat{P}_I \frac{1}{N\left(\mathcal{F}_I^l\right)} \sum_{\hat{\mathbf{j}}\left(\mathbf{x}_t^l\right) \in \mathcal{F}_I^l} \left(\hat{\mathbf{j}}\left(\mathbf{x}_t^l\right) - \mathbf{m}\left(\mathcal{F}_I^l\right)\right)\left(\hat{\mathbf{j}}\left(\mathbf{x}_t^l\right) - \mathbf{m}\left(\mathcal{F}_I^l\right)\right)^T.$$

$$\tag{6.23}$$

In the remainder of the section, $\mathbf{m}(\mathcal{X})$ denotes the mean vector of a set of vectors $\mathcal{X}$ and $N(\mathcal{X})$ denotes the cardinality of a set $\mathcal{X}$. The between-class scatter is given by

$$\mathbf{F}_B^l = \hat{P}_C \hat{P}_I \left(\mathbf{m}\left(\mathcal{F}_I^l\right) - \mathbf{m}\left(\mathcal{F}_C^l\right)\right)\left(\mathbf{m}\left(\mathcal{F}_I^l\right) - \mathbf{m}\left(\mathcal{F}_C^l\right)\right)^T, \tag{6.24}$$

where $\hat{P}_C$ and $\hat{P}_I$ are the a priori probability estimates for the genuine and impostor class, respectively.

The most commonly used criterion for linear feature vector transformation is the one that projects the feature vectors in the direction of $\psi^l$ so that the Fisher discriminant ratio

$$J(\psi^l) = \frac{\psi^{l^T} \mathbf{F}_B^l \psi^l}{\psi^{l^T} \mathbf{F}_W^l \psi^l} \tag{6.25}$$

is maximized [37]. The optimal projection $\hat{\boldsymbol{\psi}}_l$ is given by [37]

$$\hat{\boldsymbol{\psi}}_l \triangleq \frac{\mathbf{F}_W^{l\,-1}\left(\mathbf{m}\left(\mathcal{F}_I^l\right) - \mathbf{m}\left(\mathcal{F}_C^l\right)\right)}{\left\|\mathbf{F}_W^{l\,-1}\left(\mathbf{m}\left(\mathcal{F}_I^l\right) - \mathbf{m}\left(\mathcal{F}_C^l\right)\right)\right\|}. \tag{6.26}$$

It is assumed that $\mathbf{F}_W^l$ is invertible, which is true in most implementations of EGM [7, 19, 20, 22], where the feature vector has no more than 20 dimensions and most databases provide a relative large number of impostor claims. Equation (6.26) indicates that for the face verification problem, the original multidimensional feature space is projected to a one-dimensional feature space. The jet $\hat{\mathbf{j}}(\mathbf{x}_t^l)$ is projected to one dimension by

$$\hat{j}(\mathbf{x}_t^l) = \hat{\boldsymbol{\psi}}_l^T\,\hat{\mathbf{j}}\left(\mathbf{x}_t^l\right). \tag{6.27}$$

It is obvious that the one-dimensional feature space derived by Eq. (6.27) is only a very limited solution to the problem of discovering discriminant projections in a multidimensional feature space. Recently, it was shown [38] that alternative LDA schemes that give more than one discriminative dimensions in a two class classification problem, have better classification performance. In reference 30 the same criterion has been used as in references 7 and 19, which can give more than one discriminant directions. Let $\mathbf{W}^l$ and $\mathbf{B}^l$ be the matrices:

$$\mathbf{W}^l = \sum_{\hat{\mathbf{j}}(\mathbf{x}_t^l)\in\mathcal{F}_I} \left(\hat{\mathbf{j}}\left(\mathbf{x}_t^l\right) - \mathbf{m}\left(\mathcal{F}_C^l\right)\right)\left(\hat{\mathbf{j}}\left(\mathbf{x}_t^l\right) - \mathbf{m}\left(\mathcal{F}_C^l\right)\right)^T \tag{6.28}$$

and

$$\mathbf{B}^l = \sum_{\hat{\mathbf{j}}(\mathbf{x}_t^l)\in\mathcal{F}_C} \left(\hat{\mathbf{j}}\left(\mathbf{x}_t^l\right) - \mathbf{m}\left(\mathcal{F}_C^l\right)\right)\left(\hat{\mathbf{j}}\left(\mathbf{x}_t^l\right) - \mathbf{m}\left(\mathcal{F}_C^l\right)\right)^T. \tag{6.29}$$

The trace of the matrix $\mathbf{W}^l$ denotes the dispersion of the impostor jets from the center of the genuine class while the trace of the matrix $\mathbf{B}^l$ denotes the dispersion of the jets of the genuine class from the center of the genuine class. The optimal discriminant directions are the columns of the matrix $\hat{\boldsymbol{\Psi}}_l$ which is given by the maximization of the criterion:

$$J(\boldsymbol{\Psi}^l) = \frac{\mathrm{tr}[\boldsymbol{\Psi}^{l^T}\mathbf{W}^l\boldsymbol{\Psi}^l]}{\mathrm{tr}[\boldsymbol{\Psi}^{l^T}\mathbf{B}^l\boldsymbol{\Psi}^l]}, \tag{6.30}$$

where $\mathrm{tr}[\mathbf{R}]$ is the trace of the matrix $\mathbf{R}$. This criterion is well-suited for the face verification problem due to the fact that it tries to find the feature projections that maximize the distance of the impostor jets from the genuine class center, while minimizing the distance of the genuine jets from the genuine class center. If $\mathbf{B}^l$ is not singular, then Eq. (6.30) is maximized when the column vectors of the projection matrix, $\hat{\boldsymbol{\Psi}}_l$, are the eigenvectors of $\mathbf{B}^{l^{-1}}\mathbf{W}^l$.

In order to proceed to feature dimensionality reduction in $P < M$ dimensions the matrix $\acute{\boldsymbol{\Psi}}_l$ should be comprised by the eigenvectors of $\mathbf{B}^{l-1}\mathbf{W}^l$ that correspond to the $P$ greatest eigenvalues. It is obvious that $\mathbf{B}^l$ is not always invertible since the training sets usually provide less samples than required. Numerous methods have been proposed in order to solve such optimization problems, like the maximization of Eq. (6.30), when the matrix in the denominator is singular [13, 39, 40]. The feature vector projection after discriminant dimensionality reduction is given by

$$\acute{\mathbf{j}}(\mathbf{x}_t^l) = \mathbf{g}_r^l \hat{\mathbf{j}}(\mathbf{x}_t^l) = \acute{\boldsymbol{\Psi}}_l^T \hat{\mathbf{j}}(\mathbf{x}_t^l). \tag{6.31}$$

The similarity measure of the new feature vectors can be given by a simple distance metric. The $L_2$ norm for forming the new feature vector similarity measure in the final multidimensional space has been used. Other choices for the distance metric are the $L_1$ norm, the normalized correlation or the Mahalanobis distance. Another alternative distance metric that has been recently introduced for LDA subspaces is the gradient direction metric along the most discriminant direction [41].

## 6.4.2  Discriminant Weighting of the Local Similarity Measure

The second step of the DEGM is to combine the feature vector similarity measure and the node deformation in a discriminant manner in order to form the new local similarity measure. To do so, let $\mathbf{d}_t^l \in \Re^2$ be a column vector that is comprised by the two similarity measures (feature similarity and node deformation) for the node $l$ between the test person $t$ and the reference person $r$, that is,

$$\mathbf{d}_t^l = \left[ C_f \left( \hat{\mathbf{j}}(\mathbf{x}_t^l), \hat{\mathbf{j}}(\mathbf{x}_r^l) \right) \quad C_d \left( \mathbf{x}_t^l, \mathbf{x}_r^l \right) \right]^T. \tag{6.32}$$

The two similarity measures $C_f \left( \hat{\mathbf{j}}(\mathbf{x}_t^l), \hat{\mathbf{j}}(\mathbf{x}_r^l) \right)$ and $C_d \left( \mathbf{x}_t^l, \mathbf{x}_r^l \right)$ could be considered as similarity scores that occurred from different sensors for the same biometric modality (facial image in our case). Thus, its values may range in different intervals. Therefore, normalization techniques can be used for robust fusion of these scores, as in reference 42.

Let $\hat{\mathbf{d}}_t^l$ be the vector with the normalized scores. When performing discriminant local similarity measure weighting, a discriminant function $\mu_r^l$ is used that is a person- and node-specific combination of the measure of similarity between jets and the measure of local deformation. The sets of normalized local similarity vectors $\hat{\mathbf{d}}_t^l$ that correspond to genuine and impostor claims should be used in the LDA procedure. In order to form the optimization criterion, the between-class scatter matrix and the within-class scatter matrix of the normalized local similarity vectors $\hat{\mathbf{d}}_t^l$ are employed. LDA is applied again as described in Section 6.4.1 seeking for a discriminant projection vector $\acute{\mathbf{q}}_l$. The new similarity score between the $l$th node of the reference graph and the same node of the test graph is now

$$c_t^l = \acute{\mathbf{q}}_l^T \hat{\mathbf{d}}_t^l. \tag{6.33}$$

where $\acute{\mathbf{q}}_l$ is the projection vector derived by LDA.

## 6.4.3  Discriminant Node Weighting

The final step of the DEGM algorithm is to find a person-specific discriminant function $\beta_r$ of the new local similarity values and create the total similarity measure between a reference face $r$ and a test face $t$. The idea here is to weight the similarity measures of nodes that correspond to different landmarks with weights that correspond to their discriminant power. The weights should be person-specific because different persons have different discriminant landmarks. Let $\mathbf{c}_t \in \Re^L$ be a column vector comprised by the new local similarity values at every node:

$$\mathbf{c}_t = \begin{bmatrix} c_t^1 & c_t^2 & \dots & c_t^L \end{bmatrix}^T, \tag{6.34}$$

where $L$ is the number of graph nodes. The vector $\mathbf{c}_t$ is the total similarity vector between the reference face $r$ and a test face $t$. The standard EGM algorithm [6, 7] treats uniformly all the similarity values $c_t^l$. That is, the total similarity measure between a reference person $r$ and a test person $t$ is simply the sum of all node similarity measures:

$$D_t = \sum_{i=1}^{L} c_t^i = \mathbf{1}^T \mathbf{c}_t, \tag{6.35}$$

where $\mathbf{1}$ is an $L \times 1$ unity vector. The discriminant function $\beta_r$ is person specific and forms the total similarity measure between faces:

$$\acute{D}_t = \beta_r(\mathbf{c}_t). \tag{6.36}$$

The transform $\beta_r$ could be just a weighting vector or a more complicated nonlinear support vector machine. Once again, LDA can be used in order to create a total similarity measure between the reference person $r$ and a test person $t$. A modified LDA algorithm that can cope with the small sample size problem and can be applied to this step is the one presented in reference 43. Let $\mathcal{T}_C$ and $\mathcal{T}_I$ be the sets of the total similarity vectors for the genuine and impostor claims of the reference person $r$, respectively. Let $\mathbf{V}_W$ and $\mathbf{V}_B^l$ be the within-scatter and the between-scatter matrices, of the vectors $\mathbf{c}_t^l$, respectively. The $\mathbf{V}_W$ and $\mathbf{V}_B$ can be calculated using Eq. (6.23) and (6.24) for the vectors $\mathbf{c}_t^l$, respectively. The optimal weighting coefficients, which are derived from the maximization of criterion (6.25), are the elements of the vector $\acute{\mathbf{w}}$ [37]. The similarity measure between the reference person $r$ and the test person $t$, after all the successively discriminant steps, is given by

$$\acute{D}_t = \beta_r(\mathbf{c}_t) = \acute{\mathbf{w}}^T \mathbf{c}_t. \tag{6.37}$$

Alternatively, one may use support vector machines in order to find the discriminant projection vector or a nonlinear class separating surface [25]. The solution is given by the minimization of the within scatter matrix after the projection, subject to the constraints imposed by the fact that the samples should be separated after the projection. The solution is given by the saddle point of the Lagrangian:

$$L(\acute{\mathbf{w}}_r, b, \boldsymbol{\alpha}) = \acute{\mathbf{w}}_r^T \mathbf{V}_W \acute{\mathbf{w}}_r - \sum_{t=1}^{N} \alpha_t \left\{ y_t \left( \acute{\mathbf{w}}_r^T \mathbf{c}_t - b \right) - 1 \right\}, \tag{6.38}$$

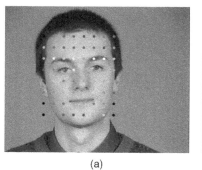
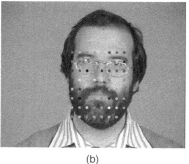

(a)                                    (b)

**Figure 6.7.** Weighting coefficients for the grid nodes in elastic graph matching. The brighter a node is, the bigger the discriminatory power it possesses.

where $\boldsymbol{\alpha} = (\alpha_1, \ldots, \alpha_N)^T$ is the vector of Lagrange multipliers and $\hat{\mathbf{w}}_r$ denotes the vector $\hat{\mathbf{w}}$ in Eq. (6.37). Kernels can be also used for calculating nonlinear class separating surfaces. In Figure 6.7, the discriminant power of each grid node is depicted for two sample images. The interested reader may refer to reference 25 for details.

## 6.5  DISCRIMINANT GRAPHS IN ELASTIC GRAPH MATCHING

In references 7, 8, 19, 20, 24, and 25, the discriminant analysis has been used either for finding the linear discriminant transforms for feature selection at preselected graph nodes or for discriminant weighting of the local node similarity measures. The use of discriminant analysis for locating the most discriminant facial features of a person's face is described in this section. To do so, a discriminant analysis that produces a graph, whose nodes correspond to discriminant facial points of a person, is presented.

In order to find such graphs, a heuristic cost optimization algorithm has been proposed in reference 44, which produces the graph that optimizes a preselected discriminant cost. The cost is formed by calculating the significance of each node using discriminant values like the ones proposed in references 7, 15, and 19. It is assumed that nodes with high discriminant values correspond to facial points with high discriminant capability. Thus, the corresponding neighborhood should be represented in more detail in the graph by adding more nodes around the discriminant one. This practically means that the nodes, which are considered to be discriminant, are expanded. This way, graphs that are person-specific and have nodes placed at discriminant facial features are obtained.

Let $\mathcal{F}_C^l$ and $\mathcal{F}_I^l$ be the sets of the jets of the $l$th node that correspond to genuine and impostor claims related to person $r$, respectively. In order to define the similarity of a test jet $\mathbf{j}(\mathbf{x}_t^l)$ with the class of reference jets for the same node, the following norm is used [19]:

$$c_t^l = \left\| \mathbf{j}\left(\mathbf{x}_t^l\right) - \mathbf{m}\left(\mathcal{F}_C^l\right) \right\|^2. \tag{6.39}$$

Let $\mathcal{L}_C^l$ and $\mathcal{L}_I^l$ be the sets of local similarity values $c_t^l$ that correspond to genuine and impostor claims, respectively. A possible measure of the discriminant power of the $l$th node is the Fisher's discriminant ratio [37]:

$$p_1^l = \frac{\left(m\left(\mathcal{L}_C^l\right) - m\left(\mathcal{L}_I^l\right)\right)^2}{\sigma^2\left(\mathcal{L}_C^l\right) + \sigma^2\left(\mathcal{L}_I^l\right)}. \tag{6.40}$$

In references 19 and 20 it has been proposed to weight the graph nodes after the elastic graph matching using the coefficients $p_1^l$ in order to form a similarity measure between graphs. By summing the discriminant coefficients for a certain graph setup $g$, we have

$$E_g = \frac{1}{L}\sum_{l=1}^{L} p^l, \tag{6.41}$$

where $L$ is the total number of graph nodes. This is the mean graph node discriminant ratio and is a characteristic measure for a particular graph setup of some reference person $r$. The measure defined in Eq. (6.41) creates an ordering relationship between graphs. That is, for two graphs $g_1$ and $g_2$ of a reference person $r$ if $E_{g_1} < E_{g_2}$, the graph $g_2$ is considered more discriminant than the graph $g_1$. Practically, the nodes of the graph $g_2$ are placed in more discriminant facial points than the nodes of $g_1$. Figure 6.8 shows two different graph setups $g_1$ and $g_2$ with different $E_g$ values. Both graphs have 64 nodes. The graph depicted in Figure 6.8b is found experimentally to be more discriminant than the rectangular graph depicted in Figure 6.8a since $E_{g_1} < E_{g_2}$.

In the following, the steps of the algorithm proposed in reference 44 are described in more detail. This procedure should be repeated for every reference person $r$ in

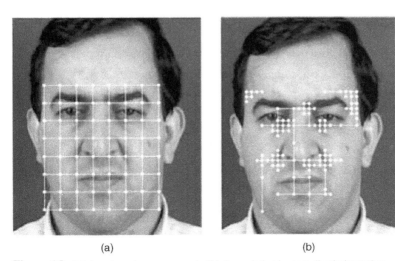

(a)                                                          (b)

**Figure 6.8.** (a) A rectangular sparse graph. (b) A graph that is more discriminant than the rectangular graph.

the database. Before starting the optimization procedure, the reference graphs for the person $r$ should be created. The reference graphs are created by overlaying a rectangular sparse graph on the facial image region in the positions indicated by a face localization algorithm.

Let the initial graph contain $L$ vertices at the first iteration $i \leftarrow 1$. Let $\mathcal{B}_i$ be the set of graph vertices at the $i$th iteration. The algorithm has the following steps:

**Step 1.** Take the reference graphs and match them in all genuine and impostor images.

**Step 2.** For each node $l$, calculate the discriminant measure $p^l$.

**Step 3.** Select a subset of the nodes with the higher discriminant value that have not been already expanded and expand them. The nodes that lie in the perimeter of the graph can be expanded only inside the facial region.

**Step 4.** Verify that the inserted nodes do not violate the graph sparseness criterion. That is, erase the new nodes that violate the criterion $||\mathbf{x}_r^l - \mathbf{x}_r^j|| < \Delta$, $\forall\, l, j$. The set of the final inserted nodes in the $i$th iteration is denoted as $\mathcal{A}_i$.

**Step 5.** Match locally the nodes of $\mathcal{A}_i$ in all the genuine and impostor facial images. Let $k \in \mathcal{A}_i$ be an inserted node and $\tilde{\mathbf{x}}_t^k$ be the initial coordinate vector for the node $k$ in a test image $t$. The local matching procedure is the outcome of the local search:

$$\grave{\mathbf{x}}_t^k = \arg\min_{\mathbf{x}_t^k} C_f \left( \mathbf{j}\left(\mathbf{x}_t^k\right), \mathbf{j}\left(\mathbf{x}_r^k\right) \right) \quad \text{subject to}$$

$$||\mathbf{x}_t^k - \tilde{\mathbf{x}}_t^k|| \leq \delta_{\max} \tag{6.42}$$

$\grave{\mathbf{x}}_t^k$ is the final coordinate vector that gives the jet $\mathbf{j}\left(\grave{\mathbf{x}}_t^k\right)$.

**Step 6.** For each node $k \in \mathcal{A}_i$, calculate its discriminant value $p^k$.

**Step 7.** Let $\mathcal{C}_i = \mathcal{A}_i \cup \mathcal{B}_i$. Order the nodes in $\mathcal{C}_i$ according to their discriminant power and obtain a graph $g_{i+1}$ by keeping only the $L$ nodes with the highest discriminant power. The set $\mathcal{B}_{i+1}$ contains the nodes of $g_{i+1}$.

**Step 8.** If $|E_{g_{i+1}} - E_{g_i}| > \tau$ then $i \leftarrow i + 1$ and goto **Step 4**, else stop.

The procedure described is a "greedy," hill-climbing algorithm for finding the graph $g$ with maximum $E_g$. It always follows the direction of the best solution, and thus it may get stuck at local maxima.

The elastic graph matching procedure of the new graphs is performed using the minimization procedure indicated in the optimization problem (6.5). The optimization problem (6.5) uses a global translation of the graph. That is, the components cannot be translated independently but only as part of the entire graph. In the second step, every node can be locally matched (deformed) independently, because it is imposed by the optimization problem (6.5).

## 6.6   FACE VERIFICATION PERFORMANCE OF ELASTIC GRAPH MATCHING

The elastic graph matching algorithm and its variants have been extensively tested in several databases. In this section we shall present the most recent results from experiments that were conducted in the XM2VTS database, which offers a strict verification protocol with more than one sample per person [45]. Thus, the XM2VTS database is chosen in more cases, instead of the FERET database, for testing face verification technologies. This is verified by the fact that many face verification competitions have been conducted in the XM2VTS database [46, 47], over the past few years.

The performance of face verification systems is measured in terms of the *false rejection rate* (FRR) achieved at a fixed *false acceptance rate* (FAR). There is a trade-off between FAR and FRR. That is, it is possible to reduce either of them with the risk of increasing the other one. This trade-off between the FAR and FRR can create a curve where FRR is plotted as a function of FAR. This curve is called *the receiver operating characteristic* (ROC) curve [15, 25]. The performance of a verification system is often quoted by a particular operating point of the ROC curve where FAR = FRR. This operating point is called *equal error rate* (EER).

In reference 27, a comparative study between linear subspace methods and elastic graph matching for frontal face verification was given. Different alignment conditions were considered. The experimental results confirmed the fact that the performance of subspace methods greatly depends on the alignment system used. On the contrary, elastic graph matching is not so sensitive to geometric distortions. That is, the major advantage of EGM against other state-of-the-art face recognition methods is the robustness to geometrical distortions. Indeed, all the subspace methods proposed in the literature are very sensitive to the misalignment of the facial images. In most cases, the images are normalized according to the eyes coordinates that are located manually. This fact renders the subspace methods unusable with automatic face detectors that are not perfect, since their verification performance greatly deteriorates under such circumstances.

On the other hand, EGM has the ability to correct misalignments due to the elastic matching step. However, the computational cost of EGM is bigger that the computational cost of subspace techniques. This fact places EGM among the techniques that cannot be easily used for face recognition task where a large number of test images should be examined in a limited time period. The outcome of the comparative study in reference 27 is given in Table 6.1. The experiments were performed in the M2VTS

**Table 6.1.** Comparison of Equal Error Rates for Subspace and Elastic Graph Matching Verification Techniques in the Aligned (A) and Attacked (by Scale (S) and Rotation (R)) M2VTS Database

| Verification Technique | EER(A) (%) | EER(R) (%) | EER(S) (%) |
|---|---|---|---|
| EGM | 6.05 | 6.65 | 7.4 |
| Eigenfaces | 10–40 | 13.1–38 | 13–39 |
| Fisherfaces | 8.3–26 | 9.5–26 | 11–31 |

database [48]. It can be easily observed that EGM is by far more robust against scaling and rotation of the test images.

EGM has also been tested in the XM2VTS database, combined with a fully automatic alignment method according to the eye position of each facial image, using the eye coordinates that have been derived from the method reported in reference 49. No other image preprocessing technique has been used. In order to simplify the approach, graphs of the same size were considered for all persons. As an alternative, the face normalization reported in reference 15 could be used in order to find the width and the height of the face and create person specific graphs.

The XM2VTS database contains 295 subjects, four recording sessions, and two shots (repetitions) per recording session. The XM2VTS database provides two experimental setups, namely, Configuration I and Configuration II [45]. Each configuration is divided in three different sets: the training set, the evaluation set, and the test set. The training set is used to create genuine and impostor probabilistic models for each person. The evaluation set is used to learn the verification decision thresholds. In the case of multimodal systems, the evaluation set is also used for training the verification fusion manager.

For both configurations, the training set has 200 clients, 25 evaluation impostors, and 70 test impostors. The two configurations differ in the distribution of client training and client evaluation data. For additional details concerning XM2VTS database, the interested reader can refer to reference 45. Recently, frontal face verification competitions using the XM2VTS [46, 47] have been conducted. The interested reader can refer to references 46 and 47 and to the references therein for the tested face verification algorithms.

When a verification technique is to be evaluated for a real application, the thresholds needed for deciding if a verification claim should be accepted or not should be set a priori. The evaluation set can be used for setting the thresholds. The same thresholds will then be used on the test set. Let FAE and FRE denote the corresponding *false acceptance rate* (FAR) and *false rejection rate* (FRR) obtained on the evaluation set. Since application requirements might constrain the FAR or FRR to stay within certain limits, the system is evaluated for three different threshold vectors that correspond to the operating points where FAE = 0, FRE = 0, and FAE = FRE. For each given threshold, the *total error rate* (TER) can be obtained as the sum of FAR and FRR.

The training set of the Configuration I contains 200 persons with three images per person. The evaluation set contains three images per client for genuine claims and 25 evaluation impostors with eight images per impostor. Thus, the evaluation set gives a total of $3 \times 200 = 600$ client claims and $25 \times 8 \times 200 = 40,000$ impostor claims. The test set has two images per client and 70 impostors with eight images per impostor and gives $2 \times 200 = 400$ genuine claims and $70 \times 8 \times 200 = 112,000$ impostor claims. The training set is used for calculating for each reference person $r$ and for each node $l$ a matrix for feature selection. In the training set, three reference graphs per person are created. The $3 \times 2 = 6$ graphs that comprise the genuine class are created by applying elastic graph matching having one image as reference (i.e., in order to create the graph) and the other two images are used as test images. The impostor class contains $3 \times 3 \times 199 = 1797$ graphs.

In reference 30, linear techniques have been used for training the different discriminant steps. The selection of linear techniques has been done due to the fact that the risk of overtraining in comparison with the nonlinear discriminant transforms is smaller and that they are less computationally complex than the nonlinear techniques. The problem of overtraining is of much greater intensity when nonlinear techniques are applied in training sets containing small and nonrepresentative data. Therefore, in many cases nonlinear techniques exhibit very poor generalization [50].

For threshold calculation the method proposed in reference 19 can be used. That is, the similarity measures for every person calculated in the training set form the distance vector $\mathbf{o}$. The elements of the vector $\mathbf{o}$ are sorted in ascending order and are used for the person specific thresholds on the distance measure. Let $T_Q$ denote the $Q$th order statistic of the vector of distances, $\mathbf{o}$. The threshold of the person $r$ is chosen to be equal to $T_Q$. Let $r_1$, $r_2$, and $r_3$ be the three instances of the person $r$ in the training set. A claim of a person $t$ is considered valid if $\min_j\{\hat{D}_t(r_j)\} < T_Q$, where $\hat{D}_t(r_j)$ is the distance between the graph of test person $t$ and the reference graph $r_j$.

In order to illustrate the contribution of each discriminant step and also show the performance of the combined discriminant approach, we present the following experiments that have been conducted in reference 30:

- EGM without discriminant analysis;
- EGM applying only discriminant feature selection, as described in Section 6.4.1 (abbreviated as EGM-FD);
- EGM applying only local discriminant weighting using LDA, as described in Section 6.4.2, without using feature vector discriminant analysis or discriminant node weighting (abbreviated as EGM-LD);
- EGM applying only discriminant node weighting using LDA, as described in Section 6.4.3, without any other discriminant step (abbreviated as EGM-ND).

The EGM without any discriminant step has given a TER = 12.9% in the test set of Configuration I. For EGM-FD the best TER has been achieved by keeping the first three discriminant projections of the solution of the maximization of the criterion (6.30) and has been estimated to be around 5.7%. The evaluation set has been used in order to estimate how many discriminant dimensions should be kept. The feature vector discriminant analysis using the Fisher's criterion (6.25) produced a projection to the one-dimensional space using Eq. (6.27) that has not improved significantly the performance, giving an TER = 10%. The EGM-LD gave a TER = 9.2%. The TER that has been obtained with node weighting using LDA has been estimated to be around 10.7% (EGM-ND). The best TER achieved was 2.8%, using successively all the discriminant steps described in Section 6.4. As can be seen the feature vector discriminant analysis step is very important since it reduces the TER from 12.9% to 5.7% (that is a 50% reduction in terms of TER). Moreover, the other two steps are also significant, and reduce the TER from 5.7% to 2.8% (another 50% reduction in terms of TER).

The error rates, computed according to the XM2VTS protocol, are illustrated in Table 6.2. Table 6.3 shows a comparison of DEGM with other methods that use

**Table 6.2.** Error Rates According to XM2VTS Protocol for Configuration I

| | Evaluation Set | | | Test Set | | | | | | | | |
| | | | | FAE = FRE | | FRE = 0 | | FAE = 0 | | Total Error Rate (TER) | | |
| Algorithm | FAE = FRE | FAE(FRE = 0) | FRE(FAE = 0) | FA | FR | FA | FR | FA | FR | FAE = FRE | FRE = 0 | FAE = 0 |
|---|---|---|---|---|---|---|---|---|---|---|---|---|
| EGM | 9.2 | 98.2 | 65.0 | 7.9 | 5.0 | 98.8 | 0.0 | 0.0 | 61.0 | 12.9 | 98.8 | 61.0 |
| EGM-ND | 6.3 | 62.8 | 56.3 | 6.7 | 4.2 | 63.8 | 0.0 | 0.0 | 61.0 | 10.7 | 63.8 | 61.0 |
| EGM-LD | 5.2 | 45.5 | 20.0 | 5.2 | 4.0 | 45.0 | 0.5 | 0.0 | 17.0 | 9.2 | 45.5 | 17.0 |
| EGM-FD | 2.5 | 29.9 | 55.3 | 2.5 | 3.2 | 11.2 | 0.2 | 0.2 | 14.7 | 5.7 | 11.4 | 14.9 |
| DEGM | 0.2 | 0.7 | 6.5 | **1.6** | **1.2** | **10.2** | 0.0 | 0.2 | **13.1** | **2.8** | **10.2** | **13.1** |

**Table 6.3.** A Comparison of TER for Configuration
I Using Fully Automatic Registration

| Algorithm | TER |
|---|---|
| IDIAP-Cardinaux [47] | 4.7 |
| UPV [47] | 3.98 |
| UNIS-NC [47] | 3.86 |
| DEGM | **2.8** |

fully automatic alignment. The results have been acquired by the most recent competition in XM2VTS database [47]. Obviously, the DEGM method outperforms all the approaches tested in reference 47 using fully automatic alignment.

The XM2VTS Configuration II differs from the Configuration I in the distribution of client training and client evaluation data. The training set of the Configuration II contains 200 persons with four images per person. The evaluation set contains two images per client for genuine claims. Thus, the evaluation set gives a total of $2 \times 200 = 400$ genuine claims. The training set contains four reference images for each client. The same approach as in Configuration I has been used for training, for accepting a claim as valid, and for threshold calculation. The ROC curves achieved for the variants of EGM are depicted in Figure 6.9. As can be seen, the DEGM achieves a very low TER = 1.7% in this Configuration. A comparison of DEGM with

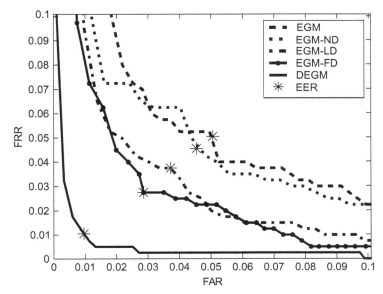

**Figure 6.9.** ROC curves for the different discriminant variants of DEGM in test set of the Configuration II experimental protocol of the XM2VTS database.

other methods that use fully automatic alignment in Configuration II highlighted that DEGM outperforms all the approaches tested in reference 47 using fully automatic alignment in Configuration II.

## 6.7  CONCLUSION

Elastic graph matching is a very powerful object recognition algorithm that has been successfully applied to face verification. Many variants and advances on the standard algorithm have been published in the last decade. The incorporation of discriminant analysis in EGM has attracted the interest of many researchers. As a result, many discriminant analysis techniques have been combined with EGM. Thus, a general method for enhancing the performance of the EGM algorithm by employing discriminant analysis techniques in all phases of EGM has been proposed. The fully discriminant EGM has been tested in the XM2VTS facial image database. The performance of DEGM has been significantly improved, and its advantages have been highlighted compared with those other techniques.

Further research on EGM is concentrated on achieving even better robustness against geometric distortions of the facial image and on improving the computational speed of the algorithm. The exploration of other pattern recognition algorithms, like support vector machines or relevance vector machines, in the various discriminant steps of the EGM algorithm in order to boost further the verification performance of DEGM is another research direction.

## REFERENCES

1. R. Chellappa, C. L. Wilson, and S. Sirohey, Human and machine recognition of faces: A survey, *Proc. IEEE* **83**(5):705–740, 1995.
2. W. Zhao, R. Chellappa, P.-J. Phillips, and A. Rosenfeld, Face recognition: A literature survey, *ACM Comput. Surv.* **35**:399–458, 2003.
3. P. J. Phillips, Matching pursuit filters applied to face identification, *IEEE Trans. Image Processing* **7**(8):1150–1164, 1998.
4. R. Brunelli and T. Poggio, Face recognition: Features versus templates, *IEEE Trans. Pattern Anal. Mach. Intell.* **15**(10):1042–1052, 1993.
5. M. Turk and A. P. Pentland, Eigenfaces for recognition, *J. Cognit. Neurosci.* **3**(1):71–86, 1991.
6. M. Lades, J. C. Vorbrüggen, J. Buhmann, J. Lange, C. v. d. Malsburg, R. P. Würtz, and W. Konen, Distortion invariant object recognition in the dynamic link architecture, *IEEE Trans. Comput.* **42**(3):300–311, 1993.
7. B. Duc, S. Fischer, and J. Bigün, Face authentication with Gabor information on deformable graphs, *IEEE Trans. Image Processing* **8**(4):504–516, 1999.
8. L. Wiskott, Phantom faces for face analysis, *Pattern Recognit.* **30**(6):837–846, 1997.
9. J. Zhang, Y. Yan, and M. Lades, Face recognition: Eigenface, elastic matching, and neural nets, *Proc. IEEE* **85**(9):1423–1435, 1997.
10. M. Kirby and L. Sirovich, Application of the Karhunen–Loeve procedure for the characterization of faces, *IEEE Trans. Pattern Anal. Mach. Intell.* **12**(1):103–108, January 1990.
11. G. W. Cottrell and M. Fleming, Face recognition using unsupervised feature extraction, in *International Neural Network Conference*, Vol. 1, Paris, July 1990, pp. 322–325.

12. Y. Adini, Y. Moses, and S. Ullman, Face recognition: The problem of compensating for changes in illumination direction, *IEEE Trans. Pattern Anal. Mach. Intell.* **19**(7):721–732, 1997.
13. P. N. Belhumeur, J. P. Hespanha, and D. J. Kriegman, Eigenfaces vs. Fisherfaces: Recognition using class specific linear projection, *IEEE Trans. Pattern Anal. Mach. Intell.* **19**(7):711–720, 1997.
14. A. Tefas, Y. Menguy, C. Kotropoulos, G. Richard, I. Pitas, and P. Lockwood. Compensating for variable recording conditions in frontal face authentication algorithms, in *Proceedings of the IEEE International Conference on Acoustics, Speech and Signal Processing (ICASSP-99)*, Phoenix, AZ, March 1999.
15. C. Kotropoulos, A. Tefas, and I. Pitas, Morphological elastic graph matching applied to frontal face authentication under well-controlled and real conditions, *Pattern Recognit.* **33**(12):31–43, 2000.
16. B. S. Manjunath, R. Chellappa, and C. v. d. Malsburg, A feature based approach to face recognition, in *Proceedings of the IEEE International Conference on Computer Vision and Pattern Recognition (CVPR-92)*, 1992, pp. 373–378.
17. L. Wiskott, J. Fellous, N. Krüger, and C. v. d. Malsburg, Face recognition by elastic bunch graph matching, *IEEE Trans. Pattern Anal. Mach. Intell.* **19**(7):775–779, July 1997.
18. R. P. Würtz, Object recognition robust under translations, deformations, and changes in background, *IEEE Trans. Pattern Anal. Mach. Intell.* **19**(7):769–775, July 1997.
19. C. Kotropoulos, A. Tefas, and I. Pitas, Frontal face authentication using discriminating grids with morphological feature vectors, *IEEE Trans. Multimedia* **2**(1):14–26, 2000.
20. C. Kotropoulos, A. Tefas, and I. Pitas, Frontal face authentication using morphological elastic graph matching, *IEEE Trans. Image Processing* **9**(4):555–560, April 2000.
21. P. T. Jackway and M. Deriche, Scale-space properties of the multiscale morphological dilation-erosion, *IEEE Trans. Pattern Anal. Mach. Intell.* **18**(1):38–51, 1996.
22. A. Tefas, C. Kotropoulos, and I. Pitas, Face verification using elastic graph matching based on morphological signal decomposition, *Signal Processing* **82**(6):833–851, 2002.
23. J. Triesch and C. v. d. Malsburg, A system for person-independent hand posture recognition against complex backgrounds, *IEEE Trans. Pattern Anal. Mach. Intell.* **23**(12):1449–1453, 2001.
24. N. Krüger. An algorithm for the learning of weights in discrimination functions using A priori constraints, *IEEE Trans. Pattern Anal. Mach. Intell.* **19**(7):764–768, July 1997.
25. A. Tefas, C. Kotropoulos, and I. Pitas, Using support vector machines to enhance the performance of elastic graph matching for frontal face authentication, *IEEE Trans. Pattern Anal. Mach. Intell.* **23**(7):735–746, 2001.
26. V. Vapnik, *The Nature of Statistical Learning Theory*, Springer-Verlag, New York, 1995.
27. S. Zafeiriou, A. Tefas, and I. Pitas, Elastic graph matching versus linear subspace methods for frontal face verification, in *International Workshop on Nonlinear Signal and Image Processing*, 2005, pp. 19–22.
28. R. M. Haralick and L. G. Shapiro, *Computer and Robot Vision*, Vol. I, Addison-Wesley, Reading, MA, 1992.
29. R. M. Haralick, Image analysis using mathematical morphology. *IEEE Trans. Pattern Anal. Mach. Intell.* **9**(4):532–550, July 1987.
30. S. Zafeiriou, A. Tefas, and I. Pitas, The discriminant elastic graph matching algorithm applied to frontal face verification, *Pattern Recognit.* **40**(10):2798–2810, 2007.
31. I. Pitas and A. N. Venetsanopoulos, *Nonlinear Digital Filters: Principles and Applications*, Kluwer Academic Publishers, Boston, MA, 1990.
32. I. Pitas and A. N. Venetsanopoulos, Morphological shape decomposition, *IEEE Trans. Pattern Anal. Mach. Intell.* **12**(1):38–45, 1990.
33. H.-C. Shin, J. H. Park, and S.-D.; Kim, Combination of warping robust elastic graph matching and kernel-based projection discriminant analysis for face recognition, *IEEE Trans. Multimedia* **9**(6):1125–1136, 2007.
34. L. Chengjun, Gabor-based kernel PCA with fractional power polynomial models for face recognition, *IEEE Trans. Pattern Anal. Mach. Intell.* **26**(5):572–581, 2004.
35. L. Juwei, K. N. Plataniotis, and A. N. Venetsanopoulos, Face recognition using kernel direct discriminant analysis algorithms, *IEEE Trans. Neural Networks* **14**(1):117–126, 2003.
36. B. Scholkopf and A. Smola, *Learning with Kernels*, MIT Press, Cambridge, MA, 2002.

37. K. Fukunaga, *Statistical Pattern Recognition*, Academic, San Diego, 1990.
38. C. Songcan and Y. Xubing, Alternative linear discriminant classifier, *Pattern Recognit.* **37**(7):1545–1547, 2004.
39. H. Yu and J. Yang, A direct LDA algorithm for high-dimensional data with application to face recognition, *Pattern Recognit.* **34**:2067–2070, 2001.
40. D. L. Swets and J. Weng, Using discriminant eigenfeatures for image retrieval, *IEEE Trans. Pattern Anal. Mach. Intell.* **18**(8):831–836, 1996.
41. Y. Li, J. Kittler, and J. Matas, On matching scores of LDA-based face verification, in *Proceedings of the British Machine Vision Conference BMVC2000*, 2000.
42. R. Snelick, U. Uludag, A. Mink, M. Indovina, and A. Jain, Large-scale evaluation of multimodal biometric authentication using state-of-the-art systems, *IEEE Trans. Pattern Anal. Mach. Intell.* **27**(3):450–455, 2005.
43. M. Kyperountas, A. Tefas, and I. Pitas, Weighted piecewise lda for solving the small sample size problem in face verification, *IEEE Trans. Neural Networks* **18**(2):506–519, 2007.
44. S. Zafeiriou, A. Tefas, and I. Pitas, Learning discriminant person-specific facial models using expandable graphs, *IEEE Trans. Inf. Forens. Secur.* **2**(1):55–68, 2007.
45. K. Messer, J. Matas, J. V. Kittler, J. Luettin, and G. Maitre, XM2VTSDB: The extended M2VTS database, in *AVBPA'99*, Washington, DC, 22–23 March 1999, pp. 72–77.
46. J. Matas, M. Hamou, K. Jonsson, J. Kittler, Y. Li, C. Kotropoulos, A. Tefas, I. Pitas, T. Tan, H. Yan, F. Smeraldi, J. Bigun, N. Capdevielle, W. Gerstner, S. Ben-Yacouba, Y. Abdelaoued, and E. Mayoraz, Comparison of face verification results on the XM2VTS database, in *ICPR*, Barcelona, Spain, 3–8 September 2000, pp. 858–863.
47. K. Messer, J. V. Kittler, M. Sadeghi, S. Marcel, C. Marcel, S. Bengio, F. Cardinaux, C. Sanderson, J. Czyz, L. Vandendorpe, S. Srisuk, M. Petrou, W. Kurutach, A. Kadyrov, R. Paredes, B. Kepenekci, F. B. Tek, G. B. Akar, F. Deravi, and N. Mavity, Face verification competition on the XM2VTS database, in *AVBPA03*, Guildford, United Kingdom, 9–11 June 2003, pp. 964–974.
48. S. Pigeon and L. Vandendorpe, The m2vts multimodal face database, in J. Bigun, G. Chollet and G. Borgefors, editors, *Lecture Notes in Computer Science: Audio and Video-Based Biometric Person Authentication*, Vol. 1206, First International Conference, AVBPA'97, Crans-Montana, Switzerland, March 12–14, 1997. Springer, Berlin 1997, pp. 403–409.
49. K. Jonsson, J. Matas, and Kittler, Learning salient features for real-time face verification, in *Proceedings, Second International Conference on Audio- and Video-Based Biometric Person Authentication (AVBPA'99)*, 1999, pp. 60–65.
50. K.-R. Muller, S. Mika, G. Ratsch, K. Tsuda, and B. Scholkopf, An introduction to kernel-based learning algorithms, *IEEE Trans. Neural Networks* **12**(2):181–201, 2001.

# Chapter 7

# Combining Geometrical and Statistical Models for Video-Based Face Recognition

Amit K. Roy-Chowdhury and Yilei Xu

## 7.1 INTRODUCTION

Low-dimensional representations of object appearance have proved to be one of the successful strategies in computer vision for applications in tracking, modeling, and recognition. Active appearance models (AAMs) [1, 2], multilinear models [3–6], and other low-dimensional manifold representations [7] fall in this genre. In all these approaches, the construction of the underlying low-dimensional manifold relies upon obtaining different instances of the object's appearance under various conditions (e.g., pose, lighting, identity, and deformations) and then using statistical data analysis and machine learning tools to approximate the appearance space. This approach requires obtaining a large number of examples of the object's appearance, and the accuracy of the method depends upon the examples that have been chosen for the training phase. Representation of appearances that have not been seen during the training phase can be inaccurate. In mathematical modeling terms, this is a *data-driven* approach.

In this chapter we show that it is possible to learn complex manifolds of object appearance using a combination of *analytically* derived geometrical models and statistical data analysis. We refer to this as a "geometry-integrated appearance manifold" (GAM). Specifically, we derive a *quadrilinear* manifold of object appearance that is able to represent the combined effects of illumination, motion, identity, and deformation. The basis vectors of this manifold depend upon the 3D geometry of the object.

*Biometrics: Theory, Methods, and Applications.* Edited by Boulgouris, Plataniotis, and Micheli-Tzanakou
Copyright © 2010 the Institute of Electrical and Electronics Engineers, Inc.

We then show how to adapt the inverse compositional (IC) algorithm to efficiently and accurately track objects on this manifold through changes of pose, lighting, and deformations. Our proposed method *significantly reduces the amount of data that needs to be collected for learning the appearance manifolds during the training phase and makes the learned manifold less dependent upon the actual examples that were used.* The process for construction of this appearance manifold is relatively simple, has a solid theoretical basis, and provides a high level of accuracy and computational speed in tracking and novel view synthesis. Depending upon the application, it may be possible to derive the manifold in a completely analytical manner, an example being tracking a rigid object (e.g., vehicle) through pose and lighting changes. In other examples, like face recognition, a combination of analytical approaches and statistical data analysis will be used for learning the manifold.

Based upon the GAM, we present a novel analysis-by-synthesis framework for pose and illumination invariant, video-based face recognition. This video-based face recognition system works by (i) learning joint illumination and motion models from video using the GAM, (ii) synthesizing novel views based on the learned parameters, and (iii) designing measurements that can compare two time sequences while being robust to outliers. We can handle a variety of lighting conditions, including the presence of multiple point and extended light sources, which is natural in outdoor environments (where face recognition performance is still relatively poor [8–10]). We can also handle gradual and sudden changes of lighting patterns over time. The pose and illumination conditions in the gallery and probe can be completely disjoint. We show experimentally that our method achieves high identification rates under extreme changes of pose and illumination.

## 7.1.1   Novel Contributions and Relation to Past Work

There are three main parts of this paper: learning GAMs using a combination of geometrical models and statistical analysis, adapting the IC algorithm for tracking and view synthesis using these manifolds, and developing the framework for video-based face recognition using the GAM.

**Learning GAMs.** The analytically derived geometrical models represent the effects of motion, lighting, and 3D shape in describing the appearance of an object [11–13]. The statistical data analysis approaches are used to model the other effects like identity (e.g., faces of different people) and nonrigidity, which are not easy to represent analytically. First, lighting is modeled using a spherical-harmonics-based linear subspace representation [11, 12]. This is then combined with a recent result by the authors that proved that the appearance of an image is bilinear in the 3D motion and illumination parameters, with the 3D shape determining the basis vectors of the space [13]. The variations of this analytically derived bilinear basis over identity and deformation are then learned using multilinear SVD [14], and they together form a *quadrilinear* space of illumination, motion, identity, and deformation. The GAM can be visualized (see Figure 7.1) as a collection of locally linear tangent planes along

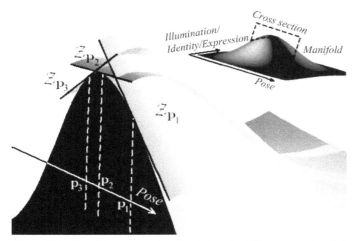

**Figure 7.1.** Pictorial representation of variation of a GAM cross section. Only two axes are shown for simplicity. At each pose, we have the manifold for illumination, identity, and deformation. Around each pose, we have the tangent plane to the manifold.

the pose dimension, where each tangent plane represents 3D motion in a local region around each pose (see Figure 7.1).

The major difference of GAMs with other methods for computing appearance manifolds and subspaces [2, 4, 5, 7] is that the object appearance space is derived using a combination of analytical models and data analysis tools, while the previous approaches rely purely on data analysis. This significantly reduces the data collection procedures for computing such manifolds and allows representations of appearances that were not included in the learning phase. We will provide some concrete numerical examples to justify this in the experimental section. Thus our method combines the precision and generalizability of model-based approaches with the robustness provided by statistical learning methods to deviations from the model predictions.

**Probabilistic Inverse Compositional Tracking and Synthesis on GAMs.** We show how to track and synthesize novel views of an object using the learned GAMs. This is done by adapting the inverse compositional (IC) algorithm to the geometry of the manifold and embedding it within a stochastic framework. This can account for changes in pose, lighting, shape, and nonrigidity of the object, as well as local errors in two-frame motion estimation. The inverse compositional (IC) approach [15] is an efficient implementation of the Lucas–Kanade image alignment method, and it works by moving the expensive computation of gradients and Hessians out of an iterative loop. Due to 3D motion estimation in our case, the expensive computations of derivatives need to take place only at a few discrete poses (not once every frame).

Our tracking algorithm provides 3D estimates of motion, illumination model parameters, and identity and deformation parameters, thus going beyond illumination-invariant 2D tracking [3, 16]. It does not require a texture mapped 3D model of the object as in [17], which can be a severe restriction in many application scenarios, like face recognition. For tracking faces, it is more computationally efficient than 3DMM approaches [18] since it approximates the pose appearance space as a series of locally linear tangent planes, while 3DMM works by finding the best fit on the nonlinear manifold (requiring computationally expensive transformations). There is a small, but not significant (for most applications), trade-off in accuracy in the process.

**Video-Based Face Recognition Using GAMs.** The probabilistic IC tracking on the GAMs described above is then used for video-based face recognition. We assume that a 3D model of each face in the gallery is available. For our experiments, the 3D model is estimated from images, but any 3D modeling algorithm, including directly acquiring the model through range sensors, can be used for this purpose. Given a probe sequence, we track the face automatically in the video sequence under arbitrary pose and illumination conditions using the probabilistic IC tracking on the GAMs. This tracking requires only a *generic* 3D shape model. The learned illumination parameters are used to synthesize video sequences for each gallery under the motion and illumination conditions in the probe. The distance between the probe and synthesized sequences is then computed for each frame. Different distance measurements are explored for this purpose. Next, the synthesized sequence that is at a minimum distance from the probe sequence is computed and is declared to be the identity of the person.

## 7.1.2    Review of Face Recognition

A broad review of face recognition is available in [8]. Recently, there have been a number of algorithms for pose and/or illumination invariant face recognition, many of which are based on the fact that the image of an object under varying illumination lies in a lower-dimensional linear subspace. In [19], the authors proposed a 3D spherical harmonic basis morphable model (SHBMM) to implement a face recognition system given one single image under arbitrary unknown lighting. Another 3D face morphable model (3DMM)-based face recognition algorithm was proposed in [20]; but they used the Phong illumination model, estimation of whose parameters can be more difficult in the presence of multiple and extended light sources. A novel method for multilinear independent component analysis was proposed in [4] for pose and illumination invariant face recognition. All of the above methods deal with recognition in a single image or across discrete poses and do not consider continuous video sequences. Video-based face recognition requires integrating the tracking and recognition modules and exploitation of the spatio-temporal coherence in the data. In [7], the authors deal with the issue of video-based face recognition, but concentrate mostly on pose variations. Similarly the authors in [21] used adaptive hidden Markov models for pose-varying video-based face recognition. A probabilistic framework that fuses the temporal information in a probe video by investigating the propagation of the posterior distribution of the motion and identity was proposed in [22]. Another work used an adaptive appearance model, an adaptive motion model, and an adaptive particle filter for simultaneously tracking and recognizing people in the video [23]. Fisher et al. [24] proposed to perform face recognition by computing the Kullback–Leibler divergence between testing image sets and a learned manifold density. Another work [25] used learned manifolds of face variations for face recognition in video. A method for video-based face verification using correlation filters was proposed in [26], but the pose in the gallery and probe have to be similar.

### 7.1.3  Organization of the Chapter

The rest of the chapter is organized as follows. Section 7.2 presents the GAM-based object representation using the analytically derived illumination and motion basis and machine learned basis of identity and deformation. Robust and efficient tracking algorithms using this object representation are presented in Section 7.3. Then, we propose an integrated tracking and recognition framework for video-based face recognition in Section 7.4. Experimental results and analysis are presented in Section 7.5. Section 7.6 concludes the chapter and highlights future work.

## 7.2  METHOD FOR LEARNING GAMs

We will start with the illumination representation of [11] and combine it with motion and shape using the results in [13] in order to derive an analytical representation of a low-dimensional manifold of object appearance with variations in pose and lighting. We will then apply N-mode SVD, a multilinear generalization of SVD, to learn the variation of this manifold due to changes of identity and object deformations. We will show that the image appearance due to variations of illumination, pose, and deformation is quadrilinear, and we will compute the basis functions of this space.

### 7.2.1  An Analytically Derived Manifold for Motion and Illumination

Recently, it was shown that for moving objects it is possible to approximate the sequence of images by a bilinear subspace of nine illumination coefficients and six motion variables [13]. Representing by $\mathbf{T} = \begin{bmatrix} T_x & T_y & T_z \end{bmatrix}^T$ the translation of the centroid of the object, by $\boldsymbol{\Omega} = \begin{bmatrix} \omega_x & \omega_y & \omega_z \end{bmatrix}^T$ the rotation about the centroid, and by $\mathbf{l} \in \mathbb{R}^{N_l}$ ($N_l \approx 9$ for Lambertian objects with attached shadow) the illumination coefficients in a spherical harmonics basis (see [11] for details), Xu and Roy-Chowdhury [13] showed that under small motion, the reflectance image at $t_2 = t_1 + \delta t$ can be expressed as

$$I(\mathbf{u}, t_2) = \sum_{i=1}^{9} l_i b_i^{t_2}(\mathbf{u}), \tag{7.1}$$

where

$$b_i^{t_2}(\mathbf{u}) = b_i^{t_1}(\mathbf{u}) + \mathbf{A}(\mathbf{u}, \mathbf{n})\mathbf{T} + \mathbf{B}(\mathbf{u}, \mathbf{n})\mathbf{\Omega}. \tag{7.2}$$

In the above equations, $\mathbf{u}$ represents the image point projected from the 3D surface with surface normal $\mathbf{n}$, and $\{b_i^{t_1}(\mathbf{u})\}$ are the original basis images before motion. $\mathbf{A}$ and $\mathbf{B}$ contain the structure and camera intrinsic parameters and are functions of $\mathbf{u}$ and the 3D surface normal $\mathbf{n}$. For each pixel $\mathbf{u}$, both $\mathbf{A}$ and $\mathbf{B}$ are $N_l \times 3$ matrices. (The exact forms of $\mathbf{A}$ and $\mathbf{B}$ are not necessary for understanding this chapter, hence we skip this. The interested reader can see [13].)

It will be useful for us to represent this result using tensor notation as

$$\hat{\mathcal{I}}_{t_2} = \left( \mathcal{B} + \mathcal{C} \times_2 \begin{pmatrix} \mathbf{T} \\ \mathbf{\Omega} \end{pmatrix} \right) \times_1 \mathbf{l}, \tag{7.3}$$

where $\times_n$ is called the *mode-n product* [14].[1] For an image of size $M \times N$, $\mathcal{C}$ is a tensor of size $N_l \times 6 \times M \times N$. For each pixel $(p, q)$ in the image, $\mathcal{C}_{klpq} = [\mathbf{A}(\mathbf{u}, \mathbf{n})\ \mathbf{B}(\mathbf{u}, \mathbf{n})]$ of size $N_l \times 6$, $\mathcal{B}$ is a subtensor of dimension $N_l \times 1 \times M \times N$, comprised of the basis images $b_i$, and $\mathcal{I}$ is a subtensor of dimension $1 \times 1 \times M \times N$, representing the image.

## 7.2.2    Learning Identity and Deformation Manifold

The above bilinear space of 3D motion and illumination is derived by using the knowledge of the 3D model of the object (tensor $\mathcal{C}$ contains the surface normals). However, the 3D shape is a function of the identity of the object (e.g., the identity of a face) and possible nonrigid deformations. The challenge now is to generalize the above analytical model so that it can be used to represent a wide variety of appearances within a class of objects.

We achieve this by learning multilinear appearance models [4, 27] directly from data. Multilinear 3D shape models have been proposed in [6] to learn the shape variation due to identity and expression. For our case, rather than directly modeling the appearance images, we will model the bilinear bases of motion and illumination derived analytically in Section 7.2.1 and will then combine all these different variations to obtain a multilinear model of object appearance.

---

[1]The *mode-n product* of a tensor $\mathcal{A} \in \mathbb{R}^{I_1 \times I_2 \times \ldots \times I_n \times \ldots \times I_N}$ by a vector $\mathbf{v} \in \mathbb{R}^{1 \times I_n}$, denoted by $\mathcal{A} \times_n \mathbf{v}$, is the $I_1 \times I_2 \times \ldots \times 1 \times \ldots \times I_N$ tensor

$$(\mathcal{A} \times_n \mathbf{v})_{i_1 \ldots i_{n-1} 1 i_{n+1} \ldots i_N} = \sum_{i_n} a_{i_1 \ldots i_{n-1} i_n i_{n+1} \ldots i_N} v_{i_n}.$$

Using $[\bullet]_v$ to denote the vectorization operation, we can vectorize $\mathcal{B}$ and $\mathcal{C}$ in Eq. (7.3), and concatenate them, as

$$\mathbf{v} = \begin{bmatrix} [\mathcal{B}]_v \\ [\mathcal{C}]_v \end{bmatrix}. \tag{7.4}$$

This $\mathbf{v}$ is the vectorized bilinear basis for one shape (i.e., one object) with dimension $I_v \times 1$, where $I_v = 7N_lMN$ ($N_lMN$ for $\mathcal{B}$ and $6N_lMN$ for $\mathcal{C}$). Given the 3D shape of $I_i$ objects with $I_e$ different deformations, we can compute this vectorized bilinear basis $\mathbf{v}$ for every combination. For faces, using the 3DMM [18] approaches, these instances can be obtained by choosing different coefficients of the corresponding linear basis functions. With the application to faces in mind, we will sometimes use the words deformation and expression interchangably.

We use $\mathbf{v}_e^i$ to represent the vectorized bilinear basis of identity $i$ with expression $e$. Let us rearrange them into a training data tensor $\mathcal{D}$ of size $I_i \times I_e \times I_v$ with the first dimension for identity, the second dimension for expression (deformation), and the third dimension for the vectorized, analytically derived bilinear basis for each training sample. Applying the *N-Mode SVD* algorithm [14], the training data tensor can be decomposed as

$$\mathcal{D} = \mathcal{Y} \times_1 \mathbf{U}_i \times_2 \mathbf{U}_e \times_3 \mathbf{U}_v$$
$$= \mathcal{Z} \times_1 \mathbf{U}_i \times_2 \mathbf{U}_e, \qquad \text{where} \quad \mathcal{Z} = \mathcal{Y} \times_3 \mathbf{U}_v. \tag{7.5}$$

$\mathcal{Y}$ is known as the core tensor of size $N_i \times N_e \times N_v$, and $N_i$ and $N_e$ are the number of bases we use for the identity and expression. With a slight abuse of terminology, we will call $\mathcal{Z}$ (which is decomposed only along the identity and expression dimension with size $N_i \times N_e \times I_v$) the core tensor. $\mathbf{U}_i$ and $\mathbf{U}_e$, with sizes of $I_i \times N_i$ and $I_e \times N_e$, are the left matrices of the SVD of

$$\mathcal{D}_{(1)} = \begin{pmatrix} \mathbf{v}_1^{1\mathbf{T}} & \cdots & \mathbf{v}_{I_e}^{1\mathbf{T}} \\ & \cdots & \\ \mathbf{v}_1^{I_i\mathbf{T}} & \cdots & \mathbf{v}_{I_e}^{I_i\mathbf{T}} \end{pmatrix} \quad \text{and} \quad \mathcal{D}_{(2)} = \begin{pmatrix} \mathbf{v}_1^{1\mathbf{T}} & \cdots & \mathbf{v}_1^{I_i\mathbf{T}} \\ & \cdots & \\ \mathbf{v}_{I_e}^{1\mathbf{T}} & \cdots & \mathbf{v}_{I_e}^{I_i\mathbf{T}} \end{pmatrix}, \tag{7.6}$$

where the subscripts of tensor $\mathcal{D}$ indicate the tensor unfolding operation[2] along the first and second dimension. According to the *N-mode SVD algorithm* and Eq. (7.5), the core tensor $\mathcal{Z}$ can be expressed as

$$\mathcal{Z} = \mathcal{D} \times_1 \mathbf{U}_i^{\mathbf{T}} \times_2 \mathbf{U}_e^{\mathbf{T}}. \tag{7.7}$$

---

[2]Assume an $N$th-order tensor $\mathcal{A} \in \mathbf{C}^{I_1 \times I_2 \times \cdots \times I_N}$. The matrix unfolding $\mathbf{A}_{(n)} \in \mathbf{C}^{I_n \times (I_{n+1}I_{n+2}\cdots I_N I_1 I_2 \cdots I_{n-1})}$ contains the element $a_{i_1 i_2 \cdots i_N}$ at the position with row number $i_n$ and column number equal to $(i_{n+1} - 1)I_{n+2}I_{n+3} \cdots I_N I_1 I_2 \cdots I_{n-1} + (i_{n+2} - 1)I_{n+3}I_{n+4} \cdots I_N I_1 I_2 \cdots I_{n-1} + \cdots + (i_N - 1)I_1 I_2 \cdots I_{n-1} + (i_1 - 1)I_2 I_3 \cdots I_{n-1} + \cdots + i_{n-1}$.

## 7.2.3 The GAM of Lighting, Motion, Identity, and Deformation

The core tensor $\mathcal{Z}$ contains the basis of identity and expression (or deformation) for $\mathbf{v}$ as

$$\mathbf{v}_i^{eT} = \mathcal{Z} \times_1 \mathbf{c}_i^{\mathbf{T}} \times_2 \mathbf{c}_e^{\mathbf{T}}, \tag{7.8}$$

where $\mathbf{c}_i$ and $\mathbf{c}_e$ are the coefficient vectors encoding the identity and expression. As $\mathbf{v}_i^e$ are the vectorized, bilinear basis functions of the illumination and 3D motion, the core tensor $\mathcal{Z}$ is *quadrilinear* in illumination, motion, identity, and expression. As an example, this core tensor $\mathcal{Z}$ can describe all the face images of identity $\mathbf{c}_i$ with expression $\mathbf{c}_e$ and motion $(\mathbf{T}, \boldsymbol{\Omega})$ under illumination $\mathbf{l}$.

Due to the small motion assumption in the derivation of the analytical model of motion and illumination in Section 7.2.1, the core tensor $\mathcal{Z}$ can only represent the image of the object whose pose is close to the pose $\mathbf{p}$ under which the training samples of $\mathbf{v}$ are computed. To emphasize that $\mathcal{Z}$ is a function of pose $\mathbf{p}$, we denote it as $\mathcal{Z}_\mathbf{p}$ in the following derivation. Since $\mathbf{v}$ is obtained by concatenating $[\mathcal{B}]_v$ and $[\mathcal{C}]_v$, $\mathcal{Z}_\mathbf{p}$ also contains two parts, $\mathcal{Z}_\mathbf{p}^\mathcal{B}$ with size $(N_i \times N_e \times N_l MN)$ and $\mathcal{Z}_\mathbf{p}^\mathcal{C}$ with size $(N_i \times N_e \times 6N_l MN)$. The first part encodes the variation of the image due to changes of identity, deformation, and illumination at the pose $\mathbf{p}$, and the second part encodes the variation due to motion around $\mathbf{p}$—that is, the tangent plane of the manifold along the motion direction. Rearranging the two subtensors according to the illumination and motion basis into sizes of $N_l \times 1 \times N_i \times N_e \times MN$ and $N_l \times 6 \times N_i \times N_e \times MN$ (this step is needed to undo the vectorization operation of Eq. (7.4)), we can represent the quadrilinear basis of illumination, 3D motion, identity, and deformation along the first, second, third, and fourth dimensions respectively. The image with identity $\mathbf{c}_i$ and expression $\mathbf{c}_e$ after motion $(\mathbf{T}, \boldsymbol{\Omega})$ around pose $\mathbf{p}$ under illumination $\mathbf{l}$ can be obtained by

$$\mathcal{I} = \mathcal{Z}_\mathbf{p}^\mathcal{B} \times_1 \mathbf{l} \times_3 \mathbf{c}_i \times_4 \mathbf{c}_e + \mathcal{Z}_\mathbf{p}^\mathcal{C} \times_1 \mathbf{l} \times_2 \begin{pmatrix} \mathbf{T} \\ \boldsymbol{\Omega} \end{pmatrix} \times_3 \mathbf{c}_i \times_4 \mathbf{c}_e. \tag{7.9}$$

Note that we did not need examples of the object at different lighting conditions and motion in order to construct this manifold—these parts of the manifold came from the analytical expressions in Eq. (7.3).

To represent the manifold at all the possible poses, we do not need such a tensor at every pose. Effects of 3D translation can be removed by centering and scale normalization, while in-plane rotation to a predefined pose can mitigate the effects of rotation about the $z$ axis. Thus, the image of object under arbitrary pose, $\mathbf{p}$, can always be described by the multilinear object representation at a predefined $(\mathbf{T}_x^{pd}, \mathbf{T}_y^{pd}, \mathbf{T}_z^{pd}, \boldsymbol{\Omega}_z^{pd})$, with only $\boldsymbol{\Omega}_x$ and $\boldsymbol{\Omega}_y$ depending upon the particular pose. Thus, the image manifold under any pose can be approximated by the collection of a few tangent planes on distinct $\boldsymbol{\Omega}_x^j$ and $\boldsymbol{\Omega}_y^j$, denoted as $\mathbf{p}_j$.

## 7.3  ROBUST AND EFFICIENT TRACKING ON GAMs

We now show how the GAMs of object appearance can be applied for estimation of 3D motion and lighting, which we broadly refer to as tracking. These estimates of motion and lighting can be used for novel view synthesis that will then be used for video-based face recognition in Section 7.4.

A simple method for estimating motion and illumination is by minimizing a cost function directly derived from Eq. (7.3) as

$$(\hat{\mathbf{l}}_t, \hat{\mathbf{m}}_t) = \arg \min_{\mathbf{l}, \mathbf{m}} \|\mathcal{I}_t - (\mathcal{B}_{\hat{\mathbf{p}}_{t-1}} + \mathcal{C}_{\hat{\mathbf{p}}_{t-1}} \times_2 \mathbf{m}) \times_1 \mathbf{l}\|^2 + \alpha \|\mathbf{m}\|^2, \qquad (7.10)$$

where $\hat{x}$ denotes an estimate of $x$. Since the motion between consecutive frames is small, but illumination can change suddenly, we add a regularization term $\alpha \|\mathbf{m}\|^2$ to the above cost function. The estimates of motion and lighting can be obtained by alternate minimization along these two directions (this is a valid local minimization due to the bilinearity of the two terms) as

$$\hat{\mathbf{l}} = (\mathcal{B}_{\hat{\mathbf{p}}_{t-1}(1)} \mathcal{B}_{\hat{\mathbf{p}}_{t-1}(1)}^T)^{-1} \mathcal{B}_{\hat{\mathbf{p}}_{t-1}(1)} \mathcal{I}_{t(1)}^T \qquad (7.11)$$

and

$$\hat{\mathbf{m}} = \left( (\mathcal{C}_{\hat{\mathbf{p}}_{t-1}} \times_1 \mathbf{l})_{(2)} (\mathcal{C}_{\hat{\mathbf{p}}_{t-1}} \times_1 \mathbf{l})_{(2)}^T + \alpha \mathbf{I} \right)^{-1}$$
$$(\mathcal{C}_{\hat{\mathbf{p}}_{t-1}} \times_1 \mathbf{l})_{(2)} (\mathcal{I}_t - \mathcal{B}_{\hat{\mathbf{p}}_{t-1}} \times_1 \mathbf{l})_{(2)}^T, \qquad (7.12)$$

where $\mathbf{I}$ is an identity matrix of dimension $6 \times 6$.

This is essentially a model-based estimation approach that requires a texture-mapped 3D model of the object to be tracked. This is expected because the method works only with the analytically derived model, which cannot represent variations of identity within a single class of objects. By using our GAMs, this restriction can be overcome. Moreover, we can achieve this in a computationally efficient manner by using the inverse compositional algorithm. As mentioned earlier, our tracking method is faster than 3DMM-based approaches [18] while sacrificing little in accuracy.

### 7.3.1  Inverse Compositional (IC) Estimation on GAMs

The iteration involving alternate minimization over motion and illumination in the above approach is essentially a gradient descent method. In each iteration, as the pose is updated, the gradients (i.e., the tensors $\mathcal{B}$ and $\mathcal{C}$) need to be recomputed, which is computationally expensive. The inverse compositional algorithm [15] works by moving these computational steps out of the iterative updating process. In addition, the constraint of knowing the 3D model of the object can be relaxed by reconstructing $\mathcal{B}$ and $\mathcal{C}$ from the core tensors $\mathcal{Z}^{\mathcal{B}}$ and $\mathcal{Z}^{\mathcal{C}}$.

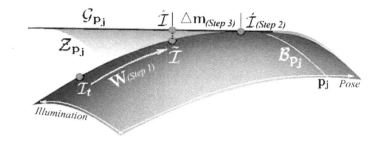

**Figure 7.2.** Pictorial representation of the inverse compositional tracking scheme on GAMs.

From Eq. (7.9), the cost function for estimation of 3D motion and lighting in Eq. (7.10) can be rewritten as

$$(\hat{\mathbf{l}}_t, \hat{\mathbf{m}}_t) = \arg \min_{\mathbf{l}, \mathbf{m}, \mathbf{c}_i, \mathbf{c}_e} \left\| \mathcal{I}_t - \left( \mathcal{Z}^{\mathcal{B}}_{\hat{\mathbf{p}}_{t-1}} + \mathcal{Z}^{\mathcal{C}}_{\hat{\mathbf{p}}_{t-1}} \times_2 \mathbf{m} \right) \times_1 \mathbf{l} \times_3 \mathbf{c}_i \times_4 \mathbf{c}_e \right\|^2 + \alpha \|\mathbf{m}\|^2.$$

(7.13)

This cost function is quadrilinear in illumination, motion, identity, and deformation variables. The optimization of Eq. (7.13) can be done by alternatively optimizing over each parameter of $\mathbf{l}$, $\mathbf{m}$, $\mathbf{c}_i$, and $\mathbf{c}_e$ while keeping the others fixed. This takes advantage of the fact that we know that the space is multilinear. Starting from an initial pose estimate (where the manifold is approximated by a tangent), we will first optimize over illumination, identity, and expression dimensions and then apply the inverse compositional algorithm for optimization over motion. In Figure 7.2 we show a pictorial scheme of this optimization process.

**IC Warping Function.** Consider an input frame $I_t(\mathbf{u})$ at time instance $t$ with image coordinate $\mathbf{u}$ (Figure 7.3). We introduce a warp operator $\mathbf{W} : \mathbb{R}^2 \to \mathbb{R}^2$ such that if the pose of $I_t(\mathbf{u})$ is $\mathbf{p}$, the pose of $I_t(\mathbf{W}_{\hat{\mathbf{p}}_{t-1}}(\mathbf{u}, \mathbf{m}))$ is $\mathbf{p} + \mathbf{m}$. Basically, $\mathbf{W}$ represents the displacement in the image plane due to a pose transformation of the 3D model. Denote the pose transformed image $I_t(\mathbf{W}_{\hat{\mathbf{p}}_{t-1}}(\mathbf{u}, \mathbf{m}))$ in tensor notation $\tilde{\mathcal{I}}_t^{\mathbf{W}_{\hat{\mathbf{p}}_{t-1}}(\mathbf{m})}$. Using this warp operator and ignoring the regularization term, we can restate the cost function (7.13) in the inverse compositional framework as

$$(\hat{\mathbf{l}}_t, \hat{\mathbf{m}}_t) = \arg \min_{\mathbf{l}, \mathbf{m}, \mathbf{c}_i, \mathbf{c}_e} \| \tilde{\mathcal{I}}_t^{\mathbf{W}_{\hat{\mathbf{p}}_{t-1}}(-\mathbf{m})} - \mathcal{Z}^{\mathcal{B}}_{\hat{\mathbf{p}}_{t-1}} \times_1 \mathbf{l} \times_3 \mathbf{c}_i \times_4 \mathbf{c}_e \|^2 + \alpha \|\mathbf{m}\|^2.$$

(7.14)

Given the other parameters of the quadrilinear manifold, the cost function can be minimized over $\mathbf{m}$ by iteratively solving for increments $\triangle \mathbf{m}$ in

$$\| \tilde{\mathcal{I}}_t^{\mathbf{W}_{\hat{\mathbf{p}}_{t-1}}(-\mathbf{m})} - \left( \mathcal{Z}^{\mathcal{B}}_{\hat{\mathbf{p}}_{t-1}} + \mathcal{Z}^{\mathcal{C}}_{\hat{\mathbf{p}}_{t-1}} \times_2 \triangle \mathbf{m} \right) \times_1 \mathbf{l} \times_3 \mathbf{c}_i \times_4 \mathbf{c}_e \|^2 + \alpha \|\mathbf{m} + \triangle \mathbf{m}\|^2.$$

(7.15)

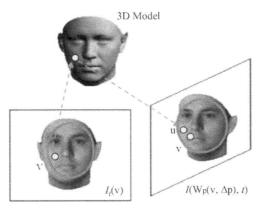

**Figure 7.3.** Illustration of the warping function $\mathbf{W}$. A point $\mathbf{v}$ in image plane is projected onto the surface of the 3D object model. After the pose transformation with $\triangle\mathbf{p}$, the point on the surface is back-projected onto the image plane at a new point $\mathbf{u}$. The warping function maps from $\mathbf{v} \in \mathbb{R}^2$ to $\mathbf{u} \in \mathbb{R}^2$. The red ellipses show the common part in both frames that the warping function $\mathbf{W}$ is defined upon.

In each iteration, $\mathbf{m}$ is updated such that $\mathbf{W}_{\hat{\mathbf{p}}_{t-1}}(\mathbf{u}, -\mathbf{m}) \leftarrow \mathbf{W}_{\hat{\mathbf{p}}_{t-1}}(\mathbf{u}, -\mathbf{m}) \circ \mathbf{W}_{\hat{\mathbf{p}}_{t-1}}(\mathbf{u}, \triangle\mathbf{m})^{-1}$.[3] Using the additivity of pose transformation for small $\triangle\mathbf{m}$, we obtain $\mathbf{W}_{\hat{\mathbf{p}}_{t-1}}(\mathbf{W}_{\hat{\mathbf{p}}_{t-1}}(\mathbf{u}, \triangle\mathbf{m})^{-1}, -\mathbf{m}) = \mathbf{W}_{\hat{\mathbf{p}}_{t-1}}(\mathbf{W}_{\hat{\mathbf{p}}_{t-1}}(\mathbf{u}, -\triangle\mathbf{m}), -\mathbf{m}) = \mathbf{W}_{\hat{\mathbf{p}}_{t-1}}(\mathbf{u}, -\triangle\mathbf{m} - \mathbf{m})$. Thus, the above update is essentially $\mathbf{m} \leftarrow \mathbf{m} + \triangle\mathbf{m}$.

Baker and Matthews [15] proved that for the inverse compositional algorithm to be provably equivalent to the Lucas–Kanade algorithm up to the first order approximation of $\triangle\mathbf{m}$, the set of warps $\{\mathbf{W}\}$ must form a group; that is, every warp $\mathbf{W}$ must be invertible. If the change of pose is small enough, the visibility for most of the pixels will remain the same; thus $\mathbf{W}$ can be considered approximately invertible. However, if the pose change becomes too big, some portion of the object will become invisible after the pose transformation, and $\mathbf{W}$ will no longer be invertible (see [17] for more details).

Since the GAM along the motion direction is composed of a set of tangent planes at a few discrete poses (see Figure 7.1), the computations for $\triangle\mathbf{m}$ need to happen only at these poses (called cardinal poses). Thus all frames that are close to a particular pose $\mathbf{p}_j$ will use the $\mathcal{B}$ and $\mathcal{C}$ at that pose, and the warp $\mathbf{W}$ should be performed to normalize the pose to $\mathbf{p}_j$. While most of the existing inverse compositional methods move the expensive update steps out of the iterations for two-frame matching, we go even further and perform these expensive computations only once every few frames. This is by virtue of the fact that we estimate 3D motion.

### 7.3.1.1  The IC Algorithm on GAMs

Consider a sequence of image frames $\mathcal{I}_t, t = 0, \ldots, N - 1$.

Assume that we know the pose and illumination estimates for frame $t - 1$, that is, $\hat{\mathbf{p}}_{t-1}$ and $\hat{\mathbf{l}}_{t-1}$.

---

[3] The compositional operator $\circ$ means that the second warp is composed into the first warp, that is, $\mathbf{W}_{\hat{\mathbf{p}}_{t-1}}(\mathbf{u}, -\mathbf{m}) \equiv \mathbf{W}_{\hat{\mathbf{p}}_{t-1}}(\mathbf{W}_{\hat{\mathbf{p}}_{t-1}}(\mathbf{u}, \triangle\mathbf{m})^{-1}, -\mathbf{m})$.

**Step 1:** For the new input frame $\mathcal{I}_t$, find the closest $\mathbf{p_j}$ to the pose estimates at $t-1$, that is, $\hat{\mathbf{p}}_{t-1}$. Assume motion $\mathbf{m}$ to be zero, and assume illumination condition $\hat{\mathbf{l}}_t = \hat{\mathbf{l}}_{t-1}$. Apply the pose transformation operator $\mathbf{W}$ to get the pose normalized version of the frame $\tilde{\mathcal{I}}^{\mathbf{W}_{\hat{\mathbf{p}}_{t-1}}(\mathbf{p_j}-\hat{\mathbf{p}}_{t-1}-\mathbf{m})}$, that is, $I_t(\mathbf{W}_{\hat{\mathbf{p}}_{t-1}}(\mathbf{u}, \mathbf{p_j} - \hat{\mathbf{p}}_{t-1} - \mathbf{m}))$. This is shown in Figure 7.2, where the input frame $\mathcal{I}_t$ on the manifold is first warped to $\tilde{\mathcal{I}}$ which is within a nearby region of pose $\mathbf{p_j}$.

**Step 2:** Use Eq. (7.8) to alternately estimate $\hat{\mathbf{l}}$, $\hat{\mathbf{c}}_i$, and $\hat{\mathbf{c}}_e$ of the pose normalized image $\mathcal{I}_t^{\mathbf{W}_{\hat{\mathbf{p}}_{t-1}}(\mathbf{u},\mathbf{p_j}-\hat{\mathbf{p}}_{t-1}-\mathbf{m})}$ as follows.

Using Eq. (7.8), $\mathcal{B}_{\mathbf{p_j}}$ can be written as

$$\mathcal{B}_{\mathbf{p_j}} = \left[ \mathcal{Z}_{\mathbf{p_j}}^{\mathcal{B}} \times_3 \mathbf{c}_i \times_4 \mathbf{c}_e \right]_v^{-1}. \tag{7.16}$$

Denoting the basis for the identity and expression as $\mathcal{E}$ and $\mathcal{F}$, we can similarly compute them as

$$\mathcal{E}_{\mathbf{p_j}} = \left[ \mathcal{Z}_{\mathbf{p_j}}^{\mathcal{B}} \times_1 \mathbf{l} \times \mathbf{c}_e \right]_v^{-1},$$

$$\mathcal{F}_{\mathbf{p_j}} = \left[ \mathcal{Z}_{\mathbf{p_j}}^{\mathcal{C}} \times_1 \mathbf{l} \times_3 \mathbf{c}_i \right]_v^{-1}. \tag{7.17}$$

Thus the illumination coefficients can be estimated using least squares (since the illumination bases after motion (7.2) are not orthogonal), while the identity and expression coefficients can be estimated by projection of the image onto the corresponding basis as

$$\hat{\mathbf{l}} = (\mathcal{B}_{\mathbf{p}_j}\mathcal{B}_{\mathbf{p}_j}^{\mathbf{T}})^{-1}\mathcal{B}_{\mathbf{p}_j}^{\mathbf{T}}\mathcal{I}_{(1)},$$

$$\hat{\mathbf{c}}_i = \mathcal{E}_{\mathbf{p}_j}^{\mathbf{T}} I_{(1)}, \hat{\mathbf{c}}_e = \mathcal{F}_{\mathbf{p}_j}^{\mathbf{T}} I_{(1)}. \tag{7.18}$$

When we iteratively solve for $\hat{\mathbf{l}}$, $\hat{\mathbf{c}}_i$ and $\hat{\mathbf{c}}_e$, the cost function Eq. (7.14) is minimized over illumination, identity, and expression directions. In Figure 7.2, the curve $\mathcal{B}_{\mathbf{p_j}}$ shows the manifold of the image at pose $\mathbf{p_j}$ with motion as zero, but varying illumination, identity, or deformation. By iteratively minimizing along the illumination, identity, and deformation directions, we are finding the point

$$\acute{\mathcal{I}} = \mathcal{Z}_{\mathbf{p_j}}^{\mathcal{B}} \times_1 \hat{\mathbf{l}} \times_3 \hat{\mathbf{c}}_i \times_4 \hat{\mathbf{c}}_e \tag{7.19}$$

on the curve $\mathcal{B}_{\mathbf{p_j}}$ which has the minimum distance to the pose normalized point $\tilde{\mathcal{I}}$.

**Step 3:** With the estimated $\hat{\mathbf{l}}$, $\hat{\mathbf{c}}_i$, and $\hat{\mathbf{c}}_e$ from Step 2, use Eq. (7.21) to estimate the motion increment $\triangle\mathbf{m}$. Update $\mathbf{m}$ with $\mathbf{m} \leftarrow \mathbf{m} + \triangle\mathbf{m}$. This can be done as follows.

Rewrite the cost function in (7.15) at the cardinal pose $\mathbf{p}_j$ as

$$\left|\left|\tilde{\mathcal{I}}_t^{\mathbf{W}_{\hat{\mathbf{p}}_{t-1}}(\mathbf{p}_j - \hat{\mathbf{p}}_{t-1} - \mathbf{m})} - \left(\acute{\mathcal{I}} + \mathcal{G}_{\mathbf{p}_j}^{\mathbf{T}} \triangle\mathbf{m}\right)\right|\right|^2 + \alpha||\mathbf{m} + \triangle\mathbf{m}||^2,$$

$$\text{where} \quad \mathcal{G}_{\mathbf{p}_j} = \left[\mathcal{Z}_{\mathbf{p}_j}^{\mathcal{C}} \times_1 \hat{\mathbf{l}} \times \hat{\mathbf{c}}_i \times \hat{\mathbf{c}}_e\right]_v^{-1}. \tag{7.20}$$

$\mathcal{G}_{\mathbf{p}_j}$ is the motion basis at pose $\mathbf{p}_j$ with fixed $\hat{l}$, $\hat{\mathbf{c}}_i$, and $\hat{\mathbf{c}}_e$. Recall that $\mathcal{Z}_{\mathbf{p}_j}^{\mathcal{C}}$ is a tensor of size $N_l \times 6 \times N_i \times N_e \times MN$; thus $\mathcal{G}_{\mathbf{p}_j}$ degenerates to a matrix of size $6 \times MN$. In Figure 7.2, we compute the tangent along the motion direction, shown as the black line $\mathcal{G}_{\mathbf{p}_j}$, from the core tensor shown as the pink surface $\mathcal{Z}$.

Taking the derivative of Eq. (7.20) with respect to $\triangle\mathbf{m}$ and setting it to be zero, we have

$$\triangle\mathbf{m} = \left[\mathcal{G}_{\mathbf{p}_j}\mathcal{G}_{\mathbf{p}_j}^{\mathbf{T}} + \alpha\mathbf{I}\right]^{-1} (\mathcal{G}_{\mathbf{p}_j}(\tilde{\mathcal{I}}_t^{\mathbf{W}_{\hat{\mathbf{p}}_{t-1}}(\mathbf{p}_j - \hat{\mathbf{p}}_{t-1} - \mathbf{m})} - \acute{\mathcal{I}}) - \alpha\mathbf{m}), \tag{7.21}$$

and the motion estimates $\mathbf{m}$ should be updated with the increments $\mathbf{m} \leftarrow \mathbf{m} + \triangle\mathbf{m}$. The overall computational cost is reduced significantly by making the gradient $\mathcal{G}_{\mathbf{p}_j}$ independent of the updating variable $\mathbf{m}$. In Figure 7.2, $\triangle\mathbf{m}$ is shown to be the distance from point $\acute{\mathcal{I}}$ to $\hat{\mathcal{I}}$, the projection of $\tilde{\mathcal{I}}$, onto the motion tangent.

**Step 4:** Use the updated $\mathbf{m}$ from Step 3 to update the pose normalized image as $\tilde{\mathcal{I}}_t^{\mathbf{W}_{\hat{\mathbf{p}}_{t-1}}(\mathbf{p}_j - \hat{\mathbf{p}}_{t-1} - \mathbf{m})}$, that is, $I(\mathbf{W}_{\hat{\mathbf{p}}_{t-1}}(\mathbf{u}, \mathbf{p}_j - \hat{\mathbf{p}}_{t-1} - \mathbf{m}), t)$.

**Step 5:** Repeat Steps 2, 3, and 4 for that input frame until the difference error $\varepsilon$ between the pose normalized image $\tilde{\mathcal{I}}_t^{\mathbf{W}_{\hat{\mathbf{p}}_{t-1}}(\mathbf{p}_j - \hat{\mathbf{p}}_{t-1} - \mathbf{m})}$ and the rendered image $\acute{\mathcal{I}}$ can be reduced below an acceptable threshold.

**Step 6:** Set $t = t + 1$. Repeat Steps 1, 2, 3, 4, and 5. Continue until $t = N - 1$.

### 7.3.2  Probabilistic IC (PIC) Estimation

To ensure that the tracking is robust to estimation errors, we embed the IC approach within a probabilistic framework. For ease of explanation, let us denote the current cardinal pose to be $\mathbf{p}_j$, and the nearby cardinal poses as $\mathbf{p}_{j-1}$ and $\mathbf{p}_{j+1}$. Denote the nearest-neighbor partition region on the multilinear manifold for cardinal pose $\mathbf{p}_j$ to be $\Theta_{\mathbf{p}_j}$. Given the estimated pose at the previous time instance $\hat{\mathbf{p}}_{t-1}$, the average velocity $\bar{\mathbf{m}}$, and variation $\sigma_m^2$ of it within a recent history, we can model the distribution of the current pose $\mathbf{p}_t \sim \mathcal{N}(\hat{\mathbf{p}}_{t-1} + \bar{\mathbf{m}}, \sigma_m^2)$, where $\mathcal{N}$ is the normal distribution. Assume that the likelihood distribution of $\varepsilon$ at pose $\mathbf{p}_j$ (difference between pose normalized image and rendered image) in step 5 of the inverse compositional algorithm is

$p(\varepsilon|\mathbf{p}_t \in \Theta_{\mathbf{p}_j}) \sim \mathcal{N}(0, \sigma)$. Using Bayes rule, we get

$$P(\mathbf{p}_t \in \Theta_{\mathbf{p}_j}|\varepsilon) = \frac{p(\varepsilon|\mathbf{p}_t \in \Theta_{\mathbf{p}_j}) \int_{\Theta_{\mathbf{p}_j}} p(\mathbf{p}_t) \, d\mathbf{p}_t}{P\varepsilon}. \qquad (7.22)$$

Similarly, we can compute $P(\mathbf{p}_t \in \Theta_{\mathbf{p}_{j-1}}|\varepsilon)$ and $P(\mathbf{p}_t \in \Theta_{\mathbf{p}_{j+1}}|\varepsilon)$. Denoting the estimate of motion, illumination, identity, and expression with the tangent at $\mathbf{p}_j$ as $\hat{\mathbf{x}}_t^{\mathbf{p}_j}$, the final estimate can be obtained as

$$\hat{\mathbf{x}}_t = E(\mathbf{x}_t|\varepsilon) = \frac{\displaystyle\sum_{i=j-1}^{j+1} \hat{\mathbf{x}}_t^{\mathbf{p}_i} P(\mathbf{p}_t \in \Theta_{\mathbf{p}_i}|\varepsilon)}{\displaystyle\sum_{i=j-1}^{j+1} P(\mathbf{p}_t \in \Theta_{\mathbf{p}_i}|\varepsilon)}. \qquad (7.23)$$

## 7.4 FACE RECOGNITION FROM VIDEO

We now explain the analysis-by-synthesis framework for video-based face recognition algorithm using GAMs. The use of GAMs is motivated by the fact that in video we will encounter changes of pose, lighting, and appearance.

In our method, the gallery is represented by a textured 3D model of the face. The model can be built from a single image [18], a video sequence [28] or obtained directly from 3D sensors [29]. In our experiments, the face model will be estimated from the gallery video sequence for each individual. Face texture is obtained by normalizing the illumination of the first frame in the gallery sequence to an ambient condition and mapping it onto the 3D model. Given a probe sequence, we will estimate the motion and illumination conditions using the algorithms described in Section 7.3. Note that the tracking does not require a person-specific 3D model—a generic face model is usually sufficient. Given the motion and illumination estimates, we will then render images from the 3D models in the gallery. The rendered images can then be compared with the images in the probe sequence. For this purpose, we will design robust measurements for comparing these two sequences. A feature of these measurements will be their ability to integrate the identity over all the frames, ignoring some frames that may have the wrong identity.

Let $I_i, i = 0, \ldots, N-1$, be the $i$th frame from the probe sequence. Let $S_{i,j}, i = 0, \ldots, N-1$, be the frames of the synthesized sequence for individual $j$, where $j = 1, \ldots, M$ and $M$ is the total number of individuals in the gallery. Note that the number of frames in the two sequences to be compared will always be the same in our method. By design, each corresponding frame in the two sequences will be under the same pose and illumination conditions, dictated by the accuracy of the estimates of these parameters from the probes sequence. Let $d_{ij}$ be the Euclidean distance between the $i$th frames $I_i$ and $S_{i,j}$. Then we obtain the identity of the probe as

$$ID = \arg \min_j \min_i d_{ij}. \qquad (7.24)$$

The measurement in Eq. (7.24) computes the distance between the frames in the probe sequence and each synthesized sequence that are the most similar and chooses the identity as the individual with the smallest distance.

As the images in the synthesized sequences are pose and illumination normalized to the ones in the probe sequence, $d_{ij}$ can be computed directly using the Euclidean distance. Other distance measurements, like those reported in [24, 30], can be considered in situations where the pose and illumination estimates may not be reliable or in the presence of occlusion and clutter. We will look into such issues in our future work.

### 7.4.1 Video-Based Face Recognition Algorithm

Using the above notation, let $I_i, i = 0, \ldots, N - 1$, be $N$ frames from the probe sequence. Let $G_1, \ldots, G_M$ be the 3D models with texture for each of $M$ galleries.

**Step 1:** Register a 3D generic face model to the first frame of the probe sequence. This is achieved using the method in [31][4]. Estimate the illumination and motion model parameters for each frame of the probe sequence using the method described in Section 7.3.1.1.

**Step 2:** Using the estimated illumination and motion parameters, synthesize, for each gallery, a video sequence using the generative model of Eq. (7.1). Denote these as $S_{i,j}, i = 1, \ldots, N$ and $j = 1, \ldots, M$.

**Step 3:** Compute $d_{ij}$ as above.

**Step 4:** Obtain the identity using a suitable distance measure as in Eq. (7.24).

## 7.5   EXPERIMENT RESULTS

As discussed above, the advantages of using the GAMs are (i) ease of construction due to the need for significantly less number of training images, (ii) ability to represent objects at all poses and lighting conditions from only a few examples during training, and (iii) accuracy and efficiency of tracking and recognition. We will now show results to justify these claims.

### 7.5.1   Constructing GAM of Faces

In the case of faces, we will need at least one image for every person. We then fit the 3DMM to estimate the face model and compute the vectorized tensor **v** at a pre-defined collection of poses $\mathbf{p}_j$. For each expression, we will need at least one image per person. Thus for $N_i$ people with $N_e$ expressions, we need $N_i N_e$ images.

---

[4]We use a semiautomatic registration algorithm to initialize the IC tracking. It requires first manually choosing seven landmark points, followed by automatically registering the 3D face model onto the image to estimate the initial pose.

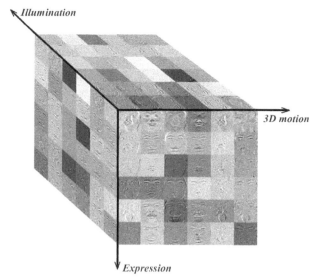

**Figure 7.4.** The basis images of the face GAM on illumination, expression, and the 3D motion around the frontal cardinal pose for a specific person.

In our experiments we have $N_i = 100$ and $N_e = 7$, thus requiring 700 images for all the people and every expression. In contrast, [7] requires 300 frames per person for training purposes while modeling only pose variation. Similarly, in [4], 225 frames of 15 poses and 15 under different illumination patterns are used for each identity (expression variation is not considered). Moreover, the GAM can model not only the appearance space at these discrete poses, but also the manifold in a local region around each pose. In our experiments, the pose collection $\mathbf{p}_j$ is chosen to be every $15°$ along the vertical rotational axis and every $20°$ along the horizontal rotational axis. In Figure 7.4 we show some basis images of the face GAM along illumination, 3D motion, identity, and expression dimensions. Because we can show only three dimensions, identity is fixed to one particular person.

### 7.5.2  Accuracy of the Motion and Illumination Estimates on GAM

We will now show some results on the accuracy of tracking on the GAM with known ground truth. We use the 3DMM [18] to randomly generate a face. The generated face model is rotated along the vertical axis at some specific angular velocity, and the illumination is changing both in direction (from right-bottom corner to the lefttop corner) and in brightness (from dark to bright to dark). In Figure 7.5, the images show the back-projection of some feature points on the 3D model onto the input frames using the estimated motion under three different illumination conditions. Figure 7.6, a

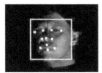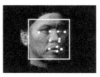

**Figure 7.5.** The back projection of the feature points on the generated 3D face model using the estimated 3D motion onto some input frames.

shows the comparison between the estimated motion (in blue) and the ground truth (in red). The maximum error in pose estimates is $3.57°$ and the average error is $1.22°$. Figure 7.6 b shows the norm of the error between the ground truth illumination coefficients and the estimated ones from the GAM, normalized with the ground truth. The maximum error is 5.5% and the average is 2.2%. The peaks in the error plot are due to the change of the cardinal pose $\mathbf{p}_j$ (the tangent planes along the pose dimension).

### 7.5.3  PIC Tracking on GAM Using Real Data

Figure 7.7 shows results of face tracking under large changes of pose, lighting, expression, and background using the PIC approach. The images in the first row show tracking under illumination variations with global and local changes. The images in the second row show tracking on the GAM with some expressions under varying illumination conditions. We did not require a texture-mapped 3D model as in [17]. Compared to 3DMM, we achieve almost the same accuracy while requiring one-tenth the computational time per frame.

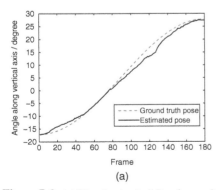

(a)

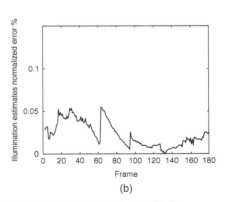

(b)

**Figure 7.6.** (a) 3D estimates (solid) and ground truth (dotted) of pose against frames. (b) The normalized error of the illumination estimates versus frame numbers.

**Figure 7.7.** Examples of face tracking using GAMs under changes of pose, lighting, and expressions.

## 7.5.4 Face Database and Experimental Setup

Our database consists of videos of 57 people. Each person was asked to move his/her head as they wished (mostly rotate their head from left to right, and then from down to up), and the illumination was changed randomly. The illumination consisted of ceiling lights, lights from the back of the head, and sunlight from a window on the left side of the face. Random combinations of these were turned on and off, and the window was controlled using dark blinds. There was no control over how the subject moves his/her head or on facial expression. An example of some of the images in the video database is shown in Figure 7.8. The images are scale normalized

**Figure 7.8.** Sample frames from the video sequence collected for our database (best viewed on a monitor).

and centered. Some of the subjects had expression changes also—for example, the last row of the Figure 7.8. The average size of the face was about $70 \times 70$, with the minimum size being $50 \times 50$. Videos are captured with uniform background. We recorded two or three sessions of video sequences for each individual. All the video sessions are recorded within one week. The first session is used as the gallery for constructing the 3D textured model of the head, while the remaining are used for testing. We used a simplified version of the method in [28] for this purpose. We would like to emphasize that any other 3D modeling algorithm would also have worked. Texture is obtained by (a) normalizing the illumination of the first frame in each gallery sequence to an ambient illumination condition and (b) mapping onto the 3D model.

As can be seen from Figure 7.8, the pose and illumination varies randomly in the video. For each subject, we designed three experiments by choosing different probe sequences:

**Experiment A:** A video was used as the probe sequence with the average pose of the face in the video being about $15°$ from frontal.

**Experiment B:** A video was used as the probe sequence with the average pose of the face in the video being about $30°$ from frontal.

**Experiment C:** A video was used as the probe sequence with the average pose of the face in the video being about $45°$ from frontal.

Each probe sequence has about 20 frames around the average pose. The variation of pose in each sequence was less than $15°$, so as to keep pose in the experiments disjoint. To show the benefit of video-based methods over image-based approaches, we designed three new Experiments D, E, and F by taking random single images from A, B, and C, respectively. We restricted our face recognition experiments to the pose and illumination variations only (which can be expressed analytically), with the bilinear representation of [13].

## 7.5.5 Recognition Results

We plot the cumulative match characteristic (CMC) [8, 9] for experiments A, B, and C with measurement (7.24) in Figure 7.9. Our proposed algorithm gives relatively high performance. In Experiment A, where pose is $15°$ away from frontal, all the videos with large and arbitrary variations of illumination are recognized correctly. In Experiment B, we achieve about 95% recognition rate, while for Experiment C it is 93% using the distance measure (7.24). Irrespective of the illumination changes, the recognition rate decreases consistently with large difference in pose from frontal (which is the gallery), a trend that has been reported by other authors [19, 20]. *Note that the pose and illumination conditions in the probe and gallery sets can be completely disjoint.*

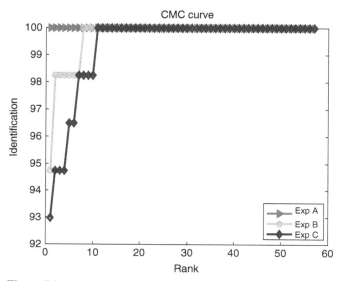

**Figure 7.9.** CMC curve for video-based face recognition experiments A to C with distance measurement in (7.24).

## 7.5.6 Comparison with Other Approaches

The area of video-based face recognition is less standardized than image-based approaches. There is no standard data set on which both image and video-based methods have been tried, thus we do the comparison on our own data set. This data set can be used for such comparison by other researchers in the future.

## 7.5.7 Comparison with 3DMM-Based Approaches

3DMM has achieved a significant impact in the biometrics area and has obtained impressive results in pose and illumination varying face recognition. It is similar to our proposed approach in the sense that both methods are 3D approaches, estimate the pose and illumination, and do synthesis for recognition. However, 3DMM method uses the Phong illumination model, thus it cannot model extended light sources (like the sky) accurately. To overcome this, Zhang and Samaras [19] proposed the SHBMM (3D spherical harmonics basis morphable model) that integrates the spherical harmonics illumination representation into the 3DMM. Although it is possible to repeatedly apply the 3DMM or SHBMM approach to each frame in the video sequence, it is inefficient. Registration of the 3D model to each frame will be needed, which requires a lot of computation and manual work. None of the existing 3DMM approaches integrate tracking and recognition. Also, 3DMM-based methods cannot achieve real-time pose/illumination estimation, which can be achieved with the inverse compositional version of our tracking method. Our proposed method, which integrates 3D motion

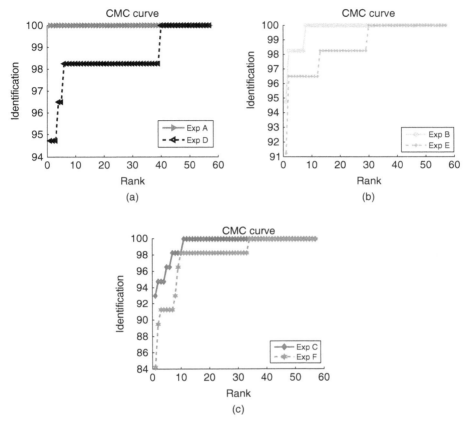

**Figure 7.10.** Comparison between the CMC curves for the video-based face experiments A to C (shown in (a) to (c) respectively) with distance measurement (7.24) against the SHBMM method in reference 19.

into SHBMM, is a unified approach for modeling lighting and motion in a video sequence.

We now compare our proposed approach against the SHBMM method of [19], which was shown give better results than 3DMM in [20]. We will also compare our results with the published results of SHBMM method [19] in the later part of this section.

Recall that we designed three new Experiments D, E, and F by taking random single images from A, B, and C, respectively. In Figure 7.10, we plot the CMC curve with measurement 1 in Eq. (7.24) (which has the best performance for Experiment A, B, and C) for the Experiments D, E, F and compare them with the ones of the Experiment A, B, and C. For this comparison, we randomly chose images from the probe sequences of Experiments A, B, C and computed the recognition performance over multiple such random sets. Thus the Experiments D, E, and F average the image-based performance over different conditions. By analyzing the plots in Figure 7.10, we see that the recognition performance with the video-based approach is consistently higher than the image-based one, both in Rank 1 performance and in the area under the CMC curve. This trend is magnified as the average facial pose becomes more nonfrontal. Also, we expect that registration errors, in general, will affect image-based methods more than video-based methods (since robust tracking maybe able to overcome some of the registration errors, as shown in Section 7.3).

It is interesting to compare these results against the results in [19], for image-based recognition. The size of the databases in both cases is close (though ours is slightly smaller). Our recognition rate with a video sequence at average 15° facial pose (with a range of 15° about the average) is 100%, while the average recognition rate for approximately 20° (called side view) in [19] is 92.4%. For Experiments B and C, [19] does not have comparable cases and goes directly to profile pose (90°), which we don't have. Our recognition rate at 45° average pose is 93%. In [19] the quoted rates at 20° is 92% and at 90° is 55%. Thus the trend of our video-based recognition results are significantly higher than image-based approaches that deal with both pose and illumination variations.

## 7.6   CONCLUSION

In this chapter, we showed how to combine geometrical and statistical models for video-based face recognition. We showed that it is possible to estimate low-dimensional manifolds that describe object appearance with a small number of training samples using a combination of analytically derived geometrical models and statistical data analysis. We derived a quadrilinear space of object appearance that is able to represent the effects of illumination, motion, identity, and deformation, and we called it the geometry-integrated appearance manifold. Based upon the GAM, we have proposed a method for video-based face recognition. We also collected a face video database consisting of 57 people with large and arbitrary variation in pose and illumination, and we demonstrated the effectiveness of the method on this new database. We showed specific examples on how to construct this manifold, analyzed the accuracy of the pose and lighting estimates, and presented the video-based face recognition results upon our own data set. Detailed analysis of recognition performance are also carried out. Future work will focus on extending GAMs to objects with large deformations and its application in video-based face recognition with large expression variations.

## REFERENCES

1. T. F. Cootes, G. J. Edwards, and C. J. Taylor, Active appearance models. *IEEE Trans. Pattern Anal. Mach. Intelli.*, **23**(6):681–685, 2001.
2. I. Matthews and S. Baker, Active appearance models revisited. *Int. J. Comput. Vis.* **60**(2):135–164, 2004.
3. D. Freedman and M. Turek, Illumination-invariant tracking via graph cuts, in *Proceedings of IEEE Conference on Computer Vision and Pattern Recognition*, 2005.

4. M. A. O. Vasilescu and D. Terzopoulos, Multilinear independent components analysis, *Proc. of IEEE Conf. on Computer Vision and Pattern Recognition*, **1**:547–553, 2005.

5. A. M. Elgammal and C. S. Lee, Separating style and content on a nonlinear manifold, *Proc. of IEEE Conf. on Computer Vision and Pattern Recognition*, **1**:478–485, 2004.

6. D. Vlasic, M. Brand, H. Pfister, and J. Popovic, Face transfer with multilinear models, *ACM Transactions on Graphics(TOG)*, 2005, pp. 426–433.

7. K. C. Lee, J. Ho, M. H. Yang, and D. J. Kriegman, Video-based face recognition using probabilistic appearance manifolds, *Proc. of IEEE Conf. on Computer Vision and Pattern Recognition*, **1**:313–320, 2003.

8. W. Zhao, R. Chellappa, P. J. Phillips, and A. Rosenfeld, Face recognition: A literature survey, *ACM Trans.* **35**(4):399–458, 2003.

9. P. J. Phillips, P. J. Grother, R. J. Micheals, D. M. Blackburn, E. Tabassi, and J. M. Bone, Face recognition vendor test 2002: Evaluation report, Technical Report NISTIR 6965, http://www.frvt.org, 2003.

10. P. J. Phillips et al. Overview of the face recognition grand challenge, *Proceedings of IEEE Conference on Computer Vision and Pattern Recognition*, **1**:947–954, 2005.

11. R. Basri and D.W. Jacobs, Lambertian reflectance and linear subspaces, *IEEE Trans. Pattern Anal. Mach. Intelli.* **25**(2):218–233, 2003.

12. R. Ramamoorthi and P. Hanrahan, On the relationship between radiance and irradiance: Determining the illumination from images of a convex Lambertian object, *J. Opt. Soc. Am. A* **18**(10), October 2001.

13. Y. Xu and A. Roy-Chowdhury. Integrating motion, Illumination and structure in video sequences, with applications in illumination-invariant tracking, *IEEE Trans. on Pattern Anal. and Mac. Intelli.*, May 2007.

14. L. D. Lathauwer, B. D. Moor, and J. Vandewalle, A multillinear singular value decomposition, *SIAM J. Matrix Anal. Appl.* **21**(4):1253–1278, 2000.

15. S. Baker and I. Matthews, Lucas-kanade 20 years on: A unifying framework, *Int. J. Comput. Vis.* **56**(3):221–255, 2004.

16. G. D. Hager and P. N. Belhumeur, Efficient region tracking with parametric models of geometry and illumination, *IEEE Trans. Pattern Anal. Mach. Intelli.*, **20**(10):1025–1039, 1998.

17. Y. Xu and A. Roy-Chowdhury. Inverse compositional estimation of 3D pose and lighting in dynamic scenes, *IEEE Trans. on Pattern Anal. and Mach. Intelli.*, July 2008.

18. V. Blanz and T. Vetter. Face recognition based on fitting a 3D morphable model, *IEEE Trans. Pattern Anal. Mach. Intelli.*, **25**(9):1063–1074, 2003.

19. L. Zhang and D. Samaras, Face recognition from a single training image under arbitrary unknown lighting using spherical harmonics, *IEEE Trans. Pattern Anal. Mach. Intell.* **28**(3):351–363, 2006.

20. V. Blanz, P. Grother, P. Phillips, and T. Vetter, Face recognition based on frontal views generated from non-frontal images, *Proc. of IEEE Conf. on Computer Vision and Pattern Recognition*, **2**:454–461, 2005.

21. X. Liu and T. Chen, Video-based face recognition using adaptive hidden markov models, *Proc. of IEEE Conf. on Computer Vision and Pattern Recognition*, **1**:340–345.

22. S. Zhou, V. Krueger, and R. Chellappa, Probabilistic recognition of human faces from video, *Computer Vision and Image Understanding (CVIU) (special issue on Face Recognition)* **91**:214–245, 2003.

23. S. Zhou, R. Chellappa, and B. Moghaddam, Visual tracking and recognition using appearance-adaptive models in particle filters, *IEEE Trans. on Image Processing (TIP)* **11**:1434–1456, 2004.

24. J. Fisher, R. Cipolla, O. Arandjelovic, G. Shakhnarovich, and T. Darrell, Face recognition with image sets using manifold density divergence, *Proc. of IEEE Conf. on Computer Vision and Pattern Recognition*, 1:581–588, 2005.

25. O. Arandjelovic and R. Cipolla, An illumination invariant face recognition system for access control using video, in *British Machine Vision Conference*, 2004.

26. C. Xie, B. V. K. Vijaya Kumar, S. Palanivel, and B. Yegnanarayana, A still-to-video face verification system using advanced correlation filters, in *First International Conference on Biometric Authentication*, 2004.

27. H. Wang and N. Ahuja, Facial expression decomposition, *IEEE Int. Conference Comput. Vision*, **2**:958 – 965, 2003.

28. A. Roy-Chowdhury and R. Chellappa, Face reconstruction from monocular video using uncertainty analysis and a generic model, *Comput. Vis. Image Understanding* **91**(1–2):188–213, 2003.

29. K.W. Bowyer and Chang, A survey of 3D and multimodal 3D+2D face recognition, in *Face Processing: Advanced Modeling and Methods*, Academic Press, New York, 2005.

30. T. Darrell, G. Shakhnarovich, and J. W. Fisher. Face recognition from long-term observations, in *European Conference on Computer Vision*, 2002.

31. Y. Xu and A. Roy-Chowdhury, Pose and illumination invariant registration and tracking for video-based face recognition, in *IEEE Computer Society Workshop on Biometrics (in association with CVPR)*, 2006.

# Chapter 8

# A Biologically Inspired Model for the Simultaneous Recognition of Identity and Expression

**Donald Neth and Aleix M. Martinez**

## 8.1 INTRODUCTION

Faces provide a wide range of information about a person's identity, race, sex, age, and emotional state. In most cases, humans easily derive such information by processes that appear rapid and automatic. However, upon closer inspection, one finds these processes to be diverse and complex. In this chapter the perception of identity and emotion is examined. We argue that the two cannot be studied independently of each other because the internal computational processes are intertwined. Next, a computational model is developed for the processing of expression variant face images. This model is then applied to matching the identity of face images with differing expression. Finally, the model is used to classify expressions from face images.

### 8.1.1 Perception of Identity and Emotion

Historically, research on human face perception has taken two perspectives. The first involves the recognition of individual identity through perception of the face. The second involves the perception of emotional expression from the face. This division between facial recognition and perception of emotional expression has its roots in

*Biometrics: Theory, Methods, and Applications.* Edited by Boulgouris, Plataniotis, and Micheli-Tzanakou
Copyright © 2010 the Institute of Electrical and Electronics Engineers, Inc.

clinical observations. In a condition known as *prosopagnosia*, patients are unable to recognize faces of people familiar to them while perception of expression remains relatively intact [1]. This condition typically results from brain injury or stroke; however, some cases of congenital prosopagnosia have been observed [2]. The preservation of emotional perception amidst a loss of recognition suggests that two relatively independent systems are involved in face perception. A condition known as Capgra's delusion offers complementary support to this theory [3]. Capgra's delusion is the belief that significant others are no longer who they were. Instead, they are thought to have been replaced by doubles, impostors, robots, or aliens. Patients with Capgra's delusion are able to recognize faces; however, they deny their authenticity. While prosopagnosia is the inability to recognize previously familiar faces, there is some evidence that the ability to discriminate familiar faces is retained outside of conscious awareness—a normal elevated skin conductance is observed in response to familiar faces. Thus, prosopagnosia can be characterized as a failure in conscious face recognition coupled with an intact unconscious or covert mechanism. Conversely, Capgra's delusion may be characterized as an intact conscious face recognition system coupled with a failure in covert or unconscious recognition. The anomalous perceptual experiences arising from failure of the covert processing system must be explained by the individual to himself or herself—the delusions arise as an attempt to explain or make sense of an abnormal experience.

While prosopagnosia and Capgra's delusion offer compelling illustrations of two major facets of face perception, there is still considerable debate as to the level of independence between face recognition and perception of expression. Nonetheless, past research has tended to treat these two aspects of face perception as involving relatively separate systems. Hence, prior research in face recognition and perception of emotional expression will first be reviewed separately. Finally, an attempt will be made to reconcile the two perspectives.

## 8.2  FACE RECOGNITION

There is evidence suggesting that the ability to accurately recognize faces relies on an innate cortical face module. The existence of discrete regions of the cerebral cortex specialized for face perception was investigated by Kanwisher, McDermott, and Chun [4]. Face perception was defined to include any higher-level visual processing of faces ranging from the detection of a face as a face to the extraction of information relative to identity, gaze, mood, or sex. A region of the fusiform gyrus that responded differentially to passive face viewing compared to passive object viewing was found and has been subsequently described as the *fusiform face area* (FFA). This region did not simply respond to animal or human images or body parts but to faces in particular. Additionally, this region generalizes to respond to images of faces taken from a different viewpoint with considerably different low-level features from the original set of face images.

In contrast to the notion that humans are hardwired for face perception, it has been suggested that face recognition is a natural consequence of extensive experience with faces. As a model of this process, a *flexible process map* was proposed by Tarr and Gauthier [5]. This model is based on the observation that a number of extrastriate areas are involved in visual object processing and recognition. Through experience with particular visual geometries, associations arise linking task-appropriate recognition strategies that automatically recruit components of the process map. The strong activation of the fusiform gyrus in face processing is thought to be a result of the extensive experience with faces common to all humans. Recognition of faces typically occurs at an individual or subcategory level. In contrast, most objects encountered in daily life are differentiated at a category level. It is suggested that the fusiform gyrus represents a cortical area in which subcategory discrimination occurs. The ubiquitous experience with faces, and the subsequent development of expertise, is reflected in the activation of the fusiform gyrus in face processing. However, this should not be interpreted to mean the fusiform gyrus is a dedicated module for face processing alone. In a study of the involvement of the fusiform gyrus with expert-level discrimination, subjects were trained to discriminate novel objects known as greebles [6]. Functional imaging revealed increased activation of the right fusiform gyrus during expert-level discrimination tasks. The authors hold that expertise is an important factor leading to the specialization of the fusiform gyrus in face processing.

An interactive specialization view in which cortical specialization is an emergent product of the interaction of both intrinsic and extrinsic factors has been proposed [7]. According to this view, the development of face recognition relies on two processes. The first process, termed *Conspec*, is a system operating from birth that biases the newborn to orient toward faces. It is mediated by primitive subcortical circuits. The second process, termed *Conlern*, relies on a system sensitive to the effects of experience through passive exposure to faces. It is mediated by the developing cortical circuits in the ventral visual pathway. Newborn infants show evidence of recognizing facial identity. Before the specialization of cortical circuits, face stimuli are processed in the same manner as other visual stimuli. This ability is then augmented as the Conlern system emerges at around 6–8 weeks of age. Newborns also exhibit preferential tracking; however, it is not specific to the fine details of facial features but relies on the arrangements of the elements comprising the face—that is, configural information. This preferential tracking declines sharply at 4–6 weeks of age, similar to the decline seen in other reflex-like behaviors thought to be due to inhibition by developing cortical circuits. In addition, it has been observed that newborns orient to patterns with a higher density of elements in the upper visual field. Infants also demonstrate the ability to recognize individual facial identity, gazing longer at the mother's face than the face of a stranger. Cortical development impacts the mental representation of facial identity. This representation is thought to be multidimensional in that it encodes multiple aspects of a face. While the specific dimensions of this face space are not clearly delineated, they are thought to be learned rather than being prespecified at birth. For an infant, the face space will contain fewer entries during development than in adulthood. Furthermore, infants and children are less likely to use a large number of dimensions since relatively few are required to distinguish the smaller number of faces in their environments. Infants develop a face-space at around 3 months of age and begin to form categories based on the faces they see.

The authors offer an alternative to the view that face processing is merely an example of acquired expertise. They propose that it is special in that the timing of particular visual inputs during development is critical for normal development. The regions of the ventral occipito-temporal cortex have the potential to become specialized for face recognition but require experience with faces for the specialization to arise.

A similar conclusion is drawn by Nelson [8], who characterizes face recognition as an important adaptive function that has been conserved across species. Monkeys have been observed to utilize a process similar to that of human adults when studying faces—the internal parts of the face are more significant than the external parts. In humans, as in monkeys, it is adaptive for the young infant to recognize potential caretakers. At around 4 months of age, human infants exhibit superior recognition performance for upright faces versus inverted faces. This suggests that they have developed a schema for faces and have begun to view faces as a special class of stimuli. Between 3 and 7 months, the ability to distinguish mother from stranger becomes more robust. It is held that the development of face recognition is an *experience-expectant* process. Such a process refers to the development of skills and abilities that are common to all members of the species and depends on exposure to certain experiences occurring over a particular period of time in development. The involvement of the inferotemporal cortex in face recognition may have been selected for through evolutionary pressures, or the properties of the neurons and synapses in this region may be particularly tuned to the task of face recognition. Such specialization occurs rapidly within the first months of life. As experience with faces increases, perceptual learning leads to further specialization of this area.

## 8.2.1  Configural Processing

Maurer, Le Grand, and Mondloch [9] identified three types of configural face processing: (1) sensitivity to first-order relations, (2) holistic processing, and (3) sensitivity to second-order relations. Sensitivity to first-order relations refers to the ability to identify a stimulus as a face based on the basic configuration of two eyes above a nose above a mouth. Holistic processing refers to the largely automatic tendency to process a face as a gestalt rather than isolated features. Second-order relations refer to the distance among internal features.

The role of the fusiform face area in the extraction of configural information from faces and non-faces was investigated by Yovel and Kanwisher [10]. Two tasks were matched for overall difficulty: Subjects were asked to discriminate sequentially presented image pairs of faces or houses that could differ in (1) only the spatial relation between parts and (2) only in the shapes of the parts. The study was extended by repeating the approach with inverted image pairs. Thus, four test conditions were used. The FFA showed a significantly higher activation to faces than houses but showed no difference between the part and configuration tasks. The inversion effect was absent for houses but was equally strong for part and configuration tasks for houses. The authors conclude that face perception mechanisms are domain-specific (i.e., engaged by faces regardless of processing type) rather than process-specific (i.e., engaged in specific process depending on task type). The similar results for configuration and part tasks is contrary to the commonly held view that face processing is largely configural and that the inversion effect results from the disruption of configural processing.

## 8.2.2   Cognitive Model of Face Recognition

In an influential paper, Bruce and Young [11] proposed a functional model to describe the process of face recognition (Figure 8.1). An abstract visual representation must be established to mediate recognition even though an identical image is rarely viewed on successive occasions. This demonstrates an ability to derive structural codes that capture aspects of the facial structure essential to distinguish one face from another. Visually derived semantic codes are useful in describing such factors as age and sex. Identity-specific semantic codes contain information about a person's occupation, where he might be encountered, and so on. It is the recovery of identity-specific semantic codes that creates the feeling of knowing. A name code exists independently of the identity-specific code. Face recognition units (FRU) are proposed that contain stored structural codes describing each face known to a person. FRUs can access identity-specific semantic codes held in associative memory known as person identity nodes. Names are accessed only through the person identity nodes. Names are thought to be abstract phonological representations stored separately from semantic representations but accessed through them.

Ellis [12] employed the Bruce and Young model to explain various blocks in facial recognition. A temporary block between semantic and name retrieval is

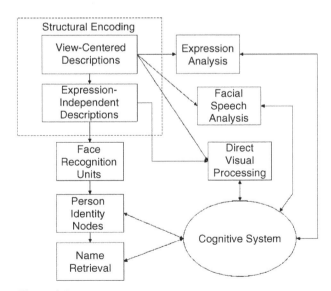

**Figure 8.1.** Cognitive model of face processing. (Adapted from Bruce and Young [11].)

responsible for errors in which the perceiver can remember everything about a person except his/her name. This theory disallows errors in which the person's name is known but the semantic information is not. While parallel access to semantics and spoken word-forms is believed to occur for the recognition of familiar written words, this does not seem to be the case for faces. Several factors influence the speed and accuracy of familiar face recognition. In repetition priming, a face will be recognized as familiar more quickly when it has been viewed previously. Repetition priming has been observed primarily in familiarity decisions and is not found in expression or sex decisions. Another factor affecting face processing is the distinctiveness of the face. In familiarity tasks, distinctiveness results in faster recognition than with more typical faces. Finally, in associative priming, past co-occurrences between familiar stimuli allow one to predict the recognition of the other. For example, if a face to be recognized is preceded by a related and familiar face, recognition will occur more rapidly.

## 8.3  FACIAL EXPRESSION OF EMOTION

Ekman and Friesen [13], expanding on the work of Darwin [14], identified six universal emotional expressions: anger, sadness, fear, surprise, happiness, and disgust. Ekman [15] extended his earlier work by compiling a list of basic emotions including amusement, anger, contempt, contentment, disgust, embarrassment, excitement, fear, guilt, pride in achievement, relief, sadness/distress, satisfaction, sensory pleasure, and shame. According to Ekman, these emotions share basic characteristics. They are distinctive universal signals with specific physiological concomitants. They provide automatic appraisal, in particular, to distinctive universals in antecedent events. Emotions typically have a quick onset, which is essential for their adaptive value. It is also adaptive for the response changes to be of brief duration unless the emotion is evoked again. In an effort to quantify facial expressions, Ekman and Friesen [13] developed the Facial Action Coding System (FACS). Facial expressions were extensively examined and their component motions were determined. Forty-four separate action units (AUs) were identified with five levels of intensity ranging from A to E. Thirty AUs are related to contraction of specific facial muscles. Eight AUs describe different movements related to head orientation, while four AUs are used to describe eye direction. While the use of FACS allows a high degree of refinement in classifying facial expressions, Ekman's approach to emotion and its expression remains categorical [15].

In contrast, a number of researchers have proposed continuous models of emotion and facial expressions [16–21]. The circumplex model proposed by Russell [17] represents emotions in two dimensions reflecting pleasure and arousal. The horizontal dimension ranges from extreme displeasure (e.g., agony) to extreme pleasure (e.g., ecstasy). The vertical dimension ranges from sleep at one extreme to frenetic excitement at the other. These two dimensions form a continuous space without clearly delineated boundaries or prototypical emotions. This model plays a central role in Russell's [21] concept of *core affect*, which is the neurophysiological state accessible as the simplest, nonreflective feelings. Core affect is always present but may subside into the background of consciousness. The prototypical emotions described in categorical approaches map into the core affect model but hold no special status. According to Russell [21], prototypical emotions are rare; what is typically categorized as proto-typical may in fact reflect patterns different from these of other states classified as the same prototype. He states that emotional life comprises the continuous fluctuations in core affect, the ongoing perception of affective qualities, frequent attribution of core affect to an external stimulus, and instrumental behaviors in response to that external stimulus. The many degrees and variations of these components will rarely fit the pattern associated with a prototype and will more likely reflect a combination of var-ious prototypes to varying extents. While Russell makes a compelling argument for the continuous nature of emotion, humans appear predisposed to experience certain continuously varying stimuli as belonging to distinct categories.

Facial expressions are controlled by both pyramidal and extrapyramidal tracts that provide voluntary and automatic control, respectively. Voluntary control over facial muscles is considered a hallmark of human nonverbal expression and may be due to the articulatory demands of human language [22]. However, there are notable differences between posed and spontaneous expressions. Such differences are particu-larly evident in smiling. The Duchenne smile is described as the combined contraction of the *zygomaticus major* and *orbicularis oculi* muscles and is thought to occur with spontaneously occurring enjoyment [23]. False smiles are described as those made to convince another that enjoyment is occurring when it is not. Masking smiles are made to conceal negative emotions. Miserable smiles denote a willingness to endure an un-pleasant situation. The Duchenne smile was found to occur during solitary enjoyment and was associated with greater left-hemisphere anterior temporal and parietal activa-tion compared to other smiles [23]. Differences in the dynamic features of social and spontaneous smiles were investigated by Cohn and Schmidt [24]. Spontaneous smiles exhibit characteristics of automatic movement. Automatic movements are thought to be preprogrammed and are characterized by a consistent relationship between max-imum duration and amplitude of movement. Posed (social) smiles exhibit a far less consistent relationship between duration and amplitude. Smiles comprise an initial onset phase, a peak, and an offset phase. The onset phase was used in this study because it provides the most conspicuous change in the face as perceived by human observers. Amplitude was found to be smaller in spontaneous smiles than in social smiles. Timing and amplitude measures were used in a linear discriminant classifier resulting in a 93% recognition rate. With timing measures alone, the recognition rate was 89%.

Gallese, Keysers, and Rizzolatti [25] suggest that mirror mechanisms in the brain allow the direct understanding of the meaning of action and emotions of others by internally replicating (or simulating) them without any reflective mediation. Thus, conceptual reasoning is not necessary for such understanding. When action is ob-served, there is concurrent activation of part of the same motor areas used to perform the action. Similarly, it is thought that mirror mechanisms allow individuals to simulate the emotional state of others. Within the cerebral cortex, the superior temporal sulcus (STS) is activated by observation of movements of the eyes and head, movements of the mouth, and meaningful hand movements. Some groups of cells respond preferentially to hand movements. Typically, the groups respond better to a particular kind of hand movement. The responsiveness of the cell group is independent of the object acted upon and the speed at which the hand moves. Additionally, the responsiveness of the cell group is greater when the movement is goal-directed. Observation of whole-body movements activates a posterior region of the STS. The STS is also activated by static images of the face and body. Taken together, this suggests that the STS is sensitive to stimuli that signal the actions of another individual [26].

Valentine [27] makes the distinction between identification and recognition in that identification requires a judgment pertaining to a specific stimulus while recognition requires only a judgment that the face has been seen before. He posits the capability to reliably distinguish friend from foe would confer an evolutionary advantage over simply knowing that a face has been seen before.

## 8.3.1 Categorical Perception of Expression and Emotion

Categorical perception is a psychophysical phenomenon that may occur when a set of stimuli ranging along a physical continuum is divided into categories. Categorical perception involves a greater sensitivity to changes in a stimulus across category boundaries than when the same change occurs within a single category [28]. Categorical perception has been observed in a variety of stimuli including colors [29] and musical tones [30], among many others. There is significant evidence that facial expressions are perceived as belonging to distinct categories. In a study by Calder et al. [31], the categorical perception of facial expressions based on morphed photographic images was investigated. Three expression continua were employed: happiness–sadness, sadness–anger, and anger–fear. Subjects were first asked to identify the individual stimuli by placing them along particular expression continua. Subjects were then asked to perform a discrimination task in which stimuli A, B, and X were presented sequentially. Subjects were asked whether X was the same as A or B. Results indicate that each expression continuum was perceived as two distinct categories separated by a boundary. It was further found that discrimination was more accurate for across-boundary rather than for within-boundary pairs.

In a classic study, Young et al. [32] investigated whether facial expressions are perceived as continuously varying along underlying dimensions or as belonging to discrete categories. Dimensional approaches were used to predict the consequences of morphing one facial expression to another. Transitions between facial expressions vary in their effects, depending on how each expression is positioned in the emotion space. Some transitions between two expressions may involve indeterminate regions or a third emotion. In contrast, a transition from one category to another may not involve passing through a region which itself may be another category. In this case, changes in perception should be abrupt. Four experiments were conducted using facial expressions from the Ekman and Friesen series [13]. All possible pairwise combinations of emotions were morphed and presented randomly. Subjects identified intermediate morphs as belonging to distinct expression categories corresponding to the prototype endpoints. No indeterminate regions or identification of a third emotion were observed. This supports the view that expressions are perceived categorically rather than by locating them along underlying dimensions. The authors suggest that categorical perception reflects the underlying organization of human categorization abilities.

## 8.3.2  Human Face Perception—Integration

Human face perception engages the visual system in processing multiple aspects of faces including form, motion, color, and depth. Visual information processing in humans has predominantly developed along two fairly segregated pathways: one for form and another for motion. Projections from the primary visual cortex form a *dorsal stream* that progresses to portions of the middle temporal lobe (MT), the medial superior temporal area (MST), and portions of the parietal lobe associated with visuospatial processing. The *ventral stream*, which is associated with object recognition tasks involving texture and shape discrimination, comprises projections from the primary visual cortex to the inferior temporal cortex. Behavioral and lesion studies support a functional distinction between the ventral and dorsal streams with motion processing occurring primarily in the dorsal stream and shape discrimination occurring primarily in the ventral stream. Ungerleider, Courtney, and Haxby [33] suggest that the functional distinction extends to the prefrontal cortex and the working memory system: Ventrolateral areas are involved primarily in working memory for objects while the dorsolateral areas are primarily involved with spatial working memory. The organization of the human visual systems reflects the importance of form and motion in the processing of visual information. Thus, it is reasonable to consider face processing from this perspective.

Many neural structures are involved in both recognition and perception of facial expressions. A distributed neural system for face perception, including bilateral regions in the lateral inferior occipital gyri (IOG), the lateral fusiform gyrus (LFG), and posterior superior temporal sulcus (STS), was investigated in an fMRI study by Hoffman and Haxby [34]. It was found that the representation of face identity is more dependent on the IOG and LFG than the STS. The STS is involved in perception of changeable aspects of the face such as eye gaze. Perception of eye gaze also activated the spatial recognition system in the intraparietal sulcus, which was thought to encode the direction of the eye gaze and to focus attention in that direction. These findings were integrated into a distributed neural model for face perception formulated by Haxby, Hoffman, and Gobbini [35]. The core system comprises three brain regions involved in separate but interconnected tasks (Figure 8.2). The lateral fusiform gyrus processes invariant aspects of faces and is involved in the perception of identity. The STS processes the dynamic aspects of faces including expression, eye gaze, and lip movement. The inferior occipital gyri are involved in the early perception of facial features. A key concept of the model is that face perception is accomplished through a coordinated participation of multiple regions.

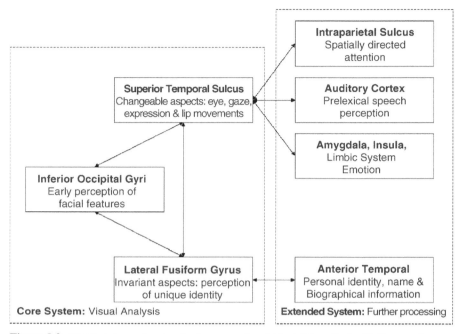

**Figure 8.2.** Distributed neural system for face perception. (Adapted from Haxby, Hoffman, and Gobbini [35].)

According to the Bruce and Young model, recognition and expression processing function independently. Much of the research reviewed above suggests a partial independence of the two processes. However, complete independence is unlikely [36, 37] and it remains to be determined whether their interaction is direct or indirect [38]. Viewed from the perspective of the visual system, invariant aspects of the face should engage the ventral stream while variable aspects or motions should engage the dorsal stream. There is also evidence that invariant aspects of the face facilitate recognition of a person's identity while the variable aspects allow inferences regarding that person's state of mind. However, Roark et al. [39] suggest that supplemental information can be derived from facial motion in the form of dynamic facial signatures that can augment recognition of familiar faces. Such signatures should be processed by the dorsal visual stream ultimately engaging the STS. The authors also speculate that motion can be useful in enhancing the representation of invariant aspects of the face. Such structure-from-motion analysis also engages the dorsal stream. They suggest that these concepts be integrated into Haxby's distributed neural model.

## 8.4  MODEL OF EXPRESSION-VARIANT PROCESSING

While Haxby's distributed neural system is a fairly comprehensive model, it is still not clear by which mechanism the brain successfully accomplishes the matching of two or more face images when differences in facial expression make the (local and global) appearance of these images different from one another. There seems to be a consensus that faces are processed holistically rather than locally, but there is not yet consensus on whether information on facial expression is passed to the identification process to aid recognition of individuals or not. As mentioned in the previous section in this chapter, some models proposed in the past suggest that to recognize people's identity we use a process that is completely decoupled from that of recognizing the facial expression [11]. Others propose that a connection must exist between the two processes [40]. Psychophysical data exist in favor of and against each view [41–47]. Martinez [38] posed a fundamental question in face recognition: *Does the identification process receive information from or interact with the process of facial expression recognition to aid in the recognition of individuals?* It has been noted that subjects are slower in identifying happy and angry faces than faces with neutral expressions. A model was proposed in which a motion estimation process is coupled with the processing of the invariant aspects of the face. Both of these processes contribute to recognition of identity and the perception of facial expressions. The key element is the addition of a deformation of the face (DF) module which calculates the apparent physical deformation between faces by computing the motion field between faces to be matched. A separate module processes the invariant aspects of the face. Both processes occur in tandem, and the outputs of both are fed into two independent processes: one for the recognition of identity and the other for analysis of expression. The addition of the DF module offers an explanation for increases in recognition time for faces with larger deformations: The more complex the deformation, the longer it takes to process the implied motion. According to this model, it is now logical to expect the identification of faces to be slower for those cases where a larger deformation of the face exists, since we need to go through the motion estimation module DF. The more complex the facial expression, the more time (generally) needed to compute an approximation of the muscle activity of the face (see *Results*). For example, the DF module shown in Figure 8.3 does not need to estimate any motion for the neutral facial expression case, but requires the computation of an approximation of the motion of a smile and other facial expressions.

We hypothesize that the motion field is necessary (or, at least, useful) to successfully match the local and global features of a set of faces when those bear distinct facial expressions. It has been shown that motion plays an important role in recognizing identity and facial expressions in a sequence of images [48–50]. In addition, uncommon deformations or uncommon sampling times disrupt identification of individuals [51] and of facial expressions [52]. This seems reasonable, because the local texture of a face changes considerably as the facial expression also changes. Facial expressions change the local texture of each of local face areas which appear quite distinct under different expressions. A classification (or identification) algorithm, however, will need to find where the invariant features are. The motion field (deformation) between the two images that one wants to match can be used to determine the features that have changed the least between the two images and, thus, which are the best candidates for matching purposes.

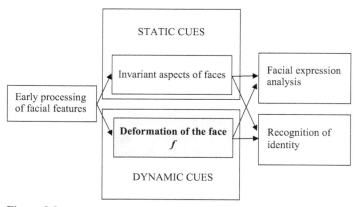

**Figure 8.3.** Depiction of the different processes of the model presented in this chapter. The modules dedicated to the recognition of identity and expression are dissociated, although they both obtain information from the common process DF (deformation of the face) and from the processes that compute static cues. This is key to explain the psychophysical date described in the past.

## 8.4.1  Recognition of Identity

Consider two different images, $\mathbf{I}_1$ and $\mathbf{I}_2$, both of $n$ pixels. We can redefine the images as vectors taking values in an $n$-dimensional space. We shall denote this as $\mathbf{V}_1$ and $\mathbf{V}_2$, with $\mathbf{V}_i \in \mathbb{R}^n$. The advantage of doing this is that it allows comparisons of the images by means of vector operations such as subtraction

$$\|\mathbf{V}_1 - \mathbf{V}_2\|, \tag{8.1}$$

where $\| \cdot \|$ denotes the $L_2$ norm (i.e., Euclidean distance). In this definition stated here, we assume that all faces have been aligned (with respect to the main facial features) in such a way that the eyes, mouths, noses, and so on, of each of the images are at roughly the same pixel coordinates (e.g., see references 53 and 54). The approach defined above, in Eq. (8.1), has proven to perform well when frontal face images with similar facial expressions are compared to each other. However, this comparison becomes unstable when matching face images bearing different facial expressions [52]; hence pixels can now carry information of different features.

The incorporation of the *DF* process in our model allows us to represent face processing as

$$\|f^{-1}(\mathbf{V}_1 - \mathbf{V}_2)\|, \tag{8.2}$$

where $f$ is a function proportional to the motion of each pixel—that is, the movement representing the facial expression of the test image. Intuitively, $f$ is a function that keeps correspondences between the pixels of the first and second images. Equation (8.2) can be interpreted as follows: Pixels (or local areas) that have been deformed largely due to local musculature activity will have a low weight, whereas pixels that are less affected by those changes will gain importance. We can formally define $f^{-1}$

as taking values linearly inverse to those of $f$, that is,

$$MAX_F - \|\mathbf{F}_i\|, \tag{8.3}$$

where $\mathbf{F}$ is the motion flow (i.e., motion between two images), $\mathbf{F}_i$ is the motion vector at the $i$th pixel, and $MAX_F = \max_{\forall i} \|\mathbf{F}_i\|$ (the magnitude of the largest motion vector in the image).

Thus the value of $f$ corresponds to the outcome of the DF process. Note that $f$ defines the face deformation (motion) between two images and, therefore, can also be used to estimate the facial expression of a new incoming face image. As mentioned earlier, experimental data support this belief.

## 8.4.2 Motion Estimation

Visual motion between two images can be expressed mathematically by local deformations that occur in small intervals of time, $\delta t$, as

$$\mathbf{I}(x, y, t) = \mathbf{I}(x + u\delta t, y + v\delta t, t + \delta t), \tag{8.4}$$

where $\mathbf{I}(x, y, t)$ is the image value at point $(x, y)$ at time $t$, $(u, v)$ are the horizontal and the vertical image velocities at $(x, y)$, and $\delta t$ is considered to be small [55]. We note that in our model we have $f = (u, v)$.

If we assume that the motion field (i.e., the pixel correspondences between the two images) is small at each pixel location, the motion estimator can be represented by the first-order Taylor series expansion as

$$E_D = \int \int \rho \left( \mathbf{I}_x u + \mathbf{I}_y v + \mathbf{I}_t \right) dxdy, \tag{8.5}$$

where $(\mathbf{I}_x, \mathbf{I}_y)$ and $\mathbf{I}_t$ are the spatial and time derivatives of the image, and $\rho$ is an *estimator*.

To resolve the above equation, it is necessary to add an additional constraint. The most common one is the spatial coherence constraint [55], which embodies the assumption that neighboring pixels in an image are likely to belong to the same surface, and therefore a smoothness in the flow is expected. The first-order model of this second constraint is given by

$$E_S = \int \int \rho \left( \nabla(u, v) \right) dxdy, \tag{8.6}$$

where $\nabla$ represents the gradient.

Visual motion is determined by minimizing the regularization problem

$$E = E_D + \lambda E_S. \tag{8.7}$$

Although the objective function $E$ is nonlinear (and a direct solution does not exist for minimizing it), a convex approximation can be obtained [56]. The global minimum can then be determined iteratively.

This procedure is most effective when the object displacements between consecutive images are small. When object displacements are large, a coarse-to-fine strategy can be used. In the current work, the pyramid method of [57] was used. In order to satisfy the small-displacement assumption, we begin with a reduced-resolution representation of the images. The optical flow is computed for the low-resolution images and then projected to the next level of the pyramid where the images in the sequence have a higher resolution. At each level of the pyramid, the optical flow computed from the previous level is used to warp the images in the sequence. This process is repeated until the flow has been computed at the original resolution. The final flow field is obtained by combining the flow information of each of the levels of the pyramid. The number of levels on the pyramid will be dictated by the largest motion in the sequence of images.

The approach to motion estimation defined above may result in biased results whenever the scene's illumination in the sample and test face images are distinct. To resolve this issue, one can include the modeling of this illumination variation in Eqs. (8.4 and 8.5). Negahdaripour [58] extends the above definition of motion flow to include radiometric changes into its computation. This definition requires an extension of the 2D motion field vector $(u, v)$ to a 3D transformation field given by $(u, v, \delta e)$. The last component, $\delta e$, describes the radiometric transformation of the image sequence. This provides us with a new model for the motion, given by

$$\mathbf{I}(x + u\delta t, y + v\delta t, t + \delta t) = \mathbf{M}(x, y, t)\mathbf{I}(x, y, t) + \mathbf{C}(x, y, t), \qquad (8.8)$$

in which the brightness at a pixel in two consecutive images is related via the motion parameters $u$ and $v$ and the radiometric parameters $\mathbf{M}$ and $\mathbf{C}$, as shown. Here, $\mathbf{M}$ defines light changes resulting in multiplier variations (e.g., change in homogenous or nonhomogeneous intensity), while $\mathbf{C}$ defines additive terms, such as cast shadows.

The data conservation constraint corresponding to Eq. (8.8) is

$$E_D = \int \int \rho(\mathbf{I}_x u + \mathbf{I}_y v + \mathbf{I}_t - (\mathbf{Im}_t + \mathbf{c}_t)), \qquad (8.9)$$

where $\mathbf{m}_t$ and $\mathbf{c}_t$ are the time derivatives of $\mathbf{M}$ and $\mathbf{C}$, respectively. Since we now have two more variables to estimate, the smoothness constraint needs also to include the following minimizations

$$E_M = \int \rho(\nabla \mathbf{m}_t) \quad \text{and} \quad E_C = \int \rho(\nabla \mathbf{c}_t). \qquad (8.10)$$

By using a robust function for $\rho(.)$, we can generate very precise estimates of the motion (i.e., DF) even under varying illumination, as we have shown in reference 59. Two examples of motion estimation between face images are shown in Figure 8.4.

## 8.4.3  Recognition of Expression

In our model, each facial expression is classified in a category according to the motion field of the face, $f$. The direction of motion is used to determine the class [60], while the magnitude of the motion can be used to specify the intensity of a given expression.

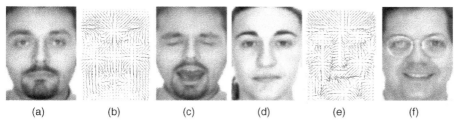

(a)          (b)          (c)          (d)          (e)          (f)

**Figure 8.4.** The motion estimation in (**b**) defines the muscle movement defining the expression change between (**a**) and (**c**). The motion estimation in (**e**) defines the expression and identity change between (**d**) and (**f**).

These two parts of the motion can be expressed mathematically as

$$S_{M_i} = \text{abs}(\|\mathbf{F_{t}}_i\| - \|\mathbf{F_{p}}_i\|) \quad \text{and} \quad S_{A_i} = \arccos \frac{\langle \mathbf{F_{t}}_i, \mathbf{F_{p}}_i \rangle}{\|\mathbf{F_{t}}_i\| \|\mathbf{F_{p}}_i\|}, \tag{8.11}$$

where $\mathbf{F_{t}}_i$ and $\mathbf{F_{p}}_i$ are the vector flows of the two expressions to be compared at the $i$th pixel, $\langle \mathbf{a}, \mathbf{b} \rangle$ represents the dot product of $\mathbf{a}$ and $\mathbf{b}$, $S_{M_i}$ is the similarity between the magnitude of the $i$th pixel in the two image flows, and $S_{A_i}$ is the similarity between the angles of the two vectors at pixel $i$.

While this method is normally used to compare two images (i.e., matching), it can also be used to classify (or identify) facial expressions within a group of prelearned categories. This comparison can be carried out at each pixel location or at specific areas that are known to be most discriminant for a given expression. We can formally express this as

$$S_M = \sum_{i=1}^{m} S_{M_i} \quad \text{and} \quad S_A = \sum_{i=1}^{m} \frac{S_{A_i}}{m_o}, \tag{8.12}$$

where $m$ is the number of pixels where comparison takes place, $m \leq n$, and $m_o$ is the total number of vectors in $m$ with magnitude greater than zero. Note that since the angle similarity can only be computed between actual vectors (of magnitude greater than zero), it is necessary to normalize $S_A$ by the number of comparisons to prevent biases toward images with associated small motions.

In order to appropriately select the value of $m$, it is convenient to search for those features (i.e., pixels) that best discriminate between categories and those that are most stable within categories. This can be accomplished by means of Fisher's linear discriminant analysis (LDA) [61] and variants [62, 63]. Formally, we define the within- and between-class scatter matrices of LDA as [61]

$$\mathbf{S}_W = \sum_{j=1}^{c} \sum_{i=1}^{N_j} (\mathbf{v}_{i,j} - \mu_j)(\mathbf{v}_{i,j} - \mu_j)^T \quad \text{and} \quad \mathbf{S}_B = \sum_{j=1}^{c} (\mu_j - \mu)(\mu_j - \mu)^T, \tag{8.13}$$

where $\mathbf{S}_W$ is the within-class scatter matrix, $\mathbf{S}_B$ is the between-class scatter matrix, $c$ is the number of classes, $N_j$ is the number of samples for class $j$, $\mathbf{v}_{i,j}$ is the $i$th sample of class $j$, $\mu_j$ is the mean vector of class $j$, and $\mu$ is the mean of all classes.

Due to singularity problems, it is generally difficult to compute the LDA transformation of large face images [60]. Additionally, $\mathbf{S}_B$ limits us to a maximum of $c - 1$ dimensions (where $c$ is the number of classes) [63]. Since we usually deal with small values of $c$ and it is known that LDA may perform poorly if the dimensionality of the space is small [64], it is convenient to only use that information which directly specifies the usefulness of each pixel. This is represented in the variances of each feature (pixel) within $\mathbf{S}_W$ and $\mathbf{S}_B$, which is given by the values at the diagonal of each of these matrices:

$$\hat{\mathbf{S}}_W = \mathrm{diag}(\mathbf{S}_W) \quad \text{and} \quad \hat{\mathbf{S}}_B = \mathrm{diag}(\mathbf{S}_B). \tag{8.14}$$

By first finding those pixels (areas) of the face that are most different among classes ($\hat{\mathbf{S}}_B$) and then selecting those that are most similar across samples of the same class ($\hat{\mathbf{S}}_W$), we can build a classifier that computes the values of $S_A$ in a smaller set of pixels. The result is a classifier that is generally more robust and efficient than one that uses all the pixels of the image.

This model allows us to predict that classification of faces into very distinct categories (e.g., happy and neutral) will be easier than when the two facial expressions are alike (e.g., angry and neutral). As a consequence, response times should be smaller for more distinct classes than for more similar classes. Since the model uses the DF procedure described above, we can also predict that when classifying faces within two distinct groups, those that involve larger motions will usually have longer RT. Similarly, those facial expressions that are more difficult to be classified or are more alike will require the analysis of additional local parts, resulting in longer RT. When a face cannot be reliably classified within one of the categories by looking at the most discriminant areas, we will need to extend our comparison to other areas of the face.

## 8.5    EXPERIMENTAL RESULTS: RECOGNITION OF IDENTITY

### 8.5.1    Computational Model

We present an analysis of the computational model defined above. This analysis will facilitate a later comparison with human performance.

#### 8.5.1.1    Performance

It is now possible to test two important points advanced in the previous section: (a) how the suppression of the DF process would affect the identification of known individuals and (b) how the identification of happy and angry faces is now slower than the recognition of neutral expression faces. In these experiments, we will use the face images of 100 individuals of the AR database [65]. The images of this database for one of the subjects are shown in Figure 8.5(a–d).

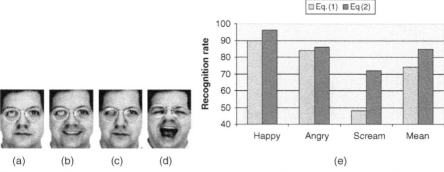

**Figure 8.5.** Examples of the following expressions: (**a**) neutral, (**b**) happy, (**c**) angry, and (**d**) scream. (**e**) The recognition rates obtained when matching: *i)* happy and neutral faces, *ii)* angry and neutral faces, and *iii)* cream and neutral faces. Note that when we incorporate the information of the DF process in our model (i.e. $f$), the results improve and the matching process becomes less sensitive to the differences in facial expression. Equation (8.1) indicates a simple Euclidean distance, and Eq. (8.2) the weighted measure given in Eq. (8.2). Adapted from Martinez [66].

As sample images we will use the neutral faces (Figure 8.5a). As test images (i.e., images to be matched with the sample ones), we will use the happy, angry, and scream faces (Figure 8.5b–d). For each of the test images, we will select the sample image that best matches it, as given by Eq. (8.2). If the retrieved image belongs to the same person (class) as the one in the testing image, we will say that our recognition was successful. Figure 8.5e shows the percentage of successful identifications. We have detailed the recognition rates for each of the facial expression images to show the dependency between the recognition of identity and facial expression. We have also shown, in this figure, what would happen if the DF process was damaged or absent. This is represented by omitting the value of $f$ in Eq. (8.2). The results of such damage as predicted by our model are obtained with Eq. (8.1) in Figure 8.5e [66].

### 8.5.1.2 *Computation Time*

As expressions increasingly diverge, the time required for the recognition of identity also increases. To calculate the time required to compute the motion field for each of the expressions, we need to determine (*i*) the number of coarse-to-fine (pyramid) levels required to compute the largest motions of the image and (*ii*) the number of iterations necessary to correctly calculate the minimum of the nonconvex function at each level of the pyramid.

For each of the facial expressions in the AR database (i.e., happy, angry, and scream) as well as for the neutral expression image, we have calculated the minimum number of iterations and levels of the pyramid required as follows. For each expression, we computed the motion fields, $f$, using levels of the pyramid that range from 1 to 4 . The results obtained when using $h + 1$ levels of the pyramid were compared to results obtained when only using $h$ levels. If the similarity in magnitude (as computed

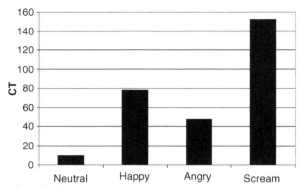

**Figure 8.6.** Shown here are the mean delays (computational time, CT) required to compute the motion fields, $f$, for each facial expression group.

by $S_M/m_o$) and angle ($S_A$) between the two ($h$ and $h + 1$) was below a threshold of one pixel, we determined that $h$ levels suffice for the computation of the motion in that image; otherwise $h + 1$ levels were necessary. This chosen value is referred to as $H$.

To determine the number of iterations required at each level of the pyramid, we compared the results obtained when using $g + 1$ and $g$ iterations. Again, if the comparison was below a threshold, we selected $g$; otherwise we selected $g + 1$. We will refer to this value as $G$. In this case, the threshold was 0.1 and $g$ was tested for the range of values from 10 to 50.

Now, we combine the two selected values into a single measure as $CT = G \times H$; that is, computational time equals the number of iterations necessary at each level multiplied by the number of levels needed. The results (mean across samples) are: *Neutral faces*: $H = 1$, $G = 10$, and $CT = 10$, *Happy faces*: $H = 3$, $G = 26$, and $CT = 78$, *Angry faces*: $H = 2.4$, $G = 20$, and $CT = 48$, *Scream faces*: $H = 4$, $G = 33$, and $CT = 152$. These results are plotted in the graphical representation of Figure 8.6. These results do not include the time necessary to compute Eq. (8.2); but since in our current implementation of the model this time is always constant, we can omit it for simplicity.

## 8.5.2 Human Performance

**Subjects:** Ten subjects normal or corrected-to-normal vision.

**Stimuli:** Eighty images of neutral, happy, angry, and scream expressions of 20 individuals were selected from the AR face database. To limit possible confounds, all 20 selections were males without glasses. The images were warped to a standard image ($165 \times 120$ pixels) and displayed on a 21-inch monitor. The viewing area corresponded to approximately 15 by 11 cm. A typical viewing distance of 60 cm corresponds to 14 by 10.4 degrees of visual angle.

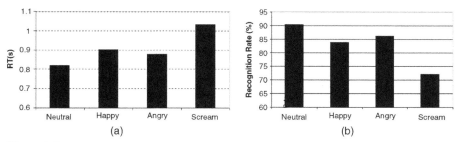

**Figure 8.7.** (a) Mean RT of the ten participants when deciding whether or not two consecutive images belong to the same individual (the prime image with a neutral expression and the target image with the expression as shown in the $x$ axes). (b) Mean recognition rate (in percentage).

**Design and Procedure:** The experiment consisted of two blocks, each with the images of 10 individuals. In each block, pairs of images were shown in sequence: First a neutral image of a randomly selected individual was displayed for 800 ms (prime face), an interstimulus interval of 300 ms followed, then a neutral, happy, angry, or screaming face (target face) was displayed. The identity of the prime and target face images as well as the facial expression of the target face were randomly selected. Participants were asked to decide whether or not the two images shown in sequence correspond to the same individual. Participants were instructed to respond as soon as they knew the answer. Responses and reaction times (RT) were recorded. Each subject viewed a total of 160 image pairs.

**Results:** Figure 8.7a shows the mean RT values of all participants when deciding whether or not the prime and target face images are of the same person. As predicted, the more the target face diverged (in muscle activity) from the prime face, the greater the RT. In Figure 8.7b, we show the percentage in recognition rate achieved by the participants for each possible sequence pair—that is, the prime image being a neutral expression face and the target as shown.

While the subjects' responses are predicted by our model, a numerical comparison is difficult: RTs include the matching time (which is not necessarily constant for all expressions) while the CTs correspond only to the time necessary to compute the deformation of the face (i.e., DF process).

## 8.6  EXPERIMENTAL RESULTS: RECOGNITION OF EXPRESSION

### 8.6.1  Computational Model

Next, we calculate the performance of the computational model in the task of expression recognition.

## 8.6.1.1 *Performance*

We now show how the motion vectors can be used to recognize facial expressions. We will calculate the similarity between pairs of images by using the value of $S_A$ described earlier in Eq. (8.12).

The first test (matching) corresponds to determining for each possible combination of two facial expressions (a total of 10 combinations) if the two images shown have the same facial expression or not. To do this, we used the neutral, happy, angry, and screaming face images of 50 randomly selected individuals of the AR face database, which gives us a total of 12,750 different pairs. For each of these pairs, we compute the motion field (i.e., face deformation, DF) that exists between the neutral image and the facial expression selected. The two resulting motion fields are then compared by using the similarity measure $S_A$. This value is expected to be low for similar motion fields (i.e., similar expressions) and large for different ones.

Once the value of $S_A$ has been obtained for each of the 12,750 pairs of images, we search for the value of $S_A$ that optimally divides the pairs with equal expression in one group and those with different expression within another group. We then use this threshold to classify the image pairs of a different set of 50 people. The correct classification in this second group (using the threshold obtained with the first group) was of 82.7%.

Results can be improved by means of a discriminant function that helps us to determine which areas of the face are most discriminant within classes (i.e., same facial expression) and which are most distinct between classes (i.e., different facial expressions) [62]. One way to do that is with Eq. (8.14). For instance, when comparing happy and scream faces, we can use the values of $\mathbf{S}_{b(happy,scream)}$ shown in Figure 8.8e and the values of $\hat{\mathbf{S}}_{w_{happy}}$ and $\hat{\mathbf{S}}_{w_{scream}}$ shown in Figure 8.8a,c to determine which pixels are most discriminant—that is, better suited for the task. We then order (rank) the pixels inversely proportional to the values of $\hat{\mathbf{S}}_w$ and proportionally to the values of $\hat{\mathbf{S}}_b$. Since most of the pixels will have an associated ranking of zero or close to zero, we can make our comparison faster by using only those pixels with a value of $\hat{\mathbf{S}}_b/\hat{\mathbf{S}}_w$ larger than a predetermined threshold [38]. This threshold can also be learned from the training data, in which case we select that value that best classifies the training data. By following this procedure, the results improved to 91.3%.

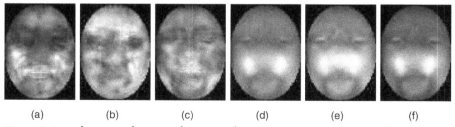

(a)          (b)          (c)          (d)          (e)          (f)

**Figure 8.8.** (a) $\hat{\mathbf{S}}_{w_{happy}}$, (b) $\hat{\mathbf{S}}_{w_{angry}}$, (c) $\hat{\mathbf{S}}_{w_{scream}}$, (d) $\hat{\mathbf{S}}_b$ including all the expressions, (e) $\hat{\mathbf{S}}_b$ for expressions happy and scream, and (f) $\hat{\mathbf{S}}_b$ for expressions angry and scream.

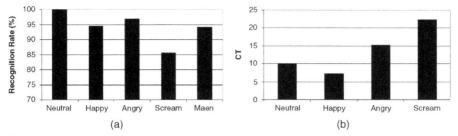

**Figure 8.9.** (a) Recognition rates obtained by our model when classifying each of the face images in four different groups: neutral, happy, angry, and scream. (b) Mean computational time (CT) required to calculate the class for those images with neutral, happy, angry, and scream facial expressions.

We used the neutral, happy, angry, and scream face images of 10 randomly selected individuals as samples and used the neutral, happy, angry and scream face images of 90 different individuals as testing images. For each of the 360 testing images, we determine the closest sample (among the 40 stored in memory) using the value of $S_A$. If the facial expression in the testing image and in the closest sample were the same, we recorded a successfully classified image. Again, we use the values of $\hat{\mathbf{S}}_b$ and $\hat{\mathbf{S}}_w$ to improve the classification results and speed up computation. These results are shown in Figure 8.9a.

### 8.6.1.2 Computation Times

According to our model, the delays observed when we recognize facial expressions can be due to (*i*) the time required to compute the motion field (DF) of the expression displayed on the (testing) image or (*ii*) the difficulty associated in classifying the facial expression of a test image in a set of preselected categories.

When classifying images as either happy or screaming, we expect to have longer RT for those images with a scream expression because it takes longer to compute the motion field (DF) of a scream face. Moreover, we would expect longer RT when classifying images as either neutral or angry than when classifying images as either happy or screaming, because the images in the first task (group) are more alike and thus a more detailed analysis will be required. While happy and screaming faces can be easily distinguish by looking at a small number of pixels (such as the eyes or the corners of the mouth), a pixel-to-pixel comparison may be necessary to decide whether an image is a neutral expression or a not-excessively-marked angry face.

In Figure 8.9b we show the computational times (CT) of Figure 8.6 multiplied by the percentage (range: 0–1) of pixels that were necessary to use in order to obtain the best classification rate when classifying the images as either neutral expressions or the expression under consideration. The pixels were selected according to the rankings given by $\hat{\mathbf{S}}_b$.

## 8.6.2  Human Performance

**Subjects:** Ten subjects with normal or corrected-to-normal vision participated in this experiment. None of the subjects had participated in the previous experiment.

**Stimuli, Design, and Procedure:** The neutral, happy, angry, and scream face images of 20 males (with no glasses) of the AR face database were selected for this experiment. To prevent recognition by shape alone, images were warped to a standard image size of 165 by 120 pixels. Subjects participated in four different tests. The first required them to classify each of the images of the AR database within one of the four categories of that data set. Subjects were told in advance of those categories, and an image for each of the expressions was shown to participants before the experiment started. The other three tests only involved two types of facial expressions. In these two-class experiments, subjects were asked to classify images within these two categories only. The two-class experiments comprise the following facial expression images: (a) happy and scream, (b) neutral and angry, and (c) neutral and happy. Reaction times (in seconds) and percentage of correct choices were recorded. Fifty images were randomly selected and displayed, one at a time, until the subject pressed a key to indicate her/his classification choice. A 2-s pause (with blank screen) separated each of the images shown to the participants.

**Results:** In Figure 8.10a we show the RT means of all the participants when classifying the images within each of the four groups. These results should be compared to the CT predicted by our model and shown in Figure 8.9b.

As discussed above, our model predicts that when classifying images into two clearly distinguishable classes, the latter will generally require longer RT because (as demonstrated in Section 8.3.1) longer time is required to estimate the *DF*. This was confirmed by our group of subjects Figure 8.10b. We also predicted that when classifying face images within two similar classes, the RT will generally increase. This is the case for neutral and angry faces, Figure 8.10b. Another particular case is that of classifying face images as either neutral or happy. This task can be readily solved by looking at a small number of pixels (such as those around the corners of

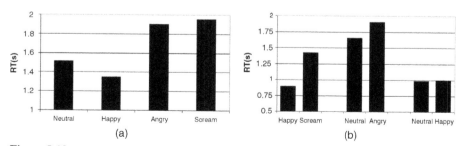

**Figure 8.10.** Mean RT when classifying the images in (**a**) four different groups (neutral, happy, angry and scream), (**b**) two categories classification (happy–scream, neutral–angry, and neutral–happy). (Reaction time in seconds.)

the lips and the eyes). Thus, in this case, similar RT are expected. This was indeed the case in our experiment (Figure 8.10b).

## 8.7 RECOGNITION OF EXPRESSION VARIANT FACES USING WEIGHTED SUBSPACE

Zhang and Martinez [67] applied the face recognition model presented above to the subspace approach for the recognition of identity under varying expressions in the appearance-based framework. By appearance-based, it is understood that the recognition system only makes use of the textural information of the face after this has been warped to a standard (prototypical) shape. Over the years, the success of appearance-based approaches, especially when applied to face recognition problems, has only increased. Appearance-based methods are attractive because the model of each class is directly defined by the selection of the sample images of that object, without the need to create precise geometrical or algebraic representations [64]. The clear disadvantage is that any image condition not included in the learning set will cause incorrect recognition results. In the pattern recognition community, it is common practice to use a minimum number of independent sample vectors of 10 times the number of classes by the number of dimensions of our original feature space. Unfortunately, it is rarely the case where one has access to such a large number of training images per class in applications such as face recognition. And, even when one does have a large number of training images, these are not generally uncorrelated or independent from each other. Hence, other solutions must be defined.

The problem with subspace techniques is that some of the learned features (dimensions) represent (encode) facial expression changes. As shown above, this problem can be resolved if we learn which dimensions are most affected by expression variations and then build a weighted-distance measure that gives less importance to these. In this formulation, a fundamental question is yet to be addressed: *Would a morphing algorithm solve the problem?* That is, rather than designing a weighted measure as we did in our model, one could utilize the motion estimation to morph the test face to equal in shape that of the sample face image. This would allow a pixel to pixel comparison. Unfortunately, morphing algorithms can fail due to occlusions (e.g., teeth and closed eyes), large deformations and textural changes due to the local deformation of the face. The last of these points is key. We note that when the face changes expression, the 3D position of several local areas also change, and therefore the reflectance angle will also change. This effect will obviously change the brightness of the image pixels (that is, the texture) in our image. The approach presented in this chapter solves this by assigning low weights to those areas with large deformations.

### 8.7.1 Learning Linear Subspace Representation

Principal component analysis (PCA), independent component analysis (ICA), and linear discriminant analysis (LDA) are three of the most popular linear subspace methods and have been largely used in face recognition applications.

PCA finds the optimal liner projection between the original space of $d$ dimensions and a low-dimensional space of $p$ dimensions (features), assuming the data are Gaussian [68]. To do this, PCA uses the first and central moments of the data—that is, the sample mean $\mu$ and the sample covariance matrix $\Sigma$. While PCA only computes the first and central moments of the data, ICA will use higher moments of the data to find those feature vectors that are most independent from each other [69]. In contrast, and as already described earlier in this chapter, LDA selects those basis vectors that maximize the distance between the means of each class and minimizes the distance between the samples in each class and its corresponding class mean [61].

## 8.7.2  Weighted Subspaces

Let the projection matrix given by each of the subspace methods mentioned in the preceding section be $\Phi_{PCA}$, $\Phi_{ICA}$, and $\Phi_{LDA}$. In this common notation, the columns in $\Phi_i$ correspond to the basis vectors of the subspace. Once these subspaces have been obtained from a training set, $\mathbf{V} = \{\mathbf{V}_1, \ldots, \mathbf{V}_n\}$, where $n$ is the number of training images, one can compare a new test image $\mathbf{T}$ using the following weighted-distance equation

$$\|\widehat{\mathbf{W}}_i (\hat{\mathbf{V}}_i - \hat{\mathbf{T}})\|, \tag{8.15}$$

where $\hat{\mathbf{V}}_i = \Phi^T \mathbf{V}_i$ which is the $i$th image projected onto the subspace of our choice of $\Phi$, $\Phi = \{\Phi_{PCA}, \Phi_{ICA}, \Phi_{LDA}\}$, $\hat{\mathbf{T}} = \Phi^T \mathbf{T}$, and $\widehat{\mathbf{W}}_i$ is the weighting matrix that defines the importance of each of the basis vectors in the subspace spanned by $\Phi$. This is a direct adaptation of our model defined in Eq. (8.2) to the subspace method.

Before one can use Eq. (8.15), we need to define the value of the weighting matrix $\widehat{\mathbf{W}}$. While it may be very difficult to do that in the reduced space spanned by $\Phi$, it is easy to calculate this in the original space and then project the result onto its corresponding subspace. Thus, we will compute the value of the weights in the original space, $\mathbf{W}$, using of the model given in Section 8.4.2 yielding $\mathbf{F}_i = DF(\mathbf{V}_i, \mathbf{T})$. The weights are given by

$$\mathbf{W}_i = \mathbf{F}_{\max} - \|\mathbf{F}_i\|, \tag{8.16}$$

where $\mathbf{F}_{\max} = \max_i \|\mathbf{F}_i\|$.

We can now project the weights onto the corresponding subspace as

$$\hat{\mathbf{W}}_i = \Phi^T \mathbf{W}_i. \tag{8.17}$$

To classify a test image, we assign the class label of the closest sample, which is given by

$$s = \operatorname{argmin}_i \|\hat{\mathbf{W}}_i (\hat{\mathbf{V}}_i - \hat{\mathbf{T}})\|, \tag{8.18}$$

and select the class label, $c^*$, of $\mathbf{V}_s$.

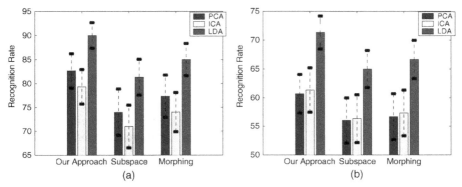

**Figure 8.11.** Recognition rates on the leave-one-expression-out test with (**a**) images from the same session and (**b**) images from different sessions.

### 8.7.3  Experimental Results

Once more, we randomly selected 100 subjects from the AR face database. From each individual we used the eight images with neutral, happy, angry, and scream expressions taken during two sessions, with each session separated by two weeks time [65]. All algorithms were tested using the leave-one-expression-out procedure. For example, when the happy face was used for testing, the neutral, angry, and scream faces were used for training.

In our first experiment, only those images taken during the first session were used. The results obtained using the proposed weighted subspace approaches as well as those of PCA, ICA, and LDA are shown in Figure 8.11a. In this figure we also show the results obtained by first morphing all faces to a neutral-expression face image and then building a PCA, ICA, and LDA subspace. The bars in this figure show the average recognition rate for each of the methods. The standard deviation for the leave-one-expression-out test is shown by the small variance line at the top of the bars.

The second test was similar to the first one, except that, this time, we used the images of the first session for training and those of the second session for testing. The results are summarized in Figure 8.11b. It is worth mentioning that the weighted-LDA approach works best for the scream face with a recognition rate of ∼84%. Other methods could not do better than 70% for this expression. In the figures shown above, this is made clear by the small variance associated to our method as compared to the others.

### 8.7.4  Recognition from Video Sequences

Compared to the large number of algorithms developed to do recognition from still images, the literature on video-based methods is relatively small. One reason for this imbalance was due to the low accessibility of high-quality video cameras that, until recently, were expensive and of limited quality. The second reason is algorithmical. While it is generally difficult to successfully do feature extraction from still images, this process has proven even more challenging over dynamic sequences [62]. This second point raises an important question: *Would the methods defined to recognize faces from a single test image perform better if they could work with multiple images or video sequences?* Note that if the answer to this question were positive, there would be less need for the design of feature extraction algorithms that can do a more direct analysis of dynamic sequences. Understanding the limitations of current algorithms when applied to video will help researchers design algorithms that can specifically solve these problems [70].

To answer our question though, we need to be able to use our computational model, originally defined to work with stills, to handle multiple images. Zhang and Martinez [70] present one such approach. In their algorithm the method of Martinez [54] is reformulated within the framework presented in this chapter. This results in a robust algorithm that can accurately recognize faces even under large expressions, pose and illumination changes, and partial occlusions. Experimental results using a database of video sequences corresponding to 50 people yielded a classification accuracy of $\sim 95\%$.

## 8.8  SUMMARY

In the model presented in this chapter and depicted in Figure 8.3, motion (dynamic) cues are processed independently from static cues. This is consistent with neurophysiological evidence that supports dorsal stream processing of dynamic cues and ventral stream processing of static cues. Although dynamic and static cues are processed separately in our model, they are combined to accomplish the tasks of recognition of identity and facial expression at the end of the hierarchy. This is also consistent with experimental data that show disruption in recognition when one of the two cues (dynamic or static) is altered [38].

The nature of this model provides a framework in which to reconcile apparently contradictory psychophysical data. The process of motion estimation (whose task is to calculate the deformation between the faces we want to match), DF, within a hierarchical model of face processing is key to explaining why in some experiments, slower recognition times are obtained when attempting to identify faces with distinct facial expression—for example, smiling versus neutral faces. At the same time, the model does not require a direct interaction between the processes of face identification and facial expression recognition. This is important, because it is consistent with the observation that some agnosic patients are impaired only with regard to one of the two tasks (either identification of people or facial expression recognition).

This model suggests that motion is useful for successful matching of face images bearing distinct facial expressions. Following references 38 and 66, we further hypothesized that the computed motion fields could be used to select the most invariant textural (appearance) features between the images we want to match. It is observed that the results that are generated by the proposed model is consistent with psychophysical and neurophysiological data. Additionally, recognition of identity is reduced by discarding the outcome of the DF module from the similarity function—for example, going from Eq. (8.2) to Eq. (8.1). These motion features could also be used to construct a motion-based feature-space for the recognition of identity and expression. Motion may be used as an alternative, independent means for identifying people and expressions. In computer vision, reasonable results have been obtained by constructing feature-spaces based solely on motion cues. These results could ultimately be used to reinforce the recognition task, or help to make a decision where other processes are not adequate.

We have demonstrated the use of our model to classify faces within a set of facial expression categories. We have also experimentally shown that the DF carries the necessary information to successfully achieve this task. By combining the DF and a linear classifier, we were able to predict the classification RT of each of the facial expressions of the AR database.

Extensions to the classical subspace approach [67] and to the recognition from video sequences [70] show the generality of the model presented in this chapter. Moreover, this chapter has illustrated how one can successfully employ the model defined herein to make predictions on how the human visual system works—predications later confirmed in a set of psychophysical experiments.

## REFERENCES

1. R. D. Adams and M. Victor, *Principles of Neurology*, McGraw-Hill, New York, 1981.
2. M. Behrmann and G. Avidan, Congenital prosopagnosia: Face-blind from birth, *Trends Cognitive Sci.* **9**:180–187, 2005.
3. H. D. Ellis and M. B. Lewis, Capgras delusion: A window on face recognition, *Trends Cognit. Sci.* **5**:149–156, 2001.
4. N. Kanwisher, J. McDermott, and M. M Chun, The fusiform face area: A module in human extrastriate cortex specialized for face perception, *J. Neurosci.* **17**:4302–4311, 1997.
5. M. J. Tarr and I. Gauthier, FFA: A flexible fusiform area for subordinate-level visual processing automatized by expertise, *Nature Neurosci.* **3**:764–769, 2000.
6. I. Gauthier, M. J. Tarr, A.W. Anderson, P. Skudlarskiand and J. C. Gore, Activation of the middle fusiform "face area" increases with expertise in recognizing novel objects, *Nature Neurosci.* **2**:568–573, 1999.
7. M. de Haan, K. Humphreys, and M. H. Johnson, Developing a brain specialized for face perception: A converging methods approach, *Dev. Psychobiol.* **40**:200–212, 2002.
8. C. A. Nelson, The development and neural bases of face recognition, *Infant Child Dev.* **10**:3–18, 2001.
9. D. Maurer, R. Le Grand, and C. J. Mondloch, The many faces of configural processing. *Trends Cognit. Sci.*, **6**:255–260, 2002.
10. G. Yovel and N. Kanwisher, Face perception: Domain specific, not process specific. *Neuron* **44**:889–898, 2004.
11. V. Bruce and A. Young, Understanding face recognition, *B. J. Psychol.* **77**:305–327, 1986.
12. A. W. Ellis, Cognitive mechanisms of face processing, *Philos. Trans. R. Soc. Lond. B* **335**;113–119, 1992.
13. P. Ekman and W. V. Friesen, *The Facial Action Coding System: A Technique for the Measurement of Facial Movement*, Consulting Psychology Press, San Diego, 1978.
14. C. Darwin, *The Expression of the Emotions in Man and Animals*, John Murray, London, 1872 (reprinted by The University of Chicago Press, 1965).

15. P. Ekman, Basic emotions, in T. Dalgleish and M. Power editors, *Handbook of Cognition and Emotion*, John Wiley & Sons, New York, 1999.

16. R. S. Woodworth and H. Schlosberg, *Experimental Psychology*, Holt, Rinehart, & Winston, New York, 1954.

17. J. A. Russell, A Circumplex model of affect, *J. Pers. Soc. Psychol.* **39**:1161–1178, 1980.

18. J. A. Russell and M. Bullock, Multidimensional scaling of emotional facial expressions: similarity from preschoolers to adults, *J. Pers. Soc. Psychol.* **48**:1290–1298, 1985.

19. E. T. Rolls, A theory of emotion, and its application to understanding the neural basis of emotion, *Cognit. Emot.* **4**:161–190, 1990.

20. J. T. Cacioppo, W. L. Gardner, and G. G. Berntson, The affect system has parallel and integrative processing components: Form follows function, *J. Pers. Soc. Psychol.* **76**:839–855, 1999.

21. J. A. Russell, Core affect and the psychological construction of emotion, *Psychol. Rev.* **110**:145–172, 2003.

22. K. L. Schmidt and J. F. Cohn, Human facial expressions as adaptations: Evolutionary questions in facial expression research, *Am. J. Phys. Anthropol.* **S33**:3–24, 2001.

23. P. Ekman, R. J. Davidson, and W. V. Friesen, The Duchenne smile: Emotional expression and brain physiology II, *J. Pers. Soc. Psychol.* **58**:342–353, 1990.

24. J. F. Cohn and K. L. Schmidt, The timing of facial motion in posed and spontaneous smiles, *Int. J. Wavelets, Multiresolut. Inf. Process.* **2**:1–12, 2004.

25. V. Gallese, C. Keysers, and G. Rizzolatti, A unifying view of the basis of social cognition, *Trends Cognit. Sci.* **8**(9):396–403, 2004.

26. T. Allison, A. Puce, and G. McCarthy, Social perception from visual cues: Role of the STS region, *Trends Cognit. Sci.*, **4**:267–278 2000.

27. T. Valentine, Face-space models of face recognition, in M. J. Wenger and J. T. Townsend, editors, *Computational, Geometric, and Process Perspectives on Facial Cognition: Contexts and Challenges*, Lawrence Erlbaum Associates, London, 2001.

28. S. Harnad, *Categorical Perception*, Cambridge University Press, New York, 1987.

29. M. H. Bornstein, Perceptual categories in vision and audition, in *Categorical Perception: The Groundwork of Cognition*, S. Harnad, editor, Cambridge University Press, New York, 1987.

30. C. L. Krumhansl, Music psychology: Tonal structures in perception and memory, *Annu. Rev. Psychol.* **42**:277–303, 1991.

31. A. J. Calder, A. W. Young, P. J. Benson, and D. I. Perrett, Categorical perception of morphed facial expressions, *Vis. Cognit.* **3**:81–117, 1996.

32. A. W. Young, D. Rowland, A. J. Calder, N. L. Etcoff, A. Seth, and D. I. Perrett, Facial expression megamix: Test of dimensional and category accounts of emotion recognition, *Cognition* **63**:271–313, 1997.

33. L. G. Ungerleider, S. M. Courtney, and J. V. Haxby, A neural system for human visual working memory, *Proc. Nat. Acad. Sci. USA* **95**:883–890, 1998.

34. E. A. Hoffman and J. V. Haxby, Distinct representations of eye gaze and identity in the distributed human neural system for face perception, *Nature Neurosci.* **3**:80–84, 2000.

35. J. V. Haxby, E. A. Hoffman, and M. I. Gobbini, The distributed human neural system for face perception, *Trends Cognit. Sci.*, **4**:223–233, 2000.

36. A. J. Calder and A. W. Young, Understanding the recognition of facial identity and facial expression, *Neuroscience* **6**:641–651, 2005.

37. M. T. Posamentier and H. Abdi, Processing faces and facial expressions, *Neuropsychol. Rev.* **13**:113–143, 2003.

38. A. M. Martinez, Matching expression variant faces, *Vis. Res.* **43**:1047–1060, 2003.

39. D. A. Roark, S. E. Barrett, M. J. Spence, H. Abdi, and A. J. O'Toole, Psychological and neural perspectives on the role of motion in face recognition, *Behavi. Cognit. Neurosci. Rev.* **2**:15–46, 2003.

40. E. C. Hansch and F. J. Pirozzolo, Task relevant effects on the assessment of cerebral specialization for facial emotions, *Brain and Language* **10**:51–59, 1980.

41. R. Bruyer, C. Laterre, X. Seron, P. Feyereisen, E. Strypstein, E. Pierrard, and D. Rectem, A case of prosopagnosia with some preserved covert remembrance of familiar faces, *Brain Cognit.* **2**:257–284, 1983.

42. J. Kurucz and G. Feldmar, Prosopo-affective agnosia as a symptom of cerebral organic-disease, *J. Am. Geriatric Soc.* **27**:225–230, 1979.

43. N. Endo, M. Endo, T. Kirita, and K. Maruyama, The effects of expression on face recognition, *Tohoku Psychol. Folia* **52**:37–44, 1992.

44. N. L. Etcoff, Selective attention to facial identity and facial emotion, *Neuropsychologia* **22**:281–295, 1984.

45. A. W. Young, D. J. Hellawell, C. Van De Wal, and M. Johnson, Facial expression processing after amygdalotomy, *Neuropsychologia* **34**:31–39, 1996.

46. S. R. Schweinberger and G. R. Soukup, Asymmetric relationship among perception of facial identity, emotion, and facial speech, *J. Exp. Psychol. Hum. Percept. Perform.*, **24**(6):1748–1765, 1998.

47. J. Baudouin, D. Gilibert, S. Sansone, and G. Tiberghien, When the smile is a cue to familiarity, *Memory*, **8**:285–292, 2000.

48. H. Hill and A. Johnston, Categorizing sex and identity from the biological motion of faces, *Curr. Biol.* **11**:880–885, 2001.

49. G. Wallis and H. H. Bulthoff, Effects of temporal association on recognition memory, *Proc. Natl. Acad. Sci. USA* **98**:4800–4804, 2001.

50. K. Lander, F. Christie, and V. Bruce, The role of movement in the recognition of famous faces, *Memory Cognit.* **27**:974–985, 1999.

51. D. C. Hay, A. W. Young, and A. W. Ellis, Routes through the face recognition system. *Q. J. Exp. Psychol. A* **43**:761–791, 1991.

52. M. Kamachi, V. Bruce, S. Mukaida, J. Gyoba, S. Yoshikawa, and S. Akamatsu, Dynamic properties influence the perception of facial expressions, *Perception* **30**:875–887, 2001.

53. D. Beymer and T. Poggio, Face recognition from one example view, *Science*, **272**:5250, 1996.

54. A. M. Martinez, Recognizing imprecisely localized, partially occluded and expression variant faces from a single sample per class, *IEEE Trans. Pattern Anal. Mach. Intell.* **24**(6):748–763, 2002.

55. B. K. P. Horn and B. G. Schunck, Determining optical flow, *Artif. Intell.* **17**:185–203, 1981.

56. A. Blake and A. Zisserman, *Visual Reconstruction*, The MIT Press, Cambridge, MA, 1987.

57. M. J. Black and P. Anandan, The robust estimation of multiple motions: Parametric and piecewise-smooth flow fields, *Comput. Vis. Image Understand.* **63**:75–104, 1996.

58. S. Negahdaripour, Revised definition of optical flow: Integration of radiometric and geometric cues for dynamic scene analysis, *IEEE Trans. Pattern Anal. Mach. Intell.* **20**(9):961–979, 1996.

59. Y. Kim, A. M. Martinez, and A. C. Kak, Robust motion estimation under varying illumination, *Image Vis. Comput.* **23**:365–375, 2005.

60. M. S. Bartlett, J. C. Hager, P. Ekman, and T. J. Sejnowski, Measuring spatial expressions by computer image analysis, *Psychophysiology* **36**:253–263, 1999.

61. R. A. Fisher, The use of multiple measurements in taxonomic problems, *Ann. Eugen.*, **7**:179–188A, 1936.

62. A. M. Martinez, and M. Zhu, Where are linear feature extraction methods applicable? *IEEE Trans. Pattern Anal. Mach. Intell.*, **27**(12), 1934–1944, 2005.

63. M. Zhu and A. M. Martinez, Subclass discriminant analysis, *IEEE Trans. Pattern Anal. Mach. Intell.* **28**(8):1274–1286, 2006.

64. A. M. Martinez and A. C. Kak, PCA versus LDA, *IEEE Trans. Pattern Anal. Mach. Intell.* **23**(2):228–233, 2001.

65. A. M. Martinez and R. Benavente, The AR-Face Database, CVC Technical Report #24, 1998.

66. A. M. Martinez, Recognizing expression variant faces from a single sample image per class. *Proc. IEEE Comput. Vis. Pattern Recognit.*, **1**:353–358, 2003.

67. Y. Zhang and A. M. Martinez, Recognition of expression variant faces using weighted subspaces, *Proc. Int. Conf. Pattern Recognit. (ICPR)* **3**:149–152, 2004.

68. I. T. Jolliffe, *Principal Component Analysis*, Springer-Verlag, New York, 2002.
69. A. Hyvärinen, J. Karhunen, and E. Oja, *Independent Component Analysis*, Wiley-Interscience, New York, 2001.
70. Y. Zhang and A. M. Martinez, A weighted probabilistic approach to face recognition from multiple images and video sequences, *Image Vis. Comput.* **24**:626–638, 2006.
71. Y. Yacoob and L. Davis, Recognizing human facial expressions from long image sequences using optical flow, *IEEE Trans. Pattern Anal. Mach. Intell.* **18**:636–642, 1996.

# Chapter 9

# Multimodal Biometrics Based on Near-Infrared Face Recognition

**Rui Wang, Shengcai Liao, Zhen Lei, and Stan Z. Li**

## 9.1 INTRODUCTION

Biometric identification makes use of the physiological or behavioral characteristics of people, such as fingerprint, iris, face, palmprint, gait, and voice, for personal identification [1], which provides advantages over nonbiometric methods such as password, PIN, and ID cards. Its promising applications as well as the theoretical challenges have gotten its heated attraction from the last decade.

Face recognition is a natural, nonintrusive and easy way for biometrics and has been one of the most popular techniques. However, most current face recognition systems are based on face images captured in visible light spectrum, which are compromised in accuracy by changes in environmental illumination. The near-infrared (NIR) face image-based recognition method [2–4] overcomes this problem. It is shown to be invariant to the changes of the visible lighting and hence is accurate and robust for face recognition.

Recent research [5–9] has pointed out that multimodal biometric fusion can significantly improve the performance of the system due to the complementary information from different modalities helpful for classification. There exists various methods for multimodal fusion. Brunelli and Falavigna [10] proposed a person identification system based on voice and face, using a HyperBF network as the best performing

---

*Biometrics: Theory, Methods, and Applications.* Edited by Boulgouris, Plataniotis, and Micheli-Tzanakou
Copyright © 2010 the Institute of Electrical and Electronics Engineers, Inc.

fusion module. Kittler et al. [11] proposed a face and voice multimodal biometric system and developed a common theoretical framework for combing classifiers in reference 5 with several fusion techniques including sum, product, minimum, and maximum rules, where the best combination results are obtained for a simple sum rule. Hong and Jain [6] proposed an identification system based on face and fingerprint, where fingerprint matching is applied after pruning the database via face matching. Ross et al. [12] combined face, fingerprint, and hand geometry biometrics with sum, decision tree, and linear discriminant-based methods, where the sum rule achieves the best. Wang et al. [13], Son and Lee [14], and Chen and Chu [15] developed face and iris multimodal biometric systems, and different fusion methods were investigated. Kumar et al. [16] described a hand-based verification system that combined the geometric features of the hand with palmprints at the feature and matching score levels. Li et al. [9] proposed a systematic framework for fusing 2D and 3D face recognition at both feature and score levels, by exploring synergies of the two modalities at these levels and achieved good performance in large database. Chang et al. [7] combined ear and face biometrics with an appearance-based method. Ribaric and Fratric [8] described a biometric identification system based on eigenpalm and eigenfinger features, with fusion applied at the matching score level.

In this chapter we present a near-infrared (NIR) face-based approach for multimodal biometric fusion. The motivations for this approach are the following: (1) NIR face recognition overcomes problems arising from uncontrolled illumination in visible light (VL) image-based face biometric and achieves significantly better results than VL face; and (2) the fusion of NIR face with VL face or iris biometrics is a natural way for multibiometrics, because it is either face-based (NIR face + VL face) or NIR-based (NIR face+ irais).

The NIR face is fused with VL face or iris modality at the matching score level. As for score level fusion, there are two common approaches. One is to treat it as a combination problem, in which the individual matching scores are combined according to some rule such as sum rule, max rule, or min rule to generate a single scalar score. The others is to formulate it as a classification problem, such as LDA [12] or a power series model (PSM)-based method [17]. The latter needs to be learned in a training set.

We evaluate these fusion methods on real large multimodal databases we collected, in which NIR face and VL face or iris image for one subject are captured simultaneously by our own image capture device. The NIR database is publicly available on the web [18]. The experimental results show that the learning-based fusion methods such as LDA and PSM are comparatively better than other conventional methods.

The rest of this chapter is organized as follows: Section 9.2 briefly introduces the near-infrared face recognition and describes the fusion of NIR face with VL face and the fusion of NIR face with iris modality respectively. Section 9.3 describes several fusion methods. The experimental results and discussions are presented in Section 9.4, and in Section 9.5 we conclude the chapter.

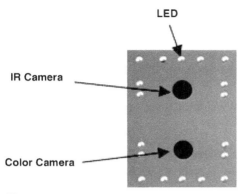

**Figure 9.1.** The capture device of NIR face images.

## 9.2  NIR FACE-BASED MULTIBIOMETRICS

### 9.2.1  NIR Face Recognition

The NIR face image is taken using the device shown in Figure 9.1, composed of NIR LEDs, an NIR camera, and a color camera. The NIR LED lights are approximately coaxial to the lens direction. For NIR camera, to minimize ambient lights in visible spectrum, a long-pass optical filter can be used with the lens to cut off visible light while allowing NIR light to pass. We choose a filter such that ray passing rates are 0%, 50%, 88%, and 99% at the wavelength points of 720, 800, 850, and 880 nm, respectively. The filter cuts off visible environmental lights ($< 750$ nm) while allowing 80–90% of the 850-nm NIR light to pass. Such NIR image is captured in a good condition regardless of visible lights in the environment and encodes intrinsic information of the face, subject only to a monotonic transform in the gray tone [2]. Based on this, we use local binary pattern (LBP) features further to compensate for the monotonic transform, thus deriving an illumination invariant face representation for face recognition.

LBP is introduced as a powerful local descriptor for microfeatures of images [19]. The LBP operator labels the pixels of an image by thresholding the $3 \times 3$ neighborhood of each pixel with the center value and considering the result as a binary number (or called LBP codes). An illustration of the basic LBP operator is shown in Figure 9.2. Note that the binary LBP code is circular.

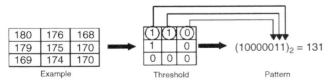

**Figure 9.2.** Calculation of LBP code from $3 \times 3$ subwindow.

**Input:**    Sequence of $N$ weighted examples:
$\{(x_1, y_1), (x_2, y_2), \ldots, (x_N, y_N)\}$;
**Initialize:**  $w_i = \frac{1}{N}$, $i = 1, 2, \ldots, N$, $F(x) = 0$
            Integer $T$ specifying number of iterations;
For  $t = 1, \ldots, T$

(a) Fit the regression function $f_t(x)$ by weighted least squares of $y_i$ to $x_i$ with weights $w_i$.
(b) Update $F(x) \leftarrow F(x) + f_t(x)$
(c) Update $w_i \leftarrow w_i e^{-y_i f_t(x_i)}$ and renormalize.

**Output:** the final classifier, $sign[F(x)] = sign[\sum_{t=1}^{T} f_t(x)]$

**Figure 9.3.** Gentle AdaBoost algorithm in reference 19.

LBP histograms over local regions provides a more reliable description when the pattern is subject to alignment errors. Hence, in our work a histogram of the base LBP codes is computed over a local region centered at each pixel, and it is considered as a set of individual features. The original LBP feature pool is of high dimensionality. Not all of them are useful or equally useful, and some of them may cause a negative effect on the performance. Therefore, we adopt the following AdaBoost algorithm [19] to select the most discriminative and complementary features and construct the powerful classifier for face recognition.

AdaBoost iteratively learns a sequence of weak classifier $f_t(x)$ and linearly combines them to construct a strong classifier $F(x)$. At each iteration, a weak classifier $f_t(x)$ is chosen to minimize the weighted squared error $J_{wse} = \sum_{i=1}^{N} w_i(y_i - f_t(x_i))^2$.

Biometric recognition is a multiclass problem, whereas the above AdaBoost learning is for two classes. To deal with this problem, we take the similar measure in reference 20 to construct intrapersonal and extrapersonal classes to convert the multiclass problem into a two-class one. Here, instead of deriving the intra- or extrapersonal variations using difference images as in reference 20, the training examples for our learning algorithm is the set of differences between each pair of LBP histogram features at the corresponding locations. The positive examples are derived from pairs of intrapersonal and the negative from pairs of extrapersonal differences.

With the two-class scheme, the face matching procedure will work in the following way: It takes the probe face image and a gallery face image as the input, computes a difference-based feature vector from the two images, and then calculates a similarity score for the feature vector using some matching function. A decision is made based on the score, to classify the feature vector into the positive class (coming from the same person) or the negative class (different persons).

## 9.2.2 Fusion with VL Face

It may be advantageous to combine information contained in different face modalities to overcome limitations in single face data so as to improve the performance of system. Several methods have been proposed to combine information from multiface modalities to achieve higher performance. Heo and co-workers [21] present two approaches to fuse thermal infrared (TIR) and visible light (VL) face images. One is to average image pixels of the two modalities, and the other is to fuse them at the decision level. In references 22 and 23, the 2D and 3D face information is dimensionally reduced, then a classifier is built and the scores are fused by sum rule. Pan and coworkers 24 capture 31 different multispectrum face images to be fused for recognition and obtain a good result. However, the image capture devices of TIR face images, 3D face images, and multispectrum face images are all complex and expensive, which is disadvantageous for practical application. The proposed modalities, NIR and VL face images, due to its complementary information and the low-cost image acquisition, may be a good choice for the fusion.

Figure 9.4 illustrates the block diagram of the fusion framework of NIR and VL multimodal faces at the score level. The input is a pair of NIR and VL face

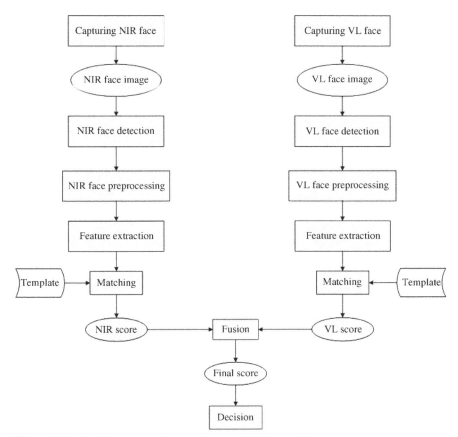

**Figure 9.4.** Algorithm structure for score fusion of NIR face and VL face.

images. After face and eye detection processes, the NIR and VL faces are cropped and normalized to a pre-fixed size. The LBP features for NIR and VL are then extracted and fed into the NIR and VL face recognition engines (e.g., AdaBoost classifiers), respectively, to produce two scores for NIR and VL. Finally, the two matching score are fused according to some rule and compared to a threshold to make the final decision.

In this paper, VL face recognition uses the same recognition algorithm as NIR, in which AdaBoost learning [25] is used to construct a powerful classifier based on a Local Binary Pattern (LBP) representation [19].

## 9.2.3   Fusion with Iris

Fusing NIR face and iris modality is another choice for NIR face-based multimodal biometrics, and it brings the following advantages [26]. (1) The NIR face and iris images can be acquired simultaneously by an improved commercial digital camera. (2) The NIR face and iris contain different or complementary information for recognition, so that the total error rate (the sum of false accept rate and false reject rate) is known to go down [27]. (3) It reduces spoof attacks on the biometric system because of the difficulty in making fake iris images.

For iris recognition, we adopt the well-known algorithm of Daugman [28], which includes the following four steps. (1) It is necessary to localize the inner and outer boundaries of the iris precisely and to detect and exclude the eyelids if they intrude. (2) The portion of the image corresponding to the iris is translated into a normalized form, so that possible dilation of the pupil does not affect the system. (3) The feature extraction process is completed by the use of 2D Gabor wavelets to perform a multiscale analysis of the iris. The information about local phase, coded with two bits corresponding to the signs of the real and imaginary parts, is obtained, which is a 256-byte IrisCode. (4) Similarity scores are obtained by computing a hamming distance between two IrisCodes.

In this chapter, NIR face and iris modalities are acquired using a single high-resolution camera with active frontal NIR lighting. This not only is a natural way for face and iris multimodal biometrics, since both NIR face and iris need active NIR nodality, but also brings convenience to the user. Figure 9.5 summarizes the structure of the algorithms of NIR face and iris biometrics fusion using a single high-resolution NIR face image. The input is a high-resolution NIR face image. The face and eyes are localized accurately using a face and eye detection algorithm [2]. After that, the left and right irises are segmented from the face, and both the face and irises are normalized into a pre-fixed sizes. The facial LBP features and iris Gabor features are extracted and fed into NIR face and iris recognition engines respectively to be compared to the corresponding templates. Finally, the three matching scores are fused following some rule, and they are compared with a threshold to make the final classification.

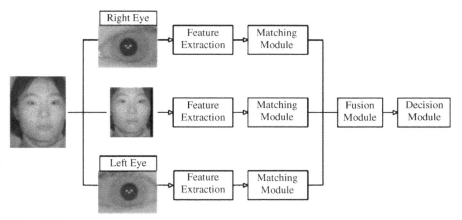

**Figure 9.5.** Algorithm structure for score fusion of face, left iris, and right iris.

## 9.3  METHOD OF MULTIBIOMETRICS FUSION

The NIR face biometric is fused with VL face or iris modality at score level. There are two common approaches for fusion at the matching score level: (1) Treat it as a combination problem, in which the individual matching scores are combined follow some rule such as sum rule, max rule, min rule, and so on, to generate a single scalar score and the other is to formulate it as a classification problem, such as the LDA- and PSM-based method.

Suppose we have $M$ scores from $M$ biometric modalities corresponding to one sample pair. The sum rule outputs the summation of the $M$ scores. The min rule outputs the minimum value of the $M$ scores, and the max rule outputs the maximum value of the $M$ ones.

For the LDA-based method, the $M$ scores are formulated as a $M$-dimension vector. The sample pairs are divided into two classes of intra and extra which denote the samples from the same persons and different persons, respectively. The purpose of LDA is to find an optimal projective direction that maximizes the between-class scatter while it minimizes the within-class scatter. The LDA-based method can be essentially considered as a weight sum rule.

Recently, Toh [17] proposed a power series model (PSM)-based fusion method. If we denote the scores from $M$ biometric modalities of one sample pair as $\bar{s} = (s_1, s_2, \ldots, s_M)$, where $s_k, k = 1, \ldots, M$, is the $k$th score corresponding to the $k$th modality, then a power series model is constructed as

$$f(\alpha, \bar{s}) = \alpha_0 + \sum_{r=1}^{R} \sum_{m=1}^{M} \alpha_{r,m} s_m^r, \tag{9.1}$$

where $f(\alpha, \bar{s})$ is the fusion score, $\alpha_0$ and $\alpha_{r,m}$ are the model parameters to be determined, and $R$ is the order of PSM. There are totally $K = 1 + RM$ parameters. The above power series model can be rewritten by matrix formulation

$$f(\bar{\alpha}, \bar{s}) = \sum_{k=0}^{K-1} \alpha_k p_k(\bar{s}) = \bar{p}(\bar{s}) \cdot \bar{\alpha}, \qquad (9.2)$$

where $\bar{p}(\bar{s}) = [p_1(\bar{s}), p_2(\bar{s}), \ldots, p_K(\bar{s})]$ and $\bar{p}_k(x)$ is a row vector corresponds to a power basis expansion term. $\bar{\alpha} = [\alpha_1, \alpha_2, \ldots, \alpha_K]^T$ denotes the parameter vector to be estimated.

Specifically, if $R = 1$, Eq. (9.1) equals

$$f(\bar{\alpha}, \bar{s}) = \alpha_0 + \sum_{m=1}^{M} \alpha_m s_m. \qquad (9.3)$$

As $\alpha_0$ is a constant, the PSM can be considered as the weight sum rule. Moreover, if we have $\alpha_m = 1$, $\alpha_0 = 0$, the PSM will be degenerated into sum rule.

We can use least square to estimate the parameter $\bar{\alpha} = [\alpha_1, \alpha_2, \ldots, \alpha_k]^T$, by minimizing the loss function:

$$J(\bar{\alpha}) = \frac{1}{2} \|\bar{y} - P\bar{\alpha}\|_2^2, \qquad (9.4)$$

where $\| \bullet \|_2$ denotes the Euclidean distance,

$$P = \begin{bmatrix} p_1(\bar{s}_1) & p_2(\bar{s}_1) & \cdots & p_K(\bar{s}_1) \\ p_1(\bar{s}_2) & p_2(\bar{s}_2) & \cdots & p_K(\bar{s}_2) \\ \vdots & \vdots & \ddots & \vdots \\ p_1(\bar{s}_n) & p_2(\bar{s}_n) & \cdots & p_K(\bar{s}_n) \end{bmatrix}$$

and $\bar{y} = [y_1, y_2, \ldots, y_n]^T$, where $y_i \in \{1, 0\}$ is the class label which denotes the sample pair from the same person or different persons.

The solution of Eq. (9.4) can be obtained as

$$\bar{\alpha} = (P^T P)^{-1} P^T \bar{y} \qquad (9.5)$$

Given a testing sample $\bar{s}_t$ as input, we can get

$$f_t = f(\bar{\alpha}, \bar{s}_t) = \bar{p}(\bar{s}_t) \cdot \bar{\alpha}, \qquad (9.6)$$

where $\bar{\alpha}$ is computed in Eq. (9.5). Assuming a threshold $\tau$, the matching result of $\bar{s}_t$ can then be determined as

$$\begin{cases} \bar{s}_t \in w_1 & \text{if } f_t \geq \tau, \\ \bar{s}_t \in w_0 & \text{if } f_t < \tau. \end{cases} \qquad (9.7)$$

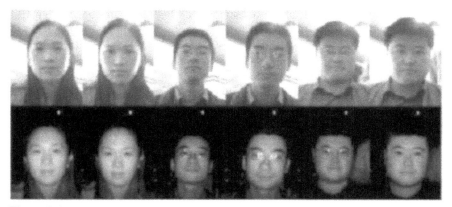

**Figure 9.6.** Typical VL face examples (upper) and NIR face examples (lower) in database.

## 9.4  EXPERIMENTS

### 9.4.1  Databases

To evaluate the performance of the proposed multimodal fusion in real-world applications, real multimodal databases are built for two fusions.

**(a) Database for NIR Face and VL Face.**  For the fusion of NIR and VL face, the capture device consists of two CMOS cameras. One is for the NIR image and the other is for the VL image, with resolution of 640*480 (in pixel). Therefore, a pair of NIR and VL face are captured from one object simultaneously.

   All the face images are taken near-frontal but in an uncontrolled indoor environment with varying pose, expression, and lighting. Some examples of typical NIR and VL face pairs in the database are shown in Figure 9.6. Both NIR and VL face images are then cropped into $144 \times 112$ according to the eye coordinates detected automatically. Figure 9.7 shows some examples of the cropped images.

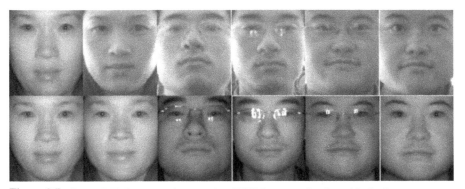

**Figure 9.7.** Cropped VL face examples (upper) and NIR face examples (lower) in database.

The NIR and VL face database is composed of 3940 pairs of images from 197 subjects, with 20 pairs per person. All the images are divided into training set and test set randomly. The training set includes 3000 pairs of images from 150 subjects, while the test set includes the left 940 pairs of images from 47 subjects. So the training set and the testing set have no intersection of persons and images either. In the training phase, we construct the AdaBoost classifiers for NIR and VL face modalities respectively and utilize the training set for LDA and PSM learning based fusion. In testing phase, each input NIR face and VL face image pair is matched with all of the other image pairs in the test set. This generates $47 \times C_{20}^2 = 8930$ intraclass (positive) and $20 \times 20 \times C_{47}^2 = 432,400$ extra-class (negative) samples.

**(b) Database for NIR Face and Iris.** To capture a high-resolution image including face and iris information sufficiently, we use a 10-megapixel CCD digital camera with up to $3648 \times 2736$ pixels. The camera is placed about 60–80 cm away from the subject. Around the camera lens, active NIR LED lights of 850 nm are mounted to provide frontal lighting. We use a band-pass optical filter on the camera lens to cut off visible light while allowing NIR light to pass.

An NIR face + iris database is built containing 560 high-resolution (2736*3648 pixels) NIR images. It includes 112 subjects of 55 females and 57 males, aged from 17 to 35, with 10 images for 76 subjects and 5 images for other 34 subjects. Figure 9.8

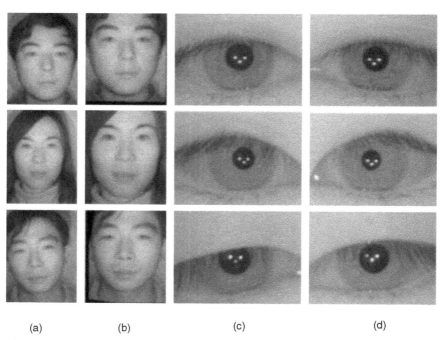

(a)            (b)            (c)            (d)

**Figure 9.8.** A high-revolution face image and separated face and both iris images. **(a)** High resolution NIR face images. **(b)** NIR image segmented from (a). **(c)** Left iris segmented from (a). **(d)** Right iris segmented from (a).

**Table 9.1.** Relationship Between GAR and the Order of the Power Series Model on Training Data

| R | 1 | 2 | 3 | 4 | 5 | 6 | 7 |
|---|---|---|---|---|---|---|---|
| GAR(%) (FAR = 0.1%) | 95.6 | 94.9 | 95.7 | 95.9 | 94.8 | 95.4 | 95.7 |
| EER(%) | 1.21 | 1.35 | 1.17 | 1.11 | 1.33 | 1.20 | 1.16 |

shows some examples of face images and the segmented iris parts. The training set includes 250 images from 50 subjects. The test set includes 310 images from 62 subjects, which are totally different from the subjects of the training set.

## 9.4.2 Results

### 9.4.2.1 Results for NIR Face and VL Face Fusion

For PSM-based fusion, the parameter order $R$ influences the performance of the fusion algorithm, so it needs to be optimized first. To determine the value of parameter $R$, we use the training set to evaluate the performance of varying the value of parameter. Table 9.1 shows the genuine acceptance rate (GAR) when the false acceptance rate (FAR) is at 0.1% and the equal error rate (EER) is at various values of $R$.

From the result, we can see that the PSM-based fusion method achieves the lowest error rate when $R$ is 4 in the training set. Therefore, in the following experiments, we choose $R = 4$ for the PSM-based method.

In this experiment, AdaBoost classifier is used in both NIR and VL face recognition. The output score of AdaBoost is a posterior probability $P(y = +1|x)$ that ranges from 0 to 1. Thus both output scores of NIR and VL face classifiers are well normalized in [0, 1] by AdaBoost, and no further score normalization process is needed when fusing them. We compare six score-level fusion methods: PSM [17], LDA [29], sum rule, product rule, min rule, and max rule [30]. Table 9.2 shows the match results of

**Table 9.2.** GAR and EER for Score Fusion of NIR Face and VL Face

| | GAR(%) (FAR = 0.1%) | EER(%) |
|---|---|---|
| PSMSF | 93.2 | 1.84 |
| LDA | 92.2 | 1.94 |
| SUM | 91.7 | 2.80 |
| PRODUCT | 91.7 | 2.81 |
| MIN | 89.4 | 4.56 |
| MAX | 90.7 | 2.04 |
| NIR | 90.1 | 2.34 |
| VIL | 84.0 | 5.27 |

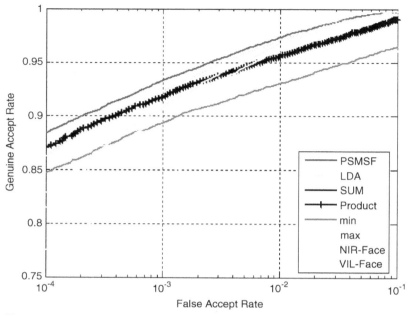

**Figure 9.9.** ROC curves for score fusion of NIR face and VL face.

six fusion methods and two single modalities, and Figure 9.9 shows the corresponding ROC curves.

### 9.4.2.2 Results for NIR Face and Iris Fusion

In this section we use the AdaBoost classifier trained from the above experiment for NIR face recognition and construct iris classifier using the method in reference 31. The method to choose $R$ is the same as fusion of NIR and VL face and the determined value of $R$ is 3 for the NIR face and iris fusion.

Since the face matching scores and iris matching scores are not in common domain, we need to normalize the scores from different modalities first. Three common normalization methods—min-max, Z-score, and tanh-score normalization—are used and compared in the experiments. Table 9.3 shows the match results for six fusion methods and three single modalities with three different normalization methods, and Figure 9.9 shows the corresponding ROC curves with different normalization methods.

## 9.4.3 Discussions

From the experimental results, we can observe that in most cases, fusion of NIR with VL faces and fusion of NIR face with iris modality can improve the recognition

**Table 9.3.** GAR and EER for Score Fusion of NIR Face and Iris

| | GAR(%) (FAR = 0.1%) | | | EER(%) | | |
|---|---|---|---|---|---|---|
| | Min–Max | Z-Score | Tanh | Min–Max | Z-Score | Tanh |
| PSM | 98.9 | 98.9 | 98.9 | 0.39 | 0.39 | 0.39 |
| LDA | 98.6 | 98.6 | 98.4 | 0.44 | 0.52 | 0.53 |
| SUM | 98.3 | 97.8 | 97.8 | 0.67 | 1.19 | 1.20 |
| MIN | 88.8 | 97.7 | 97.7 | 1.61 | 0.46 | 0.46 |
| MAX | 91.4 | 92.0 | 92.0 | 5.34 | 5.52 | 5.53 |
| NIR face | 88.2 | 88.2 | 88.2 | 1.59 | 1.59 | 1.59 |
| Left-iris | 91.1 | 91.1 | 91.1 | 3.99 | 3.99 | 3.99 |
| Right-iris | 91.8 | 91.8 | 91.8 | 5.08 | 5.08 | 5.08 |

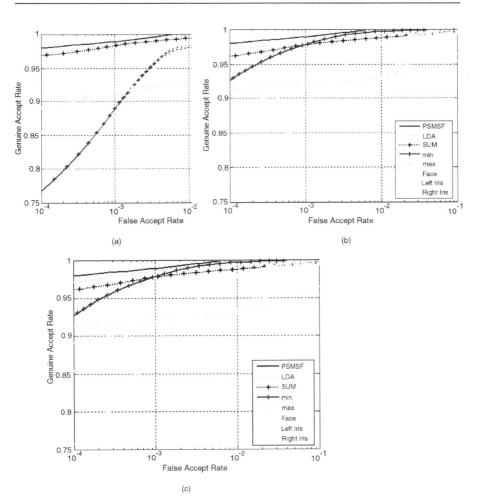

**Figure 9.10.** ROC curves for score fusion of NIR face and iris with three normalization methods: ((a) min–max, (b) Z-score, (c) Tanh.)

accuracy compared to any single modality performance, which proves the effectiveness of multimodal biometrics. The learning-based fusion methods such as LDA and PSM achieve better results than other methods, and the PSM-based method has achieved the best performance in all the cases. In the case of fusion of NIR and VL faces, the genuine accept rate (GAR) increases from 90.1% (NIR face) to 93.2%; and in the case of fusion of NIR face and iris biometric, the GAR increases from 88.2% (NIR face) to 98.9%. Moreover, comparing the results in NIR face and iris fusion, it can be seen that the PSM- and LDA-based methods have similar results with different score normalization methods, while the performance of some of the conventional methods such as min or max rule may fluctuate a little large. This indicates that the learning-based PSM and LDA methods are more robust to normalization methods and hence more suitable in practical applications.

## 9.5 CONCLUSIONS

In this chapter we explore synergies of NIR + VL faces and NIR face + iris by proposing an NIR face-based approach for multibiometrics. The NIR face is fused with VL face or iris in a natural way. This approach takes the advantages of recent progress in NIR face recognition, and it further improves the performance of biometric systems. Experimental results show that both the fusion of NIR + VL face and NIR face + iris can significantly improve the system performance in real databases. The learning-based methods such as LDA- and PSM-based fusion achieve the best results and are robust to score normalization, thus they are practical in real applications.

## ACKNOWLEDGMENTS

This work was supported by the following funding resources: National Natural Science Foundation Project #60518002, National Science and Technology Supporting Platform Project #2006BAK08B06, National 863 Program Projects #2006AA01Z192 and #2006AA01Z193, Chinese Academy of Sciences 100 people project, and the AuthenMetric Collaboration Foundation.

## REFERENCES

1. A. K. Jain, R. M. Bolle, and S. Pankanti, *Biometrics: Personal Identification in Networked Society*, Kluwer, Norwell, MA, 1999.
2. S. Z. Li, R. Chu, S. C. Liao, and L. Zhang, Illumination invariant face recognition using near-infrared images, *IEEE Trans. Pattern Anal. Mach. Intell.* **29**(4):627–639, 2007.
3. S. Z. Li, L. Zhang, S. C. Liao, X. X. Zhu, R. F. Chu, M. Ao, and R. He. A near-infrared image based face recognition system, in *Proceedings of 7th IEEE International Conference Automatic Face and Gesture Recognition (FG-2006)*, Southampton, UK, April 10–12, 2006, pp. 455–460.
4. S. Z. Li, R. F. Chu, M. Ao, L. Zhang, and R. He, Highly accurate and fast face recognition using near infrared images, in *Proceedings of IAPR International Conference on Biometric (ICB-2006)*, Hong Kong, January 2006, pp. 151–158.
5. J. Kittler, M. Hatel, R. P. W. Duin, and J. Matas, On combining classifiers, *IEEE Trans. Pattern Anal. Mach. Intell.* **20**(3):226–239, 1998.

6. L. Hong and A. K. Jain, Integrating faces and fingerprints for personal identification, *IEEE Trans. Pattern Anal. Mach. Intell.* **20**:1295–1307, 1998.

7. K. Chang, K. Bowyer, V. Barnabas, and S. Sarkar, Comparison and combination of ear and face images in appearance based biometrics, *IEEE Trans. Pattern Anal. Mach. Intell.*, **25**:1160–1165, 2003.

8. S. Ribaric and I. Fratric, A Biometric identification system based on eigenpalm and eigenfinger features, *IEEE Trans. Pattern Anal. Mach. Intell.* **27**:1698–1709, 2005.

9. S. Z. Li, C. S. Zhao, X. X. Zhu, and Z. Lei, Learning to fuse 3d+2d based face recognition at both feature and decision levels, in *Proceedings of IEEE International Workshop on Analysis and Modeling of Faces and Gestures*, Beijing, China, October 16, 2005, 44–54.

10. R. Brunelli and D. Falavigna, Person identification using multiple cues, *IEEE Trans. Pattern Anal. Mach. Intell.*, **17**:955–966, 1995.

11. J. Kittler, G. Matas, K. Jonsson, and M. Sanchez, Combining evidence in personal identity verification systems, *Pattern Recognit. Lett.* **18**:845–852, 1997.

12. A. Ross, A. K. Jain, and J. Z. Qian, Information fusion in biometrics, *Pattern Recognit. Lett.* **24**:2115–2125, 2003.

13. Y. Wang, T. Tan, and A. K. Jain, Combining face and iris biometrics for identity verification, in *Proceedings of International Conference on Audio- and Video-Based Person Authentication*, 2003, pp. 805–813.

14. B. Son and Y. Lee, Biometric authentication system using reduced joint feature vector of iris and face, in *Proceedings of International Conference on Audio- and Video-Based Person Authentication*, 2005, pp. 513–522.

15. C. Chen and C. T. Chu, Fusion of face and iris features for multimodal biometrics, in *Proceedings of IAPR International Conference on Biometric*, January 5–7, 2006, pp. 571–580.

16. A. Kumar, D. C. M. Wong, H. C. Shen, and A. K. Jain, Personal verification using palmprint and hand geometry biometric, in *Proceedings of International Conference on Audio- and Video-based Person Authentication*, 2003, pp. 668–678.

17. K.-A. Toh, Error-rate based biometrics fusion, in *ICB*, 2007, pp. 191–200.

18. S. Z. Li et al., CBSR NIR face dataset, http://www.cse.ohio-state.edu/otcbvs-bench/.

19. A. Hadid, T. Ahonen, and M. Pietikainen, Face description with local binary patterns:application to face recognition, *IEEE Trans. Pattern Anal. Mach. Intell.* **28**:2037–2041, 2006.

20. B. Moghaddam, C. Nastar, and A. Pentland, A Bayesian similarity measure for direct image matching, Media Lab Technical Report No.393, MIT, August 1996.

21. B. Abidi, J. Heo, S. Kong, and M. Abidi, Fusion of visual and thermal signatures with eyeglass removal for robust face recognition, in *IEEE Workshop on Object Tracking and Classification Beyond the Visible Spectrum in Conjunction with CVPR 2004*, 2004, pp. 94–99.

22. K. W. Bowyer K. I. Chang, and P. J. Flynn, Multi-Modal 2d and 3d biometrics for face recognition, in *IEEE Workshop on Analysis and Modeling of Faces and Gestures*, 2003.

23. K. W. Bowyer, K. I. Chang, and P. J. Flynn, Face recognition using 2D and 3D facial data, in *Workshop in Multimodal User Authentication*, 2003, pp. 25–32.

24. M. Prasad, Z. H. Pan, G. Healey, and B. Tromberg, Face recognition in hyperspectral images, *IEEE Trans. Pattern Anal. Mach. Intell.* **25**:1552–1560, 2003.

25. P. Viola and M. Jones, Robust real-time object detection, *Int. J. Comput. Vis.* **00**:000–000, 2002.

26. S. Pankanti, L. Hong, and A. Jain, Can multibiometrics improve performance?, in *Proceedings AutoID'99*, 1999, pp. 947–950.

27. A. K. Jain, Y. Wang, and T. Tan, Combining face and iris biometrics for identity verification, *AVBPA 2003 LNCS* **2688**:805–813, 2003.

28. J. G. Daugman, High confidence visual recognition of persons by a test of statistical independence, *IEEE Trans. Pattern Anal. Mach. Intell.*, **15**:1148–1161, 1993.

29. G. J. Mclachlan, *Discriminant Analysis and Statistical Pattern Recognition*, 1996.

30. R. P. W. Duin, J. Kittler, M. Hatel, and J. Matas, On combining classifiers, *IEEE Trans. Pattern Anal. Mach. Intell.* **20**(3):226–239, 1998.

31. J. Friedman, T. Hastie, and R. Tibshirani, Additive logistic regression: A statistical view of boosting, *Ann. Stat.* **28**(2):337–374, April 2000.

# Chapter 10

# A Novel Unobtrusive Face and Hand Geometry Authentication System Based on 2D and 3D Data

Filareti Tsalakanidou and Sotiris Malassiotis

## 10.1  INTRODUCTION

Research on biometric technologies has received significant attention during recent decades due to the increasing number of real-world applications requiring reliable personal authentication. Although biometric systems based on iris or fingerprint have been successfully employed in many high-security applications (e.g., providing access to secure military or citizen infrastructures and information), the use of biometrics for a wider range of everyday applications (e.g., financial services, health care, telecommunications, physical/remote access control to buildings/networks) is still limited. This is mainly attributed to lack of user acceptance, since these techniques require close cooperation of the user and follow a strict acquisition protocol using special recording devices. Other biometrics, on the other hand, such as the face or voice, are considerably less intrusive, but their performance is seriously affected by environmental conditions, such as illumination variations or background noise.

In order to enable the use of biometric technologies in a wide range of commercial and personal applications, it is important that we direct our efforts toward the development of biometric systems that will effectively combine user acceptance and convenience with highly dependable performance. Following this vision, much effort

*Biometrics: Theory, Methods, and Applications.* Edited by Boulgouris, Plataniotis, and Micheli-Tzanakou
Copyright © 2010 the Institute of Electrical and Electronics Engineers, Inc.

has been devoted to personal authentication based on user-friendly modalities such as the face and the hand, and many algorithms to this end have been proposed [1, 2].

The human face is undoubtedly the most common characteristic used by humans to recognize other people, and thus personal identification based on facial images is considered the friendliest among all biometrics. Hand geometry is another very popular biometric, and it is widely implemented for its ease of use, public acceptance, and integration capabilities.

The majority of the proposed face and hand geometry recognition techniques rely on two-dimensional (2D) intensity images, which represent the reflectance of the face or hand surface. The recorded image brightness is a function of the surface geometry, the surface material, the properties of light sources, and the camera parameters. Based on this, it is easily understood why the performance of 2D techniques can be seriously affected by illumination changes, pose variations, and use of cosmetics [3].

To alleviate limitations of traditional 2D face and hand recognition systems, three-dimensional (3D) biometrics were recently proposed based on the fact that the 3D geometry of the face and the hand offers an additional rich source of biometric information, which can be highly discriminatory. Moreover, 3D information is inherently insensitive to illumination changes and use of cosmetics and can simplify detection, localization, and face pose or hand posture estimation [4].

Although 3D authentication techniques offer significant advantages over classic 2D methods, they are not yet widespread mainly because 3D biometric research is still in the early stages and 3D sensing technologies are far from being mature compared to 2D imaging devices. This is, however, starting to change. Also, our experience from past research tells us that it is the combination of 2D and 3D that may offer a significant advantage over 2D and 3D alone, especially under relatively uncontrolled conditions [5, 6].

Much effort has been also devoted to the development of biometric systems that combine different biometric traits—for example, face combined with voice, fingerprint, and/or hand geometry [7]. Such systems are known as multimodal. Multimodal systems are more reliable because of the employment of independent sources of information, and they perform better than unimodal systems. Moreover, they overcome the problem of nonuniversality of biometric traits, and they provide more efficient antispoofing measures, since it is more difficult for an intruder to spoof multiple biometric traits of a legitimate user.

Motivated by recent advances in multimodal biometrics, as well as by the emergence of affordable 3D imaging technologies, in this chapter we present and evaluate a complete authentication system based on fusion of 2D and 3D face and hand biometrics. The system relies on a low-cost real-time sensor, which can simultaneously acquire a pair of depth and color images of the scene. By combining 2D and 3D facial and hand geometry features, as well as algorithms that compensate for environmental variations, highly accurate user authentication is achieved, as demonstrated by experiments on an extensive database recorded under real-world conditions. The proposed system presents a solution for a wide range of real-world applications, from high-security to personalization of services and attendance control.

## 10.2 PREVIOUS WORK

### 10.2.1 3D Face Recognition

Public face recognition tests demonstrated that the performance of the best 2D face recognition systems is similar to that of fingerprint recognition, when frontal neutral views recorded under controlled conditions are used, but degrades significantly for images subject to pose, illumination, or facial expressions variations [3]. These difficulties may be alleviated using the 3D geometry of the face, which is inherently insensitive to illumination changes or face pigmentation. In addition, using 3D images makes it considerably easier to cope with pose variations [8] or facial expressions [9].

Three-dimensional face recognition techniques can be roughly divided into three categories: surface-based, appearance-based, and model-based [10]. These are briefly discussed in the following.

#### 10.2.1.1 Surface-Based Methods

This class of techniques approach the problem of face recognition as one of measuring the similarity between surfaces. The similarity may be computed by means of local or global surface attributes.

In many techniques, surface curvature is used to localize facial features invariant to rigid transformations (e.g., eyes, eyebrows, nose, mouth, etc.) by making use of prior knowledge of face anatomy [11]. Face classification is usually based on the comparison of feature vectors representing the spatial relationships (distances, angles, etc.) between extracted facial features [12]. More generic transformation invariant descriptors based on mean and Gaussian curvature were also proposed [13, 14].

In reference 15, the sign of the Gaussian and mean curvature is used to segment the face in various regions and construct extended Gaussian images (EGIs) of them. The EGIs represent the distribution of the surface normal vector over each region. Face matching is performed using rotation invariant correlation between the respective EGIs. A similar approach is followed in reference 16, where an EGI of the face is computed using the maximum and minimum principal curvature and their local extrema. A recognition rate of 100% was reported in a database of 37 people.

In reference 17, the well-known point signatures method is applied for 3D face matching. Point signatures describe the structure of the face surface locally and are invariant to rigid transformations, but not to nonrigid ones, such as those caused by facial expressions. Thus, the rigid parts of the face should first be identified, before this technique is applied. Face matching is based on establishing the correspondences between the two surfaces through correlation of their signature vectors and calculating a similarity measure. In reference 18, 3D geometry features described by point signatures are fused with 2D texture features described by Gabor filters. Experiments in a database of 50 people and 300 images with viewpoint and facial expressions variations report a recognition rate close to 92%.

Although high recognition rates were reported for curvature-based techniques, in practice, these methods present several shortcomings. Their main disadvantage is that they are very sensitive to image noise (since the curvature is a second derivative) and occlusions of the face. Moreover, they are computationally expensive.

The computation of curvature features may be avoided altogether using global surface alignment techniques such as the iterative closest point (ICP) algorithm [19]. Point-to-point correspondences are established simply by searching for each point on the surface, the closest point on the other surface. Then, a rigid transformation may be computed that minimizes the sum of distances of corresponding points. This is performed iteratively; after convergence, the resulting distance between the two registered surfaces is used as a measure of similarity. This technique was tested in reference 20, and an EER better than 2% was reported in a database of 100 people with 700 images representing different poses.

The matching efficiency of the ICP can be improved by considering additional features, such as color or curvature, or by using a weighted distance [21]. The main limitation of the ICP algorithm is that its convergence is not guaranteed, unless a good initial transformation is available. As a result, this approach fails when applied on faces exhibiting pose variations. Such an initial transformation may be recovered, however, by localization of feature points such as the eyes and the nose on both probe and gallery images [22].

In order to cope with nonrigid deformation, Lu and Jain [23] extended the work in reference 22 by subdividing the face in rigid and nonrigid parts. Rigid registration is based on the ICP, while registration of nonrigid parts is based on the thin-plate spline model. Significant gains are reported using such a scheme. A combination of ICP and curvature-based approaches is presented in reference 24.

Alternative distance measures, such as the Hausdorff distance [25], the depth-weighted Hausdorff distance (DWHD) [26] and 2D approximations of the 3D Hausdorff distance [27] were also proposed.

To cope with facial expressions, many researchers have proposed the use of expression invariant representations of the face surface based on geodesic distances [28–30]. Such approaches rely on the assumption that the face is an approximately isometric surface and thus geodesic distances between face surface points are preserved with facial expressions. The intrinsic metric structure of the face surface is represented by embedding the surface into a low-dimensional 3D Euclidean space and replacing the geodesic distances by Euclidean ones [28]. Such representations are known as canonical forms and can be classified using classic rigid surface matching techniques. To address the problem of local nonisometric deformations caused by open mouths, topologically constrained Euclidean canonical forms and spherical canonical forms were also proposed in reference 29.

A computationally more efficient approach based on geodesic polar coordinates is presented in reference 30. The parameter space is built using a fast warping procedure, which avoids the embedding errors introduced by the multidimensional scaling (MDS) used in reference 29. Moreover, face matching is performed on 2D canonical images representing color or shape information, while the open-mouth problem is efficiently handled by segmenting the face in three parts and merging the distinct canonical maps.

### 10.2.1.2 Appearance-Based or Statistical Approaches

Appearance-based techniques, such as PCA, LDA, or Fisherfaces, have been widely used in 2D face recognition [1]. Extension of these techniques to 3D face recognition may be easily performed—for example, by applying them on range images, which represent the distance of each surface point from the camera plane. PCA-based classification is applied in depth data alone [31, 32] or in both 2D (color or intensity) and depth images [33, 34].

In reference 31, the PCA and ICA algorithms are applied in normalized 3D images of different dimensions. Face normalization is based on detecting the ridge of the nose and aligning it with the vertical axis. A recognition rate of 83% is reported in a database of 222 images depicting several expression variations.

A multimodal PCA scheme using two independent classifiers for color and depth images and fusion of the resulting matching scores was proposed in reference 33. Experiments were conducted on 2D, 3D, and 2D+3D images, and a recognition rate of 99% was reported for the multimodal approach in a test set of 80 images. In references 34 and 35, a database of significant size (275 subjects, 675 images) was used to produce comparative results of face identification using eigenfaces for 2D and 3D and their combination and for varying image quality. This test considered only frontal images captured under constant illumination.

In reference 6, a database with 3000 images containing several variations (pose, illumination, expressions, glasses, several recording sessions) was used. The embedded hidden Markov models (EHMM) technique was applied on both color and depth images, and low error rates were reported. To cope with intrapersonal variations due to viewpoint or lighting conditions, the face database was enriched with artificially generated examples depicting variations in pose and illumination.

In reference 36, the eigenface approach was applied in a variety of surface representations of the human face, such as range images, curvature maps, Laplacian images, surface gradient maps, and so on; and different distance metrics (Euclidean distance, Mahalanobis distance, cosine distance) were used for face matching. The same experimenting protocol was employed in reference 37, but the Fisherface method was used instead of the eigenfaces. Fisherfaces were shown to be more efficient. Fisherfaces were also examined in reference 38.

The main problem with appearance-based methods is the requirement for accurate alignment between probe and gallery images. This may be achieved by localizing facial features, such as the nose and eyes.

### 10.2.1.3 Model-Based Techniques

Model-based techniques try to capture the variability of face appearance and 3D geometry by assuming that this variability is constrained in a linear subspace, which is computed using a large example set of registered 3D face scans belonging to different subjects. Using this assumption, any novel face may be characterized by a set of appearance (texture) and geometry coefficients, which are subsequently used for face classification.

The 3D morphable model is the most known such technique successfully applied for 2D face recognition under pose and illumination variations [39]. Several similar techniques were also used for 3D face recognition. In reference 40, a set of feature points is detected in the 2D image by means of classic 2D feature extraction techniques. A generic 3D model is subsequently deformed to match the extracted 3D feature points using techniques such as the Procrustes analysis followed by local deformations [40]. Face matching is based on computing the Euclidean distances between probe and gallery face models. In reference 41, an annotated deformable face model (AFM) is used based on an average facial 3D mesh, constructed using statistical data. Anthropometric landmarks are associated with the model vertices, and the AFM is annotated into different areas. For face matching, the AFM is elastically deformed to fit a new face. The resulting deformed 3D model is used to generate a regular 2D grid, while wavelet analysis is applied to extract a set of coefficients, which are subsequently used for face classification. A 98% recognition rate is reported in the FRGC database. The AFM model can be used together with other physiological information (e.g., thermal infrared data representing facial vasculature) in a multimodal recognition scheme [42].

## 10.2.2   3D Hand Geometry Recognition

Hand geometry recognition works by comparing the 3D geometry of the palm and fingers with a previously enrolled sample. Several 2D hand geometry techniques have been proposed. These usually work by matching geometric features, such as finger width/length and palm radius [43–45] or hand silhouettes [46–48].

The use of the 3D finger surface as a biometric identifier is examined in reference 49. Depth images of the back of the hand placed on a dark surface and corresponding color images are acquired using a 3D scanner. A combination of skin and edge detection techniques is used for efficient hand segmentation and extraction of three masks corresponding to the three middle fingers. For each finger, a shape index image is computed using the principal curvatures of surface points. Recognition is based on the correlation of corresponding shape index images. A database with 688 images of 68 subjects recorded in two sessions was used for the experiments. For images acquired during the same week, the recognition rate was 99.4%, but dropped to 75% when probe and gallery images were acquired with one-week lapse.

## 10.3   SYSTEM ARCHITECTURE

In this chapter we present a novel biometric authentication system integrating 2D and 3D images of the face and the hand acquired using a novel low-cost 3D and color sensor [5]. Face and hand data are independently processed by two distinct classifiers, and the resulting matching scores are combined using state-of-the-art score fusion techniques.

The face authentication subsystem uses both 2D and 3D images. Unlike the majority of similar multimodal systems, which rely on simple fusion of scores disregarding the actual information conveyed by the two modalities, our method uses both 2D and 3D facial data in all steps of the face authentication chain: face detection, normalization, and classification. Moreover, it exploits the main advantage of 3D face geometry—that is, relative robustness to viewpoint and illumination changes—to create geometrically and photometrically aligned probe and gallery images, which are subsequently classified using a PCA-based approach [5, 50]. The combination of 2D and 3D facial data, along with treatment of illumination and pose variations, results in significant gains in terms of system performance.

Unlike techniques presented in Section 10.2.2, the hand authentication subsystem employs a contact-less approach, which facilitates unconstrained hand placement. Moreover, it works on a combination of 2D and 3D hand data, exploiting the 3D shape of fingers along with their 2D silhouette for efficient hand segmentation, localization, and feature extraction. Hand classification is based on a limited number of cross-sectional 3D finger measurements, while in reference 49, which also uses the 3D shape of fingers, "3D shape images" are used to represent each finger. In addition, our system offers a real-time, low-cost, and easy-to-use solution, while reference 49 relies on images acquired from a high-end range scanner.

Multimodal authentication based on face and hand geometry was also investigated elsewhere [7, 51], but it was only tested under ideal conditions regarding both appearance variations and environmental conditions. Moreover, face recognition was based on a CCD camera, while hand recognition relied on placement of the user's hand on a special platter with knobs or pegs. Two-dimensional images of the face and hand were used for extracting facial and hand geometry features, thus making the system sensitive to illumination changes.

Fusion of 3D face, 3D hand, and 3D ear geometry features was examined in reference 52. Face matching is performed by applying the ICP algorithm on a region of interest including the nose and eye cavity areas, while finger matching is based on the technique proposed in reference 49. For the experiments, frontal neutral views of the face and ideal hand postures were collected using a range scanner.

Our system, on the other hand, offers a low-cost, totally unobtrusive solution, using a single sensor. The additional use of 3D images offers increased robustness in illumination and pose variations, as well as face pigment, while it greatly simplifies pose or finger bending estimation. Furthermore, combining color and 3D information makes the system relatively insensitive to cluttered background, use of accessories (scarfs, hats, rings), and presence of artifacts or obstructions. Moreover, the system is evaluated in a large set of images depicting numerous variations in facial appearance and pose, as well as hand posture.

For the acquisition of 2D and 3D face and hand images, we use a novel color and 3D sensor, which consists of low cost devices: a CCTV camera and a multimedia projector, both embedded in a mechanical construction. A color-coded light pattern is projected on object surfaces. By measuring its deformation in the images captured by the camera, a 3D image of the scene can be generated using an active triangulation principle. Switching rapidly between the colored pattern and a white light, a color image may be captured as well, approximately synchronized with the depth image. A frame rate of 14 fps is achieved in a 3.2-GHz PC. The generated color and depth

**Figure 10.1.** Color and depth face and hand images acquired using the 3D sensor (see Section 10.3). In the range image, brighter colors correspond to points closer to the camera, while white pixels correspond to undetermined depth values.

images have a resolution of $780 \times 580$ pixels, while the depth accuracy of the 3D sensor is 0.5-mm standard deviation for objects standing at about 1-m distance in a working volume of 60 cm $\times$ 40 cm $\times$ 50 cm (width $\times$ height $\times$ depth) [5].

Due to the 3D acquisition principle, the acquired depth images may contain pixels where no depth values were computed. These "holes" are usually located over areas that cannot be reached by the projected light (e.g., the sides of the nose or the sides of the fingers) and/or over highly refractive (e.g., eyeglasses, rings, painted nails) or low reflective surfaces (e.g., hair, beard) (see Figure 10.1).

The authentication system consists of the 3D sensor, a monitor and a PC, where the software runs. The user stands in front of the sensor looking at the camera so that her face is inside the effective working volume. The monitor shows a real-time video of the recorded color image sequence, while it also displays directions for correct placement of the face and hand inside the working volume by tracking the face and hand of the user. After a pair of face images is acquired, the user is asked to place her hand in front of her face with the back of the hand facing the sensor, keeping her fingers straight. This posture is most convenient for all users and provides the best resolution of hand images. After capturing several pairs of hand images, the system positively identifies or rejects the user based on fusion of the matching scores provided by the face and hand classifiers.

Although there are obviously some limitations on the working conditions under which the system operates (e.g., large facial poses or large finger bending are not allowed), the proposed authentication system does not constrain user movement; at the same time, special care is taken to provide a user-friendly interface.

## 10.4 3D FACE AUTHENTICATION SYSTEM

In this section we describe the various components of the face authentication system. First, 3D data are exploited for the detection and localization of the face. Then, we compensate for the pose of the face and the illumination of the scene, thus generating frontal views with constant illumination. The normalized color and depth images are subsequently used for face classification. A block diagram illustrating the various steps of the face authentication algorithm is shown in Figure 10.2.

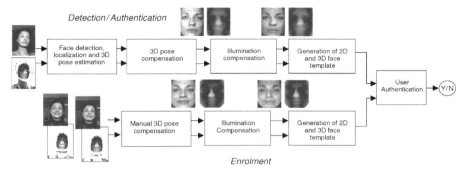

**Figure 10.2.** Block diagram illustrating the various steps of the user authentication algorithm based on color and depth facial images.

## 10.4.1 Face Detection and Feature Localization

Face detection and localization is based exclusively on 3D data, thus exhibiting robustness in illumination changes and occlusion of facial features. First, we detect the face in the 3D image using global descriptors and a priori knowledge of the geometry and relevant dimensions of the head and other body parts. Then, we localize the position of the nose using a knowledge-based technique.

Segmentation of the body from the background is achieved using the histogram of depth values and estimating the threshold separating the two distinct modes. Segmentation of the head from the body relies on statistical modeling of the head–torso points. The probability distribution of a 3D point $\mathbf{x}$ is modeled as a mixture of two Gaussians:

$$P(\mathbf{x}) = P(\text{head})P(\mathbf{x}|\text{head}) + P(\text{torso})P(\mathbf{x}|\text{torso}) \tag{10.1}$$

$$= \pi_1 N(\mathbf{x}; \boldsymbol{\mu}_1, \boldsymbol{\Sigma}_1) + \pi_2 N(\mathbf{x}; \boldsymbol{\mu}_2, \boldsymbol{\Sigma}_2), \tag{10.2}$$

where $\pi_1, \pi_2$ are the prior probabilities of the head and torso, respectively, and $N(\mathbf{x}; \boldsymbol{\mu}, \boldsymbol{\Sigma})$ is the 3D Gaussian distribution with mean $\boldsymbol{\mu}$ and covariance $\boldsymbol{\Sigma}$.

Maximum-likelihood estimation of the unknown parameters $\pi_k, \boldsymbol{\mu}_k, \boldsymbol{\Sigma}_k, k = 1, 2$, from the 3D data is obtained by means of the expectation–maximization algorithm [6]. To avoid the convergence of the algorithm to local minima, good initial parameter values are required, which may be obtained using 3D moments. Let $\mathbf{m}$ be the center of mass, let $\mathbf{S_T} = \sum_n (\mathbf{x}_n - \mathbf{m})(\mathbf{x}_n - \mathbf{m})^T$ be the scatter matrix computed from the data points $\mathbf{x}_n$, and let $\mathbf{u}_i$, $i = 1, \ldots, 3$, be the eigenvectors of $\mathbf{S_T}$, ordered according to the magnitude of the corresponding eigenvalues $\lambda_i$. Initial estimates of the unknown parameters are selected by

$$\boldsymbol{\mu}_1 = \mathbf{m} + \rho_1 s_{\min} \mathbf{u}_1, \qquad \boldsymbol{\mu}_2 = \mathbf{m} + \rho_2 s_{\max} \mathbf{u}_1,$$

$$\boldsymbol{\Sigma}_k = \mathbf{U}\boldsymbol{\Lambda}_k\mathbf{U}^T, \qquad \boldsymbol{\Lambda}_k = \text{diag}(\rho_k \lambda_1, \sigma_k \lambda_2, \lambda_3),$$

$$\pi_k = \rho_k,$$

where

$$s_{\min} = \min_{\mathbf{x}_n}\{(\mathbf{x}_n - \mathbf{m})^T \mathbf{u}_1\}, \quad s_{\max} = \max_{\mathbf{x}_n}\{(\mathbf{x}_n - \mathbf{m})^T \mathbf{u}_1\}.$$

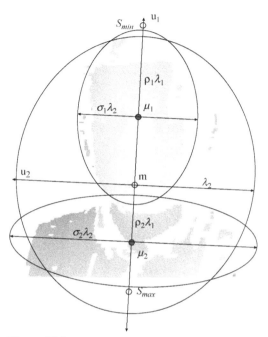

**Figure 10.3.** Illustration of knowledge-based initialization of the head and torso 3D blob distribution parameters. Ellipses represent iso-probability contours of posterior distributions. The lengths of the axes of the ellipses are selected on the basis of the iso-probability ellipse estimate computed using all 3D data.

$\mathbf{U}$ is the orthogonal eigenvector matrix of $\mathbf{S}_T$, while $\rho_1, \rho_2, \sigma_1$, and $\sigma_2$ are constants related to the relative size of the head with respect to the torso (in the experiments $\rho_1 = 1/2$, $\rho_2 = 1/2$, $\sigma_1 = 1/2$ and $\sigma_2 = 1$ were used). The physical interpretation of the above parameter selection is illustrated in Figure 10.3. The centers of the 3D blobs corresponding to the head and torso are placed along the principal axis of the full body, while their relative position and size are initialized based on prior knowledge of the human body structure.

The above algorithm provides an estimate of the center and orientation of the head, which may be used to define a bounding box in the 3D image, which safely contains the nose. The localization of the nose tip is based on the analysis of the 3D curvature of the face surface. To avoid computation of principal curvatures in all pixels inside the face bounding box, we first select a set of candidate points based on the observation that the nose tip should be close to a local minimum of the depth image. This assumption is valid if the face is the closest object to the sensor and has a medium pose. Local depth minima are detected by one-dimensional search over depth pixel values of each scan line inside the region of interest (see Figure 10.4f).

Next, we compute the minimum and maximum curvature over all local depth minima. Since surface points around the tip of the nose define a semispherical surface, we may eliminate the vast majority of candidate points by excluding those having

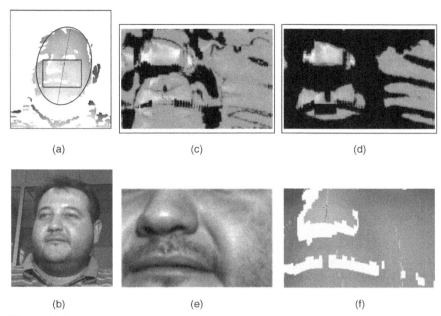

**Figure 10.4.** Nose tip localization. (**a**) Detected 3D head blob with selected region of interest containing the nose; (**b**) corresponding color image; (**c**) maximum principal curvature inside the region of interest depicted in (**e**) (negative values have been suppressed); (**d**) minimum principal curvature; (**f**) dots represent local depth minima, with black dots corresponding to minima passing the curvature threshold.

principal curvature values outside a specific range. Finally, we exploit the fact that the nose tip lies in the end of the nose ridge to exclude false candidates that pass the curvature test. Points in the nose ridge have high curvature values perpendicular to the ridge direction. Thus, an appropriate measure of ridge strength is defined by

$$C(\mathbf{p}) = \min_{\theta} \sum_{\mathbf{q} \in L(\mathbf{p}, \theta)} K(\mathbf{q})^2, \tag{10.3}$$

where $L(\mathbf{p}, \theta)$ is the set of points in the line section that starts from a candidate point $\mathbf{p}$ and has direction $\theta$ and length equal to the average nose length. $K(\mathbf{q})$ is the ratio of curvatures across this line. $C(\mathbf{p})$ is computed by searching in a small set of $\theta$ values. The nose tip is selected by first excluding candidates having $C(\mathbf{p})$ values above a threshold and then selecting from the remaining the one closest to the sensor. The nose ridge corresponds to the points along $L(\mathbf{p}, \theta)$. A root mean square error of 1–2 mm was obtained using the above nose localization algorithm [8].

## 10.4.2  Pose Estimation and Compensation

Several techniques have been proposed to recognize faces under varying pose. One approach is the automatic generation of novel views resembling the pose in the probe image. This is achieved either by using an active appearance or shape face model [41] or a deformable 3D model [39], as described in Section 10.2.1.3. Classification is subsequently based on the similarity between the probe image and the generated view. A different approach is based on building a pose-varying eigenspace by recording several images of each person under varying pose [53]. A third approach relies on pose estimation and pose compensation based on the extraction of salient features in 3D images. Face matching between normalized images is then performed using classic 2D methods, such as PCA, or 3D surface registration techniques [22, 34, 50].

The pose compensation algorithm described in this section belongs to the last category. Unlike other works, which use both 2D and 3D data for feature extraction and pose estimation, this algorithm is based solely on 3D images, thus exhibiting increased robustness in illumination changes. Moreover, it employs a fast feature extraction technique (see Section 10.4.1) and is capable, given a pair of color and depth images, to produce a new pair of frontal views accurately aligned with gallery images.

More specifically, after the nose is localized, a 3D line is fitted on the 3D co-ordinates of pixels on the ridge of the nose using a weighted least-squares fitting algorithm. The 3D line $\Lambda$ defines two of the three degrees of freedom of the face orientation. The third, which is the rotation angle $\phi$ around the nose axis, is estimated by finding the plane $\mathbf{E}(\phi)$, which bisects the face into two bilateral symmetric parts. To do this, first we define a 3D transformation $T(\phi)$, which aligns $\Lambda$ with the $Y$ axis, the symmetry plane with the $YZ$ plane, and the nose tip with the center of the axes. Next, we project the transformed 3D points of the original image in a virtual camera aligned with the coordinate system of the face, which results in the construction of a rectified depth image $I_r$. Only a very sparse sampling of the original image is performed and the projection parameters are chosen so that the projection of the central face area fits into a $32 \times 32$ image. The symmetry plane $\mathbf{E}(\phi)$ minimizes a measure of bilateral symmetry

$$S(\phi) = \sum_{(\mathbf{x}, \hat{\mathbf{x}})} |I_r(\mathbf{x}) - I_r(\hat{\mathbf{x}})| \qquad (10.4)$$

by exhaustive search in an appropriate range of values (see Figure 10.5). $\mathbf{x}$ and $\hat{\mathbf{x}}$ are pairs of symmetric image pixels that have nonzero depth values. Observing that $S(\phi)$ is a monotonic function of $\phi$, we can considerably speedup this algorithm by adopting a hierarchical approach, which starts from a very sparse sampling of $\phi$ and proceeds with finer sampling in continuously decreasing intervals of the parameter value. The average error rate produced by the above technique is less than $2°$ [8].

Using the estimated pose parameters and nose-tip location, we define a local 3D coordinate frame, which is aligned with the face and centered on the nose tip. Pose compensation relies on warping the input depth image so that the local coordinate frame is aligned with a reference coordinate frame, thus bringing the face in upright orientation (warped image). The reference frame is defined during training, as will be described below. The alignment between the two frames is further refined to pixel accuracy by applying the ICP surface registration algorithm [19] between the warped and a reference depth image of the same subject.

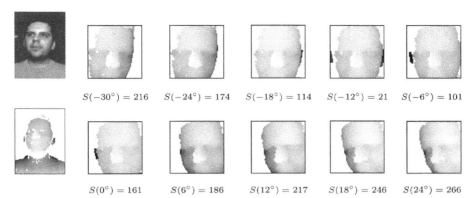

$S(-30°) = 216$    $S(-24°) = 174$    $S(-18°) = 114$    $S(-12°) = 21$    $S(-6°) = 101$

$S(0°) = 161$    $S(6°) = 186$    $S(12°) = 217$    $S(18°) = 246$    $S(24°) = 266$

**Figure 10.5.** Estimation of the plane of bilateral face symmetry. The rectified images $I_r$ obtained for different values of $\phi$ and the computed symmetry cost $S(\phi)$ are shown.

The resulting depth image contains missing pixels, some of which are filled by exploiting the face symmetry and using depth values of mirroring pixels. Remaining missing pixels are linearly interpolated from neighboring points by means of a 2D Delaunay triangulation. The interpolated depth image is finally used to rectify the associated color image, thus resulting in a pair of canonical frontal views. Figure 10.6 illustrates several examples of pose compensation.

For the training, a similar but simpler pose compensation technique is used. The face orientation is estimated by manually selecting three points on the input image, which define a local 3D coordinate frame. Then, the input color and depth images are warped to align this local coordinate frame with the coordinate frame of the camera, using the surface interpolation algorithm described above. For one of the pose-compensated depth images of each person, a simplified version of the automatic pose estimation algorithm described above is applied, thus estimating a reference coordinate frame. This last step is important, since the slant of the nose differs from person to person.

### 10.4.3  Illumination Compensation

In this section we describe an illumination compensation algorithm, which generates from the input image a novel image relit from a frontal direction. Our approach is inspired by work on image-based scene relighting used for rendering realistic images [54]. Image relighting relies on inverting the rendering equation—this is, the equation that relates the image brightness with the object material and geometry and the illumination of the scene. Given several images of the scene under different conditions, this equation may be solved (although an ill-posed problem) to recover the illumination distribution and then use this to re-render the scene under novel illumination.

The first step is therefore to recover the scene illumination from a pair of color and depth images. Assuming that the scene is illuminated by a single light source, a

**Figure 10.6.** Pose compensation examples. The original pairs of images and the resulting frontal views are shown.

technique is adopted that learns the nonlinear relationship between the image brightness and light source direction $\mathbf{L}$ using a set of artificially generated bootstrap images.

For each subject in the database, we use the reference pose compensated depth image $I_r$ to render $N$ virtual views of the face, illuminated from different known directions. To decrease the dimensionality of the problem, from each rendered image we extract a feature vector $\mathbf{q}_i$, $i = 1, \ldots, N$, comprised of locally weighted averages of image brightness over $M = 30$ locations, which were chosen to include face pixels with similar albedo. The normalized samples are subsequently used to approximate the $M$-dimensional illuminant direction function $\mathbf{L} = \mathbf{G}_j(\mathbf{q})$ of subject $j$ using support vector machines [55].

Given a pose compensated color image $I_c$ and a claimed ID $j$, the light source direction $\mathbf{L}$ can be computed by the previous formula, after extracting the feature vector $\mathbf{q}$ from $I_c$. The next step is to relight the color image with a frontal light $\mathbf{L}_0$. To do this, first we approximate the image brightness in each pixel $\mathbf{u}$ using the formula

$$I_c(\mathbf{u}) = A(\mathbf{u})R(I_d, \mathbf{L}, \mathbf{u}), \tag{10.5}$$

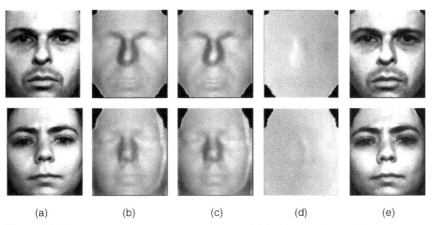

(a)          (b)          (c)          (d)          (e)

**Figure 10.7.** Illumination compensation examples. (a) Original image, (b) $R(I_d, \mathbf{L}, \mathbf{u})$, (c) $R(I_d, \mathbf{L}_0, \mathbf{u})$, (d) $R(I_d, \mathbf{L}_0, \mathbf{u})/R(I_d, \mathbf{L}, \mathbf{u})$, (e) novel image relit by frontal light.

where $I_d$ is the pose compensated depth image, $A$ is the unknown surface albedo, and $R$ is a rendering of the surface with constant albedo. Likewise, the illumination compensated color image $\tilde{I}_c$ can be written as $\tilde{I}_c(\mathbf{u}) = A(\mathbf{u})R(I_d, \mathbf{L}_0, \mathbf{u})$. From the above, it is easily drawn that the illumination compensated image $\tilde{I}_c$ can be simply computed by multiplication of the input image with a ratio image

$$\tilde{I}_c(\mathbf{u}) = I_c(\mathbf{u}) \frac{R(I_d, \mathbf{L}_0, \mathbf{u})}{R(I_d, \mathbf{L}, \mathbf{u})}. \tag{10.6}$$

An important advantage of our technique is the flexibility in coping with complex illumination conditions by adapting the rendering function $R$. For example, accounting for attached shadows may be easily achieved by activating shadowing in the rendering engine. Nonetheless, we have observed that relatively simple renderings, such as the Lambertian reflection model, where $R(\mathbf{u}) = \mathbf{n}(\mathbf{u})^T \cdot \mathbf{L}$ and $\mathbf{n}(\mathbf{u})$ is the surface normal at $\mathbf{u}$, also give good results. Figure 10.7 illustrates the relighting of side illuminated images.

## 10.4.4 Face Classification

The pair of images generated after pose and illumination compensation is subsequently used as input to the face classifier. Note that the same normalization procedure was applied to gallery images as well. Color pixel values are normalized to have zero mean and unit variance.

Several state-of-the-art face classification techniques have been examined including classic eigenfaces, probabilistic matching, embedded hidden Markov models, and elastic graph matching. A simpler version of the probabilistic matching algorithm [56] based on extra-personal eigenfaces was finally adopted because of its good performance and computational efficiency. The PM algorithm is applied to both color and depth images, independently. The two resulting matching scores are fused together to provide a single score using classic fusion techniques, as will be described in Section 10.6.3.

## 10.5  3D HAND GEOMETRY AUTHENTICATION

In this section we outline the algorithms employed by the hand geometry authentication system. First, the hand is segmented from the body using 3D moments. Then, the position of the palm and fingers is accurately localized in the 3D image. Two-dimensional information is subsequently used to localize finger boundaries using a model-based approach. Finally, we extract a set of 3D finger measurements including width and curvature information [2].

### 10.5.1  Hand Detection

According to the authentication scenario described in Section 10.3, the user stands in front of the sensor with her hand in front of the face and the back of the hand facing the sensor. Segmentation of the hand from the body is achieved by assuming that the hand does not move. Thus, we may exploit the results of face detection to form a plane that separates the face from the hand and arm. In practice, however, this may not be efficient, since the user may have moved her body. Thus, hand segmentation relies on statistical modeling of the hand, arm, and head plus torso points using a knowledge-based 3D blob approach, similar to the face segmentation algorithm described in Section 10.4.1. Similarly to Eq. (10.1), the probability distribution of a 3D point $\mathbf{x}$ can be modelled as a mixture of three Gaussians:

$$P(\mathbf{x}) = P(\text{head} + \text{torso})P(\mathbf{x}|\text{head} + \text{torso})$$
$$+ P(\text{hand})P(\mathbf{x}|\text{hand}) + P(\text{arm})P(\mathbf{x}|\text{arm}) \tag{10.7}$$
$$= \pi_1 N(\mathbf{x}; \boldsymbol{\mu}_1, \boldsymbol{\Sigma}_1) + \pi_2 N(\mathbf{x}; \boldsymbol{\mu}_2, \boldsymbol{\Sigma}_2) + \pi_3 N(\mathbf{x}; \boldsymbol{\mu}_3, \boldsymbol{\Sigma}_3), \tag{10.8}$$

where $\pi_1, \pi_2, \pi_3$ are the prior probabilities of the head/torso, hand, and arm blobs, respectively. Initialization of blob parameters is obtained in a fashion similar to that in Section 10.4.1 using prior knowledge of the relative configuration of body parts [2] (see Figure 10.8).

The parameters $\boldsymbol{\mu}_2$ and $\boldsymbol{\Sigma}_2$ that result after EM convergence correspond to the center of mass and the pose of the hand. Hand segmentation is achieved by defining a plane $(\mathbf{p} - \boldsymbol{\mu}_2)^{\mathrm{T}} \cdot \mathbf{n} = d$ that separates the hand from the face. $\mathbf{n}$ is the eigenvector of $\boldsymbol{\Sigma}_2$ corresponding to the smallest eigenvalue, and it is approximately perpendicular to the hand surface plane. $d$ is the distance of the hand plane from the cutting plane. Three-dimensional points lying in front of this plane form a mask corresponding to the hand and forearm, while the rest are discarded (see Figure 10.9a,b). The value of $d$ is chosen in accordance to allowed closeness of the hand to the face. For our experiments, the distance of the hand from the body can be as small as 10 cm. For smaller distances there are a few cases (usually exhibiting finger bending) where the algorithm fails to find a separating plane and crops part of the fingers.

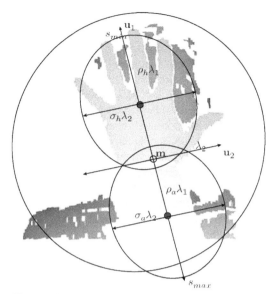

**Figure 10.8.** Illustration of knowledge-based initialization of the hand and forearm 3D blob distribution parameters.

## 10.5.2 Hand Localization

After detecting the hand blob, we localize the center and radius of the palm and fingers. An initial estimate of the palm center is obtained by projecting the center $\mu_2$ of the hand blob on the image plane. The palm radius is estimated by computing the chamfer distance transform [57] inside a bounding box centered on the palm center. This transform provides the minimum distance of each point to the object boundary. Since the palm of the hand is approximately circular, the maximum chamfer distance $r_p$ is

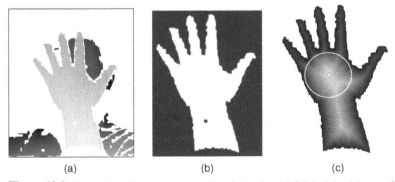

|     (a)      |     (b)      |     (c)      |

**Figure 10.9.** Estimation of the center and radius of the palm. (**a**) Original depth image, (**b**) mask of pixels corresponding to hand/forearm, (**c**) chamfer distance transform with estimated palm circle centered on the distance transform maximum.

computed near the palm center $\mathbf{c}_p$ and corresponds to the palm radius (Figure 10.9c). Finally, the 2D orientation $\theta$ of the hand is given by the slant of the vertical image axis with the hand–forearm axis. The latter is approximated by the principal eigenvector of the covariance matrix of the 2D hand–forearm pixels belonging to the mask.

To detect the fingers, first we draw circular homocentric arcs ($[\theta - \pi/2, \theta + \pi/2]$) with increasing radius $r$ ($r \in [1.2r_p, 4r_p]$) around $\mathbf{c}_p$ and obtain a set of circular segments of the fingers. After excluding segments with very large or very small length compared to the average finger width, we use the midpoints of remaining segments to estimate the finger skeletons. To do this, we should cluster skeleton points belonging to the same finger. A minimum spanning tree having as vertices these midpoints is created. By discarding edges that are longer than a threshold, we obtain an initial set of clusters, which is further refined by omitting clusters with very few points (less than three) and merging clusters that satisfy a proximity criterion. This criterion is based on the collinearity of the cluster points and is formulated as $\epsilon < \gamma(\epsilon_1 + \epsilon_2)$, where $\epsilon_1$ is the error of fitting a 2D line on the points of the first cluster, $\epsilon_2$ for the second cluster, $\epsilon$ for their union, and $\gamma$ a constant (we set $\gamma = 1$). The four longer clusters are retained. These correspond to the four fingers, excluding the thumb.

Approximate skeletons of fingers are then obtained by fitting 2D line segments on the points of each cluster. In addition, we can locate right and left finger boundaries by searching in a direction perpendicular to the finger skeleton. Unlike techniques that use the hand silhouette to detect the fingers, our approach is efficient even for noisy images with disconnected boundaries (e.g., due to rings). Moreover, it is much faster since it operates on a small set of image pixels and not the whole image. The various steps of this algorithm are illustrated in Figure 10.10a–c.

### 10.5.3 Finger Boundary Localization

The finger localization algorithm described in the previous section relies solely on 3D information, thus being sensitive in missing depth pixels along finger boundaries. In order to estimate finger boundaries more accurately, we also use the color image.

(a)                    (b)                    (c)                    (d)

**Figure 10.10.** Finger detection and localization. (**a**) Original depth image, (**b**) circular arcs used to detect finger segments, (**c**) 2D lines fitted on skeleton points and boundaries, (**d**) estimated finger boundary segments.

In this case, we have to deal with complex background and low contrast, since the hand and the face have the same color.

A deformable model approach is adopted. We create a 2D geometric finger model of each finger using the estimated finger skeleton and boundaries. $N$ points $\mathbf{q}_i$ are sampled from the model boundary; and a set of local gradient maxima $\mathbf{g}_i^j$, $j = 1, \ldots, K_i$, is computed along a line that passes from $\mathbf{q}_i$ and is perpendicular to the model boundary ($\pm$ a few pixels around $\mathbf{q}_i$). This way, we get a set of candidate boundary points located on a narrow band around the previously estimated boundary line. From these, we select an optimal set $\{\mathbf{q}_i'\}$ minimizing the cost function

$$D(\mathbf{q}_1', \mathbf{q}_2', \ldots, \mathbf{q}_N') = \sum_i^N \Delta I(\mathbf{q}_i') + \sum_i^{N-1} D(\mathbf{q}_i', \mathbf{q}_{i+1}'), \qquad (10.9)$$

where $\mathbf{q}_i' \in \{\mathbf{g}_i^j, j = 1, \ldots, K_i\}$ and $D(\mathbf{a}, \mathbf{b})$ is the length of the line segment defined by points $\mathbf{a}$ and $\mathbf{b}$.

The set of points resulting after optimization defines a polygon that approximates the finger boundary with high accuracy. The fingertip $\mathbf{t}_m$ of each finger $m$ may be easily estimated by projecting all the boundary points in the finger axis.

## 10.5.4  Feature Extraction and Classification

Hand geometry recognition is based on the measurement of 3D finger features such as finger width and curvature. More specifically, for each finger $m$ we define a set of $K$ linear segments $s_k^m$, $k = 1, \ldots, K$, which are perpendicular to the finger axis, and their endpoints lie on the estimated finger boundary (see Figure 10.10d). These segments are chosen so that their midpoints $\tilde{s}_k^m$ have specific 3D distances from the corresponding fingertips $\mathbf{t}_m$.

Then for each finger, we define two signature functions, $W^m(x)$ and $C^m(x)$, parameterized by the 3D distance $x$ from the fingertip along the finger's ridge. The first function corresponds to the width of the finger in 3D and it is computed by fitting a 3D line on the 3D points corresponding to each segment $s_k^m$, projecting the endpoints of this segment on this line and computing their Euclidian distance. The second signature corresponds to the mean curvature of the curve that is defined by the 3D points corresponding to each finger segment.

Hand classification is based on 3D geometric features of the user's fingers extracted using these signature functions. In total, 12 width and 12 curvature measurements are calculated for each of the four fingers of the user (the thumb is excluded since it provides unreliable measurements). Finger width and curvature measurements are computed by sampling $W^m(x)$ and $C^m(x)$ respectively on $\rho_i \tilde{\Lambda}^m$, $i = 1, \ldots, 12$, where $\tilde{\Lambda}^m$ is the average length of each finger, computed during training and $\rho_i \in (0.2, 0.8)$ with 0.05 step. All 96 measurements are finally concatenated in one feature vector, which is used for classification. The similarity score between two feature vectors is based on their $L1$ norm.

## 10.6  EXPERIMENTAL EVALUATION

The aim of the experimental evaluation presented in this section is to examine the efficiency of the proposed multimodal system under conditions similar to those encountered in real-world applications and compare its performance against the unimodal face and hand recognition systems, as well as against the combination of 2D and 3D facial data.

### 10.6.1  Face and Hand Database

The most common approach toward the evaluation of multimodal biometric systems is merging two or more separate databases to construct a multimodal database. Such an approach leads to the creation of the so-called *chimeric users*, who combine different biometric traits from different real users; for example, hand images of user *A* are combined with face images of user *B* [7, 51, 58]. In general, the use of such databases is based on the modality independence assumption, according to which two or more biometric traits of a single person are independent of each other. However, experimental results measuring the discrepancy in performance between the use of chimeric users and the use of real users have shown that using virtual subjects may not appropriately replace the use of real multimodal data sets [59].

For the evaluation of the performance of the proposed multimodal system, we used the setup of Section 10.3 in an office environment and recorded a face and hand database comprised of 50 subjects in two recording sessions with 10 days' lapse [2, 5]. The test population contains 15 female and 35 male subjects between 19 and 36 years of age. Each volunteer was asked to look at the camera and make several expressions (neutral face, smile, laugh). Face images depicting illumination variations (spotlight illuminating the face from one side), pose variations ($\pm 20°$ head rotation to the left or the right) and images with/without wearing eyeglasses were also acquired. Then, the user was asked to put her hand in front of the face keeping the fingers separated and several images of this posture were acquired with slight variations on palm orientation and finger bending. Examples of images belonging to the database are shown in Figure 10.11.

In each session, approximately 70 pairs of color and depth face images were recorded for each user, and about 50 pairs of hand images, thus resulting in a total of 3500 face recordings and 2500 hand recordings per session. The first session was used for training and the second for testing. Three different modalities and their combinations were examined using this data set: face reflectance data (color face images—FC), 3D face geometry (depth face images—FD), hand geometry (hand geometry measurements extracted from color and depth images—H) and combinations of the three, that is, FC + FD, FC + H, FD + H, and FC + FD + H.

### 10.6.2  Training of Classifiers

As seen in Section 10.4.4, the face classifier is comprised of two independent classifiers, one for depth and the other for color images. For the training of the face

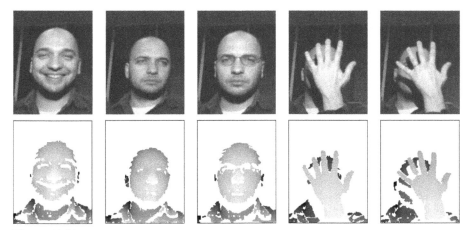

**Figure 10.11.** Examples of database images recorded during the same session.

classifiers, two frontal neutral (depth or color) views per subject were randomly selected from the first recording session and one feature vector was computed for each of them. Note that unlike Tsalakanidou et al. [5], we do not include images with facial expressions in the training set. For the training of the hand classifier, we used four pairs of hand images for each enrolled person, depicting an "ideal" posture—that is, wide-open palm approximately parallel to the camera, with extended fingers, no rings worn. For each image pair, a feature vector containing 3D finger measurements was extracted.

For a probe color or depth face image, computation of the matching score consists in calculating a similarity score between this image and the two gallery images corresponding to the claimed ID and then selecting the maximum of the two scores. For a hand probe image on the other hand, first the $L_1$ distance between the extracted feature vector and the four previously estimated gallery feature vectors is computed, and then the matching score is set equal to the minimum distance. To improve the performance of the hand classifier, we use a sequence of four input frames of the same individual instead of just one probe image, and then we combine the scores computed on the four frames by simple averaging (see reference 2). For testing, 4-tuples are generated randomly from the set of probe hand images belonging to the same individual.

### 10.6.3  Fusion of Matching Scores

The proposed multimodal system relies on fusion of the matching scores computed by the face and hand classifiers for the same enroled user. Since the output of the these classifiers is not in the same range, it is essential that the matching scores be normalized—that is, transformed in a common domain. We have experimented with five well-known normalization techniques, namely min–max, Z-score, median, tanh, and quadric-line-quadric (QLQ) [7, 58], and finally selected QLQ, which performed better than the others [60]. QLQ is an adaptive normalization procedure, proposed in reference 58, aiming to decrease the overlap of the genuine and impostor distributions while still mapping the scores in [0, 1]. First, an original score $s$ is normalized using the min–max normalization technique:

$$s_{\text{mm}} = \frac{s - \min}{\max - \min},$$ (10.10)

where max and min are the maximum and minimum values of the scores produced by the classifier. These parameters are estimated using a bootstrap set of matching scores $S = \{s_1, s_2, \ldots, s_M\}$ produced by this classifier.

Then, the following mapping function is applied to the min–max normalized score $s_{\text{mm}}$:

$$s_n = \begin{cases} \frac{1}{c - \frac{w}{2}} s_{\text{mm}}^2, & s_{\text{mm}} \leq c - \frac{w}{2} \\ s_{\text{mm}}, & c - \frac{w}{2} < s_{\text{mm}} \leq c + \frac{w}{2} \\ c + \frac{w}{2} + \sqrt{(1 - c - \frac{w}{2})(s_{\text{mm}} - c - \frac{w}{2})} & \text{otherwise,} \end{cases}$$ (10.11)

where $s_n$ is the final score and $c$ and $w$ are the center and width of the overlap zone of the min–max normalized scores of $S$.

The normalization parameters can be calculated using two different approaches: a global one and a user-specific one. In the global approach, the matching score set $S$ includes genuine and impostor scores produced by test images of all enrolled users; that is, the normalization parameters are the same for all users. In the user-specific approach, these parameters are computed for each user: The matching score set $S_k$ for user $k$ consists of genuine and impostor scores obtained when the ID of user $k$ is claimed. The second approach is more efficient for user authentication [60].

After normalization, the scores provided by different classifiers are combined in a single score, which will be used for authentication. Several score fusion techniques, such as simple sum, product, max-score, min-score, and weighted-sum [58], were used in our experiments. The weighted-sum (WS) fusion gave the best results. If $\{s_i^m\}$, $m = 1, \ldots, M$, are the normalized scores computed by $M$ different classifiers for user $i$, then the score resulting after WS fusion is given by

$$f_i = \sum_{m=1}^{M} w^m s_i^m,$$ (10.12)

where $\sum_{m=1}^{M} w^m = 1$ . The weights $w^m$ are assigned to the individual classifiers so that the total equal error rate (EER) is minimized. This way, more robust classifiers are assigned higher weights, while less accurate classifiers are assigned lower weights.

The above normalization-fusion scheme was applied to different modality combinations, that is, FC + FD and FC + FD + H. For the unimodal classifiers no normalization was required.

## 10.6.4 Experiments

The face test database consists of 3457 face image pairs of 50 persons, while the hand test database consists of 24,898 4-tuples of hand image pairs of the same individuals. Face and hand probe images were selected from the second recording session.

For each probe (face and/or hand) image the identity of all enroled users is claimed in turn, thus resulting in one genuine (user to whom this image actually belongs to) and 49 impostor claims per image. In total, 3457 genuine and 169,393 (3457 × 49) impostor matching scores are computed from the face test database and 24,898 genuine and 1,220,002 (24,898 × 49) impostor scores from the hand database.

For the evaluation of the proposed face + hand multimodal system, each pair of probe face images (depth + color) is associated with five randomly selected pairs of hand images belonging to the same person, thus resulting in 17,285 (3457 × 5) "pairs" of hand + face images—that is, 17,285 score vectors. A score vector is a triplet $\langle s_{FC}, s_{FD}, s_H \rangle$, where $s_{FC}$, $s_{FD}$, and $s_H$ are the matching scores obtained by the FC, FD, and H classifiers, respectively. From each score vector, a multimodal score is computed in the following way: First we normalize the matching scores provided by the unimodal classifiers using the QLQ normalization. Then, we consolidate the normalized scores using the weighted-sum fusion technique.

Using the above procedure, 17,285 genuine and 846,965 (17,285 × 49) impostor fusion scores were produced for evaluating the performance of the FC + FD + H authentication system. For the evaluation of the 2D + 3D face authentication system, the 3457 image pairs of the face database were used, resulting in 172,850 (3457 × 50) fusion scores (QLQ normalization and WS fusion were also applied). The performance of the proposed authentication system is presented in terms of the equal error rate (EER) values, the receiver operating characteristics (ROC) curves, and the rank-1 identification rates.

Table 10.1 summarizes the EERs of the unimodal 2D and 3D face classifiers, the 2D + 3D face authentication system (FC + FD) and the proposed face and hand multimodal system (FC + FD + H) for different appearance variations of facial images. The corresponding identification rates (IR) are also shown. It is clear that the multimodal classifier combining facial and hand data exhibits better authentication rates (lower error rates) than do the unimodal systems or the combination of 2D and 3D facial data for all facial variations. Obviously, combining facial features with hand geometry features can be more efficient, since these features are considerably less correlated than, for example, 2D and 3D facial data.

The superiority of the proposed multimodal scheme is more clearly demonstrated in the case of expressions or wearing eyeglasses. For images depicting different expressions (smile, laugh), the EER reported for the FC and FD classifiers is about 10%. By combining 2D and 3D facial data, the EER decreases to 8%. An EER of 1% is finally obtained when fusing color and depth facial data with hand geometry data. Similar statistics are observed for images with subjects wearing glasses, although in this case the decrement of the EER is smaller.

It is also interesting to observe that in the case of the unimodal face classifiers or the 2D + 3D face classifier, the EERs obtained for probe images with pose or

**Table 10.1.** EER Values and Rank-1 Identification Rates (%) Obtained for Different Facial Variations[a]

| | | Facial Variations | | | | |
|---|---|---|---|---|---|---|
| Modality | Frontal | Expression | Pose | Illumination | Glasses | All |
| FC | 3.32 (99.13) | 10.14 (95.18) | 5.79 (98.14) | 3.61 (98.36) | 5.03 (97.96) | 6.46 (97.75) |
| FD | 2.22 (99.87) | 10.73 (92.96) | 4.42 (99.00) | 2.53 (98.55) | 6.49 (98.95) | 7.55 (97.85) |
| FC + FD | 0.86 (99.72) | 8.00 (96.43) | 2.57 (98.93) | 2.00 (98.76) | 3.36 (98.59) | 4.39 (98.51) |
| FC + FD + H | 0.38 (100.00) | 1.07 (100.00) | 0.50 (100.00) | 0.80 (100.00) | 1.32 (100.00) | 0.82 (100.00) |

[a]We compare the performance of the proposed face + hand geometry authentication system (FC + FD + H), the 2D + 3D face authentication system (FC + FD), and the unimodal face classifiers.

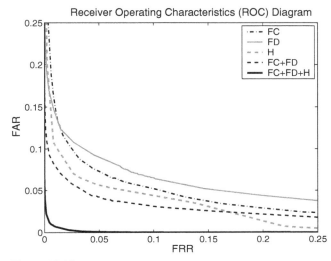

**Figure 10.12.** ROC diagrams for the unimodal systems, the 2D + 3D face recognition system, and the proposed face + hand geometry recognition system.

illumination variations are significantly lower compared to those reported for other variations, such as facial expressions. This should be attributed to the deployment of the proposed pose and illumination compensation algorithms [5]. To cope with facial expressions, the use of training images depicting representative expressions was proposed by Tsalakanidou et al. [5]. In this work, the problem of facial expressions and all other variations is effectively solved by the additional use of the hand geometry modality, which results in low EERs for all variations.

The performance of the hand classifier is affected by hand pose and hand posture variations. More specifically, the proposed system was shown to work efficiently with palm orientations up to 15° with respect to the camera and finger bending up to 15° of the knuckle joints. For larger hand poses, its accuracy deteriorates significantly due to finger occlusion, which leads to biased cross-sectional finger measurements. Finger bending, on the other hand, affects the accuracy of the finger localization algorithm.

Figure 10.12 illustrates the ROC curve of the proposed multimodal system (all image variations included in the test set). The ROC curves of the unimodal systems and the FC + FD system are also shown for comparison. It is easily perceived that the combination of face and hand geometry features for personal authentication offers high reliability and increased robustness. More specifically, an EER of 0.82% is obtained for the multimodal classifier, while the EER reported for the FC + FD classifier is 4.39%. The EERs obtained for FC, FD, and H are 6.46%, 7.55%, and 5.44%, respectively.

For user recognition applications (closed-set 1:$N$ identification), the cumulative recognition rates versus rank are illustrated in Figure 10.13, where a recognition rate of 100% is depicted for the multimodal system, while the recognition rate reported

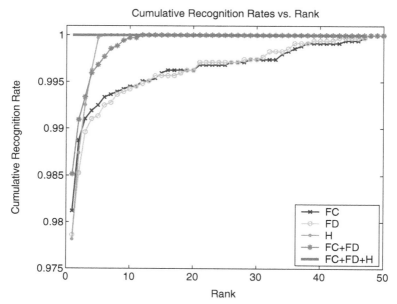

**Figure 10.13.** Cumulative recognition rates versus rank for the unimodal systems, the 2D + 3D face recognition system, and the proposed face + hand geometry recognition system.

for the FC + FD system is 98.51%. The recognition rates for the unimodal classifiers FC, FD, and H are 97.75%, 97.86%, and 97.80%, respectively.

## 10.7   CONCLUSIONS

An end-to-end biometric authentication system based on integration of 2D and 3D face and hand images was presented in this chapter. The proposed system aims to satisfy both user convenience and authentication accuracy requirements. The first requirement was achieved by selection of unobtrusive modalities, acquisition setup, and authentication scenario. High accuracy was also attained by exploiting the 3D geometry of face and hand, but also thanks to algorithms that compensate for pose and illumination variability.

Although the proposed system is also robust to other forms of variability (e.g., facial expressions or hand posture) due to the combination of the face and hand modalities, further work will be needed in this direction.

Specifically, working under completely unattended conditions, such as an outdoor ATM authentication system, would require further research in 3D face recognition to cope with large head rotations and complex illumination. Similarly, unattended 3D hand recognition would require algorithms that effectively deal with finger bending or posture variation or at least detect such situations and guide the user accordingly.

# ACKNOWLEDGMENTS

This work was supported by research projects "BioSec-Biometrics and Security" (FP6-001766) and "PASION-Psychologically Augmented Social Interaction over Networks" (FP6-027654) under the Information Society Technologies (IST) priority of the 6th Framework Programme of the European Community.

# REFERENCES

1. W. Zhao, R. Chellappa, A. Rosenfeld, and P. J. Phillips, Face recognition: A literature survey, *ACM Comput. Surv.* **35**(4):399–459, 2003.
2. S. Malassiotis, N. Aifanti, and M. G. Strintzis, Personal authentication using 3D finger geometry, *IEEE Trans. Inf. Forensics Secur.* **1**(1):12–21, 2006.
3. P. J. Phillips, P. Grother, R. J. Micheals, D. M. Blackburn, E. Tabassi, and J. M. Bone, Face Recognition Vendor Test 2002, Evaluation Report, Defense Advanced Research Projects Agency and National Institute of Justice, USA, 2003.
4. K. W. Bowyer, K. Chang, and P. J. Flynn, A survey of approaches and challenges in 3D and multi-modal 3D + 2D face recognition, *Comput. Vis. Image Understanding* **101**(1):1–15, 2006.
5. F. Tsalakanidou, F. Forster, S. Malassiotis, and M. G. Strintzis, Real-time acquisition of depth and color images using structured light and its application to 3D face recognition, *Real-Time Imaging* **11**(5–6):358–369, 2005.
6. F. Tsalakanidou, S. Malassiotis, and M. G. Strintzis, Face localization and authentication using color and depth images, *IEEE Trans. Image Processing* **14**(2):152–168, 2005.
7. A. Jain, K. Nandakumar, and A. Ross, Score normalization in multimodal biometric systems, *Pattern Recognit.* **38**(12):2270–2285, 2005.
8. S. Malassiotis and M. G. Strintzis, Robust real-time 3D head pose estimation from range data, *Pattern Recognit.* **38**(8):1153–1165, 2005.
9. A. M. Bronstein, M. M. Bronstein, and R. Kimmel, Expression-invariant 3D face recognition, in *Lecture Notes in Computer Science, International Conference on Audio- and Video-Based Biometric Person Authentication*, LNCS 2688, 2003, pp. 62–70.
10. T. Papatheodorou and D. Rueckert, 3D face recognition, in K. Delac and M. Grgic, editors, *Face Recognition*, I-Tech Education and Publishing, Vienna, pp. 417–446.
11. T. K. Kim, S. C. Kee, and S. R. Kim, Real-time normalization and feature extraction of 3D face data using curvature characteristics, in *Proceedings of the 10th International Workshop Robot and Human Interactive Communications*, pp. 74–79.
12. G. G. Gordon, Face recognition based on depth and curvature features, in *Proceedings of the International Conference on Computer Vision and Pattern Recognition*, pp. 808–810.
13. A. B. Moreno, A. Sanchez, J. F. Velez, and F. J. Diaz, Face recognition using 3D surface-extracted descriptors, in *Proceedings of the Irish Conference on Machine Vision and Image Processing*, 2003.
14. Y. Lee, H. Song, U. Yang, H. Shin, and K. Sohn, Local feature based 3D face recognition, in *Lecture Notes in Computer Science, International Conference on Audio- and Video-Based Biometric Person Authentication*, LNCS 3546, 2005, pp. 909–918.
15. J. C. Lee and E. Milios, Matching range images of human faces, in *Proceedings of the 3rd International Conference on Image Processing*, 1990, pp. 722–726.
16. H. T. Tanaka, M. Ikeda, and H. Chiaki, Curvature-based face surface recognition using spherical correlation. Principal directions for curved object recognition, in *Proceedings of the 3rd International Conference on Automatic Face and Gesture Recognition*, 1998, pp. 372–377.
17. C.-S. Chua, F. Han, and Y.-K. Ho, 3D human face recognition using point signature, in *Proceedings of the 4th International Conference on Automatic Face and Gesture Recognition*, 2000, pp. 233–238.
18. Y. Wang, C.-S. Chua, and Y.-K. Ho, Facial feature detection and face recognition from 2D and 3D images, *Pattern Recognit. Lett.* **23**(10):1191–1202, 2002.

19. P. J. Besl and H. D. McKay, A method for registration of 3-D shapes, *IEEE Trans. Pattern Anal. Mach. Intell.* **14**(2):239–256, 1992.
20. G. Medioni and R. Waupotitsch, Face modeling and recognition in 3D, in *Proceedings of the IEEE International Workshop Analysis and Modeling of Faces and Gestures*, 2003, pp. 232–233.
21. T. Papatheodorou and D. Rueckert, Evaluation of automatic 4D face recognition using surface and texture registration, in *Proceedings of the 6th International Conference on Automatic Face and Gesture Recognition*, 2004, pp. 321–326.
22. X. Lu, D. Colbry, and A. K. Jain, Matching 2.5D scans for face recognition, in *Proceedings of the International Conference on Pattern Recognition*, 2004, pp. 362–366.
23. X. Lu and A. K. Jain, Deformation modeling for robust 3D face matching, in *Proceedings of the International Conference on Computer Vision and Pattern Recognition*, 2006, pp. 1377–1383.
24. K. Chang, K. W. Bowyer, and P. J. Flynn, Multiple nose region matching for 3D face recognition under varying facial expression, *IEEE Trans. Pattern Anal. Mach. Intell.* **28**(10):1695–1700, 2006.
25. B. Achermann and H. Bunke, Classifying range images of human faces with hausdorff distance, in *Proceedings of the International Conference on Pattern Recognition*, 2000, p. 809–813.
26. Y. Lee and J. Shim, Curvature based human face recognition using depth weighted hausdorff distance, in *Proceedings of the International Conference on Image Processing*, 2004, pp. 1429–1432.
27. T. D. Russ, K. W. Koch, and C. Q. Little, A 2D range Hausdorff approach for 3D face recognition, in *Proceedings of the International Conference on Computer Vision and Pattern Recognition*, 2005, p. 169.
28. A. M. Bronstein, M. M. Bronstein, and R. Kimmel, Three-dimensional face recognition, *Int. J. Comput. Vis.* **64**(1):5–30, 2005.
29. A. M. Bronstein, M. M. Bronstein, and R. Kimmel, Expression-invariant representations of faces, *IEEE Trans. Image Processing* **16**(1):188–197, 2007.
30. I. Mpiperis, S. Malassiotis, and M. G. Strintzis, 3D face recognition with the geodesic polar representation, *IEEE Trans. Inf. Forensics Secu.* **2**(3):537–547, 2007.
31. C. Hesher, A. Srivastava, and G. Erlebacher, A novel technique for face recognition using range imaging, in *Proceedings of the 7th International Symposium on Signal Processing and Applications*, 2003, pp. 201–204.
32. G. Pan, S. Han, Z. Wu, and Y. Wang, 3D face recognition using mapped depth images, in *Proceedings of the IEEE International Conference on Computer Vision and Pattern Recognition*, 2005, p. 175.
33. F. Tsalakanidou, D. Tzovaras, and M. G. Strintzis, Use of depth and colour eigenfaces for face recognition, *Pattern Recognit. Lett.* **24**(9–10):1427–1435, 2003.
34. K. I. Chang, K. W. Bowyer, and P. J. Flynn, Face recognition using 2D and 3D facial data, in *Proceedings of the ACM Multimodal User Authentication Workshop*, 2003, pp. 25–32.
35. K. I. Chang, K. W. Bowyer, and P. J. Flynn, An evaluation of multimodal 2D + 3D face biometrics, *IEEE Trans. Pattern Anal. Mach. Intell.* **27**(4):619–624, 2005.
36. T. Heseltine, N. Pears, and J. Austin, Three-dimensional face recognition: An eigensurface approach, in *Proceedings of the International Conference on Image Processing*, 2004, pp. 1421–1424.
37. T. Heseltine, N. Pears, and J. Austin, Three-dimensional face recognition: A fishersurface approach, in *Proceedings of the International Conference on Image Analysis and Recognition*, 2004, pp. 684–691.
38. B. Gokberk, A. A. Salah, and L. Akarun, Rank-based decision fusion for 3D shape-based face recognition, in *Lecture Notes in Computer Science, International Conference on Audio- and Video-Based Biometric Person Authentication*, LNCS 3546, 2005, pp. 1019–1028.
39. V. Blanz, Face recognition based on a 3D morphable model, in *Proceedings of the 7th International Conference on Automatic Face and Gesture Recognition*, 2006, pp. 617–624.
40. A.-N. Ansari and M. Abdel-Mottaleb, 3D face modeling using two views and a generic face model with application to 3D face recognition, in *Proceedings of the International Conference on Advanced Video and Signal Based Surveillance*, 2003, pp. 37–44.
41. I. A. Kakadiaris, G. Passalis, G. Toderici, M. N. Murtuza, Y. Lu, N. Karampatziakis, and T. Theocharis, Three-dimensional face recognition in the presence of facial expressions: An annotated deformable model approach, *IEEE Trans. Pattern Anal. Mach. Intell.* **29**(4):640–649, 2007.

42. I. A. Kakadiaris, G. Passalis, T. Theocharis, G. Toderici, I. Konstantinidis, and M. N. Murtuza, Multi-modal face recognition: Combination of geometry with physiological information, in *Proceedings of the 4th International Conference on Computer Vision and Pattern Recognition*, 2005, pp. 1022–1029.

43. A. Jain, A. Ross, and S. Pankanti, A prototype hand Geometry-based verification system, in *Proceedings of the 2nd International Conference on Audio and Video-Based Biometric Person Authentication*, 1999, pp. 166–171.

44. R. Sanchez-Reillo, C. Sanchez-Avila, and A. Gonzalez-Marcos, Biometric identification through hand geometry measurements, *IEEE Trans. Pattern Anal. Mach. Intell.* **22**(10):1168–1171, 2000.

45. Y. Bulatov, S. Jambawalikar, P. Kumar, and S. Sethia, Hand recognition using geometric classifiers, in *Proceedings of the 1st International Conference on Biometric Authentication*, 2004, pp. 753–759.

46. A. Jain and N. Duta, Deformable matching of hand shapes for verification, in *Proceedings of the International Conference on Image Processing*, 1999, pp. 857–861.

47. C. Oden, A. Ercil, and B. Buke, Hand recognition using implicit polynomials and geometric features, *Pattern Recognit. Lett.* **24**(13):2145–2152, 2003.

48. G. Zheng, C. Wang, and T. E. Boult, Personal identification by cross ratios of finger features, in *Proceedings of the International Conference on Pattern Recognition, Biometrics Workshop*, 2004.

49. D. Woodard and P. Flynn, Finger surface as a biometric identifier, *Comput. Vis. Image Understanding* **100**(3):357–384, 2005.

50. S. Malassiotis and M. G. Strintzis, Robust face recognition using 2D and 3D data: Pose and illumination compensation, *Pattern Recognit.* **38**(12):2537–2548, 2005.

51. A. Ross and A. Jain, Information fusion in biometrics, *Pattern Recognit. Lett.* **24**(13):2115–2125, 2003.

52. D. L. Woodard, T. Faltemier, P. Yan, P. J. Flynn, and K. W. Bowyer, A comparison of 3D biometric modalities, in *Proceedings of the Conference on Computer Vision and Pattern Recognition*, 2006, p. 57.

53. A. Pentland, B. Moghaddam, and T. Starner, View-based and modular eigenspaces for face recognition, in *Proceedings of the International Conference on Computer Vision and Pattern Recognition*, 1994, p. 84–91.

54. L. Zhang and D. Samaras, Face recognition under variable lighting using harmonic image exemplars, in *Proceedings of the International Conference on Computer Vision and Pattern Recognition*, 2003, p. 19–25.

55. K.-R. Muller, S. Mika, G. Ratsch, K. Tsuda, and B. Scholkopf, An introduction to kernel-based learning algorithms, *IEEE Neural Networks* **12**(2):181–201, 2001.

56. B. Moghaddam, W. Wahid, and A. Pentland, Beyond eigenfaces: Probabilistic matching for face recognition, in *Proceedings of the International Conference on Automatic Face and Gesture Recognition*, pp. 30–35, 1998.

57. G. Borgefors, Distance transformations in digital images, *Comput. Vis. Graphics and Image Processing* **34**:344–371, 1986.

58. R. Snelick, U. Uludag, A. Mink, M. Indovina, and A. Jain, Large-scale evaluation of multimodal biometric authentication using state-of-the-art systems, *IEEE Trans. Pattern Anal. Mach. Intell.* **27**(3):450–455, 2005.

59. N. Poh and S. Bengio, Can chimeric persons be used in multimodal biometric authentication experiments? in *Lecture Notes in Computer Science, International Workshop on Machine Learning and Multimodal Interaction*, LNCS 3869, 2005, pp. 87–100.

60. F. Tsalakanidou, S. Malassiotis, and M. G. Strintzis, A 3D face and hand biometric system for robust user-friendly authentication, *Pattern Recognit. Lett.* **28**(16):2238–2249, 2007.

# Chapter 11

# Learning Facial Aging Models: A Face Recognition Perspective

**Narayanan Ramanathan and Rama Chellappa**

## 11.1 INTRODUCTION

Developing computational models that characterize human facial appearances has been a challenging research problem for many decades. Human faces vary in appearance due to factors such as illumination variations, head pose changes, facial expressions, aging effects, and so on. Human perception studies have often highlighted the psychosocial importance associated with one's facial appearance. Hence, modeling human faces is often driven toward tasks such as (i) extracting a biometric signature from faces that is invariant to the many factors that induce appearance variations and (ii) performing facial analysis (facial expression analysis, gender identification, age estimation, etc.).

From the perspective of deriving an illumination and pose invariant signature, most approaches adopt the three-dimensional (3D) Lambertian surface assumption in modeling human faces. Photometric stereo-based approaches such as Basri and Jacobs [1], Ramamoorthy [2], Georghiades et al. [3], Zhou and Chellappa [4], and Zhou et al. [5] were proposed to generalize across illumination variations and to derive illumination invariant face signatures. Blanz and Vetter [6] proposed the "3D morphable model"-based approach for performing recognition across illumination and pose variations. Ekman's facial action coding systems (FACS) [7] initiated a whole line of research on facial expressions analysis. Yacoob and Davis [8], Essa and Pentland [9], Martinez [10], and Liu et al. [11] propose methods to analyze facial

*Biometrics: Theory, Methods, and Applications.* Edited by Boulgouris, Plataniotis, and Micheli-Tzanakou
Copyright © 2010 the Institute of Electrical and Electronics Engineers, Inc.

expressions, to mention a few. From a face recognition perspective, how significant is it to characterize facial aging effects? In this chapter we provide a thorough analysis on facial aging effects and, furthermore, discuss in detail computational models that characterize the same. The chapter is organized as follows : We begin with describing the motivations behind working on the problem of facial aging. Next, we provide a detailed account of some of the previous work on this topic. Later, we describe a computational model that we developed to characterize facial aging effects observed during the formative years (1–18 years). We conclude the chapter by providing some insights into future work on the aforementioned topic.

### 11.1.1 Motivation

Facial aging effects induce notable variations in one's appearance across ages. During the formative years, facial aging effects are typically observed in the form of pronounced variations in facial shape, and during adulthood, they are observed in the form of subtle variations in facial shape and texture. Typically, individuals of the same gender and ethnic background exhibit similar facial aging traits during different ages. Furthermore, individuals undergoing weight gain/loss across years are observed to exhibit similar facial aging traits. Some of the significant implications of studies related to facial aging are listed below:

- **Face Recognition/Verification Across Age Progression:** Facial aging effects are known to progressively induce appearance variations. With face recognition systems getting increasingly deployed in places of high security, it is important to develop recognition algorithms that are robust to facial aging effects. In the absence of such systems, periodically updating large face databases with recent face images would be an inevitable task. Homeland security applications such as passport renewal are bound to gain from such applications.

- **Appearance Prediction Across Ages:** Computational models that characterize facial appearances at different ages can be used to predict one's appearance across ages. Apart from having direct implications to face recognition systems, appearance prediction systems can be helpful in finding missing individuals.

- **Age Estimation:** In the advent of systems that can automatically estimate an individual's age from his/her face image, age-based content management applications can be integrated into human–computer interaction (HCI) systems.

Figure 11.1 illustrates samples of age-separated face images of individuals during childhood and during adulthood.

### 11.1.2 Previous Work on Facial Aging

Researchers from psychophysics and human perception largely laid the foundations for studies related to human facial growth. Thompson [12] studied morphogenesis as an outcome of the physical forces that were acting on biological forms. Thompson

**Figure 11.1.** (a) Age-separated images of an individual taken during formative years. (b) Age-separated face images of individuals taken during adulthood.

described the geometric distortions that are often a result of morphogenetic changes by means of global geometric transformation functions which, when applied on the biological form, best describe the morphological changes. A key implication of such an approach is that it initiated numerous studies on identifying the internal forces acting on biological forms (typically, a combination of biomechanical stress and gravity) that best accounted for the resultant coordinate transformations. Figure 11.2 illustrates the geometric transformations induced on biological upon applying coordinate transformations.

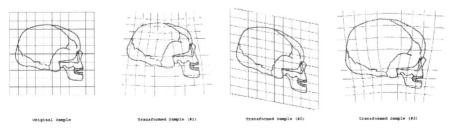

**Figure 11.2.** An illustration of using geometric transformations in the study of morphogenesis.

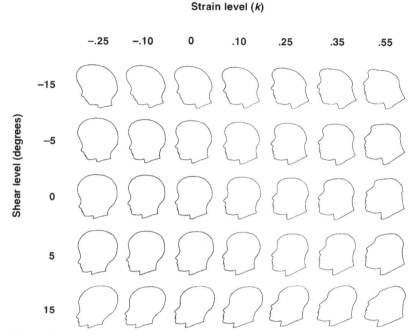

**Figure 11.3.** Transformation functions that were proposed to model craniofacial growth. The "revised" cardioidal-strain transformation was observed to be most effective in performing the task.

Pittenger and Shaw [13] examined the relative importance of the affine-shear transformation and the cardioidal-strain transformation in the global remodeling of the human skull with growth. By applying varying amounts of each transformation on the profile face of a child, they studied the relative significance of each transformation function in inducing growth related transformations on the profile face. Figure 11.3 illustrates the effects of applying combinations of strain transformations and shear transformations on profile faces. They identified the cardioidal-strain transformation to be more effective in the above task. Interestingly, when the cardioidal-strain transformations were applied on inanimate objects such as the Volkswagen "beetle," they observed that the inanimate object was perceived to be undergoing growth-related transformations. Such observations proved crucial in identifying the primary source of perceptual information for relative age judgments and subsequently in identifying the viable alternative transformation functions that were more accurate in describing facial growth.

Todd et al. [14] performed a hydrostatic analysis on the effects of gravity on a growing head. Treating a human head as an idealized system such as a fluid-filled spherical object, they characterized the distribution of pressure across different parts of the head. Such a characterization resulted in the "revised" cardioidal-strain transformation model, which was observed to be more effective in inducing growth-related transformations on face profiles of children than were other transformation models. Upon studying different transformation functions that were proposed to characterize facial growth, Mark et al. [15] identified certain geometric properties of objects that remained invariant across growth related transformations. The geometric invariants that were identified are described below:

- Preserving the angular coordinates of object features across transformations.
- Preserving the continuity of all contours and their directions of curvature across transformations.
- Preserving the bilateral symmetry of the object across transformations.

Furthermore, they suggested that only those transformation functions that preserve the aforementioned geometric properties of objects undergoing the transformation could result in transformations associated with growth. Table 11.1 illustrates some of transformation functions that were proposed to model craniofacial growth [15, 16]. Figure 11.4 illustrates the outcomes of employing the transformation functions on profile faces. The approaches discussed above limited their analysis to growth deformations induced on profile faces (silhouettes) which invariably are devoid of intricacies associated with facial structures. Hence, the effectiveness of such transformation models in inducing growth-like transformations on real 3D faces were unclear. Mark and Todd [17] extended the "revised" cardioidal-strain transformation model into three dimensions and demonstrated the effectiveness of the model in simulating facial growth on 3D head structures of children. For a concise account on the above discussed approaches toward developing a craniofacial growth model, the readers are referred to references 18 and 19. On another note, O'Toole et al. [20] studied the effects of inducing wrinkles and facial creases on 3D caricatures of human faces and observed that such variations had a direct impact on the perceived age the caricatured faces. Figure 11.5 illustrates the effects of inducing exaggerations on 3D caricatures.

From a computer vision perspective, studies pertaining to facial aging largely address the following tasks: (i) age estimation, (ii) appearance prediction, and (iii) face recognition/verification across ages.

**Table 11.1.** Some Geometric Transformations that Were Proposed to Model Craniofacial Growth

| Applied Transformation | Model |
|---|---|
| Cardioidal strain | $\theta_{t+1} = \theta_t$ |
| (polar coordinates) | $R_{t+1} = R_t(1 - k\cos(\theta_t))$ |
| Spiral strain | $\theta_{t+1} = \theta_t$ |
| (polar coordinates) | $R_{t+1} = R_t(1 + k|\theta_t|)$ |
| Affine shear | $Y_{t+1} = Y_t$ |
| (carthesian coordinates) | $X_{t+1} = X_t + kY_t$ |
| Revised cardioidal strain | $\theta_{t+1} = \theta_t$ |
| (polar coordinates) | $R_{t+1} = R_t(1 + k(1 - \cos(\theta_t)))$ |

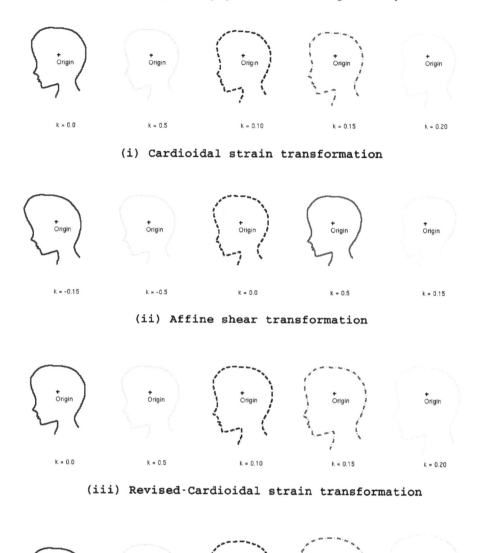

**Figure 11.4.** Strain transformations versus shear transformations : An illustration of the effects of applying varying combinations of the transformations on profile faces. (This illustration was derived from that which originally appeared in reference 13.)

**Figure 11.5.** The effects of inducing wrinkles and facial creases on 3D caricatures of human faces are illustrated. The illustration is reprinted from [20] with due permission from the authors.

**Age Estimation.** Kwon and Vitoria da Lobo [21] observed that the facial aspect ratios underwent notable changes from infancy to adulthood and performed age-based classification of faces using facial aspect ratios and the density of wrinkles on pre-designated facial regions. They classified faces as that of infants or young adults or senior adults. While facial aspect ratios were predominantly used to classify faces into that of infants or young adults, facial wrinkle density was used to classify faces into that of young adults or senior adults. Lanitis et al. [22, 23] performed a comparative study on different age-based classifiers. They represent faces by means of their shape (fiducial features) and texture (shape warped facial texture) and create an eigenspace to perform dimensionality reduction. Assuming that such a representation inherently captures the age information, they built regression functions and trained hierarchical neural-network-based classifiers to estimate the age from face images. Gandhi [24] trains a support vector regression machine to derive an age prediction function from face images. Geng et al. [25] learn the aging pattern subspace (addressed as "AGES") from a sequence of age progressed images of many individuals and use the same in estimating the age from face images.

**Appearance Prediction.** Burt and Perrett [26] created prototype faces for different age groups using face samples from the respective age groups. They studied the variations in shape and texture between face prototypes from different age groups and observed that by incorporating such variations on real face images, the perceived age of the face images could be altered. But the average textures derived by averaging across warped face images belonging to the same age group were often devoid of wrinkles and other textural variations that are commonly associated with images from different age groups. Tiddeman et al. [27] extended the above approach by compensating for the loss of textural information in the facial prototypes that occurred during the blending process. Using wavelet-based methods, they created texture enhanced prototypes by adjusting the amplitude of edges in the composite edges. Following the shape and texture transformations described in reference 26, they transformed the texture of face images using locally weighted wavelet functions at different scales and orientations and thereby increased the perceived age of a face image. Both the aforementioned studies were performed on adult face images.

Lanitis et al. [22] proposed age transformation functions for individuals in the age group 1–30 years. Representing faces by means of their shape and texture, as described earlier in this section, they proposed methods to transform the eigencoefficients in such a manner that the age of the face image could be transformed. Gandhi [24] adopted the "image-based surface detail transfer (IBDST)" [28] approach in inducing facial wrinkles in adult face images. Suo et al. [29] adopt a high-resolution grammatical face model that represents a face by means of a multilayer and-or graph. They present a dynamic Markov process that integrates the following three factors, in simulating facial aging effects: (i) global appearance changes in hair style and shape, (ii) facial deformations, and (iii) facial wrinkles.

**Face Recognition/Verification Across Age Progression.**   Ideally, the task of performing face recognition/verification across ages should not be treated separately from that of building facial appearance prediction models. Furthermore, age estimation approaches, if integrated with recognition algorithms, could prove crucial in improving recognition performance. Since face images of an individual taken across different ages invariably differ in aspects such as illumination, head pose, facial expressions, and so on, the recognition algorithms need to account for such variations prior to characterizing facial aging effects.

In one of our earlier works on this topic [30], we developed a Bayesian age difference classifier that classifies face images of individuals based on age differences and performs face verification across age progression. From a database that is comprised of pairs of age-separated face images retrieved from the passports of many individuals, we characterized the facial appearance variations that are typically observed across different age separations. We considered the following age differences in our study: 1–2 years, 3–4 years, 5–7 years, 8–9 years. Figure 11.6 illustrates the difference images from the intra-personal class (under each of the four age difference categories) and from the extra-personal class. We also studied the similarity of faces across age progression and observed that facial similarity scores dropped as the age separation increases. Haibin et al. (cited in reference 31) proposed an image gradient-based face operator that was used to perform face verification across ages, using the SVM framework.

In the next section we shall detail a craniofacial growth model that characterizes growth-related shape variations in human faces during formative years. The facial growth model has direct implications to predicting one's appearance across ages and

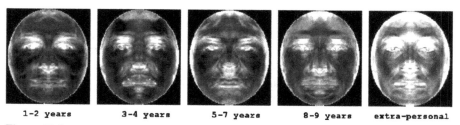

1-2 years      3-4 years      5-7 years      8-9 years      extra-personal

**Figure 11.6.** Intra-personal versus extra-personal difference images: The average difference images obtained from our training set for the different categories are illustrated. Reprinted with permission from Ref. 30.

in performing face recognition across age progression. The model was originally presented in reference 32.

## 11.2 AGE PROGRESSION DURING FORMATIVE YEARS

We propose a craniofacial growth model that draws inspiration from the "revised" cardioidal-strain transformation model proposed by Todd et al. [14]. Craniofacial growth observed during formative years is often attributed to the internal forces that act on the craniofacial complex. In mathematical terms, the "revised" cardioidal-strain transformation model can be expressed as follows:

$$P_i^{t_0} \propto R_i^{t_0} \left(1 - \cos\left(\theta_i^{t_0}\right)\right),$$

$$R_i^{t_1} = R_i^{t_0} \left[1 + k_i^{t_0 t_1} \left(1 - \cos\left(\theta_i^{t_0}\right)\right)\right], \tag{11.1}$$

$$\theta_i^{t_1} = \theta_i^{t_0}, \tag{11.2}$$

where $P_i^{t_0}$ denotes the pressure (directed radially outward) applied at the $i$th fiducial feature on the surface of the spherical object at age $t_0$ years, $\left(R_i^{t_0}, \theta_i^{t_0}\right)$ and $\left(R_i^{t_1}, \theta_i^{t_1}\right)$ denote the angular coordinates of the $i$th fiducial feature at $t_0$ years and $t_1$ years, respectively, and $k_i^{t_0 t_1}$ denotes a growth-related constant. The model assumes knowledge of the origin of reference for the transformation model. Figure 11.7a illustrates the pressure distribution within a fluid-filled spherical object. Figure 11.7b illustrates

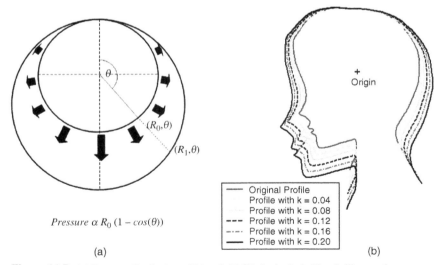

(a)

(b)

**Figure 11.7.** (a) Pressure distribution within a fluid-filled spherical object is illustrated. (b) Facial growth simulated on the profile of a child's face using the "revised" cardioidal-strain transformations. Adapted from [14].

the different face profiles that were generated upon applying the "revised" cardioidal-strain transformation on face profiles of children. With an increase in the value of parameter $k$, one can observe an increase in the perceived age of the resultant face profiles.

Interestingly, the three geometric invariants that were identified by Mark et al. [15] as those characteristic of objects undergoing growth are well-preserved in objects undergoing transformations induced by the "revised" cardioidal-strain transformation model. Reexamining the geometric invariants with respect to the "revised" cardioidal-strain transformation model, we observe the following.

- *Angular coordinates of the fiducial features on an object are preserved*: The pressure applied on fiducial features are directed radially outward, hence preserving their angular coordinates.

- *Bilateral symmetry about the vertical axis is maintained*: The pressure distribution being bilaterally symmetric about the vertical axis preserves the bilateral symmetry of objects upon transformation.

- *Continuity of object contours is preserved*: In the proposed model, the pressure distribution changes gradually throughout the object and hence continuity of object contours is preserved.

Figure 11.8 illustrates the face images obtained by applying the "revised" cardioidal strain transformation model. We observe that while the age transformation is perceivable in the initial few transformations, the aspect ratio of faces obtained for

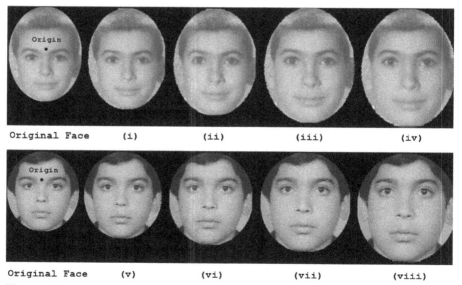

**Figure 11.8.** Age transformation results obtained by applying the "revised" cardioidal-strain transformation model (with increasing values of facial growth parameters) on the face images of two individuals.

large age transformations seem unnatural. Some of the factors that need to be taken into consideration while applying the model on real faces are:

- *Facial growth rates at different ages*: Face anthropometric studies [33] provide considerable evidences on the different growth rates observed over different facial features across years. Different facial features attain saturation in growth at different stages; hence, facial growth models should implicitly account for such variabilities. Growth parameters designated as $k_i^{t_0 t_1}$ in Eq. (11.1) play a crucial role in controlling the amount of growth observed over the $i$th fiducial feature from ages $t_0$ years to $t_1$ years; hence, identifying the growth parameters for each fiducial feature across different age transformations is crucial toward the success of the model.

- *Gender-based and ethinicity-based facial growth rates*: Again, face anthropometric studies have proven that facial growth rates depend heavily on the individual's gender and ethinicity. Hence, accounting for such factors is also crucial for developing facial growth models.

We use age-based anthropometric data (in the form of measurements extracted across different features) in developing the proposed facial growth model.

## 11.2.1 Face Anthropometry

Face anthropometric studies provide a quantitative description of the craniofacial complex by means of measurements taken between key landmarks on human faces across ages and are often used in characterizing normal and abnormal facial growth. Gender-based facial measurements collected across individuals from the same ethnic background across different ages provide significant information on facial growth patterns. We incorporate such evidences on facial growth in computing the facial growth parameters and, hence, implicitly account for factors such as gender, ethnicity, adolescence, and so on, that affect facial growth. Face anthropometry has been successfully used in computer graphics applications by DeCarlo et al. [34] in developing geometric models for human faces and by Kahler [35] in simulating growth on human head models. Next, we elaborate the nature of face anthropometric data that were used in our approach toward developing a craniofacial growth model.

Farkas [33, 36] identifies a set of facial landmarks that can be reliably located on human faces (both from real-life faces and frontal / profile face images) and extracts facial measurements across different landmarks on Caucasian faces (male/female) belonging to ages 1–18 years. For each of the ages 1–18 years, facial measurements were extracted from 50 subjects (of the same gender and ethinic origin) and the means and standard deviations across such measurements are tabulated in reference 33. Facial measurements extracted across landmarks are generally of three kinds: (i) projective measurements (shortest distance between two landmarks), (ii) tangential measurements (distance between two landmarks measured along the skin surface), and (iii) angular measurements. For the proposed application, we select 24 facial landmarks that can be reliably located on frontal faces and use a set of projective measurements

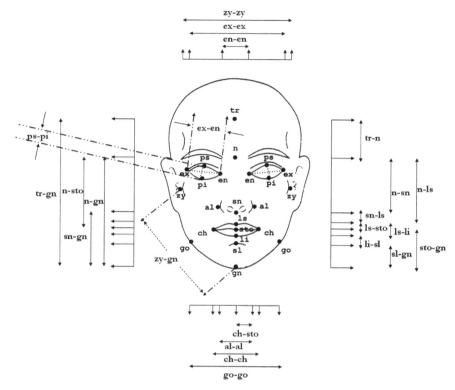

**Figure 11.9.** The 24 facial landmarks identified on frontal faces and the different facial measurements that were used in developing the model are illustrated.

extracted across these landmarks to characterize facial growth. Figure 11.9 illustrates the 24 landmarks and the relevant facial measurements that are used in our study.

Facial proportion index, defined as the ratio of a pair of facial measurements, is a commonly adopted metric in analyzing facial growth [36]. Clinical studies related to craniofacial disorders are said to identify a set of facial proportion indices while studying abnormalities in facial growth. Furthermore, an inherent advantage of using facial proportion indices in our application is that the unknown scale factor from an individual's face images can be discounted while studying the variations in facial measurements across ages. We identify 52 such facial proportion indices in developing the craniofacial growth model. Some of the proportion indices that were used are listed here: (i) facial index $\left(\frac{n-gn}{zy-zy}\right)$, (ii) mandibular index $\left(\frac{sto-gn}{go-go}\right)$, (iii) intercanthal index $\left(\frac{en-en}{ex-ex}\right)$, (iv) orbital width index $\left(\frac{ex-en}{en-en}\right)$, (v) eye fissure index $\left(\frac{ps-pi}{ex-en}\right)$, (vi) nasal index $\left(\frac{al-al}{n-sn}\right)$, and so on.

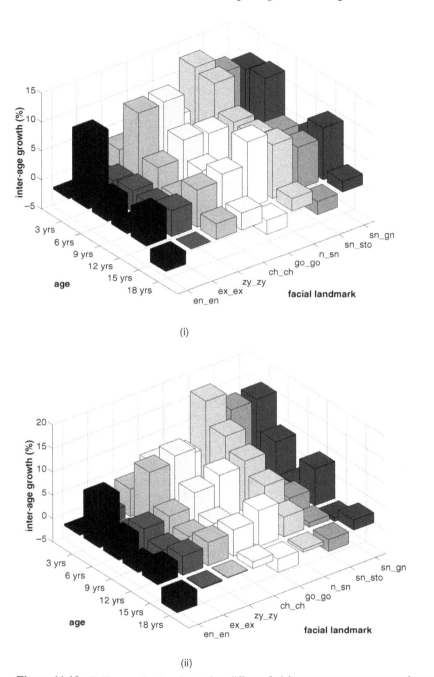

(i)

(ii)

**Figure 11.10.** (**i**) The growth rates observed on different facial measurements across ages in men. (**ii**) The growth rates observed on different facial measurements in women. The data help identify the "growth spurts" observed across different facial features in men and women.

## 11.2.2 Generic Growth Model: Computational Aspects

We propose a facial growth model that is built using average facial measurements extracted across individuals of the same age, gender, and ethnicity (tabulated in reference 33). The facial growth model characterizes population-specific growth patterns and hence is termed "generic." With the objective of characterizing the age-based flow observed over different facial features, we detail the computational aspects involved in developing the "generic" growth model in the following subsections.

### 11.2.2.1 Identifying the Origin of Reference

First, we build prototype faces for each of the ages (for boys and girls) using age-based average facial measurements provided in reference 33. Let the age-based facial measurements be denoted as $\Omega_i = (\omega_1^{(i)}, \omega_2^{(i)}, \ldots, \omega_N^{(i)})$, where $i$ corresponds to the age ($1 \leq i \leq 18$) and $N$ corresponds to the number of facial measurements used in our study. Building prototype faces amounts to identifying the coordinates of the 24 facial landmarks of interest for each of the ages: ($\Omega_i \mapsto (\mathbf{x}_i, \mathbf{y}_i)$, $1 \leq i \leq 18$). Subsequently, the facial feature drifts observed on the prototype faces (average faces) across different ages are used to determine the optimal origin of reference for the proposed craniofacial growth model. The following cues help in identifying the origin of reference for the proposed model.

- The craniofacial growth model defined in Eq. (11.2) is such that the facial features with angular coordinates $\theta = 0$ remain static and features with $\theta$ such that $|\theta| \leq \epsilon$, where $\epsilon$ is a small number, grow minimally. Furthermore, from Eq. (11.2) we observe that facial feature growth is directly proportional to the radial coordinates of feature points.

- "Relative total increment," RTI (%), is a measure that quantifies the growth observed across different landmarks. It is defined as $\frac{l_{18}-l_1}{l_1} \times 100$, where $l_1$, $l_{18}$ correspond to the facial measurements extracted across a pair of facial landmarks at ages 1 and 18 years. Farkas [33] cites that the "relative total increment" computed across landmarks "tr" and "n" (in the forehead region) is much less than that computed across other pairs of facial landmarks.

The above cues suggest that the origin of reference for the craniofacial growth model should ideally be located between landmarks "tr" and "n" on the axis of bilateral symmetry. Figure 11.11 illustrates the flow of facial features across prototype faces at different ages.

The optimal origin of reference for the craniofacial growth model is estimated as explained below. Let ($x_{ij}, y_{ij}$) correspond to the coordinates of the $i$th feature at age $j$ years ($1 \leq i \leq 24$, $1 \leq j \leq 18$). Let ($x_0, y_0$) correspond to the origin of reference for the growth model. $y_0$ corresponds to the facial mid-axis and hence is known a priori. The origin of reference for the craniofacial growth model is to be identified such that the growth constraints imposed on the radial and angular coordinates of facial features

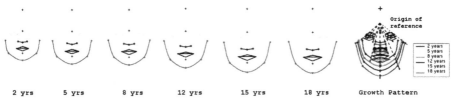

2 yrs        5 yrs        8 yrs        12 yrs        15 yrs        18 yrs        Growth Pattern

**Figure 11.11.** The figure illustrates prototype faces at different ages and helps visualize the flow of facial features with increase in age.

are best accounted for. The growth constraints imposed on the angular coordinates of facial features imply that the $x$ and $y$ coordinates of facial features across age follow a linear relationship. We compute $x_0$ and $m_i$, $1 \leq i \leq 24$, the slopes of lines that best fit the facial feature coordinates across years, by solving the underlying least squares problem:

$$\min_{w.r.t\ m_i,\ x_0} \left\{ \sum_{i=1}^{m} \sum_{j=1}^{n} (x_{ij} - m_i(y_{ij} - y_0) - x_0)^2 \right\}. \tag{11.3}$$

While solving Eq. (11.3), we observe that the optimal origin of reference for the model is located between landmarks "tr" and "n" (on the forehead). The low rates of growth observed on forehead regions for boys (11.8%) and girls (2.25%) [33] further validate the above solution. Figure 11.12 illustrates the growth observed over different facial features for boys and girls and illustrates the located origin of reference.

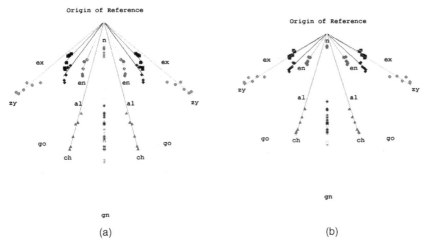

(a)                                                                                        (b)

**Figure 11.12.** The figure illustrates the drift of facial features observed on average faces at different ages, for men and women. The origin of reference that was identified for the two classes is illustrated as well.

### 11.2.2.2 Computing Facial Growth Parameters

Upon computing the origin of reference for the craniofacial growth model, the facial landmarks for different ages are represented in polar coordinates $((x_i, y_i) \leftrightarrow (r_i, \Theta_i)$ where $i$ corresponds to the feature index and $j$ corresponds to the age in years. Let the growth parameters corresponding to facial landmarks designated by [$tr$, $n$, $sn$, $ls$, $sto$, $li$, $sl$, $gn$, $en$, $ex$, $ps$, $pi$, $zy$, $al$, $ch$, $go$] be $\mathbf{k} = [k_1, k_2, \ldots, k_{16}]$, respectively. Assuming bilateral symmetry of faces, symmetric facial features share the same growth parameters and hence the 24 facial features result in 16 unique growth parameters. The 52 proportion indices that were discussed in the previous section play a fundamental role in computing the facial growth parameters. By studying the transformation in proportion indices from ages $u$ years to $v$ years, we can compute the facial growth parameters corresponding to the specific age transformation. The age-based proportion indices translate into linear and nonlinear equations in facial growth parameters. Proportion indices derived from facial measurements that were extracted across facial features that lie on the same horizontal or vertical axis result in linear equations in the respective growth parameters, and those extracted across features that do not lie on the same horizontal or vertical axis result in nonlinear equations in growth parameters.

For example, the age-based transformation observed in the proportion index $\frac{n-gn}{zy-zy}$ on features $n$, $gn$, and $zy$, for an age transformation from $u$ years to $v$ years, results in a linear equation in the relevant growth parameters. The following equations illustrate the same. ($R_n^u$, $\theta_n^u$, $R_{gn}^u$, $\theta_{gn}^u$, $R_{zy}^u$, $\theta_{zy}^u$, and $c_v$ were derived from the projective facial measurements provided in reference 33).

$$\frac{(n\_gn)_v}{(zy\_zy)_v} = c_v \Rightarrow \frac{R_{gn}^v - R_n^v}{2 \times R_{zy}^v \times \cos(\theta_{zy})} = c_v \Rightarrow \tag{11.4}$$

$$R_{gn}^u(1 + k_{gn}(1 - \cos(\theta_{gn}))) - R_n^u(1 + k_n(1 - \cos(\theta_n)))$$
$$= 2 \times c_v \times \cos(\theta_{zy}) \times R_{zy}^u(1 + k_{zy}(1 - \cos(\theta_{zy})))$$
$$\Rightarrow \alpha_1 k_{gn} + \alpha_2 k_n + \alpha_3 k_{zy} = \beta_1. \tag{11.5}$$

Similarly, the age-based transformation observed in the proportion index $\frac{sto-gn}{gn-zy}$ on features $sto$, $gn$, and $zy$, for an age transformation from $u$ years to $v$ years, results in a nonlinear equation in the relevant growth parameters, as illustrated below. (Again, $R_{gn}^u$, $\theta_{gn}^u$, $R_{sto}^u$, $\theta_{sto}^u$, $R_{zy}^u$, $\theta_{zy}^u$, and $d_v$ were derived from the projective facial measurements provided in reference 33).

$$\frac{(sto\_gn)_v}{(gn\_zy)_v} = d_v \Rightarrow$$

$$\frac{R_{sto}^v - R_{gn}^v}{\sqrt{(R_{gn}^v - R_{zy}^v \times \sin(\theta_{zy}))^2 + (R_{zy}^v \cos(\theta_{zy}))^2}} = d_v \Rightarrow$$

$$R_{sto}^u(1 + k_{sto}(1 - \cos(\theta_{sto}))) - R_{gn}^u(1 + k_{gn}(1 - \cos(\theta_{gn}))) =$$

$$\{[R_{gn}^u(1 + k_{gn}(1 - \cos(\theta_{gn}))) - R_{zy}^u(1 + k_{zy}(1 - \cos(\theta_{zy})))$$

$$\times \sin(\theta_{zy})]^2 + [R_{zy}^u(1 + k_{zy}(1 - \cos(\theta_{zy}))) \cos(\theta_{zy})]^2\}^{\frac{1}{2}} \times d_v$$

$$\Rightarrow \alpha_1 k_{sto} + \alpha_2 k_{gn} + \alpha_3 k_{zy} + \alpha_4 k_{sto}^2 + \alpha_5 k_{gn}^2$$

$$+ \alpha_6 k_{zy}^2 + \alpha_7 k_{sto} k_{gn} + \alpha_8 k_{gn} k_{zy} = \beta_2.$$

Thus, the set of 52 proportion indices that were identified for our study result in a set of linear and nonlinear equations on growth parameters solving whereby one can identify the growth parameters for specific age transformations.

Let the constraints derived using proportion indices be denoted as $r_1(\mathbf{k}) = \beta_1$, $r_2(\mathbf{k}) = \beta_2, \ldots, r_{52}(\mathbf{k}) = \beta_{52}$. The objective function $f(\mathbf{k})$ that needs to be minimized with respect to $\mathbf{k}$ is defined as

$$f(\mathbf{k}) = \frac{1}{2} \sum_{i=1}^{52} (r_i(\mathbf{k}) - \beta_i)^2. \tag{11.6}$$

The following equations illustrate the constraints that were derived using different facial proportion indices.

$$r_1: \qquad \left[\frac{n - gn}{zy - zy} = c_1\right] \equiv \alpha_1^{(1)} k_1 + \alpha_2^{(1)} k_7 + \alpha_3^{(1)} k_{12} = \beta_1$$

$$r_2: \qquad \left[\frac{al - al}{ch - ch} = c_2\right] \equiv \alpha_1^{(2)} k_{13} + \alpha_2^{(2)} k_{14} = \beta_2$$

$$r_3: \qquad \left[\frac{li - sl}{sto - sl} = c_3\right] \equiv \alpha_1^{(3)} k_4 + \alpha_2^{(3)} k_5 + \alpha_3^{(3)} k_6 = \beta_3$$

$$r_4: \qquad \left[\frac{sto - gn}{gn - zy} = c_4\right] \equiv \alpha_1^{(4)} k_4 + \alpha_2^{(4)} k_7 + \alpha_3^{(4)} k_4^2 + \alpha_4^{(4)} k_7^2$$

$$+ \alpha_5^{(4)} k_{12} + \alpha_6^{(4)} k_{12}^2 + \alpha_7^{(4)} k_4\, k_7 + \alpha_8^{(4)} k_7\, k_{12} = \beta_4$$

($\alpha_j^i$ and $\beta_i$ are constants. $c_i$ is the proportion index value computed from the ratios of mean values of facial measurements corresponding to the target age, which were obtained from reference 33.) To compute the growth parameters $\mathbf{k}$, we minimize the objective function in an iterative fashion using the Levenberg–Marquardt non-linear optimization algorithm [37]. We use the craniofacial growth model defined in Eq. (11.2) to compute the initial estimate of the facial growth parameters. The initial estimates are obtained using the age-based facial measurements provided for each facial landmark, individually. The iterative step involved in the optimization process is defined as

$$\mathbf{k}_{i+1} = \mathbf{k}_i - (\mathbf{H} + \lambda \mathrm{diag}[\mathbf{H}])^{-1} \nabla f(\mathbf{k}_i),$$

$$\nabla f(\mathbf{k}_i) = \sum_{i=1}^{N} r_i(\mathbf{k}) \nabla r_i(\mathbf{k}),$$

where $\mathbf{H}$ corresponds to the Hessian matrix of $f$ evaluated at $\mathbf{k}_i$. At the end of each iteration, $\lambda$ is updated as illustrated in reference 37. Since the computation of $\mathbf{k}$ discussed above is based on the average facial measurements tabulated in reference 33 and does not involve facial measurements from test face images, such computations can be performed offline.

### 11.2.2.3  Applying Aging Model on Faces

On each of the test face images, we locate the 24 facial features illustrated in Figure 11.9 in a semiautomatic manner. We adopt the face detection and feature localization approach proposed by Moon et al. [38] to detect facial features such as eyes, mouth, and the outer contour of the face. This operation enables the location of the following facial landmarks (*tr*, *gn*: forehead and chin), (*en*, *ex*, *ps*, *pi*: eyes) and (*ch*, *sto*, *ls*, *li*: mouth). Other features designated as *n*, *zy*, *go*, and so on, do not correspond to corners or edges on faces and hence were located manually. We enforce bilateral symmetry while locating facial features. In our observation, minor errors in feature localization do not affect the proposed method to compute facial growth parameters.

Next, using the growth parameters computed over selected facial landmarks $\mathbf{k}$, we compute the growth parameters over the entire facial region. This is formulated as a scattered data interpolation problem [39]. On a cartesian coordinate system defined over the face region, the growth parameters $\mathbf{k} = [k_1, k_2, \ldots, k_n]$ correspond to parameters obtained at facial landmarks located in $(x_1, y_1), (x_2, y_2), \ldots, (x_n, y_n)$. Our objective is to find an interpolating function $f : R^2 \rightarrow R$ such that

$$g(\mathbf{x}_i) = k_i, \quad i = 1, \ldots, n, \tag{11.7}$$

where $\mathbf{x}_i = (x_i, y_i)$ and the thin-plate energy functional $\mathbf{E}$, a measure of the amount of "bending" in the surface, is minimized. The thin-plate energy functional is defined as

$$\mathbf{E} = \iint_{\Omega} g_{xx}^2(\mathbf{x}) + 2g_{xy}^2(\mathbf{x}) + g_{xx}^2(\mathbf{x}) \, d\mathbf{x}, \tag{11.8}$$

where $\Omega$ is the region of interest (face region, in our case). Using the method of radial basis function, the interpolating function that minimizes the energy functional can be shown to take the form

$$g(\mathbf{x}) = c_0 + c_1 x + c_2 y + \sum_{i=1}^{n} \lambda_i \phi(|\mathbf{x} - \mathbf{x}_i|), \tag{11.9}$$

where $\lambda_i$'s are real numbers, $|.|$ is the Euclidean norm in $R^2$, and the linear polynomial $c_0 + c_1 x + c_2 y$ accounts for affine deformations in the system. We adopt the thin-plate splines functions defined as $\phi(\mathbf{x}) = |\mathbf{x}|^2 \log(|\mathbf{x}|)$ as the basis functions. As illustrated in reference 39, to remove affine contributions from the basis functions, we introduce additional constraints $\sum_{i=1}^{n} \lambda_i = \sum_{i=1}^{n} \lambda_i x_i = \sum_{i=1}^{n} \lambda_i y_i = 0$. Equations (11.7) and (11.9) coupled with the constraints above, results in the following linear system of

**Table 11.2.** Age Transformation Models

| Age Transformation | Growth Model |
|---|---|
| From $t_0$ years to $t_1$ years $(t_1 > t_0)$ | $R_i^{t_1} = R_i^{t_0}[1 + k_i^{t_0 t_1}(1 - \cos(\theta_i^{t_0}))]$ $\theta_i^{t_1} = \theta_i^{t_0}$ |
| From $t_0$ years to $t_1$ years $(t_1 < t_0)$ | $R_i^{t_1} = \dfrac{R_i^{t_0}}{[1 + k_i^{t_1 t_0}(1 - \cos(\theta_i^{t_0}))]}$ $\theta_i^{t_1} = \theta_i^{t_0}$ |

equations, the solution of which yields the interpolating function g. The linear system of equations is

$$\left( \begin{array}{c|c} \mathbf{A}_{n \times n} & \mathbf{P}_{n \times 3} \\ \hline \mathbf{P}_{3 \times n}^T & \mathbf{0}_{3 \times 3} \end{array} \right) \left( \begin{array}{c} \Lambda_{n \times 1} \\ \mathbf{c}_{3 \times 1} \end{array} \right) = \left( \begin{array}{c} \mathbf{k} \\ \mathbf{0} \end{array} \right), \qquad (11.10)$$

where $\mathbf{A}$ is a matrix with entries $A_{i,j} = \phi(|\mathbf{x}_i - \mathbf{x}_j|)$ $i, j = 1, \ldots, n$, $\mathbf{P}$ is a matrix with rows $(1, x_i, y_i)$, $\Lambda = (\lambda_1, \ldots, \lambda_n)^T$, and $\mathbf{c} = (c_0, c_1, c_2)^T$. Thus, the growth parameters computed at selected facial features using age-based anthropometric data is used to compute the growth parameters over the entire facial region. Upon computing the facial growth parameters over the facial region, the craniofacial growth model can be applied in a pixel-wise manner, to transform the age of faces. The transformation models for different age transformations are illustrated in Table 11.2.

The proposed craniofacial growth model finds direct applications in predicting the appearances of children across different ages. Figure 11.13 illustrates the original age-separated image pairs of different subjects and the age-transformed face image that was obtained using the "personalized" growth model. Furthermore, the facial growth parameters corresponding to the specific age transformation on each subject are illustrated, in the form of range maps. The varying intensities observed in the range maps reflect the different growth rates observed across different facial features across ages. One can identify certain gender-based facial growth patterns that are similar across subjects undergoing a similar age transformation. We evaluate the performance of the proposed facial aging model by performing face recognition across age progression on the FG-NET aging database [40]. For a detailed account on the experiments, please refer to reference 32.

## 11.3 DISCUSSIONS AND CONCLUSIONS

In the previous section we had discussed a craniofacial growth model that characterizes growth-related shape variations observed during formative years. We had illustrated the significance of incorporating anthropometric facial measurements extracted across children from different ages, in developing the growth model. We wish to offer some insights into a related, but more challenging, problem: modeling facial aging in adults.

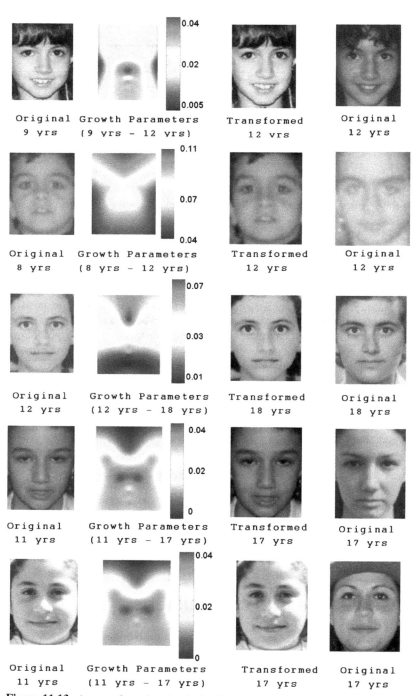

**Figure 11.13.** Age transformed results obtained by employing the proposed craniofacial growth model are illustrated.

Facial aging effects during adulthood, often a combination of subtle shape and textural variations, are primarily induced by factors such as (i) facial muscles losing elasticity, (ii) facial skin's inability to retain moisture, (iii) prolonged exposure to sunlight, (iv) dietary habits, and so on. Developing a computational model that characterizes facial aging effects in adults might involve addressing some of the aspects discussed below:

- **Shape Transformation Model:** Facial muscles tend to lose elasticity with increase in age. This invariably results in the sagging of facial features which induces subtle changes in facial shape. Furthermore, weight loss/weight gain might gradually induce facial shape variations across ages. Waters [41] identifies three types of facial muscles—namely, linear muscles, sheet muscles, and sphincter muscles—and proposes different models for the same. Would computational models that characterize facial muscles prove crucial in developing a shape transformation model for human faces that accounts for facial aging effects?

- **Texture Transformation Model:** Unlike facial aging effects during formative years when skin textural variations are minimal, during adulthood textural variations are commonly observed in the form of wrinkles and other skin artifacts. Does characterizing facial albedo (a measure of surface reflectivity) across different ages help in analyzing skin textural variations?

- **Facial Growth Statistics:** Anthropometric measurements extracted from faces of children belonging to different ages [33] proved crucial toward developing a facial growth model for children. As mentioned earlier, such data implicitly capture the facial growth patterns that are characteristic to individuals belonging to a specific ethnic group/gender. To our best knowledge, facial growth statistics of this nature are not available for adults. Initiatives that are directed toward collecting such data might benefit research pertaining to facial growth during adulthood.

- **Facial Aging Models in 3D:** 3D face models possess an inherent advantage over 2D models in their ability to characterize facial shape with better accuracy. Developing realistic 3D muscle models would help analyze the shape variations in observed in faces with increase in age. The advent of 3D data (3D scans of faces) helps the computation of the surface albedo (reflectance map) which can be used to characterize textural variations. Some of the problems encountered in 2D face models such as pose compensation, illumination compensation, and so on, can be handled with better precision by using 3D face models.

From a computer vision perspective, one can identify numerous challenges in the task of modeling one's appearance variations with increase in age. Given that facial appearances are governed by multiple factors such as illumination, pose, facial expressions, and so on, computational models that characterize facial aging effects should ideally be adaptable to the different conditions under which face images were taken. Currently, research initiatives pertaining to facial aging are severely restricted with the lack of publicly available face databases that are comprised of age-separated face images of many individuals. With the advent of such databases, research initiatives on this topic are bound to deliver.

## REFERENCES

1. R. Basri and D. W. Jacobs, Lambertial reflectance and linear subspaces, *IEEE Trans. Pattern Anal. Mach. Intell.* **25**(2): 218–233, 2003.
2. R. Ramamoorthy, Analytic pca construction for theoretical analysis of lighting variability, including attached shadows, in a single image of a convex lambertian object, *IEEE Trans. Pattern Anal. Mach. Intell.* **24**(10): 1322–1333, 2002.
3. A. S. Georghiades, P. N. Belhumeur, and D. J. Kriegman, From few to many: Illumination cone models for face recognition under variable lighting and pose, *IEEE Trans. Pattern Anal. Mach. Intell.* **23**(6): 643–660, 2001.
4. S. K. Zhou and R. Chellappa, Image-based face recognition under illumination and pose variations, *J. Opt. Soc. Am.* **22**: 217–229, 2005.
5. S. K. Zhou, G. Aggarwal, and R. Chellappa, Appearance characterization of linear lambertian objects, generalized photometric stereo and illumination-invariant face recognition, *IEEE Trans. Pattern Anal. Mach. Intell.* 2006 (to appear).
6. V. Blanz and T. Vetter, Face recognition based on fitting a 3d morphable model, *IEEE Trans. Pattern Anal. Mach. Intell.* **25**(9): 1063–1074, 2003.
7. P. Ekman and W. Friesen, *Facial Action Coding System: A Technique for the Measurement of Facial Movement*, Consulting Psychologists Press, San Francisco, 1998.
8. Y. Yacoob and L. Davis, Recognizing human facial expressions from long image sequences using optical flow, *IEEE Trans. Pattern Anal. Mach. Intell.* **18**(6): 636–642, 1996.
9. I. Essa and A. Pentland, Coding, analysis, interpretation and recognition of facial expressions, *IEEE Trans. Pattern Anal. Mach. Intell.* **19**(7): 757–763, 1997.
10. A. M. Martinez, Recognizing imprecisely localized, partially occluded and expression variant faces from a single sample per class, *IEEE Trans. Pattern Anal. Mach. Intell.* **24**(6): 748–763, 2002.
11. Y. Liu, K. L. Schmidt, J. F. Cohn, and S. Mitra, Facial asymmetry quantification for expression invariant human identification, *Comput. Vis. Image Understanding* **91**(1/2): 138–159, 2003.
12. D. W. Thompson, *On Growth and Form*, Dover Publications, Mineola, NY, 1992 (original publication, 1917).
13. J. B. Pittenger and R. E. Shaw, Aging faces as viscal-elastic events: Implications for a theory of nonrigid shape perception, *J. Exp. Psychol. Hum. Percept. Perform.* **1**(4): 374–382, 1975.
14. J. T. Todd, L. S. Mark, R. E. Shaw, and J. B. Pittenger, The perception of human growth, *Sci. Am.* **242**(2): 132–144, 1980.
15. L. S. Mark, J. T. Todd, and R. E. Shaw, Perception of growth: A geometric analysis of how different styles of change are distinguished, *J. Exp. Psychol. Hum. Percept. Perform.* **7**: 855–868, 1981.
16. L. S. Mark and J. T. Todd, Describing geometric information about human growth in terms of geometric invariants, *J. Percept. Psychophys.* **37**: 249–256, 1985.
17. L. S. Mark and J. T. Todd, The perception of growth in three dimensions, *J. Percept. Psychophys.* **33**(2): 193–196, 1983.
18. J. B. Pittenger, The early years of Robert Shaw's craniofacial growth project, *Ecol. Psychol.* **17**(3&4): 147–159, 2005.
19. L. S. Mark, Developing formative models of craniofacial growth and workplace design: Personal reflections on the work and the influence of Robert E. Shaw, *Ecol. Psychol.* **17**(3/4): 161–191, 2005.
20. A. J. O'Toole, T. Vetter, H. Volz, and E. M. Salter, Three-dimensional caricatures of human heads: Distinctiveness and the perception of facial age, *Perception* **26**: 719–732, 1997.
21. Y. H. Kwon and N. Vitoria da Lobo, Age classification from facial images, *Comput. Vis. Image Understanding* **74**: 1–21, 1999.
22. A. Lanitis, C. J. Taylor, and T. F. Cootes, Toward automatic simulation of aging effects on face images, *IEEE Trans. Pattern Anal. Mach. Intell.* **24**(4): 442–455, 2002.

23. A. Lanitis, C. Draganova, and C. Christodoulou, Comparing different classifiers for automatic age estimation, *IEEE Trans. Syst. Man Cybern. Part B* **34**(1): 621–628, 2004.

24. M. Gandhi, A method for automatic synthesis of aged human facial images, Master's thesis, McGill University, September 2004.

25. X. Geng, Z.-H. Zhou, Y. Zhang, G. Li, and H. Dai, Learning from facial aging patterns for automatic age estimation, in *International Multimedia Conference*, Santa Barbara, CA, October 2006, pp. 307–316.

26. M. Burt and D. I. Perrett, Perception of age in adult Caucasian male faces: Computer graphic manipulation of shape and colour information, *J. R. Soc.* **259**: 137–143, 1995.

27. B. Tiddeman, D. M. Burt, and D. Perret, Prototyping and transforming facial texture for perception research, *Comput. Graphics Appl. IEEE* **21**(5): 42–50, 2001.

28. Y. Shan, Z. Liu, and Z. Zhang, Image based surface detail transfer, in *IEEE Conference on Computer Vision and Pattern Recognition*, Vol. 2, Hawaii, 2001, pp. 794–799.

29. J. Suo, F. Min, S. Zhu, S. Shan, and X. Chen, A multi-resolution dynamic model for face aging simulation, in *IEEE Conference on Computer Vision and Pattern Recognition*, Minneapolis, MN, 2007, pp. 1–8.

30. N. Ramanathan and R. Chellappa, Face verification across age progression, *IEEE Trans. Image Processing*, 2006.

31. H. Ling, S. Soatto, N. Ramanathan, and D. Jacobs, A study of face recognition as people age, in *IEEE International Conference on Computer Vision*, Rio de Janeiro, Brazil, October 2007.

32. N. Ramanathan and R. Chellappa, Modeling age progression in young faces, in *IEEE Conference on Computer Vision and Pattern Recognition*, Vol. 1, New York, 2006, pp. 387–394.

33. L. G. Farkas, *Anthropometry of the Head and Face*, Raven Press, New York, 1994.

34. D. DeCarlo, D. Metaxas, and M. Stone, An anthropometric face model using variational techniques, *SIGGRAPH*, pp. 67–74, 1998.

35. K. Kahler, A head model with anatomical structure for facial modeling and animation, Master's thesis, Universitat des Saarlendes, 2003.

36. L. G. Farkas and I. R. Munro, *Anthropometric Facial Proportions in Medicine*, Charles C Thomas, Springfield, IL, 1987.

37. D. M. Bates and D. G. Watts, *Nonlinear Regression and its Applications*, John Wiley & Sons, New York, 1988.

38. H. Moon, R. Chellappa, and A. Rozenfeld, Optimal edge-based shape detection, *IEEE Trans. Image Processing*, **11**(11): 1209–1226, 2002.

39. F. L. Bookstein, Principal warps: Thin-plate splines and the decomposition of deformations, *IEEE Trans. Pattern Anal. Mach. Intell.* **11**(6): 567–585, 1989.

40. A. Lanitis. FG-Net aging database. [Online]. Available: `http://sting.cycollege.ac.cy/alanitis/fgnetaging/`

41. K. Waters, A muscle model for animating three-dimensional facial expression, *Proc. SIGGRAPH* **21**: 17–24, 1987.

# Chapter 12

# Super-Resolution of Face Images

**Sung Won Park and Marios Savvides**

## 12.1 INTRODUCTION

Super-resolution of a face image is to enhance the resolution of a face image. A high-resolution face image can be recovered from a given low-resolution face image by modeling the face image space. In particular, in video surveillance it can often be seen that the resolution of a captured facial image is not sufficient for face recognition even by a human being. Thus, we need to recover higher-resolution images by super-resolution techniques. This problem was introduced by Baker and Kanade [1] The technique of face super-resolution, also called face hallucination, has many applications in face recognition, image enhancement, and image compression.

Face super-resolution needs a different approach from general super-resolution which is applied to all kinds of images. There are two main approaches for super-resolution: reconstruction-based [2–5] and learning-based approaches [1, 6–9]. While the reconstruction-based approaches can be applied to super-resolution of a single image, the learning-based approaches require a set of training images to extract features. Particularly, for face super-resolution, learning-based approaches are more commonly applied since they are more appropriate to extract and represent facial features. Face images have similar patterns and characteristics and are distinguishable from non-face images. Thus, learning-based approaches can be especially useful to analyze the statistical distribution of face images. Face super-resolution is more challenging than general super-resolution; the slightest errors of face synthesis can be significant to human perception because of our familiarity with human faces. For these reasons, face super-resolution has become a distinguished research area different from super-resolution, and it requires different approaches and techniques.

*Biometrics: Theory, Methods, and Applications.* Edited by Boulgouris, Plataniotis, and Micheli-Tzanakou
Copyright © 2010 the Institute of Electrical and Electronics Engineers, Inc.

The methods for face super-resolution are mainly classified into two approaches: statistical inference-based approaches and subspace-based approaches. To reconstruct a high-resolution image from its low-resolution counterpart, we should estimate some parameters or features in a high-resolution image space. To solve these inference problems, statistical inference-based approaches have been applied. Statistical inference-based approaches aim to find a high-resolution image which has a maximum probability for a given low-resolution image by Bayesian or other statistical formulations. The maximum a posteriori (MAP) estimator has been one of the most widely used solution for face super-resolution [1, 8, 9]. Baker and Kanade [1, 6] developed a face hallucination method using a Bayesian formulation and image pyramids such as Gaussian, Laplacian, and feature pyramids. This approach infers the high-frequency components from a parent structure based on training samples. Finally, the high-resolution image in the Gaussian pyramid is inferred pixel by pixel so as to maximize the posterior probability given the low-resolution image.

Next, subspace-based approaches are based on the assumption that a high-resolution image and its low-resolution counterpart have similar coefficients, features, or distributions in the high- and low-resolution image spaces. So, the subspaces such as eigenfaces obtained by principal component analysis [10] in the two spaces are learned and a high-resolution image is represented by the similarity between the two subspaces. Wang and Tang [11, 12] developed an efficient face hallucination algorithm using an eigentransformation algorithm. However, all these methods have not utilized the neighborhood relationship in the distribution of face images. Facial images change appearance due to multiple factors such as pose variations, lighting acquisition conditions, and facial expressions. Most of the previous work has not considered this distribution and dealt with all the diverse images equally. In the previous work of face image analysis using manifold learning methods, it has been shown that face images lie on a manifold [13–16]. Also, it has been demonstrated that the variation of a certain facial factor such as pose or expression makes a submanifold in the manifold structure [7, 17]. Thus, it is expected that manifold learning methods can improve the tasks requiring face image analysis, such as face recognition, super-resolution, or face synthesis. Based on this idea, Chang et al. [18] developed the neighbor embedding algorithm for super-resolution of general images. They assume that the local distribution structure in sample space is preserved in smoothing and down-sampling, and they apply one of the manifold learning methods, locally linear embedding (LLE) [13].

Statistical inference-based approaches and subspace-based approaches have often been merged to solve face super-resolution problems. Liu et al. [9, 19] proposed a two-step approach integrating both the global parametric modeling and the local nonparametric modeling of face images. Their method is based on the inference using the MAP estimator and Markov network, but PCA is also applied to calculating the subspace of the high-resolution image space. Also, Park and Savvides [20, 21] applied the subspaces and features of locality preserving projections (LPP) [15] for their novel face super-resolution method, which is also employed the traditional MAP estimator.

In this chapter, several state-of-the-art methods for face super-resolution are introduced. In particular, we introduce remarkable methods focusing on enhancing the resolution of face images, not all kinds of images. We demonstrate how each method trains and models the characteristics of face images. The rest of this chapter is organized as follows. In Section 12.2 we briefly introduce statistical inference-based approaches for face super-resolution. First of all, we present the MAP estimator, which allows us to make inferences simply and effectively since various super-resolution methods have applied it. As illustrations, we briefly show two methods proposed by Baker and Kanade [1, 6] and Liu et al. [9, 19]. In Section 12.3 the subspace-based approaches for face super-resolution are presented with the methods using PCA [11, 12], LLE [18], and LPP [20, 21]. In Section 12.4 the state-of-the-art methods for face super-resolution are compared to a baseline method. Finally, Section 12.5 concludes this chapter.

## 12.2    STATISTICAL INFERENCE-BASED APPROACHES

In this section, face super-resolution methods based on statistical inference are presented. Super-resolution tasks often need to solve inference problems such as estimating some parameters or features in an output high-resolution image from an input low-resolution image. To solve these inference problems, in literature, statistical inference-based approaches have been applied to analyze the face image space as probabilistic models using various probabilistic methods such as the MAP estimator, Markov random fields, and belief propagation. First of all, we present the MAP estimator, which is one of the most widely and simply used methods for inference. Let us assume the functional relationship between a pair of high- and low-images:

$$\mathbf{l} = f(\mathbf{h}), \tag{12.1}$$

where a $M \times 1$ vector $\mathbf{l}$ and a $N \times 1$ vector $\mathbf{h}$ are low- and high-resolution counterparts, respectively, and $f(\cdot)$ is the transformation matrix for smoothing and down-sampling. In many cases, a liner transform multiplying a $M \times N$ matrix $\mathbf{A}$ is simply used as a smoothing and down-sampling function $f(\cdot)$, where each row vector of $\mathbf{A}$ smoothes a block in $\mathbf{h}$ to a pixel in $\mathbf{l}$. Equation (12.1) is therefore rewritten as

$$\mathbf{l} = \mathbf{A}\mathbf{h}. \tag{12.2}$$

We cannot analytically calculate the inverse function of $f(\cdot)$ or the inverse matrix of $\mathbf{A}$ since this reverse process is full of uncertainty. Thus, we need to reconstruct a high-resolution vectorized image $\mathbf{h}$ for an input $\mathbf{l}$ by super-resolution techniques. The maximum a posteriori (MAP) estimator is one of the widely used solutions in this case [1, 5, 9]. We calculate the optimal $\mathbf{h}^*$ maximizing the posterior probability $p(\mathbf{h}|\mathbf{l})$ based on the MAP criterion:

$$\mathbf{h}^* = \arg\max_{\mathbf{h}} p(\mathbf{h}|\mathbf{l}) = \arg\max_{\mathbf{h}} \frac{p(\mathbf{l}|\mathbf{h})p(\mathbf{h})}{p(\mathbf{l})}. \tag{12.3}$$

Since $\mathbf{l}$ is already given as an input and then $p(\mathbf{l})$ is a constant, Eq. (12.3) can be rewritten as

$$\mathbf{h}^* = \arg\max_{\mathbf{h}} p(\mathbf{l}|\mathbf{h})p(\mathbf{h}). \tag{12.4}$$

Note that Eq. (12.4) contains the prior probability of a high-resolution image $p(\mathbf{h})$. So, if we can also formulate $p(\mathbf{h})$ using reliable methods, then Eq. (12.4) can be solved. For example, Liu et al. [9] formulated the prior distribution of PCA coefficients, instead of $\mathbf{h}$, as a Gaussian distribution through eigenfaces [10] since $\mathbf{h}$ is determined by PCA coefficients. Moreover, in many cases, it is simply assumed that the likelihood $p(\mathbf{l}|\mathbf{h})$ is formulated as a Gaussian distribution function when a Gaussian noise $\eta = \mathbf{l} - \mathbf{Ah}$ is regarded in Eq. (12.2) as follows:

$$\mathbf{l} = \mathbf{Ah} + \eta. \tag{12.5}$$

Then, we can get the following equation:

$$p(\mathbf{l}|\mathbf{h}) = \frac{1}{Z} \exp\left(-\frac{1}{2\sigma^2} \| \mathbf{Ah} - \mathbf{l} \|^2\right), \tag{12.6}$$

where $Z$ is a normalization constant and $\sigma^2$ is the variance of the Gaussian noise.

In the rest of this section, several face super-resolution methods using the MAP estimator are introduced.

## 12.2.1    Face Hallucination by Baker and Kanade

Baker and Kanade [1, 6] introduced the idea of super-resolution to facial images for face recognition, and they suggested calling this idea face hallucination. Also, they proposed a novel method more appropriate to frontal face images than all kinds of images.

The basic idea is that the high-resolution image in the Gaussian pyramid is inferred pixel by pixel so as to maximize the posterior probability of the unknown high-resolution image given the low-resolution image. To do this, the prior probability of the high-resolution image should be known. In references 1 and 6, the prior probability was learned from a set of training images, so this method yields more reliable results for face super-resolution than other traditional super-resolution methods for all kinds of images.

### 12.2.1.1    Gaussian Pyramids

Face hallucination starts from constructing the Gaussian pyramids of high- and low-resolution images. For a high-resolution image $I$, $G_k$ means the $k$th image in the Gaussian pyramid, where the lowest level of the Gaussian pyramid $G_0$ is set to $I$ and other levels are set by the following equation:

$$G_k = \text{REDUCE}(G_{k-1}(I)), \tag{12.7}$$

where REDUCE($\cdot$) is an operator for smoothing and down-sampling, and it is actually chosen to be the pixel averaging function:

$$\text{REDUCE}(I)(m, n) = \frac{1}{4} \sum_{i=0}^{1} \sum_{j=0}^{1} I(2m + i, 2n + j) \tag{12.8}$$

In terms of the Gaussian pyramid, super-resolution is a function to obtain a high-resolution image $G_0(I)$ from an input low-resolution image $G_k(I)$ where $k > 0$. In reference 1, it is assumed that $G_k(I)(m, n)$, a pixel in the low-resolution image, is defined as the addition of the weighted sum of the high-resolution pixels and i.i.d. Gaussian noise $\eta(m, n)$:

$$G_k(I)(m, n) = \sum_{(p,q)} W(m, n, p, q)G_0(I)(p, q) + \eta(m, n). \tag{12.9}$$

### 12.2.1.2   Estimation of a High-Resolution Image by the MAP Estimator and the Gradient Prior

The high-resolution image $G_0$ can be inferred for a given low-resolution image $G_k$ by the MAP estimator in Eq. (12.4):

$$G_0^* = \arg\max_{G_0} P(G_0|G_k) = \arg\max_{G_0} P(G_k|G_0)P(G_0). \tag{12.10}$$

So, in the above equation, the MAP estimator can be applied if the two terms $P(G_k|G_0)$ and $P(G_0)$ are defined. The first term $P(G_k|G_0)$ can be solved by the assumption that $\eta(m, n)$ is i.i.d. Gaussian since $P(G_k|G_0) = P(\eta(m, n))$ in Eq. (12.9). Next, the prior term $P(G_0)$ is learned by a pyramid-based algorithm using a pyramids of feature vectors: Laplacian pyramids, the horizontal and vertical first derivatives of the Gaussian pyramids, and the horizontal and vertical second derivatives of the Gaussian pyramids [1]. A feature vector $\mathbf{F}_k(T_i)$ denotes a set of these pyramids for the training image $T_i$ at the $k$th level. Here, if $(m, n)$ is a pixel in the $l$th level of a pyramid, its parent at the $l + 1$th level is $\left( \lfloor \frac{m}{2} \rfloor, \lfloor \frac{n}{2} \rfloor \right)$. Thus, the parent structure vector of a pixel $(m, n)$ in the $l$th level is defined as

$$\text{PS}_l(I)(m, n) = \left( \mathbf{F}_l(I)(m, n), \ldots, \mathbf{F}_N(I) \left( \left\lfloor \frac{m}{2^{N-l}} \right\rfloor, \left\lfloor \frac{n}{2^{N-l}} \right\rfloor \right) \right). \tag{12.11}$$

Finally, the optimal feature vector $\mathbf{F}_0^*(I)(m, n)$ of the unknown high-resolution image can be chosen to be $\mathbf{F}_0(T_{i*})(m, n)$, where the training image $T_{i*}$ minimizes the $L_2$ norm error of the parent structure vectors:

$$i^* = \arg\min_{i} \left\| \text{PS}_k(I) \left( \left\lfloor \frac{m}{2^{N-l}} \right\rfloor, \left\lfloor \frac{n}{2^{N-l}} \right\rfloor \right) - \text{PS}_k(T_i) \left( \left\lfloor \frac{m}{2^{N-l}} \right\rfloor, \left\lfloor \frac{n}{2^{N-l}} \right\rfloor \right) \right\|^2. \tag{12.12}$$

The high-resolution image $G_0(m, n)$ can be easily obtained by $\mathbf{F}_0^*(I)(m, n)$.

## 12.2.2    Two-Step Approach by Liu et al.

In references 9 and 19, it is assumed that a high-resolution face image **h** is a composition of a global face image $\mathbf{h}^g$ and a local feature image $\mathbf{h}^l$:

$$\mathbf{h} = \mathbf{h}^g + \mathbf{h}^l. \tag{12.13}$$

So, the two components are recovered respectively by a two-step approach: a global parametric model and a local nonparametric model. This assumption is based on the global and local constraints. First, the global constraint is that the result of face super-resolution must have common features of a human face—for example, eyes, mouth, nose, symmetry, and so on. The first step is for the global parametric modeling of face images based on the assumption that a global face image is generated by a Gaussian distribution learned by principal component analysis (PCA) [10]. Here, the PCA coefficients of the global face image is inferred by a MAP estimator introduced in Session 12.2.

Next, the local constraint is that the result must have specific characteristics of a face image with local features that make the face look different from other faces. Thus, the second step is for the local nonparametric modeling of face images and an optimal local feature image is inferred from the optimal global image by minimizing the energy of the Markov network. Finally, an output high-resolution image is obtained by the sum of the global and local images. In sum, the novelty of this approach is that by integrating both global and local models, both common feature and individual characteristics of faces are recovered respectively, so more reliable results can be yields.

### 12.2.2.1    Global Modeling: A Linear Parametric Model

At the first step of the two-step approach, the global face image $\mathbf{h}^g$ of the high-resolution image **h** is inferred using PCA and the MAP estimator. It is assumed that the low-resolution image **l** obtained from **h** by smoothing and down-sampling loses the local feature $\mathbf{h}^l$:

$$\mathbf{l} = \mathbf{A}\mathbf{h} = \mathbf{A}\mathbf{h}^g \tag{12.14}$$

Therefore, Eq. (12.4) is rewritten as

$$p(\mathbf{l}|\mathbf{h}) = \frac{1}{Z}\exp\left(-\frac{1}{2\sigma^2}\|\mathbf{A}\mathbf{h}^g - \mathbf{l}\|^2\right) = p(\mathbf{l}|\mathbf{h}^g). \tag{12.15}$$

Also, Eq. (12.6) is defined by both $\mathbf{h}^g$ and $\mathbf{h}^l$:

$$\mathbf{h}^* = \arg\max_{\mathbf{h}} p(\mathbf{l}|\mathbf{h})p(\mathbf{h})$$

$$= \arg\max_{\mathbf{h}^g,\mathbf{h}^l} p(\mathbf{l}|\mathbf{h}^g)p(\mathbf{h}^g,\mathbf{h}^l)$$

$$= \arg\max_{\mathbf{h}^g,\mathbf{h}^l} p(\mathbf{l}|\mathbf{h}^g)p(\mathbf{h}^g)p(\mathbf{h}^l|\mathbf{h}^g). \tag{12.16}$$

To calculate $\mathbf{h}^*$ by the sum of $\mathbf{h}^{g*}$ and $\mathbf{h}^{l*}$, we should find

$$\mathbf{h}^{g*} = \arg \max_{\mathbf{h}^g} p(\mathbf{l}|\mathbf{h}^g)p(\mathbf{h}^g) \tag{12.17}$$

at the first step, and next,

$$\mathbf{h}^{l*} = \arg \max_{\mathbf{h}^l} p(\mathbf{l}|\mathbf{h}^{g*}) \tag{12.18}$$

at the second step. First, to solve for $\mathbf{h}^{g*}$, Liu et al. employed eigenfaces [10]:

$$\mathbf{h}^g = \mathbf{W}\mathbf{x}_h^g + \mu, \mathbf{x}_h^g = \mathbf{W}^T(\mathbf{h}^g - \mu), \tag{12.19}$$

where the column vectors of the matrix $\mathbf{W}$ are eigenvectors of the matrix whose column vectors are training images, a vector $\mu$ is the mean of the training set, and $\mathbf{x}_h^g$ is PCA coefficients. Since $\mathbf{h}^g$ is determined by $\mathbf{x}_h^g$, we first solve for $\mathbf{x}_h^{g*}$ instead of $\mathbf{h}^{g*}$, and next calculate $\mathbf{h}^{g*}$ by $\mathbf{h}^{g*} = \mathbf{W}\mathbf{x}_h^{g*} + \mu$ in Eq. (12.19). Thus, Eq. (12.17) defined by $\mathbf{h}^g$ can be replaced by the equation

$$\mathbf{x}_h^{g*} = \arg \max_{\mathbf{x}_h^g} p\left(\mathbf{l}|\mathbf{x}_h^g\right) p(\mathbf{h}^g), \tag{12.20}$$

defined by $\mathbf{x}_h^g$. $p(\mathbf{h}^g)$ can be replaced by $p(\mathbf{x}_h^g)$, which is

$$p(\mathbf{x}_h^g) = \frac{1}{Z'} \exp\left(-\frac{1}{2}\mathbf{x}_h^{gT}\Lambda^{-1}\mathbf{x}_h^g\right), \tag{12.21}$$

where $\Lambda$ is a diagonal matrix consisting of eigenvalues of the matrix of training images. Then, the likelihood of Eq. (12.6) is replaced by

$$p\left(\mathbf{l}|\mathbf{x}_h^g\right) = \frac{1}{Z} \exp\left(-\frac{1}{2\sigma^2} \left\|\mathbf{A}\left(\mathbf{W}\mathbf{x}_h^g + \mu\right) - \mathbf{l}\right\|^2\right). \tag{12.22}$$

From Eq. (12.20) and Eq. (12.22), Eq. (12.22) can be solved.

### 12.2.2.2 *Local Modeling: Patch-Based Nonparametric Model*

At the second step, to infer the local feature image $\mathbf{h}^l$ of the high-resolution image $\mathbf{h}$, Markov network [17, 22, 23] is applied. Markov network shown in Figure 12.1 can be applied to learning the network parameters from the examples with observed data and underlying data. In the super-resolution tasks, a low-resolution image or patch is observed but a high-resolution one is unknown, so Markov network can be successfully applied to super-resolution [7, 9, 19, 24].

In contrast to the global modeling, for the local modeling, the patch-based approach is applied as shown in Figure 12.2. $\mathbf{h}^g(\mathbf{v})$ and $\mathbf{h}^l(\mathbf{v})$ are set to the observed and latent data, respectively, since $\mathbf{h}^g(\mathbf{v})$ is already determined at the first step for the global modeling and $\mathbf{h}^l(\mathbf{v})$ is not estimated yet. $(w + h) \times (w + h)$ pixel patches overlap horizontally and vertically with each other by $h$ pixels. The patch $\mathbf{h}^l(\mathbf{v})$ has four

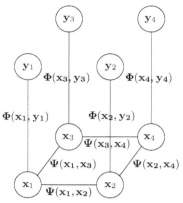

**Figure 12.1.** Markov network for vision problems. Underlying data $\mathbf{x}_i$ can be inferred from observation $\mathbf{y}_i$.

neighboring patches $N_h^l(\mathbf{v}) = \{\mathbf{h}^l(\mathbf{v} + \Delta_x), \mathbf{h}^l(\mathbf{v} - \Delta_x), \mathbf{h}^l(\mathbf{v} + \Delta_y), \mathbf{h}^l(\mathbf{v} - \Delta_y)\}$. Also, $\mathbf{h}^g(\mathbf{v})$ is another neighboring node in the Markov network. Therefore, the optimal local feature $\mathbf{h}^{l*}$ can be defined by

$$\mathbf{h}^{l*} = \arg\max_{\mathbf{h}^l} p\left(\mathbf{h}^l(\mathbf{v}) | N_h^l(\mathbf{v}), \mathbf{h}^g(\mathbf{v})\right). \qquad (12.23)$$

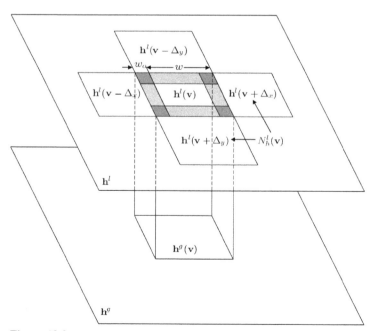

**Figure 12.2.** Illustration of the patch-based Markov network.

By introducing the Gibbs potential function $E_G(\cdot)$, it is described how likely a patch $\mathbf{h}^l(\mathbf{v})$ connects to $\mathbf{h}^g(\mathbf{v})$ and $N_h^l(\mathbf{v})$.

$$p\left(\mathbf{h}^l(\mathbf{v})|N_h^l(\mathbf{v}), \mathbf{h}^g(\mathbf{v})\right) \propto \exp\left(-E_G\left(\mathbf{h}^l(\mathbf{v}), N_h^l(\mathbf{v}), \mathbf{h}^g(\mathbf{v})\right)\right). \quad (12.24)$$

The Gibbs potential function $E_G(\cdot)$ is decoupled into two independent terms concerning $N_h^l(\mathbf{v})$ and $\mathbf{h}^g(\mathbf{v})$.

$$E_G\left(\mathbf{h}^l(\mathbf{v}), N_h^l(\mathbf{v}), \mathbf{h}^g(\mathbf{v})\right) = E_G^{int}\left(\mathbf{h}^l(\mathbf{v}), N_h^l(\mathbf{v})\right) + E_G^{exp}(\mathbf{h}^l(\mathbf{v}), \mathbf{h}^g(\mathbf{v})), \quad (12.25)$$

where $E_G^{int}(\cdot)$ is the internal potential function that describes the neighboring statistics between patches inside $\mathbf{h}^l$, and $E_G^{ext}(\cdot)$ is the external potential function that represents the connecting statistics between connecting patches in $\mathbf{h}^l$ and $\mathbf{h}^g$. In reference 9, it is described in detail how to obtain $\mathbf{h}^{l*}(\mathbf{v})$ by defining and solving the internal and external potential functions.

## 12.3  SUBSPACE-BASED APPROACHES

In this section, subspace-based approaches for face super-resolution are introduced. Subspace-based approaches assume that the high- and low-resolution images have similar coefficients, features, or distributions in the high- and low-resolution image spaces. So, in subspace-based approaches, first the subspaces in the two spaces are learned, and then a high-resolution image is represented by the similarity between the two subspaces. In this section we introduce novel methods for face super-resolution using the subspaces obtained by several kinds of dimensionality reduction methods: PCA, Locally Linear Embedding (LLE) [13], and locality preserving projections (LPP) [15, 25].

### 12.3.1  Eigentransformation by Wang and Tang

Different from most of the proposed methods based on probabilistic models, Wang and Tang [11, 12] proposed a new face super-resolution method called eigentransformation using PCA to represent the structural similarities of face images. This algorithm treats the face super-resolution problems as the mapping between two groups of training samples: high- and low-resolution facial images. In this method, it is simply assumed that the high- and low-resolution counterparts have the same PCA coefficients while each image space has its own PCA subspace. The input low-resolution image is fitted as the weighted sum of the centered low-resolution images in the training set. Next, the output high-resolution image is reconstructed with the identical weights and the high-resolution counterparts corresponding to these centered low-resolution images.

### 12.3.1.1 Principal Component Analysis for High- and Low-Resolution Training Sets

PCA represents any face image using a weighted linear combination of eigenfaces shown in Eq. (12.19). To apply the eigentransformation algorithm to face super-resolution, we need two training sets: high-resolution images $\mathbf{h}_1, \mathbf{h}_2, \ldots, \mathbf{h}_M$ and corresponding low-resolution images $\mathbf{l}_1, \mathbf{l}_2, \ldots, \mathbf{l}_M$, where each training set has $M$ images and the low-resolution training images are created by Eq. (12.2):

$$\mathbf{l}_i = \mathbf{A}\mathbf{h}_i. \tag{12.26}$$

Where a low-resolution image has $N_L$ pixels in it, the $N_L \times M$ matrix of the low-resolution training set is defined by $\mathbf{L} = [\mathbf{l}_1 - \mu_l, \mathbf{l}_2 - \mu_l, \cdots, \mathbf{l}_M - \mu_l] = [\mathbf{l}'_1, \mathbf{l}'_2, \cdots, \mathbf{l}'_M]$. By applying PCA to the low-resolution training set $\mathbf{L}$, any input low-resolution $\mathbf{l}$ can be represented by

$$\mathbf{l} = \mathbf{W}\mathbf{x}_l + \mu_l \tag{12.27}$$

as shown in Eq. (12.19). Here, $\mathbf{W}$ is the eigenvector matrix of $\mathbf{L}\mathbf{L}^T$ and $\mu_l$ is the mean of all the low-resolution training images. That is, the column vectors of $\mathbf{W}$ are the eigenfaces of the low-resolution training set sorted as the corresponding eigenvalues are decreasing. Also, by singular vector decomposition, the matrix $\mathbf{L}$ can be represented by

$$\mathbf{W} = \mathbf{L}\mathbf{V}\Lambda_l^{-\frac{1}{2}}, \tag{12.28}$$

where $\mathbf{V}$ and $\Lambda$ are the eigenvector matrix and the eigenvalue matrix of $\mathbf{L}^T\mathbf{L}$, respectively. Then, Eq. (12.27) can be reformulated as

$$\mathbf{l} = \mathbf{L}\mathbf{V}\Lambda_l^{-\frac{1}{2}}\mathbf{x}_l + \mu_l = \mathbf{L}\mathbf{c} + \mu_l, \tag{12.29}$$

where $\mathbf{c} = \mathbf{V}\Lambda_l^{-\frac{1}{2}}\mathbf{x}_l = [c_1, c_2, \cdots, c_M]^T$. Thus, the input low-resolution image $\mathbf{l}$ in Eq. (12.27) can be rewritten as

$$\mathbf{l} = \mathbf{L}\mathbf{c} + \mu_l = \sum_{i=1}^{M} c_i \mathbf{l}'_i + \mu_l. \tag{12.30}$$

This shows that the input low-resolution image is reconstructed by the weighted sum of the $M$ low-resolution training images. By applying Eq. (12.2), Eq. (12.30) can be represented by the soothing and down-sampling matrix $\mathbf{A}$:

$$\mathbf{A}\mathbf{h} = \sum_{i=1}^{M} c_i \mathbf{A}\mathbf{h}'_i + \mathbf{A}\mu_h. \tag{12.31}$$

Removing the multiplication by $\mathbf{A}$ from the left and right sides in the above equation, we can get

$$\mathbf{h} = \sum_{i=1}^{M} c_i \mathbf{h}'_i + \mu_h, \tag{12.32}$$

where $\mathbf{h}_i'$ is a high-resolution training image corresponding to $\mathbf{l}_i'$. Therefore, the output high-resolution image $\mathbf{h}$ can be reconstructed by the weighted sum of the same weights $\mathbf{c}$ obtained by PCA for $\mathbf{l}$ and the corresponding $M$ high-resolution training images.

In some, in the eigentransformation algorithm, the principal components of high-resolution face can be inferred from the principal components of the low-resolution face by mapping between the high- and low-resolution training pairs.

## 12.3.2  Super-Resolution Through Neighbor Embedding by Chang et al.

Recently, super-resolution inspired by manifold learning methods have been proposed [18, 20, 21]. Manifold learning methods allows us to analyze the geometries of data spaces which lie on nonlinear manifolds. A manifold is a natural generalization of a Euclidean space to a locally Euclidean space. Manifold learning methods are based on the observation that the local manifold structure is more important than the global Euclidean structure. Thus, manifold learning techniques often use adjacency to preserve the local neighborhood relationships.

In particular, Chang et al. [18] developed the neighbor embedding algorithm for super-resolution. The idea is inspired by locally linear embedding (LLE) [13], one of the most widely used manifold learning methods. In LLE, the local geometry is characterized by $K$ nearest neighborhoods and an image is reconstructed by the weighted linear combination of its neighbors in the image space. Chang et al. assume that the local geometry (i.e., neighborhood relationships in the sample space) is preserved even after the loss of resolution; the low- and high-resolution images are represented as the weighted sum using the identical weights and neighbors among the training images. The application of this work is not limited to face images.

### 12.3.2.1  Locally Linear Embedding

Locally linear embedding (LLE) is one of the most widely used manifold learning methods. LLE is an unsupervised learning algorithm that computes low-dimensional, neighborhood-preserving embeddings of high-dimensional data [13]. A $D$-dimensional vector $\mathbf{x}_i$ in a training set is characterized by the linear combination of its neighbors:

$$\mathbf{x}_i = \sum_{j=1}^{K} w_{ij}\mathbf{x}_j, \tag{12.33}$$

where a data point $\mathbf{x}_j$ is among $\mathbf{x}_i$'s neighbors in the training set. Consequently, in LLE, local geometry is characterized by the neighbors of each image.

In particular, LLE is useful for dimensionality reduction; by LLE, the data sampled from an underlying manifold are mapped into a lower-dimensional data space. Dimension reduction by LLE preserves the neighborhood relationships; the goal of

LLE for dimension reduction is to find a lower-dimensional embedding $\mathbf{y}_i$ characterized by the same weighted linear combination of the neighbors with $\mathbf{x}_i$.

For each point in the $D$-dimensional sample space, the LLE algorithm can be summarized as follows:

1. Using the Euclidean distance measure, find $K$ nearest neighbors of a data point $\mathbf{x}_i$ among $N$ training images: $\mathbf{x}_1, \mathbf{x}_2, \ldots, \mathbf{x}_j, \ldots \mathbf{x}_K$.

2. Calculate the optimal weights of the neighbors such that minimize the reconstruction error:

$$w_{ij}^* = \arg\min_{w_{ij}} \left\| \mathbf{x}_i - \sum_{j=1}^{K} w_{ij}\mathbf{x}_j \right\|^2 \qquad \text{subject to} \sum_{j=1} w_{ij} = 1, \quad (12.34)$$

where Eq. (12.34) can be solved by Lagrange multiplier.

3. Compute the $d$-dimensional embedding which is best reconstructed by the same neighbors and weights where $D \gg d$:

$$\mathbf{y}_i^* = \arg\min_{\mathbf{y}_i} \left\| \mathbf{y}_i - \sum_{j=1}^{K} w_{ij}\mathbf{y}_j \right\|^2 . \qquad (12.35)$$

The optimal solution of $\mathbf{y}_i^*$ in Eq. (12.35) is the smallest eigenvectors of matrix $(\mathbf{I} - \mathbf{W})^T(\mathbf{I} - \mathbf{W})$ where $\mathbf{I}$ is the $N \times N$ identity matrix and $\mathbf{W}$ is the matrix consisting of $\{w_{ij}\}$; $w_{ij}$ is 0 when $\mathbf{x}_j$ is not $\mathbf{x}_i$'s neighbor.

### 12.3.2.2  Super-Resolution Method Inspired by Locally Linear Embedding

The analysis of neighbor embedding reveals the characteristics and the underlying structure in the distribution of high-dimensional data. Neighbor embedding by manifold learning methods has been usually applied to dimensionality reduction. Chang et al. extended the idea of preserving neighborhood relationships to enhancement of resolution. By analogy with dimension reduction to find mapping between high-dimensional data and low-dimensional data, LLE can be applied to super-resolution from a low-resolution image to a high-resolution image. In reference 18, it is assumed that small image patches in the low- and high-resolution images form manifolds with similar local geometry in two different vector spaces.

In super-resolution through neighbor embedding, given a low-resolution image patch $\mathbf{l}$ as input, its neighbors $\mathbf{l}_i$'s in a low-resolution training set and their weights $w_i$'s are obtained by Eqs. (12.33) and (12.34):

$$\mathbf{l} = \sum_{i=1}^{K} w_i\mathbf{l}_i. \qquad (12.36)$$

According to the assumption that low-resolution patches and high-resolution patches have the same neighborhood relationships, the high-resolution counterpart $\mathbf{h}$

of the low-resolution patch **l** is reconstructed by the same weighted linear combination in the high-resolution data space:

$$\mathbf{h} = \sum_{i=1}^{K} w_i \mathbf{h}_i, \tag{12.37}$$

where $\mathbf{h}_i$ is a high-resolution counterpart of $\mathbf{l}_i$ in the training set.

### 12.3.3  Super-Resolution Using LPP by Park and Savvides

Park and Savvides proposed a novel super-resolution method for face images focusing on the fact that it has been shown that face images lie on a nonlinear manifold [13–16]. Manifold learning algorithms are more powerful for face image analysis than other pattern recognition methods which analyze a Euclidean space because they can reveal the underlying nonlinear distribution of the face space. PCA and linear discriminant analysis (LDA) [26] effectively see only the Euclidean structure; they fail to discover the underlying structure when the data lie on a nonlinear manifold. Thus, it is expected that manifold learning methods can improve the tasks demanding face image analysis, such as face recognition, super-resolution, or face synthesis.

However, almost all the methods for face super-resolution have not utilized the manifold in the distribution of face images. Park and Savvides [20, 21] applied another novel manifold learning method, locality preserving projections (LPP) [15, 25] to face super-resolution.

#### 12.3.3.1  Locality Preserving Projections

LPP is to find a linear projective mapping for dimensionality reduction. Compared to LPP, other manifold learning techniques such as isomap [14], LLE [13], or Laplacian eigenmap [16] define the mapping only on the training data. They successfully show the training data are distributed along manifolds, but it is unclear how to evaluate the maps for new test samples. On the other hand, by LPP, we obtain the well-defined transformation matrix that is applicable to new test images absent from the training set.

LPP is designed for optimally preserving the neighborhood structure of the data set while principal component analysis (PCA) utilizes only a global basis. LPP is a novel method for dimensionality reduction by using both the local structure and the global basis of the data set. LPP aims to find a linear projection for dimensionality reduction such that the local structure of the data space is preserved. LPP utilizes a weight which represents how close any two data points are in the data space. Using a set of these weights, we can obtain a set of eigenvectors which represent both the global basis and the neighbor embedding in the data set. When the high-dimensional data lies on a low-dimensional manifold embedded in data space, the locality preserving projections are obtained by finding the optimal linear approximations to the eigenfunctions of the Laplace Beltrami operator on the manifold. The algorithm of LPP is proposed in reference [15], which can be summarized as following:

1. Constructing the adjacency graph: Let $G$ denote a graph with $m$ nodes. One node (or a training image) has $K$ nearest neighbors in the meaning of Euclidean distance, and the neighbors are connected by edges.

2. Choosing the weights between neighbors: The weight between any two neighbors can be calculated by Gaussian kernel of the Euclidean distance. In this chapter, binary kernel is used; $W_{ij}$ is set up as 1 if the two images $\mathbf{x}_i$ and $\mathbf{x}_j$ are connected by an edge, and otherwise $W_{ij}$ is set up as 0.

3. Eigenmaps: Compute the eigenvectors and eigenvalues for the generalized eigenvector problem:

$$\mathbf{XLX}^T \mathbf{e} = \lambda \mathbf{XDX}^T \mathbf{e}, \tag{12.38}$$

where $\mathbf{D}$ is a diagonal matrix whose diagonal entries are $D_{ii} = \sum_j W_{ij}$, $\mathbf{L} = \mathbf{D} - \mathbf{W}$ is the Laplacian matrix, and the $i$th column of the matrix $\mathbf{X}$ is the $i$th vectorized training image $\mathbf{x}_i$. Now, the projective matrix $\mathbf{E}$ has the eigenvectors $\mathbf{e}_i$ as column vectors.

Note that the two matrices $\mathbf{XLX}^T$ and $\mathbf{XDX}^T$ are both symmetric and positive semidefinite since the Laplacian matrix $\mathbf{L}$ and the diagonal matrix $\mathbf{D}$ are both symmetric and positive semidefinite. The Laplacian matrix for finite graph is analogous to the Laplace Beltrami operator on compact Riemannian manifolds, and the Laplace Beltrami operator for a manifold is generated by the Riemannian geometry.

### 12.3.3.2  Patch-Based Modeling

Patch-based approaches for super-resolution using small image patches in Figure 12.3 are less dependent on person-identity than global super-resolution approaches using a whole image. Introduced in Section 12.2.2, Liu et al. [9] also employed patch-based approach. Saul and Roweis [27] shows that local areas such as the mouths in face images also can be analyzed by manifold learning methods.

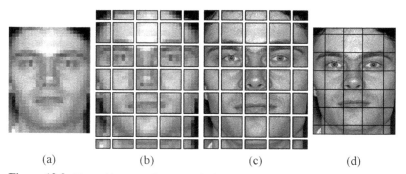

(a)                (b)                (c)                (d)

**Figure 12.3.** The architecture of super-resolution: (**a**) Input low-resolution image; (**b**) low-resolution patches generated by dividing the input image into multiple patches; (**c**) high-resolution patches created by reconstructing each patch into a high-resolution patch; (**d**) reconstructed how-resolution image.

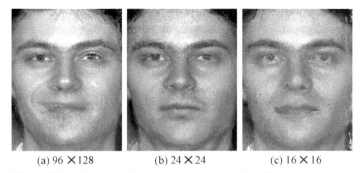

(a) 96 ✕ 128        (b) 24 ✕ 24        (c) 16 ✕ 16

**Figure 12.4.** The effect of the size of a patch when K is 100.

In reference 20 and 21, one image is divided into multiple patches and perform super-resolution for each patch. Patch-based approaches for super-resolution using small image patches are less dependent on person-identity than global super-resolution approaches using a whole image. 24 × 24 pixel patches overlap both horizontally and vertically with each other by two pixels, and the remaining pixels compose one small patch. The size of patches and overlaps were empirically concluded optimal according to experimental results. To integrate all the patches, all the pixel values at the same position are added, and then they are divided by the number of overlaps to normalize intensity. The reason why patches are overlapped is to remove strong difference of intensity at the boundary of two patches. If the overlapping area shrinks, effects of undesirable local distortions spread to neighboring patches.

Figure 12.4 shows that the size of a patch is important for getting reliable results [20, 21]. As each patch becomes larger, it needs more training images for modeling the data space of face images. In particular, if a new test image is totally different from any of the training images, a patch-based approach with large patches requires much more training images; for example, if a new person absent from the training set is given in a test image, a patch-based approach with large patches yields less reliable results than a patch-based approach with small patches. Figure 12.4a shows that when one image is used as one patch, its high-resolution image obtained by patch-based super-resolution may be significantly noisy. Thus, it is necessary to find the optimal patch size empirically. On the other hand, when each patch is too small, it loses the characteristics of human faces, thus the reconstructed images by super-resolution become blurry as we can see in Figure 12.4c.

### 12.3.3.3 Inferring the LPP Feature of the High-Resolution Image

Each patch has its own LPP model to compute the mapping between a high-resolution patch $\mathbf{h}$ and a smoothed and down-sampled patch $\mathbf{l}$. Given a high-resolution patch, the corresponding low-resolution patch $\mathbf{l}$ is computed by down-sampling by Eq. (12.2). LPP aims to find a low-dimensional embedding from a high-dimensional patch, so it is proper to be used for dimensionality reduction such as PCA and LDA. LPP has been applied to dimension reduction by projecting a high dimensional vector onto a low-dimensional subspace. On the contrary, in references 20 and 21, it is shown that LPP can be also applied to super-resolution problem by estimating the LPP feature of an output high-resolution image by the MAP estimator introduced in Section 12.2.

Given the high-resolution patch $\mathbf{h}$ taken from a training image, the LPP feature $\mathbf{x}_h$ are calculated by

$$\mathbf{x}_h = \mathbf{E}^T\mathbf{h}, \mathbf{h} = \mathbf{E}\mathbf{x}_h, \tag{12.39}$$

where $\mathbf{E}$ is the projective matrix of LPP in Eq. (12.38). Maximize $p(\mathbf{l}|\mathbf{h})p(\mathbf{h})$ in Eq. (12.4) is equivalent to maximizing the prior $p(\mathbf{x}_h)$ modeled by the Gaussian distribution function from Eq. (12.21):

$$p(\mathbf{x}_h) = \frac{1}{Z}\exp\left(-\mathbf{x}_h^T\Lambda^{-1}\mathbf{x}_h\right), \tag{12.40}$$

where $Z$ is a normalization constant and $\Lambda = \mathrm{diag}\left(\sigma_1^2, \sigma_2^2, \ldots, \sigma_1^N\right)$. Also, the likelihood is denoted by

$$p(\mathbf{l}|\mathbf{h}) = \frac{1}{Z}\exp\left(-\frac{1}{2\sigma^2}\|\mathbf{A}\mathbf{E}\mathbf{x}_h - \mathbf{l}\|^2\right). \tag{12.41}$$

To maximize $p(\mathbf{l}|\mathbf{h})p(\mathbf{x}_h)$, the optimal LPP feature $\mathbf{x}_h^*$ is selected such that it satisfies the following objective:

$$\mathbf{x}_h^* = \arg\min_{\mathbf{x}_h} 2\sigma^2\mathbf{x}_h^T\Lambda^{-1}\mathbf{x}_h + \|\mathbf{A}\mathbf{E}\mathbf{x}_h - \mathbf{l}\|^2. \tag{12.42}$$

Finally, the optimal solution is given by

$$\mathbf{x}_h^* = (\mathbf{E}^T\mathbf{A}^T\mathbf{A}\mathbf{E} + 2\sigma^2\Lambda^{-1})^{-1}\mathbf{E}^T\mathbf{A}^T\mathbf{l}, \tag{12.43}$$

where $\sigma$ is decided empirically. If $\sigma$ is too small, $\mathbf{x}_h^*$ cannot be obtained because $\mathbf{E}^T\mathbf{A}^T\mathbf{A}\mathbf{E}$ is close to singular.

The number of nearest neighbors for each patch also has significant impact on the super-resolution results. Figure 12.5 shows that the manifold structure cannot be analyzed as $K$ becomes too small or large. When $K$ is too large, we cannot analyze

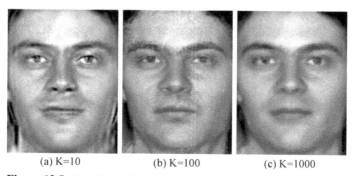

(a) K=10          (b) K=100          (c) K=1000

**Figure 12.5.** The effect of the number of nearest neighborhoods when $24 \times 24$ pixel patches are used.

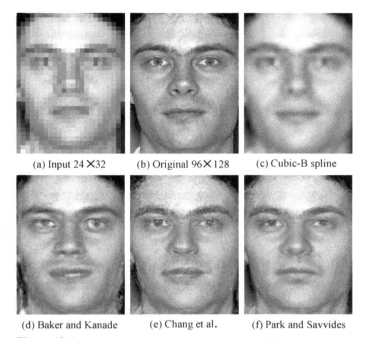

(a) Input 24 ×32        (b) Original 96× 128        (c) Cubic-B spline

(d) Baker and Kanade        (e) Chang et al.        (f) Park and Savvides

**Figure 12.6.**  The results of face super-resolution using LPP and other methods.

the local structure consisting of neighbors while too small $K$ makes it impossible to analyze the global structure in data space.

## 12.4  EXPERIMENTAL RESULTS

In this section we compare the results of several face supre-resolution methods introduced in this chapter. For experiments, a subset of the color FERET database [28] was used. We selected the images with neutral expression and frontal pose, and we used 1500 images for training and 500 images for testing. Before experiments, the face images were aligned with given eye coordinates, cropped to $96 \times 128$ pixel images, and normalized by intensity. The high-resolution images were down-sampled to a low-resolution $24 \cdots 36$ pixel images. We choose $\lambda = 1000$ and $K = 100$. Figure 12.6 shows the results of several face super-resolution methods introduced in this chapter and baseline methods: cubic B-spline and the methods proposed by Baker and Kanade [1], Chang et al. [18], and Park and Savvides [20, 21], respectively.

## 12.5  CONCLUSION

Face super-resolution needs different approaches from general super-resolution since face images can be effectively collected and trained. Also, face super-resolution has its own application such as face recognition in video surveillance. So, there is a great demand to develop robust face super-resolution methods that can significantly enhance the quality of face images.

In this chapter, recently proposed remarkable methods for face super-resolution are introduced. We analyze the trends of the literature and classify the methods as two main approaches: statistical inference-based approaches and subspace-based approaches. We also demonstrate the super-resolution results of the methods introduced in this chapter.

## REFERENCES

1. S. Baker and T. Kanade, Hallucinating faces, in *Proceedings of the International Conference on Automatic Face and Gesture Recognition,* 2000, pp. 83–88.
2. M. Elad and A. Feuer, Restoration of a single superresolution image from several blurred, noisy, and undersampled measured images, *IEEE Trans. Image Processing* **6**(12):1646–1658, 1997.
3. M. Irani and S. Peleg, Improving resolution by image registration, CVGIP: Graphics Models Image Processing, **53**:231–239, 1991.
4. R. R. Schulz and R. L. Stevenson, Extraction of high resolution frames from video sequences, *IEEE Trans. Image Processing* **5**:996–1011, 1996.
5. R. C. Hardie, K. J. Barnard, and E. E. Armstrong, Joint MAP registration and high-resolution image estimation using a sequence of undersampled images, *IEEE Trans. Image Processing* **6**:1621–1633, 1997.
6. S. Baker and T. Kanade, Limits on super-resolution and how to break them, *IEEE Trans. Pattern Anal. Mach. Intell.* **24**:1167-1183, 2000.
7. W. Freeman and E. Pasztor, Learning low-level vision, in *7th International Conference on Computer Vision*, 1999, pp. 1182–1189.
8. D. P. Capel and A. Zisserman, Super-resolution from multiple views using learnt image models, in *Proceedings of IEEE International Conference, Computer Vision and Pattern Recognition*, Vol. 2, 2001, pp. 627–634.
9. C. Liu, H. Shum and C. Zhang, A two-step approach to hallucinating faces: Global parametric model and local nonparametric model, in *Proceedings. of IEEE International Conference on Computer Vision and Pattern Recognition*, 2001, pp. 192–198.
10. M. Turk and A. Pentland, Eigenfaces for recognition, *J. Cognit. Neurosci.* **3**(1):71–86, 1991.
11. X. Wang and X. Tang, Hallucinating face by eigentransformation, *IEEE Trans. Syst. Man Cybern. Part C* (special issue on biometrics systems) **35**:425–434, 2005.
12. X. Wang and X. Tang, Face hallucination and recognition, in *Proceedings of the 4th International Conference on Audio- and Video-Based Personal Authentication*, 2003, pp. 486–494.
13. S. Roweis and L. K. Saul, Nonlinear dimensionality reduction by locally linear embedding, *Science*, **290**:2323–2326, 2000.
14. J. B. Tenenbaum, V. Silva, and J. C. Langford, A global geometric framework for nonlinear dimensionality reduction, *Science* **290**(12):2319–2323, 2003.
15. X. He, S. Yan, Y. Hu, P. Niyogi, and H. Zhang, Face recognition using laplacian faces, *IEEE Trans. Pattern Anal. Mach. Intell.* **27**(3):328–340, 2005.
16. M. Belkin and P. Niyogi, Laplacian eigenmaps and spectral techniques for embedding and clustering, *Adv. Neural Inf. Processing Syst.* **14**:585–591, 2002.
17. J. Pearl, *Probabilistic Reasoning in Intelligent Systems: Networks of Plausible Inference*, Morgan Kaufmann, San Francisco, 1988.
18. H. Chang, D. Y. Yeung, and Y. Xiong, Super-resolution through neighbor embedding, *Proceedings of IEEE International Conference on Computer Vision and Pattern Recognition*, Vol. 1, 2004, pp. 275–282.

19. C. Liu, H. Shum, and W. T. Freeman, Face hallucination: Theory and practice, *Int. J. Comput. Vis.* **75**(1):115–134, 2007.
20. S. W. Park and M. Savvides, Breaking the limitation of manifold analysis for super-resolution of facial images, in *Conference on Acoustics, Speech, and Signal Processing*, 2007, pp. 573–576.
21. S. W. Park and M. Savvides, Locality preserving projections as a new manifold analysis approach for robust face super-resolution, in *SPIE Defense and Security Symposium on Biometric Identification Technologies*, 2007.
22. S. Geman and D. Geman, Stochastic relaxation, Gibbs distribution, and the Bayesian restoration of images, *IEEE Pattern Anal. Mach. Intell.* **6**:721–741, 1984.
23. M. I. Jordan, *Learning in Graphical Models*, MIT Press, Cambridge, MA, 1998.
24. W. T. Freeman, E. C. Pasztor, and O. T. Carmichael, Learning low-level vision, *Int. Conference Comput. Vis.* **40**(1):25–47, 2000.
25. X. He and O. Niyogi, Locality preserving projections, *Adv. Neural Inf. Processing Syst.* **16**:00–00, 2003.
26. P. Belhumeur, J. Hespanha, and D. Kriegman, Eigenfaces vs. fisherfaces: Recognition using class specific linear projection, *IEEE Trans. Pattern Anal. Mach. Intell.* **19**(7):711–720, 1997.
27. L. K. Saul and S. T. Roweis, Think globally, fit locally: Unsupervised learning of low dimensional manifolds," *J. Mach. Learning Res.* **4**:119–155, 2003.
28. http://www.nist.gov/humanid/colorferet
29. J. Sun, N. Zhang, H. Tao and H. Shum, Image hallucination with primal sketch priors, in *Proceedings of IEEE International Conference on Computer Vision and Pattern Recognition*, 2003.
30. http://www.cs.toronto.edu/ roweis/lle/code.html

# Chapter 13

# Iris Recognition

**Yung-Hui Li and Marios Savvides**

## 13.1 INTRODUCTION

In the last few decades, biometric recognition has drawn significant attention due to the vast applications in the field of law enforcement, surveillance, border control, and national security. The core goal of any biometric recognition system is to recognize the identity of the target person based on his/her physiological or behavioral characteristics. Examples of such characteristics include fingerprint, face, voice, signature, hand geometry, iris, and palmprint [1].

Among all the usable characteristics for biometric recognition, the pattern of iris texture is one of the few characteristics believed to be the most distinguishable among different people [2]. The iris is the annular area between the pupil and the sclera of the eye, as shown in Figure 13.1. It consists of pigmented fibrovascular tissues that connect to the sphincter and dilator muscles that control the contraction and dilation of the pupil. It is the randomness of the structure of those tiny tissues that gives the iris pattern its uniqueness for each person. Furthermore, the iris possesses certain properties that make it a very attractive biometric measure. First and foremost, it is thought to remain relatively unchanged throughout a person's lifetime. In fact the iris pattern is formed in the third month of gestation, and the structure becomes stable around the eighth month [3]. This permanence over time makes iris recognition a reliable biometric compared to other physiological characteristics such as a face or voice, which change drastically as a person grows old. Second, the iris is rarely affected by external elements because it is well-protected behind the cornea. Even eye surgery, which is typically performed on the cornea or on the retina through the pupil, seldom hurts the iris. In comparison, fingerprints, although unique and relatively permanent, suffer significantly from external elements, such as erosion, cuts and scratches, and medical conditions (such as psoriasis) that cause thinning, and ultimately all lead to

*Biometrics: Theory, Methods, and Applications.* Edited by Boulgouris, Plataniotis, and Micheli-Tzanakou
Copyright © 2010 the Institute of Electrical and Electronics Engineers, Inc.

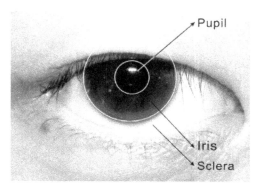

**Figure 13.1.** Pupil, iris, and sclera region on an eye image.

failures in acquisition by common fingerprint sensors. Third, although a little bit hard to acquire, iris imaging is relatively unintrusive and, as with face imaging, requires minimum effort from a subject, such as standing still or staring at a camera with no touching or physical contact, which can make its acceptance easier. Last but not least, it is believed to be one of the hardest biometrics to spoof and circumvent.

All these factors, along with small intra-class variations and large inter-class variations, make iris recognition a highly desirable biometric for identification. With adequate image preprocessing and coordinate transformation (to normalize for pupil dilation), problems that often stand in the way of other biometric modalities can be easily eliminated in iris recognition. More details will be discussed in the following subsections.

A typical iris recognition system will consist of the following stages: (1) iris image acquisition, (2) iris image preprocessing, (3) iris texture feature extraction, and (4) feature matching. Figure 13.2 shows the flow chart of a typical iris recognition system. In the following sections, we will review the literature of a variety of different implementations of each of these stages. Iris recognition first came into the spotlight in *National Geographic* magazine when it was used to identify an Afghan girl who appeared on the cover of one of their issues [4]. Sharbat Gula, fleeing the war in Afghanistan, was photographed in 1985 in a refugee camp in Pakistan by photographer Steve McCurry. Because of her sea-green eyes, she appeared on the cover of the June 1985 issue, and her picture became a symbol of the Afghan conflict and the resulting refugee situation. In January 2002, *National Geographic* sent a team to look for her again. Amazingly, the iris feature analysis used by Federal Bureau of Investigation (FBI) enabled them to successfully identify the girl from a single photograph taken 17 years earlier.

Iris recognition technology has been progressively gaining attention, and there have been several large-scale deployments. One significant large-scale deployment has taken place in the United Arab Emirates. Since 2001, the United Arab Emirates (UAE) Ministry of Interior has used iris recognition to screen foreigners entering the UAE at 17 air, land, and sea ports. Their purpose has been to detect and stop

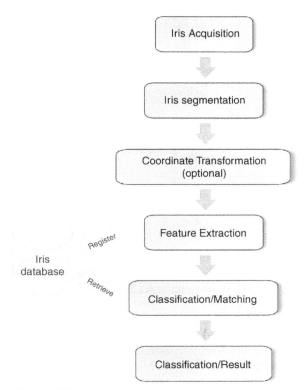

**Figure 13.2.** Functional unit and flow chart of a typical iris recognition system.

re-entry attempts by subjects previously expelled. The reported time required for an exhaustive search through the database is about 1 s. On an average day, about 6500 arriving passengers are compared against the entire watch list, which amounts to 2.7 billion comparisons per day. We will go back to the deployment case in UAE later in Section 13.6.

In several other countries, some airports have introduced biometrics systems based on iris recognition technology to process prescreened frequent flyers to reduce check-in times. All these examples are a proof of the power of iris recognition. Throughout this chapter, we will analyze what goes on behind a robust iris recognition system.

## 13.2   IRIS IMAGE ACQUISITION

Robust iris recognition is inherently related to the quality of the iris image and the acquisition mechanism. A typical high-quality iris image is shown in Figure 13.3. Upon close examination of Figure 13.3, one can clearly see the furrows, crypts, and moles distributed randomly in the pattern. If the input images are of low quality, out

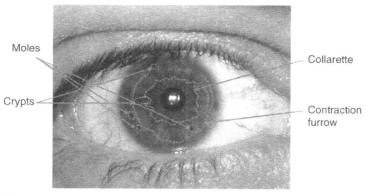

**Figure 13.3.** Illustration of crypts, furrows, collarette, and moles in an iris image.

of focus or motion-blurred, the detailed information of the iris pattern is lost. As a result, the performance of the overall recognition system will suffer, particularly if it's the enrollment or training image that is of low quality. An example of both a clear and a blurred input eye image is shown in Figure 13.4.

The necessity of good-quality images for robust iris recognition highlights the importance of the iris acquisition device. A good imaging device must capture all the detailed textural information of the iris which represents the high-frequency components in the image. However, in practice, other factors should be considered, such as the user-friendliness of the device, its acceptance, and its robustness to external elements. An ideal scenario for an acquisition device to capture the best iris image consists of an immobile user staring directly at the device for a long time without blinking or squinting or moving his/her head. Such a scenario involves a high level of user cooperation and patience. Such constraints significantly handicap the usability and acceptance of iris recognition systems in real-world applications.

In the following subsections, three different models of iris acquisition will be introduced. Each of them has its advantages and drawbacks in terms of image quality as

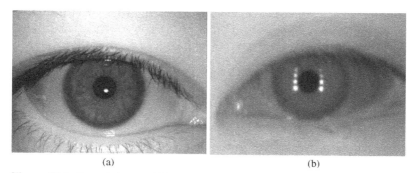

(a)                                    (b)

**Figure 13.4.** Example image of (a) a clear eye image and (b) a blurred image.

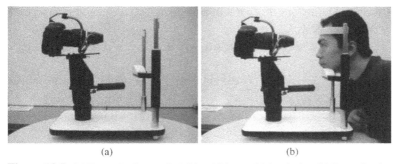

          (a)                           (b)

**Figure 13.5.** **(a)** Example picture of traditional iris acquisition device. **(b)** Example picture to illustrate how to use it.

well as user-friendliness and nonintrusiveness. These are some of the most important aspects of iris acquisition, and system designers and engineers work hard to find the optimal compromise between high-quality imagery and user-friendliness that is best suited for a particular deployment situation and context.

## 13.2.1  Traditional Iris Acquisition Devices

A traditional iris acquisition device usually consists of a high-resolution imaging device (digital camera or camcorder), one or more light sources (illuminators), and an adjustable mechanical rack to position the subject's head.

    Figure 13.5 depicts how a traditional iris acquisition device looks like and how it is operated and positioned with respect to a subject. The basic functionality of the device is shown in a block diagram in Figure 13.6.

    The advantage of such device is that the target object (the iris of the subject) is located at a predefined position, with minimal movement since the subject's head is held in position. Obviously, this model of iris acquisition demands a very high level of cooperation from subjects.

    In photography optics, there are some important formulae that define the relation between some important parameters, and they are summarized below:

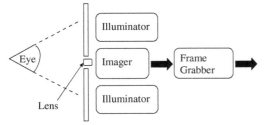

**Figure 13.6.** Block diagram of basic functional unit in traditional iris acquisition device.

- Luminance ($E$): Luminous flux per unit area; it can be considered as luminous power per unit area.
- Focal length ($f$): A measure of how strongly the lens converges or diverges light.
- $f$ number ($f\#$): The diameter of the entrance pupil in terms of the effective focal length of the lens.
- Magnification rate ($m$): the ratio between the height of the image and the height of the subject to be imaged.
- Depth of field (dof): The distance in front of and beyond the subject that appears to be in focus.

Equations (13.1) and (13.2) show the relations between these parameters. Equation (13.2) holds when the depth of field is very small.

$$E \propto \frac{1}{(f\#)^2},\qquad(13.1)$$

$$\text{dof} \approx \frac{2C \cdot (f\#)(m+1)}{m^2},\qquad(13.2)$$

where $C$ denotes the circle of confusion.

In a traditional iris acquisition setting, the camera is fixed, which means that the focal length of the system $f$ is fixed. The magnification rate $m$ is also fixed since the size of human eyeball doesn't vary too much. The circle of confusion $C$ is a fixed parameter. Therefore, according to Eq. (13.2), the depth of field is proportional to the $f$ number. For image acquisition devices like this, the depth of field dof can be small because subjects would always position their eyes at fixed distance from the camera. Therefore, the $f$ number of the system can be small. By Eq. (13.1), which shows how the luminance is inversely proportional to the square of the $f$ number, this translates into a large luminance $E$ according to the system design.

The drawbacks of such devices are, obviously, the difficulty of use and the slow turnover rate of the system. They are impractical in most real-world applications such as access control and border security where the throughput of the system is crucial. Therefore, devices like this are confined to very specific environments such as laboratories and hospitals where the turnover rate can be low.

## 13.2.2  Middle Distance Iris Capturing Devices

In the last decade, a lot of research has been done to enhance the usability of iris imaging devices by relaxing the constraints of the system as much as possible while maintaining satisfactory results. As a result, many new products of iris capturing devices have become available. Most of them have the ability to detect the location of a human face and eyes in an image. Therefore, it does not require users to place their heads in a fixed location and allow for greater distances between the users and the camera.

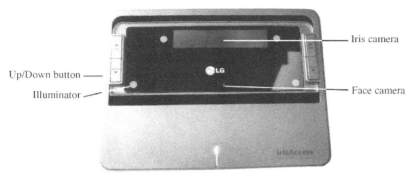

**Figure 13.7.** LG iCAM4000 iris acquisition device and description of the functional unit.

The LG iCAM4000 is one of such off-the-shelf devices that have become popular. The iris camera, face camera, and illuminator are all packaged in one box, which makes it easy to move and deployed in different places. There are also up/down buttons located on the front of the panel to allow users to adjust the angle of the camera, which compensates heights of different users.

Figure 13.7 shows a photograph of the LG iCAM4000. Figure 13.8a depicts a user interfacing with the device. Clearly, this capturing device is more user-friendly because users can stand at a distance from the camera and stare at it to capture a high-resolution iris image (shown in Figure 13.8b).

## 13.2.3  High-Speed Iris Capturing Device

As mentioned above, high identification rates and low false matching rates make iris recognition systems ideal for high-volume applications such as border control and access control in public transportation or workplaces where the number of subjects to be tested in a relatively short time is high. Therefore, the speed of acquisition

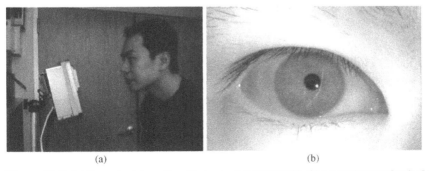

(a)                                                    (b)

**Figure 13.8.** (**a**) Example picture of a subject using LG iCAM4000. (**b**) An eye image taken by LG iCAM4000.

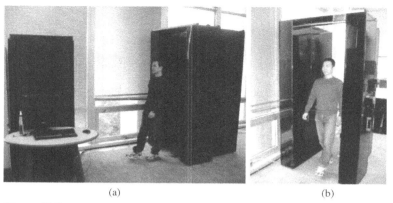

(a)                                           (b)

**Figure 13.9.** (a) IOM system. (b) Example picture of a subject walking through the portal.

becomes critical. Recently, high-speed iris capturing devices have appeared in the market. Those devices are capable of capturing iris images of both eyes in less than 3 s per person. They greatly reduce the identification time compared to traditional devices and make iris recognition technology possible for deployment in high-volume real world applications.

One example of high-speed systems is the Iris-on-the-Move (IOM) manufactured by Sarnoff Corporation, shown in Figure 13.9a. The system consists of three components: the portal where subjects walk through, the cabinet where the imaging devices reside, and a computer to control the device. The capturing process is made extremely easy. All the subjects have to do is to walk through the portal looking straight at the cabinet. The cameras inside the cabinet will automatically capture the iris images. Figure 13.9b shows the iris capturing process with a subject walking through the portal.

Figure 13.10 shows some pictures taken by the IOM system: some of them are clear and well-focused, while others appear to be blurred. This is a reasonable result since those images were taken while the subjects were moving, which represents a

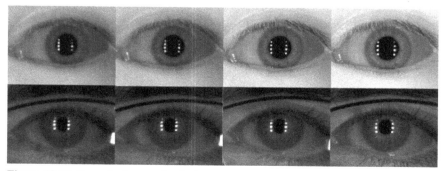

**Figure 13.10.** Example pictures taken by IOM system.

major challenge: The depth of field (dof) of the whole system should be fine-tuned to cover the entire depth of the portal. From Eq. (13.2), when dof is increased, $f$ number is increased too. From Eq. (13.1), increasing $f$ number will decrease luminance, which in turn makes the picture darker and lowers the contrast of the image: The trade-off between image quality and depth of field is inevitable, and an iris capturing system will always be fine-tuned to a operate in a specific setting.

## 13.3  IMAGE PREPROCESSING

After an eye image is taken, the next step is to locate where the iris is in the image and then crop it out. This is called "iris segmentation" or "iris localization." Since the shape of the iris is annular, segmentation consists of finding two circles in the eye image. One of them is the inner boundary of the iris region, while the other is the outer boundary. Note that that these two circles are not necessarily concentric, because sometimes the direction of the line of sight is off the axis between camera and face. This happens when the subject is looking away from the camera at the time of capture. This scenario represents a major challenge for iris segmentation.

### 13.3.1  Iris Segmentation

The most widely used iris segmentation algorithm is proposed by Dr. John Daugman [5]. This section analysizes Daugman's iris segmentation algorithm, as well as other related algorithms.

Daugman assumes that both the inner and outer boundary of the iris can be approximated by a circle in a two-dimensional (2D) plane. This is a reasonable assumption given that the line of sight of the subject is very close to the axis between the camera and the subject's face. In such cases, the eye in the picture is looking straight ahead, and the boundaries between pupil and iris and between sclera and iris are well-described by two circles.

A circle in 2D plane can be parameterized by three parameters: the coordinate of the center $(x_0, y_0)$ and the radius $r$. A very effective integrodifferential operator for determining these parameters is

$$\max_{(r,x_0,y_0)} \left| G_\sigma(r) * \frac{\partial}{\partial r} \oint_{r,\, x_0,\, y_0} \frac{I(x, y)}{2\pi r}\, ds \right| \tag{13.3}$$

where $I(x,y)$ is the eye image and $G_\sigma(r)$ is a smoothing function such as a Gaussian of scale $\sigma$. Basically, it is looking for the parameters $(x_0, y_0, r)$ which maximizes the Gaussian blurred version of the partial derivatives (with respect to a different radius $r$) of circular integral that is normalized by the length of the circle. Basically it serves as a circular edge detector, which searches through three-dimensional (3D) parameter space $(x, y, r)$ to find the most prominent circle in the image.

One important fact for iris localization is that the pupillary boundary will always be located inside the region that is bound by the limbic boundary (the boundary between sclera and iris). The reason is very obvious: The pupil is always surrounded by the iris region. If the pupilary boundary is outside or intersects with the limbic boundary, it implies that the segmentation algorithm has made a serious mistake. This constraint can be imposed during the searching for the limbic boundary if the pupilary boundary has been located successfully. This is because most of the time, the pupilary boundary is much easier to find than the limbic boundary due to the fact that limbic boundary appears softer under long-wavelength NIR illumination.

Once the two circular boundaries are found, the remaining task is to find the boundary between the iris and the eyelids. This can be done using the same optimization process as Eq. (13.3), with the circular contour integral replaced by a spline curve integral. The result of all these localization operations is the isolation of the iris tissue from all other image regions, as illustrated in Figure 13.11 by the graphical overlays on the eye image.

Wildes [5] proposed a slightly different algorithm which is mostly based on Daugman's method. Wildes performs the contour fitting in two steps. First, a gradient-based edge detector is used to generate an edge-map from the raw eye image [6]. Second, every positive point on edge-map can vote to instantiate particular circular contour parameters. This voting scheme is implemented by Hough transform [7]. In particular, given a set of edge points $(x_i, y_i)$, $i = 1, \ldots, n$, a Hough transform is defined as

$$H(x_c, y_c, r) = \sum_{i=1}^{n} h(x_i, y_i, x_c, y_c, r), \qquad (13.4)$$

where

$$h(x_i, y_i, x_c, y_c, r) = \begin{cases} 1 & \text{if } g(x_i, y_i, x_c, y_c, r) = 0, \\ 0 & \text{otherwise} \end{cases}$$

with

$$g(x_i, y_i, x_c, y_c, r) = (x_i - x_c)^2 + (y_i - y_c)^2 - r^2.$$

The function $g(x_i, y_i, x_c, y_c, r)$ will equal to zero if and only if the point $(x_i, y_i)$ is on the perimeter of the circle centered at $(x_c, y_c)$ with radius $r$. Therefore, $h(x_i, y_i, x_c, y_c, r)$ keeps track of the voting result for a particular point $(x_i, y_i)$, and $H(x_c, y_c, r)$ is a plane representing the voting results for all of the points on the edge-map. Different parameter sets $(x_c, y_c, r)$ will generate different $H$ planes, and the optimized parameter $(x_c, y_c, r)$ is defined by the maximum value of points on $H$.

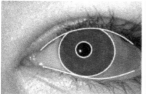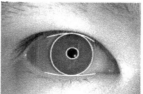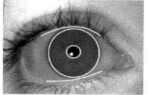

**Figure 13.11.** Example images of iris segmentation. The white curves are the identified iris boundaries.

## 13.3.2 Coordinate Transformation

After the iris boundary has been identified, we can separate the iris region from the other parts of the image. According to the iris segmentation model mentioned in the previous section, the segmented iris region should appear in an annular shape. Figure 13.12a and 13.12b show the raw eye image and the segmented iris part.

One important physical variation that affects the iris considerably is the dilation and contraction of the pupil. The pupil dilates in the absence of ambient light and contracts in the presence of a strong ambient or direct light. When the pupil dilates or contracts, the visible area of the iris region varies accordingly, which can significantly impact the pattern recognition performance. To achieve a robust and reliable recognition rate, this problem must be addressed

Daugman proposed a Cartesian to polar coordinate transformation to overcome this obstacle. A raw eye image is in Cartesian coordinate representation. After the iris boundaries are identified, every point $(a, b)$ in the iris region can be mapped into a polar coordinate representation by Eqs. (13.5) and (13.6):

$$R = \sqrt{(a - x_c)^2 + (b - y_c)^2} - r, \tag{13.5}$$

$$\theta = \arccos \frac{|a - x_c|}{R + r}, \tag{13.6}$$

where the center of the pupil region is $(x_c, y_c)$, and the radius is $r$.

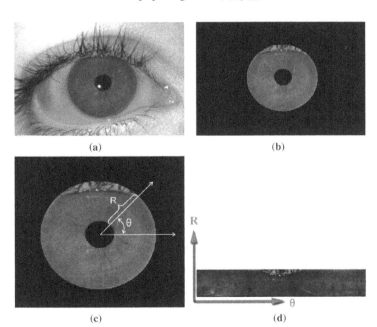

(a)          (b)

(c)          (d)

**Figure 13.12.** (a) Raw eye image and its boundary. (b) Iris region segmented out from raw image. (c) Description of how to compute R and θ from Cartesian coordinate. (d) Iris image after coordinate transformation.

If we map every point in the iris region from Cartesian to polar coordinate as $(\theta, R)$, the resulting iris pattern in polar coordinate will be inside a rectangular strip similar to the one shown in Figure 13.12d. This process is called polar coordinate transformation.

The advantage of this coordinate transformation is that it yields a normalized representation of iris region, invariant of the size of the pupil. No matter how much the pupil dilates or contracts, the normalized iris pattern would be contained in a rectangle of constant size after polar coordinate transformation. Another advantage of the polar coordinate transformation is how it deals with rotational variations; rotational variations in the iris image occur when the subject tilts his/her head. This rotational shift in Cartesian coordinate translates into a simple $x$-directional shift in polar coordinate. Therefore, if the feature extraction and matching are performed in polar domain, shifting the reference template in the horizontal direction and choosing the result with highest matching score are all that's needed to account for rotational variations in the original image. This invariance to rotations that the polar coordinate transformation brings significantly reduces the complexity of the solution and adds a great deal of robustness. Note that not all iris recognition systems perform polar coordinate transformation. For example, Wildes' system does not adopt this scheme; instead, he chooses to extract the features and perform the matching in the original Cartesian coordinate domain, and he reports equally good experimental results.

### 13.3.3 Image Enhancement

Ma et al. [8–10] proposed an image enhancement method that aims to enhance the contrast of the iris pattern in polar coordinate domain. The normalized iris image may suffer from low contrasts and nonuniform brightness due to the bad position of the light sources. These defects may affect the feature extraction and pattern matching performance. In order to alleviate the problem and enhance the image quality, Ma et al. adopt a two-step process.

The first step is to estimate the intensity variations across the whole image (in polar coordinate domain). They utilize a $16 \times 16$ window to swipe through the entire image and use the mean of these windows as the coarse estimate of the background illumination. This estimate is then expanded to the same size of the iris pattern by bicubic interpolation. The estimated background illumination pattern is subtracted from the iris pattern to compensate for the brightness variations within the pattern.

The second step is to further enhance the lighting-corrected iris pattern by using histogram equalization in windows of size $32 \times 32$. Such postprocessing deals with the problem of nonuniform illumination variations and also improves the contrast in regions of different illumination levels.

### 13.4 FEATURE EXTRACTION

After the iris region is identified and transformed into polar coordinate, the next step is to extract the features from the iris pattern. The goal of feature extraction is to extract discriminative information from the pattern so that in a later matching stage, the discriminative information from two different iris images can be compared to perform identity recognition. Another important issue is how fast these features can be computed. If the feature extraction process is slow, it makes the iris recognition system impractical.

Daugman proposed a feature extraction scheme by using 2D wavelet demodulation [2–18]. The wavelets he uses are Gabor filters. Gabor elementary functions are Gaussians modulated by oriented complex sinusoidal functions, like sine and cosine waves. Equation (13.7) shows the formula for Gabor filters.

$$G(x, y, f) = \frac{1}{2\pi\delta_x\delta_y}e^{-\frac{1}{2}\left(\frac{x^2}{\delta_x^2}+\frac{y^2}{\delta_y^2}\right)}\cos(2\pi f(x\cos\theta + y\sin\theta)), \qquad (13.7)$$

where $f$ is the frequency of the sinusoidal function, $\delta_x$ and $\delta_y$ are the space constants of the Gaussian envelope along the $x$ and $y$ axis, respectively, and $\theta$ denotes the orientation of the Gabor filter.

The encoding process is carried out by convolving the iris pattern with a 2D Gabor wavelet with multiple wavelet sizes, frequencies, and orientation, and then quantizing the result into one of the four quadrants, setting two bits of phase information. This process can be described by Eq. (13.8):

$$h_{\text{Re,Im}} = \text{sign}_{(\text{Re,Im})} \int_\rho \int_\phi I(\rho, \phi)e^{-i\omega(\theta_0-\phi)}e^{-\frac{(\gamma_0-\rho)^2}{\alpha}}e^{-\frac{(\theta_0-\phi)^2}{\beta}}\rho d\rho d\phi, \quad (13.8)$$

where $h_{(\text{Re,Im})}$ can be regarded as a complex-valued bit whose real and imaginary parts are either 1 or 0 (sign), depending on the sign of the 2D integral; $I(\rho, \phi)$ is the raw iris image in a dimensionless polar coordinate system that is size- and translation-invariant and which corrects for pupil dilation as explained before; $\alpha$ and $\beta$ are the multiscale 2D wavelet size parameters, spanning an eightfold range from 0.15 to 1.2 mm on the iris; $\omega$ is wavelet frequency, spanning three octaves in inverse proportion to $\beta$; and $(\gamma_0, \theta_0)$ represent the polar coordinates of each region of the iris for which the phasor coordinates $h_{\text{Re,Im}}$ are computed. After this quantization process, an iris code of size 2048 bits total is generated. An equal number of masking bits is also computed to indicate which parts of the iris map are obscured by something that is not an iris—for example, eyelids, eyelashes, eyeglass frames, and so on.

Ma et al. [8–10] proposed a slightly different feature extraction method based on Daugman's approach. The main difference between these two methods resides in the convolutional functions that were chosen to perform the feature extraction. Specifically, these two implementations are compared in Eq. (13.9):

$$G(x, y, f) = \frac{1}{2\pi\delta_x\delta_y}e^{-\frac{1}{2}\left(\frac{x^2}{\delta_x^2}+\frac{y^2}{\delta_y^2}\right)}M_i(x, y, f), \qquad i = 1, 2$$

$$M_1(x, y, f) = \cos(2\pi f \sqrt{x^2 + y^2}),$$

$$M_2(x, y, f) = \cos(2\pi f(x\cos\theta + y\sin\theta)),$$

$$(13.9)$$

where $M_1$ is the modulation function that Ma et al. [8–10] proposed, and $M_2$ is the Gabor filter displayed in Eq. (13.7).

For filters like $M_1$, when $\delta_x$ equals to $\delta_y$ (i.e., the Gaussian function is isotropic), one can obtain a band-pass filter with a specific center frequency. When $\delta_x$ and $\delta_y$ are different, $M_1$ picks up information along a particular direction, whose slope is determined by $\arctan(\delta_y/\delta_x)$. Since the detailed information in the iris pattern are usually spread along a radial direction, the information density in the angular direction corresponding to the horizontal direction is relatively higher than that in the other direction. Therefore, a lot of benefits can be obtained by paying more attention to the pattern variation along the angular direction.

Furthermore, Ma et al. [8–10] choose to neglect the part of iris that is close to the limbic boundary since this region is easily occluded by eyelids or eyelashes. Therefore, the region of interest (ROI) is roughly the upper 80% of the iris pattern. After picking the ROI, they apply the proposed filter described in Eq. (13.9) with two different parameters to generate an output of two channels: one set of $(\delta_x, \delta_y)$ is (3, 1.5) and the other is (4.5, 1.5). The 2D convolution between the iris image and the proposed filters can be expressed in Eq. (13.10):

$$F_i(x, y) = \iint I(x_1, y_1) G_i(x - x_1, y - y_1)\, dx_1 dy_1, \qquad i = 1, 2, \qquad (13.10)$$

where $G_i$ is the $i$th channel of the proposed filters, $I(x, y)$ denotes the ROI, and $F_i(x, y)$ the filtered image. To extract the local texture information of the iris pattern, they move across the entire filtered image with a window of size 8×8 pixels and compute the mean $m$ and the average absolute deviation $\sigma$ of the magnitude of each block, where $m$ and $\sigma$ is defined in Eq. (13.11):

$$m = \frac{1}{n} \sum_w \left| F_i(x, y) \right|, \qquad \sigma = \frac{1}{n} \sum_w \left| \left| F_i(x, y) \right| - m \right| \qquad (13.11)$$

where $w$ is an $8 \times 8$ block in the filtered image, n is the number of pixels in the block w, and m is the mean of the block $w$. These feature values are concatenated into a long 1D vector. Since the size of the ROI is $48 \times 512$, the total number of features for one iris image is $48 \times 512/(8 \times 8) \times 2 \times 2 = 1536$.

Wildes proposed a different procedure for iris feature extraction [19]. The procedure makes use of isotropic band-pass decomposition obtained by applying Laplacian of Gaussian filters to the image data [20]. This representation is derived by successively applying Laplacian operators on image to form a Laplacian pyramid. Specifically, let $w = [1\ 4\ 6\ 4\ 1]/16$ be a one-dimensional (1D) mask and let $W = w^{\mathsf{T}} w$ be a 2D mask derived by taking the outer product of $w$ with itself. Given an iris image $I$, a series of images $l_k$, $k = 1, \ldots n$, called a Laplacian pyramid can be derived by first computing $g_k$, which is obtained by convolving $I$ with $W$ and down-sampling the resulting image, as shown in Eq. (13.12):

$$g_k = (W^* g_{k-1}) \downarrow 2, \qquad (13.12)$$

where $\downarrow 2$ means down-sampling the image by a factor of 2.

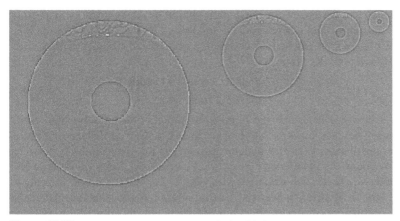

**Figure 13.13.** Example of a Laplacian pyramid of an iris image.

In fact, $g_k$ is a set of low-pass filtered images derived from the original iris pattern, with different scales. The Laplacian pyramid $l_k$ can be computed by Eq. (13.13):

$$l_k = g_k - 4W^*(g_{k+1})\uparrow 2, \qquad (13.13)$$

where $\uparrow 2$ means up-sampling the image by a factor of 2.

Figure 13.13 shows an example of a Laplacian pyramid of an iris image.

## 13.5  RECOGNITION

The classification scheme of an iris strongly depends on the scheme of the feature extraction because different features have to be manipulated in different ways. In this section, different classification schemes will be introduced according to the feature extraction methods mentioned in the previous section.

### 13.5.1  Traditional Approach

Daugman [2] proposed a highly effective matching algorithm based on the iris code feature he proposed. The iris code consists of 2048 bits. To quantify the difference between two bit streams, one simple way is to utilize an exclusive-or (XOR) operation. An XOR operator returns 1 if two bits are different and 0 if they are the same. Therefore, performing XOR on two identical iris codes will produce 2048 bits of value 0, and the XOR of two exactly opposite iris codes will give 2048 bits of value 1. Another advantage of using the XOR operator is that it is extremely fast to compute in modern computation systems, which speeds up the iris recognition process.

As mentioned in Section 13.4, each iris code comes with a mask of the same length, to indicate which part of the iris map represents real iris information and which parts corresponds to objects of occlusion. Therefore, when computing the distance between two iris codes, the noisy parts should be disregarded by inspecting with the two iris masks, and normalizing the final result by the number of valid bits. Equation (13.14) summarizes how to compute a normalized distance between iris code A and B, given masks A and B:

$$HD = \frac{\|(\text{code A} \otimes \text{code B}) \cap \text{mask A} \cap \text{mask B}\|}{\|\text{mask A} \cap \text{mask B}\|} \tag{13.14}$$

where the $\|\cdot\|$ operator measures the number of 1 bits, $\cap$ denotes bit-wise AND operation, and $\otimes$ denotes bit-wise XOR operation. The derived distance metric is called "Hamming distance" (HD), which measures normalized dissimilarity between two binary iris codes. As mentioned earlier, two identical iris codes would have HD equal zero, and two exactly opposite iris codes would have HD equal one. In general, if two irises come from different persons, the iris patterns should be uncorrelated and therefore the probability of two identical bits at a particular location of the iris code should be 0.5. Hence, the HD between two different iris patterns should be normally distributed with a mean of 0.5.

Ma et al. [10] proposed a different scheme based on the characteristics of their feature sets 20. As mentioned in Section 13.4, their feature extraction method generates a 1D vector of length 1536 for every iris pattern. The classification scheme can be described in two steps.

First, the size of the feature vector is reduced from 1536 to 200 by means of Fisher linear discriminant analysis [21]. FLDA is a dimensionality reduction method that finds a projection matrix that projects feature vectors onto a lower dimension subspace, with within-class variations being minimized and between class variations being maximized. The new feature vector $f$ can be denoted as Eq. (13.15):

$$f = W^T V, \tag{13.15}$$

where $V$ is the feature vector of length 1536, $f$ is the feature vector projected by FLDA method, and $W$ is the FLDA transformation matrix

Second, they use a nearest center classifier to perform classification based on the new feature vector $f$. There are three available distance metrics to be chosen from:

$$m = \arg \min_{1 \le i \le c} d_n(f, f_i), \quad n = 1, 2, 3,$$

$$d_1(f, f_i) = \sum_j \left| f^j - f_i^j \right|,$$

$$d_2(f, f_i) = \sum_j \left( f^j - f_i^j \right)^2, \tag{13.16}$$

$$d_3(f, f_i) = 1 - \frac{f^T f_i}{\|f\| \|f_i\|},$$

where $f$ and $f_i$ are the feature vectors of an unknown sample and the $i$th class, respectively; $f^j$ and $f_i^j$ are the $j$th component of the feature vector of the unknown sample and that of the $i$th class, repectively; and $c$ is the total number of classes, $\|\cdot\|$ i indicates the Euclidean norm, and $d_n(f, f_i)$ denotes a similarity measure. $d_1$, $d_2$, and $d_3$ are $L_1$ distance, $L_2$ distance, and cosine similarity measure, respectively.

Wildes proposed a classification scheme based on normalized correlation between two iris patterns. Let $p_1[i, j]$ and $p_2[i, j]$ be two image arrays of size $n$ by $m$. Define

$$\mu_1 = (1/nm) \sum_{i=1}^{n} \sum_{j=1}^{m} p_1[i, j],$$

$$\sigma_1 = \sqrt{\frac{1}{nm} \sum_{i=1}^{n} \sum_{j=1}^{m} (p_1[i, j] - \mu_1)^2}, \qquad (13.17)$$

where $\mu_1$ and $\sigma_1$ are, respectively, the mean and the standard deviation of the intensities of $p_1$. Let $\mu_2$ and $\sigma_2$ be similarly defined for $p_2$. Then the normalized correlation between $p_1$ and $p_2$ can be defined as

$$\frac{\sum_{i=1}^{n} \sum_{j=1}^{m} (p_1[i, j] - \mu_1)(p_2[i, j] - \mu_2)}{nm\sigma_1\sigma_2}. \qquad (13.18)$$

The advantage of the normalized correlation method is that it measures the correlation in a global sense and simultaneously accounts for the local variations in the image intensity that corrupt the standard correlation. In implementation, Wildes performs normalized correlation in local blocks of size $8 \times 8$ in each of the four spatial frequency bands derived from the Laplacian pyramid. This will result in multiple correlation values for each band. Subsequently, he chooses the median of the normalized correlation values for each of the pyramid layer, which gives four goodness-of-match values when comparing two iris patterns. These four values can be treated as a feature vector of length four to indicate whether these two irises are from the same eye or not. In the end, Wildes performs FLDA to reduce the dimensionality of the feature vector and then performs classification.

## 13.5.2  Probabilistic Graphical Model Approach

Kerekes et al. [24] proposed a novel matching algorithm based on modeling of the local deformation of iris patterns with a probabilistic distribution on a lattice-type undirected graphical model, and they used Gabor wavelet-based similarity scores and intensity statistics as observations in the model. They reported a significant improvement over Daugman's algorithm.

### 13.5.2.1  Model Description

The first assumption behind their model is that iris patterns, even from the same eye, suffer from local deformations due to pupil dilations or contractions that ultimately lead to segmentation errors. Local deformations mean that when an iris is divided into several small patches, every patch may be translated in different directions and different distances. Such deformations are not constant and therefore cannot be recovered by a global transformation. Local shifts of iris pattern are shown in Figure 13.14.

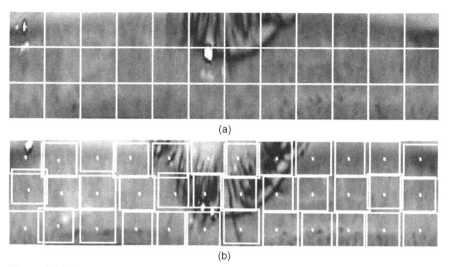

(a)

(b)

**Figure 13.14.** (**a**) Reference iris pattern. (**b**) iris pattern from the same eye, but with local deformation. Shifts of white boxes between (a) and (b) indicates how many local shifts are in each small window.

This type of local shifts can be modeled with an undirected lattice-type graphical model, depicted in Figure 13.15. Suppose the entire iris map is divided into 36 small patches. Each node $\mathbf{d}_i$ in the model ($i = 1, \ldots, 36$) represents a 2D discrete-valued shift vector for each local patch, and the true values of the shift vectors are hidden and cannot be observed from outside. The components of $\mathbf{d}_i$ are the vertical and horizontal shifts (in pixels) of the template region relative to the corresponding query region. The nodes $\omega_i$ ($i = 1, \ldots, 36$) are hidden binary-valued occlusion variables, where $\omega_i = 0$ represents an occluded region and $\omega_i = 1$ represents a valid unoccluded iris region. Nodes $\mathbf{O}_i$ represent the observations, which include the match score array $m_i(\mathbf{x})$ and the occlusion statistic $\pi_i$. The definition of $m_i(\mathbf{x})$ is given in Eq. (13.19):

$$m(x) = \frac{1}{|S_t|} \sum_{y \in S_t} c_t(y)^T c_q(y - x), \qquad (13.19)$$

where $c_t(y)$ and $c_q(y)$ are the feature vectors from the unshifted template and the query iris patterns, respectively; $S_t$ is the support of the template iris code and $|S_t|$ is the size of the template. $\pi_i$ is derived from classifying features that consist of (1) the mean intensity value in a small neighborhood of the pixel, (2) the standard deviation of the intensity values in the same neighborhood, (3) the percentage of pixels whose intensity is greater than one standard deviation above the mean of the entire iris plane, and (4) the shortest Euclidean distance to the centers of the upper and lower eyelids. This classification is done using FLDA.

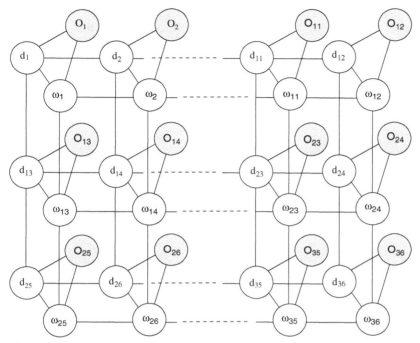

**Figure 13.15.** Probabilistic graphical model for modeling local deformation of iris patterns, proposed by Kerekes et al.

### 13.5.2.2  *Potential Functions and Density Estimation*

The next step is to define a potential function between each pair of connected nodes in the graphical model. The potential between two nodes $\mathbf{d}_i$ and $\mathbf{d}_j$ should be higher if both vectors are closer in direction and should be lower if they are opposite in direction. Similarly, the potential between node $\omega_i$ and $\omega_j$ should be higher if their values are similar and should be lower if they are dissimilar. Furthermore, the potential functions between $\mathbf{d}_i$ and $\omega_i$ should be independent from each other. Therefore, Eq. (13.20) is used to simplify the overall potential function:

$$\psi_{i,j}(\boldsymbol{h}_i, \boldsymbol{h}_j) = \psi_{\mathbf{d},i,j}(\mathbf{d}_i, \mathbf{d}_j) \cdot \psi_{\omega,i,j}(\omega_i, \omega_j),$$

$$\psi_{\mathbf{d},i,j}(\mathbf{d}_i, \mathbf{d}_j) = e^{-\frac{1}{2}(a\|\mathbf{d}_i\| + a\|\mathbf{d}_j\| + b\|\mathbf{d}_i - \mathbf{d}_j\|)},$$

$$\psi_{\omega,i,j}(\omega_i, \omega_j) = \begin{cases} \alpha_0, & \omega_i = \omega_j = 0, \\ \alpha_1, & \omega_i = \omega_j = 1, \\ \alpha_2, & \omega_i \neq \omega_j. \end{cases} \tag{13.20}$$

Parameters $a$ and $b$ represent penalties on absolute and relative deformations, respectively, while parameters $\alpha_i$ correspond to priors on their corresponding occlusion configuration $(\omega_i, \omega_j)$. The authors used $a = 0.05$, $b = 0.1$, $\alpha_1 = 0.7$, $\alpha_2 = 0.14$, and $\alpha_3 = 0.08$.

If we denote the random variable $s$ to be the probability distribution of "true" match scores and denote $\pi$ to be the probability distribution of "true" occlusion metrics, then the distributions $P(s)$ and $P(\pi)$ are assumed to be normally distributed with mean and variance $\mu_s, \sigma_s^2, \mu_\pi,$   and   $\sigma_\pi^2$, and we define

$$F(S) = P(s < S) = \int_{-\infty}^{S} N(s; \mu_s, \sigma_s^2)\, ds,$$
$$F_\pi\left(\prod\right) = P\left(\pi < \prod\right) = \int_{-\infty}^{\prod} N(\pi; \mu_\pi, \sigma_\pi^2)\, d\pi \tag{13.21}$$

to be the cumulative distribution functions (cdf) of $s$ and $\pi$. These parameters can be learned from the training data. We can compute the probabilities $F_s(m(\mathbf{d}_i))$ and $F_\pi(\pi_i)$ of having observed at least the true match score and occlusion metric for each pixel or region, respectively. We then achieve the monotonic potential function $\psi_i(h_i, O_i)$ by setting them equal to the corresponding probability for the believed state of $\omega_i$ as follows:

$$\psi_i(h_i, \mathbf{O}_i) = \begin{cases} F_s(m(d_i)), & \omega_i = 0, \\ F_\pi(\pi_i), & \omega_i = 1. \end{cases} \tag{13.22}$$

### 13.5.2.3   *Loopy Belief Propagation (LBP)*

Given a particular set of observations for nodes $\mathbf{O}_i$, the structure in Figure 13.13 reduces to a Markov random field (MRF) with potential functions described in the previous section [23, 24]. First we have to estimate the conditional distributions P($h_i$ | $\mathbf{O}$) for $i = 1, \ldots, 36$ ($\mathbf{O}$ is the set of all observations $\mathbf{O}_1, \ldots, \mathbf{O}_{36}$) in order to compute the overall match score.

One way to estimate the conditional distributions is to use loopy belief propagation [25]. It is an iterative optimization process over the joint distribution in a graphical model. In each iteration every unobserved node sends a message to each of its unobserved neighbors. The message $\delta_{j \to k}^i$ from node $j$ to neighboring node $k$ at iteration $i$ is computed according to Eq. (13.23):

$$\delta_{j \to k}^i(h_k) = \sum_{h_j} \psi_j(h_j, \mathbf{O}_j)\psi_{j,k}(h_j, h_k) \times \prod_{l \in N(j)-k} \delta_{l \to j}^{i-1}(h_j), \tag{13.23}$$

where $\psi_j$ and $\psi_{j,k}$ are define in Eqs. (13.22) and (13.20), respectively, and $N(j)$ denotes the set of all the neighbors of node $j$ in the graph. Equation (13.24) can be used to estimate the belief $\hat{P}(h_j | O)$ of the quantity $h_j$ after iteration $i$:

$$\hat{P}(h_j|\mathbf{O}) = \frac{1}{Z_j}\psi_j(h_j, \mathbf{O}_j) \prod_{k \in N(j)} \delta_{k \to j}^i(h_j),$$
$$Z_j = \sum_{h_j} \psi_j(h_j, \mathbf{O}_j) \prod_{k \in N(j)} \delta_{k \to j}^i(h_j). \tag{13.24}$$

Then the marginal beliefs for each region can be computed via Eq. (13.25):

$$\hat{P}(\mathbf{d}_j|\mathbf{O}) = \sum_{\omega_j} \hat{P}(\mathbf{h}_j|\mathbf{O}),$$

$$\hat{P}(\omega_j|\mathbf{O}) = \sum_{\mathbf{d}_j} \hat{P}(\mathbf{h}_j|\mathbf{O}). \tag{13.25}$$

### 13.5.2.4  *Score Computation*

A single match score $M_i$ for each subregion $i$ is computed once the conditional distribution $P(\mathbf{d}_i|\mathbf{O})$ has been estimated. Specifically, for each subregion, Eq. (13.26) can be used to compute the expected match score with respect to the estimated distribution:

$$M_i = \sum_{\mathbf{d}} m_i(\mathbf{d})\hat{P}(\mathbf{d}_i = \mathbf{d}|\mathbf{O}). \tag{13.26}$$

One thing to keep in mind when computing the match score for each subregion is that we don't want the probability of occlusion to interfere with the similarity score. That is the reason why we use a marginal distribution $\hat{P}(\mathbf{d}_i|\mathbf{O})$ instead of the joint distribution $\hat{P}(\mathbf{h}_j|\mathbf{O})$. The overall match score M can be computed from 36 individual subregional scores $M_i$ as a normalized weighted sum of the subregional match scores:

$$M = \frac{\sum_{i=1}^{36} \beta_i M_i}{\sum_{i=1}^{36} \beta_i}, \tag{13.27}$$

$$\beta_i = \hat{P}(\omega_i = 1|\mathbf{O}).$$

## 13.6  REAL-WORLD DEPLOYMENT OF IRIS RECOGNITION SYSTEM

There are already several real-world deployments of iris recognition systems. One of the largest-scale deployments of iris recognition is in the United Arab Emirates (UAE). The Ministry of Interior of UAE decided to use iris recognition technology to verify all passengers going into the country, through any of the 17 air, land, and sea ports. In this section, we will introduce the system deployed in the UAE. All of the text description and statistics are excerpted from the paper published by Daugman and Malhas in 2004 [26].

UAE deployed iris recognition system for border-control and security purpose. More than 6500 passengers enter the border of UAE via seven international airports, three land ports, and seven sea ports every day. When they go through customs, by looking at an iris camera for a few seconds, their irises images would be captured and sent to a centralized iris database and compared with a watchlist that contains 420,000 IrisCodes of people who were expelled from the UAE for various violations. Within 1 s, the comparison result would be reported by the system to verify whether this passenger is listed on the watchlist. The system is efficient and highly accurate. Every day, the number of iris comparisons is roughly 2.7 billion. So far, more than

9500 persons have been captured that tried to use forged document to disguise their identity and sneak into the UAE again. This system successfully prevents their reentry and therefore proves herself to be useful and effective.

The secret of highly efficient iris matching lies in the architecture of the iris database storage. They called it "IrisFarm," which is a networked distributed database system, developed by Imad Malhas of IrisGuard Inc. The system administrator can enroll new IrisCode into the centralized database while there are probe iris images being compared with images in the database. Based on its essence of distributed system, "IrisFarm" can be scaled larger very easily and still maintains the high matching speed. Here is a list of some important features of IrisFarm architecture:

- Iris Search can be done in a parallel way, with a series of search engines (called "IrisEngine"). Each IrisEngine can search a database that contains more than 500,000 irises in less than 1 s.
- Can be operated in a variety of network speed, even in a very slow network. For example, the system is able to perform iris matching in a networking environment as slow as 33.6 Kbytes/s.
- Uninterrupted search capability during iris data synchronization with enrollment devices.

Although the system has to perform 2.7 billion iris cross-matching every day, so far there is not a single false matching reported. It proves that iris recognition is extremely accurate and efficient and is practical enough for real-world application.

## 13.7 SUMMARY

In this chapter we reviewed both the theoretical and practical aspects of iris recognition. An iris recognition system usually consists of subfunctional units: (1) iris acquisition, (2) image preprocessing, (3) iris feature extraction, and (4) pattern recognition and matching. We introduced different types of iris acquisition devices and analyzed their strengths and weaknesses.

Image preprocessing is an extremely important step for all computer vision and pattern recognition problems because higher-quality images will always produce better results. For iris recognition systems, the specific characteristics of the annular shape of the iris region call for a coordinate transformation that can compensate for rotational and non-affine variations in images. Furthermore, contrast enhancement methods can improve the quality of the images by raising the contrast level locally.

The goal of feature extraction is to extract discriminant information in raw iris patterns. In this chapter we analyzed different feature extraction schemes proposed by different researchers. Wavelet analysis has been widely used due to its power in space-frequency domain analysis. Image pyramids are also used to inspect detailed information in iris patterns under different scales of image size.

The recognition algorithm strongly depends on the feature extraction scheme. Good recognition algorithms are expected to give (a) high distance scores for irises that come from different eyes and (b) low distance scores for irises that come from the same eye. Another important issue we considered is how fast the matching process can be achieved. Finally, we reviewed a recent work that takes into account the local deformations of the iris patterns, which we model with probabilistic graphical models. The reported experimental results show the superiority of local patch matching versus global pattern matching.

At the end, we also introduced one example of large-scale deployment of iris recognition system, happening in the UAE. The system can perform iris matching with 420,000 iris templates in the database in less than 1 s, and the system is scalable to allow more templates to be enrolled. The UAE iris recognition system proves that iris recognition is feasible, practical, and accurate. This example showed iris recognition has emerged as the most promising biometric technology and has been used successfully in enhancing national security and protecting a country.

## REFERENCES

1. A. K. Jain, A. Ross, and S. Prabhakar, An Introduction to biometric recognition, *IEEE Trans. Circuits and Syst. Video Technol.* **14**(1), 2004.
2. J. Daugman, Biometric personal identification system based on iris analysis, United States patent 5291560, 1994.
3. P. Kronfeld, Gross anatomy and embryology of the eye, in H. Davson, editor, *The Eye*, Academic Press, London, 1962.
4. D. Braun, How they found national geographic's "Afghan Girl," *National Geographic*, March 7, 2003.
5. R. Wildes, Iris recognition: An emerging biometric technology, *Proc. IEEE* **85**:1348–1363, 1997.
6. J. Canny, A computational approach to edge detection, *IEEE Trans. Pattern Anal. Mach. Intell.* **8**(6), 1986.
7. P. V. C. Hough, Method and means for recognizing complex patterns, U.S. Patent 3 069654, 1962.
8. L. Ma, Y. Wang, and T. Tan, Iris recognition based on multichannel Gabor filtering, *Proceedings, Fifth Asian Conference on Computer Vision*, Vol. I, 2002, pp. 279–283.
9. L. Ma, Y. Wang, and T. Tan, Iris recognition using circular symmetric filters, *Proceedings, 16th International Conference on Pattern Recognition*, Vol. II, 2002, pp. 414–417.
10. L. Ma, T. Tan, Y. Wang, D. Zhang, Personal identification based on iris texture analysis, *IEEE Trans. Pattern Anal. Mach. Intell.* **25**(12), 2003.
11. J. Daugman, Uncertainty relation for resolution in space, spatial frequency, and orientation optimized by two-dimensional visual cortical filters, *J. Opt. Soc. Am. A* **2**(7):1160–1169, 1985.
12. J. Daugman, Complete discrete 2D Gabor transforms by neural networks for image analysis and compression, *IEEE Trans. Acoust., Speech, Signal Processing* **36**:1169–1179, 1988.
13. J. Daugman, High confidence visual recognition of persons by a test of statistical independence, *IEEE Trans. Pattern Anal. Mach. Intell.* **15**(11):1148–1161, 1993.
14. J. Daugman and C. Downing, Demodulation, predictive coding, and spatial vision, *J. Opt. Soc. Am. A*, **12**(4):641–660, 1995.
15. J. Daugman, Statistical richness of visual phase information: Update on recognizing persons by iris patterns, *Int. J. Comput. Vis.* **45**(1):25–38, 2001.
16. J. Daugman, Demodulation by complex-valued wavelets for stochastic pattern recognition, *Int. J. Wavelets Multiresolution Inf. Processing* **1**(1):1–17, 2003.
17. J. Daugman, The importance of being random: Statistical principles of iris recognition, *Pattern Recognit.* **36**, 2003.
18. J. Daugman, How Iris recognition works, *IEEE Trans. Circuits Syst. Video Technol.* **14**(1):2004.
19. R. Wildes, J. Asmuth, G. Green, S. Hsu, R. Kolczynski, J. Matey, and S. McBride, A machine-vision system for iris recognition, *Mach. Vis. Appl.*, **9**:1–8, 1996.
20. B. K. P. Horn, *Robot Vision*, MIT Press, Cambridge, MA, 1986.

21. P. Belhumeur, J. Hespanha, and D. Kriegman, Eigenfaces vs. fisherfaces: Recognition using class specific linear projection, *IEEE Trans. Pattern Anal. Mach. Intell.* **19**(7):711–720, 1997.
22. R. Kerekes, B. Narayanaswamy, J. Thornton, M. Savvides, B. V. K. Vijaya Kumar, Graphical model approach to iris matching under deformation and occlusion, *IEEE Conference on, Computer Vision and Pattern Recognition, 2007. (CVPR '07), 17–22 June* 2007, pp. 1–6.
23. P. Perez, Markov random fields and images, *CWI Q*. **11**(4):413–437, 1998.
24. P. Felzenszwalb and D. Huttenlocher. Markov random fields and images. *Int. J. Comput. Vis.* **70**(1):41–54, 2006.
25. B. J. Frey and N. Jojic, A comparison of algorithms for inference and learning in probabilistic graphical models, *IEEE Trans. Pattern Anal. Mach. Intell.* **27**(9):1392–1416, 2005.
26. J. Daugman and I. Malhas, Iris recognition border-crossing system in the UAE, *Int. Airport Rev.* **2**, 2004.
27. J. Illingworth and J. Kittler, A survey of the Hough transform, *Comput. Vis. Graph. Image Processing* **44**:87–116, 1988.
28. B. Jahne, *Digital Image Processing*, 2nd edition, Springer-Verlag, Berlin, 1993.

# Chapter 14

# Learning in Fingerprints

**Alessandra Lumini, Loris Nanni, and Davide Maltoni**

## 14.1 INTRODUCTION

Fingerprint recognition is certainly one of the most used biometric techniques [1]. The first automatic algorithms, developed in the early 1950s, were inspired by the manual method used by forensic experts: Minutiae are first detected in correspondence of the ridge line terminations and bifurcations, and two fingerprint patterns are then spatially aligned to maximize the number of minutiae mates. A typical computer implementation of this approach relies on classical image processing techniques for the enhancement, segmentation, and thinning of the image and on a point pattern matching algorithm to find the minutiae correspondence. Although some learning-based strategies date back to the early 1990s, for a long time fingerprint recognition algorithms, unlike other biometric modalities such as face, have been improved by making use of classical image processing and pattern recognition instruments. One of the reasons is that manual matching performed by forensic experts is nowadays still very important because it is the only accepted procedure in the court of laws to link a latent fingerprint to a suspected person. Another reason is that a good implementation of the classical approach allows us to achieve very good performance and therefore developers focused on improving some of the basic steps (e.g., enhancement of poor quality fingerprints) instead of looking at new methods. In the last 10–15 years, biometric recognition has progressively become one of most-studied pattern recognition problem; and new issues such as quality checking, liveness detection, and multimodal authentication have gained much attention. At the same time, powerful learning-based approaches such as support vector machines (SVM) [2], boosting [3], multiclassifier systems (MCS) [4], and so on, proved to be able to obtain performance improvement with respect to traditional approaches (e.g., statistical, template-based) and started being applied to biometric systems (including fingerprint-based systems).

*Biometrics: Theory, Methods, and Applications.* Edited by Boulgouris, Plataniotis, and Micheli-Tzanakou
Copyright © 2010 the Institute of Electrical and Electronics Engineers, Inc.

**Table 14.1.** Organization of the Chapter

| Subproblem | | Subsection |
|---|---|---|
| Acquisition | Quality check | 14.2.1 |
| | Liveness detection | 14.2.2 |
| Preprocessing | Segmentation | 14.3.1 |
| | Enhancement | 14.3.2 |
| Features extraction | Minutiae detection | 14.4.1 |
| | Minutiae filtering | 14.4.2 |
| Matching | Minutiae-based matching | 14.5.1 |
| | Ridge feature-based matching | 14.5.2 |
| | Combination of matchers | 14.5.3 |
| Fingerprint classification | | 14.6 |

There are several reasons why learning-based methods might overcome traditional techniques [5]; in fact, they allow us to

- Extract hidden relationships and correlations among the data
- Automatically select the most discriminant features
- Deal with a large amount of data that cannot be effectively encoded by humans
- Take into account characteristics not completely known at design time

On the other hand, learning-based techniques suffer from two main problems: (1) A representative "labeled" training set is necessary to provide ground truth information to the system during the learning stage; (2) the risk of overtraining the systems (i.e., overfitting the data) is always present and could lead to a system that works very well on the training set but whose performance significantly degrades on unseen data. This chapter reviews the main learning-based approaches to fingerprint recognition; the chapter is organized in five subchapters, each focusing on a particular fingerprint recognition subproblem as shown in Table 14.1. Finally, Section 14.7 draws some conclusions and points out some promising research directions for the future.

## 14.2  ACQUISITION

In this step a fingerprint image is acquired through a given sensor. Apart from the hardware and software technologies used for on-line fingerprint acquisition, two important processing steps are strictly related to this phase: quality check and liveness detection. Quality check allows to control the quality of the acquired sample and to reject it in case of insufficient quality; liveness detection is aimed at detecting the presentation of fake fingerprints.

## 14.2.1  Quality Check

The performance of a fingerprint recognition system is heavily affected by the fingerprint image quality. Several factors determine the quality of a fingerprint image: skin conditions, sensor quality and conditions, user cooperation and proper use of the sensing device (see Figure 14.1).

Fingerprint quality is usually defined as a measure of the clarity of ridge and valley pattern, but it is not simple to describe it with mathematical equations. Machine learning techniques can then be exploited to train systems by examples. A taxonomy of existing approaches for fingerprint image quality computation is reported in reference 6, where they are divided into three families: (i) approaches based on local features, (ii) approaches based on global features, and (iii) approaches addressing the problem of quality assessment as a classification problem. Methods belonging to the third class make large use of learning techniques [7, 8].

The method proposed by NIST [7] operationally defines the quality as a prediction of a matcher performance: Good-quality fingerprints are likely to produce high match scores. An important advantage of this method is that it does not require a ground truth provided by a human expert; in fact, defining the ground truth by visual inspection is quite complicated, could lead to subjective evaluations, and is not necessarily the best approach when the focus is on automatic matching algorithms. Given a training data set $D$ containing $n$ different fingers $x_1, \ldots, x_n$ and 2 samples for each finger (the second sample of the finger $x_i$ is here denoted as $x_i'$), the normalized matching score of $x_i$ is defined as

$$\text{normscore}(x_i) = \frac{\text{score}(x_i, x_i') - \text{avg}_{j=1\ldots n, j \neq i}(\text{score}(x_j, x_j'))}{\text{std}_{j=1\ldots n, j \neq i}(\text{score}(x_j, x_j'))}, \qquad (14.1)$$

where $\text{score}(a, b)$ returns the matching score between the two fingerprints $a$ and $b$ according to a given automatic matcher, avg() is the average value, and std() is

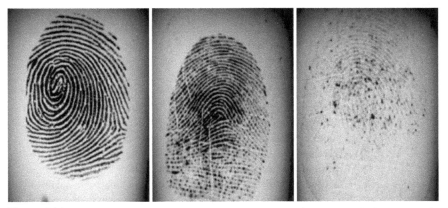

**Figure 14.1.** Examples of real fingerprints of different quality acquired by an optical sensor (good quality on the left, medium quality in the middle, and poor quality on the right).

the standard deviation. The quality $q(x_i)$ of $x_i$ is then defined as the prediction of its normalized matching score normscore$(x_i)$. Given a feature vector $\mathbf{v}_i$ extracted from $x_i$, a mapping between $\mathbf{v}_i$ and $q(x_i)$ can be found by regression over $D$ by considering the pairs $\langle \mathbf{v}_i, \text{normscore}(x_i)\rangle$, $i = 1, \ldots, n$. Tabassi et al. [7] preferred to formulate the problem as a classification problem (instead of as a regression problem) in order to quantize the quality into just five values; to this purpose a neural network classifier is trained to classify the feature vector into one among the five predefined quality classes (where class 1 means top quality and class 5 means worst quality). The features constituting the 11-dimensional feature vectors $\mathbf{v}_i$ are reported in Table 14.2. To extract these features, the method calculates a quality map of the foreground according to the consistency of local orientation, the local contrast, and the curvature. Minutiae detection is then performed and the reliability of each detected minutia point is computed according to simple pixel intensity statistics (mean and standard deviation) within the immediate neighborhood of the minutia point. The minutiae reliability is then combined with the local quality at the minutiae location (from the quality map) to produce a quality measure for each minutia.

Another neural-network-based approach is proposed in reference 8, but differently from reference 7 here the classifier is used to define the quality locally (i.e., blockwise). For each image block, 11 features are computed to characterize the local orientation correctness; in fact, the incorrect estimation of local ridge orientation typically indicates that the local ridge pattern is noisy and its structure is unrecoverable. The binary network output indicates whether the estimated local orientation is correct or not. If necessary, a global fingerprint quality can be obtained by counting the number of correct foreground blocks.

Alonso-Fernandez et al. [6] have shown that most of the existing quality algorithms behave similarly, and they have assigned well-separated quality measures to different quality groups. They pointed out that the NIST approach [7] sometimes

**Table 14.2.** Features Used in Tabassi et al. [7]

| Feature | Description |
|---------|-------------|
| 1 | Number of blocks that have quality 1 or better |
| 2 | Number of total minutiae found in the fingerprint |
| 3 | Number of minutiae that have quality 0.5 or better |
| 4 | Number of minutiae that have quality 0.6 or better |
| 5 | Number of minutiae that have quality 0.75 or better |
| 6 | Number of minutiae that have quality 0.8 or better |
| 7 | Number of minutiae that have quality 0.9 or better |
| 8 | Percentage of the foreground blocks of quality map with quality = 1 |
| 9 | Percentage of the foreground blocks of quality map with quality = 2 |
| 10 | Percentage of the foreground blocks of quality map with quality = 3 |
| 11 | Percentage of the foreground blocks of quality map with quality = 4 |

behaves differently from the others algorithms and can lead to worst results; in their judgment this may be related to the low number (i.e., 5) of quality classes used.

## 14.2.2  Liveness Detection

A recent and very interesting application of machine learning techniques in finger-prints is the detection of fake fingers [9]. In fact, fingerprint recognition systems are not totally spoof-proof [1], and several works showed that it is possible to create well-made fake fingertips and use them for spoofing the biometric systems [10, 11]. Examples of real and fake fingers (of different materials) are shown in Figure 14.2. Unlike conventional fingerprint processing and recognition where most of the existing algorithms are inspired by manual methods (e.g., point pattern matching for minutiae matching), the discrimination of a fake fingerprint image from a real one is not easy for humans and great benefit can be obtained by the application of learning-based feature selection and classification.

The fake finger detection techniques can be roughly classified as follows:

- *Analysis of skin details in the acquired images* [12]: These methods often use high-resolution sensors (e.g., 1000 dpi); in this way it is possible to analyze the skin fine details, such as sweat pores or coarseness of the skin texture.
- *Analysis of static properties of the finger* [13]: temperature, impedance or other electric measurements, odor, and spectroscopy.
- *Analysis of dynamic properties of the finger* [11, 14–16]: dynamic properties are the skin perspiration (the most studied in scientific publications), pulse oximetry, blood pulsation, and skin elasticity.

Parthasaradhi et al. [11] used several classification methods (i.e., neural networks, discriminant analysis, and OneR decision tree) to discriminate real from fake finger-prints based on skin perspiration. In order to quantify skin perspiration, a sequence of images has to be collected at closed time intervals. Both static and dynamic features are exploited; static features include the Fourier transform of the ridge signal from

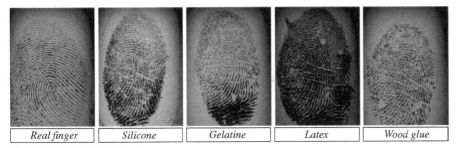

| Real finger | Silicone | Gelatine | Latex | Wood glue |

**Figure 14.2.** Fake fingertips created with different materials. (From reference 14. Copyright © 2006, IEEE.)

**Table 14.3.** Vitality Detection Features Used in Reference 16

| Feature | Description |
|---------|-------------|
| 1 | Average intra-distances among the extracted minutiae |
| 2 | Bending energy (the amount of the deformation, see reference 15 for details) |
| 3 | Average ridge width |
| 4 | Time difference of mean gray-level on the skeleton |
| 5 | Dry saturation percentage change |
| 6 | Wet saturation percentage change |
| 7 | Time variation of the gray-level average over the whole image |
| 8 | L1 distance of gray-level histogram |

the first image captured. Four dynamic features are computed from the subsequent images to quantify the specific ongoing temporal changes of the ridge signal intensity due to active perspiration. Starting from the consideration that in live fingers the gray-level along the ridges changes with a specific frequency pattern due to the presence of perspiration and pores, Tan and Schuckers [17] extracted the gray-level values along the thinned ridges. The wavelet transform is then used to analyze the signal at multiple scales, and classification trees are trained to separate the non-live subjects from the live subjects. This method obtains performance similar to that in reference 11, but a large data set of live, spoof (Play-Doh and gelatin), and cadaver fingerprints is here used. An approach based on the conjoint use of skin distortion and perspiration was introduced by Coli et al. [16]. Three skin elasticity features are extracted through an elastic model [15], and five further features are extracted from perspiration (see Table 14.3). A simple $k$-nearest-neighbor classifier is finally used for fake detection.

The authors of this chapter have studied the performance of a number of different classifiers starting from the same data set and features used in reference 16. Moreover, the Pudil's feature selection algorithm [18] has been used to identify the most discriminating features. Pudil's sequential forward floating selection (SFFS) is a top-down search that successively deletes features from a set of original candidate features in order find a smaller optimal set of $K$ features. As the number of subsets to be considered grows exponentially with the number of original features, this algorithm provides a heuristic for determining the best order to transverse the feature subset space.

In Figure 14.3 the liveness detection performance, measured as area under the ROC curve (AUC) [19], is reported as a function of the number $K$ of selected features, for four different classifiers: 1-nearest neighbor (**NN**), pseudo-Fisher support vector classifier (**PF**), linear SVM (**LS**), and radial basis SVM (**RS**).

The results show that the best performance of the different classifiers are very similar, even if the **LS** is the most stable classifier when the number of retained features varies. It is worth noting that the best result is achieved by **PF** by retaining just the four features numbered as 3, 5, 6, and 7 in Table 14.3. Hence, for this specific data set, where skin distortion was not deliberately introduced as in reference 14, skin distortion features appear to be useless.

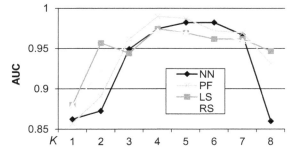

**Figure 14.3.** AUC obtained for the vitality detection, by the leave-one-out method, testing four different classifiers (**NN**, 1-nearest neighbor; **PF**, pseudo-Fisher support vector classifier; **LS**, linear SVM; **RS**, radial basis SVM).

## 14.3   PREPROCESSING

### 14.3.1   Segmentation

Fingerprint segmentation refers to the separation of the fingerprint area (foreground) from the background. The foreground is the region where the fingertip is in contact with the sensor during acquisition, while the background includes the noisy regions external to the fingerprint borders and the unrecoverable ridge regions. The segmentation process is useful to avoid the extraction of unreliable features and to save computing time, but is problematic due to the striped and oriented nature of the fingerprint image that makes the use of global or local thresholding ineffective. In fact, what really discriminates between the fingerprint foreground and its background is the presence of an oriented pattern in the foreground and an isotropic pattern in the background. Moreover, the process of fingerprint segmentation is made further complex by the presence of noise in the fingerprint image (i.e., dust or grease on the sensor surface) and by other factors, such as the movement of the finger after its placement on the sensor surface. Several approaches exist in the literature, but only few of them are learning-based. In the authors' opinion, the use of learning-based approaches for segmentation is very useful because of the possibility of deriving automatic rules from a quite small training set consisting of a few hundred small fingerprint blocks manually labeled as foreground or background.

Most of the existing methods divide the image into nonoverlapped blocks, extract a set of features from each block, and train a classifier to discriminate between foreground and background blocks (i.e., block-wise segmentation). Some authors proposed pixel-wise segmentation approaches [20, 21] which, in spite of a higher computation complexity, can be more accurate in extracting the external fingerprint silhouette.

Bazen et al. [20] introduced a coherence-based segmentation where a linear classifier discriminates between foreground and background pixels and a morphological postprocessing stage refines the result. A Hidden Markov Model (HMM)-based approach is proposed in reference 21 where gray mean, gray variance, gradient consistency, and Gabor responses are used as features. Wang et al. [22] compute four features (contrast, main energy ratio, variance, and coherence) for each block of size 16 × 16 and use a radial basis function (RBF) network for the classification step. Afsar et al.'s technique [23] is based on seven features, extracted from both the original and the enhanced image, that are projected into a one-dimensional feature space using Fisher discriminant analysis; the classification of each 16 × 16 block is carried out by learning vector quantization (LVQ) neural networks. This approach seems to be able to detect irrecoverable regions in a very effective manner due to the incorporation of the error correction capabilities of the enhancement algorithm. The error rate reported is very low (1.8%). Marques and Thome [24] observed that, since a small fingerprint fragment resembles a two-dimension sinusoid function, its Fourier spectrum must present a well-defined pattern. Their method consists, basically, in partitioning the image into blocks of 32 × 32, extracting the Fourier descriptors of each block and training a multilayer perceptron (MLP) neural network to discriminate the regions containing valid fingerprint fragments from the rest of the image.

All the above approaches perform a one-layered partition (OLP) that simply uses one binary classifier to partition the fingerprint image into background and foreground. Zhu at al. [25] proposed a multiple-layered partition (MLP) that hierarchically segments the fingerprints using multiple binary classifiers, each one for a partition stage (i.e., non-ridge region versus ridge region, visually unrecoverable region versus visually recoverable region, etc.), defining a partition tree (Figure 14.4); an advantage of this approach is the possibility of accepting as foreground also noisy but recoverable blocks. The fingerprint image is partitioned into blocks of size 15 × 15, and then each block is processed as follows:

1. *Orientation Estimation*: Computation of the orientation field using a gradient based method [25].

2. *Orientation Correctness Evaluation*: Computation of the correctness of the block orientation through a machine learning approach. A set of 11 features

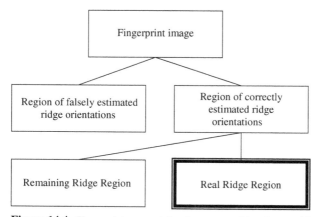

**Figure 14.4.** Fingerprint segmentation tree proposed in reference 25.

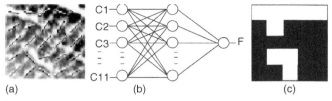

**(a)**                        **(b)**                        **(c)**

**Figure 14.5.** Orientation correctness evaluation. (**a**) Estimating orientation field. (**b**) Three-layer neural network, (**c**) Black blocks indicate a correct orientation, and white blocks indicate incorrect orientation. (From reference 25. Copyright © 2006, Elsevier.)

are extracted from each block: seven of them are independent of the orientation and are used for distinguishing ridge blocks from non-ridge blocks, and the remaining four are used for distinguishing between correct and incorrect orientation. A three-layer perceptron network (Figure 14.5) is used to learn the correctness of an estimated local orientation. The network is also able to correct the wrongly estimated ridge orientation of a block using the orientation of the valid neighboring blocks.

3. *Coarse Segmentation*: Each image block is classified into foreground or background according to its orientation correctness.

4. *Secondary Segmentation*: Further classification of the foreground produced by the coarse segmentation based on the consideration that the gray difference between the ridges and valleys for remaining ridge blocks is usually smaller than for true ridge blocks. To this purpose, a set of four features are extracted for each block and fed to a linear classifier.

5. *Orientation Correction and Segmentation Revision*: Postprocessing phase that allows us to move blocks from foreground to background and vice versa based on heuristic rules (e.g., consistency of a block with its neighboring blocks).

## 14.3.2  Enhancement

The performance of a fingerprint identification system heavily relies on the quality of the ridge–valley structures of the input fingerprint. Unfortunately, due to different skin conditions, sensor noise, incorrect finger pressure, and inherently low-quality fingerprints, several images contain poor-quality regions where the ridge pattern is very noisy and corrupted. The aim of an enhancement algorithm is to improve the clarity of the ridge structures, thus making the successive feature extraction more reliable.

The most effective fingerprint enhancement approaches proposed in the literature [1] are based on contextual filtering where the image is locally convolved with filters tuned according to the local context (i.e., ridge orientation and frequency). These are quite standard image processing techniques where the use of learning is typically limited to an initial tuning of the system aimed at finding out the best parameters. However, some isolated attempts have been introduced where the role of learning is

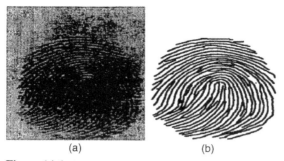

(a)                                    (b)

**Figure 14.6.** (a) A noisy fingerprint image. (b) Expert-provided corresponding ridge map. (From reference 26. Copyright © 2000, IEEE.)

central: The main drawback of these approaches is to collect a reliable training set with proper ground truth.

In the Ghosal et al. method [26] the filter coefficients are learned through a learn-by-example paradigm from a small set of training fingerprints and the corresponding set of binary ridge maps manually drawn by an expert (see Figure 14.6).

Bal et al. [27] proposed a supervised filtering technique that makes use of a recurrent neural network. Supervised filtering employs a fixed-sized filter mask and a convolution operation, as shown in Figure 14.7, where $h_{i,j}$ are the weights of the filter mask, $b$ is a scalar bias value, $f$ is a fixed nonlinear activation function, $t$ is the iteration step, and $a_{m,n}(t)$ is the pixel intensity at the step $t$. The recurrent flow of supervised filtering is described by the convolution between the input and the filter mask and then by a summation of the bias scalar value in the nonlinear activation function. The learning process consists in finding the optimal values for the weights $h_{i,j}$ and the bias value $b$ that minimize the difference between the current output and the desired output.

## 14.4   FEATURE EXTRACTION

### 14.4.1   Minutiae Detection

Minutiae (or Galton characteristics) are essentially the terminations and bifurcations of the ridges in a fingerprint image (Figure 14.8). Because of their high discriminant power, minutiae are widely used in automatic fingerprint recognition systems.

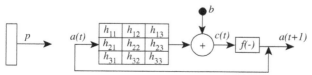

**Figure 14.7.** Supervised filtering architecture proposed by Bal et al. [27].

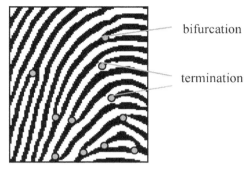

bifurcation

termination

**Figure 14.8.** Minutiae in a fingerprint portion.

Several methods exist for minutiae extraction from a gray-level fingerprint image [1] and most of them are based on traditional or adhoc image processing techniques. However some learning based minutiae detection approaches have been proposed where a sliding window (see Figure 14.9) is moved on the finger image and each local window is analyzed by a trained classifier to check whether it corresponds to a minutia or not. A set of minutiae manually extracted by a domain expert is used for the classifier training.

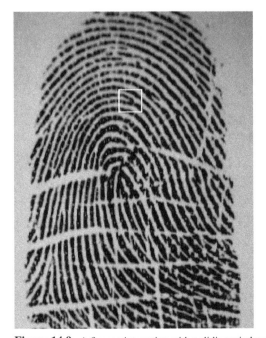

**Figure 14.9.** A fingerprint portion with a sliding window over a minutia region.

The first approaches based on neural networks date back to the early 1990s when Leung et al. [28] used a multilayer perceptron trained by the output of a bank of Gabor's filters applied to the gray-scale fingerprint and Leung et al. [29] used a multilayer perceptron trained by the minutiae extracted from skeletonized binary images. Other pioneering approaches based on artificial intelligence methods are: image exploring agents and reinforcement learning [30] and image exploring agents and genetic programming [31].

More recently, new learning approaches for minutiae detection have been proposed:

- Yang et al. [32] associate to a minutia point both the information from the point itself and also from its surrounding edges.

- Burian et al. [33] use a SVM; unlike most of the previous approaches, this method does not require a ridge thinning processing step.

- In the work by Carlson et al. [34], three different classifiers are trained and combined: a minimum distance classifier trained by principal component analysis (PCA) features extracted from gray-level data; a neural network classifier trained by PCA features (hereto extracted by gray-level data); and a neural network classifier directly trained by the gray-level data (i.e., without dimensionality reduction by PCA). The individual best result has been obtained by the second classifier; however, the combination (through clustering) of the three classifiers outperforms single classifiers.

- In the Bhanu and Tan [35] approach, a set of templates for minutiae extraction are learned from examples by optimizing a criterion function using Lagrange's method. Then for online minutiae extraction, these learned templates are applied to binarized fingerprint images to detect the presence of minutiae.

Minutiae detection through local window classification is today still not much used by state-of-the-art fingerprint recognition systems because of two main drawbacks: (i) the large amount of false alarms that they can produce especially on poor-quality images, and (ii) the high computation time that makes them unsuitable for fast detection. The same drawbacks were initially encountered also in face detection approaches [36], but nowadays the adoption of boosting techniques based on intensive training of many efficient weak classifiers (e.g., the Viola and Jones algorithms [3] based on Adaboost [37]) allows us to effectively overcome them. The same could happen in the future for fingerprint minutiae detection where the use of new learning-based technique could lead to better performance than conventional image processing-based extractors.

## 14.4.2  Minutiae Filtering

Since a large number of spurious minutiae are often located in noising fingerprint images by automatic extraction algorithms, postprocessing techniques can be useful to filter out most of them. Many minutiae filtering methods have been proposed in the literature (see reference 1 for a survey); they can be roughly classified into two groups: structural postprocessing and image-based filtering. The former mainly contains rule-based approaches that do not require any learning phase, with the only exception of reference 34 (see Subsection 14.4.1). The latter includes learning approaches similar to those developed for minutiae detection where a classifier is trained to process (i.e., labeling as *true* or *false*) image-based features extracted from a small region around each minutia. It is worth noting that here efficiency is not a concern (as for minutiae detection) because only a small number of regions have to be checked—that is, those corresponding to the minutiae detected in the previous stage.

Maio and Maltoni [38] reduce the dimensionality of the gray-scale data in the local region around each minutia through principal component analysis (PCA). Classification is then performed by a shared weights neural network that uses both positive and negative images of the minutiae neighborhood to exploit the duality of the ridge and bifurcation. Prabhakar et al. [39, 40] first enhance the region surrounding the minutia by Gabor filters, and then they use learning vector quantizer to filter the minutiae. Another method based on the PCA subspace is proposed by Chikkerur et al. [41], where the dimensionality of features extracted by steerable wedge filters is first reduced; the resulting vectors are then used to train a neural network. Santhanam et al. [42] propose using an ARTMAP neural network classifier, whose output indicates whether an input region is a termination, a bifurcation, or a false minutia. In the work by Mansukhani et al. [43] a SVM is used for filtering not directly the minutiae but the pair of mated minutiae after the matching stage.

The authors of this chapter have recently studied the performance of filtering approaches based on the fusion of different minutiae representations. The following preliminary results have been obtained on a dataset of minutiae extracted from the FVC2002 DB2 [1] by using the minutiae detection algorithm described in [44]. From the first 50 individuals of FVC2002 DB2, 1500 false positives and 1500 true positives have been manually labeled. The experiments have been carried out according to a fivefold cross-validation testing protocol. Starting from the minutiae regions, which are $33 \times 33$ pixel windows centered around each minutia, the following feature extraction methods have been evaluated:

- **DCT:** The first 100 coefficients of the discrete cosine transform [2] with higher variance are retained.
- **PCA:** Dimensionality reduction is performed through PCA [2] by preserving a variance of 0.95.
- **LEM:** Laplacian eigenmaps [45] have been used to project the image onto a lower 100-dimensional space (after the application of a PCA with preserved variance of 0.98).
- **ICA:** Independent component analysis [2] has been used to project the image onto a lower 100-dimensional space (after the application of a PCA with preserved variance of 0.98).

**Table 14.4.** AUC Obtained by the Fusion between Pairs of Feature Extraction Methods

|      | DCT  | PCA  | LEM  | ICA  | GAB  | GLBP |
|------|------|------|------|------|------|------|
| **DCT**  | 0.89 | 0.88 | 0.89 | 0.88 | 0.85 | 0.92 |
| **PCA**  | 0.88 | 0.84 | 0.88 | 0.86 | 0.83 | 0.91 |
| **LEM**  | 0.89 | 0.88 | 0.89 | 0.88 | 0.86 | **0.92** |
| **ICA**  | 0.88 | 0.86 | 0.88 | 0.83 | 0.81 | 0.90 |
| **GAB**  | 0.85 | 0.83 | 0.86 | 0.81 | 0.68 | 0.85 |
| **GLBP** | 0.92 | 0.91 | 0.92 | 0.90 | 0.85 | 0.89 |

- **GAB:** A feature vector is extracted by convolving the region with a bank of 16 Gabor filters [46] (four different wavelengths and four orientations: 0, $1/4\pi$, $1/2\pi$, $3/4\pi$).
- **GLBP:** Invariant local binary patterns histogram with 10 bins (see [47] for details) are extracted after convolution with Gabor filters.

Each feature vector has been normalized (through linear scaling) in the range [0, 1] and used to train a radial basis function SVM (with parameters $Gamma = 1$; $C = 1000$). Table 14.4 reports the AUC [48] obtained by combining through the sum rule the performance of the two classifiers located at each row–column intersection.

These results show the benefit of fusing classifiers trained on different features: the best stand-alone method (**GLBP** [46], as reported in the diagonal of Table 14.4) obtains an AUC of 0.89 while the fusion between **LEM** and **GLBP** raises AUC to 0.92. Since for minutiae filtering only the few regions classified as minutiae by the minutiae detector need to be processed, it is feasible to design complex and accurate systems, as the multiclassifier presented in this section, without compromising the whole efficiency.

## 14.5 MATCHING

Fingerprint matching is aimed at establishing if a pair of fingerprints, usually denoted as template $T$ and input $I$, belongs to the same finger (i.e., match or not). The large intra-class variability in different impressions of the same finger (due to several perturbations such as displacement, rotation, distortions, different skin conditions, noise, etc.) makes fingerprint matching a difficult problem. In this section we concentrate only on the methods based on learning; three main classes of approaches can be identified:

- *Minutiae-based matching*
- *Ridge feature-based matching*
- *Combination of matchers*

## 14.5.1  Minutiae-Based Matching

Most of the minutiae-based matching approaches address the problem as a point pattern matching problem [1]. Some researchers proposed methods based on evolutionary techniques where a learning stage is employed to optimize a given objective function for finding the best alignment between $T$ and $I$:

- Tan and Bhanu [49] used a traditional (and very time-consuming) Genetic Algorithm for finding the best alignment between two sets of minutiae.
- Le et al. [50] employed the technique of fuzzy evolutionary programming.
- Sheng et al. [51] developed a memetic fingerprint matching algorithm. In contrast to previous minutiae point pattern matching methods, this algorithm combines the use of a global search via a Genetic Algorithm with a local improvement operator used to prune the search. The fitness of individual solutions is computed by combining (according to the product rule) the globally matched minutiae pairs with the result of the minutiae's local feature similarity. Additionally, an efficient local matching operation for population initialization by examining local features of minutiae is proposed.

Another class of works [52–54] formulates the fingerprint verification problem as a standard two-class pattern recognition problem (*genuine* versus *impostor*). During the training, for each pair of fingerprints $A$ and $B$ of a given training set, a feature vector $c$ is produced from the matching between $A$ and $B$; $c$ is labeled as genuine if $A$ and $B$ belong to the same individual, as impostor otherwise. Finally, a general-purpose classifier is trained to classify as genuine or impostor a generic feature vector. Once the system has been trained, an online verification can be simply performed by classifying the feature vector obtained by the matching between $T$ and $I$. This formulation of the problem can be also conceived as a fusion (or combination) of partial scores where the learning phase is aimed at finding the optimal rules/weights for the fusion.

- Jea and Govindaraju [52] perform the classification by means of a neural network trained on the following features extracted from the optimal minutiae alignment: (i) the number of mated minutiae $n$; (ii) the number of minutiae on $T$ and $I$ ($nt$, $ni$); (iii) two widely used expressions for similarity calculation: $\frac{n^2}{ni \times nt}$, $\frac{2 \times n}{ni+nt}$ and (iv) another similarity score calculated by an heuristic method.
- Jia et al. [53] use SVM trained on five features: the number of the minutiae on $T$ and $I$, the number of mated minutiae $n$, a minutiae's weight $w$, and the score of a standard method to compare fingerprints. Based on the observation that false minutiae are usually closer to each other than real ones, the authors conjecture that if the distances between a minutia and its neighboring minutiae are much smaller than the minutia in a false one, then they define the minutia's weight $w$ according to the distance between the minutia and its nearest minutia.
- Feng [54] extracts from the matching results a 17-dimensional feature vector and trains a SVM for the classification. The features used reflect the matching

degree of minutiae, orientation image, frequency image, ridge-line associated with minutiae, and singular points.

## 14.5.2 Ridge Feature-Based Matching

These approaches are based on numerical features directly extracted from the gray-level image of the fingerprint (e.g., local orientation and frequency, ridge shape, texture information) [55, 56]. Throughout this chapter, all the methods relying on features derived from the ridge pattern will be considered in this family, even if a minutiae-based registration is performed. Most of the well-known ridge feature-based approaches published in the literature (e.g., Fingercode [56]) does not make use of a learning stage, with a few exceptions. Ceguerra and Koprinska [57] use minutiae for registration, but they base their matching on shape signatures; a Learning Vector Quantization Neural Network is trained to distinguish between matching and nonmatching fingerprints. He et al. [58] extract the texture features through the Fourier–Mellin transform and use a multiclass SVM for fingerprint identification. Nanni and Lumini [59] perform a multiresolution wavelet analysis on separate regions of the fingerprint pattern. A learning approach—that is, sequential forward feature selection (SFFS) [18]—is adopted for selecting the wavelet sub-bands containing the most useful information. The features extracted are the standard deviations of the selected sub-band images convolved with 16 Gabor filters. A learning-based variant of the Fingercode approach has been proposed in references 60 and 61: The region of interest around the core point is partitioned in four quadrants (Figure 14.10), and the features extracted from each quadrant are used for training a different classifier, in order to make the system more robust to noise and distortions. In reference 61 a distinct one-class Parzen window classifier is trained for each user, while in reference 60 a single two-class SVM is trained to discriminate between genuine and impostor.

## 14.5.3 Combination of Matchers

In the field of pattern recognition, it is well-known that combining information that are at least partially independent (i.e., uncorrelated) is very useful for improving

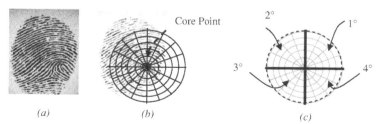

*(a)*  *(b)*  *(c)*

**Figure 14.10.** (a) An example of fingerprint. (b) FingerCode subdivision for feature extraction. (c) Partition of the region of interest into four quadrants. (From reference 60. Copyright © 2006 Elsevier.)

**Table 14.5.** EER Obtained by Two Most Uncorrelated Matchers and Their Fusion Through the Sum Rule for Each DB of FVC2004

| DB | 1st Matcher | 2nd Matcher | Fusion |
|---|---|---|---|
| DB1 | 1.97% (P047) | 2.72% (P101) | 1.45% |
| DB2 | 1.58% (P039) | 3.56% (P101) | 0.92% |
| DB3 | 1.85% (P075) | 1.2% (P101) | 0.28% |
| DB4 | 0.61% (P071) | 0.8% (P101) | 0.48% |

performance [4]; independence could be achieved here by combining matchers based on different features (e.g., a minutiae-based matcher and a ridge feature-based matcher).

Marcialis and Roli [62] propose a perceptron-based scheme for fusing two fingerprint matchers. The verification scores from two matchers (one minutiae-based and one ridge feature-based) are fused by a single-layer perceptron explicitly optimized to increase the separation between genuines and impostors. A systematic investigation on the correlation among the best performing fingerprint matchers presented at FVC2004 have been carried out in references 63–65, where learning-based approaches for combining multiple classifiers has been proposed. The similarity score of each matcher is considered as a feature; a feature pre-selection is done by SFFS leading to a reduced set of matchers. Scores from the selected matchers are then implicitly fused by a classifiers trained to separate genuine from impostor matches. Maio and Nanni [65] and Fierrez-Aguilar et al. [62] made the first studies on the combination of the different fingerprint systems submitted to FVC2004 and analyzed the benefits and the limits of the resulting multiple classifier approaches. These works show that combining systems based on heterogeneous matching strategies allows a drastic reduction of the equal error rate (see Table 14.5 and Figure 14.11).

| Preprocessing | | | Alignment | | | Features used | | | | | | | | | Comparison based on | | | | |
|---|---|---|---|---|---|---|---|---|---|---|---|---|---|---|---|---|---|---|---|
| *Algorithm* | *Segmentation* | *Enhancement* | *Before matching (B), During matching (D)* | *Displacement (D), Rotation (R), Scale (S), Non-linear (N)* | | *Minutiae* | *Singular points* | *Ridges* | *Ridge counts* | *Orientation field* | *Local ridge frequency* | *Texture measures* | *Raw/Enh. image parts* | *Minutiae (global)* | *Minutiae (local)* | *Ridge pattern (geometry)* | *Ridge pattern (texture)* | *Correlation* |
| P039 | x | x | D | N | | x | | | | x | x | | | x | | | | |
| P047 | x | | D | DRSN | | x | x | x | x | x | x | x | x | x | x | | x | |
| P071 | | x | D | N | | x | x | x | x | x | | | x | | x | x | | x |
| P075 | x | x | B | DR | | x | | | | | | | | x | | | | |
| P101 | (x) | x | BD | DRS | | | x | x | x | x | x | | x | | | x | | x |

**Figure 14.11.** High-level description of the matchers cited in Table 14.5. Note about P101: Segmentation is performed only on DB1 images.

**Table 14.6.** Performance of Our Minutiae-Based Multimatcher

|      |     | MM(2) | MM(3) | MM(4) | TICO |
|------|-----|-------|-------|-------|------|
| DB1  | AUC | 0.985 | 0.9855 | 0.9858 | 0.98 |
|      | EER | 3.8%  | 3.8%  | 4%    | 4%   |
| DB2  | AUC | 0.9975 | 0.9964 | 0.9974 | 0.9948 |
|      | EER | 1.52% | 1.52% | 1.6%  | 1.6% |
| DB3  | AUC | 0.976 | 0.9751 | 0.9736 | 0.968 |
|      | EER | 5.4%  | 5.28% | 5.86% | 6.5% |
| DB4  | AUC | 0.9787 | 0.9809 | 0.9841 | 0.9765 |
|      | EER | 6.4%  | 6.4%  | 5.78% | 7.7% |

The authors of this chapter have studied the performance of the combination of minutiae matchers based on extended minutia descriptors: In particular minutiae, data ($x$, $y$ coordinates and angles) are enriched with local orientation extracted from a neighborhood of each minutia as originally proposed by Tico and Kousmanen [66]. Each single matcher, implemented as described in reference 66, works on a different image: In fact, from the original gray-level image 17 images are extracted, the first 16 are obtained by the wavelet decomposition of the original image, while the 17th image is a block frequency image (it encodes the local ridge density). Different wavelet families have been used: Haar, Daubechies order 4, Symmlet order 2, Coiflets order 2. Before combining the matchers through the sum rule, a feature selection has been performed on a disjoint data set using SFFS.

Experiments have been conducted on the four FVC2002 databases according to the FVC2002 testing protocol. The equal error rate (EER) and AUC obtained by the following methods are reported in Table 14.6, where **TICO** denotes the original Tico and Kousmanen method as proposed in reference 66, and **MM(n)** denotes the proposed ensemble of matchers, where $n$ is the number of matchers selected through SFFS. From the results it can be concluded that **MM(2)**, **MM(3)**, and **MM(4)** outperform **TICO**; the performance of all **MM(n)** are very similar, and therefore **MM(2)** is preferable because of the lower complexity; the two images selected for **MM(2)** are the horizontal coefficients of the Haar wavelet and the frequency image (as reported in Figure 14.12).

## 14.6 FINGERPRINT CLASSIFICATION

Fingerprint exclusive classification consists in assigning a fingerprint to a predefined class and can be very useful for fingerprint identification to reduce the retrieval time and complexity by narrowing the search space to a subset of a potentially huge database. In fact, to speed-up the search in a fingerprint database, an initial coarse level selection (usually based on macro-features extracted from the fingerprint pattern) allows us to limit the accurate but also computationally demanding minutiae matching to the samples passing the initial selection.

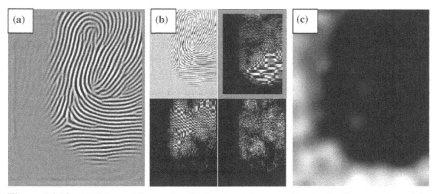

**Figure 14.12.** (a) Enhanced fingerprint, (b) One-level decomposition by the Haar wavelet of (a). (c) Frequency image of (a).

All the exclusive classification schemes currently used by police agencies and automated systems for the coarse level search of database are variants of the so-called Henry's classification scheme (see Figure 14.13 for an example of each class). The natural fingerprint distribution of the Henry five classes is 3.7% plain arch, 2.9% tented arch, 33.8% left loop, 31.7% right loop, and 27.9% whorl. Due to the small number of classes and the unevenly distribution among them, exclusive classification cannot sufficiently narrow down the search of database; therefore, continuous

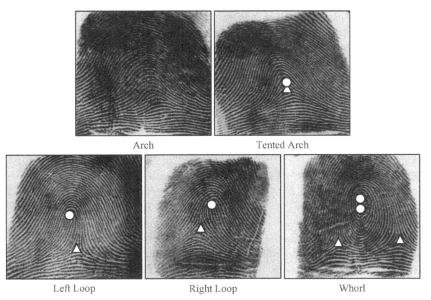

**Figure 14.13.** The five commonly used fingerprint classes marked with core (O) and delta ($\triangle$) points.

classification and other indexing technique has been proposed for the coarse level search [89][92][93]; anyway, these are not a focus of the present work.

Completely automated fingerprint exclusive classification is a difficult pattern recognition problem, due to the small inter-class variability, the large intra-class variability, and the presence of noise, which has attracted the interest of many researchers during the last 30 years (see references 67 and 68 for a survey). Because of the complexity and variability of the fingerprint pattern, the approaches based on modeling or rule-based description of the fingerprint classes proved to be unable to deal with difficult cases, and best results have been achieved with methods implementing learning by examples paradigms. Learning-based approaches will be reviewed in the following:

- *Syntactic Methods.* A syntactic method describes patterns by means of terminal symbols and production rules of a grammar. Moayer and Fu [69] associate terminal symbols to small groups of directional elements within the fingerprint directional image and use a class of context-free grammars to describe the fingerprint patterns. Learning is here implicit in the grammar inference process.

- *Approaches Based on Ridge-Line Shape.* These approaches [70, 71] extract and encode the fingerprint ridge structures and use these features as the basis for classification. Senior [71] trained a Hidden Markov Model classifier, whose input features are measured at the intersection points between some horizontal/vertical fiducial lines and the fingerprint ridge-lines (ridge angle, separation, curvature, etc.).

- *Neural Network Approaches.* Neural networks have been applied to fingerprint classification since the early 1990s and are generally based on the elements of the directional image [72–75]. Kamijo [75] proposes a pyramidal architecture constituted by several multilayer perceptrons, each of which is trained to recognize a different class. The well-known PCASYS system (Pattern-level Classification Automation System for Fingerprints) [73] developed by Candela et al. from NIST is an hybrid system that uses neural network classification followed by an auxiliary classifier (pseudoridge tracer) used to improve the reliability of classification. The directional image is first registered with respect to the centre of the fingerprint image, then its dimensionality is reduced by PCA and classified by a probabilistic neural network (PNN).

- *Other Approaches.* Several systems are based on clustering or general-purpose classifiers. Wang et al. [76] use a $k$-means clustering algorithm coupled to a three-nearest neighbors classifier. Cappelli et al. [77] use a MKL classifier [78] applied to an enhanced version of the orientation image (see Figure 14.14). Tan and Bhanu [79] propose an original approach based on feature-learning, where a set of artificial features are learned and classified by a Bayesian classifier. Genetic programming is used to discover evolved features that are obtained from combinations of primitive image processing operations.

- *Combined Approaches.* Recently, some researchers [80–82] have proposed the combination of different approaches to exploit their complementarities.

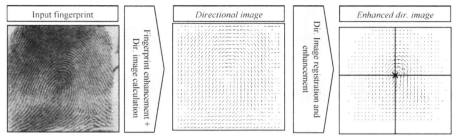

**Figure 14.14.** The main feature extraction steps of the system proposed in reference 77.

Jain et al. [83] adopt a two-stage classification strategy: A K-nearest neighbor classifier is used to find the two most likely classes from a FingerCode feature vector; then a set of ten neural networks are trained to distinguish between each possible pair of classes. Yao et al. [84] use a combination of SVMs trained by two kind of features: the FingerCode representation of the fingerprint [85] and a distributed vectorial representation of the relational graph associated with the fingerprint obtained by Recursive Neural Networks. Cappelli et al. [86] improve the results obtained by [83] using a two-stage sequential architecture based on an MKL classifier to select the two-most-likely classes and a set of 10 SPD classifiers to discriminate between selected pair of classes. In references 67, 92, and 87, some classifiers based on the MKL transform are combined.

In Table 14.7, some comparisons among different fingerprint classification methods are reported for the NIST DB4 [88]: Most of them were obtained by using the first half of the database for training and the second half for testing. Furthermore, since DB4 contains an equal number of fingerprints for each class, some authors prefer to

**Table 14.7.** Comparison Among Different Classification Approaches on DB4[a]

| | | Five Classes | | Four Classes | |
|---|---|---|---|---|---|
| Method | Category | Equal | Weighted | Equal | Weighted |
| Candela et al. [73] | Neural network | — | — | 11.4% | 6.1% |
| Senior [71] | Ridge line shape | — | — | — | 8.4% |
| Jain et al. [83] | Combined | 10.0% | 7.0% | 5.2% | — |
| Cappelli et al. [89] | Other | 7.9% | 6.5% | 5.5% | — |
| Marcialis et al. [80] | Combined | 12.1% | 9.6% | — | — |
| Yao et al. [82] | Combined | 10.7% | 9.0% | 6.9% | — |
| Senior [81] | Combined | — | — | — | 5.1% |
| Yao et al. [84] | Combined | 10% | 8.1% | 5.3% | — |
| Cappelli and Maio [67] | Combined | 7.0% | 5.9% | 4.7% | 5.4% |
| Tan et al. [79] | Other | 8.4% | 8.3% | 6.7% | 6% |

[a]Classification error is reported for the five-class and four-class problems. In the four-class problem, "Arch" and "Tented-Arch" classes are here fused into a single class.

weight the results according to the natural class distribution. All the results are reported at 0% rejection rate, with the exception of the approaches based on FingerCode feature vectors (Jain et al. [83], Marcialis et al. [80], Yao et al. [82], Yao et al. [84]), where 1.8% fingerprints are discarded during the feature extraction stage.

## 14.7   CONCLUSION

In this chapter the main learning-based approaches to fingerprint acquisition, processing, recognition, and classification have been discussed. It is not surprising that tasks where the application of learning seems to provide maximum benefit are those that are critical for humans (e.g., quality check, liveness detection, continuous and exclusive classification, etc.). Combination of classifiers (both at feature and at score level) and automatic selection of redundant features proved to be very effective to improve the accuracy of fingerprint verification; SVM and other robust classification techniques were successfully applied to fingerprint verification formulated as a two class problem. The two main factors limiting the performance of learning based techniques are still the availability of reliable large-enough training data set and the lack of efficiency of some techniques such as the exhaustive classification of small portions of the image to detect minutiae. The authors believe that important advances could arise by the availability of large sets of *ad hoc*-created synthetic fingerprints [90] and the implementation of boosted cascade of weak classifiers (such as in reference 3) that allows us to solve in real time and with good accuracy the face detection problem.

## ACKNOWLEDGMENTS

The authors want to thank F. Roli, G. Marcialis, and P. Coli for sharing the vitality data set used in this chapter.

## REFERENCES

1. D.Maltoni, D. Maio, A. K. Jain, and S. Prabhakar, in *Handbook of Fingerprint Recognition*, Springer, Berlin, 2003.
2. R. Duda, P. Hart, and D. Stork, *Pattern Classification*, John Wiley & Sons, New York, 2000.
3. P. Viola and M. Jones, Rapid object detection using a boosted cascade of simple features, in *Proceedings of the IEEE Computer Society Conference on Computer Vision and Pattern Recognition*, Kauai, Hawaii, 2001, pp. 511–518.
4. L. I. Kuncheva and C. J. Whitaker, Measures of diversity in classifier ensembles and their relationship with the ensemble accuracy, *Mach. Learning* **51**:181–207, 2003.
5. N. J. Nilsson, *Introduction to Machine Learning*, Stanford University, Palo Alto, CA, 1997.
6. F. Alonso-Fernandez, J. Fierrez-Aguilar, and J. Ortega-Garcia, A review of schemes for fingerprint image quality computation, in *COST 275—Biometrics Based Recognition of People over the Internet*, October 2005.
7. E. Tabassi, C.Wilson, and C.Watson, Fingerprint image quality, NIST Research Report NISTIR 7151, August 2004.

8. E. Zhu, J. Yin, C. Hu, and G. Zhang, Quality Estimation of fingerprint image based on neural network, in *ICNC 2005,*, 2005, pp. 65–70.

9. R. Derakhshani, S. Schuckers, L. Hornak, and L. O'Gorman, Determination of vitality from a non-invasive biomedical measurement for use in fingerprint sensors, *Pattern Recognit.* **36**(2):383–396, 2003.

10. T. Matsumoto, H. Matsumoto, K. Yamada, and S. Hoshino, Impact of artificial "gummy" fingers on fingerprint systems, in *Proceedings Optical Security and Counterfeit Deterrence Techniques IV,* 4677, 2002, pp. 24–25.

11. S. Parthasaradhi, R. Derakhshani, L. Hornak, and S. Schuckers, Time-series detection of perspiration as a vitality test in fingerprint devices, *IEEE Tran. Syst. Man Cybern. Part C,* **35**(3):335–343, 2005.

12. Y. S. Moon, J. S. Chen, K. C. Chan, K. So, and K. C. Woo, Wavelet based fingerprint liveness detection, *Electron. Lett.* **41**(20):1112–1113, 2005.

13. K. Nixon, Novel spectroscopy-based technology for biometric and liveness verification, *Proc. SPIE,* 2004, p. 5404.

14. A. Antonelli, R. Cappelli, D. Maio, and D. Maltoni, Fake finger detection by skin distortion analysis, *IEEE Trans. Inf. Forens. Secur.* **1**(3):360–373, 2006.

15. Y. Chen, A. K. Jain, and S. Dass, Fingerprint deformation for spoof detection, in *Biometric Symposium,* Crystal City, VA, 2005.

16. P. Coli, G. L. Marcialis, and F. Roli, Analysis and selection of features for the fingerprint vitality detection, in *SSPR/SPR,* 2006, pp. 907–915.

17. B. Tan and S. Schuckers, Liveness detection for fingerprint scanners based on the statistics of wavelet signal processing, in *Conference on Computer Vision and Pattern Recognition Workshop,* 2006.

18. P. Pudil, J. Novovicova, and J. Kittler, Floating search methods in feature selection, *Pattern Recognit. Lett.* **15**(11):1119–1125, 1994.

19. T. Fawcett, ROC graphs: Notes and practical considerations for researchers, Technical report, HP Laboratories, Palo Alto, CA, 2004.

20. A. M. Bazen and S. H. Gerez, Segmentation of fingerprint images, in *Workshop on Circuits, Systems and Signal Processing,* Veldhoven, The Netherlands, November 2001.

21. S. Klein, A. M. Bazen, and R. N. J. Veldhuis, Fingerprint image segmentation based on hidden Markov models, in *13th Annual Workshop on Circuits, Systems, and Signal Processing,* 2002.

22. S. Wang, W. Zhang, and Y. Wang, New features extraction and application in fingerprint segmentation, *J. Acta Automat. Sin.* **29**(4):622–627, 2003.

23. F. A. Afsar, M. Arif, and M. Hussain, An effective approach to fingerprint segmentation using Fisher basis, in *9th IEEE International Multitopic Conference,* 2005, pp. 1–6.

24. P. B. Marques and T. Gay, A neural network fingerprint segmentation method, in *Proceedings of the Fifth International Conference on Hybrid Intelligent Systems,* 2005, pp. 385–392.

25. E. Zhu, J. Yin, C. Hu, and G. Zhang, A systematic method for fingerprint ridge orientation estimation and image segmentation, *Pattern Recognit.* **39**:1452–1472, 2006.

26. S. Ghosal, R. Udupa, S. Pankanti, and N. K. Ratha, Learning partitioned least squares filters for fingerprint enhancement, in *Fifth IEEE Workshop on Applications of Computer Vision,* 2000, pp. 2–7.

27. A. Bal, A. M. El-Saba, and M. S. Alam, Improved fingerprint identification with supervised filtering enhancement, *Appl. Opt.* **44**: 647–654, 2005.

28. W. F. Leung, S. H. Leung, W. H. Lau, and A. Luk, Fingerprint recognition using neural network, in *Proceedings of the IEEE Workshop on Neural Network for Signal Processing,* 1991, pp. 226–235.

29. M. T. Leung, W. E. Engeler, and P. Frank, Fingerprint image processing using neural network, in *Proceedings of the 10th conference on Computer and Communication Systems,* Hong Kong, 1990, pp. 582–586.

30. H. Gerez, M.M.P. Bazen, and M. van Otterlo A reinforcement learning agent for minutiae extraction from fingerprints, in *Proceedings of the 13th Belgian–Dutch Conference on Artificial Intelligence,* Amsterdam, Netherlands, 2001.

31. P. G. M. van der Meulen, H. Schipper, M. Bazen, and S. H. Gerez, A distributed object-oriented genetic programming environment, in *Proceedings of ASCI Conference,* Netherlands, Heijen, 2001.

32. G. Yang, D. Shi, and C. Quek, Fingerprint minutia recognition with fuzzy neural network, *Adv. Neural Netw.* **3497**:165–170, 2005.

33. A. Burian, M. Tico, M. Lehtokangas, P. Kuosmanen, and J. Saarinen, Support vector method for minutiae detection in fingerprint images, in *European Signal Processing Conference,* Tampere, Finlande, 2000, pp. 569–572.

34. B. P. Carlson, G. Bebis, and C. Looney, Minutiae detection through classifier fusion and clustering, in *International Conference on Imaging Science, Systems, and Technology,* Las Vegas, June 2002.

35. B. Bhanu and X. Tan, Learned templates for feature extraction in fingerprint images, *Proc. IEEE Conf. Comput. Vis. Pattern Recognit.* **2**:591–596, 2001.

36. M. H. Yang, D. Kriegman, and N. Ahuja, Detecting faces in images: A survey, *IEEE Trans. Pattern Anal. Mach. Intell. (PAMI)* **24**(1):34–58, 2002.

37. G. Zhang, X. Huang, S. Li, and Y. Wang, Boosting local binary pattern-based face recognition, *LNCS* **3338**:180–187, 2004.

38. D. Maio and D. Maltoni, Neural network based minutiae filtering in fingerprints, in *Proceedings of the 14th International Conference on Pattern Recognition,* 2, 1998, pp. 1654–1658.

39. S. Prabhakar, A. Jain, J. Wang, S. Pankanti, and R. Bolle, Minutiae verification and classification for fingerprint matching, in *Proceedings of the 15th International Conference on Pattern Recognition,* 1, 2000, pp. 25–29.

40. S. Prabhakar, A. Jain, and S. Pankanti, Learning fingerprint minutiae location and type, *Pattern Recognit.* **36**(8):1847–1857, 2003.

41. S. Chikkerur, V. Govindaraju, S. Pankanti, and R. Bolle, Minutiae verification in fingerprint images using steerable wedge filters, in *2004 IEEE Workshop on Applications of Computer Vision, WACV-04,*

42. T. Santhanam, C. P. Sumathi, and K. S. Easwarakumar, Fingerprint minutiae filtering using ARTMAP, *Neural Comput. Appl.* **16**:49–55, 2007.

43. P. Mansukhani, S. Tulyakov, and V. Govindaraju, Using support vector machines to eliminate false minutiae matches during fingerprint verification, in *Proceedings of SPIE,* 2007, p. 6539.

44. D. Maio and D. Maltoni, Direct gray-scale minutiae detection in fingerprints, *IEEE Trans. Pattern Anal. Mach. Intell.* **19**(1):27–40, 1997.

45. X. He, S. Yan, Y. Hu, P. Niyogi, and H-J Zhang, Face recognition using Laplacian faces, *IEEE Trans. Pattern Anal. Mach. Intell.* **27**(3):328–340, 2005.

46. W. Zhang, S. Shan, W. Gao, X. Chen, and H. Zhang, Local Gabor binary pattern histogram sequence (LGBPHS): A novel non-statistical model for face representation and recognition, in *Tenth IEEE Int. Conf. Comput. Vis.* **1**(17–21), 786–791, 2005.

47. T. Ojala, M. Pietikainen, and T. Maeenpaa, Multiresolution gray-scale and rotation invariant texture classification with local binary patterns, in *IEEE Tran. Pattern Anal. and Mach. Intell.* **24**(7):971–987, 2002.

48. J. Swets, Measuring the accuracy of diagnostic systems, *Science* **240**, 1285–1293, 1988.

49. X. Tan and B. Bhanu, Fingerprint matching by genetic algorithms, *Pattern Recognit.* **39**(3):465–477, 2006.

50. T. V. Le, K. Y. Cheung, and M. H. Nguyen, A fingerprint recognizer using fuzzy evolutionary programming, in *Proceedings of the 34th International Conference on System Sciences,* 2001.

51. W. Sheng, G. Howells, M. C. Fairhurst, and F. Deravi, A memetic fingerprint matching algorithm, *IEEE Trans. Inf. Forens. Secur.* **3**(1):402–412, 2007.

52. T-Y. Jea and V. Govindaraju, A minutiae-based partial fingerprint recognition system, *Pattern Recognit.* **38**:1672–1684, 2005.

53. J. Jia, L. Cai, P. Lu, and X. Lu, Fingerprint matching based on weighting method and the SVM, *Neurocomputing* **70** (4–6):849–858, 2007.

54. J. Feng, Combining minutiae descriptors for fingerprint matching, *Pattern Recognit.* **41**(1):342–352, 2008.

55. J. Wayman, A. Jain, D. Maltoni, and D. Maio, *Biometric Systems: Technology, Design and Performance Evaluation*, Springer, Berlin, 2005.

56. A. Ross, A. Jain, and J. Reismanb, A hybrid fingerprint matcher, *Pattern Recognit.* **36**:1661–1673, 2003.

57. A. Ceguerra and I. Koprinska, Automatic fingerprint verification using neural networks, in *Proceedings of the International Conference on Artificial Neural Networks,* 2002, pp. 1281–1286.

58. Y. He, Z-Y Ou, and H.Guo, A method of fingerprint identification based on space invariant transforms and support vector machines, in *International Conference on Machine Learning and Cybernetics,* 2003.

59. L. Nanni and A. Lumini, A hybrid wavelet-based fingerprint matcher, *Pattern Recognit.* **40**(11): 3146–3151, 2007.

60. A. Lumini and L. Nanni, Two-class fingerprint matcher, *Pattern Recognit.* **39**(4):714–716 (2006).

61. D. Maio and L. Nanni, An efficient fingerprint verification system using integrated Gabor filters and Parzen window classifier, *NeuroComputing* **68**:208–216, 2005.

62. G. L. Marcialis and F. Roli, Fusion of multiple fingerprint matchers by single-layer perceptron with class-separation loss function, *Pattern Recognit. Lett.* **26**(12):1830–1839, 2005.

63. J. Fierrez-Aguilar, L. Nanni, J. Ortega-Garcia, R. Cappelli, and D. Maltoni, Combining multiple matchers for fingerprint verification: A case study in FVC2004, in *Proceedings 13th International Conference on Image Analysis and Processing,* Cagliari, September 2005.

64. A. Lumini and L. Nanni, When fingerprints are combined with iris, a case study: FVC2004 and CASIA, *Int. J. Network Secur.* **4**(1):27–34, 2007.

65. D. Maio and L. Nanni, Combination of different fingerprint systems: A case study FVC2004, *Sensor Rev.* **26**(1):51–57, 2006.

66. M. Tico and P. Kuosmanen, Fingerprint matching using an orientation-based minutia descriptor, *IEEE Trans. Pattern Anal. Mach. Intell.* **25**:1009–1014, 2003.

67. R. Cappelli and D. Maio, The state of the art in fingerprint classification, *N. Ratha and R. Bolle, Automatic Fingerprint Recognition Systems,* Springer, 2004.

68. N. Yager and A. Amin, Fingerprint classification: A review, *Pattern Anal. Appl.* **7**(17):77–93, 2004.

69. B. Moayer and K. S. Fu, A syntactic approach to fingerprint pattern recognition, *Pattern Recognit.* **7**:1–23, 1975.

70. M. M. S. Chong et. al., Geometric framework for fingerprint image classification, *Pattern Recognit.* **30**(9):1475–1488, 1997.

71. A. Senior, A hidden Markov model fingerprint classifier, *Asilomar Conference (31st) on Signals, Systems and Computers,* 1997, pp. 306–310.

72. S. Bernard, N. Boujemaa, D. Vitale, and C. Bricot, Fingerprint classification using Kohonen topologic map, in *Proceedings International Conference on Image Processing,* Thessaloniki, Greece, 2001.

73. G. T. Candela et. al., PCASYS—A pattern-level classification automation system for fingerprints, NIST Technical Report NISTIR 5647, August 1995.

74. P. A. Hughes and A. D. P. Green, The use of neural network for fingerprint classification, in *Proceedings of the 2nd International Conference on Neural Network,* 1991, pp. 79–81.

75. M. Kamijo, Classifying fingerprint images using neural network: Deriving the classification state, in *Proceedings 3rd International Conference on Neural Network,* 1993, pp. 1932–1937.

76. S. Wang, W. Zhang, and Y. Wang, Fingerprint classification by directional fields, in *Proceedings of the Fourth IEEE Conference on International Conference on Multimodal Interfaces,* Los Alamitos, CA, October 2002.

77. R. Cappelli, D. Maio, and D. Maltoni, Fingerprint classification based on multi-space KL, in *Proceedings, Workshop on Automatic Identification Advances Technologies,* Summit, NJ, 1999, pp. 117–120.

78. R. Cappelli, and D. Maio, and D. Maltoni, Multi-space KL for pattern representation and classification, *IEEE Trans. Pattern Anal. Mach. Intell.* **23**(9):977–996, 2001.

79. X. Tan, B. Bhanu, and Y. Lin, Fingerprint classification based on learned features, *IEEE Trans. Syst. Man Cybern. Part C: Appl. Rev.* **35**(3):287–300, 2005.

80. G. L. Marcialis, F. Roli, and P. Frasconi, Fingerprint classification by combination of flat and structural approaches, *International Conference (3rd) on Audio-and Video-Based Biometric Person Authentication,* 2001, pp. 241–246.

81. A. Senior, A combination fingerprint classifier, *IEEE Trans. Pattern Anal. Mach. Intell.* **23**(10):1165–1174, 2001.

82. Y. Yao, P. Frasconi, and M. Pontil, Fingerprint classification with combination of support vector machines, in *International Conference (3rd) on Audio- and Video-Based Biometric Person Authentication,* 2001, pp. 253–258.

83. A. K. Jain, S. Prabhakar, and L. Hong, A multichannel approach to fingerprint classification, *IEEE Trans. Pattern Anal. Mach. Intell.* **21**(4):348–359, 1999.

84. Y. Yao, G. Marcialis, M. Pontil, P. Frasconi, and F. Roli, Combining flat and structured representations for fingerprint classification with recursive neural networks and support vector machines, *Pattern Recognit.* **36**(2):397–406, 2003.

85. A. Jain, S. Prabhakar, and L. Hong, A multichannel approach to fingerprint classification, *IEEE Trans. Pattern Anal. Mach. Intell.* **21**(4):348–359, 1999.

86. R. Cappelli, D. Maio, D. Maltoni, and L. Nanni, A two-stage fingerprint classification system, in *Proceedings ACM SIGMM Multimedia Biometrics Methods and Applications Workshop,* 2003, pp. 95–99.

87. R. Cappelli, D. Maio, and D. Maltoni, A Multi-classifier approach to fingerprint classification, *Pattern Anal. Appl. (Special Issue on Fusion of Multiple Classifiers),* **5** (2):136–144, 2002.

88. C. I. Watson and C. L. Wilson, Nist Special Database 4, Fingerprint Database, U.S. National Institute of Standards and Technology, 1992.

89. R. Cappelli, D. Maio, and D. Maltoni, Fingerprint classification based on multi-space KL, in *proceedings Workshop on Automatic Identification Advances Technologies (AutoID'99),* Summit, NJ, 1999, pp. 117–120.

90. R. Cappelli, D. Maio and D. Maltoni, Synthetic fingerprint-database generation, in *Proceedings of the 16th International Conference on Pattern Recognition (ICPR2002),* Québec City, Vol. 3, August 2002, pp. 744–747.

91. R. Cappelli, D. Maio, and D. Maltoni, Combining fingerprint classifiers, in *Proceedings of the First International Workshop on Multiple Classifier Systems (MCS2000),* Cagliari, 2000, pp. 351–361.

92. M. Liu, X. Jiang, and A. C. Kot, Efficient fingerprint search based on database clustering, *Pattern Recognit.* **40**(6):1793–1803, 2007.

93. A. Lumini, D. Maio, and D. Maltoni, Continuous vs exclusive classification for fingerprint retrieval, *Pattern Recognit. Lett.* **18**(10):1027–1034, 1997.

# Chapter 15

# A Comparison of Classification- and Indexing-Based Approaches for Fingerprint Identification

Xuejun Tan, Bir Bhanu, and Rong Wang

## 15.1 INTRODUCTION

There are two kinds of biometric systems that use fingerprints for the personal identity: verification and identification. In a verification system, the input includes a query fingerprint and a known identity (ID), and the system verifies whether the ID is consistent with the input fingerprint. The output of a verification system is an answer of yes or no. In an identification system, the input only includes a query fingerprint, and the system tries to answer the following question: Are there any fingerprints in the database which resemble the query fingerprint? In this chapter, we are dealing with the identification problem. There are three kinds of approaches to solve the fingerprint identification problem:

1. The *first* approach is to repeat the verification procedure for each fingerprint in the database and select the best match. However, if the size of the database is large, this approach will be time-consuming and it is not practical for real-world applications [1].

2. The *second* approach involves fingerprint classification followed by verification. Traditional classification techniques attempt to classify fingerprints into five classes: right loop (R), left loop (L), whorl (W), arch (A), and tented

*Biometrics: Theory, Methods, and Applications.* Edited by Boulgouris, Plataniotis, and Micheli-Tzanakou
Copyright © 2010 the Institute of Electrical and Electronics Engineers, Inc.

arch (T). The most widely used approaches for fingerprint classification are based on the number and relations of singular points (SPs) [2]. The problem with this kind of approach is that it is not easy to detect SPs and some fingerprints do not have SPs. Moreover, the uncertainty in the location of SPs is large, which has an undesired effect on the classification results. Based on fingerprint's orientation field [3], other classification approaches use multispace Karhunen–Loeve transform [4] and a combination of different classifiers [5] to improve the performance. The most important problem associated with the classification technique for identification is that the number of principal classes is small and the fingerprints are unevenly distributed (31.7%, 33.8%, 27.9%, 3.7%, and 2.9% for classes R, L, W, A, and T, respectively [6]). The classification approach does not narrow down the search enough in the database for efficient identification.

3. The *third* approach consists of fingerprint indexing followed by verification. Germain et al. [7] integrate indexing and verification in their approach, in which top hypothesis generated by indexing is considered as the final identification result. They use the triplets of minutiae in their identification procedure. The features they use are: the length of each side, the angles that the ridges make with respect to the $x$-axis of the reference frame, and the ridge count between each pair of vertices. Bhanu and Tan [8] present an indexing approach using novel features of minutiae triplets. They compare the performance of their approach with Germain et al. [7] and demonstrate the improvement in result over Germain et al. [7].

In this chapter, we compare the second and third approaches (see Figure 15.1) that use minutiae features for fingerprint identification. The contributions of this chapter are as follows: (a) It provides the comparison of classification- and indexing-based approaches in a single chapter; *some* of the material is scattered in various recent papers. All the experimental results for comparison are carried out on the entire NIST-4 fingerprint database [6]. (b) It presents a technique based on learned

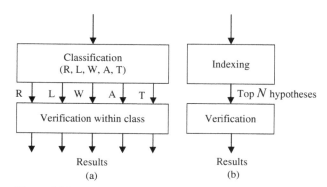

**Figure 15.1.** Block diagram of two different approaches to solve identification problem: (a) Classification followed by verification; (b) Indexing followed by verification.

masks for minutiae feature extraction and integrates newly developed classification [9] and indexing [8] techniques with the same verification algorithm that optimizes a criterion function. (c) It presents extensive comparisons between classification- and indexing-based techniques for identification.

## 15.2  TECHNICAL APPROACH

### 15.2.1  Minutiae Extraction Using Learned Feature Extraction Masks

There are many approaches in the literature for the minutiae extraction [10, 16]. As compared to the other approaches, we extract minutiae using *learned masks* for all the results reported in this chapter. For each fingerprint, first the background is removed. Local orientation is computed in each local $16 \times 16$ block. The fingerprint is adaptively smoothed, binarized, and thinned using the local orientation information. Potential minutiae are found using crossing number [2]. Finally, learned feature extractor masks obtained during offline processing are adaptively applied to purify the potential minutiae.

#### 15.2.1.1  *Offline Learning of Feature Extraction Masks*

A mask is a 2D filter that is concerned with detecting a minutia. Since a minutia can be an endpoint or a bifurcation, two masks are to be learned, one for each kind of feature. For simplicity, we use endpoints as the example to explain our learning approach. The mask for bifurcations is learned by following a similar process.

Figure 15.2 shows an ideal endpoint mask $T$ that consists of two submasks, $T_r$ (length $L_r$) and $T_g$ (length $L_g$), which denote the mask for ridge and gap, respectively. For simplicity, we assume $L_r = L_g$. $H$ and $L$ are the height and the length of the mask $T$, and $L = L_r + L_g$. The values of each pixel in $T_r$ and $T_g$ are 1 and 0, respectively. Suppose (a) a ridge end $E$ in a binary fingerprint is as ideal as the ideal mask $T$, (b) the local orientation at the ridge end is $\theta_l$, (c) the correlations between the mask $T$ and the ideal ridge end $E$ with the orientation $\theta_l$ and $\theta_l + \pi$ are $f_{\theta_l}$ and $f_{\theta_l+\pi}$, respectively, and (d) the difference between $f_{\theta_l}$ and $f_{\theta_l+\pi}$ is $\Delta_{\theta_l}$, that is,

$$\Delta_{\theta_l} = f_{\theta_l} - f_{\theta_l+\pi} \qquad (15.1)$$

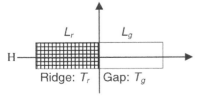

**Figure 15.2.**    Illustration of an ideal endpoint mask $T$.

where $f_{\theta_l} = \sum_{(h,l) \in (T \cap E_{\theta_l})} \{T(h,l) \times E_{\theta_l}(h,l)\}$ and $E_{\theta_l}(h,l)$ is the ridge with orientation $\theta_l$ and the mask $T(h,l)$ is applied along the ridge.

**Training Data.** Suppose (a) examples of endpoints and bifurcations are obtained from $M$ fingerprint images $FI_k$, where $k = 1,2,\ldots,M$; (b) in the $k$th fingerprint image $FI_k$, there are $N_k$ feature locations $(x_{k,i}, y_{k,i})$, where $i = 1,2,3,\ldots,N_k$; (c) in the local area around $(x_{k,i}, y_{k,i})$, $I_{k,i}(m,n)$ is the gray-scale value at pixel $(m,n)$ of the image $FI_k$, where $x_{k,i} - d_1 \leq m \leq x_{k,i} + d_1$, $y_{k,i} - d_2 \leq n \leq y_{k,i} + d_2$, $d_1$ and $d_2$ are constants; and (d) $G = \{(x_{k,i}, y_{k,i})\}$. Then, for each pixel in $G$, we carry out the following steps: (1) Estimate the local orientation $\theta_{k,i}$ at pixel $(x_{k,i}, y_{k,i})$ in the local area; (2) adaptively smooth $I_{k,i}(m,n)$ in the local area; (3) adaptively binarize $I_{k,i}(m,n)$ in the local area. The details of these steps are the same as those in the run-time minutiae extraction, which are discussed in Section 15.2.1.2.

**Optimzation for Feature Extracton Masks Learning.** Suppose (a) the mask is $T(h,l)$, where $1 \leq h \leq H$, $1 \leq l \leq L$, and $H = 2d_1 + 1$ and $L = 2d_2 + 1$; (b) $B_{k,i}(h,l)$ is the binary image of $I_{k,i}(m,n)$; and (c) $B^{\theta_{k,i}}{}_{k,i}(h,l)$ is the rotated binary image of $B_{k,i}(h,l)$, rotation angle is $\theta_{k,i}$, which is the local orientation at pixel $(x_{k,i}, y_{k,i})$. According to Eq. (15.1), the objective of learning algorithm can be defined as [11]

$$\arg \max_T \left\{ \sum_{k=1}^{M} \sum_{i=1}^{N_k} \sum_{h=1}^{H} \sum_{l=1}^{L} \left[ T(h,l) \times Q_{k,i}(h,l) \right] \right\}, \tag{15.2}$$

where $Q_{k,i}(h,l) = B_{k,i}^{\theta_{k,i}}(h,l) - B_{k,i}^{\theta_{k,i}}(h, L-l)$. If we normalize the mask's energy to one—that is, $\sum_{h=1}^{H} \sum_{l=1}^{L} T^2(h,l) = 1$—we can solve the optimization problem with Lagrange's method. Let

$$q(h,l) = \sum_{k=1}^{M} \sum_{i=1}^{N_k} Q_{k,i}(h,l). \tag{15.3}$$

Then, the optimal solution for the mask is

$$T(h,l) = \frac{q(h,l)}{\sqrt{\sum_{h=1}^{H} \sum_{l=1}^{L} q^2(h,l)}}. \tag{15.4}$$

### 15.2.1.2  Run-Time Feature Extraction

The steps are summarized below:

**Remove Background.** Since a fingerprint image usually includes some background that does not have any useful information, it is desired to eliminate it. We split an fingerprint into $16 \times 16$ blocks and compute the mean $\mu_s$ of the gray-scale value of the pixels in each block. If the mean $\mu_s$ is greater than $\delta_s$ ($\delta_s = 150$), then the block belongs to background.

**Compute Local Orientation.** The input fingerprint is first smoothed using a $5 \times 5$ Gaussian filter of $\mu = 0$ and $\sigma = 1$. Sobel operators are then applied to the smoothed image to estimate the gradient magnitude. After that, the fingerprint is split into $m \times m$ blocks ($m = 16$) with 4 pixels overlap. For each block, the local orientation $\theta$ is obtained using a mean square error (*MSE*) criterion [12].

**Adaptively Smooth Image.** The fingerprint obtained after background removal is adaptively smoothed using guidance from the local orientation. The purpose of this processing is to eliminate most fine details such as islands and pores. We perform uniform smoothing along the local ridge orientation and Gaussian smoothing normal to it. The kernel of the smoothing filter is the normalized product of a $5 \times 1$ uniform kernel and a $1 \times 3$ Gaussian kernel of $\mu = 0$ and $\sigma = 1$. Possible orientations of the smoothing filters are discretized into 16 values. An appropriate filter is selected according to the local orientation and applied to each pixel.

**Adaptively Binarize and Thin Image.** The smoothed fingerprint is split into $16 \times 16$ blocks with 8 pixels overlap. For each block, we perform histogram equalization and binarize the block by a threshold. Thinned ridges are obtained by thinning the binary image.

**Find Potential Minutiae.** The initial potential minutiae are selected by crossing number (CN) at each pixel in the thinned image. Generally, initial potential minutiae are very noisy because of binarization, thinning, and error in estimating local orientation. Two simple criteria we use to filter the initial potential minutiae are as follows: (a) In a small local area, if an endpoint and a bifurcation are chosen as the initial potential minutiae, then ignore both of them; (b) in a small local area, if more than one endpoint or one bifurcation are chosen as the initial potential minutiae, then ignore all these minutiae. The result is a relatively good set of potential minutiae.

**Adaptively Apply Feature Extraction Mask.** At this step, the learned masks are adaptively applied to the potential minutia locations obtained above. Suppose the local orientation at a potential minutia location is $\theta$, then we rotate the learned mask by $\theta$ and compute the difference in correlation using Eq. (15.1). In order to compensate for the error in estimating the local orientation, the correlations of the fingerprint are computed with five masks, which are the learned masks rotated with $\theta$, $\theta \pm 5°$ and $\theta \pm 10°$. The largest of these values is taken as the correlation at this location. (a) Let the number of potential minutiae in an image be $N_a$; (b) let the correlation of potential minutiae be $V = \{v_i\}$, where $i = 1, 2, 3, \ldots, N_a$; (c) let the mean and the standard deviation of $V$ be $\mu_v$ and $\sigma_v$, respectively; (d) let $k_r$ be a constant (taken as 1 for all the experiments in this chapter) for adjusting the threshold of rejecting false minutiae. If $v_i > (\mu_v + k_r \times \sigma_v)$, we choose the $i$th potential minutia as a true minutia, otherwise it is a false minutia.

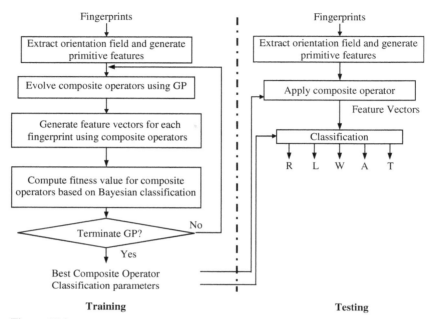

**Figure 15.3.** Block diagram of the classification approach.

## 15.2.2 Classification

Figure 15.3 shows the diagram of our classification approach using genetic programming (GP) [9, 3, 14]. During training, GP is used to generate *composite operators*, which can be viewed as a selected combination of primitive operations applied to the primitive features generated from the original orientation field. Features are computed wherever *feature generation operators* (see below) are used. These features are used to form a *feature vector* that represents a particular fingerprint image, and it is used for subsequent fingerprint classification. A Bayesian classifier is used for classification. Fitness value is computed based on the classification result and is used for evolving GP. During testing, composite operators are applied to generate feature vectors.

The individuals in our GP-based learning approach are composite operators represented by binary trees whose internal nodes represent the prespecified primitive operators and leaf nodes represent the primitive feature images. The major design considerations are explained in the following:

**The Set of Terminals.** For a fingerprint, we can estimate the orientation field [8]. The block size is $m = 32$ in our classification experiments, and $\theta \in [0, 180]$ and is measured in clockwise direction. The set of terminals used in this chapter are called primitive features, which are generated from the orientation field. Primitive features used in our experiments are: (1) original orientation image; (2) mean, standard deviation, min, max, and median images obtained by applying $3 \times 3$ and $5 \times 5$ filters on orientation image; (3) edge images obtained by applying sobel filters along horizontal and vertical directions on orientation image; (4) binary image obtained by thresholding the orientation image with a threshold of 90; and (5) images obtained by applying sine and cosine operations on the orientation image. These 16 images are input to the composite operators. GP determines which operations are applied on them and how to combine the results.

**The Set of Primitive Operators.** A primitive operator takes one or two input images, performs a primitive operation on them, and outputs a resultant image. Suppose (1) A and B are images of the same size and $c$ is a constant; and (2) for operators, which take two images as input, the operations are performed on the pixel-by-pixel basis. Currently, there are two kinds of primitive operators in our approach: *computation operators* and *feature generation operators*, which are described in references 9 and 13. For computation operators, the output is an image, that is generated by applying the corresponding operations on the input image. However, for feature generation operators, the output includes an image and a real number or vector. The output image is the same as the input image and is passed as the input image to the next node in the composite operator. The size of the feature vectors depends on the number and kind of the feature generation operators.

**Generation of New Composite Operator.** The initial population of the composite operators, represented as binary trees, is randomly generated. The search by GP is done by performing reproduction, crossover, and mutation operations. The reproduction operation used in our approach is the tournament selection. To perform crossover, two composite operators are selected based on their fitness values. One internal node in each of these two parents is randomly selected, and the two subtrees with these two nodes as root are exchanged between the parents. Once a composite operator is selected to perform mutation operation, an internal node of the binary tree representing this operator is randomly selected, and the subtree rooted at this node is replaced by another randomly generated binary tree. The resulting new binary tree replaces the old one in the population. We use *steady-state* GP [9] in our experiments.

**The Fitness Measure.** During training, at every generation for each composite operator proposed by GP, we estimate the probability distribution function (PDF) of the feature vectors for each class using all the available features. Suppose the feature vectors for each class have a normal distribution, $v_{i,j}$, where $i = 1, 2, 3, 4, 5$ and $j = 1, 2, \ldots, n_i$; $n_i$ is the number of feature vectors in the training for class $i$, $\omega_i$. Then, for each $i$, we estimate the mean $\mu_i$ and covariance matrix $\sum_i$ by all $v_{i,j}$, and the PDF of $\omega_i$ is obtained. A Bayesian classifier is used for classification. The percentage of correct classification (PCC) is taken as the fitness value of the composite operator: *Fitness value* $= \frac{n_c}{n_s} \times 100\%$, where $n_c$ is the number of correctly classified fingerprints in the training set and $n_s$ is the size of the training set.

**Parameters and Termination.** The key parameters are the population size, the number of generations, the crossover rate, and the mutation rate. The GP stops whenever it finishes the prespecified number of generations.

## 15.2.3  Indexing

Our approach for fingerprint indexing is based on the use of triplets of minutiae and ridge counts. However, for identification, the indexing and verification in our approach are separated. First, we apply indexing techniques to find the top $N$ hypotheses, and then we apply a verification technique to select a hypothesis with the best match. The hypotheses are generated according to the number of corresponding triangles between two fingerprints. Top $N$ hypotheses, sorted in a descending order of the number of potential corresponding triangles, are the indexing results.

For indexing, we use features based on minutiae triplets [8] in conjunction with the constraints on the transformation to eliminate the false corresponding triangles. Figure 15.4 shows the block diagram of our indexing approach. During the offline processing, the features of each template fingerprint are computed and used to construct the indexing space function $H(\alpha_{min}, \alpha_{med}, \phi, \eta, \lambda, \chi, \xi)$ [8].

- Angles $\alpha_{min}$ and $\alpha_{med}$. $\alpha_i$'s are the three angles in a triplet, where $i = 1, 2, 3$. $\alpha_{min} = \min\{\alpha_i\}$, $\alpha_{max} = \max\{\alpha_i\}$, $\alpha_{med} = 180° - \alpha_{min} - \alpha_{max}$.
- Triangle handedness $\phi$. Let $Z_i = x_i + jy_i$ be the complex number corresponding to the location $(x_i, y_i)$ of point $P_i$, $i = 1, 2, 3$. Define $Z_{21} = Z_2 - Z_1$, $Z_{32} = Z_3 - Z_2$, and $Z_{13} = Z_1 - Z_3$. Let triangle handedness $\phi = \mathrm{sign}(Z_{21} \times Z_{32})$. Points $P_1$, $P_2$, and $P_3$ are noncolinear points, so $\phi = 1$ or $-1$.

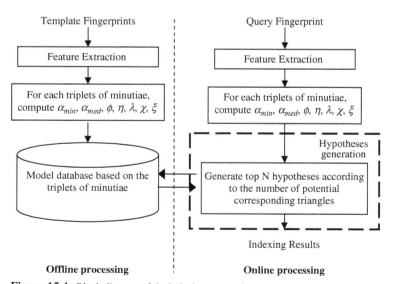

**Figure 15.4.** Block diagram of the indexing approach.

- Triangle direction $\eta$. We search the minutiae in the image from top to bottom and left to right. If a minutiae is the start point of the ridge, then $\nu = 1$; otherwise $\nu = 0$. Let $\eta = 4\nu_1 + 2\nu_2 + \nu_3$, where $\nu_i$ is $\nu$ value of point $P_i$, $i = 1, 2, 3$ and $0 \le \eta \le 7$.
- Maximum side $\lambda$. Let $\lambda = \max\{L_i\}$, where $L_1 = |Z_{21}|$, $L_2 = |Z_{32}|$, and $L_3 = |Z_{13}|$.
- Minutiae density $\chi$. In a local area ($32 \times 32$ pixels) centered at the minutiae $P_i$. If there exists $\chi_i$ minutiae, then the minutiae density for $P_i$ is $\chi_i$. Minutiae density $\chi$ is a 3D vector consisting of all $\chi_i$.
- Ridge counts $\xi$. Let $\xi_1$, $\xi_2$, and $\xi_3$ be the ridge counts of sides $P_1P_2$, $P_2P_3$, and $P_3P_1$, respectively. Then, $\xi$ is a 3D vector consisting of all $\xi_i$.

During the online processing, we compute the features for the query fingerprint and use them to search the indexing space $H(\alpha_{\min}, \alpha_{\text{med}}, \phi, \eta, \lambda, \chi, \xi)$. If the feature values of two triangles, which are from two different fingerprints, are within some error tolerance, then they are potential corresponding triangles. The criteria are: $|\alpha'_{\min} - \alpha''_{\min}| \le T_{\alpha_{\min}}$, $|\alpha'_{\text{med}} - \alpha''_{\text{med}}| \le T_{\alpha_{\text{med}}}$, $\phi' = \phi''$, $\eta' = \eta''$, $|\lambda' - \lambda''| \le T_\lambda$, $|\chi'_i - \chi''_i| \le T_\chi$, $|\xi'_i - \xi''_i| \le T_\xi$, $i = 1, 2, 3$, where $(\alpha'_{\min}, \alpha'_{\text{med}}, \phi', \eta', \lambda', \chi'_i, \xi'_i)$ and $(\alpha''_{\min}, \alpha''_{\text{med}}, \phi'', \eta'', \lambda'', \chi''_i, \xi''_i)$ are the local properties of the triangle in different fingerprints; $T_{\alpha_{\min}}$, $T_{\alpha_{\text{med}}}$, $T_\lambda$, $T_\chi$, and $T_\zeta$ are thresholds to deal with the local distortions.

## 15.2.4 Verification

Verification follows classification and indexing. It consists of the following two steps: (a) Use local information to estimate transformation between potential corresponding triangles and (b) use global information to eliminate false corresponding triangles and compute matching score. For indexing, verification is simple, since after indexing, for each hypothesis, we know the potential corresponding triangles and we may use this information in the verification directly. However, for classification, we only know the class information. So, we have to find the potential corresponding triangles between the query fingerprint and each template fingerprint that belongs to the same class.

**Step 1. Estimate Transformation Between Potential Corresponding Triangles.** Suppose the sets of minutiae in the template and the query fingerprints are $\{(t_{n,1}, t_{n,2})\}$ and $\{(q_{m,1}, q_{m,2})\}$ respectively, where $n = 1, 2, 3, \ldots, N$, $m = 1$, $2, 3, \ldots, M$. The number of minutiae in the template and the query fingerprints are $N$ and $M$, respectively. Let $\Delta_t$ and $\Delta_q$ be two potential corresponding triangles in the template and the query fingerprints, respectively. The coordinates of the vertices of $\Delta_t$ and $\Delta_q$ are $(x_{i,1}, x_{i,2})$ and $(y_{i,1}, y_{i,2})$, respectively, and $i = 1, 2, 3$. Suppose $X_i = [x_{i,1} \quad x_{i,2}]^T$, $Y_i = [y_{i,1} \quad y_{i,2}]^T$ and that the transformation $Y_i = F(X_i)$ can be expressed as

$$Y_i = s \cdot R \cdot X_i + T, \tag{15.5}$$

where $s$ is the scaling factor, $R$ is the rotation matrix with $\theta$ as the angle of rotation in counter clockwise direction between two fingerprints, and $T = [t_1 \quad t_2]^T$ is the vector of translation.

There are two possible approaches: Least squares minimization (LSM) over all hypothesized triangles correspondences or over each of the triangle pair. We prefer the second alternative since it may allow better distortion tolerance on different parts of the fingerprint. We estimate the transformation parameters by minimizing error $\varepsilon^2$, which is the sum of the squared distances between the transformed template points and their corresponding query points. That is,

$$\text{error} = \underset{(\hat{s},\hat{R},\hat{T})}{\arg \min} \{\varepsilon^2\} \qquad (15.6)$$

where $\varepsilon^2 = \sum_{i=1}^{3} ||Y_i - (\hat{s} \cdot \hat{R} \cdot X_i + \hat{T})||^2$ and $||V||$ is the $L_2$ norm of vector $V$. The solution of Eq. (15.6) is

$$\hat{\theta} = \arctan\left(\frac{B}{A}\right), \qquad \hat{s} = \frac{\sum\limits_{i=1}^{3}\{(X_i - \overline{X})' \hat{R}'(Y_i - \overline{Y})\}}{\sum\limits_{i=1}^{3}\{(X_i - \overline{X})'(Y_i - \overline{Y})\}}, \qquad \hat{T} = \overline{Y} - \hat{s}\cdot\hat{R}\cdot\overline{X},$$

where

$$A = \sum_{i=1}^{3}\{(\overline{x}_1 - x_{i,1})(y_{i,1} - \overline{y}_1) + (\overline{x}_2 - x_{i,2})(y_{i,2} - \overline{y}_2)\},$$

$$B = \sum_{i=1}^{3}\{(\overline{x}_1 - x_{i,1})(y_{i,2} - \overline{y}_2) - (\overline{x}_2 - x_{i,2})(y_{i,1} - \overline{y}_1),\}$$

$$\overline{X} = \begin{bmatrix} \overline{x}_1 \\ \overline{x}_2 \end{bmatrix} = \sum_{i=1}^{3} \overline{X}_i, \quad \overline{Y} = \begin{bmatrix} \overline{y}_1 \\ \overline{y}_2 \end{bmatrix} = \sum_{i=1}^{3} \overline{Y}_i, \quad \hat{R} = \begin{bmatrix} \cos\hat{\theta} & -\sin\hat{\theta} \\ \sin\hat{\theta} & \cos\hat{\theta} \end{bmatrix}, \quad \hat{T} = \begin{bmatrix} \hat{t}_1 \\ \hat{t}_2 \end{bmatrix}.$$

If $\hat{s}$, $\hat{\theta}$, $\hat{t}_1$, and $\hat{t}_2$ are within limits, then we take them as the parameters of the transformation between two potential corresponding triangles $\Delta_t$ and $\Delta_q$. Otherwise, they are false correspondences.

## Step 2. Eliminate False Corresponding Triangles and Compute Match Score.
Based on the above transformation $\hat{F}$ $(\hat{s}, \hat{\theta}, \hat{t}_1, \hat{t}_2)$, $\forall j, j = 1, 2, 3,$ ..., $N$, we compute:

$$d = \underset{k}{\arg \min} \left\{ \left| \hat{F}\left(\begin{bmatrix} t_{j,1} \\ t_{j,2} \end{bmatrix}\right) - \begin{bmatrix} q_{k,1} \\ q_{k,2} \end{bmatrix} \right| \right\}.$$

If $d$ is less than a threshold $T_d$, then we define the points $[t_{j,1}, t_{j,2}]'$ and $[q_{k,1}, q_{k,2}]'$ are corresponding points. If the number of corresponding points based on $\hat{F}(\hat{s}, \hat{\theta}, \hat{t}_1, \hat{t}_2)$ is greater than a threshold $T_n$, then we define $\Delta_t$ and $\Delta_q$ as the *corresponding triangles* between the template and the query fingerprints. The final identification score is the number of corresponding triangles between the query and template fingerprints.

Endpoint:
(Black ridge)

Bifurcation:
(White ridge)

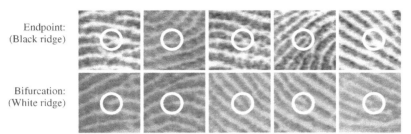

**Figure 15.5.** Examples of training data: Endpoint (**first row**) and bifurcation (**second row**).

## 15.3 EXPERIMENTAL RESULTS

NIST Special Database 4 (NIST-4) [6] with 2000 pairs of fingerprints is used in our experiments, where each pair is a different impression of the same finger. The size of the fingerprint images is $480 \times 512$ pixels with a resolution of 500 DPI. The fingerprint is coded as an $f$ or $s$ followed by six numbers, which means the fingerprint image is the first or second impression of certain finger.

### 15.3.1 Learning Feature Extraction Mask

Training data are manually obtained from 30 fingerprints based on the quality and the location of the minutiae. There are 85 endpoints and 86 bifurcations that are obtained from these 30 images. Figure 15.5 shows five examples of the training data for endpoints and bifurcations (note that each image contains at least one minutia). The masks for endpoint and bifurcation are learned from these binarized examples. Figure 15.6 shows the learned masks that are used to extract minutiae. Note that in order to show the structure of the masks clearly, the masks are normalized such that the minimum and maximum values map to 0 and 1, respectively. Figure 15.7 shows the learned masks superimposed on the examples in Figure 15.5.

**Evaluation by Goodness Value.** Suppose $M_e = \{e_i, i = 1, 2, 3, \ldots, n\}$ is the set of $n$ minutiae extracted by a feature extraction algorithm and $M_g = \{g_j, j = 1, 2, 3, \ldots, m\}$ is the set of $m$ minutiae extracted by an expert in a fingerprint. We define the following terms: (1) *Matched minutiae:* If minutia $e_i$ is located in an uncertainty

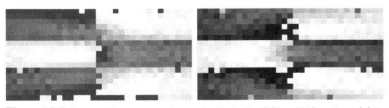

**Figure 15.6.** Learned feature extraction masks: Endpoint (**left**) and bifurcation (**right**).

Endpoint:

Bifurcation:

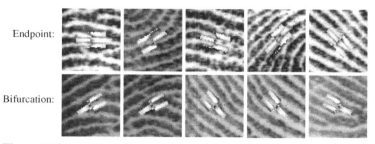

**Figure 15.7.** Learned feature extraction masks superimposed on examples in Figure 15.5.

region centered around minutia $g_j$, $e_i$ and $g_j$ are matched minutiae. (2) *Occluded minutia:* If minutia $g_j$ is not in an uncertainty region of any minutia $e_i$, then $g_j$ is an occluded minutia. (3) *Clutter minutia:* If $e_i$ is not in an uncertainty region of any minutia $g_j$, then $e_i$ is a clutter minutia.

In our experiments, the size of the uncertainty region is $8 \times 8$. goodness value (GV) of extracted feature is defined as:

$$GV = \frac{n_m}{n_m + n_o + n_c},$$

where $n_m$, $n_o$, and $n_c$ are the number of matched, occluded, and clutter minutiae, respectively. We choose 400 pairs of images from the first 1000 pairs of images in NIST-4. These images are chosen visually based on the size of overlapped areas between two images, the number of scars, translation, rotation and scale between images. Figure 15.8 shows goodness value of 15 test fingerprints images (from NIST-4 database). From this figure, we find that the learned masks work better than the fixed masks described in Bhanu et al. [15]. For example, mean of GV on these 15 images is 0.66 for learned masks, and 0.57 for fixed masks, which amounts to an improvement of 15.7%.

**Evaluation by Indexing Performance.** A query fingerprint, which has a corresponding fingerprint in the database, is said to be correctly indexed if it has enough corresponding triangles in the model database and the correct corresponding fingerprint appears in a short list of hypotheses obtained by the indexing approach. We define correct index power (CIP) as

$$CIP = \frac{N_{ci}}{N_d} \times 100\%,$$

where $N_{ci}$ is the number of correctly indexed fingerprints and $N_d$ is the number of images in the database. Figure 15.9 shows the comparison of CIP for fixed and learned masks. We observe that the performance of the learned masks is better than that of the fixed masks. CIP for the top 1 hypothesis increases by 2.8%, and by 6.5% and 5.2% when we consider the top 5 and top 10 hypotheses, respectively. Using the fixed masks, the CIP reaches 100% only when we consider the top 26 hypotheses. For learned masks, however, we only need to consider top 10 hypotheses.

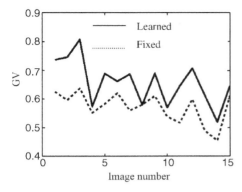

**Figure 15.8.**    Goodness value of test fingerprints.

## 15.3.2    Classification Results

We use the first 1000 pairs of fingerprints for training. In order to reduce the effect of overfitting, we use only the first 500 pairs to estimate the parameters for each class and use the entire training set to validate the training results. Since we want to compare the results of classification and indexing, we only test the second impression of the second 1000 pairs of fingerprints. The first impressions of the second 1000 pairs of fingerprints are used as templates in verification. The parameters in our experiments are: maximum size of composite operator 150, population size 100, mutation rate 0.05, crossover rate 0.6, and number of generation 100.

We performed the experiments 10 times and took the best result as the learned composite operator. Table 15.1 shows the confusion matrix of our testing results of the second 1000 pairs of fingerprint in NIST-4. The images where tented arch is confused with arch are s1037_06, s1299_07, s1486_03, s1711_02, s1745_09, and s1759_09. The images where arch is confused with tented arch are s1568_08, s1948_05, s1956_10, and s1998_07. Figure 15.10 shows these 10 images where tented arch and arch are confused. Note that because of bad quality, the ground truths of some fingerprints

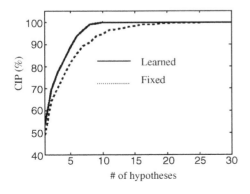

**Figure 15.9.**    Comparison of experimental results.

**Table 15.1.** Confusion Matrix for Five-Class Classifications

| True Class | Assigned Class | | | | |
|---|---|---|---|---|---|
| | R | L | W | A | T |
| R | **180** | 5 | 1 | 1 | 14 |
| L | 1 | **188** | 3 | 3 | 2 |
| W | 6 | 6 | **187** | 0 | 1 |
| A | 2 | 1 | 0 | **208** | 4 |
| T | 5 | 10 | 2 | 6 | **172** |

provided by NIST-4 contain two classes, for example, the ground-truth labels of f0008_10 include class T and L. As other researchers did in their experiments, we only use the first ground-truth label to estimate the parameters of the classifier. However, in testing, we use all the ground truth labels and consider a test as correctly classified if the output of the system matches to one of the ground truths. However, if the output of the system does not match any one of them, then we consider it as two incorrect classifications and each of them has an entry in the confusion matrix. Note that some published research work, such as reference [4], only has one entry in the confusion matrix when the input fingerprint has two ground truths and the classification result is incorrect, which inevitably reduces the error rate. Based on the confusion matrix in Table 15.1, the PCC is 92.8% for five-class classification. Considering that we have not rejected any fingerprints from NIST-4, our classification results are excellent [13].

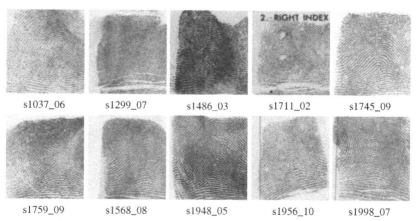

s1037_06    s1299_07    s1486_03    s1711_02    s1745_09

s1759_09    s1568_08    s1948_05    s1956_10    s1998_07

**Figure 15.10.** NIST-4 database images where tented arch and arch are confused. For the first six images (from left to right and top to bottom), the ground-truth label is tented arch and they are classified as arch. For the last four images, the ground truth is arch and they are classified as tented arch.

### 15.3.3  Indexing Results

In order to compare the results between indexing and classification, we only do indexing experiments on the second impressions of the second 1000 pairs of fingerprints. The parameters used in our experiments are: $T_{\alpha_{min}} = 2°$, $T_{\alpha_{med}} = 2°$, $T_\lambda = 20$, $T_\chi = 2$, $T_\zeta = 2$. Figure 15.11 shows the correct indexing power (CIP). We observe that CIP increases as $p$, the percentage of the database searched, increases. The CIP are 83.3%, 88.1%, 91.1%, and 92.6%, and $p$ are 5%, 10%, 15%, and 20%, respectively. As $p$ reached about 60%, the relation between CIP and $p$ becomes linear.

### 15.3.4  Identification Results

For classification, since the number of classes in fingerprint is small, we have to check more hypotheses in verification. For example, the classification result of our approach is one of the best results reported in published papers, however, we can only classify fingerprints into five classes. Since each class is uniformly distributed in NIST-4, after classification, about 200 hypotheses need to be considered in verification. And, this number cannot be tuned. As for indexing, since CIP varies according to the size of the search space, we have different performances of identification by indexing approach, depending on the percentage of the database that is searched. Conceptually, each fingerprint as a query is verified against all the stored fingerprint templates. That is 1,000,000 verifications. Among them, 999,000 verifications are estimating false acceptance rate (FAR) and 1000 verifications are for estimating genuine acceptance rate (GAR). The receiver operating characteristic (ROC) curve is defined as the plot of GAR against FAR. Based on different CIP, we can have different ROCs for identification results for the indexing-based approach and only one ROC for the classification-based approach. The parameters used in the verification step are: threshold to constrain scaling factor $\hat{s}$, $0.85 < \hat{s} < 1.15$; threshold to constrain rotation angle $\hat{\theta}$, $-30° < \hat{\theta} < 30°$; thresholds to constrain translations $\hat{t}_1$ and $\hat{t}_2$, $\left|\hat{t}_1\right| < 150$ and

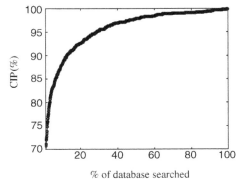

**Figure 15.11.**   Indexing performance.

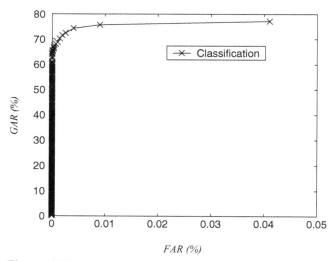

**Figure 15.12.** Identification results using classification based approach.

$|\hat{t}_2| < 100$; threshold to find the corresponding points, $T_d = 12$; threshold to find the corresponding triangles, $T_n = 8$.

Figures 15.12 and 15.13 show identification results based on classification and indexing, respectively. Note that GAR cannot reach 100.0%. One important reason is that bad-quality images do not provide enough similarity information to be used in verification, and the NIST-4 database is a very difficult database. Using the

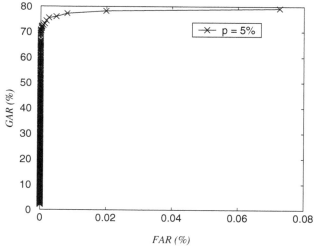

**Figure 15.13.** Identification results using indexing based approach.

classification-based approach, GAR is 77.2% when FAR is $4.1 \times 10^{-2}$%, while using the indexing-based approach with $p = 5$%, GAR is 77.2% and FAR is $8.0 \times 10^{-3}$%. It shows that in order to achieve similar GAR in identification, we only need to search 5% of the database by indexing-based approach for identification, while classification-based approach for identification may need to search 20% of the entire search space. FAR for indexing-based approach is much less than that for the classification-based approach. The classes R, L, W, A, and T are uniformly distributed in NIST-4. However, in nature, the frequencies of their occurrence are 31.7%, 33.8%, 27.9%, 3.7%, and 2.9%, respectively. So, using the classification-based approach the search space that needs to be searched will be more than 30.0%, since there are fewer fingerprints that belong to A and T classes in nature than to other classes.

## 15.4  CONCLUSIONS

In this chapter, we compared the performance of two approaches for identification. One is the traditional approach that first classifies a fingerprint into one of the five classes (R, L, W, A, T) and then performs verification. The alternative approach is based on indexing followed by verification. Using state of the art highly competitive approaches for classification, indexing, and verification, we compared the performance of the two approaches for identification using the NIST-4 fingerprint database. We found that the indexing technique performs better considering the size of search space (5% versus 20%) that needs to be examined. Also, for the same GAR (77.2%) the FAR performance ($8.0 \times 10^{-3}$% versus $4.1 \times 10^{-2}$%) of indexing-based approach is lower. Thus, the indexing based approach provides a potential alternative to the traditional classification-based approach commonly used for fingerprint identification. Also it is possible to use the indexing approach within each of the classes after the classification has been done. This will expedite the identification performance of a classification-based approach.

## REFERENCES

1. X. Tan, B. Bhanu, and Y. Lin, Fingerprint identification: classification vs. Indexing, in *IEEE International Conference on Advanced Video and Signal-Based Surveillance*, Miami, FL, July 21–22, 2003, pp. 151–156.
2. K. Karu and A. K. Jain, Fingerprint classification, *Pattern Recognit.* **29**(3):389–404, 1996.
3. R. Cappelli, A. Lumini, D. Maio, and D. Maltoni, Fingerprint classification by directional image partitioning, *IEEE Trans. Pattern Anal. Mach. Intell.* **21**(5):402–421, 1999.
4. R. Cappelli, D. Maio, and D. Maltoni, Fingerprint classification based on multi-space KL, in *Proceedings of the Workshop on Automatic identification Advances Technologies*, 1999, pp. 117–120.
5. Y. Yao, G. L. Marcialis, M. Pontil, P. Frasconi, and F. Roli, Combining flat and structured representations for fingerprint classification with recursive neural networks and support vector machines, *Pattern Recognit.* **36**(2):397–406, 2003.
6. C. I. Watson and C. L. Wilson, NIST special database 4, fingerprint database, U.S. National Institute of Standards and Technology, 1992.
7. R. S. Germain, A. Califano, and S. Colville, Fingerprint matching using transformation parameter clustering, *IEEE Comput. Sci. and Eng.* **4**(4):42–49, 1997.

8. B. Bhanu and X. Tan, Fingerprint indexing based on novel features of minutiae triplets, *IEEE Trans. Pattern Anal. Mach. Intell.* **25**(5):616–622, 2003.

9. X. Tan, B. Bhanu and, Y. Lin, Learning composite operators for fingerprint classification, *Proceeding of the International Conference on Audio- and Video-Based Biometric Person Authentication*, June 2003, pp. 318–326.

10. D. Maltoni, D. Maio, A. K. Jain, and S. Prabhakar, *Handbook of Fingerprint Recognition*, Springer, Berlin, 2003.

11. B. Bhanu and X. Tan, Learned templates for feature extraction in fingerprint images, *Proc. IEEE Conf. Comput. Vis. Pattern Recognit.* **2**:591–596, 2001.

12. A. M. Bazen and S. H. Gerez, Systematic methods for the computation of the directional fields and singular points of fingerprints, *IEEE Trans. Pattern Anal. Mach. Intell.* **24**(7):905–919, 2002.

13. X. Tan, B. Bhanu, and Y. Lin, Fingerprint classification based on learned features, *IEEE Trans. Systems, Man Cybern. Part C* (Special Issue on Biometrics) **35**(3):287–300, 2005.

14. B. Bhanu, Y. Lin, and K. Krawiec, *Evolutionary Synthesis of Pattern Recognition Systems*, Monograph in Computer Science, Springer, Berlin, 2006.

15. B. Bhanu, M. Boshra, and X. Tan, Logical templates for feature extraction in fingerprint images, *Proc. Int. Conf. Pattern Recognit.* **3**:850–854, 2000.

16. S. Prabhakar, A. K. Jain, and S. Pankanti, Learning fingerprint minutiae location and type, *Pattern Recognit.* **36**(8):1847–1857, 2003.

# Chapter 16

# Electrocardiogram (ECG) Biometric for Robust Identification and Secure Communication

**Francis Minhthang Bui, Foteini Agrafioti,
and Dimitrios Hatzinakos**

## 16.1 INTRODUCTION

As a medical diagnostic technique proposed by Willem Einthoven in the early 1900s, the electrocardiogram (ECG) has a relatively long and illustrious history. It has since been acknowledged as an indispensable tool in the detection and treatment of various cardiac disorders [1, 2]. More recently, the ECG has fulfilled a rather unlikely niche, as a purveyor of security and privacy in the form of a biometric [3, 4]. In this chapter, we examine the various implications and technical challenges of using the ECG as a biometric. Specifically, we survey and propose novel signal processing techniques that seek to not only establish the status of the ECG as an indisputable fixture in biometric research, but also reinforce its versatile utility, such as in alleviating the resource consumption in certain communication networks.

### 16.1.1 Security and Privacy Motivations

Security and privacy are intertwined issues that have long been of prime importance in society. It has even been suggested that the combination of security and privacy is

---

*Biometrics: Theory, Methods, and Applications.* Edited by Boulgouris, Plataniotis, and Micheli-Tzanakou
Copyright © 2010 the Institute of Electrical and Electronics Engineers, Inc.

tantamount to one of the cornerstones of democracy itself [5]. It is then perhaps no coincidence that we can trace the precursors of modern cryptography and steganography to as far back as—possibly even earlier than—Ancient Greece itself [6, 7], the birthplace of democracy. Methods for providing security have evolved tremendously and, to date, encompass a wide range of solutions, based mainly on number-theoretic problems [6, 8].

Despite the existence of various strong cryptographic algorithms, some with provable security or even perfect secrecy [8], the search for an applicable security solution seems to be perpetual. This is because, while a method may intrinsically demonstrate information-theoretic security, it may not be practical or suitable for a specific application. For instance, the computational requirements and the system assumptions may not be achievable in a particular scenario, due to resource scarcity or other practical issues.

## 16.1.2   Security and Privacy Solutions with Biometrics

In this context, the advent of biometric methods represents an encouraging watershed event, with the potential to deliver practical solutions to security and privacy. While certainly not a panacea, biometrics address many important issues, including cost effectiveness, user convenience, and good security.

On the other hand, biometrics differ rather significantly from conventional signals, being more noisy and variant. Despite these technical challenges, it is almost a unanimous consensus that biometrics will remain an important stakeholder in security solutions for the foreseeable future. This is because biometric systems have unique and advantageous properties, offering novelties not available with conventional password-based systems [5, 9].

In this chapter, biometric systems based on the electrocardiogram signals will be examined. The ECG biometric presents some specific difficulties, including baseline wandering and a requirement of accurate timing synchronization. At the same time, the ECG and other related cardiovascular signals have been found to be a unique class of biometrics that aptly fulfills the specific requirements of the so-called body sensor networks (BSN) [10–12].

## 16.1.3   Ethical Issues with Biometric Applications

In practice, the deployment of biometric systems has frequently encountered resistance, on the basis of user reluctance and distrust. A major goal of biometrics is to ultimately deliver user convenience, by eliminating the need to remember long passwords. But ironically, at least for the initial stages, the deployment of biometrics is inevitably disruptive and represents a major leap, since it imposes not only a technological shift, but also a psychological readjustment.

In many cases, the root problem can be ultimately linked to the responsible and ethical use of biometrics, as recorded by the acquisition and enrollment devices [5]. Moreover, for certain biometrics, such as the ECG, the original signals carry medical information about the user, with grave ethical repercussions [13, 14]. Traditionally, only physicians and qualified health-care providers have been given unrestricted access to these medical signals. Such personnel are charged with a serious duty; they are bound morally and legally by the doctor–patient confidentiality, as enunciated in the Hippocratic Oath [13, 14]. In a restricted medical environment, patient privacy is subject to high standards of human security. However, biometrics are envisioned to be much more widespread, to the extent that merely relying on human security quickly becomes a logistical predicament.

Therefore, when dealing with biometrics, a paradigm shift is needed. As noted in reference 5, a good biometric system should have built-in mechanisms to guarantee privacy and confidentiality. Such mechanisms should be robust enough to withstand certain human errors. Moreover, even in the case of data theft, no private user information should be revealed. As discussed later, these goals can be achieved using zero-knowledge hash functions [6, 8].

## 16.2 FUNDAMENTALS OF THE ELECTROCARDIOGRAM (ECG)

With the ECG being the focus of this chapter, it behooves us to first examine the fundamentals of this versatile and important class of cardiac signals.

### 16.2.1 Physiology of the ECG

ECG signals reflect the variations in electrical potential of the heart over time. The change in voltage is due to the action potentials of cardiac cells. The electrical activity is initiated when the sinoatrial (SA) node, the pacemaker of the heart, depolarizes. This electrical signal then travels rhythmically until it reaches the atrioventricular (AV) node, which is responsible for delaying the conduction rate, to properly pump blood from the atria into the ventricles.

Figure 16.1 shows the salient components of an ECG signal: the $P$ wave, the $QRS$ complex, and the $T$ wave, which together account for the sequential depolarization and repolarization of the heart. The $P$ wave describes the depolarization of the right and left atria. The amplitude of this wave is relatively small, because the atrial muscle mass is limited. The absence of a $P$ wave typically indicates ventricular ectopic focus. This wave usually has a positive polarity, with a duration of approximately 120 ms. In addition, its spectral content is limited to 10–15 Hz—that is, low frequencies.

The $QRS$ complex corresponds to the largest wave, since it represents the depolarization of the right and left ventricles, being the heart chambers with substantial mass. The duration of this complex is approximately 70–110 ms in a normal heartbeat. The anatomic characteristics of the $QRS$ complex depend on the origin of the pulse. Due to its steep slopes, the spectrum of a $QRS$ wave is higher compared to that of other ECG waves and is mostly concentrated in the interval of 10–40 Hz.

Finally, the $T$ wave depicts the ventricular repolarization. It has a smaller amplitude, compared to the $QRS$ complex, and is usually observed 300 ms after this larger

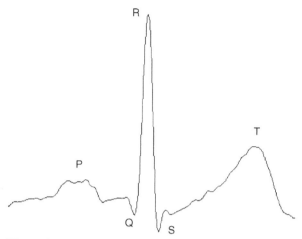

**Figure 16.1.** Main components of an ECG heartbeat.

complex. However, its precise position depends on the heart rate—for example, appearing closer to the $QRS$ waves at rapid heart rates.

The heart rate of a normal sinus rhythm is 60–100 beats/min (bpm). However, this is highly dependent on emotional factors, such as stress, anxiety, and shock, as well as on cardiovascular activities, such as running and exercising. The condition where the average heart rate is lower than the nominal value (of 60 bpm) is called sinus bradycardia; and when above, it is referred to as sinus tachycardia [1, 2].

## 16.2.2  ECG Signal Acquisition

One of the main problems in biometric signal processing is the high degree of noise and variations. In many cases, a reliable acquisition is only possible with sufficient knowledge of the spectral content, the dynamic range, and other characteristics not only of the desired signal components, but also of the noise sources involved. This is so that the appropriate filters and quantizers can be accordingly constructed to extract the desired signals, and reject the noise sources.

The previous section has highlighted the salient characteristics of ECG signal components. For instance, the $P$ wave is a lower-amplitude and lower-frequency signal, while the $QRS$ complex exhibits a larger amplitude and higher frequency variations. In addition, the following sources of noise and artifacts are relevant to ECG. The *baseline wander*, arguably one of most common artifacts, refers to a low-frequency interference in the ECG, which may be induced by cardiovascular activities. The amplitude change due to baseline wander can potentially exceed the QRS amplitude by several times, which can be highly problematic for accurate medical diagnoses based on the isoelectric line. While this distortion may exhibit higher frequencies (e.g., during strenuous exercise), its spectral content is typically limited to an interval below 1 Hz [2]. Thus, some type of low-pass filtering would be relevant to this scenario.

Another source of error is powerline interference, being 50 or 60 Hz depending on the geographical location, which occurs due to insufficient grounding or interferences from other equipments. Also present in practical ECG recordings are electrode motion artifacts, due to skin stretching which alters the impedance around the electrode. These artifacts are problematic since their spectral content, being 1–10 Hz, overlaps that of the desired signal components.

As well, there are inherent physiologically induced artifacts, namely, respiratory activity artifacts. The involved chest movements change the position of the heart and the lung conductivity, leading to not only variations in the heart rate, but also modifications of the beat morphology [2]. Clearly, as in medical applications, an ECG-based biometric system needs to take into account all these various sources of error, using the appropriate preprocessing—for example, filtering based on the specific spectral contents.

## 16.2.3  The ECG in Medical Settings

Even though the SA node is the primary pacemaker of the heart, depolarization can also be initiated by other areas with pacemaker potential—for example, by the autonomic foci: the atrial, junctional, and ventrical foci. But in such cases, the ECG may deviate from its normal healthy forms. Other conduction abnormalities may also cause disorders. For all these pathological conditions, collectively known as *arrhythmias*, the heart rhythms can become highly abnormal.

Several kinds of arrhythmias can be classified in ECG monitoring. The most commonly encountered types are the premature heart beats. These beats are not generated by the SA node, but by other cardiac cells. Depending on their origin, the geometrical characteristics of the resulting waveforms may or may not be altered. In addition, the presence of the $P$ wave is ambiguous. Two common types of premature beats are the *atrial premature contraction* (APC) and the *premature ventricular contraction* (PVC).

When multiple focal points within the atria are responsible for an impulse, atrial arrhythmias are observed. *Atrial tachycardia* and *atrial flutter* are some examples of this class of arrhythmias. For these arrhythmias, an abnormal or absent $P$ wave is found in the recorded ECG, revealing the location of the ectopic focus.

Arrhythmias originating in the ventricles are fatal rhythm disturbances that require immediate medical assistance, since they lead to cardiac arrest. Examples of these arrhythmias are the *ventricular tachycardia*, *ventricular fibrillation*, and *ventricular flutter*. In the worst case, the ventricles produce several electrical signals at such a rapid rate that the rest of the heart's mechanism cannot follow.

## 16.3  THE ECG AS A BIOMETRIC: A LITERATURE SURVEY

Biometrics are essentially signal features extracted from the human body for a number of purposes: identification, authentication, or providing network security

[3, 5, 9]. However, not every physiological or behavioral attribute is appropriate for biometric use. For instance, to be conducive to a biometric construction, the trait should be universal (present in all human beings) and yet distinct (unique for an individual) [9].

To date, the human features commonly used as biometrics comprise: fingerprint, iris, face, voice, gait, or even keystroke dynamics. By comparison, the ECG biometric represents a more recent development in biometric research. In this section, an overview of existing biometric methods and applications using the ECG will be presented.

## 16.3.1 ECG-Based Identification Using Fiducial Points

Many of the methods currently found in the ECG biometric literature can be categorized as fiducial techniques. Among the earliest works in the area is Biel et al.'s [15] proposal for a fiducial feature extraction algorithm, which demonstrated the feasibility of using ECG signals for human identification. A Siemens ECG device was used to record cardiovascular signals from 20 subjects. This apparatus was also employed for feature extraction. The feature space consisted of temporal and amplitude distances of specific heartbeat points. Further analysis was performed by analyzing the correlation matrix, for dimensionality reduction of feature vectors. A 100% subject identification rate was achieved with this methodology, for subjects of various ages.

Israel et al. [16] introduced an ECG-based identification system for temporal features extraction. According to these authors, when a subject arrives to the system to be identified, the input ECG was filtered to eliminate noise effects. The next step was to detect the peaks in the time domain by finding local maxima in regions surrounding each of the $P$, $R$, and $T$ complexes. A total of 15 time duration features were then extracted from each heartbeat. Wilks' Lamda was employed to select a set of characteristics from the feature space, followed by linear discriminant analysis for classification. The system achieved 100% subject and 81% heartbeat recognition rate for 29 subjects. In a later work by Israel et al. [17], a framework that fused face and ECG traits was reported. In this multimodal biometric method, the ECG signal analysis and feature extraction procedures are similar to those in reference 16.

Shen et al. [18] reported a two-stage framework for identity verification using one-lead ECG signals. During the first step, template matching was applied to compute the correlation coefficient among the $QRS$ complexes from the gallery set, which can be considered as candidates for a signal. A decision-based neural network (DBNN) was then used to finalize the verification from the possible candidates selected with template matching. This type of methodology achieved a verification rate of 95% for template matching, 80% for the DBNN, and 100% for integrating the two methods. The suggested methodology was extended by Shen [19] in a larger database, containing 168 healthy subjects. The highest identification rate achieved in that work was 95.3%.

Wang et al. [20] proposed an integration of analytic and appearance-based features from heartbeats. The fiducial points of ECG signals were detected in the preprocessing step, in order to to extract temporal and amplitude distances to form a feature vector. The classification performance demonstrated that even though amplitude features have discriminative ability, analytic features in general are not sufficient for identity recognition. The experimentation described in reference 20 involved extraction of appearance-based features with the help of either the principal component or linear discriminant analysis. When these two types of features were fused in a hierarchical scheme, a 100% subject and 98.9% heartbeat identification rates were achieved for 13 subjects.

Wübbeler et al. [21] addressed the issue of fluctuating anxiety states that affected the heart rate. Instead of extracting features from a heartbeat, the morphology of the *QRS* complex is utilized for feature extraction—this complex being less susceptible to rhythm variance [22]. The selected features included a two-dimensional heart vector, with embedded information from three leads, and the corresponding first and second temporal derivatives. When the method was tested on ECGs from 74 subjects, a 99% identification rates was achieved.

## 16.3.2 Nonfiducial Identification Methods Based on ECG

The detection of fiducial points increases the complexity of ECG-based applications. In addition, there are no definitive rules or methods for localizing the wave boundaries, especially in varying heart rates or heart anomalies. Motivated by these difficulties, various methods have been suggested for the nonfiducial feature extraction from ECGs. In general, the use of windowing techniques, as a precursor to the feature extraction, has been found to overcome several serious problems, due to pulse localization and synchronization, in fiducial methods.

Plataniotis et al. [23] were among the earliest to report a nonfiducial technique for extracting feature from ECG segments. The autocorrelation of nonoverlapping ECG windows was used as a source of discriminative information, followed by the discrete cosine transform for dimensionality reduction. Classification was carried out using two similarity measures, namely, the normalized Euclidean and the Gaussian log-likelihood distances. The method was tested on 14 subjects; and 100% subject and window recognition rates were achieved.

Wang et al. [24] demonstrated a systematic analysis of ECG signals for methodologies with and without fiducial points detection. A fiducial framework that combined analytic and appearance features was compared to a feature extraction technique from autocorrelated ECG windows. The proposed techniques were tested on two public data sets. It was shown that the nonfiducial methods can achieve high-recognition performance compared to the fiducial ones.

## 16.3.3 Network Security Using the ECG Biometric

The ECG biometric has also recently generated immense interest in the sensor networking research community. More specifically, it has delivered promising prospects for security in the so-called body sensor network (BSN) settings [10–12]. In this emerging area of research, the relevant ECG techniques ostensibly appear to be mere examples of fiducial methods. Indeed, the relevant ECG feature in a BSN is the so-called interpulse interval (IPI) sequence [3], which is a sequence of times between R–R intervals. In other words, it measures a sequence of times between heartbeats (similar to that in a tachogram), which is a fiducial characterization. However, as will be examined subsequently, the specific requirements for a BSN (e.g., with respect to simultaneous data acquisition) deviate significantly from those needed in standard fiducial methods. In some sense, while fiducial methods typically rely on the averaging (i.e., statistical ensemble) of values due to ECG features, it is the extraction of an instantaneous stochastic realization that is relevant to a BSN.

### 16.3.3.1  Body Sensor Network (BSN) Motivations

Representing a convergence of vast technological advances in medical instrumentation, wireless communications, and network security, among others, body sensor networks have the potential to dramatically alter the nature of medical measurements and patient monitoring. These networks, typically wireless [3, 11], consist of small sensors placed on various body locations, either noninvasively worn on or implanted in the body.

In a medical setting, which still requires scheduled visits, this BSN approach constitutes a giant leap, since it permits unsupervised and spontaneous measurements of various medical signals. The recorded data can then be transmitted, even in real-time via a mobile network, to the health-care provider as frequently as required for subsequent diagnoses. The spatiotemporal limitations in pervasive medical monitoring are effectively eliminated [3, 4, 10].

In a multimedia networking context, a BSN can also be conceived as a collection of wearable devices, including cell phones, headsets, handheld computers, and other multimedia devices [10, 25]. However, the incentive and urgency for inter-networking such multimedia devices may be less obvious and imminent (more on the convenience side), compared to those in medical scenarios (more on the necessity side).

What is evident, however, is that security needs to be given due consideration if BSNs are to be widely deployed. In both scenarios, potentially sensitive and confidential data, either medical or other personal information, are being transmitted, possibly relayed via multiple parties before reaching the final destination. Combined with the wireless broadcasting nature of the network, the threats of security compromises are very real and serious in a BSN.

### 16.3.3.2  BSN Structure

A mobile-health network topology, consisting of individual BSNs organized under several servers, is shown in Figure 16.2. Since a BSN is essentially a derivative of a sensor network, or more generally of an *ad hoc* network [25], it also suffers from the same nondefinitive system problem: The specific requirements in terms of system resources are typically not defined, until the particular *ad hoc* applications are

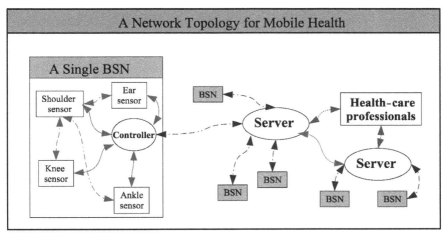

**Figure 16.2.** Model of a mobile health network, consisting of various body sensor networks.

known. Depending on the envisioned applications, the number of servers, sensors, and associated resources may vary significantly.

For the scenario considered in Figure 16.2, each BSN has a controller, which is a sensor node equipped with more advanced processing capabilities. Only the controller is destined to communicate directly with external devices. Therefore, while the individual sensors may or may not communicate with one another, they all need to communicate with the controller. Overall, this hierarchical arrangement allows for a scalable design, with more efficient resource utilization.

### 16.3.3.3  *Resource Constraints in a BSN*

According to the proposed prototypes and test beds found in the existing literature [4, 10–12], BSNs are envisioned to have computational and bandwidth resources on par with those found in the so-called microsensor networks [25, 26]. For example, the computational and storage capabilities of a BSN have been prototyped using UC Berkeley MICA2 motes [4], each of which provides an 8-MHz ATMega-128L microcontroller with 128 Kbytes of programmable flash and 4 KBytes of RAM. In fact, these motes may exceed the resources found in smaller BSN sensors. As such, to be safe, a proposed design should not overstep the capabilities offered by these prototype designs.

Energy is ultimately the limiting factor in a BSN. And according to studies assessing the energy dispensed per bit of information, it is found that the most expensive resource is the communication operation [3, 11, 12, 26, 27]. By comparison, the computational costs are typically much smaller. As such, only information bits that are truly necessary should be sent over the channel. This guideline has profound repercussions for the security protocols to be adopted in a BSN. It essentially rules out many conventional asymmetric cryptographic algorithms [6, 8]. In fact, as in a sensor network [28], a BSN cannot even handle the variables required for asymmetric cryptographic algorithms, let alone perform operations with them.

### 16.3.3.4  The ECG Biometric in a BSN

In order to address the described severe resource scarcity, the ECG biometric has been found to specifically exhibit desirable characteristics for BSN applications.

Basically, the ECG signals are used for two purposes: first, to construct good cryptographic keys; and then, to securely manage the key distribution to various sensor nodes in a BSN. To this end, the following properties are exploited.

- **Time-Variance and Key Randomness.** The ECG biometric is highly time-variant. Fortunately, for a BSN setting, it is precisely the time-varying nature of ECG that makes it a prime candidate for good security. Good cryptographic keys need a high degree of randomness; and keys derived from random time-varying signals have higher security, since an intruder cannot reliably predict the true key. As previously reported in reference 29, ECG heart rate variability is in fact characterized by a (bounded) random process.

- **Timing Synchronization and Key Recoverability.** Key randomness is only part of the security problem. The second requirement is that the ECG-generated key should be reproducible with high fidelity at various sensor nodes in the same BSN. To demonstrate the feasibility of accurate biometric reproducibility at various sensors, consider typical ECG signals from the PhysioBank [30], as shown in Figure 16.3. In this case, three different ECG signals are measured simultaneously from three different electrode or lead placements (I, AVL, VZ

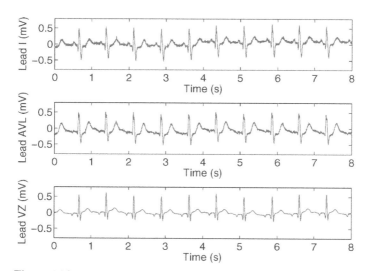

**Figure 16.3.** ECG signals simultaneously recorded from three different leads. (Taken from the PhysioBank [30]).

[30, 31]). The focus is on the sequence of R–R intervals, termed the inter-pulse interval (IPI) sequence [3]. What is noteworthy is that while the shapes of specific QRS complexes are different for each signal, the sequences of IPI for the three signals, with proper timing synchronization, are remarkably identical.

- **Interpulse Interval (IPI) Sequence.** Theoretically, the IPI sequences should be identical. This is because, physiologically, the IPI sequences capture the heart rate variations originating from the same heart, which should be the same regardless of the measurement site. This observation is completely anal-ogous to the scenario with various sensor nodes located on different sites on the human body in a BSN: Each sensor point is capable of extracting the same sequence of IPI. And interestingly, other cardiovascular signals from the same individual or BSN—including phonocardiogram (PCG), and photoplethysmo-gram (PPG)—can also be used to derive the same sequence of IPI [3]. Thus, the use of cardiovascular IPI for security has potentially a wide domain of applicability.

### 16.3.3.5 Single-Point Fuzzy Commitment Schemes

Recapitulating the implications of using an ECG biometric, we note that sensors within the same BSN have access to a common "secret" signal, namely, the IPI sequence, distributed by the physiological pathways. More importantly, from a cryptographic perspective, devices outside of a particular BSN neither have access to, nor reliably predict, the same sequence of IPI. Various strategies in the literature have exploited this phenomenon to bind an externally generated cryptographic key and distribute it to other sensors via fuzzy commitment [4, 11, 12, 32]. It should be noted that the cryptographic key intended for the entire BSN is generated at a single point and then distributed to the remaining sensors. The key is generated independently from the biometric signals, which merely act as witnesses. For these reasons, we will henceforth refer to this scheme as single-point fuzzy commitment.

Compared to other conventional key distribution schemes e.g., Diffie–Hellman multiple-session key exchange [6]), the fuzzy commitment method yields improve-ments in terms of computational complexity and information exchanged. This is made possible by exploiting the inherent transmissions of IPI sequences to various points in the BSN, as part of the body's cardiovascular system.

## 16.4 THE ECG BIOMETRIC FOR ROBUST IDENTIFICATION

For the remainder of this chapter, a number of novel signal-processing applications involving the ECG biometric will be described. These applications essentially rep-resent some of the authors' original research contributions, as reported in references 24, 33, and 34 . In this section, the problem of human identification using the ECG is investigated.

Human identification with biometrics can be regarded as a pattern recognition problem, where the goal is to create digital signatures with highly personalized power. As in other typical pattern detection problems, ECG-based identification systems consist of three main steps. The first step is preprocessing, where preliminary work is carried out to prepare the signals for further analysis. The second step is feature extraction, where the biometric is analyzed so that distinctive characteristics can be retrieved. Finally, having formed unique signatures, classification is performed to identify an individual. A variety of algorithms can enable clustering, with the purpose of measuring the degree of similarity between an input trait and the ones that are stored in the gallery set—that is, the set of subjects that the system is able to recognize.

## 16.4.1   One-Lead ECG

### 16.4.1.1   Preprocessing

In a raw form, the ECG data contain a lot of noise, which can degrade the ECG signals to such a degree that reliable feature extraction and identification may not be feasible.

To eliminate noise effects, a Butterworth bandpass filter of order 4 is applied reduce the baseline wander and the interference effects. The cutoff frequencies of the designed filter are 1–40 Hz, which were set empirically to retain as much useful ECG information as possible.

Additionally, windowing is performed on the filtered ECG signals. In this case, the design of the window to be used is quite unrestricted; for example, it is allowed to demarcate the ECG even in the middle of a pulse. The only constraint is on the window length: It needs to be larger than the average heart rate, so that multiple heartbeats are included.

### 16.4.1.2   Feature Extraction

In the existing literature, the most commonly encountered types of features for human identification are morphological characteristics of single heartbeats. It has been suggested [15–21] that amplitude and normalized time distances between successive fiducial points constitute unique patterns for different individuals. However, in these applications, it is implied that fiducial points can be successfully detected. The algorithms that perform such a task are built solely for medical applications, where the exact wave boundaries are not needed to diagnose abnormalities. This is not the case for human recognition and authentication systems, where accuracy is crucial in order to facilitate further pattern analysis. Furthermore, there is no universally acknowledged rule about the exact location of wave boundaries, which could constitute the basis of fiducial detectors [35]. Moreover, in ECG monitoring, several kinds of anomalies are met, some of which affect the morphology of the signal significantly, making the boundaries of the waves difficult to localize.

To address these problems, nonfiducial points methods can be adopted for feature extraction. The autocorrelation (AC) method has been found to be a suitable candidate [23, 24]. In general, the AC captures the repetitive property of the ECG; its shape is primarily dependent on the $P$, $QRS$, and $T$ waves. By analyzing the AC, nonrandom patterns associated with distinctive characteristics of a person's ECG can be encapsulated.

The rationale for utilizing the AC is that it extracts information from the ECG samples holistically, in a sequence of sums of products. In other words, the ECG samples do not need to be first subjected to fiducial points detection. Additionally, the AC allows a shift invariant representation of similarity features over multiple cycles.

The normalized AC is defined as

$$\widehat{R}_{yy}[m] = \frac{\sum_{i=0}^{N-|m|-1} x[i]x[i+m]}{\widehat{R}_{yy}[0]}, \tag{16.1}$$

where $x[i]$ is the windowed ECG, for $-i = 0, 1 \ldots (N - |m|1)$, and $x[i+m]$ is the time-shifted version of the windowed ECG, with a time lag of $m = 0, 1, \ldots, (M-1)$; $M << N$. Even though the major contributors to the AC are the three characteristic waves, normalization is required because large variations in amplitudes appear, even among the windows of the same subject. The fact that the AC embeds distinctive characteristics for every subject, and thus can be used to capture similarities between signals recorded at different times, can be confirmed by the AC plots in Figure 16.4.

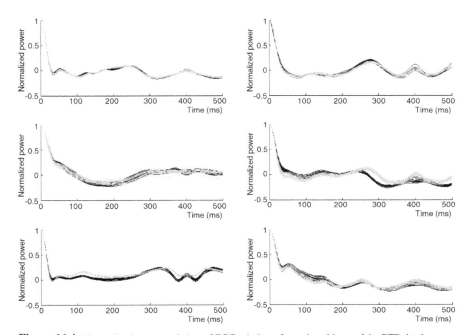

**Figure 16.4.** Normalized autocorrelation of ECG windows from six subjects of the PTB database. Two records are available for every subject, recorded at different times. Sequences from the same record are shown in the same shade.

This observation implies that an AC vector can be used directly for classification. However, depending on the sampling frequency of the ECGs, the dimensionality of an AC window can be considerably high, and dimensionality reduction is required.

**Discrete Cosine Transform for Dimensionality Reduction.** The discrete cosine transform (DCT) is applied to the normalized autocorrelation coefficients for dimensionality reduction. This methodology is referred to as AC/DCT. The DCT frequency coefficients are estimated as

$$Y[u] = G[u] \sum_{i=0}^{N-1} R[i] \cos \frac{(2i+1)\pi u}{2N}, \qquad (16.2)$$

where $N$ is the length of the signal $y[i]$ for $i = 0, 1, \ldots, (N - |m| - 1)$. For the AC/DCT method, $y[i]$ is the autocorrelated ECG obtained from Eq. (16.1). $G[u]$ is given by

$$G(k) = \begin{cases} \sqrt{\frac{1}{N}}, & k = 0, \\ \sqrt{\frac{2}{N}}, & 1 \leq k \leq N - 1. \end{cases} \qquad (16.3)$$

Due to the energy compaction property of DCT, a lower-dimension representation is obtained. Near-zero frequency components of the spectrum can be discarded. Assuming we take an $\mathcal{M}$-point DCT of the autocorrelated signal, only $\mathcal{C} << \mathcal{M}$ nonzero DCT coefficients will contain significant information for identification. From a frequency domain perspective, the $\mathcal{C}$ nonzero coefficients correspond to the frequencies between the cutoffs of the bandpass filter that is used in preprocessing. This is because after the AC operation, the bandwidth of the signal is kept.

The DCT coefficients retain the discriminative properties of the AC samples among different subjects as depicted in Figure 16.5. The refined feature space is propagated to the classification step, where every compressed input DCT vector is compared to the ones stored in the gallery set.

**Linear Discriminant Analysis for Dimensionality Reduction.** Another option to reduce the dimensionality of the feature space is the linear discriminant analysis (LDA). Supervised learning is carried out in the transformed domain, so that eventually feature dimensionality is reduced and the classes are better distinguished. This scheme is referred to as AC/LDA.

Given a training set $\mathcal{Z} = \{\mathcal{Z}_i\}_{i=1}^{U}$, with $U$ classes, where each class $\mathcal{Z}_i = \{\mathbf{z}_{ij}\}_{j=1}^{U_i}$ contains a number of autocorrelated windows $\mathbf{z}_{ij}$, a set of $K$ feature basis vectors $\{\psi_m\}_{m=1}^{K}$ can be estimated by maximizing Fisher's ratio. Maximizing this ratio is equivalent to solving the following eigenvalue problem:

$$\psi = \arg \max_{\psi} \frac{|\psi^T S_b \psi|}{|\psi^T S_w \psi|}, \qquad (16.4)$$

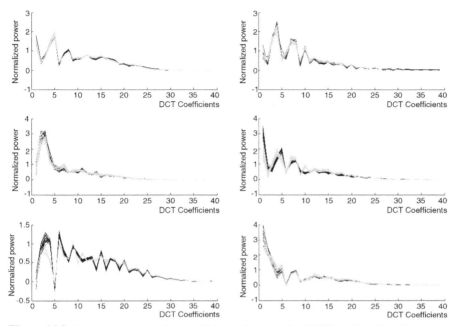

**Figure 16.5.** Discrete cosine transform coefficients of autocorrelated ECG windows from six subjects of the PTB database. Two records are available for every subject, recorded at different times. Sequences from the same record are shown in the same shade.

where $\psi = [\psi_1, \ldots, \psi_K]$, and $S_b$ and $S_w$ are the between and within-class scatter matrices respectively. These matrices are defined as

$$S_b = \frac{1}{N} \sum_{i=1}^{U} U_i (\bar{z}_i - \bar{z})(\bar{z}_i - \bar{z})^T, \tag{16.5}$$

$$S_w = \frac{1}{N} \sum_{i=1}^{U} \sum_{j=1}^{U_i} (z_{ij} - \bar{z}_i)(z_{ij} - \bar{z}_i)^T, \tag{16.6}$$

where $\bar{z}_i = \frac{1}{U_i} \sum_{j=1}^{U_i} z_{ij}$ is the mean of class $\mathcal{Z}_i$, $N$ is the total number of windows, and $N = \sum_{i=1}^{U} U_i$. Both the between- and within-class scatter matrices are symmetric and positive semidefinite.

Linear discriminant analysis finds $\psi$ as the $K$ most significant eigenvectors of $(S_W)^{-1} S_b$, which correspond to the first $K$ largest eigenvalues. A test input window $\mathbf{z}$ is subjected to the linear projection $y = \psi^T z$, prior to classification [36].

### 16.4.1.3 Classification

Classification represents the last step of the identification procedure. For this step, every input feature vector is compared to the ones stored in the gallery set in order to find the best match. The similarity measure used is the Euclidean distance, with the nearest neighbor being a classifier.

An important consideration when designing pattern recognition systems is the conversion of a large-class-number problem into a small-class-number one. This reducing procedure offers computationally functional frameworks, which are appropriate for cost-efficient applications. Template matching (TM) can be used to achieve this objective, since reducing the number of clusters is equivalent to pruning the search space. TM is based on the correlation coefficient, which is estimated between every input AC ECG window and the corresponding ones in the gallery set. The goal is to locate those subjects in the database, which can be regarded as possible candidates for a given input signal. Having obtained a reduced set of possible identities, classification can be performed in a smaller scope. The rationale for using the correlation coefficient is that it measures the morphological similarities of any two waveforms. For two autocorrelated signals **x** and **y**, the correlation coefficient is defined as

$$\rho_{xy} = \frac{\gamma_{xy}}{\sigma_x \sigma_y}, \tag{16.7}$$

where $\sigma_x$ and $\sigma_y$ are the standard deviations of the signals **x** and **y**, respectively, and $\gamma_{xy}$ is the covariance of **x** and **y**.

The correlation coefficient is a normalized statistic that reveals the degree of similarity of signals. The range of values is $[-1, 1]$, with 1 indicating a perfect match, 0 indicating nonrelated signals, and $-1$ indicating an inverse relationship. However, this measure is not exclusively sufficient to perform identification; therefore, it is used as a preclassification scheme. Thresholding on the coefficient reduces significantly the number of candidate classes among which classification is then carried out.

Furthermore, TM acts as an intruder detector. An accurate and secure recognition system needs to be able to detect an illegal entrance. Setting a threshold for the correlation coefficient, and not allowing identity decision for individuals that are below this threshold, reduces the possibility of an individual illegally penetrating the system significantly. This hierarchical method is depicted in Figure 16.6.

## 16.4.2 Twelve-Lead ECG

Most of the works in the existing literature on ECG-based human recognition take advantage of recordings from one lead only. Applying two electrodes renders the procedure less invasive to the subject. However, the standard 12-lead system offers a variety of ECG recordings that can be investigated for biometric use.

**Figure 16.6.** Block diagram of the AC/DCT and AC/LDA method in conjunction with template matching.

Information fusion is widely applied in multimodal biometric systems—that is, systems that combine more than one biometric characteristics—to increase the accuracy of the identification. For instance, ECG traits have been combined with face information to create a harder to defeat system [17]. However, fusion can also be achieved using several aspects of the same biometric trait. In fact, ECG windows that are recorded at the exact same time from different electrode configurations can be fused to generate more powerful signatures for every subject.

Employing more than one lead in the process of identifying an individual reinforces the quality and amount of useful information for every subject. Given that every lead ECG has discriminative power, a fusion of this data in the appropriate framework can manage to augment the accuracy of the output and defensibility of the system substantially.

Fusion can be performed at three different levels: the raw-data level, the feature level, and the decision level.

At the raw data level, information fusion is equivalent to combining different sources of the same trait. In the ECG case for example, the signals from different leads could be averaged. Nevertheless, there is no compelling reason why such a process would offer more information from a practical point of view.

There are two ways to combine information at the feature extraction level.

- Data collected from different aspects of the same biometric (i.e., multiple heart potential aspects) can be concatenated in one feature vector with higher dimensionality. This procedure requires that the concatenated features be in the same type of measurement scale [9].

- Combination of scores that are produced from different classifiers. Each classifier is tested on a feature vector from a different sensor. In other words, every classifier learns inputs from specific sensors, offering a distance (or score) measure when tested. Classifier fusion in this case suggests that scores are combined to make the final decision.

The third kind of fusion is decision-based. In this type of data mixture, different classifiers decide about specific feature vectors; and the final decision results in a structured synthesis, such as majority voting. An extensive description of the methodologies for combining the outcomes of classifiers can be found in reference 37.

To obtain the desired identification features, the AC/LDA method, described earlier, is applied on ECG segments from different leads. The final decision is generated based on variants of the voting principle. Specifically, $L = 12$ classifiers are trained, with each classifier operating on signals recorded from the corresponding lead.

An action where a classifier $k$ is tested on a input $x$ is denoted as $cl(x)^k$. The endmost decision where all classifiers are fused is denoted as $CL(x)$. If the system has $N$ registered subjects that can be identified, then every classifier makes a decision from the set $\Omega = 1, 2, \ldots, N$. The following characteristic function is introduced to describe of the fusion methodology [37]:

$$\Phi_k(x \in C_i) = \begin{cases} 1 & \text{if } i \in \Omega \text{ and } cl(x)^k = i, \\ 0 & \text{otherwise.} \end{cases} \tag{16.8}$$

Four rules can guide the decision fusion of different classifiers. Each one is a more or less conservative variant of the voting principle.

1. *Rule 1*: This rule can be applied to guide conservative decisions alone. In order for the system to conclude, all classifiers have to agree. In any other case, the input is rejected ($R$); that is, the subject cannot be recognized. $CL(x)$ is given from

$$CL(x) = \begin{cases} j & \text{if } j \in \Omega \text{ and } \sum_{k=1}^{L} \Phi_k(x \in C_j) = L, \\ R & \text{otherwise.} \end{cases} \tag{16.9}$$

2. *Rule 2*: Compared to the first rule, a less conservative option for decision synthesis is

$$CL(x) = \begin{cases} j & \text{if } \Psi(x, j) = \max_i \Psi(x, i) > L/2 \text{ and } j, i \in \Omega, \\ R & \text{otherwise,} \end{cases} \tag{16.10}$$

where $\Psi(x, j) = \sum_{k=1}^{12} \Phi_k(x \in C_j)$. In this case, an input $x$ is identified as subject $j$ with majority voting among the classifiers.

3. *Rule 3*: This case is a generalization of Rule 2, to accommodate decision fusions, based on the parameter $\alpha$ which takes values in $(0,1)$. This parameter shows the degree of conservatism of the system. An estimation for the subject is given from

$$CL(x) = \begin{cases} j & \text{if } \Psi(x, j) = \max_i \Psi(x, i) > \alpha * L \text{ and } j, i \in \Omega \\ R & \text{otherwise} \end{cases} \tag{16.11}$$

For $\alpha = 0.5$, Rules 2 and 3 are equivalent; therefore the current rule can be regarded as a generalization of majority voting.

4. *Rule 4*: To assist situations of equal votes for two or more subjects, or cases where the decided class is not considerably supported compared to the second maximal, the final decision can be made with

$$CL(x) = \begin{cases} j, & \text{if } \Psi(x, j) = \max_1 \text{ and } \max_1 - \max_2 \geq \alpha * L, \\ R, & \text{otherwise,} \end{cases} \tag{16.12}$$

where

$$\max_1 = \max_i \Psi(x, i), \tag{16.13}$$

$$\max_2 = \max_{i-\{j\}} \Psi(x, i), \tag{16.14}$$

When $\alpha$ is big, this rule becomes very conservative, since in order to assign an input to a class, it must be supported by an adequate number of classifiers and not have opponents [37].

However, this kind of merging rules bring up rejection $(R)$ cases. There are two main reasons why an input ECG window is rejected: Either the decision rule is too conservative, or the class of the input data is ambiguous. Rejection is generally unacceptable for biometric identification systems, because the subject has to be recognized using a different module.

On the other hand, allowing rejection to take place reduces significantly the possibility of illegal penetration. When the system is not absolutely confident about somebody's identity, it sets off the alarm rather than misidentify him/her. Nevertheless, it is important to find a fusion framework that would be conservative enough to detect intruders and at the same time have as low a rejection rate as possible.

In cases 3 and 4, where the choice is ruled by parameter $\alpha$, rejection can also take place. The degree of rejection is governed by $\alpha$, since this parameter expresses the rate of confidence about the outcome of the system. But there is a trade-off between highly confident decisions and rejection rates. The more the classifiers contribute to the voting process, the higher the probability of successful recognition, especially for large data sets.

### 16.4.3  ECG-Based Identification in Cardiac Arrhythmia Scenarios

The analysis of ECG in cardiac arrhythmia scenarios is mainly similar to the one described for healthy ECGs. The framework consists of three main steps—that is, preprocessing, feature extraction, and classification. The last two stages are adopted from the description of the methodology for healthy ECG-based identification. Autocorrelation characteristics are used, both to acquire highly personalized signatures and to avoid fiducial points detection, which in arrhythmias is even more difficult. The linear discriminant analysis reduces the dimensionality of the feature space, while rendering classes more separable.

The difference between recognizing patterns in healthy and distorted ECGs lies in the preprocessing stage. The autocorrelation of arrhythmic ECG windows deviates from a healthy appearance significantly, even when comparing healthy and arrhythmic ECG segments of the same subject. To ensure accuracy of the decided identity, the system should be able to detect and discard those segments that correspond to distorted ECG windows. This is not the case for all kinds of arrhythmias, because some deform the signal totally to such a degree that identification becomes impossible.

The methodology described here is capable of addressing identification scenarios where two kinds of arrhythmias are present: *premature ventricular contraction* (PVC) and *atrial premature contraction* (APC). These arrhythmias are not lethal. At this point, it is relevant to briefly examine the characteristics of these two kinds of anomalies.

Normally, the electrical impulse is generated from the SA node. When depolarization starts from another group of pacemaker cells, or when the conduction of the impulses is altered, the rhythm of the heartbeats becomes abnormal and arrhythmia is introduced [2].

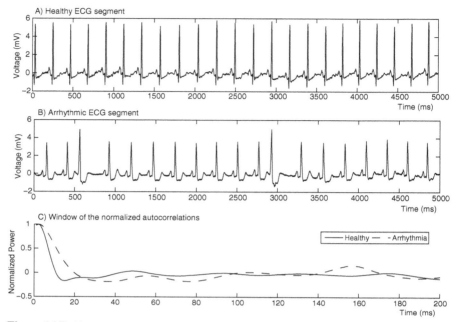

**Figure 16.7.** (**A**) A segment of healthy electrocardiogram from the MIT database. (**B**) Arrhythmic ECG segment. (**C**) Corresponding autocorrelation plots.

An ectopic heartbeat is a premature beat that can be categorized as either a supraventricular or a ventricular premature contraction, depending on the origin of the beat. A premature ventricular contraction originates in the ventricles where contraction takes place before accepting atria's electrical signal. PVCs result in distorted beats compared to the sinus ones. They usually inhibit the following normal sinus heartbeat, and force a delay of almost twice the length of a cycle. PVCs force the autocorrelation to deviate from that of a repetitive signal as demonstrated in Figure 16.7 [2].

However, cardiac arrhythmias are not caused solely by the ventricles. There are cases where rhythm disturbances originate from multiple ectopic foci in the atria. Although the ventricles are in position to respond to this electrical impulse, the heart rhythm is affected without exhibiting any abnormal morphologies. Therefore, the repetitive property of the ECG signal is not distorted. An APC results in heartbeats that are physiologically healthy, only earlier in time than expected. In such cases, the autocorrelation is not affected and the ECG segment is considered suitable for identification.

The arrhythmia screening algorithm described here is targeted at locating and discarding ECG segments that are not suitable for human recognition, from an autocorrelation point of view. Thus, the framework is robust to APC rhythm variations, but not to ventricular premature heartbeats. In the remainder of this section, ECG windows with PVCs (and not APCs) are referred to as arrhythmic. A methodology

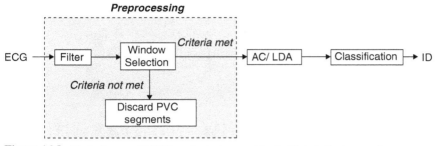

**Figure 16.8.** Block diagram AC/LDA method when combined with arrhythmia screening.

is evaluated to screen these occurrences, so that identification can proceed without accuracy losses.

Figure 16.8 describes the main steps of the described methodology. Two criteria are used to decide whether an ECG segment is arrhythmic or not. The first one is a power criterion, which is based on the power spectrum of the ECG windows. The second criterion is autocorrelation morphology dependent, showing high complexity for PVCs.

### 16.4.3.1 Power Criterion

When a premature ventricular heartbeat appears in an ECG segment, the power spectrum of the signal is corrupted by smaller frequencies. In order to define a criterion for the power distribution, the discrete cosine transform (DCT) is used because of its energy compaction property. The frequency coefficients of the AC are estimated as in Eq. (16.2).

In order to distinguish between healthy and abnormal power distributions, a criterion is defined that relates to the concentration of power. It has been observed that the autocorrelation of arrhythmic ECG segments has half of its total power concentrated in the frequency interval 0.5–7.2 Hz. For any given power distribution, the number of the DCT coefficient at which half of the total power is reached is estimated as

$$k = \min(|\sum_{i=1}^{k} Y(i) - \sum_{i=k}^{N} Y(i)|), \tag{16.15}$$

where $Y(i)$ are the coefficients of the discrete cosine transform. Figures 16.9 and 16.10 show the analysis performed to obtain the power criterion.

### 16.4.3.2 Complexity Measure

The complexity measure (CM) of finite sequences has been originally proposed by Lempel and Ziv [38]. Furthermore, some works have been reported about the suitability of this measure for ECG-based applications [39–41]. As a PVC criterion, CM is estimated for every input ECG segment because it is computationally efficient.

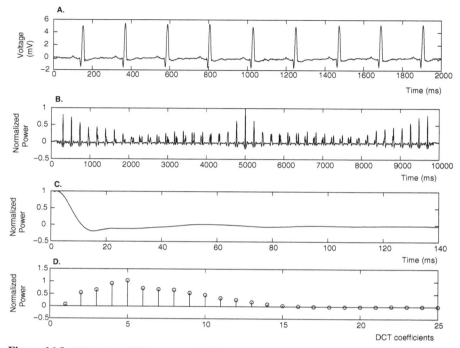

**Figure 16.9.** (A) Healthy ECG segment. (B) Corresponding autocorrelation. (C) Zoomed normalized AC. (D) DCT coefficients.

A complexity measure reveals the number of patterns that are hidden in a finite sequence as well as their frequency of appearance. In this manner, the degree of disarrangement of a signal is described. More specifically, since the autocorrelation of quasiperiodic or repetitive signals (such as healthy ECG windows) has peaks that recur periodically, the CM is expected to capture their frequency of appearance.

According to the definitions provided by Lempel and Ziv [38] to calculate CM, the autocorrelation must be translated into a binary sequence. In such a binary projection, local maxima are represented by ones and all the remaining samples by zeros. In order to detect the peaks, the AC signal is passed through a low-pass filter with cutoff frequency at 5 Hz, so that small localized peaks of less interest are eliminated. It is expected that autocorrelations obtained from arrhythmic ECG segments will have higher complexity measures, since they do not carry any repetitive patterns.

According to Lempel and Ziv [38], the algorithm for the computation of the complexity measure proceeds as described in Figure 16.11 along with the following definitions:

- $x$ is the binary autocorrelation sequence.
- $S$ and $Q$ are two binary strings.
- $SQ$ is the concatenation of $S$ and $Q$.
- $SQ\pi$ is $SQ$ where the last character is deleted.

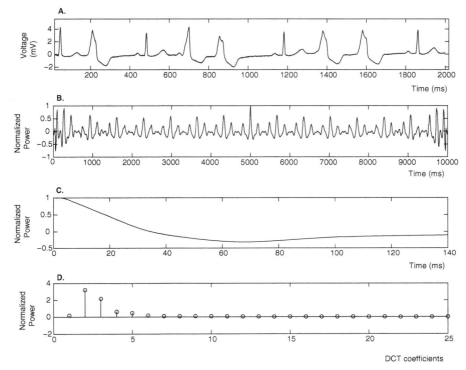

**Figure 16.10.** **(A)** Arrhythmia ECG segment. **(B)** Corresponding autocorrelation. **(C)** Zoomed normalized AC. **(D)** DCT coefficients.

- $l(SQ)$ is the length of sequence $SQ$.
- $v(SQ\pi)$ is the vocabulary of $SQ\pi$.

Initially, the complexity measure $(Cm)$ is assigned to be one. $S$ is defined to be the first character of the sequence $x$, and $Q$ the second one. In the midst of the

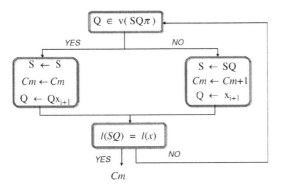

**Figure 16.11.** Flow chart showing the route of computations for the complexity measure.

computations, if word $Q$ exists in the $v(SQ\pi)$ vocabulary, then $Q$ is appended with the next symbol of $x$, while $Cm$ and $S$ remain the same. However, if $Q$ does not belong to $v(SQ\pi)$, $Cm$ is augmented by one, $SQ$ is assigned to $S$, and $Q$ becomes the next character of the $x$ sequence. This process continues until the entire sequence $x$ is scanned.

Lempel and Ziv [38] showed the upper limit of $Cm$ for a binary sequense $x$ of length $l(x) = n$ to be

$$\lim_{n \to \infty} Cm(n) = b(n) \equiv \frac{n}{\log_2(n)}. \qquad (16.16)$$

The complexity measure depends highly on the length of the sequence. In order to eliminate this effect, a normalized complexity measure $C$ is adopted instead:

$$C = \frac{Cm(n)}{b(n)} = Cm(n)\frac{\log_2(n)}{n}. \qquad (16.17)$$

Therefore, $0 \le C \le 1$, with values closer to one showing higher complexity.

## 16.5   THE ECG BIOMETRIC FOR SECURE AND RESOURCE-EFFICIENT COMMUNICATIONS IN A BSN

In this section, we consider the utility of the ECG biometric to reduce the resource consumption and provide data security for a BSN, in a practical and flexible manner.

### 16.5.1   Multipoint Fuzzy Key Management

The single-point fuzzy key management, surveyed in Section 16.3.3.5, represents a significant improvement over conventional key distribution systems, such as those based on the Diffie–Hellman scheme. However, it is still inefficient with respect to the communication rate: The length of the transmitted sequence needs to be at least as long as that of the required cryptographic key. Indeed, with the concatenation of the check code, its size is even longer. This represents an undesirable overhead, since communication transmissions consume the most energy in a BSN, compared to computational operations.

Motivated by the inherent design limitation of the single-point fuzzy management, we seek a more flexible and efficient approach to manage the keys for all sensors. The basic idea is to send only the check-code, and not a modified version of the key itself over the channel.

In a multipoint scheme, as its name suggests, all nodes would be responsible for generating the key from the obtained biometrics at various sensor points. The utility of this approach is that, unlike in a single-point scheme, a full XOR-ed version of the key no longer needs to be sent over the channel. Instead, only the check-code needs to be transmitted for verification.

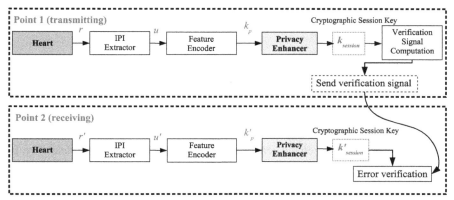

**Figure 16.12.** Multipoint fuzzy key management scheme.

### 16.5.1.1 System Modules

A high-level summary of the proposed multipoint scheme is depicted in Figure 16.12. It should be noted that, compared to a single-point scheme, no new basic modules are required. For instance, the error-correction modules and the hash function modules are already present in a single-point system. Therefore, the innovation is in the design of the roles these blocks take at various points in the transmission protocol. This is a deliberate choice, in order to ensure that our design would not overstep the resources available to a BSN, as established in previous studies for a single-point context.

In the following, the primed version of the signal (e.g., $r'$), represents the receiver counterpart of the signal found in the transmitter.

**IPI Extractor.** This front-end module represents an abstraction of the preprocessing, such as filtering and quantization, required to deliver a raw binary sequence of numbers. It should be noted that this is not an error-correcting encoder; that is, the output is a PCM binary sequence.

**Feature Encoder.** Ideally, the objective of this module is to deliver a same sequence of numbers, from two sufficiently similar signals, up to some Hamming distance. In other words, from two highly similar sequences of IPI $u$ and $u'$, the feature encoder should output an identical binary sequence at the transmitter (as $k_p$) and also at the receiver (as $k'_p$).

Since the design goal is to restrict our basic building blocks to the same ones found in a single-point scheme, it turns out that the most appropriate module to use here is an error-correcting *decoder* [42]. The reason for utilizing an error-correcting decoder, as opposed to an error-correcting encoder, to perform feature encoding is as follows. It is obvious that, for an $(n, k)$ error correction encoder, any $n$-bit binary sequence can be considered as a codeword plus some channel distortions. Therefore, an error decoder can be used to remove the dissimilar features from the signals $u$ and $u'$ in order to arrive at a common codeword. This is possible as long as the Hamming differences between these signals are within the error-correction capability of the decoder [33, 34].

**Privacy Enhancer.** This section is optional, in the sense that the obtained signals $k_p$ and $k'_p$ are already suitable to be used as cryptographic keys. However, as explained in the introduction, this is not acceptable from a privacy perspective. While the feature encoding process does result in signal modification, it may not be sufficient from a data hiding perspective. An additional processing block is needed to confidently remove obvious correlations between the generated key and the original medical data. To this end, a zero-knowledge cryptographic hash function, such as SHA-1 [6], is appropriate for this module.

**Error Verification and Transmission.** The goal of this module is to generate a verification signal to be sent to the receiver. This signal must not reveal any information regarding the session key. These requirements are also fulfilled by the same hash function SHA-1.

Compared to the single-point scheme, the transmitted signal in this case is intended mainly for error detection, as opposed to error correction. The receiver should already have all the information needed to regenerate the pre-key $k_p$.

Note that the output of SHA-1 is a 160-bit sequence. However, it is not necessary to use the entire sequence for error detection. Therefore, depending on the bandwidth constraint or the desired security performance, only some segment of the sequence is partially transmitted—for example, the first 32 or 64 bits as done in the simulation results. Possible key mismatches are detected based on the partial bits transmitted. The length of this partial sequence determines the confidence of verification and can be adapted according to the bandwidth constraints. If verification fails, then a request for retransmission needs to be sent—for example, using an ARQ-type protocol [6].

### 16.5.1.2   Scheduling and System Synchronization

Timing synchronization, between sensor nodes, is very important in the proposed protocol. This can be handled using a network broadcast [3, 4, 11]. In order that all sensors will ultimately produce the same IPI, they should all listen to an external broadcast command from the controller (see Figure 16.2), which serves to initiate, at some scheduled time instant, the ECG recording and IPI extraction process. Evidently, an intruder who is aware of the same initiation command is of inconsequential risk, since without access to the physical body of the BSN, the intruder still cannot derive the same sequence of random IPI.

This scheduling coordination also has a dual function of implementing key refreshing [3, 4, 6]. Since a fresh key is established in the BSN with each initiation command, the controller can enforce key renewal as frequently as needed to satisfy the security demand of the envisioned application: More refreshing ensures higher security, at the cost of increased system complexity.

### 16.5.1.3  *Performance and Efficiency*

Evidently, the success of the multipoint management scheme relies on the similarities of the physiological signals at the various sensors. These are the same assumptions for the single-point key management. This fact is reflected also in the similar Hamming distance requirements for the two cases. Therefore, with respect to security, the two systems are comparable for the same session key length.

More importantly, the differences involved are in the allocation of resources. With respect to spectral efficiency, the number of transmitted bits required for the single-point case is at least the length of the cryptographic key. By contrast, since the proposed system only requires the transmitted bits for error detection, the number can be made variable. Depending on the targeted amount of confidence, the number of transmitted bits can be accordingly allocated for spectral efficiency.

## 16.5.2  Multipoint Management with Key Fusion

In the system considered so far, the sole random source for key generation is the biometrics. Without requiring an external random source, a multipoint strategy has enabled a BSN to be more efficient with respect to communication resources, at the expense of computational complexity and processing delay. This is generally a desirable setup for a BSN [11, 12]. However, in operating scenarios where the longer delays and higher computational complexity become prohibitive, it is possible to resort to an intermediate case.

Suppose security requirements dictate a certain key length. Then, the key can essentially be partitioned into two components: The first one is constructed by an external random source, while the second one is derived from the biometrics. The total number of bits generated equals the required key length. Evidently, for a system with severe bandwidth restriction, most of the key bits should be derived from the biometrics. Conversely, when transmission delay is a problem, more bits should be generated by an external source.

A high-level summary of a possible key fusion approach is depicted in Figure 16.13. The key $k_{session}$ is a concatenation of two components, that is, $(k_{comp1}, k_{comp2})$. The first component $k_{comp1}$ is distributed using fuzzy commitment, while the second $k_{comp2}$ is sent using the multi-point scheme.

### 16.5.2.1  *Information Fusion and Independence*

In order to ensure that the overall cryptographic key is secured using mutually exclusive information, it is necessary to partition the output from the binary encoder properly. As a concrete example, let us consider generating a 128-bit key, half from a fuzzy commitment and half from a multipoint distribution, using a BCH(63,16,11) code. Then, the first $128/2 = 64$ bits from the raw binary output are used to bind the externally generated 64-bit sequence. The remaining 64 bits need to generated from the next $64/16 \times 63 = 252$ raw input bits. In other words, this scheme requires

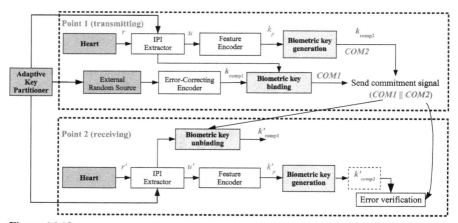

**Figure 16.13.** Multipoint management with key fusion.

waiting for $64 + 252 = 316$ bits to be recorded, as opposed to 504 bits in the nonfusion multipoint case.

### 16.5.2.2 Key Length Control and Feedback

From an implementation perspective, this fusion system allows a BSN to adaptively modify its key construction, depending on the delay requirements. But the disadvantage is the sensors need to be sufficiently complicated to carry out the adaptation in the first place. For instance, additional information needs to be transmitted for proper transceiver synchronization in the key construction. Furthermore, some form of feedback is needed to adjust the key length for true resource adaption. These requirements are conceptually represented by the key length partitioner control block. It can be practically implemented by embedding additional control data bits into the transmitted sequence to coordinate the receiver. As with most practical feedback methods, there is some inevitable delay in the system adaptive response.

Nonetheless, whenever implementable, a key fusion approach is the most general one, encompassing both the single-point and multipoint schemes as special cases, in addition to other intermediate possibilities.

## 16.5.3 INTRAS Data Scrambling

In the previous section, the general infrastructure and several approaches for generating and establishing common keys at various nodes in a secure manner have been described. The next strategy involves utilizing these keys in some symmetric encryption scheme [6].

To this end, we propose a symmetric data scrambling method that operates at the signal-sample level. The method is referred to as INTRAS [33, 34], being effectively a combination of interpolation and random sampling, which is inspired by references 43 and 44. The idea is to modify the signal after sampling, but before binary encoding.

### 16.5.3.1  *Bit-Level Versus Signal-Level Cryptography*

The proposed method is suitable for input data at the signal-level (nonbinary) form, which is typical of the raw data transmitted in a BSN. The scheme is meant to tolerate small key variations (a problem for conventional encryption: even a single-bit key error, by design, results in nonsense output), as well as to deliver a low-complexity implementation. However, the cost to be paid is a possibly imperfect recovery, due to interpolation diffusion errors with an imperfect key sequence.

It will be seen that in the presence of key variations, the resulting distortions are similar to gradual degradations found in lossy compression algorithms, as opposed to the all-or-none abrupt recovery failure exhibited by conventional encryption.

### 16.5.3.2  *INTRAS Structure*

The general high-level structure of an INTRAS scrambler is shown in Figure 16.14, with input sequence $x[n]$. At each instant $n$, the resampling block simply resamples the interpolated signal $x_I(t)$ using a delay $d[n]$ to produce the scrambled output $x_d[n]$. Security here is obtained from the fact that by properly designing the interpolating filter, the input cannot be recovered from the scrambled output $x_d[n]$, without knowledge of the delay sequence $d[n]$. Moreover, when $d[n]$ is a random sequence, as will be described next, the operation corresponds to random sampling.

In a BSN context, the available (binary) encryption key $k_{session}$ is used to generate a set of sampling instants $d[n]$, by multilevel symbol-coding of $k_{session}$ [45]. This set of sampling instants is then used to resample the interpolated data sequence. Note that, when properly generated, $k_{session}$ is a random key and that the derived $d[n]$ inherits this randomness. In other words, the resampling process corresponds effectively to random sampling of the original data sequence. Without knowledge of the key sequence, the unauthorized recovery of the original data sequence (e.g., by brute-force attack), from the resampled signal is computationally impractical. By contrast, with knowledge of $d[n]$, the recovery of the original data is efficiently performed; in some cases, an iterative solution is possible. Therefore, the proposed scheme satisfies the main characteristics of a practical cryptographic system. More importantly, it not only requires less computational resources for implementation, but also is more robust to small mismatching of the encryption and decryption keys, which is often the case in biometrics systems.

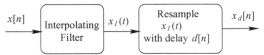

**Figure 16.14.** Interpolation and random sampling (INTRAS) structure.

### 16.5.3.3 INTRAS with Linear Interpolators

While Figure 16.14 shows an intermediate interpolated analog signal, $x_I(t)$, this is more or less a convenient abstraction only. It turns out that, depending on the filter used and the method of resampling, we can in fact bypass the continuous-time processing completely.

First, the window size or memory length $M$ needs to be selected, determining the range of time instants of over which the resampling can occur. For a causal definition, we require that the window span only the previous data symbols. Then, the current output symbol is obtained as a linear combination of the previous symbols.

Consider a simple linear interpolator with $M = 1$, so that the window size is two symbols, consisting of the current symbol and one previous symbol. Then the resampled signal $x_d[n]$ can be obtained in discrete-time form as

$$x_d[n] = a_0[n] \cdot x[n] + a_1[n] \cdot x[n-1]$$
$$= d[n] \cdot x[n] + (1 - d[n]) \cdot x[n-1], \tag{16.18}$$

where $0 \le d[n] \le 1$. The rationale for this definition is illustrated in Figure 16.15. We note that this is a causal definition. When $d = 0$, the output is the previous symbol. When $d = 1$, it is the current symbol. And for $0 < d < 1$, the filter interpolates between these values. This is precisely what a linear interpolator does, but implemented entirely in discrete-time. The iterative (16.18) needs initialization to be complete: A virtual pre-symbol can be defined with an arbitrary value $x[-1] = A$.

Also, observe that computing $x_d[n]$ actually corresponds to computing a convex combination of two consecutive symbols $x[n]$ and $x[n-1]$; that is, weighting coefficients $a_0$ and $a_1$ satisfy

$$a_0 + a_1 = 1, \tag{16.19}$$
$$a_0 \ge 0, a_1 \ge 0 \tag{16.20}$$

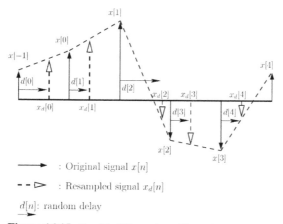

$\longrightarrow$    : Original signal $x[n]$

$--\triangleright$    : Resampled signal $x_d[n]$

$\underrightarrow{d[n]}$: random delay

**Figure 16.15.** Graphical illustration of linear interpolation followed by random sampling.

for each $n$. A convex combination is sufficient to maintain the full dynamic range (in fact, a more generalized linear combination is redundant, since it leads to unbounded output value).

The INTRAS structure is a scrambler because, depending on the random sequence $d[n]$, the output signal can differ significantly from the input. The difference can be characterized by a large MSE between $x[n]$ and $x_d[n]$. However, it is not encryption in the conventional sense, since knowing the input data and encrypted output is equivalent to knowing the key. Moreover, small mismatches in the decryption key do not lead immediately to nonsense output, but rather represent a more graceful degradation, characterized by an increasing mean-squared error (MSE). This is in stark contrast to the all-or-none criterion of conventional encryption and is thus more suitable for biometrics systems.

As the memory length $M$ is increased, a number of possibilities can be applied in interpolation. For example, (i) the simplest approach is to simply interpolate between every two successive samples (graphically, joining a straight line). Then the sampling delay determines which line should be used to pick the scrambled output. Or, (ii) linear regression can be first performed over the symbols spanning the window of interest [46]. Then, the sampling delay is applied to the best-fit regression line to produce the output. Alternatively, (iii) by revisiting the form of (16.18), which recasts interpolation as a convex combination, we can expand the formulation to incorporate multiple-symbol combination as follows:

$$x_d[n] = a_0[n]x[n] + a_1[n]x[n-1] + \cdots + a_M[n]x[n-M]$$

$$= \sum_{i=0}^{M} a_i[n]\,x[n-i], \tag{16.21}$$

where the convex combination condition, for a proper output dynamic range, requires that

$$\sum_{i=0}^{M} a_i[n] = 1, \tag{16.22}$$

$$a_0 \geq 0, a_1 \geq 0, \ldots, a_M \geq 0. \tag{16.23}$$

Therefore, the cryptographic key $k_{\text{session}}$ is used to encode $M + 1$ sequences of random coefficients. (Actually, because of the convex-combination requirement, there is a loss of degree of freedom, and only $M$ of the sequences are independent). Equivalently, the operation corresponds to a time-varying FIR filter [45] (with random coefficients).

In the receiver, an iterative solution can be used to recover the scrambled signal. Starting from the first symbol, we solve for $x[n]$, given $x_d[n]$ and knowledge of the coefficient sequences and virtual pre-symbols. For $M = 2$, we start with

$$x[0] = \frac{x_d[0] - a_1[0] \cdot x[-1] - a_2[0] \cdot x[-2]}{a_0[0]}. \tag{16.24}$$

More generally, we have

$$x[n] = \frac{x_d[n] - \sum_{i=1}^{M} a_i[n]x[n-1]}{a_0[n]}. \tag{16.25}$$

Therefore, with knowledge of the coefficient sequences and the virtual pre-symbols, the signal can be descrambled efficiently in an iterative manner.

## 16.6    SIMULATION EXAMPLES

In order to assess the efficiency and quality of the described methods, computer simulations were performed using experimental data obtained from various public databases: the MIT-BIH Normal Sinus Rhythm, the MIT-BIH Arrhythmia database, and the PTB database [30]. The results are presented in the same order as that established in Sections 16.4 and 16.5. In other words, two sets of simulation scenarios are described, highlighting respectively the robust identification strategy and the secure communication application for a BSN.

### 16.6.1    Identification

A series of experiments was conducted to test the identification performance of the described methods. The MIT-BIH Arrhythmia database has 48 ECG recordings collected between 1975 and 1979 at the Beth Israel Hospital Arrhythmia Laboratory. Each of the records is around 30 minutes long, depicting various kinds of arrhythmias. The sampling frequency of this database is 360 Hz. For the experimental setup, a subset of the database consisted of 30 subjects was formed. The selection criteria were the ECGs to show mostly premature ventricular and atrial contractions. Since only one recording for every subject is offered, the electrocardiogram signals were partitioned into two halves, one for the gallery set and one for testing.

The MIT-BIH Normal Sinus Rhythm database contains 18 electrocardiogram recordings from subjects who did not exhibit significant arrhythmias. The recordings were collected at the Laboratory of Boston's Beth Israel Hospital. The sampling frequency of this data set is 128 Hz. For our experimental setup, a subset of the database containing 13 subjects was formed. The selection was based on the length of the recordings. Waveforms with many artifacts offer limited heartbeat information and thus they were not used in our experiments. Once again, the signals were partitioned into two halves, one to build the gallery set, and one to test the system.

The PTB database is offered from the National Metrology Institute of Germany. The data set contains 549 ECG recordings from 294 subjects and every record includes the conventional 12-leads and 3 Frank leads ECG. The sampling frequency of these recordings is 1 kHz. In addition, for every subject in the PTB database, at least two recordings are offered, collected a few years apart. A subset of 14 healthy subjects was formed from the PTB database. The criteria for the selection of the records were to illustrate healthy ECG waveforms and to have at least two recordings for every subject. The older recording of every subject was used to build the gallery set, and the newer one was used to test the performance of the method.

Throughout the experimentation procedure, the three data sets were combined to achieve more general results. In order to fuse the recordings into one data set, resampling was performed when necessary.

## 16.6.2   One-Lead ECG

When a subject arrives to the system to be identified, 5 s of his/her ECG is collected and subjected to preprocessing, to eliminate the effects of noise. Having prepared the signals for further analysis, the normalized autocorrelation is computed, and several window lengths of the AC are tested for dimensionality reduction and classification, so that the optimal one is identified.

Even though its possible that windows of AC which correspond to the length of a heartbeat from the ECG offer high performance, it is important to note that not all waves of a heartbeat are invariant to stress conditions, risking this way the identification performance in anxiety situations. However, there is evidence that the $QRS$ complex is less affected by emotional conditions [22] compared to the rest of the waves; thus the corresponding AC window length is suggested to be more appropriate for feature extraction.

Table 16.1 shows the window and subject recognition rates when the system is tested on different autocorrelation window lengths $M$. The number of DCT coefficients used for identification is denoted by $C$, while the corresponding number of LDA features after dimensionality reduction depends on the size of the data set. These experiments are performed on the combined healthy data sets of the PTB and MIT healthy databases.

Splitting the available ECGs into segments of 5 s each, a test set of 506 windows from 27 subjects is generated. Both the AC/DCT and AC/LDA achieve their highest performance for an AC window length that corresponds approximately to the $QRS$

**Table 16.1.** Classification Performance of the AC/DCT and AC/LDA Method on the PTB Database

| M | C (DCT only) | Subject Rate DCT | Window Rate DCT | Subject Rate LDA | Window Rate LDA |
|---|---|---|---|---|---|
| 10 | 7 | 25/27 | 401/506 | 26/27 | 464/506 |
| 20 | 13 | 25/27 | 416/506 | 26/27 | 461/506 |
| 30 | 19 | 26/27 | 437/506 | 27/27 | 485/506 |
| 50 | 32 | 25/27 | 426/506 | 25/27 | 441/506 |
| 70 | 44 | 25/27 | 421/506 | 24/27 | 434/506 |
| 100 | 63 | 23/27 | 377/506 | 24/27 | 433/506 |
| 150 | 94 | 25/27 | 347/506 | 23/27 | 412/506 |
| 200 | 125 | 23/27 | 337/506 | 24/27 | 400/506 |

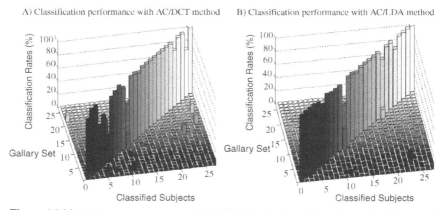

**Figure 16.16.** (**A**) Contingency matrix of the AC/DCT method applied on the combined datasets of MIT and PTB. (**B**) Corresponding AC/ LDA contingency matrix. Although it is expected the diagonal to show 100% window recognition rates, there are few missclassified windows.

complex of the electrocardiograms. However, only the LDA achieves 100% subject identification rate and 95.8% window recognition rate. This is expected because discriminant analysis embeds class information when projecting to lower dimensions therefore targeting at the same time to make clusters more separable. This is not the case for DCT where the frequency analysis is performed individually. Figures 16.16 A and 16.16B show the contingency matrices for both frameworks when simulated on the optimal $M$.

Template matching with the correlation coefficient measure is used to reduce the search space. This measure cannot be used directly to identify a subject, since high geometrical similarities exist between the AC of different subjects' ECGs if feature extraction is not performed. However, setting a threshold for the correlation coefficient value allows the system to find only those subjects from the gallery set that consist of possible identities for an input. For every newcomer, classification is carried out only among selected candidates. Figure 16.17 shows the percentage of possible identities found in the gallery set for every test subject with template matching.

It is, however, important to note that if TM is used for intruder detection as well, then a careful selection of a threshold value should be performed. The higher the threshold, the more likely to detect illegal attempts to penetrate but the less probable for the real identity to be included in the reduced subset of possible identities. This is attributed to the fact that correlation coefficient alone is not adequate to recognize a person.

## 16.6.3    Twelve-Lead ECG

The first step in merging information from 12 different leads is to investigate whether each one of them has discriminative information to offer or not. For this reason, the AC/LDA method is applied on the 12 lead electrocardiogram recordings of every

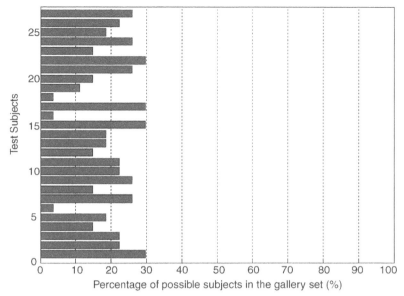

**Figure 16.17.** Percentage of candidates found for every test subject. The similarity measure is calculated only among the input and each reduced subset of the gallery set.

subject in the PTB database. The window and subject recognition rates are considerably high for every individual lead. Overall, the subject and window identification rates are in the range 85.71%–100% and 82.47%–99.39%. Figure 16.18 shows the subject and window rates of the AC/LDA method for different autocorrelation windows $M$, when tested on lead V6. The performance for that specific lead is the greatest achieved with this methodology.

Fusion at a decision level can be performed by the rules described earlier. The designer of the system can decide on how conservative the system should be in making decisions either by choosing a rule or by controlling parameter $\alpha$ in rules 3 and 4. However, the more conservative the system (i.e., the greater the number of classifier requirements to finalize a decision), the higher the rejection rates $R$.

In the current experimental setup, every subject is tested on a given number of test windows that are offered from the data set. For a subject to be rejected, it is required that all of the corresponding windows are ambiguous. Even though every rule leads to rejection, there is a drop down of 31.42% rejection rate when moving from rule number one to two. This is expected, since it is more likely that half of the total classifiers will avote for a identity rather than all of them. In addition, all subjects are identified correctly with both rules.

Rules number 3 and 4 result in 100% window and subject identification rates. It is, however, expected that for larger data sets the recognition rates will drop for lower $\alpha$ values. Rejection is introduced in these cases as well, and especially for high $\alpha$ values, the window rejection rate exceeds 30%.

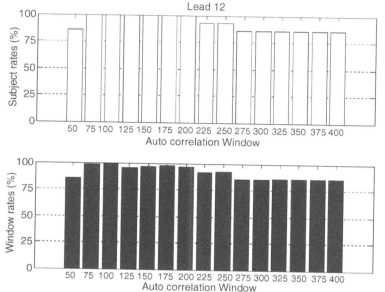

**Figure 16.18.** Window and subject classification rates of the AC/LDA method for different $M$, when applied on lead V6.

Fusion can also be performed at the feature level. Features from the LDA of autocorrelated ECGs from different leads of the same subject can be concatenated. The constructed vector is then compared to all the corresponding ones in the gallery set, and the best match is found. The window and subject recognition rates in this case is not as high as in the decision level fusion. With a window recognition rate of approximately 95%, it is suggested that specific lead information that does not offer high performance overrules the rest of the lead information significantly.

## 16.6.4 Experimental Results with Arrhythmia Screening

The recognition framework with arrhythmia screening is tested on a combination of the three data sets—that is, the PTB, MIT-BIH healthy, and MIT-BIH arrhythmia databases. In order to get comparable ECG signals, all recordings from the PTB and MIT-BIH healthy data sets were resampled to 360 Hz.

The power criterion concerns the distribution of the ECG power spectrum, when computed with DCT on autocorrelated ECG segments. Employing this criterion for arrhythmia (PVC) detection performs very well as depicted in Figure 16.19 for different power distribution thresholds.

Complexity measure is the second option for detection of arrhythmic ECG segments. As analyzed earlier, ECG windows that exhibit ventricular premature beats result in autocorrelation morphologies that correspond to high complexity since the

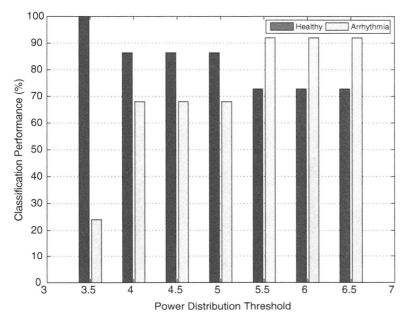

**Figure 16.19.** Arrhythmia detection rates with the power criterion.

repetitive property of the signals is lost. Several thresholds for the complexity measure are tested for their efficiency in detecting malignant recordings as shown in Figure 16.20.

Each of the criteria can be used separately for arrhythmia screening before identification. However, the misclassified windows at that step introduce an error that is propagated to the identification stage limiting the accuracy of the decision. Figures 16.21A and 16.21B demonstrate the recognition performance of the system when arrhythmia screening is performed with either the power criterion or the complexity criterion.

Finally, combining the complexity measure and DCT power criteria while utilizing strict thresholds for both, an electrocardiogram segment is classified as healthy only if both criteria are met. Thus, the propagated to the identification step error is reduced and the recognition performance is augmented. Figure 16.22 illustrates the performance of the method in terms of window recognition percentages, for several combinations of threshold values for the criteria.

## 16.6.5  Fuzzy Key Generation and Distribution

The ECG data, with R–R annotations, archived at the publicly available PhysioBank database [30] are used. ECG records are selected to include multichannel signals, recorded by placing leads at various body locations, which emulate the placements

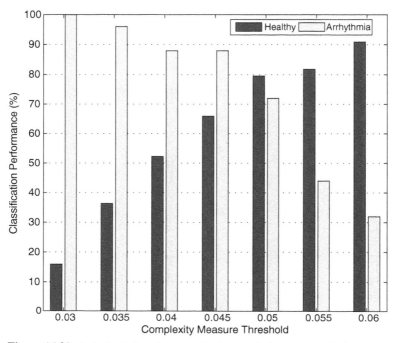

**Figure 16.20.** Arrhythmia detection rates with the complexity measure criterion.

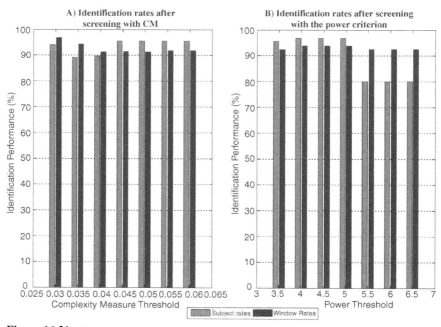

**Figure 16.21.** (**A**) Window and subject recognition rates when arrhythmia screening involves CM alone. (**B**) Corresponding rates using a power criterion for arrhythmia detection.

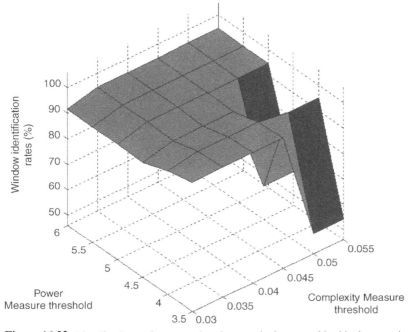

**Figure 16.22.** Identification performance when the two criteria are combined in the screening step.

of various sensors in a BSN. Since these leads are simultaneously recorded, this implicitly guarantees timing synchronization between sensors.

From the selected pool of data, a number of key distribution scenarios are investigated to illustrate the possible improvement in terms of communication resources (measured by the spectral efficiency or the effective data rate). Table 16.2 summarizes the simulation parameters and resulting findings for a targeted 128-bit cryptographic key.

**Table 16.2.** Performance of Key Generation and Distribution at Various Coding Conditions

| | Parameters | | Without Key Fusion | | With Key Fusion | |
|---|---|---|---|---|---|---|
| Number of Subjects | BCH Code | # DET Bits | FRR (%) | FAR (%) | FRR (%) | FAR (%) |
| 20 | (63,45,3) | 64 | 15.5 | 0.02 | 14.6 | 0.02 |
| 20 | (63,16,11) | 64 | 4.4 | 0.02 | 4.0 | 0.02 |
| 20 | (63,16,11) | 32 | 4.5 | 0.03 | 4.2 | 0.02 |
| 44 | (63,45,3) | 64 | 17.5 | 0.03 | 16.8 | 0.03 |
| 44 | (63,16,11) | 64 | 5.3 | 0.03 | 4.9 | 0.03 |
| 44 | (63,16,11) | 32 | 5.4 | 0.04 | 5.1 | 0.03 |

The coding parameters for error-correcting coding, with a BCH family [42], as well as the number of bits used for channel error detection (DET), were varied. Note that, compared to the single-point scheme, the amount of information actually transmitted over the channel for key distribution is lower. The results illustrate that the error-correcting stage is crucial. If key regeneration fails at the receiver (e.g., using a (63,45,3) code), then no amount of additional transmitted bits can make a difference, since no error correction is performed. On the other hand, if key regeneration is successful, then a smaller number bits (32 versus 64 bits) only negligibly degrades the key verification.

The performance metrics utilized for comparison are the standard false rejection rate (FRR) and the false acceptance rate (FAR) [3, 5]. In each case, we optimize the Hamming distance threshold of the DET bit sequence in order to give the smallest FAR, and we record the corresponding FRR. In other words, a minimum FAR is the objective, at the expense of a higher FRR. Note that this goal is not always appropriate; depending on the envisioned application a different, more balanced operating point may be more suitable. In this case, the relevant operating point is contrived instead for a particular application: to supply the cryptographic key for a conventional encryption method. Evidently, for this scenario, if accepted as a positive match, the receiver-generated cryptographic key needs to be an exact duplicate of the original key.

The results for the key fusion scheme show little change compared to key distribution from only the biometrics. This is an indication that the biometrics are already providing a good degree of randomness for key generation. If this were not the case, the external random source (which is forced to generate statistically reliable random keys) would have resulted in a significant improvement, since it would provide a much improved source of randomness for the key. But according to the obtained results, only slight changes are observed in the FAR.

## 16.6.6  INTRAS Data Scrambling

In this section, the robustness of INTRAS in the presence of key variations is investigated. Using the MSE as a performance metric, Figure 16.23 shows the results for INTRAS that combines three consecutive symbols ($M = 2$) and a key sequence $d[n]$ constructed from a 128-bit key.

In this case, the input symbols are simulated as an i.i.d. sequence of integers, ranging from $-10$ to 10. The distortions are modeled using a simple additive white Gaussian noise (AWGN) channel. Recall that, without any channel distortion, the INTRAS scheme can be summarized as follows. The scrambling step is

$$x_d[n] = \text{INTRAS}(x[n], d[n]) \quad (16.26)$$

with input $x[n]$ and key sequence $d[n]$. The corresponding descrambling step for ideal recovery of the original signal is

$$x[n] = \text{INTRAS}^{-1}(x_d[n], d[n]). \quad (16.27)$$

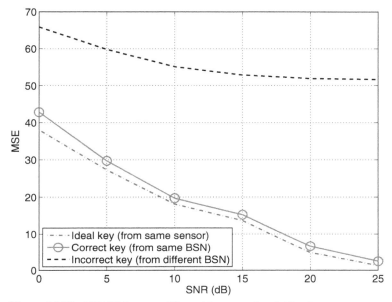

**Figure 16.23.** INTRAS data scrambling, with memory length $M = 2$.

To account for the channel distortion, the signal seen at the input to the descrambler or receiver side is

$$\widehat{x_d[n]} = x_d[n] + v[n] = \text{INTRAS}(x[n], d[n]) + v[n], \qquad (16.28)$$

where $v[n]$ is the AWGN. The associated channel signal-to-noise ratio (SNR) is computed as

$$\text{SNR} = \frac{\mathcal{E}\{|x_d[n]|^2\}}{\mathcal{E}\{|v[n]|^2\}}, \qquad (16.29)$$

where $\mathcal{E}\{\cdot\}$ represents the statistical expectation operator.

The results show that, without knowledge of the key, the signal recovered by an intruder differs significantly from the genuine signal. Moreover, an increase in the signal-to-noise ratio does not lead to a significant improvement with an incorrect key. By contrast, with the correct key, the receiver performance improves as expected with better operating environments. The gradual change in MSE is analogous to the effect caused by varying the degree of compression in a lossy compression scheme.

## 16.6.7    Remarks on the Simulation Results

It should be noted that the size of the data subsets in the scenarios examined above was modest, with fewer than 50 subjects used for performance assessment. This limitation was mainly due to various assumptions and requirements of the proposed methods. Specifically, for the robust identification with arrhythmia screening, the selected ECG signals should exhibit arrhythmic segments. Similarly, for the BSN application, only ECG signals acquired simultaneously in a multichannel manner were applicable, in order to simulate the placement of various sensor nodes on the same body.

It should also be emphasized that the experimental data were not collected originally by authors, but were retrieved from public databases [30]. The advantage of this approach is that, since these data signals have undergone critical scrutiny and were used previously in the ECG literature, one can assume reasonably that these signals faithfully represent what would be measured in the actual operating environment, using typical sensor devices. This serves to not only alleviate our need to establish a plausible experimental set up, but also demonstrate that our methods would be applicable to practical data sets. However, since these data signals were recorded using specific parameters and processing steps (which were tailored to the applications described in reference 30), the disadvantage is these signals may not be optimal for the presented methods.

Therefore, while the results presented in this section have demonstrated the feasibility of the proposed methods, for actual applications of these methods, further investigations need to be made. Several considerations should be taken into account. First, the signals used for testing the system should be recorded under conditions similar to those in the actual operating environments—for example, with the same bit resolution, dynamic range, signal-to-noise ratio and interference sources. Moreover, the number of test subjects should correspond to the typical number of users in the actual system; that is, the expected system capacity should be reflected in the simulation tests.

A practical biometric application may require several hundred users. With respect to the simulation scenarios presented in the above, this more demanding specification not only requires modifying the system setup, but also implies a loss of performance. In general, from an information-theoretic perspective, there is a limit on the supportable capacity of the system, determined by the information entropy of the biometric features. While an analysis of these issues is beyond the scope of this chapter, it can be noted that, practically, there is a trade-off between the achievable FAR and FRR, with an increased number of users. For instance, the recognition rates of the ECG identification will be decreased with more subjects. And in the BSN application, as shown in Table 16.2, the error rates are increased with more subjects.

In order to accommodate more users, the underlying processing system can be augmented—that is, trading off computational complexity for performance. For instance, the coding scheme and the number of bits transmitted in a BSN can be increased, which implies a loss in transmission efficiency. However, as noted above, this performance trade-off is only feasible when the number of users is less than the system capacity, determined by the inherent information content that can be reliably extracted from the ECG signal features.

Therefore, in practical applications of the presented methods, it is important to utilize data sets that faithfully simulate those in the actual operating environment. Then, with the corresponding simulation results, a system designer can appropriately select the various system parameters to enable suitable functionality of the proposed methods under the envisioned conditions.

## 16.7 SUMMARY

In this chapter, we study how the electrocardiogram can be used as a biometric. While it has not achieved as much prominence as other, more well-known biometrics, this versatile signal has so far proven to be a unique and promising participant. Not only can ECG deliver successful solutions in the traditional biometric arenas of human identification and authentication, it has also been instrumental in securing the resource-constrained body sensor networks in an efficient and practical manner. At the same time, there remain many challenges to be addressed. Before a successful consumer-ready product is available, a great deal of research and development is still needed to improve all aspects of the ECG-based biometric system. With a modicum of expectation, it is hoped that this chapter will play a part in further stimulating the research momentum on the ECG biometric.

## REFERENCES

1. D. B. Foster, *Twelve-Lead Electrocardiography: Theory and Interpretation*, 2nd edition, Springer, New York, 2007.
2. L. Sornmo and P. Laguna, *Bioelectrical Signal Processing in Cardiac and Neurological Applications*, Elsevier, Amsterdam, 2005.
3. C. Poon, Y.-T. Zhang, and S.-Di Bao, A novel biometrics method to secure wireless body area sensor networks for telemedicine and m-health, *IEEE Commun. Mag.*, **44**(4):73–81, 2006.
4. K. K. Venkatasubramanian and S. K. S. Gupta, Security for pervasive health monitoring sensor applications, in *Proceedings of 4th International Conference on Intelligent Sensing and Information Processing (ICISIP)*, 2006.
5. A. Cavoukian and A. Stoianov, Biometric encryption: A positive-sum technology that achieves strong authentication, security and privacy, *Information and Privacy Commissioner/Ontario*, March 2007.
6. W. Stallings, *Cryptography and Network Security: Principles and Practice*, 4th edition, Prentice-Hall, Upper Saddle River, NJ, 2006.
7. E. Cole, *Hiding in Plain Sight: Steganography and the Art of Covert Communication*, John Wiley & Sons, Hoboken, NJ, 2003.
8. A. J. Menezes, P. C. van Oorschot, and S. A. Vanstone, *Handbook of Applied Cryptography*, CRC Press, 1996.
9. A. K. Jain, A. Ross, and S. Prabhakar, An introduction to biometric systems, *IEEE Trans. Circuit Sys. Video Technol.*, **14**(1):4–20, 2004.
10. G.-Z. Yang, editor, *Body Sensor Networks*, Springer, Berlin, 2006.
11. S. Cherukuri, K. K. Venkatasubramanian, and S. K. S. Gupta, Biosec: A biometric based approach for securing communication in wireless networks of biosensors implanted in the human body, in *Proceedings, International Conference on Parallel Processing Workshops*, 2003, pp. 432–439.
12. S. D. Bao, Y. T. Zhang, and L. F. Shen, A novel key distribution of body area networks for telemedicine, in *Proceedings IEEE Workshop on Biomedical Circuits and Systems*, 2004.
13. British Medical Association Ethics Department, *Medical Ethics Today: The BMA's Handbook of Ethics and Law*, 2nd edition, BMJ Publishing Group, London, 2004.
14. J. R. Williams, *Medical Ethics Manual*, The World Medical Association, Ferney Voltaire, France, 2005.

15. L. Biel, O. Pettersson, L. Philipson, and P. Wide, ECG analysis: A new approach in human identification, *IEEE Trans. Instrume. Meas.*, **50**(3):808–812, 2001.

16. S. A. Israel, J. M. Irvine, A. Cheng, M. D. Wiederhold, and B. K. Wiederhold, ECG to identify individuals, *Pattern Recognit.*, **38**(1):133–142, 2005.

17. S. A. Israel, W. T. Scruggs, W. J. Worek, and J. M. Irvine, Fusing face and ECG for personal identification, in *Proceedings of 32nd Applied Imagery Pattern Recognition Workshop*, 2003, pp. 226–231.

18. T. W. Shen, W. J. Tompkins, and Y. H. Hu, One-lead ECG for identity verification, in *Proceedings of the 2nd Joint Conference of the IEEE Engineering in Medicine and Biology Society and the 24th Annual Conference and the Annual Fall Meeting of the Biomedical Engineering Society (EMBS/BMES'02)*, Vol. 1, 2002, pp. 62–63.

19. T. W. Shen, Biometric Identity Verification Based on Electrocardiogram (ECG), Ph.D. thesis, University of Wisconsin, Madison, 2005.

20. Y. Wang, K. N. Plataniotis, and D. Hatzinakos, Integrating analytic and appearance attributes for human identification from ECG signal, in *Proceedings of Biometrics Symposiums (BSYM)*, Baltimore, September 2006.

21. G. Wübbeler, M. Stavridis, D. Kreiseler, R. Bousseljot, and C. Elster, Verification of humans using the electrocardiogram, *Pattern Recognit. Lett.*, **28**:1172–1175, 2007.

22. D. Mücke, *Elektrokardiographie Systematisch*, Uni-Med Verlag AG, Lorch/Wurttemberg, 1996.

23. K. N. Plataniotis, D. Hatzinakos, and J. K. M. Lee, ECG biometric recognition without fiducial detection, in *Proceedings of Biometrics Symposiums (BSYM)*, Baltimore, September 2006.

24. Y. Wang, F. Agrafioti, D. Hatzinakos, and K. Plataniotis, Analysis of human electrocardiogram (ECG) for biometric recognition, *EURASIP J. Adv. Signal Processing*, vol. 2008:1–11, Article ID 148658, 2008. doi:10.1155/2008/148658.

25. M. Ilyas, editor, *The Handbook of Ad Hoc Wireless Networks*, CRC Press, Boca Raton, FL, 2003.

26. W. R. Heinzelman, A. Chandrakansan, and H. Balakrishnan, Energy-efficient communication protocol for wireless microsensor networks, in *Proceedings of the 33rd Hawaii International Conference on System Science*, Hawaii, 2000.

27. V. Shankar, A. Natarajan, S. K. S. Guptar, and L. Schwiebert, Energy-efficient protocols for wireless communication in biosensor networks, in *IEEE Personal, Indoor and Mobile Radio Communications Conference*, San Diego, 2001.

28. A. Perrig, R. Szewczyk, J. D. Tygar, V. Wen, and D. E. Culler, SPINS: Security protocols for sensor networks, *Wireless Netw.* **8**(5):521–534, 2002.

29. S. Lu, J. Kanters, and K. H. Chon, A new stochastic model to interpret heart rate variability, in *Proceedings 25th EMBS Annual International Conference of the IEEE*, 2003, pp. 17–21.

30. A. L. Goldberger, L. A. N. Amaral, L. Glass, J. M. Hausdorff, P. Ch. Ivanov, R. G. Mark, J. E. Mietus, G. B. Moody, C.-K. Peng, and H. E. Stanley, PhysioBank, PhysioToolkit, and PhysioNet: Components of a new research resource for complex physiologic signals, *Circulation*, **101**(23):e215–e220, 2000; Circulation Electronic Pages: http://circ.ahajournals.org/cgi/content/full/101/23/e215.

31. J. Malmivuo and R. Plonsey, *Bioelectromagnetism: Principles and Applications of Bioelectric and Biomagnetic Fields*, Oxford University Press, New York, 1995.

32. S. D. Bao, Y. T. Zhang, and L. F. Shen, A new symmetric cryptosystem of body area sensor networks for telemedicine, in *Proceedings of the 6th Asian-Pacific Conference on Medical and Biological Engineering*, April 2005.

33. F. M. Bui and D. Hatzinakos, Resource allocation strategies for secure and efficient communications in biometrics-based body sensor networks, in *Proceedings of Biometrics Symposiums (BSYM)*, Baltimore, September 2007.

34. F. M. Bui and D. Hatzinakos, Biometric methods for secure communications in body sensor networks: Resource-efficient key management and signal-level data scrambling, *EURASIP J. Adv. Signal Processing*, vol. 2008:1–16, Article ID 529879, 2008, doi:10.1155/2008/529879.

35. J. P. Martinez et al, A wavelet-based ECG delineator: Evaluation on standard databases, *IEEE Trans. Biomed. Eng.*, **51**(4):570–581, 2004.

36. J. Lu, Discriminant Learning for Face Recognition, Ph.D. thesis, University of Toronto, 2004.

37. L. Xu, A. Kryzak, and C. Y. Suen, Methods of combining multiple classifiers and their application to handwriting recognition, *IEEE Trans. SMC* **22**(3):418–435, 1992.

38. A. Lempel and J. Ziv, On the complexity of finite sequences, *IEEE Trans. Info. Theory* **22**(1):75–81, 1976.

39. S. W. Chen, Complexity-measure-based sequential hypothesis testing for real-time detection of lethal cardiac arrhythmias, *EURASIP J. Adv. Signal Processing* vol. 2007:1–8, Article ID 20957, 2007.

40. X. S. Zhang, Y. S. Zhu, N. V. Thakor, and Z. Z. Wang, Detecting ventrivular tachucardia and fibrillation by complexity measure, *IEEE Trans. Biomed. Eng.* **46**(5):548–555, 1999.

41. U. Ayesta, L. Serrano, and I. Romero, Complexity measure revisited: a new algorithm for classifying cardiac arrhythmias, in *Proceedings of the 23rd Annual International Conference of IEEE*, Vol. 2, Istanbul, Turkey, October 2001, pp. 1589–1591.

42. G. Kabatiansky, E. Krouk, and S. Semenov, *Error Correcting Coding and Security for Data Networks: Analysis of the Superchannel Concept*, John Wiley & Sons, Hoboken, NJ, 2005.

43. V. Valimaki, T. Tolonen, and M. Marjalainen, Signal-dependent nonlinearities for physical models using time-varying fractional delay filters, in *Proceedings International Computer Music Conference*, 1998, pp. 264–267.

44. F. Marvasti, *Nonuniform Sampling: Theory and Practice*, Kluwer Academic/Plenum Publishers, New York, 2001.

45. J. G. Proakis, *Digital Communications*, 4th edition, McGraw Hill, New York, 2001.

46. B. Noble and J. Daniel, *Applied Linear Algebra*, 3rd edition, Prentice-Hall, Englewood Cliffs, NJ, 1987.

# Chapter 17

# The Heartbeat: The Living Biometric

Steven A. Israel, John M. Irvine, Brenda K. Wiederhold, and Mark D. Wiederhold

## 17.1 WHY THE HEARTBEAT AS A BIOMETRIC

The goal of biometric authentication and verification is to uniquely characterize individuals from a population based on signatures derived from physiological attributes. The collected biometric signatures represent credentials. The biometric credentials are always resident on an individual, which is not achievable by a token-based system. Tokens have the disadvantage of being lost, stolen, forged, or subject to failure. Consequently, development of biometric methods for identification and verification is a growing area of research.

Traditional biometrics for authentication and identification include fingerprint, iris, and face. Products exploiting these signatures represent a growing commercial activity. Significant research has been conducted that documents the performance for each of the traditional biometrics over a large population [1]. Additionally, the authentication process consists of image processing implementations based upon manual processing; therefore, human confirmation of matches can be performed. However, fingerprints, iris, and face recognition technologies suffer from three basic shortcomings: Credentials can be forged [2], standoff range for acquisition is short [1], and uncooperative subjects cannot be processed [3]. Unlike token-based access systems, biometric credentials cannot be re-issued. Heartbeat biometrics offer an alternative that addresses these deficiencies and complement traditional biometrics.

Heartbeat information is observed using the three sensing modalities: electrical potential, sound, and reflection/absorption of light. Unlike traditional biometrics of

*Biometrics: Theory, Methods, and Applications.* Edited by Boulgouris, Plataniotis, and Micheli-Tzanakou
Copyright © 2010 the Institute of Electrical and Electronics Engineers, Inc.

**429**

face, fingerprint, and iris, heartbeat information can only be collected from a living individual, which makes it difficult to deceive or defeat. In order to deceive a heartbeat collection sensor, an intruder must mask the signal of his/her own body. Then, he/she must emanate the heartbeat of the target individual across electrical potential, sound, and reflection/absorption of light. Masking strategies often leave characteristic signatures themselves, such as a change in the noise floor, which would also flag the system to an intruder.

This chapter extends previous work in three areas. Previous research [4] focused mainly on analysis of the electrocardiogram (ECG). We extend the ECG results by applying our processing methods to a larger and more diverse set of individuals, demonstrating that performance remains high for a larger and a more diverse population. Second, we reviewed alternative sensing methods, using blood pressure and pulse oximetry [5], are presented and their corresponding performance is documented. Finally, we examine fusion of heartbeat information across the three modalities and quantify performance. The next section discusses the phenomenology and sensing modalities for monitoring cardiovascular function [6]. Then, we describe the experiments and data collection. Finally, we present the results and conclude with a summary of the findings and recommendation for future investigations.

## 17.2  HEARTBEAT SIGNALS

### 17.2.1  Cardiovascular Function

A heartbeat is the physical contraction of the heart muscle caused by chemical/potential differences in the component cells called myocytes. The myocytes have negatively charged interiors. The heartbeat begins with the firing of the sinoatrial (SA) node. The SA node (Figure 17.1) is the heart's dominant pacemaker. The electrical signal radiates outward causing the myocytes to depolarize and compress rapidly by a movement of sodium ($NA^+$) ions. This is expressed as P wave of the electrocardiogram (ECG) trace (Figure 17.2). The depolarization rate slows dramatically when the signal hits the atrioventricular (AV) node, where the chemical signal changes to relatively slow moving calcium ($CA^+$) ions. The change in contraction is expressed as the gap between the P and the R complexes. Once past the AV node, the signal

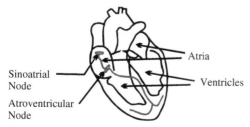

**Figure 17.1.**  The heart and its pacemakers [8]. The sinoatrial node is the heart's primary pacemaker. The atrioventricular node forces the time lag between the atrial and the ventricular contraction.

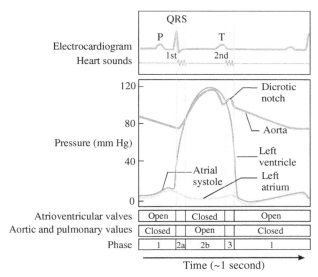

**Figure 17.2.** Heartbeat electrical, acoustical, and mechanical. (Adapted from Marieb [8].)

passes through to the cells lining the ventricles. The ventricles contract rapidly, which produces the R complex. Repolarization does not exactly mirror polarization due to the chemical agents and the lag between the end of the electrical impulse and physical displacement [7].

The heartrate is controlled by the autonomic nervous system (ANS). ANS is composed of the sympathetic and parasympathetic systems. Each of the two systems has independent ganglia and secretes neurotransmitters. The sympathetic system stimulates the cardiovascular system by increasing the rate of SA node firing, increasing the myocyte cell conductivity, and increasing the force of contraction. The results of the sympathetic secretion of neurotransmitters are: (1) the reduction of the interbeat interval due to the increased SA firing rate and (2) the reduction in the width of the P and T complexes due to increase conductivity. The parasympathetic system has the opposite effect.

Figure 17.2 shows the mechanics of a single heartbeat. The ECG and blood pressure data overlay the opening and closing of the heart valves to highlight the sensing phenomenology. The blood pressure lags the electrical firing mechanisms of the heartbeat. The contrast in the two metrics indicates the state of the heartbeat. The resultant expression of the heartbeat mechanics is captured in the synchronized electrocardiograph, blood pressure, and pulse oximetry data shown in Figure 17.3.

## 17.2.2  Sensing Electrical Potential

ECG data are traditionally acquired for clinical diagnosis of cardiac function. Dubin [7] describes the link between cardiac function and the expression of the ECG trace.

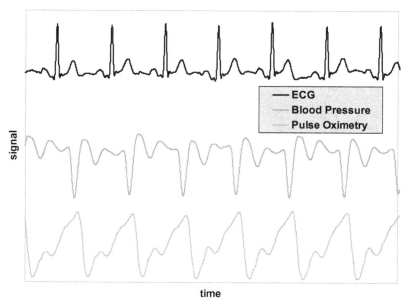

**time**

**Figure 17.3.** Synchronized ECG, blood pressure, and pulse oximetry.

In addition, he offers a set of rules for ECG interpretation. However, Dubin's work uses analog methods for applying these rules. With the advances in computational power and medical instrumentation, hardware/software systems have been developed for assisted ECG trace interpretation.

The ECG trace contains a wealth of information. Researchers have been using ECG data as a diagnostic tool since the early twentieth century. Only in the last 35 years, however, have researchers been able to apply digital analysis to the data [9]. The most common digital application is heartrate variability (HRV) [10]. Researchers have applied numerical methods to more complex diagnostic interpretation tasks such as demixing mother–fetal signals [11], identifying atrial and ventrical fibrillation [12, 13], myocardial infarction [14] and recently to characterize the uniqueness of the ECG to an individual [5, 15–18]. Except for the HRV studies, each researcher has developed *ad hoc* features from the ECG trace [19].

### *17.2.2.1 ECG*

The ECG measures the change in electrical potential over time. Each heartbeat consists of three complexes: P, R, and T. These complexes are defined by the fiducial of the peak of each complex (Figure 17.4). The ECG contains a wealth of information suitable for detailed clinical analysis. Although the electrical potential magnitudes vary directly with sensor placement, the relative temporal distances among the peaks and bases of the three complexes do not. We expanded the list of fiducials used for digital signal processing of the ECG (Figure 17.4). The additional fiducials are noted

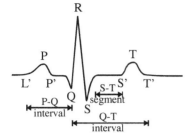

**Figure 17.4**    Expanded list of ECG fiducials with diagnostically significant intervals.

with an apostrophe ($\alpha'$) and are located at the base of the P and T complexes. Figure 17.4 also identifies segments within the ECG that cardiologists monitor for heart conditions [7].

### 17.2.2.2  Data Processing

To realize the ideal ECG data structure (Figure 17.4), the raw ECG data must be processed to remove the nonsignal artifacts. The first step is to identify the noise sources. Based upon the structure of these noise sources, a filter is designed and applied to the raw data. The filtered data are used to locate fiducials and to align the heartbeats. Figures 17.5, 17.6, and 17.7 show the processing results for a common data segment.

**Noise Sources.** Figures 17.5a and 17.5b show a sample of the high-resolution ECG data. The figures show that the raw data contain both high- and low-frequency noise components. These noise components alter the expression of the ECG trace from its ideal structure (Figure 17.4). The low-frequency noise is expressed as the slope of the overall signal across multiple heartbeat traces (Figure 17.5a). The low-frequency noise is generally associated with changes in baseline electrical potential of the device and is slowly varying. Over the 20-s segment, the potential change of the

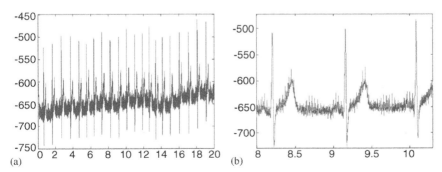

**Figure 17.5.** Raw ECG data 1000 Hz: (**a**) 20 seconds (**b**) 2 seconds. The $y$ axis is electrical potential and the $x$ axis is time in seconds.

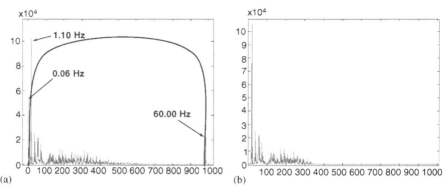

**Figure 17.6.** Power spectra of frequency filtering: (**a**) Bandpass filter of raw data. (**b**) Frequency response of filtered data. Part a shows the noise source spikes at 0.06 and 60 Hz and the information spikes between 1.10 and 35 Hz. Part b shows the filtered data with the noise spikes removed and the subject-specific information sources retained.

ECG baseline inscribes approximately 1½ wave periods. The high-frequency noise is expressed as the intrabeat noise shown in Figure 17.5b. The high-frequency noise is associated with electric/magnetic field of building power (electrical noise) and the digitization of the analog potential signal (A/D noise).

Plotting the Fourier power spectra illustrates the various elements of the ECG signal (Figure 17.6). In Figure 17.6a, three fundamental frequencies are readily identified: the 60-Hz electrical noise due to the US power line, the 1.10-Hz heartbeat information (approximately 22 heartbeats in 20 s), and the 0.06-Hz change in baseline electrical potential (approximately 1½ wave periods in 20 s). The remainder of the frequency power spectra is a combination of other noise sources and subject information. The goal of filtering is to remove the 0.06-Hz and 60-Hz noise while retaining the individual heartbeat information between 1.10 and 40 Hz. The filter

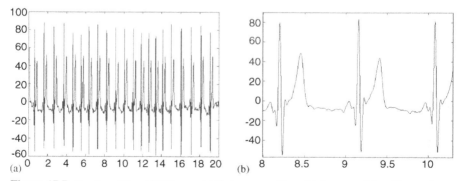

**Figure 17.7.** Bandpass filtered ECG trace. (**a**) Entire range of data. (**b**) Segment of data. The results of applying the filter (Figure 17.6) to the raw (Figure 17.5) data are shown to closely replicate the idealized (Figure 17.4) ECG without noise.

curve represents the frequency bandpass acceptance region [20, 21]. The filtering results are provided in Figure 17.6b.

Israel et al. [4] processed their high-resolution ECG data using techniques developed for standard 250-Hz ECG [21–24] and other signal processing data. Three basic technique categories that showed promise were local averaging, spectral differencing, and Fourier bandpass filtering. Filter design is constrained by both noise reduction and ability to retain the essential subject unique information that is stable across the widest population.

Each filtering technique was applied to a sample of the population. Feature extraction was performed and individuals were identified. Bandpass filtering proved to be the most efficient noise reduction technique. The frequency limits were chosen by identifying the observed high- and low-frequency noise sources from the frequency transformation plots (Figure 17.6). A considerable frequency gap exists between the subject information (43 Hz) and the 60-Hz noise. The gap at the high frequency will change with heartrate and individual. Similar factors for the collection hardware occur at the low-frequency end at approximately 2 Hz.

Our filtering solution merges heuristic and quantitative information and mathematics, using a frequency bandpass filter between 2 and 40 Hz. However, the filter is written using the equivalent of a lower-order polynomial. This filter allows 'advantageous' bleeding of information into the processed datastream (Figure 17.7b). The lower-order polynomial filter is stable at the low frequency edge. The resulting post-filtering power spectra is shown in Figure 17.6b. After filtering, the heartbeats for each data segment were aligned by their R peaks in a waterfall diagram (Figure 17.8).

R peak localization has been an interesting research focus for ECG processing [21, 25–28]. The R complex is very stable with an individual, across states of anxiety, and even across individuals. Its duration is approximately 0.2 s. To locate the R complex, we simply look for the maximum variation in electrical potential

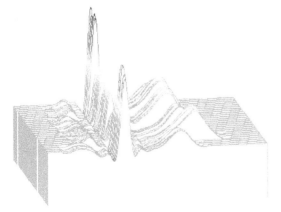

**Figure 17.8.** Waterfall diagram: Average for subjects by tasks. Each group of seven tasks is similar within each subject but visually different to other subject's seven task average.

for 0.2 s across 0.75-s overlapping windows. Double peaks or missing peaks are revealed using autocorrelation with previous and following heartbeats. Heartbeats are then cropped using the RR interval, the distance between the R peaks of adjacent heartbeats.

Figure 17.8 is a waterfall diagram where the heartbeats for each individual in a group are averaged by task [4, 5]. Differences among individuals are clearly greater than the task-to-task differences, which indicate that human identification using ECG heartbeat information is possible.

**Fiducial Points.**    After alignment, the ECG fiducial positions were located. The standard medical fiducial labels do not fully characterize the entire heartbeat trace. From pattern recognition science, additional feature attributes are rarely completely correlated or independent. However, additional attributes generally improve the scalability to larger populations [29] at the cost of reducing the tolerance to intra-subject variability.

The fiducial points were extracted in the time domain in two stages. The peaks were established by finding the local maximum in a region surrounding each of the P, R, and T complexes. The base positions were determined by tracking downhill and finding the location of the minimum radius of curvature (Figure 17.9). The minimum radius of curvature proved robust to local noise. By fixing the time difference between $x$ and $y$ and $x$ and $z$, the minimum radius of curvature is found by maximizing the value of $\delta$ using the vector cross product between the two directed line segments.

**Features.**    The expression of the ECG trace is a function of sensor placement for electrical potential magnitude only. The sensor position does not affect the observed relative timing of the individual P, R, and T complexes. Therefore, the temporal distances among the fiducial points are independent of the sensor placement. Since the heartbeat's R position was used as the origin for aligning the waterfall diagram, the distances were computed from the other fiducial points to the R position (Figure 17.10). These computational distances are unsigned.

An additional process is required to account for changes in these individual distances with changes in heartrate. The distances between the fiducial points and the R position vary with heartrate. If a linear relationship exists between heartrate and those distances, the normalized heartbeat would be computed as the extracted distance divided by the RR interval, which is the $L'T'$ distance plus the interbeat

$$\delta = \frac{|\vec{a} \times \vec{c}|}{|\vec{a}|}$$

**Figure 17.9.** Radius of curvature: By fixing the time difference between $x$ and $y$ and $x$ and $z$, the radius of curvature is computed as the vector cross product between the two directed line segments.

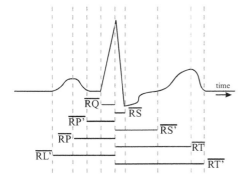

**Figure 17.10.**   Extracted distances among the ECG fiducials.

interval. This approach effectively scales the heartbeat to a unit length. The normalized features represent the relative positions of the fiducials within a heartbeat. The linear normalization has a heuristic rather than a physiological basis. The distance that an electrical impulse travels along the atrial axis is fixed, so that changes in heartrate are not evenly distributed across the P, R, and T complexes.

To better understand how normalization should occur, a review of the underlying physiology is required. The interbeat interval ($T'$ of the previous heartbeat to $L'$ of the current heartbeat) is a transition stage that is independent of the electrical timing mechanism. The R complex is a trigger for the ventricular contraction. As an electrical trigger, it is a function of distance and not heartrate. As such, it remains fairly constant with changes in heartrate. So, the principal mechanisms of heartrate changes are caused by atrial depolarization (P complex) and ventricular repolarization (T complex). These two events are the dominant causes to the changes in pressure within the heart and ventricular volume. The values for P and T complex distances were normalized by dividing by the $L'T'$ distance. Raw RQ and RS distances are used as features. In total 15, features were extracted from each heartbeat (Table 17.1).

Within each subject session, each 2-min task was divided into six 20-s segments. During feature extraction, either all features were identified for an individual heartbeat or (b) the heartbeat was removed from further analysis. Outliers were removed iteratively so that 70% of the original heartbeats were retained. Low heartbeat count

**Table 17.1.** Extracted Attributes[a]

| 1. RQ | 6. RT | 11. ST |
|---|---|---|
| 2. RS | 7. RS' | 12. PQ |
| 3. RP | 8. RT' | 13. PT |
| 4. RL | 9. P width | 14. LQ |
| 5. RP' | 10. T width | 15. ST' |

[a] The feature list labels are the normalized distance between the two fiducials. For example, RP' is the unsigned distance between the end of the P-wave and the R peak.

segments were also removed. The segregation of the task data into 20-s segments allowed for independent block training of the discriminant functions.

**Eigen Features.** The previous approach to ECG analysis relies on fiducial attributes—that is, features obtained by identifying specific landmarks from the processed signal. The fiducial-based feature extraction was unable to enroll 30% of the collected population (10% due to irregular structure of the ECG trace and 20% due to noise, such as muscle flexure). To overcome these two deficiencies, another feature extraction technique is required. The ECG data were aligned using the unsupervised procedure defined earlier.

For eigenanalysis, the entire heartbeat trace is presented to the system. This yields attributes that are always defined, even for atypical ECG traces discussed below (Figure 17.11). Due to the long feature vectors, eigen attributes are expected to characterize larger populations than fiducial-based feature vectors. Since PCA does not generate individual discriminant functions, individuals can be enrolled online without retraining. This approach has proved successful in face recognition, which has exploited eigenspace analysis for human identification [30–36].

ECG traces that depart from the idealized shape are, in fact, fairly common in the general population. Anomalies can include multiple extrema, rather than a single peak, and low contrast observable fiducials, such as the missing P wave in Figure 17.11. These exceptions, along with sensor noise, imply that fiducial processing methods are difficult to apply to a significant segment of the population.

We applied principal components analysis (PCA) for feature extraction. The technique, which we call *eigenPulse*, uses an eigenvector decomposition of the normalized ECG signal. This approach addresses the two weaknesses:

1. We are not limited to a small set of attributes; rather we use an orthonormal basis to represent the most significant features for distinguishing the ECG traces.

2. PCA features do not require fiducial extraction, which minimizes the exception handling problems and increases enrollment rates.

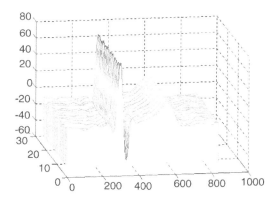

**Figure 17.11**    Missing P wave.

**Eigen Decomposition of the ECG Trace.**  The ECG trace is not a random event. It is cyclic with regularly occurring P, R, and T waves (Figure 17.4). If these common cyclic data are removed from an individual's datastream, the remaining information describes the individual's uniqueness or difference to the population norm. The fiducial features only capture information about relative position of features within the normalized heartbeat. Because the eigenvectors form an orthonormal basis for the feature space, the expression of normalized heartbeats using this decomposition provides a complete characterization of the ECG. Any normalized heartbeat can be approximated as a linear combination of a subset of the eigenvectors.

**PCA Attributes and Classifiers.**  We define the data blocks for our experiments in the following manner. The training data characterize the norm of the population. The gallery data represent the enrolled individuals. The probe data represents unlabeled information to be identified by the system. The data were block segmented into 20-s intervals in the same manner as the fiducial feature extraction analysis.

The PCA algorithm consists of four primary steps: construction of the covariance matrix from training data, calculation of the eigenvectors from the covariance matrix, projection of raw probe and gallery data into the eigenspace, and calculation of the distance between projected *probe* and *gallery* data streams. Initially, the mean heartbeat $\bar{x}_i$ is computed, where $n$ is number of heartbeats for the $i$th attribute of an $I$ length heartbeat [Eq. (17.1)]. For heartbeats, an attribute is a normalized time unit. For example, if a heartbeat is normalized to 256 intervals, we have $i = 1$ to $I$ and $I = 256$.

$$\bar{x}_i = \frac{\sum_{k=1}^{n} x_i^k}{n}. \tag{17.1}$$

Each heartbeat is then centered by subtracting its values from the mean. The centered heartbeats are then collected in matrix $w_i^k$ [Eq. (17.2)]. Matrix $w_i^k$ has attributes with zero means.

$$w_i^k = x_i^k - \bar{x}_i. \tag{17.2}$$

The next task is to find the orthogonal projections that maximize the differences within each attribute. The covariance matrix ($\Omega$) is constructed by accumulating the differences across all the examples in the training set ($k$) for each attribute ($i$) against the attribute mean [Eq. (17.3)].

$$\Omega = w_i^k \left( w_i^k \right)^T. \tag{17.3}$$

Because the covariance matrix is real-symmetric and positive semidefinite, its eigenvalues, $\lambda$, and eigenvectors, $v$, are computed using the standard eigenvalue equation [(17.4)].

$$\Omega \lambda = \lambda v. \tag{17.4}$$

Our eigen solver is a Jacobi-like method that has been applied to very large, 20k × 20k, systems [37]. The eigenvectors represent basis functions and establish the commonality of the population. The eigenvalues quantify the variance explained in each dimension corresponding to the eigenvectors.

The next task is to identify and retain the most significant classifiers by sorting the eigenvectors/eigenvalue pairs in descending order based upon the eigenvalues. Removal criteria for nonsignificant eigenvector/eigenvalue pairs can be based upon a threshold value, specific number of attributes, or estimates of information content and dimensionality achieved, $J' < I$.

The third step is to project the gallery into the basis space; i.e., bring all the data into a common basis for comparison. Projection is accomplished using Eq. (17.5).

$$\hat{w} = v_j^T w, \qquad j = 1, \ldots, J'; J' < I, \tag{17.5}$$

where $v_j$ is the $j$th eigenvector, $w$ is the gallery or probe set member, and $\hat{w}$ is the projected trace. At this stage, every individual known to the system is represented by a projection of the gallery set.

The fourth and final step is to compute the distances between each heartbeat from the probe dataset to each enrolled individual in the gallery. First, the probe traces are projected into the eigenspace using Eq. (17.5). The distance between the projected gallery traces and the projected probe traces is computed using an appropriate distance metric. Specifically, we computed the distances using the Mahalanobis cosine [Eq. (17.6)] based upon its exceptional performance with eigenFace [37].

$$s_{ij} = \frac{\hat{p} \cdot \hat{g}}{|\hat{p}||\hat{g}|}, \qquad \text{where } \frac{\hat{p}}{\hat{g}} = \frac{x_j}{\sqrt{\lambda_j}} \tag{17.6}$$

and where $\hat{p}$ and $\hat{g}$ are the probe and gallery examples of interest.

Each score for a given gallery example is normalized by the standard deviation of all scores. The normalization generates higher assignment performance than do nonnormalized values [34].

## 17.2.3 Acoustic Sensing

### 17.2.3.1 Blood Pressure

Blood pressure measures the force the blood exerts on the blood vessels. Typically, blood pressure contains two components: systolic, which is the maximum pressure during ventricular contraction; and diastolic, which occurs during ventricular relaxation. Blood pressure is used to understand narrowing of the blood vessels, hypertension/hypotension, and blood loss due to internal bleeding [8].

### 17.2.3.2 Data Processing

The blood pressure data were processed in the same manner as the ECG data; that is, the raw signal was Fourier bandpass filtered to eliminate the electrical and A to D noise. The bandpass filter designed for the ECG data was applied here. The noise

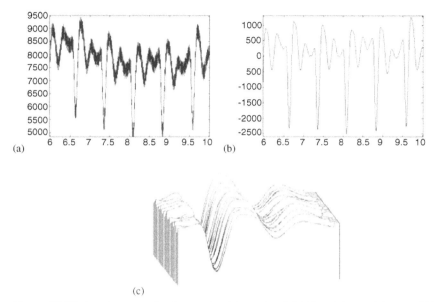

**Figure 17.12.** Blood pressure signal processing (**a**) raw signal, (**b**) filtered data, and (**c**) waterfall diagram.

sources between the two modalities are similar because both data were simultaneously digitized using the same hardware. The heartbeats were aligned using the $L'$ and $P'$ times recorded from the ECG data (Figure 17.12).

The blood pressure data contain less obvious fiducials than the ECG data (Figure 17.12). Because of this, Fourier power spectra attributes were computed to represent the blood pressure expression of the heartbeat. The first 18 power spectra attributes were extracted for each heartbeat (Figure 17.13). For most subjects, the first zero in the power spectra occurs at the 18 value. A stepwise process based on Wilks' $\lambda$ analysis selected the nine most significant power spectral components.

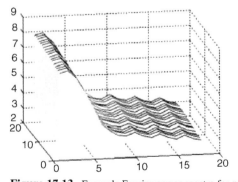

**Figure 17.13.** Example Fourier power spectra for nonstressed blood pressure data.

**Absorption Coefficient**

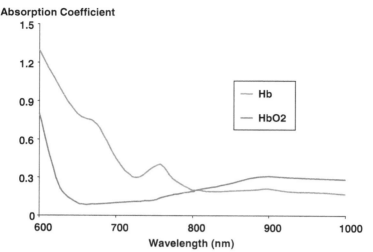

Wavelength (nm)

**Figure 17.14.** Absorption of light by wavelength by the blood.

## 17.2.4    Radiometric Sensing

### 17.2.4.1    Pulse Oximeter

Modern medical devices collect pulse oximetry data relatively easily and noninvasively [38]. The bonding of oxygen to hemoglobin affects the color properties of the blood. Specifically, differential coloring is associated with deoxyhemoglobin (Hb) and oxyhemoglobin ($HbO_2$) [39]. By illuminating the skin at the appropriate wavelengths (660-nm red light and 805-nm near-infrared light) and measuring the two signals (Figure 17.14), it is possible to estimate blood oxygenation as a function of time [40, 41].

### 17.2.4.2    Data Processing

Similar to the ECG, the Fourier bandpass filter removed the major noise artifacts and the data were aligned to the ECG data using the L′ and P′ times from the ECG traces (Figure 17.15a). Again, the ECG designed filter was applied to the pulse oximeter

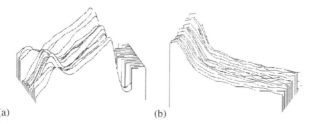

(a)                              (b)

**Figure 17.15.** (a) Raw pulse oximeter data. (b) Power spectral attributes.

data. Like the blood pressure signal, the pulse oximetry traces contain few regularly identifiable fiducials. Fourier power spectra attributes were generated to represent each heartbeat (Figure 17.15b).

## 17.3 DATA COLLECTION

The remainder of this chapter discusses a series of experiments that were performed to exploit the heartbeat signal for identification and verification. We highlight both processes that show promise for translating into the operational environment and the shortcomings of functions and procedures that should be avoided. This discussion provides a foundation for the next wave of researchers to improve the technology [42].

### 17.3.1  Baseline Experiment: Small Sample and Large Number of Tasks

In our original Phase 1 experiment, the data were collected from males and females between the ages of 22 and 48. Twenty-nine individuals were enrolled with 12 repeat sessions totaling 41 sessions within the data set. Each individual session contained data from a set of seven 2-min tasks. The tasks were designed to elicit different levels of mental and emotional stress. The low-stress tasks included the subject's baseline, a meditation task, and two recovery periods following high-stress tasks. The high-stress tasks were reading, an arithmetic stressor, and a virtual reality driving simulation (Figure 17.16) [43].

At the time of experimentation, no existing commercial-off-the-shelf (COTS) products existed to collect high-resolution information about the heart that produced an exploitable output product. Our team built specialized hardware. The hardware for this series of experiments collected data at 1000 Hz and quantized it to 12 bits, a much higher temporal resolution and bitdepth than for typical clinical instruments. The ECG data were collected at the base of the neck near the carotid artery and at the chest. The blood pressure was also acquired using the custom hardware at 1000 Hz

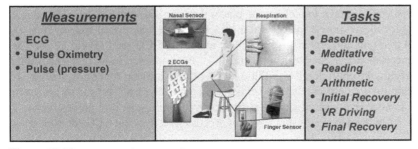

**Figure 17.16.** Data collection protocol.

using a pressure transducer. The pressure transducer was located on the index finger of the nondominant hand. The blood pressure signals were acquired simultaneously and synchronized with the ECG data. The pulse oximetry data were synchronized to the ECG and collected by a clinical device at 250 Hz. The Phase 1 collection sites were chosen to produce the highest-quality signals.

## 17.3.2   Additional Experiments: Large Sample with Simple Protocol

Four additional ECG data collection campaigns used a simplified protocol and a standard, FDA-approved ECG device. The result is an additional 75 subjects and 309 sessions. The ECG data were collected from the subject's forearms, slightly above the wrists. Some subject overlap exists between experiments (Table 17.2). For the collections identified as Phase 2 and 2b data, the subjects performed a two-task protocol: (low stress) baseline and the same arithmetic stressor that was used in the first experiment. The clinical instrument recorded the ECG data at 256 Hz and quantized it to 7 bits. The Phase 2 versus Phase 2b designations separates sessions collected by different operators using an identical protocol. For both the cardiac patients and the long duration data sets, the subjects were in a meditative state. The same commercial ECG device was used for all additional collections. The cardiac patients data sets were collected over one, two, and three sessions. No additional pulse oximetry or blood pressure data were collected.

## 17.4   IMPLEMENTATION AND PERFORMANCE

### 17.4.1   Biometric Saliency

#### 17.4.1.1   ECG Features and Sensor Location

As part of understanding the how well the ECG biometric can be exploited for identifying individuals, this section focuses on the relationship between changes in the ECG lead placement and identification performance. The hypothesis is that the extracted ECG attributes are invariant to placement of the ECG leads. To test this hypothesis, we collected ECG data at two electrode placements during each session. The sensor placement locations were at the base of the neck and fifth intercostal spacing (chest). We found a strong agreement between neck and chest ECG data (Table 17.3). The performance was determined by training the discriminant functions with the neck data and classifying the chest data. An additional set of discriminant functions was generated by training on the chest data and classifying the neck data. The scores are given for both the heartbeat and subject identification. A feature selection process chose 9 of the 15 attributes. Details of the selection process follow in the ECG Identification section.

**Table 17.2.** Summary of ECG Performance Across All Data Collections[a]

| Collection Name | Subject Count | Session Count | Total Subjects | Total Sessions | Task Count | Performance Within Task (%) | Performance Across Tasks (%) | Performance Across Sessions (%) |
|---|---|---|---|---|---|---|---|---|
| Phase 1 (1000 Hz) | 29 | 41 | 43 | 74 | 7 | 97.8 | 94.9 | 75 |
| Phase 2 | 36 | 51 | 51 | 77 | 1 | 89.2 | N/A | 82.5 (14 subjects) |
| Phase 2b | 28 | 34 | 33 | 38 | 2 | 100 | 92.5 | N/A |
| Cardiac patients | 51 session 1 | 133 | 67 total | 133 | 1 | 98.83 | N/A | 74.6 |
|  | 41 session 2 | 66 session 1 |  |  |  |  |  |  |
|  | 41 session 3 | 53 session 2 |  |  |  |  |  |  |
|  | 60 session 3 |  |  |  |  |  |  |  |
| Long duration Combined: Phase 1/ | 49 | 91 | 66 | 130 | 1 | 97.7 | N/A | 96 |
| Phase 2b/ Long Duration/ Cardiac | 104 |  |  |  | Varying | 91.5 | N/A | 88.25 (55 subjects) |

[a] Performance in the three right-hand columns is defined as the percent of individuals correctly classified.

445

**Table 17.3.** Classification Performance with Chest and Neck Data for Training and Test[a]

| Assay | Training Data | Heartbeats Classified | Individuals Classified |
|---|---|---|---|
| Locational Invariance | Neck | 82% | 100% |
| | Chest | 79% | 100% |

[a]Classification accuracies are an average of omission and commission error.

### 17.4.1.2 ECG Features and State of Anxiety

An individual's emotional state is continually changing. These changes occur naturally as a result of body chemistry, level of stress, and even time of day. The changes in emotional state are expressed in the ECG trace as changes in heartrate, noise in trace due to muscle flexor action, and variations in electrical potential gain. The hypothesis is that the normalized features extracted for human identification are invariant to the individual's state of anxiety. To prove this, four experiments were performed to test within anxiety and across anxiety states.

1. Discriminant functions trained from low-stress conditions could identify the same individuals under low-stress conditions.
2. Discriminant functions trained from high-stress conditions could identify the same individuals under high-stress conditions.
3. Discriminant functions trained from high-stress conditions could identify the same individuals under low-stress conditions.
4. Discriminant functions trained from low-stress conditions could identify the same individuals under high-stress conditions.

Table 17.4 shows the results for characterizing an individual based upon their level of anxiety. Both within and between anxiety states, nearly all the individuals were correctly classified. The results indicate that the extracted features are tolerant to anxiety state. The nominal difference of identity performance within and across levels of stress was not significantly significant.

**Table 17.4.** Classification Performance for Within and Between Anxiety State[a]

| Assay | Training Data | Heartbeats Classified | Individuals Classified |
|---|---|---|---|
| Within anxiety state | Low | 83% | 97% |
| | High | 78% | 97% |
| Between anxiety state | Low | 66% | 98% |
| | High | 63% | 98% |

[a] "Low" indicates low-stress tasks, and "High" indicates high-stress tasks.

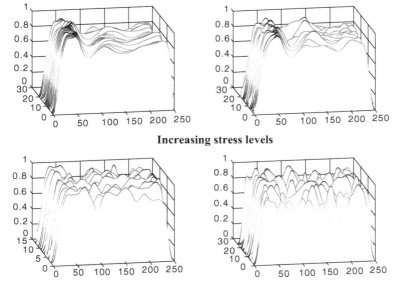

**Increasing stress levels**

**Figure 17.17.** Blood pressure waterfall diagrams baseline though higher level stressors. Due to sensitivity of the data blood pressure data with stress, classification with this modality can only be performed using low-stress tasks. The stress variance of the blood pressure data limits its utility as a biometric for verification and identification.

### 17.4.1.3   Stress and Blood Pressure

During the initial data analysis, the blood pressure data expressed a considerable amount of variation with stress. The change in wave structure with stress was not present within the ECG trace. The stressed segments exhibit higher-frequency components that are not present with the nonstressed data (Figure 17.17).

## 17.4.2   Identification

### 17.4.2.1   Background

Classification was performed on heartbeats using standard linear discriminant analysis (LDA). The LDA classified heartbeats. The heartbeat classification was converted to human identification using majority voting. The conversion was performed using contingency matrix analysis (Figure 17.18a).

The contingency matrix, Figure 17.18, is a visualization for classification performance [44]. The columns represent the known input classes. The rows indicate how the discriminant function(s) classified or assigned the data. The correctly identified samples (heartbeats) lie along the major diagonal; that is, the known input labels equal the assigned labels. If the maximum number of heartbeats within a row or

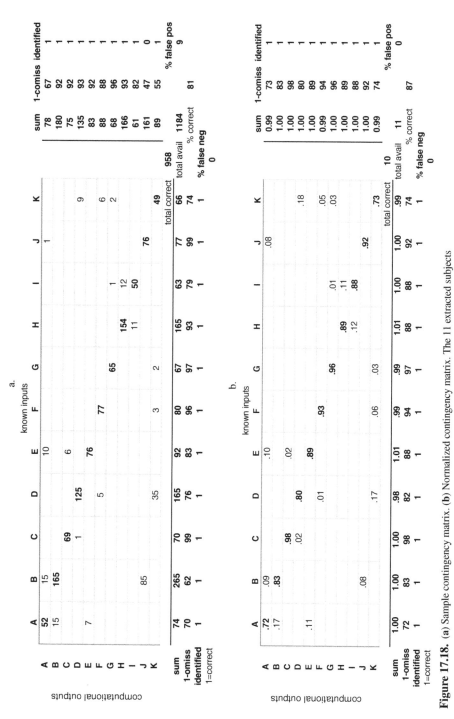

**Figure 17.18.** (a) Sample contingency matrix. (b) Normalized contingency matrix. The 11 extracted subjects illustrate the conversion between classification of heartbeats and identification of individuals. Based on voting, the marginal statistics show the classification of subjects. A "1" in the *identified* row indicates that the correct

column occurs along the major diagonal, then the subject is correctly identified—that is, voting. Errors occurring along the column are errors of omission. For a verification system, these are false-negative errors where an authorized user cannot gain access. Errors along the row are errors of commission. Commission errors are false acceptance errors, where an unauthorized user (intruder) gains access to the system. The identification error rates cited here are the average of the omission and commission values.

Figure 17.18a highlights a number of interpretation issues. First, the contingency matrix is not symmetrical. So, the rate of false acceptance between individuals is not the same. The number of heartbeats acquired is not the same for all individuals. The variable number of examples percolates through the contingency matrix. For Subject B, approximately 30% of the heartbeats have a commission error with Subject J. These heartbeats are over 50% of the total assigned to Subject J. If the two subjects contained the same number of heartbeats, then no confusion or false acceptance of Subject B to Subject J would occur. A normalization procedure, called iterative proportional fitting [45], could be applied if it were assumed that the number of heartbeats from all individuals is the same (Figure 17.18b). For these experiments, no assumptions about the relative likelihoods for assigning heartbeats were made.

### 17.4.2.2 ECG Identification

From the original 15 attributes, 9 attributes were commonly selected during the majority of experimental constraints of canonical relationships. A stepwise canonical correlation that used the Wilkes' lambda as a divergence measure provided the feature selection [46]. The feature selection process was performed to ensure stable discrimination. The nine commonly used attributes were: RQ, RS, RP', RT, Twidth, ST, PQ, LQ, and T'L' (interbeat interval), Figure 17.10.

To use ECG as a biometric, individuals will enroll their information into the security system. After enrollment, the user's ECG will be interrogated by the system. Unlike the traditional static biometrics, heartbeat signals vary with stress. The state of anxiety and the relative orientation of the ECG electrodes with respect to their heart's potential center are unknown. As the number of access controllers and individuals within a facility increases, the number of interrogations grows rapidly. To mitigate data handling issues, the number of descriptors for a given individual must be minimized.

In order to understand the extent that the data were able to generalize [47–49], discriminant functions were generated by training on the tasks individually and then block segmentation across tasks (Figure 17.19). If the features were completely invariant to anxiety state, then an operational enrollment and deployment scheme would be simplified.

The results show a high degree of agreement of generalization across the tasks, except for the VR driving. VR driving is the highest stressed task. Upon review of the VR driving data, many of the subjects' data still contained muscle flexor noise that was not removed with the current filter (Figure 17.19).

450

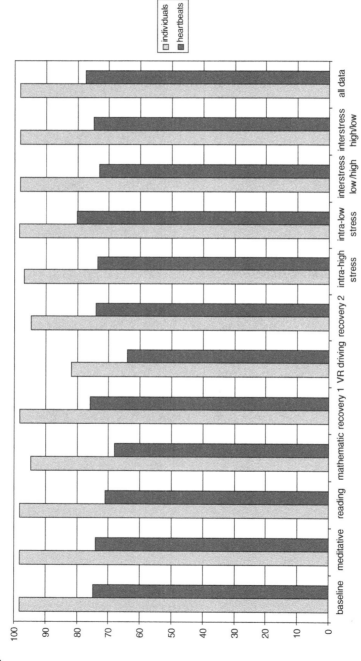

**Figure 17.19.** Classification performance for heartbeats and identification. Labels indicate training data. Test data were the remainder of the database. The "all data" was an average of segments across all tasks (i.e., train segment 1–test segments 2, 3, 4, 5, and 6).

**Other ECG Data Sets and Performance.** A large amount of additional data were collected by our team or provided to us. The additional data were collected using traditional clinical equipment. The lower temporal and quantization resolution increased the percentage of unenrollable individuals. The results consistently show that for small populations, the fiducial-based ECG performed well. When combining all the data sets, a reasonably high rate of individuals were identified. This occurred both within a given session and across time. The cost was that only 56% of the total number of heartbeats was correctly classified for the combined data set.

**Eigen ECG Performance.** The eigenspace attributes and classifier are compared to the Phase 1 fiducial attribute experiment. The results are currently being compiled and analyzed and will be reported in a forthcoming paper. The major goal of this analysis, achieving higher enrollment, was fully realized.

### 17.4.2.3 Blood Pressure Identification

Quality blood pressure information was collected from seventeen adult: males and females. Data consisted of baseline and meditative tasks alone. The heartbeats were normalized and power spectrum attributes were extracted. Six trials were performed; across segments and across tasks. Independent training and testing produced a 65% correct heartbeat classification and 93% correct classification of the individuals (Figure 17.20).

### 17.4.2.4 Pulse Oximetry Identification

Quality pulse oximetry information was collected from 17 adult, males and females. Data consisted of baseline and meditative tasks alone. The heartbeats were normalized and power spectrum attributes were extracted. Six trials were performed: across session and across tasks. Independent training and testing produced a 51% correct heart-

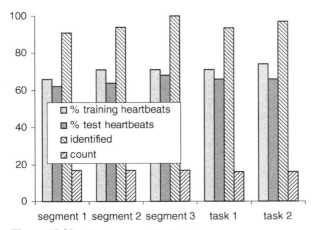

**Figure 17.20.** Blood pressure classification.

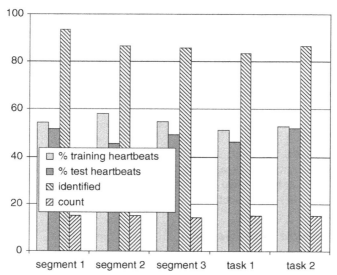

**Figure 17.21.** Pulse oximetry classification.

beat classification and 87% correct classification of the individuals (Figure 17.21). Due to the relatively poor performance, human identification using blood pressure and pulse oximetry is limited.

### 17.4.3  Heartbeats Needed

One issues with biometrics based on cardiovascular function is the amount of time required to identify an individual. The results presented in the ECG Identification Section show good identification performance based on 20-s samples of data, although correct classification of a single heartbeat may be sufficient. For an operational system, how many heartbeats are needed for identification? We are currently conducting a thorough investigation of this issue and expect to report on the findings in the near future. To give a preliminary answer to the question, one can model the classification of $N$ heartbeats with a binomial distribution with parameter $P$. The probability of classifying $K$ or more heartbeats correctly is given by Eq. (17.7).

$$P(X \geq K) = \sum_{J=K}^{N} \left( \frac{N!}{J! \cdot (N-J)!} \right) P^J (1-P)^{N-J} \qquad (17.7)$$

Based on this model, Figure 17.22 shows the probability of correct identification for varying numbers of heartbeats.

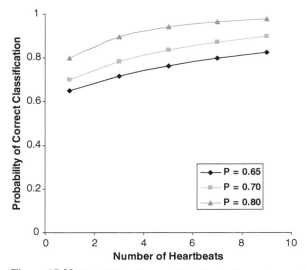

**Figure 17.22.** Probability of correct identification for varying number of heartbeats.

## 17.4.4 Fusion

### 17.4.4.1 Background

Fundamentally, any pattern recognition problem can be broken into a set of three functions: focus of attention, clutter rejection, and identification. The identification step accesses the system's knowledge base to compare the unlabeled entity features to those in the system's library. The result is a decision with the associated confidence (Figure 17.23). For cardiac function, focus-of-attention is performed by the single clock timing all of the modalities and the segmented ECG heartbeat timing applied to pulse oximetry and blood pressure. The synchronized Phase 1 data provides the inputs for this analysis. Numerically all the attributes were of the same magnitude. Fusion was performed over 16 individuals.

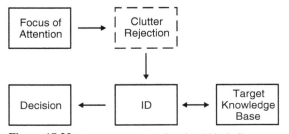

**Figure 17.23.** Pattern recognition functional block diagram.

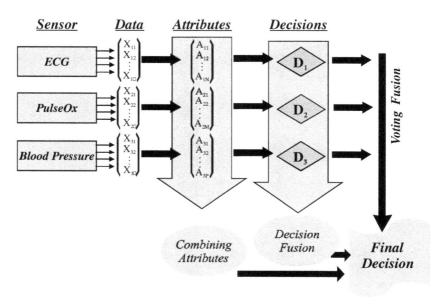

**Figure 17.24.** Fusion types.

The biggest problem facing the pattern recognition task is clutter rejection, or false-positive responses. Multimodal fusion has been shown to reduce false acceptance rate (FAR) in addition to improving probability of detection (Pd) [50]. There are three basic techniques for fusing data [51]: combining attributes, merging decisions, and voting (Figure 17.24). Combining attributes is a straightforward fusion technique. With combining attributes, a single identification algorithm is generated using feature vectors containing all of the attributes [52]. In other words, the feature vectors from all modalities are concatenated to form a new features vector, which is fed to the classifier. When we combine attribute techniques, we assume that the identification algorithms can handle (a) a relatively larger number of inputs and (b) possible differences in the input format (i.e., real, nominal, ordinal, etc.,), and we also assume that the attributes are registered and synchronized.

Decision fusion occurs when a set of classifiers generates a score from each sensor's attributes. The outputs from the individual classifiers are amalgamated using various weighting parameters based upon their belonging or membership to each output [53]. In this case, the scores were amalgamated twice: once by adding and the other by multiplying the corresponding scores from the individual analysis. Decision fusion is ideal for cases when sensor data are of different types or formats and in cases when an interaction across modalities is not expected [54].

Voting fusion is a simplification of decision fusion. With voting, each classifier makes a decision—that is, votes on the assignment for each input record generating a rank. Final assignment for each record is based the majority of output decisions [55]. Voting fusion was performed by multiplying the ranks of the

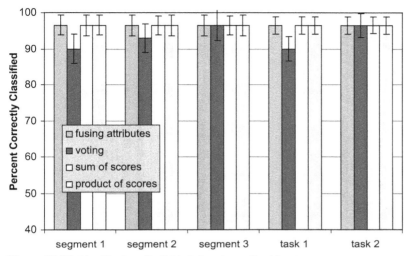

**Figure 17.25.** Identification of individuals based upon fused inputs.

corresponding values. The lowest value weighted rank determined the label for the individual. Voting fusion does not require the outputs of the individual classifiers to be calibrated.

The processing results for identifying individuals based upon the techniques described above yield inconclusive results. Figure 17.25 charts the performance of each type of fusion technique with their associated chi squared error. Each technique performs very well, with approximately 97% percent of the individuals identified. There is no significant difference among the techniques except that voting fusion generally performed worse than the rest.

However, the goal is to maximize the utility of heartbeat information to characterize larger populations. To better quantify the information gain by fusion, we present the fused heartbeat classification results. Figure 17.26 shows that most fusion techniques perform significantly better than the single modalities alone [56].

The most notable exception to fusion improvement is voting processing. This is expected since voting amalgamates a crisp discrete process that does not account for the relative magnitude of the decision of any of the classifiers. Voting, where the first and second highest classes have similar fitness scores, has the same weight as voting where the first and second highest classes for a modality are an order of magnitude different. In the former case, sufficient ambiguity exists and can be observed in the overlapping error bars, and in the latter no confusion exists. Voting fusion is not sensitive to this ambiguity. Similarly, decision fusion by product shows lower performance. This is probably caused by a single low goodness score for an individual modality that brings the fused product for the correct class below that of a competing class.

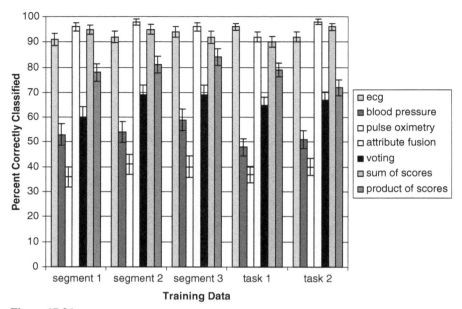

**Figure 17.26.** Heartbeat classification individual and fused modalities.

## 17.5 CONCLUSIONS

This research has extended and characterized the use of cardiovascular function as a biometric. We have extended previous work in terms of both the sensing modality and the population used for testing. Processing of ECG signals shows the strongest performance, and the results are robust across a larger and more diverse population than previously reported. In addition, alternative sensing modalities (blood pressure and pulse oximetry) are presented and the associated performance is documented.

Improved classification techniques will enable reasonable performance across higher populations, which will still likely be less than those for traditional biometrics. Heartbeat identification is ideal for verification applications [57]. These verification applications would be for unlocking tokens for access to computers and networks. Also, heartbeat information combined with traditional biometrics will reduce forgery of credentials and minimize intrusion.

The findings suggest several avenues for future investigation. Enrollment is an issue which our investigation into eigen-based methods will address [58]. We are also conducting a thorough study of the number of heartbeats required for accurate verification and identification. These results will quantify the utility of ECG biometrics in high-volume, restricted access areas. Additional topics that merit further study include:

* Characterization of the long-term (over years or decades) stability of cardiovascular biometric signatures

- Investigation of the effects of diseases and medications on the cardiovascular signatures
- Development of efficient sensing procedures to support operational use of biometrics based on cardiovascular function

## 17.6  ACKNOWLEDGMENTS

This research was sponsored by the Defense Advanced Research Projects Agency (DARPA) under contract number DABT63-00-C-1039. Additional assistance was provided by Dr. Rodney Meyer, Dr. Lauren Gavshon, Ms. Shannon McGee, Ms. Elizabeth Rosenfeld, Dr. Todd Scruggs, Mr. Will Worek, Dr. Clay Stewart, and Mr. Ted Yachik. The authors also wish to thank Dr. P. Jonathon Phillips, DARPA, for valuable comments concerning the development of this work. The view expressed here are those of the authors and do not necessarily represent the positions of DARPA or SAIC.

## REFERENCES

1. A. Jain, R. Bolle, and S. Pankanti, *BIOMETRICS Personal Identification in Networked Society*, Kluwer Academic Publishers, Norwell, MA, 1999, 411 pages.
2. D. Hawkins, Body of evidence, *US News and World Report* **18**:60–62, 2002.
3. R. Willing, Airport anti-terror systems flub tests, in *USA Today*, Internet edition, 2003.
4. S. A. Israel, J. M. Irvine, A. Cheng, M. D. Wiederhold, and B. K. Wiederhold, ECG to identify individuals, *Pattern Recognit.* **38**:138–142, 2005.
5. J. M. Irvine, S. A. Israel, M. D. Wiederhold, and B. K. Wiederhold, A new biometric: Human identification from circulatory function, in *Joint Statistical Meetings of the American Statistical Association*, San Francisco, 2003, p. 7.
6. M. J. Duggin and C. J. Robinove, Assumptions implicit in remote sensing data acquisition and analysis, *Int. J. Remote Sensing* **11**:1669–1694, 1990.
7. D. Dubin, *Rapid Interpretation of ECGs*, 6th edition, Cover, Inc., Tampa, FL, 2000.
8. E. N. Marieb, *Essential of Human Anatomy and Physiology*, 7th edition, Benjamin Cummings, San Francisco, 2003.
9. D. P. Golden, Jr., R. A. Wolthuis, and G. W. Hoffler, A spectral analysis of the normal resting electrocardiogram, *IEEE Trans. Biomed. Eng.* **BME 20**:366–373, 1973.
10. M. Malik, Heart rate variability: Standards of measurement, physiological interpretation, and clinical use, *Circulation* **93**:1043–1065, 1996.
11. L. De Lathauwer, B. De Moor, and J. Vandewalle, Fetal electrocardiogram extraction by blind source subspace separation, *IEEE Trans. Biomed. Eng.* **47**:567–572, 2000.
12. J. Carlson, R. Johansson, and B. Olsson, Classification of electrocardiographic P-wave morphology, *IEEE Trans. Biomedical Engineering*, vol. **48**:410–405, 2001.
13. E. Tatara and A. Cinar, Interpreting ECG Data by integrating statistical and artificial intelligence tools, *IEEE Eng. Med. Biol.* **January/February**:36–41, 2002.
14. M. Ohlsson, H. Holst, and L. Edenbrandt, Acute myocardial infarction: Analysis of the ECG using artificial neural networks, in *Artificial Neural Networks in Medicine and Biology (ANNIMAB-1)*, Goteborg, Sweden, 2000, pp. 209–214.
15. J. M. Irvine, B. K. Wiederhold, L. W. Gavshon, S. A. Israel, S. B. McGehee, R. Meyer, and M. D. Wiederhold, Heart rate variability: A new biometric for human identification, in *International Conference on Artificial Intelligence (IC-AI'2001)*, Las Vegas, Nevada, 2001, pp. 1106–1111.

16. L. Biel, O. Pettersson, L. Philipson, and P. Wide, ECG analysis: A new approach in human identification, *IEEE Trans. Instrum. Meas.* **50**:808–812, 2001.

17. R. Hoekema, G. J. H. Uijen, and A. van Oosterom, Geometrical aspect of the interindividual variability of multilead ECG recordings, *IEEE Trans. Biomed. Eng.* **48**:551–559, 2001.

18. J. M. Irvine, S. A. Israel, A. Cheng, B. K. Wiederhold, and M. D. Wiederhold, Validation of new biometrics for human identification, in *Joint Statistical Meeting*, New York, 2002.

19. Y. Wang, F. Agrafioti, D. Hatzinakos, and K. Plataniotis. 2008 Analysis of human electrocardiogram (ECG) for biometric recognition, *EURASIP J. Adv. Signal Processing*. 10.1155/2008/148658

20. P. S. Hamilton, A comparison of adaptive and nonadaptive filters for reduction of power line interference in the ECG, *IEEE Trans. Biomed. Eng.* **43**:105–109, 1996.

21. N. Thakor and Y. Zhu, Applications of adaptive filtering to ECG analysis: Noise cancellation and arrhythmia detection, *IEEE Trans. Biomed. Eng.* **38**:785–794, 1991.

22. A. Barros, M. Yoshizawa, and Y. Yasuda, Filtering noncorrelated noise in impedance cardiography, *IEEE Trans. Biomed. Eng.* **42**:324–327, 1995.

23. A. Koski, M. Juhola, and M. Meriste, Syntactic recognition of ECG signals by attributed finite automata, *Pattern Recognit.* **28**:1927–1940, 1995.

24. V. Afonso, W. Tompkins, T. Nguyen, and S. Luo, ECG beat detection using filter banks, *IEEE Trans. Biomed. Eng.* **46**:192–202, 1999.

25. A. H. Al-Khalidi, M. E. Lewis, J. N. Townened, R. S. Bonser, and J. H. Coote, A novel and simple technique to allow detection of the position of the R-waves from intraventricular pressure, *IEEE Trans. Biomed. Eng.* **48**:606–610, 2001.

26. R. Jane, H. Rix, P. Caminal, and P. Laguna, Alignment methods for averaging of high-resolution cardiac signals: A comparative study of performance, *IEEE Trans. Biomed. Eng.* **38**:571–579, 1991.

27. E. Laciar, R. Jane, and D. H. Brooks, Improved alignment method for noisy high-resolution ECG and holter records using multiscale cross correlation, *IEEE Trans. Biomed. Eng.* **50**:344–353, 2003.

28. A. L. Goldberger, L. A. N. Amaral, L. Glass, J. M. Hausdorff, P. C. Ivanov, R. G. Mark, J. E. Mietus, G. B. Moody, C. K. Peng, and H. E. Stanley, PhysioBank, PhysioToolkit, and PhysioNet: Components of a new research resource for complex physiologic signals, *Circulation* **101**:215–220, 2000.

29. R. O. Duda, P. E. Hart, and D. G. Stork, *Pattern Classification*, 2nd edition, John Wiley & Sons, New York, 2001.

30. T. Heseltine, N. Pears, and J. Austin, Evaluation of image pre-processing techniques for eigenface based face recognition, in *2nd International Conference on Imagery and Graphics*, Hefei, China, 2002, pp. 677–685.

31. Z. Li and X. Tang, Eigenface recognition using different training data sizes, in *Information Conference on Information Security*, Shanghai, China, 2002, p. 5.

32. X. Liu, T. Q. Chen, and B. V. K. V. Kumar, Face authentication for multiple subjects using eigenflow, *Pattern Recognit.* **36**:313–328, 2003.

33. P. J. Phillips, Matching pursuit filters applied to face identification, *IEEE Trans. Image Processing* **7**:1150–1164, 1998.

34. M. Turk and A. Pentland, Eigenfaces for recognition, *J. Cognitive Neurosci.* **3**:71–86, 1991.

35. A. Yilmaz and M. Gokmen, Eigenhill vs. eigenface and eigenedge, *Pattern Recognit.* **34**:181–184, 2001.

36. J. Zhang, Y. Yan, and M. Lades, Face recognition: Eigenface, elastic matching, and neural nets, *Proc. IEEE* **85**:1423–1435, 1997.

37. S. A. Israel, W. T. Scruggs, W. J. Worek, and J. M. Irvine, Fusing face and ECG for personal identification, in *32nd Applied Imagery and Pattern Recognition Workshop: Image and Data Fusion, Washington, 2003*, pp. 226–231.

38. M. J. Hayes and P. R. Smith, A new method for pulse oximetry possessing inherent insensitivity to artifact, *IEEE Trans. Biomed. Eng.* **48**:452–461, 2001.

39. L. G. Lindberg and P. A. Oberg, Photoplethysmography Part 2: Influence of light source wavelength, *Med. Biol. Eng. Comput.* **29**:48–54, 1991.

40. I. Yoshiya, Y. Shimada, and K. Tanaka, Spectrophotometric monitoring of arterial oxygen saturation in the fingertip, *Med. Biolog. Eng. Comput.* **18**:27–32, 1980.

41. G. Zonios, U. Shankar, and V. K. Iyer, Pulse oximetry theory and calibration for low saturations, *IEEE Trans. Biomed. Eng.* **51**:818–822, 2004.

42. M. D. Wiederhold, S. A. Israel, R. P. Meyer, and J. M. Irvine, *Human identification by analysis of physiometric variation*, SAIC, United States; 2006.

43. D. P. Jang, S. A. Israel, B. K. Wiederhold, M. D. Wiederhold, S. B. McGehee, L. W. Gavshon, R. Meyer, and J. M. Irvine, Protocols for protecting patient information within a biometric analysis, in *Biometrics Section of the International Conference on Information Security, Seoul, Korea*, 2001.

44. R. G. Congalton and K. Green, *Assessing the Accuracy of Remotely Sensed Data: Principles and Practices FL*:Lewis Publishers, Boca Raton, 1991.

45. S. E. Fienberg, An Iterative Procedure for Estimation in Contingency Tables, *The Ann. Math. Stat.* **41**:907–917, 1970.

46. D. F. Morrison, *Multivariate Statistical Methods*, 2nd edition, McGraw-Hill, New York, 1976.

47. S. C. Dass, Y. Zhu, and A. K. Jain, Validating a Biometric Authentication System: Sample Size Requirements, *IEEE Trans. Pattern Anal. Mach. Intell.* **26**:1902–1913, 2006.

48. N. Poh, A. Martin, and S. Bengio, Performance generalization in biometric authentication using joint user-specific and sample bootstrap, *IEEE Trans. Pattern Anal. Mach. Intell.* **29**:492–498, 2007.

49. J. L. Wayman, Error-rate equations for the general biometric system, *IEEE Robot. Autom. Mag.* **March**:35–48, 1999.

50. D. L. Hall and J. Llinas, An introduction to multisensor data fusion, *Proc. IEEE* **85**:6–23, 1997.

51. I. Bloch, A. Hunter, A. Appriou, A. Ayoun, S. Benferhat, P. Besnard, L. Cholvy, R. Cooke, F. Cuppens, D. Dubois, H. Fargier, H. Parade, A. Saffiotti, P. Smets, and C. Sossai, Fusion: General Concepts and Characteristics, *Int. J. Intell. Syst.* **16**:1107–1134, 2001.

52. L. I. Kuncheva, Switching between selection and fusion in combining classifiers: An experiment, *IEEE Trans. Syst. Man Cybern. Part B: Cybern.* **32**:146–156, 2002.

53. P. C. Smits, Multiple classifier systems for supervised remote sensing image classification based on dynamic classifier selection, *IEEE Trans. Geosci. Remote Sens.* **40**:801–813, 2002.

54. D. L. Hall and J. Llinas, *Handbook of Multisensor Data Fusion*, CRC Press, Boca Raton, FL, 2001.

55. J. Kittler and F. M. Alkoot, Sum versus vote fusion in multiple classifier systems, *IEEE Trans. Pattern Anal. Mach. Intell.* **25**:110–115, 2003.

56. S. A. Israel, Performance metrics: How and when, *Geocarto Int.* **21**:23–32, 2006.

57. J. M. Irvine and S. A. Israel, 2009. A sequential procedure for individual identity verification using ECG, *EURASIP J. Adv. Signal Processing*: Recent advances in Biometric systems: A signal processing perspective, 2009 (243215) 13 pp, doi:10.1155/2009/243215.

58. J. M. Irvine, S. A. Israel, M. D. Wiederhold, and B. K. Wiederhold, EigenPulse: robust human identification from cardiovascular function, *Pattern Recogn.* **41**(12), 2008.

# Chapter 18

# Multimodal Physiological Biometrics Authentication

**Alessandro Riera, Aureli Soria-Frisch, Mario Caparrini, Ivan Cester, and Giulio Ruffini**

## 18.1 INTRODUCTION

The term biometry is derived from the Greek words "bios" (life) and "metron" (measure). In the broader sense, biometry can be defined as the measurement of body characteristics. With this nontechnological meaning, this term has been used in medicine, biology, agriculture, and pharmacy. For example, in biology, biometry is a branch that studies biological phenomena and observations by means of statistical analysis.

However, the rise of new technologies since the second half of the twentieth century to measure and evaluate physical or behavioral characteristics of living organisms automatically has given the word a second meaning. In the present study, the term biometrics refers to the following definition [1]:

Biometry, however, has also acquired another meaning in recent decades, focused on the characteristic to be measured rather than the technique or methodology used [1]:

> The term biometry refers to automated methods and techniques that analyze human characteristics in order to recognize a person, or distinguish this person from another, based on a physiological or behavioral characteristic.
>
> A biometric is a unique, measurable characteristic or trait of a human being for automatically recognizing or verifying identity.

These definitions contain several important concepts that are critical to biometry:

*Unique*: In order for something to be unique, it has to be the only existing one of its type, have no like or equal, be different from all others. When trying to identify an individual with certainty, it is absolutely essential to find something that is unique to that person.

*Measurable*: In order for recognition to be reliable, the characteristic being used must be relatively static and easily quantifiable. Traits that change significantly with time, age, environment conditions, or other variables are of course not suitable for biometrics.

*Characteristic or Trait*: Measurable physical or personal behavioral pattern used to recognize a human being. Currently, identity is often confirmed by something a person has, such as a card or token, or something the person knows, such as a password or a personal identification number. Biometrics involves something a person is or does. These types of characteristics or traits are intrinsic to a person and can be approximately divided into physiological and behavioral. Physiological characteristics refer to what the person is; that is, they measure physical parameters of a certain part of the body. Some examples are fingerprints, that use skin ridges, face recognition, using the shape and relative positions of face elements, retina scanning, and so on. Behavioral characteristics are related to what a person does, or how the person uses the body. Voice recognition, gait recognition, and keystroke dynamics are good examples of this group.

*Automatic*: In order for something to be automatic it must work by itself, without direct human intervention. For a biometric technology to be considered automatic, it must recognize or verify a human characteristic in a reasonable time and without a high level of human involvement.

*Recognition*: To recognize someone is to identify them as someone who is known, or to distinguish someone because you have seen, heard, or experienced them before (to "know again"). A person cannot recognize someone who is completely unknown to them. A computer system can be designed and trained to recognize a person based on a biometric characteristic, comparing a biometric presented by a person against biometric samples stored in a database. If the presented biometric matches a sample on the file, the system then recognizes the person.

*Verification*: To verify something is to confirm its truth or establish its correctness. In the field of biometrics, verification is the act of proving the claim made by a person about their identity. A computer system can be designed and trained to compare a biometrics presented by a person against a stored sample previously provided by that person and identified as such. If the two samples match, the system confirms or authenticates the individual as the owner of the biometrics on file.

*Identity*: Identity is the answer to the question about who a person is, or about the qualities of a person or group which make them different from others—that is, being a specific person. Identity can be understood either as the distinct personality of an individual regarded as a persistent entity, or as the individual characteristics by which this person is recognized or known. Identification is the process of associating or linking specific data with a particular person.

A biometric system is essentially a pattern recognition system that operates by acquiring biometric data from an individual, extracting a feature set from the acquired data, and comparing this feature set against the template set in the database. Depending on the application context, a biometric system may operate either in authentication mode or in identification mode:

- **Authentication** (Greek: $\alpha\upsilon\theta\epsilon\nu\tau\iota\kappa\phi\varsigma$, from "authentes" = "author") is the act of proving the claim made by a person about their identity. In other words, the authentication of a person consists in verifying the identity they declare. In the authentication mode, the system validates a person's identity by comparing the captured biometric data with her own biometric template(s) stored system database. In such a system, an individual who desires to be recognized claims an identity, usually via a PIN (Personal Identification Number), a user name, a smart card, and so on, and the system conducts a one-to one comparison to determine whether the claim is true or not (e.g., "Does this biometric data belong to X?"). Identity verification is typically used for positive recognition, where the aim is to prevent multiple people from using the same identity. Authentication is also commonly referred to as verification.

- **Identification** (Latin: idem-facere, "to make the same") is the act of recognizing a person without any previous claim or declaration about their identity. In other words, the identification of a person consists in recognizing them, with that person being aware or not of this recognition task being performed. In the identification mode, the system recognizes an individual by searching the templates of all the users in the database for a match. Therefore, the system conducts a one-to-many comparison to establish an individual's identity (or fails if the subject is not enrolled in the system database) without the subject having to claim an identity (e.g., "Whose biometric data is this?"). Identification is a critical component in negative recognition applications where the system establishes whether the person is who she (implicitly or explicitly) denies to be. The purpose of negative recognition is to prevent a single person from using multiple identities. Identification may also be used in positive recognition for convenience (the user is not required to claim an identity). While traditional methods of personal recognition such as passwords, PINs, keys, and tokens may work for positive recognition, negative recognition can only be established through biometrics.

In our chapter we will describe a system that works on authentication mode, although it is quite straightforward to modify it to work on identification mode [2].

The increasing interest in biometry research is due to the increasing need for highly reliable security systems in sensitive facilities. From defense buildings to amusement parks, a system able to identify subjects in order to decide if they are allowed to pass or not would be very well accepted. This is because identity fraud nowadays is one of the more common criminal activities and is associated with large costs and serious security issues. Several approaches have been applied in order to prevent these problems. Several biometric modalities are already being used in the market: Voice recognition, face recognition and fingerprint recognition are among the more common modalities nowadays. But other types of biometrics are being studied nowadays as well: ADN analysis, keystroke, gait, palm print, ear shape, hand geometry, vein patterns, iris, retina, and written signature.

New types of biometrics, such as electroencephalography (EEG) and electrocardiography (ECG), are based on physiological signals, rather than more traditional biological traits. These have their own advantages as we will see in the following paragraphs.

An ideal biometric system should present the following characteristics: 100% reliability, user friendliness, fast operation, and low cost. The perfect biometric trait should have the following characteristics: very low intra-subject variability, very high inter-subject variability, very high stability over time, and universality. Typical biometric traits, such as fingerprint, voice, and retina, are not universal and can be subject to physical damage (dry skin, scars, loss of voice, etc.). In fact, it is estimated that 2–3% of the population is missing the feature that is required for authentication, or that the provided biometric sample is of poor quality. Furthermore, these systems are subject to attacks such as presenting a registered deceased person, presenting a dismembered body part, or introduction of fake biometric samples. Since every living and functional person has a recordable EEG/ECG signal, the EEG/ECG feature is universal. Moreover, brain or heart damage is something that rarely occurs. Finally, it is very hard to fake an EEG/ECG signature or to attack an EEG/ECG biometric system.

EEG is the electrical signal generated by the brain and recorded in the scalp of the subject. These signals are spontaneous because there are always currents in the scalp of living subjects. In other words, the brain is never at rest. Because everybody has different brain configurations (it is estimated that a human brain contains $10^{11}$ neurons and $10^{15}$ synapses), spontaneous EEG between subjects should be different; therefore a high inter-subject variability is expected [3].

A similar argument can be applied to ECG. This signal describes the electrical activity of the heart, and it is related to the impulses that travel through it. It provides information about the heart rate, rhythm and morphology. Because these characteristics are very subject-dependent, a high inter-subject variability is also expected. This has been shown in previous works [4–8].

As will be demonstrated using the results of our research, EEG and ECG present a low intra-subject variability in the recording conditions we defined: Within 1 min the subject should be relaxed and have their eyes closed. Furthermore, the system presented herein attains an improvement of classification performance by combining feature fusion, classification fusion, and multimodal biometric fusion strategies.

This kind of multistage fusion architecture has been presented in reference 9 as an advancement for biometry systems.This paper describes a ready-to-use authentication biometric system based on EEG and ECG. This constitutes the first difference with already presented works [2, 4–8, 10–14]. The system presented herein undertakes subject authentication, whereas a biometric identification has been the target of those works. Moreover, they present some results on the employment of EEG and ECG as a person identification cue, which herein becomes a stand-alone system.

A reduced number of electrodes have been already used in past works [2, 10–14] in order to reduce system obtrusiveness. This feature has been implemented in our system. There is, however, a differential trait. The two forehead electrodes are used in our system, while in other papers other electrodes configurations are used; for example, reference 11 uses electrode P4. Our long-term goal is the integration of the biometric system with the ENOBIO wireless sensory unit [15–17]. ENOBIO can use dry electrodes, avoiding the usage of conductive gel and therefore improving the user-friendliness. In order to achieve this goal, employing electrodes on hairless areas becomes mandatory, a condition our system fulfills.

In the following sections, our authentication methodology will be presented. Section 18.2 explains the experimental protocol that is common for EEG and ECG recording. Section 18.3 deals with the EEG-extracted features and the authentication algorithms, while Section 18.4 is dedicated to the ECG features and algorithms. For these two sections, the performances are also individually given. Section 18.5 explains the fusion process carried out to achieve higher performance. Finally, conclusions are drawn in Section 18.6, while Section 18.7 provides a summary of the chapter.

## 18.2 EXPERIMENTAL PROTOCOL

A database of 40 healthy subjects (30 males and 10 females, aged from 21 to 62 years) has been collected in order to evaluate the performance of our system. An informed consent along with a health questionnaire was signed and filled by all subjects.

The EEG/ECG recording device is ENOBIO, a product developed at Starlab Barcelona SL. It is wireless and implements a four-channel (plus the common mode) device with active electrodes. It is therefore quite unobtrusive, fast, and easy to place. Even thought ENOBIO can work on dry mode, in this study conductive gel has been used. In Figure 18.1, we can see the ENOBIO sensor integrated in a cap worn by a subject.

In Figure 18.2, a sample of EEG recorded with ENOBIO is shown. An ECG sample data is also shown in Figure 18.3. Notice that the EEG amplitude is typically about 60 μV, while ECG amplitude is typically about 1000 μV; therefore it is always more complicated to obtain a good EEG recording than to obtain a good ECG, because the signal-to-noise ratio is easier to maximize with a stronger signal. No preprocessing has been done on these sample signals.

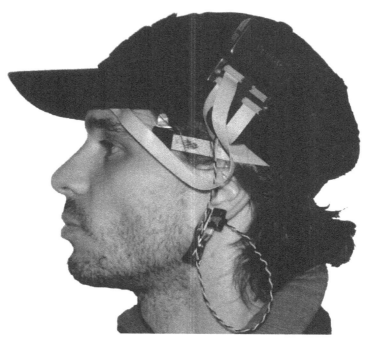

**Figure 18.1.** ENOBIO four-lead sensor integrated in a cap. In this picture, only three channels are connected (gray cables). We can also see the common mode cable connected to the left earlobe of the subject (black and yellow cable). The ENOBIO sensor is valid for recording EEG and ECG, but it can also measure electrooculogram (EOG) and electromyogram (EMG).

The electrode placement is as follows:

- Two on the forehead (FP1 and FP2) for EEG recording
- One on the left wrist for ECG recording
- One on the right earlobe as reference
- One on the left earlobe as the hardware common mode

At this time, conductive gel is used, but in the future ENOBIO will work without gel, using carbon nanotube technology. Some tests have been done using this new electrodes with very positive results [15,16], but at the moment some biocompatibility studies are being planned in order to approve their commercial use.

The recordings are carried out in a calm environment. The subjects are asked to sit in a comfortable armchair, relax, be quiet, and close their eyes. Then three 3-min takes are recorded for 32 subjects and four 3-min takes are recorded for 8 subjects, preferably on different days, or at least at different moments of the day. The 32 subject set are used as reference subject in the classification stage and the 8 subjects are the ones that are enrolled into the systems. Then several 1-min takes are recorded afterwards for these enrolled subjects, in order to use them as authentication tests. Both the enrollment takes and the authentication takes are recorded under the same conditions.

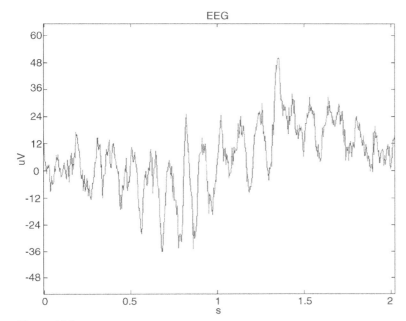

**Figure 18.2.** ENOBIO EEG recording sample of 2 s with no preprocessing. The alpha wave (10-Hz characteristic EEG wave) can be seen.

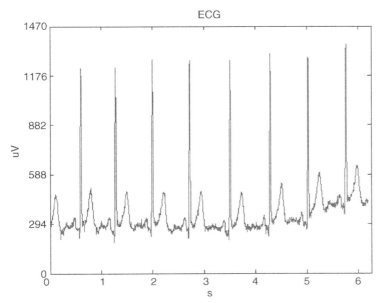

**Figure 18.3.** ENOBIO ECG recording sample of approximately 6 s with no preprocessing.

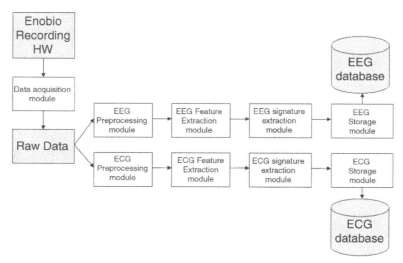

**Figure 18.4.** The data acquisition module is the software that controls the ENOBIO sensor in order to capture the raw data. Remember that four channels are recorded: two EEG channels placed in the forehead, one ECG channel placed in the left wrist and one electrode placed in the right earlobe for referencing the data. At this point the data are separate in EEG data and ECG data and sent to two parallel but different biometric modules for EEG and ECG. Each preprocessing module is explained in detail in the respective preprocessing sections. Then the features are extracted. A detailed explanation of the features used in each module is found in the features sections. For the signature extraction module, four 3-min takes are needed. The signature extraction module is explained in detail in the enrollment subsection. Once the signatures are extracted, they are both stored in their respective database for further retrieval when an authentication process takes place.

## 18.3    AUTHENTICATION ALGORITHM BASED ON EEG

We begin this section with two flowcharts that describe the whole application, in order to clarify all the concepts involved (Figures 18.4 and 18.5). As with all the other biometric modalities, our system works in two steps: enrollment and authentication. This means that for our system to authenticate a subject, this subject needs first of all to enroll into the system. In other words, their biometric signature has to be extracted and stored in order to retrieve it during the authentication process. Then the sample extracted during the authentication process is compared with the one that was extracted during the enrolment. If they are similar enough, then they will be authenticated.

### 18.3.1    EEG Preprocessing

First of all, a preprocessing step is carried on the two EEG channels. They are both referenced to the right earlobe channel in order to cancel the common interference that can appear in all the channels. This is a common practice in EEG recordings. Since the earlobe is a position with no electrical activity, and it is very easy and unobtrusive

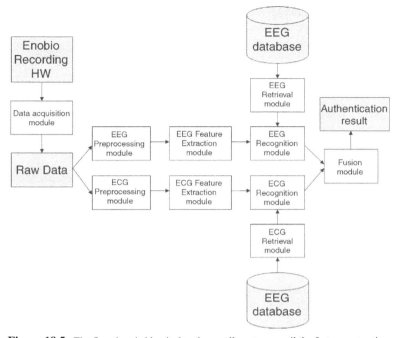

**Figure 18.5.** The flowchart is identical to the enrollment one until the feature extraction module. One difference that is not shown in the scheme is that now we only record 1 min of data. The recognition module retrieves the claimed subjects EEG and ECG signature from their respective databases. At this point we have the probability that the 1-min EEG recorded belongs to the claimed subject. We also have the probability that the 1-min ECG recorded belongs to the claimed subject. The fusion module then takes care to fusion these probabilities to obtain a very confident decision.

to place an electrode there with the help of a clip, this site appeared the better one to reference the rest of electrodes. After referencing, a second-order pass band filter with cutoff frequencies 0.5 and 40 Hz is applied.

Once the filters are applied, the whole signal is segmented in 4-s epochs. Artifacts are kept, in order to ensure that only 1 min of EEG data will be used for testing the system. We remind the reader that the subject is asked to close his/her eyes in order to minimize eye-related artifacts.

## 18.3.2 Features Extracted from EEG

We conducted an intensive preliminary analysis on the discrimination performance of a large initial set of features—for example, Higuchi fractal dimension, entropy, skewness, kurtosis, mean, and standard deviation. We chose the five ones that showed a higher discriminative power. These five different features were extracted from each 4-s epoch and input into our classifier module. All the mentioned features are simultaneously computed in the biometry system presented herein. This is what we denote as the multifeature set. The features are detailed in the following.

We can distinguish between two major types of features with respect to the number of EEG channels employed in their computation. Therefore we can group features in single-channel features and two-channels ones (the synchronicity features).

### 18.3.2.1 One Channel Features

Autoregression (AR) and Fourier transform (FT) are the implemented single-channel features. They are calculated for each channel without taking into account the other channel. The usage of these features for EEG biometry is not novel [8,10–14,19–22]. However, we describe them for the sake of completeness.

**Autoregression.** We use the standard methodology of making an autoregression on the EEG signal and the resulting coefficients as features. The employed autoregression is based on the Yule–Walker method, which fits a $p$th-order AR model to the windowed input signal, $X(t)$, by minimizing the forward prediction error in a least-square sense. The resulting Yule–Walker equations are solved through the Levinson–Durbin recursion. The AR model can be formulated as

$$X(t) = \sum_{i=1}^{n} a(i)X(t-i) + e(t). \tag{18.1}$$

We take $n = 100$ based on the discrimination power obtained in some preliminary works.

**Fourier Transform.** The well-known discrete Fourier transform (DFT) is expressed as

$$X(k) = \sum_{j=1}^{N} x(j)\omega_N^{(j-1)(k-1)}, \tag{18.2}$$

$$x(j) = \frac{1}{N} \sum_{k=1}^{N} X(k)\omega_N^{-(j-1)(k-1)}, \tag{18.3}$$

where

$$\omega_N = e^{\frac{-2\pi i}{N}}. \tag{18.4}$$

### 18.3.2.2 Synchronicity Features

Mutual information (MI), coherence (CO), and cross-correlation (CC) are examples of two-channel features related to synchronicity [23–25]. They represent some join characteristic of the two channels involved in the computation. This type of features is used for the first time here.

**Mutual Information.**  The mutual information [12,25] feature measures the dependency degree between two random variables given in bits, when logarithms of base 2 are used in its computation.

The MI can be defined as

$$MI_{xy} = E(x) + E(y) - E(xy),$$                              (18.5)

where $E$ is the entropy operator: $E(x)$ is the entropy of signal $x$, and $E(x, y)$ is the joint entropy of signals $x$ and $y$.

**Coherence.**  The coherence measure quantizes the correlation between two time series at different frequencies [23,24]. The magnitude of the squared coherence estimate is a frequency function with values ranging from 0 to 1.

The coherence $C_{xy}(f)$ is a function of the power spectral density ($P_{xx}$ and $P_{yy}$) of $x$ and $y$ and the cross-power spectral density ($P_{xy}$) of $x$ and $y$, as defined in the following expression:

$$C_{xy}(f) = \frac{|P_{xy}(f)|^2}{P_{xx}(f)P_{yy}(f)}.$$                              (18.6)

In this case, the feature is represented by the set of points of the coherence function.

**Correlation Measures.**  The well-known correlation (CC) is a measure of the similarity of two signals, commonly used to find occurrences of a known signal in an unknown one with applications in pattern recognition and cryptanalysis [27]. We calculate the autocorrelation of both channels, and the cross-correlation between them following:

$$CC_{X,Y} = \frac{\text{cov}(X, Y)}{\sigma_X \sigma_Y} = \frac{E((X - \mu_X)(Y - \mu_Y))}{\sigma_X \sigma_Y},$$                              (18.7)

where $E(\ )$ is the expectation operator, cov$(\ )$ is the covariance one, and $\mu$ and $\sigma$ are the corresponding mean and standard deviations values.

### 18.3.3  EEG Authentication Methodology

The work presented herein is based on the classical Fisher's discriminant analysis (DA). DA seeks a number of projection directions that are efficient for discrimination—that is, separation in classes.

DA is an exploratory method of data evaluation performed as a two-stage process. First the total variance/covariance matrix for all variables and then the intra-class variance/covariance matrix are taken into account in the procedure. A projection matrix is computed that minimizes the variance within classes while maximizing the variance between these classes. Formally, we seek to maximize the following expression:

$$J(W) = \frac{W^t S_B W}{W^t S_W W},$$                              (18.8)

where

- $W$ is the projection matrix
- $S_B$ is between-classes scatter matrix
- $S_W$ is within-class scatter matrix

For an $n$-class problem, the DA involves $n - 1$ discriminant functions (DFs). Thus a projection from a $d$-dimensional space, where $d$ is the length of the feature vector to be classified, into a $(n - 1)$-dimensional space, where $d \geq n$, is achieved. Note that in our particular case, the subject and class are equivalent. In our algorithm we work with four different DFs:

- *Linear*: Fits a multivariate normal density to each group, with a pooled estimate of the covariance.

- *Diagonal Linear*: Same as "linear," except that the covariance matrices are assumed to be diagonal.

- *Quadratic*: Fits a multivariate normal density with covariance estimates stratified by group.

- *Diagonal Quadratic*: Same as "quadratic," except that the covariance matrices are assumed to be diagonal.

The interested reader can find more information about DA in reference 27.

Taking into account the four DFs, the two channels, the two single-channel features, and the three synchronicity features, we have a total of 28 different classifiers. Here, we mean by classifier each of the 28 possible combinations of feature, DF, and channel. All these combinations are shown in Table 18.1.

We use an approach that we denote as "personal classifier," which is explained herein, for the identity authentication case: The five best classifiers—that is, the ones with more discriminative power—are used for each subject. When a test subject claims to be, for example, subject 1, the five best classifiers for subject 1 are used to do the classification. The methodology applied to do so is explained in the next section.

*Enrollment Process.* In order to select the five best classifiers for the $N$ enrolled subjects with four EEG takes, we proceed as follows. We use the three first takes of the $N$ subjects for training each classifier and the fourth take of a given subject is used for testing it. We repeat this process making all possible combinations (using one take for testing and the others for training). Each time we do this process, we obtain a classification rate (CR): number of feature vectors correctly classified over the total number of feature vectors. The total number of feature vectors is around 45, depending on the duration of the take (we remind the reader that the enrollment takes have a duration of approximately 3 min, and these takes are segmented in 4-s epochs). Once this process is repeated for all 28 classifiers, we compute a score measure on them, which can be defined as

$$\text{score} = \frac{\text{average(CR)}}{\text{standard deviation(CR)}}. \tag{18.9}$$

**Table 18.1.** List of Possible Classifiers Used in Our System[a]

| Classifier ID | Feature[b] | Channel | Discriminant Function |
|---|---|---|---|
| 1 | AR | 1 | Linear |
| 2 | AR | 1 | Diagonal linear |
| 3 | AR | 1 | Quadratic |
| 4 | AR | 1 | Diagonal quadratic |
| 5 | AR | 2 | Linear |
| 6 | AR | 2 | Diagonal linear |
| 7 | AR | 2 | Quadratic |
| 8 | AR | 2 | Diagonal quadratic |
| 9 | FT | 1 | Linear |
| 10 | FT | 1 | Diagonal linear |
| 11 | FT | 1 | Quadratic |
| 12 | FT | 1 | Diagonal quadratic |
| 13 | FT | 2 | Linear |
| 14 | FT | 2 | Diagonal linear |
| 15 | FT | 2 | Quadratic |
| 16 | FT | 2 | Diagonal quadratic |
| 17 | MI | — | Linear |
| 18 | MI | — | Diagonal linear |
| 19 | MI | — | Quadratic |
| 20 | MI | — | Diagonal quadratic |
| 21 | CO | — | Linear |
| 22 | CO | — | Diagonal linear |
| 23 | CO | — | Quadratic |
| 24 | CO | — | Diagonal quadratic |
| 25 | CC | — | Linear |
| 26 | CC | — | Diagonal linear |
| 27 | CC | — | Quadratic |
| 28 | CC | — | Diagonal quadratic |

[a] Note that the MI, CO, and CC features are extracted from both channels, so the field channel is omitted in these cases.

[b] AR, autoregression; FT, Fourier transform; MI, mutual information; CO, coherence; CC, crosscorrelation.

The five classifiers with higher scores out of the 28 possible classifiers are the selected ones. We repeat this process for the $N$ enrolled subjects.

It is worth mentioning that using all 28 classifiers would not improve the performance of the system, not to mention that the computational time will also increase considerably in the authentication process. Using five personal classifiers, the authentication process takes around 5 s for EEG and 4 s for ECG. If we use all the 28 classifiers, the personal classifier approach could not be implemented, since all the subjects

**Table 18.2.** Posterior Matrix of the 15 FT Feature Vectors Extracted from One-Minute EEG Recording of Subject 1[a]

| Classified as | Subject 1 | Subject 2 | Subject 3 | Subject 4 | Subject 5 |
|---|---|---|---|---|---|
| Test 1 | 0.46 | 0.28 | 0 | 0 | 0.23 |
| Test 2 | 0.40 | 0.24 | 0 | 0.23 | 0.11 |
| Test 3 | 0.99 | 0 | 0 | 0 | 0.01 |
| Test 4 | 0.99 | 0 | 0 | 0 | 0 |
| Test 5 | 0.99 | 0 | 0 | 0 | 0 |
| Test 6 | 0.91 | 0.01 | 0.04 | 0 | 0.04 |
| Test 7 | 0.99 | 0 | 0 | 0 | 0 |
| Test 8 | 0.99 | 0.01 | 0 | 0 | 0 |
| Test 9 | 0.96 | 0.02 | 0.02 | 0 | 0 |
| Test 10 | 0.99 | 0 | 0 | 0 | 0 |
| Test 11 | 0.16 | 0.04 | 0.25 | 0.53 | 0 |
| Test 12 | 0.53 | 0.35 | 0 | 0 | 0.11 |
| Test 13 | 0.92 | 0.07 | 0 | 0 | 0.01 |
| Test 14 | 0.99 | 0 | 0 | 0 | 0 |
| Test 15 | 1 | 0 | 0 | 0 | 0 |
| Average | 0.81 | 0.07 | 0.02 | 0.05 | 0.03 |

[a] Each row represents the probabilities assigned to each class for each feature vector. We see that the subject is well-classified as being subject 1 (refer to the last row). Notice that, for simplicity, this posterior matrix represents a five-class problem (i.e., four reference subjects in this case). In our real system, we work with a 33-class problem.

would use the same classifiers. We decided to use five classifiers since this number showed a good compromise between the performance and the computational time.

*Authentication Process.* Once we have the five best classifiers for all the $N$ enrolled subjects, we can then implement and test our final application. We now proceed in a similar way, but we only use 1 min of recording data; that is, we input in each one of the five best classifiers 15 feature vectors (we remind the reader that the authentication test takes have a duration of 1 min; and these takes, as we did in the enrollment case, are segmented in 4-s epochs). Each classifier outputs a posterior matrix (Table 18.2). In order to fuse the results of the five classifiers, we vertically concatenate the five obtained posterior matrices and take the column average. The resulting vector is the one we will use to take the authentication decision. In fact, it is a probability density function (PDF; see Figure 18.6 and 18.7):

- The first element is the probability that the single-minute test data come from subject 1.
- The second element is the probability that the single-minute test data come from subject 2.
- etc.

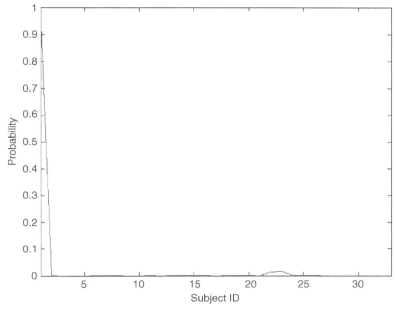

**Figure 18.6.** PDF for one of the enrolled subjects. The subject is classified against his training data set (class 1) and the training data sets of the reference subjects (from class 2 to class 33). In this example, he/she will be correctly authenticated with a high confidence level.

The last step in our algorithm takes into consideration a decision rule over the averaged PDF. We use a threshold applied on the probability of the claimed subject. If the probability of the claimed subject is higher than the applied threshold, then the authentication result is positive. Three values are output by our algorithm:

- Binary decision (authentication result)
- Score (probability of the claimed subject)
- Confidence level (an empiric function that maps the difference between threshold and score to a percentage)

In order to evaluate the performance of the system, we proceed as follows. 32 subjects with three 3-min takes are used as reference subjects, and the other eight subjects with four 3-min takes are enrolled in the system as explained in the "enrolment process" above. For the system testing, we distinguish three cases: when a subject claims to be himself (legal situation) and when a subject claims to be another subject from the database (impostor situation). We have 48 legal situations, 350 impostor situations, and 16 intruder situations. What we do, in order to take all the profit from our data, is to make all the possible combinations with the authentication takes. Subject 1 will claim to be subject 1 (legal situation), but he will also claim to be all the other enrolled subjects (impostor situation). An intruder will claim to be

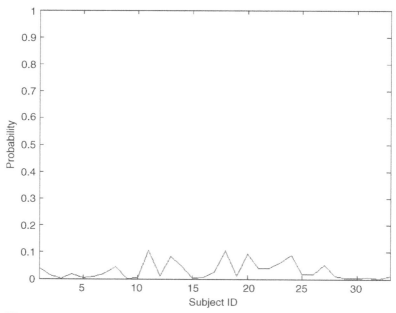

**Figure 18.7.** PDF for an impostor situation. In this case the probabilities are more or less evenly distributed among all classes: the one he claims to be (class 1) and the other reference subject classes (from class 2 to class 33), so in this case he/she will not be authenticated with a high confidence level.

all eight enrolled subjects, one by one. The false acceptance rate (FAR) is computed taking into account both the intruder and the impostor cases. By definition, the FAR is equal to the number of false instances classified as positive divided by the total number of false instances. The true acceptance rate (TAR) only takes into account the legal cases. Similarly, the TAR is defined as the number of true instances classified as positive divided by the total number true instances.

The performance of the EEG system using a probability threshold of 0.1 is

- TAR = 79.2%
- FAR = 21.8%

This threshold places our system close to the equal error rate (EER) working point. By definition, at the EER working point the following equation is valid:

$$TAR + FAR = 100\% \qquad (18.10)$$

and the compromise between the highest TAR and the lowest FAR is optimal.

## 18.4   AUTHENTICATION ALGORITHM BASED ON ECG

### 18.4.1   ECG Preprocessing

We reference the ECG channel placed in the left wrist to the right earlobe reference channel. A first difference with the EEG preprocessing is that, in this case, we are not using 4-s epochs. Now, we segment each single heartbeat waveform from the ECG signal.

### 18.4.2   Heartbeat Waveform as Unique Feature from ECG

From a large set of different features ("heart rate variability"-related features, geometric features, entropy, fractal dimension, and energy), we finally only use the heartbeat waveform as input feature in our classifiers, since it is the one that showed the higher discriminative power between subjects.

As previously said, from each minute of data we extract each single heart waveform. For defining the heartbeat waveform feature, we decimate to 144 length vectors. All these vectors in their totality are the heartbeat waveform features. Thus, the total number of feature vectors, in this case, depends on the number of heartbeats in one minute—that is, on the heartbeat rate.

### 18.4.3   ECG Authentication Methodology

The authentication methodology is very similar to the one used in EEG. The difference is that now we only have one feature, but we still have 4 DFs, so at the 'best classifier selection' stage, what we do is to select the best DF for each subject. In this modality there is no data fusion. Once the best DF is found, then the classification is made for the "heartbeat shape" feature and for the selected DF.

The outputs for this modality are the same:

- Binary decision (authentication result)
- Score (probability of the claimed subject)
- Confidence level (an empiric function that maps the difference between threshold and score to a percentage)

The performance of the ECG system using a probability threshold of 0.6:

- TAR $= 97.9\%$
- FAR $= 2.1\%$

This threshold places the performance of our system on the EER working point, as explained in the EEG authentication methodology section.

## 18.5   EEG AND ECG FUSION

At this stage, we have the elements that could lead the system to take a decision based on each of the two modalities. However, we have observed that the application of a decision fusion increases the reliability of the final system in terms of acceptance and rejection rates. In order to achieve the maximum performance of the system, we fuse the results of the EEG and the ECG authentication systems. Because both signals are independent and the recording protocols, completely compatible with each other, it is very easy to register both EEG and ECG at the same time with the ENOBIO sensor.

Figure 18.8 shows the bidimensional decision space where the scores probabilities for ECG and EEG are plotted one against the other. As can be observed, the inclusion of both modalities together with their fusion makes the two classes linearly separable. Indeed we can undertake the separation through a surface formally expressed as

$$\phi_1 = mE + c - C, \tag{18.11}$$

where $E$ and $C$ are the score probabilities of the claimed subjects respectively for the EEG and the ECG modalities, $m$ and $c$ are the parameters of the lineal decision boundary, and $\phi_1$ is the decision boundary. Values higher than $d$ will be considered as legal subjects, whereas those lower than $d$ are classified as impostors as shown in Figure 18.8, where the decision boundary labeled as 1 has been adapted to the test

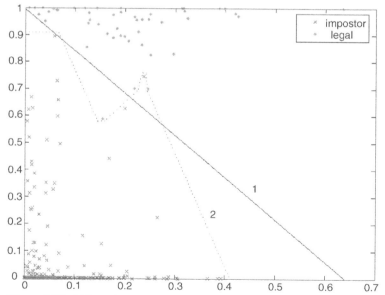

**Figure 18.8.** Bidimensional decision space. The ordinates represent the ECG probabilities, and the abscissa the EEG probabilities. Red crosses represent impostor cases, and green crosses represent legal cases. Two decision functions are represented.

**Table 18.3.** Final Results after Fusion

|                    | TAR   | FAR  |
|--------------------|-------|------|
| Decision function 1 | 97.9% | 0.82 |
| Decision function 2 | 100   | 0    |

on hand. Such a linear decision surface is easy to optimize, because it lives in a low parametrical space.

One more decision surface $\phi_2$ is depicted in Figure 18.8. The relationship between adaptation and generalization capability of a classifier system is very well known. Therefore, $\phi_2$ is much more adapted to the test data set used in the simulation presented herein. We expect such a decision boundary to present less generalization capability when new subjects enter into the system. However, the performance of $\phi_1$ is good enough for a practicable biometric system and furthermore, easier to parameterize.

From an application point of view, the decision surface 1 will be useful for an application where security issues are not critical (e.g., access to Disneyland, where we are interested that everybody is authenticated even though some intruders get also access to the facilities), while the surface 2 would be used in an application where the security issues are extremely important (e.g., access to radioactive combustible in a nuclear plant, where we really do not want any intruder to get access, even though some legal subject are not allowed to get access).

The results in terms of TAR and FAR are shown in Table 18.3.

## 18.6 CONCLUSION

We have presented the performance results obtained by a bimodal biometric system based on physiological signals, namely, EEG and ECG. The results demonstrate the validity of the multistage fusion approach taken into account in the system. In this context we undertake fusion at the feature, classification, and decision stages, thereby improving the overall performance of the system in terms of acceptance and rejection rates.

Moreover, the system presented herein improves the unobtrusiveness of other biometric systems based on physiological signals due to the employment of a wireless acquisition unit (ENOBIO). Moreover, two channels were used for the EEG modality and one channel was used for ECG.

It is worth mentioning the implementation of novel EEG features. The inclusion of synchronicity features, which take into account the data of two different channels, complement quite well the usage of one-channel features, which have been traditionally used in biometric systems. On the other hand, those two-channel features are used for the first time in such a system. The features undergo a LDA classification with different discriminant functions. Therefore we take into consideration a set of feature–classifiers combinations. This fact improves the robustness of the system and even its performance.

After testing the performance of different ECG features, we conclude that the most discriminative one is the heartbeat waveform as a whole. For its extraction, it is necessary to implement a preprocessing stage. The unique feature undergoes a classification stage similar to the one used with the modality described above. Therefore different discriminant functions of a LDA classifier present different performance for each of the subjects. The inclusion of their combination results in an improvement in the performance of the overall system.

We have demonstrated as well the suitability of including a decision fusion stage, whereby the decision between legal and impostor subjects becomes linear. Moreover, the decision fusion allows to decrease the FPR of the system, which constitutes an important feature of a reliable system. Although the corresponding decision boundary was computed from test results, its parameterization is easily attainable. Optimization procedures can be applied to fulfill this aim.

Regarding the security issues, we wish to explain that our system was developed within a European project called HUMABIO (see acknowledgment section and reference 1), in which several biometric modalities are combined to provide a highly reliable decision. All the different modalities are controlled through a central application that interfaces the different sensors with the database. A lot of security aspects have been taken into account and have been implemented in the final system (cryptography, transaction getaway, digital certificates, etc.). The details are beyond the scope of the present chapter. On the other hand, since ENOBIO has a wireless component, some additional security aspects should be taken into account during the data transmission, like data encryption. This is one development that will be implemented in the future.

We also wish to mention other possible future applications of our system. Using the ENOBIO sensor, which is unobtrusive and wearable, and through the analysis of EEG and ECG signals, we can authenticate other things in addition to the subjects. There is evidence that both EEG and ECG signals can be used to validate the initial state of the subject—that is, to detect if the subject is in normal condition and has not taken alcohol or drugs or is not suffering from sleep deprivation [28–30]. Moreover, a continuous authentication system and a continuous monitoring system could also be implemented since the sensor, as already explained, is unobtrusive and wearable.

A further step is to extract emotions from ECG and EEG [31,32]. This would be very useful for human–computer interactions. As an example, we can think on virtual reality applications where the reactions of the computer generated avatars would take into account the emotions of the subject immersed in the virtual reality environment [33].

## 18.7   SUMMARY

Features extracted from electroencephalogram (EEG) and electrocardiogram (ECG) recordings have proved to be unique enough between subjects for biometric applications. We show here that biometry based on these recordings offers a novel way to robustly authenticate subjects. In this chapter, we presented a rapid and unobtrusive authentication method that only uses two frontal electrodes (for EEG recording) and another electrode placed on the left wrist referenced to another one placed at the right earlobe. Moreover, the system makes use of a multistage fusion architecture, which has been demonstrated to improve the system performance. The performance analysis of the system presented in this chapter stems from an experiment with 40 subjects, from which 8 are used as enrolled test subjects and 32 are used as reference subjects needed for both the enrollment and the authentication process.

## ACKNOWLEDGMENTS

The authors wish to thank Starlab Barcelona S.L. for supporting this research and for providing the ENOBIO sensor. Starlab Barcelona S.L. is a research private company with the goal of transforming science into technologies with a profound and positive impact on society.

The authors also wish to thank the HUMABIO project (Contract number 026990), which funded part of the research explained in this chapter. HUMABIO is an EC co-funded "Specific Targeted Research Project" (STREP) where new types of biometrics are combined with state-of-the-art sensorial technologies in order to enhance security in a wide spectrum of applications such as transportation safety and continuous authentication in safety critical environments like laboratories, airports, and/or other buildings.

## REFERENCES

1. V. Gracia et al., State of the art in biometrics research and market survey, HUMABIO Project (EU FP6 contract no 026990), Deliverable N.1.4. www.humabio-eu.org, 2006.
2. A. Riera et al., Unobtrusive biometric system based on electroencephalogram analysis, *EURASIP J. Adv. Signal Processing*, accepted.
3. N. Sviserskaya, and T. Korolkova, Genetic features of the spatial organization of the human cerebral cortex, *Neurosci. Behav. Physiolo.* 25(5):370–376, 1995.
4. L. Biel et al., ECG analysis: A new approach in human identification, *IEEE Trans. Instrume. Meas.* 50(3):808–812, 2001.
5. C. K. Chang, Human identification using one lead ECG, Master's thesis, Department of Computer Science and Information Engineering, Chaoyang University of Technology, Taiwan, 2005.
6. S. Israel et al., EGC to identify individuals, *Pattern Recognit.* 38:133–142, 2005.
7. M. Kyoso, Development of an ECG identification system, in *Proceedings of the 23rd Annual International IEEE Conference on Engineering in Medicine and Biology Society*, Istanbul, Turkey, 2001.
8. R. Palaniappan, and S. M. Krishnan, Identifying individuals using ECG beats, in *Proceedings of the International Conference on Signal Processing and Communications, 2004*, SPCOM '04, 2004, pp. 569–572.
9. A. Ross, and A. Jain, Information fusion in biometrics, *Pattern Recognit. Lett.* 24:2115–2125, 2003.
10. G. Mohammadi et al., Person identification by using AR model for EEG signals, in *Proceedings of the 9th International Conference on Bioengineering Technology* (ICBT 2006), Czech Republic, 2006, 5 pages.
11. R. Paranjape et al., The electroencephalogram as a biometric, in *Proceedings of the Canadian Conference on Electrical and Computer Engineering*, 2001, pp. 1363–1366.

12. M. Poulos et al., Parametric person identification from EEG using computational geometry, in *Proceedings of the 6th International Conference on Electronics*, Circuits and Systems (ICECS '99), Vol. 2, 1999, pp. 1005–1008.

13. M. Poulos et al., On the use of EEG features towards person identification via neural networks, *Medical Informatics & the Internet in Medicine*, Vol. 26, 2001, pp. 35–48.

14. M. Poulos et al., Person identification from the EEG using nonlinear signal classification, *Methods Info. Med.* **41**:64–75, 2002.

15. G. Ruffini et al., A dry electrophysiology electrode using CNT arrays, *Sensors and Actuators A* **132**:34–41, 2006.

16. G. Ruffini et al., ENOBIO dry electrophysiology electrode; first human trial plus wireless electrode system, in *29th IEEE EMBS Annual International Conference*, 2007.

17. G. Ruffini et al., First human trials of a dry electrophysiology sensor using a carbon nanotube array interface, arXiv:physics/0701159.

18. S. Eischen, J. Luctritz, and J. Polish, Spectral analysis of EEG from families, *Biol. Psycholo.* **41**:61–68, 1995.

19. N. Hazarika, A. Tsoi, and A. Sergejew, Nonlinear considerations in EEG signal classification, *IEEE Trans. Signal Processing* **45**:829–836, 1997.

20. S. Marcel, and J. Mill, Person authentication using brainwaves (EEG) and maximum a posteriori model adaptation, IDIAP Research Report 05-81, 2005, 11 pages.

21. M. Poulos et al., Person identification via the EEG using computational geometry algorithms, in *Proceedings of the Ninth European Signal Processing*, EUSIPCO'98, Rhodes, Greece, September 1998, pp. 2125–2128.

22. A. Remond, editor, *EEG Informatics. A Didactic Review of Methods and Applications of EEG Data Processing*, Elsevier Scientific Publishing, New York, 1997.

23. G. Winterer et al., Association of EEG coherence and an exonic GABA(B)R1 gene polymorphism, *Am. J. Med. Genet. B Neuropsychiatr. Genet.* **117**:51–56, 2003.

24. M. Kikuchi et al., Effect of normal aging upon interhemispheric EEG coherence: Analysis during rest and photic stimulation, *Clin Electroencephalogr.* **31**:170–174, 2000.

25. R. Moddemeijer, On estimation of entropy and mutual information of continuous distributions, *Signal Processing* **16**(3):233–246, 1989.

26. M. Deriche, and A. Al-Ani, A new algorithm for EEG feature selection using mutual information, in *Acoustics, Speech, and Signal Processing, 2001*, Vol. 2, Proceedings '01, 2001, pp. 1057–1060.

27. R. Duda et al., *Pattern Classification*, John Wiley & Sons, New York, 2001.

28. X. Hogans et al., Effects of ethyl alcohol on EEG and avoidance behavior of chronic electrode monkeys, *Am. J. Physio.* **201**:434–436, 1961.

29. J. Sorbel et al., Alcohol Effects on the Heritability of EEG Spectral Power alcoholism: clinical and experimental research, 1996.

30. S. Jin et al., Effects of total sleep-deprivation on waking human EEG: Functional cluster analysis, *Clini. Neurophysiolo.* **115**(12):2825–2833, 2004.

31. K. Takahashi, Remarks on emotion recognition from biopotential signals, in *2nd International Conference on Autonomous Robots and Agents*, 2004.

32. A. Haag et al., *Emotion Recognition Using Bio-sensors: First Steps Towards an Automatic System*, ADS, LNAI 3068, Springer-Verlag, Berlin, 2004, pp. 36–48.

33. J. Llobera, Narratives within immersive technologies, arXiv:0704.2542, 2007.

# Chapter 19

# A Multiresolution Analysis of the Effect of Face Familiarity on Human Event-Related Potentials

**Brett DeMarco and Evangelia Micheli-Tzanakou**

## 19.1 INTRODUCTION

The ability of humans to recognize familiar faces everyday among a multitude of different faces is remarkable. While it is a common experience for most people, face recognition is a very complex process that is still not completely understood. A great deal of research has been performed to investigate face-specific event-related potentials. Small [1] recorded what he referred to as ERPs from occipital, parietal, and temporal regions and identified a positive peak at 300 ms (P300) that showed a significantly greater amplitude when subjects were shown faces opposed to geometric designs or pattern reversal stimuli. Furthermore, the amplitude was much greater from the right hemisphere compared to the left. Bentin et al. [2] found a negative potential at 170 ms (N170) located in a circumscribed region in the posterior–inferior aspects of the temporal lobes that responded preferentially to human faces and isolated human eyes but not to other stimuli such as human hands, animal faces, excluding apes, furniture, cars, or nonsense stimuli. Four years later, Bentin and Deouell [3] noted that it might be associated with an early face-specific structural encoding mechanism, but it was probably not related to face identification. However, Rossion et al [4] found little evidence that the N170 component was face-specific; the differences in N170 amplitude between non-face categories were sometimes as large as the differences between face and non-face categories. It must be noted, though, that they did find that the N170 was enhanced and delayed for inverted face stimuli compared to inverted object stimuli. Recently, Herrmann et al. [5] determined that face-specific processing began 70 ms earlier, with a positive peak at 100 ms (P100).

Relatively few studies have compared the differences between responses to familiar face and unfamiliar face stimuli. Bentin and Deouell [3] and Eimer [6] noted a negative peak at 400 ms from stimulus onset and named it (N400f), appending the letter "f" to distinguish the face N400 from the "classical" N400, which has been associated primarily with the semantic processing of words. They also found supporting evidence that the N170 peak was an early visual mechanism involved in face processing but was not directly associated with face identification. Eimer [6] also found an enhanced positivity at 600 ms that he termed P600f due to the apparent familiarity of faces.

Since their discoveries, wavelet and time-frequency analysis have been used extensively in analyzing EEGs and ERPs with great success; for examples see references 7–16. However, to the authors knowledge, they have not been applied to face recognition in humans. In particular, there have been no investigations into how wavelet and time-frequency analysis can be used to determine a distinction between the viewing of familiar faces compared to unknown faces. It is the aim of this study to investigate ERPs in response to familiar and unfamiliar faces in the time-frequency domain.

If such a distinction were discovered, it would be very useful toward many applications. The first applications that come to mind are in security and law enforcement. In these times of increased worries about terrorism and homeland security, a system could be devised to determine relations between potential terrorists and their associates. A similar system could be used in law enforcement as part of criminal investigations and in a court of law. Another application would be in the medical field. For example, if patients are nonverbal or unable to communicate voluntarily, a system could be devised that would allow doctors to gain some insight into whether they recognize family members or friends.

## 19.2  THEORY

The traditional time–frequency analysis method is the short-time Fourier transform (STFT); it provides time and frequency localization, but there are limitations due to the Heisenberg uncertainty principle [17, 18]. The Heisenberg uncertainty principle states that resolution in time and frequency cannot be arbitrarily small because it is meaningless to measure frequency at a moment in time because frequency is a measurement over an interval of time. Therefore, the product of time and frequency is lower bounded by

$$\Delta t \Delta f \geq 1/4\pi.$$

The advent of wavelet theory provided an apparent solution to this problem. Wavelets provide researchers with the ability to know when and to what degree transient events are taking place as well as when and how the frequency contents are changing over time [19–21]. Wavelets are band-limited, oscillating functions that are localized in both time and frequency.

A wavelet family $\Psi_{a,b}$ is the set of elemental functions generated by dilation and translation operations of a unique mother wavelet:

$$\Psi_{a,b}(t) = |a|^{-1/2} \Psi((t-b)/a),$$

where $a, b \in R, a \neq 0$, are the scale and translation parameters, respectively, and $t$ is time. As the scale parameter $a$ is increased or decreased, the wavelet is dilated or compressed; and as the translation parameter $b$ is increased or decreased, the wavelet is shifted to the right or left [21].

## 19.2.1  Continuous Wavelet Transform (CWT)

The continuous wavelet transform of a signal $x(t)$ is defined as

$$\langle x(t), |a|^{-1/2} \Psi^*((t-b)/a) \rangle = |a|^{-1/2} \int x(t) \Psi^*((t-b)/a)\, dt,$$

where "*" is the complex conjugate and "$\langle\,\rangle$" the inner product. The CWT is further defined as the correlation between the function $x(t)$ with the family wavelet $\Psi_{a,b}(t)$ for each $a$ and $b$ [19, 20, 21]. As stated by Daubechies [21], as $a$ is increased or decreased, the wavelet covers different frequency ranges, large-scale values correspond to low frequencies, and small-scale values correspond to higher frequencies.

The general operations in a CWT are as follows: The correlation between the wavelet (the first wavelet is referred to as the mother wavelet) and the signal at the signal start, is computed, the wavelet is then shifted to the right by one, and the correlation is computed again. This process is repeated for the length of the entire signal. The scale is then incremented by one, thereby dilating the mother wavelet and the process is repeated for all specified scales. The result is a set of wavelet coefficients for all times at each scale.

CWT coefficients can be plotted to yield a three-dimensional representation of the signal. The plot shows time, scale, and coefficient magnitude on the $x$, $y$, and $z$ axes, respectively. The plots allow the researcher to easily visualize maxima, minima, and transitions and where in time they occur. The plots also show at what scale/frequency (high frequency corresponds to low scale and low frequency corresponds to high scale) such maxima, minima, or transitions occur.

Theoretically, there are an infinite number of coefficients computed by the CWT, and the information displayed at proximal scales and times is highly correlated. Therefore the CWT provides a very redundant representation of the signal being analyzed and is very time-consuming when computed directly [7].

## 19.2.2  Discrete Wavelet Series

The discrete wavelet transform provides a solution to the redundancy problem inherent in the CWT. The DWT is a nonredundant representation of the signal $x(t)$, and its values make up the coefficients in a wavelet series. The conventional way of discretizing time-scale parameters is the so-called dyadic grid sampling method. In this case, time remains continuous but time-scale parameters are sampled by choosing $a = 2^i$ and $b = k2^i$, where $i, k \in Z$, so the wavelets then become

$$\Psi_{i,k}(t) = 2^{-i/2}\Psi(2^{-i}t - k),$$

Additionally, $\Psi$ must satisfy the admissibility condition:

$$\int |\Psi(\omega)|^2/|\omega|d\,\omega < \infty,$$

where

$$\Psi(\omega) = 1/(2\pi)^{1/2}\int e^{j\omega t}\Psi(t)dt.$$

If the admissibility condition is met, then a wavelet series decomposes a signal $x(t)$ onto a basis of continuous-time wavelets, or synthesis wavelets, $\alpha_{i,k}(t)$, as shown:

$$x(t) = \sum_{i\in Z}\sum_{k\in Z} C_{i,k}\,\alpha_{i,k}(t).$$

The wavelet coefficients, $C_{i,k}$ are defined as

$$C_{i,k} = \int x(t)\Psi_{i,k}^*(t)\,dt.$$

The wavelet function $\Psi(t)$ is constructed by a scale function $\phi(t)$, which is a solution of a two-scale difference equation:

$$\phi(t) = \sum_k h_k\,\phi\,(2t - k).$$

The sequence $\{h_n\}$ is called the low-pass filter or scaling sequence and is constrained to obey the regularity condition. This condition guarantees the numeric stability of a wavelet decomposition of any function in the Hilbert Space $(L^2(R))$. A scaling function with a valid $\{h_n\}$ is an admissible scaling function and can be used to construct the wavelet as

$$\Psi(t) = \sum_k g_k\,\phi\,(2t - k),$$

where $\{g_k\}$ is a high-pass filter sequence. The signal decomposition can be done using orthogonal wavelets, in which case the synthesis wavelets are time-reversed versions of the analysis wavelets [10, 22].

## 19.2.3    Discrete Wavelet Transform (DWT)

The DWT is similar to the wavelet series but is applied to discrete signals $x[n]$. It achieves a multiresolution decomposition of $x[n]$ on $I$ octaves given by $i = 1, \ldots, I$ and

$$ x[n] = \sum_{i=1} \left( \sum_{k \in Z} a_{i,k}\, g_i[2n - k] + \sum_{k \in Z} b_{i,k} h_i[2n - k] \right). $$

The DWT computes wavelet coefficients $a_{i,k}$ and scaling coefficients $b_{i,k}$ for $i = 1, \ldots, I$, which are given by

$$ a_{i,k} = \sum_n x[n]\, g_i\,[2n - k] $$

and

$$ b_{i,k} = \sum_n x[n]\, h_i[2n - k], $$

where $g_i[2n - k]$ is the discrete wavelet sequence and $h_i[2n - k]$ is the scaling sequence.

The wavelet sequence $g_i[2n - k]$ serves as a high-pass filter, and the scaling sequence $h_i[2n - k]$ serves as a low-pass filter. The decomposition of the signal into different frequency bands is achieved by successive high- and low-pass filtering operations. The output of the high-pass filter is referred to as the "detail" signal, and the output of the low-pass filter is referred to as the "approximation" signal.

The resulting sets of wavelet coefficients compose what is called an $I$th-level wavelet decomposition of the signal. The higher-numbered decomposition levels represent lower-frequency bands, as the signal is low-pass filtered repeatedly.

## 19.3    METHODS

EEG was recorded from electrode locations O1, O2, P3, P4, and Fz relative to reference electrode Cz according to the international 10–20 placement system. Stimuli were presented using a demonstration copy of Presentation, Version 9.81 (Neurobehavioral Systems Inc., Albany CA). Presentation is a fully programmable stimulus delivery software system designed for behavioral and physiological experiments. The software used to acquire the data was AcqKnowledge Version 3.5.7 by Biopac Systems Inc. Data were acquired at a rate of 500 samples/second (500 Hz). All analysis and signal processing was performed offline.

Subjects were randomly presented images of known and unknown faces with no occlusion, known and unknown faces with various degrees of noise overlaid, and finally images of composite known and unknown faces. Subjects were instructed to click a mouse button when they were presented with an image of a familiar face. Stimuli were presented for 800 ms and were separated by a 600-ms "off" sequence consisting of a $400 \times 300$ pixel black rectangle with a centered white fixation cross on an $800 \times 600$ gray background. The known and unknown images were converted to gray scale, cropped to $400 \times 300$ pixels, and centered on an $800 \times 600$ pixel gray background with a centered white fixation cross using Matlab Version 6.5. Unknown images were taken from the Psychological Image Collection at Stirling (PICS) University database [23], the Aleix database [24], and the Yale database [22]. Mean luminance for all stimuli and "off" stimulus was approximately equal.

The first trial ("Chk") stimulus was a circular checkerboard display used as a base to verify valid data collection. The second trial ("Just Faces") consisted of a set of 53 images of unknown faces taken from the previously mentioned databases and one image that the subject was familiar with (known). The known image was displayed a total of 53 times and was interspersed randomly with the unknown images. Although the unknown images were all unique, they were treated as one overall unknown image and contrasted during analysis with the known image. The third, fourth, and fifth trials ("Noise01," "Noise02," and "Noise03") consist of a set of 54 unknown images and one known image. Gaussian white noise with variance = 0.4, 0.3, and 0.05, respectively, was added to each unknown and known image using Matlab's "imnoise" command. An example is provided in Figure 19.1.

The sixth trial ("Mix01") consists of a set of four images, both_face02, both_face03, both_face04, and both_face05 (see Figure 19.2). The images are created by replacing vertical and horizontal lines in the known image with vertical and horizontal lines in the unknown image to achieve a pseudo-morphing effect. The first image of the set, both_face02.bmp, is created by replacing every other vertical and horizontal line in the known image with the corresponding vertical and horizontal lines in the unknown image. The second image of the set, both_face03.bmp, is created by replacing every third vertical and horizontal line in the known image with the corresponding vertical and horizontal lines in the unknown image. The resulting

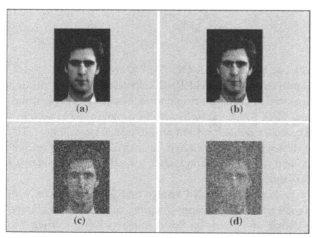

**Figure 19.1.** Example of images used in noise trials. (a) Original image, not used in trials. Images with noise added used in (b) Trial 5, 0.05 variance (c) Trial 4, 0.3 variance, and (d) Trial 3, 0.4 variance.

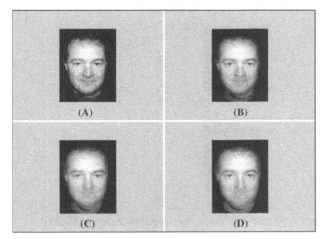

**Figure 19.2.** Images used in Trial 6—"Mix01." The images were created by replacing (**A**) every other (both_face02), (**B**) third (both_face03), (**C**) fourth (both_face04), and (**D**) fifth (both_face05) vertical and horizontal line in the known image with the corresponding vertical and horizontal line in the unknown image.

image contains two lines of the known image for every one line of the unknown image. The third, fourth, and fifth images follow a similar pattern; as the images progress from both_face02 through both_face05, the known image is exposed more.

The seventh trial ("Mix02," Figure 19.3) is created in the same manner as above; but instead of replacing both horizontal and vertical lines, only vertical lines are replaced.

The eighth trial ("Mix03," Figure 19.4) is created in the same manner as above but instead of replacing vertical lines, horizontal lines are replaced.

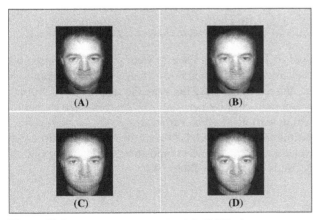

**Figure 19.3.** Images used in Trial 7—"Mix02." The images were created by replacing (**A**) every other (vert_face02), (**B**) third (vert_face03), (**C**) fourth (vert_face04), and (**D**) fifth (vert_face05) vertical line in the known image with the corresponding vertical line in the unknown image.

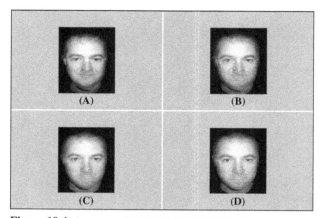

**Figure 19.4.** Images used in Trial 8—"Mix03." The images were created by replacing (**A**) every other (hor_face02), (**B**) third (hor_face03), (**C**) fourth (hor_face04), and (**D**) fifth (hor_face05) horizontal line in the known image with the corresponding horizontal line in the unknown image.

**Table 19.1.** Discrete Wavelet Decomposition Levels Used and Their Corresponding Frequency Bands and EEG Frequency Band Names

| Wavelet Decomposition Level | Frequency Band (Hz) | EEG Frequency Band Name |
|---|---|---|
| 1 | 125–250 | N/A |
| 2 | 62.5–125 | Gamma |
| 3 | 31–62.5 | High beta/gamma |
| 4 | 15.5–31 | Midrange beta/high beta |
| 5 | 7.8–15.5 | Alpha/low beta |
| 6 | 3.9–7.8 | Theta |
| 7 | 1.9–3.9 | High delta |
| 8 | 0–1.9 | Low delta |

The unknown images used in Trial 2 ("Just Faces") were previously unseen by the subject and displayed one time each. The unknown images used in Trials 3–5 ("Noise") were different from those used in Trial 2 but were the same in each "Noise" trial and contained differing amounts of noise per trial. The images were shown in order of noisiest (0.4 variance) to least noisy (0.05 variance).

To achieve the multiresolution analysis, the ERPs are decomposed into eight levels using the discrete wavelet transform. The decomposition levels correspond to conventional EEG frequency bands as shown in Table 19.1.

## 19.4 RESULTS

Three-dimensional plots of the CWT of the responses to known and unknown stimuli in Trials 2–5 are shown below. The $x$ and $y$ axes represent time and scale, respectively,

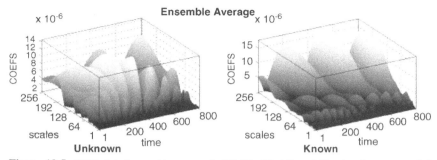

**Figure 19.5.** CWT plot of ensemble average for Trial 2—"Just Faces." The signals were recorded on electrode FZ, and a Daubechies db10 wavelet was used in the CWT.

and the $z$ axis represents the magnitude of the CWT coefficients. The ERPs analyzed in this section were detected on electrode $Fz$, and wavelet transforms were computed using Daubechies wavelet db10. Each plot reflects that of an "ensemble average," which is calculated by summing each subject signal included in a trial and then dividing by the number of signals used. For example, the ensemble average signal for Trial 2 ("Just Faces") consists of the sum of the ERPs of subjects 1–8 divided by 8.

As is seen in the known ensemble average CWT (Figure 19.5) for Trial 2 ("Just Faces"), the transition from low to high frequency (high to low scales) occurs smoothly and there are three prominent high-magnitude low-frequency (high-scale) peaks occurring at approximately 200 ms, 550 ms, and 800 ms. There are fewer, wider peaks that gradually decrease in magnitude while transitioning from low frequency (high scale) to high frequency (low scale) in the CWTs in response to known stimuli than in the CWTs in response to unknown stimuli for most subjects. Both plots display abrupt, low-magnitude peaks at high frequencies (low scales).

As we move on to Trial 3—"Noise01" (Figure 19.6), we see that the differences in CWT plots between the responses to known and unknown stimuli disappear. The

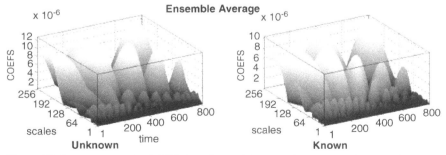

**Figure 19.6.** Three-dimensional CWT plots of ensemble average in response to known and unknown stimuli for Trial 3—"Noise01." The signals were recorded on electrode FZ and a Daubechies db10 wavelet was used in the CWT.

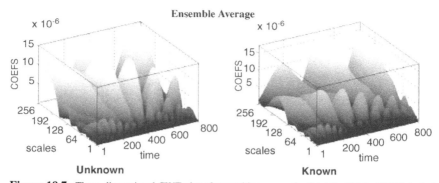

**Figure 19.7.** Three-dimensional CWT plot of ensemble average for Trial 5—"Noise02." Note that the shape of the known plot more closely resembles the known plot from Trial 2—"Just Faces."

few prominent, gradual, low-frequency (high-scale) peaks in the responses to known stimuli are less defined and they increase in number.

As we move on to Trial 4—"Noise02," a trial in which the images are more discernible than in Trial 3—"Noise01" (Figure 19.7), we see that the CWT plots change. The response to known stimuli at low frequencies (high scale) is starting to take on the few gradually decreasing peaks as seen previously.

Finally, in Trial 5—"Noise03," the differences between the responses to known and unknown stimuli are apparent (Figure 19.8), and interestingly they resemble the plots of responses to known and unknown stimuli shown in Figure 19.5 for Trial 2—"Just Faces."

The apparent return of the CWT plots in response to known stimuli to the shape of the plots seen in Trial 2 ("Just Faces") provides evidence that the CWT plot may be used to determine familiarity.

In an attempt to make a quantitative comparison of the three-dimensional CWT plots in response to known stimuli and those in response to unknown stimuli, ratios

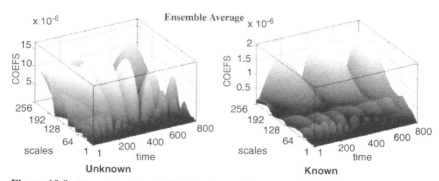

**Figure 19.8.** Three-dimensional CWT plot of ensemble average for Trial 5—"Noise03." Note that the shape of the known plot now resembles the known plot from Trial 2—"Just Faces."

**Table 19.2.** Ratios of CWT Magnitude of Known vs. Unknown for Scales 192–256 between 700 ms and 800 ms

| Trial | Known/Unknown Ratio |
|---|---|
| Just faces | 1.6895 |
| Noise01 | 1.0487 |
| Noise02 | 1.1769 |
| Noise03 | 2.3508 |
| Mix03—hor_face05vs02 | 1.5264 |
| Mix03—hor_face04vs02 | 1.2026 |
| Mix03—hor_face03vs02 | 0.9524 |

of the CWT magnitudes were computed. Based on the observation that there are concentrations of higher magnitude in response to known stimuli at high scales at approximately 200 ms, 550 ms, and 800 ms, the maximum values over the ranges of 150—250 ms, 500—600 ms, and 700—800 ms for scales 192–256 are determined and then averaged for both responses to known and unknown stimuli. The ratios computed for the 700- to 800-ms range are greater in response to more discernible known images and lesser as discernibility decreases as shown in Table 19.2.

The two highest ratios—that is, greatest differences in CWT magnitude between responses to known stimuli and responses to unknown stimuli—occur in response to the two trials in which the known image is most visible, "Just Faces" and "Noise03." As discernibility increases, as in the change from "Noise01" to "Noise03," the ratio increases, implying that the magnitude of the CWT is higher in the response to known stimuli compared to the response to unknown stimuli. The same holds true for Trial 8—"Mix03." The known image is most discernible in image hor_face05 and becomes less discernible in hor_face04, hor_face03, and hor_face02. The ratio decreases as discernibility decreases.

Lower delta activity is plotted in Figure 19.9 for each subject in Trial 2—"Just Faces." The known responses are synchronized at approximately 400 and 700 ms, which correspond to the N400f and P600f (approximately) peak observed in Eimer [6] and Bentin and Deouell [3], respectively.

In addition, phase coherent oscillations are apparent in the response to known stimuli and are not seen in the responses to unknown stimuli.

## 19.5  DISCUSSION

The results in the three-dimensional CWT plots section show the known CWT plots to have a few high-magnitude, low-frequency (high-scale) peaks occurring at approximately 200 ms, 550 ms (similar to the p600f peak found by Eimer [6]) and 800 ms, smoothly transitioning to low-magnitude, high-frequency (low-scale) peaks. As noise is added, the CWT in response to known stimuli tends to lose that characteristic shape and begins to resemble the CWT plot in response to unknown stimuli. However, as

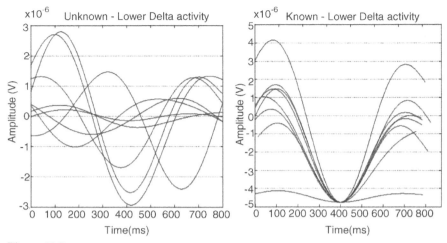

**Figure 19.9.** Lower delta activity for all (8) subjects in response to known and unknown stimuli for Trial 2—"Just Faces." ERPs are detected on electrode O2 and wavelet decomposition is computed using a Daubechies order 17 (db17) wavelet.

the trials continue and as noise is removed, as in the shift from Trial 4 ("Noise02") to Trial 5 ("Noise03"), the CWT plots in response to known stimuli regain a form much like that found in Trial 2 ("Just Faces").

The plots obtained in this section follow a logical progression: As face discernibility decreases, the shape of the CWT plot changes and resembles that of the response to unknown stimuli, then as the face becomes more discernible, the CWT plot takes a form close to that of the original. Based on the results in this section, the three-dimensional CWTs used have shown the potential to highlight differences in familiarity and may be used as a stand-alone tool or in conjunction with other methods to determine familiarity.

Finally, the superimposed lower delta activity among the responses to known stimuli shows strong phase coherence along the N400f and P600f peaks. The lower delta activity among the responses to unknown stimuli is very apparently out of phase. The observation of N400f and P600f peaks in the lower delta activity of the responses to known stimuli supports the assertions that the peaks are associated with familiar face recognition as stated in Eimer [6] and Bentin and Deouell [3]. Furthermore, the observation of these peaks in the lower delta activity in responses to known stimuli and not in responses to unknown stimuli supports the assertion in this study that the DWT is suitable to determine familiar face recognition.

## 19.6   CONCLUSION

Multiple methods were used to investigate familiar face recognition in the time-scale domain. Trends were found using discrete and continuous wavelet transform analysis. In the case of the DWT, the lower delta activity displays marked phase coherence in response to known stimuli, while the lower delta activity for the responses to unknown stimuli are out of phase. Another encouraging trend is that shown in the three-dimensional CWT plots. As face discernibility decreases, the shape of the CWT plot changes and resembles that of the response to unknown stimuli, then as the face becomes more discernible, the CWT plot takes a form close to that of the original. The same trend of discernibility is seen based on the ratio of the CWT magnitude in response to known stimuli compared to those in response to unknown stimuli.

The trends described above could potentially be applied to many real-world situations, not the least being security and law enforcement. A system can be visualized that would utilize the methods in concert to determine familiar face recognition. A subject is fitted with an electrode cap and ERPs are calculated, an eight-level DWT is performed on the ERPs, and the lower delta activity phase coherence is determined. Next, the CWT is taken for the responses to known and unknown stimuli, and the ratio of the maximum magnitudes between 700 and 800 ms is calculated. The DWT and CWT output could then be analyzed separately by an investigator or could be used as input to a trained neural network that would then output a determination of known or unknown.

## REFERENCES

1. M. Small, Asymmetrical evoked potentials in response to face stimuli, *Cortex* **19**, 441–450, 1983.
2. S. Bentin, T. Allison, E. Perez, A. Puce, and G. McCarthy, Electrophysiological studies of face perception in humans, *J. Cognitive Neurosci.* **8**, 551–565, 1996.
3. S. Bentin and L. Y. Deouell, Structural encoding and identification in face processing: ERP evidence for separate mechanisms, *Cognitive Neuropsychol.* **17**(1/2/3):35–54, 2000.
4. B. Rossion, I. Gauthier, M. J. Tarr, P. Despland, R. Bruyer, S. Linotte, and M. Crommelinck, The N170 occipito-temporal component is delayed and enhanced to inverted faces but not to inverted objects: An electrophysiological account of face-specific processes in the human brain, *Neuroreport* **11**(1):69–74, 2000.
5. M. J. Herrmann, M. C. Ehlis, H. Ellgring, and A. J. Fallgatter, Early stages (P100) of face perception in humans as measured with event-related potentials (ERPs), *J. Neural Transmission* **112**(8):1073–1081, 2005.
6. M. Eimer, Event-related brain potentials distinguish processing stages involved in face perception and recognition, *Clin. Neurophysiol.* **111**:694–705, 2000.
7. O. A. Rosso, M. T. Martin, A. Figliola, K. Keller, and A. Plastino, EEG analysis using wavelet-based information tools, *J. Neurosci. Methods* **153**: 163–182, 2006.
8. V. J. Samar, A. Bopardikar, R. Rao, and K. Swartz, Wavelet analysis of neuroelectric waveforms: A conceptual tutorial, *Brain and Language* **66**:7–60, 1999.
9. V. J. Samar, K. P. Swartz, and M. R. Raghuveer, Multiresolution analysis of event-related potentials by wavelet decomposition, *Brain and Cognition* **27**: 398–438, 1995.
10. B. Boashash, H. Carson, and M. Mesbah, Detection of seizures in newborns using time-frequency analysis of EEG signals, in *Proceedings of the IEEE Workshop on Statistical Signal and Array Processing*, Pocono Manor, PA, 2000, pp. 564–568.
11. H. E. Hanrahan, Extraction of features in auditory brainstem response (ABR) signals, *COMSIG 90, Proceedings of the third South African Conference on Communications and Signal Processing*, IEEE catalog number 90TH0314-5/90, 1990, pp. 61–66.
12. E. A. Bartnik, K. J. Blinowski, and P. J. Durka, Single evoked potential reconstruction by means of wavelet transform, *Biolo. Cybern.* **67**: 175–181, 1991.

13. V. J. Samar, M. R. Raghuveer, K. P. Swartz, S. Rosenberg, and T. Chaiyabonthanit, Wavelet decomposition of event related potentials: Toward the definition of biologically natural components, in *Sixth SSAP Workshop on Statistical Signal and Array Processing (IEEE)*, Victoria, British Columbia, *Nature* **247**:481–483, 1992.

14. F. Peyrin, B. Karoubi, P. Rubel, P. Desseigne, and P. Touboul, Time-frequency and time-scale analysis of high resolution ECGs, in *IEEE-SP International Symposium on Time-Frequency and Time-Scale Analysis*, IEEE catalog number 0-7803-0805-0/92, Victoria, British Columbia, October 4–6, 1992, pp. 143–146.

15. S. Chin and S. A. Kassam, Analysis of EEG signals using wavelet decomposition, in *Proceedings of the Conference on Information Sciences and Systems*, Johns Hopkins University, Baltimore, March, 24–26, 1993.

16. A. Ademoglu and E. Micheli-Tzanakou, Analysis of pattern reversal visual evoked potentials (PRVEP) in Alzheimer's disease by spline wavelets, *IEEE Trans. Biomed. Eng.* **44**(9):881–890, 1997.

17. T. A. C. M. Claasen and W. F. G. Mecklenbraucker, The Wigner distribution. A tool for time-frequency analysis: Part I—II, *Philips J. Res.* **35**:217–250. 276–300, 372–389, 1980.

18. M. R. Portnoff, Time-frequency representation of digital signals and systems based on short-time Fourier analysis, *IEEE Trans. ASSP*, **ASSP-28**:55–69, 1980.

19. I. Daubechies, Orthonormal bases of compactly supported wavelets, *Commun. Pure Appl. Math.* **41**:909–996, 1988.

20. S. G. Mallat, A theory for multiresolution signal decomposition: The wavelet representation, *IEEE Trans. Pattern Anal. Mach. Intelli.* **11**:674–693, 1989.

21. I. Daubechies, *Ten Lectures on Wavelets*, SIAM, Philadelphia, 1992.

22. P. N. Belhumeur, J. P. Hespanha, and D. J. Kriegman, Eigenfaces vs. fisherfaces: Recognition using class specific linear projection, *IEEE Trans. Pattern Anal. Mach. Intell.* **19**:711–720, 1997.

23. University of Stirling, Psychological Image Collection at Stirling (PICS), Department of Psychology [Online]. Available: http://pics.psych.stir.ac.uk/

24. A. M. Martinez and R. Benavente, The AR Face Database, CVC Technical Report #24, June 1998.

# Chapter 20

# On-Line Signature-Based Authentication: Template Security Issues and Countermeasures

**Patrizio Campisi, Emanuele Maiorana, and Alessandro Neri**

## 20.1 INTRODUCTION

The most emerging technology for people authentication is biometrics. It can be defined as the analysis of physiological or behavioral people characteristics for automatic people recognition. Biometric authentication relies on who a person is or what a person does, in contrast with traditional approaches, based on what a person *knows* (password, PIN, etc.) or what a person *has* (ID card, keys, token) [1, 2]. Biometric authentication is based on strictly personal traits, much more difficult to be forgotten, lost, stolen, copied, or forged than traditional data. Loosely speaking, biometric systems are essentially pattern-recognition applications, performing authentication using biometric attributes derived from physiological (like fingerprint, face, iris, retina, hand geometry, thermograms, DNA, ear shape, body odor, vein patterns, electrocardiogram (ECG), brain waves (EGG), etc.) or behavioral characteristics (like voice, signature, handwriting, gait, key stroke, lip motion, etc.) that persons possess.

Biometric authentication systems consist of two stages: the *enrollment* subsystem and the *authentication* subsystem. In the enrollment stage, biometric data are captured from a subject and checked for their quality. Then, relevant information are extracted

*Biometrics: Theory, Methods, and Applications.* Edited by Boulgouris, Plataniotis, and Micheli-Tzanakou
Copyright © 2010 the Institute of Electrical and Electronics Engineers, Inc.

and are eventually stored in a database. As for authentication, two modalities can be implemented:

- *Verification*: The subject who claims an identity presents some form of identifier (like user ID, ATM card, smart card) and a biometric characteristic. The system extracts some features from the acquired data and compares the features in the database corresponding to the provided ID and the acquired ones. It is worth pointing out that in this modality the presented biometric trait is compared only with the one stored in the centralized/distributed database, corresponding to the declared identity, which implies a *one to one* biometric comparison.

- *Identification*: The system acquires the biometric sample from the subject, extracts some features from the raw measurements, and searches the entire database for matches using the extracted biometric features. When the authentication system operates in the identification modality, *one to many* biometric comparisons are required.

In order to design a biometric-based authentication system, different issues, strictly related to the specific application under analysis, must be taken into account. As well established in the literature [3], from an ideal point of view, biometrics should be *universal* (each person should possess the characteristic), *unique* (for a given biometrics, different persons should have different characteristics), *permanent* (biometrics should be stable with respect to time variation), *collectable* (biometrics should be measurable with enough precision by means of sensors usable in real life), *acceptable* (no cultural, moral, ethical, etc., concerns should arise in the user the biometric characteristic is acquired from).

Besides the choice of the biometrics to employ, many other issues must be considered in the design stage [1]. Specifically, the authentication system must be *accurate* in the sense that it must grant access to the system to the maximum number of authorized users, whereas it must minimize the number of non authorized access to the system. The *computational speed*, which is related to the time necessary to the system to take a decision, is an important design parameter. Moreover, the system should be able to manage the *exceptions* that can occur when a user does not want to use the biometric system, when a user does not have the biometrics, or when it is not possible, for some transitory conditions, to acquire the biometrics.

When using biometric characteristics as a mean to identify people, significant *privacy* concerns arise since biometrics can be used, in a fraudulent scenario, to treat the user anonymity that must be guaranteed in many real-life situations. Moreover, in a scenario where biometrics can be used to grant physical or logical access, *security* issues regarding the whole biometric system become of paramount importance.

## 20.1.1 Contributions of this Chapter

In this chapter we focus on the security issues related to biometric templates, with application to signature-based authentication systems.

In Section 20.1.2 the main privacy and security issues are briefly summarized, and in Section 20.1.3 some approaches used to protect a biometric template are discussed. Since our contribution is presented within the context of signature biometrics, the related state of the art is presented in Section 20.1.4.

The proposed approaches are presented in Sections 20.2 and 20.3. Specifically, in Section 20.2 a user-adaptive fuzzy commitment scheme is designed with application to on-line signature-based authentication. More in detail, a cryptosystem tuned to the user signature variability is proposed, thus obtaining a user-adaptive approach able to provide the required security and renewability for the stored signature templates. The enrollment stage is described in Section 20.2.1. Specifically, the details about the chosen features extracted from the signature template are given in Section 20.2.1.1, while two metrics that drive the selection of the chosen reliable feature set are presented in Section 20.2.1.2. A detailed description of both the nonadaptive user scheme and the proposed user-adaptive scheme is given in Sections 20.2.1.3 and 20.2.1.4, respectively. The authentication stage is presented in Section 20.2.2 and extensive experimental results, including comparisons with existing approaches, are given in Section 20.2.3.

In Section 20.3 a different perspective is taken. Data hiding techniques are used to design a security scalable authentication system. Specifically, a multilevel signature-based authentication system, where watermarking is employed to hide some signature characteristics in an image of the signature itself, is proposed. Score level fusion is used to combine different types of signature properties. The proposed authentication system allows us to differentiate between two levels of security, which can be selected according to the specific application. Specifically, in Section 20.3.1 the transform domains where we can hide the chosen dynamic signature features are introduced. In Section 20.3.2 the embedding procedure is detailed. The enrollment and the authentication procedures are detailed in Section 20.3.3 and Section 20.3.4, respectively. An extensive discussion on the authentication system performance is given in Section 20.3.5. Conclusions are finally drawn in Section 20.4.

## 20.1.2  Biometric Systems: Privacy and Security Concerns

As already mentioned, biometrics represents an alternative to traditional authentication approaches, able to guarantee improved security and comfort for the users. However, the use of biometric data raises many *privacy* and *security issues* [4–6] that do not affect other methods employed for automatic people recognition.

As pointed out in [4], when an individual gives out his biometrics, either willingly or unwillingly, he discloses unique information about his identity. This implies that his biometrics can be easily replicated and misused. Also, it has been demonstrated that biometric data can contain relevant information regarding people personality and health. This information can be used, for example, to discriminate against people for hiring or to deny an insurance to people with latent health problems or undesired lifestyle preferences. Moreover, to some extent, as highlighted in [4], the *loss of anonymity* can be directly perceived by users as a *loss of autonomy*. In a scenario where a governmental agency can collect huge databases of citizens, it could monitor their behavior and actions. In this scenario, *function creep*, that is a situation where the data, collected for some specific purposes, are used for different ones, is likely to happen in the long run. The use of biometrics can also raise cultural, religious, and physical concerns, either real or unmotivated, on the invasiveness of the acquisition process.

In [7] the main security concerns related to a biometric based authentication system are highlighted: Is it possible to understand when a system becomes insecure? Can biometrics be repudiated? Can biometrics be acquired without the user authorization? How can we prevent administrator misuse? Can an operator track, identify, and then steal the identity of an individual? Which kind of side information can biometrics reveal about an individual? Can biometrics be stolen? More specifically in [8–11] the main treats to a biometric system have been identified as *repudiation* when a legitimate user denies to have accessed the system, *collusion* when a superuser grants access to an unauthorized user to fool the system, *circumvention* when an illegitimate user gains access to the system, *denial of service* when massive attacks on the system cause the system failure, *coercion* when an impostor forces a legitimate user to grant him access to the system, and *covert acquisition* when biometric traits are covertly taken from the legitimate user.

In [12] a biometric system is sketched as the cascade of the sensor for the acquisition, the feature extractor module, the module that performs matching between the output of the feature extractor and the templates stored in the database, and finally the application device. The potential attacks toward a biometric system can be perpetrated at the sensor level, where fake biometrics can be presented, at the feature extractor level that could be forced by an attacker to produce preselected features, at the matcher level, which can be attacked to produce fake scores, and at the database level that can be somehow altered. Moreover, the channels interconnecting the different parts of a biometric system, like the channel between the sensor and the feature extractor, between the feature extractor and the matcher, between the database and the matcher, and between the matcher and the application device, can be intercepted and controlled by unauthorized people.

Among the attacks that can be perpetrated against an authentication system, we can cite the *spoofing attack* and the *mimicry attack* related to physiological and behavioral biometrics, respectively. These attacks consist in copying, by means of different strategies, the biometric feature of the enrolled user and then transferring it to an impostor in order to fool the system. The *reply attack*, which consists in capturing first and in replying at a later time the stolen biometrics, in order to get unauthorized access to the system, is of primary concern. Although it was commonly believed that it is not possible to reconstruct the original biometric data starting from the corresponding extracted template, some concrete counterexamples, which contradict this assumption, have been provided for faces in [13], where a *hill climbing* attack is used to regenerate a face from face templates. In [9], a synthetic fingerprints template generator is devised using the *hill climbing* attack. A general *hill climbing* attack based on Bayesian adaption is described in [14] with application to signature verification. In [15], fingerprints are regenerated from the orientation map of the minutia template.

### 20.1.3 Biometric Template Security: State of the Art

As evident from the previous discussion, template protection is one of the key issues to face when designing a biometric based authentication system. In fact, it is highly desirable to keep secret a template, to revoke, to cancel, or to renew a template when compromised, and also to obtain from the same biometrics different keys to access different locations, either physical or logical, in order to avoid unauthorized tracking. In this section, we analyze the different possible solutions that have been investigated in the recent past to secure biometric templates and to provide the desirable cancelability and renewability properties to the employed templates. Among them, we discuss the role that classical cryptography can play in this scenario and describe the recently introduced techniques like *template distortions*, *biometric cryptosystems*, and eventually *data hiding*.

**Cryptography.** Cryptography [16] is a well-known studied solution that allows secure transmission of data over a reliable but insecure channel. Within this framework the term security is used to mean that the privacy of the message and its integrity are ensured, and the authenticity of the sender is guaranteed. However, cryptographic systems rely on the use of keys that must be stored and released on a password-based authentication protocol. Therefore, the security of a cryptographic system relies on the robustness of the password storage system with regard to brute force attacks. Moreover, the use of cryptographic techniques in a biometric-based authentication system, where templates are stored after encryption, does not solve the template security issues. In fact, at the authentication stage, when a genuine biometrics is presented to the system, the match can be performed either in the encrypted domain or in the template domain. However, because of the intrinsic noisy nature of biometric data, the match in the encrypted domain would inevitably bring to a failure, because small differences between data would bring to significant differences in the encrypted domain. Therefore, in order to overcome these problems, it would be necessary to perform the match after decryption, which, however, implies that there is no more security on the biometric templates. Recently, some activity is flourishing to properly define signal processing operations in the encrypted domain [17, 18], which could allow us, for example, to perform operations on encrypted biometric templates on nontrusted machines. However, this activity is still in its infancy and does not yet provide tools for our purposes.

**Template Distortions.** In order to obtain cancelability and renewability, techniques that intentionally apply either *invertible* or *noninvertible* distortions to the original biometrics have been recently proposed. The distortion can take place either in the biometric domain, that is before feature extraction, or in the feature domain. The distortion can be performed using either an invertible or a noninvertible transform, which is chosen on the base of a user key that must be known when authentication is performed. In the case where an invertible transform is chosen, the security of the system relies on the key, whose knowledge by an adversary can reveal total or partial information about the template. On the contrary, when noninvertible transforms are used, even if the key is known by an adversary, no significant information can be acquired on the template.

An invertible transform has been applied in [19] to face images by means of convolution with a user-defined convolution kernel. In [20], palmprint templates are hashed by using pseudorandom keys to obtain a unique code called palmhash. In [21], user's fingerprints are projected in the Fourier–Mellin domain, thus obtaining the fingerprint features, and then they are randomized using iterated inner products between biometric vectors and token-driven pseudo-number sequences. In [22], an approach similar to the one in [21] is applied to iris features. In [23], face templates are first projected in a lower-dimensional space by using Fisher discrimination analysis and are then projected on a subspace by using a user-defined random projection matrix. This approach has been generalized in [24] for text-independent speaker recognition. In [25], face templates undergo a random orthonormal transformation, performed on the base of a user-defined key, thus obtaining cancelability.

In [26], where the expression *cancelable templates* has been first introduced, noninvertible transforms have been used. In [27], Cartesian, polar, and functional noninvertible transformations are used to transform fingerprint minutiae that are projected in the minutiae space itself. In [28], noninvertible transforms are applied to face images to obtain changeable templates, which, however, allow human inspection.

In [29] a signature template protection scheme, where noninvertible transformations are applied to the functions representing users' signatures, has been presented, and its noninvertibility discussed. The renewability property of the approach proposed in [29] is also discussed in [30], where two novel transforms, defined in order to increase the number of cancelable templates generated from an original signature template, are also introduced.

Therefore, when using template distortions techniques, with either invertible or noninvertible transforms, only the distorted data are stored in the database. This implies that, even if the database is compromised, the biometric data cannot be retrieved unless, when dealing with invertible transforms, user-dependent keys are revealed. Moreover, different templates can be generated from the original data, simply by changing the parameters of the employed transform.

**Biometric Cryptosystems.** As we have already pointed out, the password management is the weakest point of a traditional cryptosystem. Many of the drawbacks risen from the use of passwords can be overcome by using biometrics. Therefore, in the recent past (see [31] for a review), some efforts have been devoted to design *biometric cryptosystems* where a classical password-based authentication approach is replaced by biometric-based authentication, which can be used for either securing the keys obtained when using traditional cryptographic schemes or providing the whole authentication system. A possible classification of the operating modes of a biometric cryptosystem is given in [31], where *key release, key binding,* and *key generation* modes are identified. Specifically, in the *key release* mode the cryptographic key is stored together with the biometric template and the other necessary information about the user. After a successful biometric matching, the key is released. However, this approach has several drawbacks, since it requires access to the stored template and then the 1-bit output of the biometric matcher can be overridden by means of Trojan horse attacks. In the *key binding* mode, the key is bound to the biometric template in such a way that both of them are inaccessible to an attacker and the key is released when a valid biometric is presented. It is worth pointing out that no match between the templates needs to be performed. In the *key generation* mode, the key is obtained from the biometric data and no other user intervention, besides the donation of the required biometrics, is needed.

Both the *key binding* and the *key generation* modes are more secure than the *key release* mode. However, they are more difficult to implement because of the variability of the biometric data.

Among the methods that can be classified as *key binding*-based approaches (see [31] and [32]) we can cite the *fuzzy commitment* scheme [33], based on the use of error correction codes and on cryptographic hashed versions of the templates, and the *fuzzy vault* scheme [34], based on polynomial-based secret sharing. More in detail, the approach proposed in [33] stems from the one described in [35], where the role of error correction codes used within the framework of secure biometric authentication is investigated and provides better resilience to noisy biometrics. The approach proposed in [33] has been applied to several biometrics: acoustic ear in [36], fingerprint in [37], 2D face in [38], and 3D face in [39]. These approaches have been generalized in [40] and [41], where user-adaptive error correction codes are used, with application to signature template protection. The *fuzzy vault* method [34] has also been widely used with applications to several biometrics. In [42] and [43], it has been applied to fingerprints protection. A modification of the original scheme was introduced in [44] and further improved in [32]. Moreover, in [45] and [46] the *fuzzy vault* scheme is described with application to signature template protection, to face protection in [47] and [48], and to iris protection in [49].

*Key generation*-based cryptosystems' major design problem is related to the variability of the biometric traits. Therefore, many efforts have been devoted to obtain robust keys from noisy biometric data. In [50] and [51], cryptographic keys are generated from voice and face, respectively. Significant activity has been devoted to the generation of keys from signature. As proposed in [52] and further detailed in [53], a set of parametric features is extracted from each dynamic signature and an interval matrix is used to store the upper and lower admitted thresholds for correct authentication. A similar approach was proposed in [54]. Both methods provide protection for the signature templates. However, the variability of each feature has to be made explicitly available, and the methods do not provide template renewability. In [55], biometric secrecy preservation and renewability are obtained by applying random tokens, together with multiple-bit discretization and permutation, to the function features extracted from the signatures. In [56], biometric keys are generated using a genetic selection algorithm and applied to on-line dynamic signature. In [57], two different primitives for generating cryptographic keys from biometrics are given: the *fuzzy extractor* and the *secure sketch*. This latter has been widely studied in [58], where the practical issues related to the design of a secure sketch system are analyzed with specific application to face biometrics.

**Data Hiding.** As already outlined, encryption can be applied to ensure the privacy, to protect the integrity, and to authenticate a biometric template. However, among the possible drawbacks, encryption does not provide any protection once the content is decrypted.

On the other hand, *data hiding* techniques [59, 60] can be used to insert additional information, namely the watermark, into a digital object, which can be used for a variety of applications ranging from copy protection, to fingerprinting, broadcast monitoring, data authentication, multimedia indexing, content-based retrieval applications, medical imaging applications, and many others. Within this respect, data hiding techniques complement encryption, since the message can remain in the host data even when decryption has been done. However, it is worth pointing out that some security requirements, in a different sense with respect to cryptography, are also needed when dealing with data hiding techniques. In fact, according to the application, we should be able to face *unauthorized embedding*, *unauthorized extraction*, and *unauthorized removal* of the watermark. Two different approaches can be taken when dealing with data hiding techniques: Either the information to hide is of primary concern, while the host is not relevant to the final user, in which case we refer to *steganography*, or the host data is of primary concern, and the mark is used to authenticate/validate the host data itself, in which case we refer to *watermarking*. In [61], both the aforementioned scenarios have been considered with applications to biometrics. Specifically, a steganographic approach has been applied to hide fingerprint minutiae, which need to be transmitted through a nonsecure channel, into a host signal. Moreover, in the same contribution, a watermarking approach has been employed to embed biometric features extracted from face into a fingerprint image. Some approaches for the protection and/or authentication of biometric data using data hiding have been proposed in [62], where robust data hiding techniques are used to embed codes or timestamps, in such a way that after the expiration date the template is useless. In [63], a fragile watermarking method for fingerprint verification is proposed in order to detect tampering while not lowering the verification performances. Also, watermarking can be used to implement multimodal biometric systems, as in [64], where fingerprints are watermarked with face features, in [65], where iris templates are embedded in face images, or in [66], where the voice pattern and the iris image of an individual are hidden in specific blocks of the wavelet transform of his fingerprint image. In [67], a steganographic approach is used to hide into a host image a template that is made cancelable before it is hidden. In [68] and [69], the authors propose a signature-based biometric system, where watermarking is applied to the signature image in order to hide and keep secret some signature features in a static representation of the signature itself.

Although a huge amount of literature has been produced on watermarking in the last years, no equal effort has been devoted to the integration between watermarking and cryptography. A first effort to formalize the points of contact between these two disciplines has been done in [70]. In [71], the commonly believed analogies between watermarking and cryptography are critically discussed, and a layered approach mimicking the open system interconnection (OSI) model, where encryption and watermarking are kept distinct, is recommended. Also, application scenarios, like content authentication and traitor tracing, are studied. However, this research field is still in its infancy and much more research effort is needed.

## 20.1.4 Signature-Based Authentication Systems: State of the Art

In this section, some introductory concepts regarding the use of signatures for biometric-based authentication are provided and a review of the state of the art, far from being exhaustive, is given.

Signature-based user recognition is one of the most accepted biometric-based authentication methods since, with signatures being part of everyday life, it is perceived as a noninvasive and nonthreatening process by the majority of the users. Moreover, a signature has a high legal value, since it has always played the role of document authentication and it is accepted both by governmental institutions and for commercial transactions as a mean of identification. Moreover, on the contrary with respect to the majority of other biometrics, a signature can be reissued, in the sense that, if compromised, with a certain degree of effort the user can change his signature. On the other hand, it can be influenced by physical and emotional conditions and it exhibits a significant variability that must be taken into account in the authentication process.

Because of the wide social and economical impact of signature-based authentication, a huge effort has been devoted to research in this fields in the last decades. A review of the state of the art covering the literature up to 1993 can be found in [72] and [73]. Survey papers quoting the more recent advances in signature recognition up to 2004 are given in [74], where also handwriting recognition is addressed, in [75], and in [76].

Signature-based authentication can be either *static* or *dynamic*. In the *static* mode, also referred to as off-line, only the spatioluminance evolution of the signature, acquired through either a camera or an optical scanner, is available. In this case, some geometric signature image characteristics can be extracted. In the *dynamic* mode, also called on-line, signatures are acquired by means of a graphic tablet or a pen-sensitive computer display, or even by means of a PDA, which can provide temporal information about the signature itself. These devices capture the spatio-temporal evolution of the signature, thus acquiring the pressure, the velocity, the acceleration, and the pen tilt signals, among the others.

Once the signature has been acquired, either off-line or on-line, some preprocessing is usually needed in order to normalize the signature dimensions, to localize the signature, to denoise the signature image in case of off-line data acquisition, to segment the signature, and so on [75].

In order to represent the signature itself, some features must be extracted. As widely accepted in the current literature, two different kinds of features can be considered: *parameters* and *functions*. The former refer to scalar values, which can be derived from either on-line or off-line signatures. The latter refer to on-line acquisitions where time functions, like pressure, velocity, acceleration, and so on, can be employed. A plethora of *parameters* have been proposed in the literature (see [75] for a survey). Some of them can be obtained by applying some operators like the average, the minimum, and the maximum operators to time functions, like velocity, acceleration, pressure, and forces. Some other typical parameters can be obtained from on-line signature acquisitions, like the number of pen-lifts, or from off-line acquired signatures, for example derived from the structural analysis of the signature, like height, width, ratio between the signature length and its width, and many others [53]. Moreover, both parameters and functions can be obtained after a preliminary projection of the data acquired either off-line or on-line in a transform domain like the Fourier, wavelet, Hadamard, or Hough, to cite a few.

Since on-line signature authentication involves dynamic features, much more difficult to forge than static ones, it is a more suitable for personal authentication in legal and commercial transactions requiring high security. However, as outlined in [77], not all the features have the same *consistency*. From an ideal point of view, a reliable feature should have values close enough for genuine signatures, but far enough when they are extracted from forged signatures. In [77], a consistency model is proposed, and the reliability of some commonly used features are analyzed.

The final step of the authentication process is the matching between the extracted features and the ones in the database. As highlighted in [78] the matching can be performed by means of *template matching*, *stochastic models*, *structural methods*, and *neural network*-based methods. Within the *template matching* methods, Dynamic Time Warping (DTW) represents one of the more flexible approaches to manage the signature length variability [79–82]. The most popular *stochastic model* is the one based on Hidden Markov Models (HMM) [83, 84]. Also *neural networks* have been widely used for matching [85, 86].

## 20.2 SIGNATURE-BASED USER-ADAPTIVE FUZZY COMMITMENT

In this section the proposed scheme for biometric templates protection is presented. As already mentioned, it is basically based on Juels' proposal of fuzzy commitment using error correcting codes [33]. The proposed approach is twofold, allowing the system both to manage cancelable biometrics [87] and to handle the intra-class variability exhibited by biometric signatures. As can be expected from behavioral biometrics, different signature realizations, taken from a user, can exhibit a lot of variability,

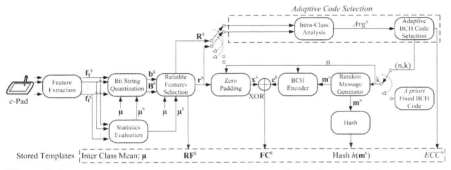

**Figure 20.1.** Signature-based fuzzy commitment: Enrollment scheme. The acquired data are analyzed, quantized and summed to error correcting codes. The stored data are $\mu$, $\mathbf{RF}^s$, $\mathbf{FC}^s$, $ECC^s$, and $h(\mathbf{m}^s)$.

mainly due to lack of user's habit and to the different conditions of execution (seated or standing position, wide or narrow area for resting the arms, etc.). The signature variability is here handled by considering the obtained templates as noisy versions of the "ideal" template, where the noise power is related to the actual signature deviation from the noise free template. The schemes of the proposed enrollment and authentication procedure are illustrated in Figures 20.1 and 20.3, respectively.

## 20.2.1 Enrollment Stage

The proposed enrollment scheme is presented in Figure 20.1. In brief, during the enrollment phase, a number $I$ of signatures are recorded for each subject $s$. Some features, properly chosen, are extracted from the signatures acquired from the user $s$ and collected in the vectors $\mathbf{f}_i^s$, $i = 1, \ldots, I$, which are then binarized using the intra-class $\mu^s$ and the inter-class $\mu$ vector mean, which are stored in the template regarding the user $s$. Then, for each subject $s$, only the most reliable features are selected, their indices are saved, and the representative binary vector $\mathbf{x}^s$ is obtained. Protection is performed by summing to $\mathbf{x}^s$ a codeword $\mathbf{c}^s$, generated as the output of a BCH encoder fed by a randomly generated binary word $\mathbf{m}^s$. The so obtained vector $\mathbf{FC}^s$ is then stored together with the hashed version $h(\mathbf{m})^s$ of $\mathbf{m}^s$ and the information regarding the BCH code employed. The stored information can be used to perform user authentication without revealing any information about the original data, as indicated in Section 20.2.2.

The proposed scheme is described in detail in the following text.

### 20.2.1.1 Feature Extraction, Statistics Evaluation, and Binarization

During enrollment, $I$ signatures are acquired from each user $s$ and from each of them $P$ parametric features are extracted and collected in the features vectors $\mathbf{f}_i^s$, $i = 1, \ldots, I$. In Table 20.1 the features employed hereafter are detailed.

**Table 20.1.** Features Extracted from On-Line Signatures

| ID | Description |
|---|---|
| 1 | Number of pen-down events |
| 2 | Writing duration |
| 3 | Sample count |
| 4 | Local maximum count |
| 5 | Aspect ratio |
| 6 | Pen-up/Pen-down ratio |
| 7–8 | $X$ and $Y$ integral |
| 9–10 | $X$ and $Y$ average absolute writing velocity |
| 11–12 | $X$ and $Y$ average absolute writing acceleration |
| 13–14 | $X$ and $Y$ distribution velocity |
| 15–24 | $X$ and $Y$ segmented areas (five equal-length segments) |
| 25 | Path length |
| 26–27 | Delta $X$ and $Y$ |
| 28 | Effective average speed |
| 29–40 | Sectors' pixel count (signature images divided in $4 \times 3$ sectors) |
| 41–42 | Cumulated integral error $X$ and $Y$ |
| 43–44 | Integral error sign $X$ and $Y$ |
| 45 | Cumulated radiant |
| 46 | Average radiant |
| 47 | Cumulated distance |
| 48 | Average distance |
| 49–50 | Average $X$ and $Y$ position |

The intra-class $\mu^s$ and the interclass $\mu$ vector mean are then estimated as

$$\mu^s = \frac{1}{I} \sum_{i=1}^{I} \mathbf{f}_i^s, \quad \mu = \frac{1}{S} \sum_{s=1}^{S} \mu^s, \tag{20.1}$$

where $S$ is the number of enrolled subjects. From the $I$ signatures acquired from the user $s$, a binary vector $\mathbf{b}^s$ representative of the considered $P$ features is then obtained comparing the intraclass $\mu^s$ with the interclass $\mu$ vectors:

$$\mathbf{b}^s[p] = \begin{cases} 0 & \text{if } \mu^s[p] \leq \mu[p] \\ 1 & \text{if } \mu^s[p] > \mu[p] \end{cases}, \quad p = 1, \ldots, P. \tag{20.2}$$

### 20.2.1.2  Reliable Feature Selection

In the proposed scheme, for the user $s$, after having determined the representative vector $\mathbf{b}^s$, a selection of the relevant features is performed in order to reduce the feature space dimensionality taken into account in the authentication stage. Only the subjects' most reliable features are selected, thus counteracting the potential instability, for the single user, of the feature vector components. In [38], where features

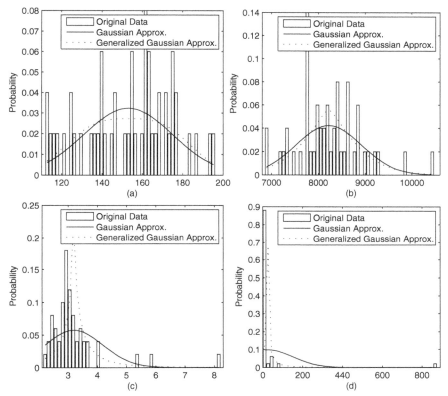

**Figure 20.2.** Fitting of four common signature features distributions to Gaussian and generalized Gaussian model: (**a**) Aspect ratio; (**b**) path length; (**c**) absolute $Y$-velocity; (**d**) average absolute $X$-acceleration.

extracted from face images are considered, this task is accomplished using a reliability measure obtained by assuming a Gaussian distribution for each considered face feature.

However, the Gaussianity assumption does not apply to the scenario under examination. In fact, extensive tests have pointed out that the majority of commonly used signature features, like mean velocity, acceleration, or pressure, cannot be properly modeled according to either a Gaussian or a generalized Gaussian distribution. In Figure 20.2, the histogram of four common features (aspect ratio, path length, average absolute $Y$-velocity, average absolute $X$-acceleration) extracted from a set of signatures is shown together with the Gaussian and the generalized Gaussian probability density functions, whose parameters are estimated from the experimental data. Testing of fit of the Gaussian and of the generalized Gaussian distribution to the data have also been performed. Specifically, the goodness-of-fit (GOF), chi-squared, Cramer–von Mises, and Anderson–Darling tests [88] have been used. The obtained results, collected in Table 20.2, highlight the poor match between the experimental data and

**Table 20.2.** Test of Fit of a Gaussian and Generalized Gaussian Distribution to the Data: Goodness-of-Fit, Chi-Squared, Cramer–von Mises, and Anderson–Darling

|  | Fitting Results | GOF | Chi-Squared | Cramer–von Mises | Anderson–Darling |
|---|---|---|---|---|---|
| Aspect ratio | Gaussian | 0.1031 | 0.0493 | 0.0463 | 0.1816 |
|  | Generalized Gaussian | 0.0823 | 0.0515 | 0.0374 | 0.1543 |
| Path length | Gaussian | 0.0683 | 0.1008 | 0.0408 | 0.1238 |
|  | Generalized Gaussian | 0.0831 | 0.1084 | 0.0454 | 0.1419 |
| $Y$ velocity | Gaussian | 0.2824 | 0.2057 | 0.1907 | 0.4001 |
|  | Generalized Gaussian | 0.3190 | 0.1514 | 0.1963 | 0.4878 |
| $X$ acceleration | Gaussian | 0.7829 | 0.2990 | 0.7624 | 2.5226 |
|  | Generalized Gaussian | 0.7638 | 0.1039 | 0.7170 | 2.2371 |

the considered distributions. Therefore, in our approach we introduce a reliability measure not directly related to the signature features distribution.

In the process of defining a reliable feature, for each user $s$, the enrolled features vectors $\mathbf{f}_i^s$, with $i = 1, \ldots, I$, are binarized by comparisons with the interclass mean $\mu$ and collected as row vectors in a binary matrix $\mathbf{B}^s$, with $I$ (signature samples) rows and $P$ (features) columns, whose generic element $\mathbf{B}^s[i, p]$ is obtained as

$$\mathbf{B}^s[i, p] = \begin{cases} 0 & \text{if } \mathbf{f}_i^s[p] \leq \mu[p] \\ 1 & \text{if } \mathbf{f}_i^s[p] > \mu[p] \end{cases}, \qquad p = 1, \ldots, P. \qquad (20.3)$$

Then, the reliability $\mathbf{R}_1^s[p]$ of the $p$th feature is defined as follows:

$$\mathbf{R}_1^s[p] = 1 - \frac{\sum_{i=1}^{I}(\mathbf{B}^s[i, p] \oplus \mathbf{b}^s[p])}{I}, \qquad p = 1, \ldots, P, \qquad (20.4)$$

where $\oplus$ represents the XOR operation and $\mathbf{b}^s$ is given by Eq. (20.2). In Eq. (20.4), the occurrence of the $p$th binary value $\mathbf{b}^s[p]$ in the corresponding elements of the binary matrix $\mathbf{B}^s$ is evaluated; in this way, a measure of the representativeness of the value $\mathbf{b}^s[p]$, with respect to the possible values obtainable from a new signature by the same user, is derived. According to this measure, components with a high reliability possess a high discrimination capability.

However, the use of the reliability measure $\mathbf{R}_1^s[p]$ can lead to components with the same reliability value. Then, in order to further discriminate among them, we introduce a second level of feature screening, according to the following reliability measure:

$$\mathbf{R}_2^s[p] = \frac{|\mu[p] - \mu^s[p]|}{\sigma^s[p]}, \qquad p = 1, \ldots, P, \qquad (20.5)$$

with $\sigma^s[p] = \sqrt{\frac{1}{I-1} \sum_{i=1}^{I} \left[ \mathbf{f}_i^s[p] - \mu^s[p] \right]^2}$ being the standard deviation of the $p$th feature of the subject $s$. A higher discriminating power is thus trusted to features with a larger difference between $\mu^s[p]$ and $\mu[p]$, with respect to the standard deviation $\sigma^s[p]$.

After the application of the reliability metrics to $\mathbf{b}^s$, we end up with the binary feature vector $\mathbf{r}^s$ containing the $P'$ most reliable components of $\mathbf{b}^s$. The indexes of the most reliable feature for the user $s$ are collected in $\mathbf{RF}^s$, which is stored, together with the inter-class vector $\mu$, being made available for the authentication process.

As already pointed out, in order to achieve both template protection and renewability, our scheme uses error correcting codes (BCH codes) [89]. The error correction capability (ECC) of the codes can be *a priori* selected, as in [38]; this approach is detailed in Section 20.2.1.3.

In this chapter we present an error correcting code selection procedure, depending on the intra-class variability of each user's signature, as detailed in Section 20.2.1.4.

### 20.2.1.3   A Priori Selection of Error Correction Capability

After having obtained the binary feature vector $\mathbf{r}^s$, BCH codes are employed to realize the fuzzy commitment. The ECC of the employed BCH encoder, and therefore the length $n$ of its codewords, is selected according to the desired false acceptance rate (FAR) or false rejection rate (FRR). In Table 20.3 the correspondences between the ECC and the values of $n$ and $k$, respectively being the length of the codewords $\mathbf{c}$ and the length of the messages to be encoded $\mathbf{m}$, are reported.

Once the BCH encoder is chosen, a codeword $\mathbf{c}^s$ is generated from a randomly selected message $\mathbf{m}^s$. Then, the binary vector $\mathbf{r}^s$, of $P'$ bits as detailed in Section 20.2.1.2 , is zero padded in order to reach the same length $n$ of the codeword $\mathbf{c}^s$, thus resulting in the vector $\mathbf{x}^s$. A XOR operation between the codeword $\mathbf{c}^s$ and $\mathbf{x}^s$ is finally performed, thus obtaining the fuzzy commitment $\mathbf{FC}$:

$$\mathbf{FC}^s = FC(\mathbf{x}^s, \mathbf{c}^s) = \mathbf{x}^s \oplus \mathbf{c}^s. \tag{20.6}$$

**Table 20.3.** Correspondences Between ECC, $n$ and $k$ values

| ECC | $n$ | $k$ | ECC | $n$ | $k$ |
|-----|-----|-----|-----|-----|-----|
| 1 | 127 | 120 | 11 | 127 | 57 |
| 2 | 127 | 113 | 12 | 255 | 163 |
| 3 | 127 | 106 | 13 | 127 | 50 |
| 4 | 127 | 99 | 14 | 127 | 43 |
| 5 | 127 | 92 | 15 | 127 | 36 |
| 6 | 127 | 85 | 16 | 511 | 367 |
| 7 | 127 | 78 | 17 | 1023 | 858 |
| 8 | 255 | 191 | 18 | 255 | 131 |
| 9 | 127 | 71 | 19 | 255 | 123 |
| 10 | 127 | 64 | 20 | 511 | 340 |

A hashed version $h(\mathbf{m}^s)$ of the random message $\mathbf{m}^s$, obtained using the SHA-1 algorithm [90], is then stored together with $\mathbf{FC}^s$.

It is worth pointing out that, as evident from Table 20.3, no restriction is introduced for the number $P'$ of the reliable features that can be considered, given that $P' < n_{min} = 127$. However, this constraint can be removed by selecting BCH codes with a longer minimum codeword length $n_{min}$.

### 20.2.1.4   Adaptive Selection of Error Correction Capability

The approach described in Section 20.2.1.3 allows obtaining renewable templates by changing the employed codeword $\mathbf{c}^s$ (i.e., the randomly generated message $\mathbf{m}^s$) associated to the user during enrollment.

In this chapter we propose an authentication method that, besides providing renewability, provides also adaptability to the user signature variability. This implies that we are able to take into account the signatures intra-variability, which is reflected in the bit differences among the enrolled feature vector $\mathbf{x}^s$ and the feature vector $\tilde{\mathbf{x}}^s$ obtained in the authentication stage from the same user $s$ (see Figure 20.3).

Adaptivity is achieved by choosing the BCH code and its ECC among the set of available codes of Table 20.3, in such a way that for users characterized by a high intra-class variability, codes with higher error correction capabilities are selected.

Therefore, in the enrollment stage, an intra-class analysis is performed as follows. Once the $P'$ reliable features are selected, as detailed in Section 20.2.1.2, the matrix $\mathbf{R}^s$, having $I$ rows and $P'$ columns, is obtained from $\mathbf{B}^s$ dropping the nonreliable features. Then, the Hamming distances $D_i^s$, with $i = 1, \ldots, I$, between any rows of $\mathbf{R}^s$ and the representative vector $\mathbf{r}^s$ are evaluated. The average $Avg^s$ of the $D_i^s$ values,

$$Avg^s = \frac{1}{I} \sum_{i=1}^{I} D_i^s, \tag{20.7}$$

is then used to characterize the intra-class variability of the user $s$.

Specifically, the BCH code whose ECC is equal to the nearest integer of $[Avg^s + \Delta_{ECC}]$, where $\Delta_{ECC}$ is a system parameter common to all the enrolled users, is chosen. The selected error correction capability $ECC^s$ for the user $s$ is stored in the database.

As described in Section 20.2.1.3, the binary vector $\mathbf{r}^s$ is zero padded in order to reach the same length $n$ of the selected BCH codewords, resulting in the vector $\mathbf{x}^s$.

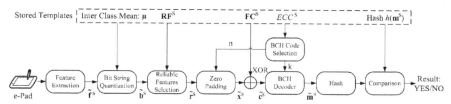

**Figure 20.3.** Signature-based fuzzy commitment: Authentication scheme. When a subject claims his identity, a response is given using the stored data $\mu$, $\mathbf{RF}^s$, $\mathbf{FC}^s$, $ECC^s$, and $h(\mathbf{m}^s)$.

The fuzzy commitment $\mathbf{FC}^s$ is then generated using a codeword $\mathbf{c}^s$ obtained from the encoding of a random message $\mathbf{m}^s$:

$$\mathbf{FC}^s = FC(\mathbf{x}^s, \mathbf{c}^s) = \mathbf{x}^s \oplus \mathbf{c}^s. \tag{20.8}$$

A hashed version $h(\mathbf{m}^s)$ of $\mathbf{m}^s$, created using the SHA-1 algorithm, is eventually stored.

The proposed framework provides security, being impossible to retrieve $\mathbf{f}^s$ from the stored templates $\boldsymbol{\mu}$, $\mathbf{RF}^s$, $\mathbf{FC}^s$, $h(\mathbf{m}^s)$, and $\mathbf{ECC}^s$. In fact, in order to infer about the extracted features, or to reconstruct their binary counterparts, it is necessary to possess, among the other data (see Figure 20.1), the BCH codeword $\mathbf{c}^s$ employed for data protection. However, neither the binary word $\mathbf{m}^s$ at the input of the BCH encoder nor its output $\mathbf{c}^s$ are stored. In fact, only the hashed value of $\mathbf{m}^s$, generated by means of the hash function $h(\cdot)$, is stored, thus guaranteeing the impossibility to recover useful information from the saved data. Then, as shown in [33], it can be concluded that the disclosure of the secret $\mathbf{x}^s$ is as difficult as finding a collision for the SHA-1 hash $h(\mathbf{m}^s)$, which leads to the observation that the security of the system is the same of the employed hash function.

However, it is worth pointing out that several attacks, being able to generate collisions when using the SHA-1 algorithm and having less computational complexity than the brute force attack, have already been proposed in the literature [91–93] . Therefore, in order to solve this problem and thus to improve the system security for practical application, two novel hash functions could be used in our scheme without affecting its architecture: either the SHA-256 with 32-bit words or the SHA-512 with 64-bit words. The cryptographic security of these hash functions has not been investigated as deeply as the SHA-1's one; however, no weakness has been found so far.

## 20.2.2 Authentication Stage

The authentication phase follows the same steps as the enrollment stage (see Figure 20.3). When a subject claims his identity, he provides his signature, which is converted in the features vector $\tilde{\mathbf{f}}^s$. Then the quantization is done using the inter-class mean $\boldsymbol{\mu}$, thus obtaining $\tilde{\mathbf{b}}^s$. The reliable features $\tilde{\mathbf{r}}^s$ are selected using $\mathbf{RF}^s$, and later extended using zero padding, generating $\tilde{\mathbf{x}}^s$. A binary vector $\tilde{\mathbf{c}}^s$, representing a possibly corrupted BCH codeword, results from the XOR operation

$$\tilde{\mathbf{c}}^s = \tilde{\mathbf{x}}^s \oplus \mathbf{FC}^s. \tag{20.9}$$

The BCH decoder is selected depending on the encoder used in enrollment, obtaining $\tilde{\mathbf{m}}^s$ from $\tilde{\mathbf{c}}^s$. Finally, the SHA-1 hashed version $h(\tilde{\mathbf{m}}^s)$ is compared to $h(\mathbf{m}^s)$: If both values are identical, the subject is authenticated.

## 20.2.3 Signature-Based Fuzzy Commitment: Experimental Results

In this section, an extensive set of experimental results, concerning the performances of the proposed system together with comparisons with other approaches proposed in the literature, are presented.

In our experimentations, on-line signatures are acquired using an Interlink Electronics ePad-ink, based on a resistive touchpad with 300 dpi resolution. The proposed approach consists in extracting a number $P$ of parametric features from the acquired signals, further processed as detailed in Section 20.2 to obtain security and renewability of the stored templates. Specifically, we have first performed experimentations in order to compare the adaptive approach detailed in Section 20.2.1.4 with the nonadaptive one described in Section 20.2.1.3.

Moreover, the proposed approach has been compared with the algorithm proposed in [54], which relies on the processing of parametric features extracted from signatures.

The selected feature set, composed by 50 parameters enumerated in Table 20.1, is the same as in [53]. Thirty subjects have been enrolled. Each of them has given 50 signatures that have been recorded at different times in a week time span. As in [53], $I = 6$ signatures are considered in the enrollment stage.

In our experiments we have tested the system performance either with an *a priori* choice of the BCH correction code or with a user-adaptive BCH code selection. The performances have been assessed using the FRR, FAR, and the receiver operating characteristic (ROC) as figures of merit. More in detail, the FRR has been estimated using for each subject the 44 signatures not used in the enrollment stage. The FAR is referred to conditions of random forgeries [76], indicated as $FAR_{RF}$, and to conditions of skilled forgeries, indicated as $FAR_{SF}$. For each subject, the 50 signatures of all the remaining 29 users are used as random forgeries. When skilled forgeries are considered, a test set of 10 skilled forgeries is created for each subject, using a training time of 10 min for each signature whose original was made available. In our experimental setup, the forgers had the ability to observe the genuine users when signing, in order to gain a better understanding of the signature dynamics.

The whole set of the employed BCH codes, with different ECC, is detailed in Table 20.3. In Figure 20.4(a) the system performances using the whole set of features for authentication ($P' = 50$), are given. In order to show the better performances obtainable using the feature selection procedure detailed in Section 20.2.1.2, in Figure 20.4(b) the system performances achieved when a lower number of features are considered ($P' = 40$) are displayed. The results are shown with respect to the ECC employed in the system. The ROC curves in Figure 20.5(a) report the $FAR_{SF}$/FRR system behavior for both $P' = 50$ and $P' = 40$. As can be seen, the achieved equal error rate (EER) is approximately 23% for $P' = 50$ and 22% for $P' = 40$ when considering skilled forgeries. As for random forgeries, the obtained EER is about 10% for $P' = 50$ and 9% for $P' = 40$.

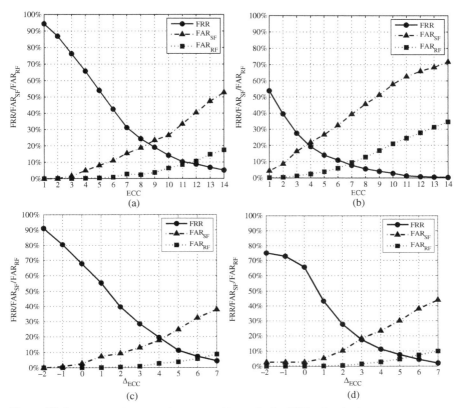

**Figure 20.4.** *First row*: System performances without adaptive BCH code selection.
(**a**) FRR/FAR$_{SF}$/FAR$_{RF}$ versus the selected ECC for $P' = 50$; (**b**) FRR/FAR$_{SF}$/FAR$_{RF}$ versus the selected ECC for $P' = 40$. *Second row*: System performances with the adaptive BCH code selection.
(**c**) FRR/FAR$_{SF}$/FAR$_{RF}$ vs. $\Delta_{ECC}$ for $P' = 50$; (**d**) FRR/FAR$_{SF}$/FAR$_{RF}$ versus $\Delta_{ECC}$ for $P' = 40$.

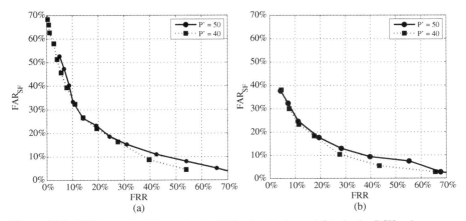

**Figure 20.5.** ROC curves for (**a**) nonadaptive BCH code selection and (**b**) adaptive BCH code selection for both $P' = 50$ and $P' = 40$.

We have also tested the proposed system using the adaptive codes selection scheme we have here proposed, which proved to be able to offer improved performances with respect to the nonadaptive approach. The ECC is selected for each user as detailed in Section 20.2.1.4. The results are shown with respect to the parameter $\Delta_{ECC}$ used to determine the proper error correction capability for each user. Figures 20.4(c) and 20.4(d) show the system performances using $P' = 50$ and $P' = 40$, respectively, while in Figure 20.5(b) the ROC curves for the adaptive codes selection scheme are illustrated. The achieved equal error rate is approximately 18,50% for $P' = 50$ and 17% for $P' = 40$, considering skilled forgeries. The performances related to random forgeries consist of an EER equal to 8% for $P' = 50$ and 6% for $P' = 40$.

The obtained experimental results highlight that the use of the adaptive code selection method improves the system performances, especially in terms of FAR. Moreover, the system performances increase when a selection of the original set of features for each user, made by means of the reliability measures introduced in Section 20.2.1.2, is done.

Finally, a performance comparison among the proposed method, the one where no template protection is taken into account and the one in [54], is reported here.

Specifically, we used a Mahalanobis distance to compute the distance of a features vector $\mathbf{f}$ from the vector $\mu^s$, representative of the user $s$:

$$D(\mathbf{f}, \mu^s) = \sqrt{\sum_{p=1}^{50} \frac{(\mathbf{f}[p] - \mu^s[p])^2}{\sigma^{s2}[p]}}, \tag{20.10}$$

where $\sigma^{s2}$ represents the feature variance for the user $s$, estimated during enrollment. If the distance is less than a threshold $T_A$, the features vector $\mathbf{f}$ is accepted as originated from the user $s$.

Then, in Figure 20.6 the ROC curves related to the $FAR_{SF}$/FRR performances of various approaches are illustrated. Specifically, Figure 20.6 shows the performances related to the following:

- A system without any template protection, where the threshold $T_A$ is continuously varied;

- A system implementing the approach in [54], where the system parameter $b$, which acts similar to a threshold, is continuously varied;

- A system implementing the nonadaptive approach here presented, using different ECC values and taking $P' = 50$ in order to present results comparable with those of the other methods;

- A system implementing the adaptive approach here presented, using different values of $\Delta_{ECC}$ and taking $P' = 50$.

As evident from Figure 20.6, the performances of the method proposed in [54] are very close to those obtainable when no protection is applied.

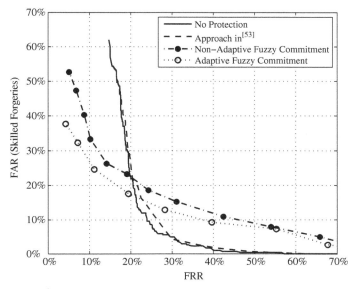

**Figure 20.6.** Comparison between the performances of the nonadaptive and adaptive template protection scheme and the performances of a system without protection, the one proposed in [54].

As far as the proposed adaptive scheme is concerned, the ROC curves obtained by varying the employed ECC differentiate with respect to the one obtained when no protection is taken into account. As shown in Figure 20.6, better performances in terms of FRR are obtained (lower value is equal to 4%), making the proposed approach more suitable to forensic applications [1] than the other considered methods. Moreover, the best achievable EER is obtained using our adaptive fuzzy commitment approach, and it is equal to 18,5%.

Finally, it is worth pointing out that, as shown in Figure 20.5(b), even better performances can be obtained by using the proposed approach when the parameters reduction is taken into account. Moreover, the proposed method is also able to provide, in addiction to template protection, template cancelability, whereas the other considered methods cannot.

## 20.3 SECURITY-SCALABLE SIGNATURE-BASED AUTHENTICATION SYSTEM USING DATA HIDING

In this section we propose a signature-based biometric system, where data hiding is applied to signature images in order to hide and keep secret some signature features in a static representation of the signature itself. The marked images can be used for user authentication, letting their static characteristics being analyzed by automatic algorithms or security attendants. When needed, the embedded features can be extracted and used to enforce the authentication procedure.

The proposed system has been designed to realize a signature-based security scalable authentication system. When higher security is needed, the embedded features can be extracted and used, thus realizing a security-scalable authentication system.

Moreover, when large-scale applications are considered, the need to use information coming from different sources and to properly combine them arises, leading to multimodal biometrics approaches [94]. Different strategies, commonly referred to as *fusion* techniques, can be implemented at different levels: fusion at the sensor level, at the feature level, at the score level, and at the decision level [95]. Fusion methods include, among others, those aiming at combining the different pieces of information embodied in one single biometric signal. Within this framework, our approach proposes the fusion of static and dynamic signature features. In [85] and [96], the fusion of complementary verification modules and the fusion of local and global characteristics have been considered for signature verification.

The enrollment procedure of the proposed security scalable signature-based authentication system is illustrated in Figure 20.7. After having acquired the signature through an electronic pad, some relevant dynamic features are extracted and then embedded into the signature image by means of watermarking techniques. Specifically, we use the pressure values of the signature as the host signal where to embed the watermark. It is worth pointing out that by considering synthetic images whose intensity is proportional to the pressure applied by the writer, a higher discriminative capability, with respect to the simple binary signature images employed by conventional methods, is obtained. More in detail, referring to Figure 20.7, the proposed enrollment scheme can be summarized as follows: First, the acquired pressure image $s[i, j]$ undergoes a two-level wavelet decomposition. The second-level subbands, namely $s_{2LL}[i, j]$, $s_{2HL}[i, j]$, $s_{2LH}[i, j]$, and $s_{2HH}[i, j]$, which represent the approximation, the horizontal detail, the vertical detail, and the diagonal detail subband, respectively, are selected for the embedding. Because signature images are typically sparse images, the subbands $s_\gamma[i, j]$, with $\gamma \in \Gamma = \{2LL, 2HL, 2LH, 2HH\}$, are then decomposed into blocks of $P_I \times P_J$ pixels in order to perform a local analysis and to identify the proper areas where the watermark has to be embedded. Two different embedding domains are then used, both derived from the Radon transform, as detailed in Section 20.3.1: The ridgelet [99] and the Radon-DCT domain. The selected blocks are projected in one of these two domains, and the most relevant projections' coefficients are chosen. Dynamic features extracted from the acquired signatures are finally embedded in the signature image by means of quantization index modulation (QIM) watermarking [97] . The whole procedure is detailed in Section 20.3.2.

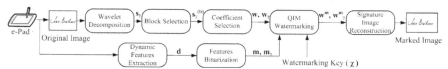

**Figure 20.7.** Security-scalable signature-based authentication system using data hiding. Proposed enrollment scheme.

Therefore, as possible application of our system, when a low security level is needed, the authentication can be performed using some selected static features extracted from the signature images. On the other hand, when a higher level of security is required, authentication is accomplished on the base of the embedded dynamic features either by themselves or together with the selected static features.

## 20.3.1  Radon Transform and Embedding Domains

Signature images are sparse images characterized by line singularities defined over a 2-D domain. Therefore, the Radon transform (RT) [98] appears to be a good tool to analyze this kind of images.

The RT is used in a wide variety of applications including tomography, ultrasound, optics, and geophysics, to cite only a few. The continuous Radon transform $R_f(\theta, t)$ of an integrable bivariate function $f(\mathbf{x}) = f(x_1, x_2)$ is defined as

$$R_f(\theta, t) = \int \int_{\mathbb{R}^2} f(x_1, x_2) \delta(x_1 \cos \theta + x_2 \sin \theta - t) \, dx_1 dx_2, \qquad (20.11)$$

where $(\theta, t) \in [0, 2\pi) \times \mathbb{R}$ and $\delta$ is the Dirac distribution. The value $R_f(\theta, t)$ thus represents the integral of $f(\mathbf{x})$ over a line oriented at an angle $\theta$ and whose distance from the origin is $t$. Therefore the Radon transform maps each line in the spatial domain $(x_1, x_2)$ into a point in the $(\theta, t)$ domain. The continuous inverse Radon transform can be expressed as

$$f(x_1, x_2) = \frac{1}{2\pi^2} \int_0^\pi \int_{-\infty}^\infty \frac{\partial R_f(\theta, t)/\partial t}{x_1 \cos \theta + x_2 \sin \theta - t} \, dt d\theta. \qquad (20.12)$$

Among the approaches that have been proposed in the literature to implement the continuous RT in the discrete domain, the finite Radon transform (FRAT) that has been used in this work was originally proposed in [99]. It is both perfectly invertible and nonredundant, and it is defined as summations of image pixels over a certain set of "lines" in a discrete 2-D space, defined in a similar way as the continuous lines in the Euclidean space. Specifically, given a real function $f[i, j]$ defined over a finite grid $Z_P^2$, where $Z_P = \{0, 1, \ldots, P - 1\}$, its FRAT is

$$\mathrm{FRAT}_f[k, l] = r[k, l] = \frac{1}{\sqrt{P}} \sum_{(i,j) \in L_{k,l}} f[i, j], \qquad (20.13)$$

where $L_{k,l}$ defines the set of points that form a line on $Z_P^2$:

$$L_{k,l} = \{(i, j) : j = ki + l \,(\mathrm{mod}\, P), i \in Z_P\},$$
$$L_{P,l} = \{(l, j) : j \in Z_P\}, \qquad (20.14)$$

where $k \in Z_{P+1}$ is the line direction and $l$ is its intercept.

The FRAT can be inverted using a finite back-projection (FBP) operator, defined as the sum of Radon coefficients of all the lines that go through a given point, that is,

$$\text{FBP}_r[i, j] = f[i, j] = \frac{1}{\sqrt{P}} \sum_{(k,l) \in O_{i,j}} r[k, l], \quad (i, j) \in Z_P^2, \quad (20.15)$$

where $O_{i,j}$ denotes the set of indices of all the lines that go through a point $(i, j) \in Z_P^2$, that is,

$$O_{i,j} = \{(k, l) : l = j - ki \ (\text{mod } P), k \in Z_{P+1}\} \cup \{(P, i)\}. \quad (20.16)$$

The proposed watermark embedding domains, which stem from the Radon transform domain, have been designed in order to allow an energy compaction for each Radon projection in few representative coefficients. Specifically, we employ the following:

- The ridgelet transform [99] obtained by applying a wavelet decomposition to the Radon projections. Watermark embedding in the ridgelet domain was already proposed in [100] by the authors and in [101];
- The Radon-DCT (R-DCT) transform obtained by applying the discrete cosine transform (DCT) to each Radon projection.

### 20.3.1.1 Ridgelet Domain

Given an integrable bivariate function $f(\mathbf{x}) = f(x_1, x_2)$, its continuous ridgelet transform (CRT) defined in [99] can be evaluated by applying the wavelet transform in the Radon domain. Specifically, the CRT can be obtained by applying a 1-D wavelet transform to $R_f(\theta, t)$ as follows:

$$CRT_f(a, c, \theta) = a^{-1/2} \int_{\mathbb{R}} \psi\left(\frac{t - c}{a}\right) R_f(\theta, t) \, dt. \quad (20.17)$$

From Eq. (20.17), it can be seen that an invertible finite ridgelet transform (FRIT) [99] can be derived from the application of a 1-D discrete wavelet transform on each FRAT projection sequence $(r[k, 0], r[k, 1], \ldots, r[k, P - 1])$, for each direction $k \in Z_{P+1}$:

$$\text{FRIT}_f[k, q] = g[k, q], \quad q \in Z_P. \quad (20.18)$$

Thanks to the wavelets' properties, the FRIT is able to concentrate the energy of each Radon projection sequence in its first coefficients.

### 20.3.1.2 Radon-DCT Domain

As an alternative to wavelet analysis, the DCT can be used to obtain energy compaction. A novel embedding domain is thus defined, indicating with Radon-DCT (R-DCT) the transform derived from application of the DCT on each FRAT projection sequence $(r[k, 0], r[k, 1], \ldots, r[k, P-1]), k \in Z_{P+1}$:

$$\text{R-DCT}_f[k, q] = c[k, q] = \omega[l] \sum_{l=0}^{P-1} r[k, l] \cos\left[\frac{\pi(2l+1)q}{2P}\right], \quad (20.19)$$

where $q \in Z_P$, $\omega[0] = \sqrt{1/N}$ and $\omega[l] = \sqrt{2/N}$, $l \neq 0$. Coefficients R-DCT $_f[k, 0] = c[k, 0]$, $k \in Z_{P+1}$, represent the DC component of each projection $k$, and are therefore connected with the mean value of each Radon projection.

## 20.3.2 Dynamic Signature Features Embedding

As already outlined, in our approach the host pressure image $s[i, j]$ undergoes a two-level wavelet decomposition and the second-level subbands $s_\gamma[i, j]$, $\gamma \in \Gamma = \{2LL, 2HL, 2LH, 2HH\}$, are then decomposed into blocks of $P_I \times P_J$ pixels in order to identify the proper areas where the watermark has to be embedded. This task is accomplished by selecting only those blocks whose energy is greater than a fixed threshold $T_E$. Specifically, indicating with $s_\gamma^{(b)}[i, j]$ the generic $b$th block extracted from the subband $\gamma$, it is then selected for watermark embedding if

$$E^{(b)} = \frac{1}{P_I P_J} \sum_{i=1}^{P_I} \sum_{j=1}^{P_J} \left|s_\gamma^{(b)}[i, j]\right| > T_E, \quad (20.20)$$

that is, if the block contains a meaningful fragment of the signature.

In our experiments we have considered $P_I = P_J = P$. In Table 20.4 we have reported the mean, the maximum, and the minimum number of blocks that can be marked according to the criterion given in Eq. (20.20) for each subband of the second wavelet decomposition level. As can be seen, each subband can provide a significant number of blocks where the mark can be embedded. Once the blocks are selected, they are projected in the ridgelet or in the R-DCT domain to choose the watermark host coefficients as detailed in Section 20.3.2.1.

**Table 20.4.** Mean, Maximum and Minimum Number of Markable Blocks for Each Second-Level Wavelet Decomposition Subband

| Wavelet Decomposition Subband | Minimum Number of Markable Blocks | Mean Number of Markable Blocks | Maximum Number of Markable Blocks |
|---|---|---|---|
| 2LL | 31 | 79,05 | 142 |
| 2HL | 10 | 58,63 | 126 |
| 2LH | 17 | 61,58 | 129 |
| 2HH | 14 | 54,76 | 114 |

The values refer to experiments with $P = 10$ and $T_E = 5$, considering 30 users, 50 signatures for each user.

### 20.3.2.1 Coefficients Selection

**Coefficients Selection in the Ridgelet Domain.** The FRIT is applied to each block selected from subband $\gamma$, whose total number is indicated as $B_\gamma$. Given the $b$th block, $P + 1$ FRIT sequences $(g_\gamma^{(b)}[k, 0], g_\gamma^{(b)}[k, 1], \ldots, g_\gamma^{(b)}[k, P - 1])$ related to each direction $k \in Z_{P+1}$ are then available. Only the two most energetic directions, namely $k_1$ and $k_2$, are selected, and from the sequences associated to them, the first $N$ values are extracted and used to build the matrix $\mathbf{M}_\gamma^{(b)}$:

$$\mathbf{M}_\gamma^{(b)} = \begin{pmatrix} g_\gamma^{(b)}[k_1, 0] \ g_\gamma^{(b)}[k_1, 1] \cdots g_\gamma^{(b)}[k_1, N - 1] \\ g_\gamma^{(b)}[k_2, 0] \ g_\gamma^{(b)}[k_2, 1] \cdots g_\gamma^{(b)}[k_2, N - 1] \end{pmatrix}. \qquad (20.21)$$

**Coefficients Selection in the Radon-DCT Domain.** The second proposed embedding method relies on the projection of the selected $B_\gamma$ blocks $s_\gamma^{(b)}[i, j]$, for each subband $\gamma$, in the R-DCT domain. As for the ridgelet domain embedding, only the sequences associated to the two most energetic directions $k_1$ and $k_2$ of each block are selected to be marked. From them, the matrix $\mathbf{M}_\gamma^{(b)}$ is then built:

$$\mathbf{M}_\gamma^{(b)} = \begin{pmatrix} c_\gamma^{(b)}[k_1, 1] \ c_\gamma^{(b)}[k_1, 2] \cdots c_\gamma^{(b)}[k_1, N] \\ c_\gamma^{(b)}[k_2, 1] \ c_\gamma^{(b)}[k_2, 2] \cdots c_\gamma^{(b)}[k_2, N] \end{pmatrix}. \qquad (20.22)$$

It is worth pointing out that the DC coefficient $c_\gamma^{(b)}[k, 0]$ of each projection $k$ is not selected to be marked. This is done in order to not modify the mean value of each Radon projection after the watermarking. As can be derived from Eq. (20.13) and reported in [99], all the FRAT projections $\text{FRAT}_f[k, l]$, $k \in Z_{P+1}$ of a function $f$ defined over $Z_P^2$ should possess the same mean value, related to the mean value of $f$. Leaving the DC coefficient unchanged after watermarking means maintaining the original mean value of the Radon sequence, that remains equal to the mean values of all the other Radon projections taken from the same block, in contrast to what happens with the mark embedding in the ridgelet domain.

The procedure is iterated for all the $B_\gamma$ blocks selected from the subband $\gamma$. The matrix $\mathbf{M}_\gamma$, having dimension $2B_\gamma \times N$ is then built:

$$\mathbf{M}_\gamma = \begin{pmatrix} \mathbf{M}_\gamma^{(1)} \\ \mathbf{M}_\gamma^{(2)} \\ \vdots \\ \mathbf{M}_\gamma^{(B_\gamma)} \end{pmatrix}. \qquad (20.23)$$

By iterating this approach for each subband $\gamma \in \Gamma$, four host vectors $\mathbf{w}_\gamma$ where the mark can be embedded are obtained by scanning the matrices $\mathbf{M}_\gamma$ column-wise.

**Table 20.5.** Dynamic Features Extracted from Each Signature

| Index | Description | Assigned Bits |
|---|---|---|
| 1 | Number of the strokes | 5 |
| 2 | Time duration | 7 |
| 3 | Final $X$ | 10 |
| 4 | Initial $X$ | 10 |
| 5 | Number of $X$ maximums | 6 |
| 6 | Final $Y$ | 10 |
| 7 | Initial $Y$ | 10 |
| 8 | Number of $Y$ maximums | 6 |
| 9 | Pen-up/pen-down ratio | 8 |
| 10 | Mean instantaneous velocity direction | 10 |
| 11 | Mean instantaneous acceleration direction | 10 |

### 20.3.2.2  *Watermark Generation*

In the enrollment stage the watermark is generated by extracting from each user's signature the dynamic features detailed in Table 20.5. Specifically, for a given user, $I$ signatures are acquired using an electronic digitizer tablet, and then the 11 dynamic features [40, 53] given in Table 20.5 are evaluated and collected in vectors $\mathbf{d}^{(i)}$, where $i = 1, \ldots, I$. A vector $\mathbf{d}$ is then calculated as the average of the dynamic feature vectors $\mathbf{d}^{(i)}$, and its elements are binarized using the bit depths, given in Table 20.5, that we have experimentally set by evaluating the average variation range of the features under examination. The so obtained binary vector, with length equal to 92 bits, is then BCH coded to provide error resilience. We have chosen to use a (127,92) BCH code, which provides an ECC equal to 5 bits. The coded binary vector $\mathbf{m}$, consisting of 127 bits, is then decomposed into three different marks $\mathbf{m}_{2LL}$, $\mathbf{m}_{2HL}$, and $\mathbf{m}_{2LH}$ with dimensions equal to 32 bits, along with a fourth mark $\mathbf{m}_{2HH}$ with dimension equal to 31 bits. These marks are separately embedded, by means of QIM [97] watermarking, in the corresponding hosts $\mathbf{w}_\gamma$, $\gamma \in \Gamma$, obtained as outlined in Section 20.3.2.1. Fewer bits are inserted in the $2HH$ subband, with respect to the others, due to its verified less reliability in the mark extraction process, as shown in Section 20.3.5.

### 20.3.2.3  *QIM Watermarking*

In its simplest implementation, a QIM watermarking system associates each bit of a message $\mathbf{m}$, namely $m_i$, to a single host element $w_i$, and let $m_i$ determine which quantizer has to be used to quantize $w_i$. Typically, the two codebooks $\mathcal{U}_0$ and $\mathcal{U}_1$ associated respectively to $m_i = 0$ and $m_i = 1$ are defined as

$$\mathcal{U}_0 = \{u_{0,z} = z\Delta + \chi, z \in \mathbb{Z}\}, \quad \mathcal{U}_1 = \{u_{1,z} = z\Delta + \frac{\Delta}{2} + \chi, z \in \mathbb{Z}\}, \quad (20.24)$$

where $\chi$ is a secret key and $\Delta$ the quantization step.

Watermark embedding is achieved by applying either the quantizer associated to $\mathcal{U}_0$ or the one associated to $\mathcal{U}_1$, depending on the bit $m_i$ that has to be embedded, respectively:

$$\mathcal{Q}_0(w_i) = \arg \min_{u_{0,z} \in \mathcal{U}_0} |u_{0,z} - w_i|, \qquad \mathcal{Q}_1(w_i) = \arg \min_{u_{1,z} \in \mathcal{U}_1} |u_{1,z} - w_i|, \quad (20.25)$$

where $u_{0,z}$ and $u_{1,z}$, with $z \in \mathbb{Z}$, are the elements of $\mathcal{U}_0$ and $\mathcal{U}_1$, respectively. Indicating with $w_i^m$ the marked element, we obtain

$$w_i^m = \begin{cases} \mathcal{Q}_0(w_i), & m = 0, \\ \mathcal{Q}_1(w_i), & m = 1. \end{cases} \qquad (20.26)$$

The complete marked sequence is indicated as $\mathbf{w}^m$. The watermarked signature image is then obtained by reversing the embedding procedure.

The watermark extraction is obtained by using a minimum distance decoder:

$$\tilde{m}_i = \arg \min_{m \in \{0,1\}} \min_{u_{m,z} \in \mathcal{U}_m} |u_{m,z} - \tilde{w}_i^m|, \qquad z \in \mathbb{Z}, \qquad (20.27)$$

where $\tilde{w}_i^m$ is the $i$th bit from the extracted marked sequence $\tilde{\mathbf{w}}^m$.

### 20.3.3  Enrollment Stage

In the enrollment procedure we extract both the dynamic features to be embedded in the signature image and some static features that will be used to perform the first level of user authentication. For a given user $u$, the 68 static features [40, 53] detailed in Table 20.6 are extracted from each of the $I$ acquired signatures and are collected in the vectors $\mathbf{s}_u^{(i)}$, where $i = 1, \ldots, I$.

We consider both global (the first 20) and local features (the last 48), calculated by dividing each signature image, of dimension $720 \times 1440$ pixels, in 12 equal-sized rectangular segments [53]. As can be seen in Table 20.6, 15 features out of 68 are

**Table 20.6.** Static Features Extracted from Each Signature Image

| Index | Description |
|---|---|
| 1 | Sample count |
| 2–4 | Height, width, and aspect ratio |
| 5–7 | Minimum, mean and maximum $X$ position |
| 8–10 | Minimum, mean, and maximum $Y$ position |
| 11–12 | $X$ and $Y$ area |
| 13–17 | Statistical moment $M_{1,1}, M_{1,2}, M_{2,1}, M_{0,3}, M_{3,0}$ |
| 18–20 | Minimum, mean and maximum pressure value |
| 21–32 | Mean pressure 12-segment |
| 33–44 | Sample count 12-segment |
| 45–68 | $X$ and $Y$ area 12-segment |

related to the signature pressure, typically considered as an on-line characteristic. In order to select, among the $I$ signatures acquired for the user $u$, a representative signature, the mean $\boldsymbol{\mu}_u$ and the variance $\boldsymbol{\sigma}_u^2$ feature vectors are calculated from vectors $\mathbf{s}_u^{(i)}$. A distance measure $D_u$ is introduced and estimated for each of the $I$ enrolled signatures of user $u$ as follows:

$$D_u^{(i)} = \sqrt{\sum_{f=1}^{68} \frac{(\mathbf{s}_u^{(i)}[f] - \boldsymbol{\mu}_u[f])^2}{\sigma_u^2[f]}},\qquad(20.28)$$

and the signature image giving the lowest value $D_u^{(i)}$, where $i = 1, \ldots, I$, is then selected for each user. The selected signature represents the one whose static features are the closest to the estimated mean, and it becomes the host image where the selected user's dynamic features can be embedded.

### 20.3.4 Authentication Stage

In the authentication stage, the user is asked to provide his signature by means of an electronic pad. His prototype signature with the embedded signature dynamic information can be stored either in a centralized database or in a card. When a low-security level is required, the authentication is performed on the base of the selected static features only. With reference to Figure 20.8, for a given user $u$ the static features given in Table 20.6 are extracted from the provided signature, collected in the vector $\mathbf{s}_u$, and compared with the static signature feature vector $\tilde{\mathbf{s}}_u$. If a higher security level is required, dynamic features are obtained from the acquired signature, collected in the vector $\mathbf{d}_u$, and compared with the dynamic signature features $\tilde{\mathbf{d}}_u$ extracted from the stored watermarked signature image.

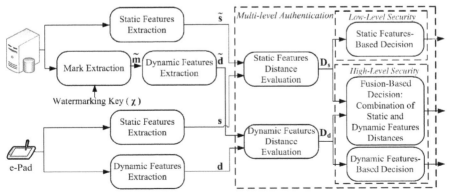

**Figure 20.8.** Security-scalable signature-based authentication system using data hiding. Proposed authentication scheme.

A Mahalanobis distance is used to compare the extracted features vectors as follows:

$$D(\tilde{\mathbf{v}}_u, \mathbf{v}_u) = \sqrt{\sum_f \frac{(\tilde{\mathbf{v}}_u[f] - \mathbf{v}_u[f])^2}{\sigma^2_{\mathbf{v}_u}[f]}},$$    (20.29)

where $\tilde{\mathbf{v}}_u$ represents either the stored static or dynamic feature vector, $\mathbf{v}_u$ represents the one obtained from the provided signature, and $\sigma^2_{\mathbf{v}_u}$ represents the variance of $\mathbf{v}_u$, estimated during enrollment. If the distance is less than a threshold $T_A$, the user is authenticated. As far as the variance $\sigma^2_{\mathbf{v}_u}$ is concerned, in order to reduce the information that has to be stored and in order to protect the data extracted from each user, it is possible to use in Eq. (20.29) the same value $\sigma^2_{\mathbf{v}}$ for all the enrolled users, taking the mean value of each individual variance $\sigma^2_{\mathbf{v}_u}$ estimated during the enrollment. This can be made for both the static and the dynamic features. In fact, the use of a common variance for all the users can increase the security of the system, thanks to the fact that less information regarding the users has to be stored.

### 20.3.4.1 Fusion Approach

When required by the application, a higher level of security can be obtained by combining both dynamic and static features using score fusion techniques [94]. In Section 20.3.5, the performances achievable using only either the static features or the dynamic features, and a combination of both, are presented.

Specifically, in order to combine the scores derived from static and dynamic features, a score normalization stage has to be implemented, followed by a score fusion stage. The first step is necessary because the matching scores at the output of the individual matchers may not be homogeneous and on the same numerical scale, or may follow different statistical distributions. Score normalization is therefore essential to transform the scores of the individual matchers into a common domain prior to combining them. Among the possible score normalization techniques, in our experiments we used the *double sigmoid* normalization technique [94], which is robust to outliers in the score distribution. The normalized score is then obtained as

$$s'_k = \begin{cases} \dfrac{1}{1 + \exp(-2((s_k - t)/r_1))} & \text{if } s_k < t, \\ \dfrac{1}{1 + \exp(-2((s_k - t)/r_2))} & \text{otherwise} \end{cases}$$    (20.30)

where $t$ is the reference operating point, and $r_1$ and $r_2$ denote respectively the left and right edges of the region in which the function is linear. In our implementation, we performed a fixed score normalization [94], which consists in using the same parameters for the normalization of the scores derived from each considered user. In order to estimate these parameters, the scores obtained considering the enrollment genuine signature, together with two skilled forgeries for each user, have been considered as evaluation test. This scheme is robust with respect to the outliers, but it requires a careful tuning of the employed parameters to obtain good efficiency. Specifically, in our implementation the reference point is selected in order to focus the double sigmoid function in the area where the EER is achieved.

After the normalization of the scores, they have to be combined in order to obtain to a single value. This can be done using different fusion methods. The most used methods include the *sum*, the *product*, the *max*, and the *min* method; in our implementations we employed only the *sum* fusion techniques, which has been proved to commonly outperform the others [94].

The performances obtainable using these fusion schemes are presented in Section 20.3.5, together with the performances achievable using only either the static features or the dynamic features.

## 20.3.5  Experimental Results

In this section an extensive set of experimental results concerning the performances of the proposed signature-based authentication system are presented. Specifically, we have characterized the system performances in terms of both the robustness of the employed watermarking methods and the authentication capabilities of the proposed system.

### 20.3.5.1  Mark Extraction

The performances of the proposed embedding methods are evaluated on the basis of 1500 signature images, taken from 30 different users. The embedding, detailed in Section 20.3.2, is performed using binary marks of 127 bits that, in our case, represent the BCH-encoded dynamic features extracted from the acquired signature. Some attacks, like JPEG compression and additive random Gaussian noise, have been performed on the watermarked signature images for testing the robustness of the proposed embedding methods. Moreover, we have tested the performances of the embedding methods varying the system's parameters $P$ and $T_E$, which are respectively the blocks dimension and the threshold for the blocks selection. These experiments are conducted trying to keep constant the number of coefficients selected for the embedding.

Figure 20.9 shows the performances of the proposed embedding methods when taking $P = 10$ pixels and $T_E = 5$, marking $N = 6$ values of each either ridgelet or R-DCT projection sequence, and using $\Delta = 100$ for the QIM watermarking algorithm. Figure 20.9(a) shows the obtained bit error rate (BER) for the proposed ridgelet and R-DCT embedding methods, as a function of the JPEG quality of the marked image. Figure 20.9(b) shows the BER obtained when considering marked images with Gaussian noise added, as a function of the PSNR between the marked and the noisy signature images. To summarize, overall better performances in terms of robustness and PSNR are obtained when the mark embedding is performed in the novel R-DCT domain, with respect to the embedding performed in the ridgelet domain.

Figure 20.10 shows the BERs obtained considering each second-level subband separately. As can be seen, the approximation subband $2LL$ performs better than the

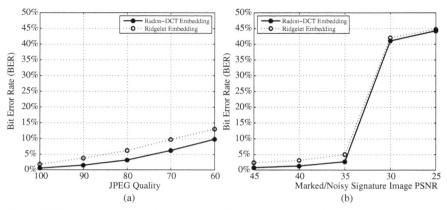

**Figure 20.9.** Mark extraction performances, considering $P = 10$ pixels, $T_E = 5$, and $N = 6$. (a) BER versus JPEG quality level. (b) BER versus marked and noisy image PSNR.

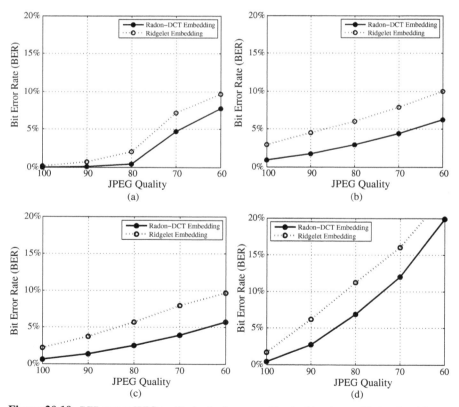

**Figure 20.10.** BER versus JPEG quality for the four second level subbands, considering $P = 10$ pixels, $T_E = 5$ and $N = 6$. (a) 2LL subband; (b) 2HL subband; (c) 2LH subband; (d) 2HH subband.

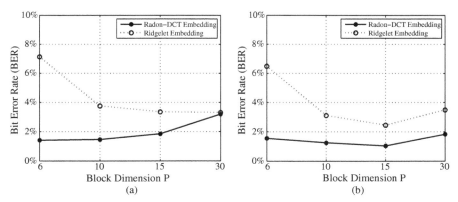

**Figure 20.11.** Mark extraction performances varying the blocks dimension $P$. (a) BER for marked signature images with JPEG quality equal to 90. (b) BER for marked signature images with Gaussian noise added, with a PSNR equal to 40 dB.

others for JPEG quality greater than 80, and as well as the subbands $2HL$ and $2LH$ for lower JPEG qualities. As mentioned earlier, the subband $2HH$ is the less reliable.

Morever, Figure 20.11 shows how the mark extraction performances vary with respect to the blocks dimension P. Figure 20.11(a) presents the BER for the ridgelet and R-DCT embedding methods, when considering images compared with a JPEG quality equal to 90. Figure 20.11(b) is related to marked images with Gaussian noise added, considering a PSNR equal to 40dB. The best performances in terms of BER are obtained when selecting P = 10 or P = 15.

In Figure 20.12 the system's performances with respect to the threshold $T_E$ given in Eq. (20.20) are illustrated. Specifically, Figure 20.12a refers to the marked images compressed with a JPEG quality equal to 90, while Figure 20.12b is related to marked images with Gaussian noise added, considering a PSNR equal to 40 dB.

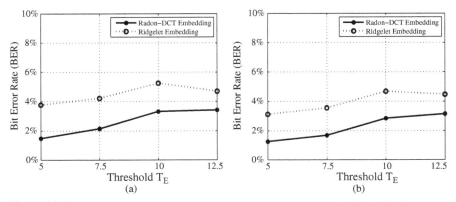

**Figure 20.12.** Mark extraction performances varying the threshold $T_E$ for the blocks selection. (a) BER for marked signature images with JPEG Quality equal to 90; (b) BER for marked signature images with Gaussian noise added, with a PSNR equal to 40 dB.

### 20.3.5.2 *Authentication System Performance*

In order to test the authentication performances of our approach, 50 signatures have been acquired from 30 users, taking for each of them 10 signatures in five different sessions during a week time span. As far as the enrollment stage is concerned, we considered both the case with $I = 5$ signatures and the case with $I = 10$ signature (taken from the first session in both cases) in order to determine the *typical* host signature image and to extract the dynamic features to be embedded, as described in Section 20.3.3. The system FRR is computed using the remaining 40 signatures for each subject, taken from sessions that are different from the one considered for the enrollment. The false acceptance rate considering random forgeries (FAR$_{RF}$) is tested taking, for each user under examination, the 50 signatures of all the remaining 29 users as random forgeries. The false acceptance rate considering skilled forgeries (FAR$_{SF}$) is evaluated on the basis of a test set of ten skilled forgeries, created using a training time of 10 min for each signature whose original was made available to the forger, for each subject.

In Figure 20.13 the performances related to the use of $I = 5$ signatures for the enrollment, with individual variances for each user in the computation of the authentication scores through Eq. (20.29), are reported. Figures 20.13(a) and 20.13(b) show the performances obtained using only static features with respect to the threshold $T_A$, considering the ridgelet and the R-DCT embedding method respectively. Figures 20.13(c) and 20.13(d) show the performances related to the use of only dynamic features, while in Figures 20.13(e) and 20.13(f) the results of the fusion of static and dynamic features are displayed through the obtained ROC curves. The fusion is implemented as detailed in Section 20.3.4.1. All the images we have considered were compressed with a JPEG quality value equal to 90. The embedding is performed using $P = 10$ pixels, $T_E = 5$, and $N = 6$. As shown, the EER achievable using only static features is approximately 15% for both R-DCT and ridgelet embedding methods considering random forgeries and is 17% considering skilled forgeries. On the other hand, the use of dynamic features results in better performances as far as R-DCT embedding is concerned, with respect to the use of ridgelet embedding: In the first case the achievable EER is approximately 10% for random forgeries and 18% for skilled forgeries, while in the latter case the EER is approximately 15% for random forgeries and 24.6% for skilled forgeries. The different behavior is due to the mark extraction capabilities of the two methods: As can be seen in Figure 20.9, the R-DCT embedding approach offers better performances in terms of BER with respect to the ridgelet embedding one. However, the application of a BCH code with ECC equal to 5 to the binarized dynamic features, as described in Section 20.3.2.2, allows us to obtain adequate performances even for the ridgelet embedding domain. Using images with worse quality, or applying ECC less than 5 in order to embed more information in the signatures, the difference between the authentication performances related to the use of R-DCT and ridgelet embedding would be even greater. Moreover, the performances obtainable from the combined systems are better than those of the individual ones, resulting in EER = 12.5% with the R-DCT embedding method and EER = 13.8% with the ridgelet embedding method, considering skilled forgeries. The performances obtained considering $I = 10$ signatures for the enrollment, with individual variances for

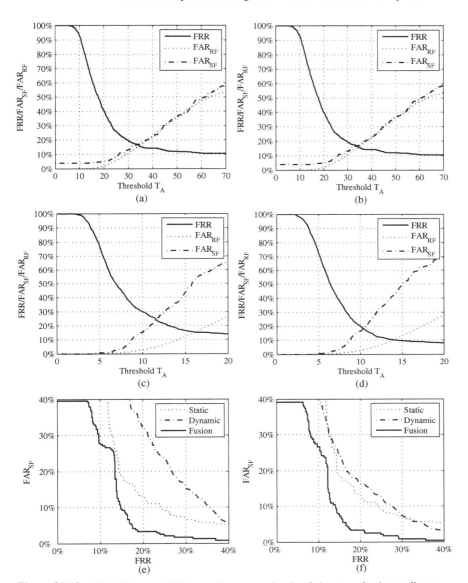

**Figure 20.13.** FRR, FAR$_{RF}$, and FAR$_{SF}$ performances using $I = 5$ signatures for the enrollment, with individual variances for each user. (**a**) Ridgelet domain embedding, static features. (**b**) R-DCT domain embedding, static features. (**c**) Ridgelet domain embedding, dynamic features. (**d**) R-DCT domain embedding, dynamic features. (**e**) Ridgelet domain embedding, individual and combined systems. (**f**) R-DCT domain embedding, individual and combined systems.

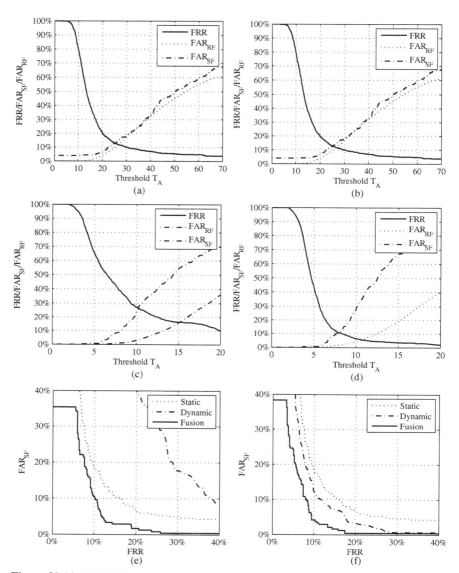

**Figure 20.14.** FRR, $FAR_{RF}$, and $FAR_{SF}$ performances using $I = 10$ signatures for the enrollment, with individual variances for each user. (**a**) Ridgelet domain embedding, static features. (**b**) R-DCT domain embedding, static features; (**c**) Ridgelet domain embedding, dynamic features; (**d**) R-DCT domain embedding, dynamic features; (**e**) Ridgelet domain embedding, individual and combined systems; (**f**) R-DCT domain embedding, individual and combined systems.

each user, are shown in Figure 20.14. Better results are obtained using $I = 10$ signatures for the enrollment, when compared to the use of $I = 5$ signatures, for both static and dynamic features. Specifically, considering the R-DCT embedding method, the obtained results consist in EER $= 13.17\%$ for the static features and EER $= 10.67\%$ for the dynamic features. The use of the *minmax* normalization method for the fusion of static and dynamic features results in EER $= 8.6\%$, considering skilled forgeries and the R-DCT embedding. Taking $I = 10$ signatures for the enrollment, with a common variance for all the user, results in worse performance when compared to the use of individual features, especially considering the ridgelet embedding method. Also in this case, in order to obtain better performances from the fusion of static and dynamic features, when compared to the performances related to their separated use, a *double sigmoid* normalization method has to be employed.

## 20.4 SUMMARY

In this chapter we present two different approaches to protect a signature biometric template.

Specifically, in the first part of the chapter a user adaptive template protection scheme applied to signature biometrics, which stems from the fuzzy commitment approach, is presented. The proposed scheme is able to provide protection to the considered signature templates. Moreover, it allows us to generate multiple templates from the same biometric data thus being able to provide also cancelability. Our protection scheme has been applied to parametric features extracted from the signatures. A user-adaptive method able to take into account the intra-class variability has been implemented, in order to customize the error correction capabilities of the employed codes for each enrolled user. Therefore, since the employed codes are selected depending on the characteristics of each user, the system performances are improved. Extensive experimental results are provided, showing that our system is able to provide performances comparable with those achievable by an unprotected system. Comparisons with other already proposed schemes for signature templates protection are also presented.

In the second part of the chapter, data hiding techniques are used to design a security scalable authentication system. Specifically, watermarking has been employed to hide some dynamic signature features into a static representation of the signature itself. Two different levels of security can be considered accordingly to the application. When low security is required, static features are the only ones to be employed, whereas when higher security is required, fusion between the modules performing authentication on the base of the static features and on the base of the extracted dynamic information is performed. Experimental results characterizing the system performance in terms of both the authentication capabilities of the proposed system and the robustness of the employed watermarking technique versus attacks are extensively reported.

# REFERENCES

1. A. K. Jain, An introduction to biometric recognition, *IEEE Trans. Circuits and Syst. Video Technol.* **14**(1):4–20, 2004.
2. R. M. Bolle, J. H. Connell, S. Pankati, N. K. Ratha, and A. W. Senior, *Guide to Biometrics*, Springer, New York, 2004.
3. R. Clarke, Human identification in information systems: Management challenges and public policy issues, *Inf. Technol. People* **7**(4):6–37, 1994.
4. A. K. Jain, R. Bolle, and S. Pankanti, editors, *Biometrics: Personal Identification in Networked society*, Kluwer Academic Publishers, Norwell, MA, 1999.
5. S. Prabhakar, S. Pankanti, and A. K. Jain, Biometric recognition: Security and privacy concerns, *IEEE Secur. Privacy* **1**:33–42, 2003.
6. M. Faundez-Zanuy, Privacy issues on biometric systems, *IEEE Aerosp. Electron. Syst. Mag.* **20**(2):13–15, 2005.
7. U. K. Biometric Working Group, Biometric security concerns, technical report, CESG, September 2003.
8. D. Maltoni, D. Maio, A. K. Jain, and S. Prabhakar, *Handbook of Fingerprint Recognition*, Springer-Verlag, Berlin, 2003.
9. U. Uludag and A. K. Jain, Attacks on biometric systems: A case study in fingerprints, in *Proceedings SPIE-EI 2004, Security, Seganography and Watermarking of Multimedia Contents VI*, San Jose, CA, January 18–22, 2004, pp. 622–633.
10. A. K. Jain, A. Ross, and U. Uludag, Biometric template security: challenges and solutions, in *Proceedings of the 13th European Signal Processing Conference (EUSIPCO 2005)*, Antalya, Turkey, September 2005.
11. C. Roberts, Biometric attack vectors and defences, *Comput. Secur.* **26**(1):14–25, 2006.
12. N. Ratha, J. H. Connell, and R. M. Bolle, An analysis of minutiae matching strength, in *Proceedings of the International Conference on Audio and Video-Based Biometric Person Authentication*, 2001, pp. 223–228.
13. A. Adler, Can images be regenerated from biometric templates?, *Proceedings of the Biometrics Consortium Conference*, 2003.
14. J. Galbally, J. Fierrez, and J. Ortega Garcia, Bayesian hill-climbing attack and its application to signature verification, *Lecture Notes Comput. Sci.* **4642**:386–395, 2007.
15. A. Ross, J. Shah, and A. K. Jain, Towards reconstructing fingerprints from minutiae points, in *Proceedings of SPIE, Biometric Technology for Human Identification II*, Vol. 5779, Orlando, FL, March 2005, pp. 68–80.
16. A. Menezes, P. van Oorschot, and S. Vanstone, *Handbook of Applied Cryptography*, CRC Press, Boca Raton, FL, 1996.
17. http://www.speedproject.eu/, EU project Signal Processing in the Encrypted Domain, funded in the framework of the IST Programme FET.
18. A. Piva and S. Katzenbeisser, editors, Signal processing in the encrypted domain, *EURASIP Journal on Information Security, Special Issue*, October 2007.
19. M. Savvides, B. V. K. Vijaya Kumar, and P. K. Khosla, Cancelable biometric filters for face recognition, in *Proceedings of the International Conference on Pattern Recognition*, 2004, pp. 922–925.
20. T. Connie, A. B. J. Teoh, M. K. O. Goh, and D. C. L. Ngo, PalmHashing: A novel approach for cancelable biometrics, *Inf. Processing Lett.* **93**(1):1–5, 2005.
21. A. B. J. Teoh, D. C. L. Ngo, and A. Goh, Biohashing: Two factor authentication featuring fingerprint data and tokenised random number, *Pattern Recognit.* **37**(11):2245–2255, 2004.
22. C. S. Chin, A. B. J. Teoh, and D. C. L. Ngo, High security iris verification system based on random secret integration *Comput. Vis. Image Understanding* **102**(2):169–177, 2006.
23. A. B. J. Teoh, D. C. L. Ngo, and A. Goh, Random multispace quantization as an analytic mechanism for BioHashing of biometric and random identity inputs, *IEEE Trans. Pattern Anal. Mach. Intell.* **28**(12):1892–1901, 2006.

24. C. L. Ying and A. B. J. Teoh, Probabilistic random projections and speaker verification, *Lecture Notes Comput. Sci.* **4662**:445–454, 2007.
25. Y. Wang and K. N. Plataniotis, Face based biometric authentication with changeable and privacy preservable templates, in *IEEE Biometric Symposium*, September Baltimore, 2007.
26. R. M. Bolle, J. H. Connell, and N. K. Ratha, Biometric perils and patches, *Pattern Recognit.* **35**:2727–2738, 2002.
27. N. Ratha, S. Chikkerur, J. H. Connell, and R. M. Bolle, Generating cancelable fingerprint templates, *IEEE Trans. Pattern Anal. Mach. Intelli.* **29**(4):561–572, 2007.
28. H. Lee, C. Lee, J. Y. Choi, J. Kim, and J. Kim, Changeable face representations suitable for human recognition, *Lecture Notes Comput. Sci.* **4662**:557–565, 2007.
29. E. Maiorana, M. Martinez-Diaz, P. Campisi, J. Ortega-Garcia, and A. Neri, Template protection for HMM-based on-line signature authentication, *CVPR Conference, Workshop on Biometrics*, Anchorage, Alaska, 23–28 June 2008.
30. E. Maiorana, P. Campisi, J. Ortega-Garcia, and A. Neri, Cancelable biometrics for HMM-based signature recognition, in *IEEE Second International Conference on Biometrics: Theory, Applications and Systems (BTAS)*, Washington DC, 29 September–1 October 2008.
31. U. Uludag, S. Pankanti, S. Prabhakar, and A. K. Jain, Biometric cryptosystems: issues and challenges, *Proc. IEEE* **92**(6):948–960, 2004.
32. K. Nandakumar, A. K. Jain, and S. Pankati, Fingerprint–based fuzzy vault: Implementation and performance, *IEEE Trans. Inf. Forens. Secur.* **2**(4):744–757, 2007.
33. A. Juels and M. Wattenberg, A fuzzy commitment scheme, *6th ACM Conference on Computer and Communication Security*, 1999, pp. 28–36.
34. A. Juels and M. Sudan, A fuzzy vault scheme, *Des. Codes Cryptogr.* **38**(2):237–257, 2006.
35. G. Davida, Y. Frankel, B. J. Matt, and R. Peralta, On the relation of error correction and cryptography to an off line biometric based identification scheme, in *Proceedings of WCC99, Workshop on Coding and Cryptography*, 1999.
36. P. Tuyls, E. Verbitsky, T. Ignatenko, D. Schobben, and T. H. Akkermans, Privacy protected biometric templates: Acoustic ear identification, *SPIE Proc.* **5404**:176–182, 2004.
37. P. Tuyls, A. Akkermans, T. Kevenaar, G. J. Schrijen, A. Bazen, and R. Veldhuis, Practical biometric template protection system based on reliable components, in *AVBPA Proceedings*, 2005.
38. M. Van der Veen, T. Kevenaar, G.-J. Schrijen, T. H. Akkermans, and F. Zuo, Face biometrics with renewable templates, in *SPIE Proceedings on Security, Steganography, and Watermarking of Multimedia Contents*, Vol. 6072, 2006.
39. E. J. C. Kelkboom, B. Gökberk, T. A. M. Kevenaar, A. H. M. Akkermans, and M. van der Veen, 3D face: Biometrics template protection for 3D face recognition, *Lecture Notes Comput. Sci.* **4642**:566–573, 2007.
40. P. Campisi, E. Maiorana; M. Gonzalez, and A. Neri, Adaptive and distributed cryptography for signature biometrics protection, in *SPIE Proceedings on Security, Steganography, and Watermarking of Multimedia Contents IX*, Vol. 6505, 28 January–1 February 2007, San Jose, CA, 2007.
41. E. Maiorana, P. Campisi, and A. Neri, User adaptive fuzzy commitment for signature templates protection and renewability, *SPIE Journal of Electronic Imaging, Special Section on Biometrics: Advances in Security, Usability and Interoperability*, Vol. 17. No. 1, January–March 2008.
42. T. C. Clancy, N. Kiyavash, and D. J. Lin, Secure smartcard-based fingerprint authentication, *ACM SIGMM Workshop on Biometrics Methods and Applications*, 2003, pp. 45–52.
43. S. Yang and I. Verbauwhede, Automatic secure fingerprint verification system based on fuzzy vault scheme, in *Proceedings of the ICASSP*, 2005, pp. 609–612.
44. U. Uludag, S. Pankati, and A. K. Jain, Fuzzy Vault for Fingerprints, in *Proceedings, Audio and Video Based Biometric Person Authentication*, 2005, pp. 310–319.
45. M. Freire-Santos, J. Fierrez-Aguilara, and J. Ortega-Garcia, Cryptographic key generation using handwritten signature, in *SPIE Defense and Security Symposium, Biometric Technologies for Human Identification*, Vol. 6202, 2006, pp. 225–231.

46. M. R. Freire, J. Fierrez, M. Martinez-Diaz, and J. Ortega-Garcia, On the applicability of off-line signatures to the fuzzy vault construction, in *Proceedings of the International Conference on Document Analysis and Recognition, ICDAR*, September 2007.

47. Y. Cheng Feng and P. C Yuen, Protecting face biometric data on smartcard with reed–solomon code, in *Proceedings on Computer Vision and Pattern Recognition Workshop*, 2006.

48. D. H. Nyang and K. H. Lee, Fuzzy face vault: How to implement fuzzy vault with weighted features, *Lecture Notes Comput. Sci.* **4554**:491–496, 2007.

49. Y. J. Lee, K. Bae, S. J. Lee, K. R. Park, and J. Kim, Biometric key binding: Fuzzy vault based on iris images, *Lecture Notes on Comput. Sci.* **4642**:800–808, 2007.

50. F. Monrose, M. K. Reiter, Q. Li, and S. Wetzel, Cryptographic Key generation from voice, in *Proceedings of the 2001 IEEE Symposium on Security and Privacy*, 2001.

51. A. Goh and D. C. L. Ngo, Computation of Cryptographic Keys from Face Biometrics, in *Lecture Notes in Computer Science. Communications and Multimedia Security*, 2003, pp. 1–13.

52. C. Vielhauer, R. Steinmetza, and A. Mayerhöfer, Biometric hash based on statistical features of on-line signatures, in *International Conference on Pattern Recognition (ICPR)*, Vol. 1, 2002, pp. 123–126.

53. C. Vielhauer and R. Steinmetz, Handwriting: Feature correlation analysis for biometric hashes, *EURASIP J. Appl. Signal Processing (Special Issue on Biometric Signal Processing)* **4**:542–558, 2004.

54. H. Feng and C. W. Chan, Private key generation from on-line handwritten signatures, *Inf. Manage. Comput. Secur.* 159–164, 2002.

55. Y. W. Kuan, A. Goh, D. Ngoa, and A. Teoh, Cryptographic keys from dynamic hand-signatures with biometric secrecy preservation and replaceability, in *Proceedings of the Fourth IEEE Workshop on Automatic Identification Advanced Technologies*, 2005, pp. 27–32.

56. M. R. Freire, J. Fierrez, J. Galbally, and J. Ortega-Garcia, Biometric hashing based on genetic selection and its application to on-line signatures, *Lecture Notes Comput. Sci.* **4642**:1134–1143, 2007.

57. Y. Dodis, L. Reyzina, and A. Smith, Fuzzy extractors: How to generate strong keys from biometrics and other noisy data, in *Advances in Cryptology-Eurocrypt Proceedings*, 2004.

58. Y. Sutcu, Q. Lia, and N. Memon, Protecting biometric templates with sketch: Theory and practice, *IEEE Trans. Inf. Forens. Secur.* **2**(3):503–512, 2007.

59. I. Cox, M. Miller, J. Bloom, M. Miller, and J. Fridrich, *Digital Watermarking and Steganography*, 2nd edition, Morgan Kaufmann, San Francisco, 2007.

60. M. Barni and F. Bartolini, *Watermarking Systems Engineering: Enabling Digital Assets Security and Other Applications*, Marcel Dekker, New York, 2004.

61. A. K. Jain and U. Uludag, Hiding biometric data, *IEEE Trans. Pattern Anal. Mach. Intelli.* **25**(11):1494–1498, 2003.

62. N. K. Ratha, J. H. Connell, and R. Bolle, Secure data hiding in wavelet compressed fingerprint images, *ACM Multimedia 2000 Workshops Proceedings*, 2000, pp. 127–130.

63. S. Pankanti and M. M. Yeung, Verification watermarks on fingerprint recognition and retrieval, *Proc. SPIE* **3657**:66–78, 1999.

64. A. K. Jain, U. Uludag, and R. L. Hsu, Hiding a face in a fingerprint image, in *International Conference on Pattern Recognition*, 2002.

65. M. Vatsa, R. Singh, P. Mitra, and A. Noore, Digital watermarking based secure multimodal biometric system, in *IEEE International Conference on Systems, Man and Cybernetics*, 2004, pp. 2983–2987.

66. A. Giannoula and D. Hatzinakos, Data hiding for multimodal biometric recognition, in *International Symposium on Circuits and Systems (ISCAS)*, 2004.

67. P. Hennings, M. Savvides, and B. V. K. Vijaya Kumar, Hiding phase-quantized biometrics: A case of steganography for reduced-complexity correlation filter classifiers, in *SPIE Proceeedings on Security, Steganography, and Watermarking of Multimedia Contents VII*, Vol. 5681, 2005, pp. 465–473.

68. E. Maiorana, P. Campisi, and A. Neri, Multi-level signature based biometric authentication using watermarking, in *SPIE Defense and Security, Mobile Multimedia/Image Processing for Military and Security Applications 2007*, Vol. 6579, Orlando, FL, 9–13 April 2007.

69. E. Maiorana, P. Campisi, and A. Neri, Biometric signature authentication using radon transform-based watermarking techniques, in *IEEE Biometric Symposium*, Baltimore, September 2007.
70. S. Katzenbeisser, On the integration of watermarks and cryptography, *Lecture Notes Comput. Sci.* **2939**:50–60, 2004.
71. I. J. Cox, G. Doerr, and T. Furon, Watermarking is not cryptography, *Lecture Notes Comput. Sci.* **4283**:1–15, 2006.
72. R. Plamondon and G. Lorette, Automatic signature verification and writer identification: The state of the art, *Pattern Recognit.* **22**(2):107–131, 1989.
73. F. Leclerc and R. Plamondon, Automatic signature verification: The state of the art 1989–1993, *IJPRAI* **8**(3):643–660, 1994.
74. R. Plamondon and S. N. Srihari, On-line and off-line handwriting recognition: A comprehensive survey, *IEEE Trans. Pattern Anal. Mach. Intelli.* **22**(1):63–84, 2000.
75. G. Dimauro, S. Impedovo, M. G. Lucchese, R. Modugno, and G. Pirlo, Recent advancements in automatic signature verification, in *Ninth International Workshop on Frontiers in Handwriting Recognition*, 26–29 October 2004, pp. 179–184.
76. M. Faundez-Zanuy, Signature recognition state-of-the-art, *IEEE Aerosp. Electron. Syst. Mag.* **20**(7):28–32, 2005.
77. H. Lei and V. Govindaraju, A comparative study on the consistency of features in on-line signature verification, *Pattern Recognit. Lett.* **15**:2483–2489, 2005.
78. A. K. Jain, R. P. W. Duin, and J. Mao, Statistical pattern recognition: A review, *IEEE Trans. Pattern Anal. Mach. Intell.* **22**(1):4–37, 2000.
79. Y. Jonghyon, L. Chulhan, and K. Jaihie, On-line signature verification using temporal shift estimated by the phase of Gabor filter, *IEEE Trans. Signal Processing* **53**(2, Part 2):776–783, 2005.
80. M. Faundez-Zanuy, On-line signature recognition based on VQ-DTW, *Pattern Recognit.* **40**:981–992, 2007.
81. G. Agam and S. Suresh, Warping-based off-line signature recognition, *IEEE Trans. Info. Forens. Secur.* **2**(3, Part 1):430–437, 2007.
82. A. Kholmatov and B. Yanikoglu, Identity authentication using improved on-line signature verification method, *Pattern Recognit. Lett.* **26**(15):2400-2408, 2005.
83. L. Yang, B. W. Widjaja, and R. Prasad, Application of hidden markov models for signature verification, *Pattern Recognit.* **28**(2):161–170, 1995.
84. J. Fierrez, J. Ortega-Garcia, D. Ramos, and J. Gonzalez-Rodriguez, HMM-based on-line signature verification: Feature extraction and signature modeling, *Pattern Recognit. Lett.* **28**(16):2325–2334, 2007.
85. M. Fuentes, S. Garcia-Salicetti, and B. Dorizzi, On-line signature verification: Fusion of a hidden Markov model and a neural network via a support vector machine, in *Eighth International Workshop on Frontiers in Handwriting Recognition*, 6–8 August 2002, pp. 253–258.
86. C. Quek and R. W. Zhou, Antiforgery: A novel pseudo-outer product based fuzzy neural network driver signature verification system, *Pattern Recognit.* **23**:1795–1816, 2002.
87. N. K. Ratha, J. H. Connell, and R. Bolle, Enhancing security and privacy of biometric-based authentication systems, *IBM Systems J.* **40**(3):614–634, 2001.
88. G. A. P. Cirrone, S. Donadio, S. Guatelli, A. Mantero, B. Mascialino, S. Parlati, M. G. Pia, A. Pfeiffer, A. Ribon, and P. Viarengo, A goodness-of-fit statistical toolkit, *IEEE Trans. Nuclear Sci.* **51**(5):2056–2063, 2004.
89. M. Purser, *Introduction to Error-Correcting Codes*, Artech House, Boston, 1995.
90. Federal Information Processing (FIP) Standards Publication 180-1, Security Hash Standard, http://www.itl.nist.gov/fipspubs/fip180-1.htm, 1995.
91. V. Rijmen and E. Oswald, Update on SHA-1, *Lecture Notes Comput. Sci.* **3376**:58–71, 2005.
92. X. Wang, Y. L. Yin, and H. Yu, Finding Collisions in the Full SHA-1, *CRYPTO*, 2005.
93. C. De Cannière and C. Rechberger, Finding SHA-1 characteristics: General results and applications, in *Advances in Cryptology, ASIACRYPT*, Vol. 4284, Springer, Berlin, 2006.
94. A. A. Ross, K. Nandakumar, and A. K. Jain, *Handbook of Multibiometrics*, Springer 2006, USA.

95. M. Faundez-Zanuy, Data fusion in biometrics, *IEEE Aerosp. Electron. Syst. Mag.* **20**(1):34–38, 2005.

96. J. Fierrez-Aguilar, L. Nanni, J. Lopez-Peñalba, J. Ortega-Garcia, and D. Maltoni, An on-line signature verification system based on fusion of local and global information, in International Conference on Audio and Video-Based Biometric Person Authentication, AVBPA, 2005, pp. 523–532.

97. B. Chen and G. Wornell, Quantization index modulation: A class of provably good methods for digital watermarking and information embedding, *IEEE Trans. Info. Theory* **47**(4):1423–1443, 2001.

98. S. R. Deans, *The Radon Transform and Some of Its Applications*, John Wiley & Sons, New York, 1983.

99. M. N. Do and M. Vetterli, The finite ridgelet transform for image representation, *IEEE Trans. Image Processing* **12**(1):16–28, 2003.

100. P. Campisi, D. Kundur, and A. Neri, Robust digital watermarking in the ridgelet domain, *IEEE Signal Processing Lett.* **11**(10), 2004.

101. L. Mao, H.-Z. Wu, Z.-H. Wei, and Y. Bao, Perceptual digital watermark of images using ridgelet transform, in *Third International Conference on Machine Learning and Cybernetics*, Shanghai, 2004.

# Chapter 21

# Unobtrusive Biometric Identification Based on Gait

**Xiaxi Huang and Nikolaos V. Boulgouris**

## 21.1 INTRODUCTION

The increasing demand for efficient security systems has created a need for novel technologies that will be able to automatically monitor wide public areas without causing inconvenience to the people who move in these areas. Gait recognition is a fairly new technology that is very suitable for the unobtrusive detection of individuals who represent a security threat or behave suspiciously. In this chapter, we present some techniques for unobtrusive biometric identification based on gait.

The common feature of most popular biometrics, such as fingerprints [1], hand geometry [2], iris [3], voice [4], and signature [5], is that their capturing can be performed only at a close distance from the recording sensor. Unlike such biometrics, gait [6] can be captured at a distance without drawing the attention or requiring the cooperation of the observed subject. For this reason, the deployment of gait as a biometric trait has a significant advantage over other biometrics.

If gait is to be used for unobtrusive identification, then its study will have to be based on video sequences captured using one or multiple video cameras. The captured video sequences have to be subjected to video processing operations for the purpose of extraction of features or gait parameters that will subsequently be used for recognition. Therefore, the accuracy with which gait can be used for identification depends not only on the inherent discriminatory power of gait but also on the accuracy with which gait features and parameters can be extracted from a video sequence. To complicate things further, it has been shown that gait changes over time and that it can be affected by attire, footwear, fatigue, or emotional condition [7]. For this

*Biometrics: Theory, Methods, and Applications.* Edited by Boulgouris, Plataniotis, and Micheli-Tzanakou
Copyright © 2010 the Institute of Electrical and Electronics Engineers, Inc.

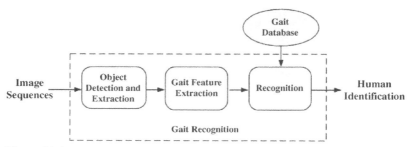

**Figure 21.1.**  A general framework for unobtrusive identification based on gait.

reason, the deployment of gait is more realistic when it takes place in combination with other biometrics, such as face [8]. In this chapter, however, we will present gait as a stand-alone biometric.

Gait recognition is a multistage process (see Figure 21.1). Although gait capturing is easier in controlled environments where the background is as uniform as possible, in practice, gait may have to be captured in crowded places—that is, under difficult conditions. Moreover, since gait recognition algorithms are not, in general, invariant to the capturing viewpoint, care must be taken so that capturing takes place from an appropriate viewpoint. Preferably, the walking subject should be walking in a direction perpendicular to the optical axis of the capturing device since the side view of walking individuals discloses most information about their gait. Once a walking sequence is captured, the walking subject is segmented from its background using an object detection and extraction process. A critical step in gait recognition is feature extraction—that is, the extraction, from video sequences depicting walking persons, of signals that can be used for recognition. This step is very important since there are numerous conceivable ways to extract signals from a gait video sequence—for example, spatial, temporal, spatiotemporal, and frequency-domain feature extraction. Therefore, one must ensure that the feature extraction process compacts as much discriminatory information as possible. Subsequently, there is a recognition step, which aims to compare the extracted gait signals with gait signals that are stored in a database.

In this chapter, we present technologies that are used in a gait recognition system. The chapter is organized as follows: In Section 21.2 we present an overview of techniques that can be used for the extraction of moving individuals from video sequences. In Section 21.3, gait analysis for feature extraction is described. Section 21.4 presents gait recognition using the features extracted previously, and Section 21.5 describes a methodology for gait recognition based on multiple views. Experimental results are presented in Section 21.6. Finally, conclusions are drawn in Section 21.7.

## 21.2   SEGMENTATION OF WALKING HUMANS IN VIDEO SEQUENCES

The first stage in an unobtrusive biometric recognition system is object detection and segmentation—that is, extraction of observed subjects from the original video sequences. This is a key step since it affects the performance of the other modules in a gait recognition system—for example, object classification or recognition. Assuming that the recording camera is stationary, the extraction of walking individuals can be achieved using background subtraction.

Background subtraction relies on the assumption that a background frame can be constructed for a given video sequence. Once a background frame is constructed, the detection and extraction of moving foreground objects is possible by comparison of a given frame with the background frame. Unfortunately, there are several facts that can cause problems during this process—for example, inaccurate background frame, shadows, and similar foreground and background colors. A variety of methods that aim to perform efficient background subtraction by tackling the above problems have been presented in the literature.

### 21.2.1 Detection and Extraction Algorithms

This section describes some basic algorithms for moving object detection and extraction [9–11] in color image sequences. In the simplest such algorithm, the detection of moving objects takes place by calculating the difference between the current frame and a background frame. If the difference between pixel $I_t(x, y)$ and the corresponding pixel $B_t(x, y)$ in the background frame is greater than a threshold $T$, that is,

$$|I_t(x, y) - B_t(x, y)| > T, \qquad (21.1)$$

then the pixel is classified as a foreground pixel. The intensities of the background frame are usually the temporal mean or median intensity, for each pixel position, throughout the entire sequence. Because some slow changes of the background often occur, a background updating process is applied to maintain the accuracy of the algorithm. An apparent limitation of this method is that the threshold must be set manually. Furthermore, the threshold is constant over the entire frame, which may not be a good strategy in cases of complicated scenes.

Another widely used method is based on a **Gaussian model** [12]. This method is based on the assumption that the intensity of each pixel $I(x, y)$ follows a Gaussian distribution (Figure 21.2) with mean $\mu_t(x, y)$ and covariance $\Sigma_t(x, y)$ at time $t$.

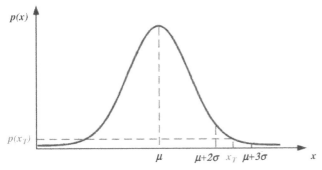

**Figure 21.2.** Gaussian distribution.

Therefore, the pixel $I_t(x, y)$ can be classified as foreground if

$$|I_t(x, y) - \mu_t(x, y)| > m\sigma_t(x, y), \tag{21.2}$$

where $\sigma_t(x, y) = |\Sigma_t(x, y)|^{1/2}$ and $m$ is usually set to be between 2 and 3. The mean $\mu_t(x, y)$ and covariance $\Sigma_t(x, y)$ of each pixel can be recursively updated by considering the current frame and using a learning rate $\alpha$.

One of the most popular methods for background subtraction uses a **mixture of Gaussian models**. This algorithm [13] models each pixel $I(x, y)$ as a mixture of $N$ Gaussian distributions, that is,

$$P(I(x, y)) = \sum_{k=1}^{N} w_k p(I(x, y), \mu_k(x, y), \Sigma_k(x, y)), \tag{21.3}$$

where $p(\cdot)$ is a Gaussian distribution and $w_k$ is the weight of the $k$th Gaussian distribution.[1] The above mixture of Gaussians is updated on the fly. For a given pixel $I(x, y)$, its value is checked with all the components in the mixture model. If $|I(x, y) - \mu_k(x, y)| < 2.5\sigma_k(x, y)$, a match in the $k$th distribution is deduced, and the distribution's parameters (i.e., $\mu_k(x, y)$, $\Sigma_k(x, y)$ and $w_k$) are updated. If there is no match, the least probable distribution is replaced by a Gaussian distribution, in which $\mu = I(x, y)$, $\sigma$ is large, and $w$ is small. Subsequently, the components are ranked in order of $w/\sigma$, and the ones with greater weight and lower variance are selected. Specifically, the first $K$ Gaussian models are considered to represent the background, while the remaining models are considered as foreground distributions. $K$ is chosen based on a prior assumption for the proportion of background data within the whole frame.

Another method, presented in reference 14, is based on a **confidence map** and **adaptive thresholding**. Initially, a block-based detection is applied. Specifically, if the average value of the difference between the current frame and the background frame is less than a threshold, then a foreground block is detected. The map obtained using this process is shown in Figure 21.3b.

Subsequently, confidence maps are calculated. The Confidence Map was firstly introduced in reference 15. It is defined as follows:

$$CM(x, y) = \begin{cases} 0\%, & D(x, y) < T_{Lo}(x, y), \\ \dfrac{D(x, y) - T_{Lo}(x, y)}{T_{Hi}(x, y) - T_{Lo}(x, y)} \times 100\%, & T_{Lo}(x, y) \le D(x, y) \le T_{Hi}(x, y) \\ 100\%, & D(x, y) > T_{Hi}(x, y), \end{cases}$$

$$\tag{21.4}$$

where $D(x, y) = |I(x, y) - B(x, y)|$ is the difference between the intensity of pixel $I(x, y)$ in the current frame and its corresponding pixel $B(x, y)$ in the background frame. In the above calculation of confidence maps in the RGB color space, two thresholds, $T_{Hi}(x, y)$ and $T_{Lo}(x, y)$, are used for each pixel. These are adaptively determined for all three components of the RGB colour space. Therefore, the confidence

---

[1]Henceforth, the subscript $t$ is dropped for notational simplicity.

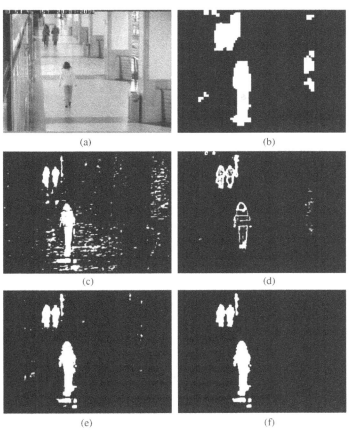

**Figure 21.3.** Adaptive thresholding foreground segmentation using a sequence from the CAVIAR database: (a) Original image, (b) Initial block-based map, (c) confidence map of RGB change detection with adaptive threshold, (d) confidence map based on Sobel edge detection, (e) combined confidence map, (f) foreground map before shadow removal.

map for color detection (Figure 21.3c) is calculated as

$$CM_c = \max(CM_R, CM_G, CM_B). \tag{21.5}$$

Similarly, confidence maps based on Sobel edge detection [16] are obtained using Eq. (21.4). This map is shown in Figure 21.3d. In order to achieve higher accuracy, the confidence maps are subsequently combined with the block-based foreground map as follows:

$$CM = \Big(\max(CM_c, CM_e) \cap M_b\Big) \cup \Big(\min(CM_c, CM_e) \cap \bar{M}_b\Big), \tag{21.6}$$

where $M_b$ is the binary block-based foreground map (0 means background, 1 means foreground), and $\bar{M}_b$ is its binary complement. The above combination ensures that the maximum confidence values appear in areas with motion, while the minimum confidence values appear in areas without motion. This approach reduces errors caused when foreground and background pixels have similar colors.

In $CM$ (Figure 21.3e), all pixels are valued between 0% and 100%. Subsequently, a *hysteresis thresholding* step [17] is applied to remove false positives by eliminating all components that are not connected to a 100% confidence region (Figure 21.3f).

## 21.2.2   Shadow Removal

The presence of shadows usually interferes with the process of moving object extraction. In moving object detection and extraction, the detection of shadow areas is one of the major difficulties, because shadow pixels have similar properties with the real foreground pixels. For example, shadow pixels also have relatively large color differences with background pixels, their colors are changing from frame to frame, and they are usually connected to the moving object areas.

By appropriately selecting the background updating parameters, we can fine-tune the sensitivity of the system to the classification of shadows. For example, if a large learning rate $\alpha$ is used, then shadow areas will be classified as background quickly; but at the same time, some foreground pixels might be misclassified as background as well. On the other hand, a small $\alpha$ usually cannot classify shadows correctly and efficiently. Therefore, more sophisticated algorithms are required for shadow removal.

So far, several approaches have been presented for identifying shadows. In reference 18, it was assumed that the intensity of an area on which shadow is cast will decrease significantly but its chromaticity will not exhibit considerable variations. Based on this assumption, frames are converted into the **normalized RGB (chromaticity)** color space. Then shadow detection is performed on the pixels that have been previously classified as foreground. A foreground pixel $I(x, y)$ is classified as shadow if both conditions below are met:

$$\left| I^R_{\text{norm}}(x, y) - \mu^R_{\text{norm}}(x, y) \right| < 3\sigma^R_{\text{norm}}(x, y), \tag{21.7}$$

$$\left| I^G_{\text{norm}}(x, y) - \mu^G_{\text{norm}}(x, y) \right| < 3\sigma^G_{\text{norm}}(x, y), \tag{21.8}$$

where $\mu^R_{\text{norm}}(x, y)$ and $\sigma^R_{\text{norm}}(x, y)$, $\mu^G_{\text{norm}}(x, y)$ and $\sigma^G_{\text{norm}}(x, y)$ are the mean and standard deviation values of the Gaussian models at pixel $I(x, y)$ in the *normalized R* and *normalized G* channels, respectively.

Based on a similar assumption, the **HSV** (**hue**, **saturation**, and **value**) color space is also used for detecting shadows [19]. A pixel is classified as shadow, if the following statements hold:

- The difference of its $H$ ($S$) component values in the current frame and the background frame is smaller than a threshold $T_H$ ($T_S$). Threshold $T_H$ ($T_S$) is set based on experimentation.

- The ratio of its $V$ component value in the current frame over the same component value on the background frame is larger than a threshold $T_{V1}$ and smaller than a threshold $T_{V2}$. Thresholds $T_{V1}$ and $T_{V2}$ are set based on experimentation.

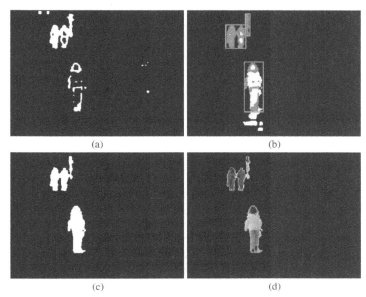

(a)                                     (b)

(c)                                     (d)

**Figure 21.4.** Shadow removal based on an edge bounding box: (**a**) Binary map for edge detection. (**b**) Edge bounding box for shadow removal. (**c**) Final foreground map. (**d**) Color image of extracted objects.

In reference 14, a shadow removal method based on an **edge bounding box** (**EBB**) was introduced. This method is very appropriate for indoor environments, especially when the shadow pixels have similar chromaticity values with the foreground pixels (for example, due to a light-reflecting floor surface). In this method, instead of pixel-based classification, a region-based classifier is used. Considering that shadows appear mainly on the floor and their boundaries are normally blurry, edge information is used to separate shadow areas from object areas. Specifically, within each foreground region in the foreground map, a *bounding box* is set which contains all the edge pixels—that is, the smallest rectangular box that includes all the edge pixels in the foreground area. This is shown in Figure 21.4b. Then, all the foreground pixels outside the *bounding box* are classified as shadows. For foreground regions in which no edge pixels are detected, all pixels are classified in those regions as shadows.

After the walking individuals are efficiently extracted, a variety of methods can be applied for their identification based on their walking style. These methods are described in the ensuing sections.

## 21.3  GAIT ANALYSIS FOR FEATURE EXTRACTION

Initial studies on gait as a discriminating trait took place in the 1970s from a medical/behavioral viewpoint [20, 21]. Later, the investigation of the gait recognition problem was attempted from the perspective of capturing and analyzing gait signals [22–26]. As shown in Figure 21.1, in a gait recognition system [6], following object detection and extraction, there is a **gait analysis** (i.e., feature extraction) process and a **gait recognition/classification** step. In the following sections, these two processes will be described in detail.

## 21.3.1  Gait Cycle Detection

Gait is a periodic activity, and this is why in a gait sequence there might be several periods (cycles) of walking. The detection of walking cycles (called gait cycles) is a very important task in gait recognition. This is because most methods for gait recognition presume the partitioning of a gait video sequence into its constituent repetitive walking cycles that will be used subsequently for feature extraction and recognition. Most common approaches for gait cycle detection are based on the calculation of the sum of foreground pixels for all frames in a gait sequence. This signal is usually quite noisy due to the existence of spurious pixels and shadows in the foreground of most frames. Therefore, appropriate techniques have to be applied for the use of this signal in gait cycle detection. One such method [25] fits a sinusoidal signal to noisy foreground sum signal using linear prediction. In reference 27 a different approach was taken by filtering the noisy foreground sum signal using an adaptive filter. The filtered signal has lower noise levels. The gait cycles can then be detected by locating the minima on the filtered signal. In another method [28], the autocorrelation of the foreground signal was calculated and was used for the determination of the walking period by observing the autocorrelation peaks. Furthermore, the above autocorrelation was used for the determination of an optimal denoising filter that was applied on the noisy foreground sum signal. Using the walking period and the denoised signal, the gait cycles were accurately detected. In the rest of this chapter, we assume that the gait cycle information—that is, the beginning and the end of each walking period in the gait sequence—is available to the gait recognition system.

## 21.3.2  Approaches to Feature Extraction from Gait Sequences

Most common methods for feature extraction are based on a holistic approach, with which feature extraction is performed directly from the video sequence depicting a walking individual. Although some such techniques use human blobs (e.g., in reference 25 *optical flow* was used for this purpose), the most popular holistic techniques in current gait recognition research are those that address the gait recognition problem using only sequences of binary maps (silhouettes) of walking human. These techniques do not presume the availability of any further information, such as color or gray-scale information, which may not be available or extractable in practical cases.

A variety of features can be extracted from a sequence of silhouettes. One such feature, which is very appropriate for deployment in gait recognition systems, is the **contour of the silhouette**. Although this feature intuitively seems to be very suitable, its deployment has two major disadvantages in practice. The first is relevant to the fact that the extracted silhouettes will not normally be noise-free and therefore the extraction of an accurate contour will usually be difficult and imperfect. The second disadvantage is the requirement for the availability of increased computational power due to processing that is required for the extraction of silhouette contours. Despite the above disadvantages, there are methods (e.g., references 29 and 30), that use the silhouette contour feature and yield good results.

Another feature that is suitable for gait recognition applications is the **width of silhouette** [31]. Essentially, the width of silhouette is the distance between the most distant contour points on the same horizontal line (see Figure 21.5a). This feature has the advantage that its extraction requires relatively low computational effort from the feature extraction system. However, this feature relies on the successful extraction of contour points and, therefore, is susceptible to noise. Some methods for dealing with the noise problem were presented in reference 31.

The **horizontal and vertical projections** of silhouettes [32] are expressed as

$$P_h(x) = \sum_{y=1}^{N_c} S(x, y), \qquad x = 1, \ldots, N_r, \tag{21.9}$$

$$P_v(y) = \sum_{x=1}^{N_r} S(x, y), \qquad y = 1, \ldots, N_c, \tag{21.10}$$

where $N_c$ and $N_r$ are the number of columns and number of rows in binary silhouette $S$, respectively. In the above definitions, it is assumed that the pixel values in the silhouettes are defined as follows:

$$S(x, y) = \begin{cases} 1 & \text{if } (x, y) \text{ is a foreground pixel,} \\ 0 & \text{otherwise.} \end{cases} \tag{21.11}$$

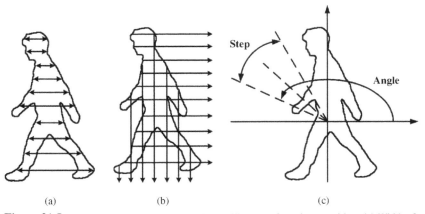

(a)                            (b)                            (c)

**Figure 21.5.** Some features extracted from binary silhouettes for gait recognition: **(a)** Width of silhouette, **(b)** vertical and horizontal projections, and **(c)** angular representation.

Considering that silhouette deformations are reflected in the horizontal or vertical silhouette projection (Figure 21.5b), this feature appears to be a very attractive choice for capturing gait information. An important advantage of this feature over the *width of silhouette* is that it is far more robust to spurious pixels. Furthermore, its calculation is straightforward and can take place in real time.

In reference 33, it was proposed that an **angular transform** is used for the robust extraction of feature from gait sequences. Specifically, each transform coefficient is calculated by dividing the silhouettes in angular sectors and by calculating the average distance between the pixels in each sector and the center of the silhouette $(x_c, y_c)$. The above process is depicted in Figure 21.5c, and is formally expressed as

$$\mathcal{A}(\theta) = \frac{1}{N_\theta} \sum_{(x,y)\in \mathcal{F}_\theta} S(x, y)\sqrt{(x - x_c)^2 + (y - y_c)^2}, \tag{21.12}$$

where $\theta$ is an angle, $\mathcal{F}_\theta$ is the set of the pixels in the circular sector $(\theta - (\Delta\theta/2),\ \theta + (\Delta\theta/2))$, and $N_\theta$ is the cardinality of $\mathcal{F}_\theta$. As shown in reference 33, the transform coefficients are linear functions of the silhouette contour. The averaging that takes place during the calculation of the transform coefficients makes this feature extraction method robust to noise.

Another method that can be used for feature extraction from gait sequences is the **Radon transform** [34]. The Radon transform of a continuous 2D function $f$ is defined as

$$R(\rho, \theta) = \int\limits_{-\infty}^{\infty} \int\limits_{-\infty}^{\infty} f(x, y)\delta(\rho - x\cos\theta - y\sin\theta)dxdy \tag{21.13}$$

By applying the discrete version of Radon transform to binary silhouettes (Figure 21.6), we can set up a mapping between the domain determined by the coordinate system $(x, y)$ and the Radon domain determined by $(\rho, \theta)$. Given a specific direction, a silhouette $S$ is projected onto the $q$ axis. In other words, pixels along a

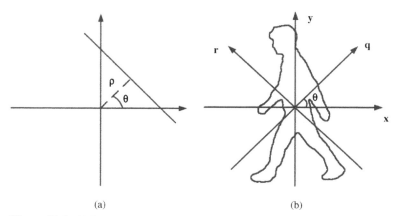

(a)            (b)

**Figure 21.6.** (a) Two parameters $(\rho, \theta)$ determining the position of the line. (b) Calculation of Radon coefficients.

set of lines parallel to the $r$ axis are summed together. A point $(\rho_i, \theta_i)$ in the Radon domain corresponds to the sum of foreground pixels along a specific line, parallel to $r$ axis, in the original silhouette; that is, the location and orientation of the summation line is determined by $\rho$ and $\theta$.

## 21.4  GAIT RECOGNITION

### 21.4.1  Calculation of the Similarity Between Different Feature Sequences

In the previous section, we described some methods for the extraction of features from binary silhouettes. After this process is completed, our original gait sequences are transformed to sequences of feature vectors. Therefore, our decisions about the identity of walking individuals will have to be based on feature vector sequences.

The comparison between different feature vector sequences requires the definition of a distance metric. In most gait recognition applications, the Euclidean distance is commonly used. However, other measures can also be used, such as the inner product distance [27] as well as the number of "ones" in the binary difference between silhouettes [35]. Other distance measures can also be used [36].

The comparison between different gait sequences is not straightforward. The reason is that these sequences might correspond to individuals walking at different pace and each gait cycle might include different numbers of silhouettes. This means that the definition of a metric for the pairwise comparison of features is not sufficient. In addition to a distance metric, some rules are needed to determine which pairs of features will be compared during the assessment of similarity between different sequences of feature vectors.

If the walking periods $T_1$ and $T_2$ of the two compared gait sequences are unequal, then the calculation of their cumulative distance would involve a warping function defined by the pairs $(w_1(t), w_2(t))$ that indicate the correspondence between frames in the two gait sequences. Using such a warping function, the cumulative distance over a gait cycle is defined as

$$D_{12} = \frac{1}{U} \sum_{t=1}^{T} u(t) D(f_1(w_1(t)), f_2(w_2(t))), \qquad (21.14)$$

where $u(t)$ is a weighting function, $U = \sum_{t=1}^{T} u(t)$, and $D(\cdot)$ denotes the distance between the feature vectors at time $t$. Based on Eq. (21.14), it becomes apparent that the calculation of the distance is dependent on the choice of the warping function.

The simplest possible way to try to compare two gait sequences is by comparing their feature vectors one-by-one by disregarding any differences in the length of the sequences [35]. This **direct matching** approach would work well in case the two sequences were of equal length. However, if the lengths of the sequences are not equal, then two gait sequences taken from the same person walking at different speeds would appear dissimilar.

Another approach for the selection of the warping path in the comparison of gait sequences is by using **dynamic time warping (DTW)** [37]. Dynamic time warping applies compensation for possible walking speed differences in the compared sequences. This is achieved by calculating the distances between all combinations of test and reference feature vectors and then determining the optimal warping path— that is, the path that yields the minimum cumulative distance. This approach was taken in references [28] and [31].

The approach that combines efficiency with computational simplicity is based on **linear time normalization**. Unlike dynamic time warping, linear time normalization determines the correspondence between frames in different sequences by applying a linear rule for the normalization on the length of the sequences before their comparison [38].

A methodology that gave excellent results for gait recognition using **Hidden Markov Models (HMMs)** was presented in reference 39. In this method, HMMs were used for the alignment of the frames in gait sequences prior to their comparison. In another method [40], Hidden Markov Models were used for the modeling of gait: Each given observation was modeled by HMMs corresponding to different subjects in a reference gait database. The model that appeared more likely to have generated the observation was assumed to correspond to the identity of the observed subject.

## 21.4.2  Construction of a Unique Gait Template

The temporal normalization process, described in the previous section, can be error-prone and computationally heavy. This is why one of the challenges in gait representation is to compact an individual's gait information on a single two-dimensional template that is suitable for use in recognition applications. Because a gait sequence is a spatiotemporal volume, its reduction to a two-dimensional template or a one-dimensional vector, without any loss of discriminatory information, is not a trivial task. In general, a template-based approach for gait recognition should:

- capture as much structural information as possible;
- capture the gait dynamics;
- condense all gait information into a relatively small number of coefficients;
- be applied directly without any need for prior compensation for speed differences between the compared walking subjects.

The simplest and one of the most widely used templates is the **average silhouette**. After an object detection and extraction step is deployed, silhouettes in a gait sequence are appropriately scaled and aligned. Then the template is calculated by simply averaging the foreground maps (silhouettes) of the sequence

$$\bar{S} = \frac{1}{N_S} \sum_{a=1}^{N_S} S_a, \tag{21.15}$$

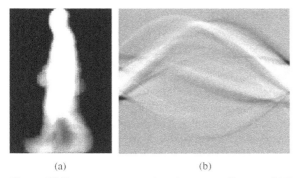

(a)                                    (b)

**Figure 21.7.** (a) Template based on the average silhouette. (b) Template for Radon transform.

where $N_S$ is the number of silhouettes and $S_a$, $a = 1, \ldots, N_S$, are the silhouettes in a gait sequence.

Figure 21.7a shows the average silhouettes of one subject in the Gait Challenge database [35]. The efficiency and recognition power of this feature was shown in references 41 and 42. Several gait recognition systems are based on such template construction, e.g., in reference 43, the average silhouette is defined as *Gait Energy Image (GEI)* and is used for further component and discriminant analysis; in reference 44, average silhouettes from multiple views are used for combined-view recognition.

Another template is based on the **Radon transform of silhouettes**. It contains both the structural and frequency information that exists in a gait cycle for each gait sequence [34]. First, each Radon-transformed silhouette $S_{R_i}$ is associated with a phase as follows:

$$\hat{S}_{R_i} = S_{R_i} \cdot (1 + \cos \phi_i + j \cdot (1 + \sin \phi_i)). \tag{21.16}$$

In the above equation, the angle $\phi_i$ is defined as

$$\phi_i = \frac{2\pi}{4N_1} \cdot i, \tag{21.17}$$

where $N_1$ is the number of frames in a gait cycle, and $i$ is an index in the range from 0 to $N_1 - 1$. Since $S$ is a two-dimensional matrix consisting of Radon coefficients, then each of its coefficients is affected in the same manner. A Radon template $T$ (see Figure 21.7b), is defined as follows:

$$T = \frac{1}{N_1} \sum_{i=0}^{N_1-1} \hat{S}_{R_i} = -S_{R_i} \cdot (1 + j) + \frac{1}{N_1} \sum_{i=0}^{N_1-1} S_{R_i} e^{j\frac{2\pi}{4N_1}i}, \tag{21.18}$$

where $N_1$ is the total number of silhouettes in a sequence.

## 21.4.3  Dimensionality Reduction

The construction of a template for gait recognition requires the availability of a video sequence depicting one walking cycle of the observed individual. In practice, however, more than one walking cycle might be available in a gait sequence. This means that recognition can be improved by focusing on the template coefficients that do not change much within templates corresponding to the same subject while they vary considerably between different subjects. Putting emphasis on the more discriminative coefficients and reducing the dimensionality of the problem are possible by using linear discriminant analysis (LDA) [45]. This is achieved by calculating a subspace protection of the original template using an appropriate matrix **W**. This matrix is calculated by maximization of Fisher's criterion

$$J(\mathbf{W}) = \frac{|\mathbf{W} \cdot \mathbf{S}_B \cdot \mathbf{W}^T|}{|\mathbf{W} \cdot \mathbf{S}_W \cdot \mathbf{W}^T|}, \tag{21.19}$$

where $\mathbf{S}_B$ is the between-class scatter matrix, and $\mathbf{S}_W$ is the within-class scatter matrix. While LDA has been extensively applied to other biometric traits, such as fingerprints and face, here we present its application on gait recognition using the templates derived in the previous section. Since the discrimination power of the template representation is expected to be unevenly distributed among template coefficients, LDA can be used in order to reduce the dimensionality of the problem and, therefore, simplify the recognition task. This is particularly important considering that the original feature vector is derived from templates and, therefore, is high-dimensional; that is, a template of dimensions of $M \times N$ is converted into a $I \times 1$ vector, where $I = M \times N$.

If only one template is available for each subject in the database, **principal component analysis (PCA)** [29, 31, 45] can be used. However, it must be noted that, unlike LDA, PCA does not emphasize the most discriminative coefficients; but instead, it uses the coefficients that best describe the templates. For this reason, PCA will generally perform worse than LDA.

## 21.5  GAIT RECOGNITION BASED ON MULTIPLE VIEWS

The gait recognition approaches that were described in the previous sections are based on the assumption that only one view of the walking individual is available. Usually, it is assumed that the side view is available since this view was shown in the past to be the view carrying most discriminatory information [46, 47]. However, there are cases in which more than one view will be available (see Figure 21.8). The investigation of such cases (e.g., reference [44]) has shown that the combination of multiple views can offer improved recognition performance in gait recognition systems. In such methods, the distance $D_{ij}$ between a test subject $i$ and a reference subject $j$ is assessed based on the distances $d_{ij}^v$ calculated for the corresponding views $v$ ($v = 1, \ldots, V$). Specifically,

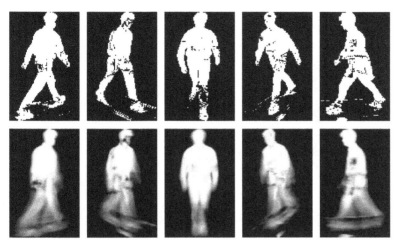

**Figure 21.8.** Silhouettes from different views for a subject in CMU gait database [48]: Original silhouettes (**upper row**) and the average silhouettes (**bottom row**).

the total distance is

$$D_{ij} = \sum_{v=1}^{V} w^v d_{ij}^v, \tag{21.20}$$

where $D_{ij}$ is the combined distance between the $i$th test subject and $j$th reference subject, $V$ is the total number of available views, $w^v$ is the weight for view $v$, and $d_{ij}^v$ is the Euclidean distance between the *average silhouettes* of the two subjects in view $v$.

The performance of a gait recognition algorithm based on Eq. (21.20) relies on the determination of appropriate weights $w^v$. The optimization of the weights—that is, in the sense of maximizing recognition performance—can be achieved by minimizing the probability of recognition error. This problem can be translated mathematically by considering that accurate recognition means that the weighed distance $D_f$ between corresponding subjects in the reference and test databases

$$D_f = \sum_{v=1}^{V} w^v d_f^v = \mathbf{w}^T \cdot \mathbf{d}_f \tag{21.21}$$

should be smaller than the weighed distance between the noncorresponding subjects

$$D_b = \sum_{v=1}^{V} w^v d_b^v = \mathbf{w}^T \cdot \mathbf{d}_b. \tag{21.22}$$

A recognition error takes place whenever $D_b < D_f$. Therefore, the probability of error is

$$P_e = P\left(D_b < D_f\right) = P\left(\mathbf{w}^T \cdot \left(\mathbf{d}_b - \mathbf{d}_f\right) < 0\right). \tag{21.23}$$

We define the random variable $z$ as

$$z = \mathbf{w}^T \cdot \left( \mathbf{d}_b - \mathbf{d}_f \right). \tag{21.24}$$

If we assume that $\mathbf{d}_b$ and $\mathbf{d}_f$ are normal random vectors, then $z$ is a normal random variable with probability density distribution given by

$$P(z) = \frac{1}{\sqrt{2\pi}\sigma_z} e^{-\frac{1}{2}\frac{(z-m_z)^2}{\sigma_z^2}}, \tag{21.25}$$

where $m_z$ is the mean value of $z$, and $\sigma_z$ is the variance of $z$.

Therefore, using Eq. (21.24) and (21.25), the probability of error in Eq. (21.23) is expressed as

$$P_e = P(z < 0) = \int_{-\infty}^{0} \frac{1}{\sqrt{2\pi}\sigma_z} e^{-\frac{1}{2}\frac{(z-m_z)^2}{\sigma_z^2}} dz. \tag{21.26}$$

Furthermore, if $q = \frac{z-m_z}{\sigma_z}$, then the above expression is equivalent to

$$P_e = \int_{-\infty}^{-\frac{m_z}{\sigma_z}} \frac{1}{\sqrt{2\pi}} e^{-\frac{1}{2}q^2} dq. \tag{21.27}$$

The probability of error can therefore be minimized by minimizing $-m_z/\sigma_z$, or equivalently by maximizing $m_z/\sigma_z$. After further calculation of $m_z$ and $\sigma_z$, $\mathbf{w}$ can be obtained by

$$\mathbf{w} = \left( \frac{m_{d_{b1}} - m_{d_{f1}}}{\sigma_{d_{b1}}^2 + \sigma_{d_{f1}}^2} \quad \frac{m_{d_{b2}} - m_{d_{f2}}}{\sigma_{d_{b2}}^2 + \sigma_{d_{f2}}^2} \quad \cdots \quad \frac{m_{d_{bV}} - m_{d_{fV}}}{\sigma_{d_{bV}}^2 + \sigma_{d_{fV}}^2} \right)^T, \tag{21.28}$$

where $V$ is the total number of available views.

The identity of a given test subject is established by comparing the distances between the test subject and the subjects in the reference database and taking the minimum:

$$\text{identity}(i) = \arg \min_{j} D_{ij}, \tag{21.29}$$

where $D_{ij}$ denotes the combined distance between the $i$th test subject and the $j$th reference subject. The interpretation of the above is that the identity of the reference subject with which the test subject has minimum distance is considered to be the identity of the test subject.

## 21.6  EXPERIMENTAL RESULTS

Gait recognition performance is usually reported in terms of cumulative match scores (CMS), in which rank $n$ results report the percentage of test subjects whose actual match in the reference database was in the top $n$ matches [49]. Specifically, Rank 1 results report the percentage of subjects in a test set that were identified exactly, and

**Table 21.1.** The Recognition Rates of Several Methods Using the Gait Challenge Database (Average on All Probe Sets)

| Gait Recognition Method | Rank 1 (%) | Rank 5 (%) |
|---|---|---|
| Baseline [35] | 42 | 64 |
| Silhouette with DTW | 47 | 70 |
| Silhouette with LTN | 50 | 72 |
| Radon template with LDA | 56 | 74 |
| Gait energy image [43] | 63 | 82 |

Rank 5 (or 10) results report the percentage of test subjects whose actual match in the reference database was in the top 5 (or 10) matches.

We use the Gait Challenge database for reaching conclusions regarding the efficiency of some gait recognition methods based on single-view gait sequences. In general, the silhouette feature has been shown [6] to work best among possible features, and this is why it is a very reasonable choice for use in a gait recognition system. So most of the methods in Table 21.1 are based on the silhouette feature. As can be seen in Table 21.1, the performance of a gait-based recognition system improves with increasing algorithmic complexity. However, even the best-performing system cannot deliver satisfactory performance that would allow the deployment of gait as the sole biometric trait in a security system. Therefore, gait-based systems are not currently considered as reliable as other biometric systems—for example, such as those based on face or fingerprints.

Recognition results, using the CMU database, for some single-view and multiple-view methods are presented in Table 21.2. We chose to use the simplest possible template—that is, the average silhouette—for the assessment of these methods since, despite its simplicity, it is very efficient. Since the average silhouettes of the side (east) view and the frontal (south) view contain more discriminative information than other views, the results using these two views are the best among the ones using single views. It can be seen that, if we combine multiple views by averaging the relevant distances, the result is worse than in the case where only the east or the south view

**Table 21.2.** The Recognition Rates of Single-View and Multiple-View Methods Using the CMU Database

| Number of Views | Direction/Combination Method | Rank 1 (%) | Rank 5 (%) | Rank 10 (%) |
|---|---|---|---|---|
| 1 | Side (east view) | 84 | 92 | 100 |
| 1 | Frontal (south view) | 88 | 96 | 100 |
| 5 | Mean Value (all views) | 80 | 92 | 92 |
| 5 | Weighed (optimal) | 92 | 96 | 100 |

is used. This happens because taking the average implicitly assumes that all views are of equal importance and therefore should contribute equally to the final decision. As a result, the inclusion of views that contain less discriminative information has an adverse impact on the recognition performance. However, when the optimal weights are applied, as shown in the previous section, greater importance is put to the side and the frontal views while the discriminative information from other views is also taken into account (but with smaller weights). Therefore, the performance of the gait recognition system is optimized.

## 21.7  CONCLUSIONS

In this chapter, we outlined several techniques that are used in unobtrusive biometric identification based on gait. Several existing methods for object detection and extraction were presented. Shadow removal techniques were also presented because object extraction is often inefficient in disregarding shadows. For the task of gait feature extraction, some holistic approaches were described, followed by appropriate template construction methods based on them. Finally, we presented an approach for gait recognition based on multiview sequences. Based on our study of gait as a biometric trait, it can be deduced that, although gait cannot, at present, be used as a stand-alone biometric, it can be a valuable complement to any biometric system, especially if unobtrusiveness is a requirement.

## REFERENCES

1. A. K. Jain, L. Hong, S. Pankanti, and R. Bolle, An identity verification system using fingerprints, *Proc. IEEE* **85**(9):1365–1388, 1999.
2. A. K. Jain and N. Duta, Deformable matching of hand shapes for verification, in *Proceedings of the IEEE Conference on Image Processing*, Kobe, Japan, October 1999, pp. 857–861.
3. J. Daugman, High confidence visual recognition of persons by a test of statistical independence, *IEEE Trans. Pattern Anal. Mach. Intell.* **15**(11):1148–1161, 1993.
4. L. Rabiner and B. Juang, *Fundamentals of Speech Recognition*, Prentice-Hall, Englewood Cliffs, NJ, 1993.
5. Y. Qi and B. R. Hunt, A multiresolution approach to computer verification of handwritten signatures, *IEEE Trans. Image Processing*, **4**(6):870–874, 1995.
6. N. V. Boulgouris, D. Hatzinakos, and K. N. Plataniotis, Gait recognition: a challenging signal processing technology for biometric identification, *IEEE Signal Processing Mag.* **22**:78–90, 2005.
7. L. Sloman, M. Berridge, S. Homatidis, D. Hunter, and T. Duck, Gait patterns of depressed patients and normal subjects, *Am. J. Psychiatry* **139**(1):94–97, 1982.
8. R. Chellappa, A. K. Roy-Chowdhury, and A. Kale, Human identification using gait and face, in *Proceedings of the IEEE Conference on Computer Vision and Pattern Recognition*, Minneapolis, MN, June 2007, pp. 1–2.
9. J. C. Nascimento and J. S. Marques, Performance evaluation of object detection algorithms for video surveillance, *Multimedia IEEE Trans.* **8**(4):761–774, 2006.
10. I. Haritaoglu, D. Harwood, and L. S. Davis, W4: Who? when? where? what? a real time system for detecting and tracking people, in *IEEE International Conference on Automatic Face and Gesture Recognition*, 1998, pp. 222–227.

11. I. Haritaoglu, D. Harwood, and L. S. Davis, W4: Real-time surveillance of people and their activities, *IEEE Trans. Pattern Anal. Mach. Intell.* **22**(8):809–830, 2000.
12. C. R. Wren, A. Azarbayejani, T. Darrell, and A. P. Pentland, Pfinder: Real-time tracking of the human body, *IEEE Trans. Pattern Anal. Mach. Intell.* **19**(7):780–785, 1997.
13. C. Stauffer, W. Eric, and L. Grimson, Learning patterns of activity using real-time tracking, *IEEE Trans. Pattern Anal. Mach. Intell.* **22**(8):747–757, 2000.
14. X. Huang and N. V. Boulgouris, Robust object segmentation using adaptive thresholding, in *IEEE International Conference on Image Processing*, San Antonio, TX, September 2007, pp. 45–48.
15. S. Jabri, Z. Duric, H. Wechsler, and A. Rosenfeld, Detection and location of people in video images using adaptive fusion of color and edge information, in *Proceedings of the 15th International Conference on Pattern Recognition*, Vol. 4, Barcelona, Spain, September 2000, pp. 627–630.
16. R. C. Gonzalez and R. E. Woods, *Digital Image Processing*, Prentice-Hall, Upper Saddle River, NJ, 2002.
17. J. F. Canny, A computational approach to edge detection, *IEEE Trans. Pattern Anal. Mach. Intell.* **8**(6):679–698, 1986.
18. S. J. McKenna, S. Jabri, Z. Duric, and A. Rosenfeld, Tracking groups of people, *Comput. Vis. Image Understanding* **80**:42–46, 2000.
19. R. Cucchiara, C. Granan, M. Piccardi, and A. Prati, Detecting moving objects, ghosts, and shadows in video streams, *IEEE Trans. Pattern Anal. Mach. Intell.* **25**:1337–1342, 2003.
20. G. Johansson, Visual perception of biological motion and a model for its analysis, *Percept. Psycophys.* **14**(2):201–211, 1973.
21. J. E. Cutting and L. T. Kozlowski, Recognizing friends by their walk: Gait perception without familiarity cues, *Bull. Psychonometric Soc.* **9**(5):353–356, 1977.
22. S. A. Niyogi and E. H. Adelson, Analyzing and recognizing walking figures in xyt, in *Proceedings of Computer Vision and Pattern Recognition*, Seattle, WA, June 1994, pp. 469–474.
23. H. Murase and R. Sakai, Moving object recognition in eigenspace representation: Gait analysis and lip reading, *Pattern Recognit. Lett.* **17**(2):155–162, 1996.
24. D. Cunado, M. S. Nixon, and J. N. Carter, Using gait as a biometric, via phaseweighted magnitude spectra, in *Proceedings of the International Conference on Audio- and Video-Based Biometric Person Authentication*, Crans-Montana, Switzerland, March 1997, pp. 95–102.
25. J. Little and J. Boyd, Recognizing people by their gait: The shape of motion, *Videre, Int. J. Comput. Vis.* **14**(6):83–105, 1998.
26. C. J. Harris P. S. Huang and M. S. Nixon, Visual surveillance and tracking of humans by face and gait recognition, in *Proceedings of the 7th IFAC Symposium on Artificial Intelligence in Real-Time Control*, Grand Ganyon National Park, AZ, October 1998, pp. 43–44.
27. A. Sundaresan, A. K. Roy Chowdhury, and R. Chellappa, A hidden Markov model based framework for recognition of humans from gait sequences, in *Proceedings of the International Conference on Image Processing 2003*, Barcelona, Spain, September 2003, pp. 14–17.
28. N. V. Boulgouris, K. N. Plataniotis, and D. Hatzinakos, Gait recognition using dynamic time warping, in *Proceedings of the IEEE International Symposium on Multimedia Signal Processing*, Siena, Italy, September 2004, pp. 263–266.
29. L. Wang, T. Tan, H. Ning, and W. Hu, Silhouette analysis-based gait recognition for human identification, *IEEE Trans. Pattern Anal. Mach. Intell.* **25**(12):1505–1518, Dec. 2003.
30. S. D. Mowbray and M. S. Nixon, Automatic gait recognition via fourier descriptors of deformable objects, in *Proceedings of the International Conference on Audio- and Video-Based Biometric Person Authentication*, Guilford, UK, June 2003, pp. 566–573.
31. A. Kale, N. Cuntoor, B. Yegnanarayana, A. N. Rajagopalan, and R. Chellappa, Gait analysis for human identification, in *4th International Conference on Audio- and Video-Based Person Authentication*, Guilford, UK, June 2003, pp. 706–714.
32. Y. Liu, R. Collins, and Y. Tsin, Gait sequence analysis using frieze patterns, in *Proceedings of the European Conference on Computer Vision*, Copenhagen, May 2002, pp. 657–671.
33. N. V. Boulgouris, K. N. Plataniotis, and D. Hatzinakos, An angular transform of gait sequences for gait assisted recognition, in *Proceedings of the IEEE International Conference on Image Processing*, Singapore, October 2004, pp. 857–860.

34. N. V. Boulgouris and Z. X. Chi, Gait recognition using radon transform and linear discriminant analysis, *IEEE Trans. Image Processing* **16**(3):731–740, 2007.
35. P. J. Phillips, S. Sarkar, I. Robledo, P. Grother, and K. W. Bowyer, The gait identification challenge problem: Data sets and baseline algorithm, in *Proceedings of the International Conference on Pattern Recognition*, Quebec City, Canada, August 2002, pp. 385–388.
36. K. N. Plataniotis, D. Androutsos, and A. N. Venetsanopoulos, Adaptive fuzzy systems for multichannel signal processing, *Proc. IEEE* **87**(9):1601–1622, 1999.
37. H. Sakoe and S. Chiba, Dynamic programming optimization for spoken word recognition, *IEEE Trans. Acoust. Speech Signal Processing* **26**(1):43–49, 1978.
38. N. V. Boulgouris, K. N. Plataniotis, and D. Hatzinakos, Gait recognition using linear time normalization, *Pattern Recognit.* **39**:969–979, 2006.
39. Z. Liu and S. Sarkar, Improved gait recognition by gait dynamics normalization, *IEEE Trans. Pattern Anal. Mach. Intell.* **28**(6):863–876, 2006.
40. A. Kale, A. Sundaresan, A. N. Rajagopalan, N. Cuntoor, A. K. Roy-Chowdhury, V. Krueger, and R. Chellappa, Identification of humans using gait, *IEEE Trans. Image Processing* **13**(9):1163–6173, 2004.
41. Z. Liu and S. Sarkar, Simplest representation yet for gait recognition: Averaged silhouette, in *International Conference on Pattern Recognition*, August 2004.
42. G. V. Veres, L. Gordon, J. N. Carter, and M. S. Nixon, What image information is important in silhouette-based gait recognition? *IEEE Computer Society Conference on Computer Vision and Pattern Recognition*, Vol. 2, 2004, pp. 776–782.
43. J. Han and B. Bhanu, Individual recognition using gait energy image, *IEEE Trans. Pattern Anal. Mach. Intell.* **28**(2):316–322, 2006.
44. X. Huang and N. V. Boulgouris, Human gait recognition based on multiview gait sequences, *EURASIP Journal on Advances in Signal Processing*, **2008**, Article ID 629102, 2008.
45. C. BenAbdelkader, R. Cutler, and L. Davis, Motion-based recognition of people in eigengait space, in *Proceedings of the IEEE International Conference on Automatic Face and Gesture Recognition*, Washington, DC, May 2002, pp. 254–259.
46. S. Sarkar, P. J. Phillips, Z. Liu, I. R. Vega, P. Grother, and K. W. Bowyer, The human id gait challenge problem: Data sets, performance, and analysis, *IEEE Trans. Pattern Anal. Mach. Intell.* **27**(2):162–176, 2005.
47. M. Ekinci, Gait recognition using multiple projections, in *Proceedings of the International Conference on Automatic Face and Gesture Recognition*, April 2006, pp. 517–522.
48. R. Gross and J. Shi, The cmu motion of body (mobo) database, Technical Report CMU-RI-TR-01-18, Robotics Institute, Carnegie Mellon University, Pittsburgh, PA, June 2001.
49. P. J. Phillips, H. Moon, S. Rizvi, and P. Raus, The FERET evaluation methodology for face recognition algorithms, *IEEE Trans. Pattern Anal. Mach. Intell.* **22**(10):1090–1104, 2000.

# Chapter 22

# Distributed Source Coding for Biometrics: A Case Study on Gait Recognition

**Savvas Argyropoulos, Dimosthenis Ioannidis, Dimitrios Tzovaras, and Michael G. Strintzis**

"There!... Look at my get-up and tell me which rich man I most resemble in my walk."

—*The Wasps*, Aristophanes

## 22.1 INTRODUCTION

The establishment of human identity has always been a field of primary concern in a variety of applications ranging from access control in secure infrastructures to customizable smart-home applications. Recognition in a robust way is a critical issue in the effective proliferation of such applications. The existing solutions are mainly based on the use of secret words (passwords), which must be entered by the user when prompted or on the possession of identification cards (tokens). However, during recent decades, recognition based on the unique physical or behavioral characteristics that describe the anatomy or behavior of individuals, called biometrics, is gaining ground. Human recognition based on biometrics has many advantages over the password-based and the ID card-based solutions. Specifically, the latter induce many problems, such as increased forgery risk, predictable or easy-to-guess password selection, loss or theft of identity cards, nonaccountability, impersonation, and repudiation.

*Biometrics: Theory, Methods, and Applications.* Edited by Boulgouris, Plataniotis, and Micheli-Tzanakou
Copyright © 2010 the Institute of Electrical and Electronics Engineers, Inc.

One of the major concerns in applications that grant access based on a password, a token, or a biometric trait is the effective protection of the stored data to prevent malicious use either from those who have authorized access to them or from those who try to access them by fraudulent means. In password-based systems, the problem of secure storage has been investigated in depth and sophisticated encryption methods have been developed. Specifically, prior to storage to the physical medium, cryptographic codes are applied to the passwords and a hash code is generated with a one-to-one relationship to the original password. The irreversibility of the employed cryptographic codes renders the hash codes useless to the potential attackers of the system since the original data cannot be revealed.

On the other hand, the use of biometrics poses novel challenges and creates open holes in terms of security. Specifically, since the representation of biometric traits is not fixed over time, the existing solutions used in password-based applications to enhance security, such as cryptography, cannot be applied. This is because existing cryptographic solutions require the exact match of the prompted and the original signatures to grant access. Thus, novel encryption methods need to be developed to take into account the noise introduced in the representation of the biometric traits and account for their inherent variability [1].

In this chapter, a novel framework for biometric authentication in secure environments is developed and a channel coding approach based on distributed source coding is proposed. First, the fundamental concepts of distributed source coding are introduced and the problem of biometric recognition is formulated as the dual of data communication over noisy channels. The main idea is that perturbations in the representation of the biometric features in different times can be modeled by a (virtual) noise channel which corrupts the initial signal. The enrollment and authentication procedures are considered as the encoding and decoding stages of a communication system, and the trade-off between security and robustness is rigorously analyzed. Advanced channel coding techniques are employed to increase the error-correcting capabilities of the decoder and enhance the performance of the biometric system.

As a case study, a biometric authentication system from gait sequences based on error-correcting codes is proposed. Depth information is utilized for enhanced silhouette segmentation, and discriminative features are extracted for the representation of gait. Moreover, the use of generalized Radon transforms and orthogonal moments is discussed. The extracted features are integrated in the distributed source coding framework, and the parameters of the dependency channel are tuned based on these features. Finally, the proposed scheme is experimentally evaluated on a large database to demonstrate the validity of the proposed method.

The contribution of this chapter is twofold. On one hand, biometric recognition is modeled as a coding problem with noisy side information and a novel framework is developed for the exploitation of side information, the noise channel statistics, and the application of advanced channel codes. In this way, the security of the stored templates is increased and privacy of personal data is ensured. Furthermore, the effective modeling of these parameters improve significantly the performance of the proposed system so that the additional security comes at the expense of a negligible cost. On the other hand, a novel gait recognition system is developed based on quite discriminative features. As a preprocessing step, a silhouette-based technique based on depth information is proposed and novel descriptors are extracted from the segmented silhouettes. These features are very resilient to noise and contribute to the robustness of the proposed algorithm.

The chapter is organized as follows. Section 22.2 presents previous research in the field of distributed source coding and gait recognition. The fundamental concepts of distributed source coding are presented in Section 22.3, and the problem of biometric recognition is formulated as a coding problem. Subsequently, Section 22.4 provides a brief analysis of the extracted features for gait representation. The employment of these features in the proposed framework for gait recognition is presented in Section 22.5, and extensive experimental results are presented in Section 22.6 to demonstrate the validity of the proposed method and the superiority over state-of-the-art algorithms for gait recognition. Finally, the chapter concludes in Section 22.7 with a discussion on the open issues and directions for future work.

## 22.2 RELATED WORK

The problem of biometric authentication based on channel codes was originally studied in reference 2, where error correcting codes were employed to tackle the perturbations in the representation of biometric signals and classification was based on the Hamming distance between two biometric representations. This concept was extended in reference 3, where a cryptographic framework, called fuzzy vault, was developed to protect data in error-prone environments, such as biometric authentication systems, and Reed–Solomon (RS) codes were employed. Similarly, a methodology based on channel codes and the Slepian–Wolf theorem [4] for secure biometric storage was presented in reference 5. Specifically, low-density parity check (LDPC) codes were utilized and security was rigorously quantified. The framework was applied on an iris authentication system. Additionally, a fingerprint recognition system based on statistical modeling of the enrolled and the measured data was presented in reference 6.

Furthermore, LDPC codes were also used for biometric authentication in reference 7. Similarly to the fuzzy vault concept, the fuzzy commitment concept was introduced and the biometric authentication problem was considered as a wire-tap problem [8]. The underlying concept in these approaches is that a biometric measurement can never be exactly the same with the measurement from the same individual at another time. Thus, it is considered as a noisy version of the original signal and error correcting codes are applied to correct the erasures caused by noise. A similar approach, but not in the context of biometric recognition, was presented in reference 9. The multimedia authentication problem in the presence of noise was investigated, the theoretical limits of the system were identified, and the trade-off among fidelity, robustness, and security was discussed. This approach provides intuition for the proposed method in this chapter; the biometric recognition problem is considered as the analogous of data transmission over a communication channel, which determines the efficiency of the system.

The main novelty of this work over the existing approaches is the effective exploitation of the noise channel statistics to improve the recognition accuracy. Analytic models are developed for authorized and unauthorized transactions, and the probability distribution is modeled for gait recognition applications. The integration of this a priori information into the channel decoder assists in correct classification. Furthermore, a complete framework is presented for biometric recognition and the integration of the biometric features into this framework is analytically discussed. In this way, the proposed scheme can be easily utilized for any biometric trait, apart from gait, with minor changes only.

Interestingly, the problem of coding correlated distributed (not colocated) sources is also addressed in the field of video coding. In the seminal work of reference 10 the DIstributed Source Coding Using Syndromes (DISCUS) system was proposed to code a source that is correlated with another source but is only available at the decoder. The source codeword space is partitioned into a bank of channel code cosets, assuming that a side information source will be available at the decoder. Upon reception of the coset at the decoder, the side information is used to disambiguate the encoded signal. Based on this work, the field of distributed video coding [11] has emerged as a new trend in video coding. This work aims at identifying the connection between the fields of distributed source coding and biometric recognition and illustrate their relationship.

## 22.3 OVERVIEW OF THE PROPOSED SYSTEM

In a biometric authentication system, the user claims an identity and the measured biometric data (probe) are compared to the corresponding templates of the claimed identity (gallery), which have been previously stored in the database, during the enrollment stage. The biometric classifier, or expert, compares the extracted biometric features (biometric signature) of the probe with the gallery signature; and based on a decision rule, the system has to decide whether the user is a client (genuine transaction, class $\omega_0$) or an impostor (unauthorized transaction, class $\omega_1$). Most biometric systems tackle this problem using conventional pattern recognition and machine learning techniques. In contrast, the proposed system relies on channel codes for this decision and, in particular, on distributed source coding principles, as illustrated in the following.

The Slepian–Wolf theorem addresses the problem of coding distributed (not colocated) sources and decoding them jointly, as depicted in Figure 22.1a. If we consider two random sequences $X$ and $Y$ that are encoded using separate conventional entropy encoders and decoders, the achievable rates are $R_X \geq H(X)$ and $R_Y \geq H(Y)$, where $H(X)$ and $H(Y)$ are the entropies of $X$ and $Y$, respectively. However, if the two sequences are jointly decoded, the achievable rate region according to the Slepian–Wolf theorem is defined as

$$R_X \geq H(X|Y), \tag{22.1}$$

$$R_Y \geq H(Y|X), \tag{22.2}$$

$$R_X + R_Y \geq H(X, Y), \tag{22.3}$$

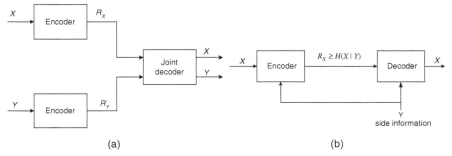

**Figure 22.1.** Conventional source coding of correlated sources.

where $H(X|Y)$ and $H(Y|X)$ are the conditional entropies and $H(X, Y)$ is the joint entropy of $X$ and $Y$. Thus, according to Eq. (22.3), the Slepian–Wolf theorem states that separate encoding and joint decoding of the two sequences can be as efficient as joint encoding. Practically, however, the equality does not hold in real-world systems.

The Slepian–Wolf theorem can be also applied in the problem of source coding with decoder side information (Figure 22.1b). Specifically, if the sequence $X$ is correlated with the sequence $Y$, which is available only at the decoder, but not at the encoder, the achievable rate for sequence $X$ is $R_X \geq H(X|Y)$. Thus, even though the encoder does not have access to the correlated sequence $Y$, it can compress source $X$ as if $Y$ were available at the encoder. However, the Slepian–Wolf theorem does not provide a practical implementation of the described system.

Biometric authentication can be formulated as a source coding with decoder side information problem if we consider the gallery and the probe signals as the random variables $X$ and $Y$, respectively. This is logical since the probe and the gallery signals are correlated and the probe is only available at the decoder (authentication) side. The architecture of the proposed biometric authentication method is illustrated in Figure 22.2. Let $x$ be the original representation of the biometric trait $b$ at the enrollment stage at time $t$.[1] In general, the probe and gallery data are not identical even in the case of client transactions due to time-related modifications in the biometric pattern, its presentation, and the sensor which captures the raw biometric data. The noise in the biometric signal $b'$ can be modeled by a (virtual) additive noise (or correlation) channel which induces noise $w$. Thus, at the authentication stage, which takes place at time $t'$, the biometric system needs to detect whether the input signal $y = x + w$ comes from a genuine or an impostor user.

This model is analogous to data communication over noisy channels and is similar to the notion that Slepian–Wolf coding protects $X$ for "transmission" over the (virtual) noise channel. At the decoder, $Y$ is regarded as if it were $X$ after transmission over

---

[1] Throughout this chapter, capital symbols will denote stochastic sequences and lowercase symbols will denote their respective realizations.

Enrollment

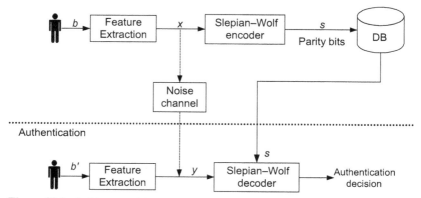

**Figure 22.2.** Architecture of the proposed authentication system based on channel codes.

the noise channel, and corrects it using error correcting codes. Let the noise induced by the channel be denoted by $W$, then

$$Y = X + W. \tag{22.4}$$

In the proposed system, the extracted biometric features are encoded using a Slepian–Wolf encoder at the enrollment stage. The biometric signature, which is stored in the database of the system, consists only of the parity bits $s$ of the generated codeword. In this way, access to the parity bits cannot reveal information about the original biometric data, and the privacy of templates is ensured.

At the authentication stage, the biometric signal $y$ comprises the systematic part of the bitstream and along with the parity bits of the claimed identity form a codeword that is decoded by the channel decoder. Intuitively, the noise $w_g$ induced by the channel in case of genuine transactions is small, whereas the noise $w_i$ in impostor transactions is relatively large. Thus, the channel decoder can decode the codeword only when the induced noise is small and the error is within the correcting capabilities of the channel code. Otherwise, if the noise of the channel corrupts the signal, the resulting codeword cannot be decoded and the transaction is rejected as unauthorized. Thus, the problem reduces to the estimation of the noise channel statistics and the exploitation of this a priori information at the channel decoder. If the selected error correcting code is suitable for error protection on this channel, the decoder will decode $X$ errorlessly.

Considering the above, the design of the system involves two critical parameters:

- The error correcting performance of the channel code.
- The level of security of the biometric template $s$.

On one hand, an encoder of high rate generates more parity bits, which increases the security of the template but also increases the risk of rejecting a genuine user. On the other hand, a low rate encoder exhibits limited error-correcting capabilities and reduces the security of the system. Thus, the design of an effective biometric system based on the channel codes involves the careful selection of the channel code rate to achieve the optimal trade-off between performance and security.

Besides the channel code rate, the error-correcting capabilities of the channel decoder also depend on the information of the noise channel and the relationship between the noise induced by the channel and the side information $y$. Accurate modeling of the distribution of the noise channel may improve the knowledge of the channel decoder, as will be analyzed in Section 22.5.3.

It must be noted that the proposed biometric authentication framework can be used with any biometric trait, provided that a robust feature extraction method exists. As a case study, a gait recognition system is developed based on the proposed framework in this chapter. The feature extraction process of the gait sequences is briefly presented in the following section.

## 22.4  GAIT REPRESENTATION

Gait recognition has emerged as a very tempting approach for unobtrusive real-time authentication method during the last years. Many methods have been proposed in the literature for the efficient representation of the human walking. These methods can be categorized into feature-based and model-based techniques. The former do not use any specific model of the human body for gait analysis [12–17], while the latter study static and dynamic body parameters [18–21] of the human locomotion.

In this chapter, three novel feature-based techniques are used for feature extraction. Two of them are based on the generalized Radon Transform, namely the Radial Integration Transform (RIT) and the Circular Integration Transform (CIT), which have been proven to provide a full analytical representation of the human silhouette using a few coefficients. The third technique is based on the Krawtchouk moments that are well known for their compactness and discrimination capability. It should be noted that the use of moments for shape identification has received increased attention [22, 23] recently. Shutler and Nixon [23] proposed the use of Zernike velocity moments to describe and analyze the motion throughout a gait sequence. Motivated by the successful use of these continuous orthogonal moments, a set of discrete orthogonal moments based on Krawtchouk moments are presented, which have been proven to offer reliable reconstruction of the original image using relatively low-order moments [24].

Since the exact description of the gait recognition system is out of the scope of this chapter, only a brief discussion is provided for sake of self-completeness in the Appendix. The interested readers are referred to reference 13 for additional details on the features for gait representation.

## 22.5  DISTRIBUTED SOURCE CODING FOR GAIT RECOGNITION

When the features for the representation of gait are extracted, the distributed source coding framework of Section 22.3 can be applied. The biometric system is divided in two stages: (a) the enrollment stage and (b) the authentication stage, which are further analyzed below.

## 22.5.1  Enrollment Stage

At the enrollment stage, the signature of the gait sequence is extracted, as described in Section 22.4. The extracted features are concatenated and form the vector $\mathbf{x} = [x_1, \ldots, x_k]^T$, thus $\mathbf{x} \in \mathbb{R}^k$. The feature vector $\mathbf{x}$ must be transformed from the continuous to the discrete domain so that it can be further processed by the channel encoder. This mapping can be represented by a uniform quantizer with $2^L$ levels. Each component of $\mathbf{x}$ is then mapped to an index in the set $\mathcal{Q}$, through the function $Q : \mathbb{R}^k \to \mathcal{Q}^k$, where $\mathcal{Q} = \{0, 1, \ldots, L - 1\}$. The resulting vector $\mathbf{q} = Q(\mathbf{x})$ is fed to the Slepian–Wolf encoder, which performs the mapping $e : \mathcal{Q}^k \to \mathcal{C}^n$, where $\mathcal{C} = \{0, 1\}$ and outputs the codeword $\mathbf{c} = e(\mathbf{q}), \mathbf{c} \in \mathcal{C}^n$.

In this work, the Slepian–Wolf encoder is implemented by a systematic LDPC encoder [25]. LDPC codes were selected due to their excellent error detecting and correcting capabilities. They also provide near-capacity performance over a large range of channels while simultaneously admitting implementable decoders. An LDPC code $(n, k)$ is a linear block code of codeword length $n$ and information block length $k$ which is defined by a sparse $(n - k) \times n$ parity matrix $H$, where $n - k$ denotes the parity bits produced by the encoder. The code rate is defined as $r = k/n$. A code is a systematic code if every codeword consists of the original $k$-bit information vector followed by $n - k$ parity bits. In the proposed system, the joint bit-plane encoding scheme of reference 26 was employed to avoid encoding and storing the $L$ bit-planes of the vector $\mathbf{q}$ separately. Alternatively, LDPC codes in a high-order Galois field could be employed, but binary LDPC codes (GF(2)) were selected due to ease of implementation.

Subsequently, the $k$ systematic bits of the codeword $\mathbf{c}$ are discarded and only the parity bits $\mathbf{s}$—that is, the $n - k$ parity bits of the codeword $\mathbf{c}$—are stored to the biometric database. Thus, the biometric template of an enrolled user consists of the parity bits $\mathbf{s}, \mathbf{s} \in \mathcal{C}^{(n-k)}$ and its size is $n - k$.

## 22.5.2  Authentication Stage

At the authentication stage, a user claims an identity $\mathcal{I}$, a new signature is extracted from the biometric features, and the vector $\mathbf{y} = [y_1, \ldots, y_k]^T, \mathbf{y} \in \mathbb{R}^k$, is constructed. The vector $\mathbf{y}$, which forms the side information corresponding to $\mathbf{x}$, is fed to the LDPC decoder. The decoding function $d : \mathcal{C}^{(n-k)} \times \mathbb{R}^k \to \mathcal{Q}^k$ combines $\mathbf{y}$ with the parity $\mathbf{s}$ which is retrieved from the biometric database and corresponds to the claimed identity $\mathcal{I}$. The decoder employs belief-propagation [27] to decode the received codewords.

If the errors introduced in the side information $\mathbf{y}$ with regard to the originally encoded signal $\mathbf{x}$ are within the error-correcting capabilities of the channel decoder, then the correct codeword is output after a number of iterations and the transaction is considered as a client transaction. Thus, the output of the LDPC decoder is the quantized vector $\hat{q} = d(s, y)$. Note that the exact reconstruction of the quantized feature vector $q = Q(x)$ is required; that is, $q = \hat{q}$. Otherwise, if the decoder cannot decode the codeword (which is indicated if the number of iterations increases over a specific number $N_{iter}$), a special symbol $\varnothing$ is output and the transaction is considered as an impostor transaction.

## 22.5.3  Noise Channel Modeling for Gait Sequences

The LDPC channel decoder uses Belief–Propagation, an iterative algorithm based on a soft-decoding approach to retrieve the original codeword. The decoder tries to compute the a posteriori probability that a given bit in the transmitted codeword equals 0 given the received side information $y$. Thus, the confidence level of each bit $c_i$ in the codeword $c$ is defined by the log-likelihood ratio as

$$\text{LLR}(c_i) = \log \left( \frac{P(x_i = 0 | Y = y)}{P(x_i = 1 | Y = y)} \right). \tag{22.5}$$

The critical point in the operation of the described system is the efficient modeling of the dependency between the side information $Y$ and the original signal $X$. From Eq. (22.4), it follows that the noise $W$ that is induced by the (virtual) dependency channel to the measured biometric signal during the authentication stage $W = Y - X$.

Empirically, the Cauchy distribution is employed to model the probability mass function of the residual signal $W$ in genuine transactions and the uniform distribution for the impostor transactions:

$$f_W(w) = \begin{cases} \dfrac{1}{\pi} \dfrac{\mu}{\mu^2 + w^2}, & \text{genuine transactions,} \\ c, & \text{impostor transactions,} \end{cases}$$

where $\mu$ and $c$ are probability distribution parameters. Let $X_i$ be the $i$th bit of the value $X$ and let $A_0$ be the set of $x$ values that have $i$th bit equal to zero; then, the probability that $X_i$ is equal to 0 is given by

$$p(X_i = 0 | Y = y) = \sum_{x \in A_0} \frac{1}{\pi} \frac{\mu}{\mu^2 + (y - x)^2}. \tag{22.6}$$

The parameter $\mu$ is estimated by plotting the residual histogram for several transactions. Figure 22.3 illustrates the components of the RIT feature vector at the enrollment stage, and at the authentication stage for a genuine (green line) and an impostor user (red line). The graphical representation of the components of the residual signal $w$ for the genuine and impostor users is illustrated in Figures 22.4a and 22.4b, respectively. Similarly, the coefficients of the CIT and the Krawtchouk feature vectors are illustrated in Figures 22.5 and 22.6. Also, the distribution of the CIT and Krawtchouk feature vectors for the genuine and impostor transactions is depicted in Figures 22.7 and 22.8.

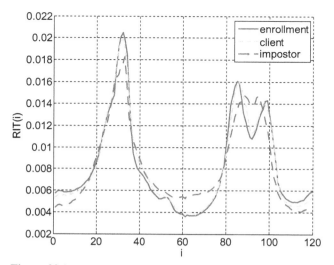

**Figure 22.3.** Graphical representation of the RIT feature vector.

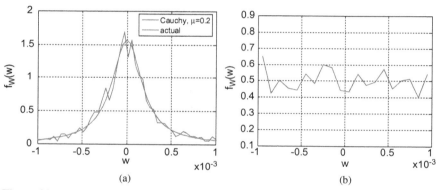

**Figure 22.4.** Probability distribution of the components of the residual signal **w** of the RIT feature vector for **(a)** a client user and **(b)** an impostor user.

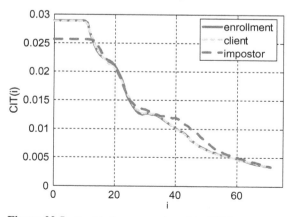

**Figure 22.5.** Graphical representation of the CIT feature vector.

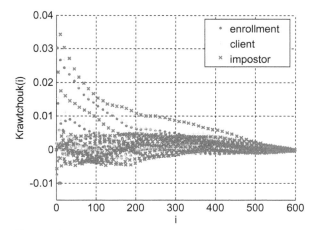

**Figure 22.6.** Graphical representation of the Krawtchouk feature vector.

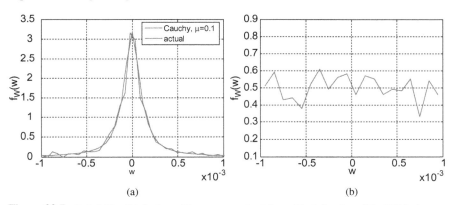

**Figure 22.7.** Probability distribution of the components of the residual signal **w** of the CIT feature vector for (**a**) a client user and (**b**) an impostor user.

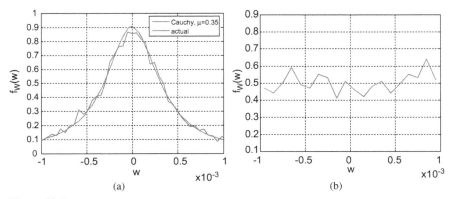

**Figure 22.8.** Probability distribution of the components of the residual signal **w** of the Krawtchouk feature vector for (**a**) a client user and (**b**) an impostor user.

It must be noted that this type of distribution is expected since, on one hand, the features from client sequences differ slightly from the enrolled features, while the features from impostor sequences differ arbitrarily. The decoder tries to decode the input codeword assuming the client model and the impostor model, successively.

## 22.6    EXPERIMENTAL RESULTS

### 22.6.1    Database Description

The validity of the proposed method was evaluated on a large-scale proprietary database acquired within the course of the HUMABIO project [28]. This is the first database that has depth data for assisted gait recognition. It was captured in an indoor environment and consists of people walking in a predefined path in a front-parallel view from the camera. This database was designed to assist in the gait recognition problem creating a large data set in an indoor environment. The main course of walking is around 6 m, and the distance from the camera varies from 4 m to 6 m. The database consists of 75 subjects. For each subject, four different conditions were captured: (a) the "normal" condition (N), (b) the "shoe" condition in which the users wear a different shoe type (slipper) (S), (c) the "hat" condition in which the users wear a hat (H), and (d) the "briefcase" condition in which the users carry a briefcase (B). The "normal" set was was used as the gallery set, and the other sets were considered as the probe tests.

### 22.6.2    Authentication Results

In an authentication scenario (or verification), the biometric system is used to grant access to individuals. Initially a subject claims his/her identity and the gait system compares the signature with the stored one in the database. Then, based on the authentication procedure, the system establishes whether the identity of the user is the claimed one. In this respect, authentication results in a one-to-one comparison and is quite different from the identification scenario, in which the system has to determine the identity of users by comparing the measured data with all the enrolled data in the database (one-to-many comparison).

Regarding the features for the gait representation, the parameter $\Delta\theta$ was selected equal to $3°$, as suggested in previous work on gait recognition [13]. Thus, the feature vector of the RIT component consists of 120 coefficients. For the CIT component $\Delta\rho = 1$, which results in 72 coefficients. Finally, the Krawtchouk feature vector consists of 600 coefficient. As a result, the concatenated feature vector that is fed to the LDPC encoder consists of 792 (120 + 72 + 600) coefficients. For the channel coding, a modified version of the Radford–Neal package was used [29] and systematic channel codes of various rates are produced.

Figure 22.9 reports the performance results of the gait recognition system for the "*shoe*" experiment as a function of the security using the proposed scheme for the

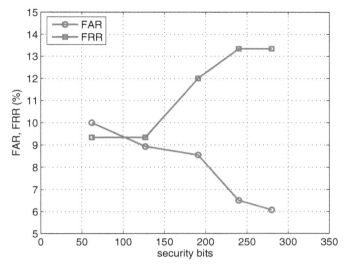

**Figure 22.9.** FRR and FAR of the "*shoe*" experiment as a function of the security bits.

protection of the templates. Thus, the horizontal axis represents the numbers of the parity bits, while the vertical axis represents the false rejection rate (FAR). Specifically, if a rate $r$ LDPC code is used, then the template **s** contains $792 \cdot (1 - r)/r$ bits. The more bits used for the template, the more secure is the template since it is more difficult to be broken. On the other hand, increasing the size of the template increases the sensitivity of the system, which results in more authentication failures of legitimate users (higher FRR). The reported results are also compared with the method presented in reference 13. Furthermore, Figure 22.9 illustrates the performance of the proposed system in terms of false acceptance rate (FAR) and the security of the biometric template **s**. For sake of brevity, the figures for the two other experiments, "hat" and "briefcase," are omitted.

It is clear that when more security bits are used (low code rate $r$), the system rejects more transactions as impostor transactions. Thus, the FRR is increased, while the FAR is decreased. Thus, it is obvious that the performance of the system can be adjusted according to the desired performance in terms of verification accuracy.

Furthermore, the proposed system was compared with state-of-the-art methods that perform authentication based on conventional pattern matching methods. The method presented in reference 13 was selected for comparison since it is the only method that performs classification in the HUMABIO database by exploiting depth data. The channel code rate of the proposed system is varied to achieve different operating points that approximate the performance of reference 13. The resulting rate operating characteristic (ROC) curve, which presents the verification rate (1-FRR) versus the FAR, is illustrated in Figure 22.10. It can be easily observed that the proposed scheme achieves substantially better performance while at the same time

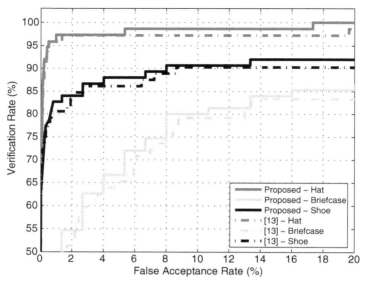

**Figure 22.10.** ROC curves for comparison of the scheme of reference 13 with the proposed scheme using variable channel code rate.

providing security to the enrolled templates. The gain in recognition performance is approximately 1–3% in all the conditions. The critical point for the effective performance of the system is mainly the effective modeling of the (virtual) noise channel as discussed in Section 22.5.3.

## 22.7  DISCUSSION

In this chapter, a novel approach for the formation of the biometric recognition problem as a distributed source coding problem was introduced. A virtual dependency channel was assumed to model the correlation between the biometric data at the enrollment and the authentication stage. In this respect, biometric recognition is regarded as a problem of source coding with side information at the decoder. As a case study, a framework for gait recognition was developed. Initially, the use of depth data was employed to enhance the silhouette segmentation algorithm and acquire more accurate features. Then, the features used for the representation of gait sequences were discussed in detail. Three quite discriminative features were extracted: RIT, CIT, and Krawtchouk. Subsequently, the integration of these features in the distributed source coding framework was described in a thorough analysis about the trade-off between security and performance of the biometric system. The experimental results validate the proposed method and demonstrate that the security of the stored templates can be increased only at a negligible penalty in performance. Future work should concentrate on the quantification of security in a more rigorous way and on the modeling of the virtual dependency channel with more accurate models.

(a)                    (b)

**Figure A.1.** Extracted silhouettes: (a) Binary silhouette and (b) geodesic silhouette.

## APPENDIX A: GENERALIZED RADON TRANSFORMATIONS

The first step in human movement analysis is the extraction of the walking subject's silhouette from the input image sequence. In the proposed framework, 2.5D information is available since the gait sequence is captured by a stereoscopic camera. Using Delaunay triangulation on the 2.5D data, a 3D triangulated hull of the silhouette is generated and is further processed using the 3D Geodesic Transform [30], thus generating the final normalized silhouettes $\tilde{S}_G(x, y)$. Figure A.1 depicts (a) a binary silhouette and (b) the corresponding geodesic silhouette.

For the representation of human gait sequences the Generalized Radon transforms, namely the Radial Integration Transform (RIT) and the Circular Integration Transform (CIT) are employed. These transforms are used, due to their aptitude to represent meaningful shape characteristics [31–33]. In particular, the RIT of a function $f(x, y)$ is defined as the integral of $f(x, y)$ in the direction of a straight line starting from the point $(x_0, y_0)$ and forming angle $\theta$ with the horizontal axis (Figure A.2). The

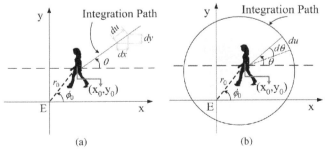

(a)                              (b)

**Figure A.2.** Applying the Radial Integration Transform and the Circular Integration Transform on a silhouette image.

coefficients for each $\theta$ are given by [31]

$$\text{RIT}_f(\theta) = \int_{0}^{+\infty} f(x_0 + u \cos \theta, y_0 + u \sin \theta) \, du, \tag{A.1}$$

where $u$ is the distance from the starting point $(x_0, y_0)$.

Practically, since there are an infinite number of angles $\theta$, the RIT transform is computed in steps of $\Delta\theta$. The angle step $\Delta\theta$ affects the level of detail of the transform. In the presented approach, the discrete form of the RIT transform is used:

$$\text{RIT}(t\Delta\theta) = \frac{1}{J} \sum_{j=1}^{J} \tilde{S}_G(x_0 + j\Delta u \cdot \cos(t\Delta\theta), y_0 + j\Delta u \cdot \sin(t\Delta\theta)), \tag{A.2}$$

where $t = 1, \ldots, T$, $\Delta u$ and $\Delta\theta$ are the constant step sizes of the distance $(u)$ and angle $(\theta)$, $J$ is the number of silhouette pixels that coincides with the line that has orientation $\theta$ and are positioned between the center of the silhouette and the end of the silhouette in that direction, $\tilde{S}_G$ represents the corresponding normalized binary silhouette image, and finally $T = 360°/\Delta\theta$.

In a similar manner, Circular Integration Transform (CIT) is defined as the integral of a function $f(x, y)$ along a circle curve $h(\rho)$ with center $(x_0, y_0)$ and radius $\rho$ and is given by

$$CIT_f(\rho) = \oint_{h(\rho)} f(x_0 + \rho \cos \theta, y_0 + \rho \sin \theta) \, du$$

$$= \int_{0}^{2\pi} f(x_0 + \rho \cos \theta, y_0 + \rho \sin \theta) \rho \, d\theta, \tag{A.3}$$

where $du$ is the arc length over the integration path and $d\theta$ is the corresponding angle.

The center of the silhouette is again used as the origin for the CIT feature extractor. The discrete form of CIT, as illustrated in Figure A.2, is given by

$$\text{CIT}(k\Delta\rho) = \frac{1}{T} \sum_{t=1}^{T} \tilde{S}_G(x_0 + k\Delta\rho \cdot \cos(t\Delta\theta), y_0 + k\Delta\rho \cdot \sin(t\Delta\theta), \tag{A.4}$$

where $k = 1, \ldots, K$, $\Delta\rho$ and $\Delta\theta$ are the constant step sizes of the radius and angle variables, $k\Delta\rho$ is the radius of the smallest circle that encloses the binary silhouette image *Sil*, and $T = 360°/\Delta\theta$.

Let $\alpha$ denote the scaling of a silhouette $S$ in both directions. Then the RIT and CIT of the scaled $S'(x, y)$ is easily found to be [31]

$$\text{RIT}_{S'}(\theta) = \alpha \cdot \text{RIT}_S(\theta), \tag{A.5}$$

$$\text{CIT}_{S'}(\rho) = \alpha \cdot \text{CIT}_S\left(\frac{1}{\alpha}\rho\right). \tag{A.6}$$

Otherwise stated, the RIT amplitude of the scaled silhouette image is only multiplied by the factor $\alpha$, while the CIT of the scaled image is scaled by $\alpha$ factor and its amplitude is also multiplied by $\alpha$. Hence, image scaling can affect the performance of the proposed technique. For this reason, all gait sequences are normalized before feature extraction, in order to overcome this scaling problem.

## APPENDIX B: ORTHOGONAL DISCRETE TRANSFORM BASED ON KRAWTCHOUK MOMENTS

Human gait can be also represented using a novel set of orthogonal moments based on the discrete classical weighted Krawtchouk polynomials [24]. These moments ensure minimal information redundancy due to their orghogonality and are mostly used to extract local shape characteristics of images. In the proposed gait system, the weighted Krawtchouk moments $Q_{nm}$ of order $(n + m)$ are estimated using the Krawtchouk polynomials for a silhouette image with intensity function $\tilde{S}_G(x, y)$ as follows:

$$Q_{nm} = \sum_{x=0}^{N-1} \sum_{y=0}^{M-1} \bar{K}_n(x; p_1, N - 1) * \bar{K}_m(y; p_2, M - 1) \cdot \tilde{S}_G(x, y), \quad (B.1)$$

$$\bar{K}_n(x; p, N) = K_n(x; p, N)\sqrt{\frac{w(x; p, N)}{\rho(n; p, N)}}, \quad (B.2)$$

where $\bar{K}_n$, $\bar{K}_m$ are the weighted Krawtchouk polynomials, and $(N - 1) \times (M - 1)$ represents the pixel size of the silhouette image. Figure B.1 shows a graphical representation of the reconstructed silhouette images using different orders of the width $N$ and the height $M$.

Krawtchouk moments can be used to extract local shape characteristics of the images by varying the parameters $N$ and $M$. Larger $N$ provides more information on the silhouette image in the horizontal axis, whereas the parameter $M$ extracts local shape information of the silhouette image in the vertical axis. For the experiments, values for $N = R/15$ and $M = C/3$ were used, where $R$ and $C$ denote the number of

**Figure B.1.** Reconstruction of silhouette images using Krawtchouk moments for various moment order values $(N, M)$, **(a)** Original silhouette ($W \times H = 188 \times 200$). **(b)** $N = W/10$, $M = H/4$, **(c)** $N = W/10$, $M = H/16$, **(d)** $N = W/30$, $M = H/2$ and **(e)** $N = W/15$, M=H/3.

rows and columns of the silhouette image, respectively. With these parameter values a satisfactory reconstruction of the initial silhouette image can be achieved as illustrated in Figure B.1e. The Krawtchouk transform is suitable for feature extraction due to its high discriminative power [24, 34]. The proposed Krawtchouk transformation is scale and rotation dependent. To remedy this issue, silhouette sequences are pre-scaled and aligned to the center; thus the Krawtchouk transform is unaffected by scaling. Furthermore, it should be noted that the input gait sequences are captured in a near fronto-parallel view and thus rotation does not affect the results of the Krawtchouk transform.

## REFERENCES

1. U. Uludag, S. Pankanti, S. Prabhakar, and A. Jain, Biometric cryptosystems: Issues and challenges, *Proc. IEEE* **92**(6):948–960, 2004.
2. G. I. Davida, Y. Frankel, and B. J. Matt, On enabling secure applications through off-line biometric identification, *Proceedings of the IEEE Symposium on Security and Privacy*, 1998.
3. A. Juels, and M. Sudan, A fuzzy vault scheme, *Proceedings of the International Symposium on Information Theory*, 2002.
4. J. D. Slepian, and J. K. Wolf, Noiseless coding of correlated information sources, *IEEE Trans. Inf. Theory* **19**:471–480, 1973.
5. E. Martinian, S. Yekhanin, and J. Yedidia, Secure biometrics via syndromes, in *43rd Annual Allerton Conference on Communications, Control, and Computing*, 2006.
6. S. C. Draper, A. Khisti, E. Martinian, A. Vetro, and J. Yedidia, Using distributed source coding to secure fingerprint biometrics, *IEEE International Conference on Acoustics, Speech and Signal Processing*, 2007.
7. G. Cohen and G. Zemor, Generalized coset schemes for the wire-tap channel: Application to biometrics, *International Symposium on Information Theory*, 2004.
8. A. Wyner, The wire-tap channel, *Bell Syst. Tech. J. 54*.
9. E. Martinian, Authenticating multimedia in the presence of noise, Master's thesis, MIT, Cambridge, MA, 2000.
10. S. S. Pradhan, and K. Ramchandran, Distributed source coding using syndromes (DISCUS): Design and construction, *IEEE Trans. Inf. Theory* **49**:626–643, 2003.
11. B. Girod, AM Aaron, S. Rane, and D. Rebollo-Monedero, Distributed video coding, *Proc. IEEE* **93**:71–83, 2005.
12. P. J. Phillips, S. Sarkar, S. I. R. Vega, P. Grother, and K. W. Bowyer, The gait identification challenge problem: data sets and baseline algorithm. *Proceedings of the International Conference in Pattern on Recognition*, 2002.
13. D. Ioannidis, D. Tzovaras, I. G. Damousis, S. Argyropoulos, and K. Moustakas, Gait recognition using compact feature extraction transforms and depth information, in *IEEE Trans. Inf. Forens. Secur.* **2**:623–630, 2007.
14. A. Kale, N. Cuntoor, A. N. Rajagopalan, B. Yegnanarayana, and R. Chellappa, Gait analysis for human identification, *Proceedings of 3rd International Conference on Audio and Video Based Person Authentication*, 2003.
15. A. Kale, A. Sundaresan, A. N. Rajagopalan, N. P. Cuntoor, A. K. Roy-Chowdhury, V. Kruger, and R. Chellappa, Identification of humans using gait, *IEEE Trans. Image Processing*, **13**:1163–1173, 2004.
16. N. V. Boulgouris, K. N. Plataniotis, and D. Hatzinakos, An angular transform of gait sequences for gait assisted recognition, in *Proceedings of the IEEE International Conference on Image Processing*, 2004.

17. N. V. Boulgouris, K. N. Plataniotis, and D. Hatzinakos, Gait recognition using linear time normalization, *Pattern Recognit.* **39**:969–979, 2006.

18. A. Johnson and A. Bobick, A multi-view method for gait recognition using static body parameters, *3rd International Conference on Audio and Video-Based Biometric Person Authentication*, 2001.

19. L. Wang, H. Ning, T. Tan, and W. Hu, Fusion of static and dynamic body biometrics for gait recognition, *IEEE Trans. Circuits Syst. Video Technol.* **14**:149–158, 2004.

20. D. Cunado, M. S. Nixon, and J. N. Carter, Automatic extraction and description of human gait models for recognition purposes, *Comput. Vis. Image Understanding* **90**:1–41, 2003.

21. H. Lu, K. N. Plataniotis, and A. N. Venetsanopoulos, A full-body layered deformable model for automatic model-based gait recognition. *EURASIP J. Adv. Signal Processing* **2008**, article ID 261317, 2008.

22. L. Lee and W. E. L. Grimson, Gait analysis for recognition and classification, in *Proceedings of the IEEE International Conference on Automatic Face and Gesture Recognition*, 2006.

23. J. Shutler and M. S. Nixon, Zernike velocity moments for sequence-based description of moving features, *Image Vis. Comput.* **24**(4):343–356, 2006.

24. P. T. Yap, R. Paramesran, and S. H. Ong, Image analysis by Krawtchouk moments, *IEEE Trans. Image Processing* **12**:1367–1377, 2003.

25. R. G. Gallager (1963). *Low-Density Parity-Check Codes,* MIT Press, Cambridge, MA.

26. D. P. Varodayan, A. Mavlankar, M. Flierl, and B. Girod, Distributed grayscale stereo image coding with unsupervised learning of disparity, *Proceedings of the Data Compression Conference*, Snowbird, UT, 2007, pp. 143–152.

27. W. E. Ryan, An introduction to LDPC codes, *CRC Handbook for Coding and Signal Processing for Recording Systems*, CRC Press, Boca Raton, FL, 2005.

28. I. G. Damousis and D. Tzovaras, Combined use of behavioural and physiological biometrics for human authentication—The HUMABIO Project, *IEEE EMBS 4th pHealth Conference*, 2007.

29. N. Radford, Software for low density parity check (LDPC) codes, *http://www.cs.toronto.edu/ radford/ldpc.software.html*.

30. D. Ioannidis, D. Tzovaras, and K. Moustakas, Gait identification using the 3D protrusion transform, in *IEEE International Conference on Image Processing*, San Antonio, TX, 2007, pp. 349–352.

31. D. Simitopoulos, D. E. Koutsonanos, and M. G. Strintzis, Robust image watermarking based on generalized Radon transformations, *IEEE Trans. Circuits Syst. Video Technol.* **13**:732–745, 2003.

32. P. Daras, D. Zarpalas, D. Tzovaras, and M. G. Strintzis, Efficient 3-D model search and retrieval using generalized 3-D radon transforms, *IEEE Trans. Multimedia* **8**:101–114, 2006.

33. N. V. Boulgouris and Z. X. Chi, Gait recognition using radon transform and linear discriminant analysis, *IEEE Trans. Image Processing* **16**:731–740, 2007.

34. A. Mademlis, A. Axenopoulos, P. Daras, D. Tzovaras, and M. G. Strintzis, 3D content-based search based on 3D Krawtchouk moments, in Proc. of the Third International Symposium on 3D Data Processing, Visualization, and Transmission, Chapel Hill, NC, Jun. 2006, pp. 743–749.

# Chapter 23

# Measuring Information Content in Biometric Features

Richard Youmaran and Andy Adler

## 23.1 INTRODUCTION

How much information is there in a face or in a fingerprint? This question is related to many issues in biometric technology. For example, one of the most common biometric questions is that of uniqueness—for example, to what extent are fingerprints unique? From the point of view of identifiability, one may be interested in how much identifying information is available from a given technology, such as video surveillance. In the context of biometric fusion [1], one would like to be able to quantify (a) the biometric information in each system individually and (b) the potential gain from fusing the systems. Additionally, such a measure is relevant to biometric cryptosystems and privacy measures. Several authors have presented approaches relevant to this question. For example, Wayman [2] introduced a set of statistical approaches to measure the separability of Gaussian feature distributions using a "cotton ball model." Another approach was developed by Daugman [3] to measure the information content of iris images based on the discrimination entropy [4], calculated directly from the match score distributions. Also, Golfarelli et al. [5] showed that the most commonly used feature representations of handgeometry and face biometrics have a limited number of distinguishable patterns, on the order of $10^5$ and $10^3$, respectively, as measured by a theoretical estimate of the equal error rate. Other authors have used information-theoretic approaches, such as the approach of Ross and Jain [1] to biometric fusion. However, none of these methods approach measurement of information content of biometric data from an information-theoretic point of view.

*Biometrics: Theory, Methods, and Applications.* Edited by Boulgouris, Plataniotis, and Micheli-Tzanakou

In this work, we elaborate an approach to address this question based on definitions from information theory [6]. We define the term "biometric information" as follows:

> *Biometric information (BI):* The decrease in uncertainty about the identity of a person due to a set of biometric features measurements.

In order to interpret this definition, we refer to two instants: (1) before a biometric measurement, $t_0$, at which time we only know a person $p$ is part of a population $q$, which may be the whole planet; and (2) after receiving a set of measurements, $t_1$, we have more information and less uncertainty about the person's identity.

$BI$ may be used to answer two different types of questions. First, given a set of measurements from a specific person, we want to know how identifiable that individual is in a population. This is the individual biometric information ($IBI$). Second, given a system that makes biometric measurements, such as fingerprint minutiae or eigenfaces, we want to know, on average, how distinguishable people are in the population, using those biometric features. This is the system biometric information ($SBI$). The difference is that $IBI$ is the information of an individual features and $SBI$ is the average information over the population.

In order to motivate our approach, we initially consider the properties that such a measure should have. Consider a soft biometric system that measures height and weight; furthermore, assume that all humans are uniformly and independently distributed in height between 100 and 200 cm and in weight between 100 and 200 lb. If a person's features were completely stable and could be measured with infinite accuracy, people could be uniquely identified from these measurements, and the biometric features could be considered to yield infinite information. However, in reality, repeated biometric measurements give different results due to measurement inaccuracies and to short- and long-term changes in the biometric features themselves. If this variability results in an uncertainty of $\pm 5$ cm and $\pm 5$ lb, one simple model would be to round each measure to $105, 115, \ldots, 195$. In this case, there are $10 \times 10$ equiprobable outcomes and an information content of $\log_2(100) = 6.6$ bits.

Such an analysis is intrinsically tied to a choice of biometric features. Thus, our approach does not allow us to answer "how much information is in a fingerprint?" but only "how much information is in the position and angle data of fingerprint minutiae?" Furthermore, for many biometrics, it is not clear what the underlying features are. Face images, for example, can be described by image basis features or landmark based features [7]. To overcome this, we may choose to calculate the information in all possible features. In the example, we may provide height in inches as well as in centimeters; however, in this case, a good measure of information must not increase with such redundant data.

This work also develops a new approach to measuring biometric image quality. Biometric sample quality is a measure of the usefulness of a biometric image [8]. One recent development is the significant level of interest in standards for measurement of biometric quality. For example, ISO has recently established a biometric sample quality draft standard [8]. According to reference 8, biometric sample quality may be considered from the point of view of character (inherent features), fidelity (accuracy of features), or utility (predicted biometrics performance). A general consensus has developed that the most important measure of a quality metric is its utility—images evaluated as higher quality must be those that result in better identification of individuals, as measured by an increased separation of genuine and impostor match score distributions. The nature of biometric sample fidelity has seen little investigation, although for specific biometric modalities, algorithms to measure biometric quality have been proposed. For example, the NFIQ algorithm [9] is a widely used measure for fingerprint image quality.

One current difficulty is that there is no consensus as to what a measure of biometric sample fidelity should give. In this work, we propose a new approach to measure this quantity, based on an information theoretic framework. We begin with the intuitive observation that a high-quality biometric image is more useful to identify the individual than is a low-quality image. This suggests that the quantity of identifiable information decreases with a reduction in quality. Given a way to measure the decrease in information caused by a given image degradation, one can measure the associated decrease in biometric information.

In this chapter, we develop a mathematical framework to measure biometric feature information in a given system for a set of biometric features. This work is based on the our previous work on this topic [6, 10]. We address ill-conditioning in the measurements using distribution modeling and regularization. We then use this algorithm to analyze the biometric information content of two different face recognition algorithms and then define the information loss due to a degradation in image quality.

## 23.2  THEORETICAL FRAMEWORK

In this section we develop an algorithm to calculate biometric information based on a set of features, using the relative entropy measure [4]. We then measure the effect of an image degradation model on biometric image quality. We explain our method in the following steps: (1) measure requirements, (2) relative entropy of biometric features, (3) Gaussian models for biometric features and relative entropy calculations, (4) regularization methods for degenerate features, (5) regularization methods for insufficient data, and (6) information loss due to degradation.

### 23.2.1  Requirements for Biometric Feature Information

In order to elaborate the requirements that a good measure of biometric feature information must have, we consider the system that measures height and weight. These values differ within the global population, but also vary for a given individual, both due to variations in the features themselves and to measurement inaccuracies. We now wish to consider the properties a measure of biometric feature information should have:

1. If an intra-person distribution $p$ is exactly equal to the inter-person $q$ distribution, then there is no information to distinguish a person, and biometric feature information is zero.

2. As the feature measurement becomes more accurate (less variability), then it is easier to distinguish someone in the population and the biometric information increases.

3. If a person has unusual feature values (i.e., far from the population mean), they become more distinguishable, and their biometric feature information will be larger.

4. The biometric information of uncorrelated features should be the sum of the biometric information of each individual feature.

5. Features that are unrelated to identity should not increase biometric information. For example, if a biometric system accurately measured the direction a person was facing, information on identity would be unchanged.

6. Correlated features such as height and weight are less informative. In an extreme example, consider the height in inches and in centimeters. Clearly, these two features are no more informative than a single value (except perhaps a reduction in noise from the averaging of repeated measurements).

Based on this definition, the most appropriate information-theoretic measure for the biometric feature information is the relative entropy $(D(p\|q))$ [4] between the intra- $(p(\mathbf{x}))$ and inter-person $(q(\mathbf{x}))$ biometric feature distributions. $D(p\|q)$, or the Kullback–Leibler distance, is defined as the measure of the information gain in moving from a prior distribution $q(\mathbf{x})$ to a posterior distribution $p(\mathbf{x})$, or to be the "extra bits" of information needed to represent $p(\mathbf{x})$ with respect to $q(\mathbf{x})$. $D(p\|q)$ is defined to be

$$D(p\|q) = \int_{\mathbf{x}} p(\mathbf{x}) \log_2 \frac{p(\mathbf{x})}{q(\mathbf{x})} \, d\mathbf{x}, \tag{23.1}$$

where the integral is over all feature dimensions, $\mathbf{x}$. $p(\mathbf{x})$ is the probability mass function or distribution of features of an individual, and $q(\mathbf{x})$ is the overall population distribution. A comment on notation: We use $p$ to refer to both an individual person and the distribution of the person's features, while $q$ represents the population and the distribution of its features.

This measure can be motivated as follows: The relative entropy, $D(p\|q)$, is the extra information required to describe a distribution $p(\mathbf{x})$ based on an assumed distribution $q(\mathbf{x})$ [4]. $D(p\|q)$ differs from the entropy, $H(p)$, which is the information required, on average, to describe features $\mathbf{x}$ distributed as $p(\mathbf{x})$. $H$ is not in itself an appropriate measure for biometric feature information, since it does not account the extent to which each feature can identify a person $p$ in a population $q$. An example of a feature unrelated to identity is the direction a person is facing. Measuring this quantity will increase $H$ of a feature set, but not increase its ability to identify a person. The measure $D(p\|q)$ corresponds to the requirements: Given a knowledge of the population feature distribution $q$, the information in a biometric feature set allows us to describe a particular person $p$.

## 23.2.2  Distribution Modeling

In a generic biometric system, $S$ biometric features are measured to create a biometric feature vector $\mathbf{x}$ $(S \times 1)$ for each person. For person $p$, we have $N_p$ features samples, while we have $N_q$ samples for the population. For convenience of notation, we sort $p$'s measurements to be the first grouping of the population. Defining $\mathbf{x}$ as an instance of random variable $X$, we calculate the population feature mean $\mu_q$

$$\mu_q = \underset{q}{E}[X] = \frac{1}{N_q} \sum_{i=1}^{N_q} \mathbf{x}_i, \tag{23.2}$$

where the feature mean of person $p$, $\mu_p$, is defined analogously, replacing $q$ by $p$. The population feature covariance $\boldsymbol{\Sigma}_q$ is

$$\boldsymbol{\Sigma}_q = \underset{q}{E}\left[(X - \mu_q)^t (X - \mu_q)\right] = \frac{1}{N_q - 1} \sum_{i=1}^{N_q} (\mathbf{x}_i - \mu_q)^t (\mathbf{x}_i - \mu_q). \tag{23.3}$$

The individuals feature covariance, $\boldsymbol{\Sigma}_p$, is again defined analogously.

One important general difficulty with direct information-theoretic measures is that of data availability. Distributions are difficult to estimate accurately, especially at the tails; and yet $\log_2 (p(\mathbf{x})/q(\mathbf{x}))$ will give large absolute values for small $p(\mathbf{x})$ or $q(\mathbf{x})$. Instead, it is typical to fit data to a model with a small number of parameters. The Gaussian distribution is the most common model; it is often a good reflection of the real-world distributions and is analytically convenient in entropy integrals. Another important property of the Gaussian is that it gives the maximum entropy for a given standard deviation, allowing such models to be used to give an upper bound to entropy values. Based on the Gaussian model, which seems to be the simplest and appropriate for $p$ and $q$, we write

$$p(\mathbf{x}) = \frac{1}{\sqrt{|2\pi \boldsymbol{\Sigma}_p|}} \exp\left(-\frac{1}{2} (\mathbf{x} - \mu_p)^t \boldsymbol{\Sigma}_p^{-1} (\mathbf{x} - \mu_p)\right), \tag{23.4}$$

$$q(\mathbf{x}) = \frac{1}{\sqrt{|2\pi \boldsymbol{\Sigma}_q|}} \exp\left(-\frac{1}{2} (\mathbf{x} - \mu_q)^t \boldsymbol{\Sigma}_q^{-1} (\mathbf{x} - \mu_q)\right), \tag{23.5}$$

from which we can calculate $D(p\|q)$.

$$D(p\|q) = \int p(\mathbf{x}) \left(\log_2 p(\mathbf{x}) - \log_2 q(\mathbf{x})\right) d\mathbf{x} \tag{23.6}$$

$$= -k \left( \ln |2\pi \boldsymbol{\Sigma}_p| - \ln |2\pi \boldsymbol{\Sigma}_q| + 1 - \underset{p}{E}\left[(\mathbf{x} - \mu_q)^t \boldsymbol{\Sigma}_q^{-1} (\mathbf{x} - \mu_q)\right]\right) \tag{23.7}$$

$$= k \left( \ln \frac{|2\pi \Sigma_q|}{|2\pi \Sigma_p|} + \text{trace} \left( (\Sigma_p + \mathbf{T}) \Sigma_q{}^{-1} - \mathbf{I} \right) \right), \tag{23.8}$$

where $\mathbf{T} = (\mu_p - \mu_q)^t (\mu_p - \mu_q)$ and $k = \log_2 \sqrt{e}$.

This expression calculates the relative entropy in bits for Gaussian distributions $p(\mathbf{x})$ and $q(\mathbf{x})$. This expression corresponds to most of the desired requirements for a biometric feature information measure introduced in the previous section:

1. If person's feature distribution matches the population, $p = q$; this yields $D(p\|q) = 0$, as required.

2. As feature measurements improve, the covariance values, $\Sigma_p$, will decrease, resulting in a reduction in $|\Sigma_p|$, and an increase in $D(p\|q)$.

3. If a person has feature values far from the population mean, $\mathbf{T}$ will be larger, resulting in a larger value of $D(p\|q)$.

4. Combinations of uncorrelated feature vectors yield the sum of the individual $D(p\|q)$ measures. Thus, for uncorrelated features $s_1$ and $s_2$, where $\{s_1, s_2\}$ represents concatenation of the feature vectors, $D(p(s_1)\|q(s_1)) + D(p(s_2)\|q(s_2)) = D(p(\{s_1, s_2\})\|q(\{s_1, s_2\}))$.

5. Addition of features uncorrelated to identity will not change $D(p\|q)$. Such a feature will have an identical distribution in $p$ and $q$. If $U$ is the set of such uncorrelated features, $[\Sigma_p]_{ij} = [\Sigma_q]_{ij} = 0$ for $i$ or $j \in U$, and $i \neq j$, while $[\Sigma_p]_{ii} = [\Sigma_q]_{ii}$ and $[\mu_q]_i = [\mu_p]_i$. Under these conditions, $D(p\|q)$ will be identical to its value when excluding the features in $U$. One way to understand this criterion is that if the distributions for $q$ and $p$ differ for features in $U$, then those features can be used as a biometric to help identify a person.

6. Correlated features are less informative than uncorrelated ones. Such features will decrease the condition number (and thus the determinant) of both $\Sigma_p$ and $\Sigma_q$. This will decrease the accuracy of the measure $D(p\|q)$. In the extreme case of perfectly correlated features, $\Sigma_p$ becomes singular with a zero determinant and $D(p\|q)$ is undefined. Thus, our measure is inadequate in this case. In the next section, we develop an algorithm to deal with this effect.

## 23.2.3  Regularization Methods for Degenerate Features

In order to guard against numerical instability in our measures, we wish to extract a mutually independent set of $W$ "important" features ($W \leq S$). To do this, we use the principal component analysis (PCA) [11, 12] to generate a mapping ($\mathbf{U}^t : X \rightarrow Y$), from the original biometric features $X$ ($S \times 1$) to a new feature space $Y$ of size $W \times 1$. The PCA may be calculated from a singular value decomposition (SVD) [13] of the feature covariance matrix, such that

$$\mathbf{U} \mathbf{S}_q \mathbf{U}^t = \text{svd}(\text{cov}(X)) = \text{svd}(\Sigma_q). \tag{23.9}$$

Since $\boldsymbol{\Sigma}_q$ is positive definite, $\mathbf{U}$ is orthonormal and $\mathbf{S}_q$ is diagonal. We choose to perform the PCA on the population distribution $q$, rather than $p$, since $q$ is based on far more data and is therefore likely to be a more reliable estimate. The values of $\mathbf{S}_q$ indicate the significance of each feature in PCA space. A feature $j$ with small $[\mathbf{S}_q]_{j,j}$ will have very little effect on the overall biometric feature information. We use this analysis in order to regularize $\boldsymbol{\Sigma}_q$ and to reject degenerate features by truncating the SVD. We select a truncation threshold of $j$, where $[\mathbf{S}_q]_{j,j} < 10^{-10}[\mathbf{S}_q]_{1,1}$. Based on this threshold, $\mathbf{S}_q$ is truncated to be $W \times W$, and $\mathbf{U}$ is truncated to $S \times W$. Using the basis $\mathbf{U}$ calculated from the population, we decompose the individual's covariance into feature space Y:

$$\mathbf{S}_p = \mathbf{U}^t \boldsymbol{\Sigma}_p \mathbf{U}, \tag{23.10}$$

where $\mathbf{S}_p$ is not necessarily a diagonal matrix. However, since $p$ and $q$ describe somewhat similar data, we expect $\mathbf{S}_p$ to have a strong diagonal component, as seen in Figure 23.4.

Based on this regularization scheme, Eq. (23.8) may be rewritten in the PCA space as

$$D(p\|q) = k \left( \beta + \mathrm{trace}\, \mathbf{U} \left( (\mathbf{S}_p + \mathbf{S}_t)\mathbf{S}_q^{-1} - \mathbf{I} \right) \mathbf{U}^t \right) \tag{23.11}$$

where $\beta = \ln \dfrac{|\mathbf{S}_q|}{|\mathbf{S}_p|}$ and $\mathbf{S}_t = \mathbf{U}^t \mathbf{T} \mathbf{U}$.

## 23.2.4 Regularization Methods for Insufficient Data

The expression developed in the previous section solves the problem caused by the ill-posed nature of $\boldsymbol{\Sigma}_q$. However, $\boldsymbol{\Sigma}_p$ may still be singular in the common circumstance in which only a small number of samples of each individual are available. Given $N_p$ images of an individual from which $W$ features are calculated, $\boldsymbol{\Sigma}_p$ will be singular if $W \geq N_p$, which will result in $D(p\|q)$ diverging to $\infty$. In practice, this is a common occurrence, since most biometric systems calculate many hundreds of features, and most biometric databases contain far less samples for each person. In order to address this issue, we develop an estimate that may act as a lower bound. In order to do this, we make the following assumptions:

1. Estimates of feature variances are valid $[\mathbf{S}_p]_{i,i}$ for all $i$.
2. Estimates of feature covariances $[\mathbf{S}_p]_{i,j}$ for $i \neq j$ are only valid for the most important $L$ features, where $L < N_p$.

Features that are not considered valid based on these assumptions are set to zero by multiplying $\mathbf{S}_q$ by a mask $\mathbf{M}$, where

$$M = \begin{cases} 1 & \text{if } i = j \text{ or } (i < L \text{ and } j < L), \\ 0 & \text{otherwise.} \end{cases} \tag{23.12}$$

Using Eq. (23.12), $[\mathbf{S}_p]_{i,j} = (\mathbf{M}_{i,j})[\mathbf{U}^t \boldsymbol{\Sigma}_p \mathbf{U}]_{i,j}$.

This expression regularizes the intra-person covariance, $\Sigma_p$, and ensures that $D(p\|q)$ does not diverge. To clarify the effect of this regularization on $D(p\|q)$, we note that intra-feature covariances will decrease $|\Sigma_p|$ toward zero, leading a differential entropy estimate diverging to $\infty$. We thus consider this regularization strategy to generate a lower bound on the biometric feature information. The selection of $L$ is a compromise between using all available measurements (by using large $L$) and avoiding numerical instability when $S_p$ is close to singular (by using small $L$).

### 23.2.5    Average Information of a Biometric System

This section has developed a measure of biometric feature information content of a biometric feature representation of a single individual with respect to the feature distribution of the population. As discussed, the biometric feature information will vary between people; those with feature values further from the mean have larger biometric feature information. In order to use this approach to measure the biometric feature information content of a biometric system, we calculate the average biometric feature information for each individual in the population (weighted by the probability of needing to identify that person, if appropriate). This is a measure of the system biometric information (SBI) that can be calculated by the average IBI over the population $q$.

$$\text{SBI} = \underset{q}{E}\left[D(p\|q)\right] \tag{23.13}$$

$$= \frac{1}{2}\log_2\left|\Sigma_q\Sigma_p^{-1}\right| + tr\left(\Sigma_p\Sigma_q^{-1} - I\right) + \underset{q}{E}\left[t^T\Sigma_q t\right] \tag{23.14}$$

$$= \frac{1}{2}\log_2\left|\Sigma_q\Sigma_p^{-1}\right| + tr\left(\Sigma_p\Sigma_q^{-1}\right). \tag{23.15}$$

### 23.2.6    Information Loss Due to Degradation

In this section, we explore the effect of image degradation and the resulting decrease in biometric quality on the relative entropy measure. Intuitively, it is expected that image degradation changes the intra- and inter-person distribution of the face features, resulting in a loss of biometric information. Given a degradation process, we wish to measure how much $BI$ is lost in the degraded images, $G$, versus the original images, $F$. This allows us to measure the severity of a degradation process.

Features, $g$, are then extracted from the degraded images $\mathbf{G}$ using three feature extraction methods given. We then compute the biometric information for the non-degraded distributions $(D(p(f)\|q(f)))$ and for the degraded distributions $(D(p(g)\|q(g)))$ using Eq. (23.11). Here $D(p(f)\|q(f))$ represents the relative entropy between the individual and population distribution prior to degradation, while $D(p(g)\|q(g))$ is the relative entropy measure between the degraded individual and population distributions, respectively. From this, we calculate the normalized mean square distance characterizing the loss of information caused by the degradation model on the underlying features as

$$\Delta BI = \frac{1}{N_f} \sum_{i=1}^{N_f} \frac{|D(p(f_i)||q(f_i)) - D(p(g_i)||q(g_i))|^2}{\sigma_{D_f}^2}, \tag{23.16}$$

where $\sigma_{D_f}^2$ is the variance of $D(p(fi)||q(fi))$. $\Delta BI$ measures the relative distance offset between the original and degraded distributions. $\Delta BI$ is a unitless measure and may be interpreted as the fractional loss in $BI$ due to a given image degradation.

In order to motivate this calculation, we initially considered calculating $D(p(g)||q(f))$ as a function of degradation. Surprisingly, this measure increases with decreasing quality. The reason is that a single person $p$ is considered to have degraded images in a population $q$ of high-quality images. The algorithm seems to be saying: Aha! I can recognize $p$. He always has a blurry face!. Therefore, it is necessary to compare a degraded person's image to the degraded population $D(p(g)||q(g))$ in order to compensate for this effect.

## 23.3 FACE RECOGNITION

Information in a feature representation of faces is calculated using our described method for different individuals. In order to test our algorithm, it is necessary to have multiple images of the same individual. Using the Aberdeen face database [14], we chose 18 frontal images of 16 persons, from which we calculate the PCA (eigenface) features using the algorithm of reference 12 and the FLD face features components using the algorithm described in reference 15. Initially, all face images were registered by rotation and scaling to have eye positions at $(50, 90)$ and $(100, 90)$. Images were then cropped to $150 \times 200$ pixels and histogram equalized to cover the intensity range $0 - 255$. The same set of operations is applied to all images using the same thresholds. This results with the same effect on all images when computing the biometric feature information.

Features are calculated from a set of $N_q$ images using different component analysis methods such as principal component analysis (PCA, also referred to as eigenface features) [12, 16] and Fisher linear discriminant (FLD) [17]. $\mu_p$ and $\mu_q$ are $S \times 1$ vectors of the population and individual mean distributions, while $\Sigma_p$ and $\Sigma_q$ are $S \times S$ matrices of the individual and population covariance matrices.

The feature decomposition process was conducted on 18 images of each of 16 persons, giving 288 total images. For PCA and Fisher feature decompositions, 288 separate vectors were computed, and the most significant 100 features used for subsequent analysis. Figures 23.1 and 23.2 illustrate PCA and FLD features, respectively. From this, $D(p||q)$ is computed for each of 16 persons using Eq. (23.11), which assumes that $p$ and $q$ have Gaussian distributions. In order to test the validity of the Gaussian model for our data, we use the following normality tests:

- *Kolmogorov–Smirnov test*: This compares the distributions of values in the two data vectors $X_1$ and $X_2$, where $X_1$ represents random samples from the underlying distribution and $X_2$ follows an ideal Gaussian with zero mean and

**Figure 23.1.** An example of PCA (eigenface) face features. *From left to right*: PCA features number 3, 15, 35, and 55 are shown. The PCA features are othonormal and fit the data in a least squares sense.

variance. The null hypothesis is that $X_1$ and $X_2$ are drawn from the same continuous normal distribution. We reject the null hypothesis at $p < 0.01$.

- *The Lilliefors test* [30]: This evaluates the hypothesis that **x** has a normal distribution with unspecified mean and variance, against the alternative that **x** does not have a normal distribution. This test compares the empirical distribution of $X$ with a normal distribution having the same mean and variance as $X$. We reject the null hypothesis at $p < 0.01$.

Using these tests, on average 89% of the marginal distribution of all the FLD and PCA computed features is normally distributed.

## 23.3.1   Biometric Information Calculations

After fitting the distributions of $p(\mathbf{x})$ and $q(\mathbf{x})$ to a Gaussian model, we initially analyze the biometric feature information in each PCA and FLD feature separately. PCA features are shown in Figure 23.3 and show a gradual decrease from an initial peak at feature 2. The form of the curve can be understood from the nature of the PCA decomposition, which tends to place higher-frequency details in higher number features. Since noise tends to increase with frequency, the biometric information in these higher-numbered PCA features will be less. A sum of biometric feature information over the first 100 PCA features gives 40.5 bits. This does not assume

  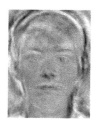 

**Figure 23.2.** An example of FLD face features. *From left to right*: FLD features number 7, 10, 30, and 50 are shown. FLD attempts to maximize class separation while minimizing the within-class scatter.

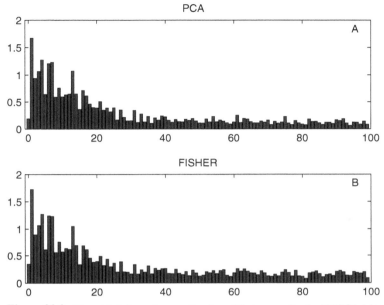

**Figure 23.3.** Biometric information as a function of feature number for (**A**) PCA (eigenface) and (**B**) FLD (bottom) face feature decomposition.

statistical independence, nor does it assume uncorrelatedness of PCA coefficients. Biometric feature information calculated using FLD features seems to be similar to PCA features such that most biometric feature information is computed for the most dominant fisherfaces.

In order to calculate $D(p\|q)$ for all features, we are limited by the available information. Since $N_p = 18$ images are used to calculate the covariances, attempts to calculate $D(p\|q)$ for more than 17 features will fail, because $\Sigma_p$ is singular. This effect is seen in the condition number (ratio of the largest to the smallest singular value), which was $4.82 \times 10^3$ for $\mathbf{S}_q$ and $1.32 \times 10^{20}$ for $\mathbf{S}_p$. The relatively small condition number of $\mathbf{S}_q$ indicates that no features are degenerate for PCA and FLD face recognition features. However, $\mathbf{S}_p$ is severely ill-conditioned. To overcome this ill-conditioning, we introduced a regularization scheme based on a mask [Eq. (23.12)] with a cutoff point $L$. This scheme is motivated by the diagonal structure of $\mathbf{S}_p$, as shown in Figure 23.4. To ensure convergence, the mask size $L$ is set to a value smaller than $N_p$.

We solve this singularity of Eq. (23.11) using a mask for $\mathbf{S}_p$ based on a parameter $L$. To further explore the effect of parameters $L$ and $N_p$, we artificially reduce the $N_p$ by randomly eliminating some images from individuals. Results for $D(p\|q)$ for PCA features for each person as a function of $L$ are shown in Figure 23.5 for $N_p = 8$, 12, 16, and 18. In these curves, we observe a "hockey stick" shape. The relative entropy measure remains stable when $L < N_p$; but if $L \geq N_p$, we observe a dramatic increase

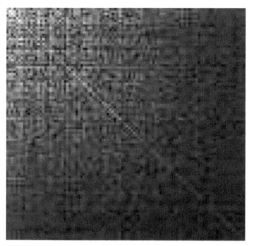

**Figure 23.4.** The regularized intra-person covariance matrix $\mathbf{S}_p$ showing dominant components along its diagonal. Since $\mathbf{\Sigma}_p$ represents similar information to $\mathbf{\Sigma}_q$, it is reasonable to expect the matrices have similar eigenvectors, resulting in strong diagonal components in $\mathbf{\Sigma}_p$.

in $D(p\|q)$ as the algorithm approaches a singularity of $\mathbf{\Sigma}_p$ and the ill-conditioning of $\mathbf{\Sigma}_q$. When $L < N_p$, $D(p\|q)$ is stable with a lower and upper bounds between 35 and 50 bits. However, when $L \geq N_p$, $D(p\|q)$ estimates start diverging and reach very large values.

Clearly, points for $L$ greater than the knee in the hockey stick do not represent accurate estimates of $D(p\|q)$. We also argue that when $L$ approaches $N_p$, the inherent ill-conditioning of $\mathbf{\Sigma}_p$ makes the our algorithm overestimate $D(p\|q)$. On the other hand, small values of $L$ will underestimate $D(p\|q)$, since these values will mask

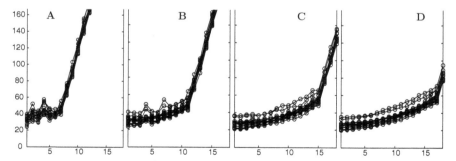

**Figure 23.5.** Biometric information (in bits) ($y$ axis) versus the mask size ($L$) ($x$ axis) for each person. Each subfigure represents a different value of $N_p$ (images of the same person): (**A**) 8, (**B**) 12, (**C**) 16, and (**D**) 18. The curves show that $D(p\|q)$ diverges as $\mathbf{\Sigma}_p$ becomes singular ($L \geq N_p$). The relative entropy increases with the size of the mask.

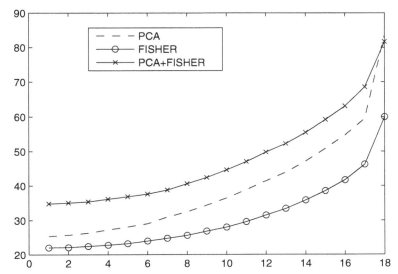

**Figure 23.6.** Average $D(p\|q)$ ($y$ axis) versus $L$ ($x$ axis) for $N_p = 18$. Each line represents the average of information calculated for a population of 16 individuals with 18 images each using PCA (*middle*), FLD (*bottom*), and a fusion of PCA and FLD features (*top*).

inter-feature correlations. This effect increases $|\mathbf{S}_p|$ as $L$ decreases. However, the results suggest that this effect is minor, especially in Figure 23.5A and 23.5B, where the "base" of the hockey stick is more flat. In order to produce an unique and stable estimate for $D(p\|q)$, it is necessary to choose a compromise between these effects. We recommend choosing $L = \frac{3}{4}N_p$, since a larger value of $L$ puts the estimate in an unstable region of Figure 23.4.

Using this algorithm and value of $L$, we calculate the overall biometric feature information for different face recognition algorithms. For PCA features, the average $D(p\|q)$ is 45.0 bits; and for FLD features, $D(p\|q)$ is 37.0 bits. If PCA and FLD features are combined (making 200 features in all), average $D(p\|q)$ is 55.6 bits (Figure 23.6). This combination of features illustrates that a biometric fusion of similar features may offer very little information above that of the individual underlying features. It is initially somewhat surprising that FLD feature information is measured to be lower than that from PCA. This result may be understood because PCA features retain unwanted information due to variations in facial expression and lighting, which are measured to contain useful information, while FLD "projects away" variations in lighting and facial expression while maintaining the discriminant features. In addition, feature decomposition using independent component analysis (ICA) [11] was also conducted on the same set of faces. ICA has the advantage that it does not only decorrelate the signals but also reduces higher-order statistical dependencies in order to make the signals as statistically independent as possible [18]. Since ICA maximizes non-Gaussianity, it fits less well to the assumptions of our model. For ICA features, an average of 39.0 bits was computed for $D(p\|q)$.

(a) (b) (c)

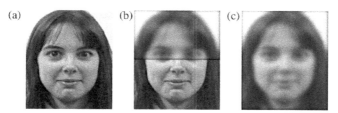

**Figure 23.7.** (a) Degraded image obtained by applying a Gaussian blur to (b) a section of the original image ($\varphi_1$) and to (c) the entire image ($\varphi_2$).

## 23.3.2 Degraded Features

In this section, $BI$ is computed for degraded features and information loss measured with respect to the original image. Equation (23.17) represents the blur degradation model used to generate degraded features where h is a space invariant Gaussian operator of size $n \times n$ and $\sigma = 3$, **F** is the original image and **G** is the resulting degraded image.

$$G(x, y) = \sum_{\alpha} \sum_{\beta} F(\alpha, \beta)h(x - \alpha, y - \beta). \tag{23.17}$$

Using the degradation model described by Eq. (23.17), two different sets of images ($\varphi_1$ and $\varphi_2$) are generated. Each set of images is composed 16 people with 18 images per individual for a total of 288. $\varphi_1$ is obtained by degrading half of each individual's face using different Gaussian operators, while $\varphi_2$ is a set of images obtained as a result of blurring the entire face region. An example of images in $\varphi_1$ and $\varphi_2$ are seen in Figure 23.7.

Using $\varphi_1$ and $\varphi_2$, new PCA, FLD, and ICA features (**g**) are extracted using the original (non-degraded) principal component vectors. From the degraded features, $\Delta BI$ is computed for the degraded individual and population distributions using Eq. (23.16). This measure represents the amount of information lost as a function of the degradation level. Figure 23.8 shows $\Delta BI$ computed as function of the blur level

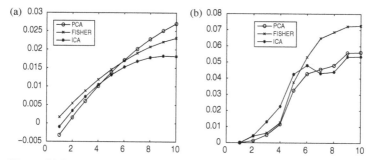

**Figure 23.8.** Normalized mean square distance ($y$ axis) as a function of an increasing blur level ($x$ axis) for images taken from (a) $\varphi_1$ and (b) $\varphi_2$.

for different images taken from $\varphi_1$ and $\varphi_2$. The $x$ axis represents nine different levels (in increasing order) of Gaussian blur. As seen in Figure 23.8, the relative information loss in an image increases with the amount of system degradation. Interestingly, $\Delta BI$ tends to reach a steady state after some level of degradation. This suggests that some features are unaffected by the degradation process and represent a lower bound of information measure of an individual distribution. PCA features extracted using the dominant eigenvalues of the system tend to be robust against blur since they preserve valuable information at a large degradation level.

## 23.4  DISCUSSION

This work describes an approach to measure biometric feature information and the changes in biometric sample quality resulting from image degradations. A definition of biometric feature information is introduced and an algorithm to measure it proposed, based on a set of population and individual biometric features, as measured by a biometric algorithm under test. Biometric information is defined in terms of the reduction in uncertainty of the identity of a person resulting from a set of biometric feature measurements. Based on this definition, we show that this concept matches the information-theoretic concept of *relative entropy* $D(p\|q)$, where $p$ is the probability distribution of the persons's features, and $q$ is the distribution of features of the population. Examples of its application were shown for two different face recognition algorithms based on PCA (eigenface) and FLD feature decompositions. Subsequently, we introduced a measure of information loss as a function of image degradation. It is shown that the normalized mean square distance measure ($\Delta BI$), based on the relative entropy, increases with the blur level but reaches a steady state after some amount of degradation that suggests that some features are unaffected by this degradation process.

Clearly, the framework developed in this work depends on accurate estimates of the population distributions $q$. Developing a good estimate of the "world model" is known to be a hard problem; in this work, we use the typical approach of assuming that our database is an adequate representation of the population.

The result of biometric feature information calculations (approximately 40 bits per face) is compatible with previous analyses of face recognition accuracy. From the FRVT results, we extrapolate the gallery size for an identification rate of 0.5 [19, 20]. This is taken to be a rough model of the population for which the algorithm can reduce the identity uncertainty to 50%. For the top three algorithms, the gallery sizes were $1.67 \times 10^8$, $3.53 \times 10^7$, and $2.33 \times 10^6$, corresponding to 27.3, 25.1, and 21.2 bits. This value is over half that calculated here and is reasonable, since the FRVT database appears to be significantly more difficult than the one used here [14], and current face recognition algorithms are not yet considered to be close to optimal. They seem to use approximately 1/2 to 2/3 of the available feature information.

As an exploration of the implications of this work, an analogy can be made between a biometric system and a traditional communication system in terms of information capacity [4]. The signal source transmits one symbol from an alphabet;

this corresponds to one person from a population to be identified. The symbol is encoded and sent across a channel and is subject to channel noise; similarly, biometric features from a person are measured and are subject to variability due to noise in the measurement system and to inherent feature variability. Thus the biometric feature measurement system corresponds to the communication channel. The communications system receiver detects a signal and must decide which symbol was sent, corresponding to the role of the biometrics identification process. In this context, $D(p\|q)$ is the differential information of a single signal, and the average $D(p\|q)$, weighted by the probability of each signal $p$, is the channel capacity. Based on this analogy, we can say that biometric feature information is the channel capacity of a biometric measurement system.

In a general biometric system, the following issues associated with biometric features must be considered:

- Feature distributions vary. Features such as minutiae ridge angles may be uniformly distributed over $0$–$2\pi$, while other features may be better modeled as Gaussian. In this work, all features are modeled as Gaussian. This is a valid model for most PCA and FLD features, but is not valid for any ICA features (since ICA is designed to maximize non-Gaussianity). On the other hand, a Gaussian model may be considered to estimate an upper bound for the entropy.

- Raw sample images need to be processed by alignment and scaling before features can be measured. Any variability in registration will dramatically increase the variability in measured features and decrease the biometric feature information measure.

- Feature dimensionality may not be constant. For example, the number of available minutiae points varies. The method presented in this work does not address this issue, since the dimensions of $p(\mathbf{x})$ and $q(\mathbf{x})$ must be the same. Generalized entropy measures exist which may allow an extension of this approach to nonconstant dimensional features.

It is interesting to note that the biometric entropy is larger for some faces. Figure 23.5 shows a range of biometric information (from 32 to 47 bits) for different individuals, which may help explain why some people are potentially easier to recognize than others. This is perhaps some evidence for the "biometrics zoo" hypothesis [21]. In order to explore this effect, we plot the biometric feature information as a function of average feature variance for each person (Figure 23.9). A significant correlation ($p < .01$) is calculated for those features, indicating that they contain less variability in those subjects with higher biometric feature information.

The *BI* measure may help address many questions in biometrics technology, such as the following:

- *Uniqueness of biometric features.* A common question is, Are fingerprints really unique? While Pankanti et al. [22] have recently provided a sophisticated analysis of this problem based on biometric feature distributions directly, a general approach based on information content would help address this question for other biometric modalities.

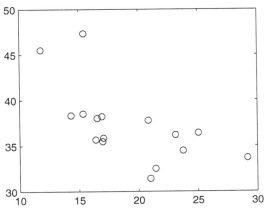

**Figure 23.9.** Average $D(p\|q)$ in bits ($y$ axis) as a function of the mean feature variance (arbitrary units) ($x$ axis) for 16 different persons. The mean feature variance is computed by summing all the diagonal components of $\mathbf{S}_p$ matrix for each person. The correlation coefficient is $-0.62$, which is significant at $p < 0.01$.

- *Inherent limits to biometric template size requirements.* A maximum compression of biometric features will be limited to the biometric feature information. This theoretical lower limit may be of use for ID card applications with limited data density.

- *Feasibility of biometric encryption.* Proposed biometric encryption systems use biometric data to generate keys [23], and thus the availability of biometric feature information limits the security of cryptographic key generation [24, 25].

- *Performance limits of biometric matchers.* While some algorithms outperform others, it clear that there are ultimate limits to error rates, based on the information available in the biometric features. In this application, the biometric feature information is related to the discrimination entropy [3].

- *Biometric fusion.* Systems which combine biometric features are well understood to offer increased performance [1]. It may be possible to use the measure of biometric feature information to quantify whether a given combination of features offers any advantage, or whether the fused features are largely redundant. The example of fusion of FLD and PCA (200 features) given here clearly falls into the latter category, since it does not necessarily offer double the amount of information.

- *Novel biometric features.* Many novel biometric features have been suggested, but it is often unclear whether a given feature offers much in the way of identifiable information. Biometric information measurement may offer a way to validate the potential of such features.

- *Privacy protection.* It would be useful to quantify the threat to privacy posed by the release of biometric feature information, and it would also be helpful to be able to quantify the value of technologies to preserve privacy, such as algorithms to de-identify face images [26, 27].

## REFERENCES

1. A. Ross and A. Jain, Information fusion in biometrics, *Pattern Recognit. Lett.* **24**:2115–2125, 2003.
2. J. S. Wayman, The cotton ball problem, *Biometrics Conference*, Washington DC, September 20–22, 2004.
3. J. Daugman, The importance of being random: Statistical principles of iris recognition, *Pattern Recognit.* **36**:279–291, 2003.
4. T. M. Cover and J. A. Thomas, *Elements of Information Theory*, John Wiley & Sons, New York, 1991.
5. M. Golfarelli, D. Maio, and D. Maltoni, On the error-reject tradeoff in biometric verification systems, *IEEE Trans. Pattern Anal. Mach. Intell.* **19**:786–796, 1997.
6. A. Adler, R. Youmaran, and S. Loyka, Information content of biometric features, in *Biometrics Consortium Conference* Washington, DC, September 19–21, 2005.
7. W. Zhao, R. Chellappa, P. J. Philips, and A. Rosenfeld, Face recognition: a literature survey, *ACM Comput. Surveys* **35**:399–458, 2003.
8. ISO JTC1 SC37 Biometrics, ISO 29794-1 biometric sample quality, Committee Draft 1, August 10, 2007.
9. E. Tabassi, C. R. Wilson, and C. I. Watson, Fingerprint image quality, NISTIR 7151, August 2004.
10. A. Adler, R. Youmaran, and S. Loyka, Towards a measure of biometric feature information, *Pattern Anal. Appli.*, 2008.
11. B. A. Draper, K. Baek, M. S. Bartlett, and J. R. Beveridge, Recognizing faces with PCA and ICA, *Comput. Vis. Image Understanding* **91**:115–137, 2003.
12. P. Grother, Software tools for an eigenface implementation, National Institute of Standards and Technology, 2000, http://www.nist.gov/humanid/feret/
13. O. Alter, P. O. Brown, and D. Botstein, Singular value decomposition for genomewide expression data processing and modeling, *Proc. Natl. Acad. Sci.* **97**:10101–10106, 2000.
14. I. Craw, N. P. Costen, T. Kato, and S. Akamatsu, How should we represent faces for automatic recognition? *IEEE Trans. Pattern Anal. Mach. Intell.* **21**:725–736, 1999.
15. C. Xiang, X. A. Fan, and T. H. Lee, Face recognition using recursive Fisher linear discriminant, *Conference on Communications, Circuits and Systems International*, June 27–29, 2004.
16. M. Turk and A. Pentland, Eigenfaces for recognition, *J. Cognit. Neurosci.* **3**:71–86, 1991.
17. S. Li and A. Jain, editors, *Handbook of Face Recognition*. Springer, Berlin, 2005.
18. T. W. Lee, Nonlinear approaches to independent component analysis, *Proceedings of the American Institute of Physics*, 1999.
19. P. J. Phillips, P. Grother, R. J. Micheals, D. M. Blackburn, E. Tabassi, and J. M. Bone, *FRVT 2002: Evaluation Report*, NIST, March 2003, http://www.frvt.org/DLs/FRVT_2002_Evaluation_Report.pdf
20. P. J. Phillips, T. W. Scruggs, A. J. O'Toole, P. J. Flynn, K. W. Bowyer, C. L. Svhott, and M. Sharpe, *FRVT 2006: Evaluation Report*, NIST, March 2007, http://www.frvt.org/FRVT2006/docs/FRVT2006andICE2006LargeScaleReport.pdf.
21. G. Doddington, W. Liggett, A. Martin, M. Przybocki, and D. Reynolds, Sheep, goats, lambs, and wolves: An analysis of individual differences in speaker recognition performance, in *Proceedings of the International Conference on Auditory–Visual Speech Processing*, Sidney, Australia, November 1998.
22. S. Pankanti, S. Prabhakar, and A. K. Jain, On the individuality of fingerprints, *IEEE Trans. Pattern Anal. Mach. Intell.* **24**:1010–1025, 2002.
23. U. Uludag, S. Pankanti, S. Prabhakar, and A. K. Jain, Biometric cryptosystems: Issues and challenges, *Proc. IEEE* **92**:948–960, 2004.
24. L. Ballard, S. Kamara, F. Monrose, and M. Reiter, On the Requirements of Biometric Key Generators, *Technical Report TR-JHU-SPAR-BKMR-090707*, John Hopkins University, 2007.

25. Y. Dodis, L. Reyzin, and A. Smith, Fuzzy extractors and cryptography, or how to use your fingerprints, *Proceedings of Eurocrypt '04*, 2004, http://eprint.iacr.org/2003/235/

26. E. M. Newton, L. Sweeney, and B. Malin, Preserving privacy by de-identifying face images, *IEEE Trans. Knowledge Data Eng.* **17**:232–243, 2005.

27. Y. Zhu, S. C. Dass, and A. K. Jain, Statistical models for assessing the individuality of fingerprints, *IEEE Trans. Info. Foren. Sec.* **2**(3, Part 1):391–401, 2007.

28. A. Adler, Vulnerabilities in biometric encryption systems, *Audio- and Video-Based Biometric Person Auth.* Tarrytown, NY, July 20–22, 2005.

29. P. N. Belhumeur, J. P. Hespanha, and D. J. Kriegman, Eigenfaces vs. Fisherfaces: Recognition using class specific linear projection, *IEEE Trans. Pattern Anal. Mach. Intell.* **19**:711–720, 1997.

30. W. J. Conover, *Practical Nonparametric Statistics*, John Wiley & Sons, New York, 1980.

31. A. Hyvärinen, Fast and robust fixed-point algorithms for independent component analysis, *IEEE Trans. Neural Net.* **10**:626–634, 1999.

32. C. Soutar, D. Roberge, A. Stoianov, R. Gilroy, and B. Vijaya, Biometric Encryption using image processing, *Proc. SPIE Int. Soc. Opt. Eng.* **3314**:178–188, 1998.

# Chapter 24

# Decision-Making Support in Biometric-Based Physical Access Control Systems: Design Concept, Architecture, and Applications

Svetlana N. Yanushkevich, Vlad P. Shmerko,
Oleg Boulanov, and Adrian Stoica

## 24.1  INTRODUCTION

This chapter presents a summary of the theoretical results and design experience obtained during the developing of a next generation of a physical access security system (PASS). The main feature of this PASS is its the efficient support of security personnel enhanced with the situational awareness paradigm and intelligent tools. Research work was conducted at the Biometric Technologies Laboratory of the University of Calgary, Canada; and at the Humanoid Robotics Laboratory at the NASA Jet Propulsion Laboratory, California Institute of Technology.

"The Guidance Package: Biometrics for Airport Access Control," developed by the Assistant Secretary of Homeland Security in consultation with representatives of the aviation industry, biometric identifier industry, and the National Institute of Standards and Technology (NIST), provides criteria for the integration of biometric devices into access control systems. In this document, access control is defined as "the examination of one or more of three factors regarding an individual's

_Biometrics: Theory, Methods, and Applications._  Edited by Boulgouris, Plataniotis, and Micheli-Tzanakou
Copyright © 2010 the Institute of Electrical and Electronics Engineers, Inc.

identity: something they know, something they have, or something they are." This document is acknowledged by other research initiatives, including the Defense Advanced Research Projects Agency (DARPA) research program, HumanID, which is aimed at the detection, recognition, and identification of humans at a distance in early warning support systems for force protection and homeland defense [1].

Most existing check-point PASSes exclusively utilize the visual appearance of customers to compare against "lookout checklists" or suspected activity and do not effectively use the time slot before or/during access authorization, or registration to collect biometric information (body temperature, surgical changes, etc.) about individuals. Significant improvement of these PASSes can be achieved by using biometric devices. However, the effectiveness of known approaches to biometric-based PASS design [1–4] is limited. The reason is that biometric devices are integrated to the PASS as separate modules. The availability of a large number of biometric devices does not mean that the officer is able to manage all of these the information streams of data captured by these devices. For example, in the advanced systems deployed in some airports, security personnel observe the customers in the monitor prior to screening, check individuals using multispectral tools, check individual data with data in databases, match the appearance of an authorized individual with a photo in his/her document and image in the database, observe the behavior of the individual during the dialogue, monitor voice features, acquire fingerprints (palmprints), and analyze his/her documents. These functions are distributed between security personnel to minimize the time of service. The integration of additional biometric devices does not improve the authorization cycle and increase performance of the system. New design paradigms and concepts are required for the next generation of PASSes to provide reliable authorization in a short time. To achieve this, security personnel must be efficiently supported in order to make reliable decisions on authorization in a limited time. These personnel must be effectively trained and prepared to make correct decisions in various authorization scenarios, including extreme situations. The new generation of PASSes should not only provide for the reliable identification of an individual, but also supply data for situational awareness and risk management support [2, 3, 5]. In particular, camouflage (plastic surgery technologies) is a particular focus of interest. It is impossible to detect these disguises for altering facial features in the visible band without prior knowledge. The infrared spectrum provides useful information for detection of disguised features [6–8].

Two directions in designing PASSes can be identified today [1–3]. The first direction includes approaches based on the expansion of data sources; and as a result, the burden of professional skills required of the officer increases. In these approaches, the problems of supporting the officer are critically simplified, allowing a cost-efficient solution, but one that is not very suitable in practice. The second direction aims at high-level automated system design, where the human factor is critically reduced. This type of system is often considered as a cognitive system [9]. Our study contributes to the fundamentals of PASS design at the system level.

The proposed concept of decision-making support in biometric-based PASSes utilizes techniques from biometrics, system design, decision-making, image understanding, human–machine interaction, and specific-area application. The PASS is a *semiautomatic* network environment, in which automatic biometric-sensing devices are used at the *local level* of an architecture hierarchy and provide information for final decisions made by the security personnel. Biometric devices are defined as tools to support decision-making on system access authorization at the *global level*. Decisions for situational awareness from the local level are translated into a *semantic* form and *propagated* to the global level [10, 11]. Prescreening is aimed at situational awareness, in addition to the primary application of biometric data, that is, *identification*. *Intelligent support* is implemented to transfer data from the biometric-sensing devices into an acceptable *semantic* form that supports an officer in dialogue with a customer. Two types of intelligent interactions are aimed at the authorization of individuals: *human–machine* interaction (officer support) and *human–human* interaction (officer–customer dialogue support). The PASS architecture is characterized by *aggregation* (can be modified by extension), *reconfiguration* (can be modified into a training system called T-PASS), and *mobility* (can be relocated and deployed in new places). In the T-PASS, *synthetic biometrics* are used to imitate various *scenarios of authorization*.

Our pre-design study showed that this enhanced support may be accomplished by effective utilization of PASS topology, advanced biometric technologies, and human–machine interaction techniques [11–13]. In this study, we introduce a systematic approach to designing such situational awareness support. A fully functional system is designed to support the officer by providing *warning data* based on visual, infrared, and other data collected during the pre-screening of an individual waiting in the line (features of changed appearance, drug and alcohol intoxication, and critical health conditions). We define two phases in the development the PASS. At the *first phase,* the biometric data are used for extraction of situational awareness information and other parameters useful for decision-making. In this phase, the *discriminative* properties of biometric data are used. In the *second phase,* biometric data will be used for *discriminative* analysis and/or *identification*. Decision-making for identification is supported by more sophisticated intelligent tools.

In this chapter, we report results of the development of the first phase. We focus on *semantic* representation of biometric data and on the architectural characteristics of the systems, including its reconfiguration into a training system.

## 24.2 FUNDAMENTAL DESIGN CONCEPTS OF THE PASS

In our pre-design study, the PASS is specified as a *semiautomated* system with distributed biometrics and intelligence functions. These concepts are specified in terms of desired functionality (*functional* design), and then they are mapped into the system resources (*system* design).

Our approach makes use of experience in designing the well-known *dialogue* systems. In particular, the architectural principles of the PASS are similar to those of the

SmartKom [14]—for example, sensor-specific input processing, modality-specific analysis and fusion, and interaction management. The differences follow from the target functionality: PASS aims at the support of a *human–human* dialogue using specific-area *human–machine* interaction, while SmartKom supports only *human–machine* interaction. For example, if the PASS detects that an individual's body temperature is high and reports this fact to the officer, one of the automatically generated questions suggested to the officer is the following: "Do you need any medical assistance?" This protocol is a response to the detected abnormal temperature. The key to the proposed concept of decision-making support in the PASS is the process of generating questions, initiated by information sensed from biometric devices. The response of the devices is associated with language—that is, a *semantic* representation of the data. In this way, the system assists the officer in access authorization.

An important feature of this approach is that a carefully chosen questionnaire strategy can alleviate some temporary errors and unreliability in biometric data. For example, unreliable data on artificial accessories in infrared facial image are transferred into a semantic form as follows: "Warning: Possible intention to change appearance; artificial hair detected; artificial implants detected." The role of *intelligence* in decision-making support is defined as the transformation of knowledge concerning the state of the information environment, obtained by means of sensors, into a sequence of operations aimed at the achievement of a predetermined goal. Such a transformation is based on a priori knowledge about the information environment and results in the protocol—that is, a linguistic representation of possible authorization scenarios.

## 24.2.1  Structural Properties and Architectural Concepts

The structure of the proposed PASS is shown in Figure 24.1. The system consists of sensors such as *cameras* in the visible and infrared bands, *processors* of preliminary information and online data, a *knowledge domain converter* and a *dialogue support* device to support conversation based on the preliminary information obtained, and a *personal file* generating module. Three-level surveillance is used in the system: surveillance of the line (pre-screening); surveillance during the walk between pre-screened and screened points, and surveillance during the authorization process at the officer's desk (screening). A personal file construction includes (a) preliminary information using the surveillance of a person undergoing screening in visible and infrared bands, and (b) information extracted from observation, conversation, and available additional sources.

Reconfiguration of the PASS into a training system can be accomplished using a minimum of extra tools, and provides a real-world conditions of training. Such a concept is called the *multitarget platform*, and forms the basis for reconfiguring the

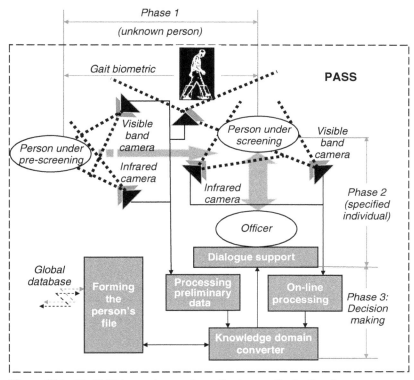

**Figure 24.1.** The PASS is a semiautomatic, application-specific distributed computer system that aims to support the officer's job in access authorization.

PASS into the T-PASS. Our architecture utilizes the *modularity* principle, the basic principle for aggregation and reconfiguration.

Screening is an adopted technique in social infrastructures for document-based checks, fingerprints, and mug-shot acquisition. A screening system possesses the following property. In terms of time, it can be divided into three phases; the time of service $T$ is divided into three subintervals $T_1$, $T_2$, and $T_3$. The first time interval, $T_1$, is the pre-screening phase of service (waiting), suitable for obtaining early warning information using surveillance. The second interval, $T_2$, is used for collecting information during an individual's movement from the pre-screened position to the officer's desk. The third time interval, $T_3$, is the time of identification (document check) and authorization based on the information collected during screening. Note that in terms of physical space, the distance between the pre-screened and screened areas can be used to obtain extra information using, for example, gait biometrics. Discriminative properties of gait biometric are useful for identifying gender, pregnancy, fatigue, injuries, affliction of the legs or feet, drunkenness, and psychological conditions [15–17].

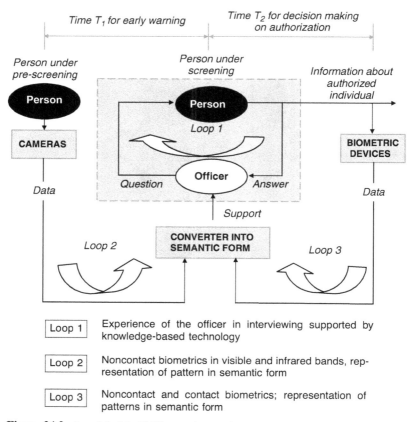

**Figure 24.2.** A model of the PASS: a semiautomatic system with information streams.

## 24.2.2 The Generic Model of the PASS

A generic model of the PASS is given in Figure 24.2. Three loops address the three main data flows: the main flow (loop 1), where the professional skills of the personnel play the key role, and the supporting flows (loops 2 and 3), where biometric data are processed, and decisions on detection or recognition of various patterns are automated. The function of loops 1 and 2 is to *propagate* the results of biometric data processing to the officer. This data must be presented to the officer in a form that is understandable and useful for for dialogue support and decision-making.

## 24.2.3 Model of a Biometric Sensor

In our design approach, each biometric device is considered as a generator of *random*, or *temporal* faults. Even with the most careful design aimed at fault and error avoidance, they will eventually occur and affect local and global decision-making. In our approach, the propagation of biometric information from the local to the global level is used to solve this problem. The propagation mechanism decreases the effect of uncertainty in data and temporal faults of biometric devices on the global level of decision-making. This effect is similar to the effect of *linguistic averaging* known in fuzzy logic. In our approach, fuzzy grammars are used to provide flexibility of fuzzy sets and in this way to utilize the opportunity to accommodate human variability in command syntax [18].

### 24.2.4    Data

Human–machine and human–human interactions are the key components of the PASS and T-PASS. In our design approach, the goal of the human–machine interface is to support the officer by providing an analysis of all sources of information in a form that is acceptable for fast and correct decision-making on authorization.

The following static and dynamic (real-time) information streams provided by various tools can be identified: (a) *static document record* and biometric data from local and global databases and (b) *online* biometric data obtained from the surveillance facilities and conversation with an individual at the desk, including behavioral biometric data such as voice, facial expressions, and signature.

Biometrics are usually classified using *physiological* and *behavioral* categories. In our design concept, we also distinguish *contact* and *noncontact* biometrics. This division is made with respect to the main functions of the PASS (early warning and service based on the screening discipline). Early warning information includes various parameters that can be obtained by *indirect* techniques (disabilities, drug and alcohol intoxication, etc.).

The PASS is a multimodal biometric system using a combination of various biometrics, including visual-band, infrared, and acoustic data for identification of both appearance (including natural aspects, such as aging, and intentional ones, such as surgical changes), physiological characteristics (temperature, blood flow rate, etc.), and behavioral features (voice and gate) (Figure 24.3). Other biometrics can be used at pre-screening and checkpoints.

### 24.2.5    Relationship of Biometric Data in Semantic Form

The relationships between biometric data are another source of information in the PASS. In particular, similarities can be measured and expressed in terms of association, resemblance, correlation, and matching. In similarity measures, various basic principles can be utilized: heuristic, probabilistic, information-theoretical, fuzzy, semantic, and so on. Figure 24.4 illustrates the relationship between biometric features and human physiological and psychological characteristics.

Biometrics represented by a feature vector is considered in multimodal systems in the form of concatenation into a single feature vector [19]. A feature-level fusion is done using matching scores and the corresponding rules. In our approach, information

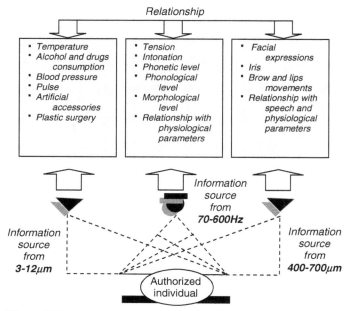

**Figure 24.3.** Relationship of biometric data in various spectral bands.

from biometric devices is transformed into a semantic form (knowledge domain), and a relationship among various biometrics is integrated through a decision-level fusion.

This relationship in semantic form is used to provoke the process of extraction of information from other sources using the questionnaire technique. This technique has been developed, in particular, for a polygraph [20]. A function similar to the objective function of polygraph can be used to extract additional information from the acoustic band and the questionnaire (information from answers and behavioral biometric data from the voice).

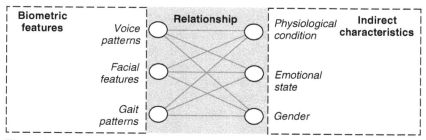

**Figure 24.4.** Example of the indirect evaluation of human physiological and psychological characteristics, and their relationships to various biometrics.

## 24.3   DECISION-MAKING SUPPORT ASSISTANT DESIGN

The devices gathered from the sensors and intelligent data processing for the situational awareness are called *decision-making support assistants*. These assistants can be based on noninvasive metrics such as

- Temperature measurement
- Artificial accessory detection
- Estimation of drug and alcohol intoxication
- Estimation of blood pressure and pulse

The basic design paradigm of these decision support assistances is the *discriminative* biometrics.

### 24.3.1   Discriminative Biometrics

We introduce several examples of discriminative biometrics using infrared thermography from medical applications—a diagnostic method that provides information about normal and abnormal functioning of the sensory and sympathetic nervous system, vascular dysfunction, myofascial trauma, and local inflammatory process. In prototyping the PASS, we studied various methods in order to choose the most efficient one. In this section, we review some of them.

An infrared image analysis component has been integrated into the prototyped PASS. It includes the recording of infrared image video, infrared image processing, and an analysis of features such as temperature and blood flow rate. The fluctuation of temperature in various facial regions is primary due to the changing blood flow rate. In reference 21, the heat-conduction formulas at the skin's surface are introduced. The thermodynamic relation between the blood flow rate $V_S$ at the skin level, blood temperature at the body core $T_{blood}$, and the skin temperature $T_{skin}$ is used to convert infrared intensity to temperature. Then, the raw thermal data are transformed into blood flow rate data.

In medical applications, infrared-based diagnostic systems provide accurate quantitative analysis of the temperature distribution on a target surface: the absolute and mean temperature of any region—in particular, of the face, and differences between the right and the left sides of the face. In reference 22, it was found that infrared thermography can be used as a screening test for distinguishing healthy subjects from patients with temporomandibular disorder. This result is used in the prototype PASS to detect the maximal and mean facial and neck region temperatures of an individual.

In reference 23, mass blind screening of potential SARS or bird flu patients was studied. In the above study, a handheld radiometric infrared ThermaCAM S60 FLIR system was used with a focal length from individual to scanner of 2 meters with a 3 second duration of scanning. The core (aural) temperature was measured around the eyes. The authors stated that contact lenses do not affect temperature profiles, since the inner corners of the eyes were scanned as well. In reference 24, the correlation between ear and eye temperatures was studied.

We also consider the monitoring of breathing function, which has been well-studied in polygraphs [20], to be potentially useful. Distance infrared measuring of the breathing function is based on the fact that exhaled air has a higher temperature than a typical background of indoor environments [25]. Infrared image processing includes skin detection and temperature evaluation [26].

Distance infrared analysis of chemical composition, such as ethanol (alcohol), acetaminophen (major ingredient of tylenol), and codeine, in body fluids is an area of particular interest in medical and other applications. However, the detection of the actions of chemicals in the infrared, such as drug applications to the skin, have not been studied enough. In the early stages of some chemical actions, capillaries near the skin surface become enlarged and hot. As the reaction increases, a warm expanding network of capillaries (the area affected) can be observed in the infrared. We are working on the hypothesis that facial infrared images are affected by specific drugs and alcohol. In addition, fusion of infrared images with images in the visible band could be useful. In reference 27, the skin color model was developed and shown to be useful for the detection of changes due to alcohol intoxication. It was reported in reference 28 that the anxious state in an individual is associated with increased blood circulation around the eyes. This phenomenon has been found useful in polygraph study [29] and can be adopted in the PASS.

## 24.3.2   Intelligent Support of Decision-Making

Intelligence is commonly considered as the ability to collect knowledge and reason with this knowledge in order to solve certain classes of problems. Experience using intelligence tools at the local level of a biometric system are well-documented, for example, in references 30–32. In the PASS, intelligence technology is used in real-time processing at the global level.

An intelligent control in the complex biometric-sensing PASS has to be designed using the following *constraints*; in particular, any solution using intelligent method must be understood by the officer, any "advice" must be formulated in a clear form, and temporary faults and uncertainty must be introduced to the officer in an acceptable form.

Consider, for example, the processing of a facial image in both the visual and infrared bands. Such processing is aimed at so-called *hyperspectral* analysis. Suppose that indirect computing results in the detection of a possible drug intoxication. This result should be considered as a hypothetical datum with high probability, because of the shortcomings of the algorithms, sensor imperfection, measurement errors, and other factors. This drawback can be alleviated using intelligent technology and, more importantly, utilized for performing more reliable authorization of the individual.

This is because the transformation of biometric data into a semantic representation is based on an assumption about the probabilistic nature of the obtained information. The problem to be solved is to construct this semantic form using appropriate target functions: to justify, to clarify, to alarm, and so on. These intelligent evaluations of the above scenario are very useful for an officer, and they can be classified as assistance in decision-making.

In our design concept, we distinguish several levels of intelligent support. In this chapter, we introduce the simplest implementation of intelligent support of human–machine interaction that is acceptable for practice, in the form of protocols (recommendations) in semantic form. These protocols generate data such as a level of warning or alarm, the reasons why these data was recognized as a warning or alarm, and recommendations to the security personnel on possible actions. The security personnel use this information for further checking, as well as for making a final decision.

Decisions based on data analysis include a set of subprocedures which can be made automatically with an acceptable risk. For example, in the fragment of training scenario below, a system generates the following data about the pre-screened person:

```
TIME 00.00.00:
PERSON UNDER PRE-SCREENING 45 WARNING LEVEL 04
SPECIFICATION: DRUG OR ALCOHOL CONSUMPTION, LEVEL 03
POSSIBLE ACTION: 1. DIRECT TO SPECIAL INSPECTION
2. REGISTER WITH CAUTION
```

This protocol means that the system detected the fourth level of alarm using measured drug or alcohol consumption. The system evaluated the risks and proposed two possible solutions. The officer can, in addition to the automatic aid, analyze the acquired raw images in the visible and infrared spectrum.

In the decision-making process, the individual's data are matched with the data in local and global databases; this process is fully automated for stationary conditions in any standard PASS. For example, the following training scenario illustrates one possible situation:

```
TIME 00.00.00:
PERSON UNDER SCREENING 45 WARNING LEVEL 04
SPECIFICATION: DRUG OR ALCOHOL CONSUMPTION, LEVEL 03
LOCAL DATABASE MATCHING: POSITIVE
POSSIBLE ACTION: 1. REGISTER 2. CLARIFY AND REGISTER
```

Note that data on the individual may not always be available in the database—this is the worst-case scenario, and intelligence-based support is vital in this case.

The above approach can be efficiently used for training personnel. Using data flows and their representations, the training system generates a set of scenarios that are ranged with respect to various criteria of training requirements. For example, the following scenario is proposed to the officer-in-training as decision-making support information:

```
TIME 00.00.00:
PERSON UNDER SCREENING 45 WARNING LEVEL 04
SPECIFICATION: DRUG OR ALCOHOL CONSUMPTION, LEVEL 03
LOCAL DATABASE MATCHING: POSITIVE
PROPOSED DIALOGUE: QUESTION 1: DO YOU NEED MEDICAL
ASSISTANCE? ...
QUESTION 10: DO YOU HAVE DRUGS IN YOUR LUGGAGE?
```

In our design concept, the results of automatically analyzing behavioral information are provided to the officer; for example, in the following form:

```
TIME 00.00.00:
PERSON UNDER SCREENING 45 ALARM, LEVEL 04
SPECIFICATION: DRUG OR ALCOHOL CONSUMPTION, LEVEL 03
LOCAL DATABASE MATCHING: POSITIVE
LEVEL OF TRUSTWORTHINESS OF QUESTION 10 IS 03: DO YOU
HAVE DRUGS IN YOUR LUGGAGE?
POSSIBLE ACTION: 1.DIRECT TO SPECIAL INSPECTION
2. CONTINUE CLARIFICATION BY QUESTIONS
```

### 24.3.3 Decision-Support Assistants for Noninvasive Temperature Measure

Consider a decision-support assistant for noninvasive temperature measurement that includes the following components (Figure 24.5):

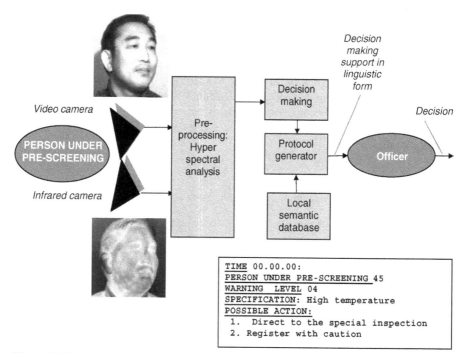

**Figure 24.5.** Decision-support assistant for noninvasive temperature measure.

- Sensor such as video and infrared cameras
- Preprocessing block for hyperspectral analysis
- Decision-making block
- Protocol generator

This decision-support assistant implements the Bayesian model of belief. In Bayesian belief estimations, input data are the results of measurement in the hyperspectral band.

## 24.3.4   Decision Support During Interviewing

Our study also concerned with studying dynamics of infrared images during interviewing. The interval of observation is used to record a thermal video and then analyze frames taken using regular intervals. The simplest analysis involves count of the number of pixels, corresponding to the low, medium, and high temperature and taken as a proportion to the total number of facial image pixels. The first image in Figure 24.6b is taken at the beginning of performing the calculation, and the second

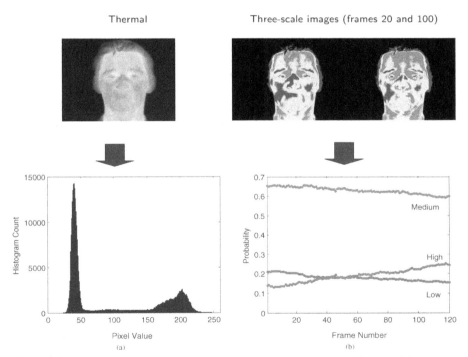

**Figure 24.6.** Dynamics of thermal images due to a mental effort: (**a**) A thermal image and the histogram in which the region between 156 and 225 pixel values corresponds to the face region; (**b**) three-scale images (the images in which the pixels are distributed according to three temperature ranges: medium, high, and low, indicated by different colors) corresponding to the 20th and 100th frames of the thermal images, and the graph of proportions (called here the probability) of the pixels from three temperature ranges.

image is taken at the end. The proportion of the number pixels in each region to the total number of pixels (called probability) is changed during thermal video recording during calculation.

We simplified our experimental study because of the complexity and high cost of real-world experiments: Instead of observing responses to questions, we asked the tested person to solve various mathematical calculations. Similarly to the questionnaire techniques, this required some intellectual effort. Based on this premise, we analyzed the dynamics of infrared images of people, participated in the study (Figure 24.6). The primary conclusion is that facial images in infrared band can distinguish people in the relaxing state and people making calculation tasks.

## 24.4  HYPERSPECTRAL ANALYSIS AND SYNTHESIS OF FACIAL SKIN TEXTURE

A decision-support assistant performs the face analysis (preprocessing phase, Figure 24.5) based on a model made up of two constituents: a face shape model (represented by a three-dimensional geometric mesh) and a skin model (generated from hyperspectral texture images in visible and infrared bands). In this section, we address the problem of skin modeling—specifically, the problem of extracting information helpful for early detection support from hyperspectral skin texture images.

### 24.4.1  Human Skin Modeling

Since the color of human skin can reveal distinct characteristics valuable for diagnostics, many authors have performed theoretical and experimental studies of the optical properties of human skin—specifically, the mechanism of skin color formation [33–37]. It has been demonstrated, in particular, that the dominant pigments in skin color formation are *melanin* and *hemoglobin*. Melanin and hemoglobin determine the color of the skin by selectively absorbing certain wavelengths of the incident light. The melanin has a dark brown color and predominates in the epidermal layer, while the hemoglobin has a reddish hue or purplish color, depending on the oxygenation, and is found mainly in the dermal layer.

The quantities of melanin and hemoglobin pigments in the human skin were experimentally determined in reference 38 using multiple regression analysis, and the accuracy of the method was estimated by Monte Carlo simulation [39]. In reference 40, the melanin and hemoglobin content of the skin was experimentally analyzed based on diffuse reflectance spectroscopy in the visible and near-infrared bands. It was confirmed that it is possible to obtain quantitative information about hemoglobin and melanin by fitting the parameters of an analytical model with reflectance spectra. An alternative, a fast-fitting procedure based on a library search, was proposed in reference 41.

Recent progress in imaging devices such as video CCD (including near-infrared and ultraviolet ranges) and thermal cameras employed in medical, surveillance, and security systems has stimulated the development of new approaches to human skin color and texture analysis, as well as skin thermodynamic and hemodynamic characteristics. For example, in reference 42, an image-based analysis technique for determining the optical properties of translucent materials was developed. In reference 43, a new method was proposed for visualizing local blood regions in the skin tissue using diffuse reflectance images. The independent component analysis (ICA) of RGB components of facial skin images was proposed in reference 44. This approach allows one to determine a spatial distribution of melanin and hemoglobin pigments in the skin and can be used to separate the components to synthesize various facial color images. It was assumed in reference 44, that the distributions of melanin and hemoglobin pigments are statistically independent and that the observed skin color is a linear function of these quantities. In practical situations, however, Fresnel reflection from the skin surface and the shadow cast can both disturb the real skin color. In references 27 and 45, a pair of polarizers was used in order to remove surface reflections; and for relaxing the effects of shadow, principal component analysis (PCA) was applied to reduce the dimensions of the color space prior to ICA. Various techniques for the analysis of thermal images of the human skin have been developed in references [46–48].

The analysis of skin color and texture based on the extraction of information about the melanin and hemoglobin content is a valuable source of information. In the infrared band, the skin temperature distribution is strongly correlated with blood flow rate and, hence, with a person's psycho-emotional state, muscle activity, or skin lesions and artificial accessories.

## 24.4.2 Preprocessing in Decision-Support Assistants Based on Skin Models in Visible and Infrared Bands

A quantitative analysis of human skin color and temperature distribution can reveal a wide range of physiological phenomena. For example, skin color and temperature can change due to drug or alcohol consumption, physical exercises, and so on. For skin analysis and synthesis, we adopt the model proposed in references 27 and 45 as basic and develop it further in order to meet its requirements in the context of an early detection support system. Specifically, we take account of the spacial and temporal structure of image data and correlate the skin color changes to the skin temperature changes obtained from the thermal camera.

## 24.4.3 3D Face Model

A 3D model-based approach offers a unified method for analysis and synthesis of face images and can help in handling changes in lighting conditions, as well as in accurately estimating facial expressions. In our approach, face shape is modeled by a polygonal mesh, while the skin is represented by a texture map image. The face image is rendered by mapping the texture image on the mesh model. Figure 24.7

3D Mesh                    Skin Texture                    Rendered Model

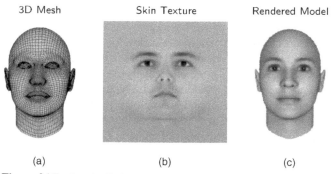

(a)                        (b)                        (c)

**Figure 24.7.** Generic 3D face model: (**a**) 3D polygonal mesh, (**b**) skin texture image, and (**c**) synthetic face image with the texture mapped to the polygonal mesh.

shows a FaceGen[1] generic 3D face model. The synthetic face image, which shown in Figure 24.7c, is rendered from the 3D polygonal mesh represented in Figure 24.7a and the skin texture image shown in Fig. 24.7b.

Any individual face shape is generated from the generic face model by specifying 3D displacements for each vertex. In FaceGen, the coordinates $x_i$ of the $i$th mesh vertex in any individual face shape are calculated from the coordinates $\bar{x}_i$ of the $i$th vertex in the average model, namely,

$$x_i = \bar{x}_i + \sum_{k=1}^{n_f} f_k \Delta u_i^k + \sum_{k=1}^{n_s} s_k \Delta v_i^k,$$

where $f_k$ and $s_k$ are the feature and expression coefficients, respectively, and $u_i^k$ and $v_i^k$ are the corresponding displacements. The generic 3D face model is fitted to the original 2D image by adjusting the coefficients $f_k$ and $s_k$.

In a similar way, the pixel values $I(i, j)$ of any particular texture image are evaluated from the corresponding pixel values $\bar{I}(i, j)$ in the generic texture model by

$$I(i, j) = \bar{I}(i, j) + \sum_{k=1}^{n_t} t_k \Delta I^k(i, j),$$

where $t_k$ are the coefficients. An individual texture map is synthesized from the generic texture map by adjusting $t_k$.

We use this approach in the assistant to model faces in the visible as well as infrared bands. An example of fitting a generic 3D face model to 2D face images is presented in Figure 24.8. The original face image in visible band (Fig. 24.8a) has

---

[1] FaceGen, software for face modeling, Singular Inversions Inc., British Columbia, Canada.

Visible Band                              Infrared Band

Original Image      3D Face Model      Original Image      3D Face Model

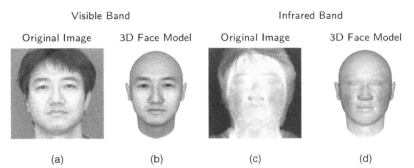

(a)                 (b)                 (c)                 (d)

**Figure 24.8.** Original face images in visible (**a**) and infrared (**c**) bands and the corresponding 3D models (**b**) and (**d**), respectively.

been fitted into the 3D model as shown in Figure 24.8b. The similar results for the infrared band are represented in Figures 24.8c and 24.8d.

## 24.4.4 Skin Color Modeling

The human skin has a layered structure, and its color is determined by how incident light is absorbed and scattered by the melanin and hemoglobin pigments in the two upper skin layers, the epidermis and dermis. Considering the specific purposes of our application, it is highly preferable to set up a skin color representation on the basis of hemoglobin and melanin pigments in order to analyze and model the diversity of skin appearance.

As far as skin color formation is concerned, we adopt the model proposed in references 27, 44, and 45 and represent colors in the optical density domain by a color vector $\mathbf{c}$ with components $c_1$, $c_2$ and $c_3$ indirectly representing red–green–blue (RGB) values, following the equation $(c_1 \ c_2 \ c_3)^T = (-\log R \ -\log G \ -\log B)^T$. We also assume that the two principal pigments determining skin color, melanin and hemoglobin, are each characterized by their own unique pure RGB components, $R_m$, $G_m$, and $B_m$ for melanin and $R_h$, $G_h$, and $B_h$ for hemoglobin. So the corresponding melanin and hemoglobin pure color vectors are

$$\mathbf{c}_1 = (-\log R_m \ -\log G_m \ -\log B_m)^T,$$
$$\mathbf{c}_2 = (-\log R_h \ -\log G_h \ -\log B_h)^T,$$

respectively. The central premise of the model is that the color vector representing the skin color can be expressed as a linear mixture

$$\mathbf{c} = x_1 \mathbf{c}_1 + x_2 \mathbf{c}_2,$$

where $x_1$ and $x_2$ are the quantities of melanin and hemoglobin pigments, respectively.

The color vectors $\mathbf{c}_1$ and $\mathbf{c}_2$ represent the intrinsic characteristics of the pigments and do not alter from one point to another; it is the changes of the quantities $x_1$ and

$x_2$ that produce all the rich variations in skin color. Despite its simplicity, this basic skin color model exhibits all the necessary characteristics that are required for our application.

## 24.4.5  Separation of Color Components by Independent Components Analysis

The quantities $x_1$ and $x_2$ in the color density vector expansion are determined by two independent physical processes—that is, by two different scattering processes. Since the sources are unrelated, color mixtures can be separated into their constituent components. Since two distinct sources, $x_1$ and $x_2$, defining the skin color arise from different underlying physical causes, we expect $x_1$ and $x_2$ to be statistically independent, and independent component analysis (ICA) can be applied for extracting these components. Hence, the color space of the skin, represented by $x_1$ and $x_2$, is two-dimensional. It forms a surface in the 3D RGB color space. We can reduce the dimensionality of the problem by applying PCA prior to ICA—that, is by projecting the color vectors $\mathbf{c}$ onto 2D subspace according to the equation

$$\tilde{\mathbf{c}} = A(\mathbf{c} - \boldsymbol{\mu}),$$

where $\tilde{\mathbf{c}} = (\tilde{c}_1 \, \tilde{c}_2)^T$ is a two-dimensional projection, $\boldsymbol{\mu}$ is a three-dimensional sample mean, and $A$ is a $2 \times 3$ matrix computed by PCA.

The next step is aimed at evaluating the relative quantities $\tilde{x}_1$ and $\tilde{x}_2$ by applying ICA to the reduced color vectors $\tilde{\mathbf{c}}$. Let $\tilde{x}_1$ and $\tilde{x}_2$ form by the vector $\tilde{\mathbf{x}} \equiv (\tilde{x}_1 \, \tilde{x}_2)^T$, and let the matrix $W$ be calculated by ICA. The unmixed components can be evaluated from the equation

$$\tilde{\mathbf{x}} = W \, \tilde{\mathbf{c}}.$$

This equation represents a model for the extraction of melanin ($\tilde{x}_1$) and hemoglobin ($\tilde{x}_2$) components from the image. Figure 24.9 illustrates the melanin and hemoglobin maps extracted from the rectangular area of skin.

We use the described method for the analysis of skin texture images generated by FaceGen from video images. An example of a 3D synthesized face model is presented in Figure 24.10: The face image rendered from the model is shown in Figure 24.10a and the RGB components of the corresponding skin texture map are presented in Figures 24.10b, 24.10c, and 24.10d, respectively.

Face images in visible and infrared bands acquired by the system constitute the input of the module for hyperspectral face analysis and synthesis. The corresponding 3D models, one for video images and one for infrared, are generated by fitting the generic model onto images.

In order to extract information about the melanin and hemoglobin content of the skin, we use the color channels of skin texture maps as source signals for ICA. For example, we applied ICA to the texture image whose color channels are shown in Figures 24.10b–24.10d. The obtained quantities are represented in separate texture images, Figures 24.11a and 24.11c. The corresponding 3D models synthesized

Techniques for Melanin and Hemoglobin Extraction Using ICA

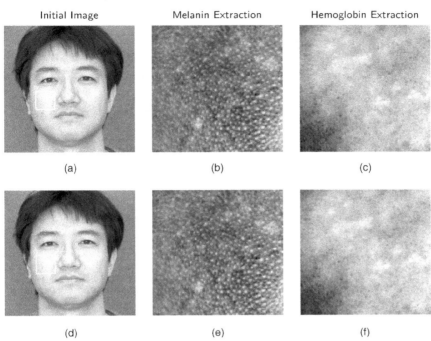

**Figure 24.9.** Extraction of melanin and hemoglobin information by ICA of the skin color: Source images with the selected region indicated by rectangle (**a, d**); melanin (**b**) and hemoglobin (**c**) components extracted from the selected region; (**e**) normalized images of the melanin and (**f**) hemoglobin components extracted from the selected region (the minimal value is set to zero and maximum to 255).

by mapping the textures on the geometric mesh are shown in Figures 24.11b and 24.11d.

The texture maps representing the hemoglobin and melanin content of the facial skin, as well as the temperature distribution, represent the output of the face analysis

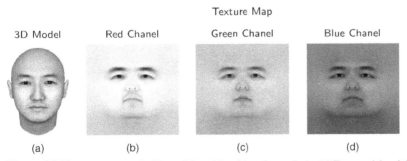

**Figure 24.10.** An example of a 3D model used for skin color analysis: (**a**) Face model and the (**b**) red, (**c**) green, and (**d**) blue components of the corresponding skin texture.

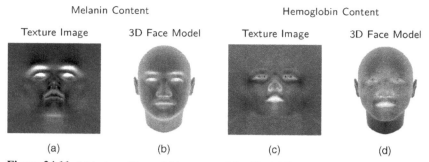

Melanin Content                      Hemoglobin Content

Texture Image        3D Face Model        Texture Image        3D Face Model

(a)                (b)                (c)                (d)

**Figure 24.11.** Melanin and hemoglobin content of the skin. (**a**) Texture map and (**b**) 3D face model representing the melanin content. The hemoglobin content is shown in (**c**) and (**d**), respectively.

and modeling module. This information is used for evaluating the physiological and psycho-emotional state of a person.

## 24.4.6    Experimental Setup

In the decision support assistant, face images are acquired throughout screening, or surveillance. A setup of the paired video and thermal cameras for acquisition of facial images in both the visual and infrared bands is shown in Figure 24.12. In our experimental setup, we use:

- Two JAI CV-M9 CL $3 \times 1/3''$ progressive scan RGB color cameras with $1034 \times 779$ 4.65 $\mu$m effective square pixels for each CCD (Figure 24.12).

*Surveillance video*        *Surveillance infrared*
*camera* JAI CV-M9        *camera* Miricle KC 307K

**Figure 24.12.** A setup of a pair of video and infrared cameras for surveillance.

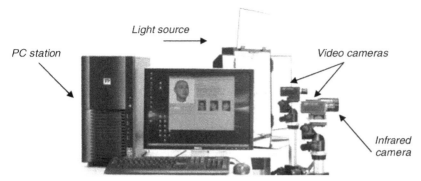

**Figure 24.13.** Experimental equipment for 3D face modeling.

These cameras can acquire full resolution images at a rate of 30 frames per second and output 24-bit RGB images via a camera link base configuration. The cameras are equipped with 16-mm lenses that allow them to capture the face images from a distance of about 2–3 m.

- A Thermoteknix MIRICLE 307K uncooled microbolometer infrared camera (Figure 24.12) with a focal plane array of $640 \times 480$ pixel size and a dynamic range of 14 bits. The spectral band of the camera is 7–14 $\mu$m and the standard frame rate is 25–30 frames per second. The camera is equipped with a 50-mm lens that allows it to capture faces from the same distance (2–3 m).

- A PC station with acquisition boards (Euresys GRABLINK Expert 2 for video cameras and Picolo Pro 2 for the thermal camera). For flicker-free illumination, two continuous light sources are used.

The experimental setup is shown in Figure 24.13. Two video cameras are used to obtain different views of a face in order to generate better 3D models. The thermal camera is paired with one of the video cameras as shown in Figure 24.12. All cameras are connected to the PC station with acquisition boards. For the flicker-free illumination, two continuous light sources are used. An example of visual information acquired by the cameras is shown in Figure 24.14. Figure 24.14a shows a thermal

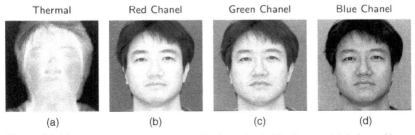

**Figure 24.14.** Visual information contained in thermal and video images: (**a**) A thermal image and the (**b**) red, (**c**) green, and (**d**) blue components of a video image.

image acquired by the system and Figures 24.14b–d demonstrate the RGB color components of a video image. The RGB components are used as input signals for ICA of the skin texture maps.

In summary, the melanin and hemoglobin content of the facial skin is analyzed based on a 3D face model generated from video images; namely, we apply ICA to the skin texture map on the 3D model. By extracting the information about melanin and hemoglobin content, we have a 3D face model with texture maps representing the pigments spacial distributions over the face. So, as we further develop our system, we could track changes in skin color in relation to certain important/key regions on the face and obtain in this way information about the physical state of a person. Note that in references 27, 44, and 45, skin color and texture analysis is performed based on 2D still images.

The main advantage of using 3D face models is that we can easily deal with variations in illumination, surface Fresnel reflection, and shading from directional light. In reference 27, this problem has been solved by processing a 2D image. We aim at 3D modeling, which allows us to control variations in appearance while the pose or illumination is changed. The main disadvantage of our approach is that the synthesis of a 3D model from images is a time-consuming procedure. For instance, the FaceGen PhotoFit tool takes about 3–5 min to generate a 3D model on a PC with Dual-Core AMD Opteron 2.21-GHz processor and ATI FireGL V3100 graphics card. This can be relaxed by reducing the level of detail of the model at the analysis phase.

## 24.5 PROTOTYPE DECISION-MAKING SUPPORT ASSISTANT DESIGN

Different decision strategies can provide distinguished for varying decisions because of their different philosophies for dealing with uncertainty.

### 24.5.1 Bayesian Decision Strategy and Belief Networks

Our motivation in the application of *Bayesian belief networks* is driven by the following: (a) decision-making in biometric-based systems in the presence of random factors can be described in *causal* form and (b) the Bayesian (probabilistic) interpretation of uncertainty provides an acceptable reliability for decision-making.

Traditionally, the semantics of Bayesian decision-making are not the focus of interest [49]. In our design concept, we extensively utilize the semantic properties of Bayesian networks in the representation and manipulation of biometric data. For this reason, we introduce a technique for computing based on *belief decision trees*.

We assume that biometric data structure can be expressed as a *causal* network with appropriate conditional probabilities. Causal knowledge is modeled as causal networks in which the nodes represent propositions (or variables), the arcs signify direct dependencies between linked propositions, and the strengths of these dependencies are quantified by conditional probabilities. Bayesian decision-making is based

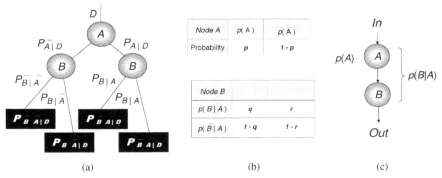

**Figure 24.15.** Belief tree (**a**), corresponding probability tables (**b**), and causal network (**c**).

on the evaluation of a *prior* probability given a *posterior* probability and *likelihood* (of an event happening given some history of previous events)

$$\overbrace{P(\text{Hypothesis}\,|\,\text{Data})}^{Prior} = \overbrace{P(\text{Data}\,|\,\text{Hypothesis})}^{Likelihood} \times \overbrace{P(\text{Hypothesis})}^{Posterior}$$

The posterior probability of $A$ is called the *belief* for $A$, $\text{Bel}(A)$. The probability $P(a|b)$ is called the *likelihood* of $b$ given $a$. In our design concept, a causal network is mapped into a *belief tree* (Figure 24.15). The belief tree is designed based on the rules for binary linguistic variables.

An arbitrary causal network can be transformed into a belief tree. An arbitrary complete belief tree with binary linguistic variables can be decomposed into two trees using evidence criteria: a tree characterized by ignorance (prior data are not available) and a tree of evidence (prior data are available). The main advantage of the belief trees is the possibility they provide for detailed description of the problem. However, belief trees can be applied only to small-size problems.

Causal knowledge can be represented in the following forms: (a) linguistic description, (b) algebraic (probabilistic) description, (c) decision tree, and (d) causal network. These data structures are useful for the representation of causal knowledge at a *high level of abstraction*. For the implementation of these data structures, the *logic level of abstraction* should be used—that is, *logic networks*. A *causal network* is a DAG in which each arc is interpreted as a direct causal influence between a parent node and a child node, relative to the other nodes in the network, so that this causal network's structure describes the dependence between associate variables and gives a concise specification of the joint probability distributions. A *node* in a causal network denotes a variable that models a feature of a process, event, state, object, agent, and so on. The causal network may contain both measured and hidden variables. Hidden variables are variables for which there are have no data. For each node, there is a probability distribution on that node given the state of its parents. In a causal network, this distribution shows how the node probabilities factor to affect a joint probability distribution over all the node. Directed edges represent causality between two nodes.

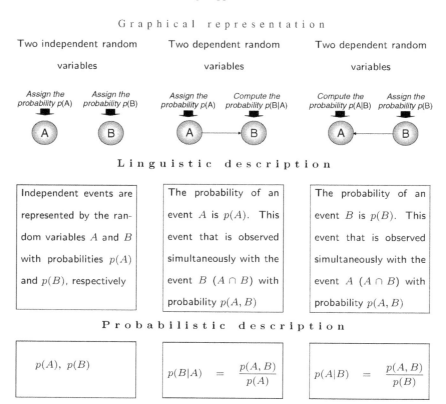

**Figure 24.16.** Graphical, linguistic, and probabilistic descriptions of the independent (**a**) and dependent (**b,c**) events $A$ and $B$.

Figure 24.16 illustrates various relationships between two nodes in graphical and probabilistic forms. Consider two nodes $A$ and $B$, interpreted as propositions. It is judged that: propositions $A$ and $B$ are not relevant (a); $A$ is relevant for $B$, so a directed link is drawn from $A$ to $B$ (b); and $B$ is relevant for $A$ (c). Another graphical representation of a causal relationship is the belief tree. In Figure 24.15, the belief tree represents the case that $A$ is relevant for $B$.

For example, given the measured temperature, M C temp, the posterior probability of Abnormal condition upon the evidence of M C temp is computed as follows:

$$p(\text{ABNORMAL}|\text{M C TEMP}) = \alpha \cdot p(\text{ABNORMAL}) \sum_{Temp} p(temp|\text{ABNORMAL})p(\text{M C TEMP}|temp)$$

$$= \alpha \cdot p(\text{ABNORMAL}) \cdot$$

$$\{p(\text{N TEMP}|\text{ABNORMAL})p(\text{M C TEMP}|\text{N TEMP})+$$

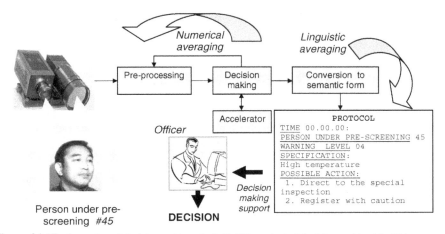

**Figure 24.17.** Averaging of decision making: the belief (the output of decision-making block) is varied during the time of surveillance while the observation conditions change.

$$p(\text{AB TEMP}|\text{ABNORMAL})p(\text{M C TEMP}|\text{Ab TEMP}) +$$

$$p(\text{C TEMP}|\text{ABNORMAL})p(\text{M C TEMP}|\text{C TEMP})\}$$

$$= \alpha \cdot 0.2 \cdot \{0.1 \cdot 0 + 0.6 \cdot 0.1 + 0.3 \cdot 0.75\}$$

$$= \alpha \cdot 0.057 = 0.429$$

Note that $\alpha = 7.519$ is computed from the equality $p(\text{ABNORMAL}|\text{M C TEMP}) + p(\text{NORMAL}|\text{M C TEMP}) = 1$.

## 24.5.2 Averaging

Data from the preprocessing block of a decision support assistant is varied during the observation of a pre-screening individual (Figure 24.17). The data variation is caused by pose, lighting, and other conditions of observation. For example, measuring the temperature of a pre-screened individual may be delayed for several minutes because of the critical angle of the individual's position with respect to the cameras. However, the equipment utilizes this time interval for processing of the other available zones— for instance, the ear. This may result in the production the supporting decision that is not reliable and cannot supply any recommendations to the officer. The processing is then continued during all pre-screening time intervals using adaptive weighted averaging.

Note that two classes of averaging procedures are distinguished: *numerical* and *linguistic* averaging. The adaptive weighted averaging is a numerical procedure resulting in the belief probability.[2] This probability is converted into linguistic form. At this

---

[2] Various statistical estimations are used at this phase, including confidence, tolerance, and prediction intervals and the quality of the point estimate (errors).

phase, linguistic averaging is performed using linguistic constructions to represent the numerical measures.

## 24.6    THE TRAINING SYSTEM T-PASS

Training of personnel naturally lags behind changes in technologies for the PASS. It is assumed that the officer obtains his/her skills through training with an instructor. Traditionally, training is implemented on a specifically designed training system. For example, training methodologies are well-developed for pilots, astronauts, surgeons [50], and the military. These are expensive professional simulation systems, which are difficult to modify or extend, since they are unique in architecture and functions.

In our approach, the design of an expensive training system is replaced by an inexpensive extension of the PASS, already deployed at the place of application [11, 12]. In this way, an important effect is achieved: a simulated environment is replaced with real-world conditions. Furthermore, long-term training is replaced by periodically repeated, short-term, intensive and computer-aided training. This means in practice that the PASS as a mobile system can be deployed in a new place (mobile border checkpoints, important public events, etc.), and the security personnel can be adapted to the new conditions by intensive and short-term training.

We propose a training paradigm utilizing a combination of various biometrics, including visual-band, IR, and acoustic acquisition data for identification of both physical appearance (including natural factors such as aging, and intentional (surgical) changes) and physiological characteristics (temperature, blood flow rate, etc.). Other biometrics can be used in pre-screening and at check-points: gait biometrics [17] and near distance noncontact and contact biometrics at the checkpoint.

The biometric-based PASS is a complex semiautomatic system. The question is, What kind of skills do secure personnel need to explore this system? The skilled PASS user possesses an ability to manipulate and efficiently utilize various sources of information in decision-making. The typical premise about the training component is that the necessary skills to employ a new system can be obtained through instruction. The PASS can be easily reconfigured into a training system. In the training system, decisions are generated by special tools according to various scenarios.

In T-PASS prototyping, we utilized the *Silicon Graphics* facilities and monitoring equipment of the *Virtual Reality Room* of the University of Calgary (Figure 24.18). We also used software tools for synthetic biometrics, such as *SFinGe*, the package for generation of synthetic fingerprints developed at the University of Bologna, Cesena, Italy, the *FaceGen* package for face modeling, and the *Comnetix Life-Scan* station for fingerprint acquisition and identification.

The PASS and T-PASS implement the concept of *multitarget platforms*; that is, the PASS can be easily reconfigured into the T-PASS, and vice versa. Using the possibilities of reconfiguration and minimal additional tools, the PASS can implement functions of the training system, T-PASS. The skills of the personnel contribute to decision-making. The skills can be gained by training (short-term) and experience (long-term). Note that traditionally, training is implemented on a unique training system.

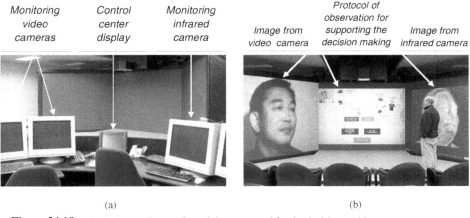

(a)   (b)

**Figure 24.18.** Monitoring equipment for training personnel for the decision-making support system: central control point (**a**) and generated test tasks (**b**) (Virtual Reality Room of the University of Calgary).

We developed an approach that alternates the known approaches with respect to several criteria, including cost-efficiency in personnel training. In the T-PASS, modeling is replaced by real-world conditions, and long-term training is replaced by *periodically repeated short-term intensive* computer-aided training.

Synthetic biometrics is understood as generated (artificial) biometric data, which is biologically meaningful for existing biometric systems [51–54]. These synthetic data replicate possible instances of otherwise unavailable data—in particular, corrupted or distorted data. For example, facial images acquired by video cameras can be corrupted due to the position and angle of observation (appearance variation) and also lighting (environmental conditions), camera resolution, and other parameters (measurement conditions). The other reason for the usage of synthetic data is the difficulty in collecting a statistically meaningful amount of samples due to privacy issues, the unavailability of large databases, and so on. Therefore, synthetic biometric data can be used as samples, or tests, generated using controllability of various parameters. This makes them useful for testing the biometric tools and devices [52]. Cancelable biometrics [51] is aimed at enhancing the security and privacy of biometric authentication through the generation of "deformed" biometric data—that is, synthetic biometrics. Instead of using a true object (finger, face), the fingerprint or face image is intentionally distorted in a repeatable manner, and this new print or image is used. The results reported in reference 55 are useful for synthetic infrared facial image generation.

As an example, a fragment of the modeling of an aging face is shown in Figure 24.19. The long-term behavior model, or age model, captures facial topology and features that change slowly through the life cycle.

This information is used in the currently developed approach to fusion of visual and infrared facial image information for evaluating the physiological and psycho-emotional state of a person.

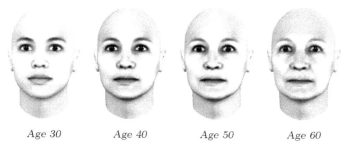

| *Age 30* | *Age 40* | *Age 50* | *Age 60* |

**Figure 24.19.** Aging modeling (neutral facial expression) in the training PASS using the package FaceGen.

## 24.7 DISCUSSION AND OPEN PROBLEMS

In this chapter, we introduced our experience and study of the prototyping of the main components of the PASS and T-PASS. These next-generation systems require novel approaches, and we focus on some of them and on their verification through prototyping.

Several problems were identified during the prototyping of the system. These problems are related to the specific-area applications as well as to fundamentals issues of biometric technologies. Motivated by the above, we grouped these problems into two classes: semantic and synthetic.

**Problem 1:** *Semantic biometrics.* The problems of decision-making in machine–human and human–human interactions that require interpretation of biometric data in semantic form without correction data are called *semantic* biometrics. These solutions are related to the classical image understanding technique, but are different in the goal: The result is not an improved image, but an understanding of the image for reasoning on possible human actions, if uncertainty is critical. Semantic *interpretability* of biometric information requires more sophisticated tools, known as the *integrated knowledge intensive approach.*

**Problem 2:** *Synthetic biometrics.* The training systems are expected to use synthetic biometrics. However, the development of solutions to inverse biometric problems (generating synthetic biometric data) and the techniques for virtual environment design demand more effort. Our prototype is based on synthetic biometric data automatically generated to "imitate" real data as described in references 53, 54, 56, and 57.

## 24.8 CONCLUSION

This chapter introduces our intermediate results in the development of a biometric-sensored PASS. It focuses on the first phase of this development, aimed at efficiently utilizing of the discriminative properties of distance biometric data (detect features and address their security personnel for clarification and decision-making). There are several features of the PASS that are attractive to industry, researchers, and academia.

The next-generation PASS is a multimode biometric system that exploits all possible aspects of biometric data. We show how to utilize discriminative properties of distance biometrics. A natural property of the PASS is the alleviation of temporary faults of biometric devices caused by poorly environment (illumination and motions). In the PASS, uncertainty in automatic decision-making at the local level (biometric device) is not transferred to the global level. This is because this uncertainty is transformed into questions that must be clarified by the officer. Hence, the PASS is a unique platform for the deployment of biometric sensors with intelligent support called a biometric assistant.

The use of various biometrics, including early detection and warning devices in the system, must involve innovative approaches, sociological, and economic considerations. The proposed PASS is considered to be a unique area to combine and prototype various methodologies, concepts, and techniques from many areas of the natural and social sciences—in particular, image processing and pattern recognition, virtual environment design and synthetic biometric data generation, distributed and multiagent systems design, human–machine interaction, integrated knowledge intensive system design, communication, medicine, and psychology.

We introduced the *fundamentals* of the next generation of PASS and T-PASS design. These are specific-area, multidisciplinary applications that require the utilization of advanced methodologies and techniques from many areas; in other words, they require a multidisciplinary approach. The specific area applications, such as PASS and T-PASS, form a suitable basis for systematic development in research laboratories and for industrial development.

Our study contributes to the development of the following design concepts:

1. *Aggregative* biometric-based PASS. In this chapter, we introduce the basic configuration (platform) with an extension using the early warning paradigm. A further extension can also be achieved by deploying various biometric subsystems to pre-screened and screened individuals, and using supporting tools. Utilization of the aggregative property addresses the progress of biometric sensors. The above addresses the *open* PASS architecture.

2. *Reconfigurable* biometric-based PASS. Using the proposed basic configuration, the PASS can be reconfigured into a training system, T-PASS. To this end, cost-efficient extensions such as additional simulators of synthetic biometric data, are utilized.

3. *Distributed topology* for the PASS. This topology involves pre-screening and screening areas, typically for airport checkpoints, facilities access, and so on. Such a distributed topology provides the conditions for the implementation of a situational awareness paradigm.

4. *Mobile* biometric-based PASS. To achieve this new operational characteristic, several design techniques, such as modularity and self-testing at local levels, can be utilized. In our design concept, the PASS is a mobile screening checkpoint. This function can be useful in many applications—for example, special event or VIP security. Many important public or high-profile settings

face a host of challenges in security, because they lack flexible screening options or need the most sophisticated security checkpoint solutions. The training system, T-PASS, inherits the mobility property as well, so personnel can be efficiently trained in a new environment, wherever the PASS is deployed.

5. *Decision-support assistants.* Our study on hyperspectral observation of the pre-screened and screened person based on facial skin texture is a particular example of such the capabilities of an assistant. We also present the results of prototyping various decision-support assistants based on noninvasive temperature measurement.

The introduced approach also contributes to the development of techniques for intelligent decision-making in the biometric-based PASS, in the following directions:

(**a**) *Biometric data understanding.* The support of security personnel is implemented in semantic form—that is, in the form of automatically generated questions recommended for the personnel to be used in dialogue with the customers. To accomplish this, we have developed a method for transferring biometric features (information in the feature domain) into a semantic representation, and then into a set of questions (information in the knowledge domain). The approach uses techniques of image understanding and human-machine interactions. Thus, decisions from the local level (biometric devices) are propagated to the global level (officer).

(**b**) *Dealing with temporal faults of biometric sensors* through the fusion at the decision-making level. Based on the fundamental properties of semiautomatic systems (where security personnel receive awareness data in support of their decision) and semantic representations, we developed a technique that alleviates temporal faults of biometric sensors.

(**c**) *Fusion of biometric data at the semantic level.* This is a new approach to the integration of biometric data evaluated in semantic form. Compared to a classical *correlation* in the feature domain, *fusion* in knowledge domain can be applied to any biometric.

## ACKNOWLEDGMENTS

This project is partially supported by the Natural Sciences and Engineering Research Council of Canada (NSERC), the Canadian Foundation for Innovations (CFI), the Government of the Province of Alberta, and the Alberta Informatics Circle of Excellence (iCore). A part of the project has been implemented as an initiative within the JPL's Humanoid Robotics Laboratory.

## REFERENCES

1. DAPRA: Total information awareness DAPRA's research program, *Info. Secur.* **10**:105–109, 2003.
2. D. N. Anderson, S. E. Thompson, C. E. Wilhelm, and N. A. Wogman, Integrating intelligence for border security, *J. Homeland Secur.* 2004, www.homelandsecurity.org.

3. J. Davis and D. Prosnitz, Technical and policy issues of counterterrorism—A primer for physicists, *Phys. Today* **56**(4):39–45, 2003.
4. Facial recognition and airport security, Imagis Technologies Inc., White Paper, 2004, www.imagisttechnologies.com.
5. B. Knerr, R. Breaux, S. Goldberg, and R. Thrurman, National defense, in K. Stanney, editor, *The Handbook of Virtual Environments Technology*, Lawrence Erlbaum Associates, Mahwah, NJ, 2002, pp. 857–872.
6. B. Bhanu and I. Pavlidis, editors, *Computer Vision Beyond the Visible Spectrum*, Springer, Berlin, 2005.
7. G. Gaussorgues, Infrared thermography, *Microwave Technology Series 5*, Chapman and Hall, London, 1994.
8. F. J. Prokoski and R. B. Riedel, Infrared identification of faces and body parts, in A. Jain, R. Bolle, and S. Pankanti, editors, *Biometrics: Personal Identification in Networked Society*, Kluwer, Dordrecht, 1999, pp. 191–212.
9. C. Forsythe, M. L. Bernard, and T. E. Goldsmith, editors, *Cognitive Systems: Human Cognitive Models in Systems Design*, Lawrence Erlbaum Associates, Mahwah, NJ, 2006.
10. S. N. Yanushkevich, A. Stoica, and V. P. Shmerko, Semantic framework for biometric-based access control systems, in *IEEE International Conference on Computational Intelligence for Homeland Security and Personal Safety*, Alexandria, VA, October 2006, pp. 11–16.
11. S. N. Yanushkevich, A. Stoica, and V. P. Shmerko, Experience of design and prototyping of a multi-biometric early warning physical access control security system (PASS) and a training system (T-PASS), *Proc. 32nd Annual IEEE Industrial Electronics Society Conf.* Paris, Nov 2006, pp. 2347–2352.
12. S. N. Yanushkevich, A. Stoica, and V. P. Shmerko, Fundamentals of biometric-based training system design, in S. N. Yanushkevich, P. Wang, S. Srihari, and M. Gavrilova, editors; and M. S. Nixon (consulting editor), *Image Pattern Recognition: Synthesis and Analysis in Biometrics*, World Scientific, Singapore, pp. 365–406, 2007.
13. S. N. Yanushkevich, A concepts of intelligent biometric-based early detection and warning system, in *Proceedings of Conference on Privacy, Security, Trust—PST2006*, Ontario, Canada, 2006, pp. 429–432.
14. G. Herzog and N. Reithinger, The SmartKom architecture: A framework for multimodal dialogue systems, in W. Wahlster, editor, *The SmartKom—Foundations of Multimodal Dialogue Systems*, Springer, Heidelberg, 2006, pp. 43–58.
15. N. V. Boulgouris, D. Hatzinakos, and K. N. Plataniotis, Gait recognition: A challenging signal processing technology for biometric identification, *IEEE Signal Processing Mag.* **22**(6):78–90, 2005.
16. G. Mather and L. Murdoch, Gender discrimination in biological motion displays based on dynamic cues, *Proc. Ro. Soc.* **258**:273–279, 1994.
17. M. S. Nixon, J. N. Carter, D. Cunado, P. S. Huang, and S. V. Stevenage, Automatic gait recognition, in A. Jain, R. Bolle, and S. Pankanti, editors, *Biometrics: Personal Identification in a Networked Society*, Kluwer, Dordrecht, 1999, pp. 231–250.
18. H. Senay, Fuzzy command grammars for intelligent interface design, *IEEE Trans. Syst., Man. Cybern.* **22**(5):1124–1131, 1992.
19. A. K. Jain, K. Nandakumar, U. Uludag, and X. Lu, Multimodal biometrics: Augmenting face with other cues, in W. Zhao and R. Chellappa, editors, *Face Processing: Advanced Modeling and Methods*, Elsevier, Amsterdam, 2006, pp. 679–705.
20. *The Polygraph and Lie Detection*, The National Academies Press, Washington, DC, 2003.
21. I. Fujimasa, T. Chinzei, and I. Saito, Converting far infrared image information to other physiological data, *IEEE Eng. Med. Biol. Mag.* **19**(3):71–76, 2000.
22. H. Fikackova and E. Ekberg, Can infrared thermography be a diagnostic tool for arthralgia of the temporomandibular joint? *OOOOE* **98**(6):643–650, 2004.
23. E. Y. K. Ng, G. J. L. Kaw, and W. M. Chang, Analysis of IR thermal imager for mass blind fever screening, *Microvasc. Res.* **68**:104–109, 2004.
24. E. Y. K. Ng, W. Muljo, and B. S. Wong, Study of facial skin and aural temperature, *IEEE Eng. Med. Biol. Mag.* 68–74, May/Jun. 2006.

25. R. Murthy and I. Pavlidis, Noncontact measurement of breathing function, *IEEE Eng. Med. Biol. Mag.* **25**(3):57–67, 2006.

26. C. K. Eveland, D. A. Socolinsky, and L. B. Wolff, Tracking human faces in infrared video, *Image Vis. Comput.* **21**:579–590, 2003.

27. N. Tsumura, N. Ojima, K. Sato, M. Shiraishi, H. Shimizu, H. Nabeshima, S. Akazaki, K. Hori, and Y. Miyake, Image-based skin color and texture analysis/synthesis by extracting hemoglobin and melanin information in the skin, *ACM Trans. Grap.* **22**(3):770–779, 2003.

28. I. Pavlidis and J. Levine, Thermal image analysis for polygraph testing, *IEEE Eng. Med. Biol. Mag.* **21**(6):56–64, 2002.

29. Y. Sugimoto, Y. Yoshitomi, and S. Tomita, A method for detecting transitions of emotional states using a thermal facial image based on a synthesis of facial expressions, *Robotics Auton. Syst.* **31**:147–160, 2000.

30. S. Y. Ho and H. L. Huang, Facial modeling from an uncalibrated face image using a coarse-to-fine genetic algorithm, *Pattern Recognit.* **34**:1015–1031, 2001.

31. L. Jain, U. Halici, I. Hayashi, S. Lee, and S. Tsutsui, Intelligent biometric techniques in fingerprint and face recognition, in L. Jain, editor, *International Series on Computational Intelligence*, CRC Press, Boca Raton, FL, 1999.

32. S. Y. Kung, W. M. Mak, and S. H. Lin, *Biometric Authentication: A Machine Learning Approach*, Prentice-Hall, Upper Saddle River, NJ, 2004.

33. R. R. Anderson and J. A. Parrish, The optics of human skin, *J. Invest. Dermatol.* **77**(1):13–19, 1981.

34. R. Chen, Z. Huang, H. Lui, I. Hamzavi, D. I. McLean, S. Xie, and H. Zeng, Monte Carlo simulation of cutaneous reflectance and fluorescence measurements—The effect of melanin contents and localization, *J. Photochem. Photobiol. B: Biol.* **86**(3):219–226, 2007.

35. J. B. Dawson, D. J. Barker, D. J. Ellis, J. A. Cotterill, E. Grassam, G. W. Fisher, and J. W. Feather, A theoretical and experimental study of light absorption and scattering by in vivo skin, *Phys. Med. Biol.* **25**(4):695–709, 1980.

36. E. A. Edwards and S. Q. Duntley, The pigments and color of living human skin, *Am. J. Anat.* **65**(1):1–33, 1939.

37. M. J. C. Van Gemert, S. L. Jacques, H. J. C. M. Sterenborg, and W. M. Star, Skin optics, *IEEE Trans. Biomed. Engi.* **36**(12):1146–1154, 1989.

38. M. Shimada, Y. Yamada, M. Itoh, and T. Yatagai, Melanin and blood concentration in human skin studied by multiple regression analysis: Experiments, *Phys. Med. Biol.* **46**:2385–2395, 2001.

39. M. Shimada, Y. Yamada, M. Itoh, and T. Yatagai, Melanin and blood concentration in a human skin model studied by multiple regression analysis: assessment by Monte Carlo simulation, *Phys. Med. Biol.* **46**:2397–2406, 2001.

40. G. Zonios, J. Bykowski, and N. Kollias, Skin melanin, hemoglobin, and light scattering properties can be quantitatively assessed in vivo using diffuse reflectance spectroscopy, *J. Invest. Dermatol.* **117**(6):1452–1457, 2001.

41. W. Verkruysse, R. Zhang, B. Choi, G. Lucassen, L. O. Svaasand, and J. S. Nelson, A library based fitting method for visual reflectance spectroscopy of human skin, *Phys. Med. Biol.* **50**:57–70, 2005.

42. H. W. Jensen, S. R. Marschner, M. Levoy, and P. Hanrahan, A practical model for subsurface light transport, *SIGGRAPH'01: Proceedings of the 28th Annual Conference on Computer Graphics and Interactive Techniques*, ACM Press, New York, 2001, pp. 511–518.

43. I. Nishidate, Y. Aizu, and H. Mishina, Depth visualization of a local blood region in skin tissue by use of diffuse reflectance images, *Opt. Lett.* **30**:2128–2130, 2005.

44. N. Tsumura, H. Haneishi, and Y. Miyake, Independent-component analysis of skin color image, *J. Opt. Soc. Am. A.* **16**:2169–2176, 1999.

45. N. Tsumura, T. Nakaguchi, N. Ojima, K. Takase, S. Okaguchi, K. Hori, and Y. Miyake, Image-based control of skin melanin texture, *Appl. Opt.* **45**:6626–6633, 2006.

46. B. F. Jones and P. Plassmann, Digital infrared thermal imaging of human skin, *Eng. Med. Biol. Mag. IEEE* **21**(6):41–48, 2002.

47. S. Karaa, J. Zhang, and F. Yang, A numerical study of a 3D bioheat transfer problem with different spatial heating, *Math. Comput. Simulation*, **68**(4):375–388, 2005.

48. J. J. Zhao, J. Zhang, N. Kang, and F. Yang, A two level finite difference scheme for one dimensional Pennes' bioheat equation, *Appl. Math. Comput.* **171**(1):320–331, 2005.

49. F. V. Jensen, *Bayesian Networks and Decision Graphs*, Springer, Berlin, 2001.

50. R. J. Lapeer, P. Chios, A. D. Linney, G. Alusi, and A. Wright, HCI: The next step towards optimization of computer-assisted surgical planning, intervention and training (CASPIT), in Q. Chen, editor, *Human Computer Interaction: Issues and Challenges*, Idea Group Publishing, Hershey, PA, 2001, pp. 232–246.

51. R. Bolle, J. Connell, S. Pankanti, N. Ratha, and A. Senior, *Guide to Biometrics*, Springer, Berlin, 2004.

52. R. Cappelli, Synthetic fingerprint generation, in D. Maltoni, D. Maio, A. K. Jain, and S. Prabhakar, editors, *Handbook of Fingerprint Recognition*, Springer, Berlin, 2003, pp. 203–232.

53. S. N. Yanushkevich, A. Stoica, V. P. Shmerko, and D. V. Popel, *Biometric Inverse Problems*, CRC Press/Taylor & Francis Group, Boca Raton, FL, 2005.

54. S. N. Yanushkevich, A. Stoica, and V. P. Shmerko, Synthetic biometrics, *IEEE Comput. Intell. Mag.* **2**(2):60–69, 2007.

55. B. A. Weber and J. A. Penn, Improved target identification using synthetic infrared images, *Proceedings of the Automatic Target Recognition XII*, Orlando, FL, pp. 93–102, 2002.

56. Y. Ma, M. Schuckers, and B. Cukic, Guidelines for appropriate use of simulated data for bio-authentication research, *Proceedings of the 4th IEEE Workshop Automatic Identification Advanced Technologies*, Buffalo, New York, 2005, pp. 251–256.

57. N. Ratha, J. Connell, and R. Bolle, Enhancing security and privacy in biometrics-based authentication systems, *IBM Syst. J.* **40**(3):614–634, 2001.

# Chapter 25

# Privacy in Biometrics

**Stelvio Cimato, Marco Gamassi, Vincenzo Piuri,
Roberto Sassi, and Fabio Scotti**

## 25.1 INTRODUCTION

Biometric features are increasingly used for authentication and identification purposes in a broad variety of institutional and commercial systems. The large diffusion of e-government, e-banking, and e-commerce applications requires more stringent methodologies to identify customers or citizens in order to prevent any malicious behavior that could lead to economic loss or fraud attempts for the involved parties. Biometric data are natural candidates to be used in authentication systems that should guarantee a higher level of security. Such kind of data are indeed unique for each person and strictly associated to its owner. They are irrevocable, in the sense that the association cannot be changed during the human life and in many cases they are hard to forge.

Many different authentication systems have been proposed taking into account different biometric traits, some physiological, some behavioral, each proposal having different advantages or drawbacks. In some cases, practical settings have been devised and different solutions are available in commercial applications or for border control. If from one side the interest in biometrics techniques is more and more increasing for their advantages (security, reliability, etc.) on the other side, the potential threat to the privacy of users, coming from the abuse of biometric information, is an object of discussion and often prevents the adoption of biometric systems on a large scale. In fact, people are not generally willing to give out biometric traits with little assurance that they cannot be stolen or used without an expressed consent. For the same reason discussed above, many people are more and more worried about the adoption of biometric systems in practical situation.

*Biometrics: Theory, Methods, and Applications.* Edited by Boulgouris, Plataniotis, and Micheli-Tzanakou
Copyright © 2010 the Institute of Electrical and Electronics Engineers, Inc.

Recently, much research work has been devoted to the construction of techniques for the protection of biometric templates. In this way, biometric authentication schemes can be devised, satisfying the increasing request for privacy coming from users. Such techniques usually enable the generation of secure identifiers after a transformation of the input biometric traits making it impossible to recover the original biometric features (thus preserving the privacy of the biometric traits). Several proposals have been formulated combining cryptography and biometrics in order to increase the confidence in the system when biometric templates are stored for verification.

The chapter reviews the privacy issues related to the use of biometrics and presents some of the most advanced techniques available up to date, providing a comparative analysis and giving an overview on future trends. This chapter is structured as follows. In the next section we present the most common biometric traits and features used in real-world applications as well as the associated risk level in the privacy for the individuals. In Section 25.3 we introduce efficient representation of biometric features in order to protect biometric templates and construct privacy compliant authentication system. In Section 25.4 we discuss privacy issues in multimodal biometric systems, when more than one biometric trait is used, and present in Section 25.5 an innovative method for building multimodal privacy-aware verification system.

## 25.2  BIOMETRIC TRAITS AND PRIVACY

In this section we discuss the privacy issues concerning the practical usage of the biometric systems. To this purpose it is important to consider both the view of users and the real risks which they could be exposed to. Different perspectives about privacy can also be given with respect to the application context in which biometrics are exploited and the particular methodology used for the collection of biometric data. Finally, privacy risks can also be evaluated considering the specific traits upon which the biometric systems are based.

### 25.2.1  User Perception and Real Risks

The users commonly perceive biometric authentication and identification techniques as a threat to their privacy rights. In particular, there are some aspects that enforce this perception [1]. The first one is related to the fact that the acquisition of the biometric traits is considered as an exact and permanent filing of the user's activities and behaviors. For example, very common is the thought that most biometric systems have 100% identification accuracy and that the biometric samples and templates are necessarily stored and/or sent over a network, exposing them to further risks of being exposed. Actually, the latter is a well-founded concern. In fact, while it should be granted to the user that the biometric information collected should not be used for any other activities than the ones expressly declared, in some cases it is harder to grant this aspect, especially if the biometric samples themselves are sent over a network. The second issue is related to the possibility of tracking down the user activities associated with the biometric acquisition, even in the far future. This produces in the user the perception of the possibility to be "tracked" in his movements or in his buying and lifestyle. Commonly, this issue is associated with a sort of "big brother" phobia, in which a superior entity is capable of observing and acquiring knowledge on each activity of the user.

In a negligible part of the population, the usage of a biometric system is also perceived as uncomfortable or dangerous. For example, the fingerprint sensor—when previously used by other people and not properly cleaned—can be considered as unpleasant or disgusting. Or face and iris acquisition systems might induce apprehension to have the eyes damaged by lasers and/or IR sources. Very interestingly, users often overlook others' privacy-related problems arising when biometrics are involved.

The first point concerns the possible usage of biometric information for operating *Proscription Lists*. For example, a user can be classified from a previous behavior or activity in a specific class, and then—as a consequence of this classification—some services and accesses can be denied. Important examples of this situation are the black lists present in call centers and service providers especially designed to identify and to manage the users considered as "offending" or "not-collaborative." Other examples are the "bad-credit" lists filled in many investor and mutual funds companies. Indeed, proscription lists can be employed also without the adoption of biometric systems (and actually they are), but the usage of biometric technologies can make the situation more and more dramatic.

The second point concerns the fact that many biometric features can be used to *obtain personal information* of the users, such as medical information of past illnesses or the current (and future) clinical trends. For example, the retinal pattern acquired by the biometric system can produce valuable information on the presence of hypertension, diabetes, and others illnesses [2]. Much more personal information can be extracted from DNA samples [3].

## 25.2.2  Applicative Contexts

The real risk of privacy-invasiveness can be analyzed in more detail with respect to both the final application which the biometric system is dedicated to and the biometric trait that is involved. Table 25.1 plots a qualitative representation of the privacy risks versus 10 different application features, according to the International Biometric Group [4].

Biometric *covert applications* (such as the surveillance systems without explicit authorization from the users) are considered to be more privacy invasive. On the other hand, the biometric systems for identification or verification that are *optional* are considered as more privacy compliant. In this case, users can decide to not be checked by a biometric system, and they can adopt a different identification/verification system.

Privacy is considered to be exposed to a greater risk when the biometric system performs an *identification* instead of a simpler verification task. This is related to the fact that the identification process encompasses a "one-to-many" comparison, which,

**Table 25.1.** Applicative Aspects Concerning the Privacy (According to the IBG)

| Lower ← Risk of Privacy Invasiveness → Greater | | |
|---:|:---:|:---|
| Overt | ↔ | Covert |
| Optional | ↔ | Mandatory |
| Verification | ↔ | Identification |
| Fixed period | ↔ | Indefinite |
| Private sector | ↔ | Public sector |
| Individual, customer | ↔ | Employee, citizen |
| Enrollee | ↔ | Institution |
| Personal storage | ↔ | Database storage |
| Behavioral | ↔ | Physiological |
| Templates | ↔ | Images |

in most cases, is not carried out in the same place of the acquisition (typically, the biometric data are sent through a network to a database for the comparisons).

Also the *duration* of the retention of the biometric data impacts the privacy risk. If retention expires in a fixed period of time, the privacy risk is reduced. Best practice notions require that every project which encompasses biometric data retention should always explicitly state its duration.

Different risks are present with respect to the sector of application: The biometric setups in the *public sector* are considered to be more susceptible to privacy-invasiveness than the same installations in the *private sector*.

Also the *role* of the individuals that use the biometric system has great impact on the privacy. There roles have an increasing privacy risk: individual, customer, employee, citizen. The most relevant privacy invasion is related to the association of the fundamental rights of the individual to a biometric identity test. The privacy risks are lower in the applications where the individuals retain usage rights over the biometric data.

Also the *storage method* of the biometric data affects the privacy risk. The worst case is when they are all stored in a central database, out of the user's control. The best case is when the user personally holds the biometric data—for example, when the personal biometric information is stored only on a smart card belonging to the users.

The distinction between behavioral and physiological traits is relevant with respect to the privacy risks. The *physiological data* (such as fingerprints, or iris templates) can be used in a more invasive manner. This is related to the fact that the physiological traits are the most stable in time, and they are characterized by very high verification/identification accuracies. On the other hand, the *behavioral traits* tend to be less accurate, and, most of the time, they request the user collaboration.

Also, the storage format is relevant: *Templates* are usually carrying much less information than the original sample/images. While they are less powerful when used as direct identifiable data, they are privacy-invasive.

**Table 25.2.** Data Collection Approaches

| Approach | Examples |
| --- | --- |
| Protective | Enterprise security, account-holder verification |
| Sympathetic | Application of the best practice notions in common applications |
| Neutral | Personal PCA, home PC, access control |
| Invasive | Surveillance, some centralized national ID services |

## 25.2.3  System Design and Data Collection

Another useful taxonomy concerns the different approaches for biometric data collection and storing. The IBG classifies four different classes concerning the privacy protection (Table 25.2): protective, invasive, neutral, sympathetic [4].

A *privacy-protective* system is designed to protect or limit the access to personal information, providing a means for an individual to establish a trusted identity. In this case, the biometric systems use biometrics data to protect personal information that might otherwise be copied, stolen, or misused.

A *privacy-sympathetic* system limits access/usage to personal data. A privacy-sympathetic approach encompasses the specific design of elements able to protect biometric data from unauthorized access and usage. Also, the storage and the transmission of biometric data must be informed, if not driven, by privacy concerns.

In a *privacy-neutral* system, privacy aspects are not important or the potential privacy impact is slight. Privacy-neutral systems are designed to be difficultly misused with regard to privacy issues, but they do not have the capability to protect personal privacy.

A *privacy-invasive* system facilitates or enables the usage of personal data in a fashion that is contrary to privacy principles. In privacy-invasive systems, personal data are used for purposes broader than what originally intended. Systems that facilitate the linkage of personal data without an individual's consent, as well as those in which personal data are loosely protected, belong to this class.

## 25.2.4  Technology Evaluation

The different biometric technologies associated to each biometric trait can produce various levels of privacy risk. Table 25.3 shows the overall risk for the user's privacy associated to the specific trait. The privacy-related aspects are summarized by taking into account the four most significant technologies features [4].

The first feature is associated with the capability of the technology to process searches in databases of biometric records. The higher this capability, the higher privacy risk.

The second feature is associated to the possibility of the technology to effectively work in an overt or covert fashion. For example, a face recognition system can be

**Table 25.3.** Privacy Risk Ranking with Respect the Available Technologies[a]

| Trait | Verif./Id. | Behav./Phys. | Ov./Cov. | DB Comp. | Overall Risk |
|---|---|---|---|---|---|
| Face | High | Medium | High | High | High |
| Fingerprint | High | High | Low | High | High |
| Retina | High | High | Low | Low | Medium |
| Iris | High | High | Low | Low | Medium |
| Hand | Low | Medium | Low | Low | Low |
| Voice | Low | Low | Medium | Low | Low |
| Keystroke | Low | Low | Medium | Low | Low |
| Signature | Low | Low | Low | Low | Low |

[a] Verif., verification; Id., identification; Behav., behavioral; Phys., physiological; Ov., overt; Cov., covert; DB Comp., database compatibility.

more likely used in a covert manner than a classical fingerprint system. The higher this capability, the higher the privacy risk.

The third feature tends to distinguish the behavioral traits from the physiological ones. The acquisition of most behavioral traits need cooperation from the user and they are less stable in time, hence they are considered to be more privacy compliant than the physiological. The higher the need of user cooperation or the variability in time, the lower the privacy risk.

The fourth feature is related to two points: (1) the technology interoperability when working with different databases and (2) the presence of numerous and/or large available databases to process comparisons. For example, a face acquisition can be used for multiple search in different databases with relatively low efforts. Similarly, many—and large—databases of fingerprints templates exist and they can be queried using fingerprints taken with different sensor and techniques. Summarizing: The higher the interoperability and the presence of available databases, the higher the privacy risk.

The last column in Table 25.3 reports the overall risk of the relative technologies obtained by qualitatively weighting all the feature scores.

## 25.2.5  Best Practice for Privacy Assessment in Biometrics

It is worth noting that the biometric features, samples, and templates cannot be considered as "secrets" since it is possible to capture them to create real or digital artifacts suitable to attack a biometric system [1]. But, in any case, the protection of the biometric data is absolutely essential from many points of view such as privacy and security issues [5].

The design and the usage of a biometric system should always respect strict guidelines in order to protect the user privacy. These notions encompass four main points [4]: (i) the scope and the capabilities of the system; (ii) the data protection;

(iii) the user control of personal data; and (iv) the disclosure, auditing, and accountability of the biometric system. In the following discussion, we refer to two main classes of actors: the users and the operators who manage the biometric system.

The first point concerns the scope and the capabilities of the system. First of all, the scope and the functionalities of the system should not be expanded without the explicit and informed consensus of all the users. From the capability point of view, the retention of the biometric information must be limited to the minimal amount. In general, the biometric system stores the enrollment data, but the verification data should always be deleted. Only templates should be recorded: Any row data, images, and recordings should be deleted as soon as possible during the functioning. Also, the collection of other information should not happen and absolutely should not not be integrated into the biometric data. In addition, the termination date of all system functionalities should be provided, or, at least, the deletion date must be communicated to the user.

The second point focus on *data protection*. The use of proper techniques to protect the biometric data should always be considered. Suitable examples are the adoption of encryption primitives and private networks that must be designed and managed using the state-of-the-art best practices. Systems should also be hosted in secure and controlled areas. These conditions must be ensured for the entire life cycle of the biometric system. It is important to note that also the result of the matching phase (the "match," "non-match," and errors cases) must be protected and considered as private information. The final issue concerns the limitation of the access of the biometric data to a well-defined and limited group of operators.

The third point is related to the *user control of personal data*. The user must keep the control on her/his biometric data. The biometric system should be used voluntarily by the user, and, in any case, the system must ensure to the user the possibility to be unenrolled. In addition, the user should be always able to correct and modify her/his personal data.

The fourth point describes the *disclosure, auditing, and accountability* of the biometric data. The exact purpose of the biometric system must be explicated to the operators and the enrollees. In particular, it must be explained if the biometric acquisition is optional or compulsory. It is important to disclose when the biometric system is used, especially when enrollment and verification or identification phases are carried on. The guidelines suggest also that each operator must be accountable for the possible missuses/errors perpetrated during the working activities. Also, suitable procedures must be considered in order to solve disputes concerning the usage of the biometric system. The owner of the biometric system and the operators must also be able to provide a clear and effective process of auditing when an institution or a third party must perform a critical review of all the modules that compose the biometric system.

A broad and rapidly growing literature is focused on the goal of protecting and augmenting the privacy protection of a biometric system. In the following part of this chapter we will focus in particular on the multidisciplinary approaches that encompass biometric and cryptographic techniques.

## 25.3 BIOMETRIC TEMPLATES PROTECTION

Much work in the literature has been devoted to the construction of techniques for the protection of biometric templates in biometric-based authentication schemes. The naive approach of storing biometric templates during the enrollment phase (for the successive identification of verification process) in a more or less secured database has a number of risks for users privacy. The strict association between each user and his biometric templates raises concerns on possible uses and abuses of such kind of sensible information, since biometrics traits cannot be replaced or modified. A stolen template after an unauthorized access to the database could help a malicious user to impersonate a legitimate user and steal private information or run applications accessing sensible resources. The loss of biometric data is then an important security issue that directly affects the valuation of a biometric authentication schema and should be carefully considered to prevent thefts of identity [5].

In many communities (in Europe see the Biometric Identification Technology Ethic (BITE Project) [6]), groups of researchers are investigating the legal background of biometric technologies, to define and consider bioethical issues arising from emerging biometric identification technologies. Different countries are adopting strict rules to limit the impact of biometric technologies on the privacy of citizens. The proposed authentication schemes often have to face the legal constraints imposed by such directives considering the risk of function creep and data misuse.

To protect users privacy, biometric templates are usually transformed before their storage during the enrollment phase, such that the authentication process can be correctly performed, but unauthorized access to the stored templates leaves the adversary with a small and unusable amount of sensible data on the biometrics of the attacked user. A natural way to protect biometric templates could be to replicate the approach used in password-based authentication schemes where users' passwords are typically stored in their hashed form (see Figure 25.1). Due to the mono-directionality of the used hash functions, the knowledge of the hashes does not give any information; so if the database has been corrupted, the passwords are not compromised. For biometric templates, things are more complicated since usable one-way transformation of the templates are not so easy to achieve. Indeed the higher variability within different readings of biometric data makes them unsuitable to be directly used as input for hash functions or as cryptographic keys.

In the literature, a wide range of techniques have been presented based on the combination of biometrics and cryptography, in order to cope with both problems: variability of biometric templates and protection of personal data. A comprehensive survey of different approaches and of the related problems can be found in reference 7. The process of generating cryptographic keys from biometrics generally relies on an error tolerant representation of the biometric features or on the selection of a distance preserving robust transformation operating on the biometric template. The transformation of biometric templates in a suitable representation that can be efficiently treated—for example, in a metric space—is itself an active research area [8]. IrisCode [9] and Fingercode [10] are techniques for the extraction of a binary string from iris and fingerprint templates, respectively. The referred model is depicted in

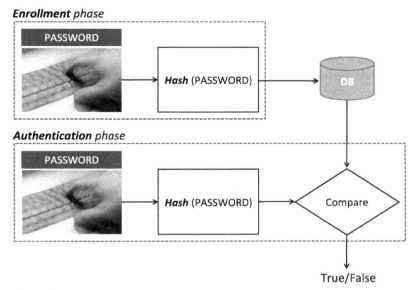

**Figure 25.1.** Password based authentication scheme.

Figure 25.2, where a string representation is extracted from the considered biometric feature and successively a noninvertible transformation is applied in order to securely store the biometric template. The same transformation is applied to the fresh biometric templates acquired during the authentication phase, and the biometric match succeeds if the two obtained transformations are equal or sufficiently close. The noninvertibility of the transformation ensures that an adversary does not get any valuable information even if he gets or steals the stored (transformed) template.

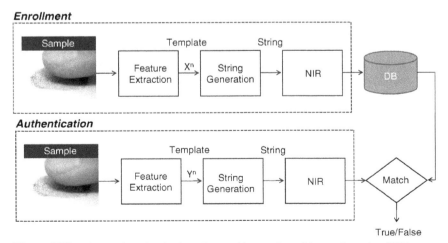

**Figure 25.2.** A biometric authentication scheme with a non invertible transformation (NIR).

Another recently developed approach relies on the extraction of *helper data* during the enrollment phase which is stored together with the hashed form of the biometrics. Such data can be made publicly available and are used in the authentication phase in combination with fresh biometric features in order to reconstruct the derived secret. The recently introduced fuzzy cryptographic primitives [11], *secure or fuzzy sketch* and *fuzzy extractor*, build on this principle and allow the secure extraction of a uniformly random string from the (biometric) input in a noise-tolerant way. Based on this primitives, recently several constructions for devising practically usable biometric authentication systems have been proposed [12, 13].

## 25.3.1    Hash Based Transformations

Hash-based biometric authentication schemes rely on variations of hash functions, ensuring a robustness property so that small changes in the input biometric samples produce the same hash value. In Davida et al. [14, 15], "robust" hash functions are used to protect the sensitive user template, avoiding the need for storing the biometric template in the database. Different kinds of comparison between the hashed templates are used in the one-way transformation combined with a secure cryptographic hash function. The one-way transformation is designed as a combination of various Gaussian functions to behave as a robust hash scheme. Then, the hash function is used to cryptographically secure the biometric templates stored in the database.

Such techniques have been applied taking into account different biometric traits. In reference 16 a similar technique has been defined for signatures. In this application a pen-based PDA is used to collect a signature that is transformed into a hash value. Then, the hash value is also used to create a key for a secure data communication channel. The authentication is not made using a typical biometric signature comparison but using a vector of hash values, composed by 24 features extracted from the signature. The method uses a statistical approach: During enrollment, four signatures per user are required to build a personal interval matrix that will be stored in the database. The final decision is made by comparing the fresh hash values in the vector with the stored interval matrix of each individual present in the database. In reference 17 palmprint biometrics has been considered. The features of palmprints are extracted from the palm images and then the Fisher discriminant analysis is applied to select the most significant ones producing a reduction of the space dimensionality. This set of features is then combined with a randomized number (the token) by the "PalmHashing" algorithm achieving a discretization process. This algorithm projects the biometric input into an orthonormal base produced by the randomized number (the token) using the well-known Gram–Schmidt process.

The *Biohashing* technique has been introduced in reference 18 and relies on the usage of a two-factor authenticator combination of pseudorandom numbers and a biometric binarized feature. The main disadvantage of the BioHashing method is that poor verification performances are displayed when an impostor steals the pseudorandom number used to build the ID of a genuine and tries to authenticates as the genuine [19].

The usage of a multimodal biometric authentication system where one or two biometric features have been "biohashed" is shown to reduce the effect of this drawback, but the proposed technique increases the overall equal error rate. In reference 20 a biohashing approach is used to produce the Facehashing algorithm. In this case, the face images are preprocessed using the Fourier–Mellin wavelet transformation in order to obtain a low-frequency face representation. The resulting representation is more robust with respect to facial expressions and small occlusions. Then, a discretization process is defined, achieved by a repeated inner product of the used data and an orthonormal base obtained with a secret number (the token) using the Gram–Schmidt process. The final hashed data are considered to be a zero-knowledge representation of the user input. In reference 21 the face is used to produce a nonreversible binary template by using a recognition of fiducial points (eyes, nose, eyebrows) and the application of a set of Gabor filters to the face images. The quantization of the extracted features is then processed using a comparison between the obtained features vector from the face and the mean features vectors present in the database. Every bit in the binary template is associated with a reliability estimate based on the standard deviation of its corresponding feature. The most reliable components of the vector after quantization are used to compose the final binary template. The matching function has been designed using a correlation quantifier.

A different approach aims at building a transformation operated on the original biometric template, which is difficult to be inverted but which can preserve similarity. In reference 22 a general scheme is proposed to produce a noninvertible function capable of transforming a point pattern (for example, the minutiae set present in a fingerprint or the frequency-amplitude parameters of a speech pattern) using high-order polynomials. Ang et al. [23] have proposed a transformation and matching algorithm for fingerprints. The transformation is based on geometric translations of the minutiae coordinates and their angles. Such transformation depends on a key and is considered not reversible. Changing the key, it is possible to produce a new transformed template from the same fingerprint. Unfortunately, the study does not provide a complete analysis of the security of the scheme, focusing only on the error rates. A deeper insight on geometrical and functional transformations in fingerprint biometrics is given in reference 24. The study compares the capability of the cartesian, radial, and functional transformations in producing cancelable biometrics. This approach provides flexibility to change the transformation from one application to another to ensure the security and privacy of biometric data. The paper demonstrates the nonreversibility by proving that it is computationally hard to recover the original biometric identifier from a transformed version. A similar approach has been proposed in reference 25 to achieve a biometric system for offline verification of certified, cryptographically secure documents. The presented technique can produce printable IDs obtained from an extracted and compressed iris feature and an arbitrary text.

In most of the presented approaches, rigorous security analysis is missing. In particular, it is not clear the real robustness of these schemes once the hash values/function are also compromised (or the transformed-templates/transformation-algorithm for the second approach), as well as the related keys and parameters (i.e., the tokens).

## 25.3.2   Cryptographic Fuzzy Primitives

A different set of techniques coping with the variability of biometric templates is based on the use of error correction codes aiming to extract an unique associated feature from each different biometric reading: The different readings are treated as corrupted codewords and are accordingly decoded. During the verification phase, the feature retrieved by a biometric reading is given as input to a hash function and is compared with the hash value stored during the enrollment phase.

A generalization of this basic approach has been proposed by a group of researchers that introduced fuzzy cryptographic primitives (i.e., fuzzy or secure sketches and fuzzy extractors) which can be used in different fields of application and biometric authentication scheme as well. Such constructions usually do not rely on a particular metric space even if most of the constructions have been given considering Hamming distance. However, set difference and edit distance metrics have also been considered, referring to the size of the symmetric difference of two input sets in the first case and referring to the number of insertions and deletions needed to convert one string into the other in the second case.

### 25.3.2.1   Fuzzy Commitment

In reference 26, Juels and Wattenberg proposed the "fuzzy commitment" scheme where a secret message is protected using a biometric template. In this case, an error correcting code is used in order to associate a codeword $c$ with a person and to compute an offset ($\delta = c \oplus x$) for the biometric template $x$. The encrypted message (the *fuzzy commitment*) is then represented by the pair ($\delta, h(c)$), where $h(c)$ is a one way hash function. It is worth noticing that neither the biometric feature nor the associated codeword is publicly stored. The authentication process is correctly performed if a fresh biometric reading $y$ allows the computation of a binary string $c' = \delta \oplus y$ sufficiently close to $c$ so that the code decodes it to $c$ and the comparison between their hash values succeeds.

A similar construction has been proposed by Hao et al. [27], with the application of an iris code feature extraction algorithm and the combined use of Hadamard and Reed–Solomon codes.

### 25.3.2.2   Fuzzy Vault

Juels and Sudan [28] proposed a "fuzzy vault scheme" relying on the polynomial interpolation technique in order to cope with variability of the stored biometric template. With such technique the problem of having an order invariant representation of the biometric template is overcome. The basic idea is to lock a secret in a vault using an unordered set. The secret could be successfully retrieved using another unordered set that substantially overlaps with the first used set. More in detail, the secret is encoded using the evaluation of a polynomial over a given set of points using the Reed–Solomon encoding scheme: that is, such points represent a codeword. To increase the security, a set of *chaff* points are added to the first set in order to form the vault. To reconstruct the codeword, the user has to provide a set of points that overlaps with the original set.

The fuzzy vault construction has been successfully applied by Uludag and Jain using fingerprint templates [29]. Clancy et al. [30] proposed a construction of a biometric identification schema using a secure smartcard to store the vault. Their construction however has been slightly modified in order to cope with real-life parameters. Finally the problem of the selection of chaff points, avoiding that the attacker get enabled to distinguish between chaff and real points, has been considered by Chang and Li [31]. Some bounds on the entropy loss have also been introduced.

### 25.3.2.3  Fuzzy Sketch and Fuzzy Extractor

An important step toward the realization of personal identification system based on a cryptographic key derived from biometric features has recently been taken by Dodis et al. [11]. In their work, novel primitives were introduced: the *secure or fuzzy sketch* and *fuzzy extractor* which find a natural application in such kind of systems.

Fuzzy sketches resolve the problem of error tolerance, enabling the computation of a public string $P$ from a biometric reading $r$, such that from another reading $r'$ sufficiently close to $r$ it is possible to reconstruct the original reading. Furthermore, the knowledge of $P$ should not reveal too much information on the original reading $r$; that is, the entropy on $r$ is enough to be useful even if $P$ is public. Fuzzy extractors address the problem of nonuniformity by associating a random uniform string $R$ to the public string $P$ and still keeping all the properties of fuzzy sketches. Indeed, fuzzy extractors can be built out of fuzzy sketches and enable the recovering of the secret uniform random string $R$ from the knowledge of the public string $P$ and a reading $r'$ sufficiently close to $r$.

To present more formally the fuzzy primitives and the associated constructions, we introduce the basic notions. In particular, even if different metric spaces have been considered in reference 32, we focus only on Hamming distance metric and the fuzzy commitment construction of Juels et al., which can be easily turned in a more robust fuzzy extractor primitive.

A metric space $\mathcal{M}$ is a finite set equipped with a nonnegative distance function $d : \mathcal{M}x\mathcal{M} \rightarrow \mathcal{R}^+$. Consider the Hamming space $\mathcal{H}$, where $\mathcal{M} = \Sigma^n$ for some alphabet $\Sigma$, and consider the Hamming distance which for two strings $w, w' \in \Sigma^n$, returns the number of bits in which the two words differ. A $(\mathcal{M}, m, m', t)$-fuzzy sketch is a pair (Fsk, Cor), where:

- Fsk is a (typically) randomized sketching function that on input $w \in H$ outputs a sketch $P \in \{0, 1\}^*$, such that for all random variable $W$ over $H$ with min-entropy $H_\infty(W) \geq m$, the average min-entropy of $W$ given Fsk(W) is a least $m'$.

- Cor is a correction function that enables the recovery of $w$ from its sketch and another vector $w'$ close to $w$: Given a word $w' \in H$ and a sketch $P$, output a word $w'' \in H$ such that for any $P = \text{Fsk}(w)$ and $d(w, w') \leq t$, it holds that $w'' = w$.

A $(\mathcal{M}, m, l, t, \epsilon)$-fuzzy extractor is a pair of procedures that generate *Gen* and *Rep*, where:

- *Gen* is a randomized generation function that on input $w \in \mathcal{M}$ extracts a private string $R \in \{0, 1\}^l$ and public string $P$ such that for all random variable $W$ over $\mathcal{M}$ with min-entropy $H_\infty(W) \geq m$, it holds that $r$ is close to uniform even for observers $P$, that is, the statistical distance $D(R, P)(U_l, P) \leq \epsilon$.

- *Rep* is a regeneration function that, given a word $w' \in H$ and a public string $P$, outputs a string $S$ such that if $d(w, w') \leq t$ and $(R, P) = \text{Gen}(w)$, it holds that $\text{Rep}(w', P) = R = S$.

The first property (security) guarantees the uniformity of the extracted secret string $R$ (remember that the min-entropy, the second property (correctness), guarantees the correctness of the reproduction.

In this setting it is possible to show that the fuzzy commitment construction of Juels and Wattenberg is a $(\mathcal{M} = \Sigma^n, n, k, t, 0)$-fuzzy extractor when a binary linear code $C$ of length $n$, dimension $k$, and correction capacity $t$ (i.e., with parameters $[n, k, 2t + 1]$) is used and when W is uniform (i.e., $m = n$). In this case, $\text{Gen}(w)$, where $s = w - C(x)$, returns $R = x$ and $P = s$. To execute $\text{Rep}(w', P)$, decode $w' - P$ to obtain $C(x)$ and apply the decoding function to obtain $x$. Notice that $s$ is random when also $w$ is random, and if $W$ is not uniform, $s$ would leak information about $x$. In general, it is possible to obtain for a given code $C$ with parameters $[n, k, 2t + 1]$ and any $m$ and $\epsilon$ a $(M, m, l, t, \epsilon)$ fuzzy extractor with $\ell = m + k - n - 2 * \log(1/\epsilon) + 2$, by using in the extraction phase pairwise independent hashing.

In a successive work, Boyen [28], pointed out how multiple use of the same fuzzy secret can cause some security problem, introducing outsider and insider attack scenarios, where an adversary tries to obtain information on the secret by performing repeatedly extractions and regenerations of the fuzzy secret. In such scenarios, with some limitations, it is possible to show that information-theoretic security can be achieved and existing constructions can be adapted to satisfy the additional requirements. More general attack models and constructions to achieve secure remote biometric authentication are proposed in reference 33.

### 25.3.2.4  *Fuzzy-Based Authentication Schemes*

Since the introduction of the fuzzy primitives, many researchers have proposed several authentication schemes based on the applications of such techniques. A general framework to design and analyze a secure sketch for biometric templates is presented in reference 12, where the face biometrics have been used as an example. Interestingly, the paper shows that theoretical bounds have their limitations in practical schemes. In particular, it has been shown that the entropy loss of the template cannot be considered a complete description of the robustness level of the scheme in practical application, while the analysis of the FAR and FRR should be always envisioned. In reference 34 a near-optimal error-correcting code is discussed (based on a two-dimensional iterative min-sum decoding algorithm) for application with iris biometrics in a fuzzy sketches scheme. The paper produces also an explicit estimation of the upper bounds on the correction capacity of fuzzy sketches on iris-based biometrics. A fuzzy-based construction for fingerprint biometrics has been discussed in reference 13, where the string representation of the biometric templates relays on Fingercodes.

## 25.4 PRIVACY IN MULTIMODAL SYSTEMS

Humans beings typically identify other individuals using a biometric approach that encompasses more than a single biometric trait. For example, we can recognize a person watching his face, but the final decision is often integrated using other biometric traits such as the voice, the stature, the gait, or the behavior. In a similar way, a multimodal biometric system uses different biometric traits and combines them efficiently [35]. More in detail, in the literature the term *multibiometric system* is used when different approaches are considerd. In particular, the term is used when one or more of the following setups are present: multiple sensors (e.g., solid state and optical fingerprint sensors), multiple acquisitions (e.g., different frames/poses of the face), multiple traits (e.g., an eye and a fingerprint), multiple instances of the same trait kind (e.g., left eye, and right eye), multiple algorithm (e.g., different preprocessing and/or matching techniques). In this framework, a multimodal system is a case of a multibiometric system.

The usage of multimodal systems has an heavier impact on the privacy of the user since the amount of the involved personal information is greater. This issue can be better understood taking into account the specific peculiarities of multimodal systems.

### 25.4.1 Pros and Cons of Multimodal Systems

The multimodal approach has several positive aspects. For example, typically, the performance of a matching system is improved with respect to the same system working with the single traits which compose the multimodal system. Using different traits, it is possible for these systems to increase the population coverage, since some individuals cannot have one or more biometric traits (illnesses, injuries, etc.). In addition, the global fault tolerance of the system is enhanced, since, if one biometric subsystem is not working properly (e.g., a sensor problem occurred), the multimodal system can keep working using the remaining biometric submodules that are correctly functioning.

The multiple acquisition of different traits at the same time (or in a very narrow time frame) achieves an effective deterring against spoofing actions. Also, the efficiencies of the database management can be improved by indexing techniques.

In particular, the performances of a multimodal system are improved when uncorrelated traits are used (for instance, an eye and a fingerprint, the right eye and the left eye).

The usage of multimodal biometric systems has also some important drawbacks. The first is related to the higher cost of the systems, since they are composed by multiple and different biometric subsystems for each trait that has been selected.

A second aspect is related to the acquisition time: A multi-acquisition is mostly longer than a single acquisition. In addition, the user can perceive the multiple acquisition as more invasive and/or inconvenient.

A third point is associated with the fact that the retention of biometric data is proportionally larger in the case of multimodal biometric systems. Hence, the privacy issues discussed in previous sections of this chapter became much more relevant [36].

## 25.4.2  Design of Privacy Compliant Multimodal Systems

Proper guidelines for the design of the multimodal systems can reduce the described drawbacks and encourage its use in a wide range of application for authentication. Hence, in addition to the guidelines described in previous sections, the following key points should be considered:

- The usage of the templates should be subjected to randomization transformation such that the derived published identifier does not suffer from information leakage.

- When designing a multimodal system, one should carefully take into account the *number* of samples and the *types* of the biometric traits. For example, less biometric traits should be acquired for a low-security application (e.g., the access to a transport system) than for a high-security application (e.g., the access to a nuclear plant). Accordingly, also the choice of the kinds of traits to be used by the multimodal system is relevant with respect to the privacy of the user as discussed in the previous sections.

- Multiple biometric readings should be combined in order to adapt the security of the authentication system to the level requested by the running application. For example, if the same multimodal biometric system is adopted on the same building/area (such as an airport terminal), each restricted area with different levels of security should be accessed by using different traits or combination of traits.

- The multimodal system should be modular in order to not rely on a proprietary algorithm. In this case, the discovery of novel techniques for biometric recognition can be easily embedded in the system—in particular, taking into account new techniques and new template formats which are more privacy-compliant.

- Proper protection techniques must be envisioned in order to avoid that each biometric sample/template/feature that is composing the multimodal acquisition might be used for other searches in different single-trait databases in an unauthorized context.

The actuation of the previous guidelines is made difficult by the fact that some of them seem to appear as discordant or in mutual exclusion (e.g., the third point can be in conflict to the fifth point), but some techniques available in the literature seem capable to effectively overcome these drawbacks.

As a matter of fact, the enhancements of the sensors and of the hardware/software architectures associated with the reduction of the system costs will produce a growing interest and diffusion of the multimodal systems in the market. The application of proper, practical, and standard privacy-compliant guidelines is becoming more and more necessary.

## 25.5   AN EXEMPLIFYING SCHEME

Building over the considerations of the previous sections, we describe the design of a multimodal verification scheme satisfying much of the discussed issues regarding privacy compliance. The discussion will point out how few biometric traits might be used to construct an identification code for a subject while still ensuring protection to the biometric templates themselves. Also, it will clarify a few problematic aspects that might be faced when constructing an actual implementation.

A typical multimodal biometric verification scheme provides two basic modules. The first, the *enroll* module, creates some sort of ID linked to a single user starting from the user's biometric samples. The ID could then be stored in, for example, a document or a smart card and must be provided during the verification phase. The second module, the *verification* one, verifies if the ID matches a new set of freshly provided biometrics.

While the number of biometric traits might in principle be increased as desired, we limit the discussion to the case of two independent biometric readings.

### 25.5.1   A Multimodal Enrollment Module

At enrollment, as in common multimodal biometric systems, two different biometric readings are collected: for example, an iris scan of one eye and a fingerprint or the fingerprints from two different fingers. The samples are then processed using the feature extraction algorithms of choice, selected among what the market or the open literature offer. Each algorithm delivers a set of features depending on the biometric trait, which are then turned into a binary string. For example, concerning fingerprints, the features describe characteristic points of the ridges' pattern; such numbers are then collected in what is called a binary "template," possibly according to a standard. An example is the ANSI INCITS 378-2004 standard.[1] Similarly, for iris, the image of the eye is processed to obtained a string of bits (the so-called iris code) directly.

In a simpler multimodal biometric system, the two templates denoted with $I_1$ and $I_2$ (Figure 25.3) would be stored in a database or a portable ID. An attacher who could somehow access the database or recover the ID might obtain with little effort the templates of the user. To avoid such a scenario, the templates are generally encrypted using a public key infrastructure (thus relaying on, for example, a network). In here,

---

[1] American National Standard for Information Technology X Finger Minutiae Format for Data Interchange.

**Enrollment**

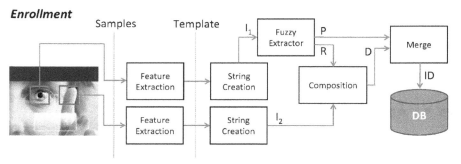

**Figure 25.3.** A multimodal biometric enroll module satisfying privacy compliance issues.

following a different approach, the biometric strings are concealed exploiting their peculiar quality of being "similar" when obtained from the same subject.

The novelty with respect to a multimodal biometric system begins in Figure 25.3 after the construction of $I_1$ and $I_2$. First, $I_1$ is fed into a "fuzzy extractor." Fuzzy extractors are cryptographic primitives that enable the extraction of a random uniform string $R$ from a given input in a noise-tolerant way. Therefore they convert a noisy nonuniform input, such as a biometric reading, into a easily and reliably reproducible binary string, allowing a certain degree of tolerance in the given input. The tolerance to variations within biometric strings is typically obtained using an $[n, k, 2t + 1]$ error-correcting code, where $n$ and $k$ are the lengths of the codeword and the message, respectively, and $t$ is the number of errors the code can correct. The code-correcting capability $t$ needs to be large enough to compensate for within-subject variability in the biometric samples. On the other hand, it must be smaller that the between-subjects variability, or otherwise the tolerance of the fuzzy extractor might be so large that impostors might be recognized as genuine ID holders.

But this is actually not a big issue in practice. In fact, usually the opposite problem arises and the error-correcting capability of typical codes is not large enough for practical applications involving biometric samples. Given the large inter-subjects variability of biometric templates, the fraction of errors the code must be able to withstand is larger than in usual ECC applications. Common ECC code, like BCH, are capable of correcting a fraction of errors $n/t$ strictly $< 0.25\%$, thus are often ruled out.[2] Others binary codes might get closer to the $t/n = 1/2$ Singleton bound, but the Plotkin bound implies [37] that a binary code can correct more than $n/4$ errors only at the expenses of reducing the length of codeword to about $\log n$. This is the route that one might pursue by deriving a binary code from a Reed–Solomon code for which time-efficient decoding routines exist.

---

[2] Actually, BCH codes could be employed in the schemes we suggested, but the construction needs to be generalized slightly. The main idea is that by injecting errors only over a restricted part of a longer codeword, a larger local error correction ratio is obtained, which in turn could easily satisfies the requirements imposed by the biometrics at hand.

The fuzzy extractor produces two binary strings. The first, $R$, must be kept secret while the second, $P$, can be made public without disclosing any information on both $I_1$ and $R$. So, the scheme started with two "secrets," $I_1$ and $I_2$, and by now we only swapped the secret $I_1$ for $R$. But the important difference is that with $R$ being uniformly random by construction if we properly compose $R$ and $I_2$ with a fuzzy commitment, we are sure that no information is disclosed on both. Along this line a possible composition function might be the binary $x$ or function.

The two strings $D$ and $P$, while derived from the biometrics provided by the subject at enrollment (and no other information), cannot be used to obtain information on the biometric templates. They might be merged and published on an ID which the user could even safely lose.

### 25.5.1.1  A Correspondent Verification Scheme

The *verification* phase enables a "strong" authentication of the subject, who has to provide both (a) the biometric traits that were requested at enrollment and (b) the ID he received. The overall structure is reported in Figure 25.4.

The verification phase follows the line of a typical multimodal biometric verification. The subject is requested the same biometric traits he provided at enrollment, and the samples are collected. From the samples, two fresh binary templates are constructed: $I_1'$ and $I_2'$.

The fuzzy reconstructor guarantees that if the distance of $I_1'$ from $I_1$ is within the tolerance of the error-correcting code, and $P$ is available (thus the ID is provided), the same secret $R$ built at enrollment can be constructed (hence the name "reconstructor"). With $R$ in hand, $I_2$ is easily decomposed from $D$. If the subject is an impostor, the distance of its biometric sample and the ID holder sample is larger than the fuzzy reconstructor tolerance and $R$ is not reconstructed. The verification scheme is positively concluded if the retrieved biometric $I_2$ matches the fresh $I_2'$.

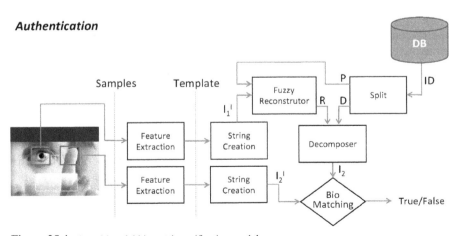

**Figure 25.4.** A multimodal biometric verification module.

In a biometric multimodal system with two inputs, we would have had two biometric comparisons. In the simple example, we offered instead the only biometric test that is performed between $I_2$ and $I_2'$ while the other enters the scheme through the fuzzy reconstructor only. While this is not an issue for biometric tests based only on Hamming distance measures (like in the case of iris codes), it is the small price that one needs to pay to enforce protection of the biometrics themselves.

## 25.6  CONCLUSIONS

In this chapter we focused on issues and relative possible solutions regarding the privacy protection in the context of biometric systems. We described (a) the risks perceived by the user approaching biometric systems and (b) the actual risks for her/his privacy.

Privacy issues are pervasive in all the design phases of a biometric system: They can be related to the applicative context, to the approaches and goals set up when collecting the biometric data, and to the involved traits and technologies. Best practice notions have been discussed to ensure a privacy compliant design and management of biometric systems.

Recent advances show that it is possible to achieve an effective biometric template protection. Most techniques present in the literature are based on methods that combine standard cryptographic techniques and biometrics for the purpose of providing a privacy-compliant and deployable identity verification system. The approaches we discussed are the fuzzy-based constructions (Fuzzy Commitment, Fuzzy Vault, Fuzzy Sketch) and the hash-based techniques. The application of these schemes offers a valid solution to the privacy protection of the user templates.

Multimodal systems revealed new privacy issues, and a set of guidelines for the design of a privacy-compliant system has been discussed. An exemplifying scheme is presented, showing a possible privacy-compliant multimodal system. In particular, the proposed method is inherently multimodal: At least two biometric traits are simultaneously used to create a secure identifier. Such an identifier combines the biometric features extracted in the enroll phase, ensuring that the verification phase can be correctly executed, but avoiding any attempt to mine the privacy of the users. Indeed, the information contained in the identifiers is not sufficient to reconstruct the biometric features of the users, and any abuse of biometric information is then prevented.

Moreover, the presented scheme satisfies the design guidelines. The security properties of the methods have been analyzed informally, and they rely on the well-investigated properties of the used fuzzy cryptographic primitives. The system is completely modular: Both the input biometric readings and the matching procedures can be selected among the different ones proposed in the open literature. Composed systems can be constructed by assembling a number of enroll and verification modules requiring a corresponding larger number of input biometric readings, in order to achieve a higher degree of security when requested by the application.

# REFERENCES

1. A. K. Jain, A. Ross, and S. Pankanti, Biometrics: A tool for information security, *IEEE Trans. Inf. Forens. Securi.* **1**(2):125–143, 2006.
2. J. A. Pugh, J. M. Jacobson, W. A. Van Heuven, J. A. Watters, M. R. Tuley, D. R. Lairson, R. J. Lorimor, A. S. Kapadia, and R. Velez, Screening for diabetic retinopathy: The wide-angle retinal camera, *Diabetes Care* **16**(6):889–895, 1993.
3. K. Inman and N. Rudin, *An Introduction to Forensic DNA Analysis*, CRC Press, Boca Raton, FL, 1997.
4. LLC International Biometric Group, Bioprivacy initiative, 2003.
5. B. Schneier, Biometrics: Uses and abuses, *Commun. ACM* **42**(8):136, 1999.
6. Society Centre for Science and Citizenship. Biometric identification technology ethic (bite project), 2006.
7. U. Uludag, S. Pankanti, S. Prabhakar, and A. Jain, Biometric cryptosystems: Issues and challenges, in *Proceedings of the IEEE, Special Issue on Enabling Security Technologies for Digital Rights Management*, Vol. 92, 2004, pp. 948–960.
8. P. Tuyls, B. Skoric, and T. Kevenaar, editors, *Security with Noisy Data*, Springer, Berlin, 2008.
9. J. G. Daugman, High confidence visual recognition of persons by a test of statistical indenpendence, *IEEE Trans. Pattern Anal. Mach. Intelli.* **15**:1148–1161, 1993.
10. A. K. Jain, S. Prabhakar, L. Hong, and S. Pankanti, Filterbank-based fingerprint matching, *IEEE Trans. Image Processing* **9**(5):846–859, 2000.
11. Y. Dodis, L. Reyzin, and A. Smith, Fuzzy extractors: How to generate strong keys from biometrics and other noisy data, in C. Cachin and J. Camenisch, editors, *Advances in Cryptology (EUROCRYPT 2004)*, Vol. 3027 of *Lecture Notes in Computer Science*, Springer-Verlag, Berlin, 2004.
12. Y. Sutcu, Q. Li, and N. Memon, Protecting biometric templates with sketch: Theory and practice, *IEEE Trans. Info. Forens. Secur.* **2**(3):503–512, 2007.
13. V. V. T. Tong, H. Sibert, J. Lecoeur, and M. Girault, Biometric fuzzy extractors made practical: A proposal based on fingercodes, in *ICB*, 2007, pp. 604–613.
14. G. I. Davida, Y. Frankel, and B. J. Matt, On enabling secure applications through off-line biometric, in *Proceedings of the IEEE International Symposium on Security and Privacy, 1998*, IEEE Press, New York, 1998, pp. 148–157.
15. G. I. Davida, Y. Frankel, B. J. Matt, and R. Peralta, On the relation of error correction and cryptography to an off line biometrics based identification scheme, in *WCC99, Workshop on Coding and Cryptography*, 1999.
16. C. Vielhauer, R. Steinmetz, and A. Mayerhöfer, Biometric hash based on statistical features of online signatures, in *ICPR (1)*, 2002, pp. 123–126.
17. T. Connie, A. T. Beng Jin, M. G. K. Ong, and D. N. C. Ling, Palmhashing: A novel approach for cancelable biometrics, *Inf. Process. Lett.* **93**(1):1–5, 2005.
18. A. T. B. Jin, D. N. C. Ling, and A. Goh, Biohashing: Two factor authentication featuring fingerprint data and tokenised random number, *Pattern Recognit.* **37**(11):2245–2255, 2004.
19. L. Nanni and A. Lumini, Empirical tests on biohashing, *NeuroComputing* **69**(16):2390–2395, 2006.
20. A. T. B. Jin, D. N, C. Ling, and A. Goh, Personalised cryptographic key generation based on face-hashing, *Comput. Secur.* **23**(7):606–614, 2004.
21. T. A. M. Kevenaar, G. Jan Schrijen, M. van der Veen, A. H. M. Akkermans, and F. Zuo, Face recognition with renewable and privacy preserving binary templates, in *AutoID*, 2005, pp. 21–26.
22. N. K. Ratha, J. H. Connell, and R. M. Bolle, Enhancing security and privacy in biometrics-based authentication systems, *IBM Syst. J.* **40**(3):614–634, 2001.
23. R. Ang, R. Safavi-Naini, and L. McAven, Cancelable key-based fingerprint templates, in *ACISP*, 2005, pp. 242–252.
24. N. K. Ratha, S. Chikkerur, J. H. Connell, and R. M. Bolle, Generating cancelable fingerprint templates, *IEEE Trans. Pattern Anal. Mach. Intell.* **29**(4):561–572, 2007.
25. D. Schonberg and D. Kirovski, Eyecerts, *IEEE Trans. Info. Forens. Secur.* **1**:144–153, 2006.

26. A. Juels and M. Wattenberg, A fuzzy commitment scheme, in *CCS '99: Proceedings of the 6th ACM Conference on Computer and Communications Security* ACM Press, New York, 1999, pp. 28–36.
27. F. Hao, R. Anderson, and J. Daugman, Combining cryptography with biometrics effectively, Technical Report UCAM-CL-TR-640, University of Cambridge, Computer Laboratory, United Kingdom, July 2005.
28. A. Juels and M. Sudan, A fuzzy vault scheme, in A. Lapidoth and E. Teletar, editors, *Proceedings of the IEEE International Symposium on Information Theory, 2002*, IEEE Press, New York, 2002, p. 408. The full version of the paper is located at http://www.rsasecurity.com/rsalabs/staff/bios/ajuels/publications/fuzzy-vault/fuzzy_vault.pdf.
29. U. Uludag, S. Pankanti, and A. K. Jain, Fuzzy vault for fingerprints, in T. Kanade, A. K. Jain, and N. K. Ratha, editors, *AVBPA*, Vol. 3546 of *Lecture Notes in Computer Science*, Springer, Berlin, 2005, pp. 310–319.
30. T. C. Clancy, N. Kiyavash, and D. J. Lin, Secure smartcardbased fingerprint authentication, in *WBMA '03: Proceedings of the 2003 ACM SIGMM Workshop on Biometrics Methods and Applications*, ACM, New York, 2003, pp. 45–52.
31. E.-C. Chang and Q. Li, Hiding secret points amidst chaff, in S. Vaudenay, editor, *EUROCRYPT*, Vol. 4004 of *Lecture Notes in Computer Science*, Springer, Berlin, 2006, pp. 59–72.
32. X. Boyen, Reusable cryptographic fuzzy extractors, in *11th ACM Conference on Computer and Communication Security (CCS 2004)*, Vol. 3027, ACM, 2004, pp. 82–91.
33. X. Boyen, Y. Dodis, J. Katz, R. Ostrovsky, and A. Smith, Secure remote authentication using biometric data, in R. Cramer, editor, *Advances in Cryptology (EUROCRYPT 2005)*, Vol. 3494 of *Lecture Notes in Computer Science*, Springer-Verlag, Berlin, 2005.
34. J. Bringer, H. Chabanne, G. Cohen, B. Kindarji, and G. Zémor, Optimal iris fuzzy sketches, in *IEEE Conference on Biometrics: Theory, Applications and Systems (BTAS 07)*, 2007.
35. R. Snelick, U. Uludag, A. Mink, M. Indovina, and A. K. Jain, Large scale evaluation of multimodal biometric authentication using state-of-the-art systems, *IEEE Trans. Pattern Anal. Mach. Intelli.* **27**(3):450–455, 2005.
36. S. Prabhakar, S. Pankanti, and A. K. Jain, Biometric recognition: Security & privacy concerns, *IEEE Secur. Privacy Mag.* **1**(2):33–42, 2003.
37. Y. Dodis, L. Reyzin, and A. Smith, Fuzzy extractors, in P. Tuyls and J. Goseling, editors, *Security with Noisy Data*, Springer-Verlag, Berlin, 2007, Chapter 5, pp. 93–111.

# Chapter 26

# Biometric Encryption: The New Breed of Untraceable Biometrics

**Ann Cavoukian and Alex Stoianov**

## 26.1 INTRODUCTION

Biometric technologies promise many benefits, including stronger user authentication, greater user convenience, improved security, and operational efficiencies. These technologies are now being deployed in a wide range of public and private sector applications, including border security control, crime and fraud prevention, attendance recording, payment systems, and access controls.

Biometric technologies are not, however, without their challenges and risks. These include several important technological challenges (such as accuracy, reliability, data security, user acceptance, cost, and interoperability), as well as challenges associated with ensuring effective privacy protections.

The term *informational* privacy refers to an individual's ability to exercise *personal* control over the collection, use, and disclosure of recorded information about themselves, as well as an organization's responsibility for data protection and the safeguarding of personally identifiable information (PII), in its custody or control. Informational privacy is key to user confidence, trust, and acceptance of new technologies, applications, deployments, and entire industries. As such, it is an essential foundation for the successful widespread deployment of biometric technologies.

A preference for building large-scale interoperable biometric databases that have identification as their primary objective has taken place in an environment defined by the predominant "zero-sum" paradigm of privacy versus security. In a zero-sum world,

*Biometrics: Theory, Methods, and Applications.* Edited by Boulgouris, Plataniotis, and Micheli-Tzanakou
Copyright © 2010 the Institute of Electrical and Electronics Engineers, Inc.

the greater the desired presence of one attribute (security), the lesser the presence of the opposing attribute (privacy). This perspective advances the view that adding privacy compromises system functionality, control, and effectiveness. Furthermore, it mistakenly believes that privacy interests can be satisfied by building system controls that seek to ensure the confidentiality and integrity of biometric data.

In this environment, building true biometric privacy into an information system is seen principally as a cost, and rarely as an enhancement. This prevailing view posits that privacy can only be improved at the expense of security.

The emerging area of privacy-enhancing biometric technologies, which we are referring to as "untraceable biometrics," challenges this paradigm by making it possible to enhance both privacy *and* security in a positive-sum model. Protecting privacy should not lead to less security and more costly business practices. In our view, biometric encryption (BE) may be classified an untraceable biometric technology, deserving of closer investigation because it demonstrates superior privacy enhancing qualities. Engineering privacy directly into biometric systems through BE is not only possible, but highly desirable.

## 26.2   THE CASE FOR BUILDING PRIVACY INTO BIOMETRIC TECHNOLOGIES

### 26.2.1   Security Vulnerabilities of Biometric Technologies

Despite all of the emphasis on security in the development of biometric technologies, they, nonetheless, have some common security vulnerabilities. These give rise to risks that can have significant impacts on the reliability, trustworthiness, and usability of the entire information system and on the privacy and security interests of individuals.

Security vulnerabilities of biometric systems include [1–3] (see Figure 26.1):

- *Spoofing*: Biometric systems can sometimes be fooled by applying fake biometrics such as fingerprints, or face or iris images.
- *Replay Attacks*: Sensors can be circumvented by injecting a recorded image into the system input.
- *Substitution Attacks*: The biometric template must be stored to allow user verification. If an attacker gets access to the storage, either local or remote, he/she can overwrite the legitimate user's template with his/her own—in essence, stealing their identity.
- *Tampering*: Feature sets on verification or in the templates can be modified in order to obtain a high verification score, no matter which image is presented to the system, or, alternatively, to bring the system down by making the score low for legitimate users.
- *Masquerade Attacks*: It has been demonstrated that a digital "artifact" [4] image can be created from a fingerprint template, so that this artifact, if submitted

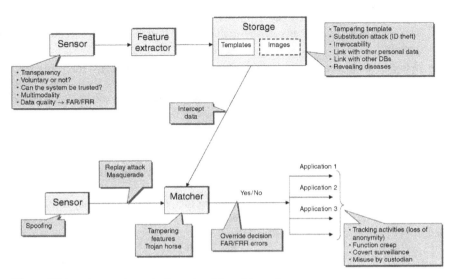

**Figure 26.1.** Privacy and security issues involving a biometric system.

to the system, will produce a match. The artefact may not even resemble the original image. As was shown by Adler [5], a masquerade image can be reconstructed from a face template using a "Hill Climbing attack" (this attack can be applied to any biometrics). In more recent publications by Ross et al. [6] and Cappelli et al. [7], a masquerade image reconstructed from a minutiae template can actually resemble the original fingerprint (see also Mohanty et al. [8] for face recognition). The masquerade attack poses a real threat to remote authentication systems, since an attacker does not even need to acquire a genuine biometric sample. All he needs to do is gain access to the templates stored on a remote server.

- *FAR Attack on a Database*: If an attacker can obtain access to all the templates stored in a database, he can run offline his own biometric against the database in the hopes of obtaining a false acceptance with at least one of the stored templates. If, for example, the system false acceptance rate (FAR) is 0.01%, which is common for one-to-one verification, and the database contains more than 10,000 templates, the attacker has a good chance of finding a matching template. The attacker's biometric will serve as a masquerade image for this template.

- *Trojan Horse Attacks*: Some parts of the system (e.g., a matcher), can be replaced by a Trojan horse program that always outputs high verification scores.

- *Overriding Yes/No Responses*: An inherent flaw of existing biometric systems is that the output of the system is always a binary Yes/No (i.e., match/no match) response. This makes the system open to potential attacks. For example, if an attacker were able to interject a false "Yes" response at a proper point of the communication between the biometrics and the application, he could pose as a legitimate user to any of the applications, thus bypassing the biometric portion.[1]

- *Insufficient Accuracy*: In many commercial biometric systems, there is a risk associated with both the false rejection rate (FRR) and the FAR. High FRR causes inconvenience for legitimate users and prompts the system administrator to lower a verification threshold. This inevitably gives rise to FAR, which, in turn, lowers the security level of the system.

## 26.2.2    Privacy Risks of Biometric Technologies

In addition to the security threats that undermine the potential reliability of biometric technologies, critics have also identified [9, 3, 10] a number of specific privacy concerns (Figure 26.1). They include:

- *Unauthorized Secondary Uses of Biometric Data ("Function Creep")*. Biometric data can be collected for one purpose, then used for other unrelated purposes without the knowledge or consent of the data subjects (or sometimes even the system owners). For example, fingerprint samples provided for payment purposes could be shared with national intelligence agencies.

- *Expanded Surveillance, Tracking, Profiling, and Potential Discrimination*. Biometric data can be matched against samples collected and stored elsewhere to calculate risk, predict and modify behavior, and make decisions about individuals. This could include, for example, employment decisions, insurance and other pricing scenarios, or police investigation and detainment.

- *Data Misuse (Data Breach, Identity Fraud and Theft)*. Misuses of biometric data represent the ultimate risk for identity theft and fraud. In the case of catastrophic or wholesale data loss or theft, the impacts on individuals and system owners can be profound and far-reaching.

- *Negative Personal Impacts of False Matches, Non-matches, System Errors and Failures*. Where biometrics are concerned, the consequences of system anomalies (especially in large-scale systems) often fall disproportionately on individuals, normally in the form of inconveniences, costs, and stigma.

- *Insufficient Oversight, Accountability, and Openness in Biometric Systems*. Biometric systems are not always designed and operated with due regard for well-established privacy principles. As a result, the purpose(s), functions, and risks of biometric systems are often not well-articulated or communicated.

- *The Potential for Collection and Use of Biometric Data Without Knowledge, Consent, or Personal Control*. The collection and use of some biometric data

---

[1]This was demonstrated by overriding Yes/No response in biometric USB flash drive: http://spritesmods.com/?art=biostick&page=1

can be carried out without the informed knowledge or consent of individuals. A clear example is the collection and use of closed-circuit television (CCTV) images for face recognition and matching purposes. In these cases, even where notice of collection is given, individuals often lack meaningful choice and control over the data.

Privacy risks threaten user confidence and may lead to a lack of acceptance and trust in biometric systems. When these risks are actualized in heavy-handed or poorly-designed biometric systems, the result can be a full-scale public backlash.

## 26.2.3  Building Privacy into Biometric Systems

Privacy concerns raised by biometric technologies can be addressed in a number of ways such as: (a) strengthening legal and regulatory oversight mechanisms (b) developing and implementing clear data usage policies and (c) improving education and awareness efforts for all stakeholders. All of these approaches aim to minimize risk, but they are band-aid solutions. More structural approaches to protecting privacy in biometric systems are also possible. For example, the design and operation of biometric technologies can be limited to authentication (one-to-one) rather than identification (one-to-many) purposes [11]. This approach not only minimizes the unnecessary collection and use of biometric data, but is also more consistent with the accuracy and performance capabilities of most biometric technologies. Indeed, the global privacy and data protection communities have consistently argued against the use of biometrics for most one-to-many identification purposes and against the creation of large, centralized, or interoperable databases of biometric data. They prefer local authentication against portable reference samples, like those stored on user-controlled smartcards or laptops [12].

These communities also encourage the development and use of privacy-enhancing technologies (PETs) that build internationally accepted fair information practices directly into the information systems. This approach minimizes privacy risks at an earlier, more granular level [13]. As such, it provides a more profound and meaningful foundation for addressing privacy in biometric systems.

PETs enable individuals to manage their own personally identifiable information (PII) within a given information system *without compromising the functionality of that system*. They express fair information practices by:

- actively *engaging the individual* in managing and controlling their own PII (i.e., effecting informed consent, accuracy, individual access, and challenging compliance);
- *minimizing* the collection, use, retention and disclosure of PII by others (i.e., limiting purposes, limiting collection, use, and retention of biometric data); and
- enhancing data *security* (i.e., safeguards).

## 26.3 INTRODUCTION TO UNTRACEABLE BIOMETRICS (UB)

In this section, we examine how untraceable biometric technologies help to minimize the privacy-invasiveness of biometric systems. "Untraceable biometrics" (UB) is the term we created to define privacy-enhancing biometric technologies.

The features of UB are as follows:

- There is no storage of biometric image or conventional biometric template.
- The original biometric image/template cannot be recreated from the stored information; that is, it is untraceable.
- A large number of untraceable templates for the same biometric can be created for different applications.
- The untraceable templates from different applications cannot be linked.
- The untraceable template can be revoked or canceled.

These features embody standard fair information principles, providing user control, data minimization, and data security.

Untraceable biometrics include two major groups of emerging technologies: biometric encryption (BE) and cancelable biometrics (CB).

BE technologies securely bind a digital key to a biometric, or generate a key from the biometric, so that neither the key nor the biometric can be retrieved from the stored BE template, also called "biometrically encrypted key" or "helper data." The key is recreated only if the correct biometric sample is presented on verification, so the output of BE verification is either a key or a failure message. Currently, any viable BE system requires that biometric dependent helper data be stored.[2] In essence, the key is "encrypted" with the biometric. This "encryption/decryption" process is fuzzy because of the natural variability of biometric samples. BE is also known by terms such as biometric cryptosystem, fuzzy extractor, secure sketch, helper data systems, biometric locking, biometric key generation, and so on.

CB technologies apply a transform (which is usually kept secret) to the original biometric and store the transformed template. The transform can be either invertible or, preferably, not. On verification, the same transform is applied to a fresh biometric sample, and the matching is done between two transformed templates. The output of CB verification is a Yes/No response, as in the conventional biometrics.

Our classification of privacy-enhancing biometric technologies, however, is somewhat different than that proposed by Ratha et al. [14]. Ratha et al. divide the technologies into the following categories: biometric salting, biometric key generation (without the use of additional information), fuzzy schemes, and noninvertible transforms. While these categories capture the most important works to date, this terminology also has some shortcomings. For example, the Mytec BE scheme [15] is

---

[2]From the present-day perspective, the only exception might be the future use of DNA testing as a biometric. However, since the DNA testing would create huge practical and privacy related problems, we will not discuss it in this chapter.

put into the salting category. While it does use the salting technique, Mytec's scheme is fundamentally a fuzzy scheme since it does a true binding of a key to biometrics without resorting to obscurity. The other salting schemes are closer to noninvertible transforms. Second, all key generation schemes have, in fact, some kind of biometric-dependent helper data (check bits in Davida et al. [16, 17]; "history file" in Monrose et al. [18–21]). And third, some CB technologies (e.g., references 22, 23, and 24) do not fall into any of these categories.

In our opinion, there are only two main categories of untraceable biometrics, BE and CB. These terminologies ascend to the pioneer works of G. Tomko et al. [25] on BE and N. Ratha et al. [1, 26] on CB. Both terms correctly reflect the most distinctive features of each category: BE is focused on biometrically managing cryptographic keys/passwords, while CB aims at making the conventional biometric template cancelable (note that BE also possesses this revocability property). We use the terms BE and CB in a broad sense and, therefore, prefer the term "biometric encryption" to "biometric cryptosystem" [27, 28] (BE is intended to be a part of a larger cryptosystem where it replaces the passwords).

## 26.3.1 Comparison of BE and CB

Both BE and CB satisfy the requirements for untraceable biometrics, since the biometric image or template is transformed to a domain from which it cannot be recovered; a large number of those transforms exists; the transformation is application-dependent; and the resulting BE or CB template is cancelable (revocable).

In general, BE and CB face similar technological challenges. First, the inherent variability of biometric samples makes it more difficult for both BE and CE to achieve good accuracy than in conventional biometrics. Since BE usually operates in a "blind" mode (i.e., the biometric template is not seen on verification, unlike CB), this could be more technologically challenging in the case of BE, although evidence so far does not show significant advantages of CB in terms of accuracy. Additionally, besides improving the system FAR/FRR performance, another challenge is making the BE or CB template secure—that is, resilient to offline attacks. These issues are discussed in more detail in Section 26.6.

It is important to note the following key differences between BE and CB:

(a) CB: A distorted template is stored on enrollment.
   BE: A "biometrically encrypted key," also called "helper data," is stored.
(b) CB: Distorting transform should be kept secret.
   BE: The cryptographic key is not kept at all; distorting transform is optional.
(c) CB: Fresh *distorted* template is compared against stored *distorted* template.
   BE: Undistorted biometric is applied to the stored biometrically encrypted key.
(d) CB: Binary Yes/No response on verification.
   BE: The verification output is either a key or a failure message.

**Table 26.1.** Comparison of the Performance, Privacy, and Security Aspects of BE, CB, and Conventional Biometrics Based on the Perception of the Authors.[a]

| | Conventional Biometrics | Cancelable Biometrics | Biometric Encryption |
|---|---|---|---|
| Accuracy | ★ ★ ★★ | ★★—★ ★ | ★★ |
| Speed | ★ ★ ★★ | ★ ★ ★ | ★★ |
| Untraceability | ★ | ★ ★ ★ | ★ ★ ★★ |
| User's control and trust | ★ | ★ ★ ★★ | ★ ★ ★★ |
| Prevention of secondary uses and abuses | ★ | ★ ★ ★ | ★ ★ ★★ |
| Revocability | ★ | ★ ★ ★★ | ★ ★ ★★ |
| Resilience to spoofing | ★ | ★—★★ | ★—★★ |
| Resilience to substitution attack and tampering | ★ | ★★ | ★ ★ ★ |
| Resilience to masquerade attack | ★ | ★★ | ★ ★ ★ |
| Resilience to Trojan horse attack | ★ | ★ | ★ ★ ★★ |
| Resilience to overriding Yes/No response | ★ | ★ | ★ ★ ★★ |
| Integration into conventional cryptosystem | ★ | ★ | ★ ★ ★★ |

[a] The scale is from one to four stars (one being least optimal).

(e) CB: Closer to a conventional biometric system (even the same matching algorithm can be used in some CB schemes [14]).

BE: Can be integrated with a conventional cryptosystem.

(f) CB: Can be attacked by overriding Yes/No response, by a Trojan horse attack, and by a substitution attack.

BE: Is immune against those attacks.

Table 26.1 compares BE, CB, and conventional biometrics in terms of performance, privacy, and security.

As illustrated in Table 26.1, both BE and CB provide overall better security and privacy protection than conventional biometrics. However, it is also shown that of the two UB technologies, BE is potentially the most secure and privacy protective. We will proceed to explain in further detail why, in our view, BE is the technology of choice for building privacy into biometric systems.

## 26.3.2 Biometric Encryption at a Glance

The original concept of biometric encryption for fingerprints was pioneered in 1994 by G. Tomko, founder of Mytec Technologies (Toronto, Canada). Since then, many research groups have published their work on developing BE and related technologies as reflected in the review papers by Uludag et al. [27] and Jain et al. [28] and in the book edited by Tuyls, Škorić, and Kevenaar [29].

The most distinct BE technologies are the following: Mytec1 and Mytec2, ECC check bits, biometrically hardened passwords, the fuzzy commitment scheme and some of its generalizations in the fuzzy extractor/secure sketch framework, shielding functions (i.e., quantization using correction vector), fuzzy vault, PinSketch, and BioHashing with key binding. Most other works are close to one of those groups.

There are two BE approaches: key generation, when a key is derived from a biometric, and key binding, when an arbitrary key (e.g., randomly generated) is securely bound to the biometric. Both approaches store biometric-dependent helper data. Some BE schemes (e.g., the fuzzy commitment or the fuzzy vault schemes) can equally work in both key generation and key binding mode; the key generation is also called "secure sketch" [30]. The latter implies that the enrolled biometric template will be recovered on verification when a fresh biometric sample is applied to the helper data (i.e., the enrolled template itself, or a string derived from it, is a key). This key is biometric-dependent rather than arbitrary, and the size of the key space is unknown. In this section, we will focus primarily on the key binding approach.

As illustrated in Figure 26.2, the digital key (password, PIN, etc.) is randomly generated on enrollment, so that neither the user, nor anybody else, knows it. The key

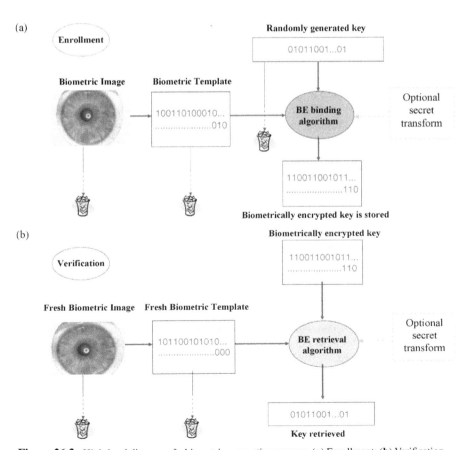

**Figure 26.2.** High-level diagram of a biometric encryption process. (**a**) Enrollment; (**b**) Verification.

itself is completely independent of biometrics and, therefore, can always be changed or updated. After a biometric sample is acquired, the BE algorithm securely and consistently binds the key to the biometric to create a protected BE template, also called "helper data, "biometrically encrypted key," "virtual PIN," "private template," and so on. In essence, the key is encrypted with the biometric. The BE template provides privacy protection and can be stored either in a database or locally (smart card, token, laptop, cell phone, etc.). At the end of the enrollment, both the key and the biometric are discarded.

On verification, the user presents her fresh biometric sample, which, when applied to the legitimate BE template, will let the BE algorithm retrieve the same key. In other words, the biometric decrypts the key. At the end of verification, the biometric sample is discarded once again. The BE algorithm is designed to account for acceptable variations in the input biometric. On the other hand, an attacker whose biometric sample is different enough will not be able to retrieve the key. This encryption/decryption scheme is fuzzy, because the biometric sample is different each time, unlike an encryption key in conventional cryptography. Of course, this presents a big technological challenge to make the system work.

After the digital key (or password, PIN, and so on) is retrieved, it can be used as the basis for any physical or logical application. The most obvious use is in the conventional cryptosystem, such as a PKI, where the password will generate a pair of public and private keys.

In order to improve the security of BE system, an optional transform (shown in the dashed square in Figure 26.2) may be applied. Preferably, the transform should be noninvertible and kept secret. One of the ways would be employing a randomization technique, such as biohashing or "salting" in more general terms [14, 28]. The best approach would be to control the transform with the user's password. It can also be stored on a token or server, always separately from the rest of helper data. This is the same approach as employed by CB. It should be noted, however, that BE, unlike CB, does not rely on the secrecy of the transform.

If properly implemented, BE is an effective, secure, and privacy-friendly tool for biometric key management, since the biometric and the key are bound on a fundamental level.

In order to have a better understanding of how BE works, let us consider a relatively simple yet real-life example, a fuzzy commitment scheme for iris [31].

The standard iris template is an ordered string of 2048 bits. As shown in Figure 26.3, a 140-bit key is generated randomly and bound to the template on enrollment. This is done through an *error correcting code* (ECC), which is an important part of most BE algorithms. ECCs are typically used in communications, data storage, and in other systems where errors can occur [32, 33], with BE being a new area for the application of ECC. An $(n, k, d)$ binary block ECC encodes $k$ bits with $n > k$ bits by adding some redundancy. Those $n$-bit strings are called *codewords*; there are $2^k$ of them in total. The minimum distance (usually a Hamming distance is implied) between the codewords is $d$. If, at a later stage (in case of BE, on verification), the errors occur, the ECC is guaranteed to correct up to $(d-1)/2$ random bit errors among $n$ bits.

| Enrollment | Verification |
|---|---|
| **Iris template, 2048 bits:**<br>100110100010...........................010 | **Fresh iris template, 2048 bits:**<br>101100101010.............................000 |
| **140 bit key:**<br>01011001...01 | **Retrieve biometrically encrypted key:**<br>110011001011.............................110 |
| **Map to 2048 bit ECC codeword:**<br>010101101001...............................100 | **XOR:**<br>011111100001...............................110 |
| **XOR:**<br>110011001011...............................110 | **If the number of errors is within the ECC capability, the ECC will decode the correct 140-bit key₁:**<br>01011001...01 |
| **Store as a biometrically encrypted key**<br>**Store** *Hash*(key) | If *Hash*(key) = *Hash*(key₁), output key |

**Figure 26.3.** Binding of a 140-bit key to a 2048-bit iris template in a fuzzy commitment scheme.

In our example with iris, the ECC is designed to encode 140 bits into 2048-bit codeword. The redundancy rate of such ECC is quite high; $2048/140 = 14.63$. On enrollment, the codeword is simply XOR-ed with the iris template, and the resulting *biometrically encrypted key* is stored. Neither the codeword nor the biometric template can be retrieved from the helper data, which is similar to a one-time-pad cryptosystem known in cryptography. It is interesting to note that there are no specific locations where the 140-bit key is hidden; it is dispersed over all 2048 bits.

On verification, a fresh 2048-bit iris template is obtained. Some bits may have errors. The fresh template is XOR-ed with the stored biometrically encrypted key. If there were no errors, the original codeword would be obtained. However, since errors are unavoidable in biometrics, the result of the XOR will differ from the correct codeword. Here the ECC decoder comes into play: If the number of errors is not too large, the ECC can correct all the errors and obtain the original codeword. Since the codewords are deterministically mapped to 140-bit keys, the correct 140-bit key will be retrieved. If, on the other hand, the number of errors exceeds the ECC's capability, the decoder will declare a failure. Therefore, the output of BE algorithm is either a key or a failure message. Ideally, the failure should be output for an impostor only; however, it could happen for a legitimate user as well—that is, the system could have a false rejection, as in conventional biometrics. As we can see, in the case of BE the ECC replaces a simple threshold-based Yes/No scheme of conventional biometrics.

Designing a good (2048, 140) ECC for BE is itself a serious technological challenge, since the error rate for a biometric template is usually high. Hao et al. [31] used a combination of Hadamard (aka 1st order Reed–Muller) and Reed–Solomon ECCs. Normally, a block ECC corrects up to 25% of errors in a *hard decoding* mode, which would be 511 errors in our example. However, the authors ran the Reed–Muller ECC in a *soft decoding* mode (i.e., the decoder always outputs the nearest codeword, even in the case of possible failure), which allowed it to achieve better error-correcting capabilities.

To make sure that the algorithm always outputs the correct key (e.g., in the soft decoding mode the ECC may output *any* key), a *hashed* value of the key is stored into the helper data, as shown in Figure 26.3. One-way hash functions are a standard tool in conventional cryptography. The key cannot be retrieved from its hashed value. On verification, the algorithm compares the hashed value of the retrieved key with the stored hashed value. If they are exactly the same, the correct key can be output to enter an application. Note that the best practice in the key/password management is not to output the key itself, nor to transmit it through an open channel, but rather to use another hashed value of the key for any application. Likewise, the biometric image/template should not be sent; the BE verification should be done locally in most scenarios.

We have just described the key binding mode of operation, which in this case can be called "fuzzy extractor." However, the fuzzy commitment scheme can be easily set up in the key generation (i.e., "secure sketch") mode: After the correct codeword is obtained, it is XOR-ed with the stored biometrically encrypted key to obtain the enrolled biometric template. This template, or rather some string derived from it (e.g., by using another hashing), serves as a *key generated from the biometric*. Note, however, that this "key" is not something inherent or absolute for this particular biometric; it will change upon re-enrollment. If the key is derived by hashing the template, the difference even in one bit with the previous version of the template would produce a completely different key. The size of the key space is defined by the intra-class variation of the biometric, as opposed to the key binding approach.

Some BE schemes (e.g., Mytec2) cannot run in the "secure sketch" mode. This is not necessarily a drawback; moreover, it is preferable from the security point of view that the original template cannot be easily recoverable if the key is compromised (see Section 26.6).

The fuzzy commitment scheme for iris demonstrates the major challenges that all BE technologies face:

- The number of errors must be made as low as possible (to accommodate natural variations of biometrics) for a legitimate user and as high as possible for an impostor.
- Powerful and efficient ECCs must be designed specifically for BE.
- The helper data (i.e., BE template) must be made resilient against attacks.

Note that the second and third challenges are not present at all in conventional biometrics. The first challenge is also emphasized differently for BE: Conventional biometrics only requires a good separation between the legitimate users and impostors, and this can be achieved even if the number of errors is high for both. BE, on the other hand, cannot operate with a number of errors exceeding the ECC capability.

## 26.3.3   What BE Is Not

Some products on the market claim to use "biometric encryption," and it is important to distinguish these from the concepts used in this chapter.

What we mean by BE is not encrypting biometric images or templates using conventional encryption. Nor is it storing a cryptographic key in a so-called trusted system (e.g., a computer, a digital signal processor (DSP), a smart card, etc.) and subsequently releasing the key upon successful biometric verification. If properly implemented, such systems may offer some security benefits. However, most problems outlined in Section 26.2 remain. For example, a binary Yes/No response is still required to release the key—this part of the algorithm is just hidden better. Most privacy issues associated with storing the biometric template are the same.

BE is also not another cryptographic algorithm, nor is it a "snake oil" [34]. Biometrics in general, and BE in particular, cannot have the same level of security as cryptographic algorithms. The overall security of a cryptographic system is fully dependent on its weakest part, the password. The vulnerabilities of password-based schemes have been well-published. The role of BE is to replace the vulnerable password-based schemes with more secure and more convenient biometrically managed keys.

## 26.4  BIOMETRIC ENTROPY

The concept of entropy is important for identifying the biometric modalities suitable for BE. Entropy is defined as a measure of the average information content. In the context of BE, the entropy of a biometric is the upper limit for the size of the key that can be securely bound to the biometric. In other words, if one tries to bind a 128-bit key to a biometric with only 40 bits of entropy, then the security strength of such a system will not be more than 40 bits.

Unlike passwords, biometrics must provide some error tolerance, since there are no two identical biometric samples. How, then, can we estimate biometric entropy? The difficulty is illustrated by the following example:

If a binary $320 \times 320$ fingerprint image has a size of $320 \times 320 = 102{,}400$ bits, does it mean that its entropy is 102,400? Technically, the answer could be Yes, if all the bits were statistically independent. However, a legitimate user will never be able to obtain a positive verification in such a system requiring that all 102,400 bits be kept unchanged. The system must be error-tolerant. In this case, the entropy will be much lower. In general, the biometric entropy is algorithm-dependent; and therefore, there is no such absolute thing as "entropy of a fingerprint."

While there are several definitions of entropy, the notion of min-entropy, $H_\infty(A)$, introduced by Dodis et al. [30] (see also reference 35), is most relevant for BE purposes:

$$H_\infty(A) = -\log_2(\max_a \Pr[A = a]). \qquad (26.1)$$

Here $A$ is a random variable (i.e., a set of features in case of biometrics) that can take any value, $a$, with a probability $\Pr[A = a]$. By taking the maximum probability, we assume that the attacker's best strategy would be to guess the most likely value (for example, of a key). This definition shows how many nearly uniform random bits can be extracted from the distribution.

In case of two variables, an average min-entropy, $\tilde{H}_\infty(A|B)$, of $A$ given $B$ is considered:

$$\tilde{H}_\infty(A|B) = -\log_2\left(E_{b\leftarrow B}\left[\max_a \Pr[A = a|B = b]\right]\right)$$

$$= -\log_2\left(E_{b\leftarrow B}\left[2^{-H_\infty(A|B=b)}\right]\right). \tag{26.2}$$

It can be interpreted for the purposes of BE in the following way: $B$ is a helper data that is available to the attacker. By knowing $B$, the attacker can predict $A$ with the maximum probability $\max_a \Pr[A = a|B = b]$. On average, the attacker's chance of success in predicting $A$ is then $E_{b\leftarrow B}[\max_a \Pr[A = a|B = b]]$, where $E_{b\leftarrow B}$ is the average over $B$. It is logical to take average rather than maximum over B, since B is not under the attacker's control. The average min-entropy $H_\infty(A|B)$ is essentially the minimum strength of the key that can be consistently extracted from A when B is known. The difference between $H_\infty(A)$ and $H_\infty(A|B)$,

$$L = H_\infty(X) - \tilde{H}_\infty(X|P), \tag{26.3}$$

is called the entropy loss, or the information leak, of a BE scheme.

In practical terms, one can estimate the biometric *discrimination* entropy as minus binary logarithm of FAR at zero "distance" (or, more exactly, at maximum similarity score),

$$H \approx -\log_2(\text{FAR}(@d = 0)), \tag{26.4}$$

meaning that it corresponds to the point where exactly the same biometric sample is presented on enrollment and verification. In other words, this FAR($@d = 0$)) is a probability of finding two identical samples among the population. However, we require that the system be realistically designed; that is, it provides a proper error tolerance for legitimate users, meaning that those samples are "identical" only within the tolerance limits. Note that the point $d = 0$ is never used itself as an operating point in any biometric system (unlike a password management scheme). There is usually no impostor data available at $d = 0$, so that FAR($@d = 0$)) can be only approximately estimated by extrapolation.

There are two basic approaches to estimating the biometric entropy: empirical estimation and theoretical modeling.

Empirical estimations are usually based on John Daugman's paper on iris recognition [36]. It computes an inter-class (i.e., impostors') distribution of Hamming distance for a large data sample. The histogram of the distribution is approximated with a normalized binomial distribution, and the total number of Bernoulli trials is called *a number of degrees of freedom*. It is estimated from the mean, $p$, and the standard deviation, $\sigma$: $N_{\text{DoF}} = p(1 - p)/\sigma^2$. For iris, Daugman obtained $N_{\text{DoF}} = 173$ bits (later upgraded to 249 bits [37]). Those numbers have been extensively quoted in many publications. The number of degrees of freedom is an adequate estimate of the discrimination entropy, as for the binomial distribution, $H \approx -\log_2(\text{FAR}(@d = 0)) = N_{\text{DoF}}$.

It should be noted that this approach, while providing a standardized and efficient method for estimating the biometric entropy, is still very algorithm- and database-dependent—it is affected by intra-class variations and the degree of error tolerance. The binomial distribution may not approximate well the "tail" (i.e., where all false acceptances occur), especially for the biometrics other than iris. The biometric database should be representative enough, which is often hard to achieve. While Daugman's system shows a very good performance in database simulations, any changes in the algorithm, including the image processing part, would result in a different estimate of $N_{DoF}$. In other words, those numbers (i.e., 173 or 249 bits) should not be interpreted as something inherently absolute for iris but rather related to the Daugman algorithm only.

A similar empirical approach was applied to fingerprints in reference 38.

The theoretical modeling approach is presented by Pankanti et al. [39] and Ratha et al. [1] for the purposes of assessing fingerprints individuality. Both scientific groups obtained formulas to calculate a probability of randomly matching a number of minutiae (not necessarily all) in two samples. In both papers an assumption was made that the number of possible minutiae locations in the overlapping area is much greater than the actual number of minutiae. For a fingerprint containing 36 minutiae, Pankanti et al. estimated a probability that two fingerprints will falsely match on all 36 minutiae as 5.5e-59. Therefore, the entropy is $-\log_2(5.5e-59) = 193$ bits.

In more recent paper by Zhu, Dass, and Jain [40], the Pankanti et al. model was improved by taking into account the clustering tendencies in the minutiae distributions and the correlation between minutiae angles and locations. The results show a significant increase in the probability of random correspondence between minutiae compared to the Pankanti et al. model (which assumed a uniform distribution). This increase would translate to the effective reduction of entropy.

The issue of fingerprint entropy is still an area of ongoing research. Even if the fingerprint entropy is not sufficient for BE, a multimodal approach (i.e., using two or more fingerprints) would result in higher entropy.

All previous works focused mostly on inter-class (i.e., impostor) distribution to estimate the uniqueness of the biometrics, while intra-class (i.e., genuine) distribution was taken into account only implicitly, through the system tolerance requirements.

Wayman [41] introduced a "cotton ball model" being developed in an attempt to obtain basic estimations of FAR and FRR in Euclidean spaces. The model assumes Gaussian within- and between-class distributions and known covariance matrix. The published results do not contain any application to a specific biometric system. In general, theoretical FAR/FRR estimations can provide little insight with respect of system performance, which can vary by 1–2 orders of magnitude for different algorithms on the same database, or for the same algorithm on different databases (compare, for example, FVC2002 and FVC2004 results [42]). On the other hand, those studies can be useful for estimating the biometric entropy.

Adler, Youmaran, and Loyka [43, 44] proposed a more rigorous approach to the biometric entropy problem. The authors introduce the notion of the relative entropy, or the Kullback–Leibler distance, $D(p||q)$:

$$D(p||q) = \int_x p(x) \log_2 \frac{p(x)}{q(x)} \, dx, \tag{26.5}$$

where $x$ is a multidimensional feature vector, $p(x)$ is the intra-class probability distribution of features of an individual, and $q(x)$ is the overall (i.e., inter-class) population distribution.

It is not easy to estimate the multidimensional distributions, especially on the tails, as a large number of samples is required. Adler et al. approximated $p(x)$, $q(x)$ with multidimensional Gaussian functions (similar to the "cotton ball model"), for which they obtained an analytical solution. The theory was applied to face recognition. For the PCA (principal component analysis) features, the authors obtained 45 bits of information. This number is sufficient for medium-security BE applications. With recent advances in the face recognition technology [45], one can hope that this number could be greater for 3D or high-resolution images, as well as for the state-of-the-art 2D algorithms.

Ballard et al. [46] argue that the biometric entropy is not sufficient to analyze BE security, and introduce a new measure, called "guessing distance" (GD). GD estimates the number of guesses that an attacker must make to retrieve the biometric or the key. The idea is somewhat similar to that of Adler et al. [43, 44], because GD is also related to a distance between two probability distributions. GD can be estimated for non-Gaussian distributions, as shown by Ballard et al.

Based on the entropy analysis, we can conclude that iris, fingerprints, and face (with some reservations) are the biometric modalities that may have sufficient amounts of information to be used for BE purposes. Other biometrics, such as voice, retina, dynamic signature, hand/finger veins, keystroke dynamics, and so on, require further research, or can be put on the list of "auxiliary" biometrics (i.e., to be combined with another biometrics or to "harden" the passwords).

In a work by Plaga [47], an upper bound for a BE key size, $k$, was obtained:

$$k \leq -\log_2 (\text{FAR}), \tag{26.6}$$

where FAR is taken at an operational threshold. For example, if $\text{FAR} = 10^{-6}$ (most biometric systems work even at higher FAR), then $k \leq 20$ bits. This places a tough and unnecessary restriction on BE in general and is worth discussing in more detail.

The inequality 26.6 was derived from an ideal model for a fuzzy commitment scheme, where all bits are random and uncorrelated. However, there is no direct connection between the *real system FAR* and the maximum key size (see references 48 and 49 for rigorous estimates of the theoretical bounds for FAR and FRR in the fuzzy commitment scheme). Plaga [47] arbitrarily extends the inequality (26.6) to any (i.e., nonideal) BE system; that is, even if the system manages to extract a biometric key with the length of $k$ bits, the achievable FAR must be maintained lower than $2^{-k}$.

This issue is closely related to a so-called "FAR attack" on a BE system (see Section 26.6). If an attacker can collect or generate (using SFinge [50], for example) a biometric database, he would need about $\text{FAR}^{-1}$ samples to break the system. If, on the other hand, the attacker chooses to cryptographically test (i.e., to run them through the hash function) all possible keys, the number would be $2^k$. The requirement (26.6) means, in fact, that the FAR attack must be made more difficult for the attacker than the cryptographic brute force search! However, it is obvious that the latter method (i.e., inverting the hash) is much more available and attractive to an ordinary attacker, and the requirement (26.6) just invites him to do so.

There is a significant difference between FAR attack and a cryptographic brute force attack. The FAR attack does not have an exact analogue in conventional cryptography and requires collection or generation of a large database of biometric samples that must be *compatible* with the samples used in the real BE system. Second, the BE algorithm is usually much slower than simply hashing the key. Image processing, features extraction, and ECC decoding parts may take longer (by six orders of magnitude or more) than hashing. Note that six orders of magnitude are equivalent to extra 20 bits of security.

Taking into account the "cost factor," CF, of collecting and maintaining the interoperable biometric database,[3] and the speed factor, SF, we will turn the over-restrictive requirement 26.6 right-side up:

$$k \geq -\log_2 (\text{FAR}) + \log_2 (\text{CF}) + \log_2 (\text{SF}). \qquad (26.7)$$

In other words, the key should be long enough to make the cryptographic brute force search less feasible than the FAR attack.

## 26.5  OVERVIEW OF UB TECHNOLOGIES

### 26.5.1  Biometric Encryption

#### 26.5.1.1  Bodo

The prior art of BE is a German patent to Bodo [51]. It suggests deriving a cryptographic key directly from a biometric (e.g., fingerprint minutiae) template without storing any helper data. The patent does not actually disclose a method for deriving a key.

Although it may be tempting to map any biometric to a unique key, there are two major problems with this approach [15, 52]:

- It is very hard to accommodate for biometric variability; and
- The key would not be revocable; that is, if compromised, this particular biometric would be lost forever.

The difficulties of handling errors in the biometric without helper data can be illustrated by the following simple example:

Let us assume that the biometric template is a random binary string, such as 100101110100100110. ... We will try to use an ECC in a decoding mode in order to map parts of that string to the nearest codeword. For example, we can choose a (9, 1)

---

[3]The "cost factor" is defined from the attacker's perspective on feasibility of the attack.

repetition code. The first 9 bits, 100101110, will be mapped to 1, because there are 5 ones and 4 zeros; and by the majority rule, the nearest codeword is 111111111. The second chunk, 100100110, is mapped to 0. However, on verification, this scheme will not tolerate even a single bit error that would change the 5:4 score to 4:5.

If, on the contrary, we use a BE fuzzy commitment scheme, then the codeword 111111111000000000... is XOR-ed with the template, and the result is stored as helper data. This scheme tolerates up to 4 arbitrary bit errors in each chunk (note that a repetition code is not a good choice for BE in general, because it creates many security problems detailed in Section 26.6, and this simple example is used for the sake of clarity only).

Key generation without helper data is more likely to succeed if the biometric is condensed to a few very robust biometric features, and the key size is small (see references 21 and 53). DNA testing is, probably, the only biometric of the future that could generate long keys with this technique.

### 26.5.1.2 Mytec1

The first BE scheme, which we call Mytec1,[4] now holds only a historical significance. Nevertheless, we think it is worth describing to illustrate major concepts and problems with BE.

The method used optical correlation and was implemented in a hardware (see references 25, 54, and 55 for details). A Fourier transform of a fingerprint image was performed in an analog way using the properties of a coherent light passing through an optical system. It is important to point out that the optical hardware did not serve an obscuration purpose; therefore, the system could be implemented digitally, as follows:

Let $f(x)$ be the input fingerprint pattern signal and let $s(x)$ be the output signal, which is designed to have the form of the sum of $n$ delta functions in the positions $x_1, x_2, \ldots, x_n$ and relative intensities $g_1, g_2, \ldots, g_n$:

$$s(x) = \sqrt{g_1}\delta(x - x_1) + \sqrt{g_2}\delta(x - x_2) + \cdots \sqrt{g_n}\delta(x - x_n). \tag{26.8}$$

The Fourier filter function, $H(u)$, is stored as a ratio of the output signal Fourier transform, $S(u)$, and the fingerprint Fourier transform $F(u) = |F(u)|\exp(i\phi(u))$:

$$H(u) = \frac{S(u)}{F(u)} = \frac{\exp(-i\phi(u))}{|F(u)|}$$
$$\times \left[\sqrt{g_1}\exp(-i2\pi ux_1) + \sqrt{g_2}\exp(-i2\pi ux_2) + \cdots\right]. \tag{26.9}$$

Thus, the stored filter, $H(u)$, is a ratio of a complex pseudo-random function (the sum of complex exponents), which is related to the key, and a fingerprint Fourier transform. At the first glance, it is impossible to derive either the key or the fingerprint from this ratio. If a correct fingerprint is submitted on verification, its Fourier

---

[4]Mytec1 and Mytec2 schemes were originally called "Biometric Encryption," which was a trademark of Toronto-based Mytec Technologies Inc., now Bioscrypt, a fully owned subsidiary of L1 Identity Solutions Inc. The Biometric Encryption trademark was abandoned in 2005.

Reference peak

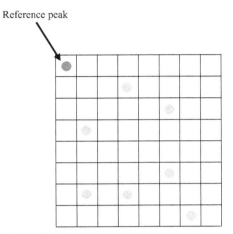

**Figure 26.4.** Central part of a correlation plane output in Mytec1 scheme.

transform, $F_1(u)$, will be multiplied by the filter $H(u)$, and, since $F_1$ and $F$ are close, the signal $s(x)$ will be reconstructed. As shown in Figure 26.4, the output signal looks like a set of a few correlation peaks. Their locations relative to a reference peak (normally, the top left one) form the key. For example, if a central part of the correlation plane is set on a $8 \times 8$ grid, each peak carries 6 bits of information, so that 7 peaks (plus one reference) are needed to encode $7 \times 6 = 42$-bit key. The magnitudes $g_i$ associated with each peak are set to 1 in the preferred embodiment. In fact, the total number of distinct keys is

$$\binom{63}{7} = 2^{29},$$

that is, much less than $2^{42}$. The authors suggest creating and storing several filters as per Eq. (26.9), so that the number of distinct keys can be greater.

The system is translation-invariant, as the output pattern moves synchronously with the input fingerprint. This is, basically, the main reason why the correlation-like processing via Fourier transform is used.

The correlation technique also provides some error tolerance, since the fresh biometric sample does not have to be exactly the same as on the enrollment. However, the accuracy of the system quickly diminishes as the number of peaks grows, so that for the 8 peaks needed to encode 42 bits with 29-bit security, as in the foregoing example, the FRR will likely be high enough.

Moreover, the stored complex filter, $H(u)$, turns out to be not very secure: As seen from Eq. (26.9), the filter magnitude contains cross-reference complex exponents,

$$|H(u)|^2 \propto \sum_{ik} \exp(-i2\pi u(x_i - x_k)),$$

so that the inverse Fourier transform of it, that is,

$$FT^{-1}(|H(u)|^2) \propto \sum_{ik} \delta(x_i - x_k), \qquad (26.10)$$

will reveal to an attacker the relative locations of all the peaks.

Even though the Mytec1 scheme is neither practical nor secure from the present-day perspective, its introduction in the mid-1990s, when the whole biometric industry was still in infancy, opened a new area of research and had a great impact on the development of privacy-enhancing biometric technologies.

### 26.5.1.3 Mytec2

The first practical BE scheme, which we call Mytec2, was developed by diverging from the optical hardware constraints of Mytec1. The patent application [56], filed in 1997, clearly establishes the priority. The work was publicly presented at the RSA Security Conference in January 1998 [57]. The most thorough description of Mytec2 algorithm was given in references 15, 58, and 59 and in the patent [56] itself, which extended the applicability of the algorithm to other biometrics, in particular, to iris scan. However, the test results and a complete security analysis of the algorithm were not published. Since 2001, biometric encryption has never been mentioned in press releases or annual reports of Bioscrypt Inc., the successor of Mytec Technologies.

Unlike Mytec1, the Mytec2 scheme uses a phase-only random function, $\exp(i\varphi_{rand}(u))$, to bind a key to the biometric. It is multiplied with a complex conjugate phase, $\exp(-i\varphi(u))$, of the fingerprint Fourier transform; the result, $H(u)$, is stored as a filter:

$$H(u) = \exp(i\varphi_{rand}(u) - i\varphi(u)). \qquad (26.11)$$

It can be shown that $H(u)$ is truly secure, because it is similar to a one-time pad cryptosystem [34]. To link a key to the biometric, $\exp(i\varphi_{rand})$ is multiplied by a magnitude part of the fingerprint "optimal" (i.e., Wiener-style) filter, and the inverse Fourier transform is performed to obtain the output complex array, $c_0(x)$:

$$c_0(x) = FT^{-1}\left(\frac{|F(u)|^2}{\alpha + |F(u)|^2} \exp(i\varphi_{rand}(u))\right), \qquad (26.12)$$

where $\alpha$ is a tunable parameter. If it is small enough, the output pattern will be random.

Then the central part of $c_0(x)$ is extracted in order to accommodate for the image displacement. The key (normally, ~128 bit long), which is generated randomly, is mapped to a codeword of an ECC. The most reliable components of $c_0(x)$ are selected and linked to the codeword via a lookup table of bit locations. The table is stored. The system described in the publications used a simple repetition code as an ECC, such as each bit is repeated an odd number of times. The decoding is done by a majority rule. The key (together with some bits from the filter) was hashed to obtain an ID check, $id_0$, which is also stored.

At the end of the enrollment process, the key, the random function, and the filter magnitude are discarded. The helper data contain $H(u)$, the lookup table, and $id_0$.

An important part of the enrollment process, which we have omitted here for the sake of clarity, was a design of the optimal filter out of multiple images. This allowed achieving a trade-off between distortion tolerance and discrimination.

On verification, a fresh biometric sample is applied to the stored filter $H(u)$ to obtain an output pattern, $c_1(x)$:

$$c_1(x) = FT^{-1}\left(\frac{|F_1(u)|^2}{\alpha + |F_1(u)|^2}\exp(i\varphi_1(u)) \cdot H(u)\right). \qquad (26.13)$$

If the image is the same as on enrollment, $c_1(x)$ and $c_0(x)$ would be exactly the same. The bits are extracted in the locations predefined by the lookup table, and the ECC decoder obtains an output key, which is run through the hash function to obtain $id_1$. If $id_1 = id_0$, then the correct key is released. If $id_1 \neq id_0$, the lookup table is moved across $c_1(x)$, and the process is repeated until the key is found or the search (up to $\sim 1000$ times normally) is exhausted. By doing that, the algorithm efficiently solves the problem of the image alignment.

The Mytec2 scheme falls under the general definition of a fuzzy extractor [30]. It is quite similar to the fuzzy commitment scheme [60] that appeared later, especially to the one with the selection of the most reliable components [61–64]. Note that the product of two phase-only functions that create $H(u)$ is an analog equivalent of XOR operation in the fuzzy commitment scheme. The linkage of the ECC codeword through a lookup table is similar to what was called a "permutation-based fuzzy extractor" [30]. The important difference between Mytec2 and those schemes is that there is an inverse Fourier transform in between the stored filter $H(u)$ and the link to the codeword. Not only does this provide translation invariance, but it can also make the system more resilient to certain types of attacks (see Section 26.6).

The Mytec2 scheme is conceptually different from what was called in references 14 and 28 "biometric salting," since the random phase is not stored anywhere. The scheme provides a true (i.e., with no obscuration) binding between the key and the biometric.

The Mytec2 scheme was sometimes criticized for the lack of formal proof of security. The simple repetition ECC, which was used in the published version, makes the scheme vulnerable to score-based attacks (see Section 26.6), such as hill climbing. However, a closer examination of the Mytec2 scheme shows that the theoretical results on fuzzy extractors [30] are applicable to Mytec2 with minor modifications. For that, both the stored filter, $H(u)$, and the output patterns, $c_0(x)$ and $c_1(x)$, must be random. $H(u)$ is made random by the system design [Eq. (26.11)], and the randomness of $c_{0,1}(x)$ can be maintained by properly implementing the image processing part (e.g., by choosing the parameter $\alpha$ in Eqs. (26.12) and (26.13)). Of course, an ECC better than a simple repetition code should be used. In terms of security, not only for Mytec2 but for most other schemes as well, the best choice would be a single block ECC.

With all those enhancements in place, the Mytec2 scheme should not be less secure than a fuzzy commitment or a permutation-based fuzzy extractor scheme.

### 26.5.1.4 ECC Check Bits (Davida et al.)

This scheme, which was originally called "private template," was proposed by Davida, Frankel, and Matt [16, 17]. It was chronologically the third (after Mytec1 and 2) BE scheme.

A biometric template itself (or, for example, a hashed value derived from it), serves as a cryptographic key. This is a key generation scheme but, unlike Bodo [51], there are helper data. Therefore, the scheme falls under the definition of "secure sketch" [30]. To account for the template variations between different biometric samples, an $(n, k, d)$ error-correcting code is used: a number of $(n - k)$ bits, called check bits, are appended to the template. Those check bits are to correct possible bit errors in the template upon verification. The check bits are stored into the helper data along with the hashed value of the appended template. The authors targeted a 10% bit error rate for iris images, and they suggested using multiple images on enrollment and verification to reduce this error rate by majority coding. No specific implementation details, such as which ECC to use, were given.

The problem with this approach is that the check bits reveal some information about the biometric template. Consider the following example: A 55-bit template is encoded into 255-bit codeword using (255, 55) BCH ECC. According to Davida et al., there will be $(255 - 55) = 200$ check bits stored into the helper data. The BCH code can correct up to 31 random errors, which is only $31/255 = 12.2\%$ of all bits. Note that most biometrics usually have a higher error rate. Even though the template size, $k = 55$, is larger than the number of correctable random errors, an attacker can run the ECC decoder in the erasure mode, which can correct up to $2 * 31 = 62$ errors (the "error" locations, i.e., the first 55 bits, are known). In other words, the stored check bits allow the complete reconstruction of the template without actually capturing a fresh biometric sample, meaning that the scheme would not have any security. Perhaps to address this issue, the authors put a requirement $n < 2k$. However, such an ECC would not be powerful enough for most biometrics, since even for iris images, a realistic bit error rate is about 25% [36, 31], and it does not decrease significantly when multiple images are used (as Davida et al. had hoped). Even if $n < 2k$, the search space still can be reduced by soft decoding. Therefore, we deem this scheme inherently not secure and impractical.

### 26.5.1.5 Biometrically Hardened Passwords (Monrose et al.)

In a series of publications by Monrose, Reiter, Wetzel, Li, and co-workers [18–21], a technique called "biometrically hardened passwords" is presented. It deals with keystroke dynamics or voice recognition. A password that the user types or says is fused with a key (via a secret sharing scheme) extracted from a biometric component, thus hardening the password with the biometrics.

This is, probably, one of a few BE schemes that, like in Bodo [51], try to extract a key, at least initially, without helper data. However, the technique is made adaptive: upon each successful authentication, a "history file" is updated to make the authentication easier to the legitimate user and more difficult to an attacker. The "history file" is, in fact, helper data.

The types of biometrics used (i.e., the keystroke dynamics and the voice recognition) did not allow for achieving good accuracy numbers: for example, the keystroke dynamics generates up to a 15-bit key with FRR = 10% and FAR = 27%. That is why the biometric is combined with a conventional password. The fusion is done on a very low level, so that the overall system security is enhanced compared to the password-only scheme. Keystroke dynamics and voice are suitable biometrics in this regard, since the biometric samples are taken at the same time while the password is typed or spoken. The idea of hardening BE with a password on a low level is very promising.

The generalization of this scheme, called "secret locking construction," was presented in reference [65] along with the security analysis.

A somewhat similar technique of key generation was proposed by Hao and Chan [66] for online signature verification. The static signature features (shape-based) are stored into the template and are used for Stage 1 matching; this is a conventional biometrics approach. The dynamic features, such as pen-down time, velocities, and so on, are used for Stage 2 feature extraction. The boundary for each feature is defined and segmented; this information is stored into the template as helper data. The authors were able to extract 40-bit keys on average without any ECC. The results were quite encouraging: FRR = 28% at FAR = 1.2%.

### 26.5.1.6  *Fuzzy Commitment*

The fuzzy commitment scheme proposed by Juels and Wattenberg [60] is the simplest, yet the most studied, among all BE schemes. A biometric template must be in the form of an ordered bit string. A key is mapped to an $(n, k, d)$ ECC codeword of the same length, $n$, as the biometric template. The codeword and the template are XOR-ed, and the resulting $n$-bit string is stored into helper data along with the hashed value of the key. On verification, a fresh biometric template is XOR-ed with the stored string, and the result is decoded by the ECC. If the codeword obtained coincides with the enrolled one (this is checked by comparing the hashed values), the $k$-bit key is released. If not, a failure is declared.

The fuzzy commitment scheme was considered from a more general point of view by Tuyls, Verbitskiy, Goseling, Denteneer, and Linnartz [61–64], who introduced "helper data systems," and by Dodis, Reyzin, and Smith [30], who created the concepts of "fuzzy extractors" and "secure sketches." In particular, the scheme was generalized to incorporate non-binary strings and permutation-based extractors. Both scientific groups delivered a formal proof of security for such systems (see also references 35 and 67). Other generalizations of fuzzy extractors were presented in references 68 and 69.

It was also shown by Dodis et al. [30] that storing the so-called ECC *syndrome* of $(n - k)$ size is, in fact, equivalent to the fuzzy commitment scheme if the ECC is linear. This syndrome scheme is a secure sketch; that is, the original template can be recovered on verification. Unlike the scheme of Davida et al. [16, 17], the syndrome scheme does not have limitations on the size of stored $(n - k)$ bits.

Tuyls et al. [61–64, 70] and Van der Veen et al. [71] modified the fuzzy commitment scheme by extracting the most reliable components out of the biometric feature vector. The selection of these components is done on enrollment, which requires multiple biometric samples. The locations of the reliable components are also stored in the helper data.

The advantage of the fuzzy commitment scheme, besides its simplicity and proven security, is that, if properly implemented, it enables accuracy of the system almost as high as that of an equivalent non-BE system. The scheme requires a biometric template in the form of an ordered string of a fixed length and, therefore, a proper alignment of biometric images. When those conditions are met, such as for iris scan and some face and fingerprint recognition systems, the fuzzy commitment scheme seems to be one of the most feasible, as described in the following subsections. Also, the fuzzy commitment is the only BE scheme that can be used in a very secure application of a homomorphic cryptosystem (see Case Scenario 5, Section 26.7 for more details).

**Fuzzy Commitment Scheme for Iris.** Hao, Anderson, and Daugman [31] applied the fuzzy commitment scheme to iris recognition. They used an efficient combination of Hadamard (aka 1st order Reed–Muller) and Reed–Solomon ECCs[5] to improve the system performance. The 2048-bit iris template is divided by 32 chunks of 64 bits. Each chunk is a Reed–Muller (64, 7) codeword mapped to 7 bits. In addition, a Reed–Solomon ECC encodes 32 seven-bit bytes to produce 20 seven-bit bytes—that is, 140 bits in total. On verification, the Reed–Muller ECC is run in a soft decoding mode (i.e., it always produces an output codeword rather than declaring a failure) in each chunk, yielding 32 seven-bit bytes. The Reed–Solomon (32B, 20B) ECC can correct up to 6-byte errors. In total, two ECCs can correct about 25–27% of bit errors. The key size of 140 bits is sufficient for most cryptographic applications.

The scheme showed excellent performance: FRR was only 0.47% at FAR = 0 (or less than 1 in 200,000). These are the best results achieved so far for a BE scheme, although the database of iris images was captured under close to ideal conditions.

However, certain nonrandomness of the iris template (i.e., 2048 bits have the entropy of 249 bits) and the small size of the Reed–Muller block (64 bits) could be a source of potential security vulnerabilities (see Section 26.6).

Bringer et al. [48, 49] used a product of two Reed–Muller ECCs (64,7) and (32, 6), to link a 42-bit key to the 2048-bit iris template. They applied iterative (i.e., soft) decoding. This construction is near-optimal in the sense that it allows achieving the accuracy close to the theoretical limits: FRR = 5.6% at FAR < $10^{-5}$ for ICE iris database. This database is more realistic than the one used by Hao et al.

**Philips Priv-ID System.** Van der Veen, Kevenaar, Schrijen, Akkermans, and Zuo presented a BE system for face recognition [71]. It is based on the fuzzy

---

[5]This combination was used in the US space program in the late 1960s and early 1970s.

commitment scheme and on "helper data systems" (HDS) proposed earlier in theoretical works [61–64]. To improve the algorithm accuracy, the authors extracted reliable components from a biometric template and applied a BCH (single block of 511 encoding bits) ECC. They obtained good results: For a key size of 58 bits, FRR = 3.5% for the Caltech database with low to medium variability of images, and FRR = 35% for the FERET database with high variability; FAR = 0 (or at least less than 1 in 100,000) in both cases. The algorithm seems to be quite secure (see Section 26.6), and has been subsequently implemented into the priv-ID system.

The first application of BE to 3D face recognition was presented in references 72 and 73. It is not trivial to adapt the 3D features to the fuzzy commitment scheme. The authors achieved FRR = 10% at FAR = 0.7% and FRR = 21% at FAR $\approx$ 0.

Tuyls, Akkermans, Kevenaar, Schrijen, Bazen, and Veldhuis [70] applied fuzzy commitment scheme to fingerprints. The feature vector was created from Gabor filters and directional fields. The authors extracted reliable components from the template and applied BCH ECC. They obtained FRR = 5.4–9.9% for 49-bit and 85-bit key, respectively. However, FAR was 3.2–2.5%.

Later, the scheme was applied to a fingerprint minutiae template [74]. Each minutia was modeled as a Gaussian dipole to take into account the minutia angle. The resulting map was transformed into a Fourier domain. The most reliable components were extracted from the Fourier power spectrum in polar-log coordinates. This allowed creating a translation- and (to a certain extent) rotation-invariant feature vector. However, the magnitude-only part of the Fourier transform may not be discriminative enough.

In reference [75], the fuzzy commitment scheme was generalized to allow the extraction of multiple bits from a biometric feature, which improved the technique previously described by Chang, Zhang, and Chen [76, 77].

Kevenaar et al. [78] also proposed several practical applications of BE technologies, such as a server access token, a 3-way check for a biometric ePassport, and a "password vault." The technology is a part of a European 3D Face project [79, 80] and of a TURBINE project [146].

### 26.5.1.7  Quantization Using Correction Vector

A quantization method called "shielding functions" was proposed by Linnartz and Tuyls [52]. For each continuously distributed biometric feature, an offset to the center of the nearest even–odd (for a key bit equal to 0) or odd–even interval (for a key bit equal to 1) is estimated. Those offsets form the correction vector and are stored in the helper data. On verification, a fresh noisy feature is added to the offset and is decoded as 1 or 0, depending on the interval it falls into. If necessary, an ECC can be added to correct remaining errors.

Lyseggen et al. [81] and Duffy and Jones [82] proposed a scheme where a continuous feature is offset to the middle of an integer interval.

Buhan et al. [83] proposed 2D hexagonal constructions using the quantization index modulation (QIM) technique. This advanced technique allows the storage of more information per feature compared to Linnartz and Tuyls [52].

In general, the schemes with a correction vector could be vulnerable to score-based attacks.

### 26.5.1.8 Fuzzy Vault

An important milestone in the development of the BE technologies was the 2002 work by Juels and Sudan [84], called "fuzzy vault," and the subsequent implementation work by Clancy, Kiyavash, and Lin [85]. This is one of the most popular BE schemes, since it is applicable to a fingerprint minutiae template, which is in the form of an unordered set with arbitrary dimensionality. The template is a key to unlock the fuzzy vault where a secret message (e.g., a cryptographic key or a password) can be stored; therefore, the scheme falls under the common umbrella of BE technologies.

The vault is created using polynomial encoding and error correction. A polynomial is selected such that its coefficients form the secret message. Each minutiae point is represented by locations; the minutiae angles were not used in early works. Those points are treated as distinct $x$-coordinate values of the polynomial. The corresponding $y$-coordinates are computed as the values of the polynomial on each $x$. Both $x$ and $y$ numbers are stored. Following the example from reference 86, the minutiae horizontal and vertical locations can be quantized so that each location is represented by a 16-bit integer, $x$. The system will operate in a Galois field, $GF(2^{16})$. If a secret is 144 bits long (that includes the 128-bit key and 16 bits for cyclic redundancy check), it can be encoded as nine coefficients of an 8-degree polynomial, $p(x)$:

$$p(x) = c_8 x^8 + c_7 x^7 + \cdots + c_1 x + c_0.$$

To make the system secure, a number of *chaff points* are added to hide the real $x, y$ points. The chaff points do not lie on the polynomial and are more or less randomly distributed. The number of chaff points should be bigger than the number of minutiae by at least one order of magnitude (e.g., if there are on average 38 minutiae, then 313 chaff points or more are required). The idea of chaff points (also known as "ghost points") was first introduced in the Bjorn patent [102]). The chaff points are stored along with the real $(x, y)$ points, so that it is believed that an attacker cannot distinguish them. Unlike most other BE schemes, fuzzy vault usually does not store a hashed value of the key, although this can be done.

On verification, if a correct minutiae template is presented, some minutiae, but not necessarily all of them, coincide with the genuine stored points. In this case, it is possible to reconstruct a full polynomial using an ECC (Reed–Solomon ECC is the prime choice; some works used Lagrange interpolation with 16-bit cyclic redundancy check instead). This means that the secret message would be successfully decrypted, since the polynomial coefficients are the secret message.

For the above example, to reconstruct the 8-degree polynomial, $(8 + 1) = 9$ minutiae must coincide with the enrolled set.

Juels and Sudan gave a proof of the security of the system against a brute force attack, meaning that an attacker does not use the biometric information in a sophisticated way but checks all possible polynomials instead.

Unlike most other BE schemes, fuzzy vault uses *stored*, not fresh, minutiae to actually retrieve the key. Fresh minutiae are applied to the stored data only to find genuine minutiae among the chaff points. This allows better accuracy, since stored minutiae are not distorted, but may also pose a security threat.

Another fuzzy vault construction was proposed in reference [30]. Instead of storing chaff points, the top-degree coefficients of a high-degree polynomial are stored. This can be understood as interpolating through minutiae and chaff points to obtain a new "chaff" polynomial. According to Dodis et al., the chaff points need not be chosen at random. They can instead be evaluated as $y_i = p(x_i)$ for some polynomial $p$, and represent the entire list of pairs $(x_i, y_i)$ implicitly, using only a few of the coefficients of $p$. This scheme provides better security, but may be more difficult to implement for a fingerprint minutiae system (where it is harder to decode the vault since minutiae are not stored anymore).

The mathematically rich fuzzy vault scheme presents many attractive research opportunities. However, there are some implementation difficulties and security shortcomings of the fuzzy vault:

- Even though the minutiae set does not have to be ordered, there is still a problem of fingerprint alignment. Many published results assume that the fingerprints were manually prealigned. However, storing alignment data may leak some information to an attacker;
- If minutiae angles are not used as features, it is hard to achieve good accuracy. On the other hand, storing the angles may leak too much information;
- The real minutiae points are actually stored, which presents security challenges (see Section 26.6 for details).

Uludag et al. [86, 112] and Yang and Verbauwhede [87] further developed the fuzzy vault scheme for fingerprint minutiae. In reference 87, the minutiae are aligned relative to the reference minutiae pair found on enrollment. A similar approach using minutiae triangles and other structures for alignment was presented in reference 88. However, storing reference minutiae pairs or triangles may reveal too much information to an attacker.

The most advanced version of the fingerprint fuzzy vault is presented in references 89, 90 and 155. The system in reference 89 works in a fully automatic mode and is characterized by the following improvements:

- The fingerprints are aligned using high curvature points. Those points are identified from the ridge orientation field and stored in the template. The method allows compensation for both displacement and rotation. This alignment method is more accurate than using a fingerprint core/delta and more secure than storing minutiae pairs or triangles;
- Both minutiae coordinates and angles are stored within 16-bit integers. Adding minutiae angles improves the accuracy and allows more flexibility in placing chaff points during enrollment (i.e., a chaff point can be placed close to a real minutia if it has a different angle);

- A minutiae matcher that can compensate nonlinear distortions is used. This allows elimination of almost all chaff points during the verification of a legitimate user and improvement of the system accuracy;

- Other features include: selecting the most reliable minutiae; user-dependent numbers of minutiae, chaff points, and key size.

The tests were performed on two fingerprint databases, FVC2002-DB2 (half of all images modeling uncooperative users were removed) and MSU-DBI. The results show FRR in the range of 6–17% at FAR = 0.02%. Those results are among the best for all fingerprint-based BE schemes.

In our opinion, storing minutiae angles alongside with the high curvature points may leak some information to an attacker. It is known that minutiae angles are not random, they follow the ridge orientation field, and the angle $= 0°$ is most probable. High curvature points may reveal the ridge orientation field in some parts of the image, so that the attacker can discard a substantial number of chaff points. Adding more chaff points that are consistent with the orientation field, as suggested by the authors [89], would allow the attacker to even better reconstruct the orientation field and would also likely reduce the accuracy.

As Section 26.6 details, the fuzzy vault scheme is vulnerable to a reusability attack and, perhaps, to a "hill climbing" attack.

To overcome the security vulnerabilities of fuzzy vault, Nandakumar et al. [90] suggest hardening the vault with the user's password. This approach, which can (and should) be applied to any BE system, is stronger than the more common two-factor authentication (i.e., first password, then fingerprint). Hardening means that the password and the fuzzy vault are integrated on a low level. The password controls a permutation that is applied to the minutiae template; after that, the vault is constructed. For the same databases as in reference 89, the authors report a relatively minor increase in FRR, whereas FAR goes to 0 even for low-degree ($n = 7$) polynomials. It is not clear, though, whether both the impostors and the legitimate user were assigned the same password in the "stolen token" scenario (this is a frequent problem in results reporting, especially for CB). Reference 155 combines minutiae fuzzy vault with a fuzzy commitment scheme that uses non-minutiae information. This improves the overall system accuracy and security.

Freire-Santos, Fierrez-Aguilar, and Ortega-Garcia [91] applied the fuzzy vault scheme to online signature verification, Feng and Yuen applied it to face [92], and Lee et al. [93] applied it to iris.

Wang and Plataniotis [94] proposed another fuzzy vault system for face recognition. The method is based on 2D quantization of distance vectors between biometrics features and pairs of random vectors. The $N$-dimensional face features are mapped to $M$ 16-bit binary features (they can be called pseudo-minutiae). This transformation can be controlled by a password. The resulting 2D image plane looks like a fingerprint minutiae map (without angles). After chaff points are added, a coding/decoding procedure developed by Uludag et al. [86] is applied (it was not actually implemented in the paper). Unlike the fuzzy commitment scheme for face [71], the method does not require the biometric input to be in the form of an ordered string. The authors reported 4% for the equal error rate for the scenario when the attacker knows the transform, and EER $= 0$ (i.e., full separation) when the transform is kept secret. Basically, this work tries to integrate the CB approach of noninvertible transforms with BE. Such a scheme will likely be more secure against the nonrandomness and the reusability attacks (see Section 26.6).

Kholmatov et al. [95] developed the fingerprint fuzzy vault as a secret sharing scheme—that is, when a few users (or different fingers of the same user) can unlock the same secret. This can be done since the number of chaff points exceeds the number of real minutiae by at least one order of magnitude, so that the authors were able to enrol three users. However, this should increase the system FAR, which was not measured in reference 95 over a sufficient data sample. Nandakumar and Jain [156] developed the first multibiometric fuzzy vault.

### 26.5.1.9  *BioHashing (with Key Binding)*

BioHashing is a technique that can be used both for CB and BE. It transforms the biometric feature set to a new space of a lower dimension by generating a random set of orthogonal vectors and obtaining an inner product between each vector and the biometric feature set. The result is binarized to produce a bit string. The random feature vectors are generated from a random seed that is kept secret—for example, by storing it in a token.

For CB, the resulting binary string is the transformed template. On verification, a new string is obtained using the same secret set of orthogonal vectors, and the Hamming distance is computed between two strings.

The scheme can be applied to BE by adding one step of key binding. This is done via Shamir secret sharing with linear interpolation [96, 97], or within the framework of a standard fuzzy commitment scheme with Reed–Solomon ECC [98] (fingerprints and face). Both methods provide some error tolerance (although not very powerful). The authors report very good results: FRR $= 0.93\%$ at FAR $= 0$ (face recognition) [96], and FRR $= 0.11$–$1.35\%$ at FAR $= 0$ for fingerprints (FVC2002 databases were used) [42]. The latter results are better than those of the FVC2002 winner (i.e., among non-BE algorithms). However, those results were obtained simply because each impostor was assigned a different set of the secret random vectors, which made FAR artificially equal to 0 (this is typical of a "nonstolen token" scenario; see discussion in Section 26.5.2). In other words, the good results are rather attributed to a secret nonbiometric component of the system.

In general, the BioHashing approach (also called "salting" in more general terms [14]) of transforming the biometric feature set is promising in terms of improving the security of BE algorithm.

### 26.5.1.10  *Graph-Based Coding*

In a series of recent publications by Martinian et al. and Draper et al. [99–101], a new approach based on modern advances in the theory of ECCs is presented. The authors use low-density parity check (LDPC) codes, which are the state-of-the-art channel codes. They seem to be quite suitable for BE purposes because

- the LDPC codes can be designed as a single block $(n, k)$ ECC with large numbers of $n$ and $k$, which makes the system secure;

- high error rates can be handled;
- efficient decoding algorithms are available;
- LDPC coding is well represented graphically, which allows implementation of the graphical model movement. In other words, it is possible to model features of various biometrics—for example, to accommodate minutiae distortions.

In reference 99, the iris biometric is considered. First, unreliable bits are discarded from the iris template, which leaves 1806 bits available. Second, a random parity check matrix of the LDPC code is selected. Third, a LDPC syndrome is computed from the matrix and the biometric 1806-bit vector. This syndrome is stored as helper data. On verification, a fresh biometric template is applied to the syndrome. A belief propagation (BP) decoding algorithm is used. If the decoder succeeds (i.e., the number of error is within the decoder limit), the enrolled 1806-bit vector is recovered. The authors achieved good results for iris, with FRR varying from $\sim 0.1\%$ to $\sim 10\%$ and the system security varying from 50 to 110 bits, respectively. This ECC syndrome scheme falls under the definition of "secure sketch" [30], which is the key generation technique.

In references 100 and 101, an even more advanced technique is applied to fingerprint minutiae. The minutiae variability is modeled as movement, erasure, or insertion (i.e., spurious generation) of minutiae. This can be represented by a factor graph. At the same time, the graph is used to connect the biometric template to a LDPC syndrome. The scheme does not use minutiae angles as features (this is a potential area for future improvement).

For the preliminary tests, the authors had to limit the number of enrolled minutiae in the range from 31 to 35 in order to maintain the system security; otherwise, the variable LDPC encoding rate should be applied to each template (a potential subject of future work). The FRR varies from 11.6% to 32.3% at corresponding FAR from 1% to 0.03%.

The graph-based scheme, which is the most notable generalization of a fuzzy commitment (or its spinoff, the ECC syndrome [30]) scheme, seems to be quite secure and, in our opinion, is one of the most promising developments in the evolution of BE technologies.

### 26.5.1.11  Other Works

The U.S. patent to Bjorn [102] describes a process that falls under the definition of BE. It introduces an interesting idea: a number of ghost points (called "chaff" points in later works on fuzzy vault) are added to a fingerprint minutiae template to hide real minutiae. The ghost points are hashed to create a cryptographic key. However, the patent does not disclose the most important part—that is, a method for differentiating the ghost points from real minutiae on verification.

Burnett et al. [103] suggested using fuzzy extractors (or any other BE scheme) in a biometric identity-based signature scheme. A key string is generated from a biometric and then is used to create a *public key* and corresponding *private key*. One of the main applications of these schemes is in the area of nonrepudiation of documents.

Voderhobli, Pattinson, and Donelan [104] suggested using the secure sketch/fuzzy extractor scheme to combine multiple biometrics, such as fingerprint, iris, face, and voice. A password can be also seamlessly added to the scheme. This combination would improve both the system's accuracy and security. No specific implementation details or results were disclosed, however.

Martini and Beinlich [105] proposed a Virtual PIN scheme, which is practically identical to the fuzzy commitment scheme [60] and [70]. Gabor filters were used for feature extraction. The authors suggested using low-density parity check (LDPC) codes for error correction. The ability of these codes to handle very large block sizes may be beneficial for BE development (compare to Martinian et al. [99]). The equal error rate of 12% was achieved on an unspecified database.

Li, Niu, and Sun [106] proposed a "biometric key scheme" based on modular secret sharing, known in conventional cryptography. They applied the scheme to irises and obtained very good results: FRR = 5.7% and FAR = 0 (the sample size was not specified).

The publications by Sutcu, Li, and Memon [35, 107] further theoretically and experimentally examine the security aspects of BE systems—in particular, a "secure sketch" scheme of Dodis et al. [30]. The scheme with quantization using correction vector was applied to face biometrics [107]. For E94 database, good results were obtained: FRR = 4.5% at FAR $\approx$ 0.1%; the average key size was about 73 bits.

Zheng, Li, and Zhan [108] replaced an ECC in the fuzzy commitment scheme with a lattice mapping. This is, in fact, a quantization of the feature vector and storing the offset to a binary codeword. It is unclear if the scheme is capable of providing necessary error tolerance. Another quantization scheme was presented in references 76 and 77 but, as shown in reference 69, it may be not secure.

Schipani and Rosenthal [109] proposed several ECC constructions for the fuzzy commitment scheme. In order to handle large block sizes, the authors consider a product of Goppa codes with small size codes, such as a repetition or Hamming code.

The U.S. patent to Layton [110], which is assigned to the U.S. National Security Agency, basically describes the fuzzy commitment scheme with extraction of the most reliable components for iris. However, the patent does not cite the most important prior art [56, 60] and, therefore, may be challenged.

Sheng et al. [53] proposed a novel method for key generation without helper data. They employed an unsupervised clustering algorithm to separate the biometric feature space into clusters. The method was tested for signature verification and showed promising results. The template-free system would be inherently resilient to most of the attacks described in Section 26.6. However, it is not clear at this point if the technique is applicable to the "mainstream" biometric modalities (i.e., fingerprints, iris, and face).

Korte et al. [67] designed a fuzzy commitment scheme for DNA testing and reported good results. Socek et al [150] describe a new approach (called SFINX$^{TM}$) using a minutiae set intersection as a similarity measure, which is somewhat similar to the improved fuzzy vault [30]. It seems that the major practical challenge faced by this scheme is that it requires the exact coincidence (in terms of coordinates and angles) of a number of minutiae in two sets.

Buhan et al [151] come up with a notion of "fuzzy embedder," which is just another term for a key binding mode of BE for continuous distributions. They also propose adding noise (which is called dithering) to the input features to improve the system security.

Arakala et al [152] report the first practical implementation of PinSketch BE scheme [30] for fingerprint minutiae.

## 26.5.2   Cancelable Biometrics

This subsection provides a brief overview of some CB technologies primarily for the purpose of analyzing the security issues of CB (Section 26.6). A more detailed examination may be found in Ratha et al. [14] and in the references cited there (see also [29]).

### 26.5.2.1   Problem of Results Reporting

When evaluating the performance of cancelable biometrics, it is important to bear in mind the results reporting issue that is common in CB and sometimes in BE.

For any biometric system, the main performance indicator is the "receiver operating characteristic" (ROC) curve, which is a plot of true acceptance rate, TAR = 1 − FRR, versus false acceptance rate, FAR. The closer the curve is to the top left corner, the better. In most cases, ROC curves are generated offline from a database of biometric images or templates (i.e., not from live data).

CB applies a transform (usually secret) to each image or template in the database. When the ROC curve is calculated, the question arises: Should these transforms be the same or different for all impostors' attempts against a particular template? In our view, the impostors' transforms should be the same as the transform applied to the enrolled template.

Indeed, consider a real-life scenario: an impostor tries to get an access to the system by applying his biometric sample to somebody's cancelable template (it is assumed that the impostor does not possesses the true biometric). However, when the impostor presents the stolen token, the CB system will always recognize the token and apply the transform associated with it, i.e., the one belonging to the legitimate user. This is often called the "stolen token" scenario. It should be noted that the impostor does not necessarily have to be an active attacker stealing the token; it could be that the tokens are switched, for example, by mistake among legitimate users: FAR sometimes is defined such that the impostor makes "zero effort" to obtain a match [111, 112]. The most notable exception to the "stolen token" scenario is when the transform is controlled with the user's password and is not stored anywhere in the system. In this case there might be a "non-stolen token," or rather a "naïve/innocent impostor" scenario: The impostor applies both wrong biometric and wrong password (again, this is more or less likely if, for example, the users' tokens are switched by mistake).

When the templates are stored in a database, the system usually knows which transform is associated with a particular template. If the attacker steals the templates from the database but does not steal the transforms, he can try to obtain offline a false match with a wrong biometric *and* a wrong transform. However, the benefits for the attacker are quite limited without having knowledge of the correct transform. The attacker has to forge both the biometrics and the transform (stored, for example, on a token).

More likely is the "wrong biometrics, plurality of transforms" scenario: The attacker tries to obtain a false match using *his own* biometrics but with many different transforms. If successful, the attacker may forge the token that stores the transform. In this case, the "nonstolen token" scenario can be used to roughly estimate the number of transforms that the attacker has to test on average (for example, if FAR $= 10^{-6}$, the attacker will likely have to test about $10^6$ transforms). However, it would be more appropriate to run a direct test in the "wrong biometrics, plurality of transforms" scenario. We are unaware of such works.

Another realistic scenario for CB is "same biometrics, different transforms," which may take place when the user applies correct biometrics but wrong password, or (more serious) when there is an attempt to link CB templates created for the same user in different applications. This scenario has been considered in some publications.

Unfortunately, many works on CB apply different transforms to all impostors without specifically mentioning it—that is, using the "nonstolen token" scenario as a default. The ROC curve often becomes better than in conventional biometrics; sometimes even full separation (i.e., FAR = FRR = 0) is achieved. Those results leave one wondering how it is possible that applying the transform so dramatically improves the system's performance. The reason is that the "improvement" is related to the randomness brought by a nonbiometric component of the system, which has very little in common with real-life scenarios.

In our opinion, the main mode of performance estimation should be that the impostors are assigned the same transform as the legitimate user ("stolen token" scenario). When different transforms are assigned to all impostors in the "nonstolen token" scenario, it should be explicitly stated. The same guidelines should be applied to BE with a secret optional transform.

### 26.5.2.2  *Distorting Transforms*

The concept of CB using distorting transforms was introduced by Ratha et al. in 2001 [1, 26]. A parameterized, one-way *geometric distortion function* is applied to a biometric image or template. Only the distorted images/templates are stored, and they are matched also in the distorted form. If the distorted template is compromised, it can be "canceled" simply by choosing another transform. A large number of those transforms exist, so that each application uses different transforms, which prevents the linkage between databases.

The original works [1, 26, 113] contain examples of geometric transforms for fingerprints, face, iris, and voice biometrics. Preferably, the transform should be one-way—that is, noninvertible, such as a "many-to-one" function. However, in practice this property often causes accuracy degradation, so that some trade-off should be maintained.

The most advanced version of CB for fingerprint minutiae with distorting transforms is presented in references 14 and 114. The authors consider three types of transforms: Cartesian, polar, and functional ("folding"). The best balance in terms of accuracy and security is achieved with the functional transforms. It can be viewed as a surface folding transformation, as if the minutiae are embedded in a sheet that is then crumpled. Both the position and the orientation of the minutiae are changed by the parametric transfer function, which is locally smooth but not globally. In other words, the function tends to preserve the local minutiae similarity but moves the minutiae blocks globally. About 8.3% of minutiae changed their nearest neighbors.

The important feature of Ratha et al. technology is that it can use the standard minutiae matching algorithms to perform the verification in the distorted domain, which allows for seamless integration with existing biometric systems. The test results [14] showed only minor accuracy degradation compared to the nondistorted minutiae set, and even some improvement for the left part (i.e., at low FAR) of the ROC curve. However, those results were obtained when all the impostors were assigned different transforms, which is, as we already discussed, a scenario unlikely in real life.

As shown in Section 26.6, this CB scheme may be vulnerable to a reverse lookup attack, so that the original template can be approximately reconstructed.

### 26.5.2.3  BioHashing

The BioHashing technique is used more often for CB than BE, where there is no last step of key binding. A review of various BioHashing techniques can be found in reference 115.

The BioHashing was applied to face, fingerprints, palmprint recognition, and signature verification [116–119]. Two recent versions [120–122] are more advanced both in terms of accuracy and security. The authors also report results for the "stolen token" scenario, thus addressing the earlier criticism [123] of their work.

In a series of publications by Lumini and Nanni [124, 125], the accuracy of BioHashing is improved by fusing scores obtained for several BioHashing transforms ("spaces augmentation") or for several binarization thresholds ("$t$ variation") or for several biometrics (fingerprints and face). The authors reiterate the importance of the "stolen key scenario" and also show that the original BioHashing scheme is an instable classifier: Changes to the parameters of the classifier may cause dramatic changes in output classification.

Some modifications and improvements of the BioHashing technique were presented in reference 126.

### 26.5.2.4  Template Permutation

Braithwaite et al. [127] suggested application-specific permutation of the iris template. The permutation is kept secret. This transform is fully invertible; there are no changes to the matching algorithm, and the accuracy is preserved. The permutation can be made even transaction-dependent. The system completely relies on the secrecy of the permutation.

In another version proposed by Braithwaite et al. [127], the iris template is XOR-ed with a secret random mask. This is similar to a one-time pad cryptosystem [34]. The same idea is described in a Swedish patent to Tiberg and in a follow-up U.S. Patent Application [128].

### 26.5.2.5  Convolution with a Random Kernel (Savvides et al.)

Savvides, Vijaya Kumar, and Khosla [129] proposed a method for CB similar to Mytec2 BE processing—that is, using a convolution of a biometric image with a random kernel. The important differences are that, unlike BE,

- the random kernel must be kept secret (e.g., controlled by a password); and
- there is no key binding step.

After the convolution, a minimum average correlation energy (MACE) filter is created and stored as a cancelable template. The authors showed that the correlation outputs of the system with and without the random kernels are nearly identical; it was confirmed by experiments with the face images. In other words, the accuracy of a correlation-based system is preserved.

The transform is invertible and, therefore, must be kept secret.

### 26.5.2.6  Revocable Biotokens

This CB scheme [22], also called Biotope$^{TM}$ [23], transforms the biometric template and also changes the way in which the distance is calculated. The first part is necessary for privacy protection (creating a cancelable template), while the second part is done for accuracy improvement. This is likely the only CB scheme that claims to have better accuracy in the transformed domain for the "stolen token" scenario. The scheme is applicable only to distance-based biometric classifiers.

Each biometric feature value, $v$, is translated by $t$ and scaled by $s$, $v' = (v - t)s$. The resulting data $v'$ are separated into the integer, $g$, and the residual, $r$, parts: $v' = g + r$. The residual part, which is similar to the correction vector in references 52, 81, and 82, is stored into the template, but the integer part is transformed to $w$. This can be done through either public key (PK) encryption or a one-way hash. PK is a preferred method, since it can be fused with a user's password and allows controllable reversibility, so that the template may be changed even for each transaction (compare to reference 127). If the system requires higher security, hashing can be used instead. The system stores $t$, $s$, $r$, and $w$ into the template (called "revocable biotoken"). The attacker cannot technically obtain $g$ from $w$ if he does not know the private key.

When two biometric samples are matched, $w_1$ and $w_2$ must exactly coincide. For the residuals, $r_1$ and $r_2$, the distance is set to a constant, $c$, outside a fixed window, $b$. Ideally, a legitimate user has $w_1 = w_2$ and an impostor has $w_1 \neq w_2$. In reality, however, both the legitimate user and the impostor are penalized, so that for some features, $w_1 \neq w_2$. The average penalty tends to be larger for the impostors; this is claimed to be a prime source of accuracy improvement.

The ROC curves for face recognition [22] show a sharp increase of FRR at some FAR, which might be a manifestation of an instable classifier, such as the example that is discussed in reference 124. There are four main parameters associated with each biometric feature: $t$, $s$, $c$, and $b$. It is unclear if the system remains robust if changes are made to these parameters or to the settings of the image acquisition and processing steps.

As shown in Section 26.6, it is possible to exactly reconstruct the original biometric template with a reverse lookup attack. The system may also be vulnerable to score-based attacks.

### 26.5.2.7 Other Works

In reference 130, a minutiae template was transformed using algebraic hash functions applied to minutiae triplets. The authors showed that their transform is, at least technically, noninvertible.

In reference 131, the fingerprint minutiae are not distorted but hardened by adding a number of chaff points on both enrollment and verification. Those points are selected from a chaff pool unique for each user; this pool is secret and stored, for example, on a smartcard. The transform in this scheme is invertible if the attacker knows the chaff pool. The scheme is also vulnerable to the reusability attack (Section 26.6).

## 26.6    SECURITY ISSUES WITH UB: ATTACKS

By providing stronger binding of user biometrics and identifier, BE technologies offer improved authentication security over CB. The identifiers are bound with the biometric and recomputed directly from it on verification. This results in much longer and, therefore, stronger identifiers (keys/passwords), which do not require user memorization and, in general, are less susceptible to security attacks.

There are two types of attacks: high level and low level. In high level attacks the attacker can access the stored helper data but is not familiar with the algorithm and rather tests it as a black box. These attacks are basically the same as in conventional biometrics. In low-level attacks the attacker is familiar with the algorithm and can access offline all intermediate steps of it. The attacker can also collect or generate a biometric database.

A BE system is more resilient to many high-level attacks listed in Figure 26.1:

*Substitution Attack:* An attacker cannot create his own template since he, or anybody else, does not know the digital key and other transitory data that had been used to create the legitimate template.

*Tampering:* Since the extracted features are not stored, the attacker has no way to modify them.

*Masquerade Attack:* The system does not store the conventional biometric template, so the attacker cannot create a digital artifact image to submit to the system, as described in references 4, 6–8. However, a masquerade attack may still be possible on a lower level—for example, by using the hill climbing attack against BE (see below). In general, BE can provide better protection against the masquerade attack.

*Trojan Horse Attacks:* A BE algorithm does not use any score, either final or intermediate, to make a decision; it just retrieves (or does not retrieve) a key.

Therefore, the attacker has no means to fool the system by outputting a high score.

*Overriding Yes/No Response:* The output of a BE algorithm is a digital key, as opposed to the binary Yes/No response. The attacker does not know the key.

The security of CB, on the other hand, almost completely depends on the system's ability to maintain the secrecy of the transform that is applied to the image or template. If an attacker learns this transform, he can create a template for the substitution attack or tamper with the existing CB template. If the transform is invertible (fully or partially), the masquerade attack becomes possible. Like any conventional biometric system, CB still has a verification score (which can be modified by a Trojan horse program) and a Yes/No response (which can be overridden).

As previously mentioned, the security of a BE system can also be augmented by a secret transform, preferably controlled by a password. Moreover, there are BE and CB schemes very similar to each other that use the same type of transform (e.g., Mytec2 BE and Savvides et al. CB, or BioHashing with and without key binding). However, even if an attacker learns the secret transform in the case of BE, the impact on the system security will be less significant, since BE system does not rely, in general, on the secrecy of the transform.

BE or CB can address, to a certain extent, the problem of spoofing or a replay attack, which are common for all biometrics. To address these types of attacks, the system should use a secret transform, preferably controlled by a password.

The other group of attacks, which will be the main focus of this section, is of a low level, when the attacker is familiar with the algorithm. The security of the BE algorithm means that neither the digital key nor the biometric, which was used on enrollment, can be extracted from a stored helper data. As in conventional cryptography, it is implied that the attacker has complete knowledge of the BE algorithm and can access the helper data; however, the attacker does not have a legitimate user's biometrics. Assuming that the attacker is a smart adversary, rather than counting on security by obscurity, sets a very high benchmark for BE. A CB system should be analyzed according to the same standard: The attacker may know all the details of the algorithm, including the secret transform, and has access to the transformed CB template. The CB system is considered secure if the attacker cannot obtain a biometric image or conventional template from this information.

In trying to crack a BE system, an attacker can pursue one or more of the following objectives:

- Obtain the key linked to the biometrics.
- Obtain the exact biometric template used on enrollment.
- Obtain an approximate version of the template that, nonetheless, would defeat the system (masquerade template).
- Obtain a masquerade image of the biometrics.
- Link BE templates across different applications or databases.

The same holds for CB, except that there is no key involved.

Here an important question arises: If the key is known, does it automatically expose the biometric template? The answer is Yes for some BE schemes, such as fuzzy commitment and fuzzy vault. Other schemes, such as Mytec2 and some BioHashing, do not reveal the biometric template in full, although obtaining the key would make other attacks (e.g., hill climbing) easier. Ballard et al. [46] put a "strong biometric privacy" requirement on a BE system; that is, an attacker should not be able to obtain the biometric even if the key is compromised. For most BE schemes, this requirement is unrealistic; moreover, the very design of many fuzzy extractor/secure sketch schemes implies that the two modes are interchangeable.

Some BE schemes are accompanied by a theorem that delivers a formal proof of security, claiming, for example, that the stored data leak no or little information. However, the schemes reveal vulnerabilities later on. Then what is the place and value of those theorems? The answer is that the theorems usually assume that an attacker deals with just one set of the helper data. If the conditions of the theorem are met, for example, the biometric template is random (which is rarely the case), the attacker will not be able to retrieve a key from this particular helper data other than by a brute force search in the key space. However, the truth is that the attacker does not have to be bound by the constraints of the theorem or even by the BE algorithm. The attacker can use any biometric data, either real or computer-generated (such as SFinge [50]). In fact, most attacks against BE have come from the biometric, not cryptographic, side. In reality, the theorems provide only necessary, but not sufficient, conditions for the system security. As Sutcu et al. [107] conclude, "known theoretical results become not very useful and the exact security of the system needs to be further investigated."

In terms of security, the most studied is the fuzzy commitment scheme and some of its generalizations. As we already mentioned, this is the simplest of all BE schemes and, therefore, is easier to analyze. The main result of all the studies is that if the biometric template is a random $n$-bit string, and it is XOR-ed with a $n$-bit codeword of an $(n, k)$ ECC to obtain the helper data, then the entropy loss is not more than $(n - k)$ bits (in reference 67, this result was extended to any arbitrary bit string). In other words, the system still securely holds $k$ bits (i.e., the size of the key). Even though this information-theoretical proof is only a necessary condition, we think that the fuzzy commitment scheme remains, if properly implemented, one of the most secure out of all BE schemes.

## 26.6.1   Description of the Attacks

There is little information in the literature (see, for example, reference 46 focused primarily on signature verification) about the practical feasibility of the attacks against BE or CB systems. The following is an overview of possible attacks, both published and unpublished, and their applicability to various BE and CB systems.

### 26.6.1.1   False Acceptance Attack

One of the easiest methods for breaking BE, which we call *false acceptance attack,* does not require a knowledge of the BE algorithm. If, for example, FAR equals $10^{-6}$, the attacker can run a database of about $10^6$ biometric images or templates against the helper data with a good chance of obtaining a false acceptance—that is, to retrieve a digital key. The attacker can either acquire a database of real images or use a computer-generated database. The image or template that generated a false acceptance could serve as a masquerade image/template, although it will not necessarily break the same user's helper data for another application (or after the user is re-enrolled).

The false acceptance attack is applicable to CB if the attacker knows the secret transform. Out of all CB schemes, the earlier versions of BioHashing may be especially vulnerable [123], because the separation of genuine and impostor distributions can be very poor when the same transform is applied to both. We already mentioned the problem of results reporting for CB. The effectiveness of the false acceptance attack should be measured when the same transform is applied to both genuine and impostor attempts ("stolen token" scenario).

As we already mentioned in Section 26.4, breaking a BE algorithm in, say, $10^6$ attempts is not equivalent to searching $10^6$ keys in cryptography. A BE algorithm is much slower than cryptographic hash algorithms and is usually slower than most conventional biometric algorithms. Besides setting FAR at low level ($<10^{-6}$–$10^{-5}$), it makes sense to keep the BE verification algorithm deliberately slow, for example, at 1 second level. The approach similar to *one-way slowdown functions* that are known in cryptography [132] could be applied. The reduced efficiency would not be an issue for one-to-one applications, but would require more processing time to get a false acceptance. Moreover, the number of slowdown iterations could be a tunable characteristic of a system. The slowdown functions can be placed in different parts of a BE algorithm, such as the template transformation stage, or within the ECC. Slowing the hash at the end of the BE algorithm is not sufficient (although desirable), since the ECC output already provides a clue to the likelihood of the success.

A multimodal approach (e.g., using more than one finger) would definitely help to reduce the false acceptance [156].

The false acceptance attack, which is one of the "brute force" attacks, is conceptually the simplest (besides inverting the hash) but also a cumbersome way to break a BE system. Unlike cryptography, collecting and maintaining a large database of biometric images (compatible with the BE system under attack) is not always the easiest and the most economical approach. There are other, more sophisticated attacks that may not even require a biometric database or may require a much smaller database.

### 26.6.1.2  Pseudo False Acceptance Attack on CB

If the CB secret transform is not known, the attacker may try to obtain a false acceptance by varying transforms. If successful, the attacker may forge a token storing the transform and use it with his own biometrics. The attack requires more computations than obtaining a false match with a known transform; however, the attacker does not need to collect or generate a biometric database. The FAR in the "nonstolen token" scenario may provide an estimate for the average number of transforms required, although a more direct method would be to generate a pseudo-FAR curve by varying the transforms only.

### 26.6.1.3  Inverting the Hash

This is another "brute force" attack. If a hashed key is stored into the helper data, the attacker may try to cryptographically invert the hash. As we already discussed, this attack should always be made more computationally expensive for an attacker than other attacks.

### 26.6.1.4  Nearest Impostors Attack

Unlike conventional biometrics or CB, a BE algorithm does not have a verification score: Its output is either a correct key or a failure message. However, an attacker may try to derive an intermediate score based on the knowledge of the algorithm. This score may be either global or partial—that is, dealing with some parts of the helper data. This is usually the case when an ECC divides the helper data into smaller chunks, such as in Mytec2 [15] with a simple repetition code in $k$ chunks, or in the Hao et al. fuzzy commitment scheme for iris [31] with Reed–Muller ECC in 32 chunks. The partial score would be a length of the chunk minus a distance to the nearest codeword.

   The attacker may run a small (starting from a few hundred) database of images/templates against the helper data to obtain a partial score for each chunk and a global score as the sum of the partial scores. The attacker identifies several "nearest impostors" [153]—that is, the attempts with the highest global score or, alternatively, with the highest partial score for a given chunk. If, for any impostor's attempt, the partial score is large enough for a particular chunk, the attacker may assume that the correct codeword has been decoded for this chunk. Other impostors' attempts may decode other chunks. Then a voting technique is applied to several of the nearest impostors' attempts to make the process more robust. The attacker does not need to decode "all or nothing"—he can do it chunk by chunk instead.

   A scheme that uses a simple repetition code, such as Mytec2, is especially vulnerable to this attack. If an $(m, L)$ ECC is used, the success rate of the attack quickly diminishes when the $L$ value (i.e., the number of codewords) increases [153].

### 26.6.1.5  Hill Climbing Attack

This is one of a few published practical attacks. It was developed by Adler [133, 134] against Mytec2 BE. The scheme was deliberately weakened and altered[6] to make the attack easier and to prove the concept (note that this is a common practice in cryptography).

   Similar to the nearest impostors attack, the hill climbing attack is also based on the ability of the attacker to derive an intermediate score during the verification process.

---

[6]The author omitted the second Fourier transform from the Mytec2 algorithm and did binary encoding in the filter domain rather than for the output array $c_0(x)$.

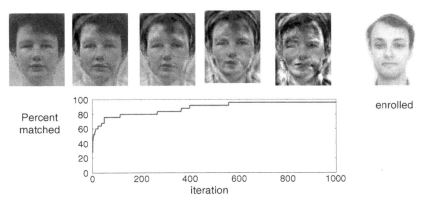

enrolled

**Figure 26.5.** Hill climbing attack on Mytec2 BE system. (Courtesy of A. Adler.)

However, the hill climbing attack is more sophisticated than the nearest impostors attack, although the latter is usually more efficient.

For a BE chunk of $(m, 1)$ repetition code, the partial score is derived in the same way as described for the nearest impostors attack. Then a global matching score is constructed as a sum of all chunk partial scores. By making small changes in the input impostor's image, the attacker watches how the score changes. If it increases, the change is retained; if not, the attacker tries a different change. After a number of iterations, the attacker may be able to retrieve a key. The details of the attack, which uses "quantized hill climber," are thoroughly described in references 133 and 134. As shown in Figure 26.5, the attack converges quite quickly toward the correct key; the impostor face image becomes looking somewhat similar to the enrolled image.

If successful, the hill climbing attack retrieves the key and creates a masquerade image/template.

There are two conditions necessary for the hill climbing attack:

1. The attacker must be able to obtain a global, or a partial/intermediate matching score. The score must be meaningful; that is, a higher score means closer similarity.

2. Small changes in the input cause relatively small changes in the score (although Adler's algorithm is able to handle score quantization to some extent).

Most vulnerable to the hill climbing attack are the schemes with short ECCs, such as Mytec2 with a repetition code. A BE scheme with a single block ECC is much better protected against this and the nearest impostors attack. Most CB schemes are inherently vulnerable to the hill climbing attack, since, unlike BE, the CB algorithm always outputs a verification score. A successful hill climbing attack on CB would create a masquerade image/template.

It is likely that an intermediate score can be derived for the fuzzy vault scheme, which stores real fingerprint minutiae buried among chaff points. The applicability of a hill climbing attack to the fuzzy vault has been claimed by Adler [133]. The advanced fuzzy vault scheme [89], which stores minutiae angles and is able to eliminate most chaff points during verification of a legitimate user, may allow the attacker to derive a matching score and, therefore, could also be vulnerable to the hill climbing or other score-based attacks.

For BE and CB schemes with a correction vector [22, 52, 81, 82], the attacker may derive a partial score based on the distance to the nearest integer. A global score will be a sum of the partial scores. Whether this score is discriminative enough to run a hill climbing or a nearest impostors attack depends on the specifics of the scheme.

### 26.6.1.6    Using Statistics of ECC Output (ECC Histogram Attack)

The ECC histogram attack is applied to the relatively small ECC chunks of the helper data [153]. In particular, the Reed–Muller (64, 7) ECC, which was used in reference 31, is a good candidate. The attack is performed by running a relatively small database of images (usually with various distortions, rotations, and shifts applied) against the helper data and by counting the number of appearances of each possible output codeword for all impostor attempts. For example, the (64, 7) ECC has $2^7 = 128$ possible output codewords, so that the result will be a histogram with 128 bins. The bin corresponding to the histogram maximum is declared a winner, thus yielding a likely codeword. This attack is very simple and does not require a deep knowledge of the properties of the ECC or the BE algorithm.

The attack works because the bit error probability for an impostor distribution is below 0.5 (e.g., 0.46 in reference 31). Therefore, a correct codeword has a slightly higher probability of appearance.

Note that most codes proposed in reference 109, which are the product of Goppa code and a repetition or other code with a small number of codewords, would likely be vulnerable to the ECC histogram attack and to the hill climbing attack. The ECC histogram attack may also work for the product codes proposed in reference 48.

The remedy for the ECC Histogram attack is to increase the $L$ size of the $(m, L)$ ECC, such that $2^L$ becomes so large that the bin content for all output codewords would be either 0 or 1. At some $L$, the ECC histogram attack becomes less feasible than the false acceptance attack.

### 26.6.1.7    Nonrandomness Attack

This attack exploits possible nonrandomness of the helper data. It does not require a biometric database. The attack is done manually and requires a thorough knowledge of the BE algorithm.

As we already mentioned, the fuzzy commitment scheme is proven to be secure if the helper data are random. The same is desirable for all other BE schemes, even without a formal proof. However, it is difficult to satisfy this condition in real life, because most biometric traits are inherently nonrandom. Extracting random components from the biometric would likely hike false rejection, as the nonrandomness often provides needed redundancy.

For example, in the Mytec2 scheme, the key is linked to the output 2D pattern. If the algorithm is not properly implemented, this pattern will consist of clusters; that is, it will be nonrandom. Every key bit is encoded by $m$ bits of the same parity, if $(m, 1)$ repetition code is used. The locations of those $m$ bits within the 2D array are known. If the array contains clusters, the attacker can interconnect different bits as having the same parity. By creating the lists of adjacent bits and using the voting technique, it is possible to completely recover the key [153]. Note that the $c_0(x)$ pattern in Mytec2 scheme [Eq. (26.12)] can easily be made random. However, this is not always true for the fuzzy commitment and some other BE schemes.

In reference 135, an attack on fuzzy vault exploiting nonrandomness of chaff points is presented. The method is based on the fact that chaff points should have a minimum distance to real minutiae. The chaff points in reference 85 are generated one-by-one, and the point generated later in the process tends to have more neighboring points. Therefore, an attacker may assume that the points with larger "free area" are more likely to be real minutiae. Chang et al. showed that the attacker would obtain a speed gain compared to the brute force search, but did not actually demonstrate cracking a real fuzzy vault scheme.

In the advanced version of fuzzy vault [89], the minutiae angles are stored alongside the coordinates. This makes the system more robust to the Chang et al. [135] attack, since chaff points can be placed closer to real minutiae by assigning a different random angle. However, storing the minutiae angles itself may pose some security threats (the minutiae angles are not randomly distributed).

### 26.6.1.8  *Reusability Attack*

While a BE scheme may be secure for one particular key, there is a possibility that an attacker would compare helper data created from the same biometric but with different keys. This may occur when the same biometrics is reused for different applications/keys.

The reusability attack was introduced by Boyen [68], although without giving detailed recipes. Boyen showed that if a fuzzy extractor scheme is poorly designed (e.g., in terms of ECC), then every next usage of the same biometric may leak a certain amount of information to the attacker, so that after a number of times all the keys may be cracked. The fact that the biometric sample slightly varies from application to application provides very little relief, since the system's tolerance (such as an ECC) works to the advantage of the attacker.

An important result of Boyen's work is the proof that the fuzzy commitment scheme is secure against the reusability attack if the ECC is *linear*. Linearity of the ECC means that the sum (i.e., XOR for binary codes) of any two codewords is always another codeword. Fortunately, most practical ECCs are linear.

Among all BE schemes, fuzzy vault turns out to be one of the most vulnerable to the reusability attack [90, 136, 150, 154]. For example, a fuzzy vault scheme containing 20 real fingerprint minutiae, 300 chaff points, and an 8- or higher-degree polynomial is secure against a brute force search, as shown in reference 85. However, if the same biometric is reused in two or more fuzzy vaults, they will have different keys and different sets of chaff points. The only thing in common will be genuine minutiae, which can be obtained by using a minutiae matcher of the type described in reference 89. The successful attack recovers minutiae sets and the keys in both fuzzy vaults [154].

To improve the resilience of fuzzy vault against the re-usability attack, Nandakumar et al. [90] suggest applying an application-dependent secret transform to the minutiae set. Another example of the transform for face biometrics can be found in reference 94. In the latter case, the scheme may be more secure against the re-usability attack even if the attacker knows the transform. The reason is that the transform of reference 94 is designed in such a way that each pseudo-minutia is derived from all input features (rather than simply permuting the minutiae set [90]).

Reference 136 also states that the phase-only filter of Mytec2 scheme (see Eq. (26.11)) is not secure against the re-usability attack. In our opinion, this analysis is inadequate.[7] Let us assume that the attacker has access to two filters, $H_1(u)$ and $H_2(u)$, created from the same biometric but with different random phases, $\varphi^{(1)}_{rand}(u)$ and $\varphi^{(2)}_{rand}(u)$. Those filters are random and completely uncorrelated. All the attacker can get from this information, as follows from Eq. 26.11, is $\exp(i\varphi^{(1)}_{rand}(u) - i\varphi^{(2)}_{rand}(u))$, which is yet another random phase-only function. No information is revealed about $\varphi^{(1)}_{rand}(u)$ or $\varphi^{(2)}_{rand}(u)$. In general, all known vulnerabilities of the Mytec2 scheme are related to the lookup table (that links the key and the output pattern), but not to the filter $H(u)$.

The re-usability attack can help facilitate all other attacks. For example, two masquerade templates obtained by the hill climbing attack can be compared to rectify the result. Accordingly, the re-usability attack will be effective for CB as well.

In the CB scheme of Kanak and Sogukpinar [131], the re-usability attack works even if the attacker does not know the secret chaff pools in two applications: he just finds common minutiae in both templates.

The re-usability attack may be also applicable to BioHashing [137].

### 26.6.1.9 Blended Substitution Attack

If the attacker knows *the key and the biometric template*, he can create a blended template that would work both for the attacker and the legitimate user [136], so that it would be harder to detect such an attack compared to a simple substitution with the attacker's template. The attack works for fuzzy vault: The attacker can override a number of chaff points to make them coincide with his own minutiae, so that both the legitimate user and the attacker will be able to retrieve the key on verification. This basically exploits the earlier idea of secret sharing via the fuzzy vault [95] (i.e., now the secret is "shared" with the attacker). It should be pointed out that the fuzzy commitment and Mytec2 schemes are much more robust to the attack, since the attacker would need to alter a significant percentage of bits to have it work for both

---

[7]For example, reference 136 claims that two complex phase-only products (for genuine users and impostors) have different magnitudes, even though the magnitude of both products is 1—that is, exactly the same.

users. It can be shown that the errors introduced into the system would make FRR very high (actually, close to 100%) for both users, so that the attack would be infeasible.

Considering this attack from another angle, it should be noted that it is not fair to put a requirement on BE to keep the key secure outside of the BE system. After the key is retrieved, it enters a conventional cryptosystem which should keep the key secure; otherwise, the cryptosystem does not make sense. The key is not stored anywhere in the BE system nor is it needed for verification; the key is recreated only upon successful verification (this is different from CB, where a secret transform is stored). A good practice would be not to release the key but rather some derivative of it—for example, yet another hashed version of the key. This hashed version can in turn serve as a cryptographic key for any application. With this architecture, the attacker would not be able to obtain the original key outside of the BE system.

The blended substitution could make sense as a secondary attack—that is, if the attacker was able to crack BE by other attacks and to obtain both the key and the biometric. Of course, in this case, the attacker would have many other options with respect to using the obtained information.

### 26.6.1.10   Inverting CB Transform

This attack is obvious for some CB schemes that have an invertible transform. For example, in the Savvides et al. scheme [129] that uses Mytec2 type processing—that is, a convolution of the image with a random kernel—the attacker can multiply the stored filter with a complex conjugate of the kernel Fourier transform and do the inverse Fourier transform. The result will be an almost exact biometric image, with some minor differences caused by the processing of the Fourier intensity and quantization in the MACE filter. Other examples include inverting the permutation table for the iris template [127], and possibly inverting a BioHashing transform [138]. In reference 131, if the attacker knows the chaff pool, he can completely reconstruct the real minutiae. The security of these schemes fully depends on the secrecy of the transform. The privacy protection is even more limited if the transforms are controlled by the database custodian.

A BE scheme that uses a secret transform in the middle [31, 90, 94, 139, 151] still remains secure even if the transform is invertible and known to the attacker (with possible exception of the earlier BioHashing schemes with key binding [96, 97]). Moreover, such a transform may improve, in some cases, resilience against the reusability and the nonrandomness attacks. The reason is that the transform, such as in references 94 and 126, is applied to the biometric template only, and the key is bound to the transformed template. The result will be more secure if the transform in the middle is properly designed (at least more complex than a simple permutation or mapping).

### 26.6.1.11   Reverse Lookup of CB Template

Even if a CB scheme uses a transform that is technically noninvertible, the attacker may exploit the fact that biometric features have a finite range of values. By knowing the range from a training biometric data set and then quantizing the feature, the attacker applies the forward (i.e., known) transform to the features and creates a lookup table for all transformed features. Then, by doing a reverse lookup, the attacker may retrieve the original features from a CB template.

In Ratha et al. cancelable biometrics [14], the most promising transform is functional folding. The transform preserves local, but not global, minutiae similarity. In order to achieve a reasonable accuracy, the transform is designed in a way that only 8.3% minutiae change their nearest neighbors.

The reverse lookup attack does the following:

The attacker divides the minutiae space by cells in the same way—for example, $16 \times 16$, as in the CB algorithm [14]. By knowing the forward transform, the attacker creates a lookup table for all 256 cells. The same is done for the minutiae angles. The reverse lookup will correctly retrieve all but 8.3% of cells that changed their nearest neighbors. For those cells, the attacker is faced with an ambiguity as to which of the two distinct regions the cells should be assigned. However, the minutiae matcher can easily accommodate 8.3% errors, so that the attacker can either delete those minutiae in question or assign them (i.e., in random) to either region. The attacker can also use the information from minutiae angles, since each region should contain minutiae with close angles. The resulting template will not be the exact copy of the original, but rather a masquerade template. The effectiveness of the attack can be further improved if the attacker has access to another CB template created from the same biometric, since the ambiguous cells will be different for the second template.

In the revocable biotokens CB scheme [22], each biometric feature value, $v$, is translated and scaled, $v' = (v - t)s$. The resulting data $v'$ is separated into two parts, the integer number $g$ (i.e., the result of quantization) and the residual $r$. Then $g$ is mapped to $w$ via public key (PK) encryption (preferred embodiment) or a one-way hash. The system stores $t$, $s$, $r$, and $w$. The attacker technically cannot obtain $g$ from $w$ (it is reasonable to assume that the attacker does not know the private key). However, the attacker does not have to break a strong PK or hash algorithm. By knowing the transformation parameters $t$ and $s$ and the forward cryptographic algorithm (i.e., a public key or a hash function), the attacker can obtain $g$ from $w$ using the reverse lookup. Indeed, by running a small training biometric database, the attacker determines a range of $v'$ and, therefore, all possible numbers for $g$. This range is not very broad; otherwise, the system accuracy would degrade due to overquantization. The lookup table is built by applying the forward cryptographic algorithm to all possible numbers of $g$. The reverse lookup attack will reconstruct the exact biometric template from the stored data, meaning that the system is not much stronger in terms of privacy/security protection than other CB systems with invertible transforms.

The possibility of inverting a CB transform, either directly or via the reverse lookup, along with the inherent vulnerability to a substitution attack, necessitates keeping the CB transform secret, even if it is technically noninvertible.

### 26.6.1.12 Linkage Attack

If the same biometric is used for several BE applications, the attacker may try to link the BE templates without actually cracking them [140], which makes the attack different from the re-usability attack. If successful, this attack affects privacy rather than the security of the system.

Suppose that there are two BE applications or databases, 1 and 2, that contain BE templates (helper data), $W_1$ and $W_2$, created from the biometric samples, $X_1$ and $X_2$. Those samples were taken from the same user; that is, $X_1$ and $X_2$ are close. However, different keys, $k_1$ and $k_2$, were bound to $X_1$ and $X_2$. A person may be enrolled in databases 1 and 2 under different user names or pseudonyms. The attacker tries to link $W_1$ and $W_2$ without knowing $X_1$ or $X_2$ or having any other user information.

For the simple fuzzy commitment scheme (i.e., without the component selection), the attack can be done in the following way:

Let $C_1$ and $C_2$ be the ECC codewords corresponding to $k_1$ and $k_2$. They are XOR-ed with the binary templates $X_1$ and $X_2$ to create BE templates $W_1$ and $W_2$:

$$W_1 = C_1 \oplus X_1, \quad W_2 = C_2 \oplus X_2, \quad \text{where } \oplus \text{ denotes the bitwise XOR operation.}$$

The attacker XORs both templates: $W_1 \oplus W_2 = (C_1 \oplus C_2) \oplus (X_1 \oplus X_2) = C_3 \oplus (X_1 \oplus X_2)$, where $C_3 = C_1 \oplus C_2$. If the ECC is linear, $C_3$ is just another codeword.

If, by running an ECC decoder, the attacker obtains a codeword $C_3$ with a small number of errors, he can assume that $X_1$ and $X_2$ are close—that is, belong to the same user.

The scheme with the selection of the most reliable components will be more resilient to the attack, since $X_1$ and $X_2$ will differ in a larger number of bits. Also, the "transform in the middle" approach [31, 90, 94, 139, 151] would thwart the threat of this attack.

### 26.6.1.13  *Learning from Vulnerabilities*

The broad spectrum of attacks on BE (and CB) described in this section may leave an impression that BE is not secure. We believe this is not the case. There are just particular steps in some BE schemes that make them vulnerable to the attacks. The purpose of this section was to outline known and new attacks, so that necessary remedies may be taken.

Many vulnerabilities are related to the schemes that divide the biometric template by smaller chunks and run $(m, L)$ ECCs, where $m$ and $L$ are relatively small, in each of them. At present, it looks like one of the most secure BE schemes would be a fuzzy commitment (or an ECC syndrome, such as in reference [99]) scheme with a single block $(n, k)$ ECC, where $n > {\sim}1000$, $k > {\sim}100$, applied to iris (or, even better, two irises of the same person).

While BE and CB must be made resilient against attacks, we think it is unrealistic to expect the same level of security as found in cryptography. To begin with, any conventional biometric system is not cryptographically secure. It can be attacked at many points, from spoofing the sensor to overriding the final Yes/No response. The security of a biometric system is achieved through the hardware (e.g., liveness detection, smartcards, secure storage and communication), and procedures (e.g., supervised enrollment/verification, time stamps, passwords, conventional encryption). In a nontrusted environment—that is, when an attacker can gain access to a stored template and/or to the algorithm, the security of a biometric system diminishes.

On the other hand, BE offers a certain level of security even in a nontrusted environment, with the addition of greatly enhanced privacy benefits. Instead of applying a cryptographic yardstick to BE, we view it along the lines of a key management scheme, or a stronger replacement for conventional passwords. Passwords do not possess, in general, cryptographic security, because they can be broken with a dictionary attack, and so on.

For a BE system, nothing would prevent the same protection measures (i.e., hardware and procedures) from being implemented, as presently used in conventional biometrics. For example, storing helper data on a smart card, or even running the whole BE algorithm on card, would add an additional layer of security. Even more, those measures may be applied in a manner that is unique to BE. For example, using a password to recreate, on-the-fly, some part of the helper data would integrate the biometric and the knowledge-based approaches at a more fundamental level. The password/token can control part of the helper data: For example, a permutation table [31], a transform of a minutiae [90] or a face [94] template will be regenerated on-the-fly each time. This is similar to the CB approach, where a secret transform is controlled by the password or token and, in a way, is a *merger of BE and CB* (see also discussion in reference 139). Thus, the password/token may become an essential part of the BE process on a fundamental level.

While such a system would not offer full cryptographic security, it could be more secure than either a conventional biometric system or a password-based system, or even two-tier authentication involving password/token and conventional biometrics.

If BE is used within a framework of a homomorphic cryptosystem [142], it will allow biometric authentication in the encrypted domain (see Case Scenario 5 in Section 26.7 for more details). This would provide an ultimate solution to most BE security issues.

## 26.7  PRIVACY AND SECURITY ADVANTAGES OF BE

In the following subsections, we consider several BE case scenarios (see also reference 3) which demonstrate the great potential of BE technologies as a tool that enhances both privacy and security. Note that CB technologies are less suitable or not suitable at all for these scenarios, since CB outputs a binary Yes/No response instead of a key.

### 26.7.1  Case Scenarios

#### 26.7.1.1  Biometric Ticketing

A promising BE application is one-time-use biometric tickets or tokens, for events, boarding passes, and so on. A BE template (i.e., helper data) can be stored on a ticket as a 2D bar code, and a database stores the hashed value of a key for each enrolled user.

The key and the ticket are used only for this particular application. On a verification terminal:

   **(a)** The user presents her ticket to the system which reads the BE template from the bar code.

   **(b)** The live biometric sample is taken.

   **(c)** The system applies the biometric to the BE template to retrieve the key.

   **(d)** The hashed key is sent to the database where it is compared to the stored version.

Notably, the database does not store biometric information or even helper data. The hashed version of the key is secure and meaningless for anything but one-time authentication of the user, such that it can be sent through unsecured channels. The ticket is disposed after its use. If BE has a secret transform, it can be also stored in the database and sent to the verification terminal when the user presents the ticket. This would significantly increase the security level of the system.

With conventional biometrics, the danger of such a one-time-use system is that the person's biometrics could be lost or stolen and later used by thieves to access more secure applications—for example, a bank account. The consequences of *biometric identity theft* are significant since the conventional biometric template is nonrevocable. BE also reduces the risk of linkage when the same biometrics are used in multiple applications.

### 26.7.1.2 Remote Authentication (Challenge–Response Scheme)

The following case illustrating biometric authentication (remote or local) with third-party certification is a simplified description from Boyen's paper [68] (see also reference 3).

Suppose that Alice wishes to authenticate herself to Bob using biometrics. Due to privacy concerns, she does not wish to reveal any biometric information to Bob. We assume that there is a third party, Trent (often called the Trusted Authority), whom Bob trusts to honestly certify Alice's biometrics, and to whom Alice will temporarily grant access to her biometrics for the purpose of generating such a certificate. Alice will want to be able to obtain as many or as few of those certificates as she wants, and to reuse as many of them with multiple Bobs, some of whom may even be dishonest, without fear of privacy leaks or impersonation.

Enrollment and certification takes place under Trent's supervision and using Alice's own biometric. Alice's PIN, which is bound to her biometric, is used to generate a pair of public and private keys. On verification, Bob verifies Alice using a challenge/response scheme, such that Alice signs a random challenge (sent by Bob) with her private key, which is obtained from her live biometric applied to the BE template.

The protocol [68] does not require Alice to remember or store her PIN or her private key. The BE template may be stored on a smart card or in Alice's laptop that also has a biometric sensor. For different applications ("multiple Bobs"), a new pair of public and private keys is generated from the PIN. Those keys are periodically updated. Some applications may require different PINs, in which case several BE templates can be stored. A proper template can be automatically recognized by the application. The system based on digital signatures may be adopted for both remote and local access. The important point is that the most critical part of any cryptosystem, the PIN (or a password), is securely bound to the biometrics.

To summarize, Alice has in her possession and under her control as many BE templates as necessary. She can use them to digitally sign in, either for remote authentication or for logical or physical access. The authentication is done simply by checking the validity of her digital signature using standard cryptographic means. Neither Alice's biometric nor her PIN are stored or revealed. As a result, the system is both secure and highly privacy-protective.

Note that BE can be seamlessly integrated into public key infrastructure (PKI) or other cryptographic scheme. This is an important advantage of BE over CB, since the latter does not bind a key to biometrics.

### 26.7.1.3  Travel Documents

To illustrate how BE can protect the user's privacy when using biometrics for travel documents and, at the same time, improve the level of security, we will consider a system (Figure 26.6) proposed by van der Veen et al. [71] (see also reference 3).

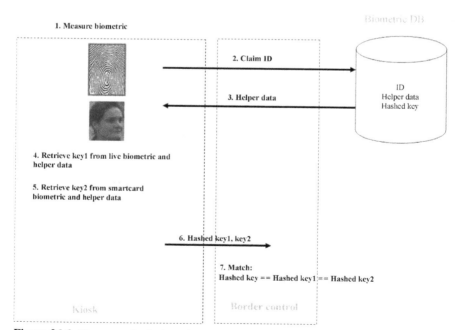

**Figure 26.6.**  Three-way check of travel documents using BE (Adapted from reference 71).

The International Civil Aviation Organization (ICAO) develops the standards for machine-readable travel documents (MRTD) including the so-called ePassport. Among the recommendations is the three-way check for secure verification at the border. This involves comparing data originating from (i) the biometric sensor, (ii) the biometric image stored on the ePassport, and (iii) biometric data stored in external (centralized) databases.

BE technology provides the opportunity to do this in a privacy-preserving way [3, 71]. In addition to biometric templates stored on the ePassport, their secure versions (i.e., helper data and hashed keys) are also stored in a third-party database. The biometric images or conventional templates are not stored in the database. A three-way check is then performed by matching the helper data from the database with the live biometric measurements and the biometric data on the ePassport. As shown in Figure 26.6, a key is obtained from the live biometric (key1) and from the image stored on ePassport (key2). A positive authentication is achieved when all three hashed versions are exactly the same.

The database is inherently secure, meaning that there is no need for complicated encryption and key management protocols. The ePassport is protected against tampering, since neither a potential attacker nor anybody else knows the key that was used to create the helper data.

### 26.7.1.4 Anonymous DB [141]

Suppose that a clinic, a hospital, or a network of hospitals maintains a database of medical records. Alice does not want her record to be accessed by unauthorized personnel or third parties, even for statistical purposes. To address this, her record is made anonymous and encrypted (by conventional means). The only public entry in the database is her personal identifier, which may be her real name or, in certain cases (e.g., drug addiction clinic), an alias ("Jane Doe"). The link between Alice's identifier and her medical record is controlled by BE.

As shown in Figure 26.7, a BE template (helper data) is created on enrollment from Alice's biometrics and a randomly generated PIN (Alice does not even know the PIN). The PIN is used to generate a pointer to Alice's medical record and a symmetric key that encrypts the record, and also a pair of public and private keys (similar to the Case Scenario 2). The helper data and the public key are associated with Alice's ID and stored in the database (they can also be stored on Alice's smart card). Other temporary data, such as Alice's biometrics, the PIN, the private key, the pointer, and the symmetric key, are discarded.

Suppose that Alice visits a doctor, to whom she wants to grant remote access to her medical record, or part of it, if the record is structured. From the doctor's office, Alice makes a request to the database administrator, Bob. The authentication procedure using a challenge/response scheme is similar to that in Case Scenario 2 (see reference 3 for more details):

Alice applies her live biometric sample to the helper data and recovers her PIN on-the-fly. This allows Bob to verify Alice's identity using a challenge–response

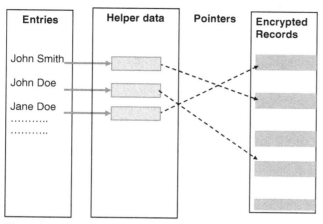

**Figure 26.7.** Anonymous database controlled by BE.

scheme. Then the pointer to Alice's medical record is regenerated from the PIN. Bob recovers Alice's encrypted medical record (or a part of it, also encrypted) and sends it to Alice. She decrypts it using the symmetric key that was also regenerated from her PIN.

Bob (the database administrator) has an assurance that Alice is, in fact, who she claims to be (she was able to unlock her helper data in the doctor's office); he is also assured that her medical record was sent to the right person. At the same time, Alice retains full control over her medical record, so that even Bob (the database administrator) has no access to it, since he does not have the symmetric key to decrypt it. The privacy protection is embedded into the system at a very low technological level.

There might be many other versions and potential applications of BE-based anonymous databases. For example, in an application that requires somewhat lower level of security, Alice uses a fully anonymous database as a repository of her personal data. The data are encrypted by conventional means. Both the symmetric key(s) and the pointer to the data are controlled by BE. The helper data are stored on Alice's smart card. When Alice wants to remotely access her data, she presents a fresh biometric sample to recover her key. The key is used to regenerate the pointer, which is sent to the database to retrieve the Alice's data. The encrypted data are sent back to Alice. She can decrypt the data by using the symmetric key, which is also regenerated from the key that she recovered from her biometric. The advantages of such a system over a password-based system are that:

- It provides the "who you are" (as opposed to "what you know") user authentication.

- The key bound to the biometric is much longer than a password, thus providing a cryptographic-level strength to the rest of the system.

### 26.7.1.5    *Biometric Matching in Encrypted Domain [142]*

Conventional cryptography does not tolerate a key with even a single bit error. Therefore, because of the natural variability of biometric samples, matching in the encrypted domain has been deemed impossible. However, in a recent publication [142], Bringer and Chabanne showed that this can be achieved using a combination of BE with a Goldwasser–Micali *homomorphic encryption*. In this encryption scheme, a pair of public, *pk*, and secret (private), *sk*, keys is generated. One bit at a time is encrypted, so that, in order to encrypt a binary string, *m*, every bit must be encrypted individually. The Goldwasser–Micali scheme possesses a homomorphic property:

$$\mathrm{Enc}(m) \times \mathrm{Enc}(m') = \mathrm{Enc}(m \oplus m'),$$

where $\oplus$ denotes the bitwise XOR operation.

This encryption can be combined with the fuzzy commitment BE scheme in the following way:

The biometric system consists of three major components: a service provider, a sensor client, and a storage. On enrollment, the service provider generates a Goldwasser–Micali (*pk, sk*) key pair and publishes *pk*. The client captures the user's biometric and creates the binary biometric template, *b*. A random ECC codeword, *c*, is generated and XOR-ed with the template, $c \oplus b$. The result is encrypted with *pk* to obtain $\mathrm{Enc}(c \oplus b)$ and is put into the storage. Also, a hashed codeword, $\mathrm{Hash}(c)$, is stored separately by the service provider.

On verification, a fresh template, $b'$, is obtained by the client. The encrypted (with *pk*) template, $\mathrm{Enc}(b')$, is sent to the storage. Alternatively, $\mathrm{Enc}(c \oplus b)$ can be retrieved from the storage by the client. Then, using the homomorphic property of the Goldwasser–Micali encryption, the product is computed: $\mathrm{Enc}(c \oplus b) \times \mathrm{Enc}(b') = \mathrm{Enc}(c \oplus b \oplus b')$. The result is sent to the service provider, where it is decrypted with the private key *sk* to obtain $c \oplus b \oplus b'$. Then the ECC decoder obtains a codeword $c'$. Finally, the service provider checks if $\mathrm{Hash}(c) = \mathrm{Hash}(c')$.

Neither the service provider nor the storage ever obtain the biometric data, which stay encrypted during the whole process. The BE template, $c \oplus b$, is stored in the encrypted form. Since the codeword, *c*, is not stored anywhere, the BE template cannot be substituted or tampered. Overall, this system would solve most security problems mentioned in Section 26.6. Bringer and Chabanne [142] also proposed using yet another homomorphic encryption, Paillier, on top of Goldwasser–Micali to further enhance the privacy and security protection for the database application.

It should be noted that the XOR-based fuzzy commitment is the only BE scheme suitable for this system. There are difficulties in the practical implementation of the proposed system [142] relating to the large size of the encrypted template and to the computation costs.

A somewhat similar biometric system that uses a homomorphic encryption but without BE was proposed by Schoenmakers and Tuyls [143]. It can be viewed as a method for cancelable biometrics and, like any other CB scheme, is vulnerable to a substitution attack: If the attacker knows the public key, *pk*, he can substitute the encrypted template, Enc(*b*).

## 26.8  BE CURRENT STATE AND CHALLENGES

As we have seen, many different approaches have been developed for BE, but currently few systems have been deployed or implemented into products. The following developments of BE technologies are the most noticeable:

- Philips (the Netherlands) priv-ID$^{TM}$ for the face recognition (2D and 3D) and fingerprints (see Section 26.5 for details).
- EU TURBINE (TrUsted Revocable Biometric IdeNtitiEs) project [144–146]. This 3-year project has been given significant funding and aims at piloting a fingerprint-based BE technology at an airport in Greece;
- The Genkey BioCryptic® technology [147] has been deployed for a Rickshaw project in New Delhi (India). Unfortunately, not much information about the technology is available.

Technologically, BE is more challenging than conventional biometrics. Although BE has already approached the phase of creating and testing a prototype, there are issues that still need to be addressed:

### 26.8.1  Choose a Biometric Modality Suitable for BE

The most promising results in terms of accuracy have been obtained for irises. Low variability of image samples, along with the presence of a natural alignment feature (eye pupil), makes this biometric the number one candidate for UB.

Face recognition is one of the most publicly accepted types of biometric. At the present time, one of the drawbacks of the face-based BE system, however, is the relatively small size ($\sim$ 45–60 bits or less) of the encryption key that may be securely bound to the biometrics. Using high-resolution or 3D face recognition would likely improve the system performance.

Fingerprints, for which both BE and CB were originally pioneered, are also a prime choice. Fingerprint biometrics are used more widely than the iris or face, and most privacy concerns relate to fingerprints. At the same time, using fingerprints for BE turns out to be more challenging. The reasons are that high skin distortions can be introduced when the finger presses upon the sensor, and the difficulty of aligning a fingerprint on verification with the one enrolled. As mentioned before, the situation is more difficult for BE than for a conventional fingerprint verification or for CB, since most BE schemes (except fuzzy vault) work in a "blind" mode (the enrolled fingerprint or its minutiae template is not seen). Some of these issues can be overcome with a free-air image. Although this would present other optical issues, we believe they could be resolved by current technology. In general, face and especially iris are less vulnerable to distortion and alignment problems.

Other biometrics (e.g., voice, signature, veins, palmprints, etc.) may not have enough entropy to support a long cryptographic key. They could possibly be put on the list of "auxiliary" biometrics—that is, used for BE in combination with irises, faces, fingerprints, or passwords.

## 26.8.2   Improve the Image Acquisition Process

For fingerprints, this means choosing a proper fingerprint sensor that is less susceptible to skin distortions (e.g., a free air sensor), or changing the existing sensor ergonomics to keep the distortions under control. Image quality can also be improved at the algorithm level (i.e., through software). A promising approach would be to algorithmically remove fingerprint distortions ("unwarping" the image [148, 149]). In general, the requirements for image quality are tougher for BE than for conventional biometrics.

## 26.8.3   Make BE Resilient Against Attacks

This area of research—that is, the analysis of the potential vulnerabilities of BE against attacks—has been largely overlooked. A sophisticated attacker, fully familiar with the algorithm and exploiting its weaknesses, will not be doing just a brute force search in order to break the BE system. Instead, he will devise the attacks that can be run in a realistic time frame. As we have shown in this chapter, various attacks are possible against BE and CB. The BE algorithm must be made resilient against those offline attacks. The same requirement (i.e., resilience against attacks) is adopted in conventional cryptography; however, BE is not a cryptographic algorithm but rather a part of a key management scheme.

## 26.8.4   Improve Accuracy and Security of BE Algorithms

There have been substantial advances in algorithm development in conventional biometrics in the past few years, as demonstrated by a series of international competitions. Many of those advances are applicable to both BE and CB.

In the case of BE, a crucial step, in terms of both accuracy and security, is the selection of a proper ECC. For the past 10–13 years, there have been major advances in the area of ECC, which should be applied to BE.

The security of BE can be improved by applying a secret transform, preferably, controlled by a user's password. This is, in fact, a merger of BE and CB.

## 26.8.5   Exploit Multimodal Approaches

The performance of a biometric system is significantly improved when different algorithms, or different fingers, or different biometrics (e.g., fingerprints and face) are combined. The modes that are combined should be "orthogonal" (i.e., statistically independent) as much as possible. It has already been shown that the multimodal approach works also for BE [155, 156].

### 26.8.6  Develop BE Applications

The applications, such as those described in the case scenarios, should clearly demonstrate the benefits for privacy and security brought about by the use of BE.

## 26.9  SUMMARY AND CONCLUSIONS

UB technologies offer the promise of exploiting the utility of biometric technologies, but without their privacy-invasive aspects. This chapter has explored the privacy-enhancing benefits of primarily one of the categories of untraceable biometrics—biometric encryption—making it a fruitful area for research, prototype development, and consideration of applications.

We believe that BE technologies exemplify the fundamental privacy and data protection principles that are endorsed around the world, such as data minimization, user empowerment, and security, better than any other biometric technology solution in existence.

While introducing biometrics into information systems may result in considerable benefits, it can also introduce many new security and privacy vulnerabilities, risks, and concerns. However, novel BE techniques have been developed that can overcome many of those risks and vulnerabilities, resulting in a win–win, positive-sum scenario.

One can only hope that the biometric portion is done well, and preferably not modeled on a zero-sum paradigm, where there must always be a loser. A positive-sum model, in the form of BE, presents distinct advantages to both security AND privacy.

## REFERENCES

1. N. K. Ratha, J. H. Connell, and R. M. Bolle. Enhancing security and privacy in biometrics-based authentication systems, *IBM Syst. J.* **40**(3):614–634, 2001.
2. U. Uludag and A. K. Jain, Attacks on biometric systems: A case study in fingerprints, in *Proceedings of SPIE-EI 2004, Security, Steganography and Watermarking of Multimedia Contents VI*, San Jose, CA, January 18–22, Vol. 5306, pp. 622–633, 2004.
3. A. Cavoukian and A. Stoianov, Biometric encryption: A positive-sum technology that achieves strong authentication, security and privacy, March 2007. Available at www.ipc.on.ca/images/Resources/up-1bio_encryp.pdf; and A. Cavoukian, A. Stoianov, and F. Carter, *Biometric encryption: Technology for strong authentication, security and privacy*, in E. de Leeuw, S. Fischer-Hübner, J. Tseng, and J. Borking, editors, *IFIP International Federation for Information Processing. Policies and Research in Identity Management*, Vol. 261, Springer, Boston, 2008, pp. 57–77.
4. C. J. Hill, Risk of masquerade arising from the storage of biometrics, B. S. thesis, Australian National University, 2001 (Dr. Roger Clarke, supervisor), http://chris.fornax.net/biometrics.html.
5. A. Adler, Sample images can be independently restored from face recognition templates. in *Proceedings of the Canadian Conference on Electronic and Computer Engineering*, 2003, pp. 1163–1166.

6. A. Ross, J, Shah, and A. K. Jain, From templates to images: Reconstructing fingerprints from minutiae points, *IEEE Trans. Pattern Anal. Mach. Intell.* **29**(4):544–560, 2007.

7. R. Cappelli, A. Lumini, D. Maio, and D. Maltoni, Fingerprint image reconstruction from standard templates, *IEEE Trans. Pattern Anal. Mach. Intell.* **29**(9):1489–1503, 2007.

8. P. Mohanty, S. Sarkar, and R. Kasturi, Privacy and security issues related to match scores, in *IEEE Workshop on Privacy Research In Vision*, CVPRW, 2006.

9. OECD Directorate for Science, Technology and Industry, Committee for Information, Computer and Communications Policy: Biometric-Based Technologies (June 2004) at http://appli1.oecd.org/olis/2003doc.nsf/linkto/dsti-iccp-reg(2003)2-final.

10. www.bioprivacy.org/bioprivacy_main.htm.

11. See, for example, the 27th International Conference of Data Protection and Privacy Commissioners, Montreux (16 September 2005), Resolution on the use of biometrics in passports, identity cards and travel documents: www.privacyconference2005.org/fileadmin/PDF/biometrie_resolution_e.pdf

12. See, for example, European Union Article 29 Working Party, Working document on biometrics (August 2003) at: http://ec.europa.eu/justice_home/fsj/privacy/docs/wpdocs/2003/wp80_en.pdf

13. See UK Information Commissioner, Data Protection Technical Guidance Note: Privacy enhancing technologies (November 2006) at http://tinyurl.com/23b6kc; and European Commission Supports PETs: Promoting Data Protection by Privacy Enhancing Technologies (2 May 2007) at: http://ec.europa.eu/information_society/newsroom/cf/itemlongdetail.cfm?item_id=3402; and Information and Privacy Commissioner of Ontario & Dutch Registratierkamer, Privacy-Enhancing Technologies: The Path to Anonymity (Volume I, August 1995): www.ipc.on.ca/index.asp?layid=86&fid1=329.

14. N. K. Ratha, S. Chikkerur, J. H. Connell, and R. M. Bolle, Generating cancelable fingerprint templates, *IEEE Trans. Pattern Anal. Mach. Intelli.* **29**(4):561–572, 2007.

15. C. Soutar, D. Roberge, A. Stoianov, R. Gilroy and B. V. K. Vijaya Kumar, Biometric encryption, in *ICSA Guide to Cryptography*, McGraw-Hill, New York, 1999.

16. G. I. Davida, Y. Frankel, and B.J. Matt, On enabling secure applications through off-line biometric identification, in *Proceedings of the IEEE 1998 Symposium on Security and Privacy*, Oakland, CA, 1998, pp. 148–157.

17. G. I. Davida, Y. Frankel, B. J. Matt, and R. Peralta, On the relation of error correction and cryptography to an off line biometrics based identification scheme, in *Workshop on Coding and Cryptography*, 1999, pp. 129–138.

18. F. Monrose, M. K. Reiter, and R. Wetzel, Password hardening based on keystroke dynamics, in *Proceedings of Sixth ACM Conference on Computer and Communications Security (CCCS 1999)*, 1999, pp. 73–82.

19. F. Monrose, M. K. Reiter, Q. (Peter) Li, and S. Wetzel, Cryptographic key generation from voice (extended abstract), in *Proceedings of the 2001 IEEE Symposium on Security and Privacy*, May 2001.

20. F. Monrose, M. K. Reiter, and S. Wetzel, Password hardening based on keystroke dynamics, *Int. J. Inf. Secur.* **1**(2):69–83, 2002.

21. F. Monrose, M. K. Reiter, Q. Li, D. P. Lopresti, and C. Shih, Toward speech-generated cryptographic keys on resource constrained devices, in *Proceedings of the 11th USENIX Security Symposium*, 2002, pp. 283–296.

22. T. Boult, Robust distance measures for face recognition supporting revocable biometric tokens, in *Proceedings of the 7th International Conference on Automatic Face and Gesture Recognition* (April 10–12, 2006), IEEE Computer Society, Washington, DC, 2006, pp. 560–566.

23. T. E. Boult, W. J. Scheirer, and R. Woodworth, Revocable fingerprint biotokens: Accuracy and security analysis, *IEEE Conference on Computer Vision and Pattern Recognition*, June 2007.

24. S. Tulyakov, F. Farooq, and V. Govindaraju, Symmetric hash functions for fingerprint minutiae, in *Lecture Notes in Computer Science*, Vol. 3687, Springer, Berlin, 2005, pp. 30–38.

25. G. J. Tomko, C. Soutar, and G. J. Schmidt, Fingerprint controlled public key cryptographic system, U.S. Patent 5541994, July 30, 1996 (Priority date: September 7, 1994); and G. J. Tomko, C. Soutar,

and G. J. Schmidt, Biometric controlled key generation, U.S. Patent 5680460, October 21, 1997 (Priority date: September 7, 1994).

26. R. M. Bolle, J. H. Connel, and N. K. Ratha, System and method for distorting a biometric for transactions with enhanced security and privacy, US Patent 6,836,554, December 28, 2004 (Priority date: June 16, 2000).

27. U. Uludag, S. Pankanti, S. Prabhakar, and A. K. Jain, Biometric cryptosystems: Issues and challenges, *Proc. IEEE* **92**(6):948–960, 2004.

28. A. K. Jain, K. Nandakumar, and A. Nagar, Biometric template security, *EURASIP J. Adv. Signal Processing* **2008**:1–17, 2008, Article ID 579416.

29. P. Tuyls, B. Škorić, and T. Kevenaar, editors, *Security with Noisy Data: Private Biometrics, Secure Key Storage and Anti-Counterfeiting*, Springer-Verlag, London, 2007.

30. Y. Dodis, L. Reyzin, and A. Smith, Fuzzy extractors: How to generate strong keys from biometrics and other noisy data, in *Proceedings, Eurocrypt 2004*, 2004, pp. 523–540.

31. F. Hao, R. Anderson, and J. Daugman, Combining crypto with biometrics effectively, *IEEE Trans. Comput.* **55**(9): 1081–1088, 2006. (See also: Technical report No. 640, University of Cambridge, Computer Laboratory, July 2005, http://www.cl.cam.ac.uk/TechReports/).

32. S. Lin and D. J. Costello, Jr., *Error Control Coding: Fundamentals and Applications*, 2nd edition, Prentice Hall, Englewood Cliffs, NJ, 2005.

33. S. B. Wicker, *Error Control Systems for Digital Communication and Storage*, Prentice Hall, Englewood Cliffs, NJ, 1995.

34. B. Schneier, *Applied Cryptography*, 2nd edition, John Wiley & Sons, New York, 1996.

35. Q. Li, Y. Sutcu, and N. Memon, Secure sketch for biometric templates, in *Advances in Cryptology—ASIACRYPT 2006, Lecture Notes in Computer Science*, Vol. 4284, Springer, Berlin, 2006, pp. 99–113.

36. J. G. Daugman, High confidence visual recognition of persons by a test of statistical independence, *IEEE Trans. Pattern Anal. Mach. Intelli.* **15** (11): 1148–1161, 1993.

37. J. Daugman. The importance of being random: Statistical principles of iris recognition, *Pattern Recognit.* **36**(2):279–291, 2003.

38. P. Tu and R. Hartley, Statistical significance as an aid to system performance evaluation, in *Lecture Notes in Computer Science*, Vol. 1843/2000, Springer, Berlin, 2000, pp. 366–378.

39. S. Pankanti, S. Prabhakar, and A. Jain, On the individuality of fingerprints, *IEEE Trans. Pattern Anal. Mach. Intell.* **24**(8):1010–1025, 2002.

40. Y. Zhu, S. C. Dass, and A. K. Jain, Statistical models for assessing the individuality of finger-prints, *IEEE Trans. Inf. Forens. Secur.* **2**(3, Part 1):391–401, 2007. also http://www.cse.msu.edu/cgi-user/web/tech/reports?Year=2006.

41. J. S. Wayman, The cotton ball problem, in *Biometric Consortium Conference*, Crystal City, Arlington VA, 20–22 September 2004. Available at http://www.biometrics.org/bc2004/program.htm.

42. http://bias.csr.unibo.it/fvc2002/; http://bias.csr.unibo.it/fvc2004/.

43. A. Adler, R. Youmaran, and S. Loyka, Information content of biometric features, in *Biometric Consortium Conference* 2005, September 19–21, Washington, DC. Available at http://www.sce.carleton.ca/faculty/adler/publications/2005/adler-2005-biometrics-conf-entropy.pdf.

44. R. Youmaran, A. Adler, and S. Loyka, Towards a measure of biometric information, in *Canadian Conference on Computer Electronics and Engineering* (CCECE), Ottawa, Canada, May 7–10, 2006. Available at http://www.sce.carleton.ca/faculty/adler/publications/2006/youmaran-ccece2006-biometric-entropy.pdf. See also Chapter 23 by Youmaran and Adler in the present book.

45. FRVT 2006 and ICE 2006 large-scale results, in *NISTIR 7408*, National Institute of Standards and Technology, Gaithersburg, MD 20899, March 2007. Available at http://www.frvt.org/FRVT2006/docs/FRVT2006andICE2006LargeScaleReport.pdf.

46. L. Ballard, S. Kamara, F. Monrose, and M. Reiter, *On the requirements of biometric key generators, Technical Report TR-JHU-SPAR-BKMR-090707*, John Hopkins University, September 7, 2007. Available at http://www.cs.jhu.edu/~seny/pubs/bkg-req.pdf.

47. R. Plaga, Biometrics and cryptography—On biometric keys, their information content and proper use, in *Conference on Biometric Feature Identification and Analysis*, Göttingen, 7.9.2007. Available at http://www.stochastik.math.uni-goettingen.de/biometrics2007/talks/Plaga.pdf; and U. Korte, R. Plaga, Cryptographic Protection of Biometric Templates: Chance, Challenges and Applications,

in *Proceedings of BIOSiG 2007*, Darmstadt, Germany, July 2007, pp. 33–45. Available at http://gi.ioport.net/lni276658/GI-Proceedings108.pdf.

48. J. Bringer, H. Chabanne, G. Cohen, B. Kindarji, and G. Zemor, Optimal iris fuzzy sketches, in *IEEE First International Conference on Biometrics: Theory, Applications, and Systems*, BTAS'07, 2007.

49. J. Bringer, H. Chabanne, G. Cohen, B. Kindarji, and G. Zemor, Theoretical and practical boundaries of binary secure sketches, *IEEE Trans. Inf. Forens. Secur.* 3(4): 673–683, 2008.

50. R. Cappelli, A. Erol, D. Maio, and D. Maltoni, Synthetic fingerprint-image generation, in *Proceedings 15th International Conference on Pattern Recognition* (ICPR2000), Barcelona, Vol. 3, September 2000. pp. 475–478, See also http://biolab.csr.unibo.it/research.asp.

51. A. Bodo, Method for producing a digital signature with aid of a biometric feature, German patent DE 42 43 908 A1, June 30, 1994 (Priority date: Dec. 23, 1992).

52. J.-P. Linnartz and P. Tuyls, New shielding functions to enhance privacy and prevent misuse of biometric templates, in *Proceedings of the 4th International Conference on Audio and Video Based Biometric Person Authentication*, Guildford, UK, 2003, pp. 393–402.

53. W. Sheng, G. Howells, M. Fairhurst, and F. Deravi, Template-free biometric-key generation by means of fuzzy genetic clustering, *IEEE Trans. Inf. Forens. Secur.* 3(2):183–191, 2008.

54. C. Soutar and G. J. Tomko, Secure private key generation using a fingerprint, in *CardTech/SecurTech Conference Proceedings*, Vol. 1, May 1996, pp. 245–252.

55. G. J. Tomko and A. Stoianov, Method and apparatus for securely handling a personal identification number or cryptographic key using biometric techniques, U.S. Patent 5712912, January 27, 1998 (Priority date: July 28, 1995).

56. C. Soutar, D. Roberge, A. V. Stoianov, R. Gilroy, and B. V. K. Vijaya Kumar, Method for secure key management using a biometric, U.S. Patent 6219794, April 17, 2001 (Priority date: April 21, 1997).

57. C. Soutar, Biometric encryption for secure key generation, presentation at the 1998 *RSA Data Security Conference, San Francisco*, January 1998.

58. C. Soutar, D. Roberge, A. V. Stoianov, R. Gilroy, and B. V. K. Vijaya Kumar, Biometric encryption using image processing, in *Proc. SPIE, Optical Security and Counterfeit Deterrence Techniques II*, Vol. 3314, 1998, pp. 178–188.

59. C. Soutar, D. Roberge, A. V. Stoianov, R. Gilroy, and B. V. K. Vijaya Kumar, Biometric encryption—enrollment and verification procedures, in *Proceedings of SPIE, Optical Pattern Recognition IX*, Vol. 3386, 1998, pp. 24–35.

60. A. Juels and M. Wattenberg, A fuzzy commitment scheme, in *Sixth ACM Conference on Computer and Communications Security*, ACM Press, New York, 1999, pp. 28–36.

61. E. Verbitskiy, P. Tuyls, D. Denteneer, and J.-P. Linnartz, Reliable biometric authentication with privacy protection, in *Proceedings of the 24th Symposium on Information Theory in the Benelux*, Veldhoven, The Netherlands, 2003, pp. 125–132.

62. P. Tuyls and J. Goseling, Capacity and examples of template protecting biometric authentication systems, in *Biometric Authentication Workshop*, Prague (ECCV2004), May 2004, pp. 158–170.

63. P. Tuyls, E. Verbitskiy, J. Goseling, and D. Denteneer, Privacy protecting biometric authentication systems: an overview, in *XII European Signal Processing Conference* (EUSIPCO 2004, Vienna, Austria), 2004, pp. 1397–1400.

64. P. Tuyls, Privacy protection of biometric templates: Cryptography on noisy data, in H. F. Revue editors, No. 3, 2004, pp. 55–64.

65. S. Kamara, B. de Medeiros, and S. Wetzel, Secret locking: Exploring new approaches to biometric key encapsulation, in *Proceedings of the Second International Conference on E-business and Telecommunication Networks (ICETE 2005)*, Reading, U.K., 2005, pp. 254–261. Available at http://www.cs.jhu.edu/~seny/pubs/locking.pdf.

66. F. Hao, C. W. Chan, Private key generation from on-line handwritten signatures, *Inf. Management Comput. Secur.* 10(2):159–164, 2002.

67. U. Korte, M. Krawczak, U. Martini, J. Merkle, R. Plaga, M. Niesing, C. Tiemann, and H. Vinck, A cryptographic biometric authentication system based on genetic fingerprints, in *Lecture Notes of Informatics*, LNI P-128, Springer-Verlag, Berlin, 2008, pp. 263–276.

68. X. Boyen, Reusable cryptographic fuzzy extractors, in *11th ACM Conference on Computer and Communications Security (CCS 2004)*, Washington, DC, October 2004, pp. 82–91. Available at http://crypto.stanford.edu/~xb//ccs04/fuzzysecure.pdf.

69. I. R. Buhan, J. M. Doumen, P. H. Hartel, and R. N. J. Veldhuis, Fuzzy extractors for continuous distributions, in *Proceedings of the 2nd ACM Symposium on Information, Computer and Communications Security (ASIACCS)*, Singapore, March 2007, pp. 353–355. See also http://eprints.eemcs.utwente.nl/7693/01/main.pdf.

70. P. Tuyls, A. H. M. Akkermans, T. A. M. Kevenaar, G.- J. Schrijen, A. M. Bazen, and R. N. J. Veldhuis, Practical biometric authentication with template protection, in *5th International Conference*, AVBPA 2005, Hilton Rye Town, NY, July 20–22, 2005, *Lecture Notes in Computer Science*, Vol. 3546, Springer, Berlin, 2005, pp. 436–446.

71. M. van der Veen, T. Kevenaar, G.- J. Schrijen, T. H. Akkermans, and Fei Zuo, Face biometrics with renewable templates, in *Proceedings of SPIE*, Vol. 6072: *Security, Steganography, and Watermarking of Multimedia Contents VIII*, 2006.

72. X. Zhou, T. A. M. Kevenaar, E. Kelkboom, C. Busch, M. van der Veen, and A. Nouak, Privacy enhancing technology for a 3D-face recognition system, in *BIOSIG 2007: Biometrics and Electronic Signatures, Proceedings of the Special Interest Group on Biometrics and Electronic Signatures*, 12–13, July 2007, Darmstadt, Germany, 2007, pp. 3–14. Available at http://www.3dface.org/files/papers/zhou-CAST2007-TemplateProtection.pdf.

73. X. Zhou, Template protection and its implementation in 3D face recognition systems, in *Proceedings of SPIE, Biometric Technology for Human Identification IV*, Vol. 6539, April 2007. Available at http://www.3dface.org/files/papers/zhou-SPIE2007-template-protection.pdf.

74. H. Xu, A. M. Bazen, R. N. J. Veldhuis, T. A. M. Kevenaar, and A. H. M. Akkermans, Spectral representation of fingerprints, in *Proceedings of the 28th Symposium on Information Theory in the Benelux*, 24–25 May 2007, Enschede, The Netherlands. 2007, pp. 313–319.

75. C. Chen, R. Veldhuis, T. Kevenaar, and T. Akkermans, Multi-bits biometric string generation based on the likelihood ratio, in *IEEE Conference on Biometrics: Theory, Applications and Systems*, September 27–29th, 2007, Washington DC.

76. Y. J. Chang, W. Zhang, and T. Chen, Biometrics-based cryptographic key generation, in *IEEE International Conference on Multimedia and Expo (ICME)*, Vol. 3, June 2004, pp. 2203–2206.

77. Y. J. Chang, T. Chen, and W. Zhang, Biometrics-based cryptographic key generation system and method, US Patent Application 20060083372, Filing Date: 03/11/2005.

78. T. Kevenaar, G. J. Schrijen, A. Akkermans, M. Damstra, P. Tuyls, and M. van der Veen, Robust and secure biometrics: Some application examples, in *Information Security Solutions Europe (ISSE) Conference*, Rome, 10–12 October, 2006.

79. www.3Dface.org.

80. C. Busch, A. Nouak, X. Zhou, M. van der Veen, F. Deravi, and J.- M. Suchier, Towards unattended and privacy protected border control, in *Proceedings of Biometrics Consortium Conference*, Baltimore, September 2007. Available at http://www.3dface.org/files/papers/busch-BSYM2007-towards-unattended-border-control.pdf.

81. J. Lyseggen, R. A. Lauritzsen, and K. G. S. Oyhus, System, portable device and method for digital authenticating, crypting and signing by generating short-lived cryptokeys, US Patent Application 2006/0198514 A1, September 7, 2006 (Priority date: October 1, 2001).

82. G. D. Duffy and W. A. Jones, Data processing apparatus and method, PCT Patent Application PCT/GB02/00626 (WO02/098053), December 5, 2002 (Priority date: May 31, 2001).

83. I. R. Buhan, J. M. Doumen, P. H. Hartel, and R. N. J. Veldhuis, Constructing practical fuzzy extractors using QIM, Technical Report TR-CTIT-07-52 Centre for Telematics and Information Technology, University of Twente, Enschede, 2007. Available at http://eprints.eemcs.utwente.nl/10785/01/quantizers.pdf.

84. A. Juels and M. Sudan, A fuzzy vault scheme, in *Proceedings, 2002 IEEE International Symposium on Information Theory*, Piscataway, NJ, 2002, p. 408.

85. T. C. Clancy, N. Kiyavash, and D. J. Lin, Secure smartcard-based fingerprint authentication, in *Proceedings, ACMSIGMM 2003 Multimedia*, Biometrics Methods and Applications Workshop (WBMA'03), Berkeley, CA, November 2003, pp. 45–52.

86. U. Uludag, S. Pankanti, and A. K. Jain, Fuzzy vault for fingerprints, in *AVBPA 2005:Audio- and Video-Based Biometric Person Authentication* (Hilton Rye Town, NY, 20–22 July 2005), Vol. 3546, Springer, Berlin, 2005, pp. 310–319.
87. S. Yang and I. Verbauwhede, Secure fuzzy vault based fingerprint verification system. in *Thirty-Eighth Asilomar Conference on Signals, Systems, and Computers* (2004), Vol. 1, 2004, pp. 577–581.
88. J. Jeffers and A. Arakala, Fingerprint alignment for a minutiae-based fuzzy vault, in *Biometric Consortium Conference*, Baltimore, September 2007.
89. K. Nandakumar, A. K. Jain, and S. C. Pankanti, Fingerprint-based fuzzy vault: Implementation and performance, *IEEE Trans. Inf. Forens. Secur.* 2(4):744–757, 2007. Available at http://biometrics.cse.msu.edu/Publications/SecureBiometrics/NandakumarJainPankanti_FpFuzzyVault_TIFS07.pdf.
90. K. Nandakumar, A. Nagar, and A. K. Jain, Hardening fingerprint fuzzy vault using password, in *Proceedings of ICB 2007*, Seoul, Korea, August 27–29, 2007, *Lecture Notes in Computer Science*, 4642/2007, Springer, 2007, pp. 927–937. Available at http://biometrics.cse.msu.edu/Publications/SecureBiometrics/NandakumarNagarJain_FpFuzzyVaultHardening_ICB2007.pdf.
91. M. Freire-Santos, J. Fierrez-Aguilar, and J.Ortega-Garcia, Cryptographic key generation using handwritten signature, in *Defense and Security Symposium, Biometric Technologies for Human Identification (BTHI), Proc. SPIE*, Vol. 6202, Orlando, FL, April 2006, pp. 225–231. Available at http://atvs.ii.uam.es/files/2006_SPIE_KeyGenSignature_Freire.pdf.
92. Y. C. Feng and P. C. Yuen, Protecting face biometric data on smartcard with Reed–Solomon code, in *Proceedings of the Conference on Computer Vision and Pattern Recognition Workshops (CVPRW '06)*, New York, June 2006, p. 29.
93. Y. J. Lee, K. Bae, S. J. Lee, K. R. Park, and J. Kim, Biometric key binding: Fuzzy vault based on iris images, in *Proceedings of 2nd International Conference on Biometrics*, Seoul, South Korea (August 2007), *Lecture Notes in Computer Science*, Vol. 4642, 2007, pp. 800–808.
94. Y. Wang and K. N. Plataniotis, Fuzzy vault for face based cryptographic key generation, in *Biometric Consortium Conference*, Baltimore, September 2007.
95. A. Kholmatov, B. Yanikoglu, E. Savas, and A. Levi, Secret sharing using biometric traits, in *Biometric Technology for Human Identification III*, Orlando, FL (April 17, 2006), *Proceedings of SPIE*, Vol. 6202, 2006, pp. 62020W1–9.
96. A. Goh and D. C. L. Ngo, Computation of cryptographic keys from face biometrics, in *International Federation for Information Processing 2003. Lecture Notes in Computer Science (LNCS)*, Vol. 2828, Springer, Berlin, 2003, pp. 1–13.
97. A. B. J. Teoh, D. C. L. Ngo, and A. Goh, Personalised cryptographic key generation based on FaceHashing, *Comput. Secur.* 23:606–614, 2004.
98. O. T. Song, A. Teoh, and D. C. L. Ngo, Application-specific key release scheme from biometrics, *Int. J. Network Secur.* 6(2):127–133, 2008; and A. B. J. Teoh and Kar-Ann Toh, Secure biometric-key generation with biometric helper, in *3rd IEEE Conference on Industrial Electronics and Applications (ICIEA 2008)*, pp. 2145–2150.
99. E. Martinian, S. Yekhanin, and J. S. Yedidia, Secure biometrics via syndromes, in *Allerton Conference on Communications, Control and Computing.* Monticello, IL, September 2005. Available at http://www.merl.com/reports/docs/TR2005-112.pdf.
100. S. C. Draper, A. Khisti, E. Martinian, A. Vetro, and J. S. Yedidia, Secure storage of fingerprint biometrics using Slepian-Wolf codes, in *Inform. Theory and Apps. Work*, UCSD, San Diego, CA, Jan. 2007. Available at http://www.merl.com/reports/docs/TR2007-006.pdf.
101. S. C. Draper, A. Khisti, E. Martinian, A. Vetro and J. S. Yedidia, Using distributed source coding to secure fingerprint biometrics, in *Proc. of IEEE International Conference on Acoustics, Speech and Signal Processing (ICASSP)*, Vol. 2, April 2007, pp. 129–132. Available at http://www.merl.com/reports/docs/TR2007-005.pdf.
102. V. Bjorn, Cryptographic key generation using biometric data, U.S. Patent 6035398, March 7, 2000 (Priority date: November 14, 1997).
103. A. Burnett, F. Byrne, T. Dowling, and A. Duffy, A biometric identity based signature scheme, in *Applied Cryptography and Network Security Conference*, Columbia University, New York, 2005.

104. K. Voderhobli, C. Pattinson, and H. Donelan, A schema for cryptographic keys generation using hybrid biometrics, in *7th Annual Postgraduate Symposium: The Convergence of Telecommunications, Networking and Broadcasting*, 26–27 June 2006, Liverpool, UK.

105. U. Martini and S. Beinlich, Virtual PIN: Biometric encryption using coding theory, in *Proceedings of the 1st Conference on Biometrics and Electronic Signatures of the GI Working Group* BIOSIG, 24th July 2003, Darmstadt, Germany, 2003, pp. 91–99.

106. Q. Li, X. Niu, and S. Sun, A novel biometric key scheme, *Chinese J. Electron.* 2005. Available at http://www.paper.edu.cn.

107. Y. Sutcu, Q. Li, and N. Memon, How to protect biometric templates, in *SPIE Conference on Security, Steganography and Watermarking of Multimedia Contents IX*, January 2007, San Jose, CA, *Proc. of SPIE*, Vol. 6505, 2007; and Y. Sutcu, Q. Li, and N. Memon, Design and analysis of fuzzy extractors for faces, in *Proc. of SPIE*, 7306: 73061X-1 - 73061X-12, 2009.

108. G. Zheng, W. Li, and C. Zhan, Cryptographic key generation from biometric data using lattice mapping, in *18th International Conference on Pattern Recognition (ICPR 2006)*, 20–24 August 2006, 4, 2006, pp. 513–516.

109. D. Schipani and J. Rosenthal, Coding solutions for the secure biometric storage problem, Technical report, 2007, http://arxiv.org/PS_cache/cs/pdf/0701/0701102v1.pdf.

110. W. J. Layton, Method of biometric authentication, US Patent 7272245 September 18, 2007 (Priority date: 05/13/2004).

111. A. J. Mansfield and J. L. Wayman, Best practices in testing and reporting performance of biometric devices, NPL Report CMSC 14/02, August 2002. http://www.cesg.gov.uk/site/ast/biometrics/media/BestPractice.pdf.

112. A. K. Jain, A. Ross, and S. Pankanti, Biometrics: A tool for information security, *IEEE Trans. Info. Forens. Secur.* **1**(2):125–143, 2006.

113. R. M. Bolle, J. H. Connel, and N. K. Ratha, Biometric perils and patches, *Pattern Recognit.* **35**(12):2727–2738, 2002.

114. N. K. Ratha, J. Connell, R. M. Bolle, and S. Chikkerur, Cancelable biometrics: A case study in fingerprints, in *Proceedings of the 18th International Conference on Pattern Recognition (ICPR 2006)*, 20–24 August 2006, Hong Kong, China, ICPR (4), 2006, pp. 370–373.

115. A. Kong, K.- H. Cheung, D. Zhang, M. Kamel, and J. You, An analysis of Biohashing and its variants, *Pattern Recognit.* **39**(7):1359–1368, 2006.

116. A. Teoh, D. Ngo, and A. Goh, Biohashing: Two factor authentication featuring fingerprint data and tokenised random number, *Pattern Recognit.* **37**:2245–2255, 2004.

117. T. Connie, A. Teoh, M. Goh, and D. Ngo, PalmHashing: A novel approach for cancelable biometrics, *Inf. Processing Lett.* **93**:1–5, 2005.

118. D. C. L. Ngo, A. B. J. Teoh, and A. Goh, Biometric hash: High-confidence face recognition, *IEEE Transactions on circuits and systems for video technology* **16**(6):771–775, 2006.

119. D. C. L. Ngo, A. Goh, and A. B. J. Teoh, Recognition using robust bit extraction, *J. Electron. Imaging* **14**(4):043016-1–043016-11, 2005.

120. W. K. Yip, A. B. J. Teoh, and D. C. L. Ngo, Replaceable and securely hashed keys from online signatures. *IEICE Electronics Express* **3**(18):410–416, 2006.

121. W. K. Yip, A. B. J. Teoh, and D. C. L. Ngo, Secure hashing of dynamic hand signatures using wavelet-Fourier compression with BioPhasor mixing and 2N discretization, *EURASIP J. Adv. Signal Processing*, Vol. 2007, Article ID 59125, 8 pages, 2007.

122. A. B. J. Teoh and C. T. Yuang, Cancelable biometrics realization with multispace random projections, *IEEE Trans. Syst. Man. Cybern. Part B: Cybernetics* **37**(5):1096–1106, 2007.

123. K. H. Cheung, B. Kong, D. Zhang, M. Kamel, and J. You, Revealing the secret of FaceHashing, in *Proceedings of International Conference on Biometrics (ICB 2006), Lecture Notes in Computer Science*, Vol. 3832, Springer, Berlin, 2006, pp. 106–112. Available at http://staffx.webstore.ntu.edu.sg/personal/adamskong/Shared%20Documents/publication/FaceHashingICBA2006.pdf.

124. A. Lumini and L. Nanni, An improved BioHashing for human authentication, *Pattern Recognit.* **40**(3): 1057–1065, 2006. Available at http://bias.csr.unibo.it/gpubs/_docs_/2006_BioH.zip.

125. A. Lumini and L. Nanni, An advanced multi-modal method for human authentication featuring biometrics data and tokenised random numbers, *NeuroComputing* **69**(13):1706–1710, August 2006. Available at http://bias.csr.unibo.it/gpubs/_docs_/2006_AMM_NeuroC.zip.

126. Y. Wang and K. N. Plataniotis, Face based biometric authentication with changeable and privacy preservable templates, in *Biometric Consortium Conference*, Baltimore, September 2007.

127. M. Braithwaite, U. C. von Seelen, J. Cambier, J. Daugman, R. Glass, R. Moore, and I. Scott, Application-specific biometric templates, in *IEEE Workshop on Automatic Identification Advanced Technologies*, Tarrytown, NY, March 14–15, 2002, pp. 167–171.

128. M. Tiberg, A method and a system for biometric identification or verification, Swedish Patent 0202147-5. Priority date: July 9, 2002. PCT Patent Application WO 2004/006495, PCT/SE2003/001181. US Patent Application US2005/0210269 A1, September 22, 2005.

129. M. Savvides, B. V. K. Vijaya Kumar, and P. K. Khosla, Cancelable biometric filters for face recognition, in *Proceedings of the 17th International Conference on Pattern Recognition (ICPR'04)*, Cambridge, England, Vol. 3, 2004, pp. 922–925.

130. S. Tulyakov, F. Farooq, and V. Govindaraju, Symmetric hash functions for fingerprint minutiae, in *Lecture Notes in Computer Science*, Vol. 3687, Springer, Berlin, 2005, pp. 30–38.

131. A. Kanak and I. Sogukpinar, Fingerprint hardening with randomly selected chaff minutiae, in *Computer Analysis of Images and Patterns (CAIP 2007), Lecture Notes in Computer Science*, Vol. 4673, Springer, Berlin, 2007, pp. 383–390.

132. S. Buss and P. N. Yianilos, Secure short-key cryptosystems: Forty bits is enough, NEC Research Institute Technical Report, 1999. Available at http://www.intermemory.org/pny/papers/sk/sk.pdf.

133. A. Adler,Vulnerabilities in biometric encryption systems, in *NATO RTA Workshop: Enhancing Information Systems Security—Biometrics* (IST-044-RWS-007), 2004. Available at http://www.sce.carleton.ca/faculty/adler/publications/2004/adler-2004-NATORTA-biometric-encryption-vulnerabilities.pdf.

134. A. Adler, Vulnerabilities in biometric encryption systems, in *Audio- and Video-Based Biometric Person Authentication* (AVBPA2005), Tarrytown, NY. *Lecture Notes in Computer Science*, Vol. 3546, Springer, Berlin, 2005, pp. 1100–1109 . Available at http://www.sce.carleton.ca/faculty/adler/publications/2005/adler-2005-AVBPA-biometric-encryption.pdf.

135. E.-C. Chang, R. Shen, and F. W. Teo, Finding the original point set hidden among chaff, in *Proceedings of the 2006 ACM Symposium on Information, Computer and Communications Security (ASIACCS'06)*, March 21–24, 2006, Taipei, Taiwan, 2006, pp. 182–188.

136. W. J. Scheirer and T. E. Boult, Cracking fuzzy vaults and biometric encryption, in *Biometric Consortium Conference*, Baltimore, September 2007. Available at http://vast.uccs.edu/~tboult/PAPERS/Scheirer-Boult-BCC07-Crack-Fuzzy-Vault.pdf.

137. K.-H. Cheung, A. Kong, J. You, and D. Zhang, An analysis on invertibility of cancelable biometrics based on biohashing, in *Proceedings of the 2005 International Conference on Imaging Science, Systems, and Technology*, 2005, pp. 40–45. Available at http://staffx.webstore.ntu.edu.sg/personal/adamskong/Shared%20Documents/publication/IMCSE2005_paperCIS3056.pdf.

138. K. Liu, H. Kargupta, and J. Ryan, Random projection-based multiplicative data perturbation for privacy preserving distributed data mining, *IEEE Trans. Knowledge and Data Eng.* **18**(1):92–106, 2006.

139. J. Bringer, H. Chabanne, and B. Kindarji, The best of both worlds: applying secure sketches to cancelable biometrics, in *2nd Benelux Workshop on Information and System Security (WISSec'07)*, Luxembourg, September 20–21, 2007. *Science of Computer Programming*, **74**(1-2):43–51, 2008.

140. F. Carter and A. Stoianov, Implications of Biometric Encryption on wide spread use of biometrics. Presentation at the EBF Biometric Encryption Seminar, Amsterdam, NL, 24 June 2008. http://www.eubiometricsforum.com/pdfs/be/BE-Carter_Stoianov.pdf.

141. The concept of anonymous database using BE was proposed by Tomko: Method and apparatus for securely handling data in a database of biometrics and associated data. U.S. Patent 5790668 to G. J. Tomko, August 4, 1998 (Priority date: December 19, 1995).

142. J. Bringer and H. Chabanne, An authentication protocol with encrypted biometric data, in *AFRICACRYPT*, Casablanca, Morocco, June 11–14, 2008, *Lecture Notes in Computer Science*, Vol. 5023, Springer, Berlin, 2008, pp. 109–124.

143. B. Schoenmakers and P Tuyls, Computationally secure authentication with noisy data, in P. Tuyls, B. Škorić, and T. Kevenaar, editors, *Security with Noisy Data: Private Biometrics, Secure Key Storage and Anti-Counterfeiting*, Springer-Verlag, London, 2007, pp. 141–149.

144. http://www.turbine-project.org/.

145. C. Busch, TURBINE: background and status—ISO standardization initiative, in *EBF Biometric Encryption Seminar*, Amsterdam, June 24, 2008. http://www.eubiometricsforum.com/pdfs/be/BE-Busch.pdf.

146. N. Delvaux, J. Bringer, J. Grave, K. Kratsev, P. Lindeberg, J. Midgren, J. Breebaart, T. Akkermans, M. van der Veen, R. Veldhuis, E. Kindt, K. Simoens, C. Busch, P. Bours, D. Gafurov, B. Yang, J. Stern, C. Rust, B. Cucinelli, and D. Skepastianos, Pseudo identities based on fingerprint characteristics, in *IEEE 4th International Conference on Intelligent Information Hiding and Multimedia Signal Processing (IIH-MSP 2008)*, August 15–17, Harbin, China, pp. 1063–1068, 2008.

147. http://genkey.no/file.php?n=12&id=1.

148. A. Senior and R. Bolle, Improved fingerprint matching by distortion removal, *IEICE Trans. Inf. Syst.* **E84–D**(7):825–831, 2001.

149. A. Ross, S. C. Dass, and A. K. Jain, Fingerprint warping using ridge curve correspondences, *IEEE Trans. Pattern Anal. Mach. Intell.* **28**(1):19–30, 2006.

150. D. Socek, D. Ćulibrk and V. Božović. Practical Secure Biometrics Using Set Intersection as a Similarity Measure. In *International Conference on Security and Cryptography (SECRYPT 2007)*, July 2007, Barcelona, Spain, pp. 25–32, 2007.

151. I. R. Buhan, J. M. Doumen, and P. H. Hartel, Controlling leakage of biometric information using dithering, in *16th European Signal Processing Conference (EUSIPCO)*, Aug 2008, Lausanne, Switzerland.

152. A. Arakala, K. J. Horadam, and S. Boztas, Practical considerations for secure minutiae based templates, in *Biometrics Symposium (BSYM)*, September, 2008, Tampa, FL.

153. A. Stoianov, T. Kevenaar, and M. van der Veen, Security Issues of Biometric Encryption, in *IEEE TIC-STH Symposium on Information Assurance, Biometric Security and Business Continuity*, September, 2009, Toronto, Canada.

154. A. Kholmatov and B. Yanikoglu, Realization of correlation attack against fuzzy vault scheme, in *Proc. of SPIE*, Vol. 6819, 2008. pp. 68190O-1 - 68190O-7.

155. A. Nagar, K. Nandakumar and A. K. Jain, Securing Fingerprint Template: Fuzzy Vault with Minutiae Descriptors, in *Proc. of Int. Conf. on Pattern Recognition*, Tampa, FL, December 2008.

156. K. Nandakumar and A. K. Jain, Multibiometric Template Security Using Fuzzy Vault, in *Proc. of IEEE Second Int. Conf. on Biometrics: Theory, Applications and Systems*, Washington DC, Sept. 2008.

# Index

256-byte IrisCode, 230

**A**

AC/DCT method, 416
  block diagram of, 398
  classification performance, 416
  contingency matrix, 416
AC/LDA method, 398, 418
  block diagram, 398
  contingency matrix, 416
  window/subject classification rates, 418
Active appearance models (AAMs), 171
Ad hoc network, applications, 390
AdaBoost algorithm, 96, 228
AdaBoost classifier, 234, 235, 236
  usage, 235
AdaBoost ensemble, 98
AdaBoost learning, classes, 228
Adaptive appearance model, 175
Adaptive motion model, 175
Adaptive thresholding, 542
  foreground segmentation, 543
Additive white Gaussian noise (AWGN), 422
Affine-shear transformation, 274
AFM model, 246
Age-based transformation, 286
Age estimation, 277
  hierarchical neural-network-based classifiers, 277
Age transformation models, 289
Aging face modeling, 625
Algebraic hash functions, 690
Algorithms of pattern extraction (ALOPEX), 52
  algorithm optimization procedure, 68
  equation, 68

Alternative sensing methods, 430
Ambient-light set, 130
Analog-to-digital conversion, 52
AND rule fusion, 104
  ensemble design, 104–107
  favorable statistical dependence analysis, 93
  monotonic decision fusion rules, 107
    ROCs of, 107
  NIST 24 plastic distortion fingerprint database, 104
  PIE pose/illumination database, 104
Angle markings, 129
Angular transform, 548
Appearance-based techniques, 217, 245
  Fisherfaces, 245
  LDA, 245
  PCA, 245
AR database facial expressions, 211
Arrhythmia ECG segment, 405
Arrhythmia screening, 418, 419, 420
  algorithm, 387, 402
  data sets, combination of, 418
  identification performance, 421
  recognition framework, 418
  window/subject recognition rates, 420
Arrhythmic ECG segments, autocorrelations, 404
Artificial neural network (ANN)-based distance measurement, 49
ARTMAP neural network classifier, 351
Assistive face recognition system, 115
Assistive technology application, 115
Asymmetric cryptographic algorithms, 391, 392
Atrial premature contraction (APC), 387, 401

---

www.ingramcontent.com/pod-product-compliance
Lightning Source LLC
Chambersburg PA
CBHW070833040225
21358CB00001B/5